map pages

Orkney Islands

153
• Kirkwall

Shetland Islands

153
• Lerwick

Western Isles

WITHDRAWN

• Steornabhagh (Stornoway)

152

148 | **149** | Thurso **150** | **151**
Wick

144 | Ullapool **145** | **146** | **147**
• Gairloch | Tain

136 • Uig **137** | Dingwall • | Elgin • **141** | Banff
Portree • | **138** | **139** | **140** | Inverness • | **142** | Peterhead • **143**
Kyle of Lochalsh

128 | **129** | **130** | **131** | Aviemore • | Aberdeen •
• Mallaig | • Fort William | **132** | **133** | **134** | **135**
Pitlochry •

120 | **121** | **122** | **123** | **124** | **125** | **126** | **127**
Oban • | Crianlarich • | Perth • | Dundee •

112 | **113** | **114** | Stirling • **115** | Edinburgh • | **118** | **119**
Largs • | **262** **263** | Berwick-upon-Tweed
116 | **117**

104 | **105** | Kilmarnock • | Peebles • | **110** | **111**
Campbeltown • | **106** | **107** | **108** | **109** | Alnwick •
Ayr • | Moffat •

98 | **99** | **100** | **101** | **102** | **103**
Stranraer • | Dumfries • | Newcastle upon Tyne •
Carlisle • | **266** **267**
92 | **93** | **94** | **95** | **96** | **97**
Workington • | Penrith • | Middlesbrough •

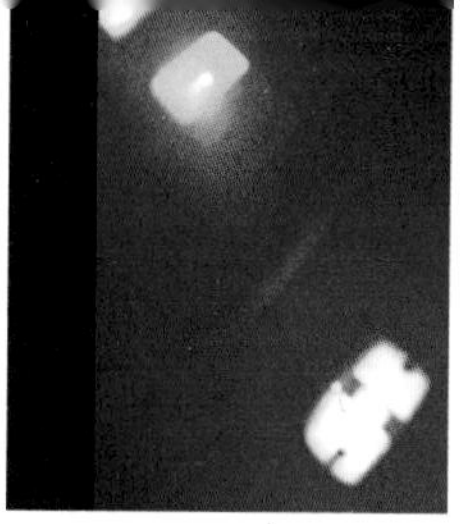

Kendal • | Thirsk • | Scarborough •
86 | **87** | **88** | **89** | **90** | **91**
Lancaster • | Settle •

York •
Blackpool • | Burnley • | Leeds • | Hull •
80 | **81** | **82** | **83** | **84** | **85**
Grimsby •

Liverpool • | **264** | Manchester • | Sheffield •
78 | **79** | **74** | **75** | **76** | **77**
265 | Lincoln •
Holyhead • | Colwyn Bay •
68 | **69** | **70** | **71** | Chester • | Newark-on-Trent •
Caernarfon • | Stoke-on-Trent •
72 | **73** | Nottingham • | Boston •
56 | **57** | Shrewsbury • | Stafford • | **62** | **63** | King's Lynn • | **66** | **67**
Dolgellau • | **58** | **59** | **60** | **61** | Leicester • | **64** | **65** | Norwich • | Great Yarmouth
Aberystwyth • | Newtown • | Birmingham • | **50** | **51** | Peterborough •
42 | **43** | Ludlow • | **260** **261** | Coventry • | Northampton • | Bury St Edmunds
Cardigan • | **44** | **45** | **46** | **47** | Stratford-upon-Avon | Bedford • | **52** | **53** | **54** | **55**
Fishguard • | Worcester • | **48** | **49** | Cambridge • | Ipswich •
30 | **31** | Brecon • | Hereford • | **38** | Luton • **39** | Felixstowe •
Carmarthen • | Abergavenny • | Gloucester • | Oxford • | **26** | Watford • | Chelmsford • | **41**
Pembroke • | **32** | Swansea • | **34** | **35** | **36** | **37** | Reading • | **27** | **40**
33 | Cardiff • | Bristol • | Swindon • | LONDON | Maidstone •
Bath • | 256 - 259 | **28** | **29**
Basingstoke • | **25** | Sevenoaks • | Dover •
20 | **21** | **22** | Andover • **23** | **24** | Guildford • | **14** | **15** | **16** | **17** | Folkestone •
Barnstaple • | Salisbury • | Brighton • | Hastings •
18 | **19** | Taunton • | Yeovil • | Southampton • | Chichester • | Newhaven •
Bude • | **10** | **11** | **12** | **13**
Lyme Regis • | Bournemouth •
8 | Exeter • **9** | Weymouth •
4 | Bodmin • **5** | Torquay •
Truro • | **6** | **7**
2 | **3** | Plymouth •

154
• Sligo

155
Larne •
Londonderry •
Belfast •

• Westport
• Cavan | • Newry

158
Douglas •
Isle of Man

• Galway | • Athlone | DUBLIN ■

Limerick •

156 | **157**
Tralee •
Killarney • | Waterford • | Rosslare •
Cork •

Isles of Scilly **2**

The Channel Islands **158**

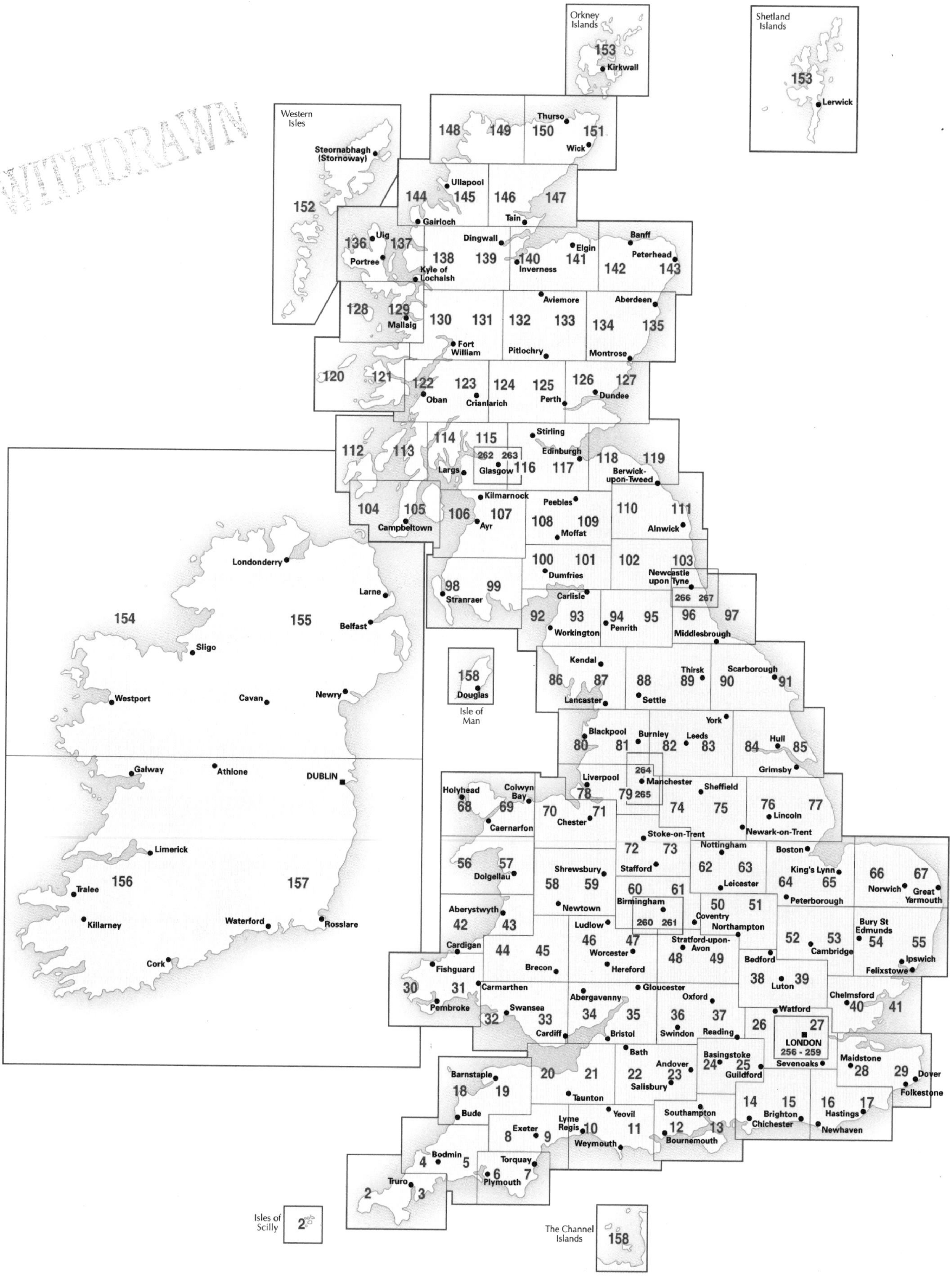

GREAT BRITAIN ROAD ATLAS 2001

contents

Scale 1:200,000
or 3.15 miles to 1 inch

15th edition July 2000

© Automobile Association Developments Limited 2000

Automobile Association Developments Limited retains the copyright in the original edition © 1986 and in all subsequent editions, reprints and amendments.

Published by AA Publishing (a trading name of Automobile Association Developments Limited, whose registered office is Norfolk House, Priestley Road, Basingstoke, Hampshire RG24 9NY. Registered number 1878835).

Mapping produced by the Cartographic Department of The Automobile Association. This atlas has been compiled and produced from the Automaps database utilising electronic and computer technology.

ISBN 0 7495 2520 7

A CIP catalogue record for this book is available from The British Library.

Printed in Italy by Pizzi, Milan.

The contents of this atlas are believed to be correct at the time of the latest revision. However, the publishers cannot be held responsible for loss occasioned to any person acting or refraining from action as a result of any material in this atlas, nor for any errors, omissions or changes in such material. The publishers would welcome information to correct any errors or omissions and to keep this atlas up to date. Please write to the Cartographic Editor, Publishing Division, The Automobile Association, Fanum House, Basing View, Basingstoke, Hampshire RG21 4EA.

Information on National Parks provided by the Countryside Commission for England and the Countryside Council for Wales.

Information on National Scenic Areas in Scotland provided by Scottish Natural Heritage.

Information on Forest Parks provided by the Forestry Commission.

The RSPB sites shown are a selection chosen by the Royal Society for the Protection of Birds.

National Trust properties shown are a selection of those open to the public as indicated in the handbooks of the National Trust and the National Trust for Scotland.

Traffic signs © Crown copyright. Reproduced with the permission of the Controller of HMSO.

Distances, journey times and map pages	inside front cover
Information for motorists–air ambulance	IV–V
Route planner	VI–XI
Road signs	XII–XIII
Motorways	
Restricted junctions	XIV–XV
M25 London orbital motorway	XVI
M60 Manchester orbital motorway	XVII
Map symbols	XVIII–1
Road maps	**2–153**
Scottish islands	152–153
Ireland	154–157
The Channel Islands & The Isle of Man	158
Town plans	159–232
Key to town plans	159
Central London	238–248
Central London street index	249–255
Ports and airports	
Major ports	233
Major airports	234–236
Channel Tunnel	237
District maps	
London district	256–259
Birmingham district	260–261
Glasgow district	262–263
Manchester district	264–265
Tyne & Wear district	266–267
Index to place names	268–318
County map	268
Distances, journey times and map pages	inside back cover

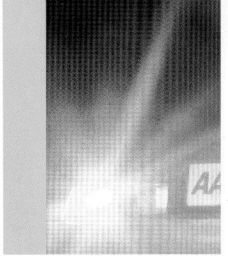

information for motorists

The AA is Britain's largest motoring organisation, providing accurate and up-to-date information services for all motorists – just give us a call

All 09003 prefixed numbers are charged at 60p per minute at all times (correct at time of going to press)

Traffic information

To check the latest road conditions before you travel call **08705 500 600** (AA members only) or visit our website at **www.theaa.co.uk** for more information.

AA Roadwatch on 09003 401 100 You can access one of the most detailed and accurate traffic reports available in the UK.

Select the latest traffic information for your local area or any other region of the UK. You can also request information on specific motorways and A-roads.

VODAFONE DIGITAL MOBILE USERS – call '1800' ... For an up-to-the-minute, location-specific traffic report, with the option to obtain information on a specific road or motorway. This service also gives you the opportunity to speak to an experienced AA Traffic and Travel Information Adviser for details about a particular incident or advice on an alternative route.

Calls to 1800 are charged at 45p per minute (59p per minute for Pay-as-you-Talk customers and operator service). Average call time 1 minute.

Need expert advice?

Access the expertise of the AA **– call 09003** followed by the numbers shown

Motoring hints and advice

401 505 Checks before you start, route planning and motorway driving
401 506 Child seats and harnesses
401 508 Safe motorway driving

401 509 Motoring for disabled drivers
401 522 Towing: matching the vehicle to the load
401 526 Motorway breakdowns

The material contained in these 09003 recorded information services has been researched by the AA. While every effort is made to ensure that it is accurate, no liability can be accepted arising from inaccuracies or omissions. © Automobile Association Developments Limited 2000.

Useful numbers

AA The Driving School 0800 60 70 80
Book your driving lessons anywhere in mainland Britain

Road User Information Line (Highways Agency) 0845 750 40 30
For information on motorways and trunk roads, to make a complaint or comment on road conditions or roadworks, for MoT and vehicle licence enquiries

Exclusive services for AA Members

All 08705 prefixed numbers are charged at BT's National Rate

AA Hotel Booking Service 08705 05 05 05 (9am–6pm, Mon–Fri; 9am–1pm, Sat) Free reservation service for business or leisure travel covering over 8,000 AA-inspected establishments in Britain and Ireland

UK Route Planning visit **www.theaa.co.uk** or call **08705 500 600** (24 hours, 7 days a week) Free personalised itineraries for routes within Great Britain and Ireland

Special Offers and AA Services 08705 500 600 (24 hours, 7 days a week) Expert advice and assistance on legal and technical aspects of motoring Details of discounts on AA services and other exclusive offers and savings

AA Membership Administration 08705 444 444 (7am–11pm, 7 days a week) For all Membership enquiries

If you are not an AA Member and would like to be – call 0800 444 999 for details on how to join

air ambulance

The Road User's Guide to Calling an Air Ambulance

Air ambulances are a vital part of emergency medical services, providing a rapid response and swift transfer from incident to hospital, free of traffic congestion. An airlift is of particular benefit in cases of head or spinal injuries, where a high level of patient comfort is necessary, or when a patient has to be taken to a specialist unit.

If you witness an accident, dial 999 and tell the operator an ambulance is needed.

Description of the incident: this information will help the ambulance control to decide whether an air ambulance is needed. For example: 'There are four cars involved in an accident, and it looks like there are three casualties.'

Location: try to give as accurate a location as you can. For example: 'A40 southbound carriageway, two miles south of the M50 exit for Ross-on-Wye.'

Relevant landmarks: look around for anything that might be visible from the air. For example: 'There's a petrol station near by.' or 'There's a farmhouse on the left.'

Dangers: try to spot potential hazards for an incoming aircraft, such as overhead wires, pylons and telegraph poles.

Other information: tell the operator other details that will help the crew locate you or that will help them to plan their landing. For example: 'We will be waving a red blanket.' or 'There is a flat field next to the road.'

The air ambulance pilot will use the information you provide to decide where to land. It might be necessary for the helicopter to land some distance from the accident, but this is to ensure the safety of the aircraft. You can assist the air ambulance by doing the following:

Wear something highly visible: a brightly coloured scarf, or anything that will make you easy to spot.

Stand with your back to the wind: it is very helpful to the pilot to know in which direction the wind is blowing as the helicopter must land into the wind.

Face the proposed landing area: choose somewhere as flat as possible. Air ambulances can manoeuvre very easily, but they need to land somewhere level.

Raise and outstretch your arms: if you have your back to the wind, this will indicate the wind direction and landing site to the crew. When the aircraft lands, stay well clear of the blades and tail rotor and wait for them to stop before approaching.

For more information about the work of the National Association of Air Ambulance Services, or to make a donation, please call **0800 3 899899**.

route planner

Port Nis
(Port of Ness)

A857

Tolsta Head

Steornabhagh
(Stornoway)

Isle of
Lewis

A859

The Minch

O u t e r   H e b r i d e s

Taransay

Tairbeart
(Tarbert)

Harris

Gairloch

Uibhist a Tuath
(North Uist)

Loch nam Madadh
(Lochmaddy)

Uig

Kinloch

A87

Beinn na Faoghla
(Benbecula)

Dunvegan

Portree

A865

Uibhist a Deas
(South Uist)

Isle
of
Skye

Kyle of
Lochalsh

A87

Loch Baghasdail
(Lochboisdale)

Barraigh
(Barra)

Rum

Mallaig

Eigg

I n n e r   H e b r i d e s

A830

Coll

Tobermory

A861

A884

Lochaline

Tiree

Craignure
Isle of Mull

Obar

Fionnphort

A849

A816

Colonsay

Lochgilphead

Port
Askaig

Jura

Tarbert

A846

Kennac

Islay

Port Ellen

A83

Campbeltown

Arn
Bro

BALLYCASTLE
summer only

▭▭▭	Motorway
▭▭▭	Primary route dual carriageway
▭▭▭	Primary route single carriageway
▬▬▬	Other A roads

0   10   20   30 miles
0 10 20 30 40 kilometres

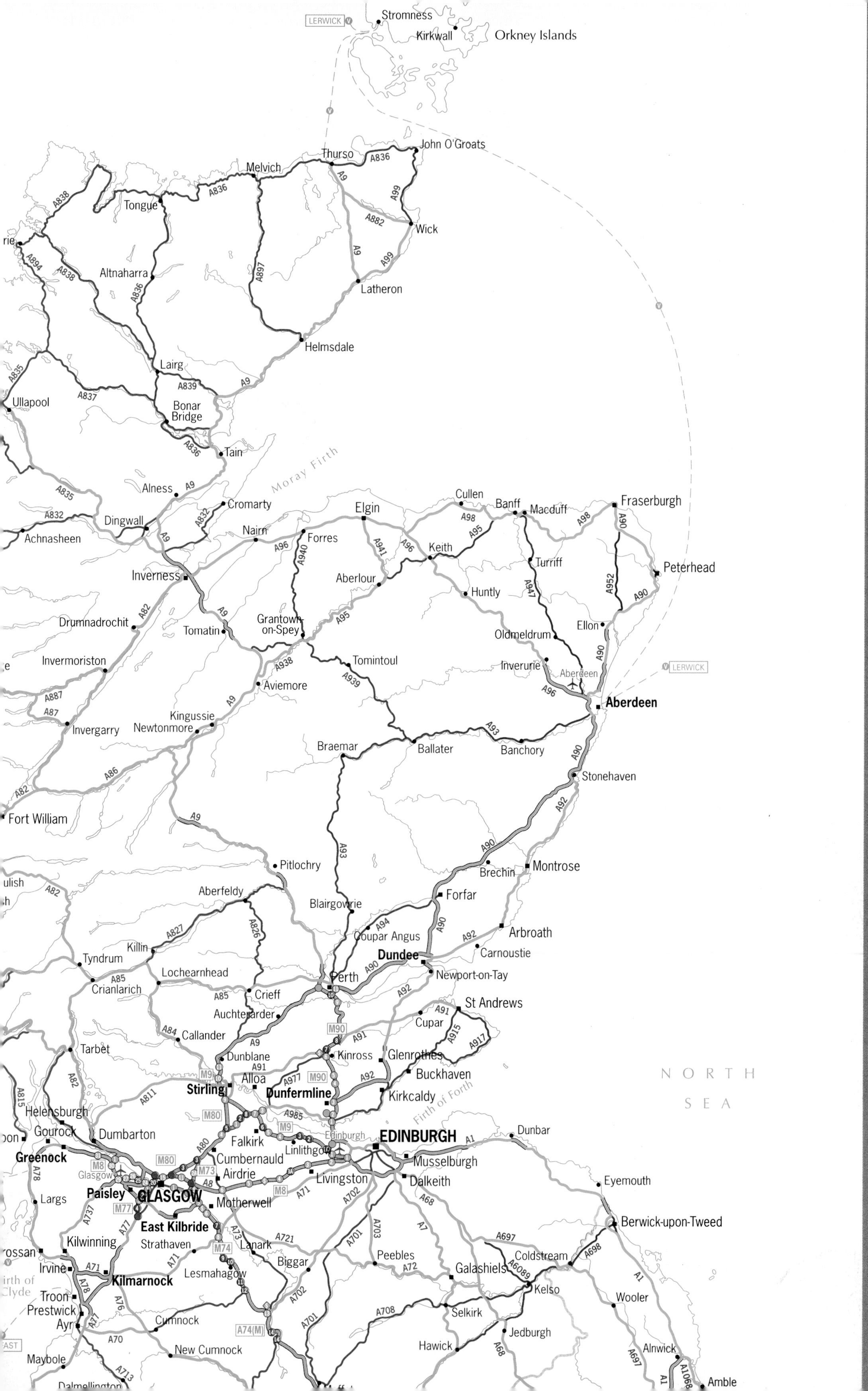

Orkney Islands

Stromness
Kirkwall
LERWICK

Thurso · John O'Groats
Melvich
A836
A9 · A99 · Wick
A882
Tongue
Altnaharra · A897 · Latheron
A838 · A836
A894
Helmsdale
Lairg
Bonar Bridge · A839 · A9
Ullapool · A837
Tain
Alness · A9 · Moray Firth
Achnasheen · A835 · Dingwall · Cromarty
A832 · Nairn · Elgin · Cullen · Banff · Macduff · Fraserburgh
A96 · Forres · A98 · A95
Inverness · A940 · A941 · Keith · A90
Aberlour · Turriff · Peterhead
Drumnadrochit · A82 · A96 · Huntly · A947 · A952
Tomatin · Grantown-on-Spey · A95 · Oldmeldrum · Ellon · A90
Invermoriston · A9 · Inverurie · Aberdeen · LERWICK
A887 · A938 · Tomintoul · A96
A87 · Aviemore · A939
Invergarry · Kingussie · Newtonmore · Aberdeen
A86 · Braemar · Ballater · A93 · Banchory · A90
Fort William · A9 · Stonehaven
A82 · A92
Pitlochry · Brechin · Montrose
Aberfeldy · A93 · Forfar
A827 · A826 · Blairgowrie · A94 · A90 · A92 · Arbroath
Killin · Coupar Angus · Carnoustie
Tyndrum · A85 · Crieff · Dundee · Newport-on-Tay
Crianlarich · A85 · Auchterarder · Perth · A92
Tarbet · A84 · Callander · A9 · M90 · A91 · St Andrews
Dunblane · Cupar · A915 · A917
A82 · M9 · Kinross · Glenrothes
Helensburgh · A811 · Alloa · A977 · M90 · Buckhaven
Gourock · Dumbarton · Stirling · Dunfermline · A92 · Kirkcaldy
Greenock · A815 · M80 · Falkirk · Linlithgow · Firth of Forth
A78 · M8 · M80 · M73 · Cumbernauld · Edinburgh · EDINBURGH · Dunbar
Glasgow · Airdrie · Livingston · Musselburgh · Eyemouth
Paisley · GLASGOW · Motherwell · A8 · A71 · Dalkeith · A1
Largs · M77 · East Kilbride · M73 · A702 · A68 · Berwick-upon-Tweed
Kilwinning · A721 · Lanark · A703 · Peebles · A697
Strathaven · M74 · Biggar · A701 · A72 · Galashiels · Coldstream · A698
Irvine · A71 · Lesmahagow · A708 · Selkirk · Kelso · Wooler
Troon · A76 · Cumnock · A74(M) · A701 · Hawick · Jedburgh · A68 · A1
Prestwick · A77 · A70 · New Cumnock · A697 · Alnwick · A1068
Ayr · Maybole · A713 · Amble

NORTH SEA

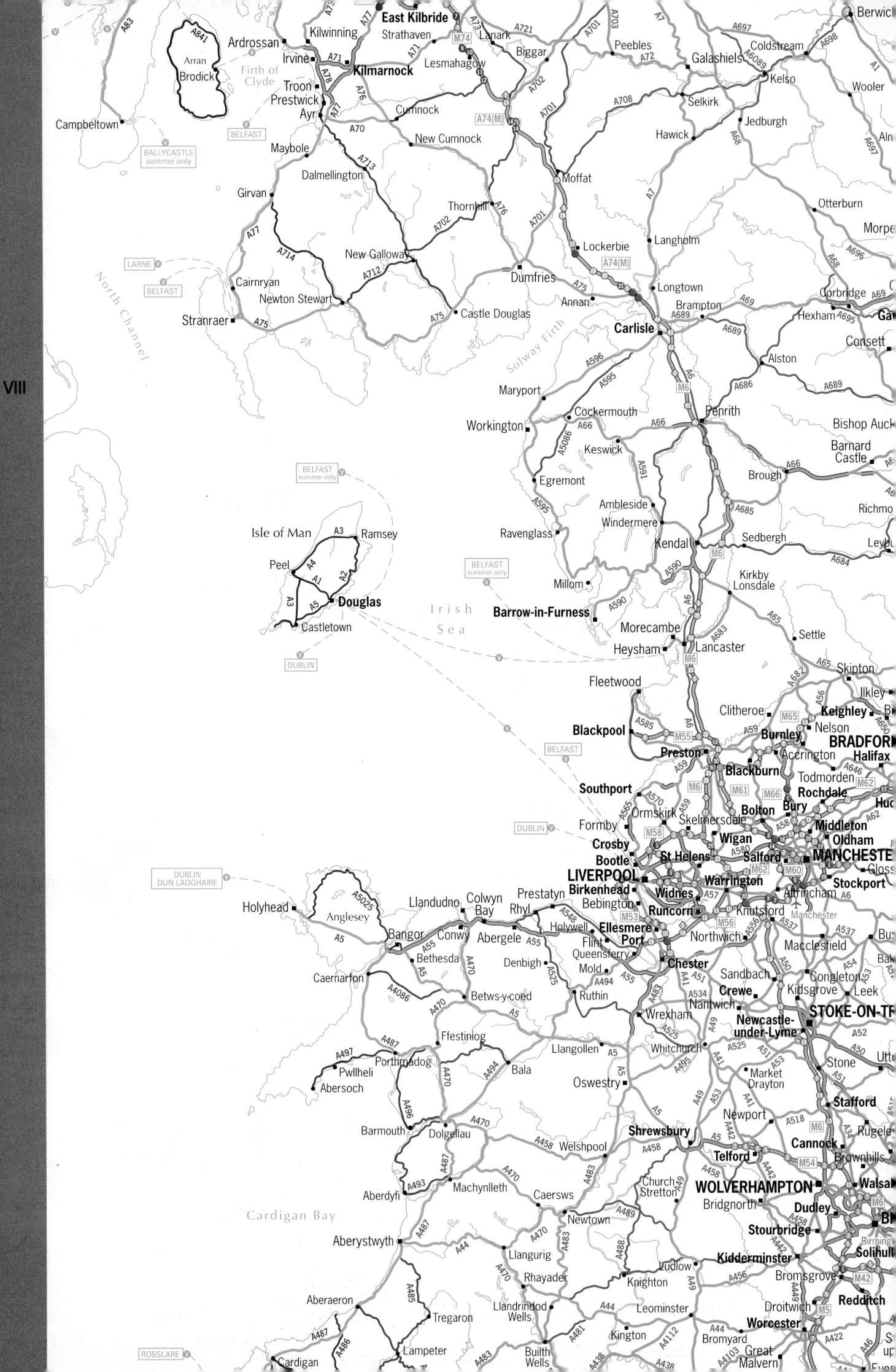

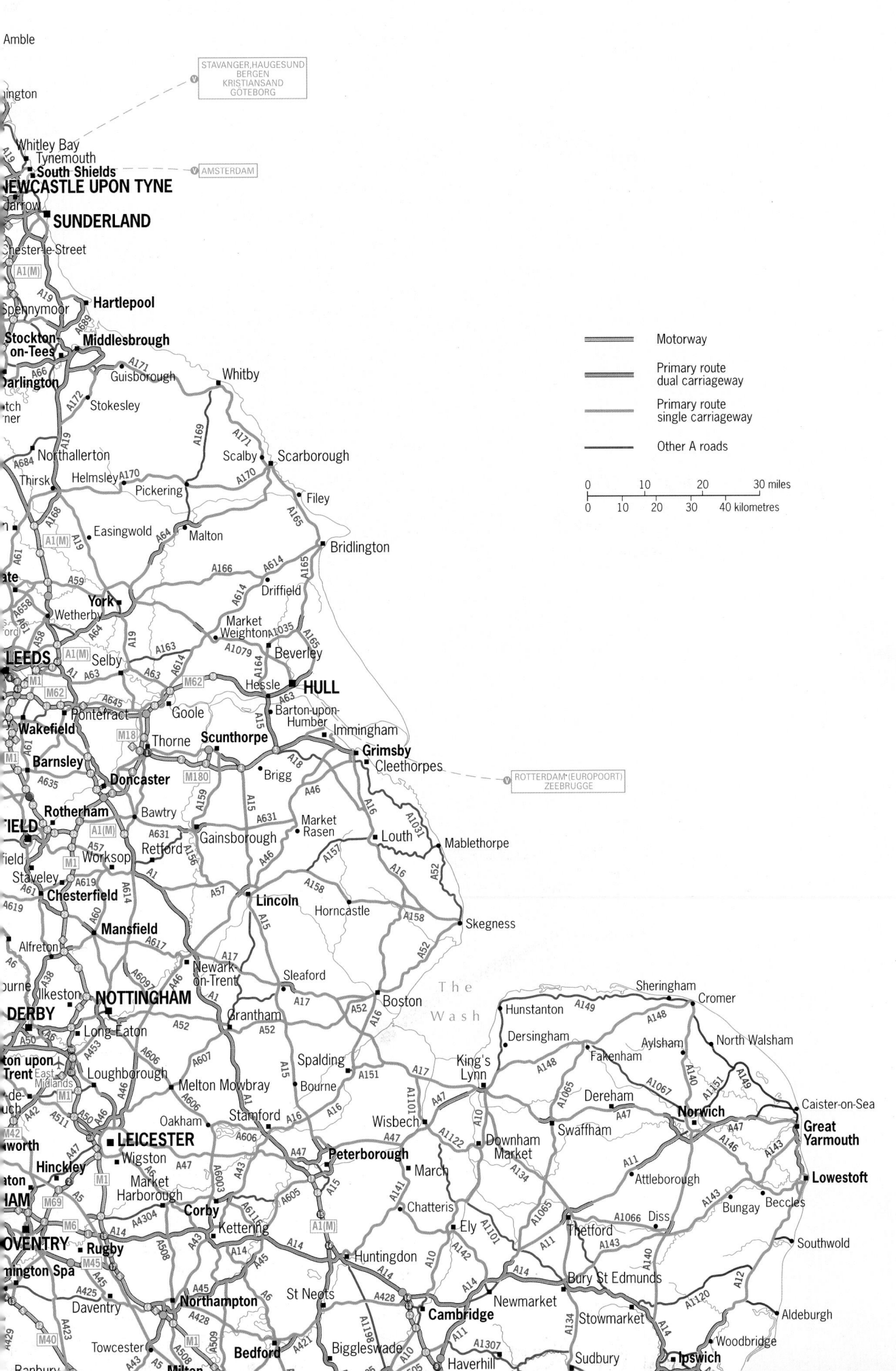

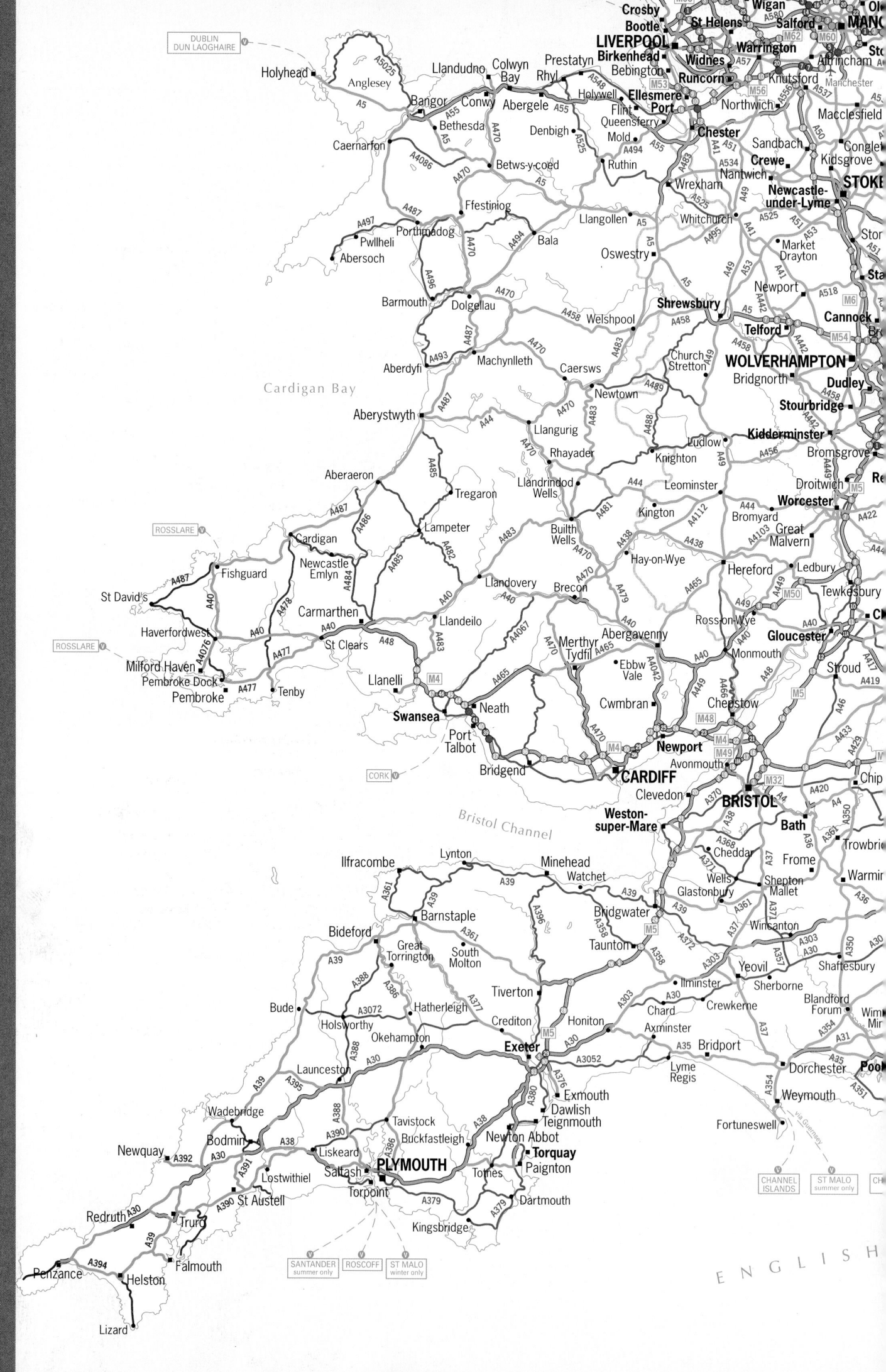

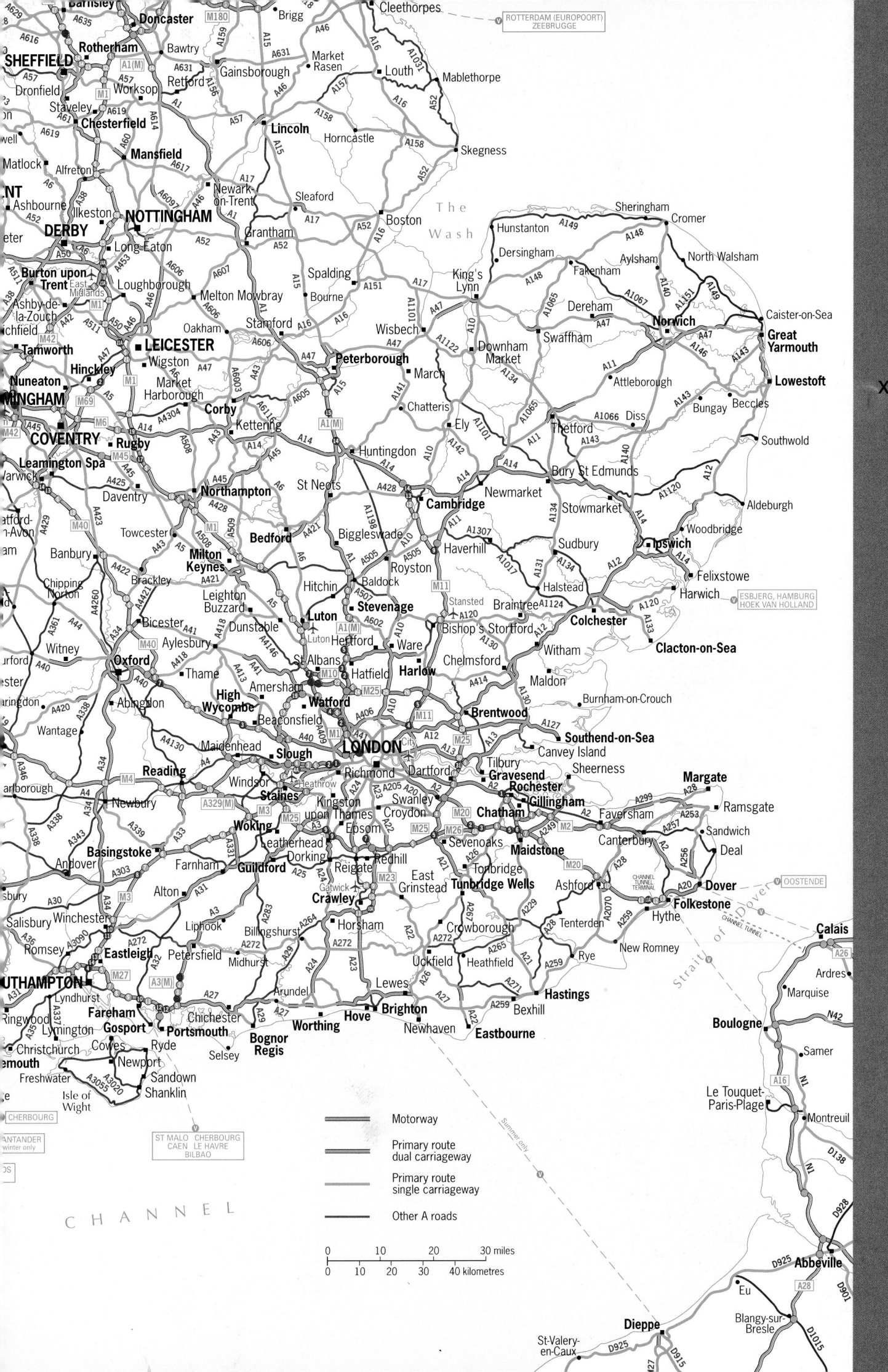

 # road signs

Classes of signs

Our road system has a consistent and comprehensive set of road signs that provide you with information, instructions and warnings.

Circles order and prohibit

Triangles warn

Rectangles provide information

 XII

Junctions and roundabouts

These signs provide you with important information about the nature of the junction or the roundabout ahead.

| Distance to 'STOP' line ahead | Distance to 'GIVE WAY' line ahead | Give way to traffic on major road | Stop and give way | Crossroads | T-junction | Staggered junction | Roundabout | Mini-roundabout (roundabout circulation) | No through road |

Traffic behaviour

Signs which must be obeyed. They indicate the speed or action you are required to take in particular situations.

| No stopping (clearway) | National speed limit applies | Maximum speed | Give priority to vehicles from opposite direction | No overtaking | Motor vehicles prohibited except for access | No entry for vehicular traffic | No U-turns | No right turn | No left turn |

| Turn left ahead | One-way traffic | Turn left | Vehicles may pass either side to reach same destination | Ahead only | Keep left |

The road ahead

Advance warning of the road layout ahead enables you to plan a safe approach.

| Bend to left | Double bend, first to left | Bend to right | Double bend, first to right | Road hump or series of road humps ahead | Worded warning sign | Dual carriageway ahead | Steep hill downwards | Steep hill upwards |

| No goods vehicles over maximum gross weight shown (in tonnes) | No vehicles over width shown | No vehicles over height shown | Sharp deviation of route | Two-way traffic straight ahead | Traffic merges from left | Traffic merges from right | Road narrows on left | Road narrows on both sides |

Hazards ahead

These signs warn you of potential hazards on the road ahead.

| Hospital ahead with accident and emergency facilities | Traffic queues likely ahead | Cycle route ahead | Slippery road | Road works | Uneven road | Wild animals | Falling or fallen rocks | Other danger |

| School crossing patrol ahead | School crossing patrol | Pedestrian crossing | Trams crossing ahead | Risk of grounding | Hump bridge | Opening or swing bridge ahead | Quayside or river bank |

On the motorway

These signals are used to warn you of conditions ahead and the lanes affected. They may be located overhead, on the central reservation or over the nearside lane. Drivers must observe the advisory speed limits and should remember that the red circle means a mandatory speed control.

| Temporary maximum speed limit and information message | Change lane | Leave motorway at next exit | Do not proceed further in this lane |

 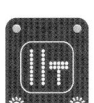       

| Reduced visibility ahead | Lane ahead closed | Temporary maximum speed limit | End of restriction | National speed limits apply | Traffic building up ahead. Reduce speed to a maximum of 60mph to help maintain flow | Traffic getting heavier ahead. Reduce speed to a maximum of 50mph or lower if incidents occur | Traffic improving. Maximum speed increased to 60mph | Traffic is lighter. Flow easier. Return to national speed limits. This will appear for 3 minutes before going blank |

Motorway diversions

Where the motorway is closed, special signs advise you of the recommended diversion route around the incident.

  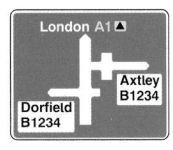

Symbols showing emergency diversion route
for motorway and other main road traffic

motorways – restricted junctions

Diagrams of selected motorway junctions which have entry and exit restrictions
(Motorways and Service Areas booklet also available tel: **08705 500 600**)

XIV

M1 London–Leeds

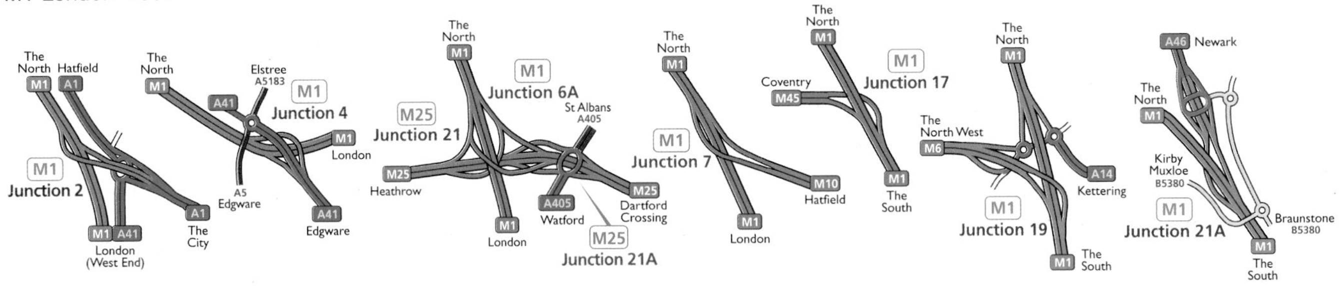

M1 London–Leeds | M2 Rochester–Faversham | M3 Sunbury–Southampton

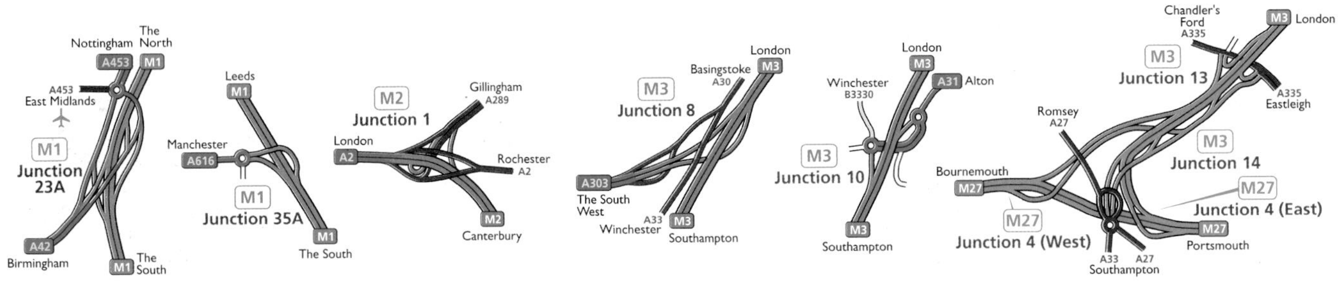

M4 London–South Wales | M5 Birmingham–Exeter

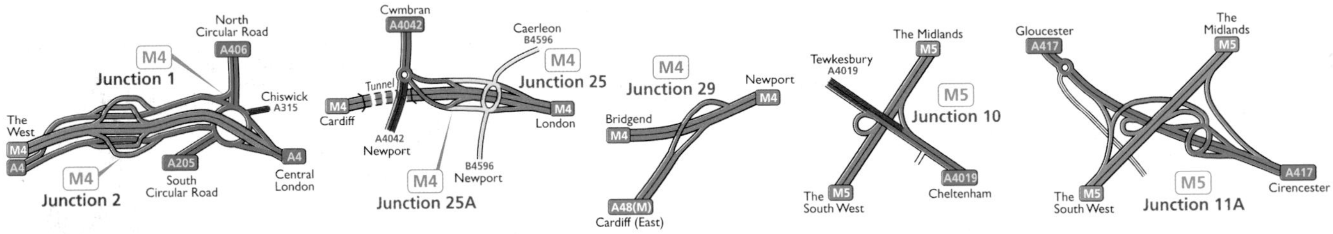

M5 Birmingham–Exeter | M6 Rugby–Carlisle

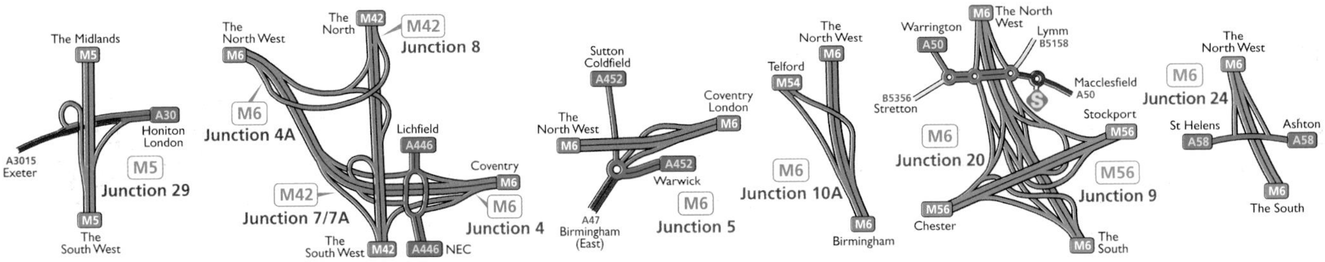

M6 Rugby–Carlisle | M8 Edinburgh–Bishopton

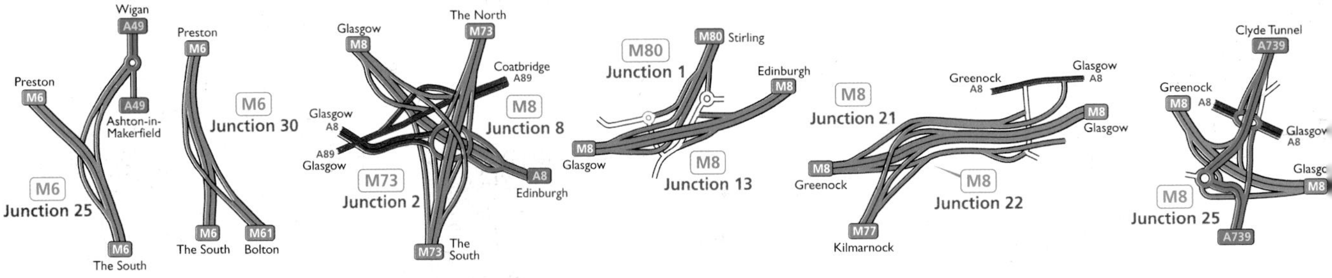

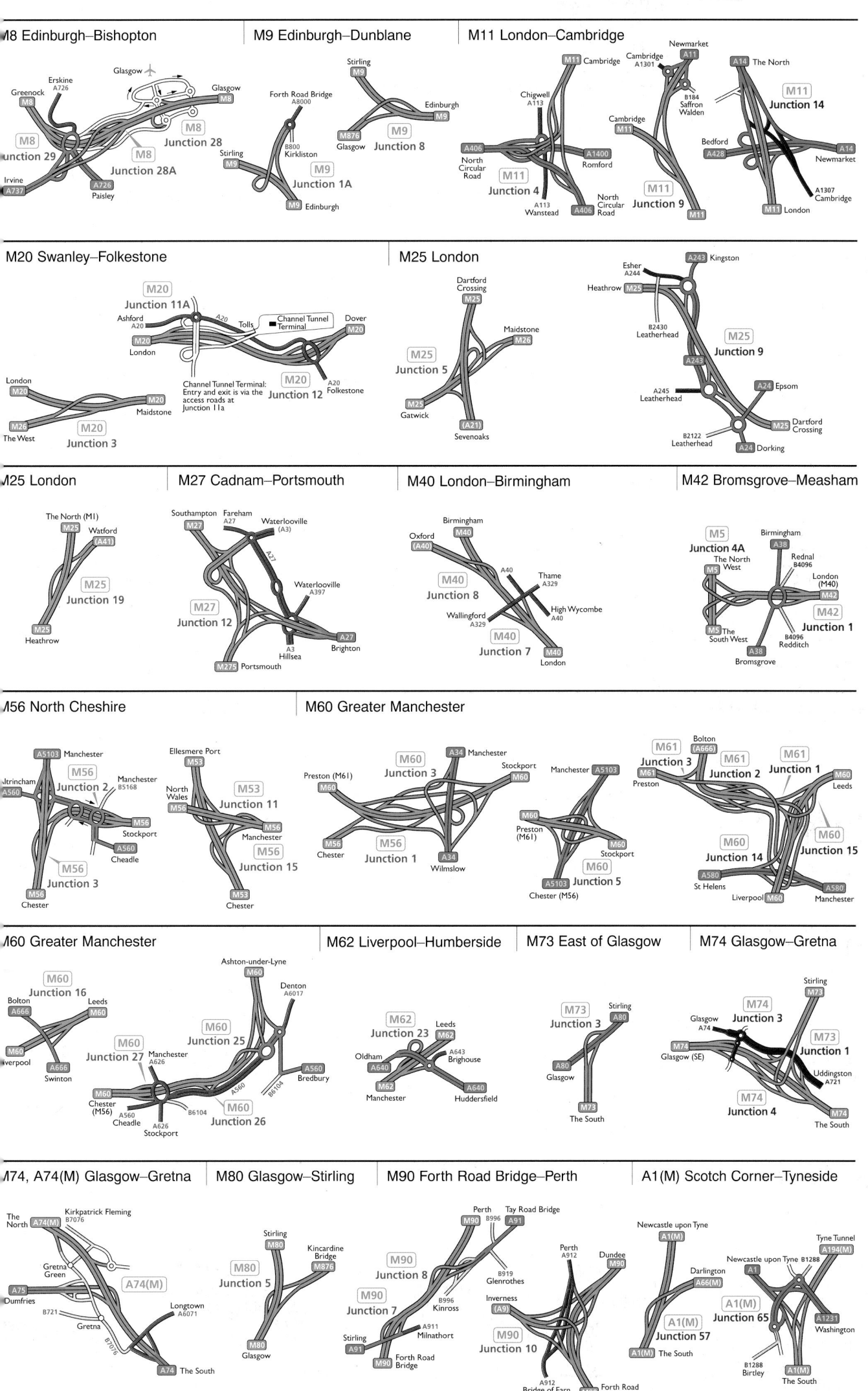

M25 London orbital motorway

Refer also to atlas pages 26–27

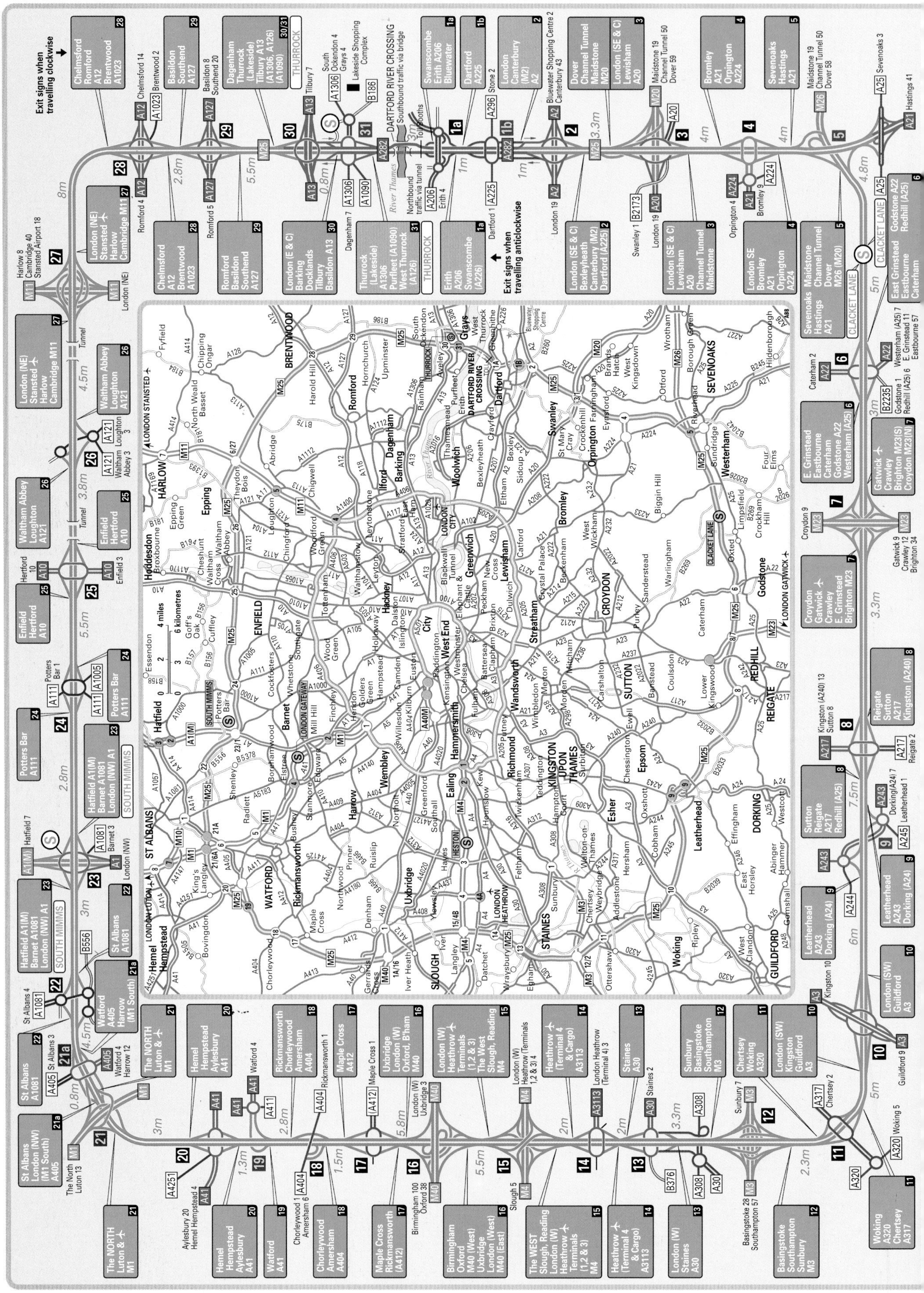

M60 Manchester orbital motorway

Refer also to atlas page 79

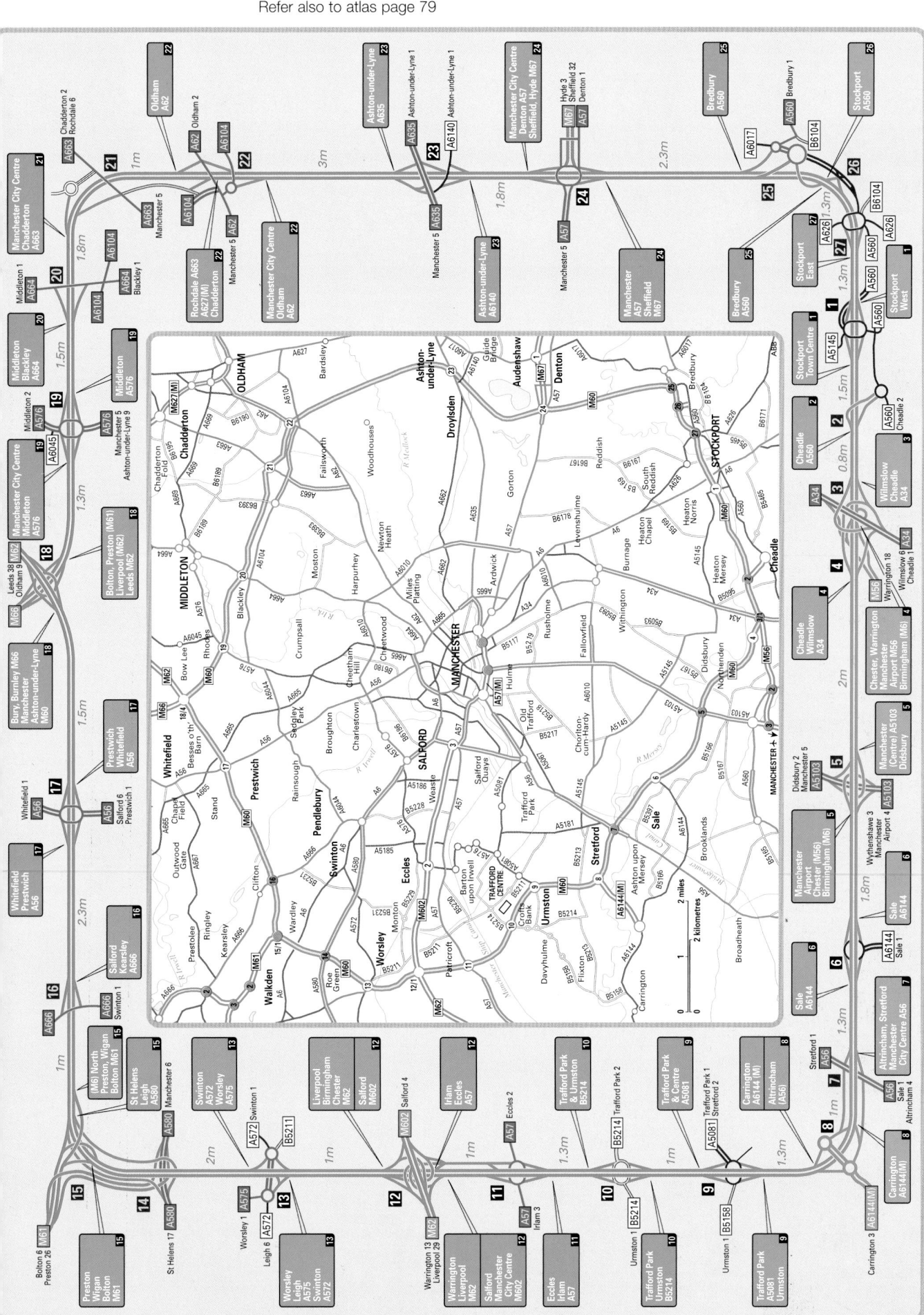

map symbols

Motoring information

M4	Motorway with number
11	Motorway junction with and without number
3	Restricted motorway junctions
S Fleet	Motorway service area
	Motorway and junction under construction
A3	Primary route single/dual carriageway
S Grantham North	Primary route service area
BATH	Primary route destination
A1123	Other A road single/dual carriageway
B2070	B road single/dual carriageway
	Unclassified road single/dual carriageway
	Roundabout
	Interchange
	Narrow primary/other A/B road with passing places (Scotland)
	Road under construction
⊨════⊨	Road tunnel
→	Steep gradient (arrows point downhill)
Toll	Road toll
▽ 5 ▽	Distance in miles between symbols
— ⓥ — —	Vehicle ferry – Great Britain
BERGEN ⓥ	Vehicle ferry – continental
- - - - -	Railway line/in tunnel
—○—✕—	Railway station and level crossing
+++++++	Tourist railway
✈	Airport
Ⓗ	Heliport
Ⓕ	International freight terminal
★	Major shopping centre
P+R	7-day Park and Ride locations
☎	AA telephone
	Urban area and village
628 ▲	Spot height in metres
	River, canal, lake
	Sandy beach
	County/County Borough/Council Area boundary
	National boundary
85	Page overlap and number

Tourist information

Places of interest are also shown on town plans. See pages 159–232

🄸	Tourist Information Centre
🄸	Tourist Information Centre (seasonal)
🄸	Visitor or heritage centre
	Abbey, cathedral or priory
	Ruined abbey, cathedral or priory
♜	Castle
	Historic house or building
Ⓜ	Museum or art gallery
	Industrial interest
�	Aqueduct or viaduct
❋	Garden
♣	Arboretum
❀	Vineyard
Ⴑ	Country park
♜	Agricultural showground
	Theme park
	Farm or animal centre
	Zoological or wildlife collection
	Bird collection
	Aquarium
	Nature reserve
RSPB	RSPB site
·········	Forest drive
- - - - -	National trail
☼	Viewpoint
	Picnic site
	Hill-fort
	Roman antiquity
	Prehistoric monument
✕ 1066	Battle site with year
	Steam centre (railway)
	Cave
✖	Windmill
	Monument
⚑	Golf course
	County cricket ground
	Rugby Union national stadium
	International athletics stadium
	Horse racing
	Show jumping/equestrian circuit
	Motor-racing circuit
	Air show venue
	Ski slope – natural
	Ski slope – artificial
NT	National Trust property
NTS	National Trust for Scotland property
★	Other place of interest
☐	Boxed symbols indicate attractions within urban areas
	National Park (England & Wales)
	National Scenic Area (Scotland)
	Forest Park
	Heritage Coast
	Little Chef Restaurant (7am–10pm)
	Travelodge
	Little Chef Restaurant and Travelodge
BURGER KING	Granada Burger King sites
Ⓖ	Granada service area

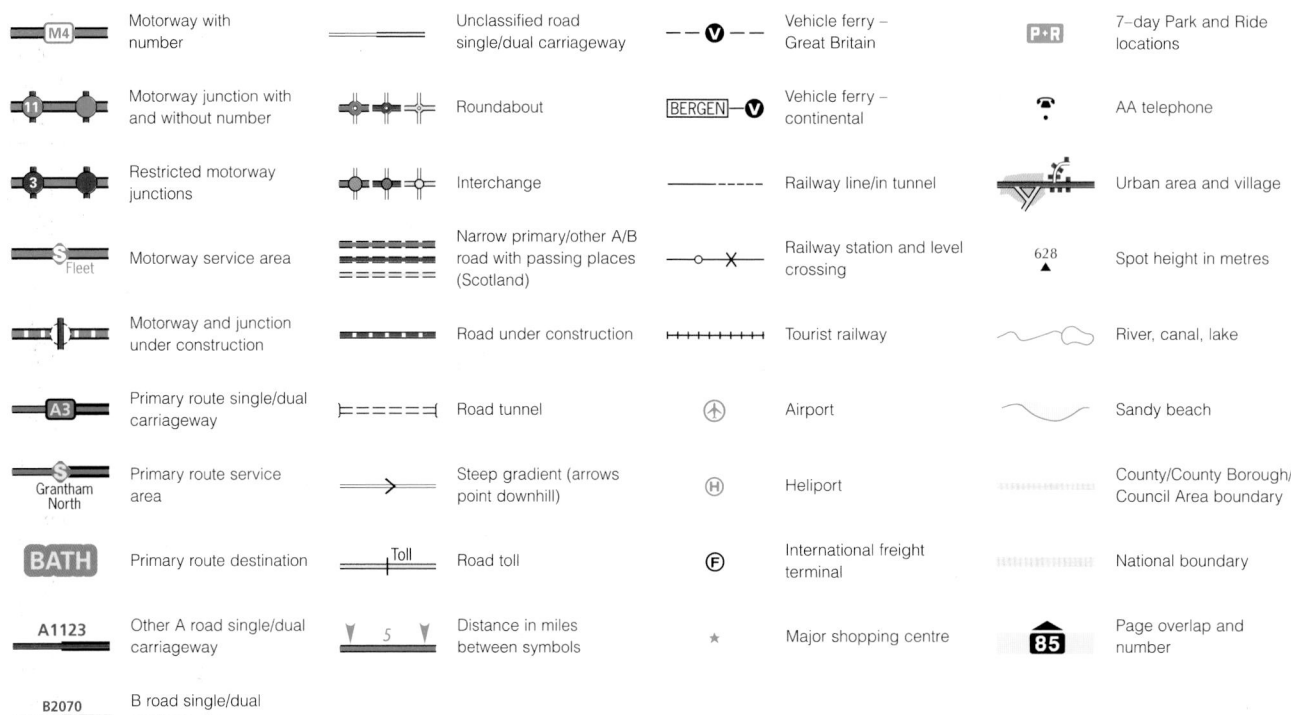

Ireland (see pages 154–157) For tourist information see opposite page

▭ M1 ▭ Motorway	▭ N17 ▭ National primary route (Republic of Ireland)	▭ A4 ▭ Primary route (Northern Ireland)	▬▬ Road under construction
Motorway junction with and without number	N54 National secondary route (Republic of Ireland)	A21 A road (Northern Ireland)	Distance in miles between symbols
Restricted motorway junctions	R182 Regional road (Republic of Ireland)	B75 B road (Northern Ireland)	International boundary

1

Central London (see pages 238–248)

Motorway	Restricted road (access only/private)	Banned turn (restricted periods only)	PO Post Office
Primary route single/dual	- - - - - - - Footpath	Ahead only	POL Police station
Other A road single/dual	========= Track	Mini-roundabout	Steps
B road single/dual	::::::::: Pedestrian street	Barrier	† Church
Unclassified road single/dual	- - - - - Railway line/in tunnel	⇌ Railway station	i Tourist Information Centre
Unclassified road wide/narrow	← One-way street	London Regional Transport (LRT) station	i Tourist Information Centre (seasonal)
Road under construction	Compulsory turn	Docklands Light Railway (DLR) station	
Road tunnel wide/narrow	Banned turn	P Parking	

Royal Parks (opening and closing times for traffic)
Green Park   Constitution Hill: closed Sundays, 08.00–dusk
Hyde Park   Open 05.00–midnight
Regent's Park   Open 05.00–midnight
St James's Park   The Mall: closed Sundays, 08.00–dusk

Traffic regulations in the City of London include security checkpoints and restrict the number of entry and exit points.

Note: Oxford Street is closed to through-traffic (except buses & taxis) 07.00–19.00, Monday–Saturday. Restricted parts of Frith Street/Old Compton Street are closed to vehicles 12.00–01.00 daily.

District maps (see pages 256–267) For tourist information see opposite page

Motorway	Unclassified road single/dual	Inner London Regional Transport (LRT) station	H Hospital
Motorway under construction	- - - - - Road under construction	Outer London Regional Transport (LRT) station	Crem Crematorium
Primary route single/dual	- - - - - - - Restricted road	Railway station/LRT interchange	
Other A road single/dual	— - - - Railway line/in tunnel	Light railway/tramway station	
B road single/dual	● Railway station	Sports stadium	

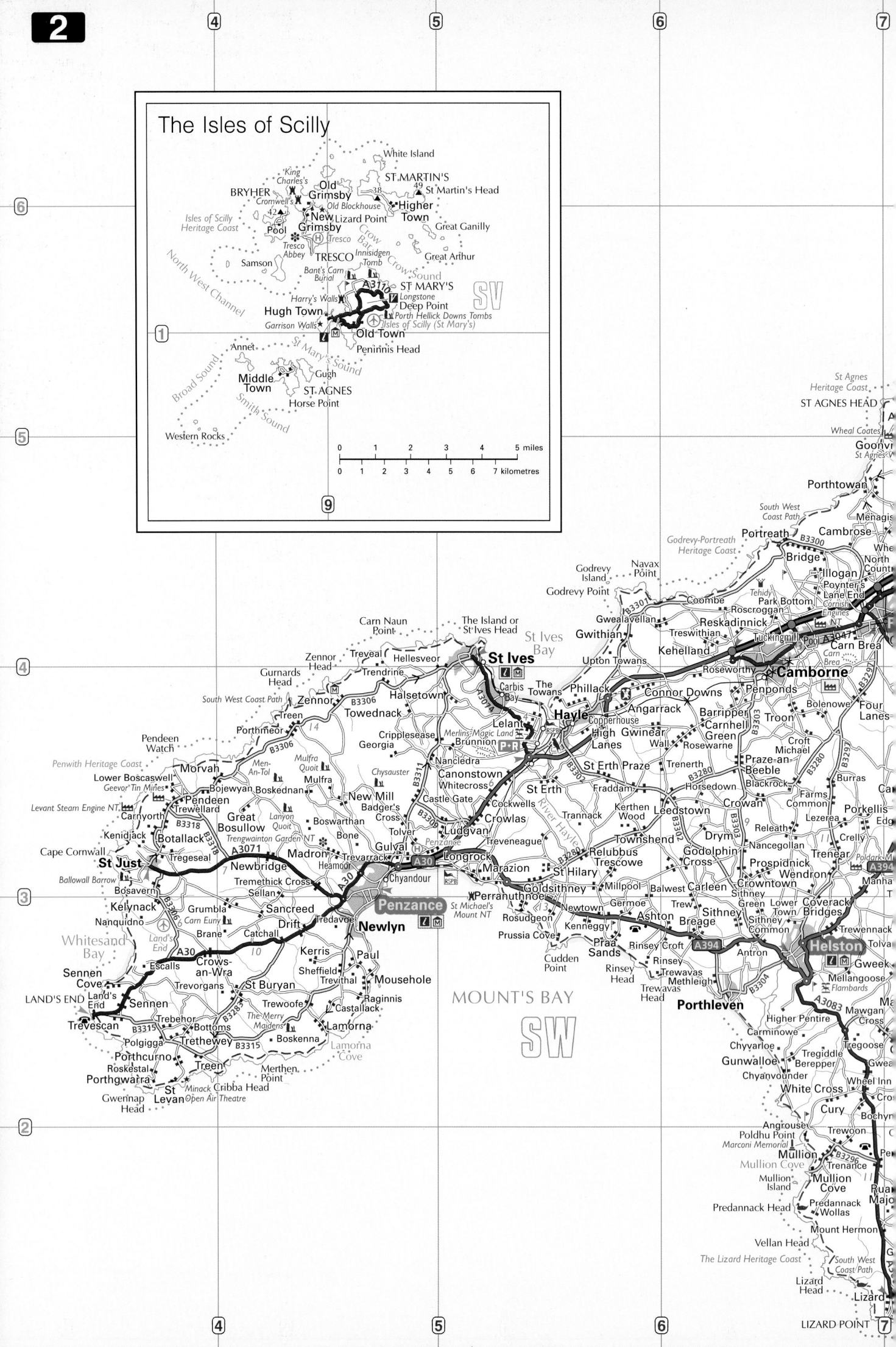

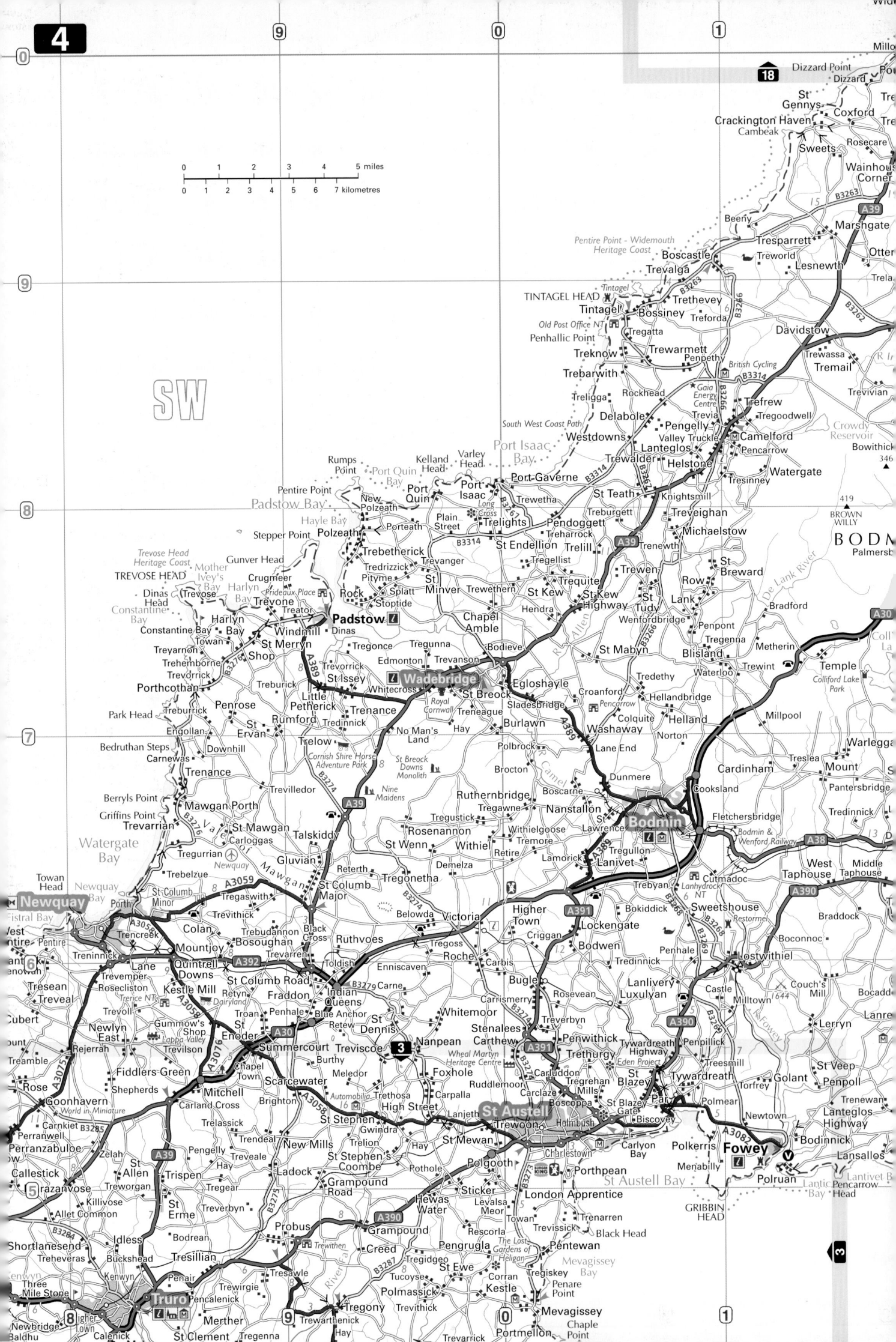

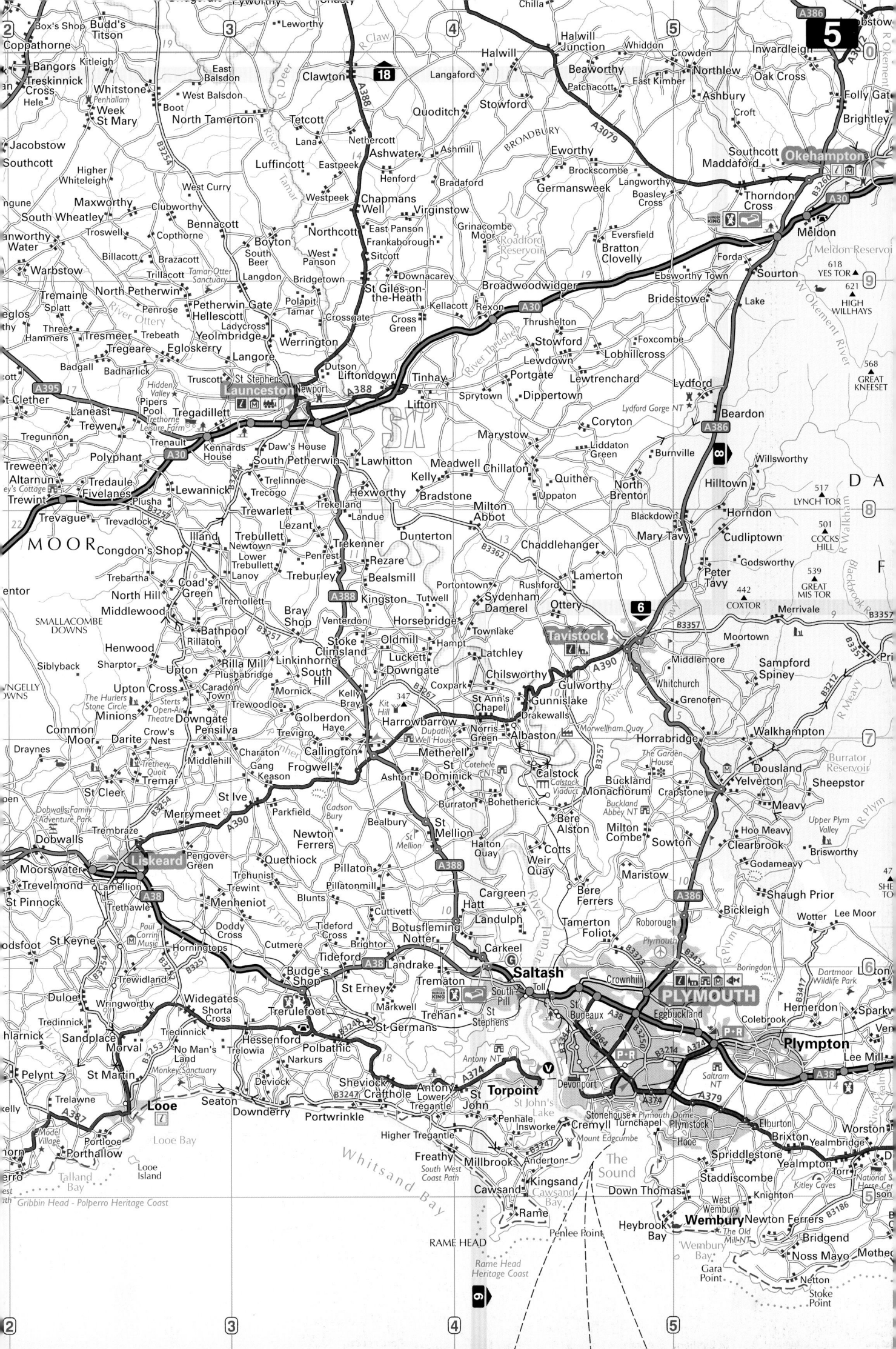

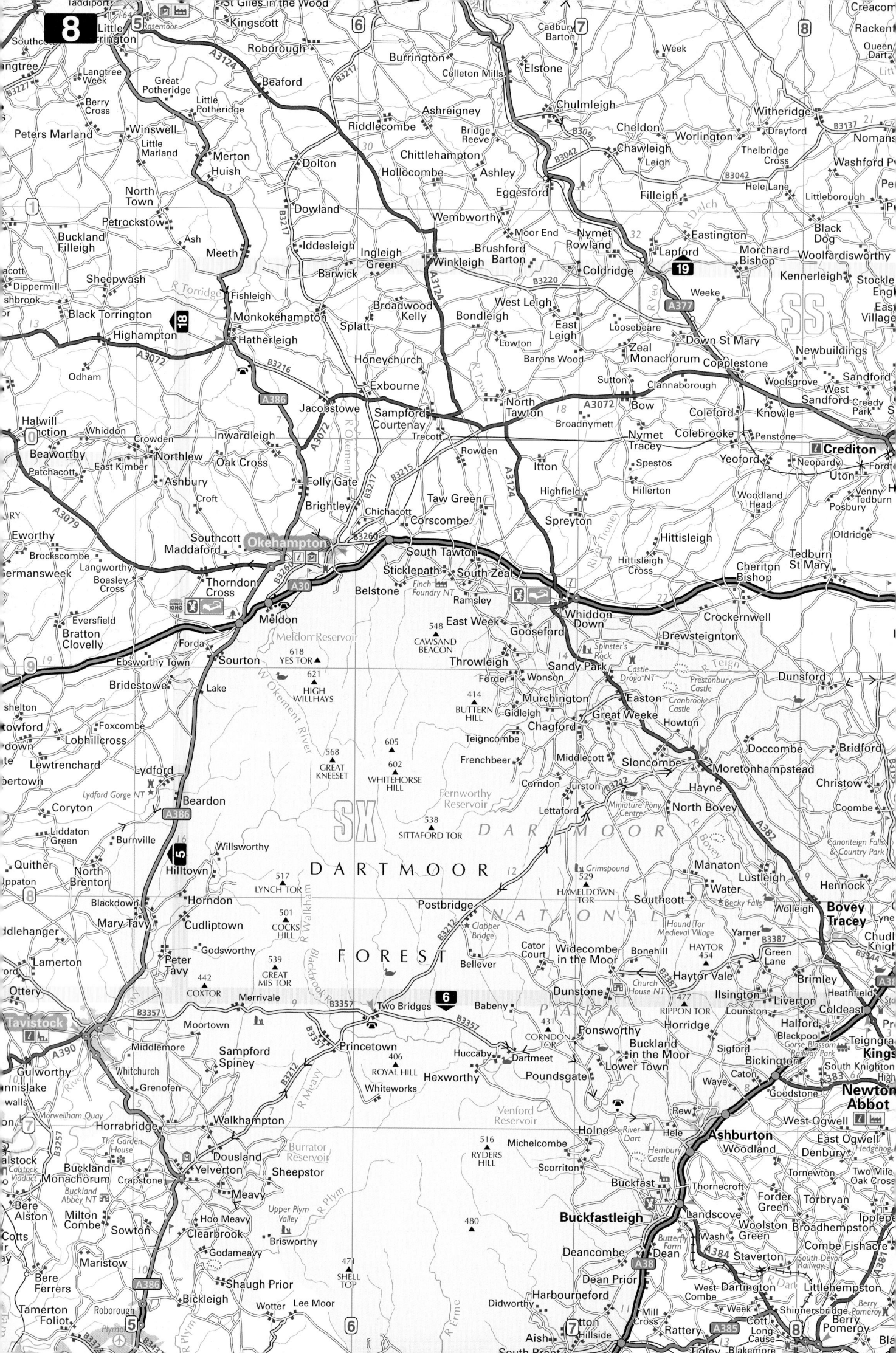

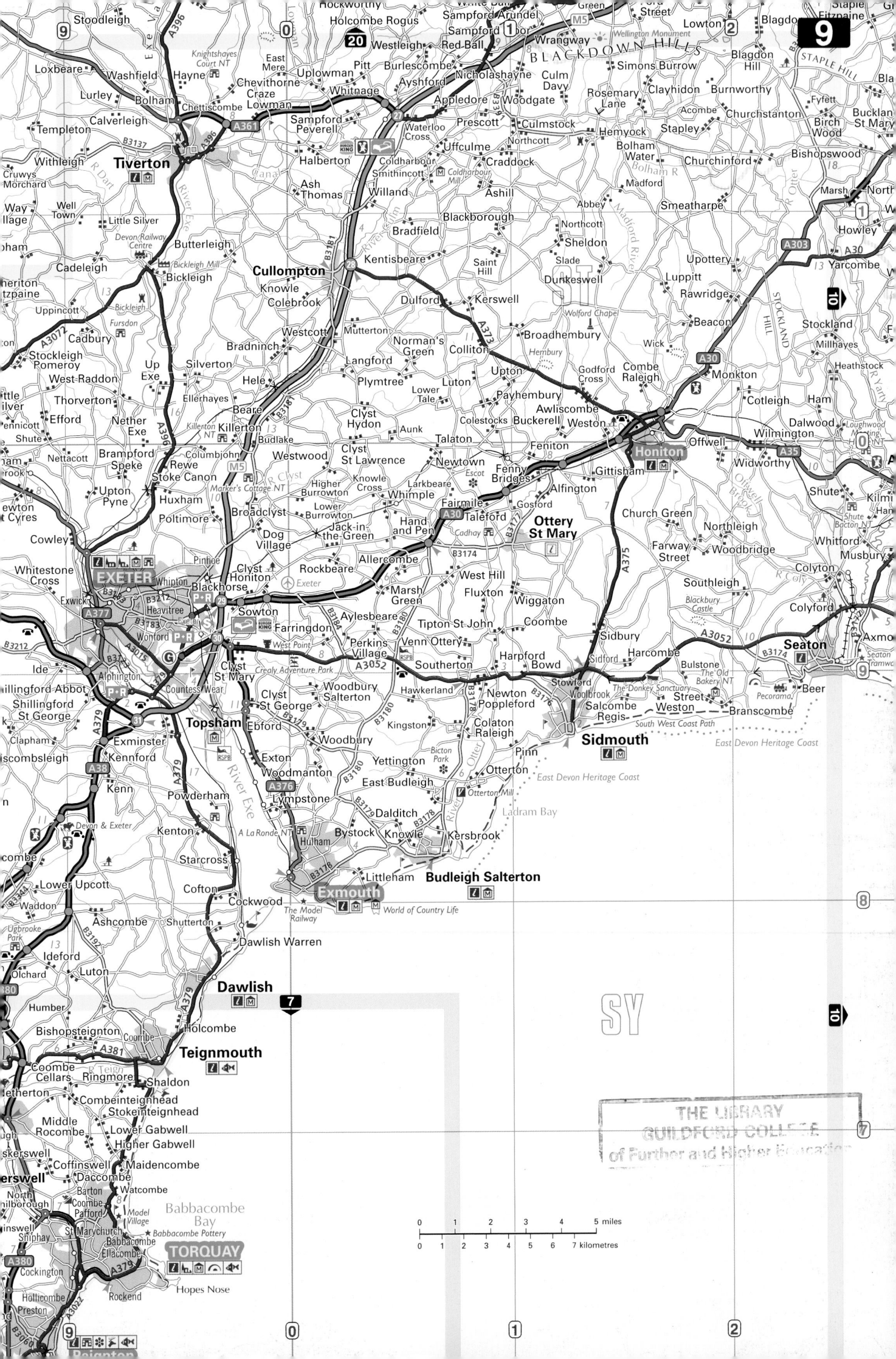

SY

EXETER

Tiverton

Cullompton

Honiton

Ottery St Mary

Sidmouth

Seaton

Budleigh Salterton

Exmouth

Topsham

Dawlish

Teignmouth

TORQUAY

BLACKDOWN HILLS

STAPLE HILL

Babbacombe Bay

East Devon Heritage Coast

South West Coast Path

0 1 2 3 4 5 miles

0 1 2 3 4 5 6 7 kilometres

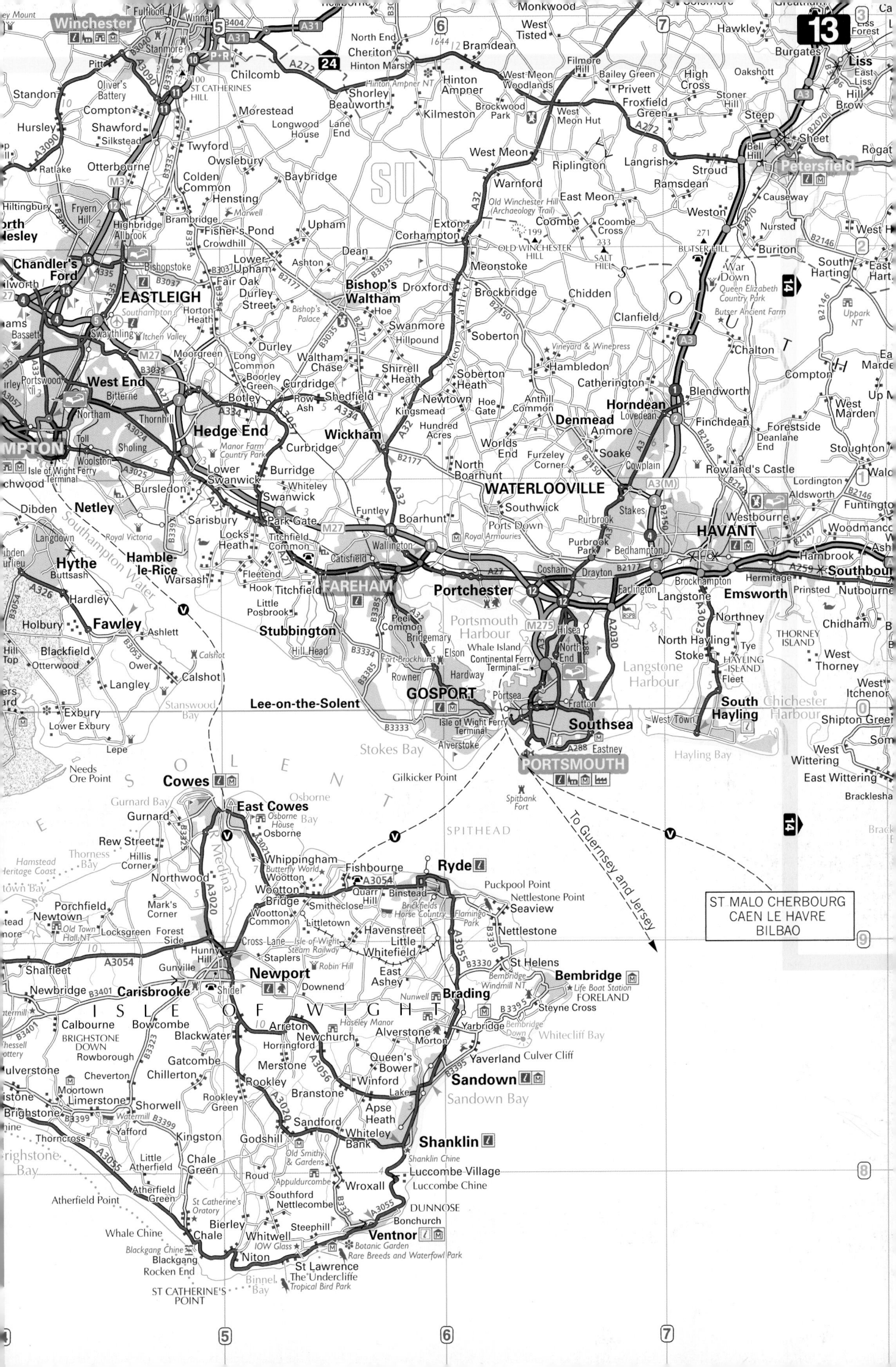

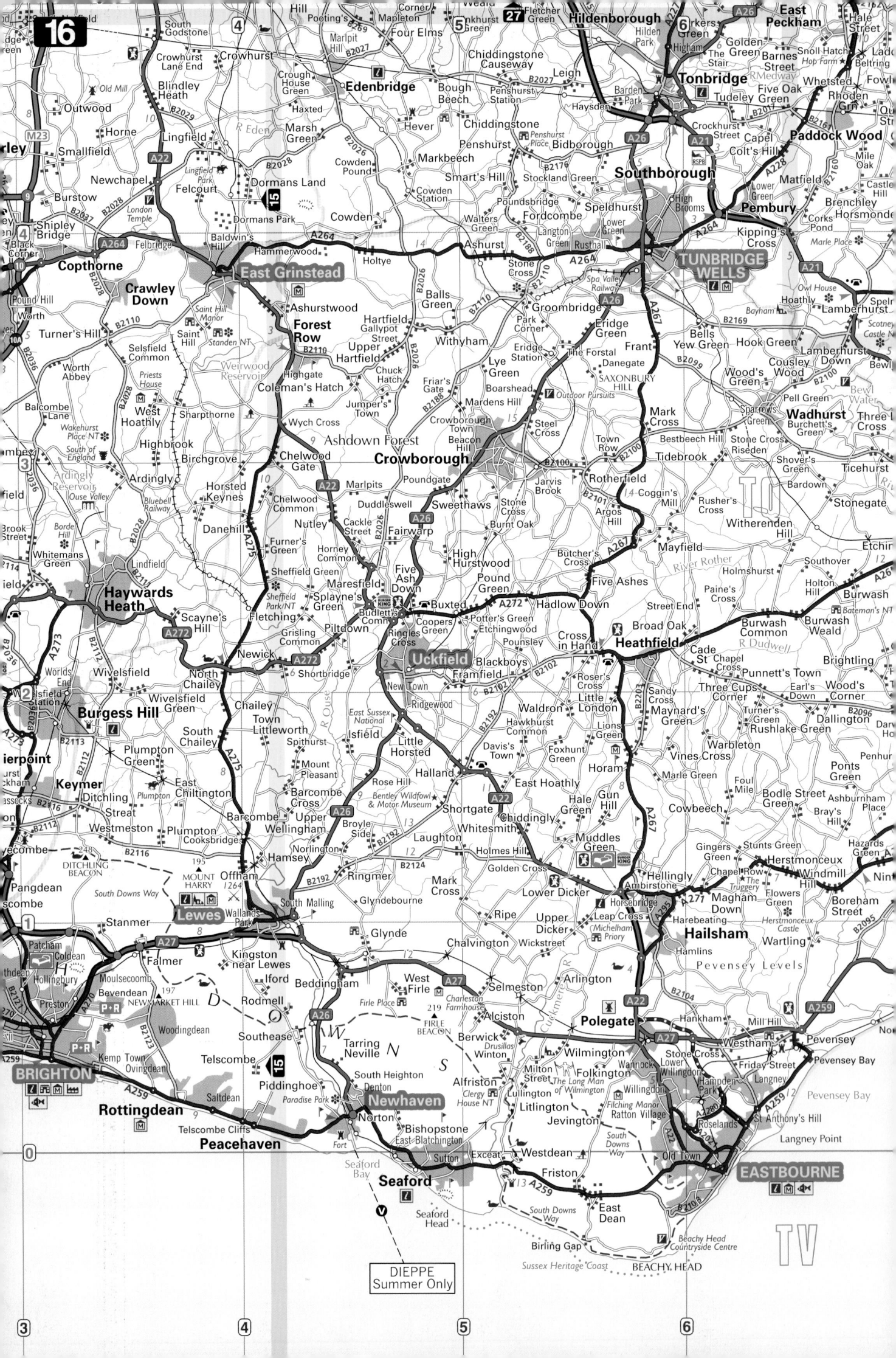

North West
Point

*Lundy
Heritage Coast*

LUNDY

142 ▲

Marisco

Surf Point

Shutter Point

0 1 2 3 4 5 miles
0 1 2 3 4 5 6 7 kilometres

B A R N S T A P L E

O R

B I D E F O R D   B A Y

Bull
Point

Rockham
Bay

Morte
Point

Morte
Bay

Woolacombe

Baggy
Point
Putsborough

Pickwell

Croyde Bay

Croyde Bay

Georgeham
Croyde
B3231

Saunton

Braunton

Darraco
Know

Lobb

*North Devon
Heritage Coast*

Appledore

Westward Ho!   **Northam**

B3236

Eastleigh

HARTLAND POINT

*Shipload
Bay*

Titchberry

Damehole
Point

Brownsham

Stoke

Hartland Quay

*Spekes Mill
Mouth*

Hartland

Velly

Clovelly

*Hartland
Heritage Coast*

Higher
Clovelly

B3248

4

B3233

Buck's
Mills

Fairy Cross

Horns
Cross

Ford

The Big
Sheep

Bideford

Abbotsham

East-the-Wat

Milford
Philham

Woodtown

Yeo
Vale

Elmscott

Buck's
Cross

A39

Milky Way

11

Goldworthy

Littleham

Landcross

Saltrens

Woolfardisworthy

Cranford

Parkham

Parkham
Ash

Melbury

Cabbacott

Buckland
Brewer

Monkleigh

A386

Frithelstock

Hardisworthy

South
Hole

Welcombe

Ashmansworthy

East
Putford

Thornehillhead

West
Putford

Frithelstock Stone

Taddipo

Southcott

Torr

Langtree

Lang
Wee

Mead

Darracott

Woolley

Meddon

East
Youlstone

Dinworthy

Colscott

Haytown

B3227

Gooseham

Eastcott

16

Morwenstow

Higher Sharpnose Point

Shop

*Killarney
Springs*

West-Youlstone

Bradworthy

Abbots
Bickington

Newton
St Petrock

Berr
Cros

Stibb
Cross

Peters Marland

*South West
Coast Path*

Lower Sharpnose Point

Steeple Point

Kilkhampton

Stibb

*Tamar
Lakes*

Darracott

Kimworthy

Sutcombe

Bulkworthy

A388

Venngreen

Milton
Damerel

Alfardisworthy

Sutcombemill

Soldon

River

Waldon

Shebbear

Buckland
Filleigh

She

*Sandy
Mouth*

A39

B3254

Thurdon

Soldon
Cross

Dunsdon

Holsworthy
Beacon

Thornbury

Brendon

Little
Lashbrook

Bradford

Priestacott

Hole

Dippermill

Black

*Northcott
Mouth*

Maer

Poughill

Venn

Hersham

Lana

Chilsworthy

Cookbury

Lashbrook

Holemoor

13

Bush

Flexbury

Stratton

Grimscott

Launcells

Launcells
Cross

Kingford

10

Pancrasweek

Anvil
Corner

Cookbury
Wick

Neet

Bude

Bude
Bay

Lynstone

Upton

A3072

Red Cross

Derril

Derriton

A3072

Holsworthy

A3072

Hollacombe

Brandis
Corner

Chilla

Odham

Helebridge

Buttsbear
Cross

Pyworthy

Whimble

Chasty

Marhamchurch

Bridgerule

Leworthy

R Claw

Widemouth
Bay

19

Box's Shop

Budd's
Titson

Halwill
Junction

Beaworthy

Halwill

Patchacott

A3079

Millook

Coppathorne

Kitleigh

Dizzard Point

Poundstock

Bangors

Dizzard

Penlean

Treskinnick
Cross

Whitstone

East
Balsdon

West Balsdon

Clawton

A388

Langaford

Patchacott

St
Gennys

Tregole

Hele

Penhallam

Boot

Stowford

Cambeak

ackington Haven

Coxford

Trencreek

Week
St Mary

North Tan**3**ton

Tetcott

Quoditch

Nethercott

Jacobstow

Sweets

Rosecare

Lana

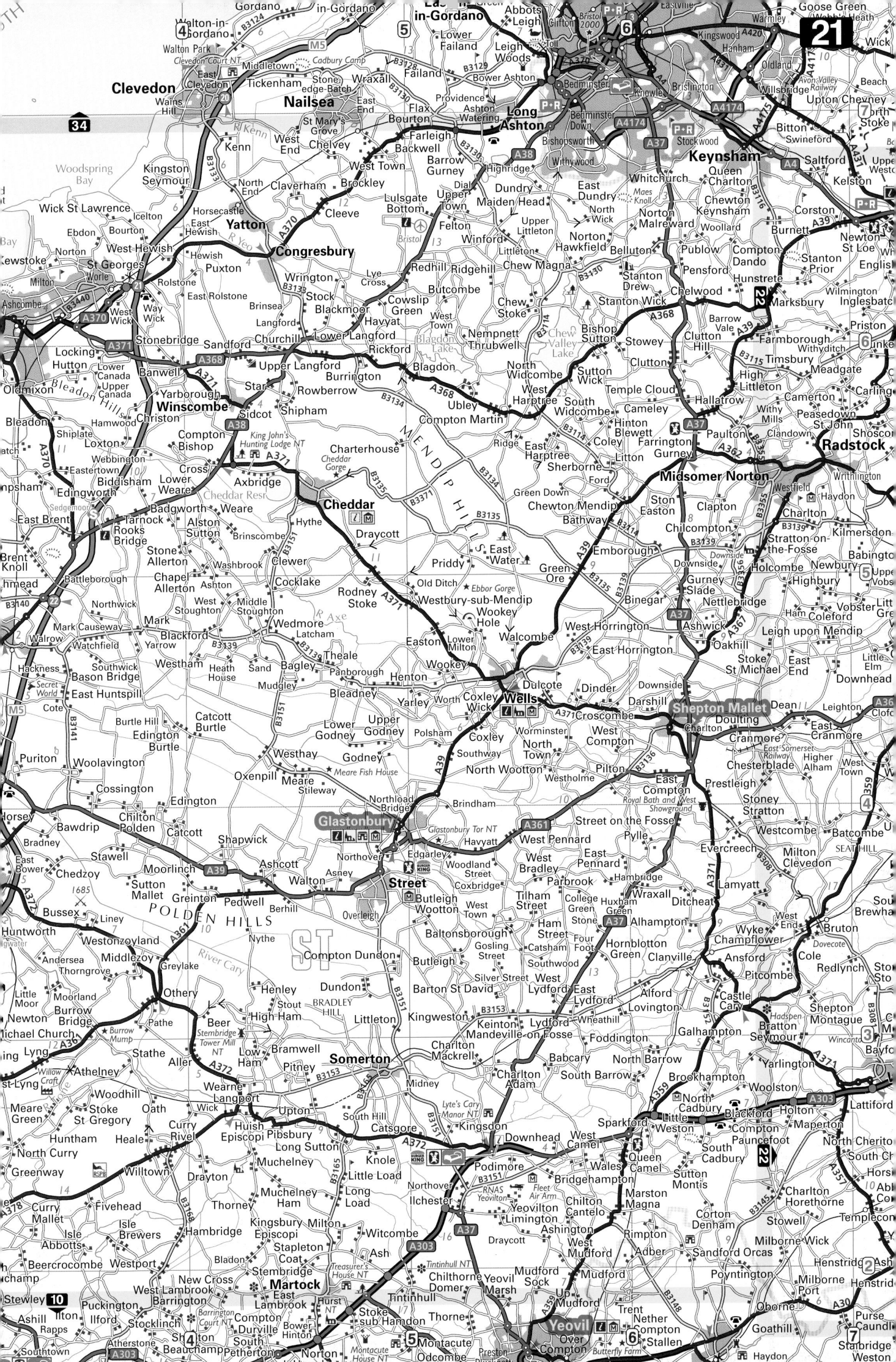

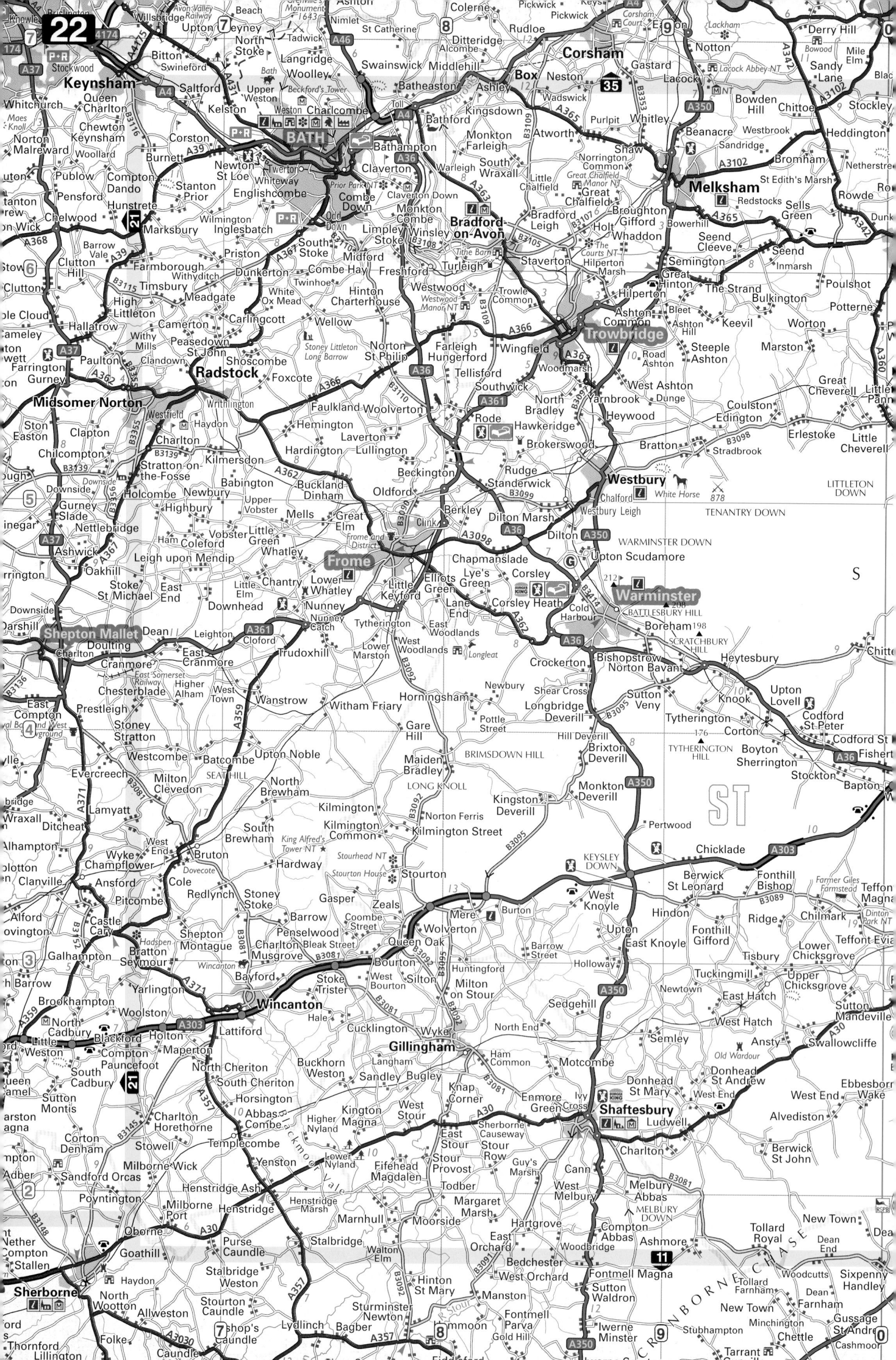

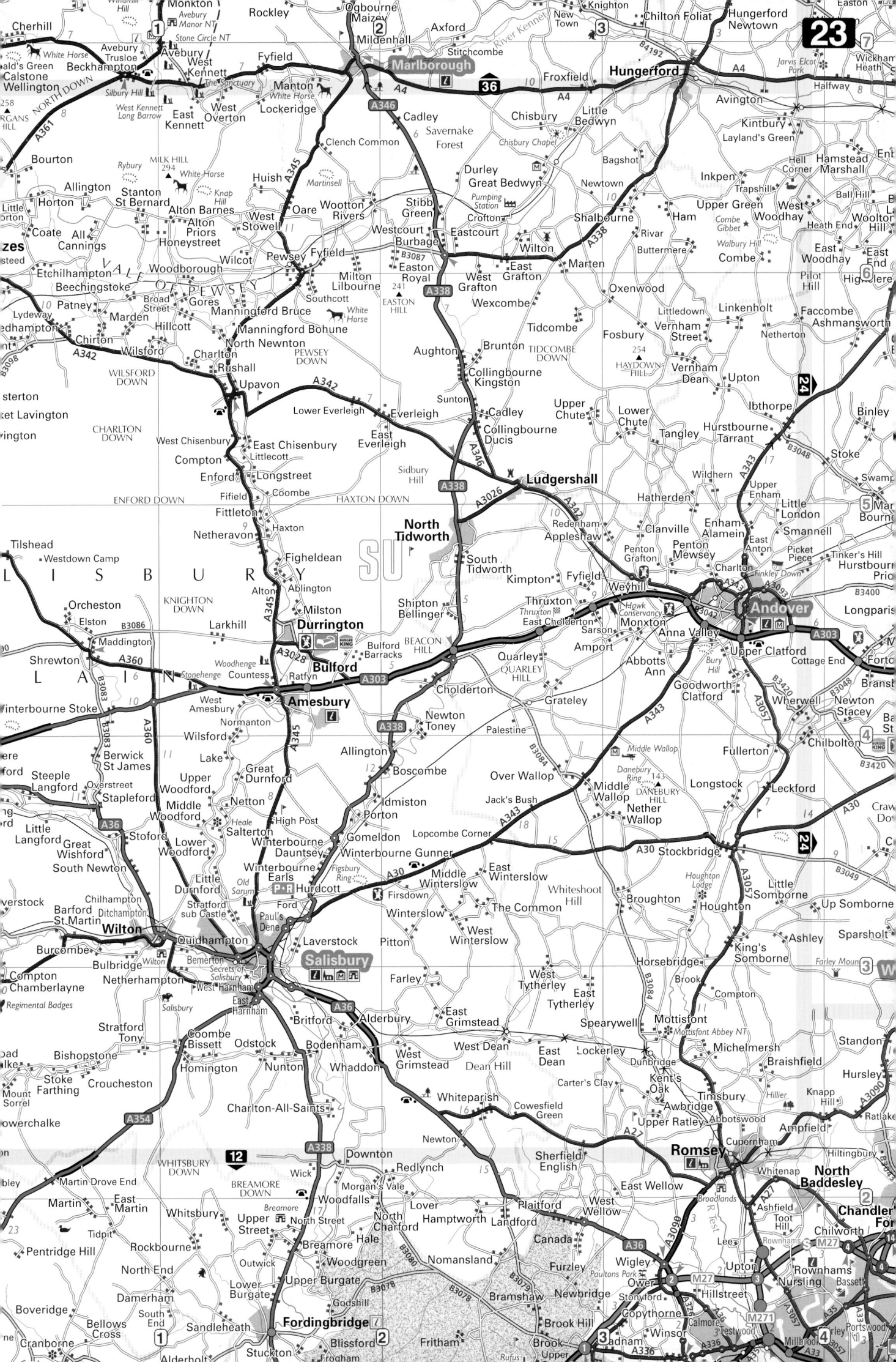

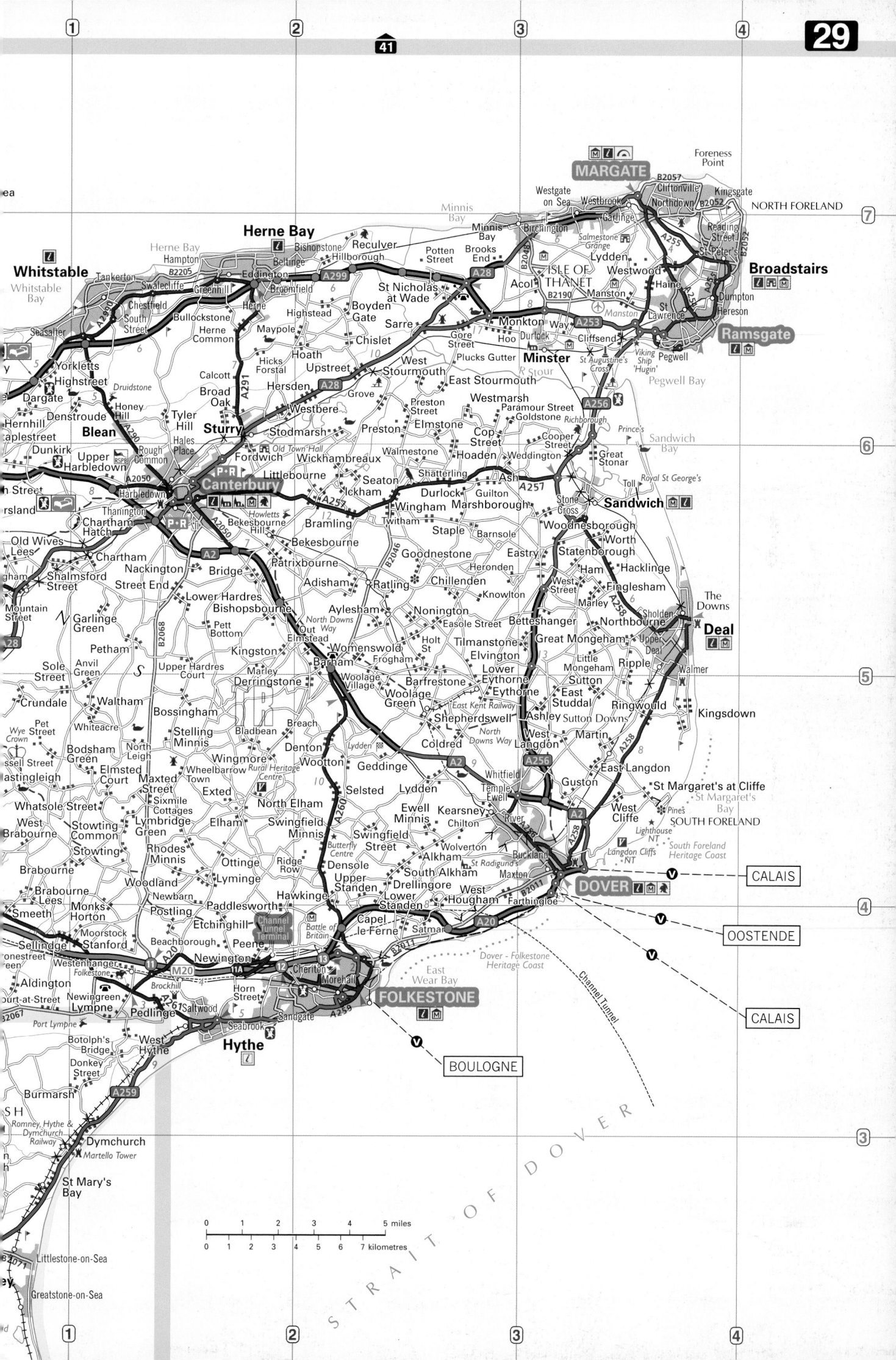

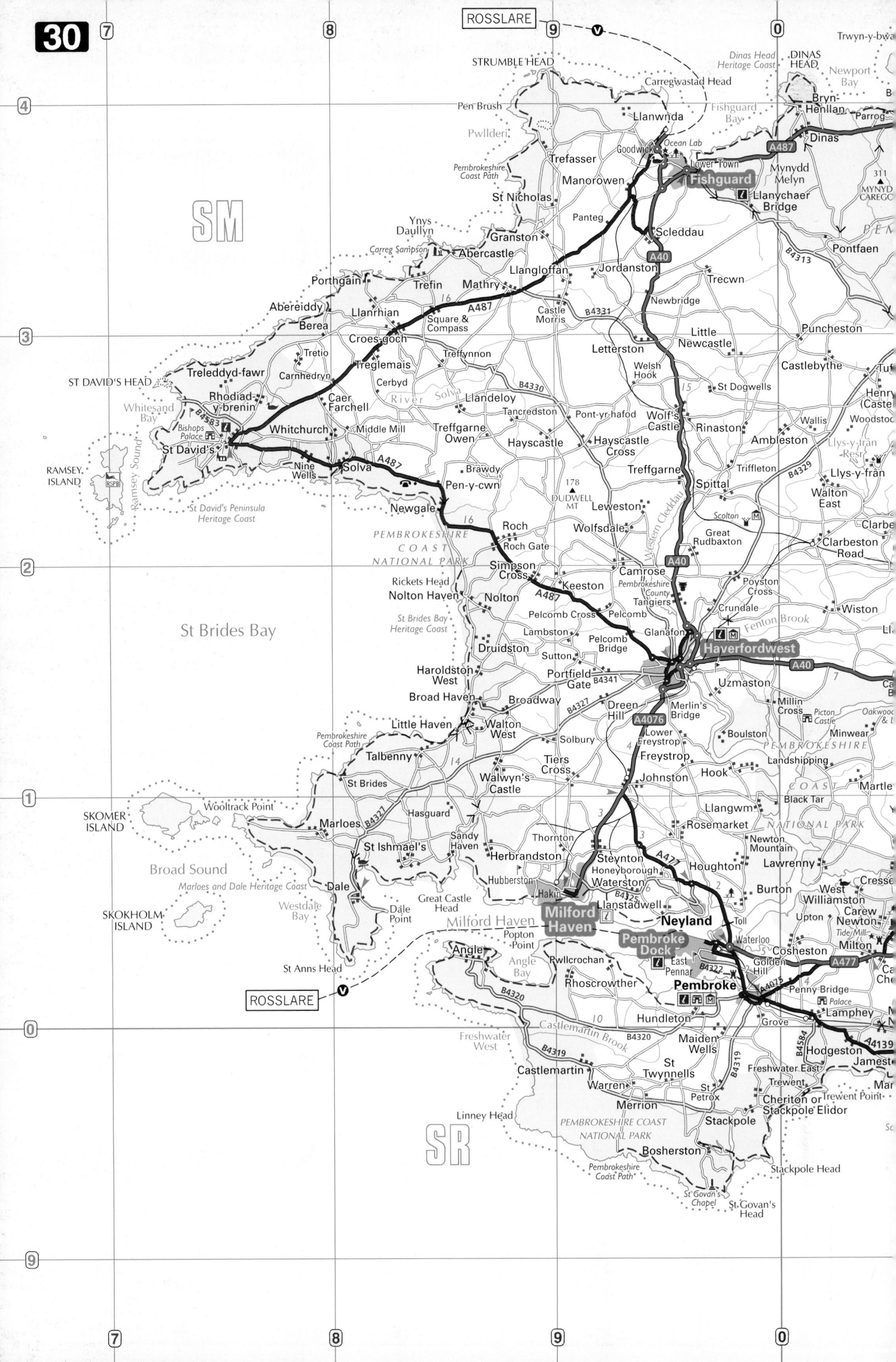

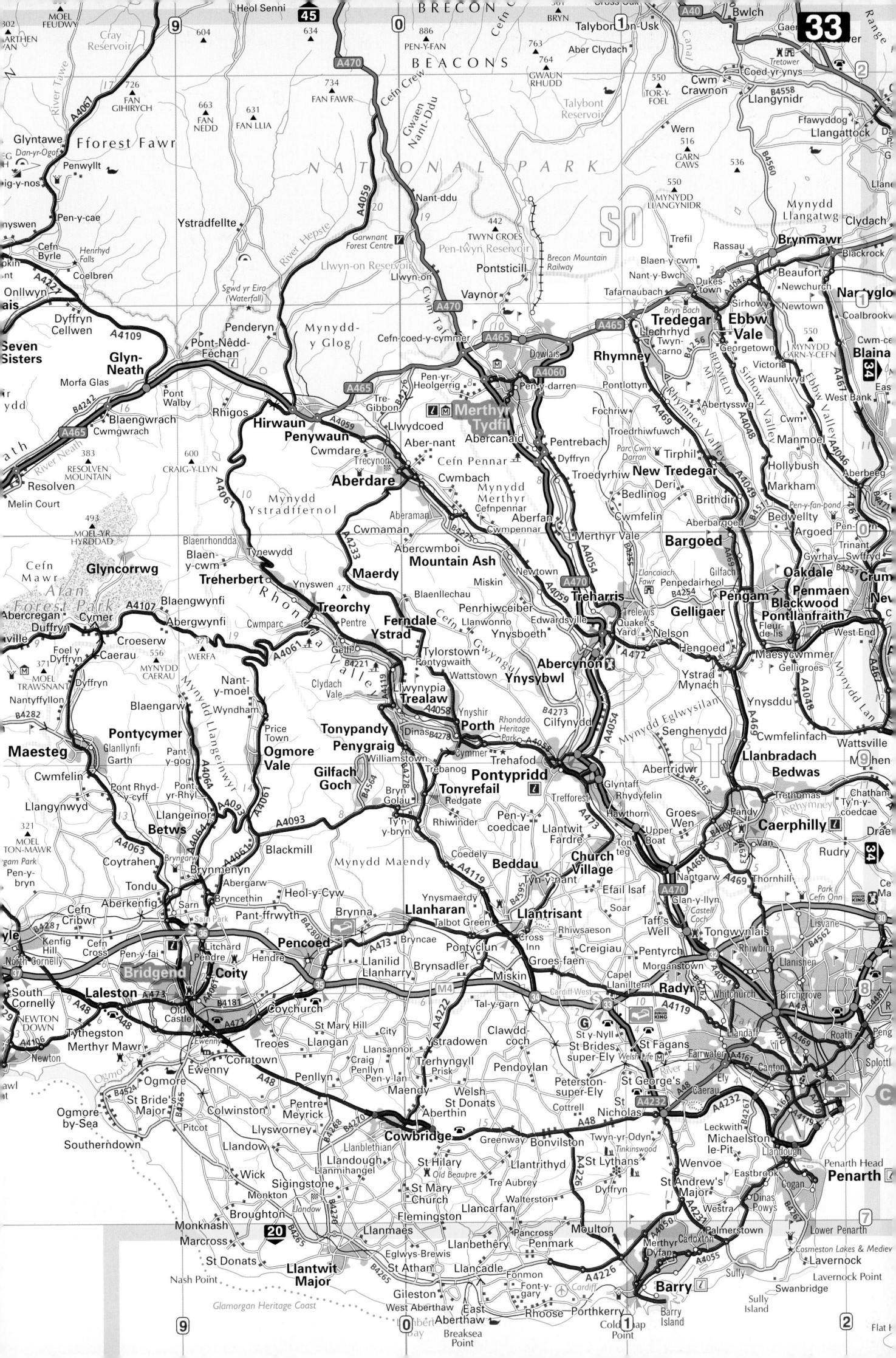

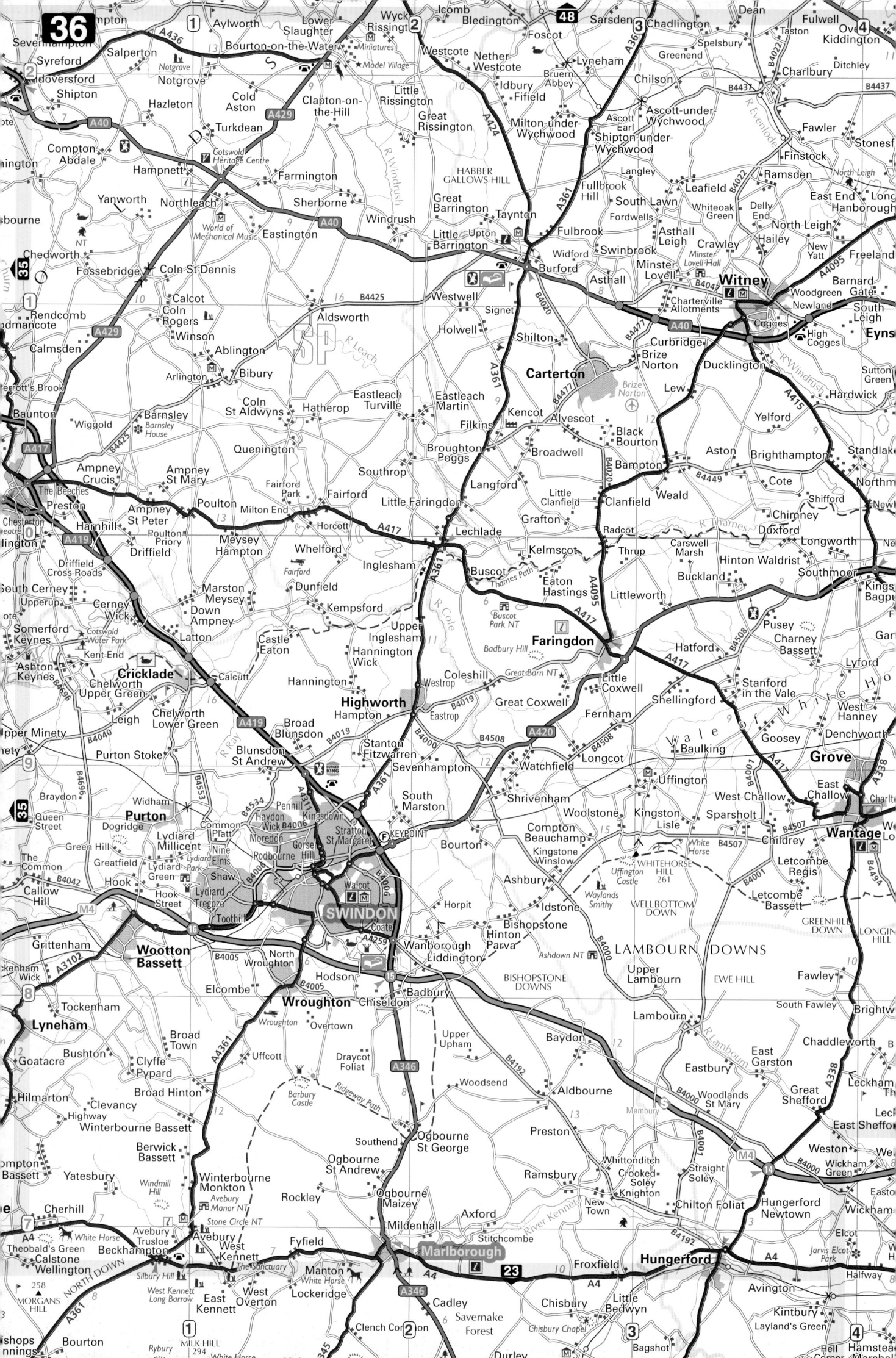

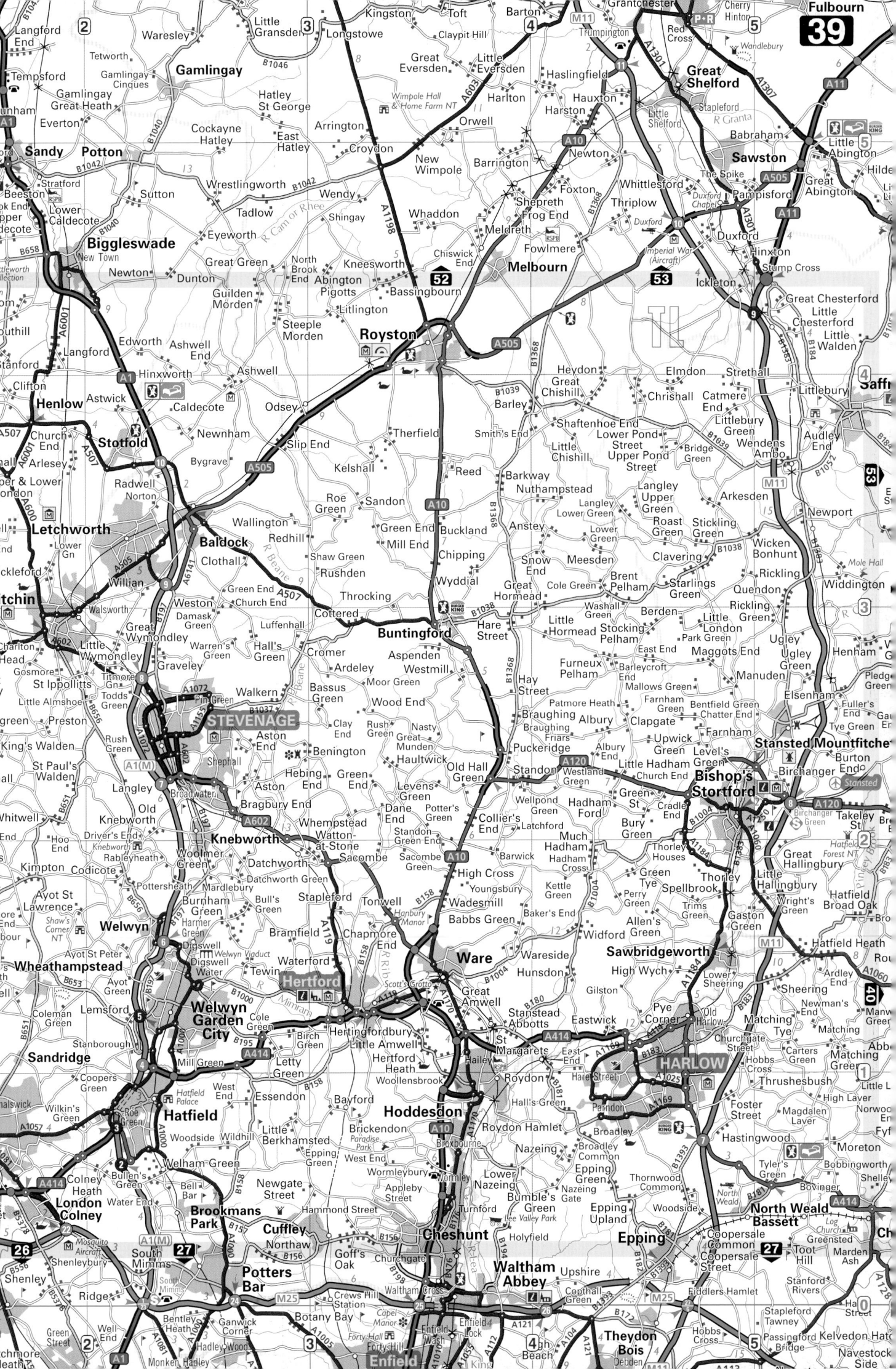

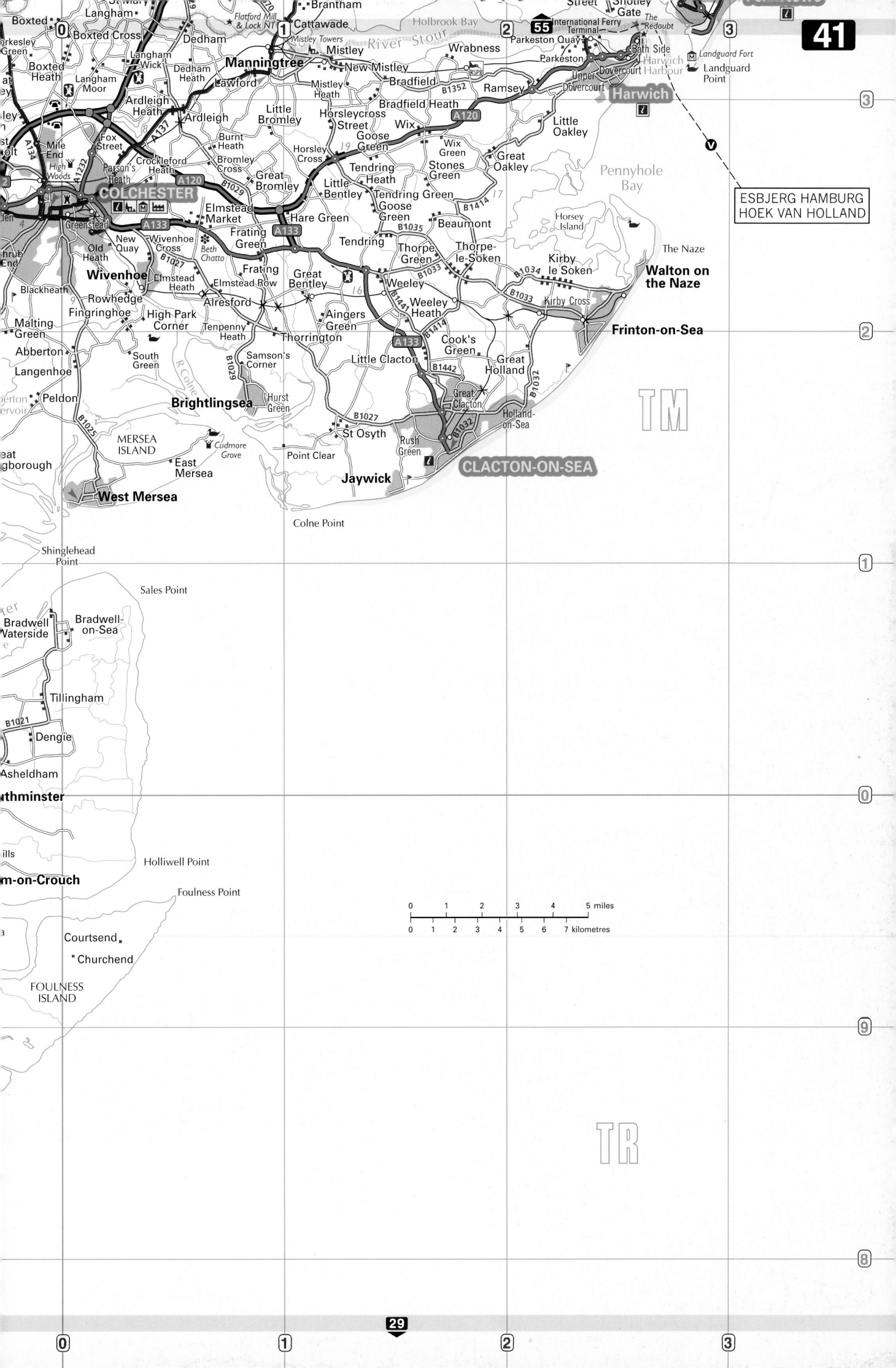

C A R D I G A N

B A Y

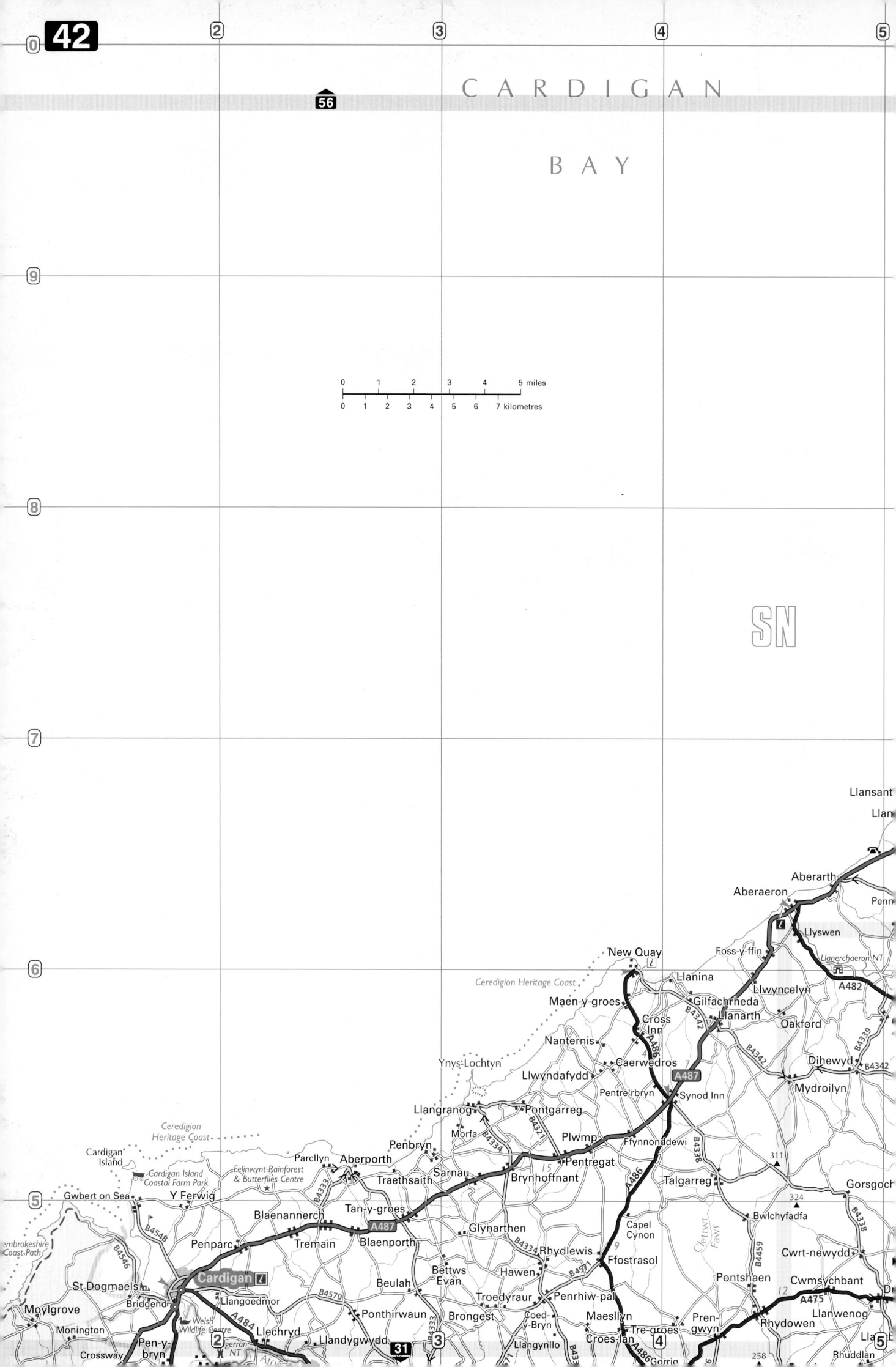

0   1   2   3   4   5 miles

0 1 2 3 4 5 6 7 kilometres

SN

Llansant

Llan

Aberarth

Aberaeron

Penn

Llyswen

New Quay

Foss-y-ffin

Llanerchaeron NT

A482

Ceredigion Heritage Coast

Llanina

Llwyncelyn

Maen-y-groes

Gilfachrheda

Oakford

Cross Inn

Llanarth

Nanternis

A486

B4342

A487

Ynys-Lochtyn

Caerwedros   7

Dihewyd

B4342

Llwyndafydd

Pentre'rbryn

Synod Inn

Mydroilyn

A487

Llangranog

Pontgarreg

Plwmp

Ffynnonddewi

B4338

Morfa

B4334

B4321

311

Penbryn

Pentregat

A486

Talgarreg

Gorsgoch

Parcllyn

Aberporth

Sarnau

15

Brynhoffnant

324

Ceredigion Heritage Coast

Cardigan Island

Felinwynt Rainforest & Butterflies Centre

Bwlchyfadfa

B4338

Cardigan Island Coastal Farm Park

B4332

Traethsaith

Glynarthen

Capel Cynon

Gwbert on Sea

Y Ferwig

Tan-y-groes

A487

B4334

Rhydlewis

Cwrt-newydd

Blaenannerch

A486

B4459

Pembrokeshire Coast Path

Penparc

Tremain

Blaenporth

Ffostrasol

Pontshaen

B4546

B4548

Cwmsychbant

St Dogmaels

Cardigan

Bettws Evan

Hawen

B4571

9

Prengwyn

A475

Llanwenog

Bridgend

Llangoedmor

Beulah

Troedyraur

Penrhiw-pal

Rhydowen

Lla

Moylgrove

Welsh Wildlife Centre

B4570

Brongest

Coed-y-Bryn

Maesllyn

Tre-groes

258

Rhuddlan

Monington

A484

Ponthirwaun

Croes-lan

A486

Pen-y-bryn

Llechryd

Llandygwydd

Llangynllo

Crossway

Gorrig

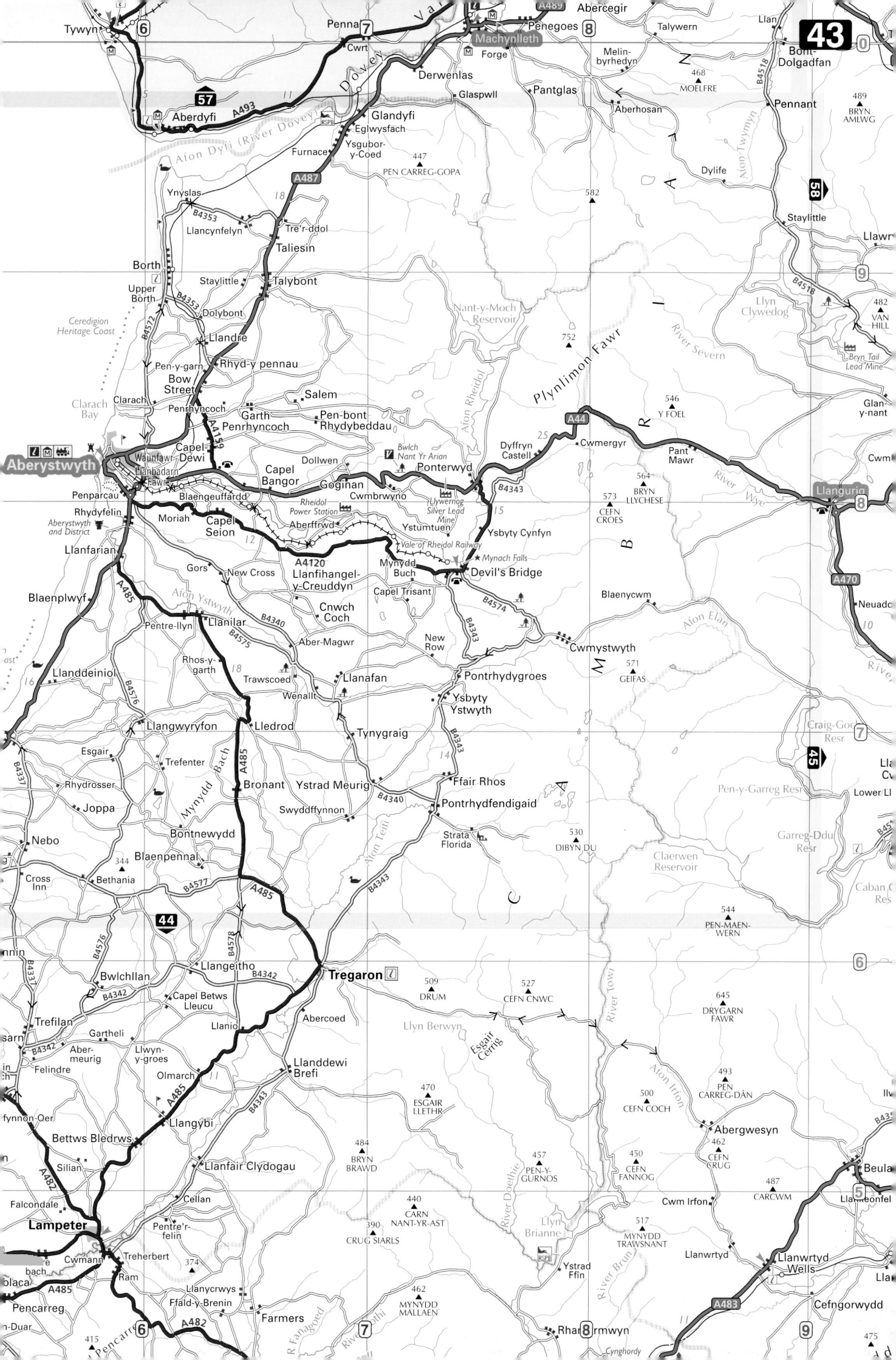

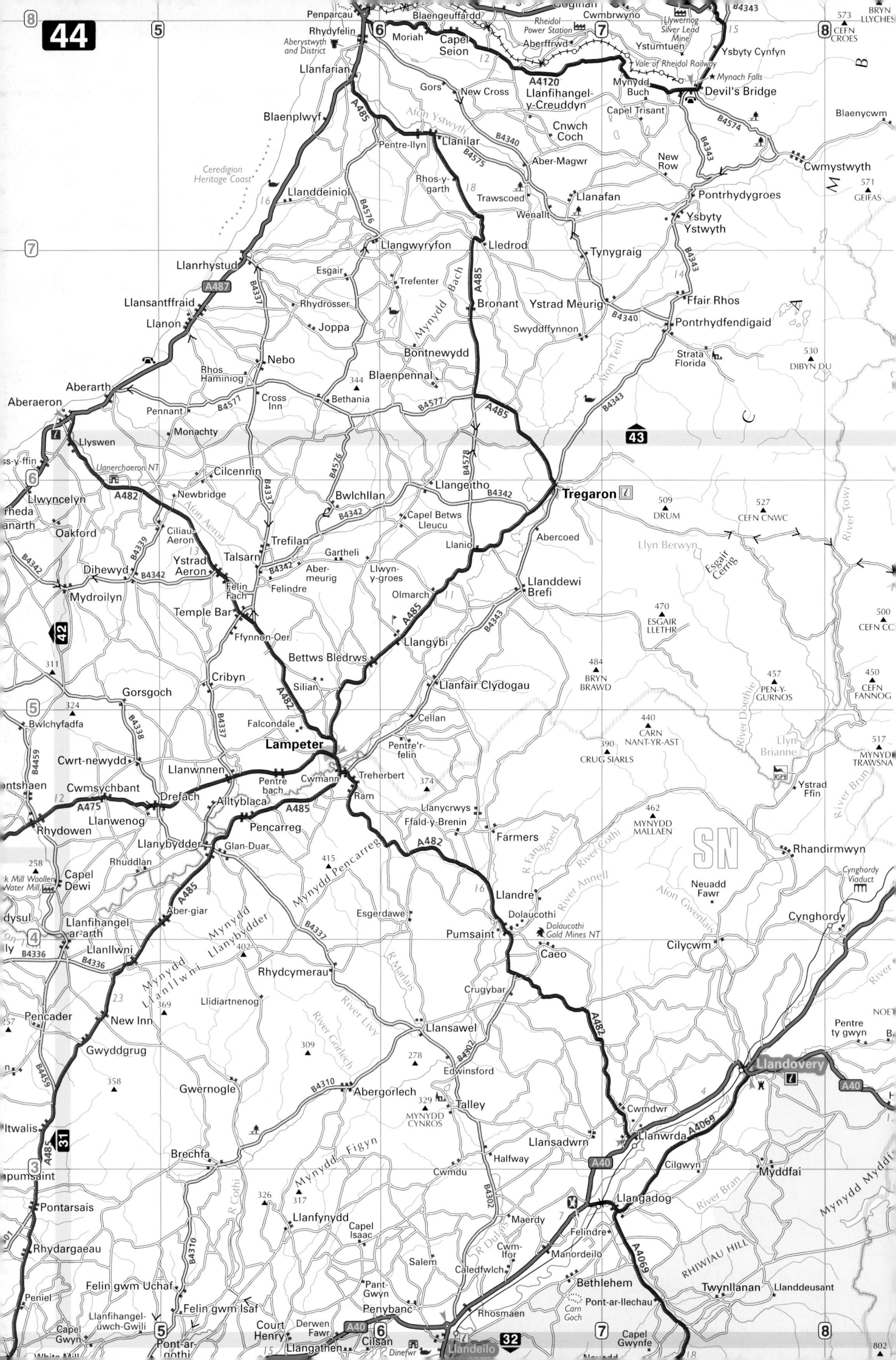

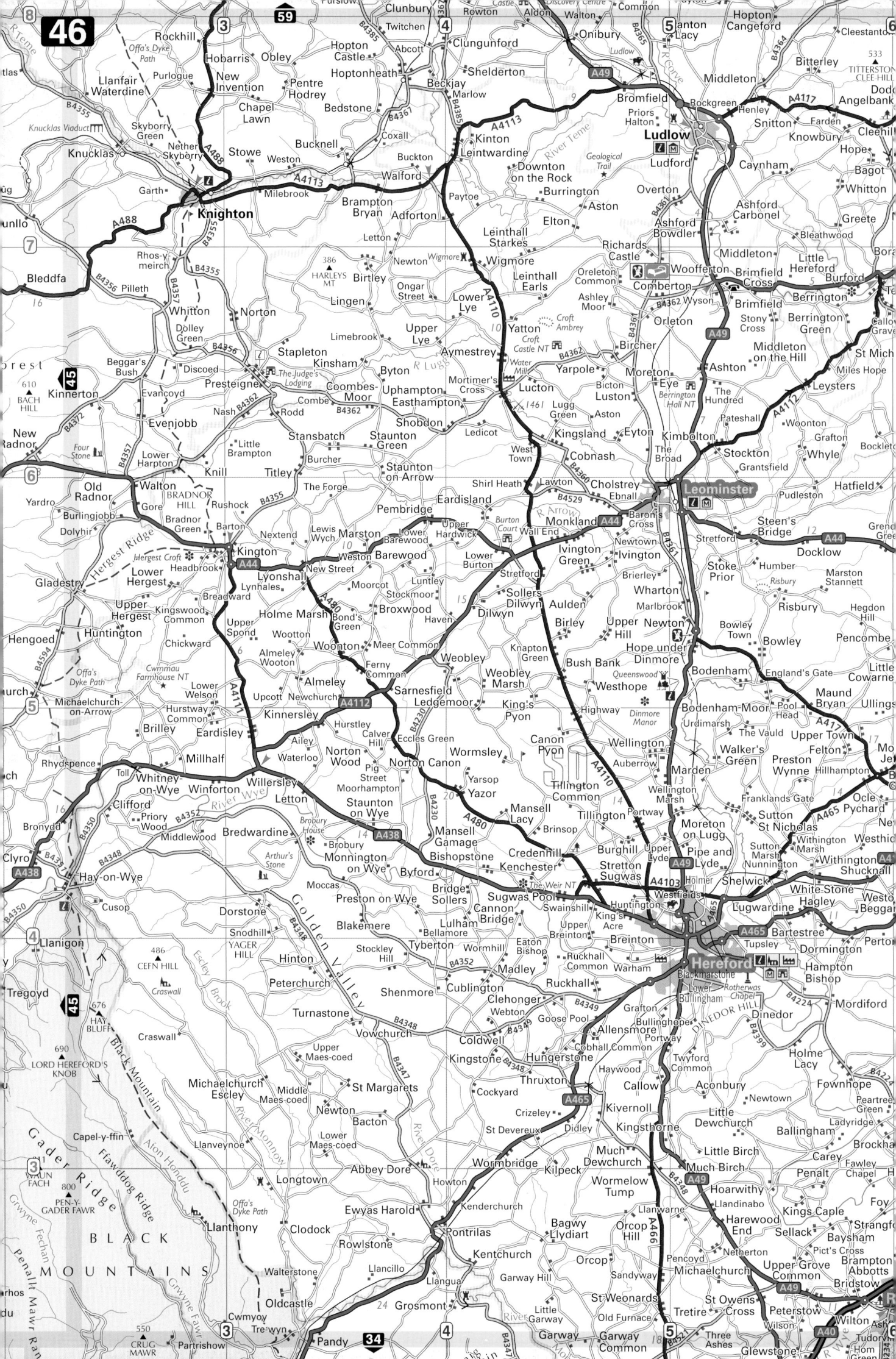

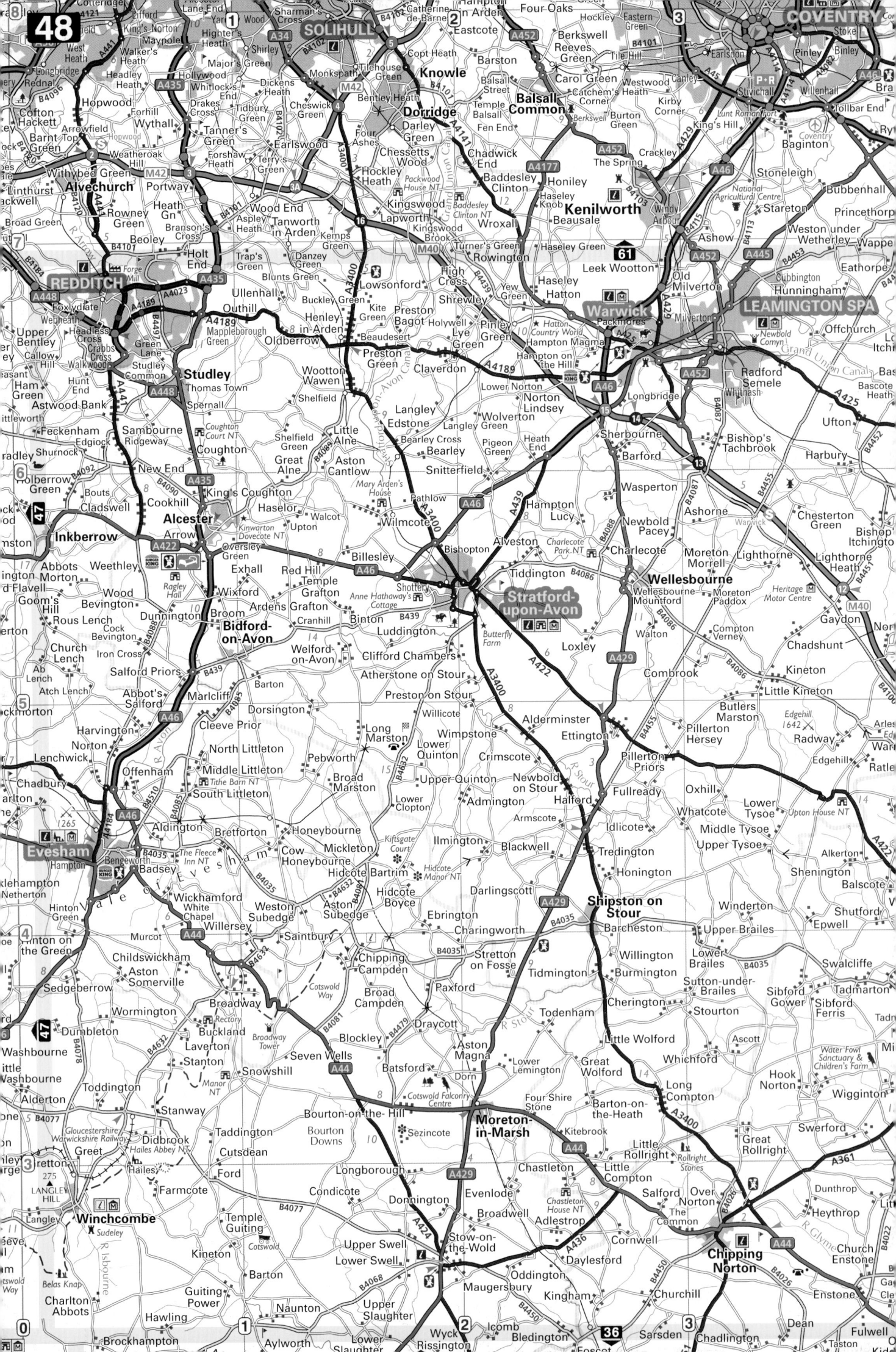

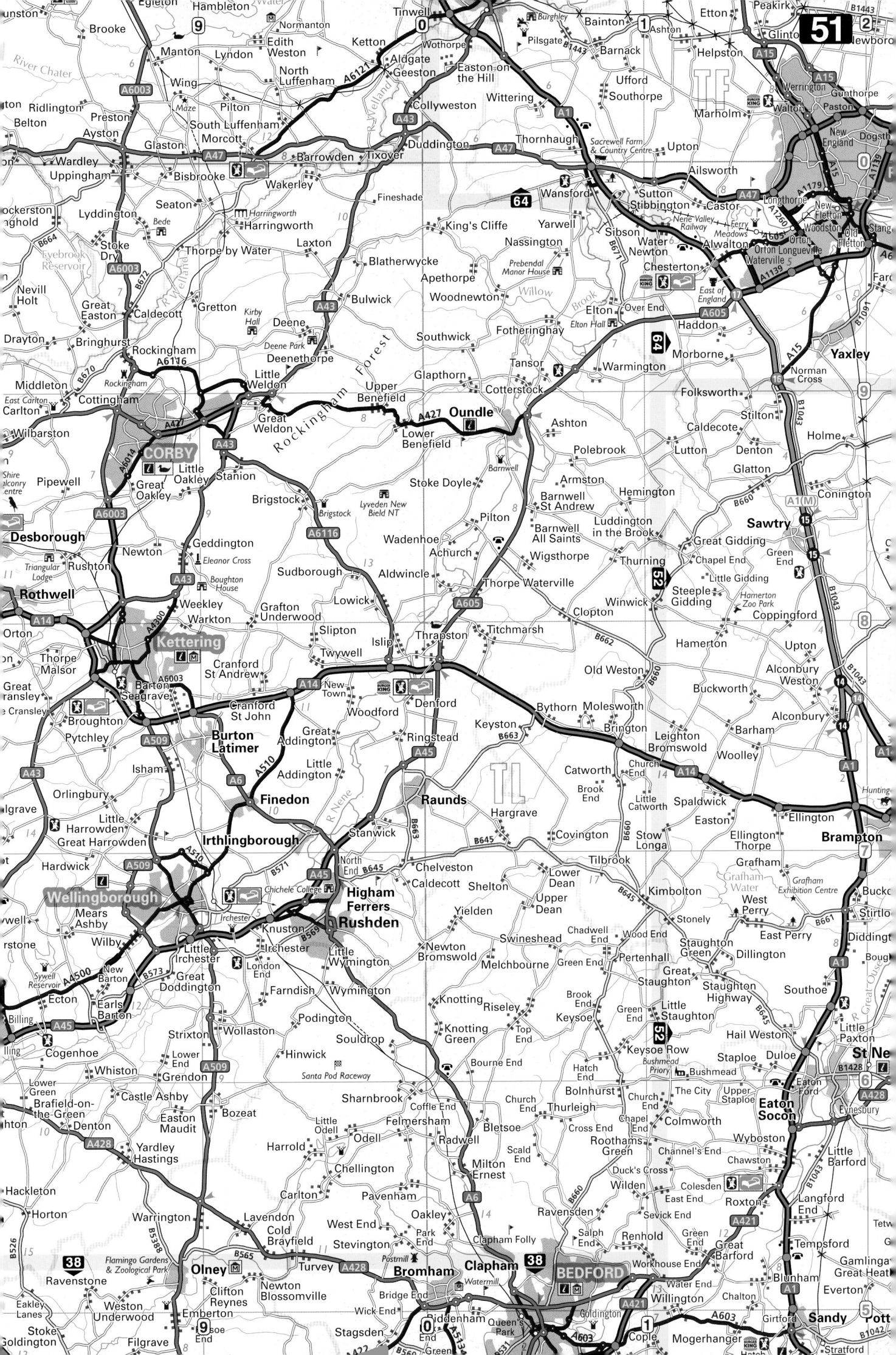

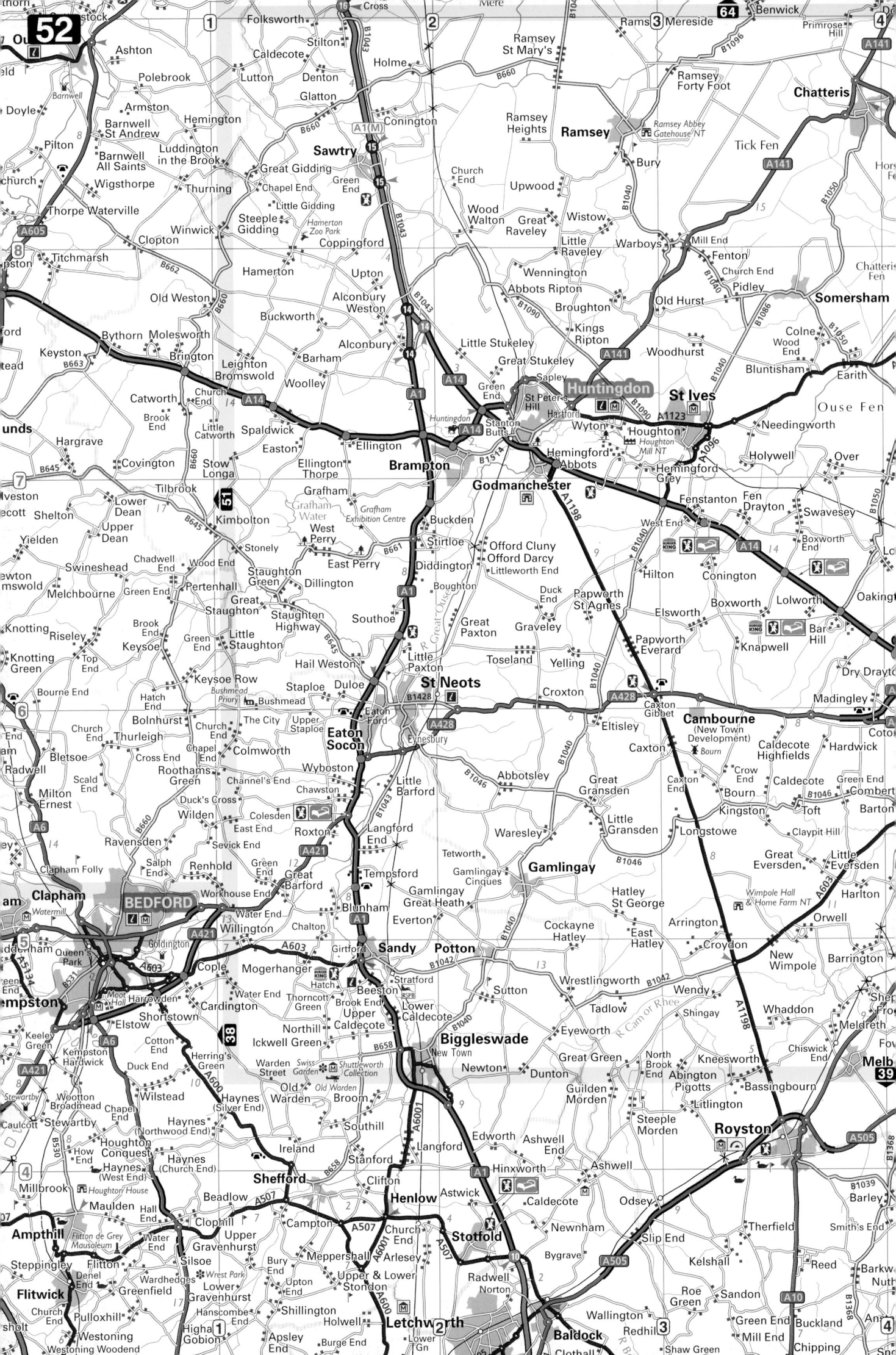

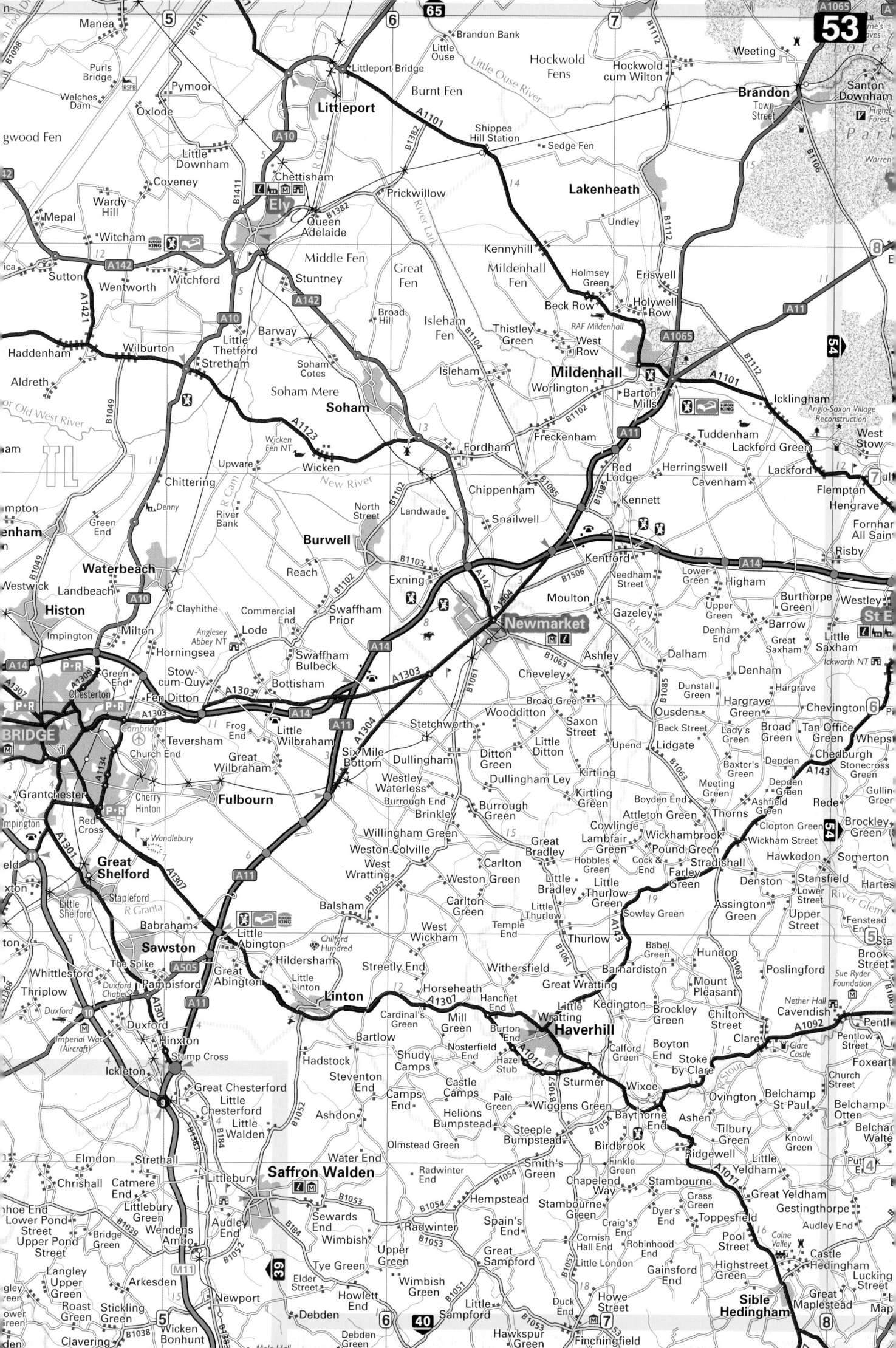

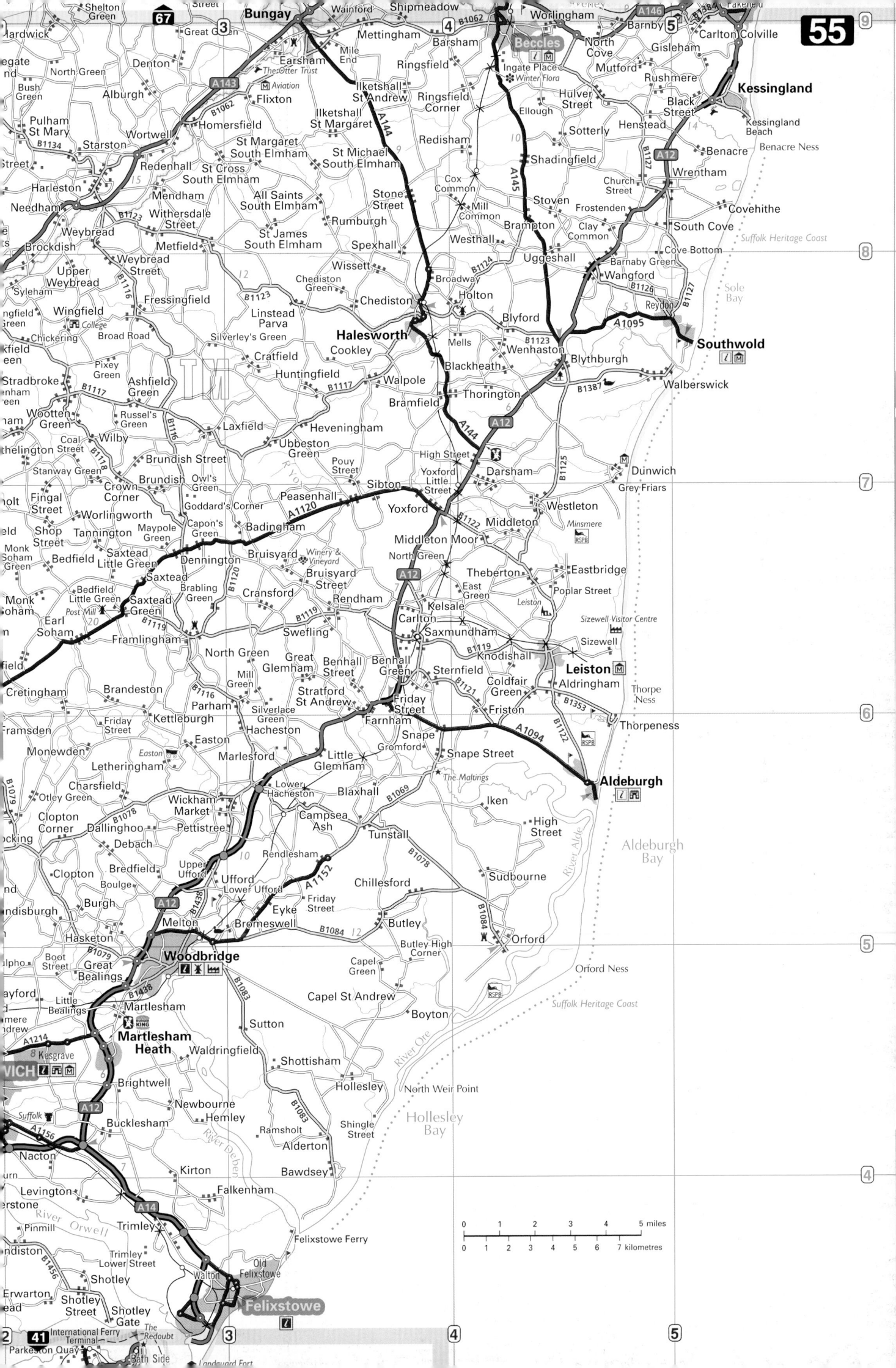

68

Aberdesach
Fontuyrni
Llanlly
Neb
Nasare

Clynnog-fawr
Capeluchaf

Gyrn-gôch
Pant
Glas

Y GYRN-DDU
522
Upper
Clynnog

Trefor
Tre'r Ceiri
19

Lleyn Heritage
Coast
YR EIFL
564
Llanaelhaearn
A487

Trwyn y
Grolech
B4417
20
21
Bryncir
Glan-Dwyfach

Llithfaen
PENINSULA
St Cybi's
Well

Carreg Ddu
Porth
Nefyn
Pistyll
A499
Pencaenewydd
Llangybi
Rhoslan
B4411

Morfa
Nefyn
Nefyn
Llwyndyrys
Y Ffor
Llanarmon
Llanystumdwy

Porth Dinllaen
Groesffordd
Edern
Bodfuan
A497
Fron
B4354
Rhos-fawr
B4354
Chwilog
13
M

Porth Ysgaden
Rhos-y-llan
Tudweiloig
Llandudwen
LLEYN
Llannor
Abererch
Pennarth Fawr
R Erch

Porth
Colman
Dinas
371
Carn
Fadrum
Garn
A497
Efailnewydd
Denio
Pen-ychain

Pen-y-graig
B4417
14
Bryn-
mawr
Llaniestyn
B4415
Rhyd-y-clafdy
Penrhos
A499
Pwllheli

Llangwnnadl
Meyllteyrn
Sarn
Botwnnog
B4413
17
Nanhoron
B4413
Mynytho
Llanbedrog

Porthor
Rhydlios
Rhoshirwaun
Bryncroes
Llandegwning
Trwyn Llanbedrog

Anelog
B4413
Penycaerau
Plas-Yn-
Rhiw NT
Llangian
St Tudwal's
Road

Uwchmynydd
Aberdaron
Y Rhiw
Llanfaelrhys
Llanengan
Abersoch
SH

Bardsey Sound
Aberdaron
Bay
Porth
Ysgo
Porth Neigwl
Bwlchtocyn
Sarn-bach
Marchros
St Tudwal's
Island East

St Mary's
Lleyn Heritage
Coast
Porth
Geiriad
St Tudwal's
Island West

BARDSEY ISLAND

0   1   2   3   4   5 miles
0 1 2 3 4 5 6 7 kilometres

C A R D I G A N

42

B A Y

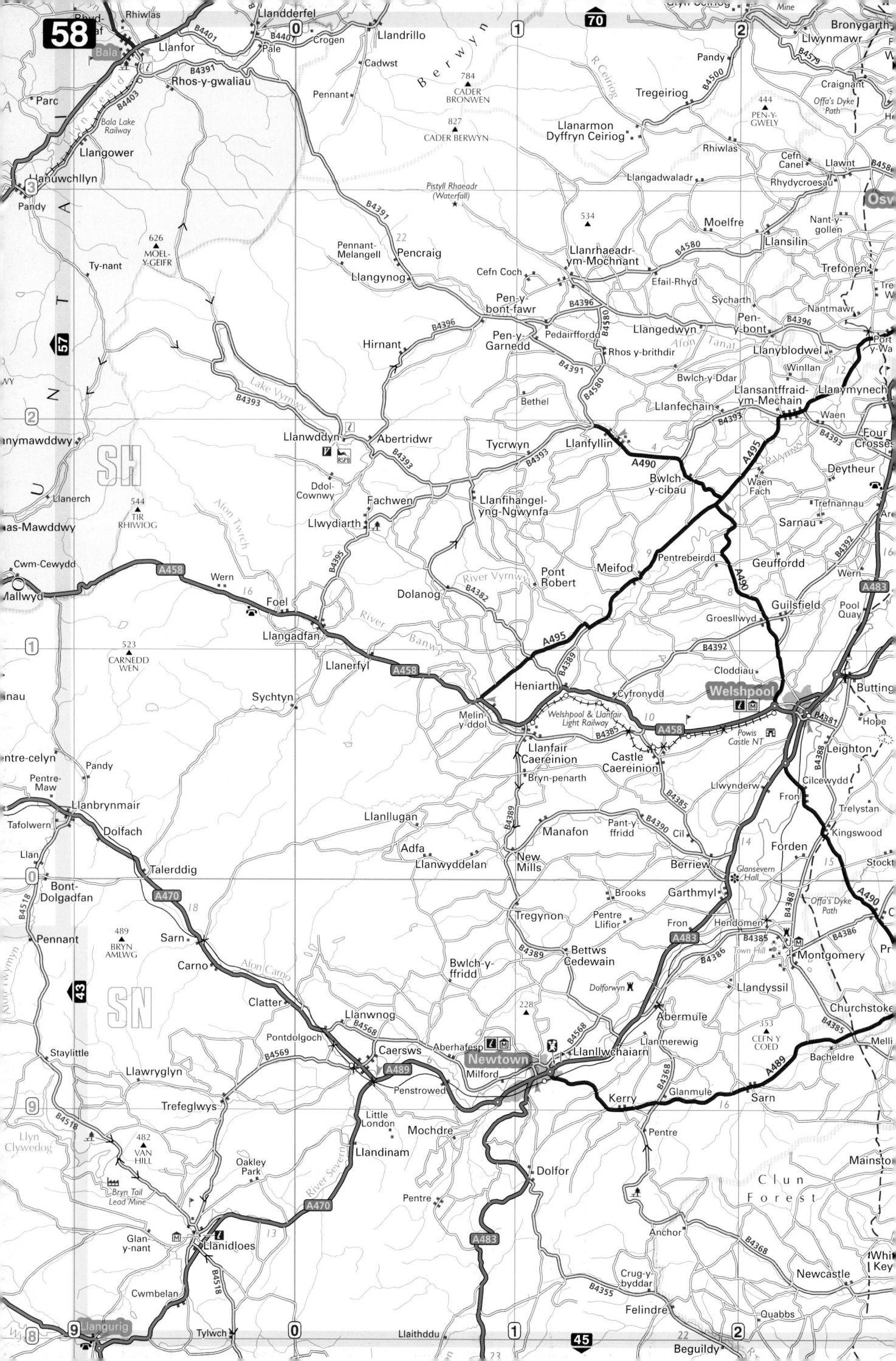

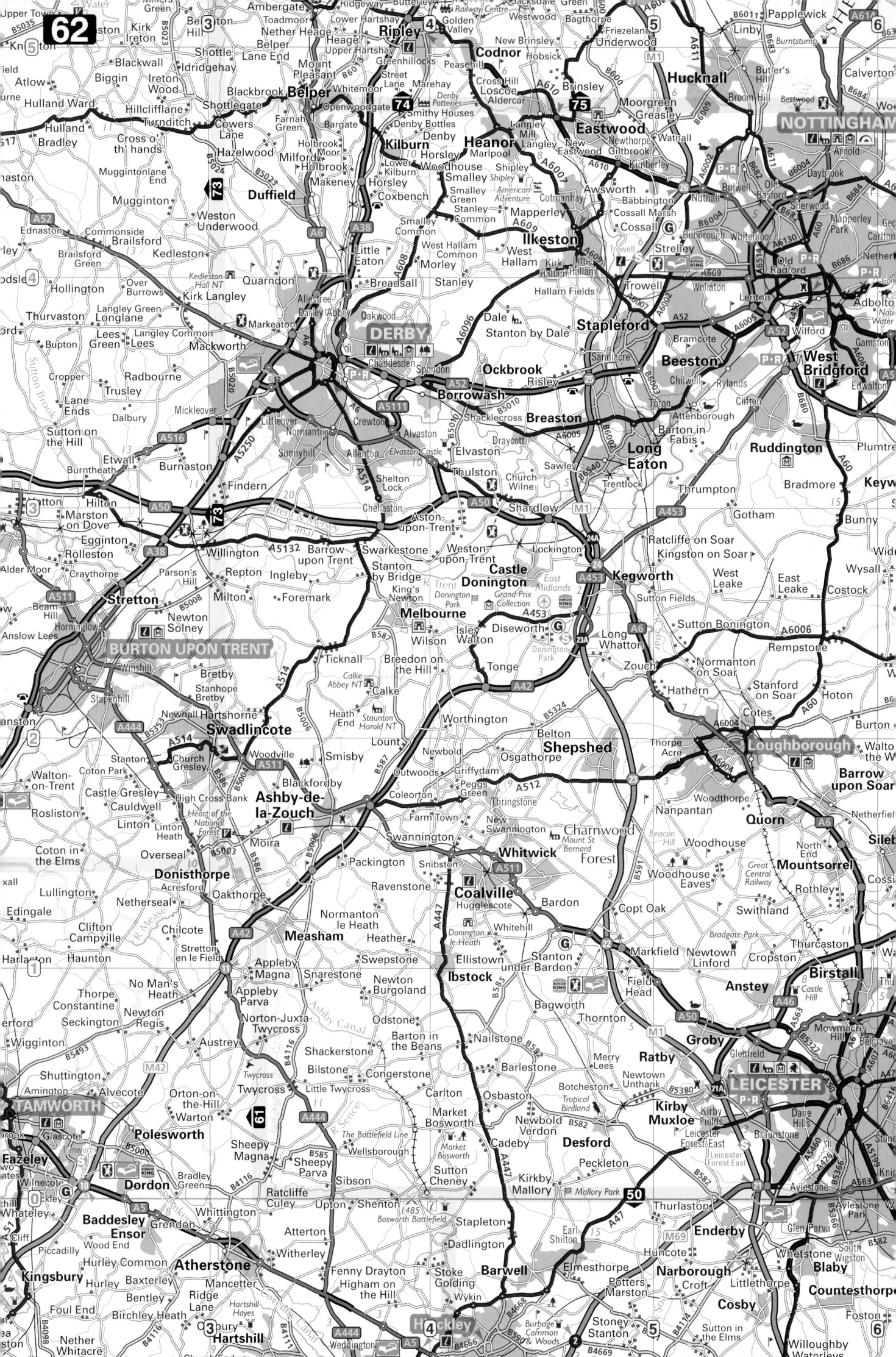

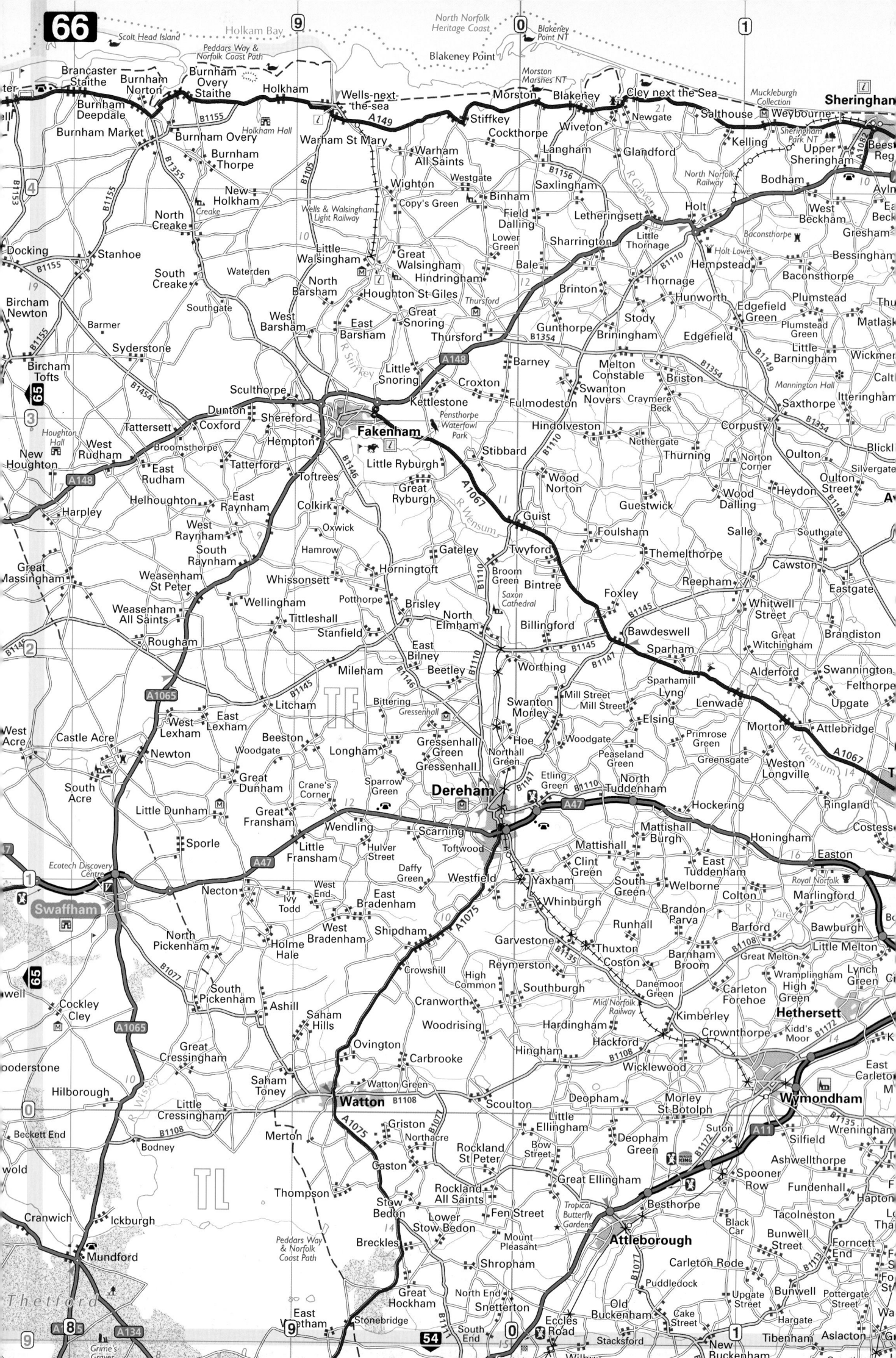

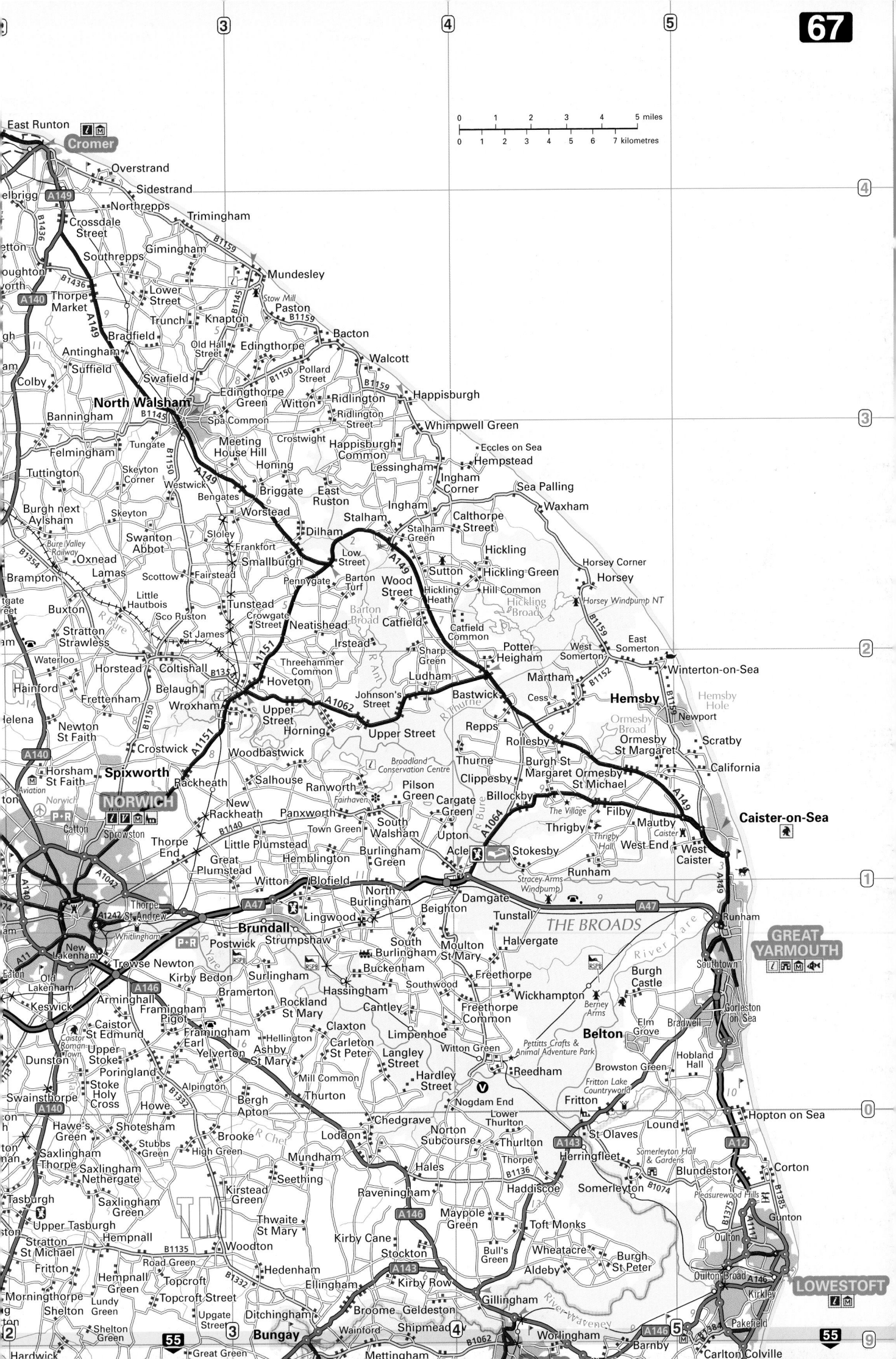

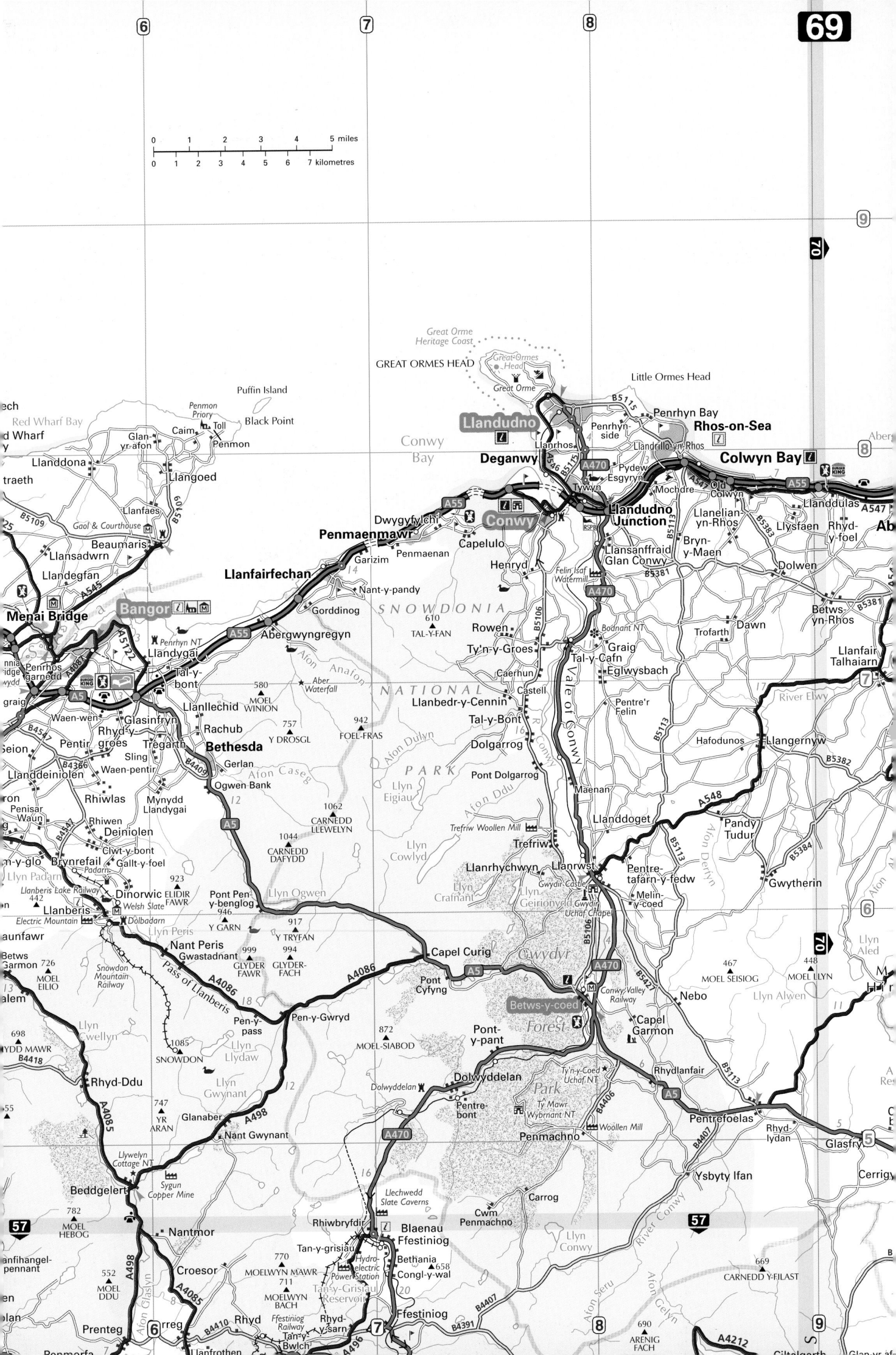

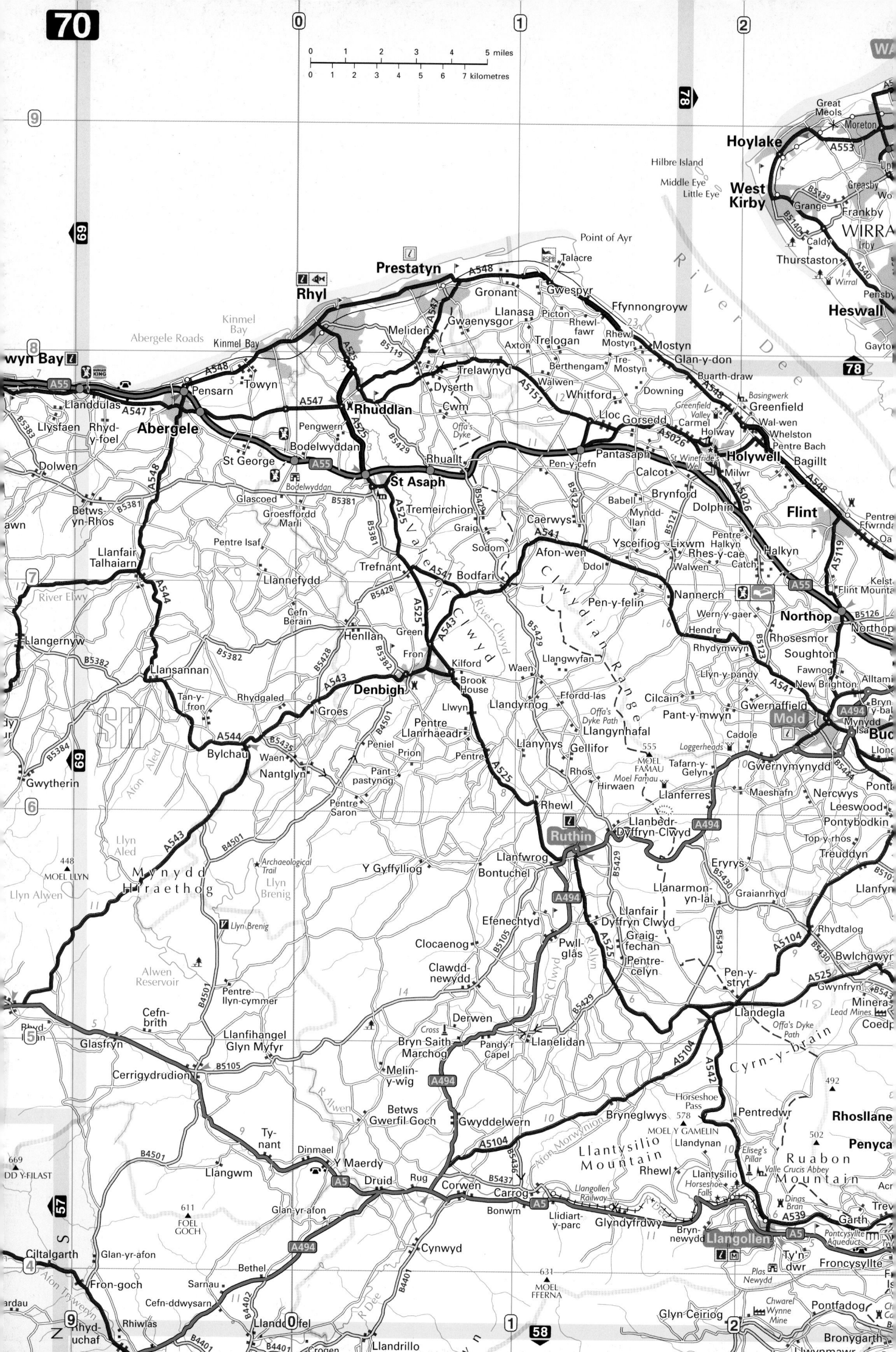

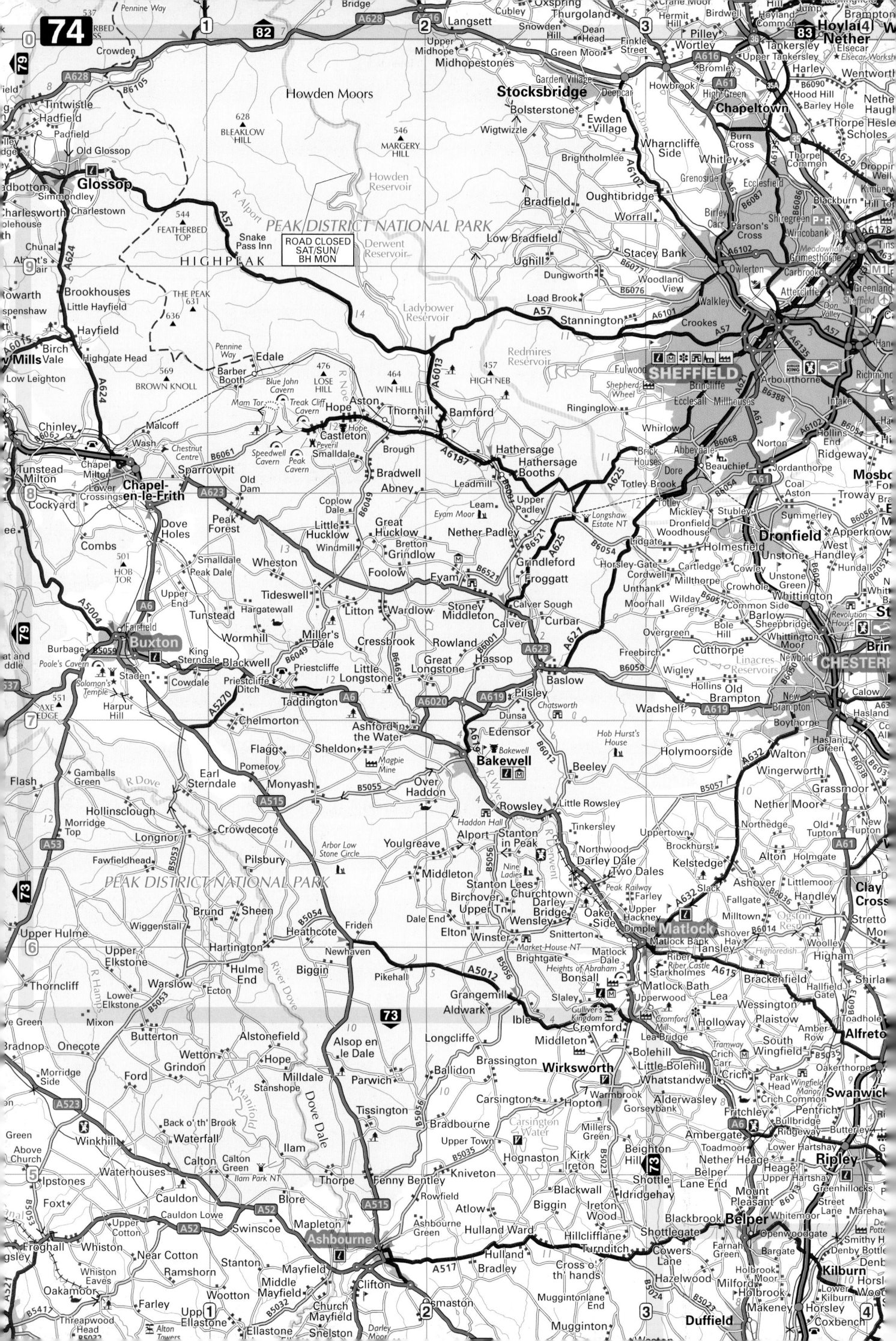

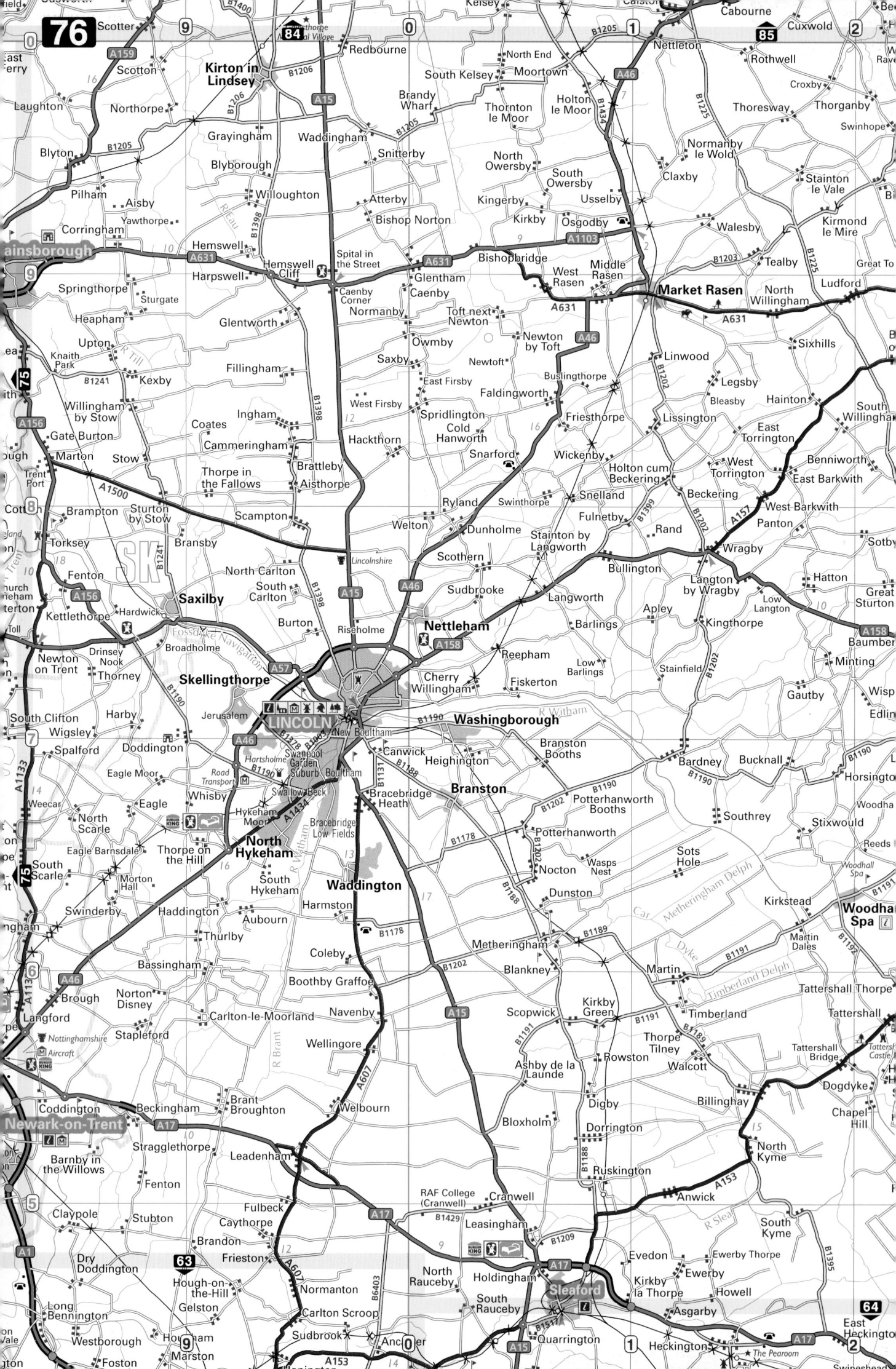

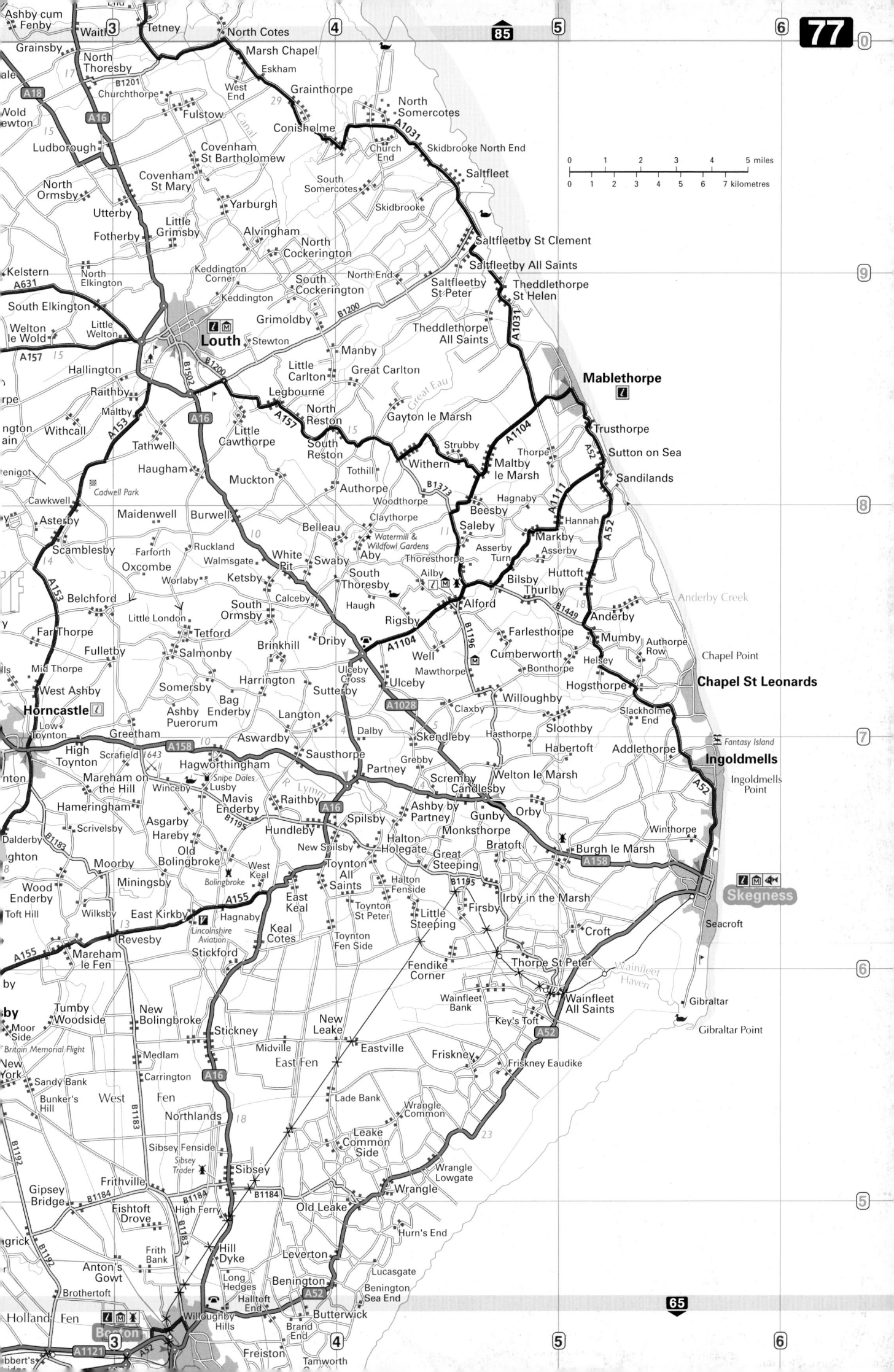

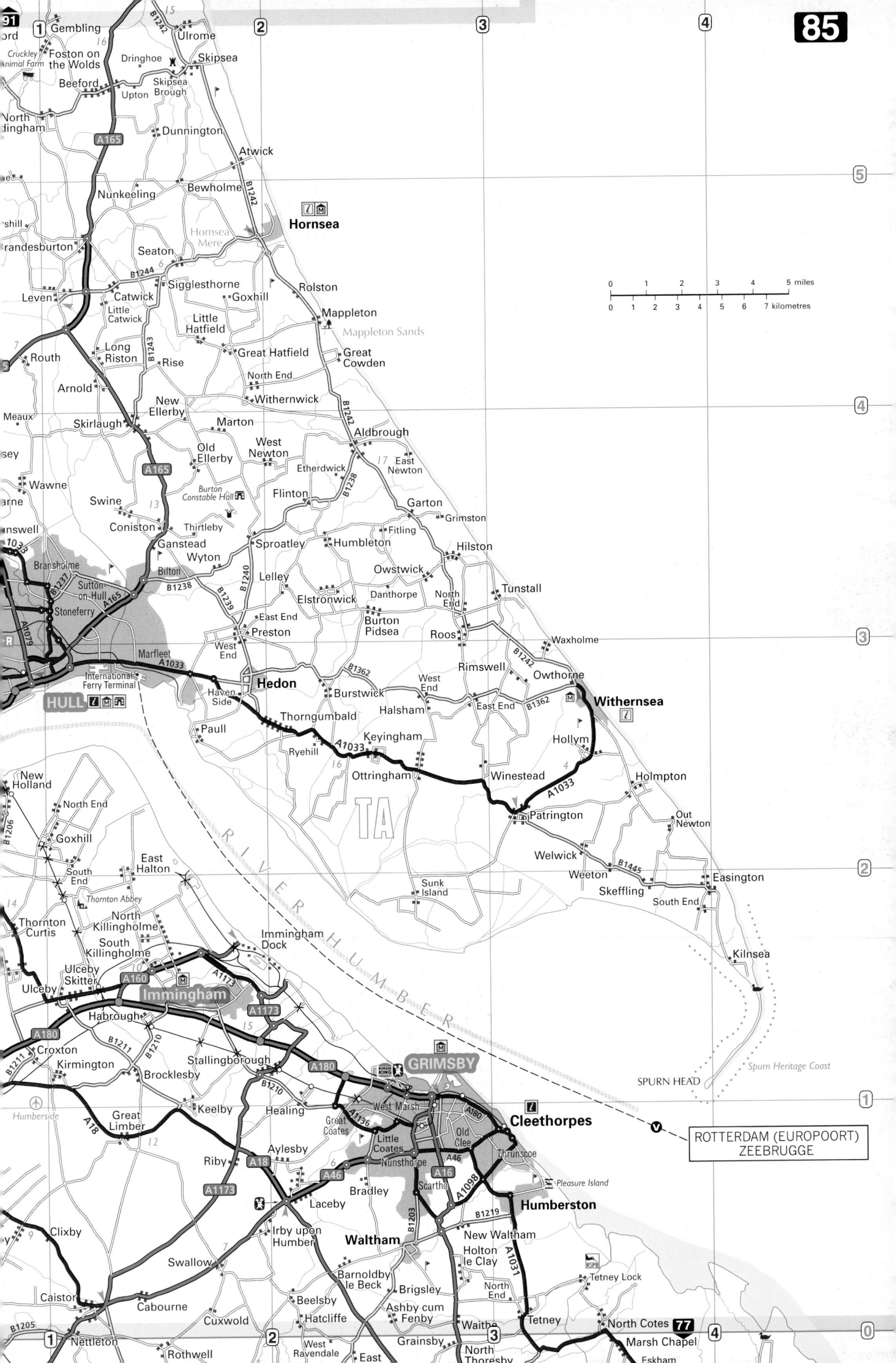

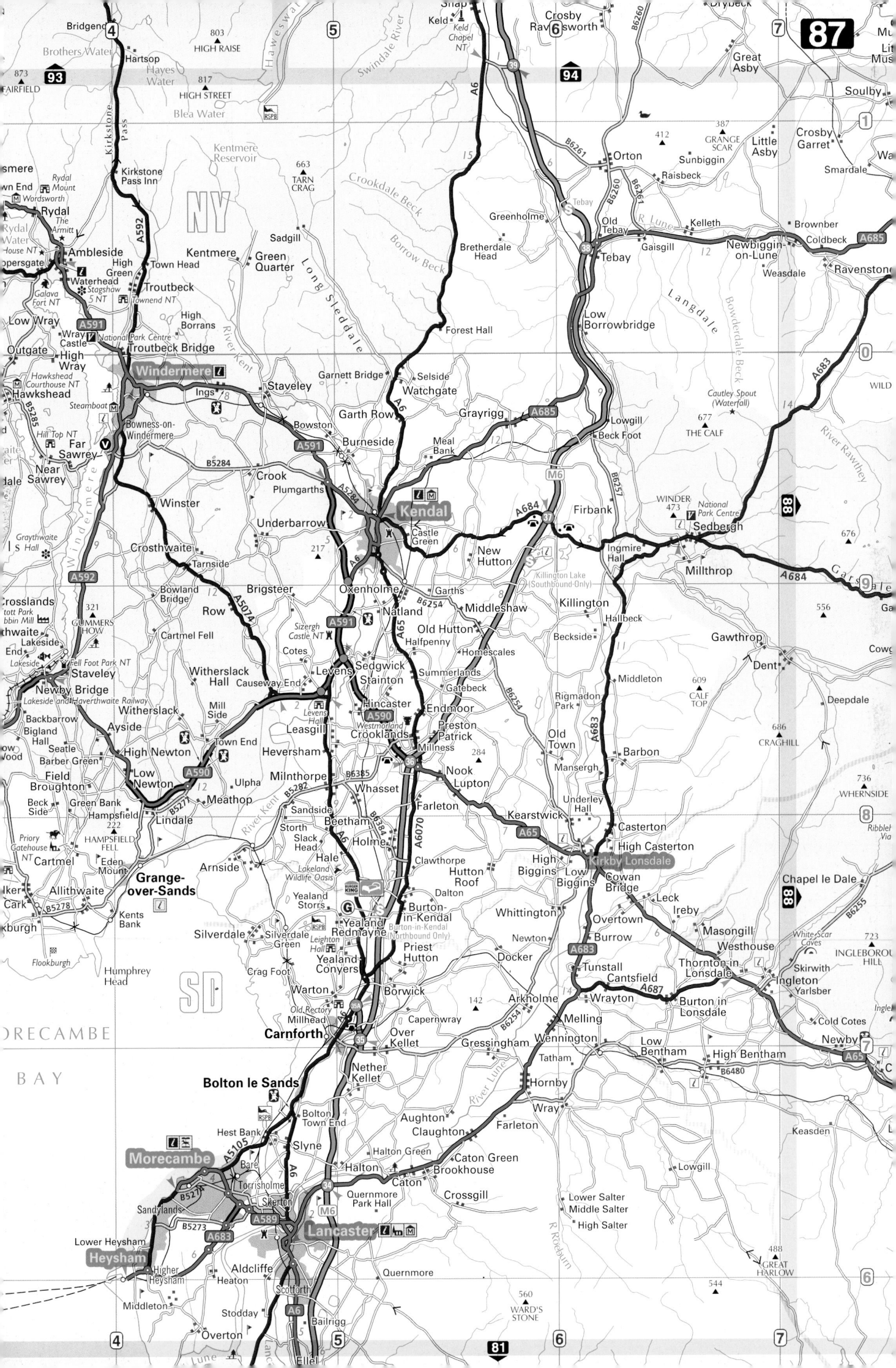

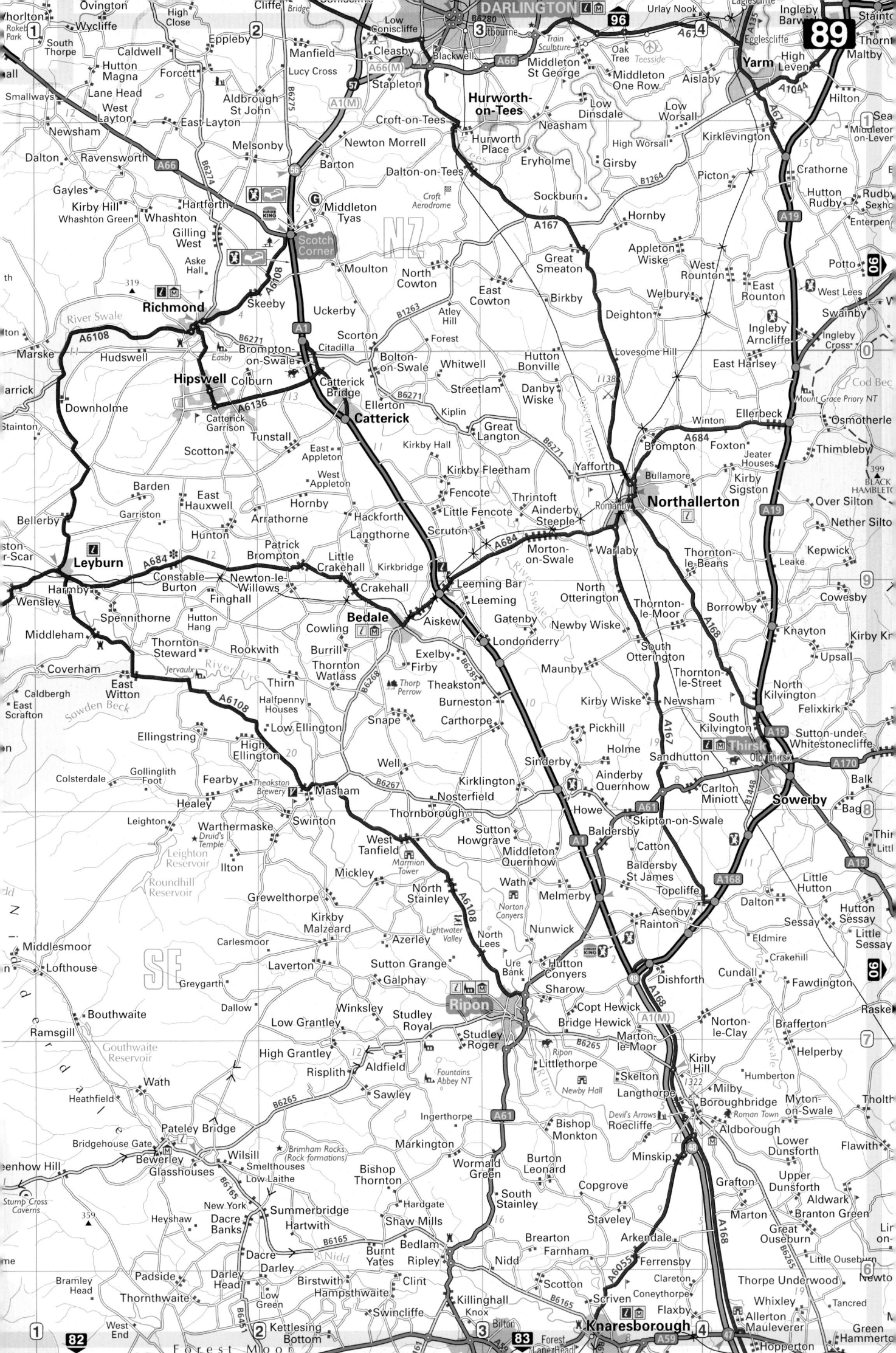

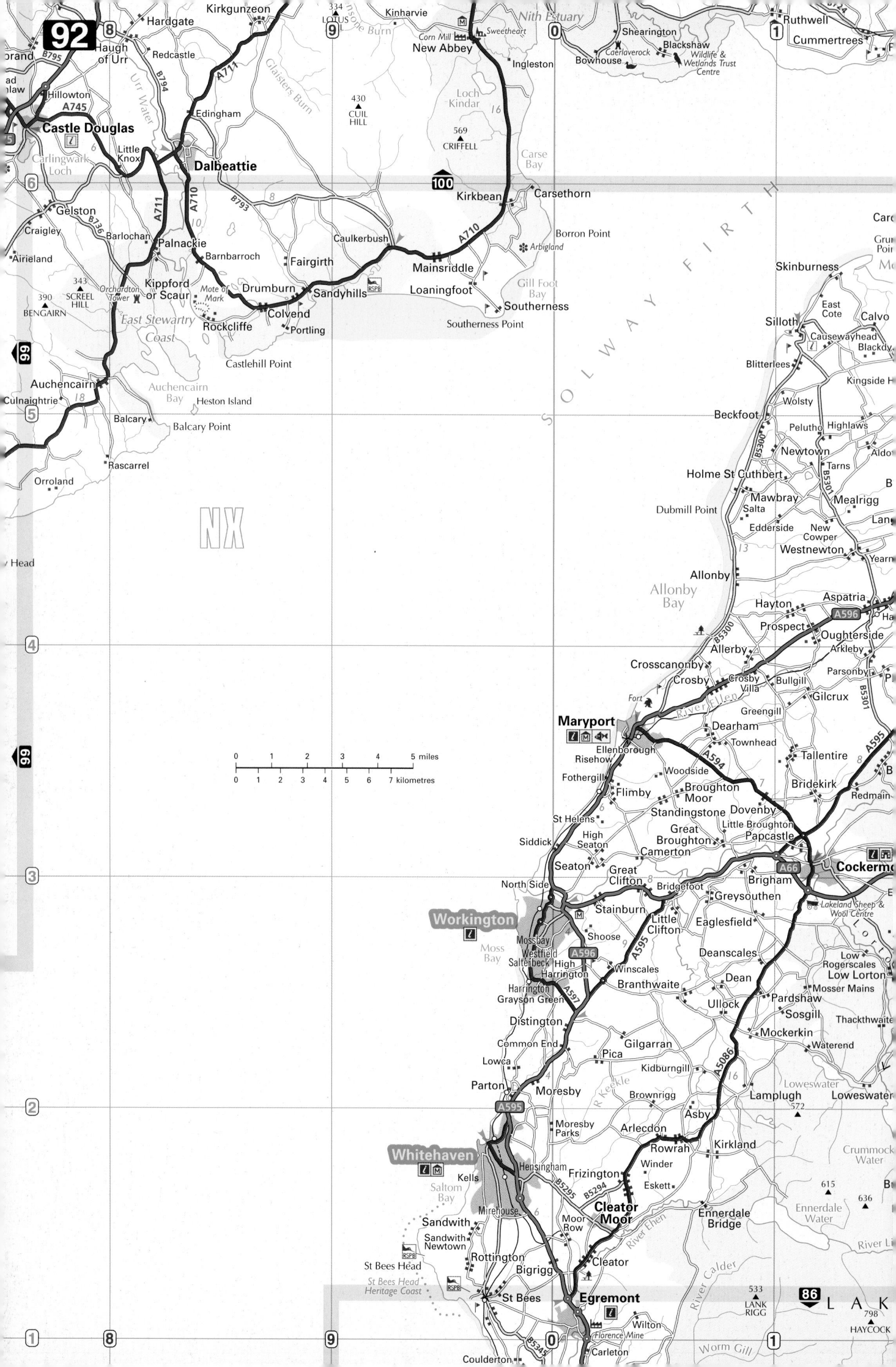

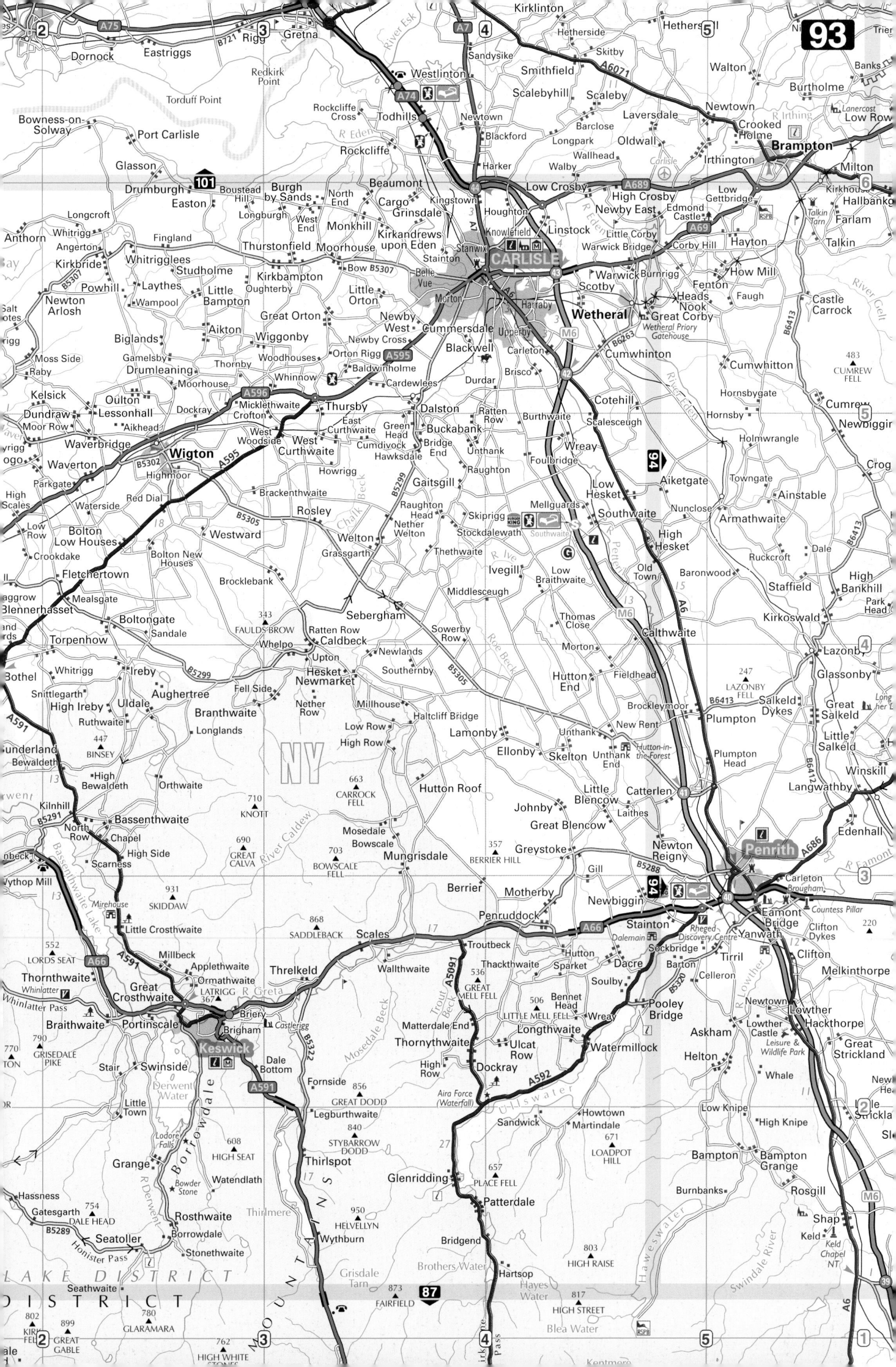

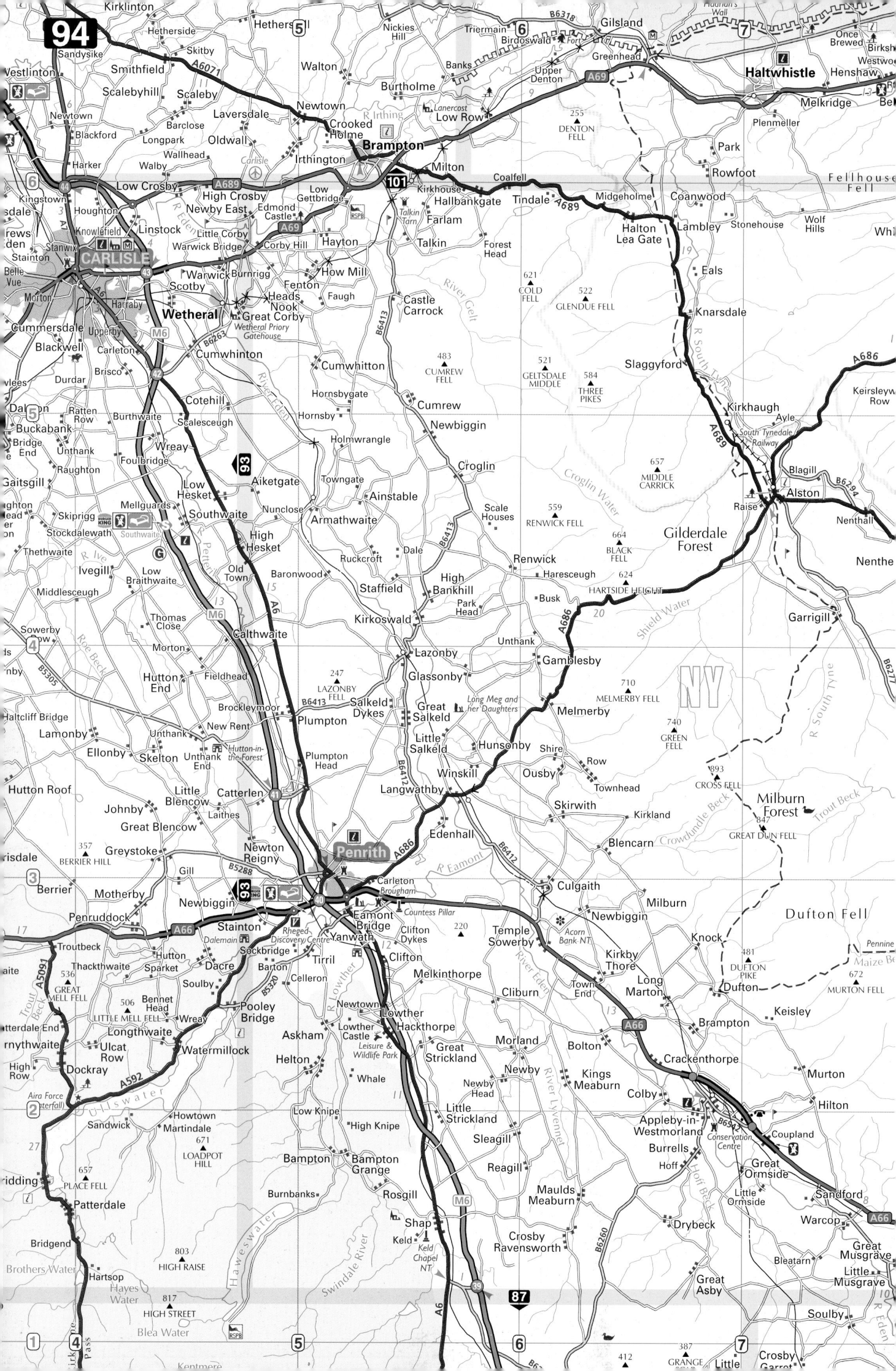

STAVANGER
HAUGESUND
BERGEN

KRISTIANSAND
GÖTEBORG

AMSTERDAM

97

NZ

...ton Colliery

...erlee

Blackhall Colliery
Blackhall Rocks
...khall
...en
...y
...on
A1086
Hart Station
Hart
79
High
Throston
...wick
Dalton
Piercy
Brierton

Historic
Quay
Headland
HARTLEPOOL
Hartlepool Bay

B1277

Seaton
Carew
6
B1277

A689
Greatham
Graythorpe
Tees Bay
Newton
Bewley
A178
Hartlepool Power
Station Visitor
Centre
Billingham
A1185
Coatham
Cowpen
Bewley
Seal
Sands
Warrenby
Redcar
9
Haverton Hill
River Tees
A1042
Teesport
Marske-by-
the-Sea
B1275
Port
Clarence
Toll
A66
South Grangetown
North
Ormesby
Lazenby
Wilton
Kirkleatham
Old Hall
Yearby
A174
Saltburn-by-the-Sea
Saltburn Smugglers
8
New Brotton
Hummersea Scar
A1086
MIDDLESBROUGH
A171
Teesside Park
Acklam
A172
A174
Normanby
Ormesby
Eston
Dunsdale
B1269
**New
Marske**
Upleatham
A174
Brotton
Skelton
New
Skelton
North
Skelton
Carlin
How
Kilton
Skinningrove
Street
Houses
Boulby
Loftus
A173
Tocketts
7
Boosbeck
Lingdale
Kilton
Thorpe
Liverton
Mines
Dalehouse
Easington
Staithes
Heritage Centre
Port Mulgrave
Runswick
Bay
North Yo
Clevelan
A19
A1032
B1380
Stainton
Hemlington
5
Marton
Ormesby Hall NT
A171
Nunthorpe
Pinchinthorpe
Newton
6
Guisborough
Hutton Hall
A171
90
Margrove
Park
Stanghow
Handale
Liverton
7
Liverton
Roxby
Newton
Mulgrave
Borrowby
Hinderwell
Runswick
Kettleness
Ellerby
Goldsbor
B1266
...ythe

0   1   2   3   4   5 miles
0 1 2 3 4 5 6 7 kilometres

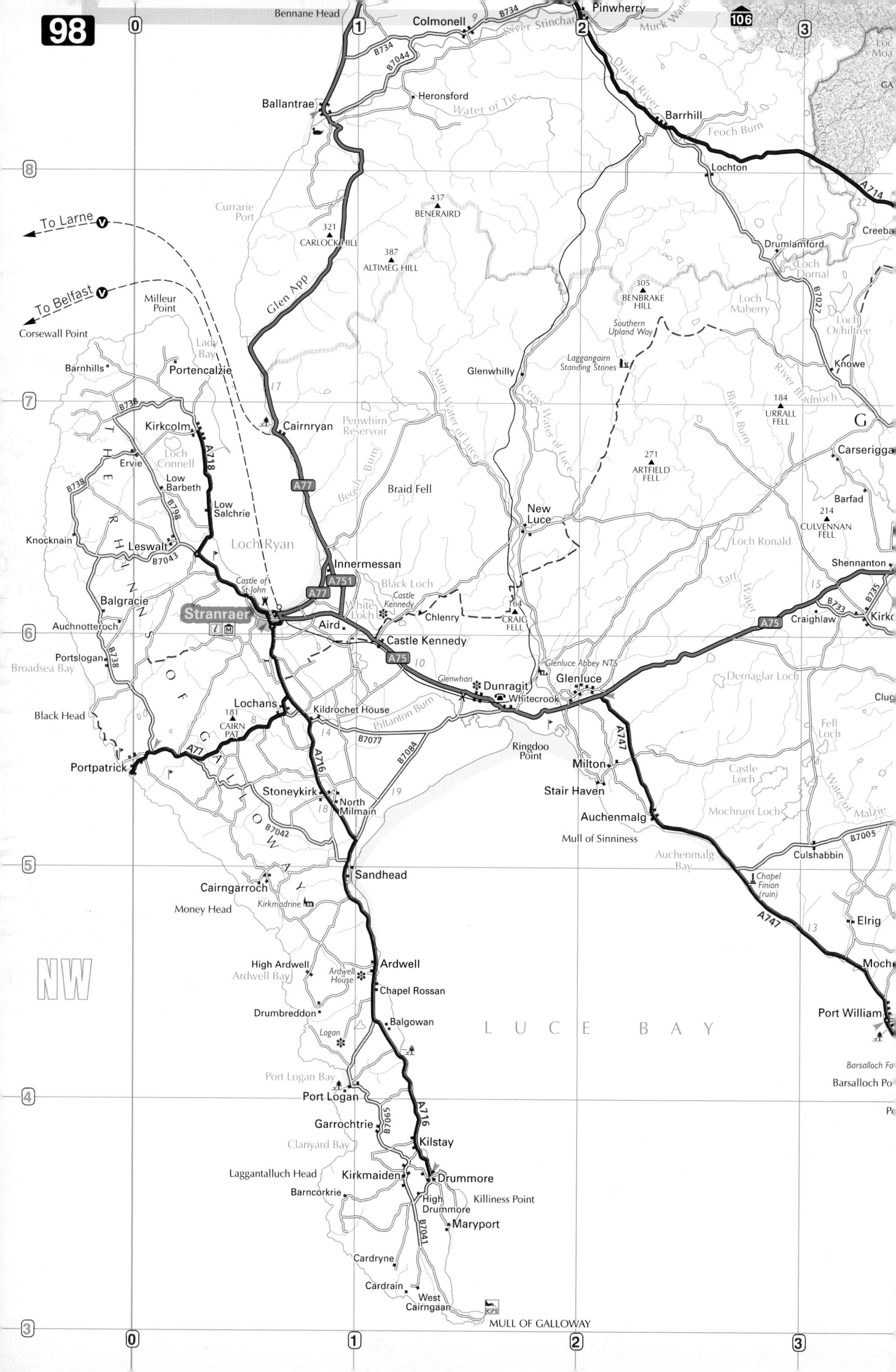

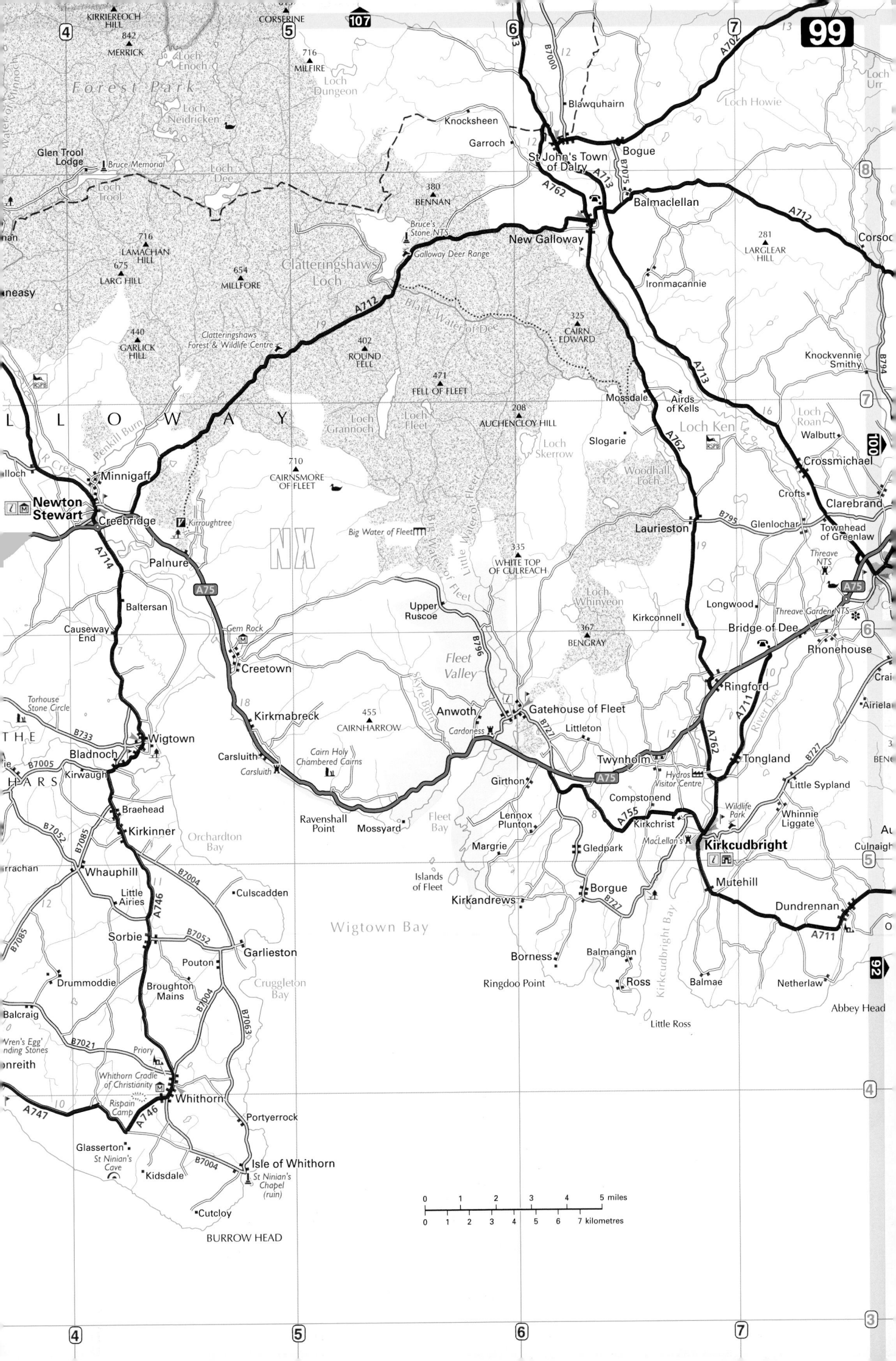

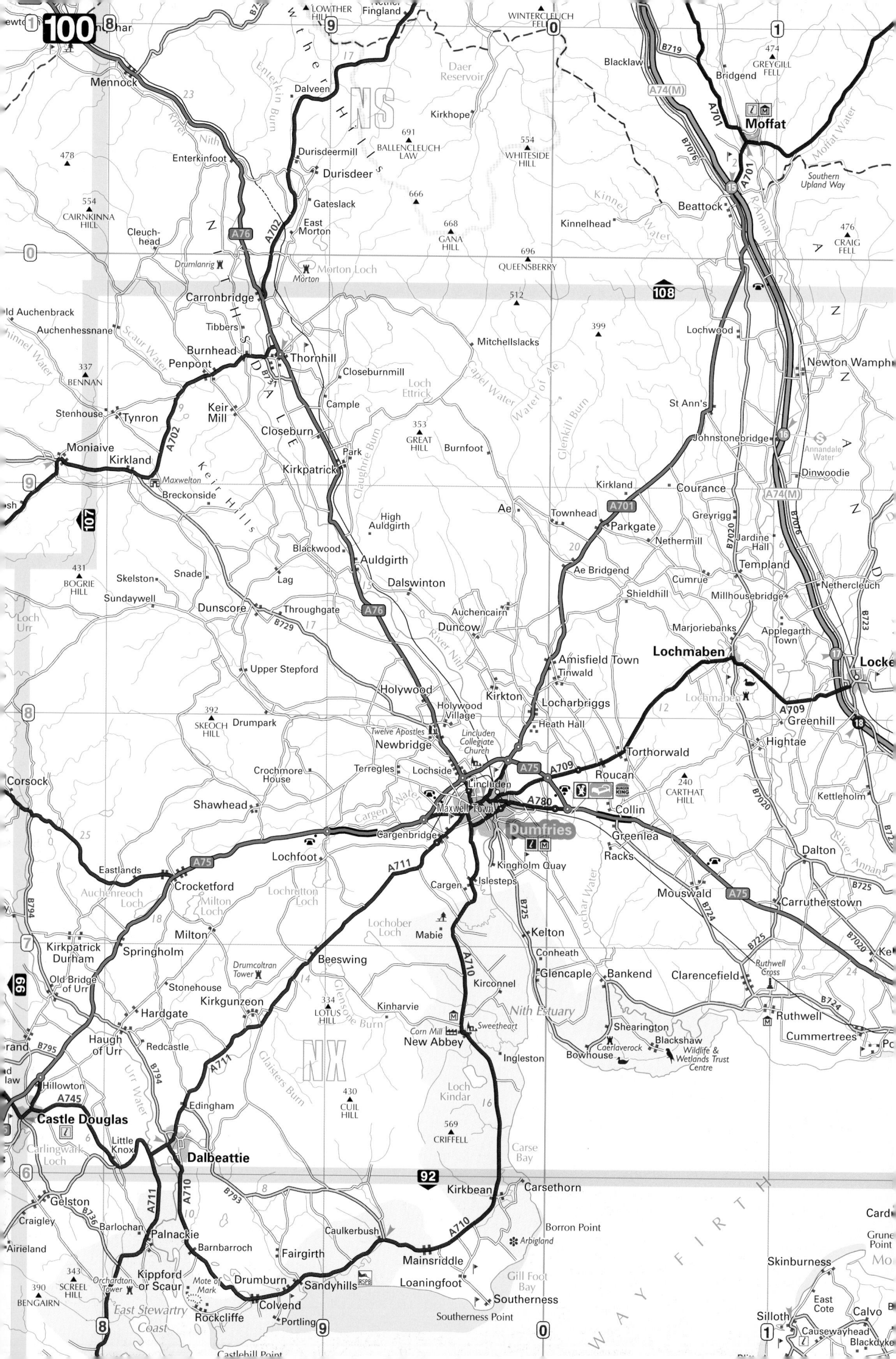

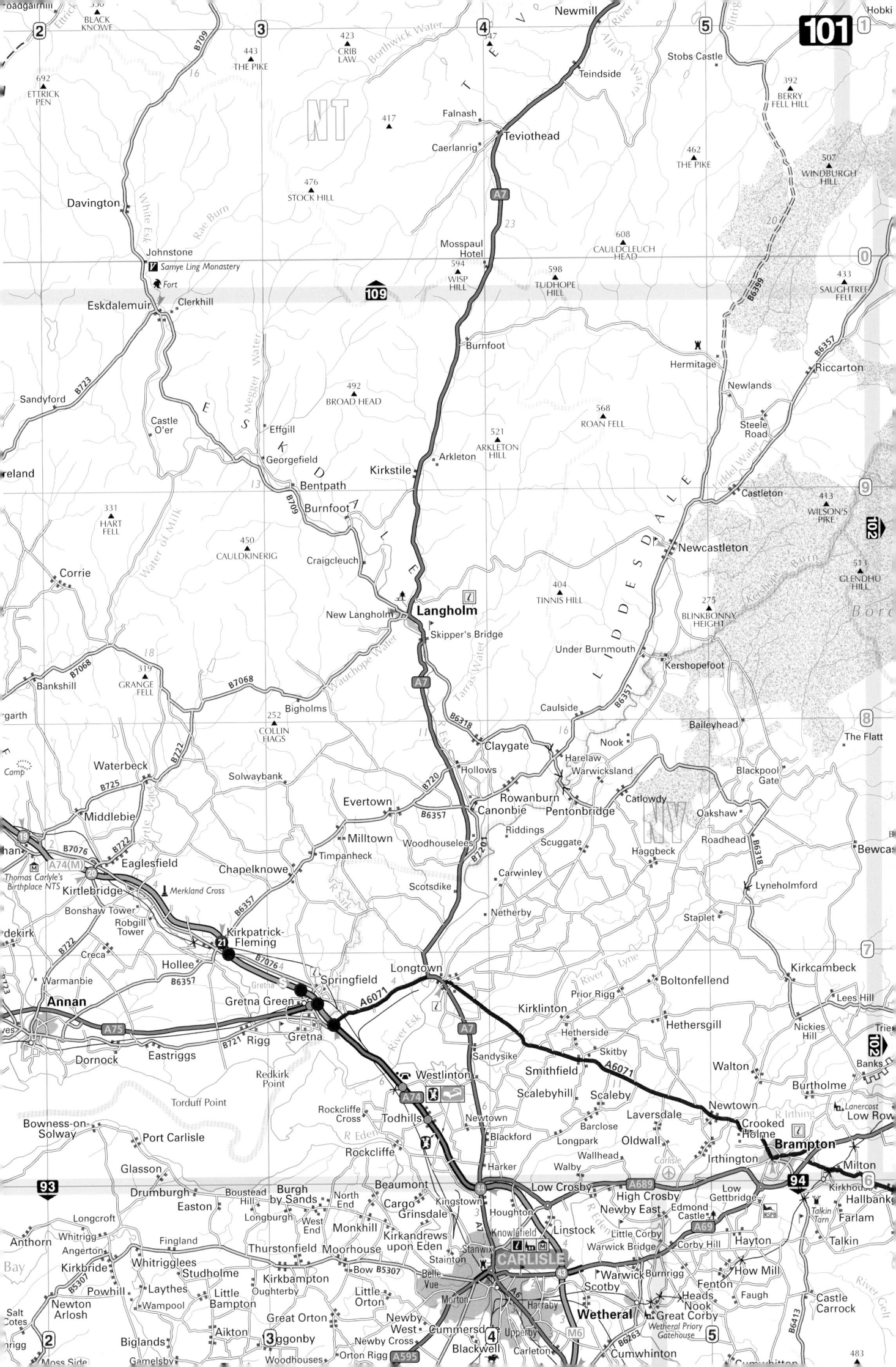

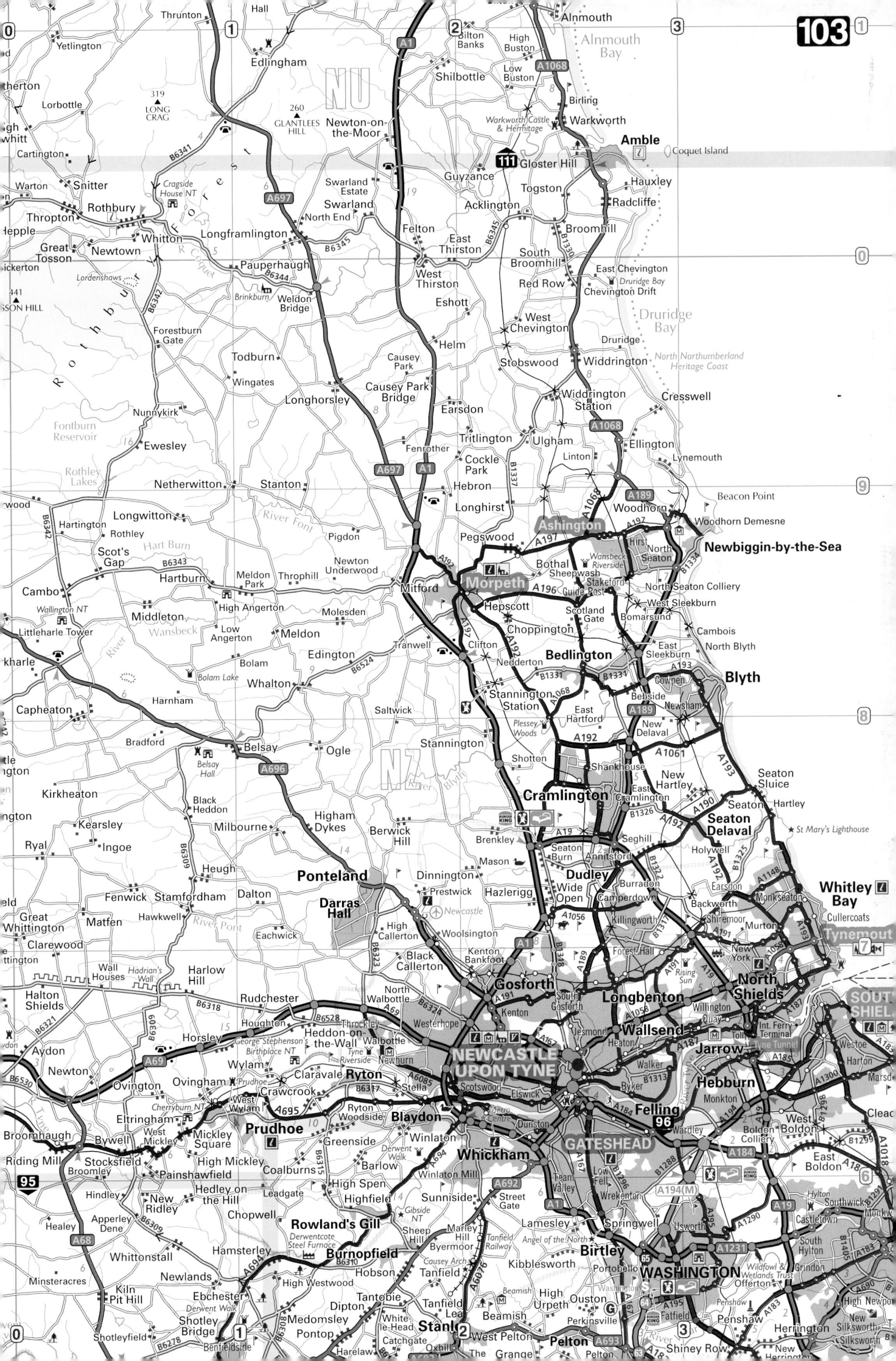

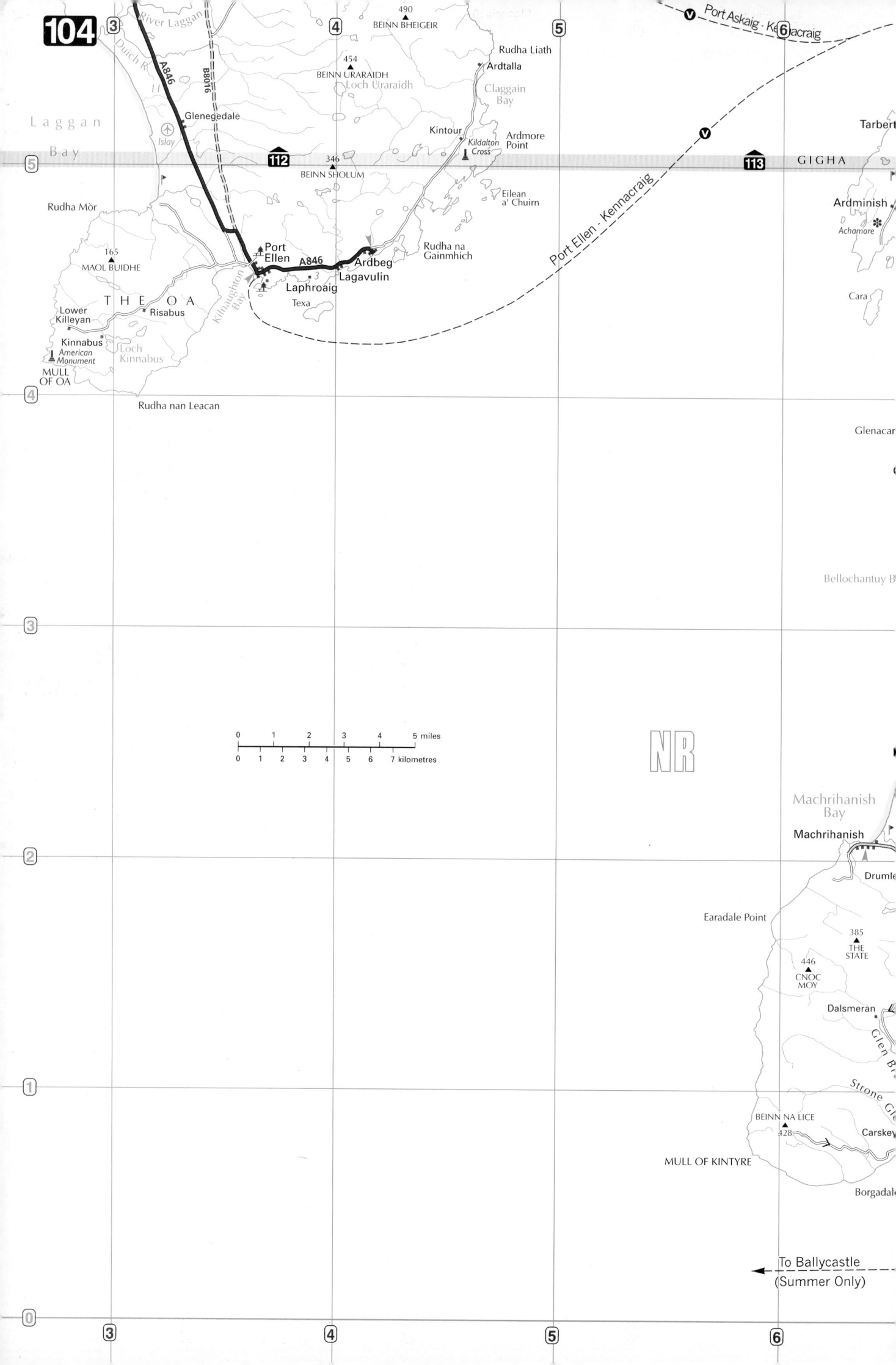

3

River Laggan

Duich R

490
BEINN BHEIGEIR

4

5

Port Askaig - Ke**6**acraig

Rudha Liath
Ardtalla

A846

B8016

454
BEINN URARAIDH
Loch Uraraidh

Claggain
Bay

Glenegedale

Islay

Laggan

Bay

5

112

Kintour

Ardmore
Point

Kildalton
Cross

346
BEINN SHOLUM

v

113

GIGHA

Rudha Mòr

Eilean
a' Chuirn

Port Ellen - Kennacraig

Ardminish

Achamore

165
MAOL BUIDHE

Port
Ellen

A846

Ardbeg
Lagavulin

Rudha na
Gainmhich

Cara

Kilnaughton Bay

Laphroaig

T H E   O A

Risabus

Texa

Lower
Killeyan

Kinnabus
American
Monument

Loch
Kinnabus

MULL
OF OA

4

Rudha nan Leacan

Glenacar

3

Bellochantuy B

0   1   2   3   4   5 miles

0   1   2   3   4   5   6   7 kilometres

NR

Machrihanish
Bay

Machrihanish

2

Drumle

Earadale Point

385
THE
STATE

446
CNOC
MOY

Dalsmeran

Glen B

1

Strone Gle

BEINN NA LICE
428

Carskey

MULL OF KINTYRE

Borgadal

To Ballycastle
(Summer Only)

0

3

4

5

6

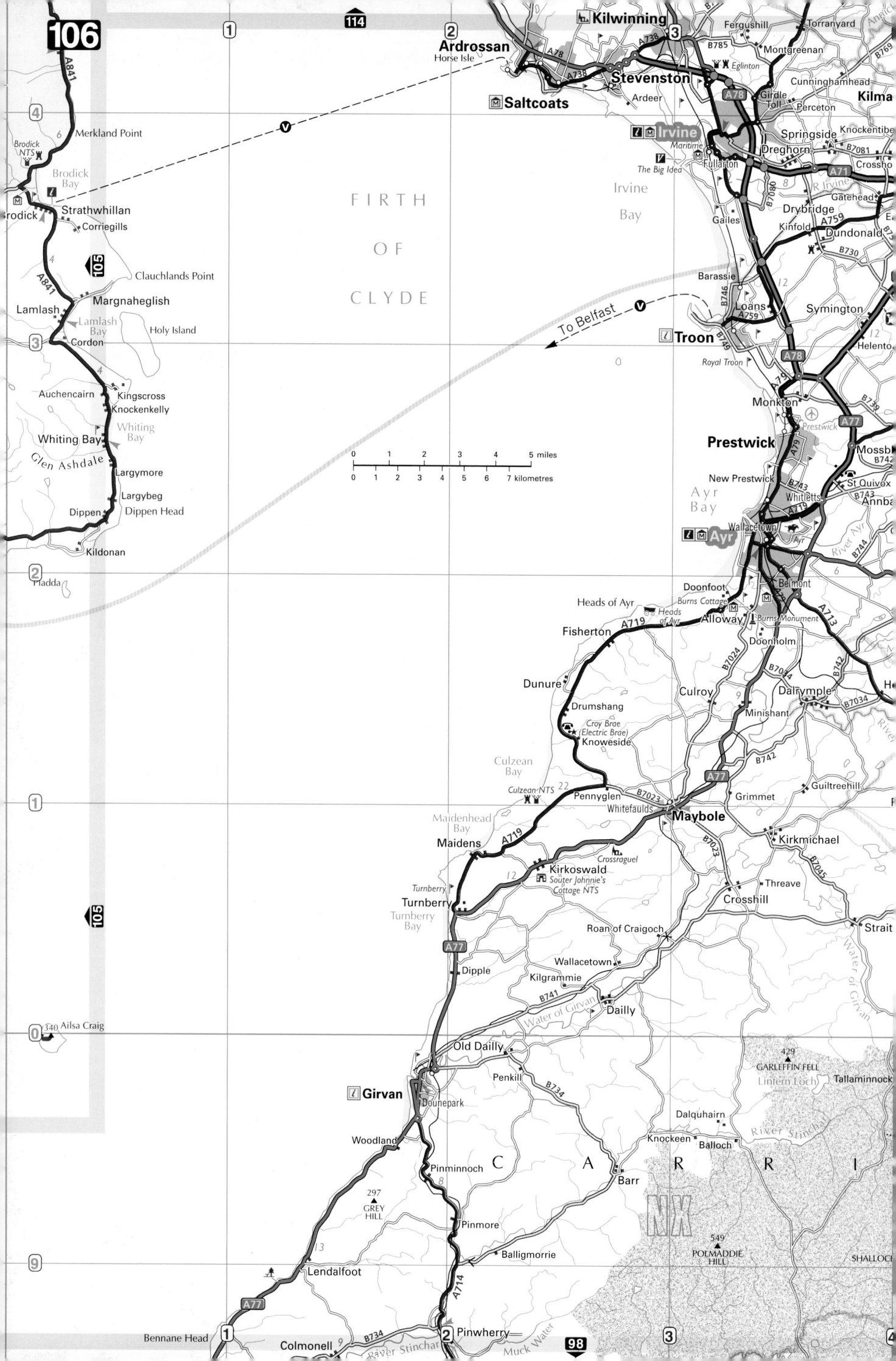

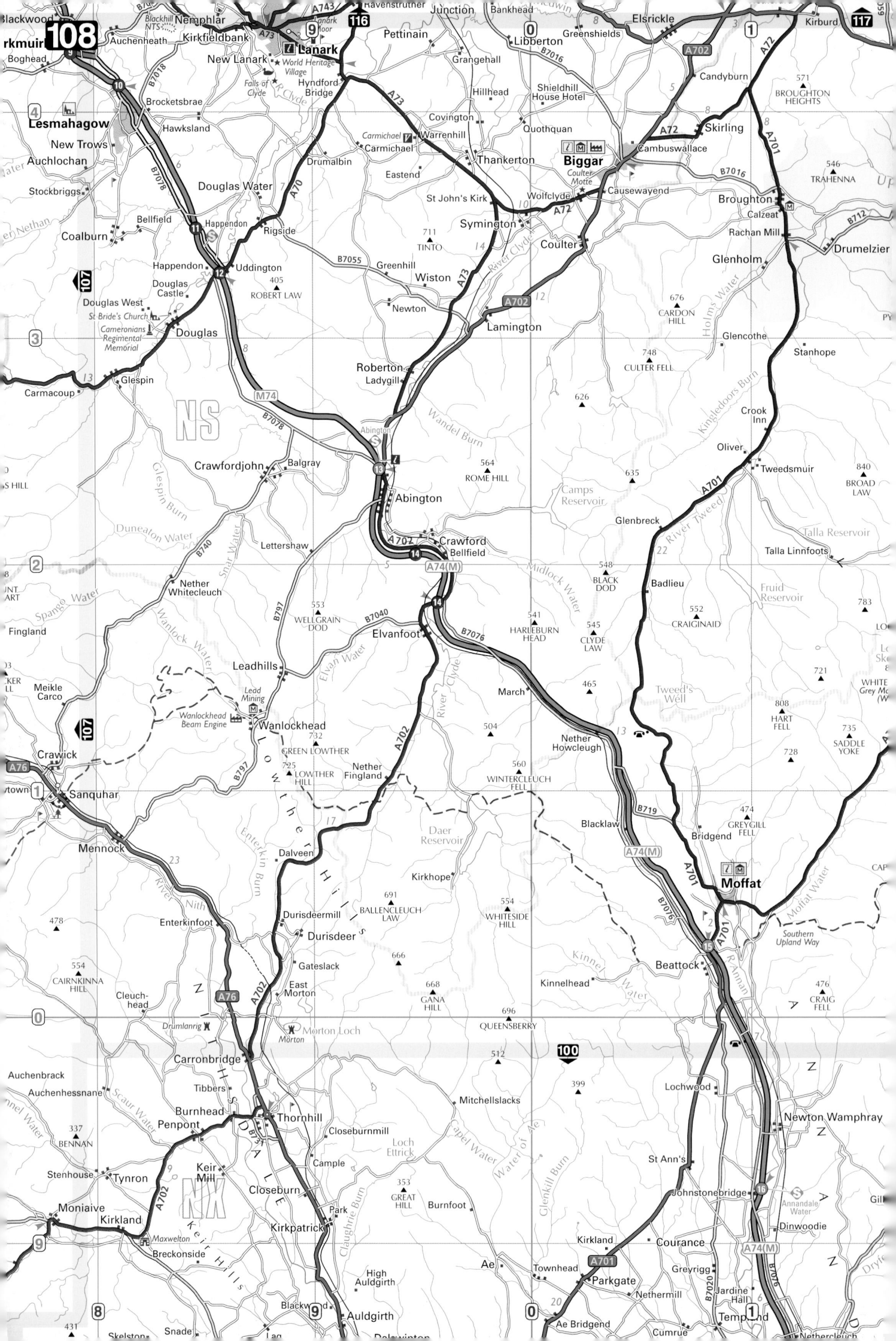

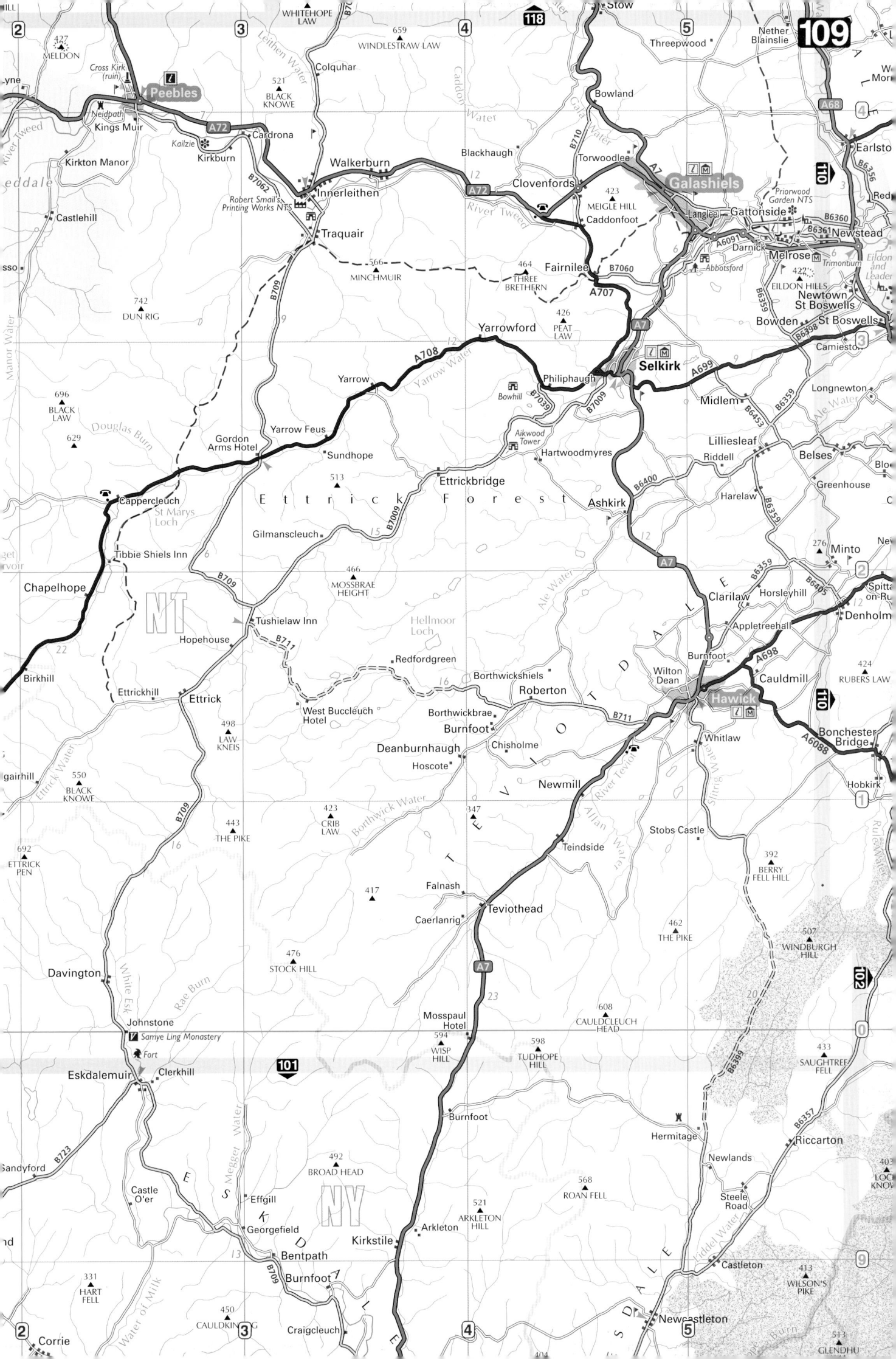

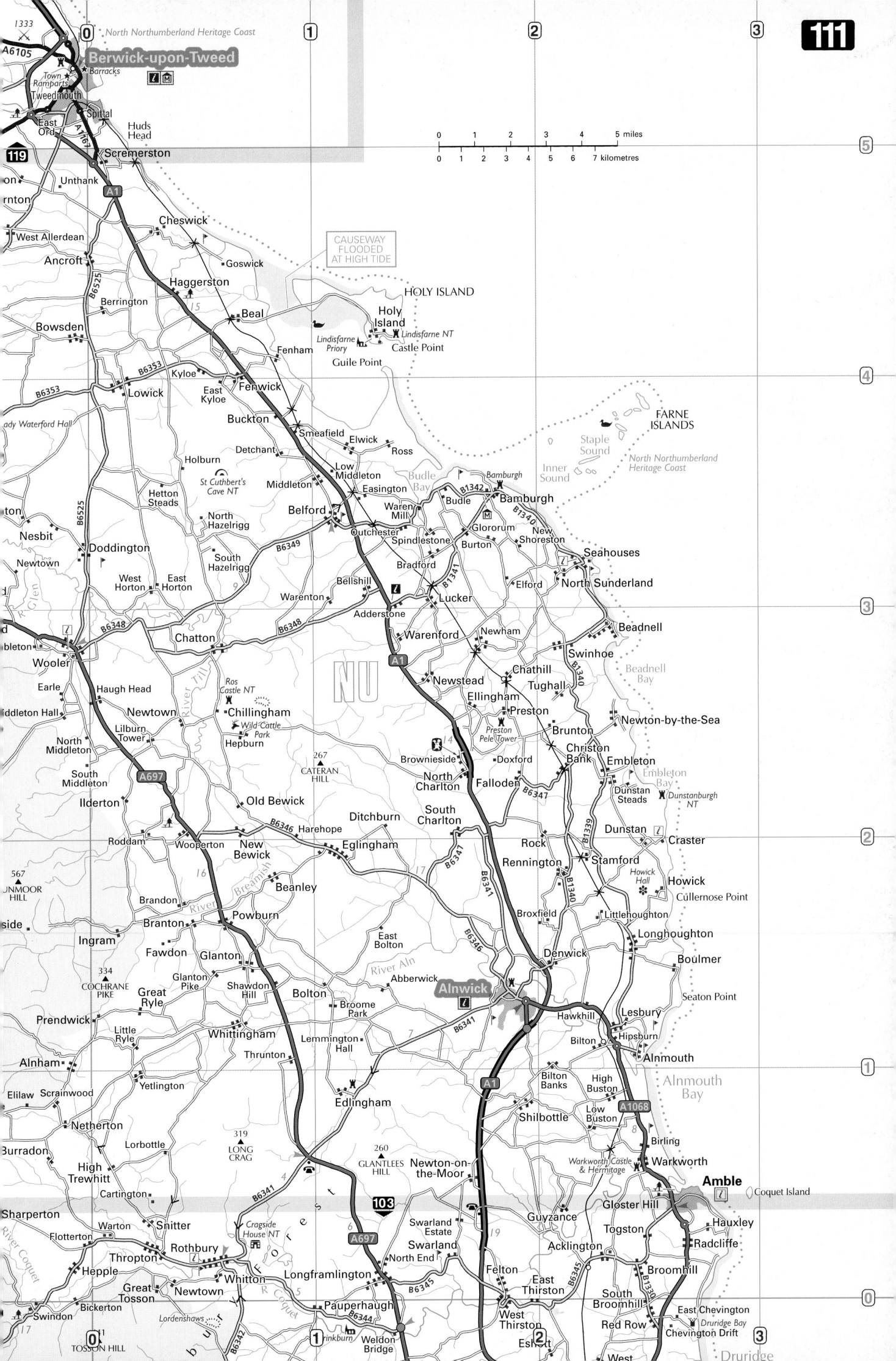

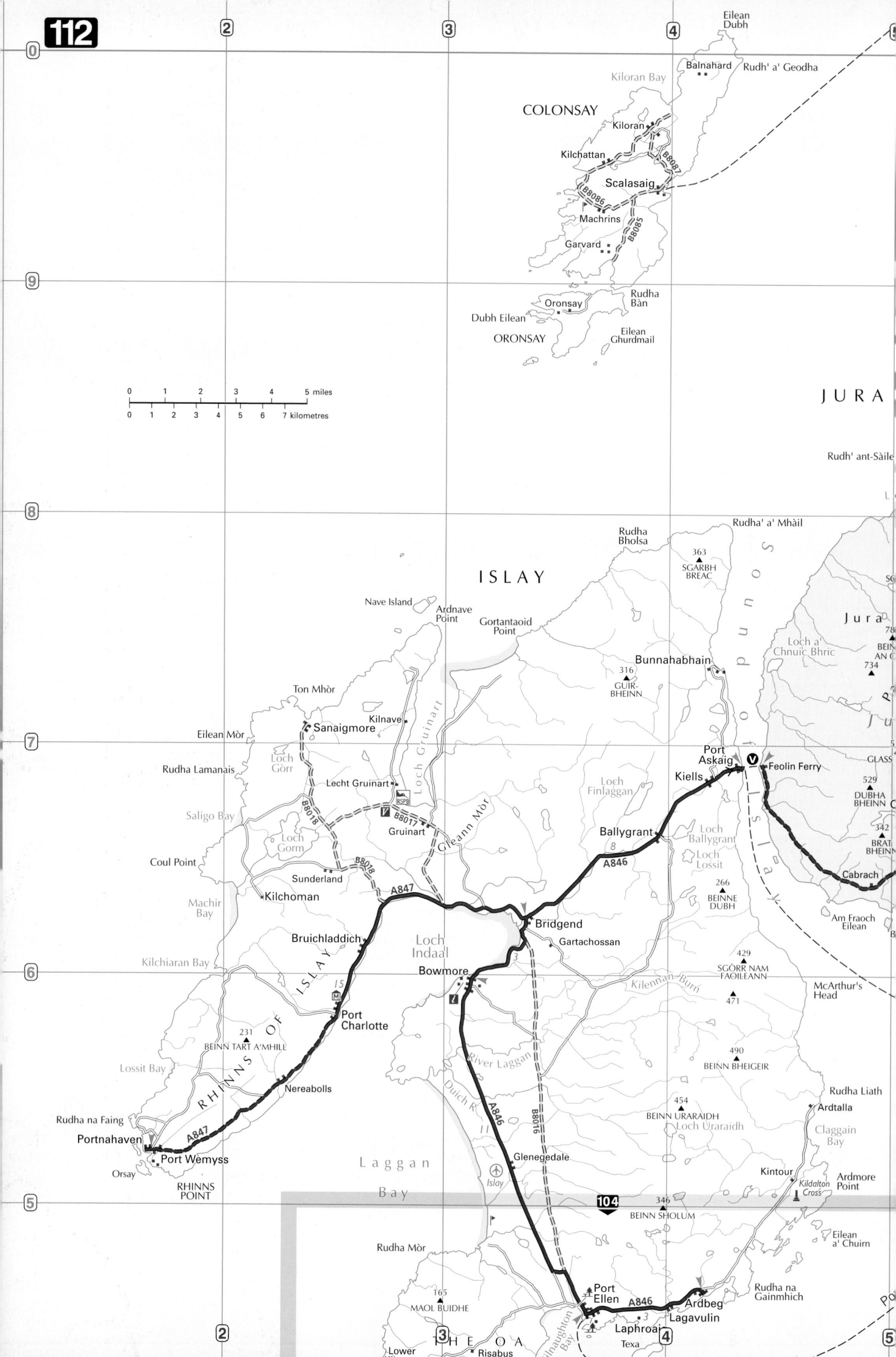

COLONSAY

Eilean
Dubh

Balnahard   Rudh' a' Geodha

Kiloran Bay

Kiloran

Kilchattan

B8087

Scalasaig

B8086   Machrins

B8085

Garvard

JURA

Oronsay   Rudha
Bàn

Dubh Eilean

Eilean
Ghurdmail

ORONSAY

Rudh' ant-Sàile

0   1   2   3   4   5 miles
0   1   2   3   4   5   6   7 kilometres

Rudha
Bholsa   Rudha' a' Mhàil

363
SGARBH
BREAC

ISLAY

Nave Island   Ardnave
Point   Gortantaoid
Point

Bunnahabhain

316
GUIR-
BHEINN

Loch a'
Chnuic Bhric

Jura

78

BEIN
AN C

734

Ton Mhòr   Kilnave

Eilean Mòr   Sanaigmore

Rudha Lamanais

Loch
Gòrr   Lecht Gruinart

RSPB

Port
Askaig

Kiells

Feolin Ferry

GLASS

529

DUBHA
BHEINN

V

Loch
Finlaggan

B8017   B8017

Saligo Bay

Gruinart

Gleann Mòr

Ballygrant

8

A846

Loch
Ballygrant

Loch
Lossit

342
BRAT
BHEINN

Loch
Gorm

B8018

Cabrach

Coul Point

Sunderland   A847

266
BEINNE
DUBH

Am Fraoch
Eilean

Machir
Bay   Kilchoman

Bridgend

Gartachossan

429
SGÒRR NAM
FAOILEANN

McArthur's
Head

Kilchiaran Bay

Bruichladdich   Loch
Indaal

Bowmore

Kilennan Burn

471

Port
Charlotte

15

M

231

BEINN TART A'MHILL

River Laggan

Duich R

490
BEINN BHEIGEIR

Rudha Liath

Ardtalla

Lossit Bay

Nereabolls

A846

B8016

454
BEINN URARAIDH

Loch Uraraidh

Claggain
Bay

Rudha na Faing   A847

Portnahaven

Port Wemyss

Orsay

RHINNS
POINT

Laggan

Bay

Glenegedale

Islay

Kintour   Kildalton
Cross

Ardmore
Point

104

346

BEINN SHOLUM

Rudha Mòr

Eilean
a' Chuirn

165
MAOL BUIDHE

Port
Ellen   A846   Ardbeg

Lagavulin   Rudha na
Gainmhich

Laphroaig

Texa

Lower
Risabus   THE O A

Kilnaughton Bay

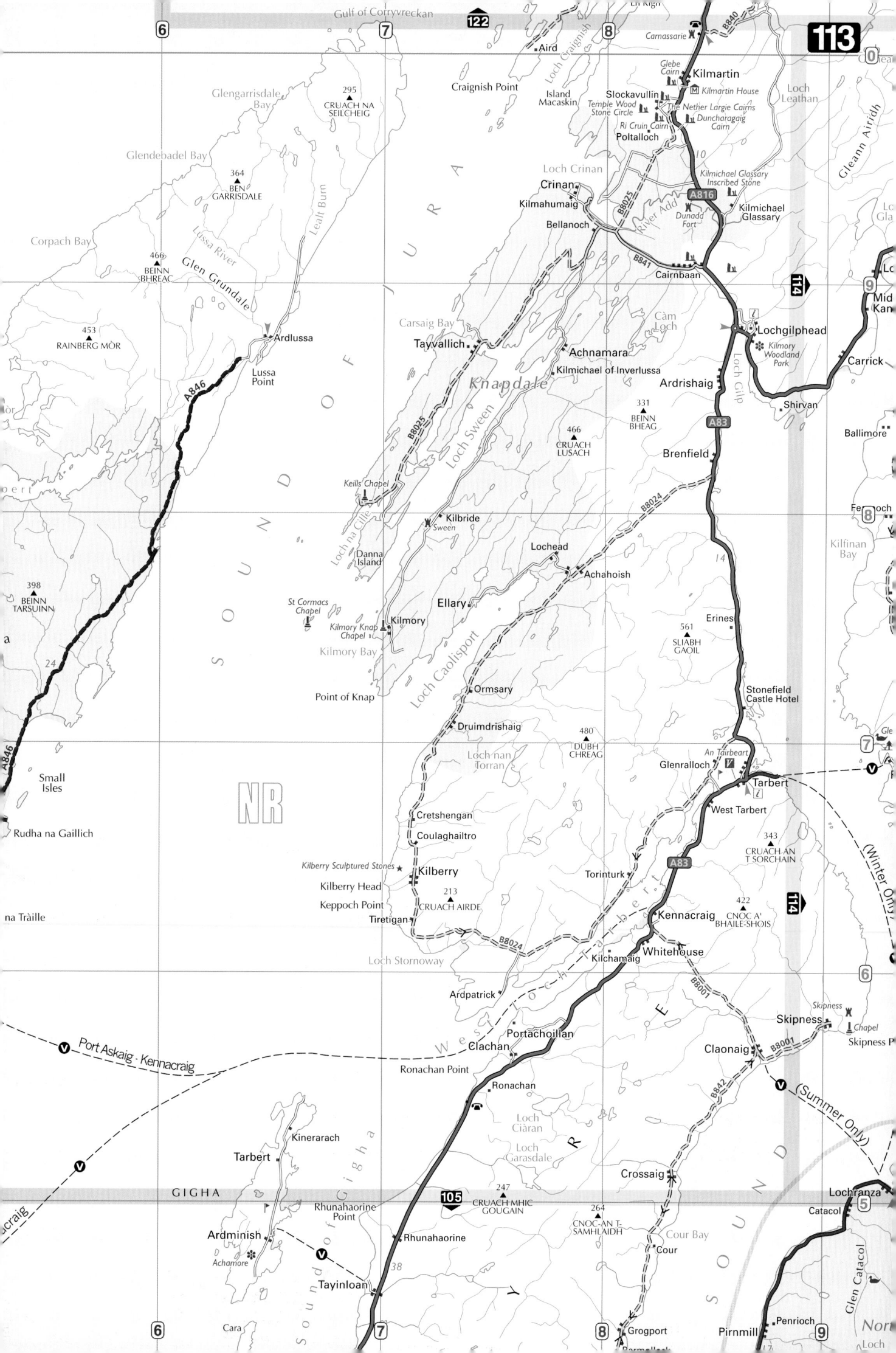

Gulf of Corryvreckan

6   7   122   8   113   0

Ln Righ
Carnassarie
B840
Aird
Craignish Point
Loch Craignish
Glebe Cairn   Kilmartin
Island   Kilmartin House
Macaskin   Slockavullin
Temple Wood   The Nether Largie Cairns
Stone Circle   Duncharagaig
Ri Cruin Cairn   Cairn
Poltalloch   Loch Leathan
Kilmichael Glassary
Inscribed Stone
Loch Crinan   A816
Crinan   Kilmichael
Kilmahumaig   B8025   Glassary
Bellanoch   River Add   Dunadd
Fort
B841
Cairnbaan   114   Gleann Airidh
9
Mid
Kan
Carsaig Bay   Càm   Lochgilphead
Loch
Taynallich   Kilmory
Woodland
Achnamara   Park   Carrick
Kilmichael of Inverlussa   Ardrishaig
K n a p d a l e   Shirvan
331   A83   Ballimore
BEINN   Brenfield
BHEAG
466
Keills Chapel   CRUACH
LUSACH   B8024
Loch Sween   14   Fe   och
8
Kilbride   Kilfinan
Sween   Lochead   Bay
Danna   Achahoish
Island   561
St Cormacs   SLIABH
Chapel   Ellary   GAOIL
Kilmory Knap   Erines
Chapel   Kilmory   Stonefield
Kilmory Bay   Castle Hotel
Ormsary
Point of Knap   Druimdrishaig   480
DUBH   An Tairbeart   7
Loch nan   CHREAG   Glenralloch
Torran   Tarbert
Cretshengan   West Tarbert
Coulaghailtro   343
CRUACH AN
Kilberry Sculptured Stones   T SORCHAIN
Kilberry   Torinturk   114
Kilberry Head   422
Keppoch Point   213   CNOC A'
Tiretigan   CRUACH AIRDE   Kennacraig   BHAILE-SHOIS
Whitehouse
Loch Stornoway   B8024   Kilchamaig   B8001
Ardpatrick   Skipness
Clachan   Skipness
Portachoillan   Claonaig   B8001   Chapel
Ronachan Point   Skipness P

Port Askaig - Kennacraig   Ronachan   B842
Loch Ciaran   Crossaig
Kinerarach   Loch
Garasdale   Lochranza
Tarbert   105   247   5
GIGHA   CRUACH MHIC   Catacol
GOUGAIN   264
Rhunahaorine   CNOC AN T-
Point   SAMHLAIDH   Cour Bay
Ardminish   Cour
Achamore   Rhunahaorine
Cara   Tayinloan   Grogport   Pirnmill
6   7   8   9

A846
Glengarrisdale   295
Bay   CRUACH NA
SEILCHEIG
Glendebadel Bay   364
BEN
Corpach Bay   GARRISDALE
466
BEINN
BHREAC   Glen Grundale
Lussa River   Ardlussa
453   Lussa
RAINBERG MÒR   Point
Lealt Burn
S O U N D   O F   J U R A
398
BEINN
TARSUINN
a
NR
Small
Isles
Rudha na Gaillich
na Tràille
acraig
V
V

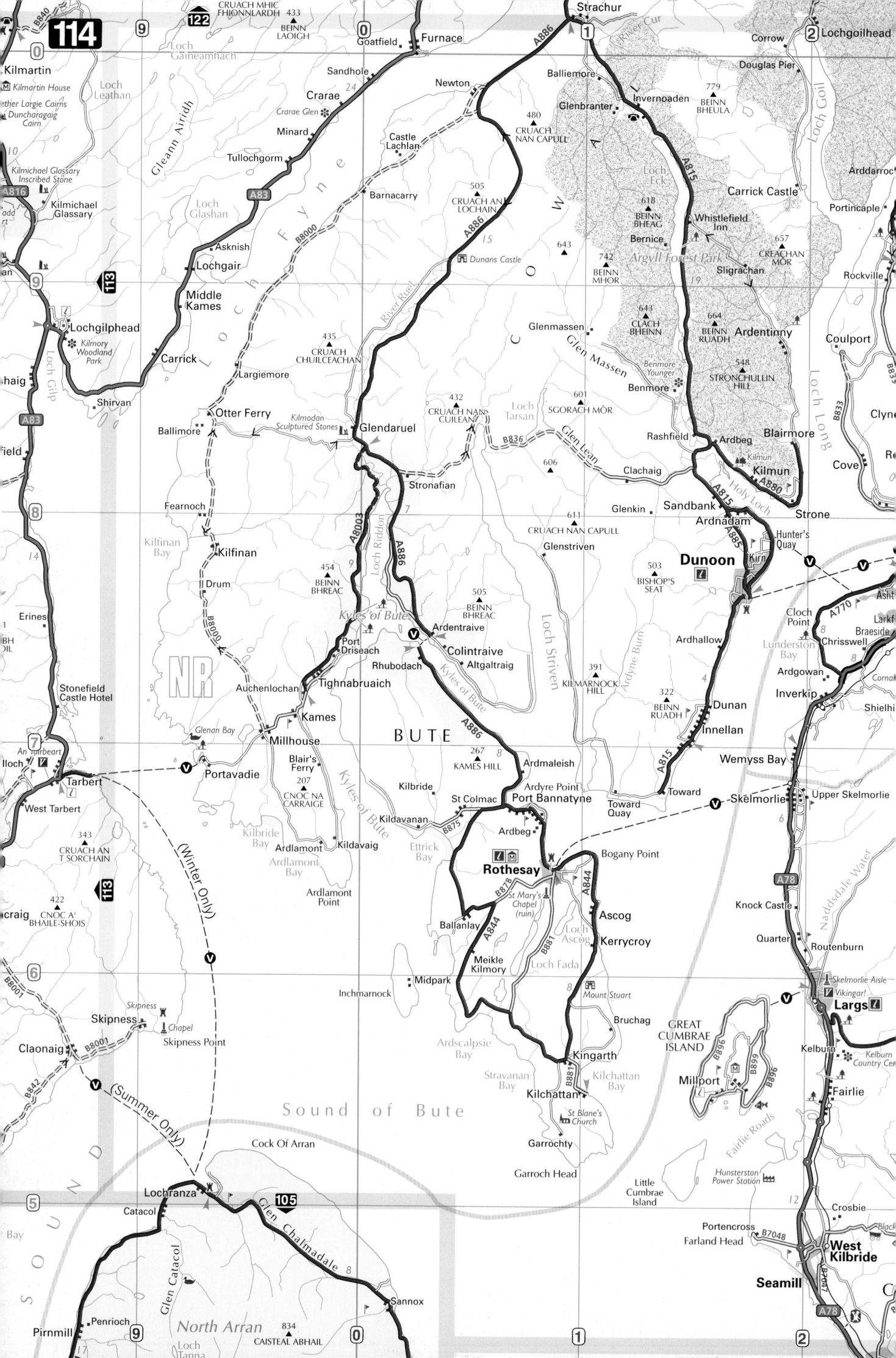

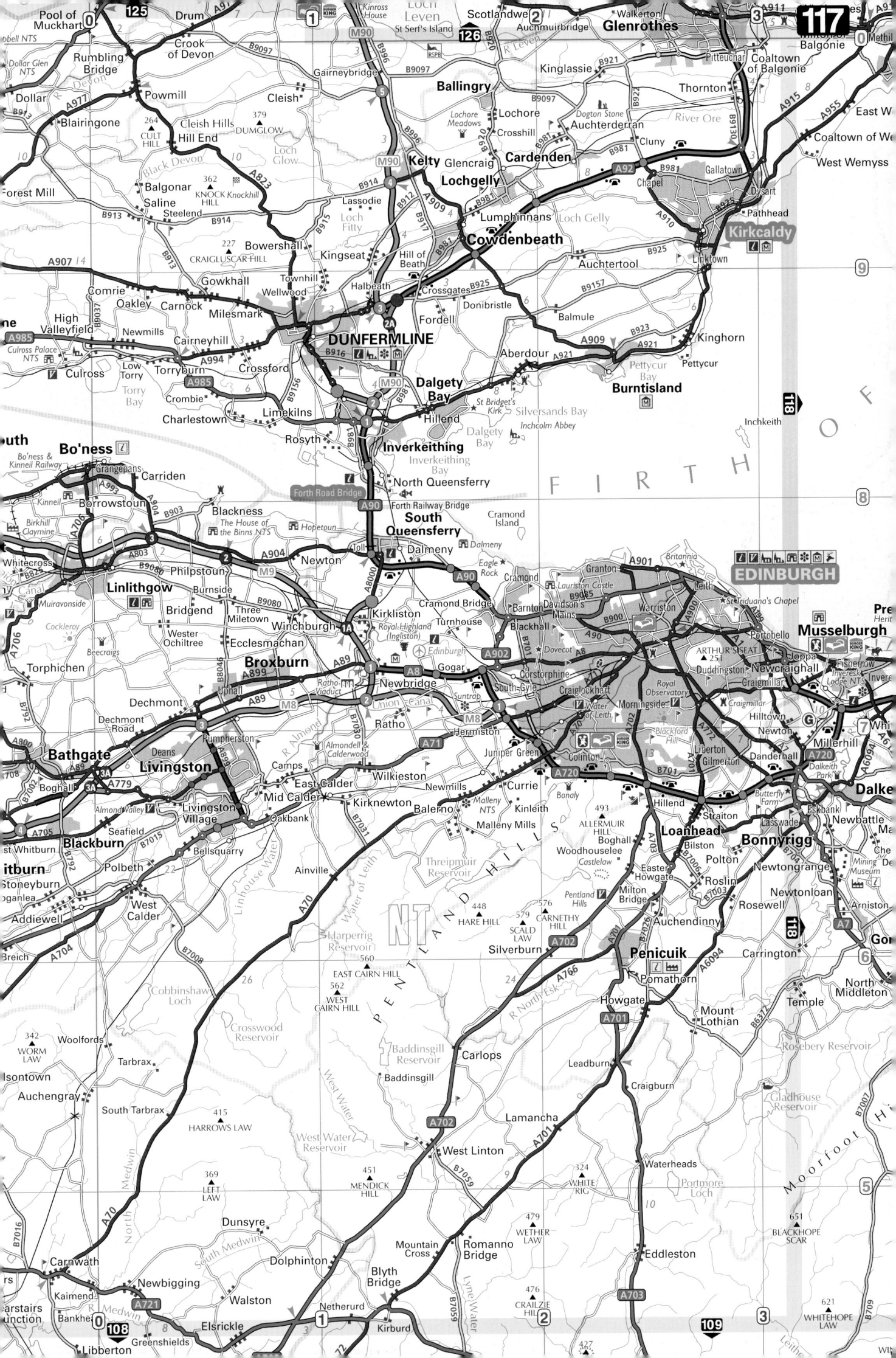

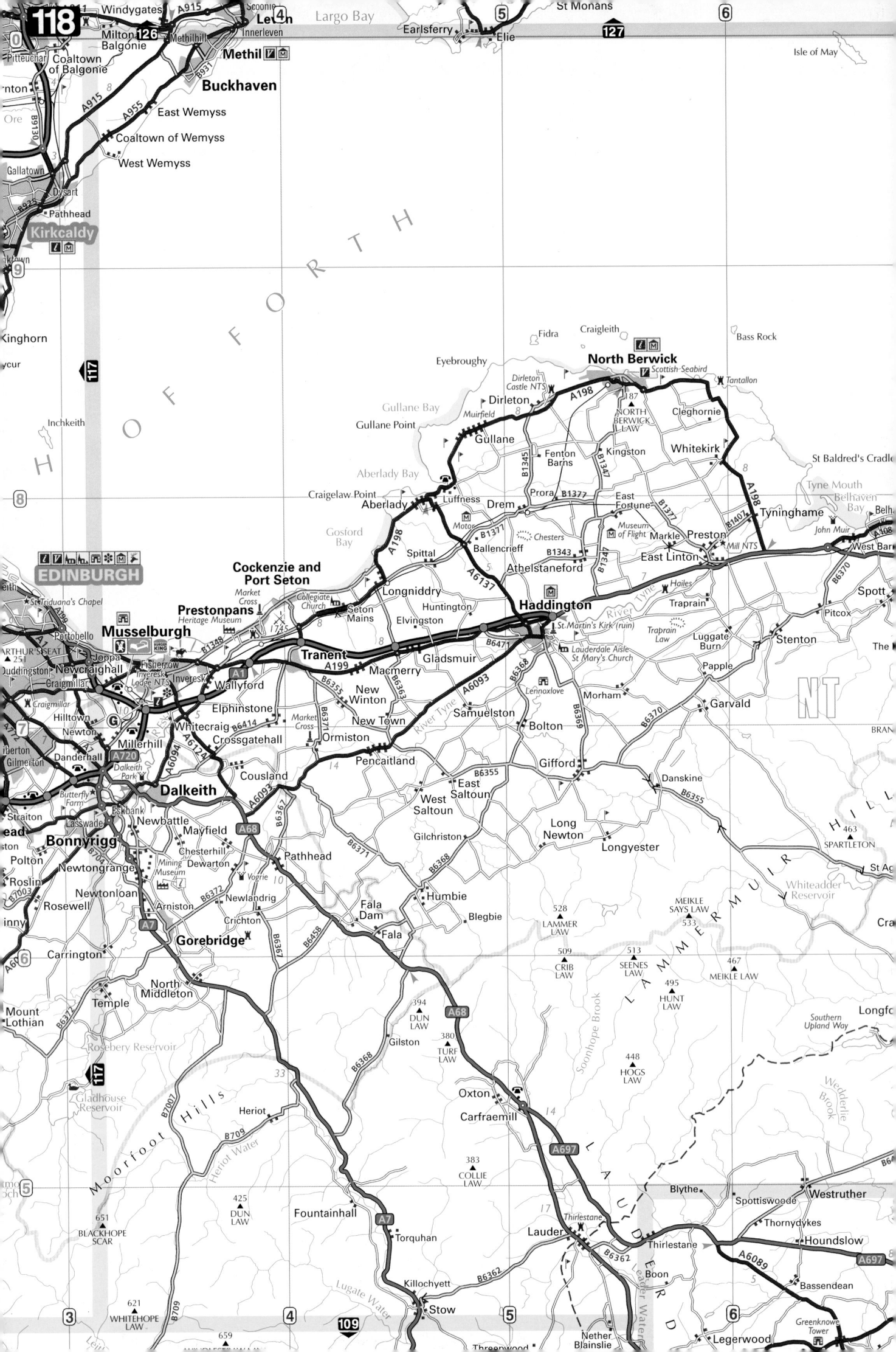

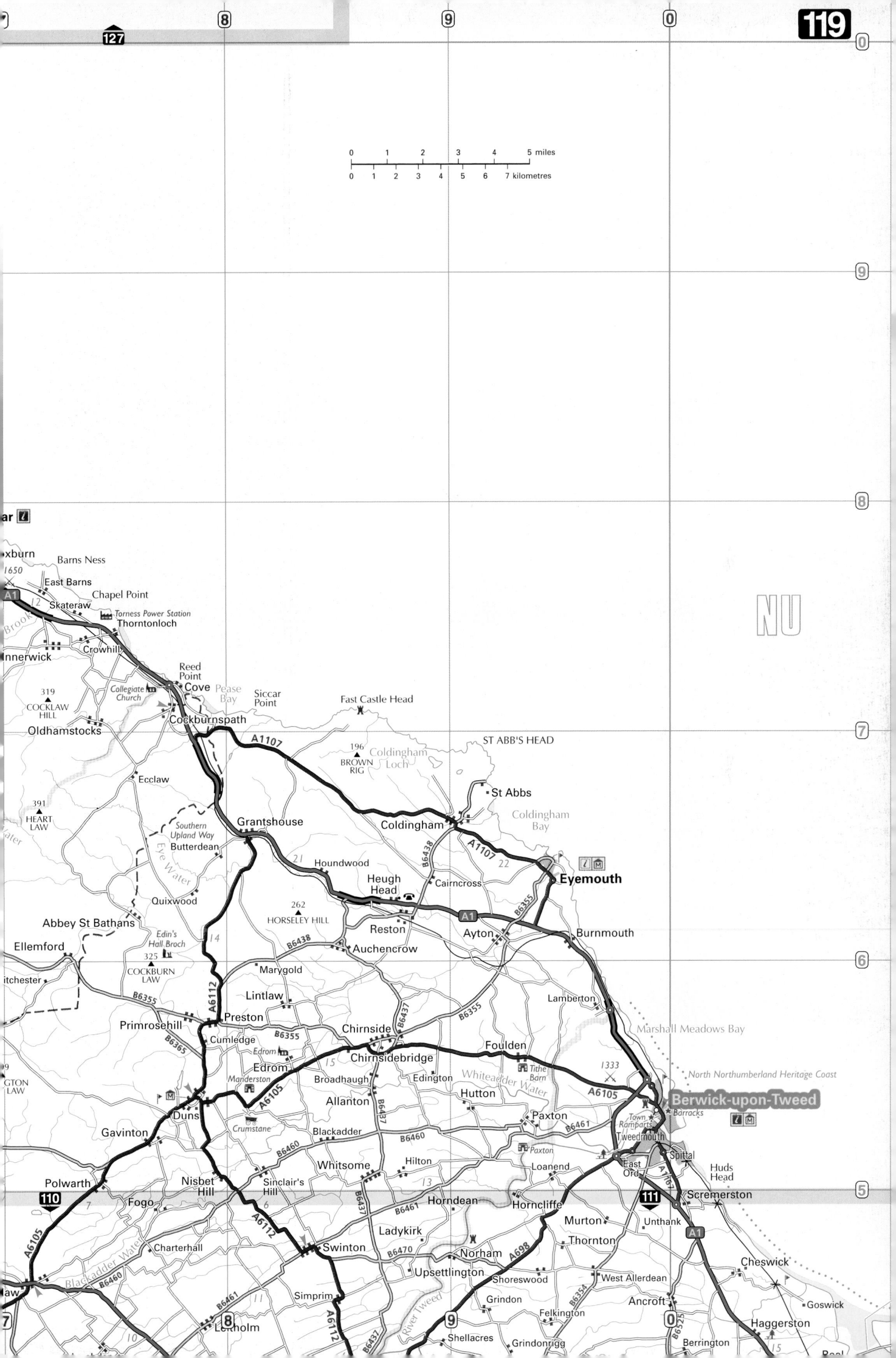

Eilean Mòr

Rudha Mòr

Rudha Sgor-innis

Bousd

Sorisdale

Cliad Bay

B8072

Arnabost

Grishipoll

Clabhach

Loch Cliad

B8071

Hogh Bay

Ballyhaugh

Arinagour

COLL

Totronald

Acha

B8070

Co

Feall Bay

Arileod

Uig

Eilean Ornsay

V

Friesland Bay

V

Calgary Point

Crossapol Bay

Loch Breachacha

Rudha Fàsachd

V

Gunna

Tiree - Oban

Rudha Port Bhiosd

Clachan Mòr

Caoles

Rudha Dubh

Balephetrish Bay

B8069

Ruaig

Loch Bhasapoll

B8068

Fladda

Haugh Bay

Gott Bay

Ballevullin

Cornoigmore

Kenovay

V

Kilkenneth

B8068

Tiree

Lunga

Moss

Heylipoll

B8055

Scarinish

TRESHNISH ISLES

Middleton

Crossapoll

TIREE

Barrapoll

B8065

Hynish Bay

Balemartine

Bac Mòr or Dutchmans Cap

B8067

Mannel

Bac Beag

Rinn Thorbhais

Balephuil Bay

Hynish

NL

IONA

Abbey

Baile Mòr

Macleans Cross

Fio

0 1 2 3 4 5 miles

0 1 2 3 4 5 6 7 kilometres

Soa Island

Erraid

Torran Rocks

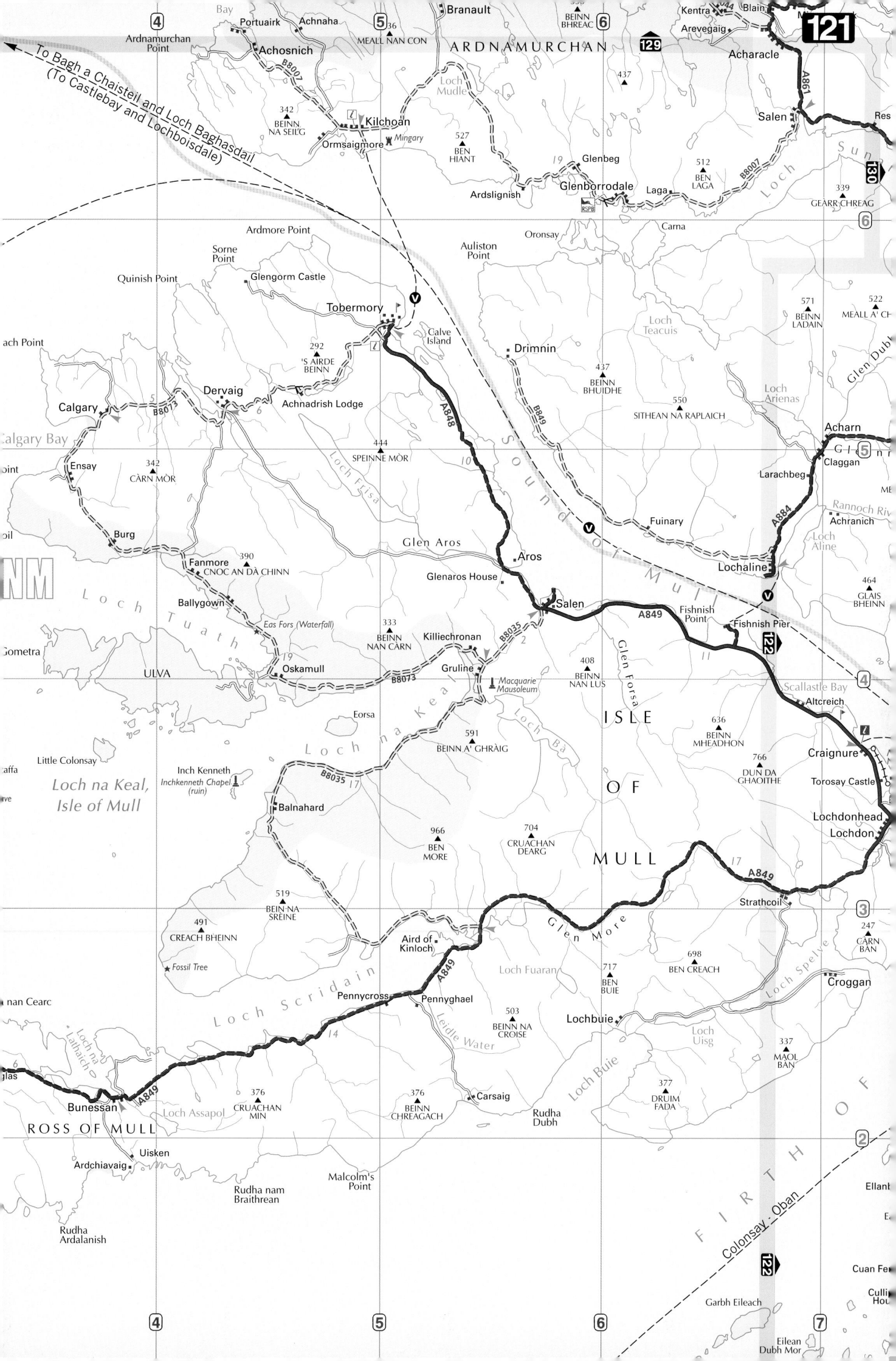

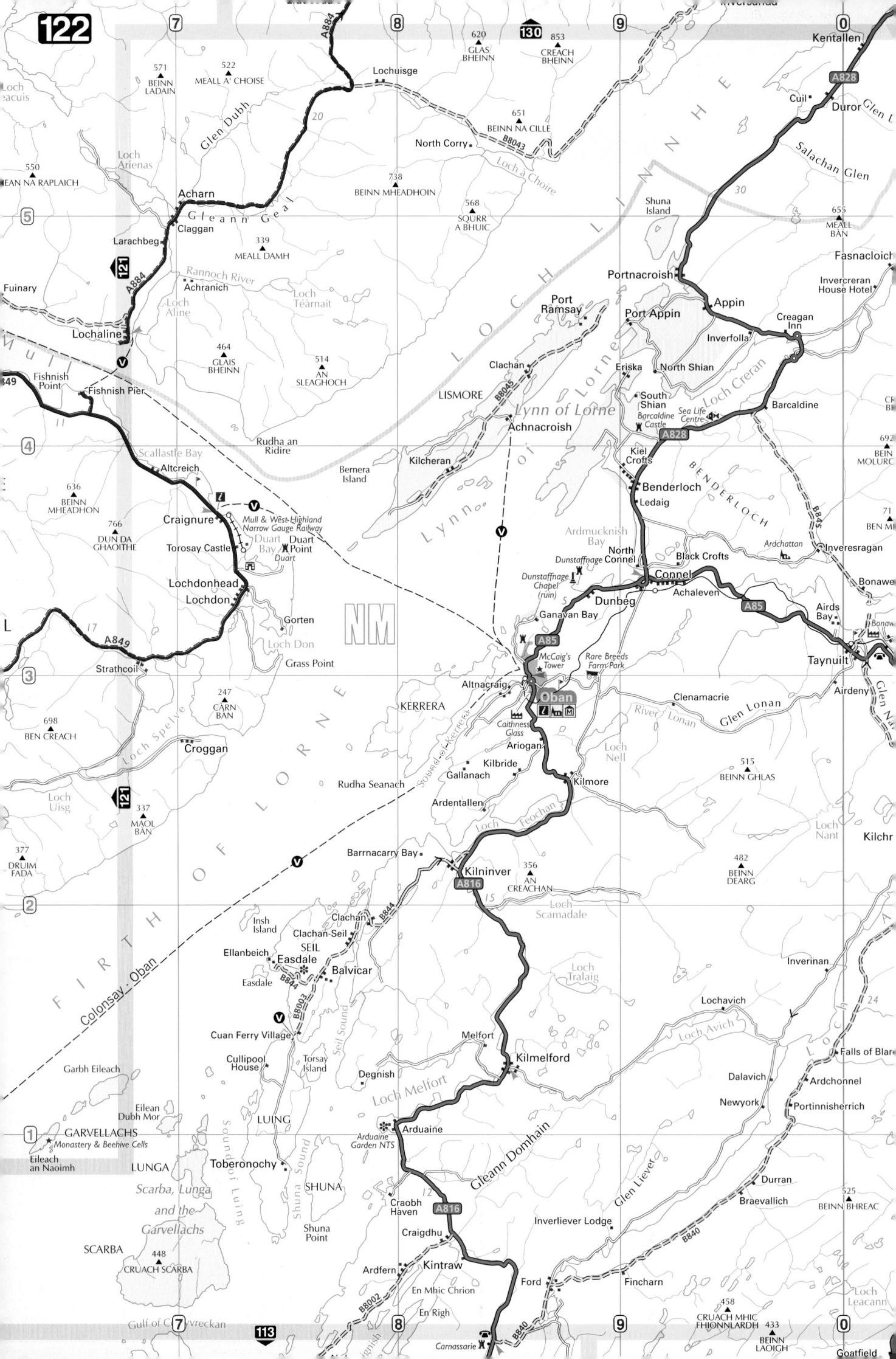

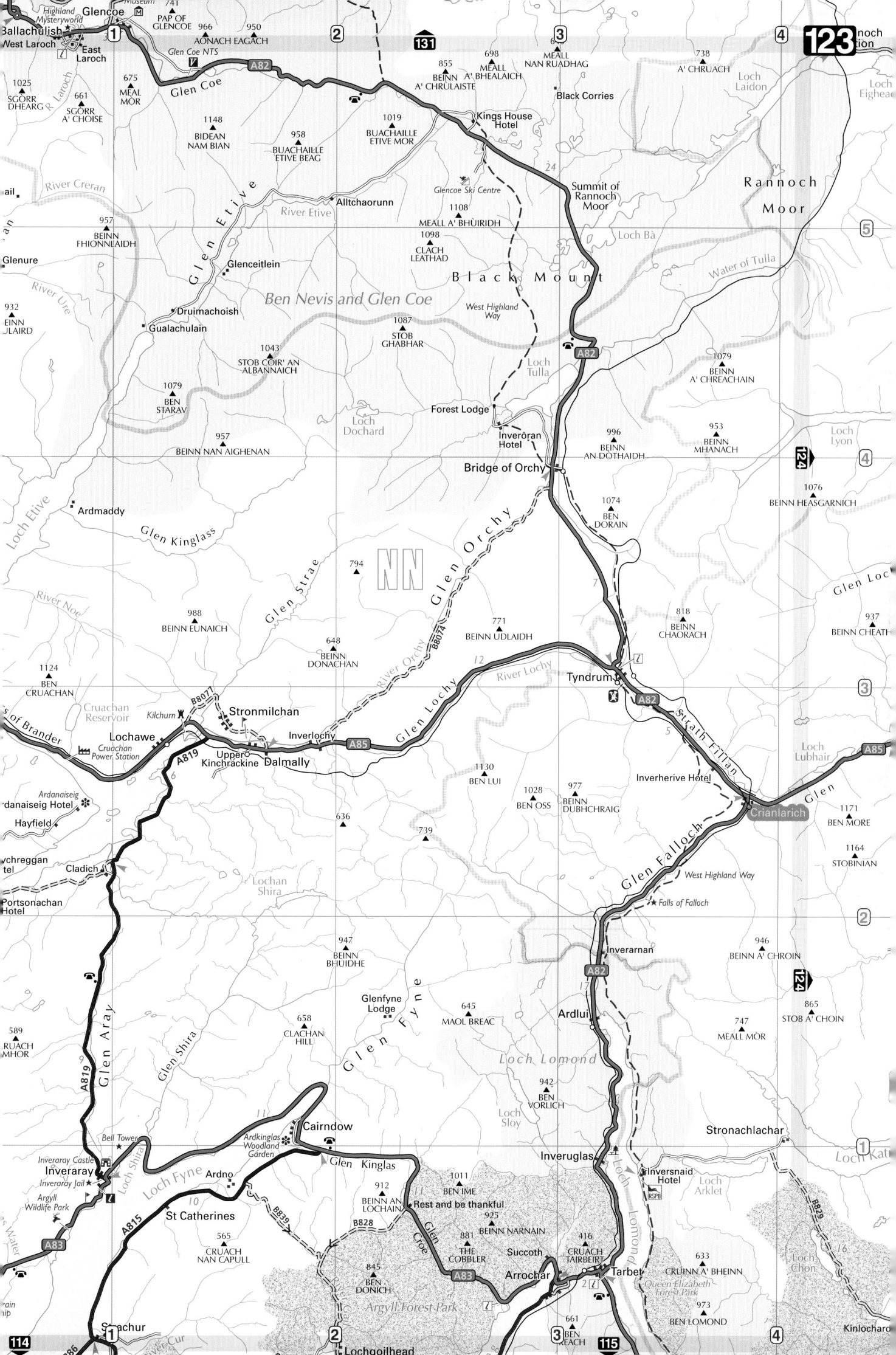

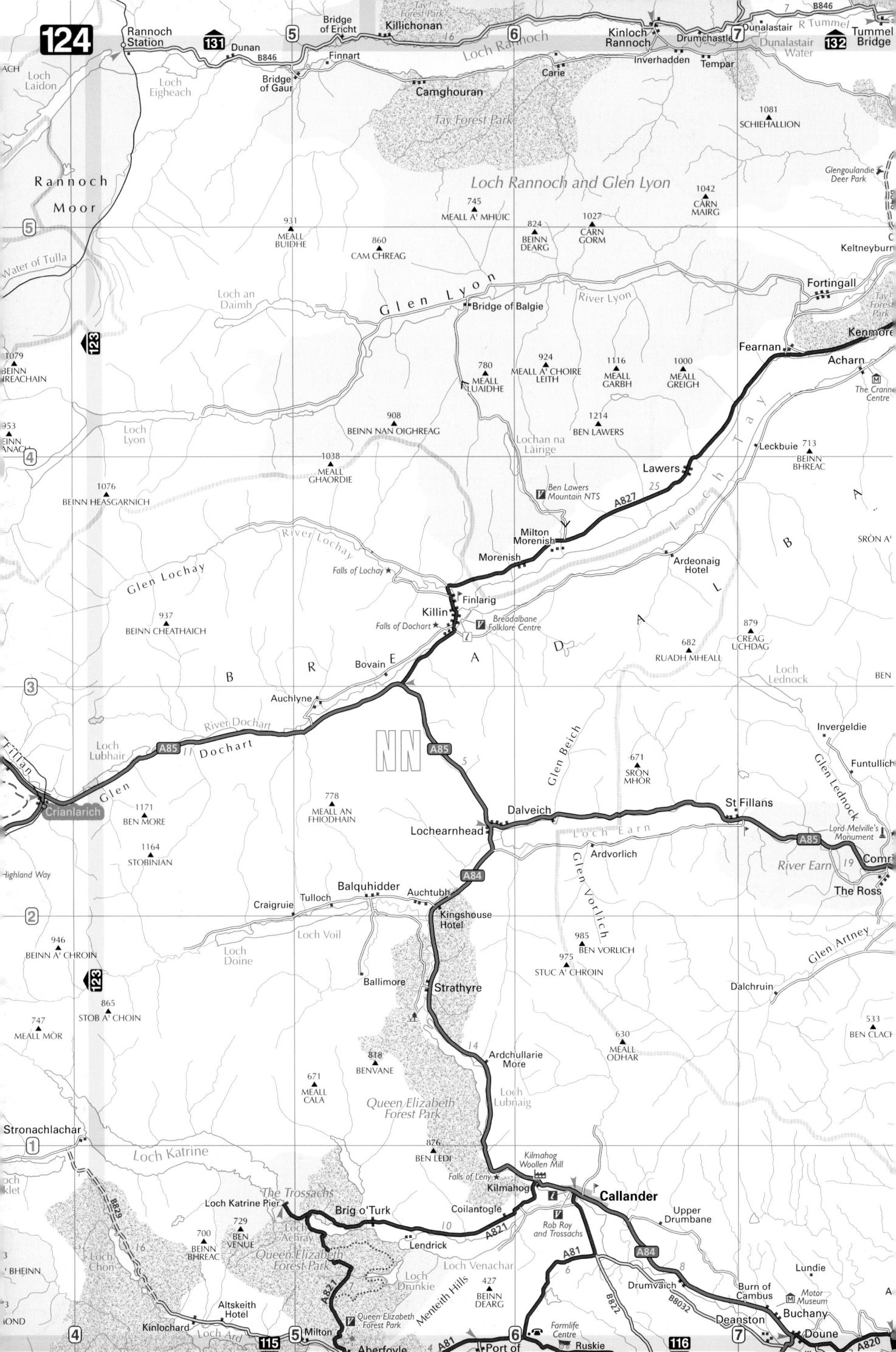

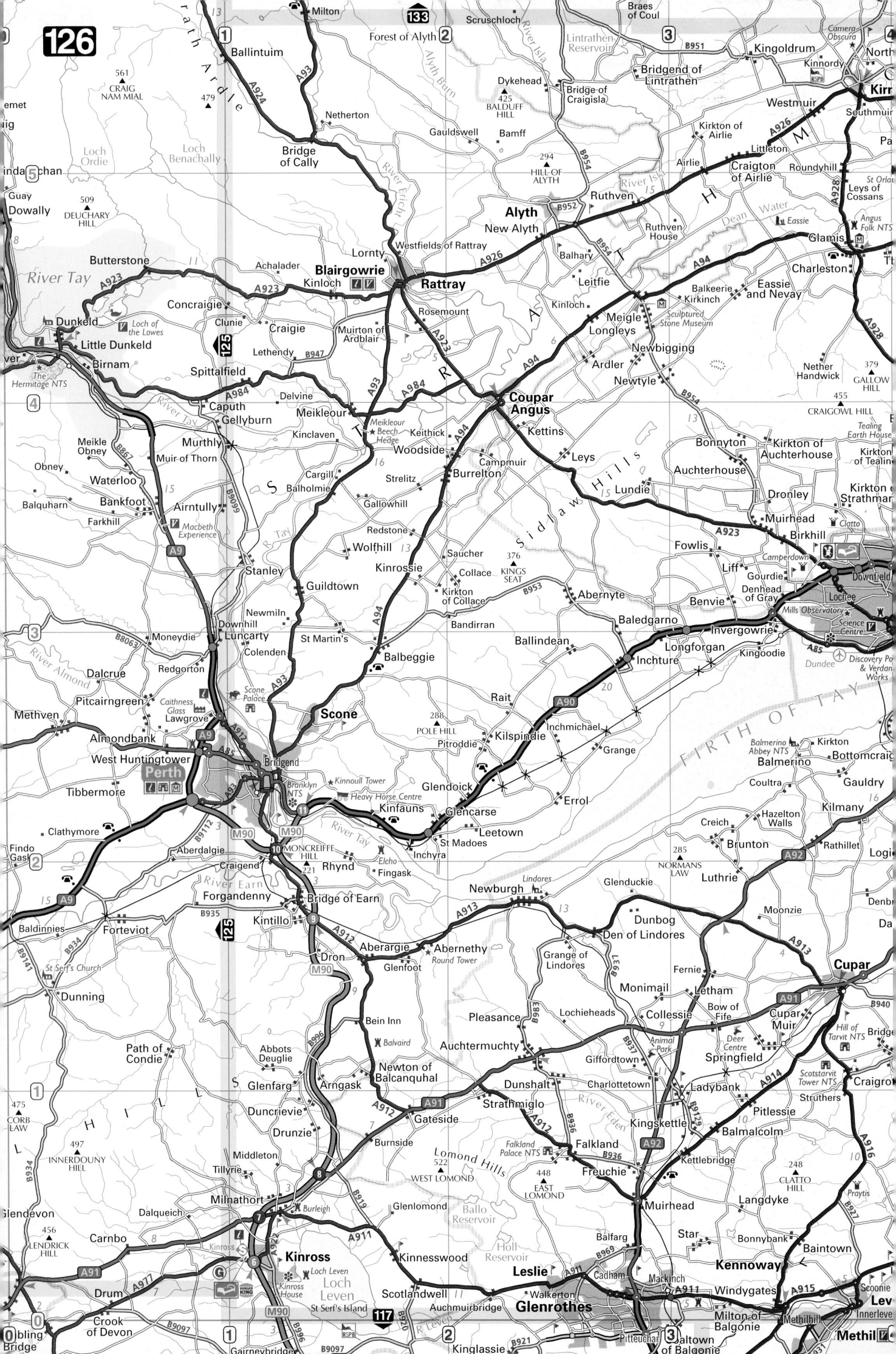

Loch Eynort

The Cuillin Hills

SGÙRR
A' GHEADAIDH 974

AN CRUACHIN 434
Glenbrittle House
Bualintur

Cuillin Hills

SGÙRR
ALASDAIR 1009

Loch
Coruisk

Loch Crèithe

BLA

225
CEANN NA BEINNE

GARS
BHEINN 894

Loch
Scavaig

Loch Brittle

Rudh' an Dùnain

Soay Sound

BEINN
BHREAC 139

Mol-chlach

SOAY

E

Rudh'
Aonghais

CANNA

CÀRN A' GHAILL 210

A'Chill

Garrisdale Point

Canna
Harbour

Rudha
Shamhnan Insir

C
U
I
L
L
I
N

S
O
U
N
D

NG

Sanday

Sound of Canna

MULLACH
MÒR 302

Rudha na Roinne

Oigh-sgeir

A Bhrideanach

ORVAL 570

Kinloch

Loch
Scresort

RUM

ASKIVAL 810

Sound of Rum

SGÙRR NAN
GILLEAN 763

The Small Isles

Rudha nam
Meirleach

Bay of
Laig

Cleadale

AN
CRUACHAN 299

Rudha an Fhasaidh

Laig

EIGG

Kildonnan

Sound of Eigg

AN SGÙRR 393

Sandavore

Eilean
Chathastail

Eilean
nan Each

MUCK

Port Mor

0   1   2   3   4   5 miles

0 1 2 3 4 5 6   7 kilometres

Sanna Point

Kilmory

Sanna
Bay

Sanna Bay

Achnaha

B

Portuairk

MEALL NAN CON 436

Ardnamurchan
Point

Achosnich

B8007

To Bagh a Chaisteil
(To Castleb

Eilean Mòr

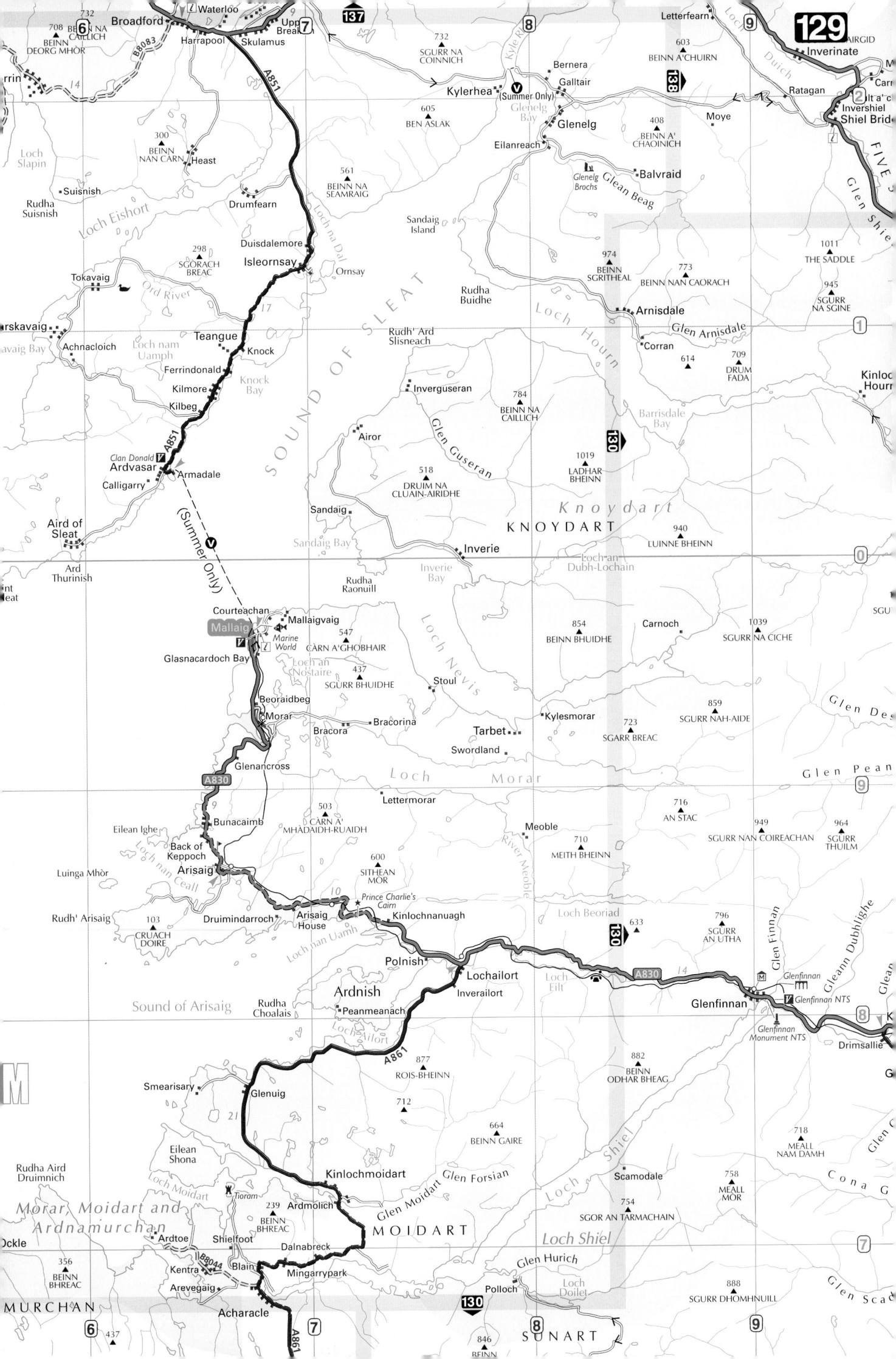

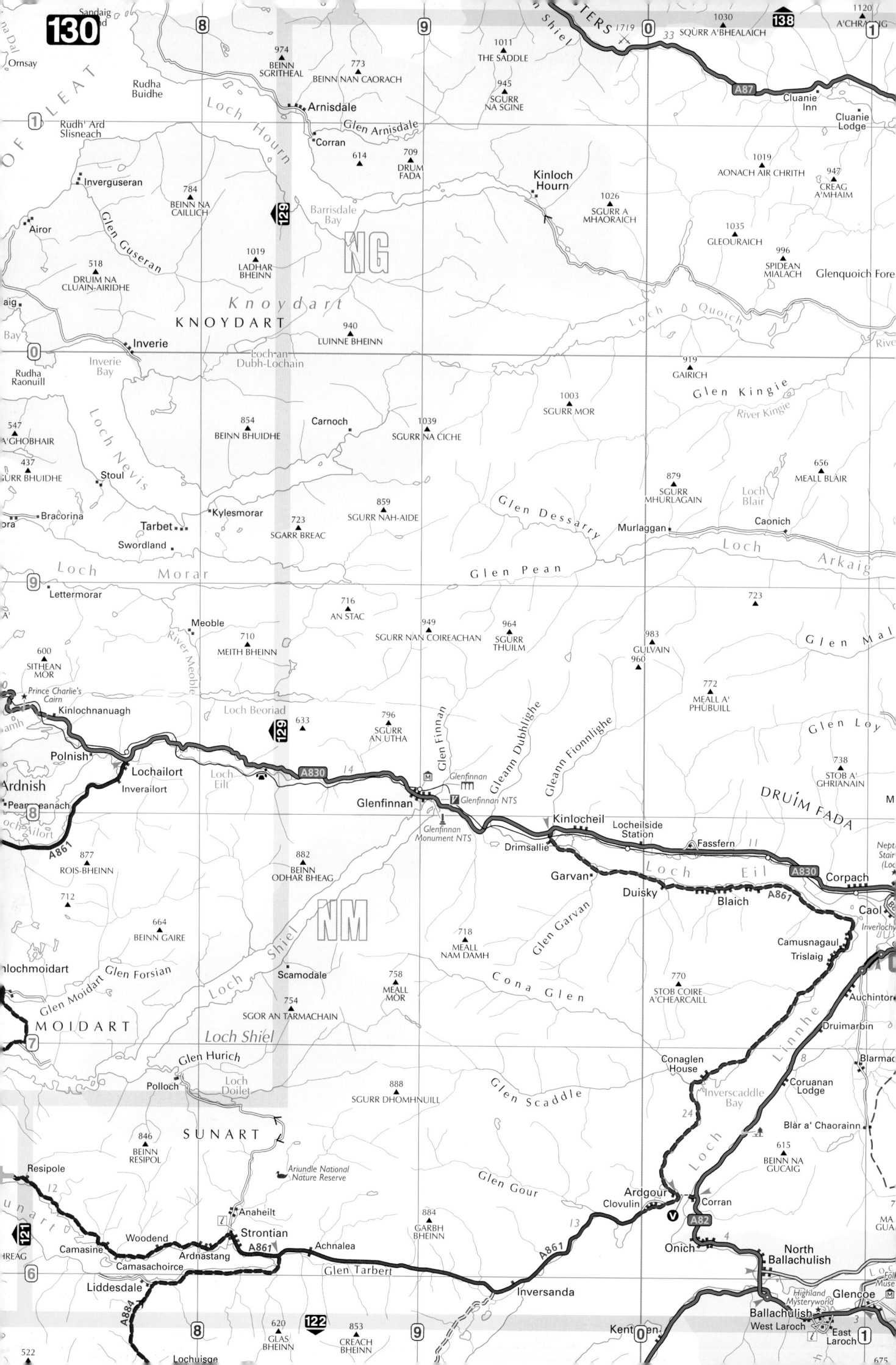

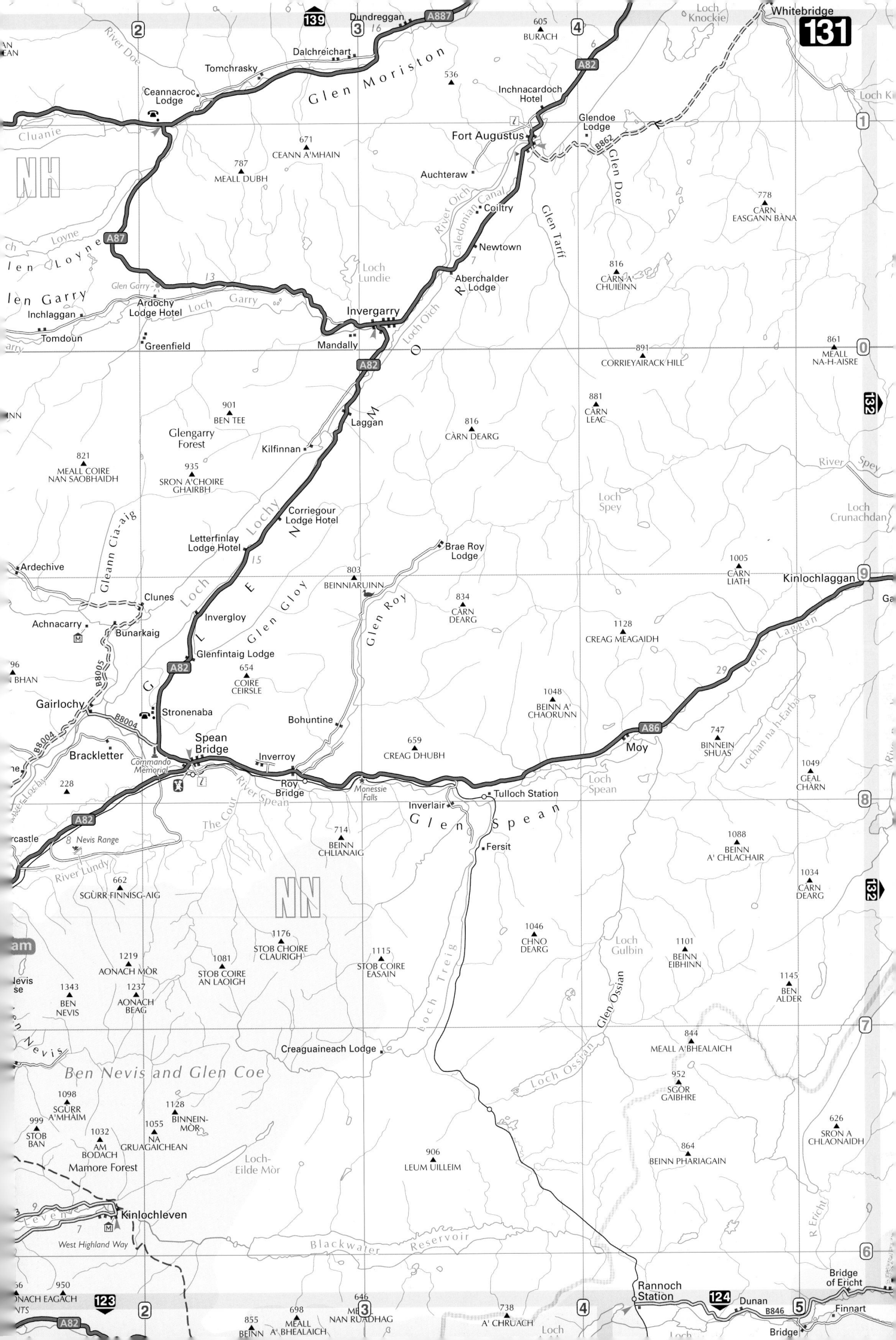

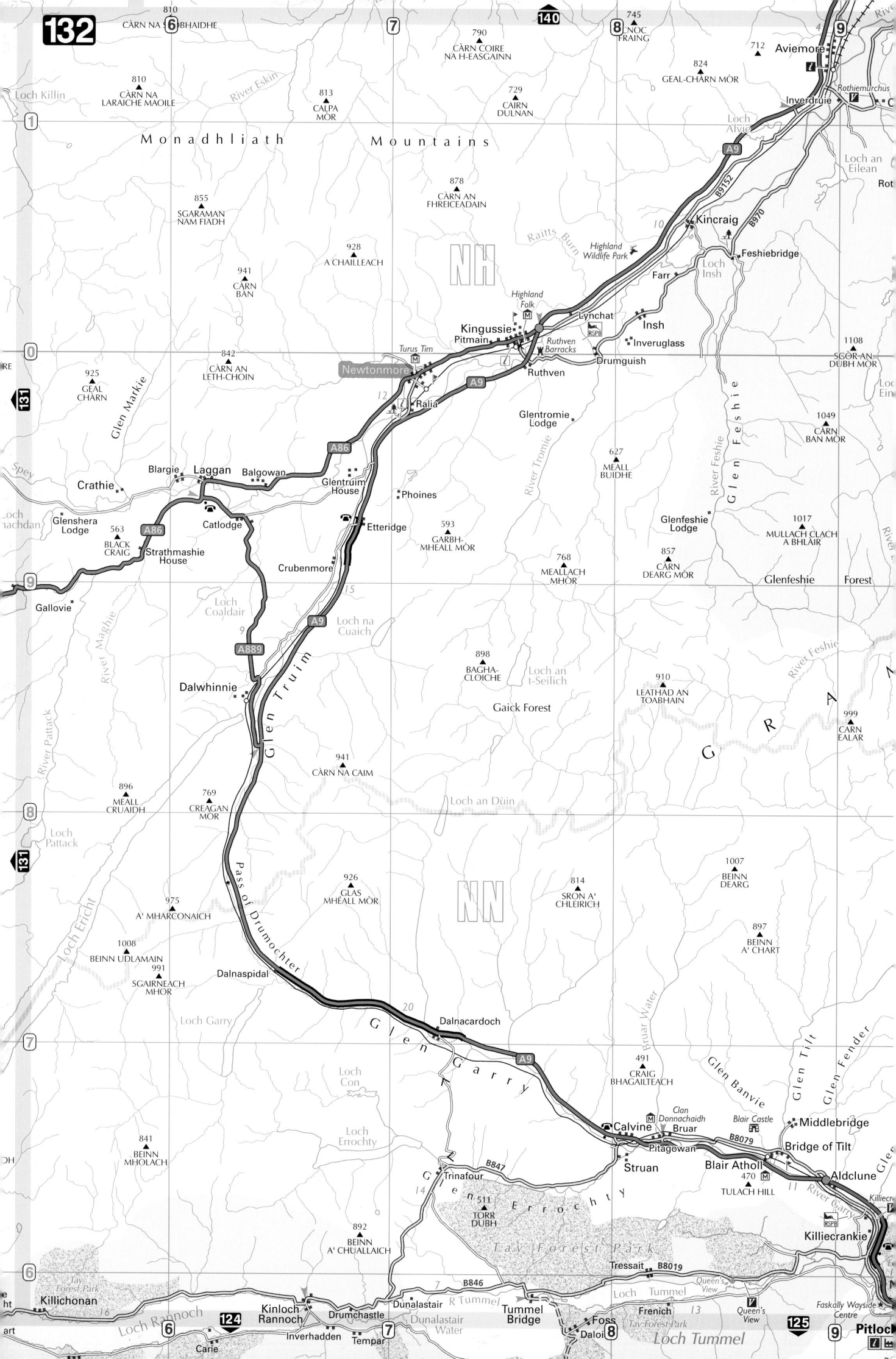

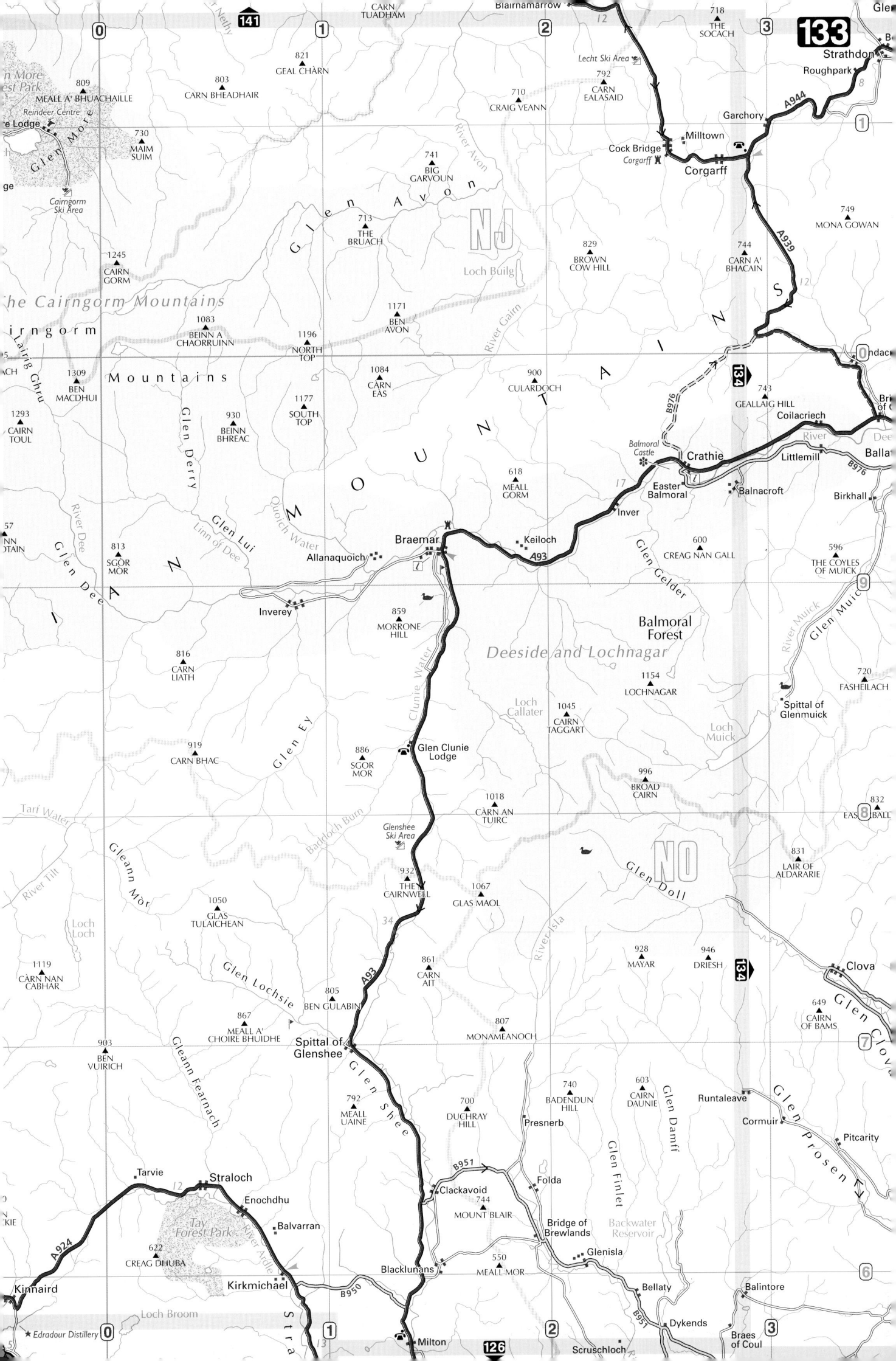

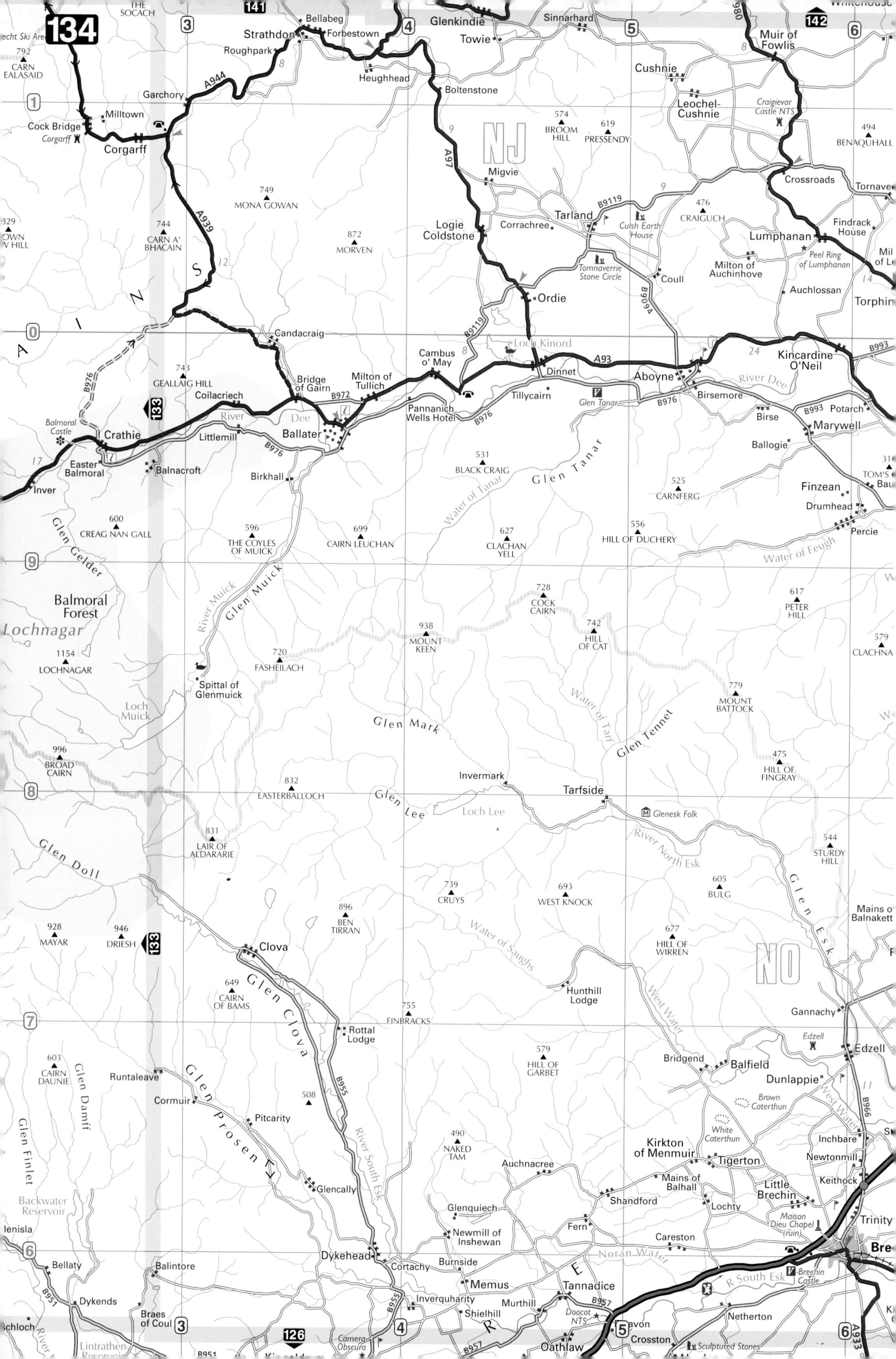

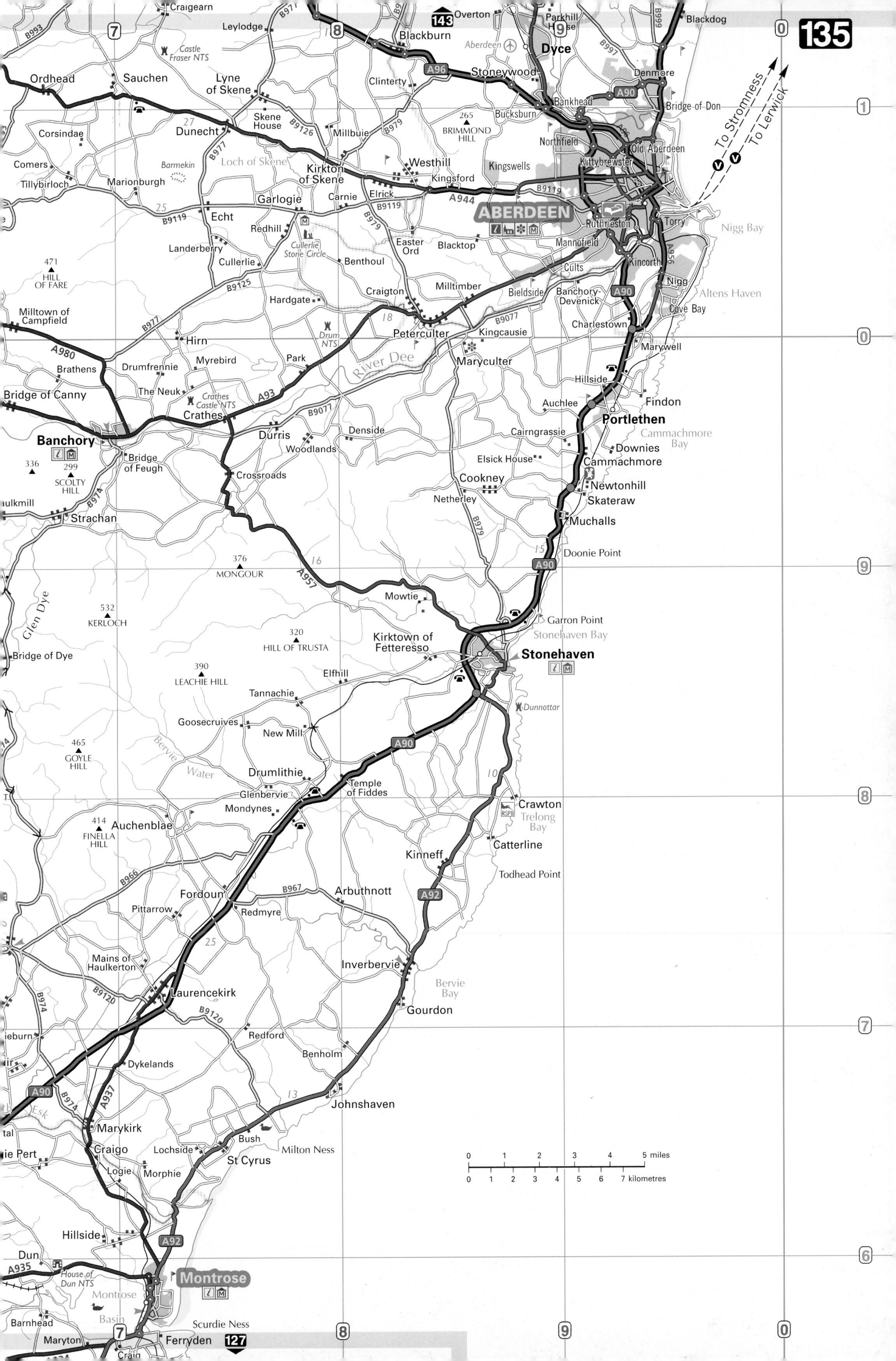

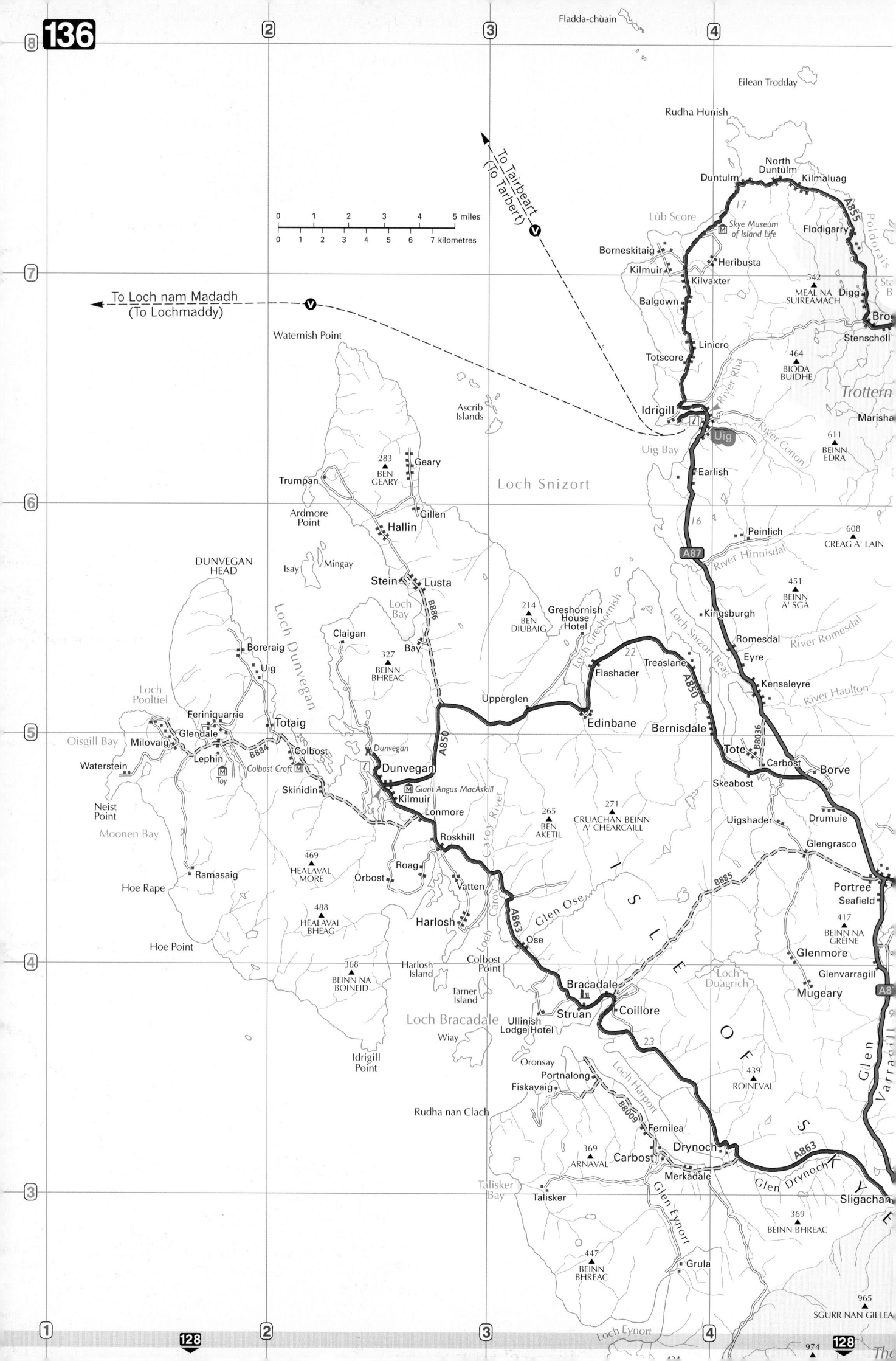

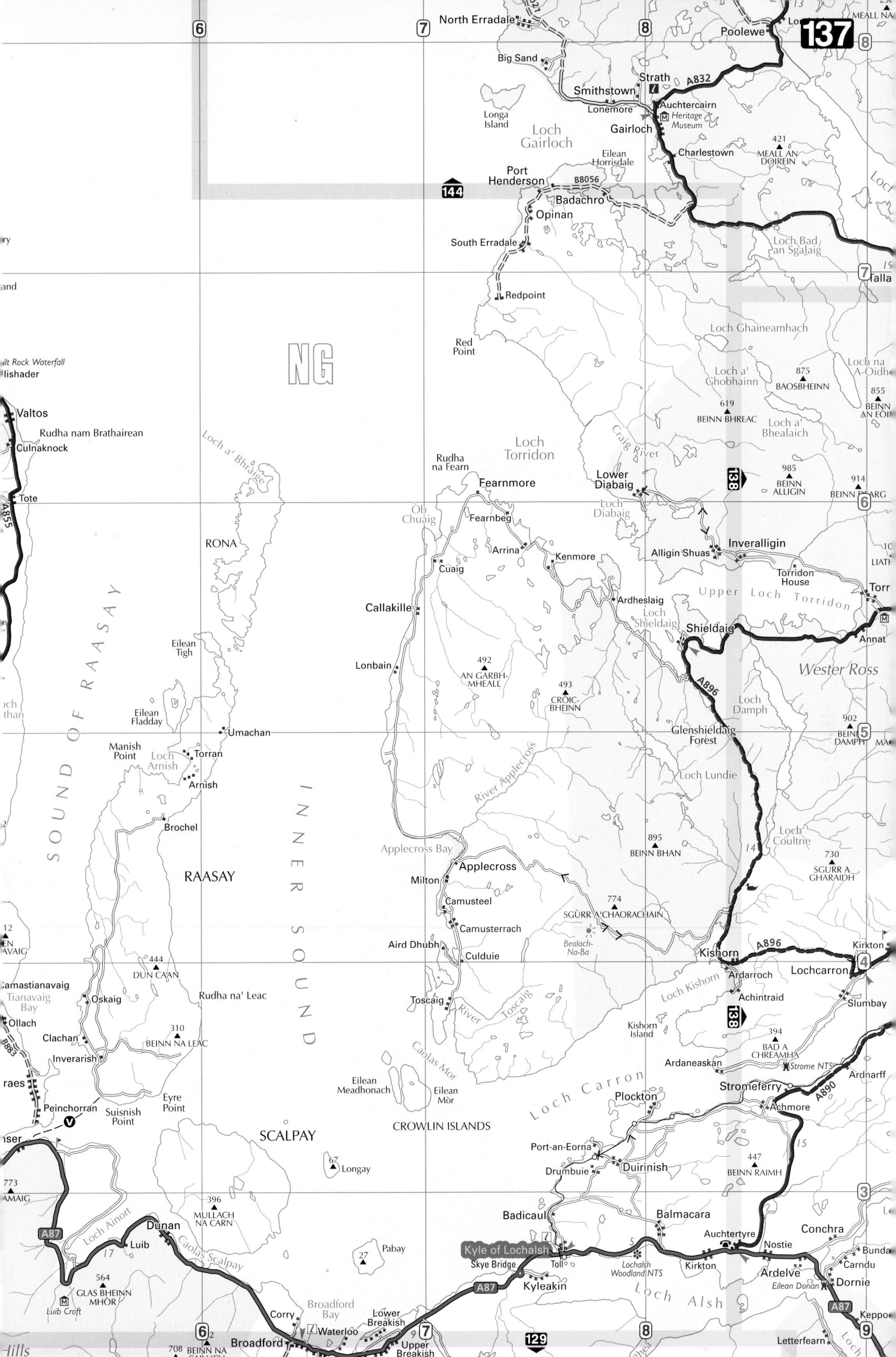

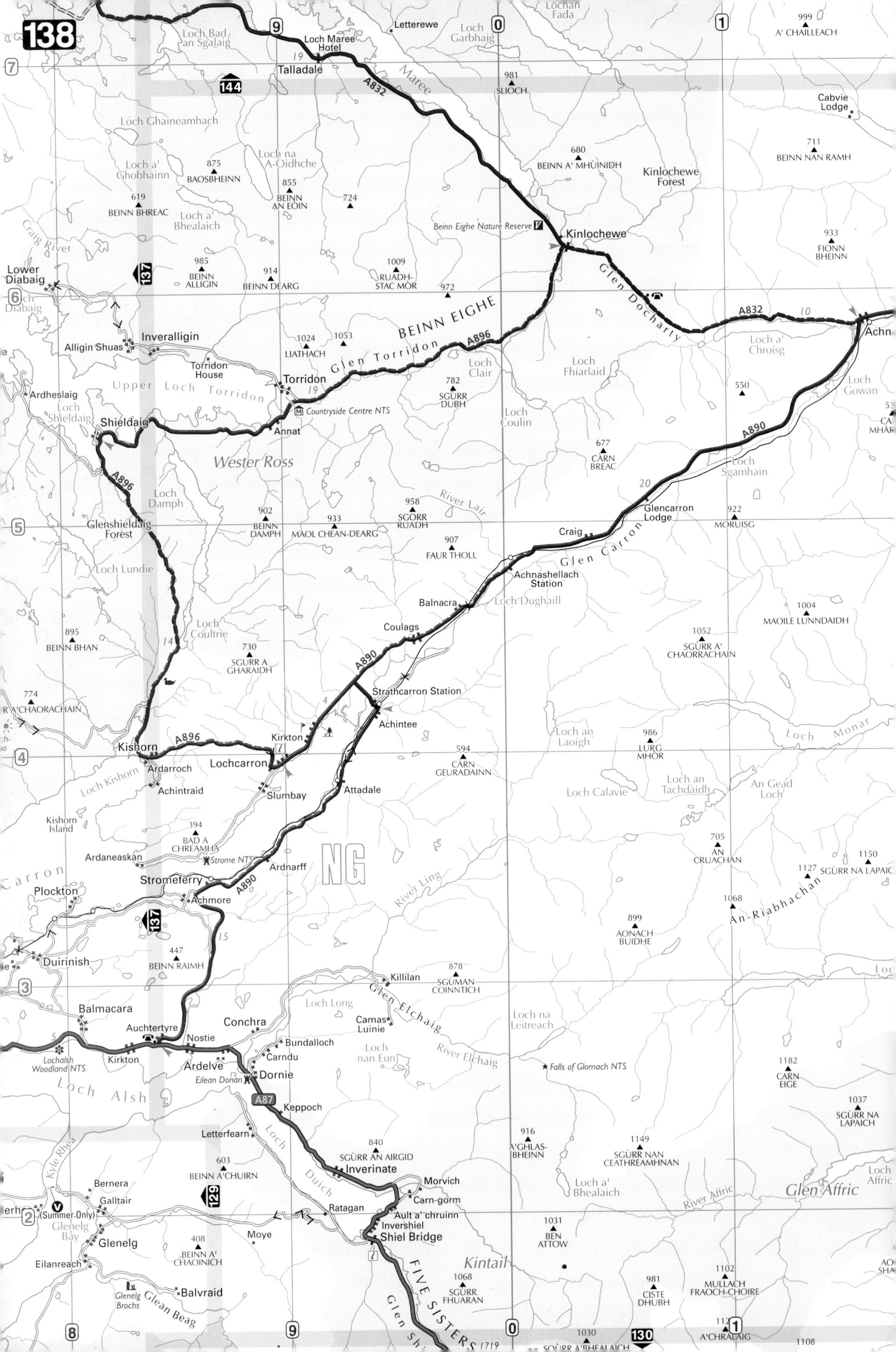

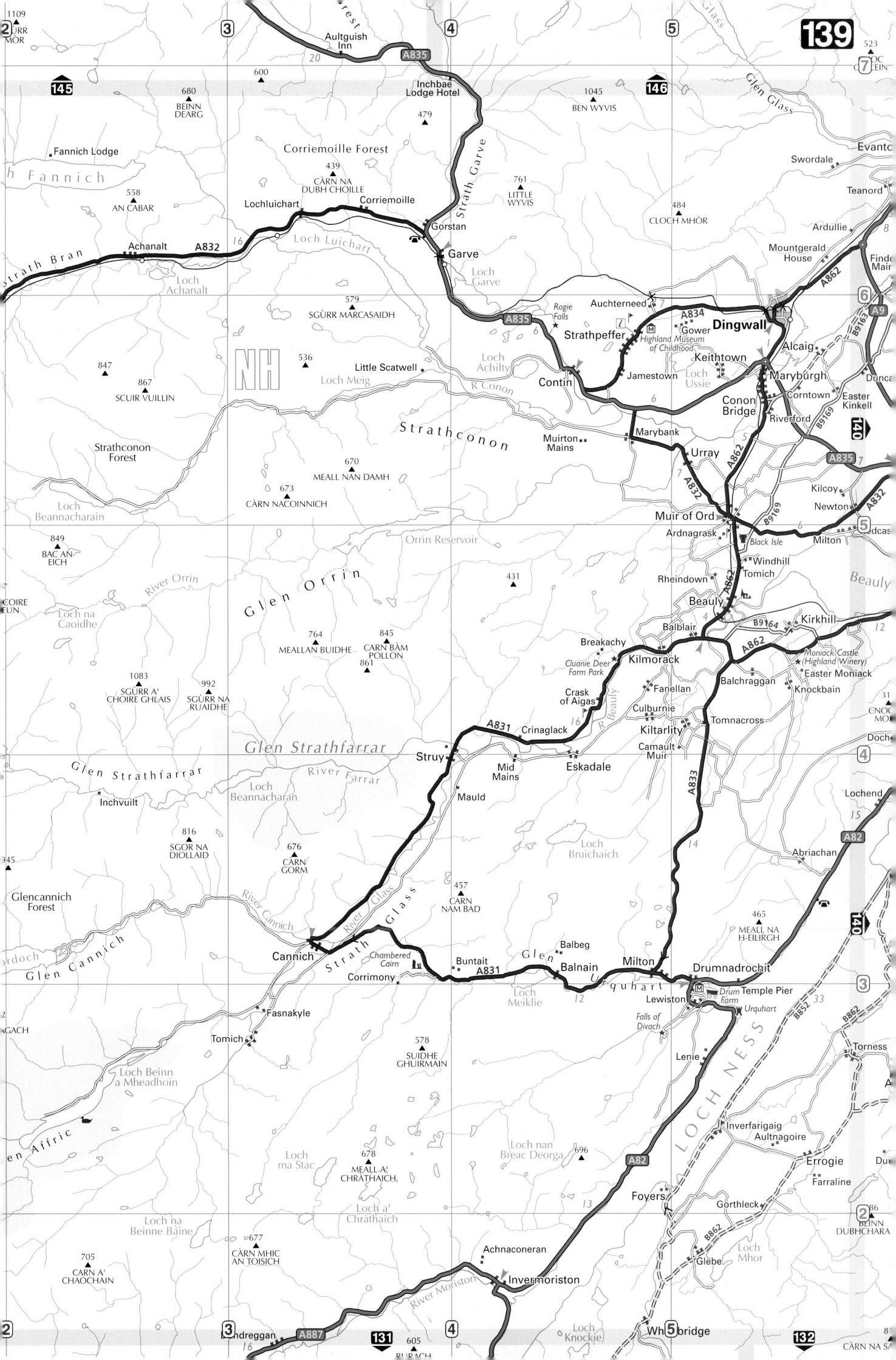

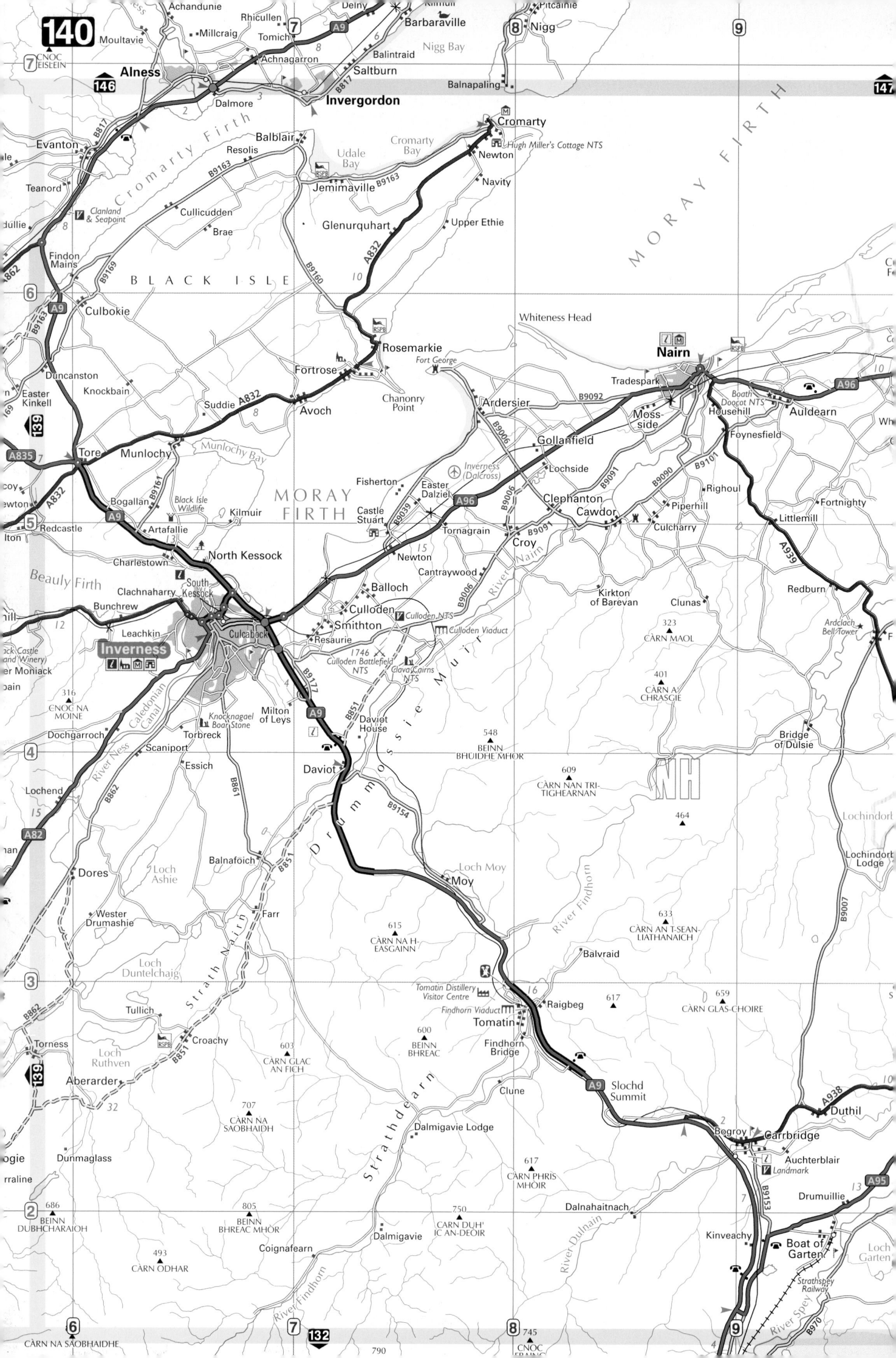

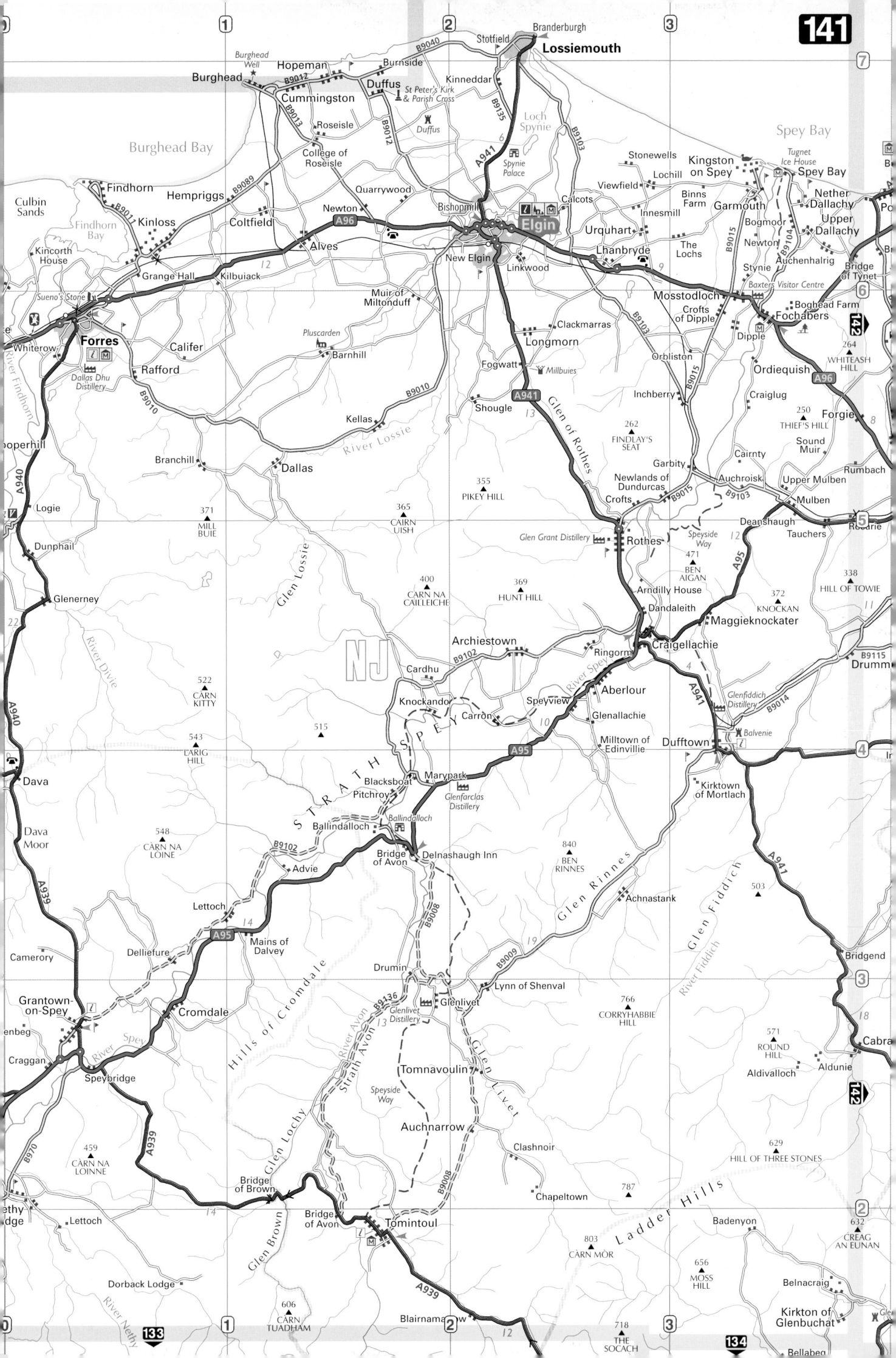

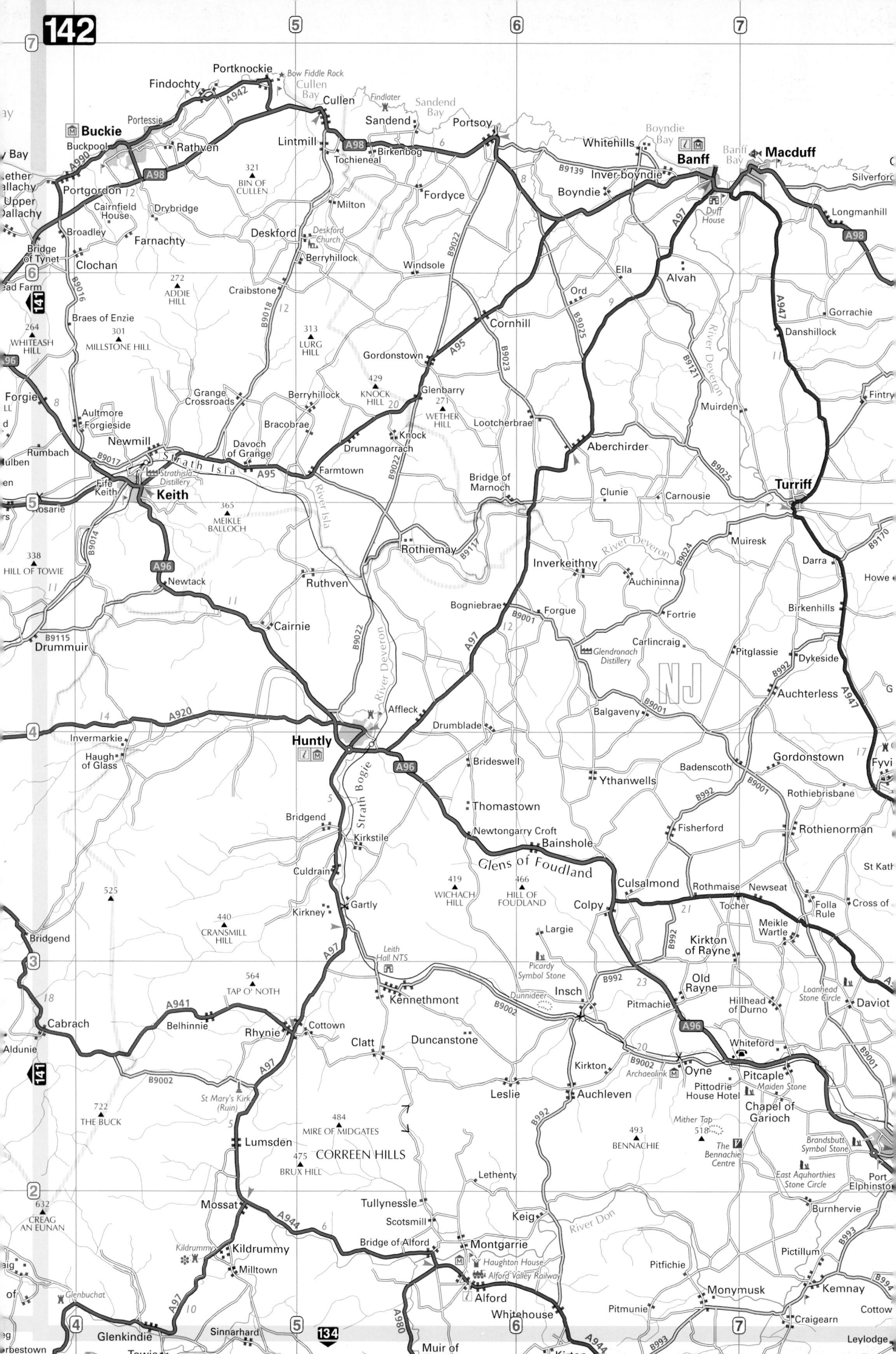

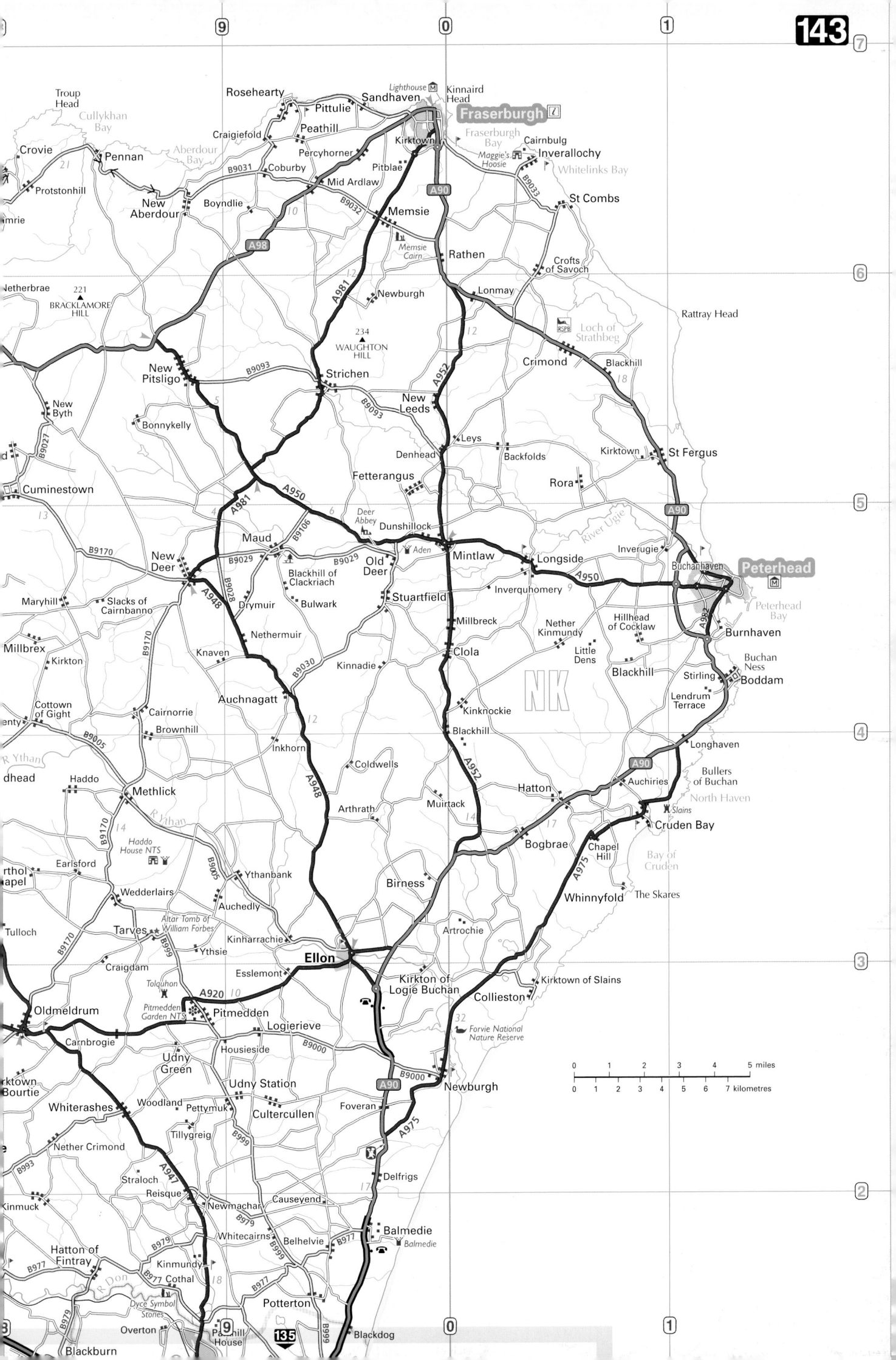

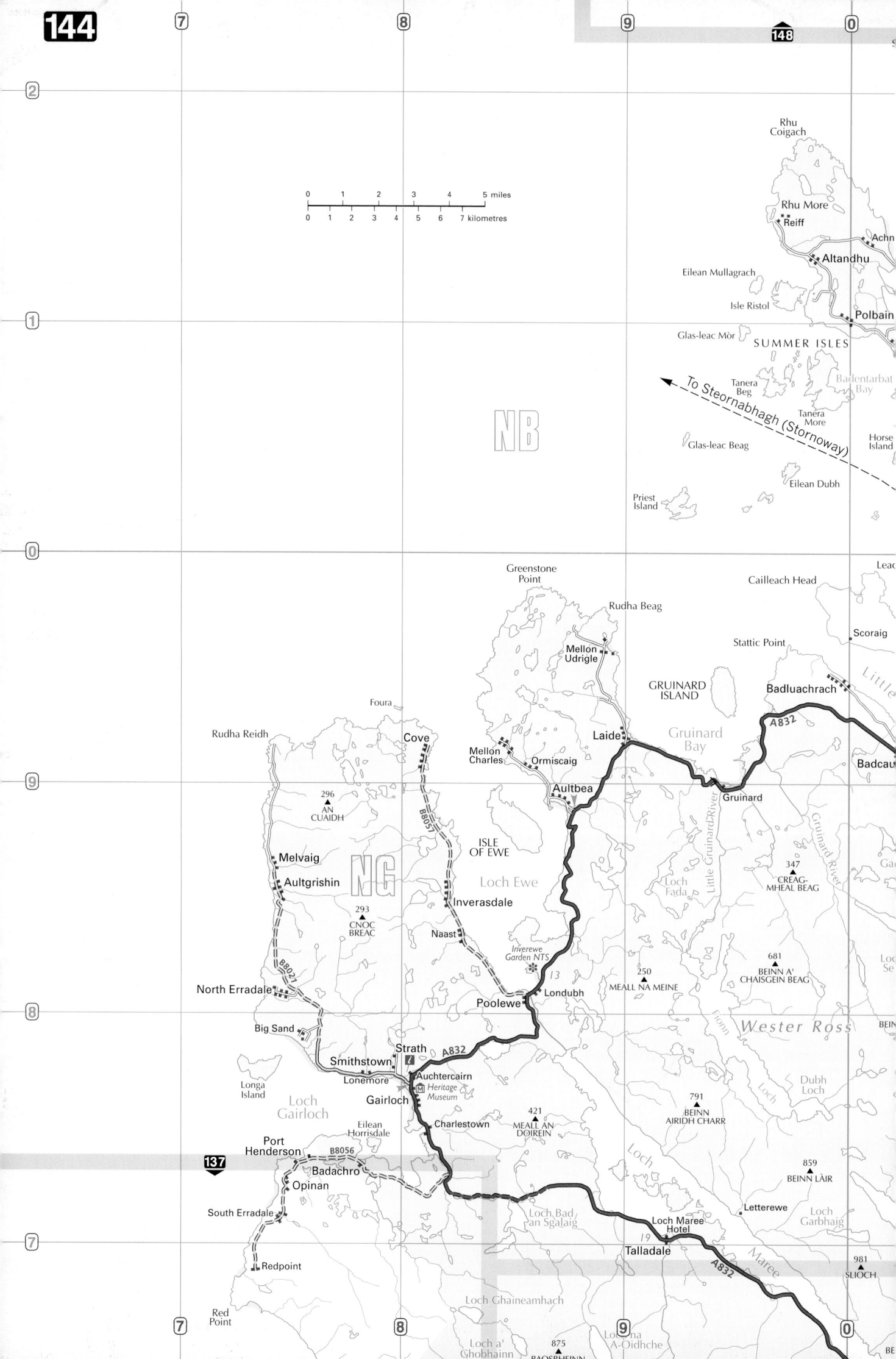

Scale:
0 1 2 3 4 5 miles
0 1 2 3 4 5 6 7 kilometres

NB

Rhu Coigach
Rhu More
Reiff
Achn
Altandhu
Eilean Mullagrach
Isle Ristol
Polbain
Glas-leac Mòr   SUMMER ISLES
Badentarbat Bay
Tanera Beg
To Steornabhagh (Stornoway)
Tanera More
Glas-leac Beag
Horse Island
Eilean Dubh
Priest Island

Greenstone Point
Cailleach Head
Leac
Rudha Beag
Stattic Point
Scoraig
Mellon Udrigle
GRUINARD ISLAND
Badluachrach
Little
Foura
Gruinard Bay
A832
Rudha Reidh
Cove
Mellon Charles
Laide
Badcau
296 AN CUAIDH
Ormiscaig
Gruinard
Aultbea
B8057
ISLE OF EWE
347 CREAG-MHEAL BEAG
Ga
Melvaig
NG
Loch Ewe
Aultgrishin
293 CNOC BREAC
Inverasdale
Loch Fada
Naast
681 BEINN A' CHAISGEIN BEAG
Lo Se
B8021
Inverewe Garden NTS
13
250 MEALL NA MEINE
North Erradale
Londubh
Poolewe
Wester Ross
BEIN
Big Sand
Strath
A832
Dubh Loch
Smithstown
Auchtercairn
Longa Island
Lonemore
Heritage Museum
791 BEINN AIRIDH CHARR
Loch Gairloch
Gairloch
Charlestown
421 MEALL AN DOIREIN
Loch
Eilean Horrisdale
Port Henderson
137
B8056
Badachro
859 BEINN LÀIR
Opinan
Loch Bad an Sgalaig
Letterewe
Loch Garbhaig
South Erradale
Loch Maree Hotel
Redpoint
19
Talladale
A832
981 SLIOCH
Red Point
Loch Ghaineamhach
Maree
Loch a' Ghobhainn
875
Loch na A-Oidhche
BE

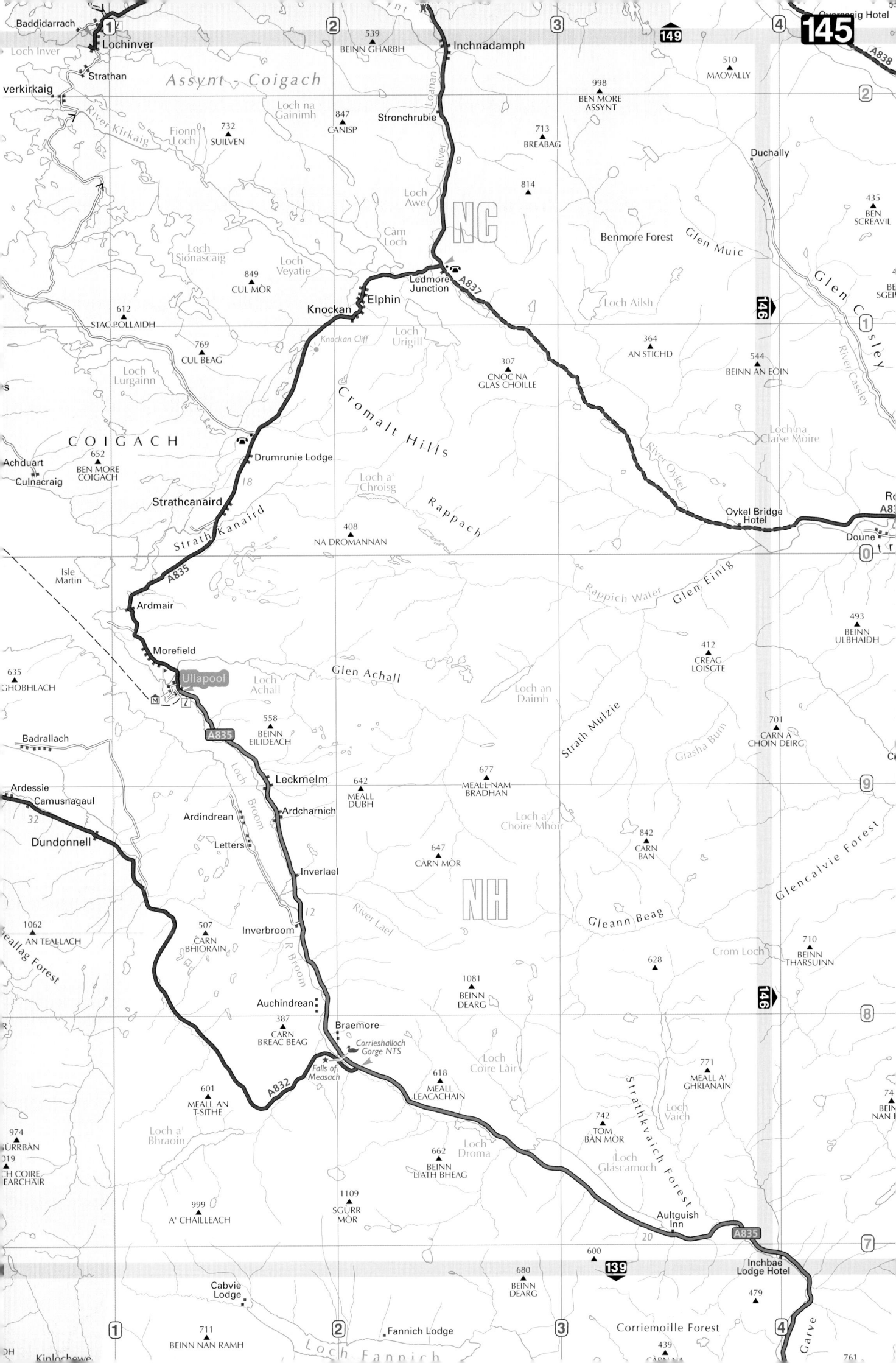

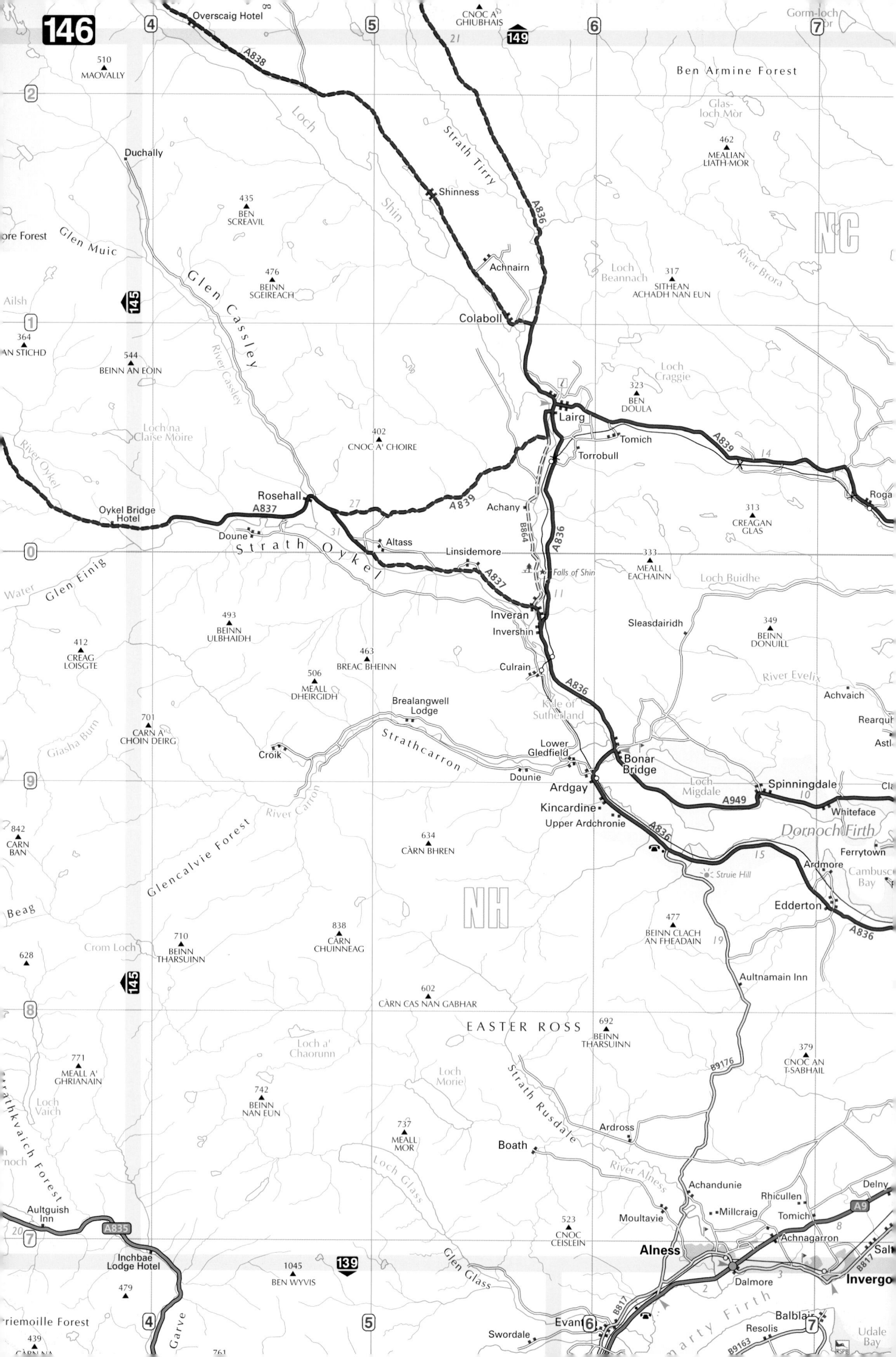

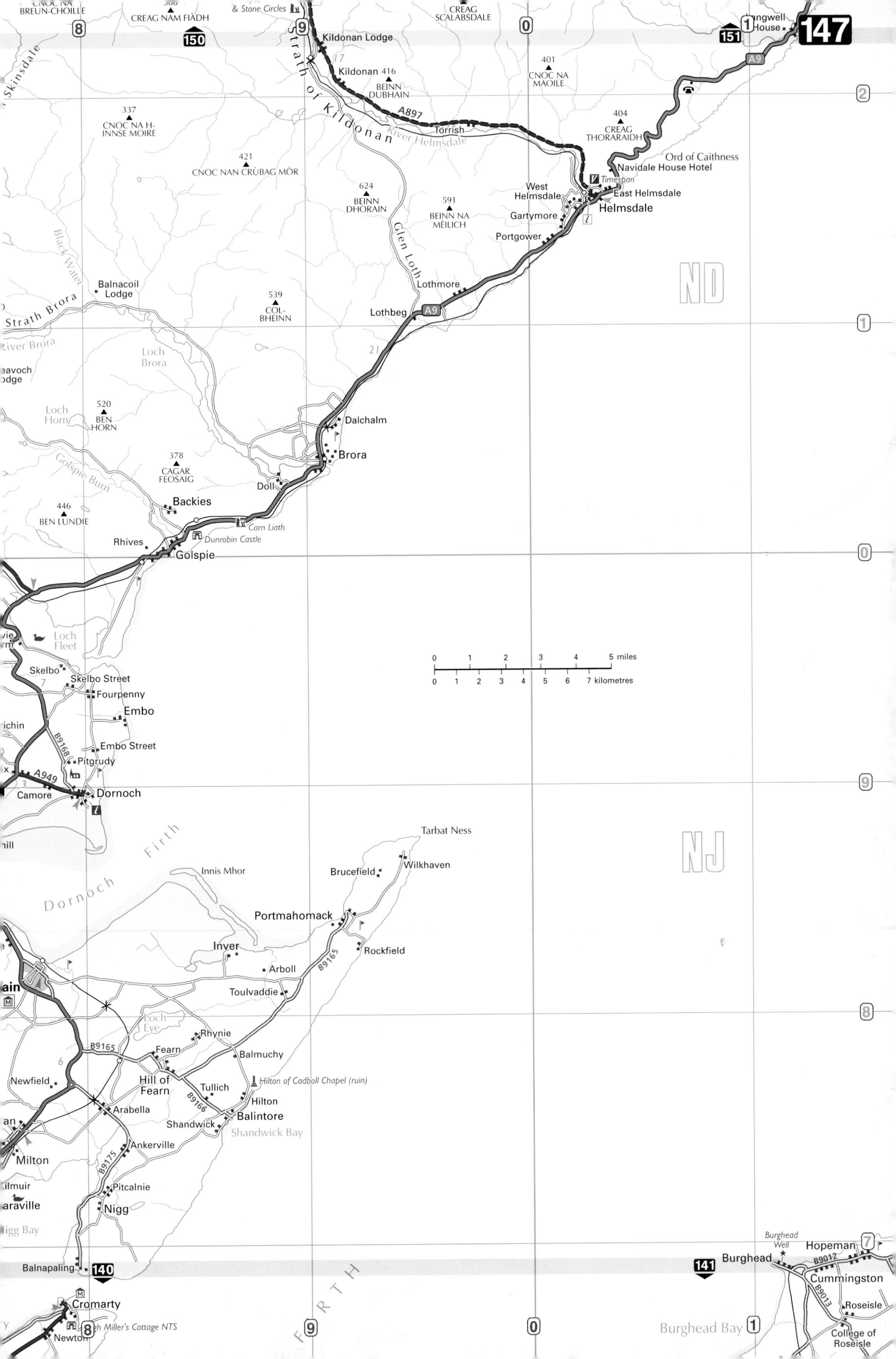

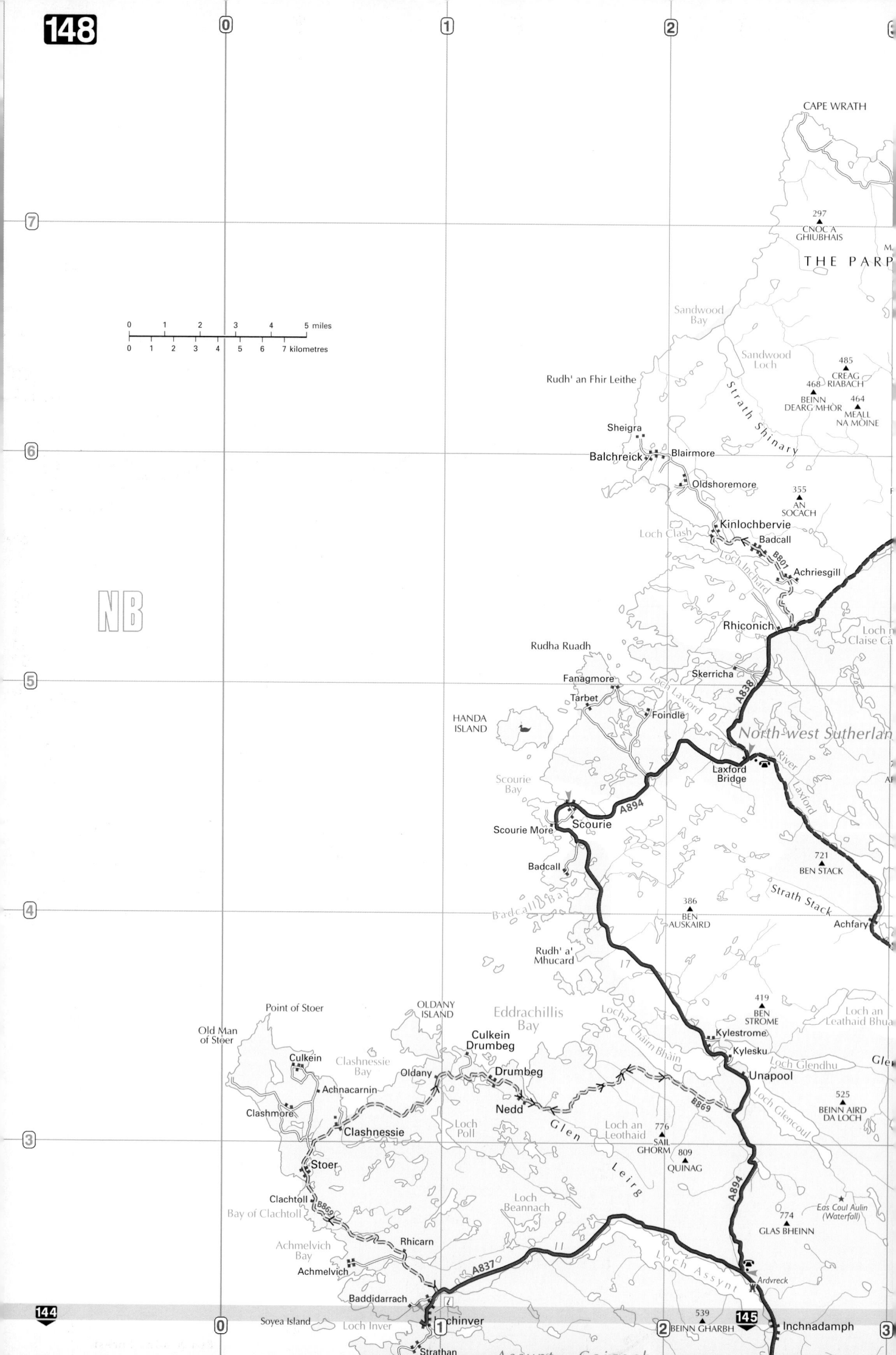

NB

0   1   2   3   4   5 miles
0 1 2 3 4 5 6 7 kilometres

THE PARP

CAPE WRATH

297
CNOC A
GHIUBHAIS

Sandwood
Bay

Sandwood
Loch

485
CREAG
RIABACH
468

464
MEALL
NA MOINE

BEINN
DEARG MHOR

Strath Shinary

Rudh' an Fhir Leithe

Sheigra

Balchreick   Blairmore

Oldshoremore

355
AN
SOCACH

Kinlochbervie

Loch Clash

Badcall

B801

Achriesgill

Loch Inchard

Rhiconich

Loch n
Claise C

Rudha Ruadh

Skerricha

Loch Laxford

A838

Fanagmore

Tarbet

Foindle

North-west Sutherlan

HANDA
ISLAND

Scourie
Bay

River Laxford

Laxford
Bridge

Scourie More   Scourie

A894

Badcall

721
BEN STACK

Badcall Bay

386
BEN
AUSKAIRD

Strath Stack

Achfary

Rudh' a'
Mhucard

17

Point of Stoer

OLDANY
ISLAND

Eddrachillis
Bay

Loch a Chairn Bhain

419
BEN
STROME

Loch an
Leathaid Bhua

Old Man
of Stoer

Culkein

Clashnessie
Bay

Culkein
Drumbeg

Kylestrome

Kylesku

525
BEINN AIRD
DA LOCH

Oldany

Drumbeg

Achnacarnin

Loch Glendhu

Gle

Clashmore

Nedd

Unapool

B869

Loch Glencoul

Clashnessie

Loch
Poll

Glen

Loch an
Leothaid

776
SAIL
GHORM

Leirg

809
QUINAG

Stoer

A894

Clachtoll

B869

Loch
Beannach

774
GLAS BHEINN

Eas Coul Aulin
(Waterfall)

Bay of Clachtoll

Achmelvich
Bay

Rhicarn

11

A837

Loch Assynt

Ardvreck

Achmelvich

Baddidarrach

Soyea Island   Loch Inver

chinver

539
BEINN GHARBH

Inchnadamph

Strathan

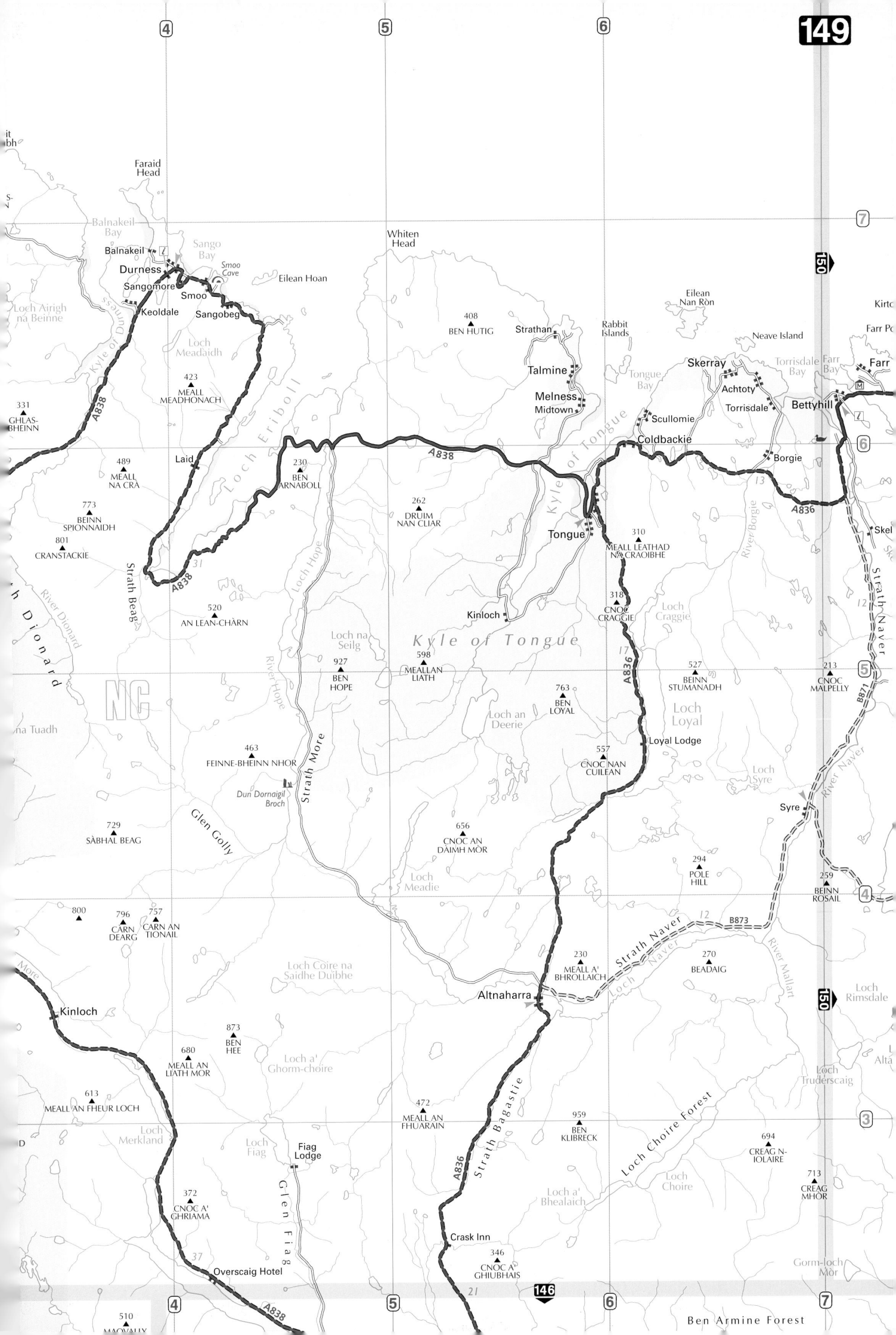

Faraid
Head

Balnakeil
Bay

Balnakeil

Durness

Sangomore

Keoldale

Smoo

Sangobeg

Sango
Bay

Smoo
Cave

Eilean Hoan

Whiten
Head

Loch Airigh
na Beinne

331
GHLAS-
BHEINN

Loch Dhuis Dhuris

423
MEALL
MEADHONACH

Loch
Meadaidh

489
MEALL
NA CRÀ

Laid

773
BEINN
SPIONNAIDH

801
CRANSTACKIE

Strath Beag

A838

230
BEN
ARNABOLL

Loch Eriboll

Strath Dionard

River Dionard

NC

520
AN LEAN-CHÀRN

Loch Hope

River Hope

262
DRUIM
NAN CLIAR

A838

Kyle of Tongue

Tongue

Kinloch

408
BEN HUTIG

Strathan

Talmine

Melness

Midtown

Rabbit
Islands

Tongue
Bay

Eilean
Nan Ròn

Skerray

Achtoty

Torrisdale

Scullomie

Coldbackie

Torrisdale
Bay

Neave Island

Bettyhill

Borgie

A836

13

River Borgie

Strath Naver

150

Farr
Bay

Farr

Kirto

Farr Po

Skel

Skel

12

310
MEALL LEATHAD
NA CRAOIBHE

318
CNOC
CRAGGIE

A836

17

Loch
Craggie

Loch
Loyal

527
BEINN
STUMANADH

213
CNOC
MALPELLY

5

na Tuadh

598
MEALLAN
LIATH

927
BEN
HOPE

Loch na
Seilg

763
BEN
LOYAL

Loch an
Deerie

557
CNOC NAN
CUILEAN

Loyal Lodge

463
FEINNE-BHEINN NHOR

Strath More

Dun Dornaigil
Broch

729
SÀBHAL BEAG

Glen Golly

656
CNOC AN
DÀIMH MÒR

Loch
Meadie

Loch
Syre

Syre

River Naver

294
POLE
HILL

259
BEINN
ROSAIL

4

800

796
CÀRN
DEARG

757
CARN AN
TIONAIL

Loch Coire na
Saidhe Duibhe

230
MEALL A'
BHROLLAICH

Strath Naver

12

270
BEADAIG

B873

River Mallart

150

Loch
Rimsdale

More

Kinloch

873
BEN
HEE

680
MEALL AN
LIATH MOR

Loch a'
Ghorm-choire

Altnaharra

Loch Naver

Strath Bagastie

613
MEALL AN FHEUR LOCH

Loch
Merkland

Loch
Fiag

Fiag
Lodge

472
MEALL AN
FHUARAIN

959
BEN
KLIBRECK

Loch Choire Forest

694
CREAG N-
IOLAIRE

Loch
Truderscaig

Loch
Alt

3

372
CNOC A'
GHRIAMA

Glen Fiag

37

Overscaig Hotel

A838

4

Crask Inn

346
CNOC A'
GHIUBHAIS

A836

21

146

5

Loch a'
Bhealaich

Loch
Choire

713
CREAG
MHOR

Gorm-loch
Mòr

6

Ben Armine Forest

7

510
MAOVALLY

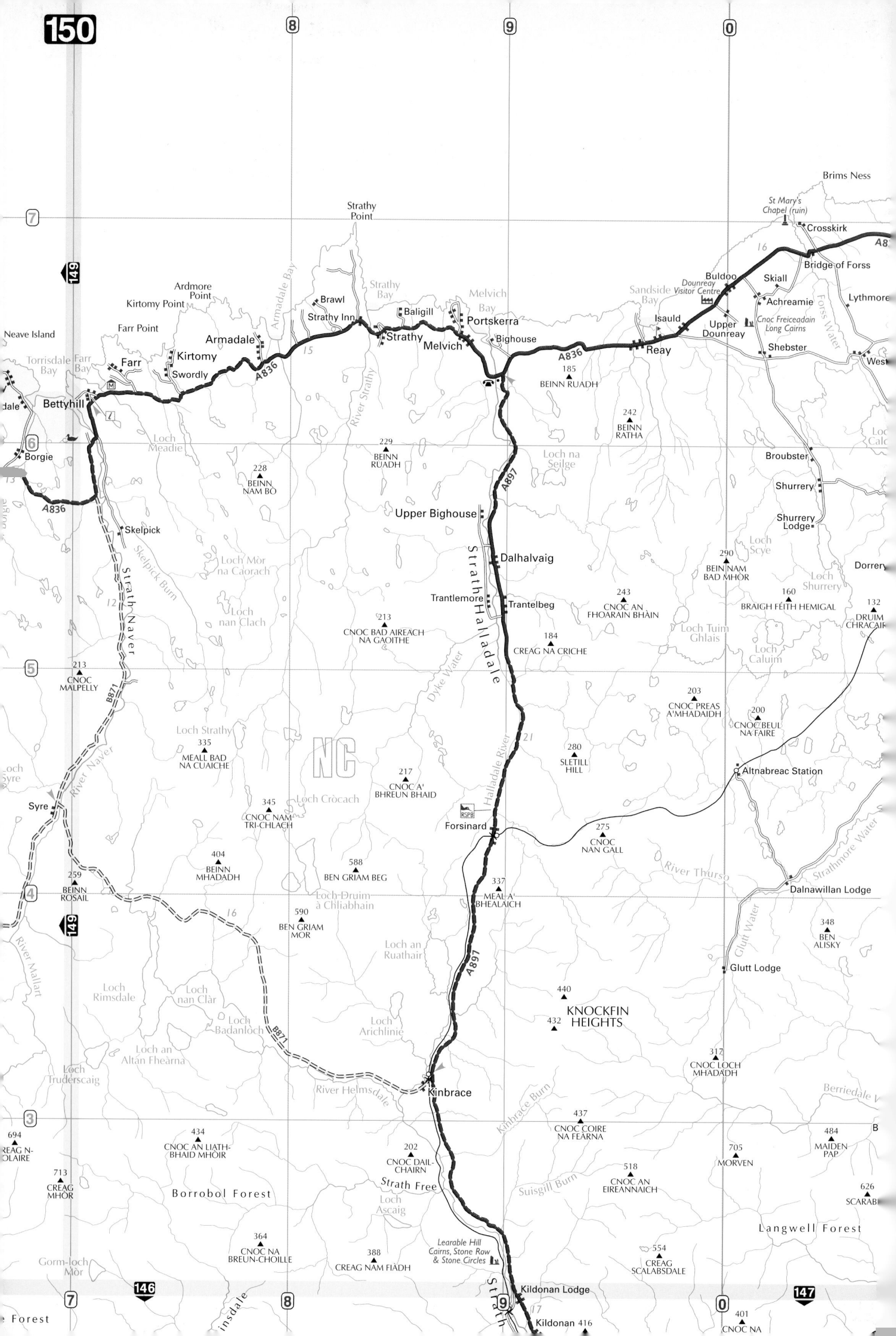

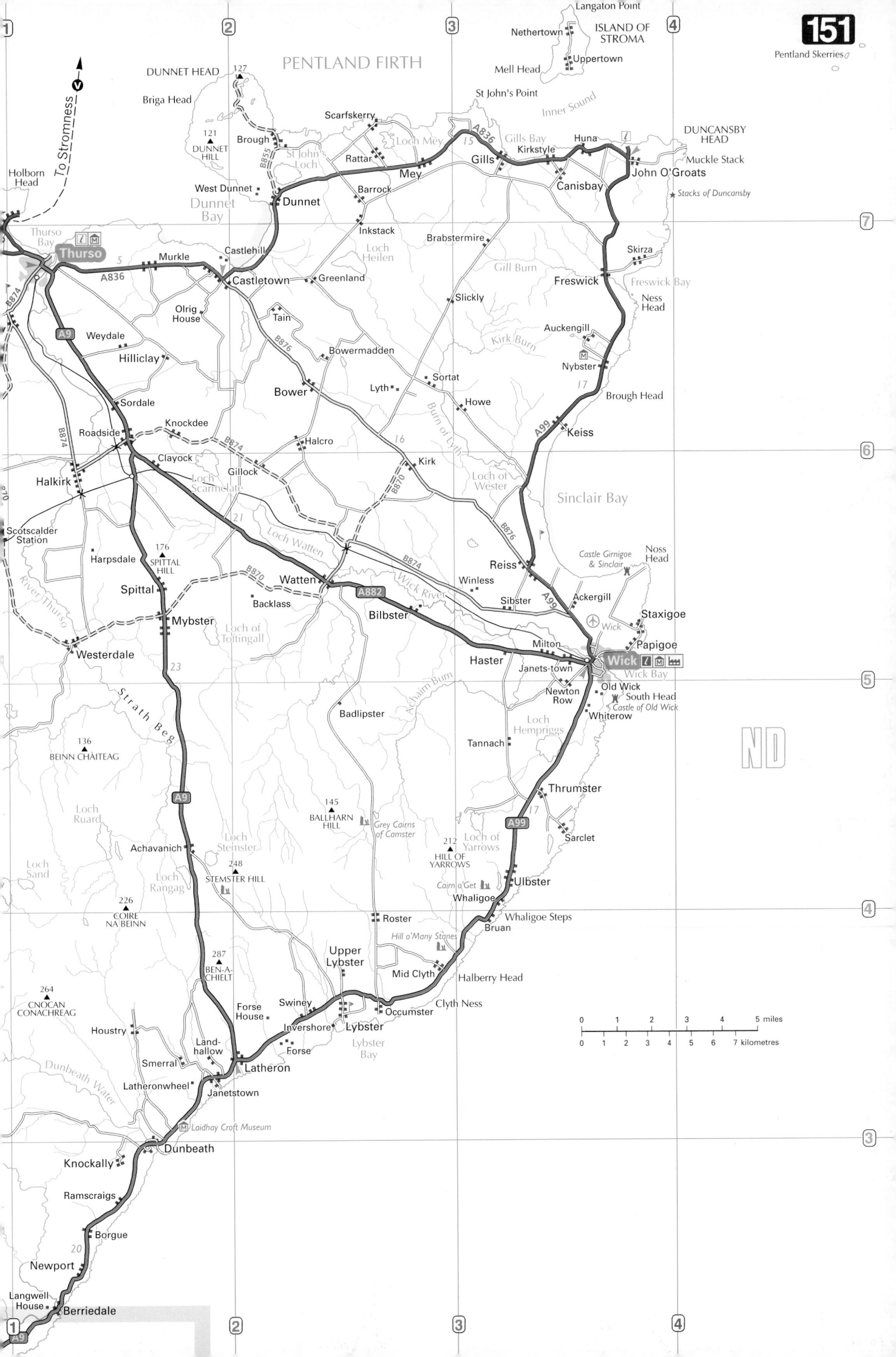

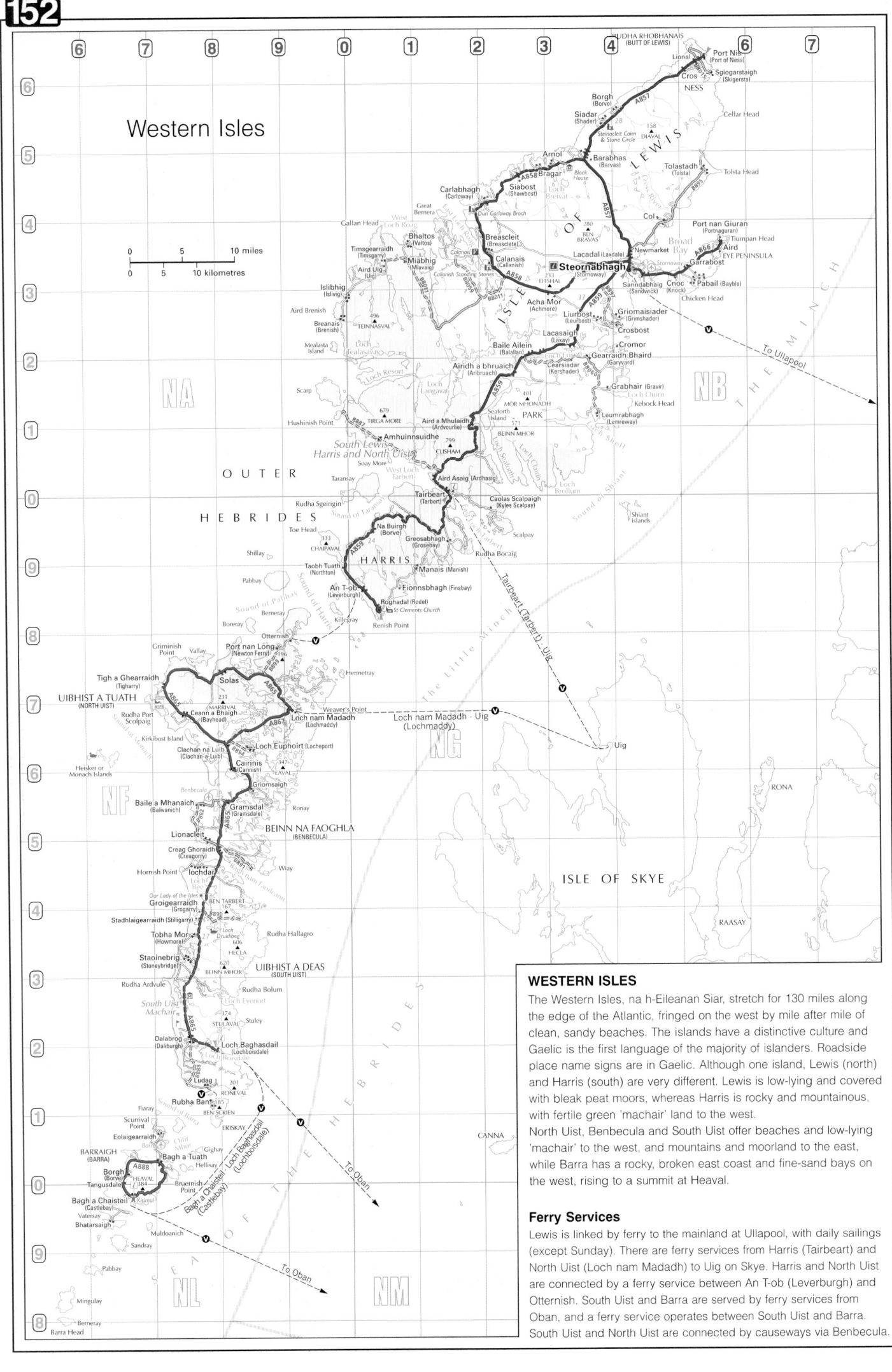

Western Isles

WESTERN ISLES

The Western Isles, na h-Eileanan Siar, stretch for 130 miles along the edge of the Atlantic, fringed on the west by mile after mile of clean, sandy beaches. The islands have a distinctive culture and Gaelic is the first language of the majority of islanders. Roadside place name signs are in Gaelic. Although one island, Lewis (north) and Harris (south) are very different. Lewis is low-lying and covered with bleak peat moors, whereas Harris is rocky and mountainous, with fertile green 'machair' land to the west.

North Uist, Benbecula and South Uist offer beaches and low-lying 'machair' to the west, and mountains and moorland to the east, while Barra has a rocky, broken east coast and fine-sand bays on the west, rising to a summit at Heaval.

Ferry Services

Lewis is linked by ferry to the mainland at Ullapool, with daily sailings (except Sunday). There are ferry services from Harris (Tairbeart) and North Uist (Loch nam Madadh) to Uig on Skye. Harris and North Uist are connected by a ferry service between An T-ob (Leverburgh) and Otternish. South Uist and Barra are served by ferry services from Oban, and a ferry service operates between South Uist and Barra. South Uist and North Uist are connected by causeways via Benbecula.

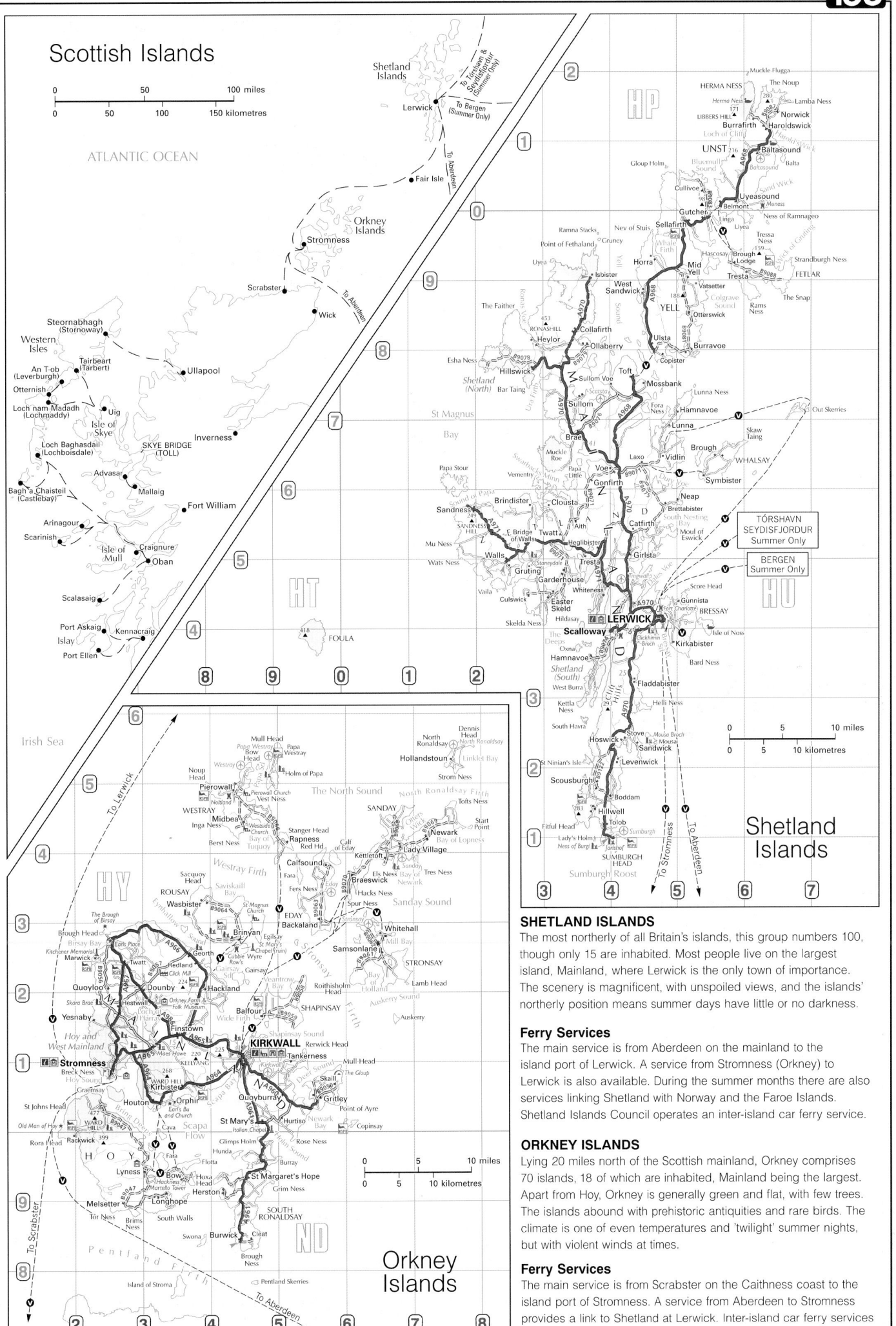

SHETLAND ISLANDS

The most northerly of all Britain's islands, this group numbers 100, though only 15 are inhabited. Most people live on the largest island, Mainland, where Lerwick is the only town of importance. The scenery is magnificent, with unspoiled views, and the islands' northerly position means summer days have little or no darkness.

Ferry Services

The main service is from Aberdeen on the mainland to the island port of Lerwick. A service from Stromness (Orkney) to Lerwick is also available. During the summer months there are also services linking Shetland with Norway and the Faroe Islands. Shetland Islands Council operates an inter-island car ferry service.

ORKNEY ISLANDS

Lying 20 miles north of the Scottish mainland, Orkney comprises 70 islands, 18 of which are inhabited, Mainland being the largest. Apart from Hoy, Orkney is generally green and flat, with few trees. The islands abound with prehistoric antiquities and rare birds. The climate is one of even temperatures and 'twilight' summer nights, but with violent winds at times.

Ferry Services

The main service is from Scrabster on the Caithness coast to the island port of Stromness. A service from Aberdeen to Stromness provides a link to Shetland at Lerwick. Inter-island car ferry services are also operated (advance reservations recommended).

Ireland

Abbeydorney B3
Abbeyfeale B3
Abbeyleix D3
Adamstown D3
Adare B3
Adrigole B2
Ahascragh C4
Ahoghill E6
Allihies A2
Anascaul A2
Annalong E5
Annestown D2
Antrim E6
Ardagh B3
Ardara C6
Ardcath E4
Ardee D5
Ardfert B3
Ardfinnan C3
Ardglass E5
Ardgroom A2
Arklow E3
Arless D3
Armagh D6
Armoy E7
Arthurstown D2
Arvagh D5
Ashbourne E4
Ashford E4
Askeaton B3
Athboy D5
Athea B3
Athenry C4
Athleague C4
Athlone C4
Athy D4
Augher D6
Aughnacloy D6
Aughrim E3
Avoca E3

Bagenalstown D3
(Muine Bheag)
Bailieborough D5
Balbriggan E4
Balla B5
Ballacolla D3
Ballaghaderreen C5
Ballina C3
Ballina B3
Ballinafad C5
Ballinagh D5
Ballinakill D3
Ballinalee C5
Ballinamore C3
Ballinamallard D6
Ballinascarty B2
Ballinasloe C4
Ballindine B5
Ballineen B2
Ballingarry C3
Ballingarry B3
Ballingeary B2
(Béal Átha an Ghaorthaidh)
Ballinhassig C2
Ballinlough C5
Ballinrobe B5
Ballinspittle C2
Ballintober C5
Ballintra C6
Ballivor D4
Ballon D3
Ballybaun C4
Ballybay D5
Ballybofey C6
Ballybunion B3
Ballycanew E3
Ballycarry E6
Ballycastle B6
Ballycastle E7
Ballyclare E6
Ballyconneely A4
Ballycotton C2
Ballycumber C4
Ballydehob B1
Ballydesmond B2
Ballyduff C2
Ballyduff B3
Ballyfarnan C5
Ballygalley E6
Ballygar C4
Ballygawley D6
Ballygowan E6
Ballyhaise D5
Ballyhale D3
Ballyhaunis C5
Ballyhean B5
Ballyheige B3
Ballyjamesduff D5
Ballykeeran C4
Ballylanders C3
Ballylongford B3
Ballylooby C3
Ballylynan D3
Ballymahon C4
Ballymakeery B2
Ballymena E6
Ballymoe C5
Ballymoney D7
Ballymore C4
Ballymore Eustace D4
Ballymote C5
Ballynahinch E6
Ballynure E6
Ballyporeen C3
Ballyragget D3
Ballyroan D4
Ballyronan D6
Ballysadare C5
Ballyshannon C6
Ballyvaughan B4
Ballywalter E6
Balrothery E4
Baltimore B1
Baltinglass D3
Banagher C4
Banbridge E6
Bandon B2
Bangor E6
Bangor Erris B5
Bansha C3

Banteer B2
Bantry B2
Beaufort B2
Belcoo C6
Belfast E6
Belgooly C2
Bellaghy D6
Belleek C6
Belmullet B6
(Béal an Mhuirhead)
Belturbet D5
Benburb D6
Bennett's Bridge D3
Beragh D6
Birr C4
Blacklion C6
Blackwater E3
Blarney C2
Blessington D4
Boherbue B2
Borris B3
Borris-in-Ossory C4
Borrisokane C4
Borrisoleigh C3
Boyle C5
Bracknagh D4
Bray E4
Bridgetown D2
Brittas D4
Broadford C3
Broadford B3
Broughshane E6
Bruff C3
Bruree C3
Bunclody D3
Buncrana D7
Bundoran C6
Bunmahon D2
Bunnahowen B6
Bunnyconnellan B5
Burnfort C2
Bushmills D7
Butler's Bridge D5
Buttevant B2

Cadamstown C4
Caherconlish C3
Caherdaniel A2
Cahersiveen A2
Cahir C3
Caledon D6
Callan D3
Caltra C4
Camp A3
Cappagh White C3
Cappamore C3
Cappoquin C2
Carlanstown D5
Carlingford E5
Carlow D3
Carndonagh D7
Carnew D3
Carnlough E7
Carracastle C5
Carrick C6
(An Charraig)
Carrickfergus E6
Carrickmacross D5
Carrickmore D6
Carrick-on-Shannon C5
Carrick-on-Suir D3
Carrigahorig C4
Carrigaline C2
Carrigallen D5
Carriganimmy B2
Carrigans D7
Carrigart C7
(Carraig Airt)
Carrigtohill C2
Carrowkeel D7
Carryduff E6
Cashel C3
Castlebar B5
Castlebellingham E5
Castleblayney D5
Castlebridge D3
Castlecomer D3
Castlederg D6
Castledermot D3
Castleisland B3
Castlemaine B2
Castlemartyr C2
Castleplunket C5
Castlepollard D5
Castlerea C5
Castlerock D7
Castleshane D5
Castletown D4
Castletown
Bearhaven A2
Castletownroche C2
Castletownshend B1
Castlewellan E6
Causeway B3
Cavan D5
Celbridge D4
Charlestown C5
Charleville B3
(Rath Luirc)
Clady D6
Clane D4
Clara C4
Clarecastle B3
Claremorris B5
Clarinbridge B4
Clashmore C2
Claudy D7
Clifden A4
Cliffoney C6
Clogh D3
Cloghan C4
Cloghen C3
Clogher D6
Clohamon D3
Clonakilty B2
Clonard D4
Clonaslee D4
Clonbulloge D4
Clonbur B5
(An Fhairche)
Clondalkin E4

Clones D5
Clonmany D7
Clonmel C3
Clonmellon D5
Clonmore D3
Clonony C4
Clonoulty C3
Clonroche B3
Clontibret D5
Cloondara C5
Cloonlara B3
Clough E6
Cloughjordan C4
Cloyne C2
Coagh D6
Coalisland D6
Cobh C2
Coleraine D7
Collinstown D5
Collon D5
Collooney C5
Comber E6
Cong B5
Conna C2
Cookstown D6
Coole D5
Cooraclare B3
Cootehill D5
Cork C2
Cornamona B4
Corofin B4
Courtmacsherry B2
Courtown Harbour E3
Craigavon E6
Craughwell C4
Creeslough C7
Creggs C5
Croagh B3
Crolly (Croithli) C7
Crookedwood D4
Crookhaven B1
Crookstown B2
Croom B3
Crossakeel D5
Cross Barry C2
Crosshaven C2
Crossmaglen D5
Crossmolina B5
Crumlin E6
Crusheen B4
Culdaff D7
Culleybackey E6
Curracloe D3
Curraghboy C4
Curry C5
Cushendall E7

Daingean D4
Delvin D5
Derrygonnelly C6
Derrylin D5
Dervock E7
Dingle A2
(An Daingean)
Doagh E6
Donaghadee E6
Donaghmore C3
Donegal C6
Doneraile C2
Doon C4
Doonbeg B3
Douglas C2
Downpatrick E6
Dowra C5
Draperstown D6
Drimoleague B2
Dripsey B2
Drogheda E5
Dromahair C6
Dromcolliher B3
Dromod C5
Dromore D6
Dromore D6
Dromore West C6
Drum D6
Drumcliff C6
Drumconrath D5
Drumkeeran C5
Drumlish C5

Drumquin D6
Drumshanbo C5
Drumsna C5
Duagh B3
Dublin E4
Duleek E5
Dunboyne D4
Duncormick D2
Dundalk E5
Dunderrow C2
Dundrum E5
Dunfanaghy C7
Dungannon D6
Dungarvan C2
Dungarvan D3
Dungiven D7
Dunglow C7
(An Clochan Liath)
Dungourney C2
Dunkineely C6
Dun Laoghaire E4
Dunlavin D3
Dunleer E5
Dunloy E7
Dunmanway B2
Dunmore C5
Dunmore East D2
Dunmurry E6
Dunshauglin E4
Durrow D3
Durrus B2
Dysart C4

Easky B6
Edenderry D4
Edgeworthstown D5
Eglinton D7
Elphin C5
Emyvale D6
Enfield D4
Ennis B3
Enniscorthy D3
Enniscrone B6
Enniskean B2
Enniskillen D6
Ennistymon B4
Eyrecourt C4

Farnaght C5
Farranfore B2
Feakle C4
Fenagh C5
Ferbane C4
Fermoy C2
Ferns D3
Fethard D2
Fethard C3
Finnea D5
Fintona D6
Fivemiletown D6
Fontstown D4
Foxford B5
Foynes B3
Freemount B3
Frenchpark C5
Freshford D3
Fuerty C5

Galbally C3
Galway B4
Garrison C6
Garristown E4
Garvagh D7
Geashill D4
Gilford E6
Glandore B1
Glanworth C2
Glaslough D6
Glassan C4
Glenamaddy C5
Glenarm E7
Glenavy E6
Glenbeigh A2
Glencolumbkille C6
(Gleann Cholm Cille)
Glendalough E4
Glenealy E3
Glengarriff B2

Glenmore D3
Glenties C6
Glin B3
Glinsk B4
(Glinsce)
Golden C3
Goleen B1
Goresbridge D3
Gorey E3
Gort B4
Gortin D6
Gowran D3
Graiguenamanagh D3
Granard D5
Grange C6
Greyabbey E6
Greystones E4
Gulladuff D6

Hacketstown D3
Headford B4
Herbertstown C3
Hillsborough E6
Hilltown E5
Hospital C3
Holycross C3
Holywood E6
Howth E4

Inch A2
Inchigeelagh B2
Inishannon B2
Irvinestown D6

Johnstown C3

Kanturk B2
Keadue C5
Keady D6
Keel A5
Keenagh C5
Kells D5
Kells D5
Kenmare B2
Kesh C6
Kilbeggan D4
Kilberry D5
Kilbrittain B2
Kilcar C6
(Cill Charthaigh)
Kilcock D4
Kilcolgan B4
Kilconnell C4
Kilcoole E4
Kilcormac C4
Kilcullen D4
Kilcurry E5
Kildare B4
Kildavin D3
Kildorrery C2
Kilfenora B4
Kilgarvan B2
Kilkee B3
Kilkeel E5
Kilkelly C5
Kilkenny D3
Kilkieran B4
Kilkinlea B3
Kill D2
Killadysert B3
Killala B6
Killaloe C3
Killarney B2
Killashee C5
Killeigh D4
Killenaule C3
Killeshandra D5
Killimer B3
Killimor C4
Killiney E4
Killinick D2
Killorglin B2
Killough E5
Killucan D4
Killybegs C6
Killyleagh E6
Kilmacanoge E4
Kilmacrenan C7
Kilmacthomas D2

Kilmaganny D3
Kilmaine B5
Kilmallock C3
Kilmanagh D3
Kilmeadan D2
Kilmeage D4
Kilmeedy B3
Kilmichael B2
Kilmore Quay D2
Kilnaleck D5
Kilrea D7
Kilrush B3
Kilsheelan C3
Kiltealy D3
Kiltegan D3
Kiltimagh B5
Kiltoom C4
Kingscourt D5
Kinlough C6
Kinnegad D4
Kinnitty C4
Kinsale C2
Kinvarra B4
Kircubbin E6
Knock B5
Knockcroghery C4
Knocklofty C3
Knocktopher D3

Lahinch B4
Laragh E4
Larne E6
Lauragh A2
Laurencetown C4
Leap B2
Leenane B5
Leighlinbridge D3
Leitrim C5
Leixlip D4
Lemybrien C2
Letterfrack B5
Letterkenny D7
Lifford D7
Limavady D7
Limerick B3
Lisbellaw D6
Lisburn E6
Liscannor B4
Liscarroll B3
Lisdoonvarna B4
Lismore C3
Lisnaskea D6
Lisryan D5
Listowel B3
Loghill B3
Londonderry D7
Longford C5
Loughbrickland E6
Loughgall D6
Loughglinn C5
Loughrea C4
Louisburgh B5
Lucan D4
Lurgan E6
Lusk E4

Macroom B2
Maghera E5
Maghera D6
Magherafelt D6
Maguiresbridge D6
Malahide E4
Malin D7
Malin More C6
Mallow C2
Manorhamilton C6
Markethill D6
Maynooth D4
Mazetown E6
Middletown D6
Midleton C2
Milford D7
Millstreet B2
Milltown B2
Milltown Malbay B3
Mitchelstown C3
Moate C4
Mohill C5
Monaghan D5

Monasterevin D4
Moneygall D3
Moneymore D6
Monivea C4
Mooncoin D2
Moorfields E6
Mount Bellew C4
Mount Charles C6
Mountmellick D4
Mountrath D4
Mountshannon C4
Moville D7
Moy D6
Moynalty D5
Moyvore C4
Muckross B2
Muff D7
Mullinavat D2
Mullingar D4
Mulrany B5
Myshall D3

Naas D4
Naul E4
Navan D4
Neale B5
Nenagh C3
Newbliss D5
Newbridge D4
(Droichead Nua)
Newcastle E5
Newcastle West B3
Newinn C3
Newmarket B2
Newmarket-on
Fergus B3
Newport D3
Newport B5
New Ross D3
Newry E5
Newtown D3
Newtownabbey E6
Newtownards E6
Newtownbutler D6
Newtownhamilton D5
Newtown-
mountkennedy E4
Newtownstewart D6
Newtown Forbes C5
Nobber D5

Oilgate D3
Oldcastle D5
Omagh D6
Omeath E5
Oola C3
Oranmore B4
Oughterard B4
Ovens B2

Pallas Grean C3
Parknasilla A2
Partry B5
Passage East D2
Passage West C2
Patrickswell C3
Paulstown D3
Pettigo C6
Plumbridge D6
Pomeroy D6
Portadown E6
Portaferry E6
Portarlington D4
Portavogie E6
Portglenone E6
Portlaoise D4
Portmarnock E4

Portrane E4
Portroe C3
Portrush D7
Portstewart D7
Portumna C4
Poulgorm Bridge B2
Poyntzpass E6

Raharney D4
Randalstown E6
Rasharkin E7
Rathangan D4
Rathcoole D4
Rathcormack C2
Rathdowney C3
Rathdrum E3
Rathfriland E5
Rathkeale B3
Rathmelton D7
Rathmolyon D4
Rathmore B2
Rathmullan D7
Rathnew E4
Rathowen D5
Rathvilly D3
Ratoath D4
Ray D7
Ring (An Rinn) C2
Ringaskiddy C2
Rockcorry D5
Roosky C5
Rosapenna C7
Rosbercon D3
Roscommon C4
Roscrea C4
Ross Carbery B1
Rosscor C6
Rosses Point C6
Rosslare Harbour D2
Rosslea D5
Rostrevor E5
Roundstone B4
Roundwood E4
Rush E4

St Johnstown D7
Saintfield E6
Sallins D4
Scarriff C4
Scartaglen B2
Scarva E6
Schull B1
Scramoge C5
Seskinore D6
Shanagarry C2
Shanagolden B3
Shannonbridge C4
Shercock D5
Shillelagh D3
Shinrone C4
Shrule B4
Silvermines C3
Sion Mills D6
Sixmilebridge B3
Skerries E4
Skibbereen B1
Slane D5
Sligo C6
Smithborough D5
Sneem A2
Spiddal B4
(An Spideal)
Stewartstown D6
Stonyford D3
Strabane D6
Stradbally D4
Stradone D5

Strandhill C6
Strangford E6
Stranorlar C6
Strokestown C5
Summerhill D4
Swanlinbar C5
Swatragh D6
Swinford B5
Swords E4

Taghmon D3
Tagoat D2
Tahilla A2
Tallaght E4
Tallow C2
Tallowbridge C2
Tandragee E6
Tang C4
Tarbert B3
Templemore C3
Templetouhy C3
Termonfeckin E5
Thomastown D3
Thurles C3
Timahoe D3
Timoleague B2
Tinahely D3
Tipperary C3
Tobercurry C5
Tobermore D6
Toomyvara C3
Toormore B1
Tralee B3
Tramore D2
Trim D4
Tuam B4
Tuamgraney C3
Tulla B3
Tullamore D4
Tullow D3
Tulsk C5
Turlough B5
Tyrellspass D4

Urlingford C3

Virginia D5

Warrenpoint E5
Waterford D2
Watergrasshill C2
Waterville A2
Westport B5
Wexford D3
Whitegate C2
Whitehead E6
Wicklow E4
Woodenbridge E3
Woodford C4

Youghal C2

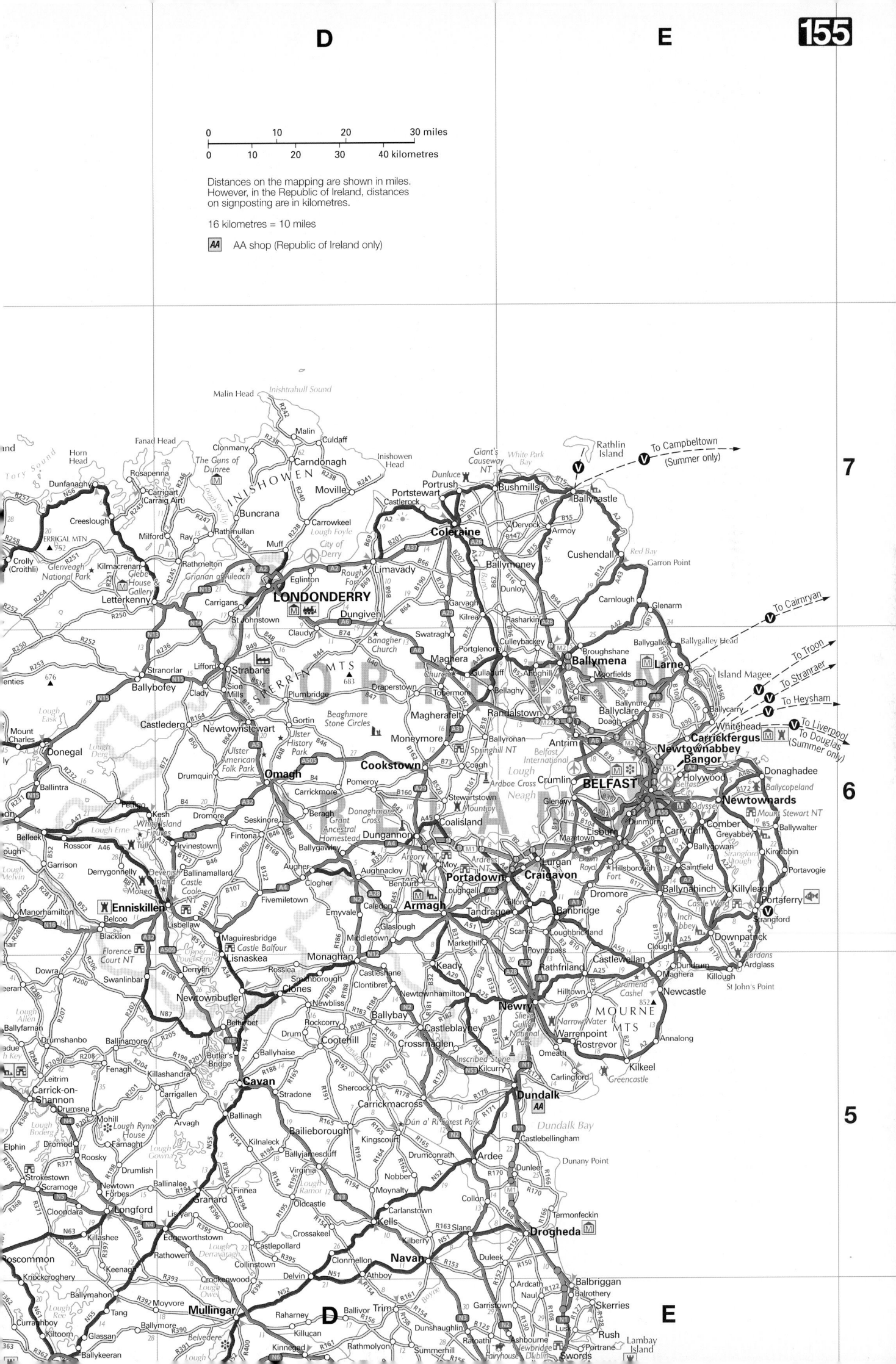

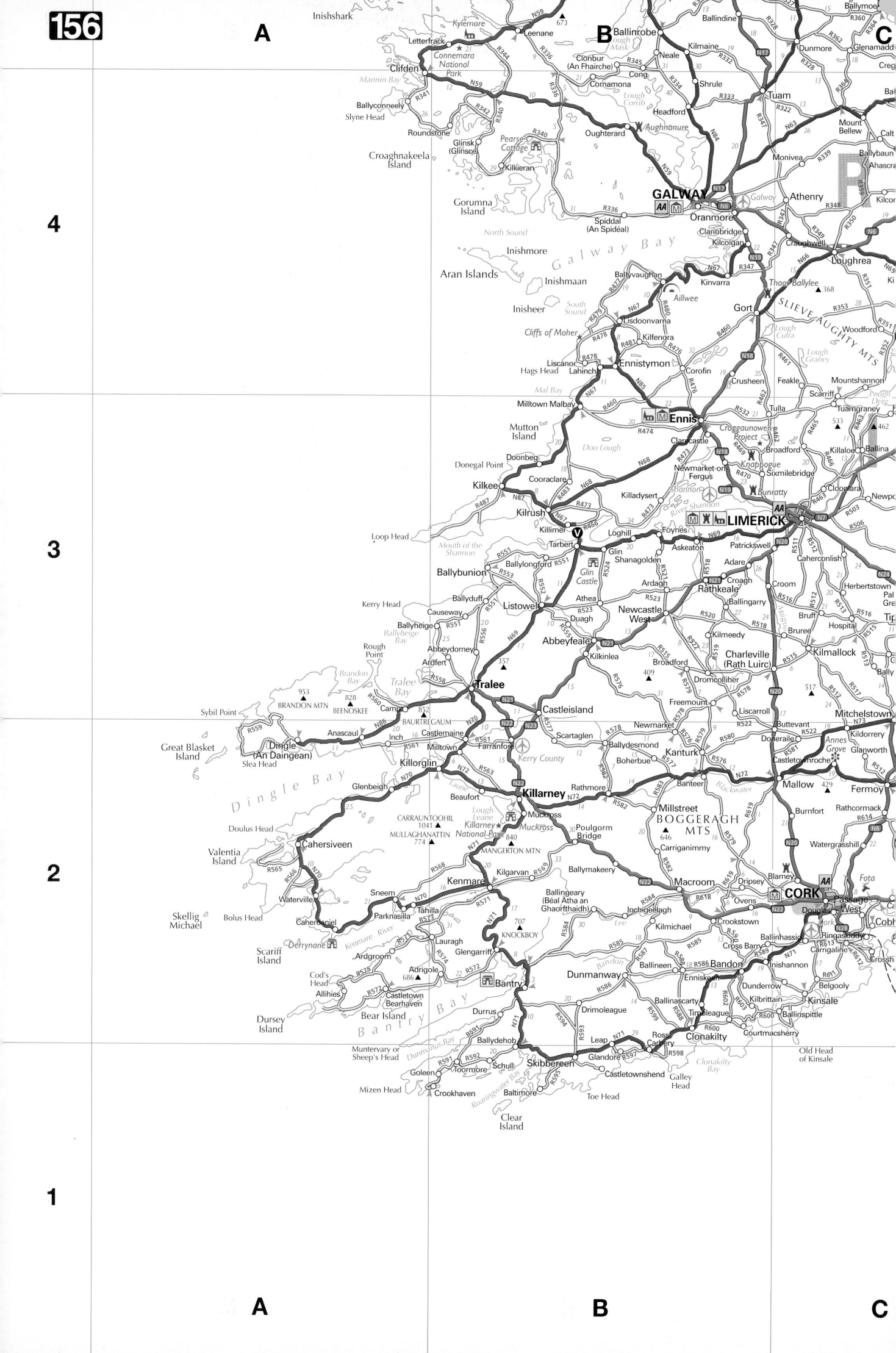

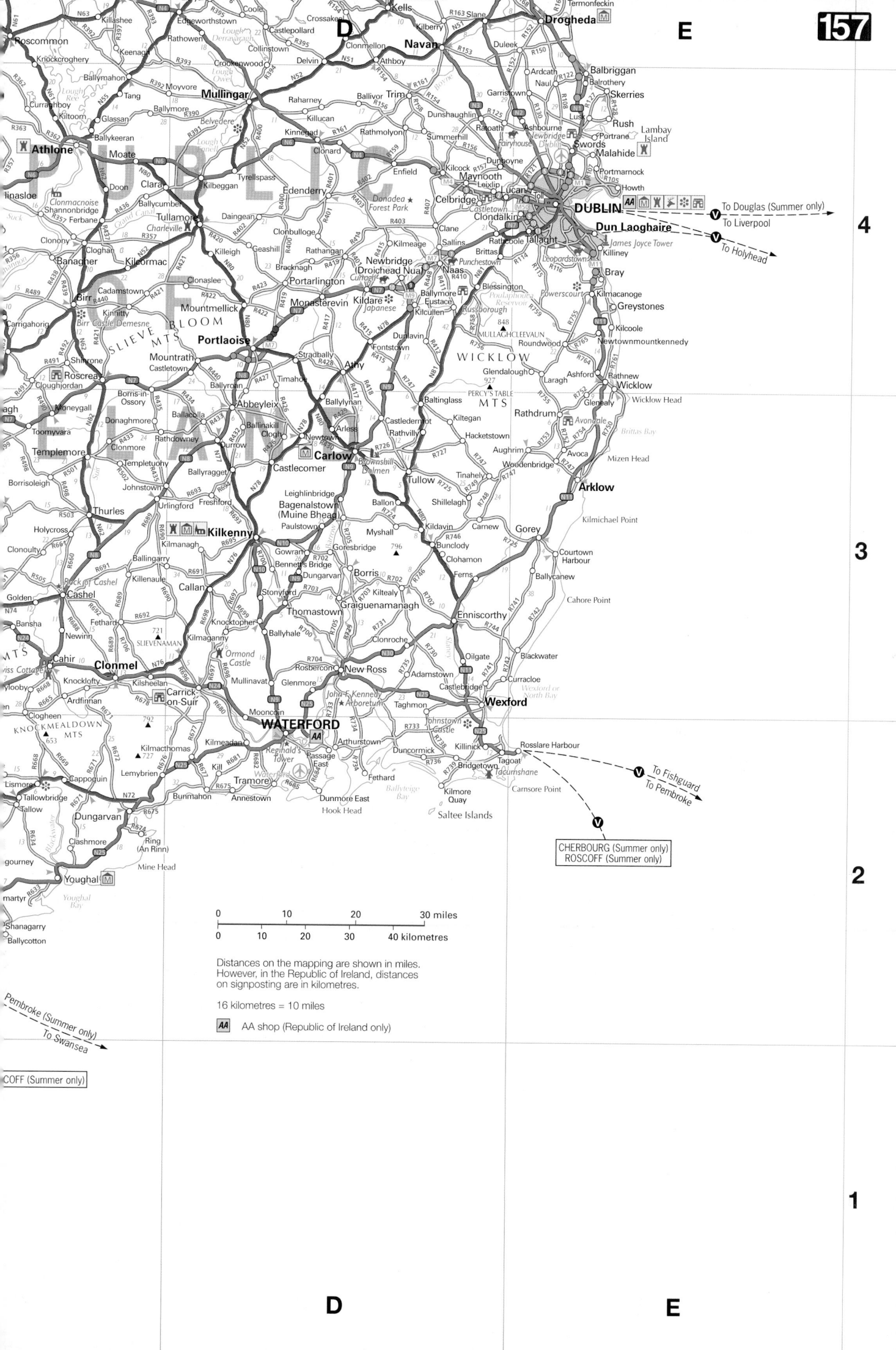

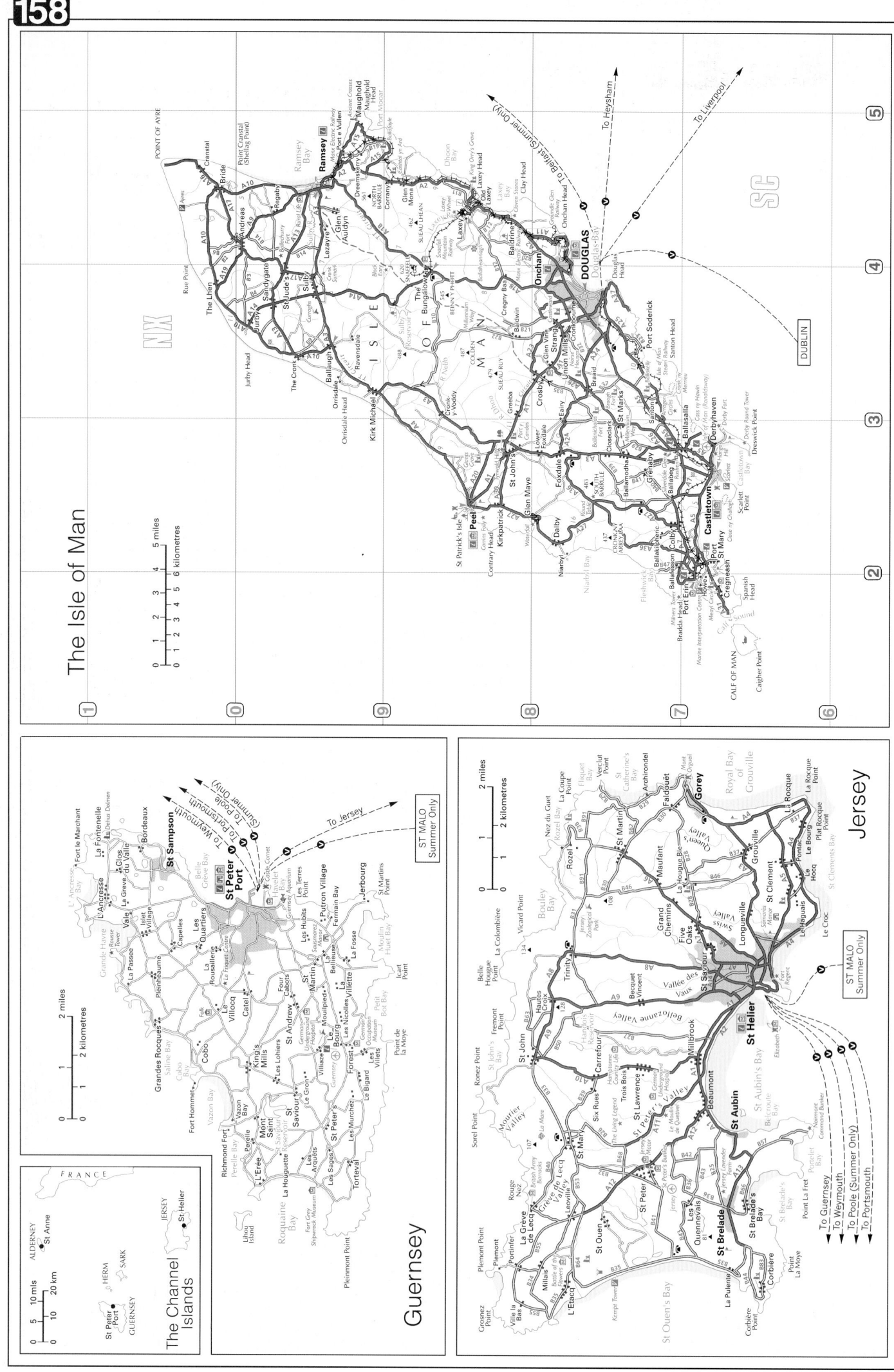

The Isle of Man

DUBLIN

To Heysham

To Liverpool

To Belfast (Summer Only)

The Channel Islands

FRANCE

ALDERNEY
St Anne

JERSEY
St Helier

HERM

SARK

St Peter Port
GUERNSEY

10 mls   20 km
5   10

Guernsey

ST MALO
Summer Only

To Jersey

To Weymouth

To Portsmouth (Summer Only)

St Sampson

St Peter Port

Jersey

Gorey

Royal Bay of Grouville

St Helier

St Aubin

St Brelade

ST MALO
Summer Only

To Guernsey
To Weymouth
To Poole (Summer Only)
To Portsmouth

key to town plans

Aberdeen.................Page 160	Luton.......................Page 191
Andover............................161	Maidstone..........................193
Ashford............................162	Manchester.......................198
Basingstoke.....................162	Margate............................195
Bath.................................163	Middlesbrough.................197
Birmingham.....................164	Milton Keynes..................200
Blackpool.........................166	Newcastle upon Tyne........201
Bournemouth...................165	Newport...........................199
Bradford...........................167	Newquay...........................202
Brighton...........................170	Northampton....................202
Bristol..............................168	Norwich............................203
Cambridge.......................172	Nottingham......................204
Canterbury.......................169	Oldham.............................206
Cardiff.............................171	Oxford..............................207
Carlisle.............................173	Perth................................205
Cheltenham.....................177	Peterborough...................208
Chester............................174	Plymouth..........................209
Coventry..........................175	Poole................................211
Darlington........................178	Portsmouth.......................210
Derby...............................176	Preston.............................212
Doncaster........................178	Ramsgate..........................212
Dover...............................179	Reading............................213
Dundee............................179	St Andrews.......................219
Durham............................180	Salisbury...........................214
Eastbourne......................180	Scarborough.....................215
Edinburgh........................181	Sheffield...........................216
Exeter..............................182	Shrewsbury.......................217
Glasgow...........................184	Southampton....................218
Gloucester........................182	Stirling.............................221
Great Yarmouth................183	Stoke-on-Trent (Hanley)...222
Guildford..........................183	Stratford-upon-Avon..........222
Harrogate.........................185	Sunderland.......................220
Huddersfield.....................185	Swansea............................223
Hull.................................186	Swindon............................224
Inverness.........................187	Taunton............................225
Ipswich............................188	Torquay............................226
Lancaster.........................189	Tunbridge Wells................227
Leeds...............................190	Warwick............................227
Leicester..........................192	Watford............................228
Lincoln.............................196	Weston-Super-Mare..........229
Liverpool..........................194	Windsor............................230
Llandudno........................189	Wolverhampton.................231
LONDON...................238-248	Worcester.........................230
	York.................................232

159

Central London

PADDINGTON		ISLINGTON	
238 — **239**	**240**	**241**	
	SOHO	CITY	
		246 **247**	DOCK LANDS
KENSINGTON		SOUTHWARK	**248**
242	**243** **244**	**245**	BERMONDSEY
CHELSEA	WESTMINSTER		
	KENNINGTON		

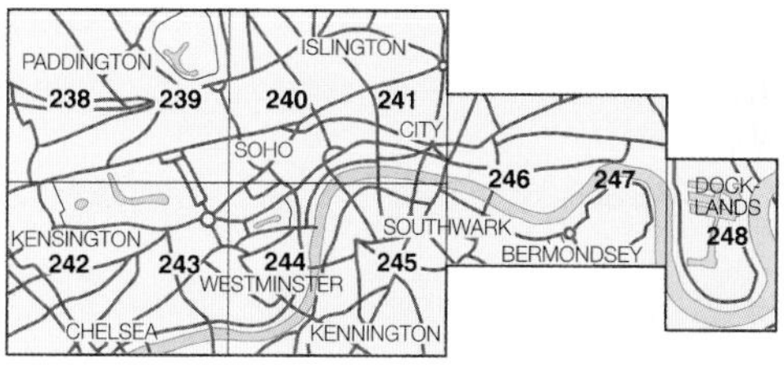

Ports and airports

⛴	Ports.................................233
✈	Airports.....................234–236
Ⓐ	Channel Tunnel.................237

Town plan legend

▨	AA-recommended routes
▢	Restricted roads / pedestrians only
= =	Other roads
COLLEGE ▨	Buildings of interest
†	Churches
▢	Parks and open spaces
P	Car parks
C/S C	Toilets
←	One-way streets
♿	Shopmobility
P+R	Park and ride
M	Metrolink stations

Map labels: Inverness, Aberdeen, Dundee, Perth, St Andrews, Stirling, Glasgow, Edinburgh, Newcastle upon Tyne, Carlisle, Sunderland, Durham, Middlesbrough, Darlington, Scarborough, Lancaster, Harrogate, Leeds/Bradford, York, Blackpool, Bradford, Leeds, Hull, Preston, Huddersfield, Oldham, Liverpool, Manchester, Doncaster, Sheffield, Holyhead, Llandudno, Chester, Stoke-on-Trent (Hanley), Lincoln, Shrewsbury, Derby, Nottingham, East Midlands, Wolverhampton, Leicester, Peterborough, Norwich, Great Yarmouth, Birmingham, NEC/Birmingham, Coventry, Northampton, Warwick, Cambridge, Ipswich, Worcester, Stratford-upon-Avon, Milton Keynes, Stansted, Cheltenham, Harwich, Gloucester, Oxford, Luton, Swansea, Newport, Swindon, Watford, Cardiff, Reading, LONDON, City, Bristol, Windsor, Heathrow, Margate, Bath, Basingstoke, Maidstone, Ramsgate, Weston-Super-Mare, Andover, Guildford, Canterbury, Taunton, Salisbury, Ashford, Dover, Gatwick, Tunbridge Wells, Channel Tunnel Terminal, Southampton, Portsmouth, Brighton, Eastbourne, Exeter, Poole, Bournemouth, Newquay, Torquay, Plymouth

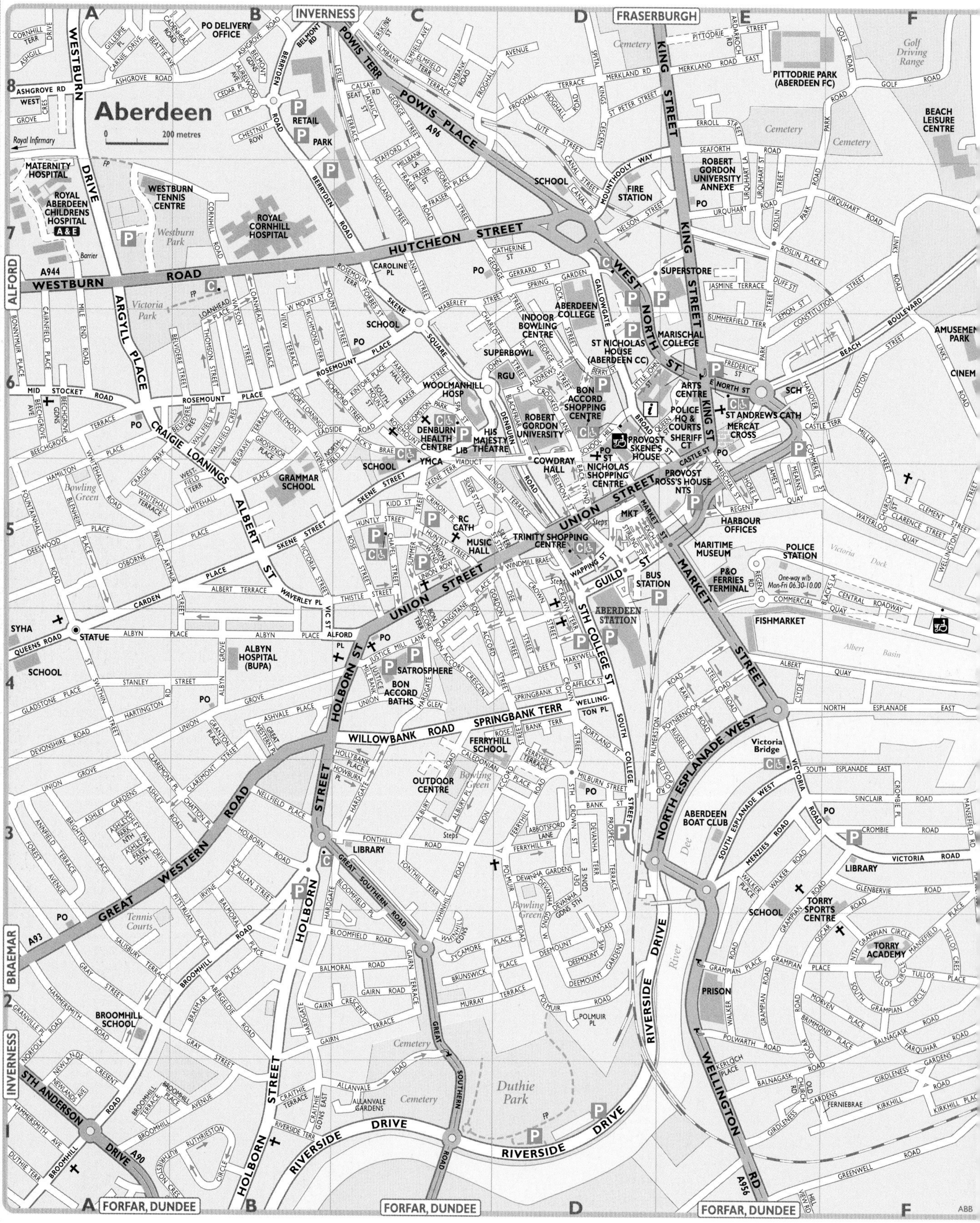

Aberdeen

0 200 metres

Grid references: A B C D E F, rows 1–8

INVERNESS
FRASERBURGH
FORFAR, DUNDEE

Major labels:

PO DELIVERY OFFICE
RETAIL PARK
MATERNITY HOSPITAL
ROYAL ABERDEEN CHILDRENS HOSPITAL A&E
WESTBURN TENNIS CENTRE
ROYAL CORNHILL HOSPITAL
Royal Infirmary
Westburn Park
Victoria Park
WESTBURN ROAD
HUTCHEON STREET
POWIS PLACE
POWIS TERR
BERRYDEN ROAD
CORNHILL ROAD
ARGYLL PLACE
CRAIGIE LOANINGS
ALBERT ST
ROSEMOUNT PLACE
GRAMMAR SCHOOL
SKENE STREET
SKENE SQUARE
WOOLMANHILL HOSP
DENBURN HEALTH CENTRE
HIS MAJESTY'S THEATRE
YMCA
ROBERT GORDON UNIVERSITY
RGU
MUSIC HALL
RC CATH
UNION STREET
HOLBORN ST
SATROSPHERE
BON ACCORD BATHS
ALBYN HOSPITAL (BUPA)
SYHA
QUEENS ROAD
Statue
GREAT WESTERN ROAD
BRAEMAR
A93
A90
STH ANDERSON DRIVE
BROOMHILL SCHOOL
RIVERSIDE DRIVE
GREAT SOUTHERN ROAD
HOLBORN STREET
SPRINGBANK TERR
WILLOWBANK ROAD
FERRYHILL SCHOOL
OUTDOOR CENTRE
LIBRARY
Bowling Green
Duthie Park
Cemetery
SKENE STREET
ROSEMOUNT
KING STREET
PITTODRIE PARK (ABERDEEN FC)
Golf Driving Range
BEACH LEISURE CENTRE
Cemetery
ROBERT GORDON UNIVERSITY ANNEXE
FIRE STATION
MARISCHAL COLLEGE
ABERDEEN COLLEGE
ST NICHOLAS HOUSE (ABERDEEN CC)
BON ACCORD SHOPPING CENTRE
ARTS CENTRE
ST ANDREWS CATH
MERCAT CROSS
PROVOST SKENE'S HOUSE
COWDRAY HALL
NICHOLAS SHOPPING CENTRE
POLICE HQ & COURTS
SHERIFF CT
PROVOST ROSS'S HOUSE NTS
HARBOUR OFFICES
MARITIME MUSEUM
P&O FERRIES TERMINAL
POLICE STATION
Victoria Dock
TRINITY SHOPPING CENTRE
ABERDEEN STATION
BUS STATION
GUILD ST
MARKET STREET
STH COLLEGE ST
FISHMARKET
Albert Basin
NORTH ESPLANADE WEST
NORTH ESPLANADE EAST
Victoria Bridge
ABERDEEN BOAT CLUB
RIVERSIDE DRIVE
River Dee
WELLINGTON RD
A956
TORRY SPORTS CENTRE
TORRY ACADEMY
PRISON
LIBRARY
AMUSEMENT PARK
CINEM
Cemetery
AMUSEMENT PARK

ABB

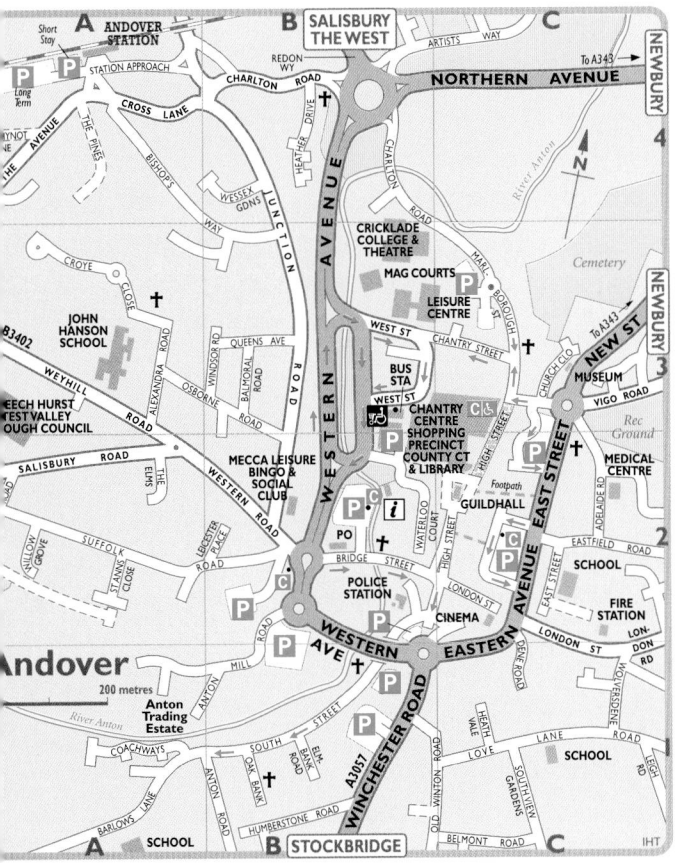

Andover

Andover is found on atlas page **23**,
grid reference **3645**

Adelaide Road	C2-C3	High Street	B2-C2-C3	The Avenue	A4
Alexandra Road	A3	Humberstone Road	B1	The Elms	A2
Anton Mill Road	A1-B1-B2	Junction Road	B2-B3-B4	The Pines	A4
Anton Road	B1	Leicester Place	B2	Vigo Road	C3
Artists Way	B4-C4	Leigh Road	C1	Waterloo Court	B2
Balmoral Road	B3	London Road	C1	Wessex Gardens	B4
Barlows Lane	A1	London Street	C1	Western Avenue	B1-B2-B3
Belmont Road	B1-C1	Love Lane	C1-C2	Western Road	A2-B2
Bishop's Way	A4-B4-B3	Marlborough Street	C3	West Street	B2-B3
Bridge Street	B2	Mead Road	A2	Weyhill Road	A3
Chantry Street	B3-C3	New Street	C3	Whynot Lane	A4
Charlton Road	B4-B3-C3	Northern Avenue	B4-C4	Winchester Road	B1
Church Close	C3	Oak Bank Road	B1	Windsor Road	B3
Coachways	A1	Old Winton Road	B1-C1	Willow Grove	A2
Cross Lane	A4	Osborne Road	A3-B3	Wolversdene Road	C1
Croye Close	A3	Queens Avenue	B3		
Dene Road	C1	Redon Way	B4		
Eastfield Road	C2	St Anns Close	A2		
East Street	C2-C3	Salisbury Road	A2		
Eastern Avenue	C1-C2	South Street	B1-B2		
Elmbank Road	B1	Southview Gardens	C1		
Heath Vale	C1	Station Approach	A4		
Heather Drive	B4	Suffolk Road	A2-B2		

161

berdeen

erdeen is found on atlas page **135**,
reference **9306**

otsford Lane	D3	Belvidere Crescent	B6	Claremont Street	B3-B4
geldie Road	B2	Belvidere Street	B6	Clarence Street	F5
t Quay	D4	Berry Street	D6	Clyde Street	E4
rt Quay	E4-F4	Berryden Road	B8-B7-C7	Commerce Street	E5-E6
rt Street	B5	Blackfriar Street	D6	Commercial Quay	E5-F5-F4
rt Terrace	B5	Blacks Lane	F5	Constitution Street	E6-E7-F7
ry Place	C3	Blenheim Place	A5	Cornhill Road	B7
ry Road	C3-C4	Bloomfield Place	C2-C3	Cotton Street	F6
n Grove	B4	Bloomfield Road	B2-C2	Craigie Loanings	A6-B6-B5
n Place	A4-B4	Bon Accord Crescent	C4	Craigie Park	A5-A6
d Place	B4-C4	Bon Accord Street	C3-D4-C4-C5	Craithie Gardens East	B1
Street	B3	Bon Accord Terrace	C4-C5	Craithie Terrace	B1
vale Gardens	C1	Bonnymuir Place	A6	Crimon Place	C5
vale Road	B1-C1-C2	Braemar Place	B2	Crombie Place	F3
Street	C7	Brighton Place	A3	Crombie Road	F3
ield Terrace	A3	Brimmond Place	E2-F2	Crooked Lane	D6
rroch Road	E8	Broad Street	D6-E6	Crown Street	D3-D4-D5
ll Place	A6-A7	Broomhill Avenue	A1-B1	Crown Terrace	D4-D5
gill Drive	A8	Broomhill Place	A1-B1	Dee Place	D4
grove Road	A8-B8	Broomhill Road	A1-A2-B2-B3	Dee Street	D4-D5
grove Road West	A8	Broomhill Terrace	A1	Deemount Avenue	D2
ey Gardens	A3	Brunswick Place	C2-D2	Deemount Gardens	D2
ey Park Drive	A3	Cadenhead Road	A8-B8	Deemount Road	D2
ey Park North	A3	Cairnfield Place	A6-A7	Deeswood Place	A3
ey Park South	A3	Caledonian Place	C4-C3-D3	Denburn Road	D5-D6
Place	A3-B3	Calsay Seat Road	C8	Devanha Gardens	D3
vale Place	B4	Canal Place	D7	Devanha Gardens East	D3
Wynd	D5-D6	Canal Street	D7-D8	Devanha Gardens South	D3
r Street	C6	Carden Place	A4-A5-B5	Devanha Gardens West	D2-D3
noral Place	B2-B3	Carnie Drive	A8	Devanha Terrace	D3
noral Road	B2-C2	Caroline Place	C7	Devonshire Road	A3-A4
agask Road	E1-F2	Castle Street	E5-E6	Duff Street	E7
k Street	D3	Castle Terrace	E6-F6	East North Street	E6
ch Boulevard	E6-F6-F7	Catherine Street	C7-D7	Elm Place	B8
tie Avenue	A8-B8	Cedar Place	B8	Elmbank Road	C8
hgrove Avenue	A6	Central Roadway	F5	Elmbank Terrace	C8
hgrove Gardens	A6	Chapel Street	C5	Elmfield Avenue	C8
hgrove Terrace	A5-A6	Charlotte Street	C7-C6-D6	Elmfield Terrace	C8
rave Terrace	B5-B6	Chatton Place	B3	Erroll Street	E8
nont Gardens	B8	Chestnut Row	B8	Erskine Street	D5
nont Road	B8	Church Street	F5	Esslemont Avenue	B6-B5-C5
nont Street	D5	Claremont Place	A4-A3-B3	Exchange Street	D5
				Farmers Hall	C6
				Farquhar Road	F2
				Ferniebrae	E1-F1
				Ferryhill Place	D3
				Ferryhill Road	D3
				Ferryhill Terrace	D3-D4
				Fonthill Road	C3

Fonthill Terrace	C3	Loanhead Place	B6-B7	St Swithin Street	A4
Forest Avenue	A2-A3	Loanhead Terrace	B6-B7	Salisbury Terrace	A2-B2
Forbes Street	C6-C7	Lock Street	D6-D7	School Hill	D6
Fountainhall Road	A4-A5	Maberley Street	C7-D7	Seaforth Road	E8
Fraser Place	C7-C8	Mansefield Place	F2-F3	Shore Lane	E5
Fraser Road	C7	Mansefield Road	F2-F3	Short Loanings	B6
Fraser Street	C7	Marischal Street	E5-E6	Silver Street North	C5
Frederick Street	E6	Market Street	D5-E5-E4	Silver Street South	D5
Froghall Avenue	C8-D8	Marywell Street	D4	Sinclair Road	E3-F3
Froghall Road	D8	Mearns Street	E5	Skene Square	C6-C7
Froghall Terrace	D8	Menzies Road	E3	Skene Street	B5-C5
Gairn Crescent	B2-C2	Merkland Road	D8	Skene Terrace	C5
Gairn Road	C2	Merkland Road East	E8	South Anderson Drive	A1
Gairn Terrace	B2-C2	Mid Stocket Road	A6	South College Street	D3-D4-D5
Gallowgate	D6-D7	Milburn Street	D3	South Crown Street	D3
George Street	C8-C7-D7-D6	Mile End Road	A6-A7	South Esplanade East	E3-F3
Gerrard Street	D7	Millbank Lane	C7-C8	South Esplanade West	E3
Gillespie Place	A8	Miller Street	F5-F6	South Grampian Circle	F2
Gilsomston Park	C6	Morven Place	E2-F2	South Mount Street	C6
Girdleness Gardens	E1-F1-F2	Mount Street	B7-C6	Spa Street	C6
Gladstone Place	A4	Mounthooly Way	D7-D8-E8	Spital Kings Crescent	D7-D8
Glenbervie Road	F3	Murray Terrace	C2-D2	Spring Garden	D7
Golf Road	F8	Nellfield Place	B3	Springbank Street	D4
Gordon Street	D4-D5-C5	Nelson Street	D7-E7	Springbank Terrace	C4-D4
Grampian Place	E2-F2	Newlands Avenue	A1	Stafford Street	C7-C8
Grampian Road	E2-E3-F3	Newlands Crescent	A1-A2	Stanley Street	A4-B4
Granton Place	A3	Norfolk Road	A1-A2	Stell Road	E4
Granville Place	A2	North Esplanade East	E4-F4	Stirling Street	D5
Gray Street	A2-B2-B1	North Esplanade West	E3-E4	Summer Street	C5
Great Southern Road	C1-C3-B3	North Grampian Circle	F2	Summerfield Terrace	E6
Great Western Place	C3	Northfield Place	B5-C6	Sycamore Place	C2-D2
Great Western Road	A2-A3-B3-B4	Northfield Place	B5-C6	Thistle Street	C5
Greenwell Road	E1-F1	Old Church Road	E1	Thomson Street	B6
Grosvenor Place	B6	Old Ford Road	E3-E4	Tullos Circle	F2
Grove Crescent	A8	Osborne Place	A5-B5	Tullos Crescent	F2
Guild Street	D5-E5	Oscar Road	E2-F2-F3	Tullos Place	F2
Hamilton Place	A5-A6	Palmerston Road	D3-D4-E4	Union Glen	C4
Hammersmith Avenue	A1	Park Road	E7-E8-F8	Union Grove	A3-A4-B4-C4
Hammersmith Road	A2	Park Street	E6-E7	Union Row	C5
Hanover Street	E6	Pitstruan Place	A3-B3-B2	Union Street	C4-C5-D5
Hardgate	B2-B3-C3-C4	Pittodrie Street	E8	Union Terrace	C5-D5
Hartington Road	A4	Polmuir Place	D2	Union Wynd	C5
Holborn Road	B3	Polmuir Road	D2-D3	Urquhart Lane	E7-E8
Holborn Street	B1-B2-B3-C4	Polwarth Road	E2	Urquhart Road	E7-F7
Holland Street	C7	Portland Street	D4	Urquhart Street	E7-E8
Hollybank Place	C3-C4	Powis Place	C8-D7	Victoria Road	E4-E3-F3
Howburn Place	C3	Powis Terrace	C8	Victoria Street	B4-B5
Huntly Street	C5	Poynernook Road	E4	View Terrace	B6-B7
Hutcheon Street	C7-D7	Prince Arthur Street	A5-B5-B4	Walker Place	E3
Irvine Place	B3	Prospect Terrace	D2-D3	Walker Road	E2-E3
Jack's Brae	C6	Queen Street	D6-E6	Wallfield Crescent	B6
Jamaica Street	C8	Queens Road	A4	Wallfield Place	B6
James Street	E5	Raik Road	E4	Wapping Street	D5
Jasmine Terrace	E7	Regent Quay	E5	Waterloo Quay	F5
John Street	C6-D6	Regent Road	E5	Watson Street	B6-B7
Justice Mill Lane	C4	Richmond Street	B6-C6	Waverley Place	B5
Justice Mill Bank	C4	Richmond Terrace	B6-B7	Wellington Place	D4
Jute Street	D8	Riverside Drive	B1-C1-D1-E2	Wellington Road	E1-E2-E3
Kerloch Place	E1-E2	Riverside Terrace	B1	Wellington Street	F5-F6
Kidd Street	C4	Rose Street	C4-C5	West Mount Street	B7
King Street	E6-E7-E8-D8	Rosebank Terrace	C4-D4	West North Street	D7-D6-E6
Kintore Place	C6	Rosemount Place	A6-B6-C6	Westburn Drive	A7-A8
Kirkhill Place	F1	Rosemount Terrace	C7	Westburn Road	A7-B7-C7
Kirkhill Road	E1-F1	Rosemount Viaduct	C6-C5	Westfield Terrace	B5
Langstane Place	C4-C5	Roslin Place	E7-F7	Whinhill Gardens	C2
Laurelwood Avenue	B8	Roslin Street	E7-E8	Whinhill Road	C2-C3
Leadside Road	B6-C6	Russell Road	E4	Whitehall Place	A5-B5-B6
Lemon Street	E6-E7	Ruthrieston Circle	B1	Whitehall Road	A5-A6
Leslie Terrace	C8	Ruthrieston Crescent	A1-B1	Whitehall Terrace	A5
Links Road	F6-F7	St Andrew Street	D6	Willowbank Road	C4
Little John Street	D6	St Clement Street	F5	Windmill Brae	D5
		St Peter Street	D8		

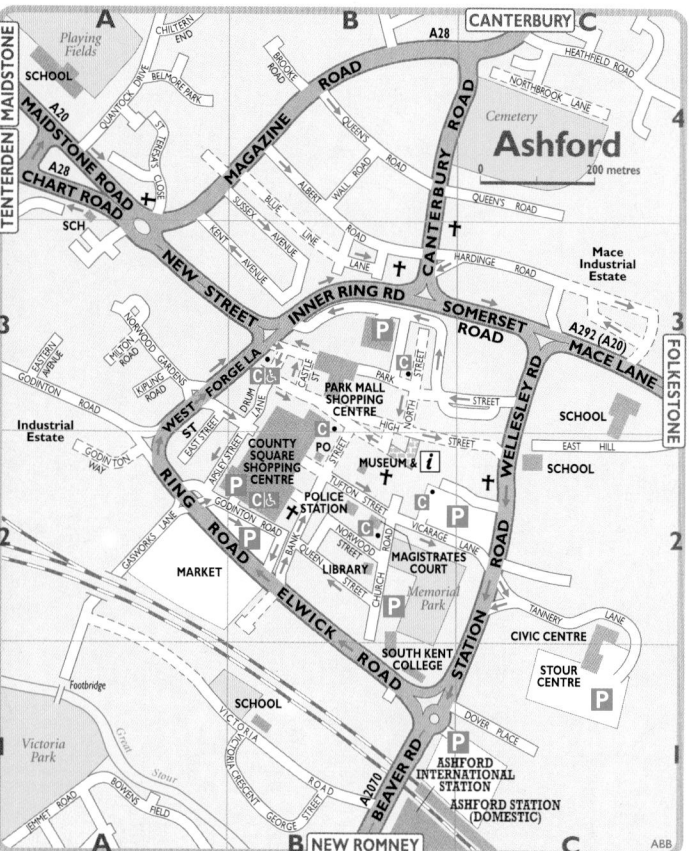

Ashford

Ashford is found on atlas page **28**,
grid reference **0142**

Albert Road	B3-B4
Apsley Street	A2-B2
Bank Street	B2-B3
Beaver Road	B1
Belmore Park	A4
Blue Line Lane	B3-B4
Bowens Field	A1
Brooke Road	B4
Canterbury Road	B3-B4-C4
Castle Street	B3
Chart Road	A4
Chiltern End	A4
Church Road	B2
Dover Place	B1-C1
Drum Lane	B3
East Hill	C2
East Street	A2-A3
Eastern Avenue	A3
Elwick Road	B1-B2
Forge Lane	A3-B3
Gasworks Lane	A2
George Street	B1
Godinton Road	A3-A2-B2
Godinton Way	A2
Hardinge Road	B3-C3
Heathfield Road	C4
High Street	B3-B2-C2
Inner Ring Road	B3
Jemmet Road	A1
Kent Avenue	A4-A3-B3
Kipling Road	A3
Mace Lane	C3
Magazine Road	A4-B4
Maidstone Road	A4
Milton Road	A3
New Street	A3-B3
North Street	B3
Northbrook Lane	C4
Norwood Gardens	A3
Norwood Street	B2
Park Street	B3-C3
Quantock Drive	A4
Queen Street	B2
Queen's Road	B4-C4
Ring Road	A2-B2

St Teresa's Close	A4
Somerset Road	B3-C3
Station Road	B1-C1-C2
Sussex Avenue	A4-B4-B3
Tannery Lane	C1-C2
Tufton Street	B2
Vicarage Lane	B2-C2
Victoria Crescent	B1
Victoria Road	A1-B1
Wall Road	B4
Wellesley Road	C2-C3
West Street	A2-A3

Basingstoke

Basingstoke is found on atlas page **24**,
grid reference **6352**

Alencon Link	A3-A4-B4
Allnutt Avenue	C3
Applegarth Close	C1
Basing View	C4
Beaconsfield Road	B1
Blair Road	A1
Bounty Rise	A1
Bounty Road	A1-B1-B2
Bramblys Close	A2
Bramblys Drive	A2
Budds Close	A2
Bunnian Place	B4
Burgess Road	A4
Castle Road	B1
Chapel Hill	A4-B4
Chequers Road	B3-C3
Chester Place	A2
Chesterfield Road	C1
Church Square	A3-B3
Church Street	B2-B3
Churchill Way	A3-B3
Churchill Way East	C3-C4
Churchill Way West	A3
Cliddesden Road	B1
Clifton Terrace	B4
Cordale Road	A1
Council Road	B1-B2
Cross Street	B3
Crossborough Hill	C1-C2
Culver Road	A1
Eastfield Avenue	C2-C3
Eastrop Lane	C2-C3
Eastrop Way	C3
Essex Road	A3
Fairfields Road	B1
Flaxfield Court	A3
Flaxfield Road	A3-A2-B2
Frances Road	A1-A2
Frescade Crescent	A1
Goat Lane	B3-C3
Gresley Road	C4
Hackwood Road	B1-B2-C1
Hammond Road	A1
Jubilee Road	B1-B2
Kingsclere Road	A4

London Road	B2-C2
London Street	B2
Lytton Road	C3
Montague Place	C1
Mortimer Lane	A3
New Road	B2-B3
New Seal Road	B3
New Street	B2-B3
Norn Hill	C4
Old Market Square	B2
Old Reading Road	B4-C4
Parkside Road	C1
Penrith Road	A1-A2
Phoenix Park Terrace	B4
Rayleigh Road	A3
Red Lion Lane	B2
Rochford Road	A3
St Mary's Court	C3
Sarum Hill	A2
Southend Road	A3
Southern Road	B2
Sylvia Close	A1
Timberlake Road	A3-B3-C3
Victoria Street	B2
Vyne Road	B4
Wallis Road	B1
White Hart Lane	C2
Winchester Road	A1-A2-B2
Winchester Street	B2
Winterthur Way	A4-B4
Worting Road	A3
Wote Street	B2-B3

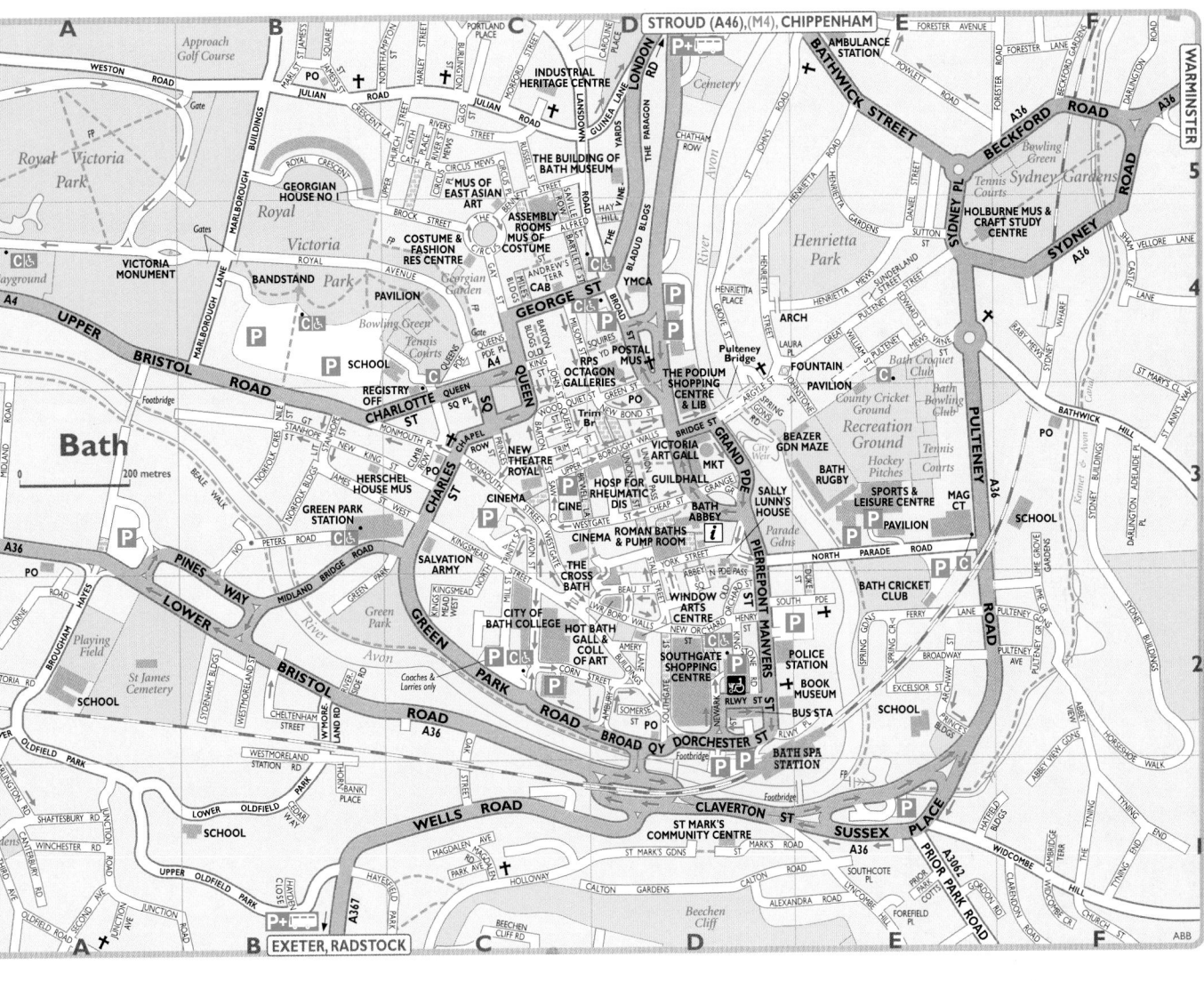

ath

h is found on atlas page **22**,
d reference **7464**

...ey Square	D2-D3	Cambridge Terrace	F1	Gordon Road	E1-F1
...ey View	F2	Canterbury Road	A1	Grand Parade	D3
...ey View Gardens	F1-F2	Caroline Place	D5	Grange Grove	D3
...aide Place	F3	Catherine Place	C5	Great Pulteney Street	E4
...andra Road	D1-E1	Cedar Way	B1	Great Stanhope Street	B3
...ed Street	C4	Chapel Row	C3	Green Park	B2-C3
...bury	D2	Charles Street	C3	Green Park Road	C2-C3
...ery Lane Buildings	D2	Charlotte Street	B3-C3	Green Street	D3-D4
...hway Street	E2	Chatham Row	D5	Grove Street	D4
...yle Street	D3-D4	Cheap Street	D3	Guinea Lane	D5
...ngton Road	A1	Cheltenham Street	B2	Harley Street	C5
...n Street	C2-C3	Church Street	F1	Hatfield Buildings	E1-F1
...dlett Street	C4	Circus Mews	C5	Hay Hill	D4
...ton Buildings	C4	Circus Place	C5	Hayden Close	B1
...ton Street	C3	Clarendon Road	F1	Hayesfield Park	B1-C1
...h Street	D3	Claverton Street	D1	Henrietta Gardens	E4-E5
...nwick Hill	E4-F4-F3	Corn Street	C2-D2	Henrietta Mews	D4-E4
...nwick Street	E5	Crescent Lane	B5-C5	Henrietta Place	D4
...u Street	D2	Cumberland Row	C3	Henrietta Road	D4-E5
...kford Gardens	F5	Daniel Street	E4-E5	Henrietta Street	D4
...kford Road	E5-F5	Darlington Place	F3	Henry Street	D2
...chen Cliff Road	C1	Darlington Road	F5	Holloway	C1
...nnett Street	C4-C5	Dorchester Street	D2	Horseshoe Walk	F1-F2
...lud Buildings	D4	Duke Street	E2-E3	Ivo Peters Road	B3
...ge Street	D3	Edward Street	E4	James Street West	B3-C3
...gewell Lane	C3	Excelsior Street	E2	John Street	C3-C4
...ad Quay	D2	Ferry Lane	E2	Johnstone Street	E3
...ad Street	D4	Forefield Place	E1	Julian Road	B5-C5
...adway	E2	Forester Avenue	E5-F5	Junction Avenue	A1
...ck Street	B4-C4	Forester Lane	F5	Junction Road	A1-B1
...ugham Hayes	A2-A3	Forester Road	F5	Kingsmead North	C2-C3
...lington Street	C5	Gay Street	C4	Kingsmead Street	C3-C2
...ton Gardens	C1-D1	George Street	C4-D4	Kingsmead West	C2
...ton Road	D1-E1	Gloucester Street	C5	Kingstone Road	D2
				Lansdown Road	C5-D5-D4
				Laura Place	D4
				Lime Grove	F2
				Lime Grove Gardens	F2-F3
				Little Stanhope Street	B3
				London Road	D5
				Lorne Road	A2

Lower Borough Walls	D2	Pulteney Gardens	F2	Sunderland Street	E4
Lower Bristol Road	A3-B2-C2-C1	Pulteney Grove	F2	Sussex Place	E1
Lower Oldfield Park	A2-A1-B1	Pulteney Mews	E4	Sutton Street	E4
Lyncombe Hill	E1	Pulteney Road	E2-E3-E4	Sydenham Buildings	B2
Magdalen Avenue	C1	Queen Square	C3-C4	Sydney Buildings	F2-F3
Magdalen Road	C1	Queen Square Place	C3-C4	Sydney Place	E4-E5
Manvers Street	C4	Queen Street	C3	Sydney Road	E4-F4-F5
Marlborough Buildings	B4-B5	Queens Parade	C4	Sydney Wharf	F3-F4
Marlborough Lane	B4	Queens Parade Place	C4	The Circus	C4
Midland Bridge Road	B2-B3-C3	Quiet Street	C3-D3	The Paragon	D5
Midland Road	A3-A4	Raby Mews	F4	The Tyning	F1
Miles Buildings	C4	Railway Place	D2-E2	The Vineyards	D4-D5
Mill Street	C2	Railway Street	D2	Third Avenue	A1
Milsom Street	C4-D4	River Street Mews	C5	Thornbank Place	B1
Monmouth Place	B3-C3	Rivers Street	C5	Trim Street	C3-D3
Monmouth Street	C3	Riverside Road	B2	Trinity Street	C3
Morford Street	C5	Royal Avenue	B4-C4	Tyning End	F1
New Bond Street	D3	Royal Crescent	B5	Union Pass	D3
New King Street	B3-C3	Russell Street	C5	Union Street	D3
New Orchard Street	D2	St Andrew's Terrace	C4	Upper Borough Walls	C3-D3
Newark Street	D2	St Ann's Way	F3	Upper Bristol Road	A4-B4-B3
Nile Street	B3	St James's Square	B5	Upper Church Street	C5
Norfolk Buildings	B3	St James's Street	B5	Upper Oldfield Park	A1-B1
Norfolk Crescent	B3	St John's Road	D4-D5-E5	Vane Street	E4
North Parade Passage	D2-D3	St Mark's Gardens	D1	Vellore Lane	F4
North Parade Road	D3-E3	St Mark's Road	D1-E1	Victoria Road	A2
Northampton Street	B5-C5	St Mary's Close	F3-F4	Wells Road	B1-C1-D1
Oak Street	C1-C2	Savile Row	C4-C5	Westgate	C2-C3
Old King Street	C4	Saw Close	C3	Westgate Street	C3-D3
Old Orchard Street	D2	Second Avenue	A1	Westmoreland Road	B2
Oldfield Road	A1	Sham Castle Lane	F4	Westmoreland Station Road	B1-B2
Park Avenue	C1	Somerset Street	D2	Westmoreland Street	B2
Pierrepont Street	D2-D3	South Parade	D2-E2	Weston Road	A5-B5
Pines Way	A3-B3-B2	Southcote Place	E1	Widcombe Crescent	F1
Portland Place	C5	Southgate Street	D2	Widcombe Hill	E1-F1
Powlett Road	E5	Spring Crescent	E2	William Street	E4
Prince's Buildings	E2	Spring Gardens	E2	Winchester Road	A1
Princes Street	C3	Spring Gardens Road	D3	Wood Street	C3
Prior Park Cottages	E1	Squires Yard	D4	York Street	D3
Prior Park Road	E1	Stall Street	D2-D3		
Pulteney Avenue	F2				

164

Birmingham

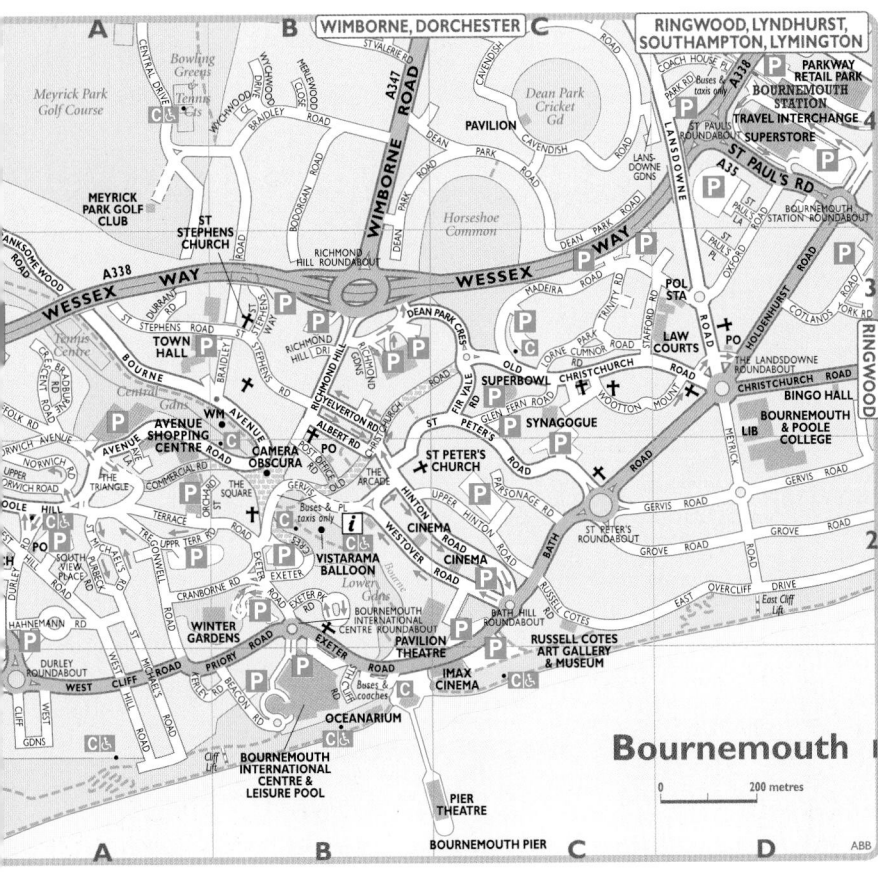

Bournemouth

Bournemouth is found on atlas page 12, grid reference **0890**

Albert Road	B2-B3	Orchard Street	A2-B2
Avenue Lane	A2	Oxford Road	D3-D4
Avenue Road	A2-A3-B2	Park Road	D4
Bath Road	C2-D2-D3	Parsonage Road	C2
Beacon Road	B1	Poole Hill	A2
Bodorgan Road	B3-B4	Post Office Road	B2
Bourne Avenue	A3-B3-B2	Priory Road	A1-B1-B2
Bradburne Road	A3	Purbeck Road	A2
Braidley Road	B3-B4	Richmond Gardens	B3
Branksome Wood Road	A3-A4	Richmond Hill	B3
Cavendish Road	C4	Richmond Hill Drive	B3
Central Drive	A3-A4	Russell Cotes Road	C2
Christchurch Road	D3	St Michael's Road	A1-A2
Coach House Place	D4	St Paul's Lane	D4
Commercial Road	A2-B2	St Paul's Place	D3
Cumnor Road	C3	St Paul's Road	D4
Cotlands Road	D3	St Peter's Road	B2-B3-C3-C2
Cranborne Road	A2-B2	St Stephens Road	A3-B3
Crescent Road	A3	St Stephens Way	B3
Dean Park Crescent	B3-C3	St Valerie Road	B4
Dean Park Road	B3-B4-C4	South Cliff Road	B1
Durley Road	A2	South View Place	A2
Durrant Road	A3	Stafford Road	C3-D3
East Overcliff Drive	C2-D2	Suffolk Road	A3
Exeter Crescent	B2	Terrace Road	A2-B2
Exeter Park Road	B2	The Square	B2
Exeter Road	B1-B2	The Triangle	A2
Fir Vale Road	C3	Tregonwell Road	A1-A2
Gervis Place	B2	Trinity Road	C3
Gervis Road	C2-D2	Upper Hinton Road	B2-C2
Glen Fern Road	C3	Upper Norwich Road	A2
Grove Road	C2-D2	Upper Terrace Road	A2-B2
Hahnemann Road	A2	Wessex Way	A3-B3-C3-D4
Hinton Road	B2-C2	West Cliff Gardens	A1
Holdenhurst Road	D3-D4	West Cliff Road	A1
Kerley Road	A1-B1	West Hill Road	A1-A2
Lansdowne Gardens	C4-D4	Westover Road	B2-C2
Lansdowne Road	C4-D4-D3	Wimborne Road	B3-B4
Lorne Park Road	C3	Wootton Mount	C3-D3
Madeira Road	C3	Wychwood Close	B4
Merlewood Close	B4	Wychwood Drive	B4
Meyrick Road	D2-D3	Yelverton Road	B3
Norwich Avenue	A2-A3	York Road	D3
Norwich Road	A2		
Old Christchurch Road	B2-C3-D3		

165

Birmingham

Birmingham is found on atlas page 61, grid reference **0786**

orn Grove	A4-A5	Cambridge Street	B4-C4	Five Ways	A1	Kent Street	E1-E2	Newhall Hill	B5	Smith Street	B8
ert Street	E5-F5	Camden Drive	A5-B5	Fleet Street	C5	Kenyon Street	B7	Newhall Street	B6-C6-C5	Snow Hill Queensway	D6
ion Street	A5-A6-B6	Camden Street	A6-A5-B5	Florence Street	D2	Key Hill	A8	Newton Street	E6-E5	Southacre Avenue	E1
gate Grove	C8	Cannon Street	D4-E4	Fox Street	F5	King Edward's Road	A4-B4	Northwood Street	B6-C6-C7	Spencer Street	A7-B7
thur Place	A5	Caroline Street	B7-B6-C6	Frederick Road	A1	Kingston Row	B4	Nova Scotia Street	F6	Staniforth Street	E7-E8
ison Street	F3-F4	Carrs Lane	E4	Frederick Street	A6-B6	Ladywell Walk	E3	Old Square	E5	Station Street	D3
ton Road	F8	Carver Street	A5-A6	Freeman Street	F4	Ladywood Middleway	A1-A2	Oozel's Street	B3	Steelhouse Lane	E6
ton Street	E6-F6-F7	Cecil Street	D7-D8-E8	Gas Street	B3-C3	Lancaster Circus Q'way	E6-E7	Oxford Street	F3	Stephenson Street	D4-E4
gusta Street	B7	Centenary Square	C4	George Road	B1	Lancaster Street	E7	Paradise Circus Q'way	C4-C5	Stoke Way	B2
got Street	E7-E8	Chamberlain Square	C4	George Street	B5-B6	Lawson Street	E7	Park Street	F4-F5	Suffolk Street Q'way	C4-C3-D3
nbury Street	F5	Chapel Street	F5	Gooch Street North	E1-E2	Lee Bank Middleway	B1-C1	Pemberton Street	A6-A7	Summer Hill Road	A5
rford Street	F1-F2-F3	Chapmans Passage	D2	Gough Street	D3	Legge Lane	A5-B5	Pershore Street	E3-E2-F2	Summer Hill Street	A4-A5
r Street	A8-B8-B7-C7	Charles Henry Street	F1-F2	Graham Street	B5-B6	Legge Street	E8-F8	Pinfold Street	D4	Summer Hill Terrace	A5-B5
rtholomew Row	F5	Charlotte Street	B5-C5-C6	Grant Street	C1-D1	Lionel Street	C5-C6	Pitsford Street	A7	Summer Lane	D7-D8
rtholomew Street	F5	Cheapside	F2	Granville Street	B3-B2-C2	Lister Street	F7-F8	Pope Street	A5-A6	Summer Row	B5-C5
rwick Street	D5	Church Street	D5	Great Charles Street Q'way	C5	Livery Street	C7-C6-D5	Powell Street	A5	Swallow Street	C4-D4
th Row	B1-C2	Claybrook Street	E2	Great Colmore Street	C1-D1	Louisa Street	B4	Price Street	E7	Temple Row	D5-E5
th Street	D7-E7	Clement Street	A4-A5-B5	Great Hampton Row	C7-C8	Love Lane	F8	Princip Street	D7-E7	Temple Row West	D5
ak Street	D3	Cleveland Street	D7-E7-D8	Great Hampton Street	B8-B7	Loveday Street	D7-E7	Printing House Street	E6	Temple Street	D4
ll Barn Road	C1	Coleshill Street	F6-F7	Great King Street	A8-B8	Lower Essex Street	E1-E2	Pritchett Street	E8	Tenby Street	A6
nnetts Hill	C5-D5-D4	Colmore Circus Q'way	D5-E6	Grosvenor Street	F5-F6	Lower Loveday Street	D7	Rake Way	B2	Tenby Street North	A6
rkley Street	B3-C3	Colmore Row	D4-D5	Grosvenor Street West	A2-A3	Lower Severn Street	D3	Rea Street	F2-F3	Tennant Street	A1-B2-B3
shop Street	E1-F1-F2	Commercial Street	C2-C3	Hadfield Croft	B8	Lower Tower Street	D8-E8	Rea Street South	F1-F2	The Priory Queensway	E5
shopsgate Street	A2-B2-B1	Constitution Hill	C7-D7	Hagley Road	A1	Ludgate Hill	C5-C6	Regent Parade	B6	Thorpe Street	D2-E2-E3
ssell Street	F1	Cornwall Street	C5-D5-D6	Hall Street	B7	Macdonald Street	E1-F1	Regent Place	B6	Tower Street	C8-D8
ucher Street	C3-D3-D2	Corporation Street	E4-E5-E6	Hampton Street	C7-D7	Manchester Street	E8	Regent Street	B6	Townsend Way	A4-B4
and Street	C7	Corporation Street	E7-F8	Hanley Street	D7	Margaret Street	C5	Rickman Drive	D1	Unett Street	B8-C8
rdesley Street	F4	Coventry Street	F4	Harbourne Road	A1	Marshall Street	C2-D2	Ridley Street	C2	Upper Gough Street	C2-D2
w Street	D2	Cox Street	C6	Harford Street	B7-B8	Martineau Square	E5	Roseland Way	B1-B2	Upper Marshall Street	C2
adford Street	F3	Cregoe Street	C1-C2	Heaton Street	A8	Mary Ann Street	C6	Royal Mail Street	C3-D3	Uxbridge Street	C8
anston Street	A8-B8-B7	Dale End	E5	Helena Street	B5	Mary Street	B6-B7-C6	Ruston Street	A2	Vesey Street	E7
earley Street	C8-D8	Dalton Street	E6	Henrietta Street	C6-C7-D7	Masshouse Circus Q'way	E5-F5	Ryland Street	A2	Victoria Square	D4
rewery Street	E8	Dartmouth Middleway	F8	Henstead Street	E1-E2	Meriden Street	F3-F4	St Chad's Circus Q'way	D6	Vittoria Street	B6
idge Street	B3-C3	Digbeth	F3	High Street	E4	Midford Grove	C1	St Chad's Queensway	D6-E7-E7	Vyse Street	A6-A7-A8
indley Drive	B4	Dudley Street	E3	Hill Street	C4-D4-D4	Milford Croft	C8	St George's Street	C7-C8	Ward Street	D8
indley Place	B3	Eden Place	C4-C5	Hinckley Street	D3-E3	Mill Lane	F3	St Mark's Crescent	A4	Warstone Lane	A6-B6-B7
istol Street	D1-D2	Edgbaston Street	E3	Hockley Hill	A8	Mill Street	F8	St Martin's Lane	E3-F3	Warstone Parade East	A6-A7
road Street	A2-B2-B4-C4	Edmund Street	C5	Hockley Street	B7-B8	Moat Lane	F3	St Martin's Street	A2	Washington Street	C2
omsgrove Street	D1-D2-E2	Edward Street	A4-B4-B5	Holland Street	B5	Moland Street	E7-E8	St Martins Circus Q'way	E3-E4	Water Street	C6-D6
rook Street	B6-C6	Ellis Street	D2-D3	Holliday Street	B2-C2-C3	Moor Street Q'way	E4-F4-F5	St Paul's Square	C6	Waterloo Street	D4
owning Street	A3	Elvetham Road North	C1	Holloway Circus Q'way	D2-D3	Moreton Street	A6	St Philips Place	D5-E5	Weaman Street	D6
ownsea Drive	D2	Ernest Street	D2	Holloway Head	C2-D2	Morville Street	A3	St Vincent Street	A3-A4	Well Lane	F4
runel Street	C4-D4-D3	Essex Street	D2-E2	Holt Street	F7-F8	Moseley Street	F2	Sand Pitts Parade	A5-B5	Well Street	B8
uckingham Street	C7-C8	Essington Street	A2-A3	Howard Street	C7	Mott Street	C7	Sandy Way	B2	Wheeleys Lane	B1-C1
ll Ring	E4	Ethel Street	D4	Hurst Street	E2-F2-F1	Navigation Street	D3-D4	Scotland Street	B4	Wheeleys Road	B1
ull Street	E5	Exeter Street	D2	Hylton Street	A8	Needless Alley	D4	Severn Street	C3-D3	Whittal Street	D6-E6
althorpe Road	A1	Fazeley Street	F5	Icknield Street	A6-A7-A8	Nelson Street	A4-A5	Shadwell Street	D6-D7	William Street	B1-B2
				Inge Street	E2	New Bartholomew Street	F4-F5	Shaws Passage	F4	William Street North	D7
				Irving Street	D2	New Canal Street	F4-F5	Sheepcote Street	A4-A3-B3-B2	Windmill Street	D2
				Islington Row Middleway	A1-B1	New Market Street	C5-D5	Sherbourne Street	A2-A3	Woodcock Street	F7-F8
				James Street	B6	New Street	D4-E4	Sherlock Street	E1-E2-F2	Wrentham Street	D1-E1
				Jennens Road	F5-F6	New Summer Street	C8-D8	Skinner Lane	E2	Wynn Street	D1
				John Bright Street	D3	New Town Row	D8-E8	Smallbrook Queensway	D3-E3		

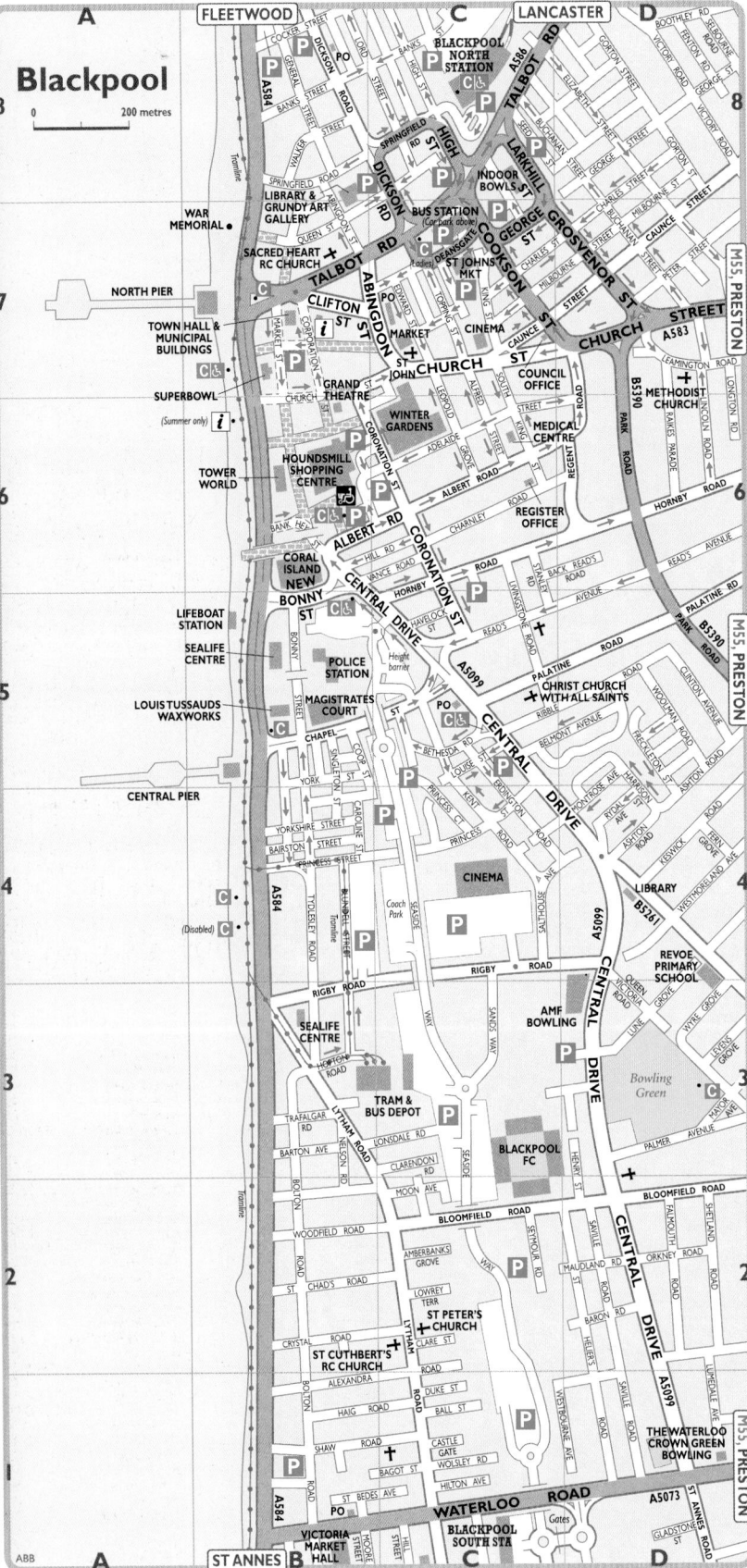

Blackpool

Blackpool is found on atlas page **80**, grid reference **3036**

Abingdon Street	B8-B7-C7
Adelaide Street	C6-D6
Albert Road	B6-C6
Alexandra Road	B1-C1-C2
Alfred Street	C6-C7
Amberbanks Grove	C2
Ashton Road	D4-D5
Back Read's Avenue	C6-D6
Bagot Street	B1-C1
Bairston Street	B4
Ball Street	C1
Bank Hey Street	B6
Banks Street	B8-C8
Baron Road	D2
Barton Avenue	B3
Belmont Avenue	C5-D5
Bethesda Road	C5
Bloomfield Road	C2-D2
Blundell Street	B4
Bolton Street	B1-B2-B3
Bonny Street	B5
Boothley Road	D8
Buchanan Street	C8-D8-D7
Caroline Street	B4
Castle Gate	C1
Caunce Street	C7-D7-D8
Central Drive	B6-C5-D4-D1
Chapel Street	B5-C5
Charles Street	C7-D7-D8
Charnley Road	C6-D6
Church Street	B6-B7-C7-D7
Clare Street	C2
Clarendon Road	C3
Clifton Street	B7
Clinton Avenue	D5
Cocker Street	B8
Cookson Street	C7
Coop Street	B4-B5
Coronation Street	B6-C6-C5
Corporation Street	B6-B7
Crystal Road	B2-C2
Deansgate	C7
Dickson Road	B8-C8-C7
Duke Street	C1
Edward Street	C7
Elizabeth Street	C8-D8
Erdington Road	C4-C5
Falmouth Road	D2
Fenton Road	D8
Fern Grove	D4
Freckleton Street	D4-D5
General Street	B8
George Street	C7-D8
Gladstone Street	D1
Gorton Street	D8
Grosvenor Street	C7-D7
Haig Road	B1-C1
Harrison Street	D4-D5
Havelock Street	C5
Henry Street	D2-D3
High Street	C8
Hill Road	B6-C6
Hill Street	C1
Hilton Avenue	C1
Hopton Road	B3
Hornby Road	C5-C6-D6
Kent Road	C4-C5
Keswick Road	D4-D5
King Street	C7
Larkhill Street	C8
Leamington Road	D7
Leopold Grove	C6-C7
Levens Grove	D3
Lincoln Road	D6-D7
Livingstone Road	C5-C6
Longton Road	D6-D7
Lonsdale Road	B3-C3
Lord Street	B8-C8
Louise Street	C5
Lowrey Terrace	C2
Lumedale Avenue	D1-D2
Lune Grove	D3-D4
Lytham Road	B3-C2-C1
Market Street	B7
Maudland Road	C2-D2
Mayor Avenue	D3
Milbourne Street	C7-D7-D8
Montrose Avenue	D4-D5
Moon Avenue	C2
Moore Street	B1
Nelson Road	B2-B3
New Bonny Street	B5-B6
Orkney Road	D2
Palatine Road	C5-D5-D6
Palmer Avenue	D3
Park Road	D5-D6-D7
Peter Street	D7
Princess Court	C4-C5
Princess Street	B4-C4
Queen Street	B7
Queen Victoria Road	D3-D4
Raikes Parade	D6-D7
Read's Avenue	C5-D5-D6
Regent Road	D6-D7
Ribble Road	C5-D5
Rigby Road	B3-C4-D4
Rydal Avenue	D4
St Annes Road	D1
St Bedes Avenue	B1-C1
St Chad's Road	B2-C2
St Helier's Road	D1-D2
Salthouse Avenue	C4-D4
Sands Way	C3-C4
Saville Road	D1-D2
Seaside Way	C1-C3-C5
Seed Street	C8
Selbourne Road	D8
Seymour Road	C2
Shaw Road	B1-C1
Shetland Road	D2
Singleton Street	B4-B5
South King Street	C6-C7
Springfield Road	B8-C8
Stanley Road	C5-C6
Talbot Road	B7-C7-C8
Topping Street	C7
Trafalgar Road	B3
Tydesley Road	B3-B4
Vance Road	B6-C6
Victory Road	D8
Walker Street	B8
Waterloo Road	B1-C1-D1
Westbourne Avenue	C1-D1
Westmoreland Avenue	D4
Wolsley Road	C1
Woodfield Road	B2-C2
Woolman Road	D5
Wyre Grove	D3
York Street	B5
Yorkshire Street	B4

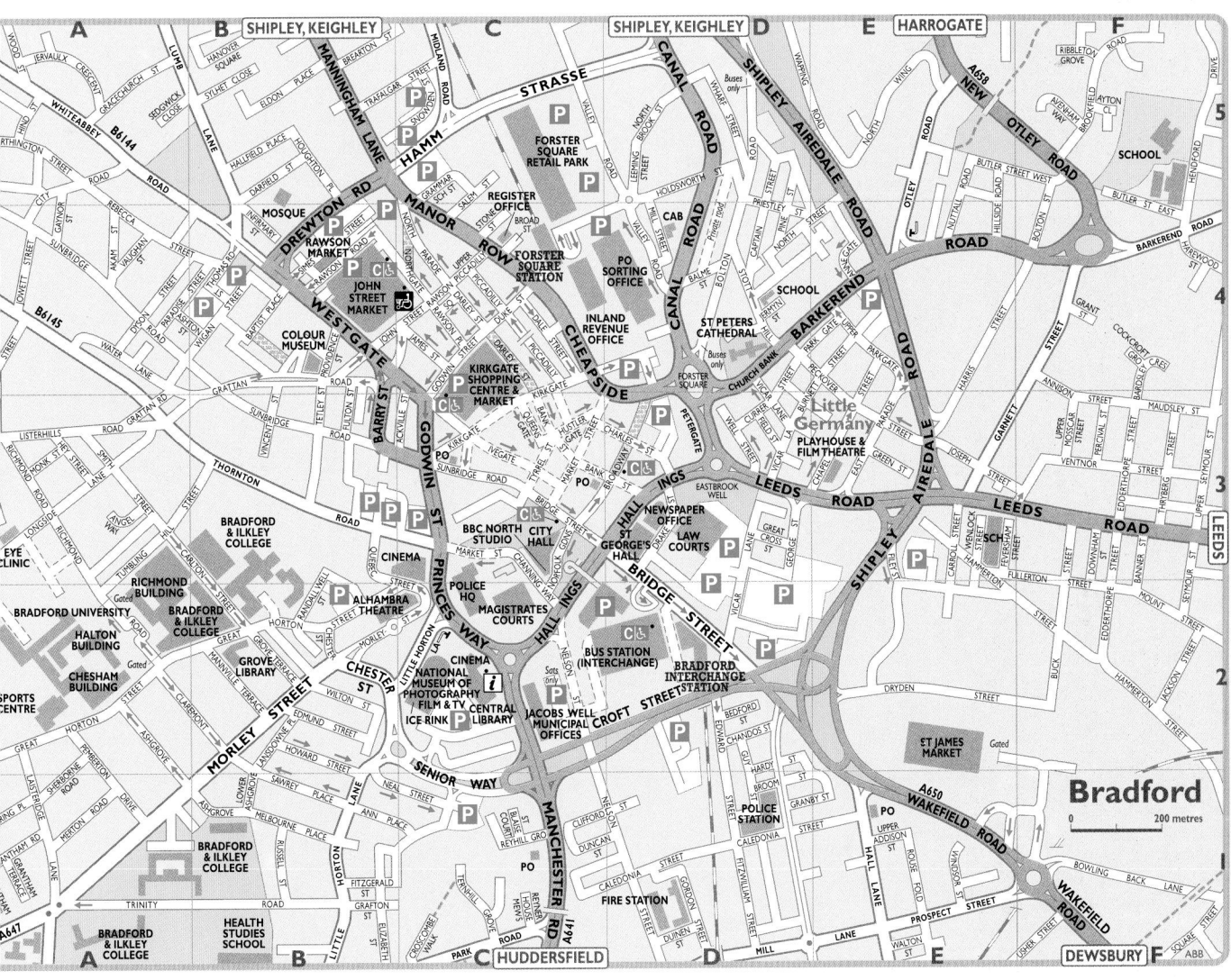

167

Bradford

Bradford is found on atlas page **82**,
d reference 1632

xville Street	C3-C4	Carroll Street	E2-E3	Fitzgerald Street	B1	Ivegate	C3	Northgate	C4	Snowden Street	C5
am Street	A4	Chandos Street	D2	Fitzwilliam Street	D1	Jackson Street	F2	Nuttall Road	E4-E5	Spring Place	A1
gel Way	A3	Channing Way	C2-C3	Fullerton Street	E3-F2	James Street	C4	Otley Road	E4-E5	Square Street	F1
Place	B1-C1	Chapel Street	D3-E3-E4	Fulton Street	B3-B4	Jermyn Street	D4	Oxley Street	A4-A5	Stone Street	C4
ne Gate	E4	Charles Street	C3-D3	Garnett Street	E3-F3-F4	Jervaulx Crescent	A5	Paradise Street	A4-B4	Stott Hill	D4
nison Street	F3-F4	Cheapside	C4-D4-D3	Gaynor Street	A4-A5	John Street	B4-C4	Park Gate	D4-E4	Sunbridge Road	A4-B4-C3
grove	A2-A1-B1	Chester Street	B2	George Street	D3	Joseph Street	E3-F3	Park Road	C1	Sylhet Close	B5
ton Street	A4-B4	Church Bank	D3-D4	Godwin Street	C3-C4	Jowett Street	A4	Peckover Street	D4-E4-E3	Ternhill Grove	C1
enham Way	F5	City Road	A4-A5	Gordon Street	D1	Kirkgate	C3-C4	Pemberton Drive	A1-A2	Tetley Street	B3-B4
ton Close	F5	Claremont	A2-B2	Gracechurch Street	A5	Laisteridge Lane	A1-A2	Percival Street	F3	Thornton Road	A3-B3-C3
ne Street	D4	Clifford Street	C1-D1	Grafton Street	B1	Lansdowne Place	B2	Petergate	D3	Thryberg Street	F3
k Street	C3-D3	Cockcroft Grove	F4	Grammar School Street	C5	Leeds Road	D3-E3-F3	Piccadilly	C4	Trafalgar Street	B5-C5
ner Street	F2-F3	Croft Street	C2-D2	Granby Street	D1-E1	Leeming Street	D5	Pine Street	D4-D5	Trinity Road	A1-B1
nett Street	D3-E4	Croscombe Walk	C1	Grant Street	F4	Listerhills Road	A3	Priestley Street	D4-D5	Tumbling Street	A2-A3-B3
dsley Crescent	B4	Currer Street	D3-D4	Grantham Place	A1	Little Horton Lane	B1-B2-C2	Princes Way	C2-C3	Tyrrel Street	C3
rry Street	B3-B4	Dale Street	C4	Grantham Road	A1	Longside Lane	A3	Prospect Street	E1-F1	Upper Addison Street	E1
kerend Road	D4-E4-F4	Darfield Street	B5	Grantham Terrace	A1	Lower Ashgrove	B1	Providence Street	B4	Upper Mosscar Street	F3
ford Street	D2	Darley Street	C4	Grattan Road	A3-B3-B4	Lumb Lane	A5-B5	Quebec Street	B3-C2	Upper Parkgate	E4
ton Road	D4-D5	Downham Street	F3	Great Cross Street	D3	Manchester Road	C1	Queens Gate	C3	Upper Piccadilly	C4
F4-F5	Drake Street	D3	Green Street	E3	Manningham Lane	B5	Randall Well Street	B2-B3	Upper Seymour Street	F3-F4
wling Back Lane	F1	Drewton Road	B4-B5	Great Horton Street	A2-B2-C2	Mannville Terrace	B2	Rawson Place	C4	Usher Street	E1-F1
arton Street	B5-C5	Dryden Street	E2-F2	Grove Terrace	B2	Manor Row	B5-C4	Rawson Road	B4	Valley Road	C5-D5-D4
dge Street	C3-D3-D2	Duinen Street	D1	Guy Street	D1-D2	Market Street	C3	Rawson Square	C4	Vaughan Street	A4
ad Street	C4	Duke Street	C4	Hall Ings	C2-C3-D3	Maudsley Street	F3	Rebecca Street	A5-A4-B4	Ventnor Street	F3
adway	C3-D3	Duncan Street	C1-D1	Hall Lane	E1	Melbourne Place	B1	Reyhill Grove	C1	Vicar Lane	D2-D3-D4
ookfield Road	F5	Dyson Street	A4	Hallfield Place	B5	Merton Road	A1	Reyner House Mews	C1	Vincent Street	B3-B4
oom Street	D1	East Parade	E3-E4	Hamm Strasse	B5-C5-D5	Midland Road	C5	Ribbleton Grove	F5	Wakefield Road	E1-F1
ck Street	F2-F3	Edderthorpe Street	F2-F3	Hammerton Road	E3-E2-F2-F1	Mill Lane	D1-E1	Richmond Road	A2-A3	Walton Street	E1
nett Street	D3-E4	Edmund Street	B2	Hanover Square	B5	Mill Street	D4	Rouse Fold	E1	Wapping Road	D5-E5
ler Street East	F4-F5	Edward Street	D1-D2	Hardy Street	D2	Monk Street	A3	Russell Street	B1	Water Lane	A4
ler Street West	E5-F5	Eldon Place	B5	Harewood Street	F4	Morley Street	A1-B1-B2-C2	St Blaise Court	C1	Well Street	D3
edonia Street	C1-D1-E1	Elizabeth Street	B1	Harris Street	E3-E4-F4	Mount Street	F2	St Thomas Road	B4	Wenlock Street	E3
nal Road	D4-D5	Feversham Street	E3	Hendford Drive	F4-F5	Neal Street	B2-B1-C1	Salem Street	C4-C5	Westgate	B4-C4
otain Street	D4-D5	Field Street	D3	Hey Street	A3	Nelson Street	C2-C1-D1	Sawrey Place	B1-B2	Wharf Street	D5
lton Street	A3-B3-B2	Filey Street	E3	Hillside Road	E4-E5	New Otley Road	E5-F5-F4	Sedgwick Close	A5	Whiteabbey Road	A5-B4
				Hind Street	A5	Norcroft Street	A3-A4	Senior Way	C1-C2	Wigan Street	A4-B4
				Holdsworth Street	D5	Norfolk Gardens	C2-C3	Seymour Street	F2-F3	Wilton Street	B2
				Houghton Place	B5	North Brook Street	D5	Sherborne Road	A1-A2	Windsor Street	E1
				Howard Street	B2	North Parade	C4	Shipley Airedale Road	D5-E5-E3-E2	Wood Street	A5
				Hustler Gate	C3	North Street	D4-E4-E5	Simes Street	B4	Worthington Street	A5
				Infirmary Street	B4	North Wing	E5	Smith Street	A3		

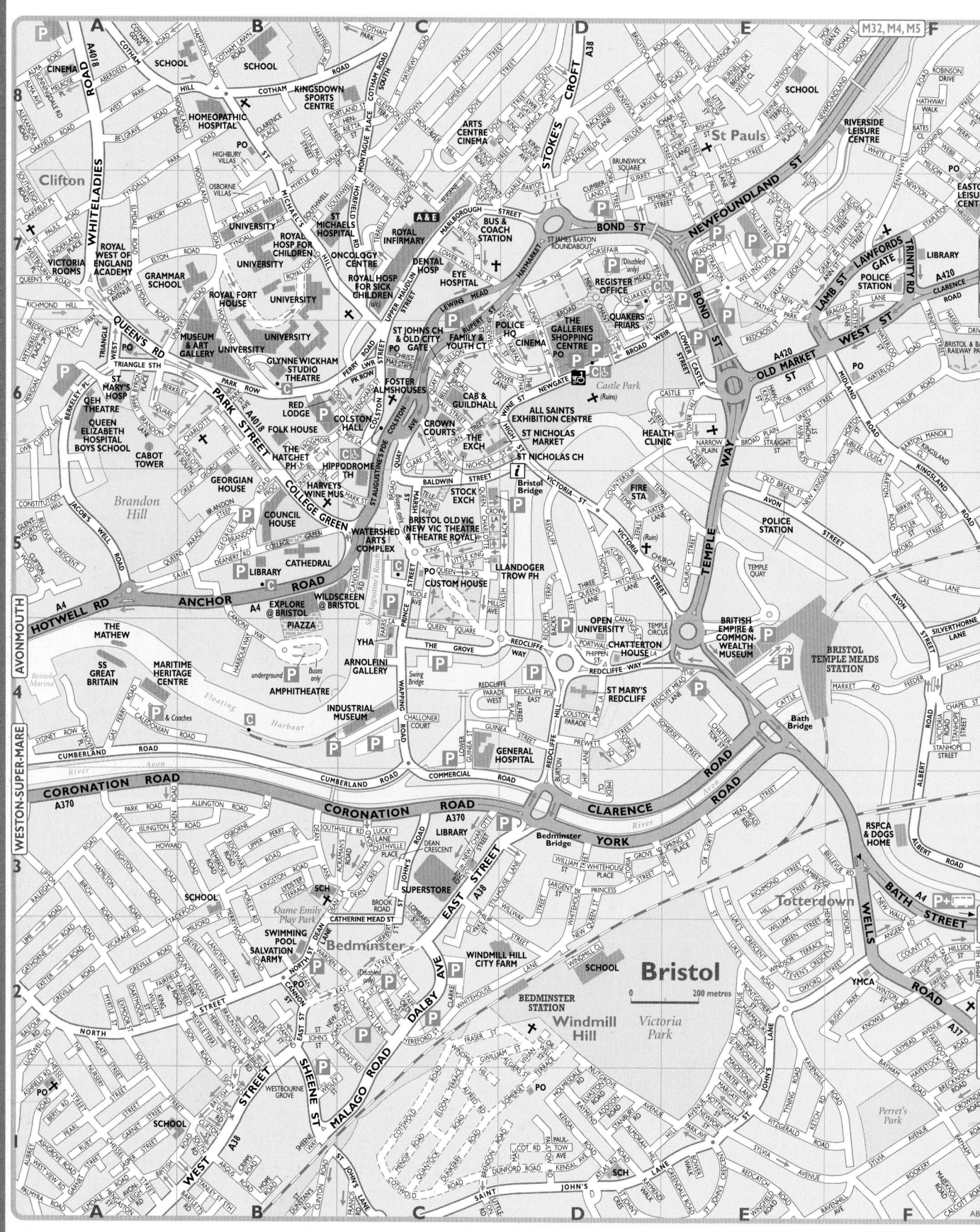

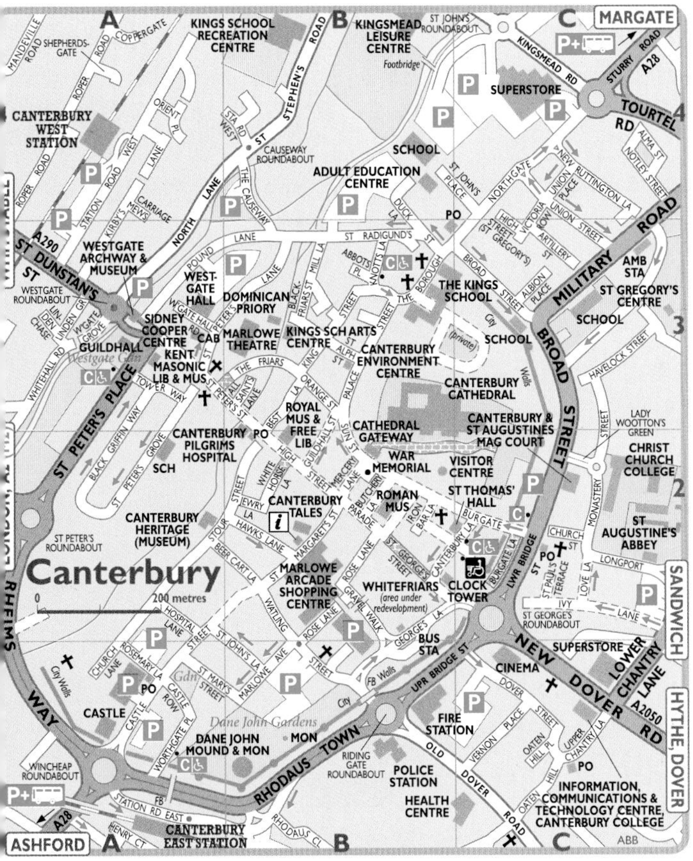
A
B
C
MARGATE
KINGS SCHOOL RECREATION CENTRE
KINGSMEAD LEISURE CENTRE
ST JOHN'S ROUNDABOUT
SUPERSTORE
TOURTEL RD
CANTERBURY WEST STATION
SCHOOL
ADULT EDUCATION CENTRE
CAUSEWAY ROUNDABOUT
WESTGATE ARCHWAY & MUSEUM
ST DUNSTAN'S
WESTGATE ROUNDABOUT
WEST-GATE HALL
DOMINICAN PRIORY
THE KINGS SCHOOL
MILITARY ROAD
AMB STA
ST GREGORY'S CENTRE
SCHOOL
SIDNEY COOPER CENTRE
CAB
MARLOWE THEATRE
KINGS SCH ARTS CENTRE
CANTERBURY ENVIRONMENT CENTRE
GUILDHALL
KENT MASONIC LIB & MUS
CANTERBURY CATHEDRAL
ROYAL MUS & FREE LIB
CATHEDRAL GATEWAY
CANTERBURY & ST AUGUSTINES MAG COURT
LADY WOOTTON'S GREEN
CHRIST CHURCH COLLEGE
CANTERBURY PILGRIMS HOSPITAL
WAR MEMORIAL
VISITOR CENTRE
ST PETER'S PLACE
SCH
CANTERBURY TALES
ROMAN MUS
ST THOMAS' HALL
ST AUGUSTINE'S ABBEY
CANTERBURY HERITAGE (MUSEUM)
ST PETER'S ROUNDABOUT
BROAD STREET
Canterbury
200 metres
MARLOWE ARCADE SHOPPING CENTRE
WHITEFRIARS (area under redevelopment)
CLOCK TOWER
ST GEORGE'S ROUNDABOUT
SANDWICH
BUS STA
SUPERSTORE
CINEMA
NEW DOVER RD
LOWER CHANTRY LANE
A2050
HYTHE, DOVER
RHEIMS WAY
CASTLE
PO
DANE JOHN MOUND & MON
Dane John Gardens
FIRE STATION
WINCHEAP ROUNDABOUT
RIDING GATE ROUNDABOUT
POLICE STATION
HEALTH CENTRE
RHODAUS TOWN
INFORMATION, COMMUNICATIONS & TECHNOLOGY CENTRE CANTERBURY COLLEGE
STATION RD EAST
CANTERBURY EAST STATION
ASHFORD
A28
ABB

Canterbury

Canterbury is found on atlas page **29**, grid reference **1457**

Abbots Place	B3
Albion Place	C3
All Saints Lane	B3
Alma Street	C4
Artillery Street	C3
Beer Cart Lane	A2-B2
Best Lane	B3
Black Griffin Way	A2-A3
Blackfriars Street	B3
Broad Street	C2-C3
Burgate	C2
Burgate Lane	C2
Butchery Lane	B2
Canterbury Lane	B2-C2
Carriage Mews	A4
Castle Row	A1
Castle Street	A1-A2
Church Lane	A1
Church Street	C2
Coppergate	A4
Cossington Road	C1
Dover Street	C1
Duck Lane	B4
George's Lane	B2
Gravel Walk	B2
Guildhall Street	B2-B3
Havelock Street	C3
Hawks Lane	B2
Henry Court	A1
High Street	B2
High Street (St Gregory's)	C4
Hospital Lane	A2
Iron Bar Lane	B2
Ivy Lane	C2
Jewry Lane	B2
King Street	B3
Kingsmead Road	C4
Kirby's Lane	A3-A4
Knotts Lane	B3
Lady Wootton's Green	C2
Linden Chase	A3
Linden Green	A3
Longport	C2
Love Lane	C2
Lower Bridge Street	C2
Lower Chantry Lane	C1-C2
Mandeville Road	A4
Marlowe Avenue	B1
Mercery Lane	B2
Military Road	C3-C4
Mill Lane	B3
Monastery Street	C2-C3
New Dover Road	C1-C2
New Ruttington Lane	C4
North Lane	A3-A4-B4
Northgate	C3-C4
Notley Street	C4
Oaten Hill	C1
Oaten Hill Place	C1
Old Dover Road	B1-C1
Orange Street	B3
Orient Place	A4
Palace Street	B3
Parade	B2
Pound Lane	A3-B4
Rheims Way	A1-A2
Rhodaus Close	B1
Rhodaus Town	B1
Roper Road	A4
Rose Lane	B2
Rosemary Lane	A1
St Alphege Street	B3
St Dunstan's Street	A3-A4
St George's Street	B2
St John's Lane	A2-B1
St John's Place	B4-C4
St Margaret's Street	B2
St Mary's Street	A1-B1
St Paul's Terrace	C2
St Peter's Grove	A2-A3
St Peter's Lane	A3-B3
St Peter's Place	A2-A3
St Peter's Street	A3-B3
St Radigund's Street	B3
St Stephen's Road	B4
Shepherd's Gate	A4
Station Road East	A1-B1
Station Road West	A3-A4-B4
Stour Street	A2-B2
Sturry Road	C4
Sun Street	B2-B3
The Borough	B3
The Causeway	B3-B4
The Friars	B3
Tourtel Road	C4
Tower Way	A3
Union Place	C4
Union Street	C3-C4
Upper Bridge Street	B1-B2
Upper Chantry Lane	C1
Vernon Place	C1
Victoria Row	C3-C4
Watling Street	B1-B2
Westgate Grove	A3
Westgate Hall Road	A3
White Horse Lane	B2
Whitehall Road	A3
Worthgate Place	A1

169

Bristol

ristol is found on atlas page **34**, rid reference **5972**

erdeen Road	A8-B8
gate Street	A1-A2
bert Road	F3-F4
fred Hill	C7
fred Place	B8-C8
fred Place	D4
lington Road	B3
ma Road	A8
morah Hill	D1
pha Road	C3
nchor Road	A5-B5-C5
ngers Road	F2-F3
gus Road	B1
las Road	D1
ubrey Road	A1
von Street	E5-F5-F4
ackfields	D8
aldwin Street	C5-D6
arton Road	F5-F6
arton Street	D7
ath Street	F2-F3
eauley Road	A3-B3
elgrave Road	A8
ell Lane	C6
ellevue Road	E3-F3
erkeley Place	A6
erkeley Square	A6-B6
rch Road	A2-A3
shop Street	E8
ond Street	D7-E7-E6
aggs Lane	E7-F7
andon Steep	B5
andon Street	B5
aunton Road	B2
endon Road	C1-D1
idewell Street	C6-C7
ighton Street	E8
igstocke Road	D8-E8
itish Road	A1-B1-B2
oad Mead	D6-D7
oad Plain	E6
oad Quay	C5-C6
oad Street	C6
oad Weir	D6-E6
ook Road	C3
unswick Square	D7
unswick Street	D8
uton Place	A6
ushy Park	E2-F2
aledonian Road	A4-B4
amden Road	A3
annon Street	B2
anons Road	C5
anons Way	B4-B5
Castle Street	D6-E6
Catherine Mead Street	B2-C2
Cattle Market Road	E4-F4
Cave Street	D8-E8
Chapel Street	F4
Charles Street	D7-D8
Charlotte Street	B6
Charlotte Street South	B6
Chatterton Street	E4
Chessel Street	A1-A2
Christmas Steps	C6
Church Lane	C2
Church Street	E5
City Road	D8-E8
Clare Street	C6
Clarence Road	D3-E3-E4
Clarence Road	F7
Clevedon Terrace	C8
Clifton Street	B1
Clifton Wood Road	A5
Clinton Road	B1
College Green	B5-C5
Colston Avenue	C6
Colston Parade	D4
Colston Street	C6
Commercial Road	C3-D3
Constitution Hill	A5
Corn Street	C6
Coronation Road	A3-B3-C3-D3
Cotham Hill	A8-B8
Cotham Lawn Road	B8
Cotham Road	B8-C8
Cotham Road South	C8
Cotswold Road	C1-C2
Cottage Place	C7
Counterslip	D5-D6-E6
Cripps Road	B1
Cumberland Road	A4-B3-C3-C4
Dalby Avenue	C2
Dale Street	E7
Dean Lane	B2-B3-C3
Dean Street	B2
Dean Street	E8
Deanery Road	B5
Denmark Street	B5-C5
Diamond Street	B2
Dighton Street	C7-C8-D8
Dove Lane	E8
Dove Street	C8-D8
Dove Street South	C8-D8
Dunford Road	C1-D1
Dunkerry Road	C1
Earl Street	C7
East Street	B2-C2-C3-D3
Elmdale Road	A1
Elmdale Road	A6-A7
Elton Road	A7-B7
Elton Street	E7-E8
Eugene Street	F7
Exeter Road	A2
Fairfax Street	D6
Farrs Lane	C4-C5
Feeder Road	F4
Ferry Street	D5
Firfield Street	F2
Fitzgerald Road	E1-F1
Fraser Street	C1-D1
Frog Lane	B5-B6
Frogmore Street	B6-C6
Garnet Street	A1
Gas Ferry Road	A4
Gas Lane	F5
Gathorne Road	A2
Goodhind Street	F8
Great George Street	A5-B5-B6
Great George Street	E7
Greendale Road	E1
Greville Road	A2
Greville Street	B2
Grosvenor Road	E8
Guinea Street	C4-D4
Halston Drive	E8
Hamilton Road	A2-A3
Hampton Road	B8
Hanover Place	A4
Harbour Way	B4
Hartfield Avenue	B8
Haymarket	D7
Henry Street	E2-F2
Herbert Street	C2
Hereford Street	C2
High Street	D6
Highgrove Street	F2
Hill Avenue	D1-E1-E2
Hill Street	B5-B6
Hill Street	E3
Hillgrove Street	D8
Holmesdale Road	D1
Horfield Road	C7
Horton Street	F6
Hotwell Road	A4-A5
Houlton Street	E7
Howard Road	A3-B3
Islington Road	A3-B3
Jacob Street	E6
Jacob's Well Road	A5
Jamaica Street	D8
Jubilee Street	F6
Kensal Road	D1
King Square	C8-D8
King Square Avenue	D8
King Street	C5
King William Street	A2
Kingsdown Parade	C8
Kingsland Road	F5-F6
Kingston Road	B3
Knowle Road	F2
Lamb Street	E7-F7
Lawfords Gate	F7
Leighton Road	A3
Lewins Mead	C7-D7
Lilymead Avenue	F2
Lime Road	A2-A3
Little Ann Street	F7
Little Bishop Street	E8
Little George Street	E7-F7
Little King Street	C5
Little Paradise	C2
Lodge Street	B6-C6
Lombard Street	C2-C3
Louisa Street	F6
Lower Castle Street	E6
Lower Clifton Hill	A6
Lower Guinea Street	C4
Lower Maudlin Street	C7
Lower Park Row	C6
Luckwell Road	A2
Maidstone Street	E1-E2
Malago Road	B1-C1-C2
Margate Street	E1
Marlborough Hill	C7-C8
Marlborough Street	C7-D7
Marsh Street	C5
Mead Street	E3
Meadow Street	E7
Melrose Place	A8
Merchant Street	D6-D7
Meridian Place	A6
Merrywood Road	B2-B3
Middle Avenue	C5
Midland Road	F6
Milford Street	B2-B3
Mill Avenue	C5
Mill Lane	C2
Milsom Street	F7-F8
Mitchell Lane	D5
Montague Hill	C8
Montague Place	C8
Montgomery Street	E2
Moon Street	D8
Morley Road	B2-B3
Mount Pleasant Terrace	A2-B2
Myrtle Road	B7-B8
Narrow Plain	E6
Nelson Street	C6-D6
New Charlotte Street	C3
New Kingsley Road	E5-F6
New Queen Street	D2-D3
New Street	E7
Newfoundland Road	E8-F8
Newfoundland Street	E7-E8-F8
Newgate	D6
Newport Street	E1
Newton Street	F7
North Street	A2-B2
Nutgrove Avenue	D2-D1-E1
Oakfield Road	A8
Old Bread Street	E5
Old Market Street	E6
Osborne Road	B3
Oxford Street	E2-F2-F3
Oxford Street	F5
Park Avenue	E1
Park Place	A6-A7
Park Road	A3
Park Row	B6
Park Street	B6
Paultow Road	D1
Pearl Street	A1
Pembroke Street	D7-E7
Penn Street	D7-E7
Pennywell Road	F7-F8
Perry Road	C6
Philip Street	C3-C2-D2
Portland Square	E7-E8
Portland Street	B8-C8
Portwall Lane	D4
Prewett Street	D4
Prince Street	C4-C5
Princess Street	D3
Priory Road	A7-B7
Pritchard Street	E7
Pump Lane	D4
Quakers Friars	D6-D7
Quay Street	C6
Queen Charlotte Street	C4-C5
Queen Square	C4-C5
Queen Street	D6-E6
Queen's Avenue	A7
Queen's Road	A6-A7
Queens Parade	A5-B5
Raleigh Road	A2-A3
Ravenhill Road	E2-E1-F1
Raymend Road	D1
Redcatch Road	E1
Redcliff Mead Lane	D4-E4
Redcliffe Backs	D4-D5
Redcliffe Parade East	D4
Redcliffe Parade West	C4-D4
Redcliff Street	D4-D5
Redcliffe Way	D4
Regent Road	C3
Richmond Hill	A7
Richmond Street	E3
River Street	E7
Royal Fort Road	B7
Ruby Street	C2
Rupert Street	C6-C7-D7
Russ Street	E6
Saint George's Road	A5-B5
Saint John's Lane	C1-D1-E1-E2
St Augustine's Parade	C5-C6
St John's Crescent	D1-E1
St John's Road	C2-C3
St John's Street	B2
St Luke's Road	E2-E3
St Mathews Road	C8
St Mathias Park	E7
St Michael's Hill	B8-B7-C7
St Michael's Park	B7
St Nicholas Street	C6-D6
St Paul's Street	E7
St Pauls Road	A7
St Phillips Road	F6
St Stephen's Street	C5-C6
St Thomas Street	D4-D5
Sargent Street	D3
Sheene Street	B1-B2
Ship Lane	D3-D4
Silverthorne Lane	F4-F5
Sion Road	B1-B2
Small Street	C6
Somerset Square	D4
Somerset Street	C8-D8
Somerset Street	D4-E4
Somerset Terrace	C1-D1-D2
South Road	B1
South Street	B1-A1-A2
Southville Road	B3-C3
Southwell Street	B7-C7
Spring Street	D3-E3
Stackpool Road	A2-B3
Stafford Street	C2
Stanley Hill	F2
Stanley Street South	B1
Stapleton Road	F7-F8
Steven's Crescent	E2-F2
Stillhouse Lane	C3-D3
Stoke's Croft	D7-D8
Stratton Street	E7
Summer Hill	F2
Surrey Street	D7-D8-E8
Sydney Row	A4
Sylvia Avenue	E1-F1
Temple Back	D5-E5
Temple Quay	E5
Temple Street	D5
Temple Way	E5-E6
Terrell Street	C7
The Grove	C4
The Horsefair	D7
The Nursery	A1-A2
The Pithay	D6
Thrissell Street	F7
Tower Hill	E6
Trenchard Street	C6
Triangle South	A6
Triangle West	A6
Trinity Road	F7
Trinity Street	F6-F7
Tyndall Avenue	B7
Tyndall's Park Road	A7-A8-B8
Tyning Road	E1-E2
Union Road	F5
Union Street	D6-D7
Unity Street	B5-B6
Unity Street	E6-F6
University Road	A6-B7
Upper Byron Place	A6
Upper Maudlin Street	C7
Upper Perry Hill	B3
Upton Road	A2-A3
Vicarage Road	A2
Victoria Street	D5-E5
Vivian Street	D2
Wade Street	E7-F7
Walker Street	B8-C8
Wapping Road	C4
Waterloo Road	F6
Waterloo Street	F6
Wellington Road	E7
Wells Road	F2-F3
Welsh Back	D4-D5
Wesley Street	B1-C1
West Park	A8
West Street	A1-B1-B2
West Street	F6-F7
Westbourne Grove	B2
Whitehouse Lane	C2-D2
Whitehouse Place	D3
Whitehouse Street	D2-D3
Whiteladies Road	A7-A8
Whitson Street	C7
Wilder Street	D8-E8
William Street	E2-E3
Wilson Street	E8
Windmill Close	D2
Windmill Hill	C1-C2
Windsor Terrace	E2
Wine Street	D6
Woodland Road	B6-B7-B8-A8
York Road	D3-E3-E4
York Street	D7-D8

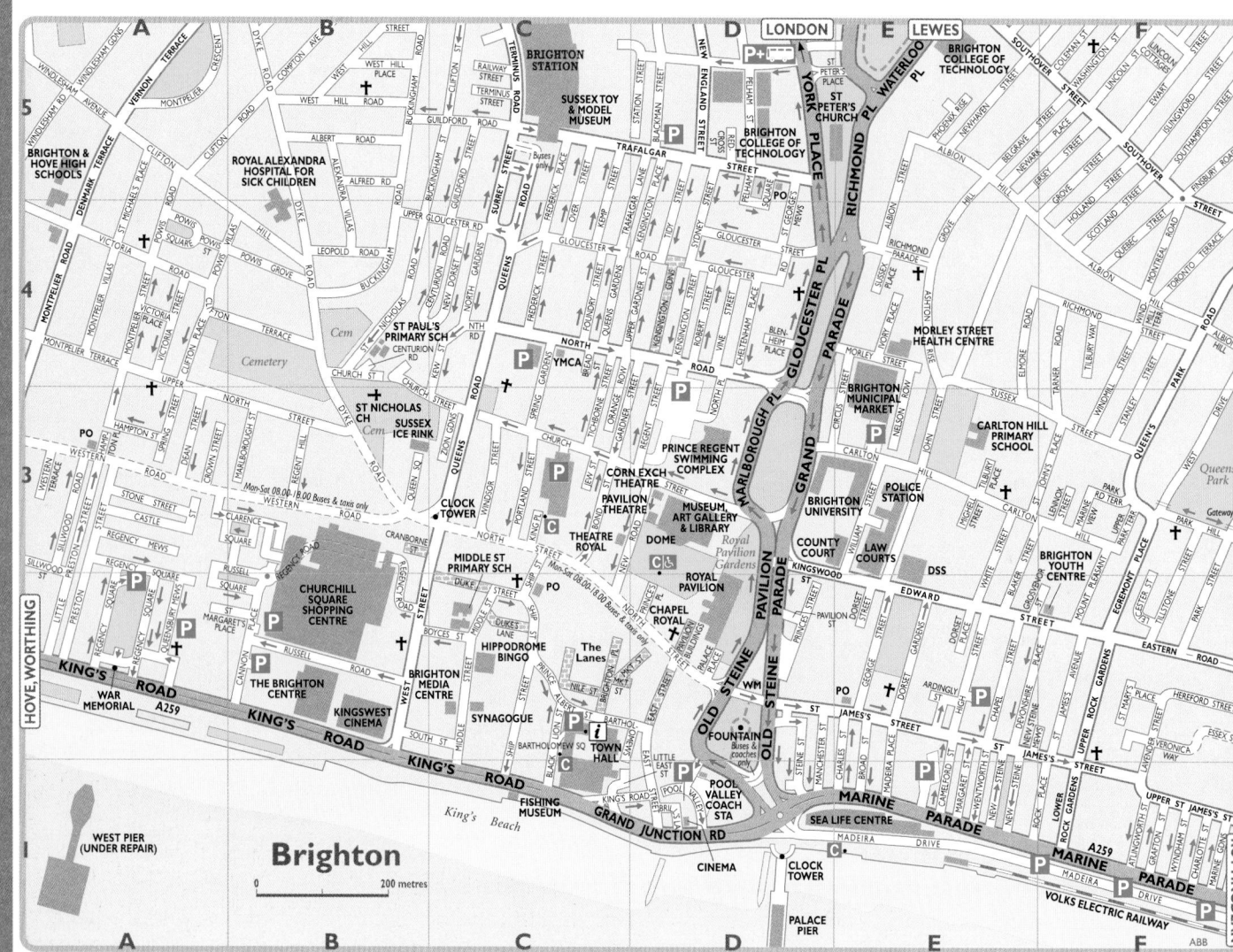

Brighton

Brighton is found on atlas page **15**,
grid reference 3104

Albert Road	B5	Clifton Street	C5	Guildford Road	B5-C5	Montpelier Terrace	A4	Queen's Park Road	F3-F4	Tarner Road	F3-
Albion Hill	E5-E4-F4	Clifton Terrace	A4-B4	Guildford Street	C4-C5	Montpelier Villas	A4	Queens Gardens	C4	Terminus Road	C
Albion Street	E4-E5	Coleman Street	F5	Hampton Place	A3	Montreal Road	F4	Queens Road	C3-C4-C5	Terminus Street	C
Alexandra Villas	B4-B5	Compton Avenue	B5	Hampton Street	A3	Morley Street	E4	Queensbury Mews	A2	Tichborne Street	C3-C
Alfred Road	B5	Cranborne Street	B3	Hereford Street	F2	Mount Pleasant	F2-F3	Railway Street	C5	Tidy Street	D4-D
Ardingly Street	E2	Crown Street	A3	High Street	E2	Nelson Row	E3-E4	Red Cross Street	D5	Tilbury Place	F
Ashton Rise	E4	Dean Street	A3	Holland Street	F4-F5	New Dorset Street	C4	Regency Mews	A3	Tilbury Way	F
Atlingworth Street	F1	Denmark Terrace	A4-A5	Islingword Street	F5	New England Street	D5	Regency Road	B2-B3	Tillstone Street	C
Bartholomews	C2-D2	Devonshire Place	E2-F2	Ivory Place	E4	New Road	C2-C3-D3	Regency Square	A2-A3	Toronto Terrace	F
Belgrave Street	E5-F5	Dorset Gardens	E2	Jersey Street	E5-F5	New Steine	E1-E2	Regent Hill	B3	Trafalgar Lane	C4-D4-D
Black Lion Street	C1-C2	Dorset Place	E2	Jew Street	C3	New Steine Mews	E2-F2	Regent Street	D3-D4	Trafalgar Street	C5-D
Blackman Street	D5	Dorset Street	E2	John Street	E3-E4	Newark Place	E5-F5	Richmond Parade	E4	Upper Gardner Street	C4-D
Blaker Street	E2-E3	Duke Street	C2	Kemp Street	C4-C5	Newhaven Street	E5	Richmond Place	E4-E5	Upper Gloucester Road	B4-C
Blenheim Place	D4	Dukes Lane	C2	Kensington Gardens	D4	Nile Street	C2	Richmond Street	F4	Upper North Street	A4-A3-B
Bond Street	C3	Dyke Road	B3-B4-B5	Kensington Place	D4-D5	North Gardens	C4	Robert Street	D4	Upper Park Terrace	F
Boyces Street	B2-C2	East Street	D1-D2	Kensington Street	D4	North Place	D3-D4	Rock Place	E1-F1	Upper Rock Gardens	F
Bread Street	C4	Eastern Road	F2	Kew Street	C3-C4	North Road	C3-C4	Russell Road	B2	Upper St James's Street	F
Brighton Place	C2	Edward Street	E2-F2	King Place	C3	North Street	B3-C3-C2-D2	Russell Square	A3-A2-B2-B3	Vernon Terrace	A
Brill's Lane	D1	Egremont Place	F2-F3	King's Road	A2-B2-C1-D1	Old Steine	D1-D2	St George's Mews	D4-D5	Veronica Way	F
Broad Street	E1-E2	Elmore Road	E3-E4	Kingswood Street	D2-D3	Orange Row	C3-C4	St James's Avenue	F2	Victoria Place	A
Buckingham Road	B4-B5	Essex Street	F2	Lavender Street	F1-F2	Over Street	C4-C5	St James's Street	D2-E2-F2-F1	Victoria Road	A
Buckingham Street	B4-C5	Ewart Street	F5	Leicester Street	F2-F3	Palace Place	D2	St John's Place	E3-F3	Victoria Street	A
Camelford Street	E1-E2	Finsbury Road	F5	Lennox Street	F3	Park Hill	F3	St Margaret's Place	A2-B2	Vine Street	D
Cannon Place	B2	Foundry Street	C4	Leopold Road	B4	Park Road Terrace	F3	St Mary's Place	F2	Washington Street	E1-E
Carlton Hill	D3-E3-F3	Frederick Place	C4-C5	Lincoln Cottages	F5	Park Street	F2-F3	St Michael's Place	A4-A5	Waterloo Place	D
Castle Street	A3	Frederick Street	C4	Lincoln Street	F5	Pavilion Buildings	D2	St Nicholas Road	B4	Wentworth Street	E1-F
Centurion Road	B4-C4	Gardner Street	C3-D3-D4	Little East Street	C1	Pavilion Parade	D2-D3	St Peter's Place	D5-E5	West Drive	F3-F
Chapel Street	E2	George Street	E2	Little Preston Street	A2-A3	Pavilion Street	D2	Scotland Street	F4-F5	West Hill Place	E
Charles Street	E1-E2	Gloucester Place	D4	Lower Rock Gardens	F1	Pelham Square	D5	Ship Street	C1-C2-C3	West Hill Road	B
Charlotte Street	F1	Gloucester Road	C4-D4	Madeira Drive	D1-E1-F1	Pelham Street	D5	Sillwood Road	A3	West Hill Street	C
Cheltenham Place	D4	Gloucester Street	D4	Madeira Place	E1-E2	Phoenix Rise	E5	Sillwood Street	A2-A3	West Street	B2-C
Church Street	B4-B3-C3-D3	Grafton Street	F1	Manchester Street	D1-D2	Pool Valley	D1	South Street	B2-C2	Western Road	A3-B
Circus Street	D3-E3-E4	Grand Junction Road	C1-D1	Margaret Street	E1-E2	Portland Street	C3	Southampton Street	F5	Western Terrace	A
Clarence Square	A3-B3	Grand Parade	D3-D4-E4	Marine Gardens	F1	Powis Grove	B4	Southover Street	E5-F5-F4	White Street	E2-F
Clifton Hill	A5-A4-B4	Grosvenor Street	E2-F2	Marine Parade	D1-E1-F1	Powis Road	A4-A5	Spring Gardens	C3-C4	William Street	F
Clifton Place	A4	Grove Hill	E4-E5	Marine View	F3	Powis Square	A4	Spring Street	A3	Windlesham Avenue	A
Clifton Road	A5-B5	Grove Street	F4-F5	Market Street	C2-D2	Powis Villas	A4-B4	Stanley Street	F3-F4	Windlesham Gardens	A
				Marlborough Place	D3	Preston Street	A2-A3	Station Street	D5	Windlesham Road	A
				Marlborough Street	B3	Prince Albert Street	C2	Steine Street	D1-D2	Windmill Street	F3-F
				Middle Street	C1-C2	Princes Place	D2	Stone Street	A3	Windmill Terrace	F
				Mighell Street	E3	Princes Street	D2	Surrey Street	C4-C5	Windsor Street	C
				Montpelier Crescent	A5	Quebec Street	F4	Sussex Place	E4	Wyndham Street	F
				Montpelier Road	A3-A4	Queen Square	B3	Sussex Street	E4-E3-F3	York Place	D4-D
				Montpelier Street	A4	Queen's Park Road	F3-F4	Sydney Street	D4-D5	Zion Gardens	B

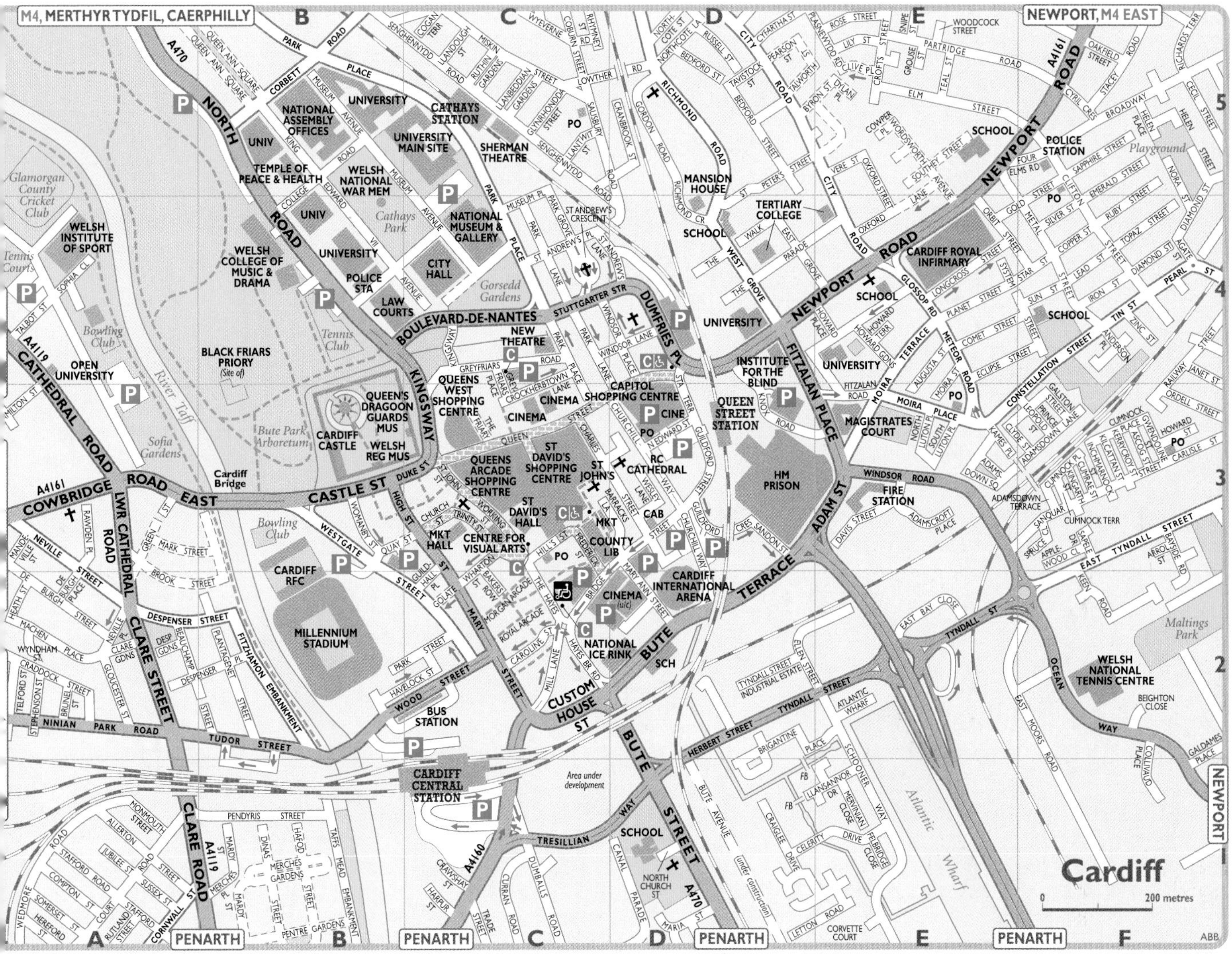

Cardiff

ardiff is found on atlas page **33**,
id reference **1876**

am Street	D3-E3
amscroft Place	E3
amsdown Lane	F3
amsdown Square	E3
amsdown Terrace	F3
ate Street	F4
erton Street	A1
derson Place	F4
plewood Close	F3
rol Street	F3
cog Street	F3
antic Wharf	E2
gusta Street	E3-E4
kers Row	C2
rracks Lane	C3-D3
yside Road	F2-F3
auchamp Street	A2-B2
dford Street	D5
ighton Close	F2
ulevard de Nantes	B4-C4
dge Street	C2-D3
gatine Place	D2-E2
oadway	F5
ook Street	A3-A2-B2
unel Street	A2
ce Avenue	D1
te Street	D1-D2
te Terrace	D2-D3
on Street	D5-E5
nal Parade	D1
rlisle Street	F3
roline Street	C2
stle Street	B3
thedral Road	A3-A4
cil Street	F5
lerity Drive	D1-E1
arles Street	C3-D3
urch Street	C3
urchill Way	D2-D3
y Road	D5-E5-E4
are Gardens	A2
are Road	A2-A1-B1
Clare Street	A2
Clifton Street	F4-F5
Clive Place	E5
Clyde Street	E3-F3
Coburn Street	C5
Cogan Terrace	C5
College Road	B4-B5
Collivaud Place	F1-F2
Comet Street	E4-F4
Compton Street	A1
Constellation Street	E3-F3-F4
Copper Street	F4
Corbett Road	B5
Cornwall Street	A1
Court Road	A1
Cowbridge Road East	A3-B3
Cowper Place	E5
Craddock Street	A2
Cranbrook Street	D5
Crawshay Street	C1
Craiglee Drive	D1
Crockherbtown Lane	C3-C4
Crofts Street	E5
Cumnock Place	F3
Cumnock Terrace	F3
Cumrae Street	F3
Curran Road	C1
Custom House Street	C2
Cyfartha Street	D5
Cyril Crescent	F5
Davis Street	E3
De Burgh Place	A2
De Burgh Street	A2-A3
Despenser Gardens	A2
Despenser Place	A2-B2
Despenser Street	A2-B2
Diamond Street	F4
Dinas Street	B1
Duke Street	B3-C3
Dumballs Road	C1
Dumfries Place	D4
Dylan Place	E5
East Bay Close	E2
East Grove	D4-E4
East Moors Road	E2-F2-F1
East Tyndall Street	F2-F3
Eclipse Street	E4-F4
Ellen Street	D2-E2
Elm Street	E5-F5
Emerald Street	F4-F5
Felbridge Close	E1
Fitzalan Place	D4-D3-E3
Fitzalan Road	E3
Fitzhamon Embankment	B2
Four Elms Road	E5-F5
Frederick Street	C2-C3
Galston Street	F3
Glossop Road	E4
Gloucester Street	A2
Glynrhondda Street	C5
Golate	C2
Gold Street	E4-F4-F5
Gordon Road	D5
Green Street	A3
Greyfriars Place	C3-C4
Greyfriars Road	C3-C4
Grouse Street	E5
Guildford Crescent	D3
Guildford Street	D3
Guildhall Place	C2
Gwendoline Street	F3
Hafod Street	B1
Hamilton Street	A3
Harpur Street	C1
Havelock Street	B2-C2
Hayes Bridge Road	C2
Heath Street	A2
Helen Place	F5
Helen Street	F5
Herbert Street	D1-D2
Hereford Street	A1
High Street	B3-C3
Hill's Street	C3
Howard Gardens	E4
Howard Place	E4
Howard Street	F3
Howard Terrace	E4
Inchmarnock Street	F3
Iron Street	F4
Janet Street	F3-F4
Jubilee Street	A1
Kames Place	E3
Keen Road	F2
Kerrycroy Street	F3
Kilcattan Street	F3
King Edward VII Avenue	B5-B4-C4
Kingarth Street	F3
Kingsway	C3-C4
Knox Road	D3
Lead Street	F4
Letton Road	D1-E1
Lily Street	E5
Llanbeddian Gardens	C5
Llandough Street	C5
Llansannor Drive	D1-E1
Llantwit Street	C5
Longcross Street	E4
Lower Cathedral Road	A2-A3
Lowther Road	C5-D5
Machen Place	A2
Mardy Street	B1
Maria Street	D1
Mark Street	A3-B3
Mary Ann Street	D2
Merches Gardens	B1
Merches Place	B1
Mervinian Close	E1
Metal Street	F4
Meteor Road	E3-E4
Mill Lane	C2
Miskin Street	C5
Moira Place	E3
Moira Street	E3-E4
Moira Terrace	E3-E4
Monmouth Street	A1
Morgan Arcade	C2
Museum Avenue	B5-C4
Museum Place	C4
Neville Place	A2
Neville Street	A2-A3
Newport Road	D4-E4-E5-F5
Ninian Park Road	A2
Nora Street	F4-F5
North Church Street	D1
North Edward Street	D3
North Luton Place	E3
North Road	A5-B5-B4
Northcote Lane	D5
Northcote Street	D5
Oakfield Street	F5
Ocean Way	F1-F2
Orbit Street	E4-F4
Ordell Street	F3
Oxford Lane	E4-E5
Oxford Street	E4-E5
Park Grove	C4
Park Lane	C4-D3
Park Place	B5-C5-C4-C3
Park Street	B2-C2
Partridge Road	E5-F5
Pearl Street	F4
Pearson Street	D5
Pendyris Street	B1
Pentre Gardens	B1
Planet Street	E4
Plantaganet Street	B2
Plasnewydd Road	D5-E5
Prince Leopold Street	F3
Quay Street	B3-C3
Queen Ann Square	A5-B5
Queen Street	C3
Railway Street	F3-F4
Rawden Place	A3
Richards Terrace	F5
Richmond Crescent	D4-D5
Richmond Road	D4-D5
Rose Street	E5
Royal Arcade	C2
Ruby Street	F4-F5
Russell Street	D5
Ruthin Gardens	C5
St Andrews Crescent	C4
St Andrews Lane	C4-D4
St Andrews Place	C4
St John Street	C3
St Mary Street	C2-C3
St Peter's Street	D4-D5
Salisbury Road	C5-D5-D4
Sandon Street	D3
Sanquar Street	E3-F3
Sapele Drive	F3
Sapphire Street	F5
Schooner Way	E1-E2
Senghennydd Road	B5-C5-D4
Silver Street	F4
Somerset Street	A1
Sophia Close	A4
South Luton Place	E3
Southey Street	E5
Spruce Close	F3
Stacey Road	F5
Stafford Road	A1
Star Street	F4
Station Terrace	D3-D4
Stephenson Street	A2
Stuttgarter Strasse	C4-D4
Sun Street	F4
Sussex Street	A1
System Street	E4-F4
Taffs Mead Embankment	B1
Talbot Street	A4
Talworth Street	D5
Tavistock Street	D5
Teal Street	E5
Telford Street	A2
The Friary	C3
The Hayes	C2
The Parade	D4-E4
The Walk	D4
Tin Street	F4
Topaz Street	F4
Trade Street	C1
Tresillian Way	C1-D1
Trinity Street	C3
Tudor Street	A2-B2-B1
Tyndall Street	D2-E2
Tyndall Street Industrial Estate	D2
Vere Street	E5
Wedmore Road	A1
Wesley Lane	D3
West Canal Wharf	C1
West Grove	D4
Westgate Street	B3-B2-C2
Wharton Street	C2-C3
Windsor Lane	C4-D4
Windsor Place	C4-D4
Windsor Road	E3
Womanby Street	B3
Wood Street	B2-C2
Wordsworth Avenue	E4-E5
Working Street	C3
Wyeverne Road	C5
Wyndham Street	A2
Zinc Street	F4

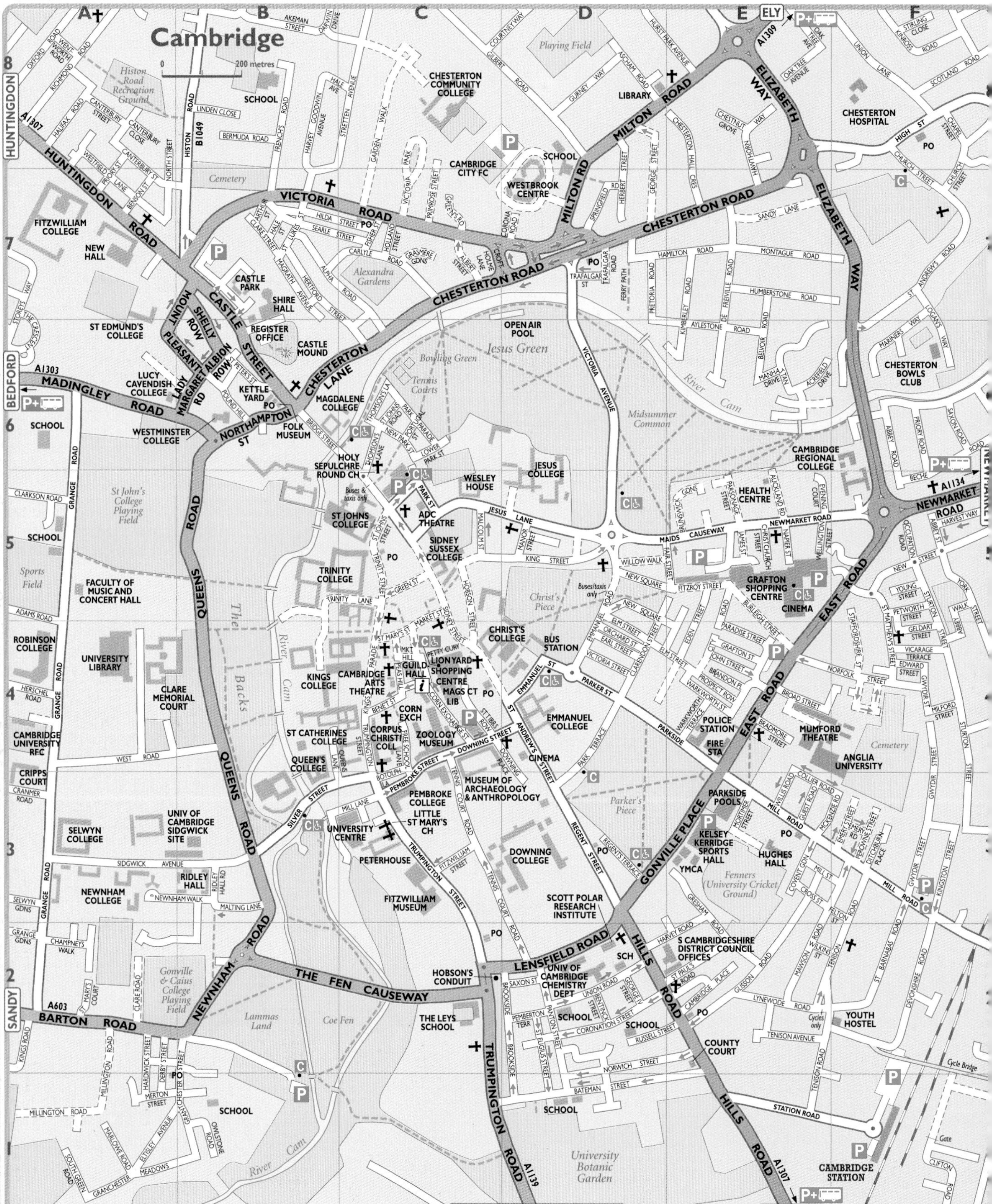

Cambridge

200 metres

Roads and places:

HUNTINGDON A1307 · HUNTINGDON ROAD · MADINGLEY ROAD A1303 · BEDFORD · QUEENS ROAD · NORTHAMPTON ST · CASTLE STREET · VICTORIA ROAD · CHESTERTON ROAD · CHESTERTON LANE · MILTON ROAD · ELIZABETH WAY · ELY A1309 · CHESTERTON ROAD · NEWMARKET ROAD A1134 · EAST ROAD · MILL ROAD · GONVILLE PLACE · LENSFIELD ROAD · HILLS ROAD A1307 · TRUMPINGTON ROAD A1309 · THE FEN CAUSEWAY · NEWNHAM ROAD · BARTON ROAD · SANDY A603 · TRUMPINGTON, LONDON (M11) · HAVERHILL

Colleges and institutions:

FITZWILLIAM COLLEGE · NEW HALL · ST EDMUND'S COLLEGE · LUCY CAVENDISH COLLEGE · WESTMINSTER COLLEGE · ROBINSON COLLEGE · FACULTY OF MUSIC AND CONCERT HALL · UNIVERSITY LIBRARY · CLARE MEMORIAL COURT · CAMBRIDGE UNIVERSITY RFC · CRIPPS COURT · SELWYN COLLEGE · UNIV OF CAMBRIDGE SIDGWICK SITE · NEWNHAM COLLEGE · RIDLEY HALL · ST JOHNS COLLEGE · TRINITY COLLEGE · KINGS COLLEGE · ST CATHERINES COLLEGE · QUEEN'S COLLEGE · CORPUS CHRISTI COLL · CAMBRIDGE ARTS THEATRE · UNIVERSITY CENTRE · PETERHOUSE · PEMBROKE COLLEGE · LITTLE ST MARY'S CH · FITZWILLIAM MUSEUM · MUSEUM OF ARCHAEOLOGY & ANTHROPOLOGY · DOWNING COLLEGE · SCOTT POLAR RESEARCH INSTITUTE · MAGDALENE COLLEGE · FOLK MUSEUM · HOLY SEPULCHRE ROUND CH · ADC THEATRE · SIDNEY SUSSEX COLLEGE · WESLEY HOUSE · JESUS COLLEGE · CHRIST'S COLLEGE · EMMANUEL COLLEGE · ZOOLOGY MUSEUM · CORN EXCH · GUILD HALL · LION YARD SHOPPING CENTRE · MAGS CT LIB · BUS STATION · POLICE STATION · FIRE STA · GRAFTON SHOPPING CENTRE · CINEMA · CAMBRIDGE REGIONAL COLLEGE · HEALTH CENTRE · NEWMARKET ROAD · CHESTERTON COMMUNITY COLLEGE · LIBRARY · CHESTERTON HOSPITAL · CAMBRIDGE CITY FC · WESTBROOK CENTRE · CHESTERTON BOWLS CLUB · MUMFORD THEATRE · ANGLIA UNIVERSITY · PARKSIDE POOLS · KELSEY KERRIDGE SPORTS HALL · YMCA · HUGHES HALL · S CAMBRIDGESHIRE DISTRICT COUNCIL OFFICES · COUNTY COURT · YOUTH HOSTEL · UNIV OF CAMBRIDGE CHEMISTRY DEPT · HOBSON'S CONDUIT · THE LEYS SCHOOL · FENNERS (University Cricket Ground) · CAMBRIDGE STATION

Open spaces:

Histon Road Recreation Ground · Cemetery · Alexandra Gardens · Castle Park · Jesus Green · Open Air Pool · Bowling Green · Tennis Courts · Midsummer Common · River Cam · St John's College Playing Field · Sports Field · The Backs · Christ's Piece · New Square · Parker's Piece · Gonville & Caius College Playing Field · Lammas Land · Coe Fen · Sheep's Green · University Botanic Garden · Cycle Bridge · Station Road

OXFORD ROAD · RICHMOND ROAD · HALIFAX ROAD · WESTFIELD ROAD · CANTERBURY STREET · CANTERBURY CLOSE · NORTH STREET · HISTON B1049 · AKEMAN STREET · LINDEN CLOSE · BERMUDA ROAD · FRENCHS ROAD · GARDEN WALK · STRETTEN AVENUE · HARVEY GOODWIN AVENUE · GILBERT ROAD · COURTNEY WAY · MOORE CLOSE · HURST PARK AVENUE · AROTHAM WAY · GURNEY WAY · HIGH ST · SCOTLAND ROAD · UNION LANE · STIRLING CLOSE · CHURCH STREET · GRANGE ROAD · CLARKSON ROAD · ADAMS ROAD · HERSCHEL ROAD · WEST ROAD · SELWYN GDNS · GRANGE GDNS · CHAMPNEYS WALK · MALTING LANE · NEWNHAM WALK · SIDGWICK AVENUE · SILVER ST · MILL LANE · TRUMPINGTON STREET · TENNIS COURT RD · REGENT STREET · PARK TERRACE · PARKSIDE · WARKWORTH ST · EMMANUEL ROAD · DRUMMER ST · JESUS LANE · KING STREET · WILLOW WALK · MAIDS CAUSEWAY · SHORT ST · MANOR ST · PARK ST · MAGDALENE ST · BRIDGE STREET · SIDNEY ST · MARKET ST · ST ANDREWS STREET · DOWNING STREET · PEMBROKE STREET · BENE'T ST · ST JOHNS ST · TRINITY ST · KINGS PARADE · NORWICH STREET · BATEMAN STREET · BROOKSIDE · SAXON ST · PEMBERTON TERR · RUSSELL STREET · CORONATION ST · CORONATION STREET · ST PAUL'S RD · GLISSON ROAD · TENISON ROAD · TENISON AVENUE · DEVONSHIRE ROAD · LYNEWODE ROAD · STATION ROAD · CLIFTON ROAD · GWYDIR ST · STURTON ST · MILL ROAD · GELDART STREET · PETWORTH ST · YORK ST · GRAFTON ST · BURLEIGH ST · FITZROY STREET · JAMES ST · NEWMARKET ROAD · ABBEY ROAD · PRIORY ROAD · BECHE ROAD · SAXON ROAD · GARLTON WAY · MARINERS WAY · LOGANS WAY · ST ANDREWS ROAD · EDWARD STREET · VICARAGE TERRACE · NORFOLK STREET · BROAD STREET · MILFORD ST · YOUNG ST · ST MATTHEWS ST · KINGSTON ST · COVENTRY ST · CROSS ST · CATHARINE ST · HARVEY ROAD · GRESHAM ROAD · ELTISLEY AVENUE

Railways and boundaries shown.

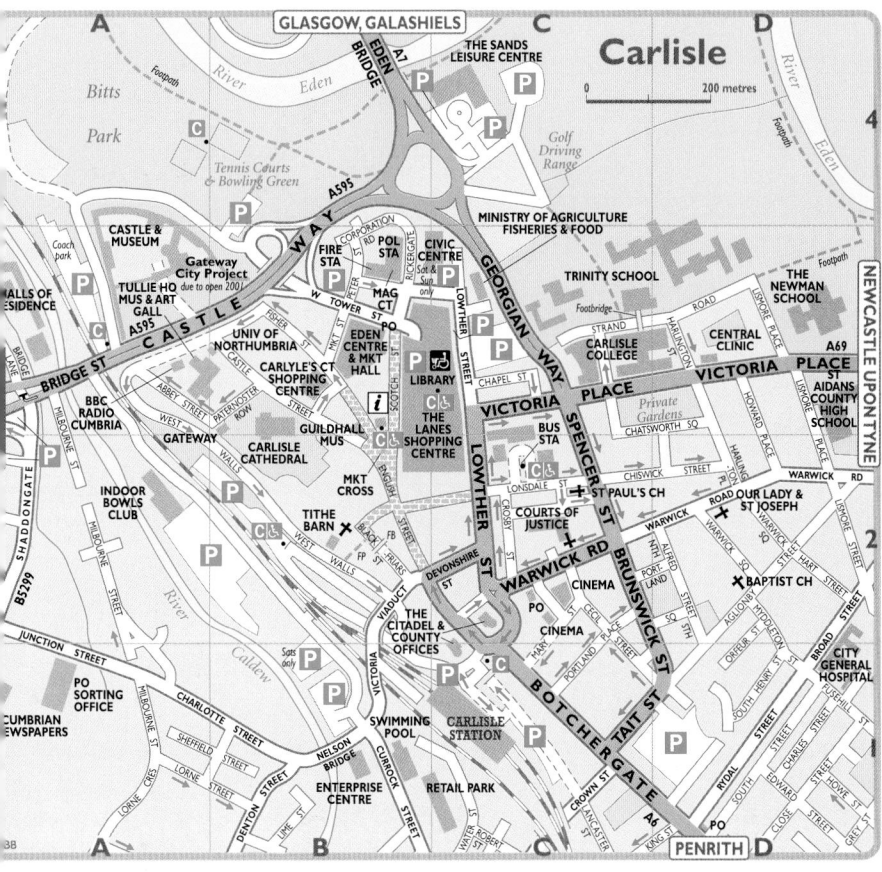

Carlisle

Carlisle is found on atlas page **93**,
grid reference **3956**

Abbey Street	A3	Lorne Street	A1-B1
Aglionby Street	D1-D2	Lowther Street	C2-C3
Alfred Street North	D2	Market Street	B3
Alfred Street South	D2	Mary Street	C1-C2
Blackfriars Street	B2	Milbourne Street	A1-A2-A3
Botchergate	C1-D1	Myddleton Street	D1-D2
Bridge Lane	A3	Nelson Bridge	B1
Bridge Street	A3	Orfeur Street	D1-D2
Broad Street	D1-D2	Paternoster Row	B3
Brunswick Street	D1-C2	Peter Street	B3
Castle Street	B2-B3	Portland Place	C1-C2
Castle Way	A3-B3-B4	Portland Square	C2-D2
Cecil Street	C1-C2	Rickergate	B3
Chapel Street	C3	Robert Street	C1
Charles Street	D1	Rydal Street	D1
Charlotte Street	A1-B1	Scotch Street	B2-B3
Chatsworth Square	C3-D3	Shaddongate	A2
Chiswick Street	C2-D2	Sheffield Street	A1-B1
Close Street	D1	South Henry Street	D1
Corporation Road	B3-B4	South Street	D1
Crosby Street	C2	Spencer Street	C2-C3
Crown Street	C1	Strand Road	C3-D3
Currock Street	B1	Tait Street	C1-D1
Denton Street	B1	Victoria Place	C3-D3
Devonshire Street	B2-C2	Victoria Viaduct	B1-B2
Eden Bridge	B4	Warwick Road	C2-D2
Edward Street	D1	Warwick Square	D2
English Street	B2	Water Street	B1-C1
Fisher Street	B3	West Tower Street	B3
Fusehill Street	D1	West Walls	A3-B2
Georgian Way	C3-C4		
Grey Street	D1		
Harlington Place	D2		
Harlington Street	D3		
Hart Street	D2		
Howard Place	D2-D3		
Howe Street	D1		
Junction Street	A1-A2		
King Street	C1-D1		
Lancaster Street	C1		
Lime Street	B1		
Lismore Place	D2-D3		
Lismore Street	D2		
Lonsdale Street	C2		
Lorne Crescent	A1		

173

Cambridge

Cambridge is found on atlas page **53**,
grid reference **4558**

...ey Road	F5-F6	Clare Road	A2	George IV Street	D2	Kingston Street	F3	Oxford Road	A8	Scotland Road	F8
...ey Street	F5	Clarendon Street	D4-D5	George Street	D7-D8	Kinross Road	F8	Panton Street	D1-D2	Searle Street	B7-C7
...ey Walk	F4-F5	Clare Street	B7	Gilbert Road	C8-D8	Lady Margaret Road	B6	Paradise Street	E4	Selwyn Gardens	A3
...efield Drive	E6	Clarkson Road	A5	Glisson Road	E2-E3	Lensfield Road	C2-D2-D3	Park Parade	C6	Shelly Row	B6-B7
...ams Road	A5	Clifton Road	F1	Gonville Place	D3-E3	Linden Close	B8	Park Street	C5-C6	Sidgwick Avenue	A3-B3
...man Street	B8-C8	Collier Road	E3-F3	Grafton Street	E4	Logan's Way	F6-F7	Park Terrace	D3-D4	Sidney Street	C4-C5
...ert Street	C7	Corn Exchange Street	C4	Grange Gardens	A2	Lower Park Street	C6	Parker Street	D4	Silver Street	B3-C3
...on Row	B6	Corona Road	D7	Grange Road	A2-A4-A6	Lynewode Road	E2	Parkside	D4-E4	South Green Road	A1
...ha Road	B7-C7-C6	Coronation Street	D2	Granchester Meadows	A1-B1	Madingley Road	A6-B6	Parsonage Street	E5	Springfield Road	D7
...hur Street	B7	Courtney Way	C8-D8	Granchester Street	B1-B2	Magrath Avenue	B7	Peas Hill	C4	Staffordshire Street	F4-F5
...ham Road	D8	Covent Garden	E3	Grasmere Gardens	C7	Maids Causeway	D5-E5	Pemberton Terrace	D2	Station Road	E1-F1
...ton Road	E5	Cranmer Road	A3	Green Street	C5	Malcolm Street	C5	Pembroke Street	C3-C4	Stirling Close	F8
...estone Road	D7-E6	Croftholme Lane	C7-D7	Green's Road	C7	Malting Lane	B3	Perowne Street	F3	Storeys Way	A6-A7
...ton Road	A2-B2	Cross Street	E3	Gresham Road	E2-E3	Manhattan Drive	E6	Petty Cury	C4	Stretten Avenue	C8
...eman Street	C1-D1-E1-E2	Darwin Drive	B8	Guest Road	E3	Manor Street	D5	Petworth Street	F5	Sturton Street	F3-F4-F5
...he Road	F5-F6	De Freiville Road	E6-E7	Gurney Way	D8	Mariners Way	F6-F7	Portugal Street	C6	Tenison Avenue	E2
...voir Road	E6-E7	Derby Street	A1-A2	Gwydir Street	F3-F4	Market Hill	C4	Pound Hill	B6	Tenison Road	E1-E2-F2-F3
...e't Street	C4	Devonshire Road	F2-F3	Hale Avenue	B8-C8	Market Street	C4-C5	Pretoria Road	D7	Tennis Court Road	C4-C3-D3-D2
...son Road	A7	Ditchburn Place	E3	Hale Street	B7	Marlowe Road	A1	Primrose Street	C7-C8	The Fen Causeway	B2-C2
...tinck Street	D2	Downing Place	C4-D4-D3	Halifax Road	A8	Mawson Road	E2-E3	Priory Road	F6	Thomson's Lane	C6
...muda Road	B8	Downing Street	C4-D4	Hamilton Road	D7-E7	McKenzie Road	E3-F3	Priory Street	A7-A8	The Crescent	A6-A7
...olph Lane	C3	Earl Street	D4	Hardwick Street	A1-A2	Merton Street	A1	Prospect Row	E4	Trafalgar Road	D7
...dmore Street	E4	East Road	E4-E5-F5	Harvest Way	F5	Milford Street	F4	Queens Lane	B3-B4	Trafalgar Street	D7
...ndon Place	E4	Eden Street	E4-E5	Harvey Goodwin Avenue	B8	Mill Lane	B3-C3	Queens Road	B3-B4-B5-B6	Trinity Lane	B5-C5
...lge Street	B6-C6-C5	Edward Street	F4	Harvey Road	D2-E2-E3	Mill Road	E3-F3	Regent Street	D3	Trinity Street	C5
...ad Street	E4	Elizabeth Way	E8-E7-F7	Hawthorn Way	E7-E8	Mill Street	E3-F3	Regents Terrace	D3	Trumpington Road	C2-C1-D1
...okside	C2-D2-D1	Elm Street	D5-D4-E4	Herbert Street	D7-D8	Millington Road	A1-A2	Richmond Road	A8	Trumpington Street	C2-C3-C4
...nswick Gardens	E5	Eltisley Avenue	A1	Herschel Road	A4	Milton Road	D7-D8-E8	Ridley Hall Road	B3	Union Lane	F8
...leigh Street	E4-E5	Emery Road	F3	Hertford Street	B7-C6	Montague Road	E7-F7	Russell Street	D2-E2	Union Road	D2
...nbridge Place	E2	Emery Street	F3	High Street	E8-F8	Mount Pleasant	B7-A6-B6	St Andrew's Road	F6-F7	Vicarage Terrace	E4
...terbury Close	A8	Emmanuel Road	D4-D5	Hilda Street	B7-C7	Napier Street	E5	St Andrew's Street	C4-D4-D3	Victoria Avenue	D5-D6-D7
...terbury Street	A7-A8	Emmanuel Street	D4	Hills Road	D3-D2-E2-E1	New Park Street	C6	St Barnabas Road	F2-F3	Victoria Park	C7-C8
...yle Road	B7-C7	Evening Court	E5	Histon Road	B7-B8	New Square	D5	St Eligius Street	D1-D2	Victoria Road	B7-C7-D7
...tle Street	B6-B7	Fair Street	D5-E5	Hobson Street	C4-C5	New Street	F5	St Johns Road	C6	Victoria Street	E4
...mpneys Walk	A2	Felton Street	F3	Holland Street	C7	Newmarket Road	E5-F5	St Johns Street	C5	Warkworth Street	E4
...pel Street	F8	Ferry Path	D7	Humberstone Road	E7-F7	Newnham Road	B2-B3	St Lukes Street	B7	Warkworth Terrace	E4
...esterton Hall Crescent	E7-E8	Fisher Street	C7	Huntingdon Road	A8-A7-B7	Newnham Walk	A3-B3	St Mary's Court	A2	Wellington Street	E5
...esterton Lane	B6-C6	Fitzroy Street	E5	Hurst Park Avenue	D8-E8	Norfolk Street	E4-F4	St Mary's Street	C4	Wentworth Road	A8
...esterton Road	C6-C7-D7-E7	Fitzwilliam Street	C3	James Street	E4	North Street	A7-A8	St Matthew's Street	F4-F5	West Road	A4-B4
...estnut Grove	E8	Free School Lane	C3-C4	Jesus Lane	C5-D5	Northampton Street	B6	St Paul's Road	E2	Westfield Lane	A7-A8
...ristchurch Street	E5	French's Road	B7-B8	John Street	E4	Norwich Street	D1-D2-E2	St Peter's Street	B6	Wilkins Street	E2
...urch Street	F7-F8	Garden Walk	C7-C8	Kimberley Road	E6-E7	Oak Tree Avenue	E8	St Tibbs Row	C4	Willis Road	E3
...e Road	E4-E5	Geldart Street	F4	King Street	C5-D5	Occupation Road	F5	Sandy Lane	E7	Willow Walk	D5
				Kings Parade	C4	Orchard Street	D4	Saxon Road	F6	York Street	F4-F5
				Kings Road	A2	Owlstone Road	B1	Saxon Street	D2	Young Street	F5

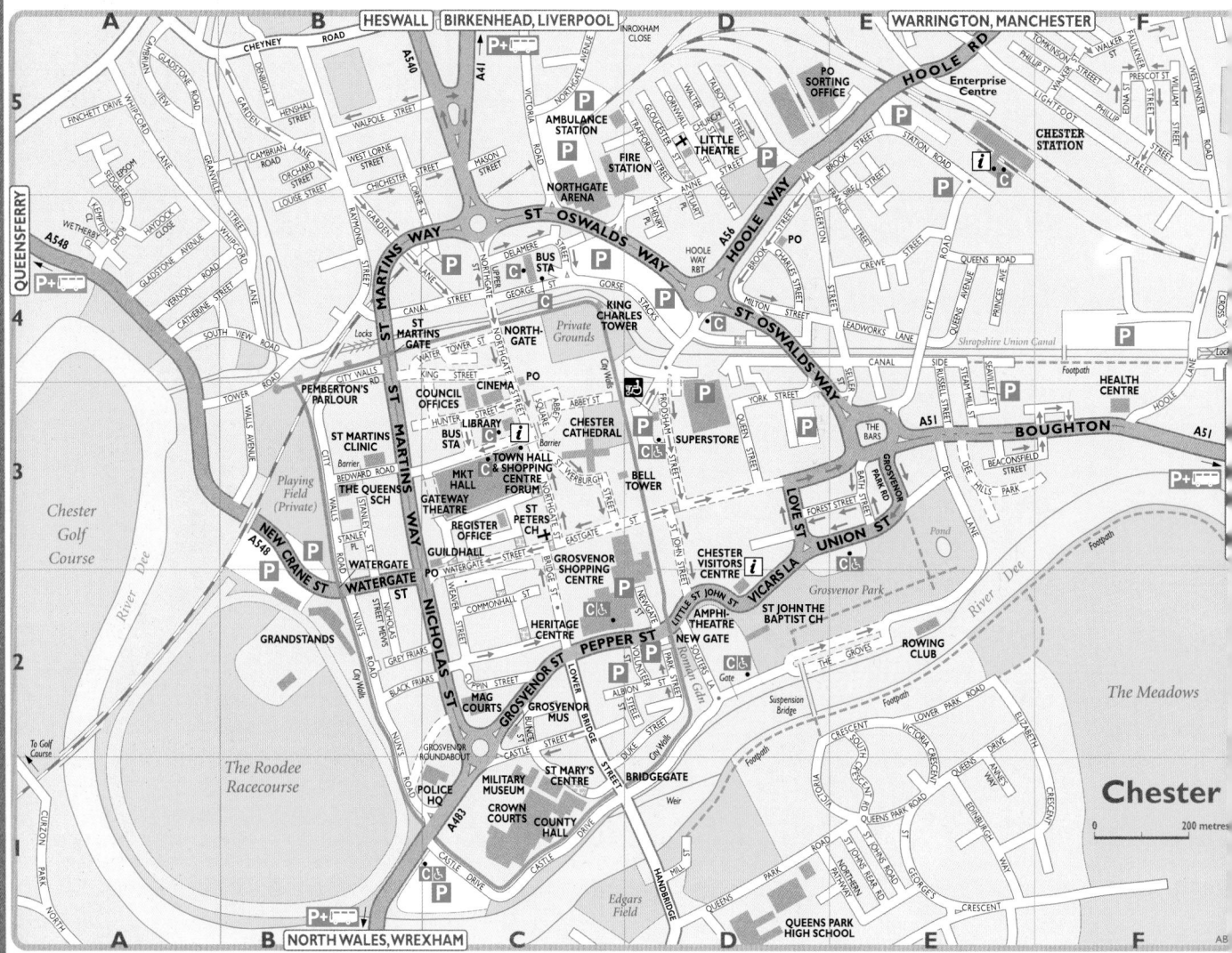

Chester

Chester is found on atlas page **71**,
grid reference **4066**

Abbey Square	C3	Dee Hills Park	E3-F3	Hoole Lane	F3-F4	Prescot Street	F5	Talbot Street	D5
Abbey Street	C3	Dee Lane	E2-E3	Hoole Road	E5	Princes Avenue	E4	The Groves	D2-E2
Albion Street	C2-D2	Delamere Street	C4	Hoole Way	D4-D5	Queen Street	D3	Tomkinson Street	E5-F5
Anne's Way	E1-E2	Denbigh Street	B5	Hunter Street	B3-C3	Queens Avenue	E4	Tower Road	A3-B3-B4
Bath Street	E3	Duke Street	C1-D2	Kempton Close	A4	Queens Drive	E1-E2	Trafford Street	C5-D5
Beaconsfield Street	E3-F3	Eastgate Street	C3-D3	King Street	B4-C4	Queens Park Road	D1-E1	Union Street	D3-E3
Bedward Road	B3	Edinburgh Way	E1	Leadworks Lane	E4	Queens Road	E4	Upper Northgate Street	C4
Black Friars	B2-C2	Edna Street	F5	Lightfoot Street	E5-F5-F4	Raymond Street	B4	Vernon Road	A4-B4
Boughton	E3-F3	Egerton Street	D4-E4	Little St John Street	D2	Russell Street	E3-E4	Vicars Lane	D2-D3
Bridge Street	C2-C3	Elizabeth Crescent	E2-F2-F1	Lorne Street	B5-B4-C4	St Anne Street	D4-D5	Victoria Crescent	D1-D2-E2-E1
Brook Street	D4-D5-E5	Epsom Court	A5	Louise Street	B4-B5	St George's Crescent	E1	Victoria Road	C4-C5
Bunce Street	C2	Faulkner Street	F5	Love Street	D3	St John Street	D2-D3	Volunteer Street	D2
Cambrian Road	B5	Finchett Drive	A5	Lower Bridge Street	C1-C2	St Johns Rear Road	E1	Walker Street	F5
Cambrian View	A5	Forest Street	D3-E3	Lower Park Road	E2	St Johns Road	E1	Walls Avenue	B3
Canal Side	D4-E4	Francis Street	D5-E5-E4	Lyon Street	D4-D5	St Martins Way	B3-B4-C4	Walpole Street	B5-C5
Canal Street	B4-C4	Frodsham Street	D3-D4	Mason Street	C5	St Oswalds Way	C4-D4-D3-E3	Walter Street	D5
Castle Drive	C1	Garden Lane	A5-B5-B4-C4	Mill Street	D1	St Werburgh Street	C3	Water Tower Street	B4-C4
Castle Street	C1-C2	George Street	C4	Milton Street	D4	Seaville Street	E3-E4	Watergate Street	B2-C2-C3
Catherine Street	A4-B4	Gladstone Avenue	A4	New Crane Street	B2-B3	Sedgefield Road	A4-A5	Weaver Street	C2
Charles Street	D4	Gladstone Road	A5	Newgate Street	D2	Seller Street	E3-E4	West Lorne Street	B5
Cheyney Road	A5-B5	Gloucester Street	D5	Nicholas Street	B2-C2	Sibell Street	E4-E5	Westminster Road	F4-F5
Chichester Street	B5-C5	Gorse Stacks	C4-D4	Nicholas Street Mews	B2	Souters Lane	D2	Wetherby Close	A4
Church Street	D5	Granville Street	A5-B4	Northern Pathway	D1-E1	South Crescent Road	E1-E2	Whipcord Lane	A5-A4-B4
City Road	E3-E4-E5	Grey Friars	B2-C2	Northgate Avenue	C5	South View Road	A4-B4	William Street	F5
City Walls Road	B2-B3-B4	Grosvenor Park Road	E3	Northgate Street	C3-C4	Stanley Place	B3	York Street	D3
Commonhall Street	C2	Grosvenor Street	C2	Nun's Road	B2-B1-C1	Stanley Street	B2-B3		
Cornwall Street	D5	Handbridge	D1	Orchard Street	B5	Station Road	E4-E5		
Crewe Street	E4	Haydock Close	A4	Park Street	D2	Steam Mill Street	E3-E4		
Cross Street	F4	Henry Place	D4	Pepper Street	C2-D2	Steele Street	D2		
Cuppin Street	C2	Henshall Street	B5	Phillip Street	E5-F5	Stuart Place	D4-D5		

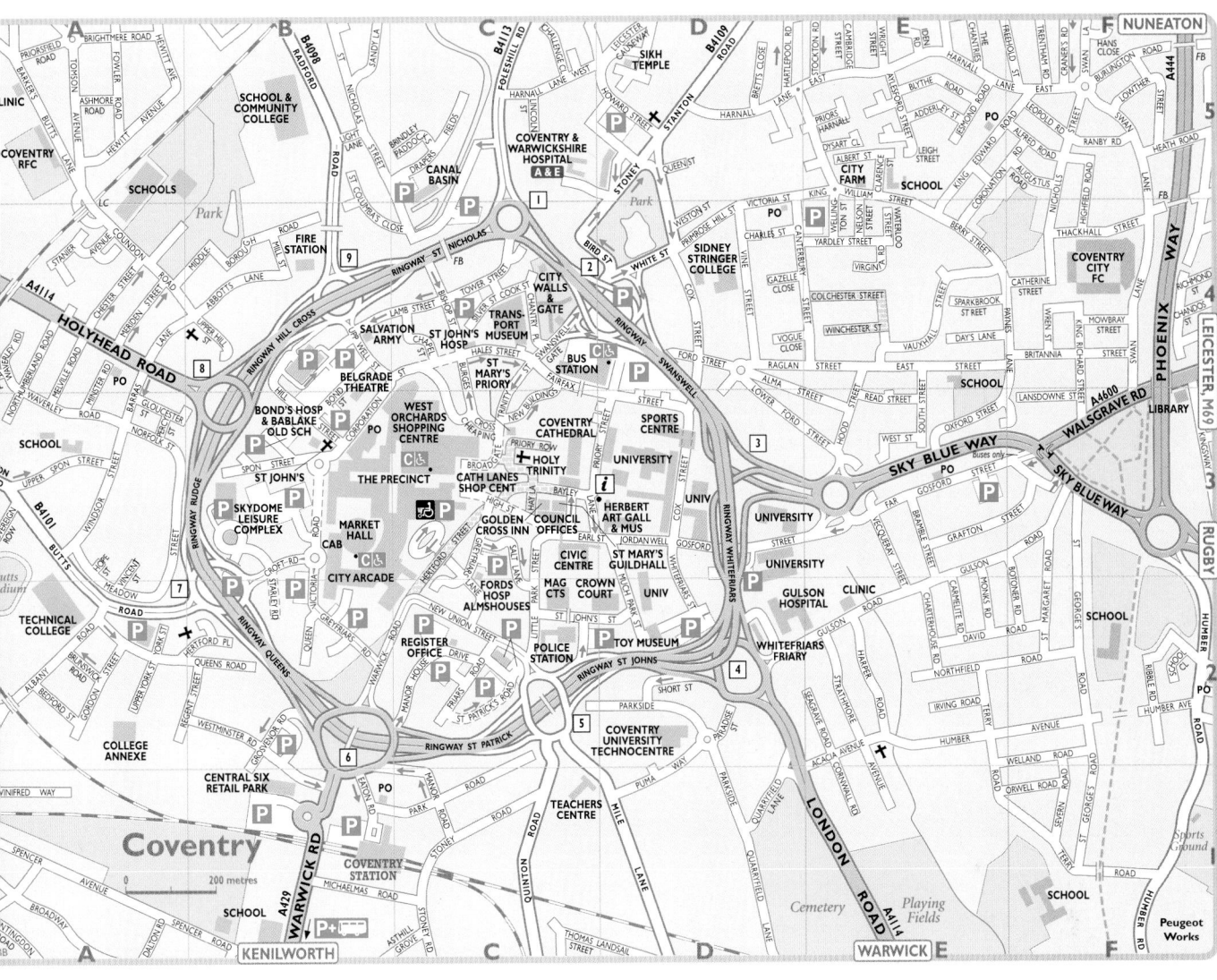

Coventry

Coventry is found on atlas page **61**,
and reference **3378**

botts Lane	B4	Challenge Close	C5	Gordon Street	A2	Lincoln Street	C5	Queens Road	A2-B2	Stoney Stanton Road	C4-D4-D5
cia Avenue	E2	Chandos Street	F4	Gosford Street	D3-E3	Little Park Street	C2-C3	Quinton Road	C1-C2	Strathmore Avenue	E1-E2
derley Street	E5	Chantry Place	C4	Grafton Street	E3-F3	London Road	D2-D1-E1	Radford Road	B4-B5	Swan Lane	F4-F5
any Road	A2	Chapel Street	C4	Greyfriars Lane	C2-C3	Lower Ford Street	D4-D3-E3	Raglan Street	D4-E4	Swanswell Gate	C4
ert Street	E5	Charles Street	D4	Greyfriars Road	B2	Lowther Street	F5	Ranby Road	F5	Terry Road	E2-E1-F1
ed Road	F5	Charterhouse Road	E2	Grosvenor Road	B1-B2	Manor House Drive	C2	Read Street	E3	Thackhall Street	F4
na Street	D4-E3	Chester Street	A4	Gulson Road	D2-E2-E3-F3	Manor Road	B2-C1	Regent Street	A2-B2	The Chantries	E5
more Road	A5	Clarence Street	E5	Hales Street	C4	Meadow Street	A2-A3	Ribble Road	F2	Thomas Landsail Street	C1-D1
hill Grove	B1-C1	Colchester Street	E4	Hans Close	F5	Melville Road	A3-A4	Richmond Street	F4	Tomson Avenue	A5
gustus Road	F5	Cook Street	C4	Harnall Lane East	D5-E5-F5	Meriden Street	A4	Ringway Hill Cross	B4	Tower Street	C4
esford Street	E5	Cornwall Road	E1-E2	Harnall Lane West	C5	Michaelmas Road	B1-C1	Ringway Queens	B2	Trentham Road	F5
ras Lane	A3-A4-B4	Coronation Road	E4-E5-F5	Harper Road	E2	Middleborough Road	A4-B4	Ringway Rudge	B3	Trinity Street	C3-C4
ley Lane	C3	Corporation Street	B3-B4-C4	Hartlepool Road	D5	Mile Lane	C2-C1-D1	Ringway St Johns	C2-D2	Upper Hill Street	B4
fford Street	A2	Coundon Road	A4	Hay Lane	C3	Mill Street	B4	Ringway St Nicholas	B4-C4	Upper Spon Street	A3
ry Street	E4	Cox Street	D3-D4	Heath Road	F5	Minster Road	A3-A4	Ringway St Patrick	C2	Upper Well Street	B4
	C4-D4	Craner's Road	F5	Hertford Place	A2-B2	Monks Road	E2-E3	Ringway Swanswell	C4-D4-D3	Upper York Street	A2
nop Street	C4	Croft Road	B2-B3	Hertford Street	C2-C3	Mowbray Street	F4	Ringway Whitefriars	D2-D3	Vauxhall Street	E4
the Road	E5	Cross Cheaping	C3	Hewitt Avenue	A5	Much Park Street	D2-D3	St Columba's Close	B5-B4-C4	Vecquaray Street	E2-E3
d Street	B3-B4	Cumbria Close	A3-A4	High Street	C3	Nelson Street	E4	St George's Road	F1-F2-F3	Victoria Street	D4-D5
toner Road	F2-F3	Dalton Road	A1	Highfield Road	F4-F5	New Buildings	C3-C4	St John's Street	C2-D2	Vincent Street	A2-A3
mble Street	E3	David Road	E2-F2	Hill Street	B3-B4	New Union Street	C2	St Margaret Road	F2-F3	Vine Street	D4
tts Close	D5	Day's Lane	E4	Holyhead Road	A4-B4	Nicholls Street	F4-F5	St Nicholas Street	B5-C5-C4	Virginia Road	E4
ghtmere Road	A5	Drapers Fields	C5	Hood Street	E3-E4	Norfolk Street	A3	St Patrick's Road	C2	Vogue Close	D4
ndley Paddocks	C5	Dysart Close	E5	Hope Street	A3	Northfield Road	E2-F2	Salt Lane	C2-C3	Walsgrave Road	F3
annia Street	F4	Earl Street	C3-D3	Howard Street	D5	Northumberland Road	A3-A4	Sandy Lane	B5	Warwick Road	B1-B2-C2
adgate	C3	East Street	E4	Humber Avenue	E2-F2	Orwell Road	E1-F1	School Close	F2	Waterloo Street	E4
adway	A1	Eaton Road	B1	Humber Road	F1-F2-F3	Oxford Street	E3	Seagrave Road	E2	Waverley Road	A3-A4
nswick Road	A2	Fairfax Street	C4-D3	Huntingdon Road	A1	Paradise Street	D2	Severn Road	F1-F2	Welland Road	E2-F2
ges	C3-C4	Far Gosford Street	E3	Iden Road	E5	Park Road	B1-C1-C2	Short Street	D2	Wellington Street	E4-E5
lington Road	F5	Foleshill Road	C5	Irving Road	E2	Parkside	C2-D2-D1	Silver Street	C4	West Street	E3
rts Road	A3-A2-B2	Ford Street	D4	Jesmond Road	E5	Paynes Lane	E4-F4	Sky Blue Way	E3-F3	Westminster Road	B2
mbridge Street	E5	Fowler Road	A5	Jordan Well	D3	Percy Street	A3	South Street	E3-E4	Weston Street	D4
nterbury Street	D4-E4	Freehold Street	E5-F5	King Edward Road	E4-E5-F5	Phoenix Way	F3-F4-F5	Sovereign Row	A3	White Street	D4
rmelite Road	E2	Friars Road	C2	King Richard Street	F3-F4	Primrose Hill Street	D4	Sparkbrook Street	E4	Whitefriars Street	D2-D3
therine Street	F4	Gazelle Close	D4	King William Street	E4-E5	Priors Harnall	E5	Spencer Avenue	A1	Winchester Street	E4
		Gloucester Street	A3	Kingsway	F3	Priorsfield Road	A5	Spencer Road	A1-B1	Windsor Street	A3
				Lamb Street	B4-C4	Priory Row	C3	Spon End	A3	Winifred Way	A1
				Lansdowne Street	F3	Priory Street	C3-D3	Spon Street	B3	Wren Street	E5
				Leicester Causeway	D5	Puma Way	D1-D2	Stanier Avenue	A4	Wright Street	E5
				Leigh Street	E5	Quarryfield Lane	D1-D2	Starley Road	B2-B3	Yardley Street	E4
				Leopold Road	F5	Queen Street	D5	Stockton Road	E5	York Street	A2
				Light Lane	B5	Queen Victoria Road	B2-B3	Stoney Road	C1		

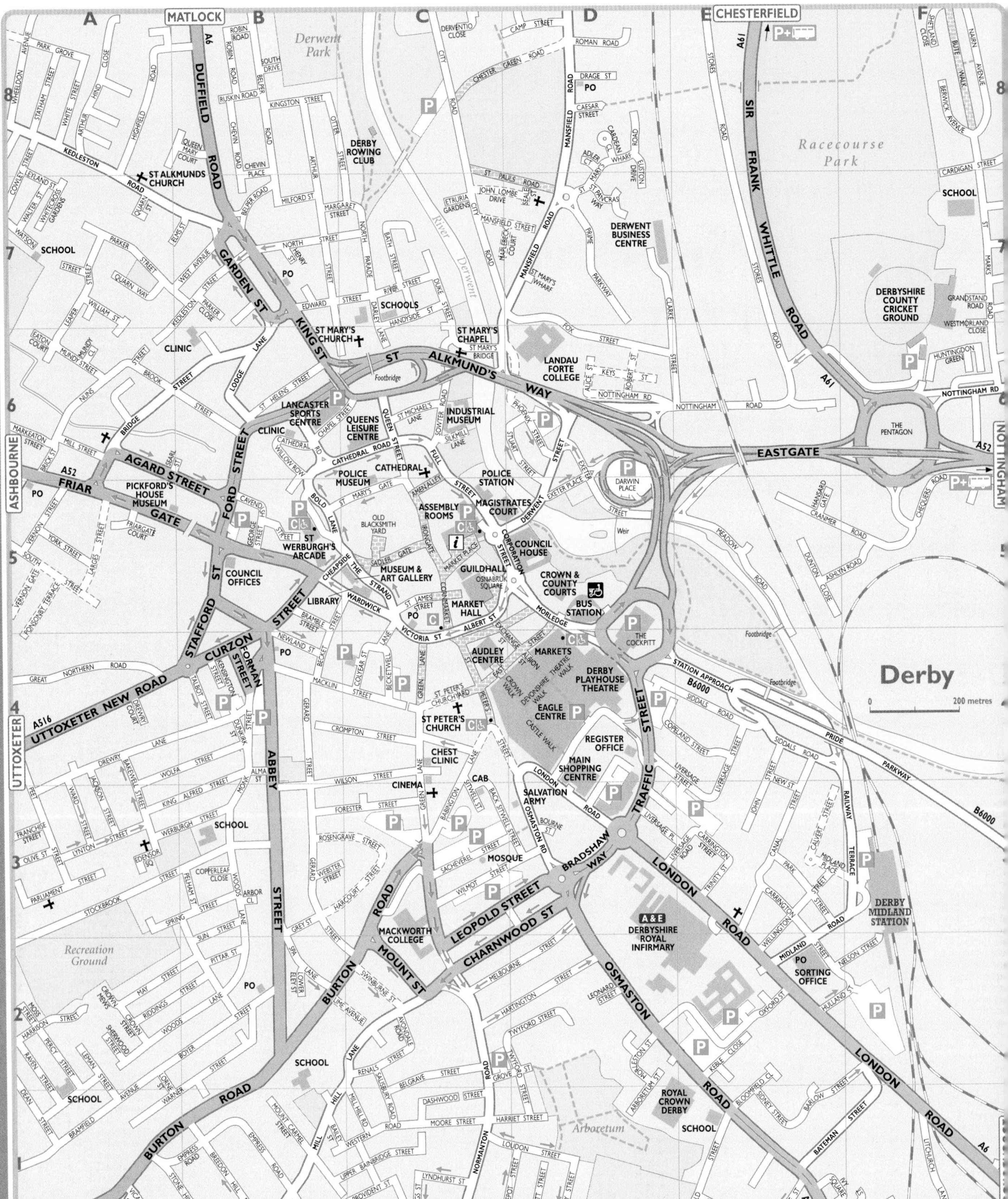

MATLOCK · CHESTERFIELD · BURTON · MELBOURNE · NOTTINGHAM · ASHBOURNE · UTTOXETER

Derby

0 · 200 metres

Derwent Park · Racecourse Park · Recreation Ground · Arboretum

River Derwent

St Alkmunds Church · St Mary's Church · St Mary's Chapel · Derby Rowing Club · Landau Forte College · Derwent Business Centre · Derbyshire County Cricket Ground · The Pentagon

Lancaster Sports Centre · Queens Leisure Centre · Industrial Museum · Police Museum · Cathedral · Police Station · Magistrates Court · Council House · Darwin Place · Weir

Pickford's House Museum · Council Offices · Library · Museum & Art Gallery · St Werburgh's Arcade · Old Blacksmith Yard · Assembly Rooms · Guildhall · Market Hall · Crown & County Courts · Bus Station · The Cockpitt

Audley Centre · Markets · Derby Playhouse Theatre · Eagle Centre · Register Office · Main Shopping Centre · St Peter's Church · Chest Clinic · Cinema · CAB · Mosque · Salvation Army

Mackworth College · Charnwood St · Leopold Street · Derbyshire Royal Infirmary (A&E) · Royal Crown Derby · Derby Midland Station · Sorting Office

Duffield Road · Garden St · King St · Ford Street · Stafford St · Curzon Street · Forman Street · Uttoxeter New Road · Abbey Street · Mount St · Burton Road · Friar Gate · Agard Street · St Alkmund's Way · Eastgate · Sir Frank Whittle Road · Traffic Street · London Road · Osmaston Road · Bradshaw Way · Pride Parkway

ABB

Cheltenham

Cheltenham is found on atlas page **35**,
grid reference **942**2

Albion Street	B3-C3	King Street	A4	Royal Well Place	A3
Ambrose Street	A4	Knapp Lane	A4	Royal Well Road	A3-B3
Bath Parade	B2-C2-C1	Knapp Road	A4	St Anne's Road	C2-C3
Bath Road	B1-B2-C2	London Road	C1-C2	St George's Place	A3-B3-B4
Bath Street	B2-C2	Milsom Street	A4	St George's Road	A3
Bayshill Lane	A2	Monson Avenue	B4	St George's Street	A4-B4
Bayshill Road	A2-A3	Montpellier Drive	B1	St James Square	A3
Bennington Street	B3-B4	Montpellier Parade	A1-B1	St James Street	C2
Berkeley Street	C2	Montpellier Spa Road	A1-A2	St John's Avenue	C3
Burton Street	A4	Montpellier Street	A1-A2	St Luke's Place	B1-B2-C2
Cambray Place	B2-B3-C3	Montpellier Terrace	A1-B1	St Luke's Road	B1
Cedar Court Road	B1	Montpellier Walk	A1-A2	St Margaret's Road	B4-C4
Clarence Road	C4	New Street	A4	St Paul's Street South	A4
Clarence Street	A4-A3-B3	North Place	B3-B4-C4	Sandford Road	A1-B1
College Road	B1-C1-C2	Northfield Terrace	B4-C4	Sandford Street	B2
Devonshire Street	A4	Oriel Road	B2	Sherbourne Place	C3
Fauconberg Road	A2	Orrisdale Terrace	C1	Sherbourne Street	C3-C4
Gloucester Place	C3	Park Street	A4	Station Street	A4
Grosvenor Street	C2-C3	Pittville Lawn	C4	Suffolk Parade	A1
Grove Street	A4	Pittville Street	B3	Suffolk Square	A1
Henrietta Street	B4	Portland Square	C4	The Broadwalk	A2-B2-B1
Hewlett Road	C2	Portland Street	C4	Trafalgar Street	A1-B1-B2
High Street	A4-B4-B3-C2	Prestbury Road	C4	Union Street	C3
Imperial Lane	B2	Promenade	A2-B3	Vittoria Walk	B1-B2
Imperial Square	A2-B2	Regent Street	B2-B3	Wellington Street	B2
Jersey Street	C3-C4	Rodney Road	B2-B3	Winchcomb Street	B3-C3-C4
Jessop Avenue	A3	Royal Crescent	A3-B3	York Street	C4
Keynsham Road	C1	Royal Well Lane	A3		

Derby

Derby is found on atlas page **62**,
grid reference **353**6

Abbey Street	B2-B3-B4	Canal Street	E3-E4	Duke Street	C7	Kedleston Road	A8-A7-B7	Nottingham Road	D6-E6-F6	Siddals Road	D4-E4
Abbott Court	D8	Cardean Close	D8	Dunkirk Street	B4	Kedleston Street	A6-B7	Nuns Street	A6	Sidney Street	E1
Agard Street	A6-B5	Cardigan Street	F7-F8	Dunton Close	E5	Kensington Street	B4	Old Blacksmith Yard	C5	Silkmill Lane	C6
Albert Street	C5	Carrington Street	D3-E3	East Street	C4-D4-D5	Keys Street	D6	Olive Street	A3	Sir Frank Whittle Road	E8-E7-E6-F6
Albion Street	D4	Castle Walk	D4	Eastgate	A6	King Alfred Street	A3-B3-B4	Osmaston Road	D3-D2-E1	Sitwell Street	C3
Alice Street	D6	Cathedral Road	B6-C6	Eaton Court	A6	King Street	B6-B7	Osnabrük Square	C5	Society Place	C1
Alma Street	B4	Cavendish Street	B5	Edensor Square	A3	Kingston Street	B8	Otter Street	B8-C7	South Drive	B8
Amen Alley	C5	Chapel Street	B6-C6	Edward Street	B7-C7	Larges Street	A5	Oxford Street	E2	South Street	A5
Arbor Close	B3	Charnwood Street	C2-D3	Elms Street	A7-B7	Leaper Street	A6-A7	Park Grove	A8	Sowter Road	C6
Arboretum Street	D1-D2	Cheapside	B5	Empress Road	A1-B1	Leman Street	A1-A2	Park Street	E3	Spa Lane	B2-B3
Ashlyn Road	A8	Chequers Road	F5-F6	Etruria Gardens	C7	Leonard Street	D2	Parker Close	B7	Spring Street	A3-B3
Arthur Hind Close	A8	Chester Green Road	C8-D8	Euston Drive	D7-D8	Leopold Street	C2-C3-D3	Parker Street	A7-B7	Stafford Street	B4-B5
Arthur Street	B6-B7-B8	Chestnut Avenue	C1	Exchange Street	C5-D4	Leyland Street	A7-A8	Parliament Street	A3	Statham Street	A8
Ashlyn Road	E5-F5	Chevin Place	B8	Exeter Place	D5	Lime Avenue	B2-C2	Peet Street	A3-A4	Station Approach	D4-E4
Avondale Road	C2	Chevin Road	B7-B8	Exeter Street	D5-D6	Litchurch Lane	F1	Pelham Street	B3	Stockbrook Street	A2-A3-B3
Babington Lane	C3-C4	City Road	C7-C8	Ford Street	B5-B6	Liversage Place	D3	Percy Street	A2	Stone Hill Road	A1-B1
Back Sitwell Street	C3-D3	Clarke Street	D6-D7	Forester Street	B3-C3	Liversage Road	D3-E3	Phoenix Street	D6	Stores Road	E6-E7-E8
Bailey Street	B1	Colyear Street	C4	Forman Street	B4	Liversage Street	D4-E3-E4	Pittar Street	B2	Strutt Street	D1
Bakewell Street	A3-A4	Copeland Street	D4-E4	Fox Street	D6-D7	Lodge Lane	B6	Ponsonby Terrace	A5	Stuart Street	D6
Barlow Street	E1-F2	Copperleaf Close	B3	Franchise Street	A3	London Road	D4-D3-E2-F1	Pride Parkway	E4-F4-F3	Sun Street	B2-B3
Bateman Street	E1-F1-F2	Cornmarket	C5	Friar Gate	A6-A5-B5	Lorne Street	A2	Prime Parkway	D7	Swinburne Street	C2
Beech Street	C7	Corporation Street	C5	Friargate Court	A5	Loudon Street	C1-D1	Provident Street	C1	Talbot Street	B4
Becket Street	B4-B5	Cowley Street	A7-A8	Full Street	C5-C6	Lower Eley Street	B2	Quarn Street	A7	The Cockpitt	D4-D5
Becketwell Lane	C4-C5	Cranmer Road	E5-F5	Garden Street	B7	Lyndhurst Street	C1	Quarn Way	A7	The Pentagon	F6
Belgrave Street	C2	Crompton Street	B4-C4	George Street	B5	Lynton Street	A3	Queen Mary Court	A8-B8	The Strand	C5
Belper Road	B7-B8	Crown Mews	A2	Gerard Street	B4-B3-B2-C2	Macklin Street	B4-C4	Queen Street	C6	Theatre Walk	D4
Berwick Avenue	F8	Crown Street	A2	Grandstand Road	F7	Madeley Street	D1	Railway Terrace	E4-F3	Traffic Street	D3-D4
Bloomfield Close	E1-E2	Crown Walk	C4-D4	Grange Street	E1	Mansfield Road	D7-D8	Raven Street	A1-A2	Trinity Street	E3
Boden Street	E1	Cummings Street	C1	Grayling Street	E1	Mansfield Street	C7-D7	Reginald Street	E1	Twyford Street	D1-C2-D2
Bold Lane	B5	Curzon Street	B4-B5	Great Northern Road	A4	Maplebeck Court	C7	Renals Street	C2	Upper Bainbridge Street	B1-C1
Bourne Street	D3	Darley Lane	C6-C7	Green Lane	C3-C4	Margaret Street	B7-C7	Riddings Street	A2-B2	Uttoxeter New Road	A4
Bradshaw Way	D3	Darwin Place	D5-D6	Grey Street	B3	Markeaton Street	A6	River Street	C7	Vernon Gate	A5
Bramble Street	B5	Dashwood Street	C1	Grove Street	C2-D2	Market Place	C5	Robert Street	D6	Vernon Street	A5
Bramfield Avenue	A1-A2	Dean Street	A1-A2	Handyside Street	C7	May Street	A2-B2	Robin Road	B8	Vicarage Avenue	A1-B1
Breedon Hill Road	B1	Depot Street	C1-D1	Hansard Gate	E5	Meadow Road	E5	Roman Road	D8	Victoria Street	C4-C5
Brick Street	A6	Derventio Close	C8	Harcourt Street	B3-C3	Melbourne Street	C2-D2-D3	Rose Hill Street	C1-D1	Walter Street	A7
Bridge Street	A5-A6-B6	Derwent Street	C5-D5-D6	Harriet Street	C1-D1	Midland Place	E3	Rosengrave Street	B3-C3	Ward Street	A3
Brook Street	A6-B6	Devonshire Walk	D4	Harrison Street	A2	Midland Road	E2-E3-F3	Ruskin Road	B8	Wardwick	B5-C5
Burton Road	A1-B1-B2-C3	Dexter Street	E1-F1	Hartington Street	C2-D2	Milford Street	B7	St Alkmund's Way	B6-C6-D6	Warner Street	A1-B2
Bute Walk	F8	Drage Street	D8	Henry Street	B7	Mill Hill Lane	B1-C2	St Helens Street	B6	Watson Street	A7
Caesar Street	D8	Drewry Court	A4	Highfield Road	A8-B8	Mill Hill Road	C1	St James Street	C5	Webster Street	B3
Calvert Street	E3	Drewry Lane	A3-A4-B4	Howard Street	B1	Mill Street	A6	St Marks Road	F6-F7	Wellington Street	E2-E3
Camp Street	D8	Duffield Road	B7-B8	Hulland Street	E2	Monk Street	B3-B4	St Mary's Bridge	C6	Werburgh Street	A3-B3
				Huntingdon Green	F6	Moore Street	C1	St Mary's Gate	B5-C5	West Avenue	A7-B7
				Irongate	C5	Morledge	D4-D5	St Mary's Wharf	D7	Western Road	B1-C1
				Ivy Square	E1	Morleston Street	D2	St Mary's Wharf Road	D7-D8	Westmorland Close	F6
				Jackson Street	A3-A4	Moss Street	A2	St Michael's Lane	C6	Wheeldon Avenue	A8
				John Lombe Drive	C7-D7	Mount Carmel Street	B1	St Pancras Way	D7	Whitaker Road	A1
				John Street	E3-E4	Mount Street	C2	St Pauls Road	C8-D7	White Street	A8
				Keble Close	E2	Mundy Close	A6	St Peter's Churchyard	C4	Whitecross Gardens	A7
						Mundy Street	A6	St Peter's Street	C4-D4	William Street	A7
						Nairn Avenue	F8	Sacheverel Street	C3	Willow Row	B6
						Nelson Street	E2-F2	Sadler Gate	C5	Wilmot Street	C3-D3
						New Street	E3-E4	Salisbury Road	C1-C2	Wilson Street	B3-C4
						Newland Street	B4	Seale Street	D7	Wolfa Street	A4-B4
						Normanton Road	C1-C2	Searl Street	A6	Woods Lane	A2-B2-B3
						North Parade	C7	Sherwood Street	A2	York Street	A5
						North Street	B7-C7	Shetland Close	F8		

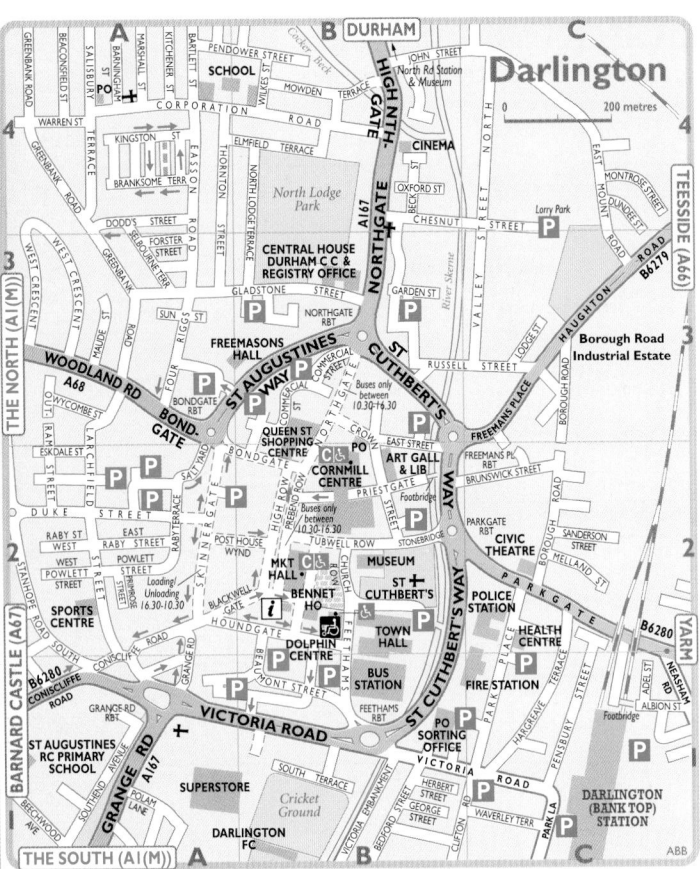

Darlington

Darlington is found on atlas page **89**,
grid reference **2814**

Adelaide Street	C1	John Street	B4-C4	Victoria Road	A1-B1-C
Albion Street	C1	Kingston Street	A4	Warren Street	A
Barningham Street	A4	Kitchener Street	A4	Waverley Terrace	C
Bartlett Street	A4	Larchfield Street	A2-A3	West Crescent	A3-A
Beaconsfield Street	A4	Lodge Street	C3	West Powlett Street	A
Beaumont Street	B1-B2	Marshall Street	A4	Wilkes Street	B
Beck Street	B4	Maude Street	A3	Woodland Road	A
Bedford Street	B1	Melland Street	C2	Wycombe Street	A
Beechwood Avenue	A1	Montrose Street	C4		
Blackwell Gate	A2-B2	Mowden Terrace	B4		
Bondgate	A3-A2-B2	Neasham Road	C1		
Borough Road	C2-C3	North Lodge Terrace	B3-B4		
Branksome Terrace	A4	Northgate	B2-B3-B4		
Brunswick Street	B2-C2	Outram Street	A2-A3		
Chestnut Street	B4-C4	Oxford Street	B4		
Church Row	B2	Park Lane	C1		
Clifton Road	B1-C1	Park Place	C1-C2		
Commercial Street	B2-B3	Parkgate	C2		
Coniscliffe Road	A1-A2	Pendower Street	A4-B4		
Corporation Road	A4-B4	Pensbury Street	C1-C2		
Crown Street	B2-B3	Polam lane	A1		
Dodd's Street	A4	Post House Wynd	A2-B2		
Duke Street	A2	Powlett Street	A2		
Dundee Street	C4	Prebend Row	B2		
Easson Road	A3-A4	Priestgate	B2		
East Mount Road	C3-C4	Primrose Street	A2		
East Raby Street	A2	Raby Street West	A2		
East Street	B2-B3	Raby Terrace	A2		
Elmfield Terrace	A4-B4	Russell Street	B3-C3		
Eskdale Street	A2	St Augustines Way	A3-B3		
Feethams	B1-B2	St Cuthbert's Way	B1-B2-B3		
Forster Street	A3	Salisbury Terrace	A4		
Four Riggs	A3	Salt Yard	A2		
Freemans Place	C3	Sanderson Street	C2		
Garden Street	B3	Selbourne Terrace	A3-A4		
George Street	B1	Skinnergate	A2		
Gladstone Street	A3-B3	South Terrace	B1		
Grange Road	A1-A2	Southend Avenue	A1		
Greenbank Road	A3-A4	Stanhope Road South	A1-A2		
Hargreave Terrace	C1-C2	Stonebridge	B2		
Haughton Road	C3-C4	Sun Street	A3		
Herbert Street	B1	Thornton Street	A3-A4		
High Northgate	B4	Tubwell Row	B2		
High Row	B2	Valley Street North	C3-C4		
Houndgate	A2-B2	Victoria Embankment	B1		

Doncaster

Doncaster is found on atlas page **83**,
grid reference **5703**

Apley Road	B2-C2	Prospect Place	B1
Baxter Gate	A3-B3	Queens Road	C4
Beechfield Road	B2-C2	Rainton Road	C1
Broxholme Lane	C4	Ravensworth Road	C1-C2
Carr House Road	A1-B1-C1	Rectory Gardens	C4
Carr Lane	B1	Regent Square	C3
Chequer Avenue	C4	Roberts Road	A1
Chequer Road	B2-C2-C1	Royal Avenue	C4
Childers Street	C1	Rutland Street	C4
Christchurch Road	B4-C4-C3	St James's Bridge	A2
Church View	A4	St James Street	A1-A2-B2-B1
Church Way	A4-B4	St Sepulchre Gate	A3
Clark Avenue	C1	St Sepulchre Gate West	A1-A2
Cleveland Street	A1-A2-B3	St Vincent Road	C4
College Road	B2	Scot Lane	B3
Cooper Street	C1	Silver Street	B3
Coopers Terrace	B4	Somerset Road	C1-C2
Copley Road	B4-C4	South Parade	C3-C2
Cunningham Road	B1-C1	South Street	C1
Dockin Hill Road	B4-C4	Spring Gardens	A3-A2
Duke Street	A3-B3	Stewart Street	A2
East Laith Gate	B3-C3	Stirling Street	A1
Elmfield Road	C2-C1	Thorne Road	C3-C4
Exchange Street	B1	Trafford Way	A3-A2-B2-B1
French Gate	A3	Vaughan Avenue	C4
Glyn Avenue	C4	Waterdale	B2-B3
Grey Friar's Road	A4-B4	West Laith	A2-A3
Grove Place	A2	West Street	A2-A3
Hallgate	B3	Whitburn Road	C2
High Street	A3-B3	Wood Street	B3
Highfield Road	C4		
Jarratt Street	B1		
King's Road	C4		
Lawn Avenue	C3		
Lawn Road	C3		
Low Fisher Gate	B4		
Market Road	B4		
Milton Walk	A2-B2-B1		
Netherhall Road	B4-C4		
North Bridge Road	A4		
North Street	C1		
Oxford Place	A1		
Palmer Street	C1		
Park Road	B3-C3-C4		
Park Terrace	B3-C3		

178

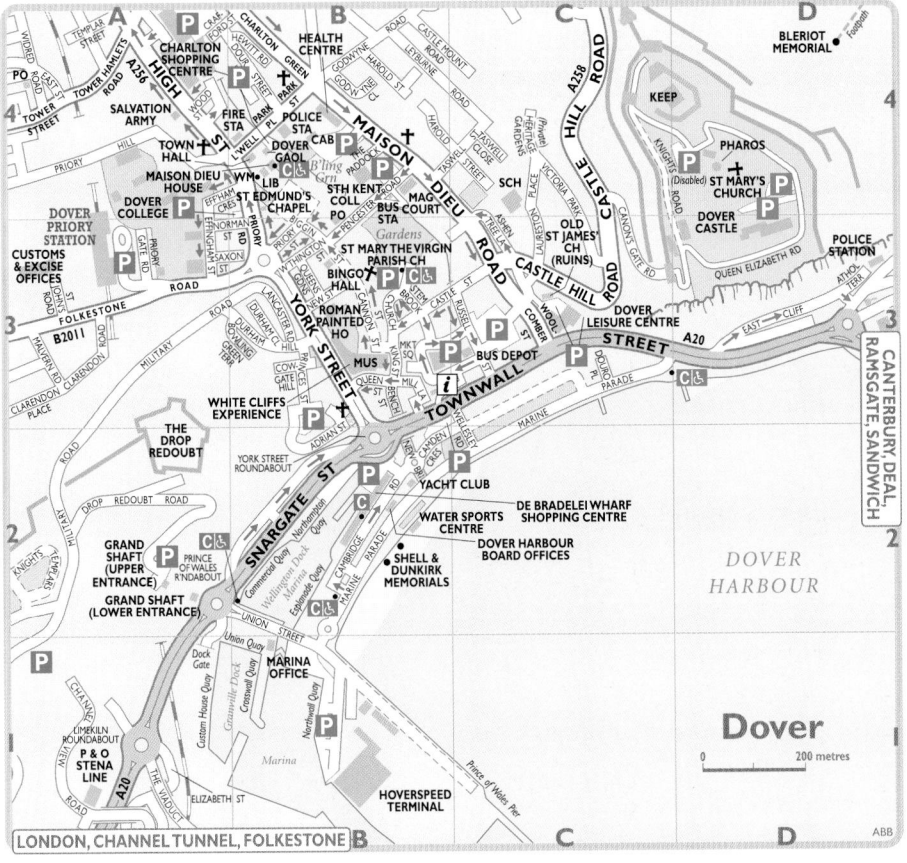

Dover

Dover is found on atlas page **29**, grid reference **3241**

Adrian Street	B2-B3	Maison Dieu Road	B4-C4-C3
Ashen Tree Lane	C3-C4	Malvern Road	A3
Athol Terrace	D3	Marine Parade	B2-C2-C3
Bench Street	B3	Market Square	B3
Biggin Street	B3-B4	Military Road	A2-A3-B3
Bowling Green Terrace	B3	Mill Lane	B3
Bulwark	A1	New Bridge	B2
Cambridge Road	B2	New Street	B3
Camden Crescent	B2-C3	Norman Street	A3-B3-B4
Cannon Street	B3	Park Place	B4
Canon's Gate Road	C3-C4	Park Street	B4
Castle Hill Road	C3-C4	Pencester Road	B3-B4
Castle Mount Road	B4-C4	Princes Street	B3
Castle Street	B3-C3	Priory Gate Road	A3
Channel View Road	A1-A2	Priory Hill	A4
Charlton Green	B4	Priory Road	B3-B4
Church Street	B3	Priory Street	B3
Clarendon Road	A3	Queen Elizabeth Road	D3
Cowgate Hill	B3	Queen Street	B3
Crafford Street	A4-B4	Queens Gardens	B3
De Burgh Street	A4	Russell Street	C3
Dour Street	B4	St John's Road	A3
Douro Place	C3	Saxon Street	A3-B3
Drop Redoubt Road	A2	Snargate Street	B2
Durham Close	B3	Stem Brook	B3
Durham Hill	B3	Taswell Close	C4
East Cliff	D3	Taswell Street	B4-C4
East Street	A4	Templar Street	A4
Effingham Crescent	A4-B4	The Paddock	B4
Effingham Street	A3-A4	The Viaduct	A1
Elizabeth Street	A1	Tower Hamlets Road	A4
Folkestone Road	A3-B3	Tower Street	A4
Godwyne Close	B4	Townwall Street	B3-C3
Godwyne Road	B4	Union Street	B1-B2
Harold Street	B4-C4	Victoria Park	C3-C4
Heritage Gardens	D6	Wellesley Road	C2-C3
Hewitt Road	B4	Widred Road	A4
High Street	A4-B4	Wood Street	A4
King Street	B3	Woolcomber Street	C3
Knights Road	C3-C4	Worthington Street	B3
Knights Templars	A2	York Street	B3
Ladywell	B4		
Lancaster Road	B3		
Laureston Place	C3-C4		
Leyburne Road	B4-C4		

179

Dundee

Dundee is found on atlas page **126**, grid reference **4030**

Airlie Place	A1	Meadowside	B3-C3-C4
Balfour Place	A1-A2	Middle Street	D4
Bank Street	B2-B3-C3	Miln Street	A3
Barrack Road	A4	Nethergate	A1-B1-B2
Barrack Street	B2-B3	Nicoll Street	B3
Bell Street	B3-C3	North Lindsay Street	B2-B3
Blackscroft	D4	North Marketgait	A3-B3-B4-C4
Blinshall Street	A2-A3	Panmure Street	B3-C3
Brown Street	A2-A3	Panmure Terrace	A4
Candle Lane	C3-D3	Park Place	A2-A1-B1
Castle Street	C2-C3	Park Wynd	B3
Commercial Street	C3	Perth Road	A1
Constable Street	D4	Princes Street	D4
Constitution Road	A4-B4-B3	Prospect Place	A4-B4
Constitution Terrace	A4	Queen Street	C4-D4
Cowgate	C4	Rattray Street	B3
Crichton Street	C2	Reform Street	B3-C3-C2
Cross Lane	A2-B2	Riverside Drive	B1-C1
Dens Street	D4	Roseangle	A1
Dock Street	C2-C3	St Andrews Street	C3-C4
Douglas Street	A3	St Roques Lane	D4
Dudhope Street	B4	Seabraes Court	A1
East Dock Street	D3-D4	Seagate	C3-D4
East Marketgait	C4-D4-D3	Session Street	A2
Euclid Crescent	B3	Small's Lane	A2
Euclid Street	B3	Small's Wynd	A1-A2
Exchange Street	C2-C3	Somerville Place	A4
Forebank Road	C4	South Marketgait	B2-C2-D2-D3
Foundry Lane	D4	South Tay Street	B1-B2
Gellatly Street	C3-D3	South Victoria Dock Road	D2-D3
Greenmarket	B1	South Ward Road	B2-B3
Guthrie Street	A2-A3	Trades Lane	C3-D3
Hawkhill	A2	Union Street	B2-C2
High Street	C2-C3	Union Terrace	A4-B4
Hilltown	B4-C4	Victoria Road	B4-C4-D4
Hilltown Terrace	B4	Ward Road	A3-B3
Horsewater Wynd	A2	West Bell Street	A3-B3
Irvine's Square	B3-B4	West Marketgait	A3-A2-B2
Johnston Street	A2-B3	West Port	A2
King Street	C4-D4	Whitehall Crescent	C2
Ladywell Avenue	C4-D4	Whitehall Street	C2
Laurel Bank	B4	Willison Street	B2
Lochee Road	A3		
Mary Anne Lane	D3-D4		
McDonald Street	B4		

180

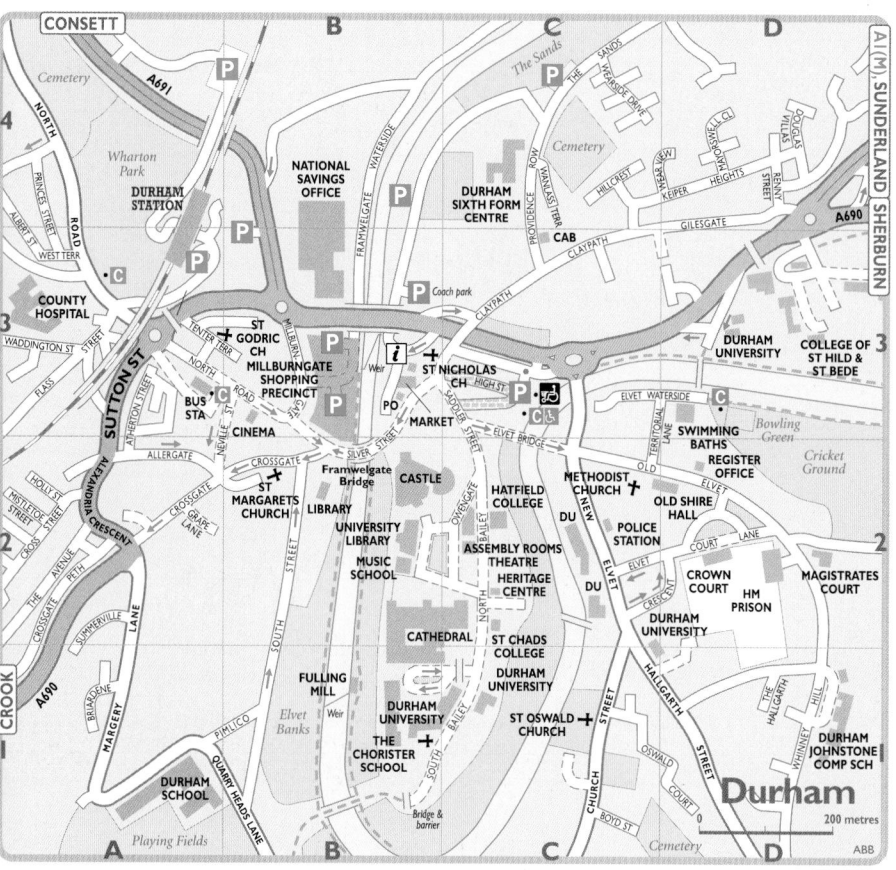

Durham

Durham is found on atlas page **96**,
grid reference **2742**

Albert Street	A3-A4	Summerville	
Alexandria Crescent	A2	Sutton Street	A2
Allergate	A2	Tenter Terrace	A3
Atherton Street	A2-A3	Territorial Lane	C2
Boyd Street	C1	The Avenue	
Briardene	A1	The Hallgarth	
Church Street	C1-C2	The Sands	
Claypath	C3-C4	Waddington Street	
Court Lane	D2	Wanlass Terrace	
Cross Street	A2	Wear View	C4
Crossgate	A2-B2	Wearside Drive	
Crossgate Peth	A1-A2	West Terrace	
Douglas Villas	D4	Whinney Hill	
Elvet Bridge	C2-C3		
Elvet Crescent	C2-D2		
Elvet Waterside	C3-D3		
Flass Street	A3		
Framwelgate Waterside	B3-B4		
Gilesgate	C4-D4		
Grape Lane	A2		
Hallgarth Street	C1-D1		
High Street	C3		
Hillcrest	C4		
Holly Street	A2		
Keiper Heights	C4-D4		
Margery Lane	A1-A2		
Mayorswell Close	D4		
Millburngate	B3		
Mistletoe Street	A2		
Neville Street	A2-B3		
New Elvet	C2		
North Bailey	C1-C2		
North Road	A4-A3-B3		
Old Elvet	C2-D2		
Oswald Court	C1-D1		
Owengate	C2		
Pimlico	A1-B1		
Princes Street	A3-A4		
Providence Row	C3-C4		
Quarry Heads Lane	A1-B1		
Renny Street	D4		
Saddler Street	B3-C3-C2		
Silver Street	B2-B3		
South Bailey	B1-C1		
South Street	B1-B2		

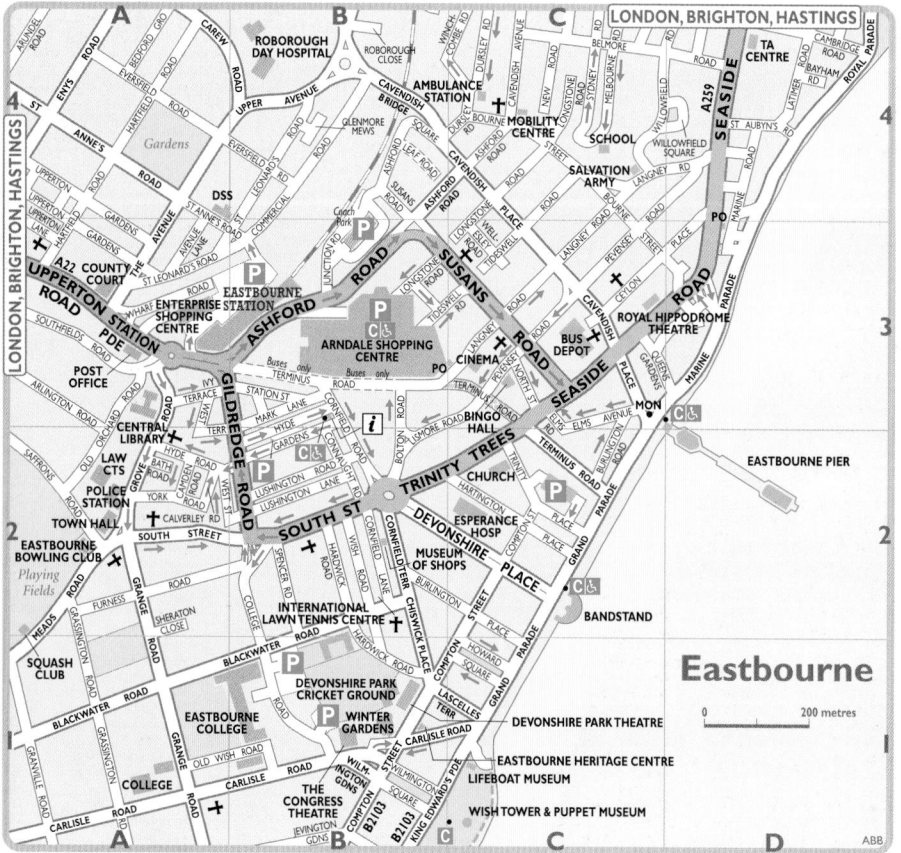

Eastbourne

Eastbourne is found on atlas page **16**,
grid reference **6199**

Arlington Road	A2-A3	Latimer Road	
Ashford Road	B3-B4-C4	Lismore Road	B2
Ashford Square	B4	Longstone Road	B3-C3
Bedford Road	A4	Lushington Lane	
Belmore Road	C4-D4	Lushington Road	
Blackwater Road	A1-B1-B2	Marine Parade	
Bolton Road	B2-B3	Marine Road	D3
Bourne Street	C4-C3-D3	Mark Lane	B2
Burlington Place	B2-C2	Meads Road	A1
Burlington Road	C2-C3	Melbourne Road	
Carew Road	A4-B4	New Road	
Carlisle Road	A1-B1-C1	North Street	
Cavendish Avenue	C4	Old Orchard Road	A2
Cavendish Bridge	B4	Old Wish Road	A1
Cavendish Place	C3-C4	Pevensey Road	C3-C4
Ceylon Place	C3-D3-D4	Queens Gardens	C3
Chiswick Place	B1-B2	Royal Parade	
College Road	B1-B2	St Anne's Road	A4
Commercial Road	B3-B4	St Aubyn's Road	
Compton Street	B1-C1-C2	St Leonard's Road	A3
Connaught Road	B2	Saffrons Road	
Cornfield Road	B2-B3	Seaside	D3
Cornfield Terrace	B2	Seaside Road	C3
Devonshire Place	B2-C2	South Street	A2
Dursley Road	C4	Southfields Road	
Elms Avenue	C2-C3	Spencer Road	
Enys Road	A4	Station Parade	
Eversfield Road	A4-B4	Station Street	
Furness Road	A2-B2	Susan's Road	B4-B3
Gildredge Road	A3-B2	Sydney Road	
Grand Parade	C1-C2	Terminus Road	B3-C3
Grange Road	A1-A2	The Avenue	A3
Granville Road	A1	Tideswell Road	B3-C3
Grassington Road	A1-A2	Trinity Place	
Grove Road	A2-A3	Trinity Trees	B2
Hardwick Road	B1-B2	Upper Avenue	
Hartfield Road	A3-A4	Upperton Gardens	A3
Hartington Place	C2	Upperton Road	
Howard Square	C1	West Terrace	A2
Hyde Gardens	B2-B3	Wharf Road	
Hyde Road	A2	Willowfield Road	C4
Junction Road	B3	Willowfield Square	C4
King Edward's Parade	B1-C1	Wilmington Square	
Langney Road	C3-C4-D4	Wish Road	
Lascelles Terrace	B1-C1	York Road	

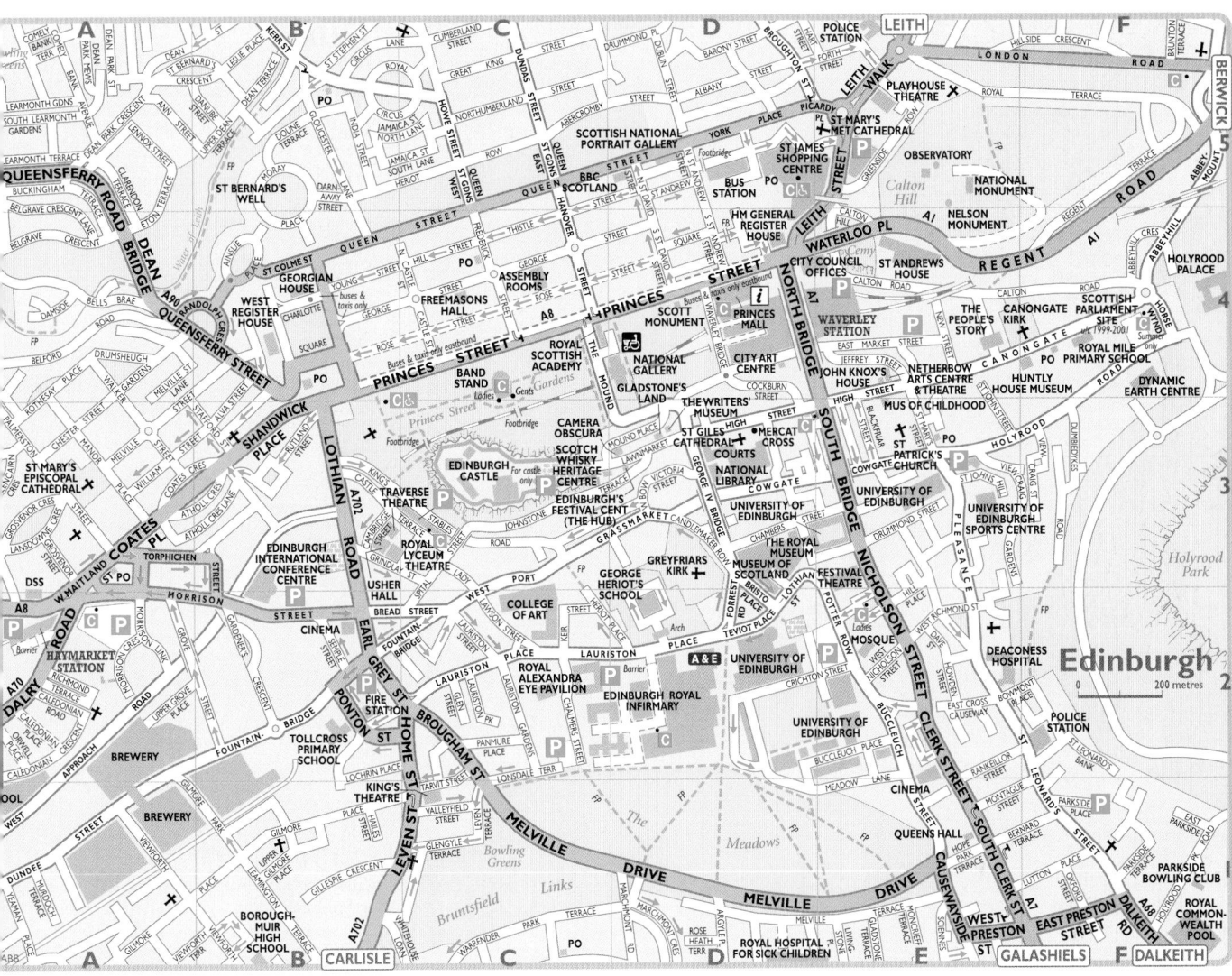

Edinburgh

Edinburgh is found on atlas page 117,
grid reference 2573

Abbeyhill	F4	Causewayside	E1	East Cross Causeway	E2	India Street	B5	Morrison Link	A2
Abbeyhill Crescent	F4	Chalmers Street	C2	East Market Street	E4	Jamaica Street North Lane	B5-C5	Morrison Street	A3-A2-B2
Abbeymount	F5	Chambers Street	D3-E3	East Parkside	F1	Jamaica Street South Lane	B5-C5	Mound Place	C3-D3
Abercromby Street	C5-D5	Charlotte Square	B4	East Preston Street	E4	Jeffrey Street	E4	Murdoch Terrace	A1
Aleslie Place	B4	Chester Street Gardens	A3-A4	Eton Terrace	A4-A5	Johnstone Terrace	C3-D3	New Street	E4
Albany Street	D5	Circus Lane	B5-C5	Forth Street	D5-E5	Keir Street	C2	Nicholson Street	E2-E3
Ann Street	B3-B4	Clarendon Terrace	A4-A5	Fountainbridge	A2-B2-C2	Kerr Street	B5	North Bridge	D4-E4
Ann Street	A5-B5	Clerk Street	E1-E2	Frederick Street	C4	King's Stables Road	B3-C3	North Castle Street	B4-C4
Argyle Place	D1	Coates Crescent	A3-B3	Gardener's Crescent	B2	Lady Lawson Street	C2-C3	North St Andrew Street	D4
Atholl Crescent	A3-B3	Coates Place	A3	George IV Bridge	D3	Lansdowne Crescent	A3	North St David Street	D4-D5
Atholl Crescent Lane	A3-B3	Cockburn Street	D3-D4	George Street	B4-C4-D4	Lauriston Gardens	C2	Northumberland Street	C5
Barony Street	D5	Comely Bank Avenue	A5	Gillespie Crescent	B1	Lauriston Park	C2	Orwell Place	A2
Bell's Brae	A4	Comely Bank Terrace	A5	Gilmore Park	A2-A1-B1	Lauriston Place	C2-D2	Oxford Street	F1
Belgrave Crescent	A4	Cowgate	D3-E3	Gilmore Place	A1-B1-C1	Lauriston Street	C2	Palmerston Street	A3-A4
Belgrave Crescent Lane	A4-A5	Crichton Street	D2-E2	Gladstone Terrace	E1	Lawnmarket	D3	Panmure Place	C2
Bells Brae	A4	Cumberland Street	C5	Glen Street	C2	Leamington Terrace	B1	Parkside Place	F1
Bernard Terrace	E1-F1	Dalkeith Road	F1	Glencairn Crescent	A3	Learmonth Gardens	A5	Parkside Terrace	F1
Blackfriar Street	E3	Dalry Road	A2	Glengyle Terrace	C1	Learmonth Terrace	A5	Picardy Place	D5-E5
Blackwmont Place	E2-F2	Damside	A4	Gloucester Lane	B4-B5	Leith Street	D4-E5	Pleasance	E2-E3
Bread Street	D5	Danube Street	A5-B5	Grassmarket	C3-D3	Leith Walk	E5	Ponton Street	B2
Bristo Place	D2-D3	Darnaway Street	B5	Great King Street	C5	Lennox Street	A5	Potter Row	E2-E3
Broughton Street	C2	Dave Street	E2	Greenside Row	E5	Leslie Place	B5	Princes Street	B4-C4-D4
Broughton Street	D5	Dean Bridge	A4	Grindlay Street	B3-C3	Leven Street	B1-C1	Queen Street	B4-C4-C5-D5
Brunton Terrace	F5	Dean Park Crescent	A5	Grosvenor Crescent	A3	Leven Terrace	C1	Queen Street Gardens East	C5
Buccleuch Place	D2-E2	Dean Park Mews	A5	Grosvenor Street	A3	Livingstone Place	E1	Queen Street Gardens West	C5
Buccleuch Street	E1-E2	Dean Park Street	A5	Grove Street	A2-B2	Lochrin Place	B2	Queensferry Road	A4-A5
Buckingham Terrace	A4-A5	Dean Street	A5-B5	Hailes Street	B1	London Road	E5-F5	Queensferry Street	A4-B4
Caledonian Crescent	A2	Dean Terrace	B5	Hanover Street	C4-C5	Lonsdale Terrace	C1-C2	Randolph Crescent	A4-B4
Caledonian Place	A2	Doune Terrace	B5	Hart Street	D5-E5	Lothian Road	B2-B3	Rankeillor Street	E2
Caledonian Road	A2	Drummond Place	D5	Heriot Place	C2-D2	Lothian Street	D2-D3	Regent Road	E4-F4-F5
Calton Hill	E4-E5	Drummond Street	E3	Heriot Row	B5-C5	Lutton Place	E1-F1	Regent Terrace	F4-F5
Calton Road	E4-F4	Drumsheugh	A4	High Street	D3-E3-E4	Manor Place	A3-A4	Richmond Terrace	A2
Cambridge Street	B3	Dublin Street	D5	Hill Place	E2-E3	Marchmont Crescent	D1	Rose Heath Terrace	D1
Candlemaker Row	D3	Dumbiedykes Road	F3	Hill Street	C4	Marchmont Road	D1	Rose Street	B4-C4-D4
Canongate	E4-F4	Dundas Street	C5	Hillside Crescent	E5-F5	Meadow Lane	E1-E2	Rothesay Place	A3-A4
Castle Street	C4	Dundee Street	A1	Holyrood Park Road	F1	Melville Drive	C1-D1-E1	Royal Circus	B5-C5
Castle Terrace	B3-C3	Earl Grey Street	B2-C2	Holyrood Road	E3-F3-F4	Melville Street	A3-B4	Royal Terrace	E5-F5
				Home Street	C1-C2	Melville Street Lane	A4	Rutland Street	B3
				Hope Park Terrace	E1	Melville Terrace	D1-E1	St Andrew Square	D4-D5
				Horse Wynd	F4	Moncrieff Terrace	E1	St Bernard's Crescent	A5-B5
				Howden Street	E2	Montague Street	E1-F1	St Colme Street	B4
				Howe Street	C5	Moray Place	B4-B5	St John Street	E3-E4
						Morrison Crescent	A2	St Johns Hill	E3

St Leonard's Bank	F2
St Leonard's Street	E2-F2-F1
St Mary's Street	E3
St Stephen Street	B5
Sciennes	E1
Semple Street	B2
Shandwick Place	B3
South Bridge	E3
South Clerk Street	E1-F1
South Learmonth Gardens	A5
South St Andrew Street	D4
South St David Street	D4
Spital Street	C2-C3
Stafford Street	B3
Tarvit Street	C1-C2
Teviot Place	D2
The Mound	C4-D3
Thistle Street	C4-C5-D5
Torphichen Street	A3-B3
Upper Dean Terrace	B5
Upper Gilmore Place	B1
Upper Grove Place	A2
Valleyfield Street	C1
Victoria Street	D3
Viewcraig Gardens	E3
Viewcraig Street	F3
Viewforth	A1-B1
Viewforth Terrace	A1-B1
Walker Street	A3-A4
Warrender Park Terrace	C1-D1
Waterloo Place	D4-E4
Waverley Bridge	D4
West Bow	D3
West Maitland Street	A2-A3
West Nicholson Street	E2
West Port	C2-C3
West Preston Street	E1
West Richmond Street	E2
Whitehouse Loan	B1-C1
William Street	A3-B3
Yeaman Place	A1
York Place	D5
Young Street	B4

182

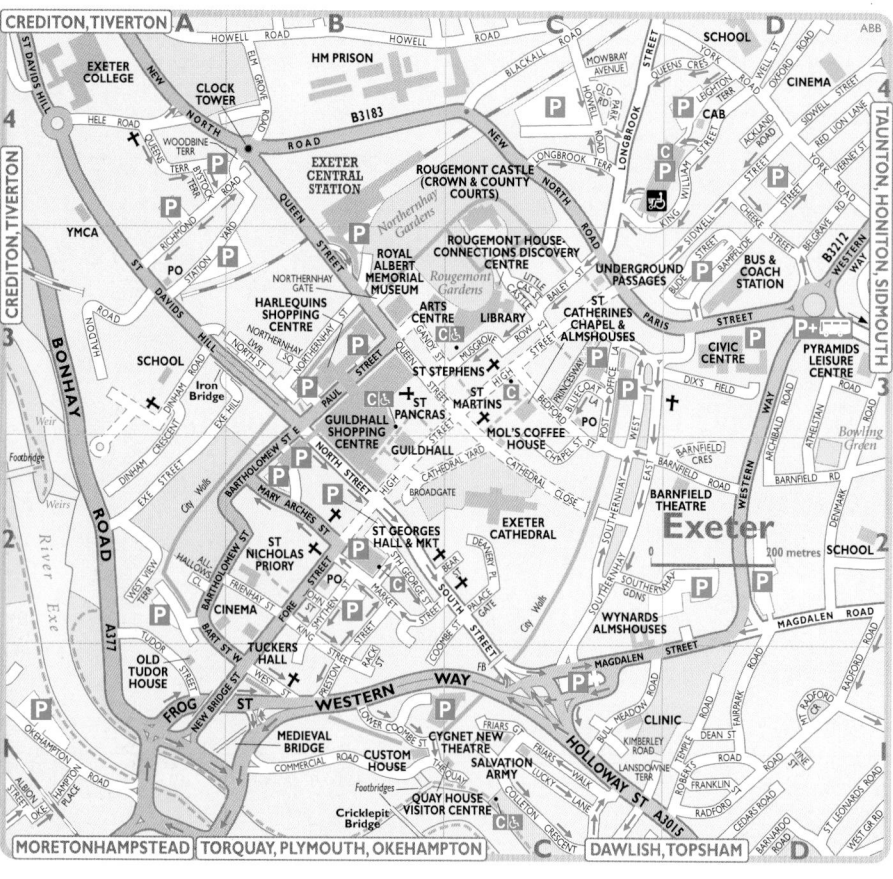

Exeter

Exeter is found on atlas page **9**,
grid reference **9292**

Archibald Road	D2-D3	Lower Coombe Street	B1
Athelstan Road	D2-D3	Lower North Street	B3
Bailey Street	C3	Lucky Lane	C1
Bampfylde Street	D3-D4	Magdalen Road	D2
Barnfield Road	C2-D2	Magdalen Street	C1-D1-D2
Bartholomew Street	A2-B2	Market Street	B2
Bartholomew Street East	B2	Mary Arches Street	B2
Bartholomew Street West	A1-A2	Musgrove Row	B3-C3
Bedford Street	C2-C3	New Bridge Street	A1-B1
Belgrave Road	D3-D4	New North Road	A4-B4-C4-C3
Blackall Road	C4	North Street	B2
Bluecoat Lane	C1	Northernhay Street	B3
Bonhay Road	A1-A2-A3-A4	Okehampton Place	A1
Bull Meadow Road	C1	Okehampton Road	A1
Castle Street	C3	Old Park Road	C4
Cathedral Close	C2-C3	Oxford Road	D4
Cathedral Yard	B2-C2	Palace Gate	C3
Cedars Road	D1	Paris Street	C3-D3
Chapel Street	C2-C3	Paul Street	B3
Cheeke Street	D3-D4	Post Office Lane	C2-C3
Colleton Crescent	C1	Preston Street	B1-B2
Commercial Road	B1	Princesway	C3
Coombe Street	B1-B2-C2	Queen Street	B4-B3-C3
Deanery Place	C2	Queens Crescent	C4-D4
Denmark Road	D2-D3	Queens Terrace	A4
Dinham Crescent	A2-A3	Radford Road	D1-D2
Dinham Road	A3	Richmond Road	A3-A4-B4
Dix's Field	D3	Roberts Road	D1
Elm Grove Road	B4	St Davids Hill	A4-A3-B3
Exe Hill	A3-B3	St Leonards Road	D1
Exe Street	A2	Sidwell Street	C3-D3-D4
Fairpark Road	D1-D2	Smythen Street	B2
Fore Street	B1-B2	South George Street	B2
Friars Walk	C1	South Street	B2-C2-C3
Frienhay Street	B2	Southernhay East	C1-C2-C3
Frog Street	A1-B1	Southernhay Gardens	C2-D2
Haldon Road	A3	Southernhay West	C2-C3
Hele Road	A4	Station Yard	A3-B3-B4
High Street	B2-B3-C3	Temple Road	D1
Holloway Street	C1-D1	Tudor Street	A1-A2
Howell Road	A4-B4-C4	West Street	B1
King Street	B1-B2	West View Terrace	A2
King William Street	C3-C4-D4	Western Way	B1-C1
Longbrook Street	C3-C4	Western Way	D2-D3-D4
Longbrook Terrace	C4	York Road	C4-D4

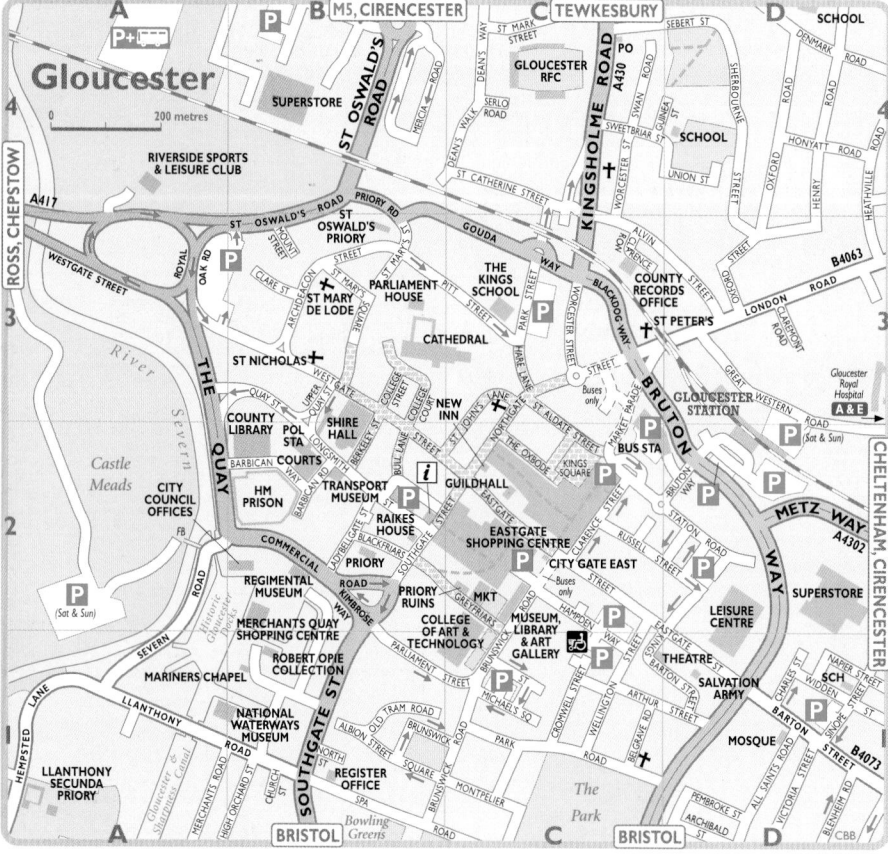

Gloucester

Gloucester is found on atlas page **35**,
grid reference **8318**

Albion Street	B1	Longsmith Street	B2
All Saints Road	D1	Market Parade	C2-C3
Alvin Street	C3-D3	Merchants Road	A1-B1
Archdeacon Street	B3	Mercia Road	B4
Arthur Street	C1-D1	Metz Way	D2
Barbican Road	B2	Montpelier	C1
Barbican Way	B2	Napier Street	D1
Barton Street	D1	Northgate Street	C2-C3
Belgrave Road	C1	Old Tram Road	B1
Berkeley Street	B2-B3	Oxford Road	D3-D4
Blackdog Way	C3	Oxford Street	D1
Blackfriars	B2	Park Road	C1
Brunswick Road	B1-C1-C2	Park Street	C3
Brunswick Square	B1-C1	Parliament Street	B2-B1-C1
Bruton Way	C3-D2-D1	Pembroke Street	C1
Bull Lane	B2	Pitt Street	B3-C3
Charles Street	D1	Priory Road	B4
Clare Street	B3	Quay Street	A3-B3
Clarence Street	C2	Royal Oak Road	A3
College Court	B3	Russell Street	C2-D2
College Street	B3	St Aldate Street	C2-C3
Commercial Road	B2	St Catherine Street	C4
Cromwell Street	C1	St John's Lane	B2-C2-C3
Dean's Walk	C4	St Mary's Square	B3
Dean's Way	C4	St Mary's Street	B3
Denmark Road	D4	St Michael's Square	C1
Eastgate Street	C2-D1	St Oswald's Road	B3-B4
Gouda Way	B3-B4-C3	Sebert Street	C4-D4
Great Western Road	D2-D3	Severn Road	A1-A2
Greyfriars	B2-C2	Sherbourne Street	D3-D4
Guinea Street	C4-D4	Sinope Street	D1
Hampden Way	C1-C2	Southgate Street	B1-B2-C2
Hare Lane	C3	Spa Road	B1-C1
Heathville Road	D3-D4	Station Road	D2
Hempsted Lane	A1	Swan Road	C4
Henry Road	D3-D4	Sweetbriar Street	C4-D4
High Orchard Street	A1-B1	The Oxbode	C2
Honyatt Road	D4	The Quay	A2-A3
Kimbrose Way	B2	Union Street	C4-D4
Kings Barton Street	C1-D1	Upper Quay Street	B2-B3
Kings Square	C2	Victoria Street	D1
Kingsholme Road	C3-C4	Wellington Street	C1-C2
Ladybellgate Street	B2	Westgate Street	A3-B3-B2
Llanthony Road	A1-B1	Widden Street	D1
London Road	D3	Worcester Street	C3, C4

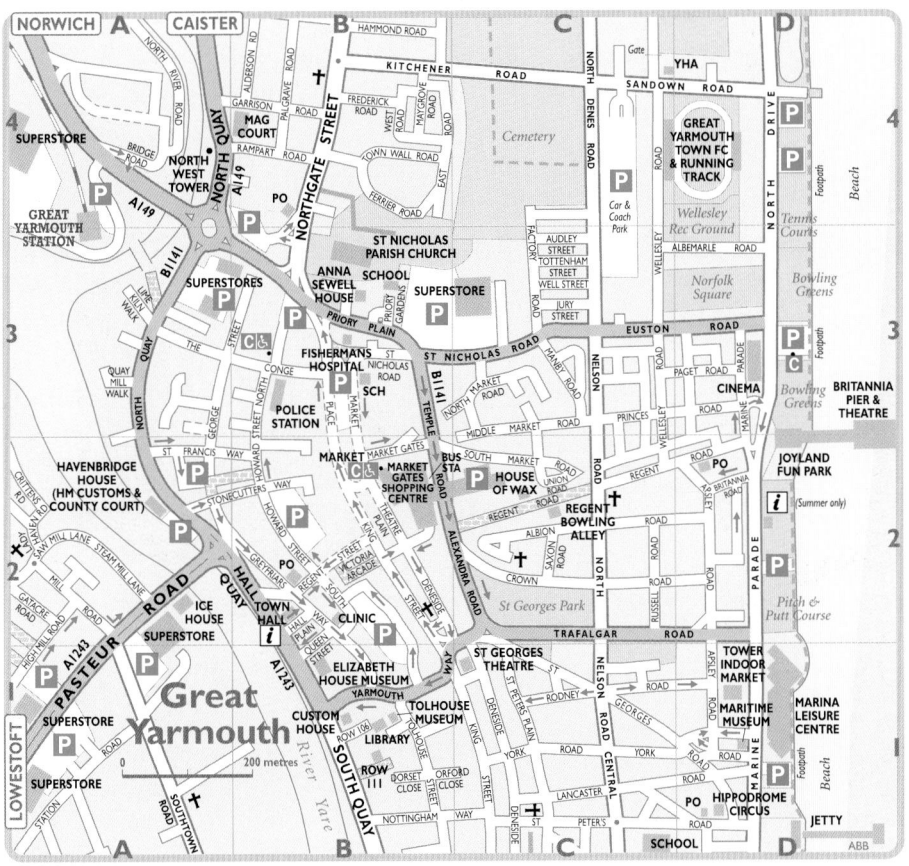

Great Yarmouth

Great Yarmouth is found on atlas page **67**,
grid reference **5207**

Albemarle Road	C3-D3	North River Road	A4
Albion Road	C2-D2	Northgate Street	B3-B4
Alderson Road	B4	Nottingham Way	B1-C1
Alexandra Road	C2	Orford Close	B1-C1
Apsley Road	D1-D2	Paget Road	C3-D3
Audley Street	C3	Palgrave Road	B4
Bridge Road	A4	Pasteur Road	A1-A2
Britannia Road	D2	Princes Road	C3-D3
Crown Road	C2-D2	Priory Gardens	B3
Deneside	B2-C1	Priory Plain	B3
Dorset Close	B1	Quay Mill Walk	A3
East Road	B4	Queen Street	B1-B2
Euston Road	C3-D3	Rampart Road	B4
Factory Road	C3-C4	Regent Road	C2-D2
Ferrier Road	B4	Regent Street	B2
Frederick Road	B4	Rodney Road	C1-D1
Garrison Road	A4-B4	Row 106	B1
Gatacre Road	A2	Russell Road	C2
George Street	A2-A3-B3	St Francis Way	A2-B2
Greyfriars Way	A2-B2-B1	St Georges Road	C1-D1
Hall Plain	B2	St Nicholas Road	B3-C3
Hall Quay	B2	St Peter's Road	C1-D1
Hammond Road	B4	St Peters Plain	C1
High Mill Road	A1-A2	Sandown Road	C4-D4
Howard Street North	B2-B3	Saw Mill Lane	A2
Howard Street South	B2	South Market Road	B2-C2
Jury Street	C3	South Quay	B1
King Street	B2-C1	Southtown Road	A1
Kitchener Road	B4-C4	Station Road	A1
Lady Haven Road	A2	Steam Mill Lane	A2
Lancaster Road	C1-D1	Stonecutters Way	A2-B2
Lime Kiln Walk	A3	Temple Road	B3-B2
Manby Road	C3	The Conge	A3-B3
Marine Parade	D1-D2-D3	Theatre Plain	B2
Market Gates	B2	Tolhouse Street	B1
Market Place	B2-B3	Tottenham Street	C3
Maygrove Road	B4	Town Wall Road	B4
Middle Market Road	C2-C3	Trafalgar Road	C2-D2
Mill Road	A2	Union Road	C2
Nelson Road Central	C1	Victoria Arcade	B2
Nelson Road North	C2-C3	Well Street	C3
North Denes Road	C4	Wellesley Road	C2-C3-C4
North Drive	D3-D4	West Road	B4
North Market Road	B3-C3	Yarmouth Way	B1-C1-C2
North Quay	A2-A3-A4	York Road	C1-D1

183

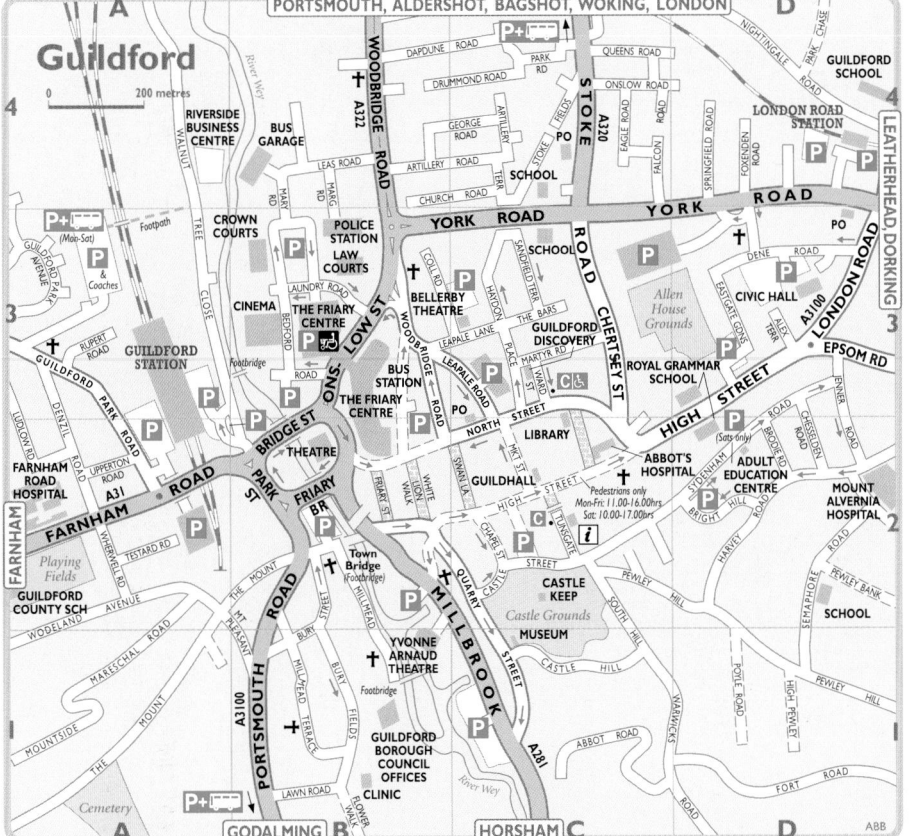

Guildford

Guildford is found on atlas page **25**,
grid reference **9949**

Abbot Road	C1	Mareschal Road	A1-A2
Alexandra Terrace	D3	Margaret Road	B3-B4
Artillery Road	B4-C4	Market Street	C2
Artillery Terrace	C4	Martyr Road	C3
Bedford Road	B3	Mary Road	B3-B4
Bridge Street	B2-B3	Millbrook	B2-C2-C1
Bright Hill	D2	Millmead	B1-B2
Brodie Road	D2	Millmead Terrace	B1
Bury Fields	B1	Mount Pleasant	B1-B2
Bury Street	B1-B2	Mountside	A1
Castle Hill	C1	Nightingale Road	D4
Castle Street	C2	North Street	B2-C2-C3
Chapel Street	C2	Onslow Road	C4
Chertsey Street	C3	Onslow Street	B3
Chesselden Road	D2-D3	Park Chase	D4
Church Road	B4-C4	Park Road	C4
College Road	B3-C3	Park Street	B2
Dapdune Road	B4-C4	Pewley Bank	D2
Dene Road	D3	Pewley Hill	C2-D2-D1
Denzil Road	A2-A3	Portsmouth Road	B1-B2
Drummond Road	B4-C4	Poyle Road	D1
Eagle Road	C4	Quarry Street	B2-C2-C1
Eastgate Gardens	D3	Queens Road	C4
Epsom Road	D3	Rupert Road	A3
Falcon Road	C4	Sandfield Terrace	C3
Farnham Road	A2	Semaphore Road	D1-D2
Fort Road	C1-D1	South Hill	C1-C2
Foxenden Road	D4	Springfield Road	D4
Friary Bridge	B2	Stoke Fields	C4
Friary Street	B2	Stoke Road	C3-C4
George Road	B4-C4	Swan Lane	B2-C2
Guildford Park Avenue	A3	Sydenham Road	C2-D2-D3
Guildford Park Road	A2-A3	Testard Road	A2
Harvey Road	D2	The Bars	C3
Haydon Place	C3	The Mount	A1-A2-B2
High Pewley	D1	Tunsgate	C2
High Street	C2-D3	Upperton Road	A2
Jenner Road	D2-D3	Walnut Tree Close	A4-A4-B3
Laundry Road	B3	Ward Street	C3
Lawn Road	B1	Warwicks Road	C1-D1
Leapale Lane	B3-C3	Wherwell Road	A2
Leapale Road	B3-C3	White Lion Walk	B2
Leas Road	B4	Wodeland Avenue	A1-A2
London Road	D3	Woodbridge Road	B2-B3-B4
Ludlow Road	A2-A3	York Road	B3-C3-D3-D4

184

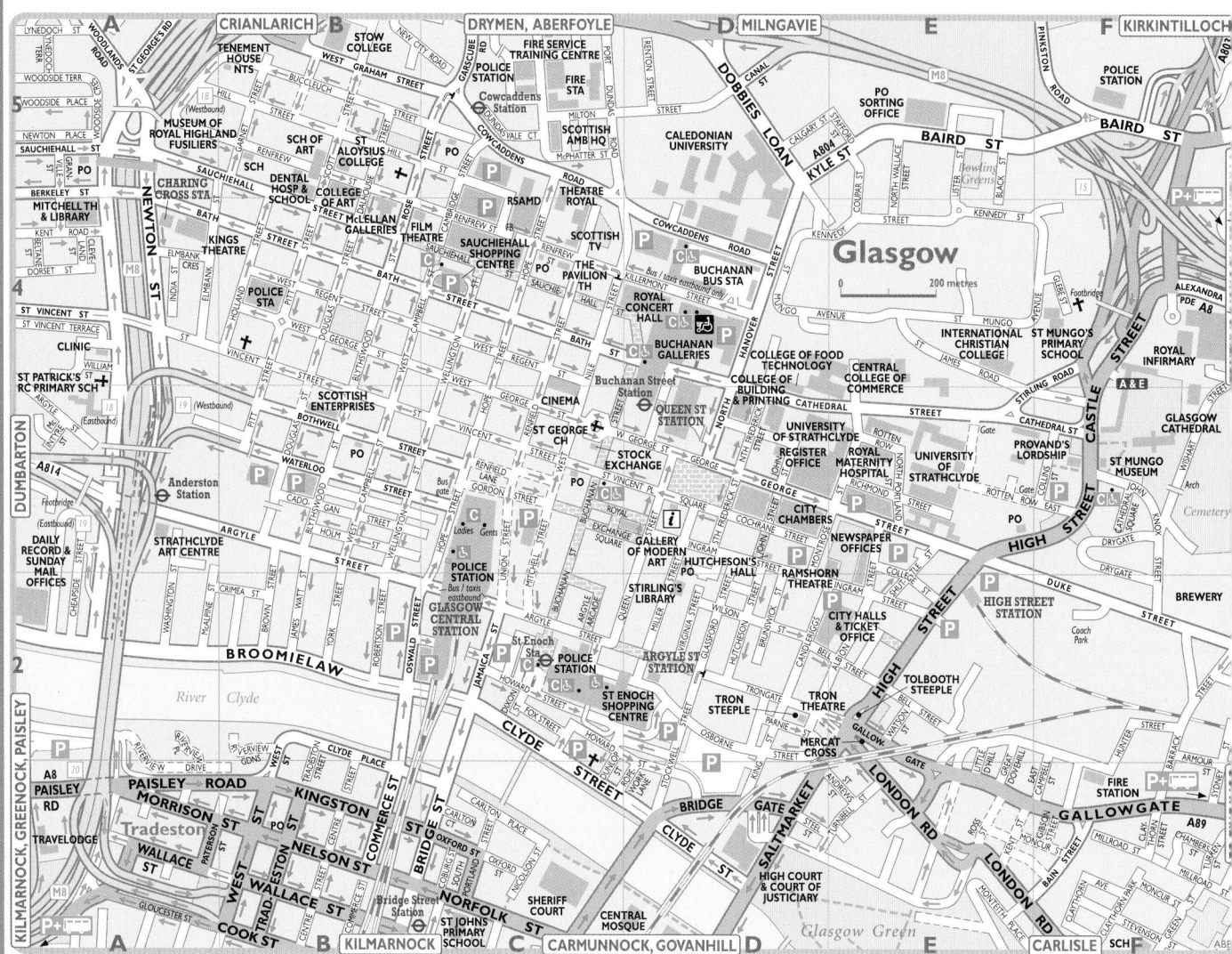

Glasgow

Glasgow is found on atlas page **115**,
grid reference **5865**

Albion Street	D2-E2-E3	Centre Street	BI	Garscube Road	C5	Lister Street	E4-E5	Pinkston Road	F5	Steel Street	
Alexandra Parade	F4	Chambers Street	FI	George Square	D3	Little Dovehill	EI-E2	Pitt Street	B3-B4	Stevenson Street	
Argyle Arcade	C2	Cheapside Street	A2-A3	George Street	D3-E3	London Road	EI-FI	Port Dundas Road	C5	Stirling Road	E3-
Argyle Street	A3-B3-C2-D2	Claythorn Avenue	FI	Gibson Street	FI	Lynedoch Street	A5	Queen Street	C2-D2-D3	Stockwell Street	DI-
Armour Street	FI-F2	Claythorn Park	FI	Glassford Street	D2-D3	Lynedoch Terrace	A5	Renfield Street	C3-C4	Sydney Street	FI-
Bain Street	EI-FI	Claythorn Street	FI	Glebe Street	F4	McAlpine Street	A2-A3	Renfrew Street	A5-B5-B4-C4	Tradeston Street	BI-
Baird Street	E5-F5	Cleveland Street	A4	Gloucester Street	AI	McIntyre Street	A3	Renton Street	D5	Trongate	
Barrack Street	FI-F2	Clyde Place	BI-B2	Gordon Street	C3	McPhatter Street	C5	Richmond Street	E3	Turnbell Street	DI-
Bath Street	A4-B4-C4-D4	Clyde Street	C2-CI-DI	Granville Street	A5	Miller Street	D2-D3	Riverview Drive	A2-AI-BI	Union Street	C2-
Bell Street	D2-E2	Coburg Street	CI	Great Dovehill	EI-E2	Millroad Street	FI	Riverview Gardens	B2	Virginia Street	
Beltane Street	A4	Cochrane Street	D3	Green Street	FI	Milton Street	C5-D5	Riverview Place	A2-AI	Wallace Street	AI-
Berkeley Street	A4-A5	College Street	E2-E3	High Street	E2-E3-F3	Mitchell Street	C2-C3	Robertson Street	B2	Washington Street	A2-
Black Street	E4-E5	Collins Street	F3	Hill Street	A5-B5-C5	Monteith Place	EI	Ropework Lane	CI-DI	Waterloo Street	B3-
Blythswood Street	B3-B4	Commerce Street	BI	Holland Street	B4	Montrose Street	D3-E3	Rose Street	B4-B5-C5	Watson Street	
Bothwell Street	B3-C3	Coupar Street	E4-E5	Holm Street	B3	Morrison Street	AI-BI	Ross Street	EI	Wellington Street	B3-C3-
Bridge Gate	DI	Cowcaddens Road	C5-C4-D4	Hope Street	C2-C3-C4-C5	Nelson Street	BI	Rotten Row	E3	West Campbell Street	B3-B4-
Bridge Street	BI-CI	Crimea Street	A2-B2	Howard Street	C2-DI	New City Road	B5-C5	Rotten Row East	E3-F3	West George Street	B4-C4-N
Broomielaw	A2-B2	Dalhousie Street	B4-B5	Hunter Street	FI-F2	Newton Place	A5	Royal Exchange Square	C3-D3	West Graham Street	B5-
Brown Street	B2-B3	Dixon Street	C2	Hutcheson Street	D2	Nicholson Street	CI	St Andrews Street	DI-EI	West Nile Street	C3-C4-N
Brunswick Street	D2	Dobbies Loan	D4-D5	India Street	A4	Nile Street	C3-C4	St Georges Road	A5	West Regent Street	B4-
Buccleuch Street	B5-C5	Dorset Street	A4	Ingram Street	D3-D2-E2	Norfolk Street	BI-CI	St James Road	E3-E4	West Street	BI-
Buchanan Street	C2-C3	Douglas Street	B3-B4	Jamaica Street	C2	North Frederick Street	D3	St Mungo Avenue	D4-E4-F4	William Street	
Cadogan Street	B3-C3	Drygate	F2-F3	James Watt Street	B2-B3	North Hanover Street	D3-D4-D5	St Vincent Place	C3-D3	Wilson Street	
Calgary Street	D5	Duke Street	E3-E2-F2	John Knox Street	F2-F3	North Portland Street	E3	St Vincent Street	A4-B4-B3-C3	Wishart Street	
Cambridge Street	C4-C5	Dundasvale Court	C5	John Street	D3	North Wallace Street	E4-E5	St Vincent Terrace	A4	Woodlands Road	
Canal Street	D5	Dunlop Street	CI	Kennedy Street	D4-E4	Osborne Street	DI-D2	Saltmarket	DI	Woodside Crescent	
Candleriggs	D2-E2	East Campbell Street	FI	Kent Road	A4	Oswald Street	B2	Sauchiehall Street	A5-B4-C4-D4	Woodside Place	
Carlton Court	CI	Elmbank Crescent	A4	Kent Street	EI	Oxford Street	CI	Scott Street	B4-B5	Woodside Terrace	
Carlton Place	CI	Elmbank Street	A4-A5	Killermont Street	C4-D4	Paisley Road	AI-BI	Shuttle Street	E2-E3	York Street	B2-
Castle Street	F3-F4	Fox Street	C2	King Street	DI-D2	Parnie Street	D2	South Frederick Street	D3		
Cathedral Square	F3	Gallowgate	E2-EI-FI	Kingston Street	BI	Paterson Street	AI	South Portland Street	CI		
Cathedral Street	D3-E3-F3	Garnet Street	B5	Kyle Street	D5-E5			Stafford Street	E5		

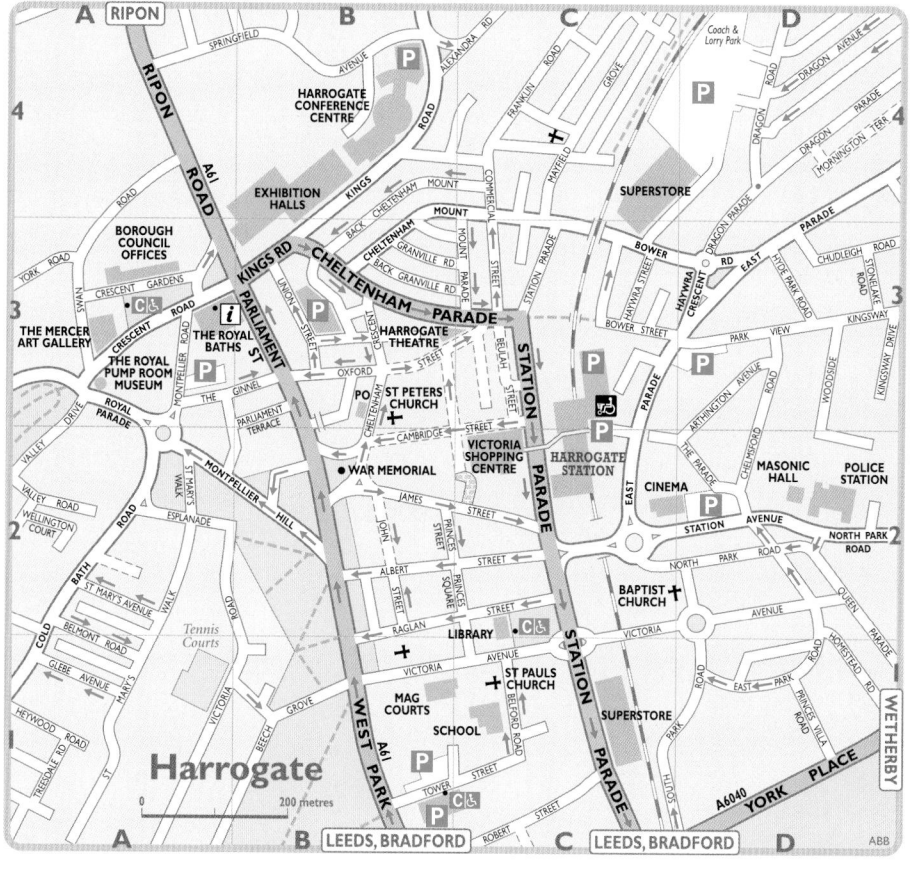

Harrogate

Harrogate is found on atlas page **82**, grid reference **3054**

Albert Street	B2-C2	North Park Road	C2-D2
Alexandra Road	B4-C4	Oxford Street	B3-C3
Arthington Avenue	D2-D3	Park View	D3
Back Cheltenham Mount	B3-B4-C4	Parliament Street	B3
Back Granville Road	B3	Parliament Terrace	B3
Beech Grove	A1-B1	Princes Square	B2-C2
Belford Road	C1	Princes Street	B2-C2
Belmont Road	A1-A2	Princes Villa Road	D1
Beulah Street	C3	Queen Parade	D1-D2
Bower Road	C4-C3-D3	Raglan Street	B1-B2-C2
Bower Street	C3	Ripon Road	A3-A4
Cambridge Street	B2-C3	Robert Street	C1
Chelmsford Road	D2-D3	Royal Parade	A3
Cheltenham Crescent	B2-B3	St Mary's Avenue	A2
Cheltenham Mount	B3-B4-C4	St Mary's Walk	A1-A2
Cheltenham Parade	B3-C3	South Park Road	C1-D1
Chudleigh Road	D3	Springfield Avenue	A4-B4
Cold Bath Road	A1-A2	Station Avenue	C2-D2
Commercial Street	C3-C4	Station Parade	C1-C2-C3
Crescent Gardens	A3	Stonelake Road	D3
Crescent Road	A3	Swan Road	A3-A4
Dragon Avenue	D4	The Ginnel	A3-B3
Dragon Parade	D3-D4	The Parade	D2
Dragon Road	D4	Tower Street	B1-C1
East Parade	C2-C3-D3-D4	Treesdale Road	A1
East Park Road	D1-D2	Union Street	B3
Esplanade	A2	Valley Drive	A2-A3
Franklin Road	C4	Valley Road	A2
Glebe Avenue	A1	Victoria Avenue	B1-C1-C2-D2
Granville Road	B3	Victoria Road	A1-B1-B2-A2
Haywra Crescent	D3	Wellington Court	A2
Haywra Street	C3	West Park	B1
Heywood Road	A1	Woodside	D2-D3
Homestead Road	D1-D2	York Place	D1
Hyde Park Road	D3	York Road	A3
James Street	B2-C2		
John Street	B2		
Kings Road	B3-B4		
Kingsway	D3		
Kingsway Drive	D3		
Mayfield Grove	C4		
Montpellier Hill	A2-B2		
Montpellier Road	A3		
Mornington Terrace	D4		
Mount Parade	C3		

185

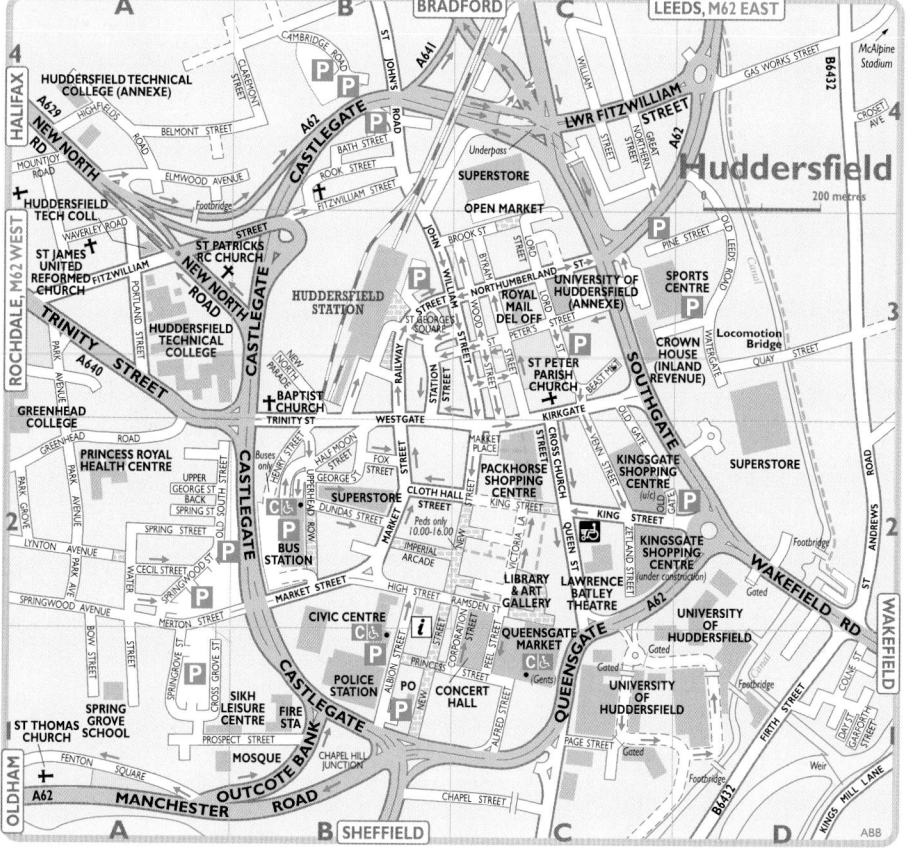

Huddersfield

Huddersfield is found on atlas page **82**, grid reference **1416**

Albion Street	B1-B2	Market Street	B2
Alfred Street	C1	Merton Street	A1-A2-B2
Back Spring Street	A2	New North Parade	B3
Bath Street	B4	New North Road	A4-A3-B3
Beast Market	C3	New Street	B1-B2-C2
Belmont Street	A4-B4	Northumberland Street	C3
Bow Street	A1-A2	Old Leeds Road	D3-D4
Brook Street	B3-C3	Old Gate	C2-C3
Byram Street	C3	Old South Street	A2
Cambridge Road	B4	Outcote Bank	A1-B1
Castlegate	B1-B2-B3-B4	Page Street	C1
Cecil Street	A2	Park Avenue	A2-A3
Chapel Street	B1-C1	Peel Street	C1-C2
Claremont Street	B4	Pine Street	C3-D3
Cloth Hall Street	B2-C2	Portland Street	A3
Colne Street	D1	Princess Street	B1-C1
Corporation Street	B1-C1-C2	Prospect Street	A1-B1
Cross Church Street	C2	Quay Street	D3
Crossgrove Street	A1	Queen Street	C2
Day Street	D1	Queensgate	C1-C2-D2
Dundas Street	B2	Railway Street	B3
Elmwood Avenue	A4-B4	Ramsden Street	C2
Fenton Square	A1	Rook Street	B4
Firth Street	D1	St Andrews Road	D2-D3-D4
Fitzwilliam Street	A3-B3-B4	St John's Road	B4
Fox Street	B2	St Peter's Street	C3
Garforth Street	D1	Southgate	C3-C2-D2
Gasworks Street	D4	Springrove Street	A1
George Street	B2	Spring Street	A2
Great Northern Street	C4	Springwood Avenue	A2
Greenhead Road	A2	Springwood Street	A2
Half Moon Street	B2	Station Street	B3
Henry Street	B2	Trinity Street	A3-A2-B2
High Street	B2	Westgate	B2-C2
Highfields Road	A4	Upper George Street	A2
Imperial Arcade	B2	Upperhead Row	B2
John William Street	B3-C3	Venn Street	C2-C3
King Street	C2	Victoria Lane	C2
Kings Mill Lane	D1	Wakefield Road	D1-D2
Kirkgate	C2-C3	Water Street	A1-A2
Lord Street	C3	Watergate	D3
Lower Fitzwilliam Street	C4-D4	Waverley Road	A3
Lynton Avenue	A2	William Street	C4
Manchester Road	A1-B1	Wood Street	C3
Market Place	C2	Zetland Street	C2

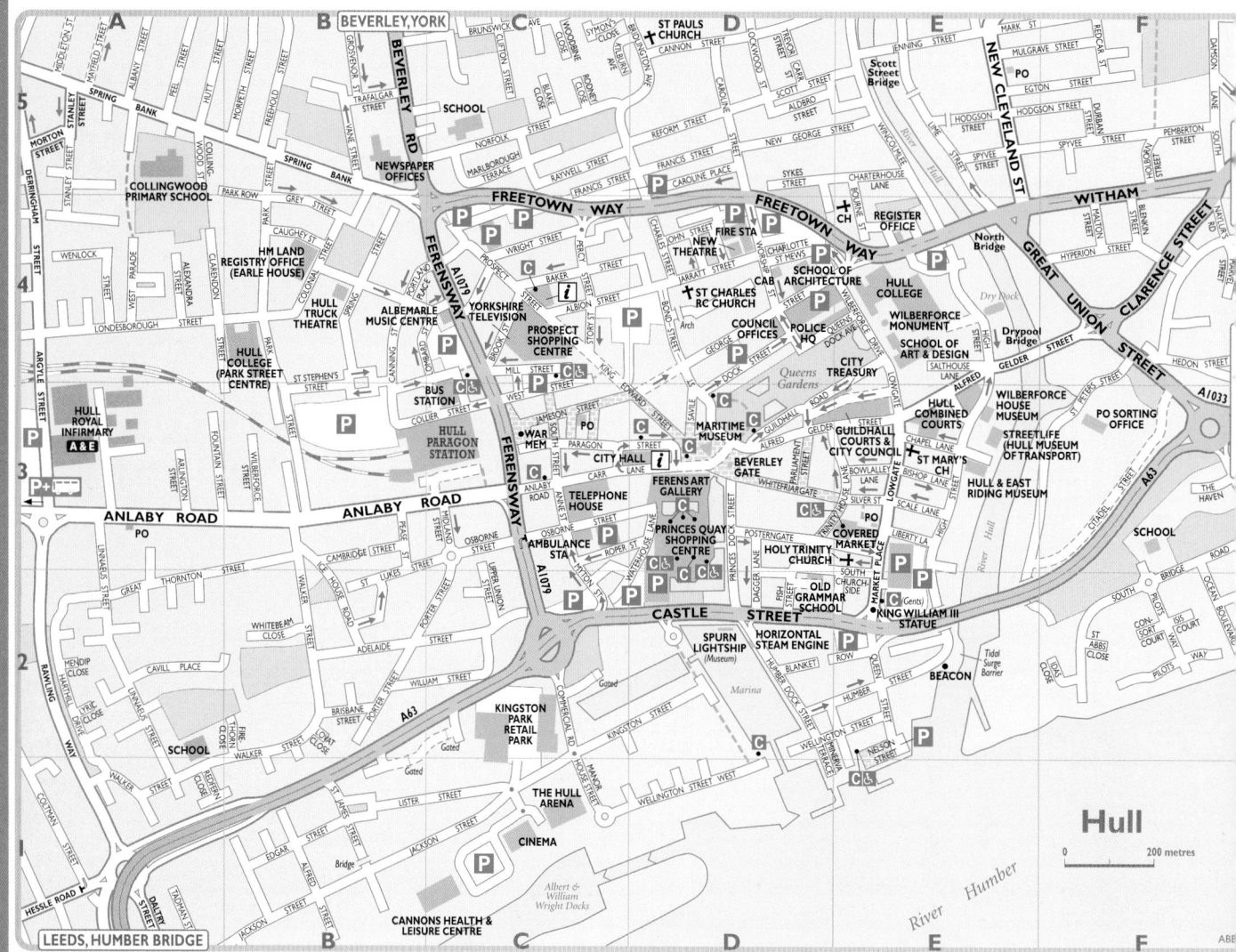

186

Hull

Hull is found on atlas page **85**,
grid reference **0829**

Adelaide Street	B2-C2	Carr Street	D5	Francis Street	C5-D5
Albany Street	A5	Castle Street	C2-D2-E2	Freehold Street	B5
Albion Street	C4-D4	Caughey Street	B4	Freetown Way	C4-D4-E4
Aldbro Street	D5	Cavill Place	A2-B2	George Street	D4
Alexandra Street	A4	Chapel Lane	E3	Great Thornton Street	A2-B3
Alfred Gelder Street	D3-E3-E4-F4	Charles Street	D4	Great Union Street	E4-F4-F3
Alfred Street	B1	Charlotte Street Mews	D4	Grey Street	B4
Anlaby Road	A3-B3-C3	Charterhouse Lane	E5	Grosvenor Street	B5
Anne Street	C3	Citadel Street	F3	Guildhall Road	D3-E4
Argyle Street	A3-A4	Clarence Street	F4-F5	Harthill Drive	A1-A2
Arlington Street	A3	Clarendon Street	A4-B3	Hedon Street	F4
Baker Street	C4-D4	Clifton Street	C5	Hessle Road	A1
Beverley Road	B5	Collier Street	B3-C3	High Street	E2-E3-E4
Bishop Lane	E3	Collingwood Street	A5	Hodgson Street	E5-F5
Blake Close	C5	Colonial Street	B4	Holborn Street	F5
Blanket Row	D2-E2	Coltman Street	A1-A2	Humber Dock Street	D2
Blenkin Street	F4	Commercial Road	C2	Humber Street	D2-E2
Bond Street	D4	Consort Court	F2	Hutt Street	A5-B5
Bourne Street	E4-E5	Dagger Lane	D2-D3	Hyperion Street	F4
Bowlalley Lane	E3	Daltry Street	A1	Ice House Road	B2-B3
Bridlington Avenue	C5-D5	Damson Lane South	F5	Idas Close	F2
Brisbane Street	B2	Derringham Street	A4-A5	Isis Court	F2
Brook Street	C4	Dock Street	D3-D4	Jackson Street	B1-C1
Brunswick Avenue	C5	Durban Street	F5	Jameson Street	C3
Cambridge Street	B3	Edgar Street	B1	Jarratt Street	D4
Canning Street	B4	Egton Street	E5-F5	Jenning Street	E5
Cannon Street	D5	Ferensway	B4-C4-C3-C2	John Street	D4
Caroline Place	D5	Firethorn Close	B2	Kilburn Avenue	B1
Caroline Street	D5	Fish Street	D2	King Edward Street	C4-D3
Carr Lane	C3-D3	Fountain Street	A3-B3	Kingston Street	C2-D2
				Liberty Lane	E3
				Lime Street	E4-E5
				Linnaeus Street	A1-A2-A3

Lister Street	B1-C1	Parliament Street	D3	Spring Bank	A5-B5-B4
Lockwood Street	D5	Pease Street	B3	Spring Street	B4
Lombard Street	B4-C4	Peel Street	A5	Spyvee Street	E5-F5
Londesborough Street	A4	Pemberton Street	F5	Stanley Street	A4-A5
Lovat Close	B2	Percy Street	C4	Story Street	C4
Lowgate	E3-E4	Pilots Way	F2	Sykes Street	D5
Lyric Close	A2	Porter Street	B2-C2-C3	Symon's Close	C5
Malton Street	F4	Portland Place	B4-C4	Tadman Street	A1
Manor House Street	C1	Posterngate	D3	The Haven	F3
Mark Street	E5-F5	Princes Dock Street	D2-D3	Trafalgar Street	B5
Market Place	E2-E3	Prospect Street	C4	Trevor Street	D5
Marlborough Terrace	C5	Queen Street	E2	Trinity House Lane	D3-E3
Marvel Street	F4	Queens Dock Avenue	D4-E4	Upper Union Street	C2-C3
Mayfield Street	A5	Rawling Way	A1-A2	Vane Street	B5
Mendip Close	A2	Raywell Street	C5	Walker Street	A1-B2-B3
Middleton Street	A5	Redcar Street	F5	Waterhouse Lane	C2-D3
Midland Street	C3	Redfern Close	A1	Wellington Street	D2-E2
Mill Street	C4	Reform Street	D5	Wellington Street West	C1-D1
Minerva Terrace	D1-D2	Rodney Close	C5	Wenlock Street	A4
Morpeth Street	B5	Roper Street	C3-D3	West Parade	A4
Morton Street	A5	St Abbs Close	F2	West Street	C3-C4
Mulgrave Street	E5-F5	St James Street	B1	Whitebeam Close	B2
Myton Street	C2-C3	St Lukes Street	B2-C3	Whitefriargate	D3-E3
Naylur's Road	F4	St Peters Street	F3-F4	Wilberforce Drive	E4
Nelson Street	E1-E2	St Stephen's Street	B3-B4	Wilberforce Street	B3
New Cleveland Street	E4-E5	Salthouse Lane	E4	William Street	B2-C2
New George Street	D5-E5	Savile Street	D3-D4	Wincolmlee	E4-E5
Norfolk Street	B5-C5	Scale Lane	E3	Witham	F4-F5
Ocean Boulevard	F2-F3	Scott Street	D5-E5	Woodbine Close	C5
Osborne Street	C3-D3	Silver Street	E3	Worship Street	D4
Paragon Street	C3-D3	South Bridge Road	F2-F3	Wright Street	C4
Park Row	A5-B4	South Churchside	E2-E3		
Park Street	B3-B4-B5	South Street	C3		

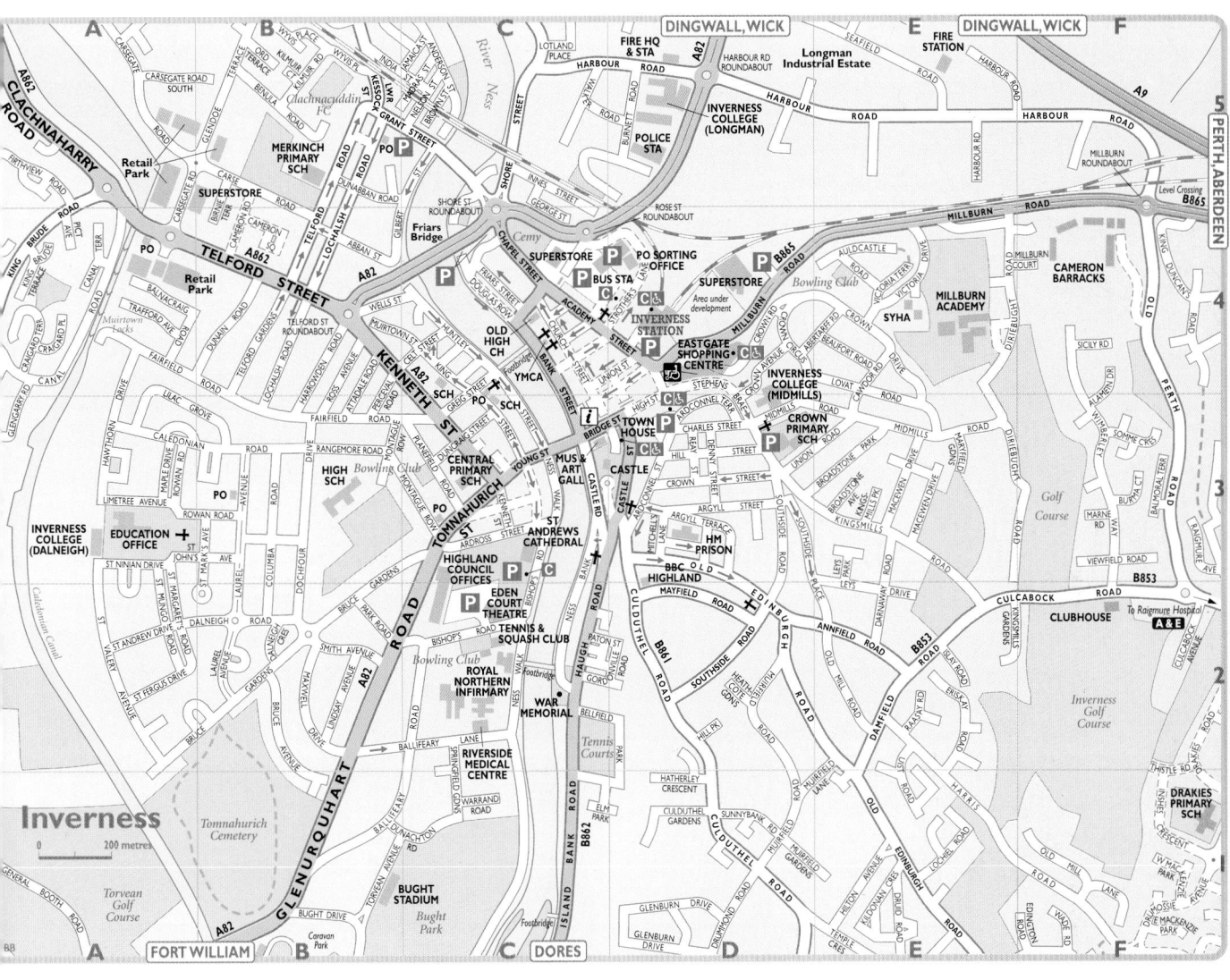

nverness

verness is found on atlas page **140**,
d reference **6645**

ban Street	B4	Burma Court	F3	Dalneigh Crescent	B2	Haugh Road	C2-C3	Madras Street	B5-C5	St Margaret's Drive	A2
ertarff Road	D4-E4	Burnett Road	D5	Dalneigh Road	A2-B2	Hawthorn Drive	A3-A4	Maple Drive	A3	St Mary's Avenue	B2-B3
ademy Street	C4-D4	Caledonian Road	A3-B3	Damfield Road	E1-E2	Heathcote Gardens	D2	Marne Road	F3	St Mungo Road	A2
dross Street	C3	Cameron Road	B4	Darnaway Road	E2-E3	High Street	D3	Maryfield Gardens	E5	St Ninian Drive	A3
mein Drive	F3-F4	Cameron Square	B4	Denny Street	D3	Hill Park	D2	Maxwell Drive	B2	St Valery Avenue	A2-A3
derson Street	C5	Canal Road	A4	Diriebught Road	E2-E3-F3-E4	Hill Street	D3	Mayfield Road	D2	Seafield Road	D5-E5
nfield Road	D2-E2	Canal Terrace	A4	Dochfour Drive	B2-B3	Hillburn Road	D4-E4-F4	Midmills Road	D3-E3	Shore Street	C4-C5
lconnel Street	D3	Carse Road	B4-B5	Douglas Row	C4	Hilton Avenue	E1	Millburn Court	F4	Sicily Road	F4
lconnel Terrace	D3	Carsegate Road	A4-A5	Drakies Road	F1-F2	Huntly Street	C3-C4	Millburn Road	D4-E4-F4	Smith Avenue	B2
gyll Street	D3	Carsegate Road South	A5-B5	Druid Road	E1	India Street	B5-C5	Mitchells Lane	D3	Somme Crescent	F3
gyll Terrace	D3	Castle Road	C3	Drummond Road	D1	Innes Street	C4-C5	Montague Row	B3-C3	Southside Place	D3-E2
adale Road	B3-B4	Castle Street	D3	Drumossie Avenue	F1	Inshes Crescent	F1	Muirfield Gardens	D1-E1	Southside Road	D2-D3
dcastle Road	E4	Cawdor Road	E3-E4	Dunabban Road	B4-B5	Island Bank Road	C1-C2	Muirfield Lane	D1-E1	Springfield Gardens	C1-C2
ifeary Lane	B2-C2	Celt Street	C4	Dunachton Gardens	B1-C1	Islay Road	E2	Muirfield Road	D1-D2	Stephens Brae	D3
ifeary Road	B1-C1-C2	Chapel Street	C4	Dunain Road	B4	Jamaica Street	C5	Muirtown Street	B4-C4	Strother's Lane	D4
moral Terrace	F3	Charles Street	D3	Duncraig Street	C3	Kenneth Street	B4-C3	Nelson Street	C5	Sunnybank Road	D1
nacraig Road	A4	Church Street	C3-C4	East Mackenzie Park	F1	Kildonan Crescent	E1	Ness Bank	C2-C3	Telford Gardens	B3-B4
nk Street	C3-C4	Clachnaharry Road	A5	Edington Road	E1-F1	Kilmuir Court	B5	Ness Walk	C2-C3	Telford Road	B4-B5
aufort Road	E4	Columba Road	B2-B3	Elm Park	C1-D1	Kilmuir Road	B5	Old Edinburgh Road	D3-D2-E2-E1	Temple Crescent	E1
lfield Park	C2-D2-D1	Craigard Place	A4	Eriskay Road	E1-E2	King Brude Road	A4-A5	Old Mill Lane	F1	Thistle Road	F1
nula Road	B5	Craigard Terrace	A4	Fairfield Road	A4-B3-C3	King Brude Terrace	A4	Old Mill Road	E2	Tomnahurich Street	C3
nie Terrace	B4-B5	Crown Avenue	D3-D4	Firthview Road	A5	King Duncan's Road	F4	Old Perth Road	F2-F3-F4	Torvean Avenue	B1
dge Street	C3-D3	Crown Circus	D4	Friars Street	C4	King Street	C3-C4	Ord Terrace	B5	Trafford Avenue	A4
dstone Avenue	E3	Crown Drive	D4-E4	General Booth Road	A1	Kingmills Road	D3-E3-E2	Park Road	B2	Uist Road	E1-E2
dstone Park	D3-E3	Crown Road	D3	George Street	C4-C5	Kingsmills Gardens	E2-F2	Paton Street	C2-D2	Union Road	D3-E3
wn Street	C5	Crown Street	D3	Gilbert Street	B4-C5	Kingsmills Park	E3	Perceval Road	B3-B4	Union Street	C3-C4-D4
uce Avenue	B1-B2	Culcabock Avenue	F2	Glenburn Drive	D1	Laurel Avenue	B2-B3	Pict Avenue	A4	Victoria Drive	E4
uce Gardens	A1-A2-B2-B3	Culcabock Road	E2-F2	Glendoe Terrace	B5	Leys Drive	E2	Planefield Road	C3	Victoria Terrace	E4
ght Drive	B1	Culduthel Gardens	D1	Glengarry Road	A3	Leys Park	E2-E3	Raasay Road	E2	Viewfield Road	F3
		Culduthel Road	D1-D2-D3	Glenurquhart Road	B1-B2-C2	Lilac Grove	A3-B3	Raigmore Avenue	F3	Wade Road	F1
				Gordonville Road	C2-D2	Lindsay Avenue	B2	Rangemore Road	B3	Walker Road	C5-D5
				Grant Street	B5-C5	Lochalsh Road	B3-B4-B5	Reay Street	D5	Warrand Road	C1
				Greig Street	C3-C4	Lochiel Road	E1	Ross Avenue	B3-B4	Wells Street	B4-C4
				Harbour Road	C5-D5-E5-F5	Lotland Place	C5	Rowan Road	A3-B3	West Mackenzie Park	F1
				Harris Road	E2-F1-F1	Lovat Road	E3-E4	St Andrew Drive	A2	Wimberley Way	F2-F3-F4
				Harrowden Road	B3-B4	Lower Kessock Street	B5	St Fergus Drive	A2	Wyvis Place	B5
				Hatherley Crescent	D1	Macewen Drive	E3	St John's Avenue	A3-B3		

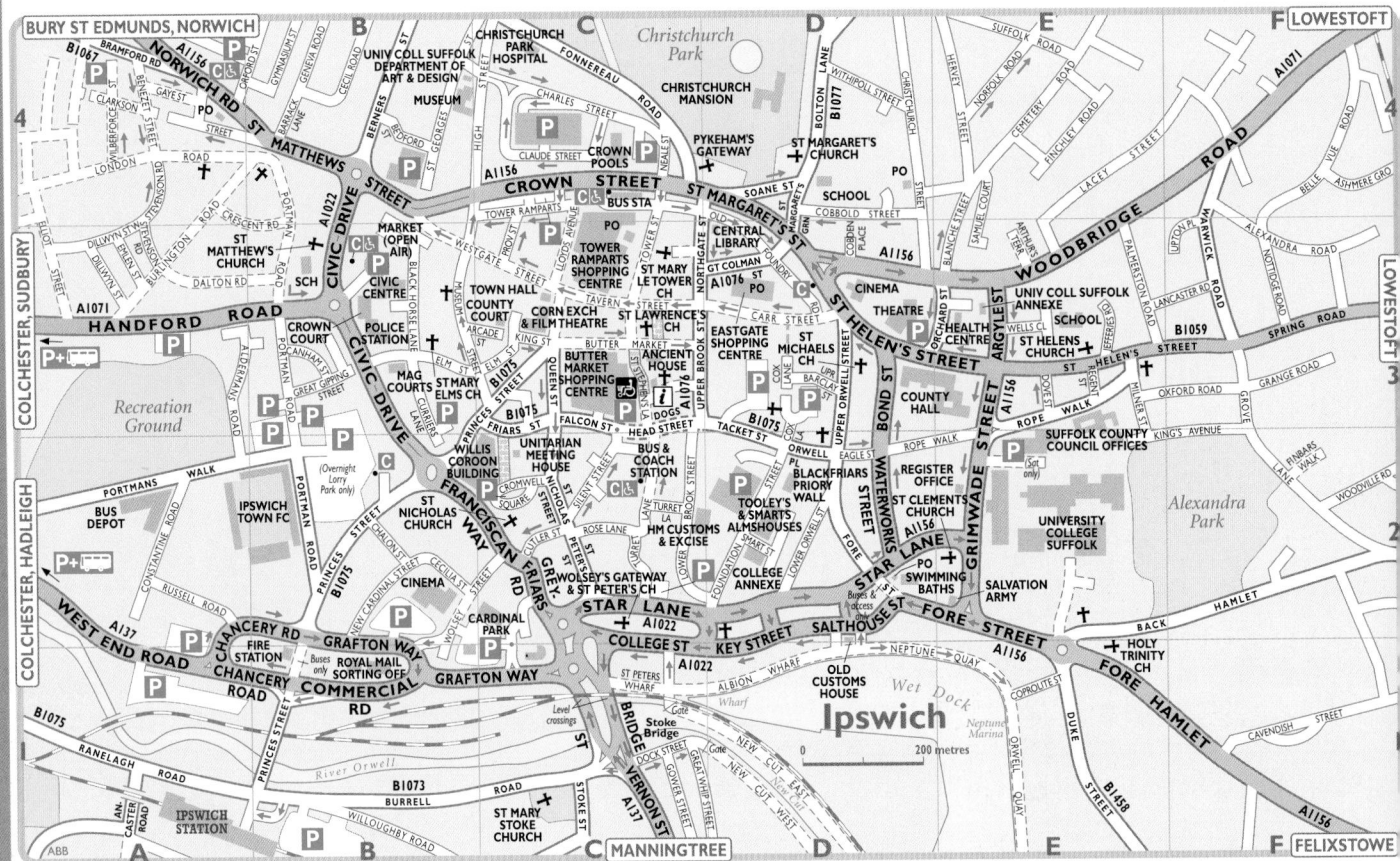

Ipswich

Ipswich is found on atlas page **54**,
grid reference **1644**

Albion Wharf	C1-D1	Cox Lane	D3	Jefferies Road	E3	St Matthews Street	B4
Aldermans Road	A2-A3	Crescent Road	A4	Key Street	C1-D2	St Nicholas Street	C2
Alexandra Road	F3-F4	Cromwell Square	C2	King's Avenue	E2-F3	St Peter's Street	C2
Ancaster Road	A1	Crown Street	B4-C4	King Street	C3	St Peters Wharf	C1
Arcade Street	B3-C3	Curriers Lane	B2-B3	Lacey Street	E3-F4	St Stephen's Lane	C3
Argyle Street	E3	Cutler Street	C2	Lancaster Road	E3-F3	Salthouse Street	D2
Arthur's Terrace	E3	Dalton Road	A3-B3	Lloyds Avenue	C3-C4	Samuel Court	E3-E4
Ashmere Grove	F4	Devonshire Road	A2	London Road	A4-B4	Silent Street	C2
Back Hamlet	E2-F2	Dillwyn Street	A3	Lower Brook Street	C2-C3	Smart Street	D2
Barrack Lane	B4	Dillwyn Street West	A3-A4	Lower Orwell Street	D2	Soane Street	D4
Bedford Street	B4	Dock Street	C1	Milner Street	E2-E3	Spring Road	F3
Bellevue Road	F3-F4	Dogs Head Street	C3	Museum Street	B3-C3	Star Lane	C2-E2
Benezet Street	A4	Dove Street	E3	Neale Street	C4	Stevenson Road	A3-A4
Berners Street	B4	Duke Street	E1	Neptune Quay	D1-E1	Stoke Street	C1
Black Horse Lane	B3	Eagle Street	D2	New Cardinal Street	B2	Suffolk Road	E4
Blanche Street	E3-E4	Elliot Street	A3-A4	New Cut East	C1-D1	Tacket Street	D2-D3
Bolton Lane	D4	Elm Street	B3-C3	New Cut West	C1-D1	Tavern Street	C3
Bond Street	D2-D3	Emlen Street	A3	Norfolk Road	E4	Tower Ramparts	B4-C4
Bramford Road	A4	Falcon Street	C3	Northgate Street	C3-D4	Tower Street	C3-C4
Bridge Street	C1	Finbars Walk	F2	Norwich Road	A4-B4	Turret Lane	C2
Burlington Road	A3-B4	Finchley Road	E4	Nottidge Road	F3	Upper Barclay Street	D3
Burrell Road	B1-C1	Fonnereau Road	C4	Old Foundry Road	D4-D3	Upper Brook Street	C3
Butter Market	C3	Fore Hamlet	E1-F1	Orchard Street	D3-E3	Upper Orwell Street	D2-D3
Canham Street	B3	Fore Street	D2-E1	Orford Street	A4-B4	Upton Place	F3-F4
Carr Street	D3	Foundation Street	D2	Orwell Place	D2	Vernon Street	C1
Cavendish Street	F1	Franciscan Way	B2-C2	Orwell Quay	E1	Warwick Road	F3-F4
Cecil Road	B4	Friars Street	C3	Oxford Road	E3-F3	Waterworks Street	D2
Cecilia Street	B2	Gaye Street	A4	Palmerston Road	E3	Wells Close	E3
Cemetery Road	E4	Geneva Road	B4	Portman Road	B2-B4	West End Road	A1-A2
Chalon Street	B2	Gower Street	C1	Portmans Walk	A2-B2	Westgate Street	B4-C3
Chancery Road	B1-A1-A2-B2	Grafton Way	B2-B1-C1	Princes Street	A1-C3	Wilberforce Street	A4
Charles Street	C4	Grange Road	F3	Queen Street	C3	Willoughby Road	B1
Christchurch Street	D3-D4	Great Colman Street	D3	Ranelagh Road	A1	Withipoll Street	D4
Civic Drive	B2-B4	Great Gipping Street	B3	Regent Street	E3	Wolsey Street	B1-C2
Clarkson Street	A4-B4	Great Whip Street	C1-D1	Rope Walk	D2-E3	Woodbridge Road	D3-F4
Claude Street	C4	Grey Friars Road	C2	Rose Lane	C2	Woodville Road	F2
Cobbold Street	D4	Grimwade Street	E2-E3	Russell Road	A2		
College Street	C1-C2	Grove Lane	F2-F3	St Georges Street	B4		
Commercial Road	B1	Gymnasium Street	B4	St Helen's Street	D3-F3		
Constantine Road	A2	Handford Road	A3-B3	St Margaret's Green	D4		
Coprolite Street	E1	Hervey Street	E4	St Margaret's Street	C4-D3		
		High Street	B4-C4				

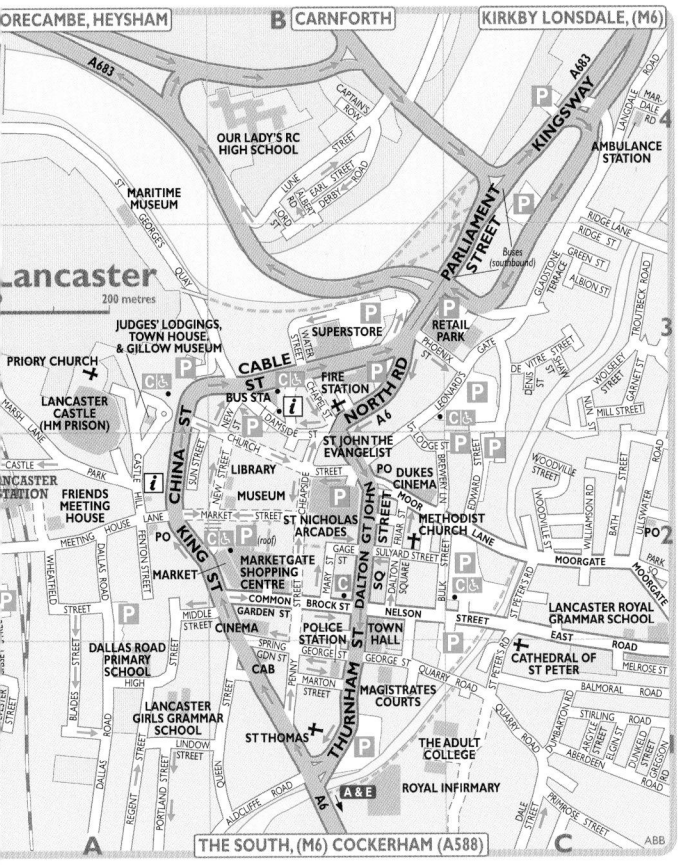

Lancaster

Lancaster is found on atlas page **87**,
grid reference **476**I

Aberdeen Road	C1	Langdale Road	C4	Wheatfield Street	A2
Albert Road	B4	Lindow Street	A1-B1	Williamson Road	C2
Albion Street	C3	Lodge Street	B2-B3	Wolseley Street	C3
Aldcliffe Road	B1	Long Marsh Lane	A2-A3	Woodville Street	C2
Argyle Street	C1	Lord Street	B4		
Balmoral Road	C1	Lune Street	B4		
Bath Street	C2	Mardale Road	C4		
Blades Street	A1-A2	Market Street	A2-B2		
Brewery Lane	B2	Marton Street	B1		
Brock Street	B2	Mary Street	B2		
Bulk Street	B2-C2	Meeting House Lane	A2		
Cable Street	B3	Melrose Street	C1		
Captain's Row	B4	Middle Street	A2-B2		
Castle Hill	A2	Mill Street	C3		
Castle Park	A2	Moor Lane	B2-C2		
Chapel Street	B3	Moorgate	C2		
Cheapside	B2	Nelson Street	B2-C2		
China Street	A2-A3	New Street	B2-B3		
Church Street	A3-B2	North Road	B3		
Common Garden Street	B2	Nun Street	C2-C3		
Dale Street	C1	Park Square	C2		
Dallas Road	A1-A2	Parliament Street	C3-C4		
Dalton Square	B2	Penny Street	B1-B2		
Damside Street	B2-B3	Phoenix Street	B3-C3		
De Vitre Street	C3	Portland Street	A1		
Denis Street	C3	Primrose Street	C1		
Derby Road	B4	Quarry Road	B1-C1		
Dumbarton Road	C1	Queen Street	B1		
Dunkeld Street	C1	Regent Street	A1		
Earl Street	B4	Ridge Lane	C3-C4		
East Road	C1-C2	Ridge Street	C3		
Edward Street	C2	St George's Quay	A4-A3-B3		
Elgin Street	C1	St Leonard's Gate	B2-B3-C3		
Fenton Street	A2	St Peter's Road	C1-C2		
Friar Street	B2	Shaw Street	C3		
Gage Street	B2	Sibsey Street	A1-A2		
Garnet Street	C3	Spring Garden Street	B1-B2		
George Street	B1	Stirling Road	C1		
Gladstone Terrace	C3	Sulyard Street	B2		
Great John Street	B2	Sun Street	A2		
Green Street	C3	Sylvester Street	A1		
Gregson Road	C1	Thurnham Street	B1-B2		
High Street	A1-A2	Troutbeck Road	C3		
King Street	A2-B2	Ullswater Road	C2-C3		
Kingsway	C4	Water Street	B3		

189

Llandudno

Llandudno is found on atlas page **69**,
grid reference **788**2

Abbey Road	A3-C4	Herkomer Road	A2
Albert Street	B2-C3	Hill Terrace	B4-C4
Anglesey Road	A3-A4	Howard Road	C2
Argyll Road	C2	Hywell Place	C2
Arvon Avenue	B3-B4	King's Avenue	B3
Augusta Street	C2-C3	King's Road	B1-B2
Bodafon Street	C3	Knowles Road	B1-B2
Bodnant Road	C1	Lees Road	B2
Brookes Street	B3-C3	Lloyd Street	B3-C3
Bryniau Road	A2-B1	Lloyd Street West	A2
Builder Street	C2	Llwynon Road	A4-B4
Builder Street West	B1-C2	Madoc Street	B3-C3
Cae Mawr	B1	Maelgwn Road	B3
Caroline Road	B3-C3	Maesdu Road	B1-C1
Chapel Street	B3	Mostyn Street	B3-C3
Charlton Street	C3	Mowbray Road	B1
Church Close	A2	Norman Road	C2
Church Walks	A3-B4	North Parade	C4
Clement Avenue	B3	Oxford Road	C2
Clifton Road	B3	Plas Road	B4
Clonnel Street	C3	Rectory Lane	B3-B4
Conwy Road	C2-C3	St Andrew's Avenue	B2-B3
Council Street West	C2	St Andrew's Place	B3
Cwlach Road	B3-B4	St David's Road	B2-B3
Cwm Road	C1-C2	St George's Place	C3
Dale Road	A2	St Mary's Road	B3-C2
Deganwy Avenue	B3	St Seiriol's Road	B2-B3
Denness Place	B2	Somerset Street	C3
Dinas Road	B2	South Parade	B4-C3
Dyffryn Road	B1-B2	The Oval	A2-B3
Eryl Place	B2	The Parade	C3
Fford Dewi	C1	Thorpe Street	C2
Fford Dulyn	B1-B2	Trevor Street	B3
Fford Dwyfor	C1	Trinity Avenue	B1-C3
Fford Elisabeth	C1	Trinity Crescent	A1-B1
Fford Gwynedd	C1	Trinity Square	C3
Fford Penrhyn	C1-C2	Tudno Street	B4
Fford yr Orsedd	C1	Ty-Gwyn Road	B4
Fford Ysbyty	B1-C1	Ty Isa Road	C3-C4
Garage Street	C2-C3	Tyn-y-Coed Road	A4
Gloddaeth Avenue	A2-B3	Upper Mostyn Street	B4
Gloddaeth Street	B3	Vaughan Street	C2-C3
Great Ormes Road	A1-A3	West Parade	A2-A3
Haulfre Gardens	A3	Winllan Avenue	A2-B2
Herkomer Crescent	A1-A2	York Road	B3

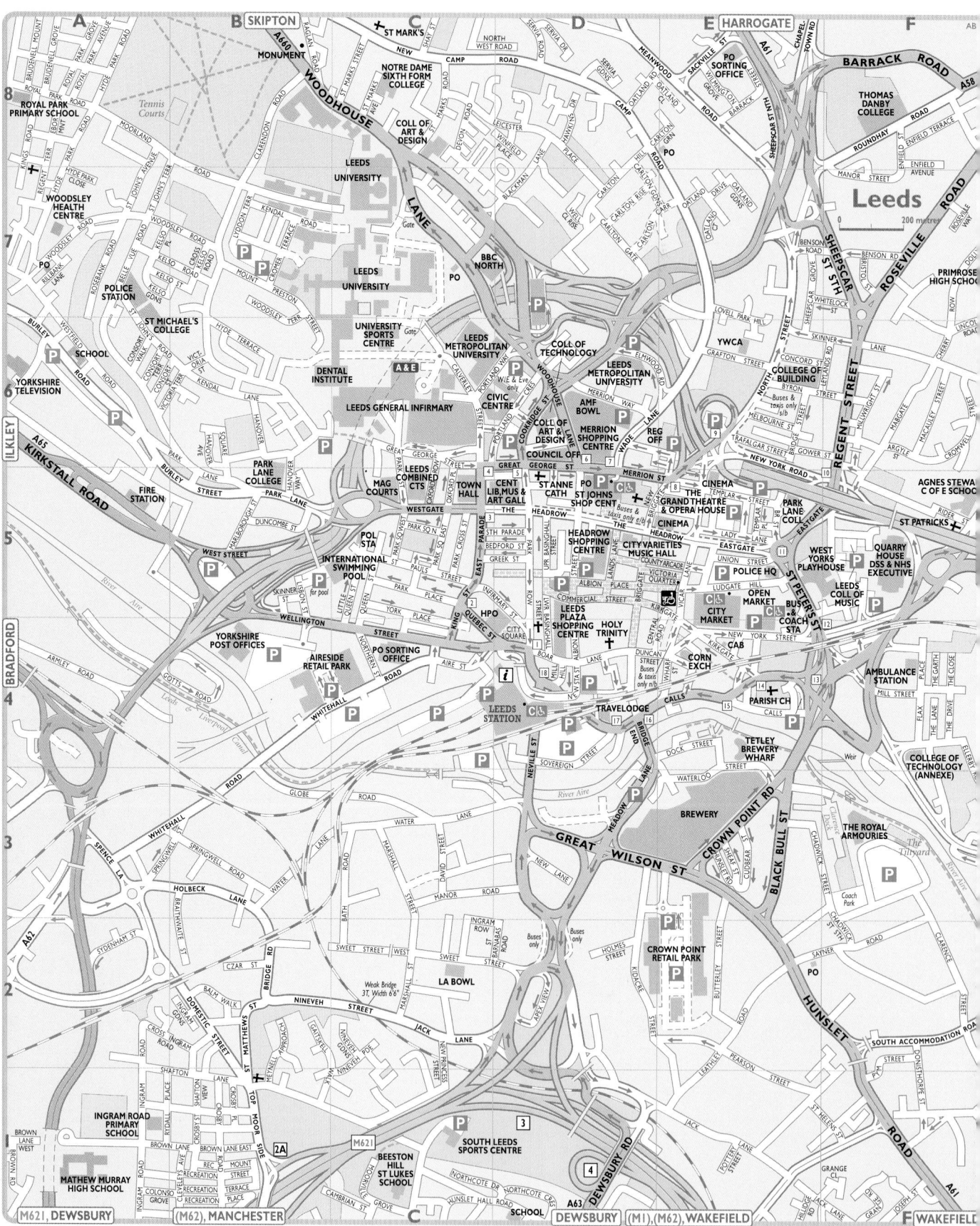

Luton

Luton

Luton is found on atlas page **38**,
grid reference **0921**

Adelaide Street	A2-B2	Guildford Street	B3-C3	Strathmore Avenue	C1
Albert Road	B1-C1	Hart Hill Drive	C3	Studley Road	A4
Alma Street	A2-B3	Hartley Road	C3-C4	Surrey Street	C1
Back Street	C4	Hastings Street	A1-B2	Tavistock Street	B1
Biscot Road	A4	Havelock Street	B4-C4	Taylor Street	C4
Boyle Close	B4	Hibbert Street	B1	Telford Way	A3
Bridge Street	B3	High Town Road	B3-C4	The Shires	A4
Brook Street	A4	Hillside Road	A4	Union Street	B1
Brunswick Street	C4	Hitchin Road	C3-C4	Upper George Street	A2-B2
Burr Street	C3-C4	Holly Street	B1	Vestry Close	A3
Buxton Road	A2	Inkerman Street	A2-A3	Vicarage Street	C2
Cardiff Grove	A2	John Street	B2-C3	Villa Road	A4-B4
Cardiff Road	A2	Jubilee Street	C4	Wellington Street	A1-B2
Cardigan Street	A3	King Street	B2	Wenlock Street	B4-C4
Castle Street	B1-B2	Kingsland Road	C1	William Street	B4
Chapel Street	B1-B2	Latimer Road	B1-C1	Windsor Street	A1-B1
Charles Street	C4	Liverpool Road	A3	Winsdon Road	A1-A2
Chequer Street	C1	Manor Road	C1-C2	York Street	C4
Chiltern Rise	A1	Meyrick Avenue	A2		
Church Street	B2-C2	Midland Road	D3-C3		
Cobden Street	C4	Mill Street	B3		
Collingdon Street	A3	Milton Road	A1		
Concorde Street	C4	Moor Street	A4		
Crawley Green Road	C2	Moulton Rise	C3		
Crawley	A3-A4	Napier Road	A2		
Crescent Rise	C3-C4	New Bedford Street	A4-B3		
Crescent Road	C3	New Town Street	B1-C1		
Cromwell Road	A4	North Street	B4-C4		
Cumberland Street	C1-C2	Old Bedford Road	A4-B3		
Dallow Road	A3	Park Street	C1-C2		
Dudley Street	B3-B4	Park Street West	B2-C2		
Duke Street	C3-C4	Power Court	C2		
Dumfries Street	A2-B1	Princess Street	A2		
Duns Place	A2-B2	Regent Street	B1-B2		
Dunstable Road	A4-C2	Reginald Street	B4		
Elizabeth Street	A1-B1	Rothesay Road	A2		
Essex Close	C1	Russell Rise	A1		
Farley Hill	A1-B1	Russell Street	A1-B1		
Francis Street	A3-A4	St Mary's Road	C2-C3		
Frederick Street	B4	St Saviours Crescent	A1		
George Street	B2	Salisbury Road	A1-A2		
George Street West	B2	Silver Street	B3		
Gloucester Road	C2	South Road	B1		
Gordon Street	B2-B3	Stanley Street	A1-A2		
Grove Road	A2-A3	Station Road	B3-C3		

191

Leeds

Leeds is found on atlas page **82**,
grid reference **2932**

e Street	C4	Chadwick Street	E3-F3	Flax Place	F4	Lovell Park Hill	E6-E7	Park Row	D4-D5	Sheaf Street	E3
ion Place	D5	Chadwick Street South	F2-F3	Gaitskell Walk	B2-C2-B1	Lower Basinghall Street	D4-D5	Park Square East	C5	Sheepscar Grove	E6-E7
ion Street	D4-D5	Chapeltown Road	E8	Globe Road	B3-C3	Ludgate Hill	E4	Park Square North	C5	Sheepscar Street North	E8
ex View	D2	Cherry Row	F6-F7	Gotts Road	A4-B4	Lyddon Terrace	B7	Park Square West	C5	Sheepscar Street South	E7-F7
gyle Street	F6	City Square	D4	Gower Street	E6-F6	Mabgate	F5-F6	Park Street	C5-C6	Skinner Lane	E6-F6
nley Road	A4	Clarence Street	F2-F3	Grafton Street	E6	Macauley Street	F6	Pearson Street	E1-E2	Skinner Street	B5
m Walk	B2	Clarendon Road	B7-B8	Grange Close	F1	Manor Road	C3-D3	Portland Crescent	C6-D6	South Accommodation Road	F2
rack Road	F8	Cleveleys Avenue	B1	Grange Road	F1	Manor Street	F7	Portland Way	C6-D6	South Parade	C5-D5
rack Street	E8	Colonso Grove	A1-B1	Great George Street	C6-D6	Marlborough Street	B5	Pottery Street	E1	Sovereign Street	D4
h Road	C2-C3	Commercial Street	D5	Great Wilson Street	D3-E3	Marshall Street	C2-C3	Pym Street	F1-F2	Spence Lane	A3
dford Street	C5-D5	Concord Street	E6	Greek Street	C5-D5	Meadow Lane	D3-D4	Quebec Street	C5-C4-D4	Springwell Road	B3
le Vue Road	A7	Consort Street	A6-B6	Hanover Avenue	B5-B6	Meanwood Road	D8-E8-E7	Queen Street	C4-C5	Springwell Street	A3-B3
nson Road	E7-F7	Consort Terrace	A6	Hanover Square	B6	Melbourne Street	E6	Raglan Road	B8	Sweet Street	C2-D2
ck Bull Street	D4	Consort Walk	A6	Hanover Way	B5-B6	Merrion Street	D6-E5	Recreation Mount	B1	Sweet Street West	B2-C2
ckman Lane	C7-D7-D8	Cookridge Street	D6	Hawkins Drive	D8	Merrion Way	D6	Recreation Place	B1	Sydenham Street	A2
ar Lane	D4	County Arcade	D5-E5	Hillidge Road	E1	Meynell Approach	B1-B2	Recreation Street	B1	Templar Place	E5
aithwaite Street	B2-B3	Cromer Terrace	B7	Holbeck Lane	A3-B3-B2	Mill Hill	D4	Recreation Terrace	B1	Templar Street	E5
dge End	D4	Cromwell Street	F6	Holmes Street	D2	Mill Street	F4	Regent Street	F5-F6	The Close	F4
dge Road	B2	Crosby Place	B1	Hunslet Hall Road	C1-D1	Millwright Street	F6	Regent Terrace	A7-A8	The Drive	F4
dge Street	E5-E6	Crosby Road	B1	Hunslet Road	E2-F2-F1	Moorland Road	A8-B8-B7	Rider Street	F6	The Garth	F4
ggate	D4-D5	Crosby Street	B1	Hyde Park Close	A7	Moorville Grove	C1	Rillbank Lane	A7	The Headrow	D5-E5
stol Street	F7	Cross Ingram Road	A2-B2	Hyde Park Road	A7-A8	Mount Preston Street	B6-B7	Rosebank Road	A7	The Lane	F4
own Lane	A1-B1	Cross Kelso Road	B7	Hyde Terrace	B6	Neville Street	D3-D4	Roseville Road	F7-F8	Top Moor Side	B1
own Lane East	B1	Crown Point Road	E3	Infirmary Street	C5-D5-D4	New Briggate	D5-E5	Roseville Way	F7	Trafalgar Street	E6
own Lane West	A1	Cudbear Street	E3	Ingram Gardens	B2	New Camp Road	C8-D8	Roundhay Road	F8	Union Street	E5
own Road	A1	Czar Street	B2	Ingram Road	A1-A2	New Lane	D3	Royal Park Avenue	A8	Upper Basinghall Street	D5
udenell Grove	A8	David Street	C3	Ingram Row	C2-C3	New Princess Street	C1-C2	Royal Park Grove	A8	Vicar Lane	E5
udenell Mount	A8	Devon Road	C8	Jack Lane	C2-D1-E1-F1	New Station Street	D4	Royal Park Road	A8	Victoria Quarter	D5-E5
A6-A7		Dewsbury Road	D1	Joseph Street	F1	New York Road	E5-E6	Rydall Place	A1-B1	Victoria Street	B6
rley Road	A6-A5-B5	Dock Street	D4-E4	Kelso Gardens	A7	New York Street	E4	St Barnabas Road	D2	Victoria Terrace	A6-B6
rley Street	E2-E3	Dolly Lane	F7	Kelso Place	A7	Nineveh Gardens	C2	St Helens Street	E1-F1	Wade Lane	D6
tterley Street	E6-F6	Domestic Street	B1-B2	Kelso Road	A7-B7	Nineveh Parade	C1-C2	St John's Avenue	A7-A8	Water Lane	B3-C3-D3
ron Street	D4-E4	Donisthorpe Street	F1-F2	Kelso Street	A7-B7	Nineveh Street	B2-C2	St John's Terrace	A7-B8	Waterloo Street	E3-E4
lls	C6	Duncan Street	D4-E4	Kendal Lane	B6	North Street	E6-E7	St John's Road	A7-A6-B6	Well Close Rise	D7
lverley Street	B1-C1	Duncombe Street	B5	Kendal Road	B7-C7	North West Road	C8-D8	St Marks Avenue	C8	Wellington Street	B5-B4-C4
mbrian Street	D8-E7	East Parade	C5	Kidacre Street	D2-E2-E1	Northcote Crescent	D1	St Marks Road	C8	West Street	B5
mp Road	D8-E7	Eastgate	E5	King Street	C4-C5	Northcote Drive	C1-D1	St Marks Street	C8	Westfield Road	A6-A7
rlton Carr	D7-E7	Ebor Mount	A8	Kings Road	A7-A8	Northern Street	C4	St Matthews Street	B1-B2	Westgate	C5
rlton Gardens	D8-D7-E7	Ellerby Road	F3-F4	Kirkgate	D5-E5-E4	Oatland Close	D8-E8	St Pauls Street	C5	Wharf Street	E4
rlton Gate	D7	Elmwood Road	D6-E6	Kirkstall Road	A5-A6	Oatland Court	E7	St Peter's Street	E4-E5	Whitehall Road	A3-B3-B4-C4
rlton Green	D8-E8	Enfield Avenue	F8	Lady Lane	E5	Oatland Drive	E7	Sackville Street	E8	Whitelock Street	E7-F7
rlton Hill	D7-D8	Enfield Street	F8	Lands Lane	D5	Oatland Gardens	E7	Sayner Road	E2-F2	Wilmington Grove	E8
rlton Rise	D7	Enfield Terrace	F8	Leathley Road	E1-E2	Oatland Road	D8	Servia Drive	D8	Winfield Place	C8-D8
entral Road	D4-E4			Leicester Place	C8-D8-D7	Oxford Place	C5	Servia Gardens	D8	Woodhouse Lane	B8-C8-C7-D6
				Leylands Road	E6-F6	Oxford Row	C5-C6	Servia Road	D8	Woodsley Road	A7-B7
				Lincoln Road	F6-F7	Park Cross Street	C5	Shafton Lane	A2-A1-B1	Woodsley Terrace	B6-B7
				Lisbon Street	B5	Park Lane	A6-B6-B5	Shafton View	B1	York Place	C4-C5
				Little Queen Street	C4-C5	Park Place	C5	Shay Street	C8		

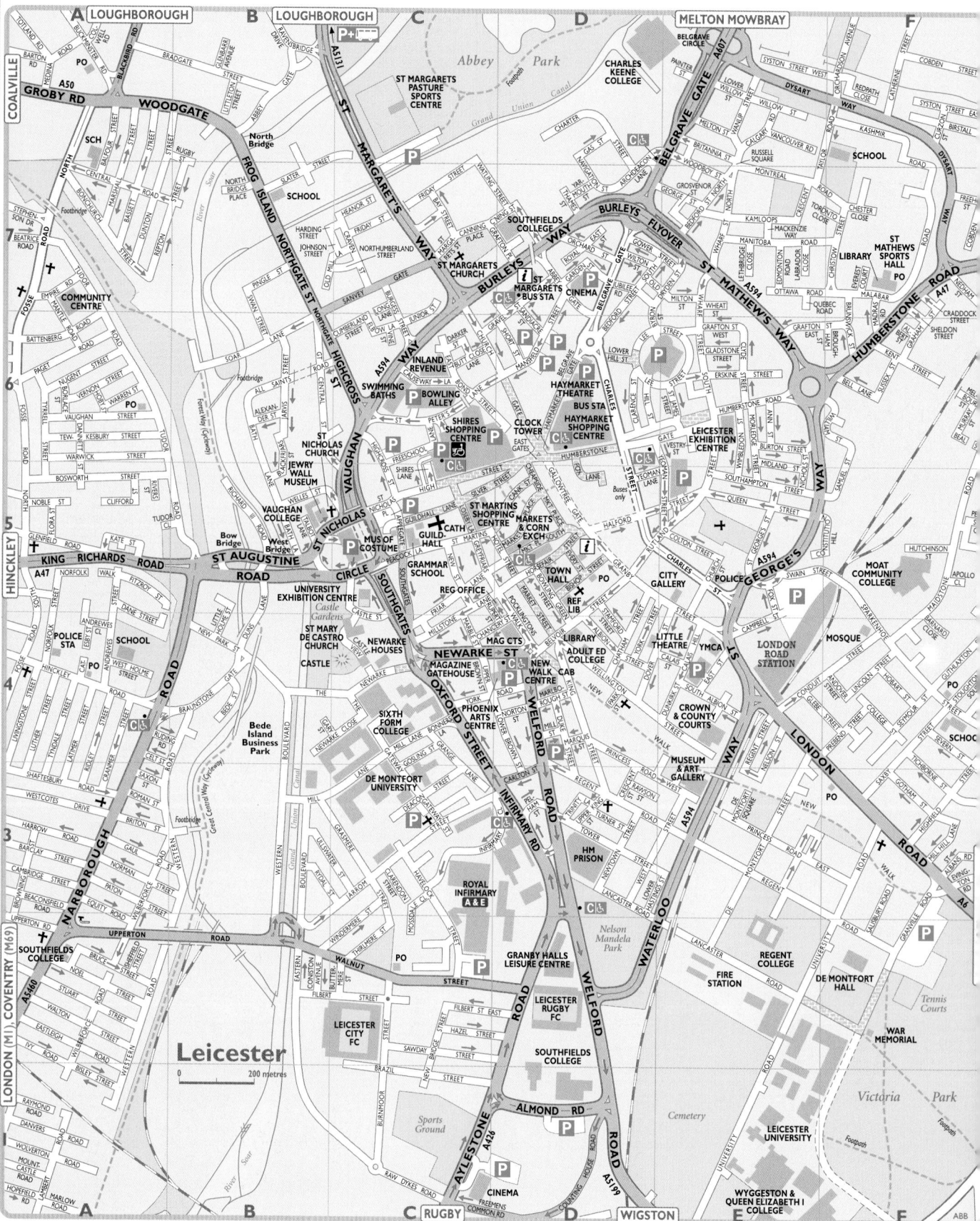

Leicester

Maidstone

Maidstone is found on atlas page **28**, grid reference **7555**

Allen Street	C4	George Street	C1	Queen Anne Road	C2-C3
Bank Street	B2	Hart Street	A1-B1-B2-A2	Reginald Road	A1
Barker Road	A1	Hastings Road	C1-C2	Romney Place	C2
Bishops Way	B2	Hayle Road	B1	St Faiths Street	B3
Bluett Street	C4	Headley Street	C4	St Peter's Street	A2-A3
Brewer Street	B3-C3-C4	High Street	B2	Sandling Road	B4
Brunswick Street	C1	Holland Road	C4	Staceys Street	B4
Buckland Hill	A3-A4	James Street	C4	Station Road	B3-B4
Buckland Road	A2-A3	James Whatman Way	A4	Terrace Road	A2
Camden Street	C4	King Street	B3-C2	Tonbridge Road	A1-A2
Charles Street	A1	Kingsley Road	C1-C2	Tufton Street	C3
Church Street	C3	Knightrider Street	B2-B1-C1	Union Street	B3-C3
College Avenue	B1	London Road	A2	Upper Stone Street	C1
College Road	B1	Lower Boxley Road	B4	Walmer Street	C4
County Road	B4-C4	Lower Stone Street	C2	Watt Tyler Way	C2
Cromwell Road	C3	Marsham Street	C3	Week Street	B3
Douglas Road	A1	Medway Street	B2	Well Road	C4
Earl Street	B3	Melville Road	C1	Westree Road	A1
Florence Road	A1	Mill Street	B2	Wheeler Street	C3-C4
Foley Street	C4	Mote Road	C1-C2	Wollett Street	C4
Foster Street	C1	Priory Road	B1-C1	Wyatt Street	C3
Gabriel's Hill	B2-C2	Pudding Lane	B2-B3	Wyke Manor Road	C3

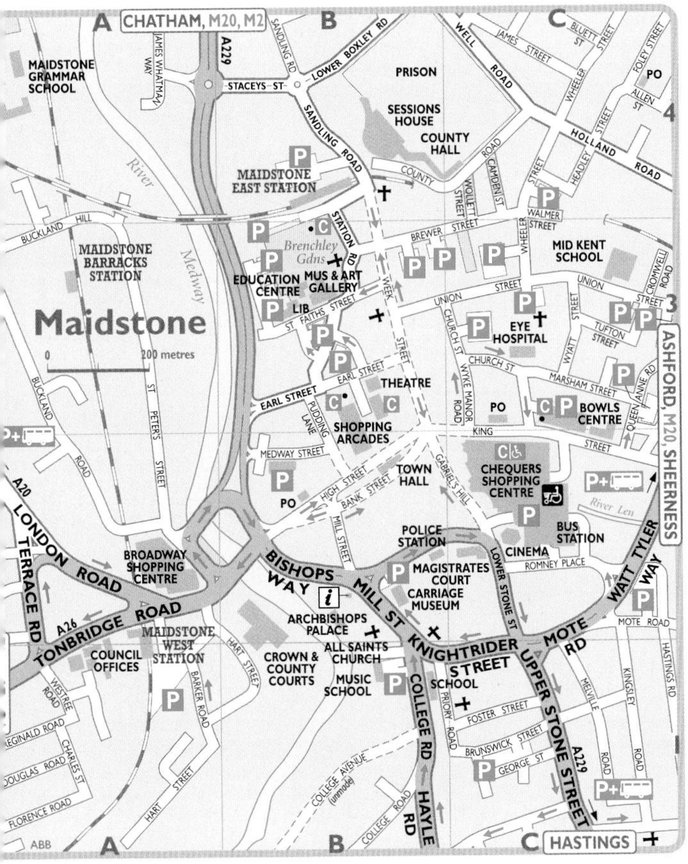
CHATHAM, M20, M2
A229
MAIDSTONE GRAMMAR SCHOOL
JAMES WHATMAN WAY
STACEYS ST
LOWER BOXLEY RD
PRISON
SESSIONS HOUSE
COUNTY HALL
SANDLING ROAD
MAIDSTONE EAST STATION
River Medway
MAIDSTONE BARRACKS STATION
BUCKLAND HILL
Brenchley Gdns
EDUCATION CENTRE
MUS & ART GALLERY
LIB
Maidstone
200 metres
MID KENT SCHOOL
EYE HOSPITAL
THEATRE
BOWLS CENTRE
SHOPPING ARCADES
TOWN HALL
CHEQUERS SHOPPING CENTRE
BUS STATION
POLICE STATION
CINEMA
MAGISTRATES COURT
CARRIAGE MUSEUM
BROADWAY SHOPPING CENTRE
LONDON ROAD
TONBRIDGE ROAD
BISHOPS WAY
ARCHBISHOPS PALACE
MAIDSTONE WEST STATION
COUNCIL OFFICES
ALL SAINTS CHURCH
CROWN & COUNTY COURTS
MUSIC SCHOOL
SCHOOL
KNIGHTRIDER STREET
UPPER STONE STREET
MOTE RD
WATT TYLER WAY
COLLEGE RD
HAYLE RD
ASHFORD, M20, SHEERNESS
HASTINGS

Leicester

Leicester is found on atlas page **62**, grid reference **5804**

bbey Gate	B8
bbey Gate	D6-D7
bert Street	F6
bion Street	D4
exander Street	B6
l Saints Road	B6
mond Road	D1
ndover Street	F4
ndrewes Close	A4
ndrewes Street	A4-A5
nn Street	E6
pollo Close	F5
pplegate	C5
rchdeacon Lane	D7-D8
ylestone Road	C1-D1-D2
alfour Street	A7-A8
arclay Street	A3
arnard Close	F4-F5
arton Road	A8
assett Street	A7-A8
ath Lane	B5-B6
attenberg Road	A6
ay Street	C7
eaconsfield Road	A3
eal Street	F6
eatrice Road	A7
ede Street	B4
edford Street North	E7
edford Street South	D6-D7
elgrave Circle	E8
elgrave Gate	D6-D7-E8
ell Lane	F6
elvoir Street	D4-D5
rstall Street	F8
shop Street	D5
isley Street	A1
lackbird Road	A8
lackfriars Street	B5-B6
onchurch Street	A7
onners Lane	C4
orlace Street	A6
osworth Street	A5
owling Green Street	D4-D5
radgate Street	A8-B8
raunstone Gate	A4-B4
razil Street	C1-C2
ritannia Street	E8
riton Street	A3
rougham Street	F6
rowning Street	A3
ruce Street	A2
runswick Street	E6-F6
uckminster Road	A8
urgess Street	C6-C7
Burleys Flyover	D7-E7
Burleys Way	C7-D7
Burnmoor Street	C1-C2
Burton Street	E6
Butt Close Lane	C6
Buttermere Street	C2
Byron Street	D6-D7
Calais Hill	E4
Calais Street	E4
Calgary Road	E8
Cambridge Street	A3
Campbell Street	E4-E5
Cank Street	D5
Canning Place	C7
Canning Street	C7-D7
Carlton Street	D3
Castle Street	C4-C5
Castle View	C4
Catesby Street	A4
Catherine Street	F8
Causeway Lane	C6
Celt Street	A4
Central Road	A7-B7
Chancery Street	C4-D4
Charles Street	D6-D5-E5
Charter Street	D8
Chatham Street	D4-D5
Cheapside	D5
Chester Close	F7
Christow Street	F7
Church Gate	C7-C6-D6
Church Street	E5
Clarence Street	D6
Clarendon Street	C3
Clifford Street	A5
Clyde Street	E6
Cobden Street	F7-F8
College Street	F4
Colton Street	E5
Colwell Road	A8
Conduit Street	E4-F4
Coniston Avenue	B2
Constitution Hill	E5-F5
Counting House Road	D1
Craddock Street	F7
Cranmer Street	A3-A4
Craven Street	C7
Crescent Street	D3
Cumberland Street	C6
Curzon Street	F8
Dane Street	A4-A5
Dannett Street	A5-A6
Danvers Road	A1
Darker Street	C6
De Montfort Square	E3
De Montfort Street	E2-E3-E4
Deacon Street	C3
Dover Street	D4-E4-E5
Dryden Street	D7-E7
Duke Street	D3-D4
Dunkirk Street	E4
Duns Lane	B4-B5
Dunton Street	A7-A8-B8
Dysart Way	E8-F8-F7
East Bond Street	C6-D6
East Gates	D6
East Street	E4
Eastern Boulevard	B2-B3
Eastleigh Road	A1-A2
Edmonton Road	E7
Elbow Lane	C6
Empire Road	A7
Equity Road	A2-A3
Erskine Street	E6
Everest Court	F7
Every Street	D5
Evington Road	F3
Filbert Street	B2-C2
Filbert Street East	C2-D2
Fitzroy Street	A5
Flora Street	A5
Fosse Road North	A5-A6-A7-A8
Fosse Road South	A4-A5
Fox Lane	D5-D6
Fox Street	E5
Freehold Street	F7
Freemens Common Road	C1-D1
Freeschool Lane	C6
Friar Lane	C4-C5-D5
Friday Street	C7-C8
Frog Island	B7-B8
Gallowtree Gate	D5-D6
Garden Street	D7
Gary Street	B4
Gas Street	D8
Gateway Street	C3
Gaul Street	A3-B3
George Street	D7-E7
Gladstone Street	E6
Glebe Street	E4-F4
Glenbarr Avenue	B8
Glenfield Road	A5
Gosling Street	C4
Gotham Street	F3
Gower Street	D7-E7
Grafton Place	C7-D7
Grafton Street East	E6-F6
Grafton Street West	E6
Graham Street	F7-F8
Granby Street	D5-E5-E4
Grange Lane	C3-C4
Granville Road	F2-F3
Grasmere Street	B3-C3
Gravel Street	C6-D6-D7
Great Central Street	B6
Greyfriars	C5
Groby Road	A8
Grosvenor Street	E7
Guildhall Lane	C5
Guthlaxton Street	F4
Halford Street	D5-E5
Harding Street	B7-C7
Harrow Road	A3
Havelock Street	C2-C3
Haymarket	D6
Hazel Street	C2-D2
Heanor Street	C7
High Street	C5-D5-D6
Highcross Street	C5-C6
Highfield Street	F3-F4
Hill Street	D6
Hinckley Road	A4
Hobart Street	F4
Hoby Street	A6
Hopefield Road	A1
Horsefair Street	D5
Hotel Street	C5-D5
Humberstone Gate	D6-E6
Humberstone Road	E6-F6-F7
Hutchinson Street	F5
Infirmary Close	C3-D3
Infirmary Road	D3
Ivy Road	A2
Jarrom Street	B2-C3
Jarvis Street	B6
Johnson Street	B7-C7
Jubilee Road	D7
Junior Street	C6-C7
Kamloops Crescent	E7
Kashmir Road	F7-F8
Kate Street	A5
Kent Street	F6
King Richards Road	A5-B5
King Street	D3-D4
Labrador Close	E7
Lambert Road	A1
Lancaster Road	D3-E2
Latimer Street	A3-A4
Lee Street	D6-E6
Lethbridge Close	E7
Lincoln Street	F4
Little Holme Street	B4-B5
Littleton Street	B8
Livingstone Street	A3-A4
London Road	E4-F3
Long Lane	C7
Loseby Lane	C5
Lower Brown Street	D3-D4
Lower Hastings Street	D3-E3
Lower Hill Street	D6
Lower Willow Street	E8
Luther Street	A3-A4
Mackenzie Way	E7
Madras Road	F6-F7
Maidstone Road	F4-F5-F6
Malabar Road	F7
Manitoba Road	E7-F7
Mansfield Street	D6-D7
Mantle Road	A6-A7
Marble Street	C4
Market Place	D5
Market Place South	D5
Market Street	D4-D5
Marlborough Street	D4
Marlow Road	A1
Marquis Street	D4
Marshall Street	A7-A8
Medina Road	A8
Melbourne Street	F6
Melton Street	E8
Midland Street	E5-E6
Mill Hill Lane	F3
Mill Lane	B3-C3-C4
Mill Street	D4
Millstone Lane	C4-C5
Montreal Road	E7-F7
Morledge Street	E5-E6
Mossdale Close	C2-C3
Mountcastle Road	A1
Murray Street	F6
Narborough Road	A2-A3-A4-A5
Navigation Street	D7-D8
Nedham Street	F7
Nelson Street	E3-E4
New Bridge Street	C1-C2
New Park Street	B4
New Street	C5
Newarke Close	B4-C4
Newarke Street	C4-D4
Newtown Street	D3
New Walk	D4-E3-F3
Nichols Street	E5-E6
Noble Street	A5
Noel Street	A2
Norfolk Street	A4-A5
Norfolk Walk	A5
Norman Street	A3-B3
North Bridge Place	B7
Northgate	B6
Northgate Street	B7
Northumberland Street	C7
Norton Street	D4
Nugent Street	A6
Old Mill Lane	B7-C7
Old Milton Street	D7-E7
Orchard Street	D7
Orchardson Avenue	F8
Ottawa Road	E7
Oxford Street	C3-C4
Paget Road	A6
Painter Street	E8
Park Street	D4
Paton Street	A2-A3
Peacock Lane	C5
Pegasus Close	F5
Pelham Street	D3
Pingle Street	B7
Pocklingtons Walk	D4-D5
Prebend Street	F4
Princess Road East	E3-F3
Princess Road West	D4-D3-E3
Quebec Road	E7
Queen Street	E5
Ravensbridge Drive	B8
Raw Dykes Road	C1
Rawson Street	D3
Raymond Road	A1
Redpath Close	F8
Regent Road	D3-E3-F3-F2
Regent Street	E3-E4
Repton Street	A7-B7
Richard I I I Road	B5
Ridley Street	A3-A4
Rivers Street	A5
Roman Street	A3
Royal East Street	D7
Ruding Road	A4
Rugby Street	B7-B8
Rupert Street	D4-C5
Russell Square	E7-E8
Rutland Street	D5-E5-E6
Rydal Street	B3-C3
St Albans Road	F3
St Augustine Road	B5
St George's Street	E5
St George's Way	E4-E5-E6
St James Street	E6
St Margaret's Way	B8-C8-C7
St Margarets Street	C7
St Martins	C5
St Mathew's Way	E6-E7
St Nicholas Circle	B5-C5
St Nicholas Place	C5
St Peter's Lane	C6
Salisbury Road	F2-F3
Samuel Street	F5-F6
Sandiacre Street	D6-D7
Sanvey Gate	B7-C7
Sawday Street	C2-D2
Saxby Street	F3-F4
Saxon Street	A3
Severn Street	F4
Seymour Street	F4
Shaftesbury Road	A3
Sheffield Street	A2
Sheldon Street	F6-F7
Shires Lane	C5
Short Street	D6
Silver Street	C5-D5
Slater Street	B7-B8-C8
Soar Lane	B6
South Albion Street	E4
Southampton Street	E5
Southgates	C4-C5
Sparkenhoe Street	F4-F5
Stamford Street	D4-D5
Stephenson Drive	A7
Stoughton Street South	F4
Stuart Street	A2
Sussex Street	F6
Swain Street	E5-F5
Swan Street	B6-B7
Syston Street East	F8
Syston Street West	E8-F8
Talbot Lane	B5
Taylor Road	E7-E8-F8
Tewkesbury Street	A6
Thames Street	D7
The Gateway	C3-C4
The Newarke	B4-C4
Thirlmere Street	C2
Tichborne Street	F3-F4
Toronto Close	E7-F7
Totland Road	A8
Tower Street	D3-E3
Trinity Lane	D3
Tudor Close	A5-B5
Tudor Road	A7-A6-A5-B5
Turner Street	D3
Tyndale Street	A3-A4
Tyrrell Street	A5-A6
Ullswater Street	B3-C3
University Road	E1-E2-F2-F3
Upper Brown Street	C4
Upper King Street	D3
Upperton Road	A2-B2
Vancouver Road	E8
Vaughan Street	A6
Vaughan Way	C5-C6-C7
Vernon Street	A6
Vestry Street	E6
Vine Street	C6
Walnut Street	B2-C2-D2
Walton Street	A2
Wanlip Street	E8
Warren Street	A6
Warwick Street	A6
Waterloo Way	D2-E3-E4
Watling Street	C8-C7-D7
Welford Road	D1-D2-D3-D4
Welles Street	B5-C5
Wellington Street	D4-E4
West Holme Street	A4
West Street	D3-E3
Westcotes Drive	A3
Western Boulevard	B2-B3-B4
Western Road	A1-A2-B3-B4
Wharf Street North	E7
Wharf Street South	E6-E7
Wheat Street	E7
Wilberforce Road	A1-A2-A3
William Street	F6
Willow Street	E8
Wilton Street	D7
Wimbledon Street	E5-E6
Windermere Street	B2-C2-C3
Wolverton Road	A1
Woodboy Street	E7-E8
Woodgate	A8-B8
Yarmouth Street	D7
Yeoman Lane	D5
Yeoman Street	D6-E6-E5
York Road	C4-D4
York Street	D4-D5

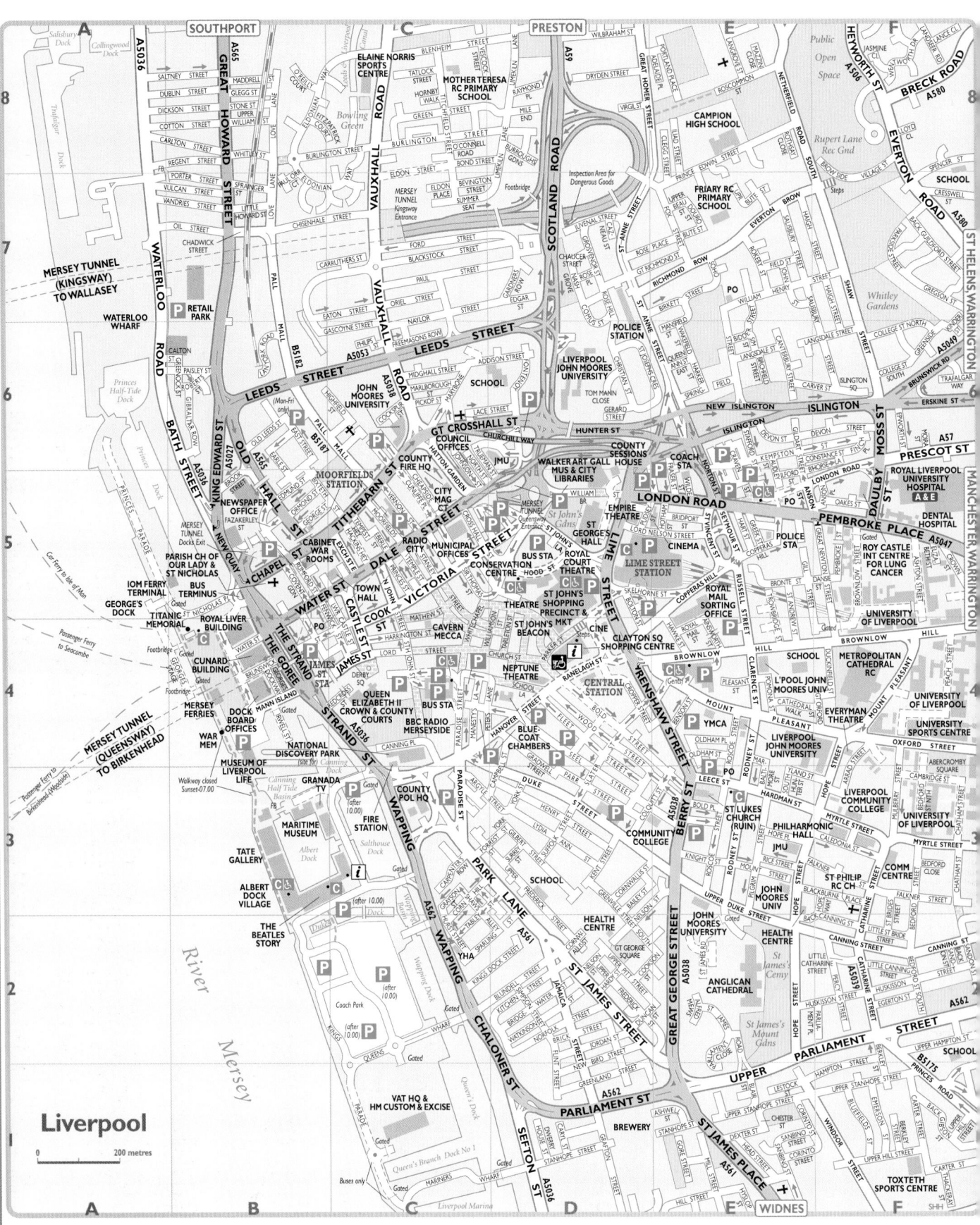

Liverpool

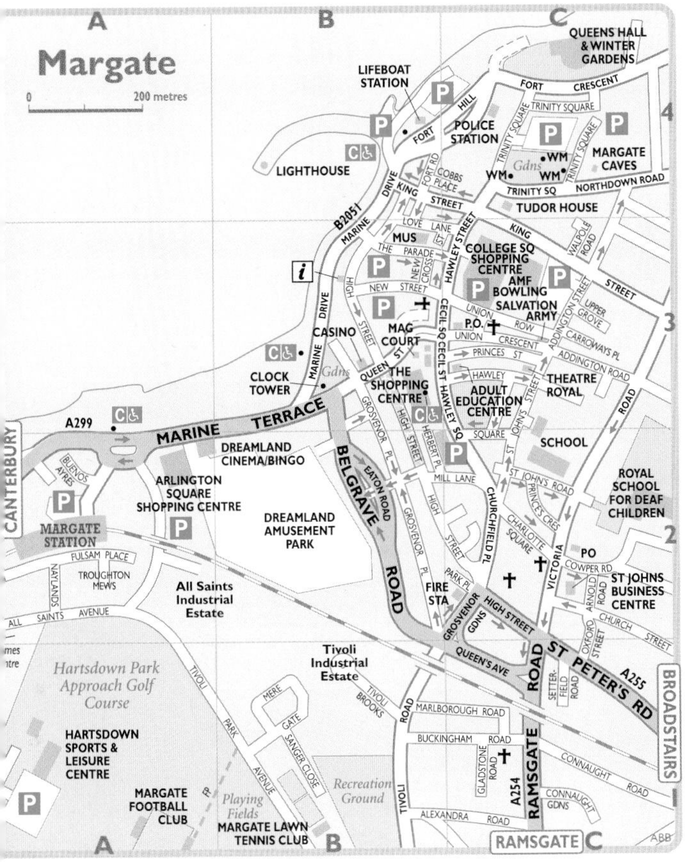

Margate

Margate is found on atlas page **29**, grid reference **3571**

Addington Road	C3
Addington Street	C3
Alexandra Road	B1-C1
All Saints Avenue	A2
Arnold Road	C2
Belgrave Road	B2-B3
Buckingham Road	B1-C1
Buenos Ayres	A2
Carroways Place	C3
Cecil Square	B3-C3
Cecil Street	B3-C3
Charlotte Square	C2
Church Street	C1-C2
Churchfield Place	C2
Cobbs Place	B4-C4
Connaught Gardens	C1
Connaught Road	C1
Cowper Road	C2
Eaton Road	B2
Fort Crescent	C4
Fort Hill	B4-C4
Fort Road	B4
Fulsam Place	A2
Gladstone Road	C1
Grosvenor Gardens	C2
Grosvenor Place	B2-B3
Hawley Square	C2-C3
Hawley Street	C3
Herbert Place	B2
High Street	B3-B2-C2
King Street	B4-C4-C3
Love Lane	B3-C3
Marine Drive	B3-B4
Marine Terrace	A2-B3
Marlborough Road	B1-C1
Mere Gate	B1
Mill Lane	B2-C2
Naylands	A2
New Cross Street	B3
New Street	B3
Northdown Road	C4
Oxford Street	C1-C2
Park Place	C2
Prince's Crescent	C2
Princes Street	C3
Queen Street	B3
Queens Avenue	C1
Ramsgate Road	C1
St John's Road	C2
St John's Street	C2-C3
St Peter's Road	C1
Sanger Close	B1
Setterfield Road	C1
The Parade	B3
Tivoli Brooks	B1
Tivoli Park Avenue	A2-A1-B1
Tivoli Road	B1
Trinity Square	C4
Troughton Mews	A2
Union Crescent	C3
Union Row	C3
Upper Grove	C3
Victoria Road	C2-C3
Walpole Road	C3

Liverpool

iverpool is found on atlas page **78**, id reference **3490**

ercromby Square	F3-F4
dison Street	C6-D6
elaide Place	E8
nsworth Street	E4-E5
red Mews	E2
son Place	F5
son Street	E5
gyle Street	C3-D3
rad Street	F3-F4
hton Street	F4-F5
hwell Street	E1
udley Street	E5-E6
ck Canning Street	E2-F2
ck Gibson Street	F1
ck Guildford Street	F7
ck Sandon Street	F2
iley Street	D3
ltimore Street	E3
th Street	A6-B5
yhorse Lane	E5-F6
dford Close	F3
dford Street	F2-F3
dford Street North	F3
dford Street South	F2
nson Street	E4
rkley Street	F1-F2
rry Street	E3
vington Street	C7-D7
dder Street	E6-E7
rchfield Street	E6
rkett Street	D7
xteth Street	B5-C5
ackburne Place	E3-F3
ackstock Street	C7-D7
air Street	E1
enheim Street	C8-D8
uefields Street	F1
undell Street	C2-D2
old Place	E3
old Street	D4-E3
olton Street	D4-D5
ond Street	C8-D8
eck Road	F8
ick Street	D2
idgewater Street	D2
idport Street	E5
onte Street	E5
ook Street	B5
ow Side	F7-F8
ownlow Hill	E4-F4
ownlow Street	F4-F5
unswick Road	F6
unswick Street	B4
Burlington Street	B8-D8
Burroughs Gardens	D8
Bute Street	E7
Caledonia Street	F3
Calton Street	B6
Cambridge Street	F3
Campbell Street	D3-D4
Canning Place	C4
Canning Street	E2-F2
Canterbury Street	E6
Carlton Street	A8-B8
Carpenter's Row	C3
Carruthers Street	B7-C7
Carter Street	F1
Carver Street	E6-F6
Caryl Street	D1
Castle Street	C4-C5
Catharine Street	F2-F3
Cathedral Walk	E4
Cazneau Street	D7
Chadwick Street	B7
Chaloner Street	C2-D1
Chapel Street	B5
Chatham Street	F3
Chaucer Street	D7
Cheapside	C5-C6
Chester Street	E1
Chisenhale Street	B7-C7
Christian Street	D6
Church Street	C4-D4
Churchill Way	C6-D6
Clarence Street	E4
Clegg Street	E7-E8
Cockspur Street	C6
College Street North	F6
College Street South	F6
Colquitt Street	D3-E3
Comus Street	D6-D7
Constance Street	E6-F6
Cook Street	C4-C5
Cookson Street	D2-E2
Copperas Hill	D4-E5
Corinto Street	E1-F1
Corn Hill	C3
Cornwallis Street	D2-D3
Cotton Street	A8-B8
Covent Garden	B5
Craven Street	E5-E6
Cresswell Street	F7
Cropper Street	D4-E4
Cross Hall Street	C5-D5
Crown Street	F5
Cunliffe Place	C5
Dale Street	C5-D5
Dansie Street	E5-F5
Daulby Street	F5
Derby Square	C4
Devon Street	E6-F6
Dexter Street	E1
Dickson Street	A8-B8
Douro Street	E7
Dryden Street	D8
Dublin Street	A8-B8
Duckinfield Street	F4
Duke Street	C4-D3-E3
Duncan Street	D2
Dwerry House Street	D1
Earle Street	B5-B6
East Street	B6
Eaton Street	B7-C7
Eberle Street	C5
Edgar Street	D7
Edmund Street	B5
Egerton Street	F2
Eldon Place	C7
Eldon Street	C7-C8
Eldonian Way	B8-C8
Elizabeth Street	F5
Emerson Street	F1
Epworth Street	F6
Erskine Street	F6
Everton Brow	E7
Everton Road	F7-F8
Exchange Street East	C5
Falkner Street	E3-F3
Fazakerley Street	B5
Fenwick Street	B5-C4
Field Street	E7
Finch Place	F6
Fitzpatrick Court	B8-C8
Fleet Street	D3-D4
Flint Street	D1-D2
Fontenoy Street	D6
Ford Street	C7-D7
Forrest Street	C3-D3
Fox Street	D8-E7
Fraser Street	E5-E6
Freemasons Row	C6
Gardners Row	D7
Gascoyne Street	B7-C6
George Street	B5
George's Dockway	B4
Georges Stage	A4-B4
Gerard Street	D6
Gibraltar Row	B6
Gilbert Street	D3
Gildart Street	E5-E6
Gill Street	E5-F4
Glegg Street	B8
Gore Street	E1
Gradwell Street	D3-D4
Grafton Street	D1
Grayson Street	C3
Great Crosshall Street	C6-D6
Great George Square	D2
Great George Street	E1-E3
Great Homer Street	D8-E8
Great Howard Street	B6-B8
Great Newton Street	F4-F5
Great Orford Street	F4
Great Richmond Street	D7-E7
Greek Street	E5
Green Street	C8-D8
Greenland Street	D1
Greenock Street	B6
Greenside	F6
Gregson Street	F7
Grenville Street South	D3-E2
Grosvenor Street	D7
Hackins Hey	C5
Haigh Street	E7-F7-F6
Hampton Street	E1-F1-F2
Hanover Street	C3-D4
Hardman Street	E3
Hardy Street	D2
Harker Street	E6
Harrington Street	C4
Hart Street	E5
Hatton Garden	C5-C6
Hawke Street	E4-E5
Head Street	E1
Henry Street	D3
Heyworth Street	F8
Highfield Street	B6-C6
Hill Street	E1
Hood Street	D5
Hope Place	E3
Hope Street	E2-E3-F4
Hope Way	F3
Hornby Walk	C8
Hotham Street	E5
Hunter Street	D6
Hurst Street	C2-C3
Huskisson Street	E2-F2
Hyslop Street	E1
Ilford Street	E5
Iliad Street	E8
Irwell Street	B4
Islington	E6-F6
Islington Square	F6
Jamaica Street	D1-D2
James Street	B4-C4
Jasmine Close	F8
John Street	E7
Johnson Street	C5-C6
Jordan Street	D2
Juvenal Street	D7
Kempston Street	E6-F6
Kent Street	D3
Kinder Street	F6-F7
King Edward Street	B5-B6
Kings Dock Street	C2-D2
Kings Parade	B2-C2-C1
Kitchen Street	D2
Knight Street	E3
Lace Street	C6-D6
Lance Close	F8
Landseer Road	F8
Langrove Street	E8
Langsdale Street	E6-F6
Lanyork Road	B6
Leece Street	E3
Leeds Street	B6-D6
Lestock Street	E1
Lime Street	D4-D5
Limekiln Lane	D7-D8
Little Canning Street	F2
Little Catharine Street	F2
Little Howard Street	B7
Little St Bride Street	F2
Lloyd Close	F8
London Road	D5-E5-F5-F6
Lord Nelson Street	D5-E5
Lord Street	C4
Love Lane	B7-B8
Lower Castle Street	C4-C5
Lydia Ann Street	D3
Maddrell Street	B8
Manesty's Lane	C4
Mann Island	B4
Mansfield Street	E6-E7
Mariners Wharf	C1-D1
Marlborough Street	C6
Marybone	C6
Maryland Street	E4-E3-F3
Mathew Street	C4-C5
Mazzini Close	E8
Midghall Street	C6
Mile End	D8
Mill Street	E1
Moira Street	F6
Moorfields	C5
Moss Street	F6
Mount Pleasant	E4-F4
Mount Street	E3
Mulberry Street	F3-F4
Myrtle Street	F3
Nash Grove	D7
Naylor Street	C6-D7
Nelson Street	D2-E3
Netherfield Road South	E8-F7
New Bird Street	D1-D2
New Islington	E6
New Quay	B5
Norfolk Street	D2
North John Street	C4-C5
North Street	C5-C6
Norton Street	E5-E6
O'Connell Road	C8
O'Reilly Court	B8
Oakes Street	F5
Oil Street	A7-B7
Old Hall Street	B5-B6
Old Leeds Street	B6
Oldham Place	E4
Oldham Street	E4
Oriel Street	C7
Ormond Street	B5
Oxford Street	F4
Paisley Street	B6
Pall Mall	B7-B6-C5
Paradise Street	C3-C4
Park Lane	C3-D2
Parker Street	D4
Parkside Street	F7
Parliament Close	E1-E2
Parliament Place	F2
Parliament Street	D1-E1
Parr Street	D3
Paul Orr Court	B7
Paul Street	C7-D7
Peach Street	F4
Pembroke Place	E5-F5
Pembroke Street	F5
Percy Street	F2
Peter's Lane	C4-D4
Pickop Street	C6
Philips Street	C6
Pilgrim Street	E3
Pleasant Street	E4
Pomona Street	E4
Porter Street	A7-B7
Portland Place	E8
Prescot Street	F6
Prince Edwin Street	E7-E8
Princes Parade	A5-A6
Princes Road	F1-F2
Princes Street	C5
Pudsey Street	D5-E5
Queen Ann Street East	E6
Queens Wharf	C2
Ranelagh Street	D4
Raymond Place	D8
Redcross Street	B4-C4
Regent Street	A8-B8
Renshaw Street	D4-E4
Rice Street	E3
Richmond Row	D7-E7
Roberts Street	B6
Rodney Street	E3-E4
Rokeby Street	E7
Roscoe Street	E3-E4
Roscommon Street	E8
Rose Hill	D6-D7
Rose Place	D7-E7
Rothsay Close	E8
Royal Mail Street	E4-E5
Rumford Street	B5
Russell Street	E4-E5
St Andrew Street	E4-E5
St Anne Street	D7-E6
St Brides Street	F2-F3
St James Place	E1
St James Road	E1-E2
St James Street	D2-E2
St John's Lane	D5
St Josephs Crescent	D6-E6
St Nicholas Place	B5
St Vincent Street	E5
Salisbury Street	E7-F6
Saltney Street	A8-B8
Sanbino Street	E1
Sandon Street	F2
School Lane	D4
Scotland Road	D6-D8
Seel Street	D4-E3
Sefton Street	D1
Seymour Street	E5
Shaw Street	F6-F7
Shaws Alley	C3-D2
Sim Street	E6
Simpson Street	D2
Sir Thomas Street	C5-D5
Skelhorne Street	D5-E5
Slater Street	D3-D4
Soho Street	E6-E7
South Hunter Street	E3
South John Street	C4
Sparling Street	C2-D2
Spencer Street	F7-F8
Sprainger Street	B7
Springfield	E6
Stafford Street	E5-E6
Stanhope Street	D1-E1
Stanley Street	C4-C5
Stone Street	B8
Strand Street	B4-C4
Suffolk Street	D3
Summer Seat	C7-D7
Surrey Street	D3
Tabley Street	C2-D3
Tarleton Street	D4-D5
Tatlock Street	C8
Tempest Hey	C5
Temple Street	C5
Thackeray Street	F1
The Goree	B4-B5
The Strand	B4-B5
Titchfield Street	C7-C8
Tithebarn Street	C5-C6
Tom Mann Close	D6
Trafalgar Way	F6
Trowbridge Street	E4-E5
Trueman Street	C6-D5
Upper Beau Street	E7
Upper Bute Street	E7
Upper Duke Street	E2-E3
Upper Frederick Street	C3-E2
Upper Hampton Street	F2
Upper Hill Street	F1
Upper Parliament Street	E1-F2
Upper Pitt Street	D2
Upper Stanhope Street	E1-F1
Upper William Street	B8
Vandries Street	A7-B7
Vauxhall Road	C6-C8
Vernon Street	C5
Vescock Street	C8-D8
Victoria Street	C5-D5
Village Street	F7-F8
Virgil Street	D8
Vulcan Street	A7-B7
Wakefield Street	E6
Wapping	C2-C3
Water Street	B4-B5-C5
Waterloo Road	A6-A8
Watkinson Street	D2
Wentworth Drive	F8
Whitechapel	C4-D5
Whitley Street	B8
Wilbraham Street	D8
Wilde Street	E5
William Brown Street	D5
William Henry Street	E7-F7
Williamson Street	C4-D5
Windsor Street	E1-F1
Wood Street	D3-D4
York Street	D3

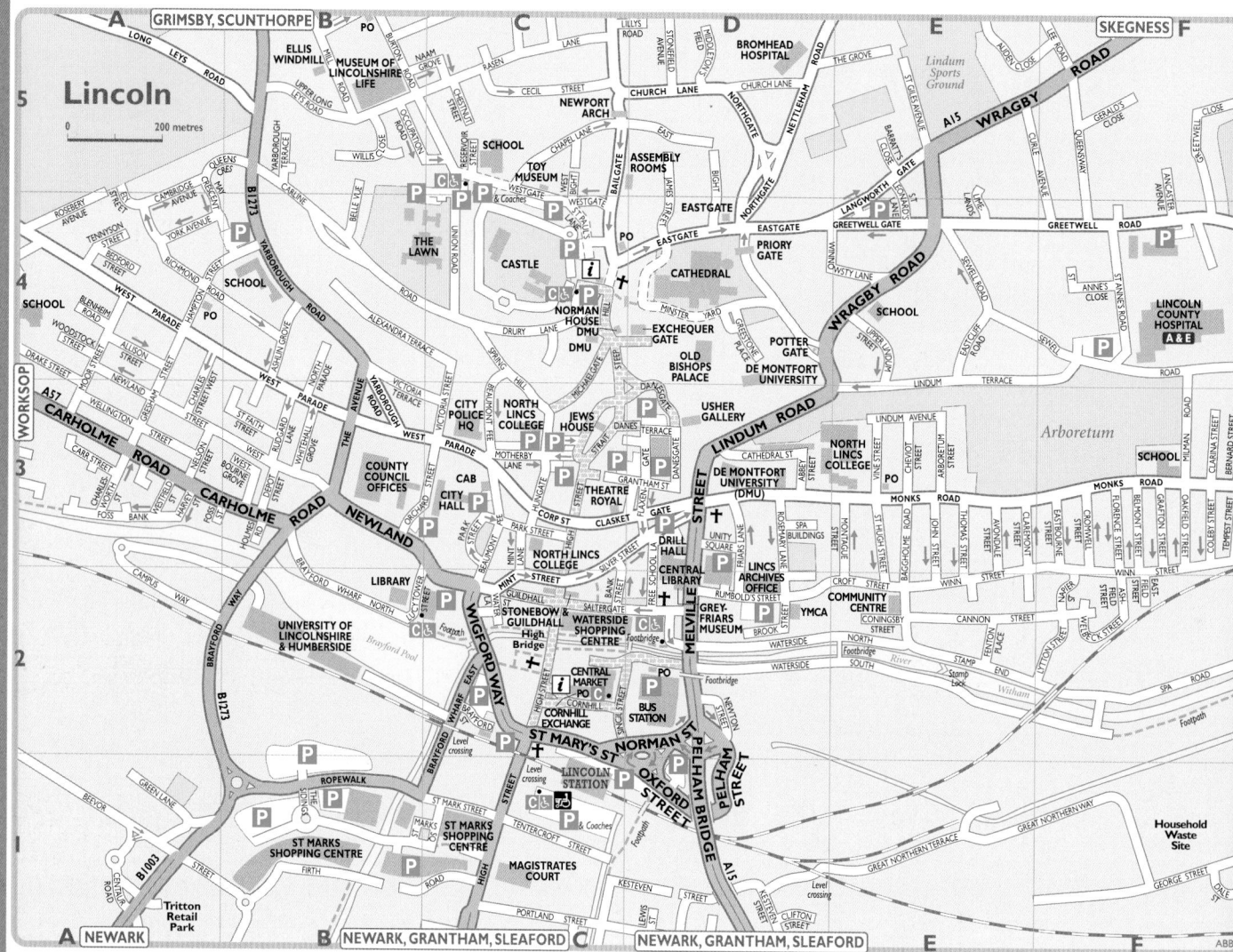

Lincoln

Lincoln is found on atlas page **76**,
grid reference **9771**

Abbey Street	D3	Carline Road	B5-B4-C4	Eastcliff Road	E4	Lewis Street	D1	Oxford Street	D1	Strait	
Alexandra Terrace	B4-C4	Carr Street	A3	Eastfield Street	F2	Lillys Road	C5-D5	Park Street	C3	Tempest Street	
Allison Street	A4	Cathedral Street	D3	Eastgate	C4-D4	Limelands	E4-E5	Pelham Bridge	D1-D2	Tennyson Street	
Ancaster Avenue	F4-F5	Cecil Street	C5	Ely Street	A4-A5	Lindum Avenue	E3	Pelham Street	D1-D2	Tentercroft Street	
Arboretum Street	E3	Centaur Road	A1	Fenton Place	E2	Lindum Road	D3	Portland Street	C1	The Avenue	B3-
Ashfield Street	F2	Chapel Lane	C5	Firth Road	B1-C1	Lindum Terrace	E3-E4-F4	Queens Crescent	A5-B5	The Grove	D5-
Ashlin Grove	B4	Charles Street West	A3-A4	Flaxengate	D3	Long Leys Road	A5-B5	Queensway	F4-F5	The Sidings	
Auden Close	E5-F5	Charles Worth Street	A3	Florence Street	F3	Lucy Tower Street	B2	Rasen Lane	C5	Thomas Street	
Avondale Street	E3	Chestnut Street	C5	Foss Bank	A3	Lytton Street	F2	Reservoir Street	C5	Union Road	C4-C
Baggholme Road	E2-E3	Cheviot Street	E3	Foss Street	A3-B3	May Crescent	A5-A4-B4	Richmond Road	A4-B4	Unity Square	D
Bailgate	C4-C5	Church Lane	C5-D5	Free School Lane	D2-D3	Melville Street	D2-D3	Ropewalk	B1	Upper Lindum Street	
Bank Street	C2-C3	Claremont Street	E3	Friars Lane	D3	Michaelgate	C3-C4	Rosebery Avenue	A4-A5	Upper Long Leys Road	
Barratts Close	E5	Clarina Street	F3	George Street	F1	Middleton's Field	D5	Rosemary Lane	D3	Victoria Street	B
Beaumont Fee	C2-C3-C4	Clasket Gate	C3-D3	Gerald's Close	F5	Mill Road	B5	Rudgard Lane	B3	Victoria Terrace	B4-B3-C
Bedford Street	A4	Clifton Street	D1	Grafton Street	F3	Milman Road	F3-F4	Rumbold's Street	D2	Vine Street	
Beevor Street	A1-B1	Coleby Street	F3	Grantham Street	C3-D3	Minster Yard	D4	St Anne's Close	F4	Water Lane	
Belle Vue	B4-B5	Coningsby Street	E2	Great Northern Terrace	D1-E1	Mint Lane	C3	St Anne's Road	F4	Waterside North	D2-
Belmont Street	F3	Cornhill	C2	Great Northern Way	E1-F1	Mint Street	C2	St Faith Street	B3	Waterside South	D2-
Bernard Street	F3	Corporation Street	C3	Green Lane	A1	Monks Road	D3-E3-E3	St Giles Avenue	E5	Welbeck Street	
Blenheim Road	A4	Croft Street	D2-E2	Greestone Place	D4	Montague Street	E2-E3	St Hugh Street	E2-E3	Wellington Street	A
Brayford Street	C2	Cromwell Street	F3	Greetwell Close	F5	Moor Street	A3-A4	St Leonard's Lane	E4-E5	West Bight	
Brayford Way	A1-A2-B2-B3	Curle Avenue	E5-F5-F4	Greetwell Gate	E4	Motherby Lane	C3	St Mark Street	C1	West Parade	A4-B4-B3-C
Brayford Wharf East	B1-C1-C2	Dale Street	F1	Greetwell Road	E4-F4	Naam Grove	B5-C5	St Marks Square	B1-C1	Westbourne Grove	
Brayford Wharf North	B2-B3	Danes Terrace	C3-D3	Gresham Street	A3-A4	Napier Street	F2	St Mary's Street	C1-C2	Westfield Street	
Brook Street	D2	Danesgate	D3-D4	Guildhall Street	C2	Nelson Street	A3	St Paul's Lane	C4	Westgate	C4-C
Burton Road	B5	Depot Street	B3	Hampton Street	A4-B4	Nettleham Road	D5	Saltergate	C2-D2	Whitehall Grove	
Cambridge Avenue	A4-A5	Drake Street	A3-A4	Harvey Street	F3	Newland	B3	Sewell Road	E4-F4	Wigford Way	C
Campus Way	A2-A3	Drury Lane	C4	High Street	C1-C2-C3	Newland Street West	A4-A3-B3	Silver Street	C2-C3-D3	Willis Close	
Cannon Street	E2-F2	East Bight	D4-D5	Holmes Road	B3	Newton Street	D2	Sincil Street	C2-D2	Winn Street	E2-
Carholme Road	A3-B3	Eastbourne Street	F3	Hungate	C3	Norman Street	C2-D2	Spa Buildings	D3	Winnowsty Lane	D4-
				James Street	D4-D5	North Parade	B3-B4	Spa Road	F2	Woodstock Street	
				John Street	E2-E3	Northgate	D4-D5	Spring Hill	C3-C4	Wragby Road	D4-E4-E5-F
				Kesteven Street	C1-D1	Oakfield Street	F3	Stamp End	E2	Yarborough Road	B5-B4-E
				Langworth Gate	E4-E5	Occupation Road	B5-C5	Steep Hill	C4	Yarborough Terrace	
				Lee Road	F5	Orchard Street	B3-C3	Stonefield Avenue	D5	York Avenue	

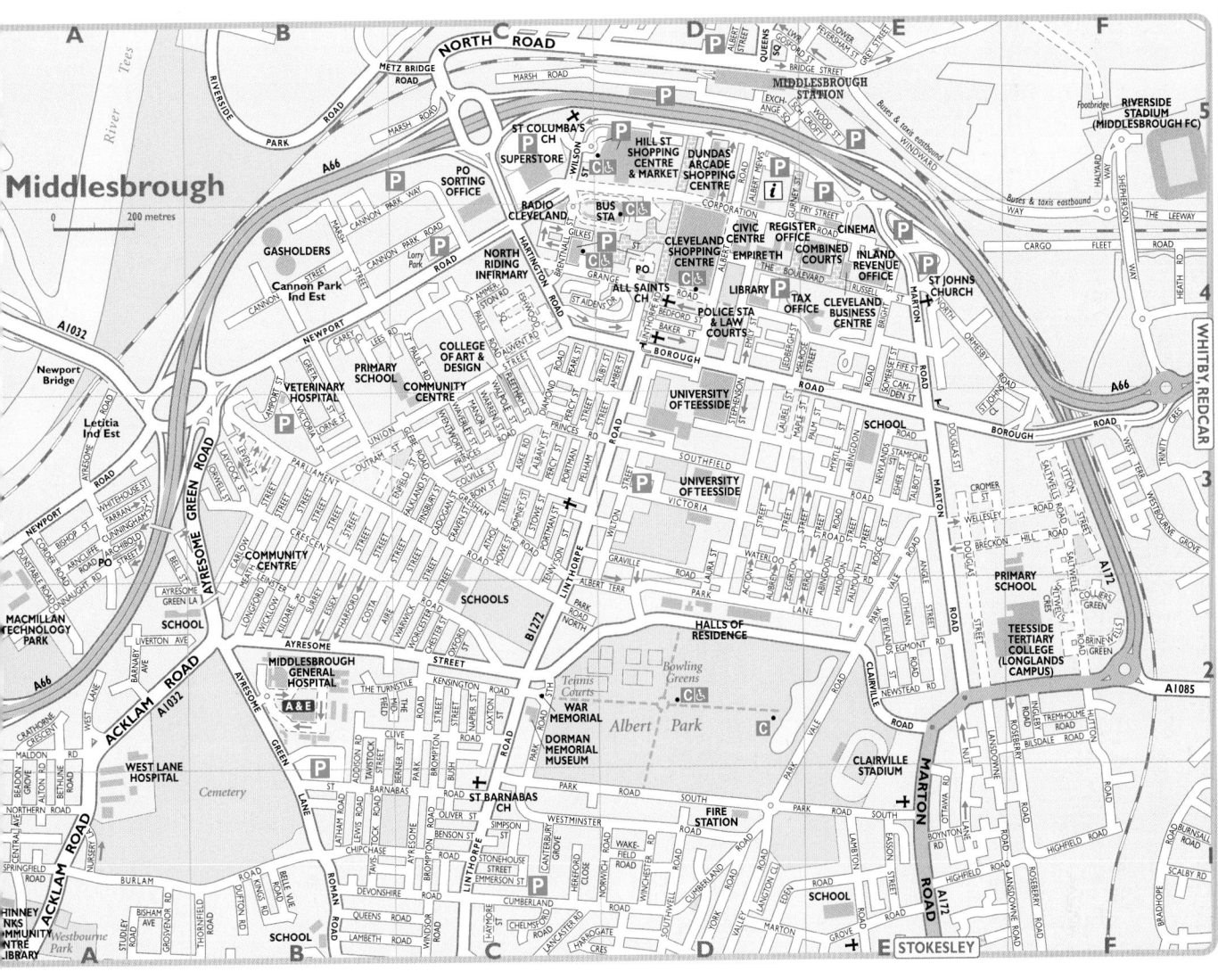

Middlesbrough

Middlesbrough is found on atlas page **97**,
grid reference **4919**

ngdon Road	E2-E3-E4	Bow Street	C3	Crescent Road	B3-C2	Howe Street	C3	North Road	C5	Stephenson Street	D3-D4

ngdon Road E2-E3-E4
lam Road A1-A2-B2
on Street D2-D3
dison Road B1-B2
e Street B2-C2-C3
any Street C3
ert Mews D5
ert Road D4-D5
ert Street D5
ert Terrace C2-D2
on Road A1-A2
vent Road C4
ber Street D4
merston Road C4
gle Street E2-E3
chibold Street A3
ncliffe Road A3
ke Road C3
nol Street C3
brey Street D2-D3
resome Green Lane A2-B2-B1
resome Green Road B2-B3
resome Park Road C1-C2
resome Street A3-A4
resome Street B2-C2
ker Street D4
rnaby Avenue A2
adon Grove A1-A2
dford Street D4
l Street A3-A2-B2
le Vue Road B1
nson Street C1
rner Road C1-C2
dale Road A1-A2
gham Avenue F2
sham Avenue A1
shop Street A3
rough Road C4-D4-E3-F3

Bow Street C3
Boynton Road E1
Bradhope Road F1
Breckon Hill Road E3-F3
Brentnall Street C4
Bridge Street D5-E5
Bright Street E4
Brinewells Green F2
Brompton Road C1
Brompton Street C1-C2
Burlam Road A1-B1
Burnsall Road F1
Bush Street C1-C2
Byelands Street E2
Cadogan Street C3
Camden Street E3-E4
Cannon Park Road B4-C4
Cannon Park Way B4-C5
Cannon Street B4
Canterbury Grove C1
Carey Close B4
Cargo Fleet Road E4-F4
Carlow Street B2-B3
Caxton Street C2
Central Avenue A1
Chelmsford Road C1
Chester Street C2
Chipchase Road B1-C1
Clairville Road E2
Clive Road B2-C2
Colliers Green F2
Colville Street C3
Connaught Road A2-A3
Corder Road A2-A3
Corporation Road D5-D4-E4
Costa Street B2-B3-C3
Crathorne Crescent A2
Craven Street C3

Crescent Road B3-C2
Cromer Street E3
Cumberland Road C1-D1
Cunningham Street A3
Devonshire Road B1-C1
Diamond Road C3-C4
Douglas Street E2-E3
Dufton Road B1
Dunstable Road A2-A3
Easson Street E1
Eden Road D1-E1
Egerton Street D2-D3-E3
Egmont Road E2
Emily Street D4
Emmerson Street C1
Enfield Street C3
Errol Street D2-E2-E3
Esher Street E3
Eshwood Square C4
Essex Street B2-B3
Exchange Square D5
Falkland Street C3
Falmouth Street E2-E3
Fife Street E4
Finsbury Street C3
Fleetham Street C3-C4
Fry Street E4
Gilkes Street C4-D4
Glebe Road B3-C3
Grange Road C4-D4
Graville Road C3-D3-D2
Gresham Road C3
Greta Street B3-B4
Grey Street E5
Grosvenor Road A1
Gurney Street D4-D5-E5
Haddon Street E2-E3
Halyard Way F5
Harford Street B2-B3-C3
Harrogate Crescent C1-D1
Hartington Road C4
Haymore Street C1
Heath Road F4
Hereford Close C1
Highfield Road E1-F1

Howe Street C3
Hutton Road F1-F2
Ingleby Road F2
Jedburgh Street D4
Kensington Road C2
Kildare Street B2-B3
Kings Road B1
Lambeth Road B1-C1
Lambton Road E1
Lamport Street B3-B4
Lancaster Road C1
Langton Close D1
Lansdowne Road E2-E1-F1
Latham Road B1
Laura Street D2-D3
Laurel Street D3
Laycock Street B4-C4
Lees Road B4-C4
Leinster Road B2-B3
Leven Street B3
Lewis Road B1
Linthorpe Road C1-C2-C3-D4
Liverton Avenue A2-B2
Longford Street B2-B3
Lorne Street B3
Lothian Road E2
Lower Feversham Street E5
Lower Gosford Street D5-E5
Lytton Street F3
Maldon Road A2
Manor Street C3
Maple Street D3-E3
Marsh Road B5-C5
Marsh Street B4-B5
Marton Grove Road D1-E1
Marton Road E1-E2-E3-E4
Meath Street B2-B3
Melrose Street D4-E4
Metz Bridge Road B5-C5
Myrtle Street E3
Napier Street C2
Newlands Road B1
Newport Road A3-B4-C4
Newstead Road E2
North Ormesby Road E4-F4-F3

North Road C5
Northern Road A1
Norwich Road C1-D1
Nursery Lane A1
Nut Lane E1-E2
Oliver Street C1
Orwell Street B3
Ottawa Road E1
Outram Street B3-C3
Oxford Street C2
Palm Street E3
Park Lane D2-E2
Park Road North C2
Park Road South C2-C1-D1-E1
Park Vale Road D1-D2-E2-E3
Parliament Road B3-C3-C2
Pearl Street C4
Pelham Street C3-D3
Percy Street C3-C4
Portman Street C3
Princes Road C3-D3
Queens Road B1-C1
Queens Square D5
Riverside Park Road B5
Roman Road B1
Romney Street C3
Roscoe Street E3
Roseberry Road F1-F2
Ruby Street D4
Russell Street E4
St Aidens Drive C4-D4
St Barnabas Road B1-C1
St Johns Close E3
St Pauls Road C4
Saltwells Crescent F2
Saltwells Road F2-F3
Scalby Road F1
School Croft D5-E5
Shepherson Way F4-F5
Simpson Street C1
Somerset Street E3-E4
Southfield Road D3-E3
Southwell Road D1
Springfield Road A1
Stamford Street E3

Stephenson Street D3-D4
Stonehouse Street C1
Stowe Street C3
Studley Road A1
Surrey Street B2-B3
Talbot Street E3
Tarran Street A3
Tavistock Road B1
Tavistock Street B1-B2
Tennyson Street C2-C3
The Boulevard D4-E4
The Leeway F5
The Midfield B2-C2
The Turnstile B2-C2
Thornfield Road B1
Tremholme Road F2
Trinity Crescent F3
Union Street B3-C3-C4
Valley Road D1
Victoria Road D3-E3
Victoria Street B3-B4
Wakefield Road D1
Walpole Street C3-C4
Warren Street C3-C4
Warwick Street B2-C2-C3
Waterloo Road D3-E3-E2
Waverley Street C3
Wellesley Road E3-F3
Wentworth Street C3
West Lane A2
West Terrace F3
Westbourne Grove F3
Westminster Road C1-D1
Whitehouse Street A3
Wicklow Street B2-B3
Wilson Street C5
Wilton Street D3
Winchester Road D1
Windsor Road C1
Windward Way E5-F5
Wood Street E5
Worcester Street C2-C3
York Road D1

Manchester

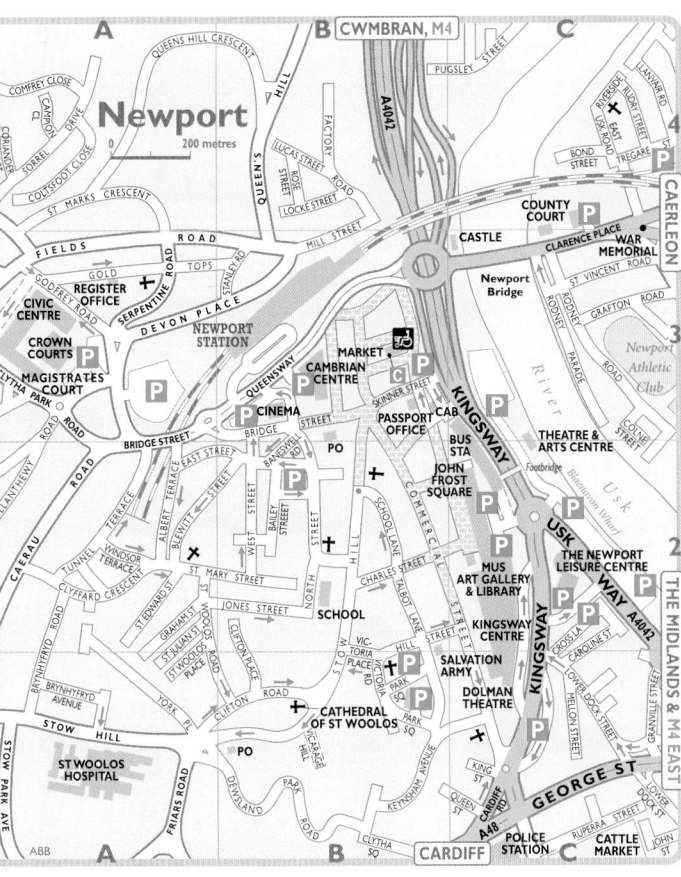

Newport

Newport is found on atlas page **34**, grid reference **3188**

Albert Terrace	A2	Fields Road	A3-B3	Rodney Road	C3
Bailey Street	B2	Friars Road	A1	Rose Street	B4
Baneswell Road	B2-B3	George Street	C1	Rudry Street	C4
Blewitt Street	A2-B2	Godfrey Road	A3	Ruperra Street	C1
Bond Street	C4	Gold Tops	A3-B3	St Edward Street	A2
Bridge Street	A2-A3-B2-B3	Grafton Road	C3	St Julian Street	A1-A2
Brynhyfryd Avenue	A1	Graham Street	A1-A2	St Marks Crescent	A3-A4
Brynhyfryd Road	A1-A2	Granville Street	C1	St Mary Street	A2-B2
Caerau Road	A2	Hill Street	B1-B2-C2	St Vincent Road	C3
Campion Close	A4	John Street	C1	St Woolos Place	A1-A2
Cardiff Road	C1	Jones Street	A2-B2	St Woolos Road	A2-A1-B1
Caroline Street	C1-C2	Keynsham Avenue	B1	School Lane	B2
Charles Street	B2	King Street	C1	Serpentine Road	A3
Clarence Place	C3-C4	Kingsway	C1-C2-C3-B3	Skinner Street	B3
Clifton Place	B2-B1	Llanthewy Road	A2-A3	Sorrel Drive	A4
Clifton Road	A1-B1	Llanvair Road	C4	Stanlet Road	B3
Clyffard Crescent	A2	Locke Street	B4	Stow Hill	A1-B1-B2
Clytha Park Road	A3	Lower Dock Street	C1	Stow Park Avenue	A1
Clytha Square	B1	Lucas Street	B4	Talbot Lane	B2
Colne Street	C3-C2	Mellon Street	C1	Tregare Street	C4
Coltsfoot Close	A4	Mill Street	B3-B4	Tunnel Terrace	A2
Comfrey Close	A4	North Street	B2	Usk Way	C2
Commercial Street	B2-C2-C1	Park Square	B1	Vicarage Hill	B1
Coriander Close	A4	Pugsley Street	B4-C4	Victoria Place	B1
Cross Lane	C1-C2	Queen's Hill	B3-B4	Victoria Road	B1
Devon Place	A3-B3	Queens Hill Crescent	A4-B4	West Street	B2
Dewsland Park Road	A1-B1	Queen Street	C1	Windsor Terrace	A2
East Street	A2-B2	Queensway	A3-B3	York Place	A1-A2
East Usk Road	C4	Riverside	C4		
Factory Road	B4	Rodney Parade	C3		

199

Manchester

Manchester is found on atlas page **79**, grid reference **8497**

Addington Street	E7-F7-F6	Bromley Street	E8-F8	Cornell Street	F6
Albert Square	D4-D5	Brook Street	E2	Corporation Street	D6-D7-E7-E8
Albion Street	C2-C3	Brotherton Drive	A6-B6	Cottenham Lane	B8
Anaconda Drive	B7	Brown Street	D5	Cotton Street	F6
Angel Street	E7	Browning Street	A6-B6	Cross Keys Street	F7
Angela Street	A2	Burstock Street	F8	Cross Street	D5
Angora Drive	A7	Bury Street	B6-C6	Crown Street	B2
Arlington Street	A6-A7	Byrom Street	B4-C4	Dale Street	E5-F5
Artillery Street	C4	Cable Street	E7-E6-F6	Dalley Avenue	A8
Aspin Lane	E7-E8	Cambridge Street	B8	Dalton Street	F8
Atherton Street	B4	Cambridge Street	D3-D2-E1	Dantzic Street	E6-E7-E8-F8
Atkinson Street	C4	Camp Street	C4	Dean Road	B7-C7
Aytoun Street	E5-E4-F4	Canal Street	E4	Dean Street	F5-F6
Back George Street	D4-E4-F5	Cannon Street	A7	Deansgate	C3-C4-C5-C6
Back Piccadilly	E5-F5	Cannon Street	D6-E6	Dearman's Place	C6
Bank Street	A6	Carnarvon Street	D8	Dickenson Street	C3-C4
Barker Street	C8	Castle Street	B3	Downing Street	F2-F3
Barrack Street	A1-A2	Cateaton Street	D6	Ducie Street	F4-F5
Barrow Street	A5	Caygill Street	C7	Dutton Street	D7-D8
Bendix Street	F7	Chapel Street	A6-B6-C6-D6	Dyche Street	E7-F7
Berry Street	F3	Chapel Walks	D5	East Ordsall Lane	A4-A5
Blackburn Street	A7	Charles Street	E2-E3	East Philip Street	B8
Blackfriars Road	A8-B7-C6	Charlotte Street	D5-D4-E4	Edge Street	E6
Blackfriars Street	C6	Charter Street	C8-D8	Edward Street	B8
Blantyre Street	B2-C3	Chase Street	E8	Eliza Street	B1
Bloom Street	B6	Chatham Street	E4-E5-F5	Ellesmere Street	A2
Bloom Street	E4	Cheetham Hill Road	D7-D8	Elton Street	B8
Blossom Street	F6	Chepstow Street	D3	Exchange Street	D5-D6
Boad Street	F4	Chester Road	A1-A2-B2-C3	Fairfield Street	F3-F4
Bonsall Street	D1	Chester Street	D2-E2	Faulkner Street	D4-E4
Bond Street	C7	Chevassut Street	B1	Fennel Street	D6
Booth Street	C6	Chevril Close	D1	Fenwick Street	C1
Booth Street	D4-D5	Chiffon Way	A7	Fernie Street	D8
Booth Street West	E1-F1	China Lane	F5	Ford Street	A6
Bootle Street	C4-C5	Chorlton Road	B1-B2	Fountain Street	D4-D5-E5
Boundary Lane	C1	Chorlton Street	E4	Francis Street	C8
Boundary Street West	E1	Church Street	E6	Garden Lane	B6
Brazenose Road	E2	City Road	A1-B1	Gartside Street	B4-B5-C5
Brazenose Street	C5-C4-D4	City Road East	C2	George Leigh Street	F6
Brewer Street	F5	Clarendon Street	C1	George Street	D4-E4-E5
Bridge Street	B5-C5	Cleminson Street	A6-B6	Gould Street	E8-F8-F7
Bridgewater Street	B3-C3	Clowes Street	C6	Goulden Street	F6-F7
Bridgewater Street	B7-B8	Cobourg Street	F3-F4	Granby Row	E3
Briggs Street	A7	Commercial Street	C2	Gravel Lane	C6-C7
Brocade Close	A7	Copperas Street	E6	Great Ancoats Street	F5-F6
				Great Bridgewater Street	C3-D3
				Great Ducie Street	D7-C7-C8
				Great Jackson Street	B2-C2
				Great Marlborough Street	D2-D3
				Greengate	C7
				Greengate West	B7-C7
				Grosvenor Street	E2-F2
				Hampson Street	A4
				Hanover Street	D7-E7-E6

Hanworth Close	F2	Middlewood Street	A4	St John Street	C4
Hardman Street	C4	Miller Street	E7	St Mary's Gate	D6
Hargreaves Street	E8	Minshull Street	E4-F4	St Mary's Parsonage	C5
Harrison Street	A8	Mirabel Street	C7-D7	St Mary's Street	C5
Hatton Avenue	A8	Mosley Street	D4-D5-E5	St Simon Street	A8-B8-B7
Henry Street	F6	Mount Street	D4	St Stephen Street	B6-B7
High Street	E5-E6	Museum Street	C4-D4	St Wilfrid's Street	B1
Higher Chatham Street	D2-E1	Nancy Street	A1	Sackville Street	F3-E3-E4
Hilton Street	E6-F6-F5	Nathan Drive	B6	Samuel Ogden Street	E3
Hope Street	E5	New Bridge Street	C7	Sharp Street	E7-F7
Houldsworth Street	F5-F6	New Elm Road	A3	Shaw Street	D8
Hulme Hall Road	A2	New Market	D5	Sherborne Street West	B8-C8
Hulme Street	C1-C2-D2-E2	New Quay Street	B4-B5	Sherratt Street	F6
Humberstone Avenue	C1	New Wakefield Street	D3	Shortcroft Street	C2
Hunmanby Avenue	C1	New Welcome Street	C1	Shudehill	E6-E7
Hunts Bank	D7	Newcastle Street	D1-D2	Sidney Street	D3
Inchley Road	F1	Newton Street	E5-F5-F6	Silk Street	A7
Islington Way	A5-A6	Nicholas Street	D4-E4	Sillavan Way	B6
Jackson Crescent	C1-C2	Norfolk Street	D5	Silvercroft Street	B2
Jackson's Row	C4	North George Street	A6-A7	Simpson Street	E7-F7
James Street	A5	North Hill Street	A7	Skerry Close	F2
John Dalton Street	C5-D5	North Star Drive	A5	Sorrel Street	B1
John Street	E6	Norton Street	C6-C7	South King Street	C5-D5
Jordan Street	C2-C3	Oak Street	E6	Southall Street	C8-D8
Julia Street	C8-D8	Oldham Road	F6-F7	Southmill Street	C4-D4
Jutland Street	F4-F5	Oldham Street	E5-E6-F6	Sparkle Street	F4
Kays Gardens	A6-B6	Overbridge Road	C8	Spaw Street	B5-B6
Kennedy Street	C5-D4	Oxford Road	E3-E2-E1	Spear Street	E5-E6-F6
Kincardine Road	F1-F2	Oxford Street	D3-D4	Spring Gardens	D5
King Street	B7-C7-C6	Pall Mall	D5	Stocks Street	E8
King Street	C5-D5	Park Place	D8	Stocks Street East	E8
King Street West	C5	Park Street	D8	Store Street	F4
Laystall Street	F5	Parker Street	E5	Stretford Road	C1-D1
Leaf Street	C1	Parsonage	C5-C6	Sussex Street	A8-B8
Lena Street	F5	Paton Street	F5	Swan Street	E7-E6-F6
Lever Street	E5-F5-F6	Peary Street	F8	Tariff Street	F5
Linby Street	B1-B2	Peru Street	A6	Tatton Street	A1
Little John Street	B4	Peter Street	C4-D4	Thompson Street	F6
Little Peter Street	C3	Piccadilly	E5-F5-F4	Tib Street	E5-E6-F6
Liverpool Road	A4-B4-B3-C3	Pimblett Street	D8	Todd Street	D6-D7
Lloyd Street	C4-C5	Port Street	F5-F6	Tonman Street	B3-C3
Lockton Close	F2	Portland Street	D3-D4-E4-E5	Trafford Street	C3
London Road	F3-F4	Potato Wharf	A3-B3	Travis Street	F3
Long Millgate	D6-D7	Prince's Bridge	A4	Trinity Way	B5-B6-C7-D7
Longworth Street	C3-C4	Princess Street	E3-E4-D4-D5	Turner Street	E6
Lord Street	D8-E8	Quay Street	B4-C4	Tysoe Gardens	A6-B6
Lordsmead Street	A1	Queen Street	B7-C7	Upper Brook Street	F1-F2
Lower Broughton Road	A8	Queen Street	C4	Viaduct Street	C6
Lower Byrom Street	B4	Quenby Street	A1	Victoria Street	D6-D7
Lower Mosley Street	C3-D3-D4	Red Bank	E8	Victoria Bridge Street	C6-D6
Lower Moss Lane	A1-A2	Reilley Street	C1	Walkers Croft	D7
Lower Ormond Street	D2-E2-E1	Richmond Street	E4	Water Street	A3-A4-B4
Loxford Street	D1	River Place	C2	Watson Street	C3-C4
Ludgate Hill	E7-F7	River Street	C2	West King Street	B7
Ludgate Street	E7	Riverside	A8	West Mosley Street	C4-D5-E5
Major Street	E4	Robert Street	D8	Whitekirk Close	F1
Mancunian Way	B2-D2-E2-F3	Rochdale Road	E7-F7-F8	Whitworth Street	D3-E3-F4
Manson Avenue	A1	Rockdove Avenue	C1	Whitworth Street West	C3-D3
Marble Street	D5-E5	Rodney Street	A5	William Street	B6
Market Street	D6-D5-E5	Roger Street	E8	Wilmott Street	D2
Marsden Street	D5	Rosamond Drive	A6	Windmill Street	C4-D4
Marshall Street	E7-F7-F6	Rosamond Street West	C1	Withy Grove	D6
Mary France Street	B1	Royce Road	A1-B1-C1	Wood Street	C5
Mary Street	C7-C8	St Ann Street	C5-D5	Worsley Street	A2
Mayan Avenue	A6	St Chad's Street	E8	York Street	D5-E5-E4
Mayes Street	E6-E7	St George's Avenue	A1	York Street	E1-E2
Medlock Street	C2	St James Street	D4	Young Street	B4-B5

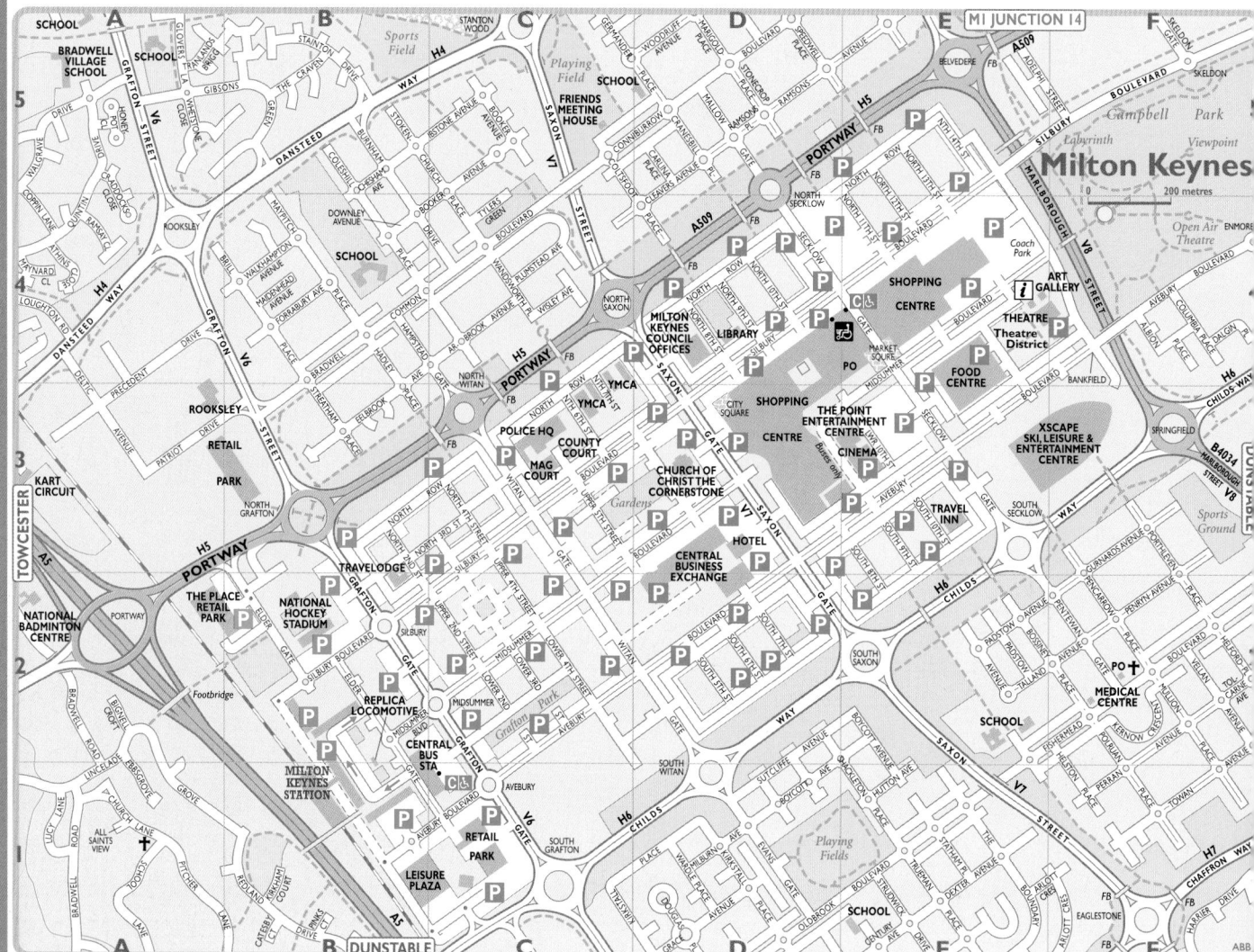

Milton Keynes

Milton Keynes is found on atlas page **38**,
grid reference **8537**

Adelphi Street	E5-F5	Cranesbill Place	D5	Kirkstall Place	C1-D1	North Row	B3-C3-D4-E5	South 8th Street	E2-E3	Woodruff Avenue	D
Albion Place	F4	Dalgin Place	F4	Lincelade Grove	A2-A1-B1	Oldbrook Boulevard	D1-E1	South 9th Street	E3
All Saints View	A1	Dansteed Way	A3-A4-B5-C5	Loughton Road	A4	Padstow Avenue	E2	South 10th Street	E3
Arbrook Avenue	C4	Deltic Avenue	A3-A4	Lower 2nd Street	C2	Patriot Drive	A3-B3	Speedwell Place	D5
Arlott Crescent	E1-F1	Dexter Avenue	E1	Lower 3rd Street	C2	Pencarrow Place	F2	Stainton Drive	B5
Athins Close	A4	Douglas Place	D1	Lower 4th Street	C2	Penryn Avenue	F2	Statham Place	E1
Avebury Boulevard	B1-C2-E3-F4	Downley Avenue	B4	Lower 10th Street	E3	Pentewan Gate	F2	Stokenchurch Place	B5-C5-C4
Bignell Croft	A2	Ebbsgrove	A1-A2	Lucy Lane	A1	Perran Avenue	F1-F2	Stonecrop Place	D5
Booker Avenue	B4-C4-C5	Eelbrook Avenue	B3-B4	Maidenhead Avenue	B4	Pitcher Lane	A1-B1	Streatham Place	B3
Bossiney Place	E2-F2	Elder Gate	B2-B1-C1	Mallow Gate	D5	Pinks Court	B1	Strudwick Drive	E1
Boycott Avenue	D1-E1-E2	Evans Gate	D1	Marigold Place	D5	Plumstead Avenue	C4	Sutcliffe Avenue	D1-D2-E2
Bradwell Common		Fishermead Boulevard	E2-F2	Marlborough Street	E5-F4-F3	Polruan Place	F1-F2	Talland Avenue	E2-F2
Boulevard	B3-B4-C4-C5	Forrabury Avenue	B4	Maynard Close	A4	Porthleven Place	F2-F3	The Boundary	E1
Bradwell Road	A1, A2	Germander Place	C5-D5	Maypitch Place	B4	Portway	A2-B3-C4-E5	The Craven	B5
Brill Place	A4-B4	Gibsons Green	A5-B5	Midsummer		Precedent Drive	A3-A4	Tolcarne Avenue	F2
Burnham Drive	B5-B4-C4	Glovers Lane	A5	Boulevard	B2-C2-D3-E4	Quintin Drive	A4-A5	Towan Avenue	F1-F2
Caruna Place	D5	Grace Avenue	D1	Milburn Avenue	D1	Ramsay Close	A4	Tranlands Brigg	A5
Catesby Court	B1	Grafton Gate	B3-B2-C2-C1	Mullion Place	F1-F2	Ramsons Avenue	D5-E5	Trueman Place	E1
Century Avenue	E1	Grafton Street	A5-A4-B4-B3	North 2nd Street	B2-B3	Ramsons Place	D5	Tylers Green	C4-C5
Chaffron Way	F1	Gurnards Avenue	F3	North 3rd Street	B3-C3	Redland Drive	B1	Upper 2nd Street	C2
Chesham Avenue	B5	Hadley Place	B3-B4	North 4th Street	C3	Saxon Gate	D4-D3-D2-E2	Upper 4th Street	C2-C3
Childs Way	C1-D2-E3-F5	Hampstead Gate	B4-C4-C3	North 6th Street	C3	Saxon Street	C5-C4, E2-E1-F1	Upper 5th Street	C3
Church Lane	A1	Harrier Drive	F1	North 7th Street	C3-C4	School Lane	A1	Vellan Avenue	F2
Cleavers Avenue	D4-D5	Helford Place	F2	North 8th Street	D4	Secklow Gate	D4-E4-E3	Walgrave Drive	A5
Coleshill Place	B4-B5	Helston Place	F1-F2	North 9th Street	D4	Shackleton Place	D2-E1	Walkhampton Avenue	B4
Coltsfoot Place	C5-D4	Honey Pot Close	A5	North 10th Street	D4	Silbury Boulevard	B2-C3-D4-F5	Wandsworth Place	C4
Columbia Place	F4	Hutton Avenue	E1-E2	North 11th Street	E4	Skeldon Gate	F5	Wardle Place	D1
Conniburrow Boulevard	C5-D5	Ibstone Avenue	B5-C5	North 12th Street	E4-E5	South 5th Street	D2	Whetstone Close	A5
Coppin Lane	A4	Kernow Crescent	F2	North 13th Street	E4-E5	South 6th Street	D2	Wisley Avenue	C4
Craddocks Close	A4-A5	Kirkham Court	B1	North 14th Street	E5	South 7th Street	D2	Witan Gate	C3-C2-D2

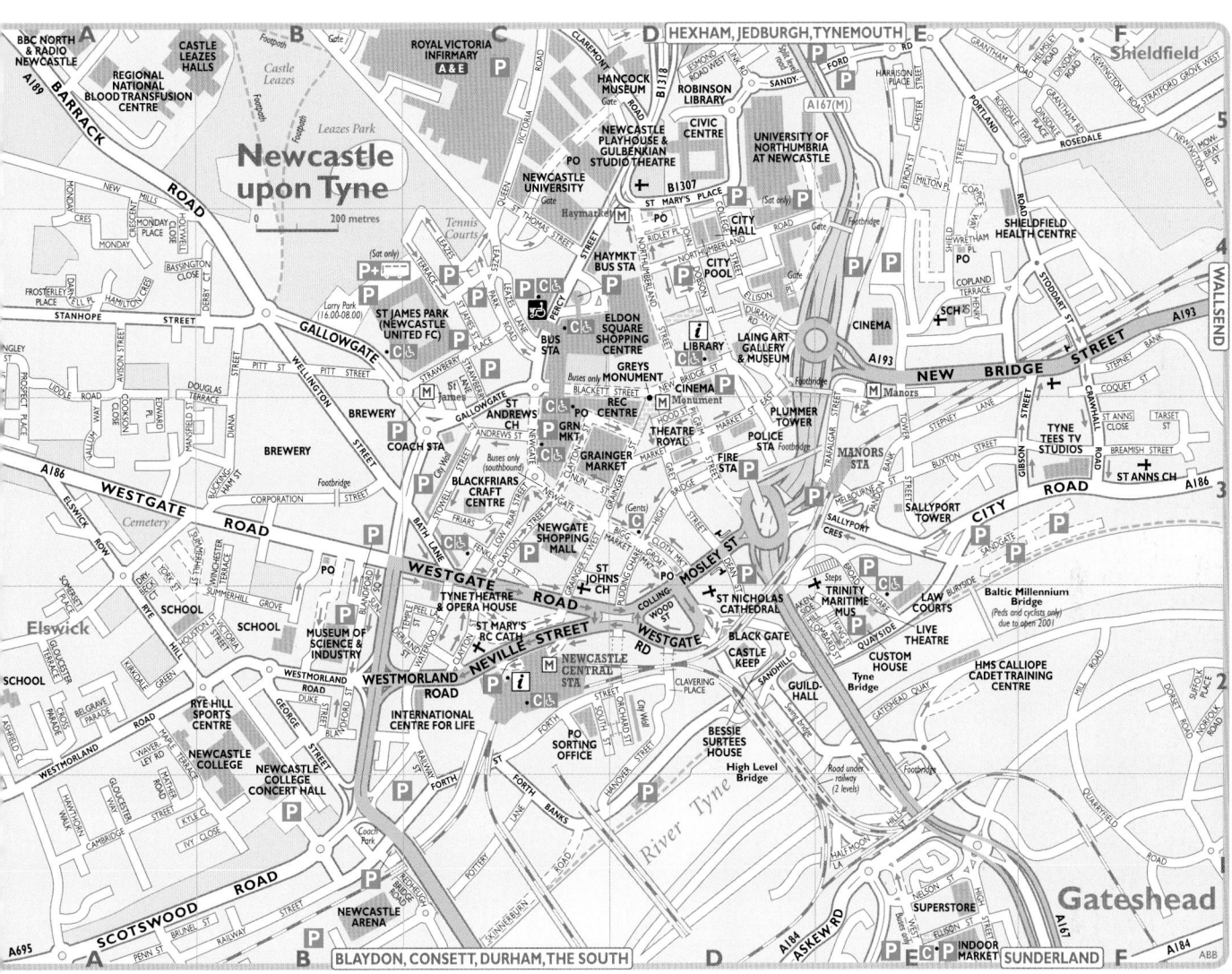

Newcastle upon Tyne

Newcastle upon Tyne is found on atlas page **103**,
id reference **2464**

...enside Hill	D2-E2	Corporation Street	B3	Grantham Road	E5-F5	*Melbourne Street	E3	Portland Road	E5-F5-F4	Stoddart Street	F4
...hfield Close	A2	Crawhall Road	F3-F4	Grey Street	D3	Mansfield Street	A3	Pottery Lane	C1	Stowell Street	C3
...kew Road	D1-E1	Cross Parade	A2	Groat Market	D3	Maple Terrace	A2-B1	Prospect Place	A3-A4	Stratford Grove West	F5
...son Street	A4	Darnell Place	A4	Half Moon Lane	E1	Market Street	D3	Pudding Chare	D2-D3	Strawberry Lane	C3-C4
...rrack Road	A5-B4	Dean Street	D2-D3	Hamilton Crescent	A4	Market Street East	D3-D4	Quarryfield Road	F1-F2	Strawberry Place	C4
...ssington Close	A4-B4	Derby Court	B4	Hanover Street	C1-D1-D2	Mather Road	A1-A2	Quayside	E2	Suffolk Place	F2
...h Lane	C3	Diana Street	B3-B4	Harrison Place	E5	Mill Road	F2	Queen Victoria Road	C4-C5	Summerhill Grove	B2
...grave Parade	A2	Dinsdale Place	F5	Hawthorn Walk	A1	Milton Place	E5	Railway Street	A1-B1-C1-C2	Summerhill Street	A3-B3
...ndford Square	B2-B3	Dinsdale Road	F5	Helmsley Road	E5-F5	Monday Crescent	A4-A5	Redheugh Bridge Road	B1-C1	Sunderland Street	B2-C2
...ndford Street	B2	Dorset Road	F2	Henry Square	E4	Monday Place	A4	Ridley Place	D4	Tarset Street	F3
...eamish Street	F3	Douglas Terrace	A4-B3	High Bridge	D3	Mosley Street	D3	Rosedale	F5	Temple Street	B2-C2
...oad Chare	E2-E3	Drybeck Court	A2-A3	High Street	E1	Mowbray Street	F5	Rosedale Terrace	E5-F5	Tower Street	E3
...ckingham Street	B3	Duke Street	B2	Hills Street	E1	Nelson Street	E1	Rye Hill	A3-A2-B2	Trafalgar Street	E3-E4
...xton Street	E3	Durant Road	D4	Holiston Street	A2-B2	New Bridge Street	D4	St Andrews Street	C3	Vallum Way	A3
...nel Street	E5	Edward Place	A3	Holywell Close	A4	New Bridge Street	E4-F4	St Anns Close	F3	Victoria Street	B2
...mbridge Street	A1	Ellison Place	D4	Hood Street	D3	New Mills	A5-A4	St James Street	C4	Waterloo Street	C2
...ron Street	E5	Elswick Row	A3	Ivy Close	A1-B1	Newgate	C3	St Mary's Place	D5	Waverley Road	A2
...mbridge Street	A1	Fenckle Street	C3	Jesmond Road West	D5	Newington Road	F5	St Thomas Street	C4-C5	Wellington Street	B3-B4
...ester Street	E5	Forth Banks	C1-C2	John Dobson Street	D4	Norfolk Road	F2	Sallyport Crescent	E3	West Ellison Street	E1
...y Road	E3-F3	Forth Street	C1-C2-D2	King Street	E2	Northcote Street	A3-A4	Sandgate	E3	Westgate Road	A3-B3-C3-D2
...remont Road	C5-D5	Friars Street	C3	Kirkdale Green	A2	Northumberland Road	D4-E4	Sandhill	D2	Westmorland Road	A1-A2-B2-C2
...yton Street	C2-C3	Frosterley Place	A4	Kyle Close	A1-B1	Northumberland Street	D4	Sandyford Road	D5-E5	Winchester Terrace	B2-B3
...oth Market	D3	Gallowgate	B4-C3-C4	Leazes Lane	C4	Nun Street	C3	Scotswood Road	A1-B1	Wretham Place	E4
...llege Street	D4-D5	Gateshead Quay	E2	Leazes Park Road	C4	Orchard Street	D2	Shield Street	E4-E5	York Street	A2-A3
...llingwood Street	D2	George Street	B1-B2	Leazes Terrace	C4	Pandon Bank	E3	Skinnerburn Road	C1	
...ookson Close	A3	Gibson Street	F3-F4	Liddle Road	A3-A4	Peel Lane	C2	Somerset Place	A2	
...pland Terrace	E4	Gloucester Terrace	A2	Link Road	D5	Penn Street	A1	South Street	C2-D2	
...ppice Way	E4-E5	Gloucester Way	A1	Lombard Street	D2-E2	Percy Street	C4	Stanhope Street	A4-B4	
...quet Street	F4	Grainger Street	C3-D3	Longley Street	A4	Pilgrim Street	D3	Stepney Bank	F3-F4	
		Grainger Street West	C2-C3	Low Friar Street	C3	Pitt Street	B4	Stepney Lane	E3-E4	

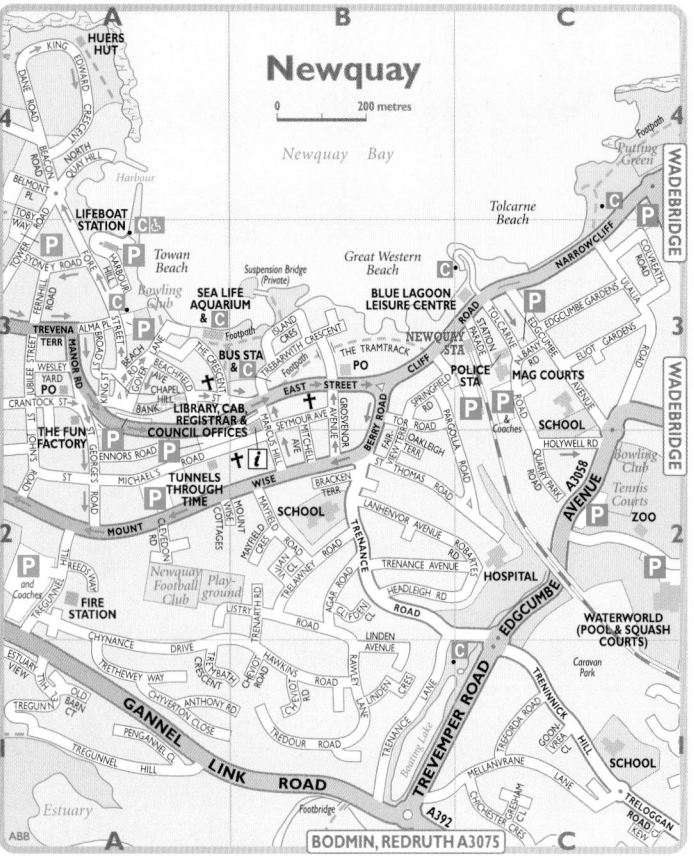

Newquay

Newquay is found on atlas page **4**,
grid reference **8161**

Agar Road	B2	King Street	A3	Trenance Lane	B1
Albany Road	C3	Lanhenvor Avenue	B2	Trenance Road	B2
Alma Place	A3	Linden Avenue	B1-B2	Trenarth Road	
Anthony Road	A1-B1	Linden Crescent	B1	Treninnick Hill	
Bank Street	A3-B3	Listry Road	A2-B2	Trethewey Way	
Beach Road	A3	Manor Road	A3	Trevemper Road	B1
Beachfield Avenue	A3	Marcus Hill	B2-B3	Trevena Terrace	
Beacon Road	A4	Mayfield Crescent	B2	Ulalia Road	
Belmont Place	A4	Mayfield Road	B2	Vivian Close	
Berry Road	B2-B3	Mellanvrane Lane	B1-C1	Wesley Yard	
Bracken Terrace	B2	Mitchell Avenue	B2-B3		
Broad Street	A3	Mount Wise	A2-B2		
Chapel Hill	A3	Mount Wise Cottages	A2-B2		
Cheviot Road	B1	Narrowcliff	C3-C4		
Chichester Crescent	C1	North Quay Hill	A4		
Chynance Drive	A1-A2	Oakleigh Terrace	B2		
Chyverton Close	A1	Old Barn Court	A1		
Clevedon Road	A2	Pargolla Road	B3-C2		
Clifden Close	B2	Pengannel Close	A1		
Cliff Road	B3-C3	Quarry Park Road	C2		
Colvreath Road	C3	Rawley Lane	B1		
Crantock Street	A3	Reeds Way	A2		
Dane Road	A4	Robartes Road	C2		
East Street	B3	St George's Road	A2-A3		
Edgcumbe Avenue	C2-C3	St John's Road	A2-A3		
Edgcumbe Gardens	C3	St Michael's Road	A2-B2		
Eliot Gardens	C3	St Thomas Road	B2-C2		
Ennors Road	A2	Seymour Avenue	B3		
Estuary View	A1	Springfield Road	B3		
Fairview Terrace	B2-B3	Station Parade	C3		
Fernhill Road	A3	Sydney Road	A3		
Fore Street	A3-A4	The Crescent	A3		
Gannel Link Road	A2-A1-B1	The Tramtrack	B3		
Goonvrea Close	C1	Toby Way	A4		
Gover Lane	A3	Tolcarne Road	C3		
Gresham Close	C1	Tor Road	B3		
Grosvenor Avenue	B2-B3	Tower Road	A3-A4		
Harbour Hill	A3	Trebarwith Crescent	B3		
Hawkins Road	B1	Tredour Road	B1		
Headleigh Road	B2	Treforda Road	C1		
Holywell Road	C2	Tregunnel Hill	A1-A2		
Island Crescent	B3	Trelawney Road	B2		
Jubilee Street	A3	Treloggan Road	C1		
Kew Close	C1	Trembath Crescent	A1-B1		
King Edward Crescent	A4	Trenance Avenue	B2-C2		

Northampton

Northampton is found on atlas page **49**,
grid reference **7560**

Abington Square	C3	Grafton Street	A4	Upper Bath Street	
Abington Street	B2-B3-C3	Great Russell Street	C4	Upper Mounts	B3
Albion Place	B1-B2	Greyfriars	A3-B3-C3	Upper Priory Street	
Alcombe Road	C4	Guildhall Road	B1-B2	Victoria Gardens	
Alexandra Road	C2-C3	Hazelwood Road	C2	Victoria Promenade	B1
Althorp Street	A3	Herbert Street	A3	Victoria Street	B3
Angel Street	B2	Horsemarket	A2-A3	Wellington Street	B3
Arundel Street	A4	Horseshoe Street	A1-A2	William Street	
Ash Street	B4	Hunter Street	C4	York Road	C2
Bailiff Street	B4	King Street	A2		
Barrack Road	A4-B4	Kingswell	A1-A2		
Bath Street	A3	Ladys Lane	A3-B3-C3		
Bedford Road	C1	Lower Harding Street	A4		
Bidders Close	B1	Lower Mounts	C3		
Billing Road	C2	Lower Priory Street	A4		
Bradshaw Street	A2-A3	Margaret Street	B4		
Bridge Street	A1-A2	Market Square	B2		
Broad Street	A3-A4	Mayor Hold	A3		
Campbell Street	A4-B4	Mercer's Row	B2		
Castillian Street	B2	Newland	B3		
Castle Street	A3	Oak Street	B4		
Cattlemarket Road	B1	Overstone Road	C3-C4		
Charles Street	B4-C4	Pike Lane	A2-A3		
Cheyne Walk	C1-C2	Quorn Way	A4		
Church Lane	A3-B3-B4	Regent Street	A4		
Clare Street	C4	Robert Street	B4		
Cloutsham Street	C4	St Andrew's Street	A3-A4		
College Street	A2	St Giles Square	B2		
Commercial Street	A1	St Giles Street	B2-C2		
Connaught Street	B4	St Giles Terrace	C2-C3		
Cranstoun Street	B4-C4	St James Street	A1		
Craven Street	B4-C4	St John's Street	B1		
Crispin Street	A3	St Katherine's Street	A2		
Deal Street	B4	St Mary's Street	A2		
Derngate	C1-C2-B2	St Michael's Road	C3		
Duke Street	B4-C4	St Peter's Way	A1		
Dunster Street	C3-C4	Sheep Street	A3-A4		
Earl Street	B3-C4	Silver Street	A3		
Elm Street	B4	Somerset Street	C4		
Fetter Street	B1-B2	Spencer Parade	C2		
Foundry Street	A1	Spring Gardens	C2		
Gas Street	A1	Swan Street	B1-B2		
George Row	B2	The Drapery	A2-B2		
Georges Street	A4	The Riding	B2-C2		
Gold Street	A2	Tower Street	A3		

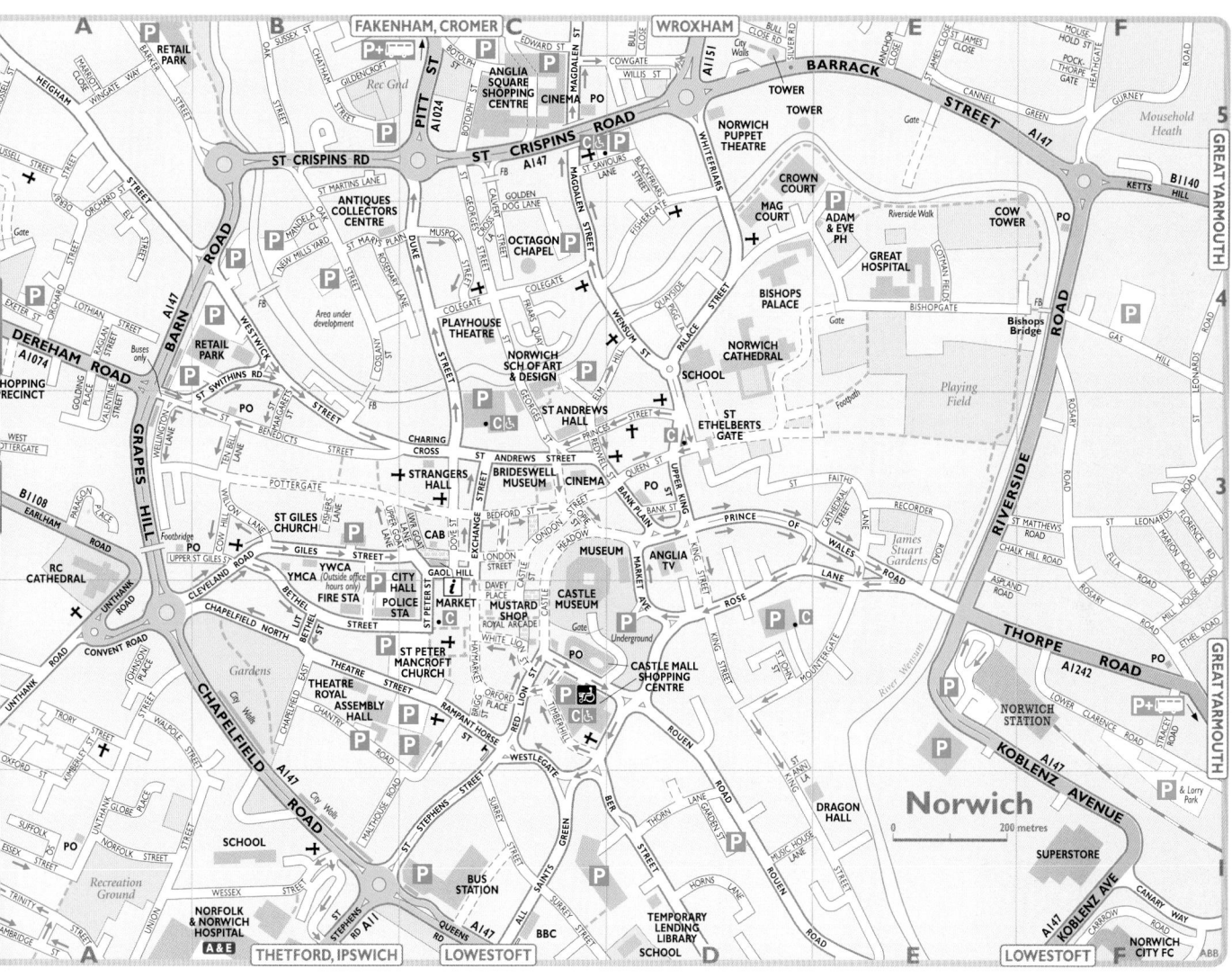

Norwich

orwich is found on atlas page **67**,
d reference **2308**

Saints Green	C1	Chatham Street	B5	Gildencroft	B5	Muspole Street	C4	Russell Street	A5
chor Close	E5	Cleveland Road	A2-B2-B3	Giles Street	B3-C3	New Mills Yard	B4	St Andrews Street	C3
land Road	E3-F2	Colegate	C4	Globe Place	A1	Norfolk Street	A1	St Ann Lane	D1-D2
k Plain	D3	Convent Road	A2	Golden Dog Lane	C4-C5	Oak Street	B4-B5	St Benedicts Street	B3
k Street	D3	Coslany Street	B4	Golding Place	A3-A4	Opie Street	C3	St Crispins Road	B5-C5-D5
ker Street	A5-B5	Cotman Fields	E4	Grapes Hill	A3	Orchard Street	A4-A5	St Faiths Lane	D3-E3
n Road	A4-B4-B5	Cow Hill	B3	Gurney Road	F5	Orford Place	C2	St Georges Street	C3-C4-C5
rack Street	D5-E5-F5	Cowgate	C5-D5	Haymarket	C2	Oxford Street	A1-A2	St James Close	E5
fford Street	C3	Cross Lane	C4	Heathgate	F5	Palace Street	D4	St John Street	D2
Street	D2-D1	Davey Place	C2	Heigham Street	A5-A4-B4	Paragon Place	A3	St Leonards Road	F3-F4
hel Street	B3-B2-C2	Derby Street	A4-A5	Hill House Road	F2-F3	Pigg Lane	D4	St Margarets Street	B3-B4
aopgate	E4-F4	Dereham Road	A4	Horns Lane	D1	Pitt Street	C5	St Martins Lane	B5
ckfriars Street	D5	Dove Street	C3	Johnson Place	A2	Pockthorpe Gate	F5	St Marys Plain	B4-C4
olph Street	C5	Duke Street	C3-C4-C5	Ketts Hill	F5	Pottergate	A3-B3-C3	St Matthews Road	E3-F3
g Street	C2	Earlham Road	A3	Kimberley Street	A1-A2	Prince of Wales Road	D3-E3	St Peter Street	C2-C3
Close	D5	Edward Street	C5	King Street	D3-D2-D1-E1	Princes Street	C3-D3	St Saviours Lane	C5-D5
vert Street	C4-C5	Ella Road	F2-F3	Koblenz Avenue	E2-F2-F1	Quayside	D4	St Stephens Street	B1-C1-C2
ary Way	F1	Elm Hill	C3-D4	Little Bethel Street	B2	Queen Street	D3	St Swithins Road	B3-B4
nbridge Street	A1	Ely Street	A4-A5	London Street	C3-D3	Raglan Street	A4	Stracey Road	F2
nell Green	E5-F5	Essex Street	A1	Lothian Street	A4	Rampant Horse Street	C2	Suffolk Square	A1
rrow Road	F1	Ethel Road	F2	Lower Clarence Road	F1-F2	Recorder Road	E3	Surrey Street	C1-D1
tle Meadow	C2-C3-D3	Exchange Street	C3	Lower Goat Lane	C3	Red Lion Street	C2	Ten Bell Lane	B3
tle Street	C2-C3	Exeter Street	A4	Magdalen Street	C4-C5	Redwell Street	C3-D3	Theatre Street	B2-C2
hedral Street	E3	Fishergate	D4-D5	Malthouse Road	B1-C1	Riverside	E1-E2	Thorn Lane	D1
alk Hill Road	E3-F3	Fishers Lane	B3	Mandela Close	B4	Riverside Road	E3-F3-F4-F5	Thorpe Road	E2-F2
antry Road	B2-C2-C1	Florence Road	F3	Marion Road	F3	Rosary Road	F2-F3-F4	Timberhill	C2
apelfield East	B2	Friars Quay	C4	Market Avenue	D2-D3	Rose Lane	D2-D3-E3	Trinity Street	A1
apelfield North	B2	Gaol Hill	C3	Marriott Close	A5	Rosemark Lane	B4-C4	Trory Street	A2
apelfield Road	A2-B2-B1	Garden Street	D1	Mountergate	D2-E2	Rouen Road	D2-D1-E1	Union Street	A1-B1
aring Cross	C3	Gas Hill	F4	Music House Lane	D1-E1	Royal Arcade	C2	Unthank Road	A2-A3
								Unthank Street	A1-A2
								Upper Goat Lane	B3-C3
								Upper King Street	D3
								Upper St Giles Street	A3-B3
								Valentine Street	A3-A4
								Walpole Street	A2-B2
								Wellington Lane	A3
								Wensum Street	C4-D4
								Wessex Street	A1-B1
								West Pottergate	A3
								Westlegate	C1-C2
								Westwick Street	B3-B4
								White Lion Street	D4-D5
								Whitefriars	D4-D5
								Willis Street	D5
								Willow Lane	B3
								Wingate Way	A5

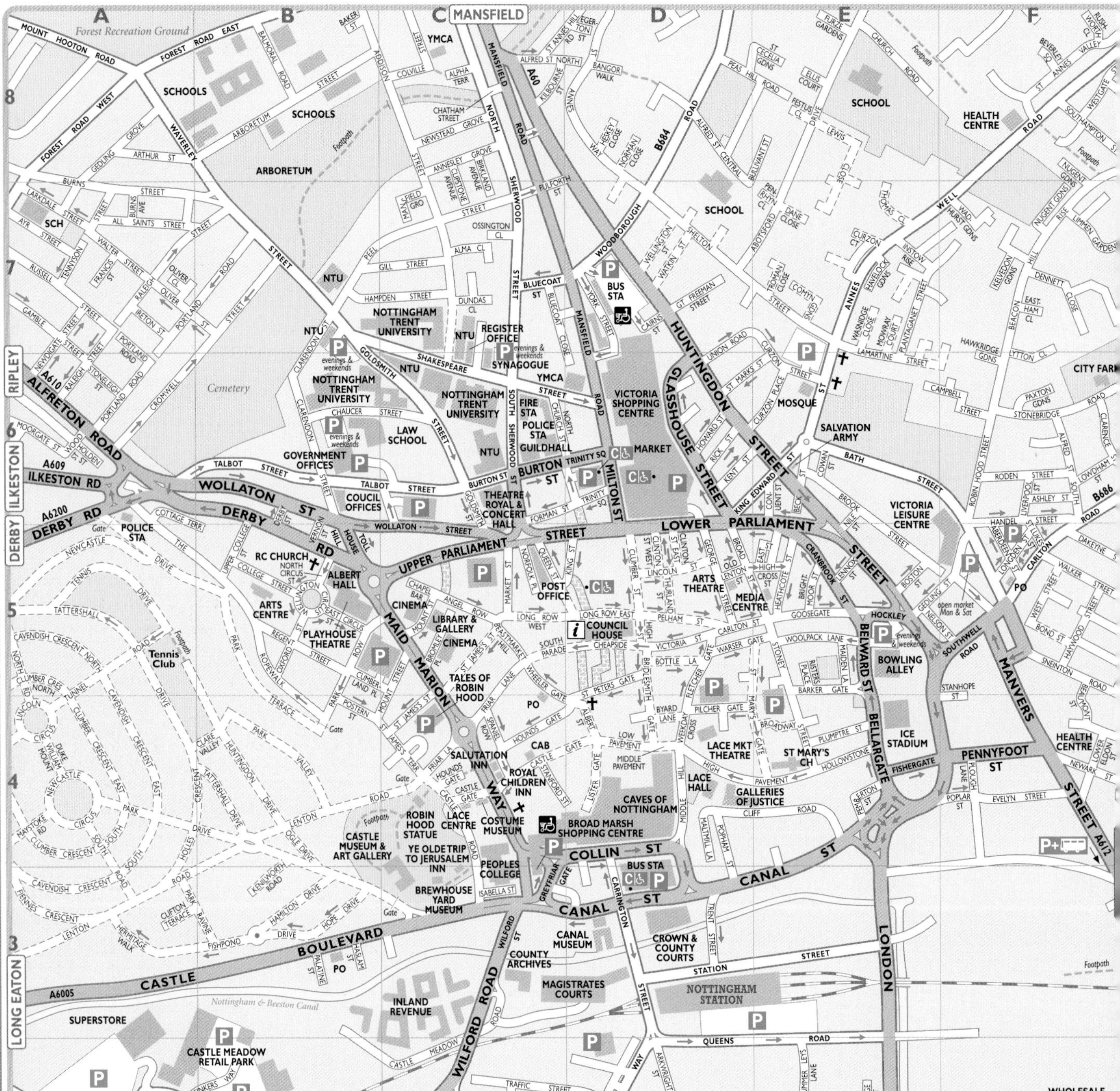

Nottingham

MANSFIELD

ASHBY

LOUGHBOROUGH

Forest Recreation Ground

RIPLEY
ILKESTON
DERBY
LONG EATON

SCHOOLS
SCHOOLS
ARBORETUM
NTU
NOTTINGHAM TRENT UNIVERSITY
NTU
NOTTINGHAM TRENT UNIVERSITY
NOTTINGHAM TRENT UNIVERSITY
LAW SCHOOL
Cemetery
GOVERNMENT OFFICES
COUCIL OFFICES
WOLLATON ST
DERBY RD
POLICE STA
RC CHURCH
ALBERT HALL
ARTS CENTRE
PLAYHOUSE THEATRE
CINEMA
LIBRARY & GALLERY
CINEMA
TALES OF ROBIN HOOD
UPPER PARLIAMENT
MAID MARION WAY
SALUTATION INN
ROBIN HOOD STATUE
LACE CENTRE
COSTUME MUSEUM
CASTLE MUSEUM & ART GALLERY
YE OLDE TRIP TO JERUSALEM INN
PEOPLES COLLEGE
BREWHOUSE YARD MUSEUM
ROYAL CHILDREN INN
BROAD MARSH SHOPPING CENTRE
COLLIN ST
BUS STA
CANAL
CAVES OF NOTTINGHAM
GALLERIES OF JUSTICE
LACE HALL
LACE MKT THEATRE
ST MARY'S CH
ICE STADIUM
BOWLING ALLEY
VICTORIA LEISURE CENTRE
HEALTH CENTRE
MANVERS
PENNYFOOT ST
CITY FARM
SCHOOL
HEALTH CENTRE
MOSQUE
SALVATION ARMY
VICTORIA SHOPPING CENTRE
MARKET
LOWER PARLIAMENT STREET
MEDIA CENTRE
ARTS THEATRE
POST OFFICE
COUNCIL HOUSE
THEATRE ROYAL & CONCERT HALL
FIRE STA
POLICE STA
GUILDHALL
REGISTER OFFICE
SYNAGOGUE
YMCA
BUS STA
HUNTINGDON STREET
GLASSHOUSE STREET
BELLARGATE
BELWARD ST
CANAL MUSEUM
COUNTY ARCHIVES
MAGISTRATES COURTS
INLAND REVENUE
CROWN & COUNTY COURTS
NOTTINGHAM STATION
CASTLE BOULEVARD
SUPERSTORE
CASTLE MEADOW RETAIL PARK
CASTLE MARINA ROAD
POLICE STATION
WILFORD ROAD
LONDON ROAD
WHOLESALE FRUIT & FLOWER MARKET
NOTTS COUNTY FOOTBALL GROUND
CATTLE MARKET RD
SCHOOL
SCHOOLS
QUEENS DRIVE
DRIVE
Nottingham & Beeston Canal
Tennis Club

Nottingham
0   200 metres

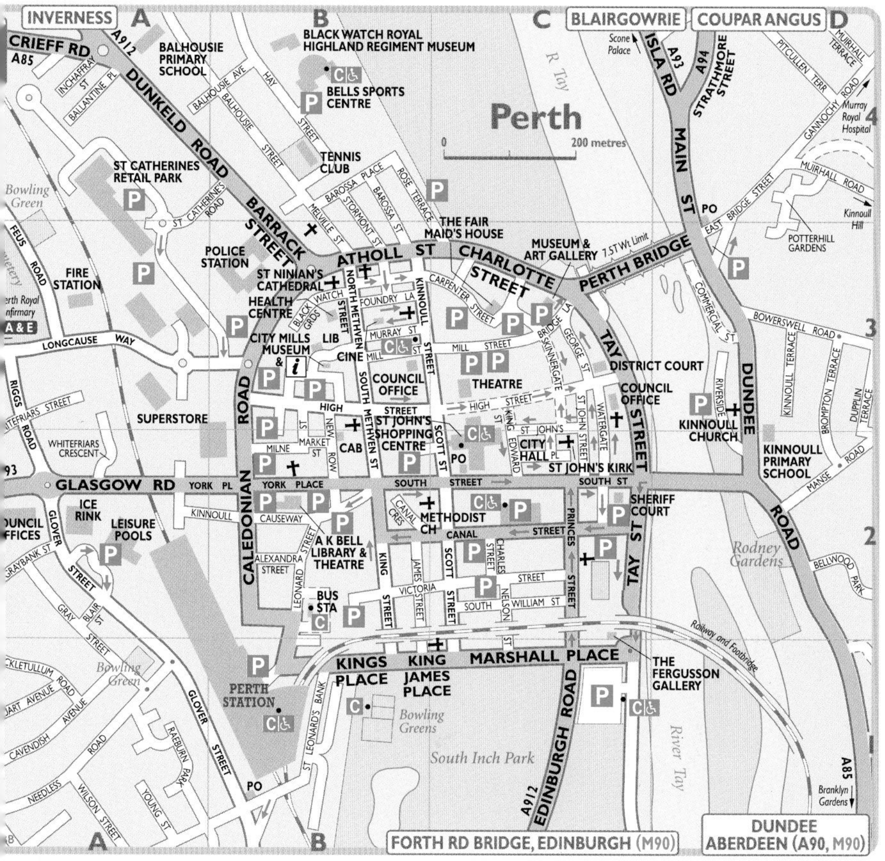
INVERNESS
A
B
C
D
BLAIRGOWRIE
COUPAR ANGUS
CRIEFF RD
A85
A912
DUNKELD ROAD
BALHOUSIE PRIMARY SCHOOL
BLACK WATCH ROYAL HIGHLAND REGIMENT MUSEUM
BELLS SPORTS CENTRE
Perth
200 metres
Scone Palace
ISLA RD
A93
A94
STRATHMORE STREET
MAIN ST
R Tay
TENNIS CLUB
ST CATHERINES RETAIL PARK
Bowling Green
BARRACK STREET
ATHOLL ST
CHARLOTTE STREET
THE FAIR MAID'S HOUSE
MUSEUM & ART GALLERY
PERTH BRIDGE
POLICE STATION
FIRE STATION
ST NINIAN'S CATHEDRAL
HEALTH CENTRE
CITY MILLS MUSEUM
LIB
CINE
COUNCIL OFFICE
THEATRE
DISTRICT COURT
COUNCIL OFFICE
KINNOULL CHURCH
LONGCAUSE WAY
SUPERSTORE
WHITEFRIARS CRESCENT
ST JOHN'S SHOPPING CENTRE
CAB
CITY HALL
ST JOHN'S KIRK
KINNOULL PRIMARY SCHOOL
DUNDEE ROAD
GLASGOW RD
YORK PL
YORK PLACE
SOUTH STREET
ICE RINK
LEISURE POOLS
CALEDONIAN ROAD
METHODIST CH
SHERIFF COURT
TAY ST
A K BELL LIBRARY & THEATRE
Rodney Gardens
BUS STA
KINGS PLACE
KING JAMES PLACE
MARSHALL PLACE
THE FERGUSSON GALLERY
Railway and Footbridge
PERTH STATION
Bowling Greens
South Inch Park
EDINBURGH ROAD
A912
River Tay
GLOVER STREET
A85
Branklyn Gardens
FORTH RD BRIDGE, EDINBURGH (M90)
DUNDEE
ABERDEEN (A90, M90)
PO
1
2
3
4

Perth

Perth is found on atlas page **126**, grid reference **1123**

Alexandra Street	B2
Atholl Street	B3-C3
Balhousie Avenue	A4-B4
Balhousie Street	A4-B4
Ballantine Place	A4
Barossa Place	B4
Barossa Street	B3-B4
Barrack Street	B3-B4
Bellwood Park	D2
Black Watch Gardens	B3
Blair Street	A2
Bowerswell Road	D3
Bridge Lane	C3
Brompton Terrace	D2-D3
Caledonian Road	B2-B3
Canal Crescent	B2
Canal Street	B2-C2
Carpenter Street	B3-C3
Cavendish Avenue	A1
Charles Street	C2
Charlotte Street	C3
Commercial Street	D3
Crieff Road	A4
Dundee Road	D1-D2-D3
Dunkeld Road	A4-B4
Dupplin Terrace	D2-D3
East Bridge Street	D3-D4
Edinburgh Road	C1
Feus Road	A3-A4
Foundry Lane	B3
Gannochy Road	D4
George Street	C3
Glasgow Road	A2
Glover Street	A2-A1-B1
Gray Street	A1-A2
Graybank Street	A2
Hay Street	B4
High Street	B3-C3
Inchaffray Street	A4
Isla Road	C4-D4
James Street	B2
King Edward Street	C2-C3
King James Place	B1-C1
King Street	B2
Kings Place	B1
Kinnoull Causeway	A2-B2
Kinnoull Street	B3-C3
Kinnoull Terrace	D3
Leonard Street	B1-B2
Longcause Way	A3
Main Street	D3-D4
Manse Road	D2
Market Street	B2
Marshall Place	C1
Melville Street	B3-B4
Mill Street	B3-C3
Milne Street	B2-B3
Muirhall Road	D4
Muirhall Terrace	D4
Murray Street	B3
Needless Road	A1
Nelson Street	C2
New Row	B2-B3
North Methven Street	B3
Perth Bridge	C3-D3
Pickletullum Road	A1
Pitcullen Terrace	D4
Potterhill Gardens	D3-D4
Raeburn Park	A1-B1
Riggs Road	A2-A3
Riverside	D2-D3
Rose Terrace	B4-C3
St Catherine's Road	A3-A4-B4
St John Street	C2-C3
St John's Place	C2-C3
St Leonard's Bank	B1
Scott Street	C1-C2-C3
Skinnergate	C3
South Methven Street	B2-B3
South Street	B2-C2
South William Street	C2
Stormont Street	B3-B4
Strathmore Street	D4
Stuart Avenue	A1
Tay Street	C2-C3
Victoria Street	B2-C2
Watergate	C2-C3
Whitefriars Crescent	A2-A3
Whitefriars Street	A2-A3
Wilson Street	A1
York Place	A2-B2
Young Street	A1

Nottingham

Nottingham is found on atlas page **62**, grid reference **5739**

rdeen Street	F5
tsford Drive	D7-E7-E8
son Street	B8-C8-C7
rt Street	D4
rmans Close	C1
ed Street Central	D7-D8
ed Street North	C8-D8
ed Street South	F6
eton Road	A6
aints Street	A7
Close	C7
a Terrace	C8
el Row	C5
esley Grove	C8
oretum Street	B8
wright Street	D2
wright Walk	D2
ur Street	A8
ey Street	F6
Street	A7
n Crescent	C1
oral Road	B8
or Walk	D8
er Gate	E5
Street	E6-F6-F5
on Hill Rise	F7-F8
dsley Gardens	B1
tmarket Hill	C5
mont Street	F4-F5
Street	E6
rgate	E4
ard Street	E5
rley Square	F8
and Avenue	C7-C8
coat Close	C7-D7-D6
coat Street	C7
l Street	F5
on Street	E5
e Lane	D5
esmith Gate	D4-D5
tmoor Street	E5
d Street	D5-E5
dway	E4
nley Place	C5
k Street	E6-E5-F5
ant Street	E8
e Close	D2
s Street	A8-A7-B7
on Street	C6
d Lane	D4
ns Street	D7
pbell Street	E6-F6
Canal Street	C3-D3-E3-E4
Carlton Road	F5-F6
Carlton Street	D5-E5
Carrington Street	D3-D4
Castle Boulevard	A3-B3-C3
Castle Bridge Road	A2-B2-B1
Castle Gate	C4-D4
Castle Marina Road	A2
Castle Meadow Road	B3-C2-C3
Castle Road	C3-C4
Castlefields	C2
Cattle Market Road	E2-F2
Cavendish Crescent East	A5-A4
Cavendish Crescent North	A5
Cavendish Crescent South	A3-A4
Chapel Bar	C5
Chatham Street	C8
Chaucer Street	B6-C6
Cheapside	D5
Church Road	E8
Clare Valley	A4-B4
Clarence Street	F6
Clarendon Street	B6-B7
Clarke Road	F2
Cliff Road	D4-E4
Clinton Street East	D5
Clinton Street West	D5
Clipstone Avenue	C7-C8
Clumber Crescent East	A4
Clumber Crescent North	A5
Clumber Crescent South	A4
Clumber Street	D5
College Street	B5
Collin Street	C4-D4
Colville Street	C8
Comyn Gardens	E7
Conuent Street	E6
Cottage Terrace	A6-B5
Cowan Street	E6
Cranbrook Street	E5
Crocus Street	C2-D2-E2
Cromwell Street	A6-B6-B7
Cumberland Place	B5-C5
Curzon Court	E7
Curzon Place	D6-E6
Curzon Street	E6-E7
Dakeyne Street	F5
Dane Close	E7
Dennett Close	F7
Derby Road	A5-A6-B6-B5
Derby Street	B6
Duke William Mount	A4
Dundas Close	C7
East Circus Street	B5
East Street	E5
Edge Street	E2
Ellis Court	E8
Eugene Gardens	E1
Evelyn Street	F4
Festus Close	E8
Fiennes Crescent	A3
Fishergate	E4
Fishpond Drive	A3-B3
Fletcher Gate	D4-D5
Forest Road East	A8-B8
Forest Road West	A8
Forman Street	C6-D6
Francis Street	A7
Friar Lane	C4-C5
Fulforth Street	C7-D8
Furze Gardens	E8
Gamble Street	A6-A7
Gedling Grove	A8
Gedling Street	E5-F5
George Street	D5
Gill Street	B7-C7
Glasshouse Street	D6
Goldsmith Street	B7-B6-C6-C5
Goosegate	E5
Great Freeman Street	D7
Greyfriars Gate	C3
Gritley Mews	C1-C2
Hamilton Drive	B3
Hampden Street	B7-C7
Handel Street	F5-F6
Haslam Street	B3
Havelock Gardens	E7
Hawkridge Gardens	F6
Haywood Street	F5
Heathcote Street	E5
Hermitage Walk	A3
Heskey Close	D8
High Cross Street	E5
High Pavement	D4-E4
High Street	D5
Hockley	E5
Holles Crescent	A3-A4-B4
Hollowstone	E4
Hope Drive	B3
Hounds Gate	C4-D4
Houseman Gardens	C1-D1
Howard Street	D6
Humber Close	D1
Huntingdon Drive	B4
Huntingdon Street	C8-D7-E6
Ilkeston Road	A6
Incinerator Road	F2
Instow Rise	E7
Iremonger Road	E2-E1-F1
Ireton Street	A7
Isabella Street	C3
Kelso Gardens	B1
Kelvedon Gardens	F7
Kent Street	D6-E6
Kilbourne Street	C8
King Edward Street	D6-E6
King Street	D5
Kinglake Place	C2
Kirkby Gardens	D1-E1
Kirtley Drive	A2
Lamartine Street	E6-E7
Lammas Gardens	D2-E2
Larkdale Street	A7
Launders Street	C1
Lawrence Way	A2
Lennox Street	E5
Lenton Road	A3-B4-C4
Lewis Close	E7-E8
Limmen Gardens	F7
Lincoln Circus	A4
Lincoln Street	D5
Lister Gate	D4
Liverpool Street	F6
London Road	E1-E2-E3-E4
Long Row East	D5
Long Row West	C5
Longden Street	F5
Low Pavement	D4
Lowdham Street	F6
Lower Parliament Street	D5-D6-E5
Lytton Close	F6-F7
Mabel Street	E2
Maid Marion Way	B5-C5-C4
Maiden Lane	E5
Maltmill Lane	D4
Manifold Gardens	D1
Mansfield Road	C8-C7-D7-D6
Manvers Street	F4-F5
Market Street	C5
Maystoke Road	A4
Meadow Lane	F1-F2
Meadows Way	B1-C2-D2-E1
Mickledon Close	C1
Middle Hill	D4
Middle Pavement	D4
Milton Street	D6
Moorgate Street	A6
Mount Hooton Road	A8
Mount Street	B4-C4-C5
Mowray Court	E7
Nelson Street	E5-F5
Newark Street	F4
Newcastle Circus	A4
Newcastle Drive	A5-B5
Newdigate Street	A6-A7
Newstead Grove	C8
Nile Street	E5-E6
Norfolk Place	C5
Norman Close	D8
North Church Street	C6-D6
North Circus Street	B5
North Road	A4-A5
North Sherwood Street	C6-C7-C8
Nugent Gardens	F7-F8
Ogle Drive	B4
Old Lenton Street	D5
Oliver Street	A7-B7
Osier Road	C1
Ossington Close	C7
Oxford Street	B5
Palatine Street	B3
Park Drive	A4-B4
Park Ravine	A3-B3
Park Row	B4-B5-C5
Park Terrace	B4-B5
Park Valley	B4
Paxton Gardens	F6
Peas Hill Road	D8-E8
Peel Street	B7-C7
Pelham Street	D5
Pemberton Street	E4
Pennyfoot Street	F4
Penrhyn Close	E7
Pilcher Gate	D4
Plantaganet Street	E7
Plough Lane	F4
Plumptre Street	E4
Popham Street	D3-D4
Poplar Street	F4
Portland Road	A6-A7-B7
Postern Street	B4
Queen Street	C5
Queens Drive	B1-B2-C2
Queens Road	D2-E2-E3
Raleigh Street	A6-A7-B7
Regent Street	B5
Rick Street	D6
Risley Drive	B1
Risters Place	E5
Robin Hood Street	F6
Robin Hood Way	C1-D1
Roden Street	F6
Russell Street	A7
St Annes Hill Road	C8-D8
St Annes Valley	F8
St Annes Way	D7-D8
St Annes Well Road	E6-E7-F7-F8
St Cecelia Gardens	E8
St George's Drive	C2
St James's Street	C4-C5
St James's Terrace	C4
St Lukes Street	F5
St Marks Street	D6-E6
St Mary's Gate	D5-D4-E4
St Peters Gate	D4-D5
St Saviours Gardens	E1
Saffron Gardens	D1
Shakespeare Street	B7-C7-C6-D6
Shelton Street	D7-E7
Sheriff's Way	D2
Sneinton Road	F4-F5
South Parade	C5-D5
South Road	A3-A4
South Sherwood Street	C6
Southampton Street	F8
Southwell Road	F5
Spaniel Row	C4
Stanford Street	C4-D4
Stanhope Street	F4-F5
Station Street	D3-E3
Stonebridge Road	F6
Stoneleigh Street	A6
Stoney Street	E4-E5
Strome Close	C1
Summer Leys Lane	E2
Talbot Street	A6-B6-C6
Tattershall Drive	A5-A4-B4
Tennis Drive	A5
Tennyson Street	A7
The Ropewalk	A6-A5-B5-B4
Thomas Close	E7
Thrumpton Drive	B1
Thurland Street	D5
Tinkers Way	A2-B2
Toll House Hill	B5
Traffic Street	C2-D2
Trent Street	D3
Trinity Square	D6
Troman Close	E7
Tunnel Road	A4-A5
Union Road	D6-D7
Upper College Street	B5-B6
Upper Parliament Street	C5-D5
Uppingham Gardens	E2
Vernon Street	B5-B6
Victoria Street	D5
Wadhurst Gardens	F7
Waldron Close	E1
Walker Street	F5
Wallett Street	E2
Walter Street	A7
Warser Gate	D5-E5
Wasnidge Close	E7
Waterway Street	D2
Watkin Street	D7
Waverley Street	A8-B8-B7
Weekday Cross	D4
Wellington Circus	B5
Wellington Street	D7
West Street	F5
Westgate Street	F8
Wheeler Gate	C4-C5
Wilford Crescent West	D1
Wilford Grove	D1-D2
Wilford Road	C2-C3
Wilford Street	C3
Willesley Drive	D1
Wollaton Street	A6-B6-B5-C5
Wood Street	A6
Woodborough Road	D7-D8
Woolpack Lane	E5
York Street	D6-D7

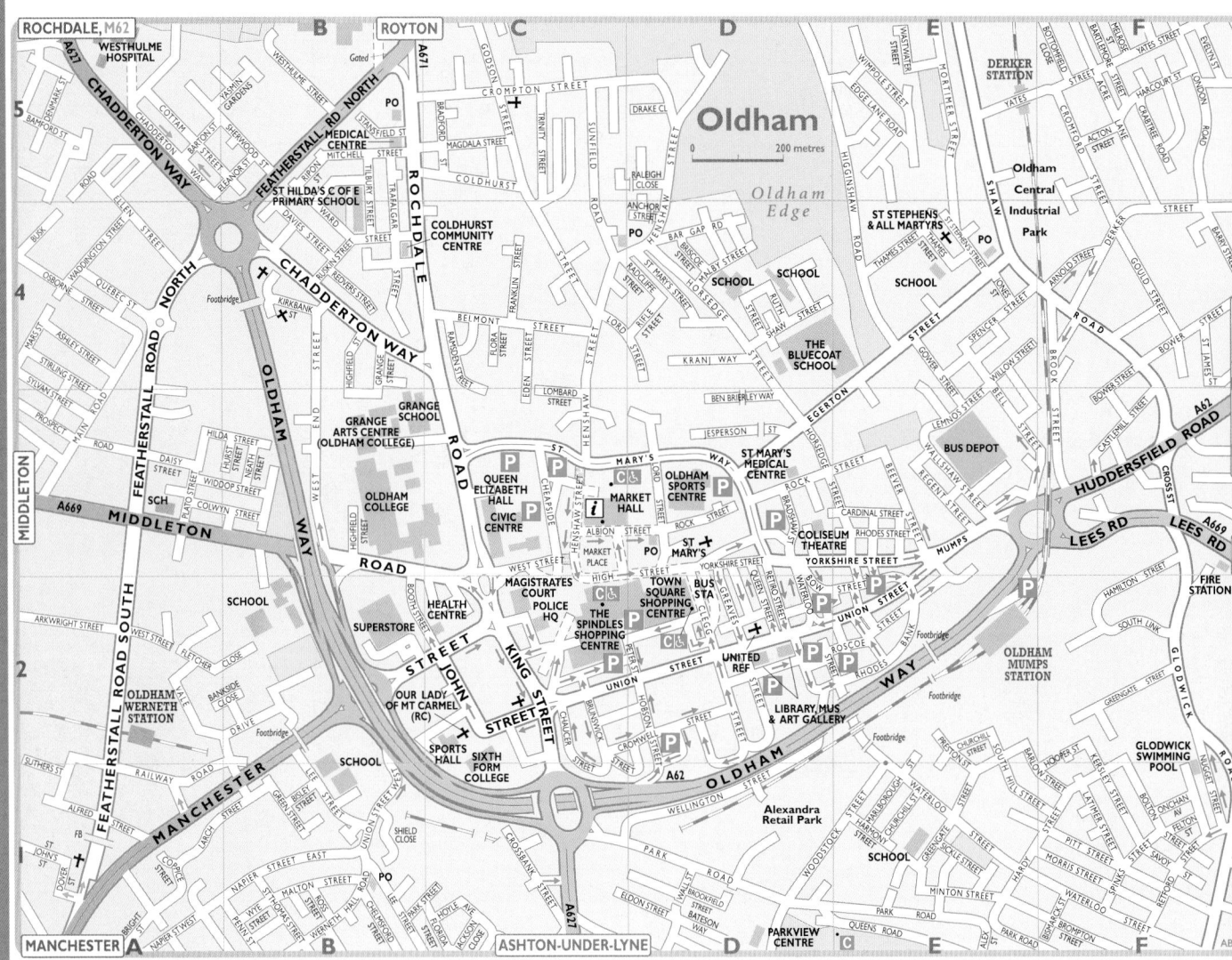

206

Oldham

Oldham is found on atlas page **79**, grid reference **9204**

Acre Lane	F4-F5	Brompton Street	E1-F1	Egerton Street	D3-E3-E4	John Street	C2	Peter Street	C2-D2	Sickle Street	
Acton Street	F5	Brook Street	F3-F4	Eldon Street	C1-D1	Jones Street	E4	Pitt Street	E1-F1	South Hill Street	E2-E
Albion Street	C3-D3	Brookfield Street	D1	Eleanor Street	A5-B5	Kersley Street	F1-F2	Plato Street	A3	South Link	
Alex Street	E1	Brunswick Street	C2-C1-D1-D2	Ellen Street	A4-A5	King Street	C2	Preston Street	E1-E2	Spencer Street	
Alfred Street	A1	Busk Road	A4-A5	Evelyn Street	F5	Kirkbank Street	B4	Prospect Road	A3	Spinks Street	
Anchor Street	D4	Cardinal Street	D3-E3	Featherstall Road North	A3-B4-B5	Kranj Way	D4	Quebec Street	A4	Stansfield Street	
Arkwright Street	A2	Castlemill Street	F3	Featherstall Road South	A1-A3	Larch Street	A1-B1	Queen Street	D3-D2	Stirling Street	A
Arnold Street	F4	Chadderton Way	A5-B4	Felton Street	F1	Latimer Street	F1	Queens Road	D1-E1	Sunfield Road	
Ashley Street	A4	Chaucer Street	C1-C2	Fletcher Close	A2-B2	Lee Street	B1-B2	Railway Road	A2-A1-B2	Sylvan Street	
Bamford Street	A5	Cheapside	C3	Flora Street	C4	Lees Road	F3	Raleigh Close	D5	Thames Street	
Bankside Close	A2-B2	Chelmsford Street	B1	Florida Street	B1-C1	Lemnos Street	E3-E4	Ramsden Street	C3-C4	Tilbury Street	B
Bar Gap Road	D4	Churchill Street	E1-E2	Franklin Street	C4	Lombard Street	C3	Redvers Street	B4	Trafalgar Street	B
Barlow Street	E2-E1-F1	Clegg Street	D2	Glodwick Road	F1-F2-F3	London Road	F5	Regent Street	E3	Trinity Street	B
Bartlemore Street	F5	Coldhurst Street	C4-C5	Godson Street	C5	Lord Street	C4-D4-D3	Retford Street	F1	Union Street	C2-D2-E
Barton Street	A5	Colwyn Street	A3-B3	Gould Street	F4	Magdala Street	C5	Retiro Street	D3-D2	Union Street West	E
Bateson Way	D1	Coppice Street	A1	Gower Street	E3-E4	Main Road	A3-A4	Rhodes Bank	E2	Vale Drive	
Beever Street	E3	Cottam Street	A5-B5	Grange Street	B3-B4	Malby Street	D4	Rhodes Street	E3	Waddington Street	
Bell Street	E3-F3	Crabtree Road	F5	Greaves Street	D3-D2	Malton Street	B1	Rifle Street	D4	Wall Street	
Belmont Street	C4	Cromford Street	F4-F5	Green Street	B1	Manchester Street	A1-B1-B2-C2	Ripon Street	B5	Wallshaw Street	
Ben Brierley Way	D3	Crompton Street	B5-C5-D5	Greengate Street	E1-F2	Marlborough Street	E1-E2	Roscoe Street	E2	Ward Street	
Bisley Street	B1	Cromwell Street	C2-D2	Hamilton Street	F2-F3	Mars Street	A4	Rochdale Road	B5-B4-C4-C3	Wastwater Street	
Bismarck Street	F1	Cross Street	F3	Harcourt Street	F5	Melrose Street	F5	Rock Street	D3-E3	Waterloo Street	D3-D2-E
Bolton Street	F1-F2	Crossbank Street	C1	Hardy Street	E1-F1	Middleton Road	A3-B3-C3	Roscoe Street	E2	Wellington Street	C1-D
Booth Street	B2-C2	Daisy Street	A3	Harmony Street	E1	Minton Street	E1	Ross Street	B1	Werneth Hall Road	
Bottomfield Close	F5	Davies Street	B4	Henshaw Street	C3-C4-D4-D5	Mitchell Street	B5	Ruskin Street	B4	West End Street	
Bow Street	D3-D2-E2	Denmark Street	A5	Higginshaw Road	D5-E5-E4	Morris Street	E1-F1	Ruth Street	D4	West Street	
Bower Street	F3-F4	Derker Street	F4	High Street	C2-D3	Mortimer Street	E4-E5	St James Street	F4	West Street	
Bradford Street	C5	Dover Street	A1	Highfield Street	B3-B4	Mumps	E3	St John's Street	A1	Westhulme Street	
Bradshaw Street	D3	Drake Close	D5	Hilda Street	A3-B3	Napier Street East	B1	St Mary's Street	D4	Widdop Street	
Bright Street	A1	Eden Street	C3-C4	Hobson Street	D1-D2	Napier Street West	A1	St Mary's Way	C3-D3	Willow Street	
Briscoe Street	D4	Edge Lane Road	E5	Hooper Street	F1-F2	Neath Street	B3	St Stephen's Street	E4	Wimpole Street	
				Horsedge Street	D4-D3-E3	Oldham Way	B4-C1-D1-E3	St Thomas Street	B1	Woodstock Street	
				Hoyle Avenue	C1	Onchan Avenue	F1	Savoy Street	F1	Wye Street	
				Huddersfield Road	F3	Osborne Street	A4	Shaw Road	E5-E4-F4-F3	Yasmin Gardens	
				Hurst Street	B3	Park Road	C1-D1-E1-F1	Shaw Street	D4	Yates Street	
				Jackson Close	C1	Park Street	B1-C1	Sherwood Street	A5-B5	Yorkshire Street	
				Jesperson Street	D3	Penn Street	B1	Shield Close	B1		

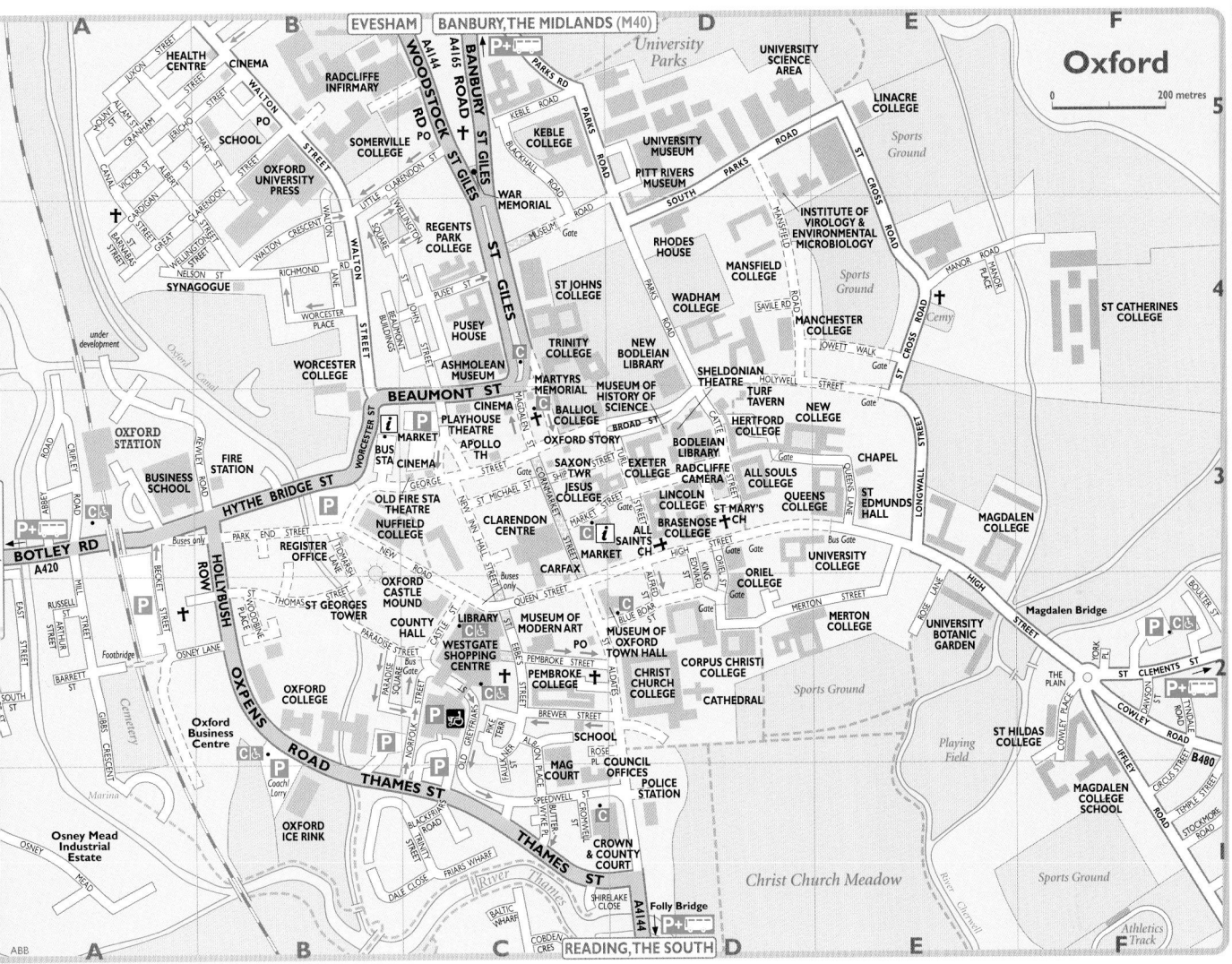

Oxford

Oxford is found on atlas page **37**,
grid reference **5106**

Abbey Road	A3	Cranham Street	A5-B5	Mill Street	A2-A3	St Giles	C4-C5
Abingdon Road	D1	Cripley Road	A3	Mount Street	A5	St John Street	C3-C4
Albert Street	A5-B4	Cromwell Street	C1	Museum Road	C4	St Michael Street	C3
Albion Place	C1-C2	Dale Close	B1-C1	Nelson Street	A4-B4	St Thomas Street	B2
Alfred Street	D2-D3	Dawson Street	F2	New Inn Hall Street	C2-C3	Savile Road	D4
Allam Street	A5	East Street	A2-A3	New Road	B3-C3-C2	Ship Street	C3-D3
Arthur Street	A2	Faulkner Street	C1-C2	Norfolk Street	C1-C2	Shirelake Close	C1
Beltic Wharf	C1	Friars Wharf	C1	Old Greyfriars Street	C1-C2	South Parks Road	D4-D5-E5
Banbury Road	C5	George Street	B3-C3	Oriel Street	D2-D3	South Street	A2
Barrett Street	A2	Gibbs Crescent	A1-A2	Osney Lane	A2-B2	Speedwell Street	C1-D1
Beaumont Buildings	B4-C4	Great Clarendon Street	A4-B4-B5	Osney Mead	A1	Stockmore Road	F1
Beaumont Street	B3-C3-C4	Hart Street	B5	Oxpens Road	B1-B2	Temple Street	F1-F2
Becket Street	A2-A3	High Street	C2-D3-E2-F2	Paradise Square	B2	Thames Street	B1-C1-D1
Blackfriars Road	C1	Hollybush Row	B2-B3	Paradise Street	B2-C2	The Plain	F2
Blackhall Road	C4-C5	Holywell Street	D4-E4-E3	Park End Street	A3-B3	Tidmarsh Lane	B2-B3
Blue Boar Street	D2	Hythe Bridge Street	B3	Parks Road	C5-D5-D4	Trinity Street	C1
Botley Road	A3	Iffley Road	F1-F2	Pembroke Street	C2	Turl Street	D3
Boulter Street	F2	Jericho Street	A5-B5	Pike Terrace	C2	Tyndale Road	F2
Brewer Street	C2	Jowett Walk	D4-E4	Pusey Street	C4	Victor Street	A5
Bridge Street	A2	Juxon Street	A5	Queen Street	C2	Walton Crescent	B4
Broad Street	C3-D3	Keble Road	C5	Queens Lane	E3	Walton Lane	B4-B5
Butterwyke Place	C1	King Edward Street	D2-D3	Rewley Road	A3-B3	Walton Street	B4-B5
Canal Street	A4-A5	Little Clarendon Street	B4-B5-C5	Richmond Road	B4	Wellington Square	B4-C4
Cardigan Street	A4-A5-B5	Longwall Street	E3	Rose Lane	E2-E3	Wellington Street	A4-B4
Castle Street	C2	Magdalen Street	C3	Rose Place	C2	Woodbine Place	B2
Cattle Street	D3	Manor Place	E4	Russell Street	A2	Woodstock Road	C5
Circus Street	F1-F2	Manor Road	E4-F4	St Aldates	C2-D2-D1	Worcester Place	B4
Cobden Crescent	C1	Mansfield Road	D4-D5	St Barnabas Street	A4	Worcester Street	B3
Cornmarket Street	C3	Market Street	C3-D3	St Clements Street	F2	York Place	F2
Cowley Place	F2	Marlborough Road	C1	St Cross Street	E3-E4-E5		
Cowley Road	F2	Merton Street	D2-E2-E3	St Ebbe's Street	C2		

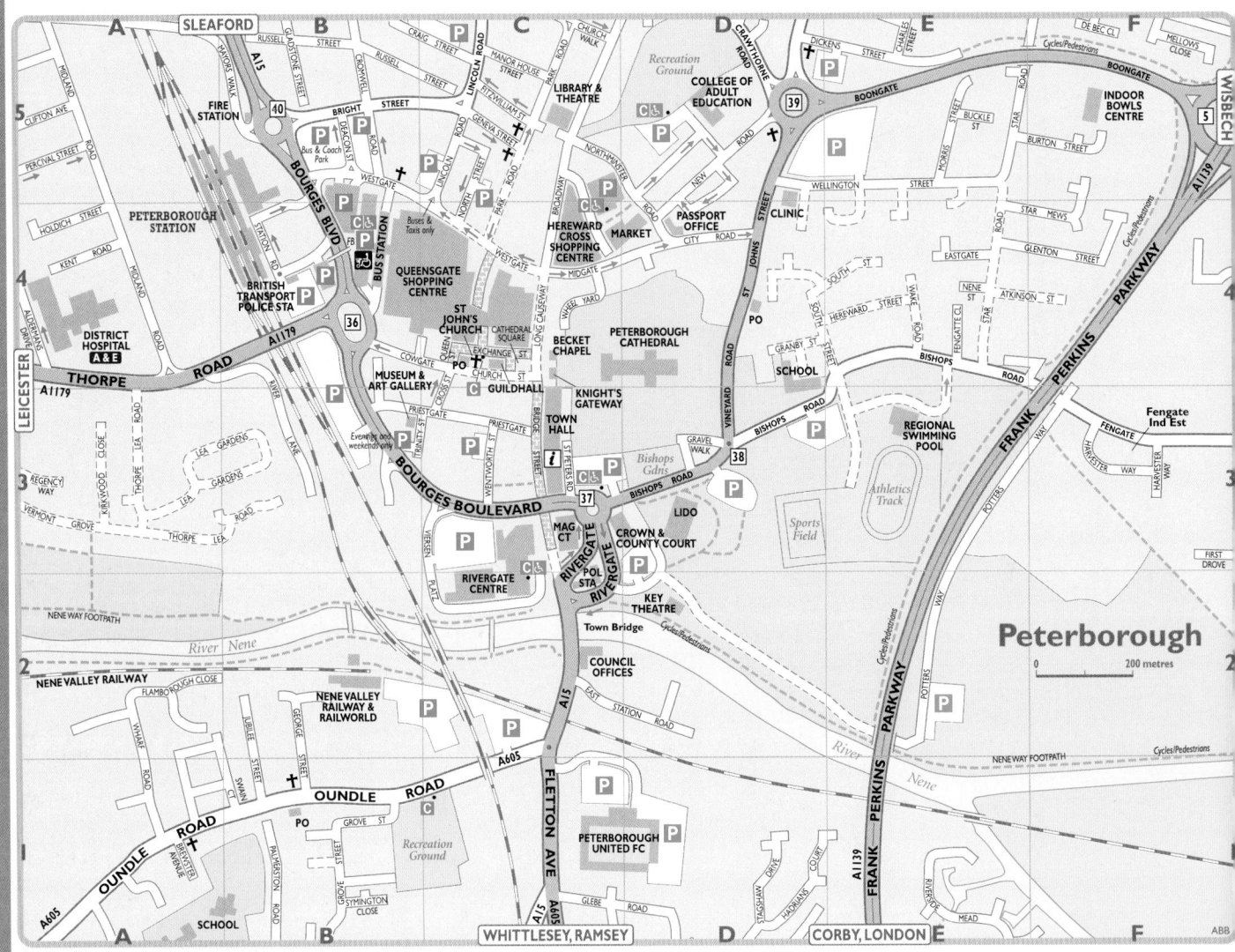

208

Peterborough

Peterborough is found on atlas page **64**,
grid reference **1998**

Aldermans Drive	A4	Fitzwilliam Street	C5	North Street	C4-C5	Wellington Street	D5-E5
Atkinson Street	E4-F4	Flamborough Close	A2	Northminster Road	C5-D5-D4	Wentworth Street	C3
Bishops Road	C3-D3-E4-F3	Fletton Avenue	C1-C2	Oundle Road	A1-B1-C1-C2	Westgate	B5-B4-C4
Boongate	D5-E5-F5	Frank Perkins		Palmerston Road	B1	Wharf Road	A1-A2
Bourges Boulevard	C3-B3-B4-B5	Parkway	E1-E3-F3-F5	Park Road	C4-C5	Wheel Yard	C4
Brewster Avenue	A1	Geneva Street	C5	Percival Street	A5		
Bridge Street	C3-C4	George Street	B1-B2	Potters Way	E2-E3-F3		
Bright Street	B5-C5	Gladstone Street	B5	Priestgate	B3-C3		
Broadway	C4-C5	Glebe Road	C1-D1	Queen Street	C4		
Buckle Street	E5	Glenton Street	E4-F4	Regency Way	A3		
Burton Street	E5-F5	Granby Street	D4	River Lane	A4-B4-B3		
Cathedral Square	C4	Gravel Walk	D3	Rivergate	C2-C3		
Church Street	C5	Grove Street	B1	Riverside Mead	E1		
Church Walk	C5	Hadrians Court	D1	Russell Street	B5-C5		
City Road	D4	Harvester Way	F3	St Johns Street	D4-D5		
Clifton Avenue	A5	Hereward Street	E4	St Peters Road	C3		
Cromwell Road	B5	Holdich Street	A4	South Street	E4-D4		
Cowgate	B4-C4	Jubilee Street	B1-B2	Stagshaw Drive	D1		
Craig Street	B5-C5	Kent Road	A4	Star Mews	E4-F4-F5		
Crawthorne Road	D5	Kirkwood Close	A3	Star Road	E4-E5		
Cross Street	C3-C4	Lea Gardens	A3-B3	Station Road	B4		
De Bec Close	F5	Lincoln Road	C4-C5	Swain Court	B1		
Deacon Street	B5	Long Causeway	C4	Symington Close	B1		
Dickens Street	D5-E5	Manor House Street	C5	Thorpe Lea Road	A3-B3		
East Station Road	C2-D2	Mayors Walk	B5-A5	Thorpe Road	A4-B4		
Eastgate	E4	Midgate	C4-D4	Trinity Street	B3-C3		
Exchange Street	C4	Midland Road	A4-A5	Vermont Grove	A3		
Fengate	F3	Morris Street	E5	Versen Platz	C3-C2		
Fengate Close	E4	Nene Street	E4	Vineyard Road	D3-D4		
First Drove	F3	New Road	D4-D5	Wake Road	E4		

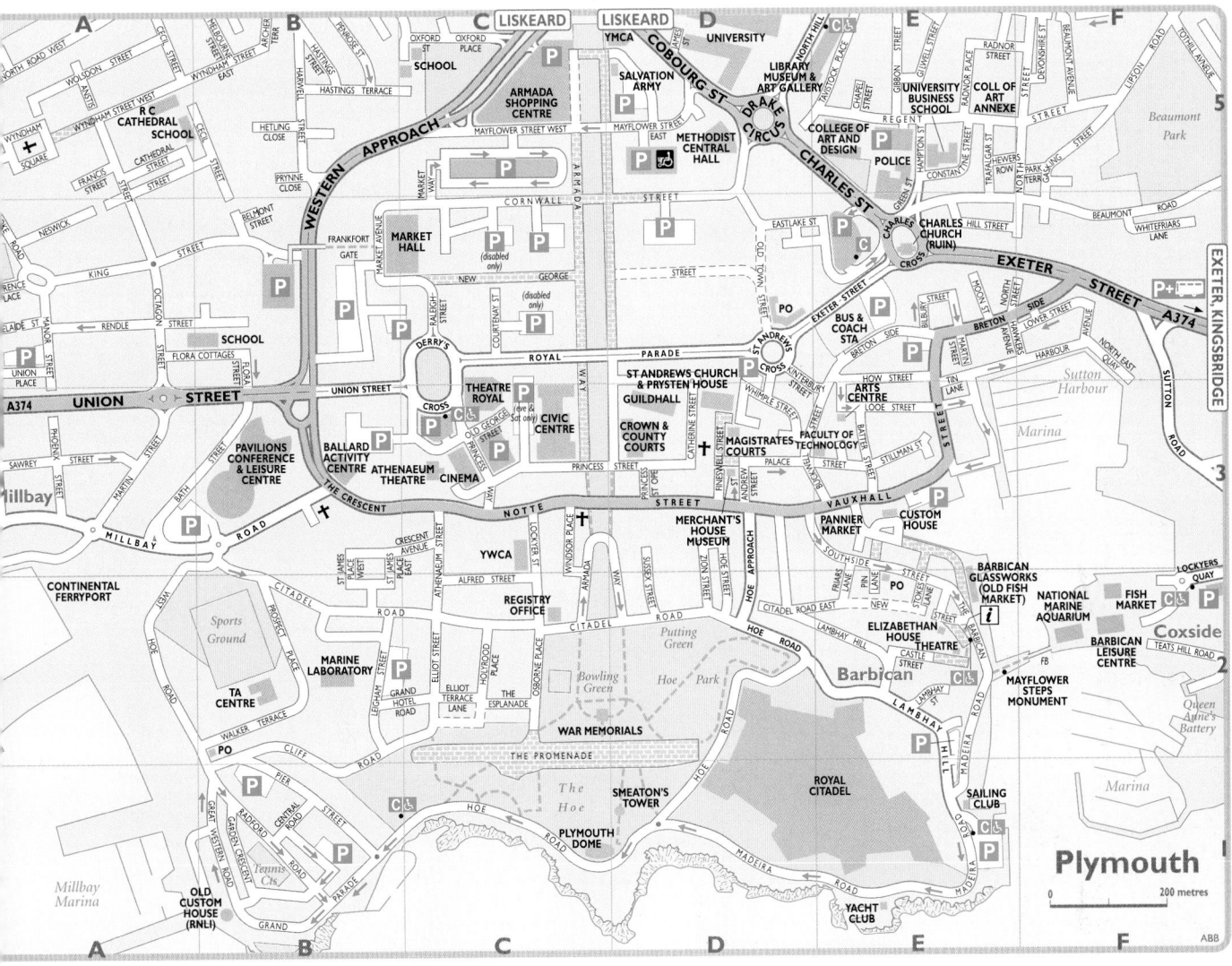

Plymouth

Plymouth is found on atlas page **6**,
grid reference **4754**

Adelaide Street	A4	Courtenay Street	C4	Hewers Row	E5	New George Street	C4-D4	Royal Parade	C4-D4	Wolsdon Street	A5
Alfred Street	C2	Crescent Avenue	B3-C3	Hill Street	E4	New Street	E2	St Andrew Street	D3	Wyndham Square	A5
Austis Street	A4-A5	Derry's Cross	C3-C4	Hoe Approach	D2-D3	North East Quay	F3-F4	St Andrews Cross	D4	Wyndham Street East	A5-B5
Archer Terrace	B5	Devonshire Street	F5	Hoe Road	B1-C1-D1-D2	North Hill	D5-E5	St James Place East	B2-B3	Wyndham Street West	A5
Armada Way	C2-C3-D3-D2	Drake Circus	D5	Hoe Street	D2-D3	North Road West	A5	St James Place West	B2-B3	Zion Street	D2-D3
Armada Way	C3-C4-C5	Eastlake Street	D4-E4	Holyrood Place	C2	North Street	E4-F4-F5	Sawrey Street	A3		
Athenaeum Street	C2-C3	Elliot Street	C2	How Street	E3-E4	Notte Street	C3-D3	Southside Street	D3-E3-E2		
Bath Street	A3-B3	Elliot Terrace Lane	C2	James Street	D5	Octagon Street	A4	Stillman Street	E3		
Batter Street	E3	Exeter Street	D4-E4-F4	King Street	A4-B4	Old George Street	C3	Stoke Road	A4-A5		
Beaumont Avenue	F5	Fineswell Street	D3	Kinterbury Street	D4-D3-E3	Old Town Street	D4	Stokes Lane	E3		
Beaumont Road	F4-F5	Flora Cottages	A4-B4	Lambhay Hill	D2-E2-E1	Osborne Place	C2	Sussex Street	D2-D3		
Belmont Street	B4	Flora Street	B4	Lambhay Street	E2	Oxford Place	C5	Sutton Road	F3-F4		
Bilbury Street	E4	Francis Street	A5	Leigham Street	B2	Oxford Street	B5-C5	Tavistock Place	D5-E5		
Breton Side	E4-F4	Frankfort Gate	B4	Lipson Street	F5	Palace Street	D3-E3	Teats Hill Road	F2		
Brackwell Street	D3-E3	Friars Lane	E2-E3	Lockyer Street	C3	Park Terrace	F5	The Barbican	E2		
Castle Street	E2	Garden Crescent	B1	Lockyers Quay	F2	Penrose Street	B5	The Crescent	B3-C3		
Cathedral Street	A5	Gasking Street	F5	Looe Street	E3	Phoenix Street	A3	The Esplanade	C2		
Catherine Street	D3	Gibbon Street	E5	Lower Street	F4	Pier Street	B1-B2	The Promenade	C2-D2		
Cecil Street	A5-B5-B4	Gilwell Street	E5	Madeira Road	D1-E1-E2	Pin Lane	E2	Tin Lane	E3-E4		
Central Road	B1	Grand Hotel Road	B2-C2	Manor Street	A3-A4	Princess Street	C3-D3	Tothill Avenue	F5		
Chapel Street	E5	Grand Parade	B1	Market Avenue	B4	Princess Street Ope	D3	Trafalgar Street	E5		
Charles Cross	E4	Great Western Road	B1	Market Way	C4-C5	Princess Way	C3	Union Place	A4		
Charles Street	D5-E5-E4	Green Street	E4-E5	Martin Street	A3	Prospect Place	B2	Union Street	A3-C3		
Citadel Road	B3-B2-C2-D2	Hampton Street	E5	Martin Street	E4	Prynne Close	B5	Vauxhall Street	E3		
Citadel Road East	D2-E2	Harbour Avenue	F4	Mayflower Street East	D5	Radford Road	B1	Walker Terrace	B2		
Clarence Place	A4	Harwell Street	B5	Mayflower Street West	C5	Radnor Place	E5	West Hoe Road	A2-A3-B3		
Cliff Road	B1-B2-C2	Hastings Street	B5	Melbourne Street	B5	Radnor Street	E5-F5	Western Approach	B4-B5-C5		
Cobourg Street	D5	Hastings Terrace	B5-C5	Millbay Road	A3-B3	Raleigh Street	C4	Whimple Street	D3		
Constantine Street	E5	Hawkers Avenue	E4-F4	Moon Street	E4	Regent Street	E5-F5	Whitefriars Lane	F4		
Cornwall Street	B4-C4-D4-D5	Hetling Close	B5	Neswick Street	A4-A5-B5	Rendle Street	A4-B4	Windsor Place	C3		

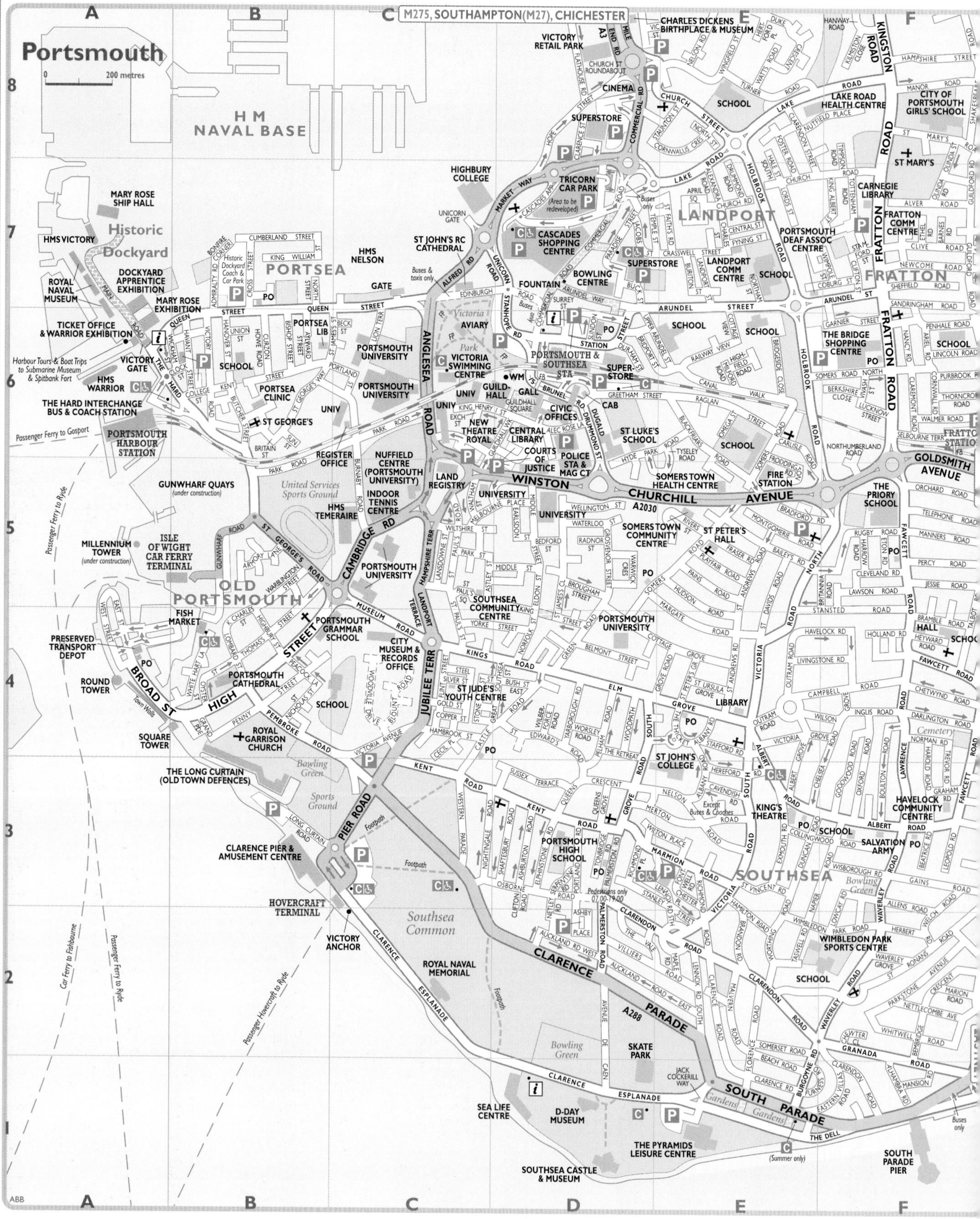

Portsmouth

0   200 metres

HM NAVAL BASE

M275, SOUTHAMPTON(M27), CHICHESTER

CHARLES DICKENS BIRTHPLACE & MUSEUM

KINGSTON ROAD

VICTORY RETAIL PARK

CINEMA

SUPERSTORE

SCHOOL

CITY OF PORTSMOUTH GIRLS' SCHOOL

LAKE ROAD HEALTH CENTRE

ST MARY'S

CARNEGIE LIBRARY

HIGHBURY COLLEGE

TRICORN CAR PARK (Area to be redeveloped)

LANDPORT

FRATTON COMM CENTRE

FRATTON

Unicorn Gate

CASCADES SHOPPING CENTRE

ST JOHN'S RC CATHEDRAL

SUPERSTORE

LANDPORT COMM CENTRE

SCHOOL

PORTSMOUTH DEAF ASSOC CENTRE

THE BRIDGE SHOPPING CENTRE

SCHOOL

FRATTON STATION

MARY ROSE SHIP HALL

HMS VICTORY

Historic Dockyard

ROYAL NAVAL MUSEUM

DOCKYARD APPRENTICE EXHIBITION

MARY ROSE EXHIBITION

HMS NELSON Gate

PORTSEA

BOWLING CENTRE

FOUNTAIN

Victoria Park AVIARY

PORTSMOUTH & SOUTHSEA STA

SCHOOL

SCHOOL

TICKET OFFICE & WARRIOR EXHIBITION

VICTORY GATE

HMS WARRIOR

THE HARD INTERCHANGE BUS & COACH STATION

Harbour Tours & Boat Trips to Submarine Museum & Spitbank Fort

Passenger Ferry to Gosport

PORTSMOUTH HARBOUR STATION

Portsea Lib

PORTSMOUTH UNIVERSITY

ST GEORGE'S

PORTSEA CLINIC

UNIV

VICTORIA SWIMMING CENTRE

UNIV

GUILD-HALL

WM GALL

BRUNEL

CAB

SUPER-STORE

ST LUKE'S SCHOOL

SOMERS TOWN HEALTH CENTRE

SCHOOL

FIRE STATION

GOLDSMITH AVENUE

REGISTER OFFICE

NUFFIELD CENTRE (PORTSMOUTH UNIVERSITY)

LAND REGISTRY

NEW THEATRE ROYAL

CENTRAL LIBRARY

COURTS OF JUSTICE

POLICE STA & MAG CT

WINSTON CHURCHILL AVENUE

THE PRIORY SCHOOL

ORCHARD ROAD

GUNWHARF QUAYS (under construction)

United Services Sports Ground

HMS TEMERAIRE

INDOOR TENNIS CENTRE

UNIVERSITY

SOMERS TOWN COMMUNITY CENTRE

ST PETER'S HALL

TELEPHONE ROAD

MILLENNIUM TOWER (under construction)

ISLE OF WIGHT CAR FERRY TERMINAL

OLD PORTSMOUTH

PORTSMOUTH UNIVERSITY

SOUTHSEA COMMUNITY CENTRE

PORTSMOUTH UNIVERSITY

LIBRARY

Passenger Ferry to Ryde

FISH MARKET

PORTSMOUTH GRAMMAR SCHOOL

CITY MUSEUM & RECORDS OFFICE

ST JUDE'S YOUTH CENTRE

PRESERVED TRANSPORT DEPOT

PORTSMOUTH CATHEDRAL

SCHOOL

ST JOHN'S COLLEGE

HAVELOCK COMMUNITY CENTRE

ROUND TOWER

BROAD ST

HIGH

ROYAL GARRISON CHURCH

KING'S THEATRE

SCHOOL

SALVATION ARMY

SQUARE TOWER

THE LONG CURTAIN (OLD TOWN DEFENCES)

Bowling Green

PORTSMOUTH HIGH SCHOOL

SOUTHSEA

Car Ferry to Fishbourne

Passenger Ferry to Ryde

Bowling Green

WIMBLEDON PARK SPORTS CENTRE

SCHOOL

CLARENCE PIER & AMUSEMENT CENTRE

PIER ROAD

Footpath

Sports Ground

Footpath

HOVERCRAFT TERMINAL

Passenger Hovercraft to Ryde

VICTORY ANCHOR

Southsea Common

CLARENCE ESPLANADE

ROYAL NAVAL MEMORIAL

CLARENCE PARADE

A288

SKATE PARK

Bowling Green

JACK COCKERILL WAY

SOUTH PARADE

Gardens

CLARENCE ESPLANADE

SEA LIFE CENTRE

D-DAY MUSEUM

THE PYRAMIDS LEISURE CENTRE

SOUTHSEA CASTLE & MUSEUM

SOUTH PARADE PIER

(Summer only)

ABB

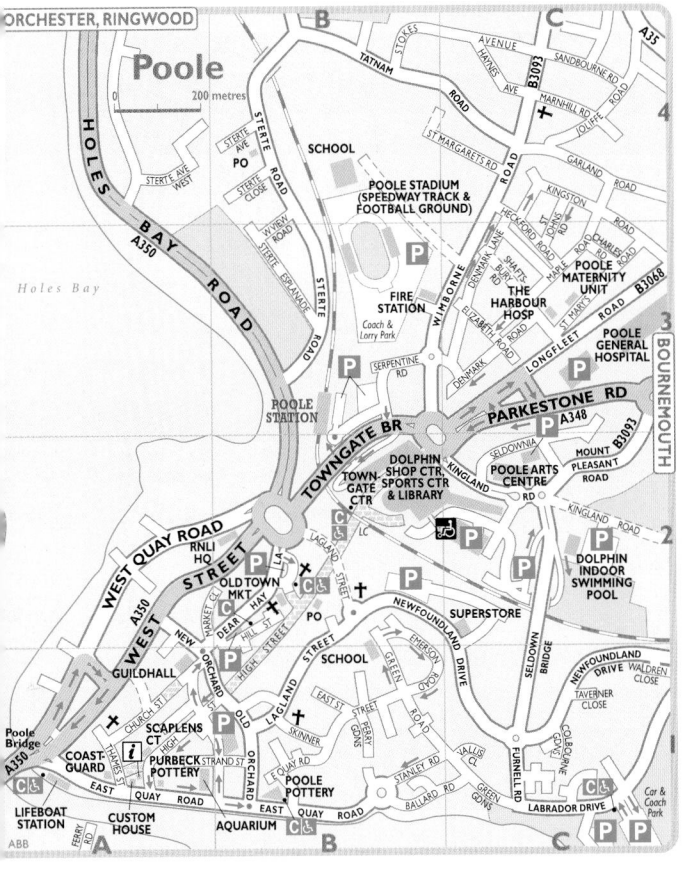

Poole

Poole is found on atlas page **11**,
grid reference **0090**

Ballard Road	B1-C1	Maple Road	C3-C4	Strand Street	A1-B1
Charles Road	C3	Market Close	A2	Tatnam Road	B4-C4
Church Street	A1	Marnhill Road	C4	Taverner Close	C1
Colbourne Gardens	C1	Mount Pleasant Road	C2	Thames Street	A1
Dear Hay Lane	B2	New Orchard	A2-A1	The Quay	A1-B1
Denmark Lane	C3	Newfoundland Drive	C1	Towngate Bridge	B2-B3
Denmark Road	C3	North Street	B2	Vallis Close	C1
East Quay Road	B1	Old Orchard	B1	Waldren Close	C1
East Street	B1	Parkstone Road	C3	West Quay Road	A1-A2-B2
Elizabeth Road	C3	Perry Gardens	B1	West Street	A1-A2-B2
Emerson Road	B2-B1	St Johns Road	C3-C4	West View Road	B3-B4
Ferry Road	A1	St Margarets Road	B4-C4	Wimborne Road	B3-C3-C4
Garland Road	C4	St Mary's Road	C3		
Green Gardens	C1	Sandbourne Road	C4		
Green Road	B1	Seldown Bridge	C1-C2		
Haynes Avenue	C4	Seldown Lane	C2		
Heckford Road	C3-C4	Serpentine Road	B3		
High Street	A1-B1-B2	Shaftsbury Road	C3		
Hill Street	B2	Skinner Street	B1		
Holes Bay Road	A4-B3-B2	Stanley Road	B1		
Jolliffe Road	C4	Sterte Avenue	B4		
Kingland Road	C2	Sterte Avenue West	A4		
Kingston Road	C3-C4	Sterte Close	B4		
Labrador Drive	C1	Sterte Esplanade	B3		
Lagland Street	B1-B2	Sterte Road	B4-B3		
Longfleet Road	C3	Stokes Avenue	B4-C4		

211

Hanway Road	F8	Nightingale Road	C3-D3	South Parade	E1-F1
Harold Road	F3-F4	Norfolk Street	D4	Stafford Road	E4
Harrow Road	F5	Norman Road	F4	Stamford Street	F7
Havant Street	B6	North Street	B7	Stanhope Road	D6-D7
Havelock Road	E4-F4	North Street	E8	Stanley Street	D3-E3-E3-E2
Herbert Road	F2	Northiam Street	E7	Stansted Road	E5-F5
Hereford Road	E3	Northumberland Road	F5-F6	Station Street	D6
Hertford Place	E8	Nutfield Place	E8-F8	Staunton Street	D8-E8
Heyward Road	F4	Olinda Road	F7	Steel Street	C4
High Street	B4	Olinda Street	F7-F8	Stone Street	C4
Highbury Street	B4	Omega Street	E6	Sun Street	B6
Highfield Road	E6	Orchard Road	F5	Surrey Street	D6
Holbrook Road	E8-E7-E6-F5	Osborne Road	C3-D3	Sussex Terrace	D3
Holland Road	F4	Outram Road	E4	Talbot Road	F4-F5
Hope Street	D7-D8	Oxford Road	F3-F4	Taswell Road	E2
Hudson Road	E4-E5	Oyster Street	B4	Telephone Road	F5
Hyde Park Road	D5-D6-E6	Pains Road	E5	Temple Street	D7
Inglis Road	F4	Palmerston Road	D2-D3	The Dell	E1-F1
Isambard Brunel Road	D6	Paradise Street	D7	The Hard	A6-B6
Jacobs Street	D7	Park Road	B5-B6-C6	The Retreat	D4
Jessie Road	F5	Park Street	C5	The Thicket	E4
Jubilee Terrace	C4	Parkstone Avenue	F2	The Vale	D2-E2
Kent Road	C3-D3	Peacock Lane	B4	Thorncroft Road	F6
Kent Street	B6	Pelham Road	D3-D4	Timpson Road	F7-F8
Kilmston Close	F8	Pembroke Road	B4-C4	Tonbridge Road	D3
King Albert Street	F7	Penhale Road	F6	Tottenham Road	F7
King Charles Street	B4	Penny Street	B4	Trevor Road	F3-F4
King Henry I Street	C6-D6	Percy Road	F5	Turner Road	E8
King Street	D4-D5	Pier Road	C3	Tyseley Road	D6-D5-E5-E6
King William Street	B7	Playfair Road	E5	Unicorn Gate	C7
Kings Road	C4-D4	Portland Road	D3	Unicorn Road	C7-D7
Kingston Road	E7-E8-F8	Portland Street	C6	Union Street	B6
Lake Road	E7-E8-F8	Purbrook Road	F6	Upper Arundel Street	D6-E6
Landport Street	E7	Queen Street	A6-B6-B7-C7	Victoria Avenue	C4
Landport Terrace	C4-C5	Queens Crescent	D3	Victoria Grove	E4-F4
Lansdowne Street	C5	Queens Grove	D3	Victoria Road North	E4-E5-F5
Lawrence Road	F3-F4	Radnor Street	D5	Victoria Road South	E2-E3-E4
Lawson Road	F5	Raglan Street	E6	Victoria Street	D8-E8
Lennox Road South	D3-E3-E2	Railway View	E6	Victory Road	B6
Leopold Street	F3	Richmond Place	D3	Villiers Road	D2-E2
Lincoln Road	F6	Richmond Road	E2-E3	Vivash Street	F6
Lion Terrace	C6	Rivers Street	E5	Walmer Road	F6
Livingstone Road	E4-F4	Rugby Road	F5	Waltham Street	C5
Lombard Street	B4	St Andrews Road	E4-E5	Warblington Street	B5
Long Curtain Road	B3	St Davids Road	E4-E5	Warwick Crescent	D5
Lords Street	E7	St Edward's Road	D3-D4	Waterloo Street	D5
Lowcay Road	F2-F3	St Faith's Road	E7	Watts Road	E8
Lucknow Street	F6	St George's Road	B5	Waverley Grove	F2
Main Road	A6-A7	St George's Way	B6	Waverley Road	F2-F3
Malvern Road	E2	St James's Close	D4-D5	Welch Road	F2-F3
Manners Road	F5	St James's Street	B6-C6	Wellington Street	D5
Manor Road	F8	St Mary's Road	F8	West Street	A4-A5
Mansion Road	F1	St Nicholas Street	B4	Western Parade	C3
Maple Road	E2	St Paul's Road	C5	White Hart Lane	B4
Margate Road	D5-E5-E4	St Paul's Square	C5	Whitwell Road	F2
Marion Road	F2	St Paul's Street	C4-C5	Wickham Street	A6-B6
Market Way	C7-D7	St Peter's Grove	E4	Wilberforce Road	D4
Marmion Road	D3-E3	St Ronans Road	F2-F3	Wilson Grove	E4-F4
Melbourne Place	C5-D5	St Thomas's Street	B4-B5	Wilton Place	D3-E3
Merton Road	D3-E3	St Ursula Grove	E4	Wiltshire Street	C5
Middle Street	D5	St Vincent Road	E3	Wimbledon Park Road	E2-F2
Mile End Road	D8	Sandringham Road	F7	Wimpole Street	F7
Milford Road	E6	Selbourne Terrace	F6	Wingfield Street	E8
Montgomerie Road	E5	Serpentine Road	D3	Winston Churchill	
Museum Road	C4-C5	Shaftsbury Road	D3	Avenue	C5-D5-E5
Nancy Road	F6	Shakespeare Road	F8	Wisborough Road	F3
Napier Road	E2-E3-F3	Sheffield Road	F7	Woodpath	D4
Nelson Road	D3-E3	Silver Street	C4	Woodville Drive	C4
Nelson Road	E8	Slindon Street	D6	Worsley Road	D4
Netley Road	D2-D3	Somers Road	D4-D5-E5-E6	Worthing Road	E2-E3
Nettlecombe Avenue	F2	Somers Road North	E6-F6	Yarborough Road	D4
Newcome Road	F7	Somerset Road	E2	Yorke Street	C4-D4

ortsmouth

rtsmouth is found on atlas page **13**,
d reference **6400**

miralty Road	B7	Buck Street	D7	Curzon Howe Road	B6
any Road	E3-E4	Burgoyne Road	E1-E2	Darlington Road	F4
ert Grove	E3-E4	Burnaby Road	C5-C6	Drummond Road	E7
ert Road	E4-E3-F3	Burton Street	E7	Dugald Drummond Street	D5-D6
Rose Lane	D6	Bush Street East	D4	Duke Crescent	E8
xandra Road	E7	Butcher Street	B6	Duncan Road	E3
ed Road	C7	Cambridge Road	C5	Durham Street	D6
ambra Road	F1	Campbell Road	E4-F4	Earlsdon Street	D5
ns Road	F2-F3	Canal Walk	E6	East Street	A4-A5
er Road	F7	Carlisle Road	E5-E6	Eastern Villas Road	E1-F1
glesea Road	C6-C7	Cascades Approach	D7	Edinburgh Road	C7-D7
il Square	E7	Castle Road	C3-C4-D4	Eldon Street	D5
il Road	F6	Cavendish Road	E3	Elm Grove	D4-E4
nory Lane	B5	Cecil Place	C4	Elphinstone Road	D3
ndel Street	D7-E7-F7	Central Street	E7	Ethel Road	F7
ndel Way	D7	Charles Street	E7	Eton Road	F5
urton Road	D3	Chelsea Road	E3-F3-F4	Exchange Street	C6
aby Place	D2	Chester Place	E7	Exmouth Road	E3
ley Street	C5	Chetwynd Road	F4	Fawcett Road	F3-F4-F5
ckland Road East	D2-E2	Chewter Close	F2	Flathouse Road	D8
ckland Road West	D2	Church Road	E7-F7	Flint Street	C4
enue De Caen	D1-D2	Church Street	D8-E8	Florence Road	E1-E2
ward Street	B6	Claremont Road	F6	Fontwell Road	E3
ey's Road	E5	Clarence Esplanade	C3-C2-D1-E1	Foster Road	E7-E8
rnes Road	F7	Clarence Parade	D2-E2-E1	Fraser Road	E5
ach Road	E1-E2	Clarence Road	E1-E2	Fratton Road	F6-F7-F8
ford Street	F3	Clarence Street	D8	Froddington Road	E5-E6
ck Street	C6	Clarendon Road	D3-E2-F2-F1	Furness Road	E1-F1
dford Street	D5	Clarendon Street	E7-E8	Fyning Street	E7
mont Street	D4	Cleveland Road	F5	Gains Road	F3
mbridge Crescent	F2	Clifton Road	D3	Garnier Street	F6
rkshire Close	F6	Clifton Street	F7	Gold Street	C4
hop Street	B6	Clive Road	F7	Goldsmith Avenue	F5-F6
kfriars Road	E5-E6	Clock Street	A6-B6	Goodwood Road	F3-F4
unt Road	C4	Coburg Street	E7-F7	Graham Road	F3
nfire Corner	B7	College Street	B6	Granada Road	F1-F2
ulton Road	F3-F4	Collingwood Road	E3-F3	Grand Parade	B4
adford Road	E5-F5	Commercial Road	D6-D7-D8	Great Southsea Street	C4-D4
amble Road	F4	Copper Street	C4	Green Road	D4-D5
andon Road	E2	Cornwall Road	F6	Greetham Street	D6-E6
dgeside Close	E6	Cornwallis Crescent	D8-E8	Grosvenor Street	D5
dport Street	D6	Cottage Grove	D5-D4-E4	Grove Road	D4-E4
tain Street	B6	Cottage View	E7	Grove Road South	D3-D4
tannia Road	E5-F5	Crasswell Street	E7	Guildford Road	F7-F8
oad Street	A4-B4	Cross Street	B7	Guildhall Square	D6
ougham Street	D5	Cumberland Street	B7	Guildhall Walk	C6-D6
				Gunwharf Road	B5
				Hale Street South	E7-E8
				Hambrook Street	C4
				Hamilton Road	E2-E3
				Hampshire Street	F8
				Hampshire Terrace	C5
				Hanover Street	B6

ABB

212

Preston

Preston is found on atlas page **80**,
grid reference **5329**

Adelphi Street	A3-A4	Ladywell Street	A2	Walker Street	A3
Appleby Street	B4	Lancaster Road	B4-B3-C3-C2	Warwick Street	A4
Ashmoor Street	A4	Lancaster Road North	B4	Winckley Square	
Avenham Lane	C1	Laurel Street	C1-C2	Winckley Street	
Avenham Road	B1-C1	Lawson Street	B3-B4		
Avenham Street	C1-C2	Lord Street	C2		
Bairstow Street	B1	Lune Street	B2		
Berwick Road	C1	Main Spritweild	C1-C2		
Birley Street	B2	Manchester Road	C2		
Bolton's Court	C1-C2	Market Street	B2		
Butler Street	A1	Market Street West	B3		
Cannon Street	B1-B2	Marsh Lane	A2-A3		
Carlisle Street	C3	Maudland Road	A3		
Chaddock Street	B1	Meadow Street	C3-C4		
Chapel Street	B1	Melling Street	B4		
Charlotte Street	C1	Moor Lane	A3-A4		
Christian Road	A1	Mount Street	B1		
Church Row	C2	Noor Street	C4		
Church Street	B2-C2	North Road	B4-C4-C3		
Constable Street	C4	North Street	B3		
Corporation Street	A1-A2-A3	Oak Street	C1		
Craggs Row	B4	Old Vicarage	C3		
Cross Street	B1	Orchard Street	B2		
Crown Street	B4	Ormskirk Road	C3		
Derby Street	C2	Oxford Street	C1		
Edward Street	A3	Pole Street	C2-C3		
Egan Street	C3	Pump Street	C3		
Elizabeth Street	B3	Ringway	B2-B3-C3		
Fishergate	A1-B1-B2	Rose Street	C2		
Fleet Street	A2-B2	Saint Ignatius Square	C3-C4		
Fox Street	B1-B2	St Paul's Road	C3-C4		
Friargate	A3-B2	St Paul's Square	C3		
Fylde Road	A3-A4	St Peter's Square	A3-A4		
Fylde Street	A3	St Peter's Street	A4		
Garden Street	B1	St Wilfred Street	A2		
Glover Street	C1	Sedgwick Street	C4		
Glovers Court	B1-B2	Shepherd Street	C1-C2		
Great George Street	B4-C4	Snow Hill	B3		
Great Shaw Street	A3-B3	Stanleyfield Road	C4		
Guildhall Street	B1-B2	Stoney Gate	C1-C2		
Harrington Street	A4	Syke Street	C1		
Heatley Street	A2	Theatre Street	A1		
Hope Street	A3	Tithebarn Street	C2-C3		
Hudson Street	C1	Turner Street	C4		
Kent Street	C4	Victoria Street	A4		

Ramsgate

Ramsgate is found on atlas page **29**,
grid reference **3865**

Abbot's Hill	B3	Duncan Road	A2	Royal Road	A2-B2
Addington Place	B2	Eagle Hill	A3	Ryton Road	
Addington Street	B2	Edith Road	A1	St Luke's Avenue	A4
Albert Road	C4	Effingham Street	B3	St Augustine's Road	A1
Albert Street	B2	Elizabeth Road	C3	St Benedict's Lawn	A1
Albion Place	B3-C3	Ellington Road	A2-A3	St Mildred's Road	
Albion Road	C4	Elms Road	B2	School Lane	B3
Alexandra Road	A4	Finsbury Road	A4	Spencer Square	B1
Alma Place	B4	George Street	B3	Spencer Street	
Alma Road	A4	Grange Road	A1	Station Approach Road	A3
Alpha Road	A2	Grove Road	A2-A3	Sundew Grove	
Anns Road	A4	Harbour Parade	B3-C3	Sussex Street	
Archway Road	B2	Harbour Street	B3	The Cloisters	A1
Arklow Square	B4	Hardres Road	B4	Townley Street	
Artillery Road	B4	Hardres Street	B3-B4	Truro Road	
Augusta Road	B4-C4	Hatfield Road	A3	Turner Street	
Avenue Road	B4	Hereson Road	B4	Unity Place	
Belgrave Close	A3	Hertford Place	B2	Upper Dumpton Park Road	
Bellevue Avenue	B4	Hibernia Street	B3	Vale Place	
Bellevue Road	B4-C4	High Street	A3-B3	Vale Road	A1-A4
Belmont Road	A3	Hollicondane Road	A4	Vale Square	A2
Belmont Street	B4	Holly Road	A4	Vereth Road	A1-A4
Beresford Road	A2-B2	King Street	B3-B4	Victoria Parade	C
Boundary Road	A4-B4	Lawn Villas	B3	Victoria Road	B4-C
Brights Place	B4	Leopold Street	B2-B3	Waterloo Place	C3-C
Broad Street	B3	Liverpool Lawn	B2	Wellington Crescent	C3-C
Brunswick Street	B3	London Road	A1	West Cliff Road	A1-A
Camden Road	B3	Madeira Walk	B3-C3	Willsons Road	A1-A
Camden Square	B3	Margate Road	A4	York Street	
Cannon Road	A3	Marlborough Road	A2-B2		
Cannonbury Road	A1	Meeting Street	A3-B3		
Carlton Avenue	A2	Monkton	A3		
Cavendish Street	B3	Nelson Crescent	B2		
Chapel Place	A2-A3	North Avenue	A2		
Chatham Place	A3-A4	Paragon Street	B1-B2		
Chatham Street	A3	Percy Road	A4		
Church Hill	B3	Plains of Waterloo	B3-C3		
Church Road	B3-B4	Poplar Road	A3		
Clifton Lawn	B1	Priory Road	B1		
Codrington Road	A2	Queen Street	A2-B2-B3		
Coronation Road	A2	Richmond Road	A2		
Cottage Road	B3-C3	Rodney Street	B2		
Crescent Road	A2	Rose Hill	B2		
D'Este Road	C4	Royal Crescent	B1-B2		
Denmark Road	A4-B4	Royal Esplanade	A1		

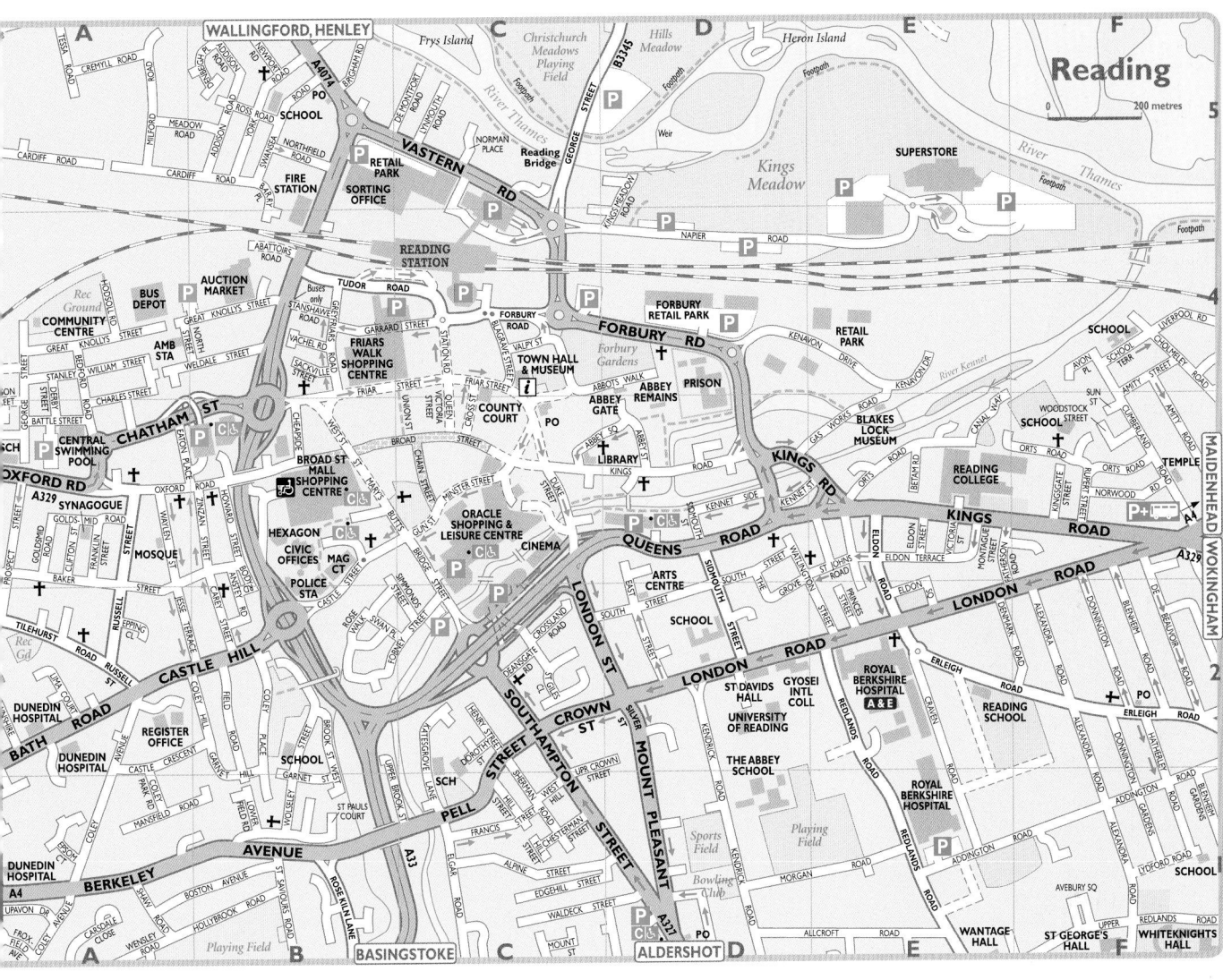

Reading

ading is found on atlas page **24**,
d reference **7173**

attoirs Road	B4	Castle Crescent	A2-B2	Eldon Road	E2-E3	Kenavon Drive	D4-E4	Queen Victoria Street	C3-C4
bey Square	C3-D3	Castle Hill	A2-B2	Eldon Square	E2-E3	Kendrick Road	D1-D2	Queens Road	D3
bey Street	D3	Castle Street	B2-B3	Eldon Street	E3	Kennet Side	D3	Redlands Road	E1-E2
bots Walk	C4-D4	Chain Street	C3	Eldon Terrace	E3	Kennet Street	D3-E3	Rose Kiln Lane	B1
dington Road	E1-F1-F2	Charles Street	A3-A4	Elgar Road	C1	Kings Meadow Road	D4-D5	Rose Walk	B2
dison Road	B5	Chatham Street	A3-B3	Epping Close	A2	Kings Road	C3-D3-E3-F3	Ross Road	B5
exandra Road	F1-F2	Cheapside	B3	Epsom Court	A1	Kingsgate Street	F3	Rupert Street	F3
croft Road	D1-E1	Chesterman Street	C1	Erleigh Road	E2-F2	Lima Court	A2	Russell Street	A2-A3
ine Street	C1-D1	Cholmeley Road	F3-F4	Fatherson Road	E2-E3	Liverpool Road	F4	St Giles Close	C2
ity Road	F3-F4	Clifton Road	A3	Field Road	B2	London Road	D2-E2-F2-F3	St Johns Road	E3
ity Street	F4	Coley Avenue	A1-A2	Forbury Road	C4-D4	London Street	C3-C2-D2	St Mary's Butts	B3-C3
stey Road	B2-B3	Coley Hill	A2-B2	Forney Street	B2-C2	Lower Field Road	B1	St Pauls Court	B1
ebury Square	F1	Coley Park Road	A1-A2	Francis Street	C1	Lydford Road	F1	St Saviours Road	B1
on Place	F4	Coley Place	B1-B2	Franklin Street	A3	Lynmouth Road	C5	Sackville Street	B4
ker Street	A2-A3	Craven Road	E1-E2	Friar Street	B3-B4-C4	Mansfield Road	A1-B1	School Terrace	F4
ry Place	B4-B5	Cremyll Road	A5	Froxfield Avenue	A1	Mason Street	A3-A4	Shaw Road	A1
h Road	A2	Cross Street	C3-C4	Garnet Hill	B1-B2	Meadow Road	A5-B5	Sherman Road	C1-C2
tle Street	A3	Crossland Road	C2	Garnet Street	B1-B2	Milford Road	A5	Sidmouth Street	D2-D3
dford Road	A3-A4	Crown Street	C2-D2	Garrard Street	B4-C4	Minster Street	C3	Silver Street	D2
keley Avenue	A1-B1	Cumberland Road	F3-F4	Gas Works Road	D3-E3-E4	Montague Street	E3	Simmonds Street	B3-C2
am Road	E3	De Beauvoir Road	F2-F3	George Street	A3-A4	Morgan Road	D1-E1	South Street	C2-D2-D3
grave Street	C4	De Montfort Road	B5-C5	George Street	C4-C5-D5	Mount Pleasant	D1-D2	Southampton Street	C2-C1-D1
nheim Gardens	F1	Deansgate Road	C2	Goldsmid Road	A3	Mount Street	C1	Stanley William Street	A4
nheim Road	F2-F3	Denbeigh Place	B5	Great Knollys Street	A4-B4	Napier Road	C4-D4-E4	Stanshawe Road	B4
dy Road	B2-B3	Denmark Road	E2-F2	Greyfriars Road	B4	Newport Road	B5	Station Road	C4
ston Avenue	A1-B1	Derby Street	A3-A4	Gun Street	C3	Norman Place	C5	Sun Street	F3
dge Street	C2-C3	Donnington Gardens	F1-F2	Hatherley Road	F1-F2	North Street	A4-B4	Swan Place	B2-C2
gham Road	B5	Donnington Road	F2-F3	Henry Street	C2	Northfield Road	B5	Swansea Road	B5
ad Street	B3-C3	Dorothy Street	C2	Hill Street	C1	Norwood Road	F3	Tessa Road	A5
ook Street West	B1-B2	Downshire Square	A2	Hodsoll Road	A4	Orts Road	E3-F3	The Grove	D2-D3
nal Way	E3	Duke Street	C3	Hollybrook Road	A1-B1	Oxford Road	A3-B3	Tilehurst Road	A2
rdiff Road	A5-B5	East Street	D2-D3	Howard Street	B3	Pell Street	C1-C2	Tudor Road	B4-C4
rey Street	B2-B3	Eaton Place	A3-B3	Jesse Terrace	A2-B2	Princes Street	E2	Union Street	C3-C4
rsdale Close	A1	Edgehill Street	C1-D1	Katesgrove Lane	C1-C2	Prospect Street	A2-A3	Upavon Drive	A1

Upper Brook Street	B2-C1
Upper Crown Street	C1-D2
Upper Redlands Road	F1
Vachel Road	B4
Valpy Street	C4
Vastern Road	B5-C5-C4
Victoria Street	E3
Waldeck Street	C1-D1
Watlington Street	D3-E2
Waylen Street	A3
Weldale Street	A4-B4
Wensley Road	A1
West Hill	C1
West Street	B3
Wolseley Street	B1-B2
Woodstock Street	F3
York Road	B5
Zinzan Street	B3

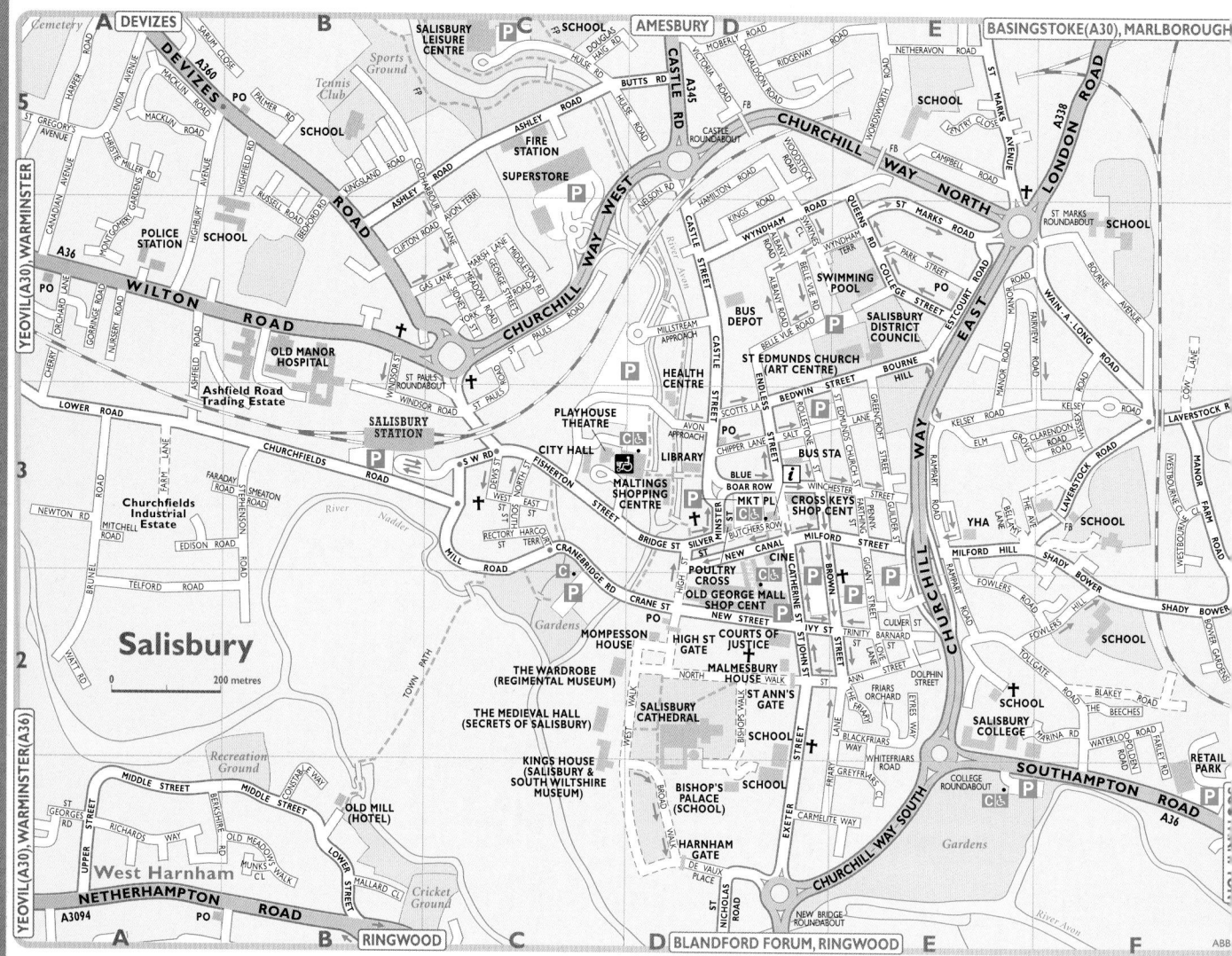

Salisbury

Salisbury is found on atlas page **23**,
grid reference **1429**

Albany Road	D4	Cherry Orchard Lane	A3-A4	Fairview Road	E4-E3-F3	Love Lane	E2	Old Meadows Walk	B1	Southampton Road	E2-E1-
Ashfield Road	A3-A4	Chipper Lane	D3	Faraday Road	A3-B3	Lower Road	A3	Palmer Road	B5	Stephenson Road	B2-
Ashley Road	B4-B5-C5	Christie Miller Road	A5	Farley Road	F1-F2	Lower Street	B1	Park Street	E4	Swaynes Close	A2-
Avon Approach	D3	Churchfields Road	B3-C3	Farm Lane	A3	Macklin Road	A5	Pennyfarthing Street	E3	Telford Road	A2-
Avon Terrace	C4-C5	Churchill Way East	E2-E3-E4	Fisherton Street	C3	Mallard Close	B1	Polden Road	F1-F2	The Avenue	
Barnard Street	E2	Churchill Way North	D5-E5-E4	Fowlers Hill	E2-F2	Manor Farm Road	F3	Queens Road	E4	The Beeches	
Bedford Road	B4	Churchill Way South	D1-E1	Fowlers Road	E3-E2-F2	Manor Road	E3-E4	Rampart Road	E2-E3	The Friary	
Bedwin Street	D3-D4-E4	Churchill Way West	C4-C5-D5	Friars Orchard	E2	Marina Road	F2	Rectory Street	C3	Tollgate Road	E2-F2-
Bellamy Lane	E3	Clarendon Road	E3-F3	Friary Lane	D1-E1-E2	Marsh Lane	C4	Richards Way	A1	Trinity Street	
Belle Vue Road	D4	Clifton Road	B4-C4	Gas Lane	B4-C4	Meadow Road	C4	Ridgeway Road	D5-E5	Upper Street	
Berkshire Road	A1-B1	Coldharbour Lane	B5-C4	George Street	C4	Middle Street	A1-B1	Rollerstone Street	D3	Ventry Close	
Bishops Walk	D1-D2	College Street	E4	Gigant Street	E2-E3	Middleton Road	C4	Russell Road	B4-B5	Victoria Road	D
Blackfriars Way	E2	Constable Way	B1	Gorringe Road	A4	Milford Lane	E3	St Ann Street	D2-E2	Wain a Long Road	F3-F
Blakey Road	F2	Cow Lane	F3-F4	Greencroft Street	E3-E4	Milford Street	D3-E3	St Edmunds Church Street	E3	Waterloo Road	
Blue Boar Row	D3	Crane Street	D2	Greyfriars Close	E1	Mill Road	C3	St Georges Road	A1	Watt Road	
Bourne Avenue	F4	Cranebridge Road	C2-C3	Guilder Street	E3	Millstream Approach	D4	St Gregory's Avenue	A5	Wessex Road	F3-F
Bourne Hill	E4	Culver Street	E2	Hamilton Road	D4-D5	Minster Street	D3	St John Street	D2	West Street	
Bower Gardens	F2	De Vaux Place	D1	Harcourt Terrace	C3	Mitchell Road	A3	St Marks Avenue	E5	West Walk	D1-D
Bridge Street	D3	Dews Street	C3	Harper Road	A5	Moberly Road	D5	St Marks Road	E4	Westbourne Close	
Broad Walk	D1	Dolphin Street	E2	High Street	D2-D3	Montgomery Gardens	A4-A5	St Nicholas Road	D1	Whitefriars Road	E1-
Brown Street	D3-E2	Donaldson Road	D5-E5	Highbury Avenue	A4-A5	Munks Close	B1	St Pauls Road	C3-C4	Wilton Road	A4-B4-C
Brunel Road	A2-A3	Douglas Haig Road	C5-D5	Highfield Road	B5	Nelson Road	D4-D5	Salt Lane	D3-E3	Winchester Street	D3-
Butchers Row	D3	East Street	C3	Hulse Road	C5-D5	Netheravon Road	E5	Sarum Close	A5-B5	Windsor Road	B3-C
Butts Road	C5-D5	Edison Road	A3-B3	India Avenue	A5	Netherhampton Road	A1-B1	Scotts Lane	D3	Windsor Road	B3-C
Campbell Road	E5	Elm Grove Road	E3-F3	Ivy Street	D2	New Canal	D3	Shady Bower	F2-F3	Woodstock Road	
Canadian Avenue	A4-A5	Endless Street	D3-D4	Kelsey Road	E3-F3	New Street	D2	Sidney Street	C4	Wordsworth Road	
Carmelite Way	D1-E1	Estcourt Road	E4	Kings Road	D4-D5	Newton Road	A3	Silver Street	D3	Wyndham Road	D4-F
Castle Road	D5	Exeter Street	D1-D2	Kingsland Road	B5	North Street	C3	Smeaton Road	B3	Wyndham Terrace	D4-F
Castle Street	D3-D4-D5	Eyres Way	E2	Laverstock Road	F3	North Walk	D2	South Street	C3	York Road	
Catherine Street	D2-D3			London Road	E4-F5	Nursery Road	A4	South West Road	C3		

214

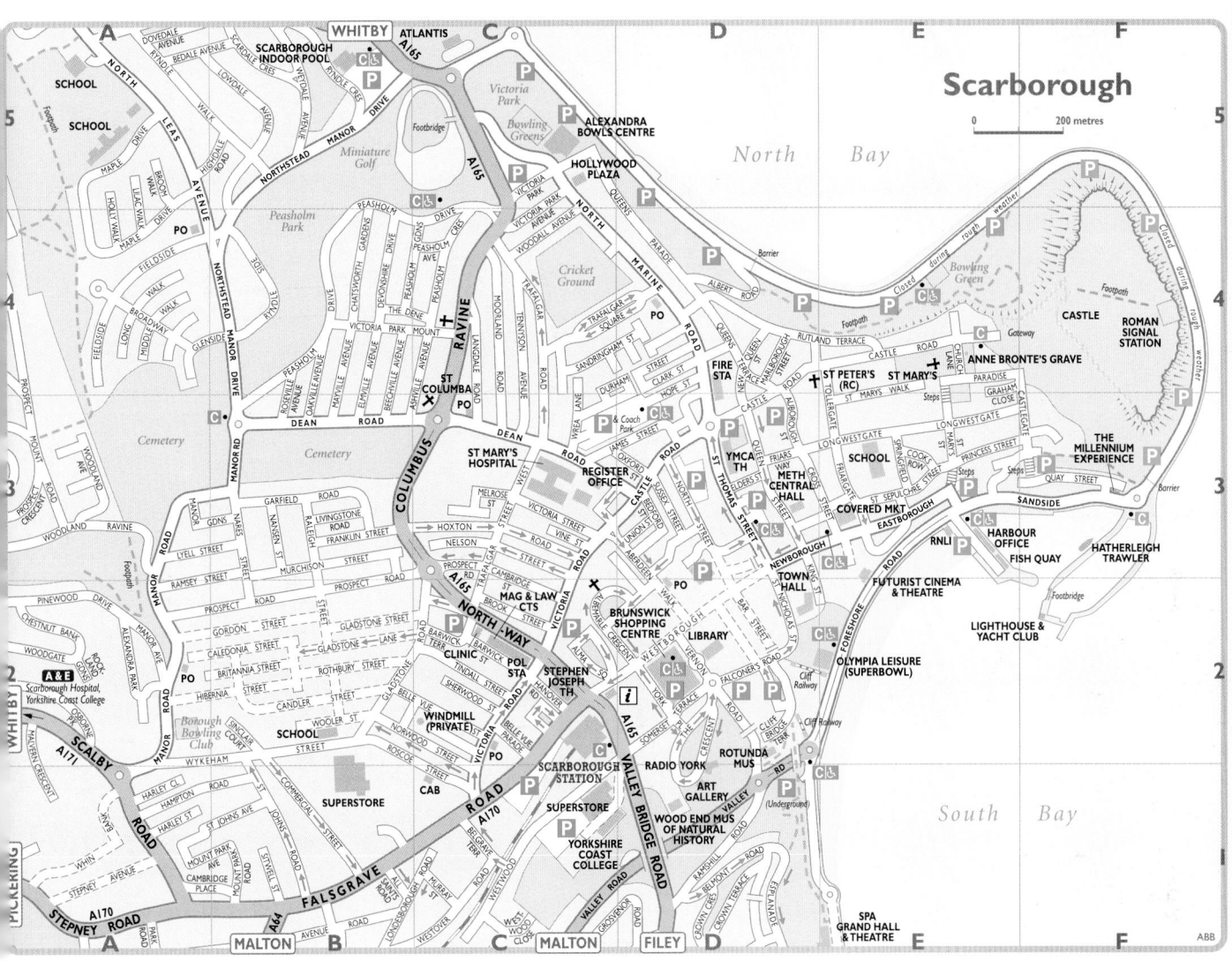

Scarborough

Scarborough is found on atlas page **91**,
grid reference **0488**

Aberdeen Walk	C3-D3-D2	Chestnut Bank	A2	Graham Close	E3-E4	Mount Park Avenue	A1-B1	Queens Terrace	D3-D4	The Dene	B4-C4
Albemarle Crescent	C2-D2	Church Lane	E4	Grosvenor Road	C1-D1	Mount Park Road	B1	Raleigh Street	B4-B5	Tindall Street	C2
Albert Road	D4	Clark Street	D3-D4	Hampton Road	A1-B1	Murchison Street	B2-B3	Ramsey Street	A2-B2-B3	Tollergate	E3-E4
Alexandra Park	A2	Cliffbridge Terrace	D2	Hanover Road	C2	Murray Street	C1	Ramshill Road	D1	Trafalgar Road	C3-C4
All Saints Road	B1	Columbus Ravine	B3-C3-C4	Harley Close	A3	Nansen Street	B3	Rockland Gardens	A2	Trafalgar Square	C4-D4
Alma Square	C2	Commercial Street	B1	Harley Street	A1	Nares Street	B2-B3	Roscoe Street	B2-C1	Trafalgar Street West	C2-C3
Ashville Avenue	B3-C3-C4	Cooks Row	E3	Hibernia Street	A2-B2	Nelson Street	C3-C2	Roseville Avenue	B3-B4	Union Street	D3
Auborough Street	D3	Cross Street	D3-E3	Highdale Road	A5-B5	New Queen Street	D3-D4	Rothbury Street	B2	Valley Bridge Road	C2-D2-D1
Avenue Road	B1	Crown Crescent	D1	Holly Walk	A4-A5	Newborough	D3-E3	Rutland Terrace	D4-E4	Valley Road	C1-D1-D2
Bar Street	D2	Crown Terrace	D1	Hope Street	D3-D4	North Leas Avenue	A5-A4-B4	Ryndle Crescent	B5	Vernon Road	D2
Barwick Street	C2	Dean Road	B3-C3-D3	Hoxton Road	B3-C3	North Marine Road	C5-D4-D3	Ryndle Side	B4	Victoria Park	C5
Barwick Terrace	C2	Devonshire Drive	B4	Huntriss Row	D2	North Street	D3	Ryndle Walk	A5-B5	Victoria Park Avenue	C4-C5
Bedale Avenue	A5-B5	Dovedale Avenue	A5	James Street	C3-D3	Northstead Manor Drive	B3-B5	St Johns Avenue	A1-B1	Victoria Park Mount	B4-C4
Bedford Street	D3	Durham Street	C3-C4-D4	King Street	D3-D2-E2	Northway	A3	St Johns Road	B1	Victoria Road	C1-C2-C3
Beechville Avenue	B3-B4	Eastborough	E3	Langdale Road	C3-C4	Norwood Street	B2-C2-C1	St Mary's Street	E3	Victoria Street	C3
Belgrave Terrace	C1	Elders Street	D3	Lilac Walk	A4-A5	Oakville Avenue	B3-B4	St Marys Walk	E3	Vine Street	C3
Belle Vue Parade	C2	Elmville Avenue	B3-B4	Livingstone Road	B3	Osborne Park	A2	St Nicholas Street	D2	Westborough	C2-D2
Belle Vue Street	B2-C2	Falconer's Road	D2	Londesborough Road	B1-C1	Oxford Street	C3-D3	St Sepulchre	E3	Westover Road	B1-C1
Belmont Road	D1	Falsgrave Road	A1-B1-C1-C2	Long Walk	A4	Paradise	E4	St Thomas Street	D3	Westwood	C1
Britannia Street	A2-B2	Fieldside	A4	Longwestgate	D3-E3	Park Road	A1	Sandringham Street	C4-D4	Westwood Close	C1
Broadway	A4	Foreshore Road	D2-E2-E2-E3	Lowdale Avenue	A5-B5	Peasholm Avenue	C4	Sandside	E3-F3	Weydale Avenue	B5
Brook Street	C2	Franklin Street	B3	Lyell Street	A3-B3	Peasholm Crescent	C4	Scalby Road	A1-A2	Whin Bank	A1
Broom Walk	A4-A5	Friargate	E3	Malvern Crescent	A1-A2	Peasholm Drive	B3-B4-C4	Scardale Crescent	B5	Woodall Avenue	C4
Caledonia Street	A2-B2	Friars Way	D3	Manor Avenue	A2	Peasholm Gardens	B4-C4	Sherwood Street	C2	Woodgate	A2
Cambridge Place	A1-B1	Garfield Road	B3	Manor Gardens	A3-B3	Pinewood Drive	A2	Sinclair Court	B2	Woodland Avenue	A3
Cambridge Street	C2-C3	Gladstone Lane	B2-C2	Manor Road	A1-A2-A3-B3	Princess Street	E3	Sitwell Street	B1	Woodland Ravine	A3
Candler Street	B2	Gladstone Road	B2-C2	Maple Drive	A4-A5	Prospect Crescent	A3	Somerset Terrace	D2	Wooler Street	B2
Castle Road	D3-D4-E4	Gladstone Street	B2-C2	Marlborough Street	D4	Prospect Mount Road	A3-A4	Springfield	E3	Wrea Lane	C3-C4
Castlegate	F3	Glenside	A4-B4	Mayville Avenue	B3-B4	Prospect Road	A2-B2-C3	Stepney Avenue	A1	Wykeham Street	A1-B2
Chatsworth Gardens	B4	Gordon Street	A2-B2	Melrose Street	C3	Quay Street	F3	Stepney Road	A1	York Place	D2
				Middle Walk	A4	Queen Street	D3	Tennyson Avenue	C3-C4		
				Moorland Road	C3-C4	Queens Parade	C5-D4	The Crescent	D1-D2		

Sheffield

Grid references (top): A B C D E F

BARNSLEY
THE NORTH, M1, ROTHERHAM
THE SOUTH, M1, WORKSOP
CHAPEL-EN-LE-FRITH
CHESTERFIELD
CHESTERFIELD

Major roads and streets:
A61 PENISTONE ROAD
NETHERTHORPE ROAD
GIBRALTAR STREET
CORPORATION STREET
NURSERY STREET
WICKER
BLONK ST
CASTLEGATE
SPITAL HILL
SAVILE STREET
A57
BROAD LANE
WEST BAR
BRIDGE ST
UPPER HANOVER STREET
A57 BROOK HILL
GLOSSOP ROAD
HANOVER WAY
ECCLESALL ROAD
A625
ST MARYS GATE
ST MARY'S ROAD
BRAMALL LANE
A621
SHOREHAM STREET
SUFFOLK ROAD
QUEEN'S ROAD
A61
MATILDA ST
SHREWSBURY

Landmarks and points of interest:
LIBRARY
PO
SUPERSTORE
SHEFFIELD INDUSTRIAL MUSEUM
KELHAM ISLAND (for Museum)
River Don
POLICE STA
SCHOOL
POLICE STATION
WEST BAR GREEN
LAW COURTS
POLICE HQ
MAG COURT
CASTLE MARKET
OPEN MARKET
CASTLE EXCHANGE
SHEAF MARKET
MEDICAL CENTRE
VICTORIA QUAYS
CATHEDRAL
NEWSPAPER OFFICES
VICTORIA HALL
ST MARIE PO RC CATH
POST SORTING OFFICE
PONDS FORGE INTERNATIONAL SPORTS CENTRE
SHEFFIELD UNIVERSITY
BROOK HILL
JESSOP HOSPITAL FOR WOMEN
UNIVERSITY LECTURE THEATRE
SHEFFIELD UNIVERSITY
RUSKIN GALLERIES
CRUCIBLE THEATRE
CINEMA
BUS AND COACH STATION
PARK HILL PRIMARY SCHOOL
CITY HALL
LYCEUM THEATRE
CENTRAL LIB & GRAVES ART GALLERY
TOWN HALL
SHU
MEDICAL CENTRE
S YORKS FIRE SERVICE HQ
COUNCIL OFFICES
REGISTER OFFICE
MILLENNIUM GALLERY & WINTER GARDEN
SHEFFIELD HALLAM UNIVERSITY
ST ANDREWS CHURCH
SPRINGFIELD SCHOOL
YORKS TV STUDIO
NATIONAL MUSIC CENTRE
CINEMA
SHEFFIELD MIDLAND STATION
SHEAF SQUARE
DUKE MEDICAL CENTRE
INLAND REVENUE OFFICE
PO
DFEE
MOORE STREET ROUNDABOUT
ICE SPORTS CENTRE
SHEFFIELD COLLEGE (NORTHSIDE)
SHEFFIELD COLLEGE (SOUTHSIDE)
ALL SAINTS RC SCHOOL
Brewery
SUPERSTORE
ST MARY'S CHURCH
BRAMALL LANE ROUNDABOUT
BAPTIST CHURCH
MEDICAL CENTRE
SHEFFIELD UNITED AFC
SHEFFIELD COLLEGE (TALBOT)
NORFOLK PARK SCHOOL
ST JOHN'S CH

0 200 metres

ABB

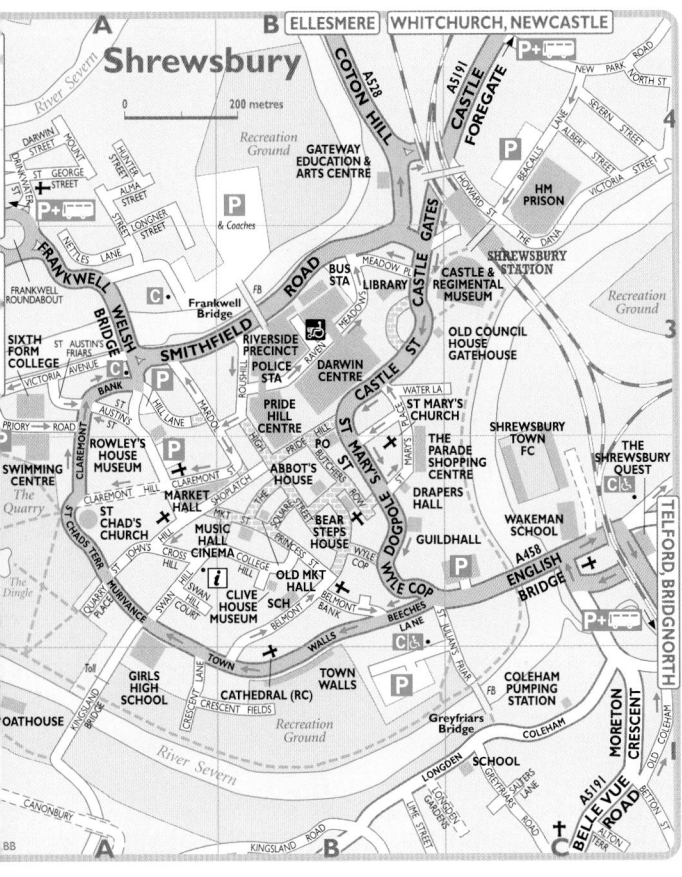

Shrewsbury

Shrewsbury is found on atlas page **59**,
grid reference **4912**

Albert Street	C4	Frankwell	A3	Quarry Place	A2
Alma Street	A4	Greyfriars Road	C1	Raven Meadows	B3
Beacalls Lane	C4	High Street	B2-B3	Roushill	B3
Beeches Lane	B2	Hill Lane	A3	St Austin's Friars	A3
Belle Vue Road	C1	Howard Street	C4	St Austin's Street	A3
Belmont	B1-B2	Hunter Street	A4	St Chads Terrace	A2
Belmont Bank	B2	Kingsland Bridge	A1	St George Street	A4
Butchers Row	B2	Kingsland Road	A1-B1	St John's Hill	A2
Canonbury	A1	Lime Street	B1	St Julian's Friar	B2-C2-C1
Castle Foregate	C4	Longden Coleham	B1-C1	St Mary's Place	B2-B3
Castle Gates	B3-B4	Longden Gardens	B1-C1	St Mary's Street	B2-B3
Castle Street	B3	Longner Street	A3-A4	Severn Street	C4
Claremont Bank	A2-A3	Mardol	A3-B2	Shoplatch	A2-B2
Claremont Hill	A2	Market Street	A2-B2	Smithfield Road	A3-B3
Claremont Street	A2-B2	Meadow Place	B3	Swan Hill	A2
College Hill	B2	Moreton Crescent	C1	Swan Hill Court	A2
Coton Hill	B4	Mount Street	A3-A4	The Dana	C3-C4
Crescent Fields	A1-B1	Murivance	A2	The Square	B2
Crescent Lane	A1	Nettles Lane	A3	Town Walls	A2-A1-B1-B2
Cross Hill	A2	New Park Road	C4	Victoria Avenue	A3
Darwin Street	A4	Old Coleham	C1	Victoria Street	C4
Dogpole	B2	Pride Hill	B2-B3	Water Lane	B3-C3
Drinkwater Street	A4	Princess Street	B2	Welsh Bridge	A3
English Bridge	C2	Priory Road	A3	Wyle Cop	B2

Sheffield

Sheffield is found on atlas page **74**,
grid reference **3587**

...orn Street	C7	Broomhall Road	A2	Cross Gilpin Street	A8
...elphi Street	A7	Broomhall Street	A2-A3	Cross Smithfield	B6-C6
...bert Terrace	A7-A8	Broomspring Lane	A3-A4	Cumberland Street	C2
...en Street	B6-C6	Brown Street	D3	Cumberland Way	C2-C3
...ma Street	C7-D7	Brownell Street	B6	Cupola	C6
...dover Street	E8	Brunswick Road	E7-E8-F8	Daisy Bank	A6
...ley Street	C1	Brunswick Street	A3-A4	Denby Street	C1
...undel Gate	D4-D5	Burgess Street	C4	Denholme Close	D8
...undel Lane	D3	Burton Road	B8-C8	Devonshire Street	B4
...undel Street	C2-D2-D3-D4	Cambridge Street	C4	Division Street	C4
...ley Lane	C5	Campo Lane	C5-D5	Dixon Lane	E5
...ley Street	C5	Carlisle Street	F7-F8	Dixon Street	B8
...l Street	C7-C8	Carver Lane	C4	Doncaster Street	B7-B6-C6
...m Green	C4-C5	Carver Street	C4	Dorking Street	F8
...nk Street	D6	Castle Street	D6-E6	Dover Street	A6-B6
...rd Street	F5	Castlegate	E6	Duchess Road	D2-D1-E1
...rker's Pool	C4	Cavendish Court	B3	Duke Street	F3-F4-F5
...rnes Court	E3	Cavendish Street	B3-B4	Dun Street	B7-C7
...ron Street	D1	Cemetery Road	A1-B1	Dunfields	C7
...dford Street	B8	Chapel Walk	D5	Earl Street	C3-C2-D2
...et Street	A5-B5	Charles Street	D3-D4	Earl Way	C3
...llefield Street	A6	Charlotte Road	C2-D2-D1-E1	Earsham Street	F8
...nnett Street	B1-C1	Charter Row	C3	East Bank Road	E1
...rnard Street	F4-F5-F6	Charter Square	C3-C4	Ebenezer Street	C7
...ackwell Place	F5	Church Street	C5-D5	Ecclesall Road	A1-A2-B2
...onk Street	E6	Clarke Street	A3	Edmund Road	D1-D2
...lsover Street	A5	Claywood Drive	E3-F3	Edward Street	B5-B6
...wer Spring	C6	Cleveland Street	A8	Effingham Street	F7
...wling Green Street	C1-C2	Cliff Street	B1	Egerton Close	B3
...amall Lane	A6	Clinton Place	A2	Egerton Street	B3
...amwell Street	A6	Clough Road	C1-D1-D2	Eldon Street	B3-B4
...idge Street	D6-D7	Club Garden Road	B1	Ellis Street	B6
...oad Lane	B5-C5	Collegiate Crescent	A3	Exchange Street	E6
...oad Street	E5	Commercial Street	D5-E5	Exeter Drive	A2-B2
...oad Street	F5	Copper Street	C6	Eyre Lane	C2-C3-D3
...occo Street	B6	Cornish Street	B7-B8	Eyre Street	C2-C3-D3
...ook Drive	A5	Corporation Street	D6-D7	Fargate	D5
...ook Hill	A5	Cotton Mill Road	D7	Farm Bank Road	F2
...oom Close	B1	Countess Road	C1	Farm Road	E1-E2
...oom Green	B3	Cream Street	E1	Fawcett Street	A6
...oom Street	A2	Cromford Street	D1	Filey Street	A3-A4
...oomhall Place	A2	Cross Bedford Street	A8-B8	Fitzwilliam Gate	C2-C3
				Fitzwilliam Street	B4-B3-C3
				Fox Hill	D8
				Fox Street	D8
				Furnace Hill	C6
				Furnival Road	E6-F6
				Furnival Street	D3
				Garden Street	B5-C5

Gell Street	A3-A4-A5	Milton Street	B2-B3-C3	Shoreham Street	D1-D2-D3
George Street	D5	Mitchell Street	A5	Shrewsbury Road	E2-E3
Gibraltar Street	C6-C7	Montfort Drive	E8	Siddall Street	B5
Gilpin Street	A8	Montgomery Terrace Road	A7-B8	Sidney Street	D2-D3
Glencoe Drive	F3	Moore Street	B2-B3-C3	Silver Street Head	C5-C6
Glencoe Road	F3	Morpeth Street	B6	Smithfield	C6
Glossop Road	A4-B4	Mount Street	B1	Snig Hill	D6
Gower Street	F8	Mowbray Street	C8-C7-D7	Snow Lane	C6
Grafton Street	F3	Napier Street	A1-B1	Solly Street	B5-B6-C6
Granville Road	F1-F2	Neepsend Lane	B8-C8	Sorby Street	F8
Green Lane	B7-C7	Netherthorpe Place	B7	South Lane	C2
Hallcar Street	F8	Netherthorpe Road	A5-A6-B6-B7	South Parade	C7
Hammond Street	A6	Neville Close	D8	South Street	E3-E4-E5
Hanover Way	A3-B3-B2	Newcastle Street	B5	Spital Hill	E7-E8-F8
Harmer Lane	E4	Norfolk Park Drive	E1	Spital Lane	E8-F8
Harrow Street	B2	Norfolk Park Road	E1-F1-F2	Spital Street	E8
Hartshead	D5	Norfolk Road	F2-F3	Spitalfields	D7
Harvest Lane	C8	Norfolk Row	D4-D5	Spring Street	D6
Harwood Street	C1	Norfolk Street	D4-D5	Stafford Street	F3-F4
Havelock Street	A3	North Church Street	D5-D6	Stanley Lane	E7
Hawley Street	C5	Nursery Lane	D7-E7-E6	Stanley Street	E6-E7
Haymarket	D5	Nursery Street	D7-D6-E6	Stockton Close	E8
Headford Gardens	A3-B3	Old Street	F5	Sudbury Street	B7
Headford Grove	A3-B3	Orchard Lane	C5	Suffolk Road	E2-E3
Headford Mews	A3-B3	Orchard Square	C5-D5	Summerfield Street	A1-A2
Headford Street	B3	Oxford Street	A7	Sunny Bank	A2
Henry Street	B7	Paradise Square	C5-D5	Surrey Street	D4
Hicks Street	C8	Paradise Street	D5-D6	Sutton Street	A5
High Street	D5	Park Grange Croft	F1	Sylvester Street	C2-D2
High Street Lane	F5	Park Square	E5-F5	Talbot Place	F3
Hill Street	B1-C1	Paternoster Row	D3	Talbot Road	F4
Hodgson Street	B2-B3	Pear Street	A1	Talbot Street	F3-F4
Holberry Close	A3	Pearl Street	A1	Terrace Road	A8-B8
Holberry Gardens	A3	Penistone Road	A8-B8-B7	The Moor	C2-C3
Holland Street	B4	Percy Street	C8	Thomas Street	B3
Hollis Croft	B6-C5	Philadelphia Gardens	A8	Townhead Street	C5
Holly Street	C4-C5	Pinfold Street	C5	Trafalgar Street	B4-C4-C3
Hounsfield Road	A4	Pinstone Street	C3-C4-D4	Travis Place	A3
Hyde Park Terrace	F4-F5	Pitt Street	B4	Trinity Street	C6
Infirmary Road	A8-B8-B7	Platt Street	C8	Trippet Lane	C5
Jericho Street	A6	Plum Lane	D6	Tudor Square	D4
Jessop Street	C2	Pomona Street	A1-A2	Union Lane	C3
John Street	B1-C1-D1	Portland Street	A8	Union Street	C3-D4
Johnson Street	D7-E7	Portobello Street	B4-B5	Upper Allen Street	B5-B6
Kelham Island	C7	Powell Street	A5-A6	Upper Hanover Street	A3-A4-A5
King Street	D5-E5	Priestley Street	D1-E1	Upperthorpe Road	A7
Kirk Street	F8	Pye Bank Road	D8	Verdon Street	D8-E8
Lambert Street	C6	Queen Street	C6-D6	Vicar Lane	C5
Lancing Road	D1	Queen's Road	E1-E2	Victoria Road	A2
Leadmill Road	D3-E3	Radford Street	A6-B6	Victoria Street	A3-A4
Leavygreave Road	A4	Regent Street	B4	Waingate	E6
Lee Croft	C5	Regent Terrace	B4	Walker Street	E7
Lenton Street	D2	Rhodes Street	F4	Washington Road	A1-B1
Leopold Street	C4-C5	Rock Street	D8	Watery Street	B7
Leverton Gardens	B1	Rockingham Lane	C4	Well Meadow Drive	B6
London Road	B1-B2	Rockingham Street	B5-C5-C4-C3	Wellington Street	B3-C4
Lopham Close	E8	Roscoe Road	B7	West Bar	D6
Lopham Street	E8	Rowland Street	C8	West Bar Green	C6
Mackenzie Crescent	A3	Russell Street	C7	West Don Street	A8
Malinda Street	B7	Rutland Road	B8	West Street	B4-C4-C5
Manor Oaks Road	F4	Rutland Way	B8	Westfield Terrace	B4
Mappin Street	B4-B5	St George's Close	A5	Westmoreland Street	A8
Margaret Street	D2	St Mary's Road	C2-D2-E2	Weston Street	A5-A6
Martin Street	A7	St Marys Gate	B2-C2	Wharncliffe Road	A2-A3
Mary Street	C2-D2	St Philip's Road	B7	Wicker	E6-E7
Mathew Street	B7	St Philip's Street	A6	Wicker Lane	E6-E7
Matilda Lane	D2-D3	Savile Street	E7-F7	Wilkinson Lane	A4
Matilda Street	C3-D3-D2	Scotland Street	B6-C6	Wilkinson Street	A4
Meadow Street	B6-B7	Sharrow Street	B1	Willey Street	E6
Midland Street	D2	Sheaf Gardens	D2-E2	William Street	A2-A3
Midvale Avenue	A8	Shepherd Street	B6-C6-C7	York Street	D5
Milton Lane	B3	Shipton Street	A7	Young Street	B2-C2

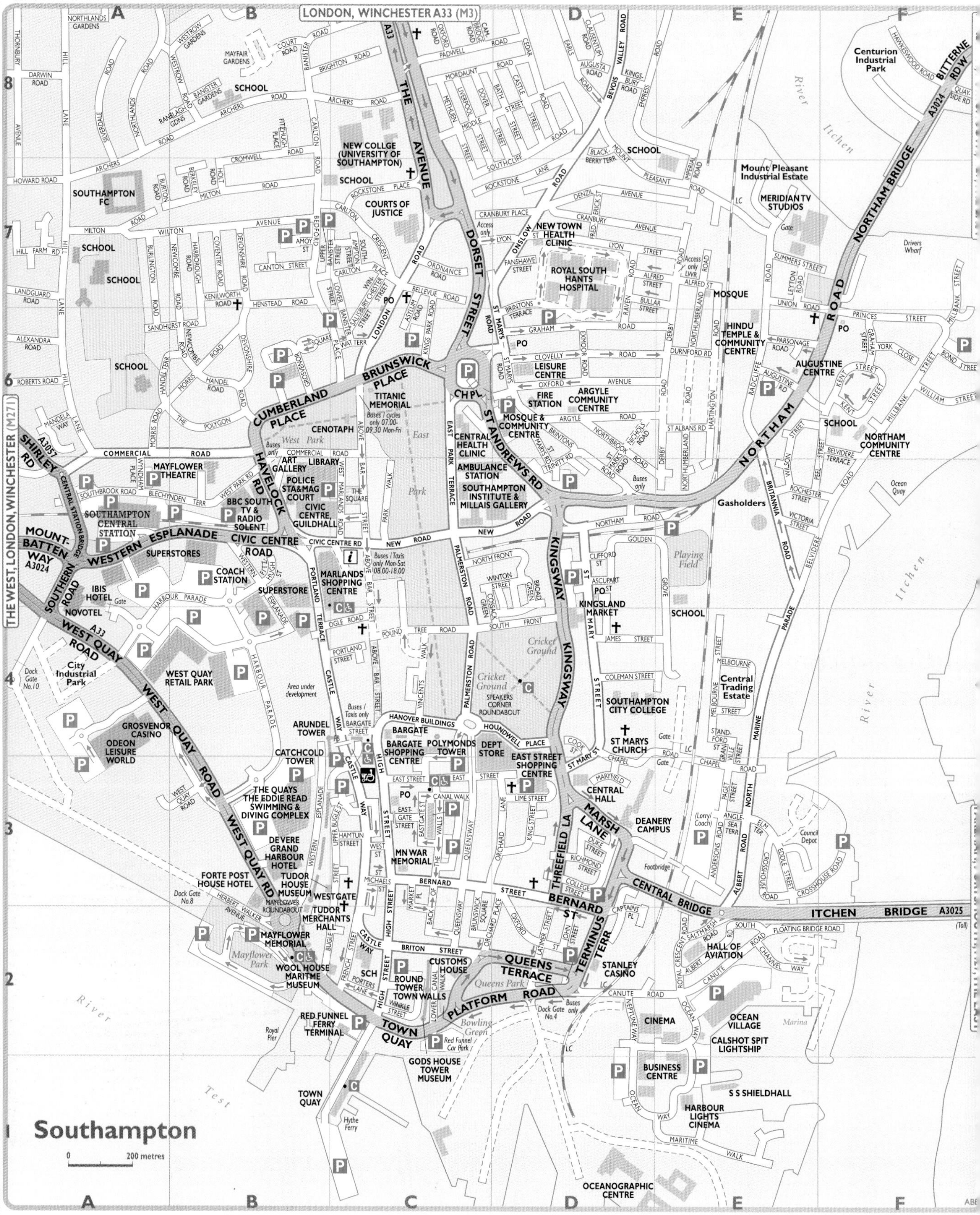

Southampton

0   200 metres

LONDON, WINCHESTER A33 (M3)

THE WEST, LONDON, WINCHESTER (M271)

Map of Southampton city centre showing streets and landmarks including:

Southampton FC, New College (University of Southampton), Courts of Justice, Royal South Hants Hospital, Mount Pleasant Industrial Estate, Meridian TV Studios, Centurion Industrial Park, Northam Bridge, Mayflower Theatre, Southampton Central Station, Civic Centre, Titanic Memorial, Cenotaph, Art Gallery, Library, Police Sta & Mag Court, BBC South TV & Radio Solent, Marlands Shopping Centre, Fire Station, Argyle Community Centre, Central Health Clinic, Ambulance Station, Southampton Institute & Millais Gallery, Mosque, Hindu Temple & Community Centre, Augustine Centre, Northam Community Centre, Ibis Hotel, Novotel, West Quay Retail Park, City Industrial Park, Grosvenor Casino, Odeon Leisure World, West Quay Shopping, Arundel Tower, Catchcold Tower, The Quays The Eddie Read Swimming & Diving Complex, De Vere Grand Harbour Hotel, Tudor House Museum, Forte Post House Hotel, Bargate Shopping Centre, Polymonds Tower, Dept Store, East Street Shopping Centre, Central Hall, Deanery Campus, St Marys Church, Southampton City College, Central Trading Estate, Kingsland Market, Mayflower Memorial, Westgate, Tudor Merchants Hall, Wool House Maritime Museum, Customs House, Round Tower Town Walls, Red Funnel Ferry Terminal, Gods House Tower Museum, Town Quay, Queens Terrace, Platform Road, Stanley Casino, Hall of Aviation, Ocean Village, Calshot Spit Lightship, Cinema, Business Centre, Harbour Lights Cinema, S S Shieldhall, Oceanographic Centre, Itchen Bridge A3025 (Toll), Central Bridge, Marsh Lane, Terminus Terr, Bernard St

River Itchen, River Test

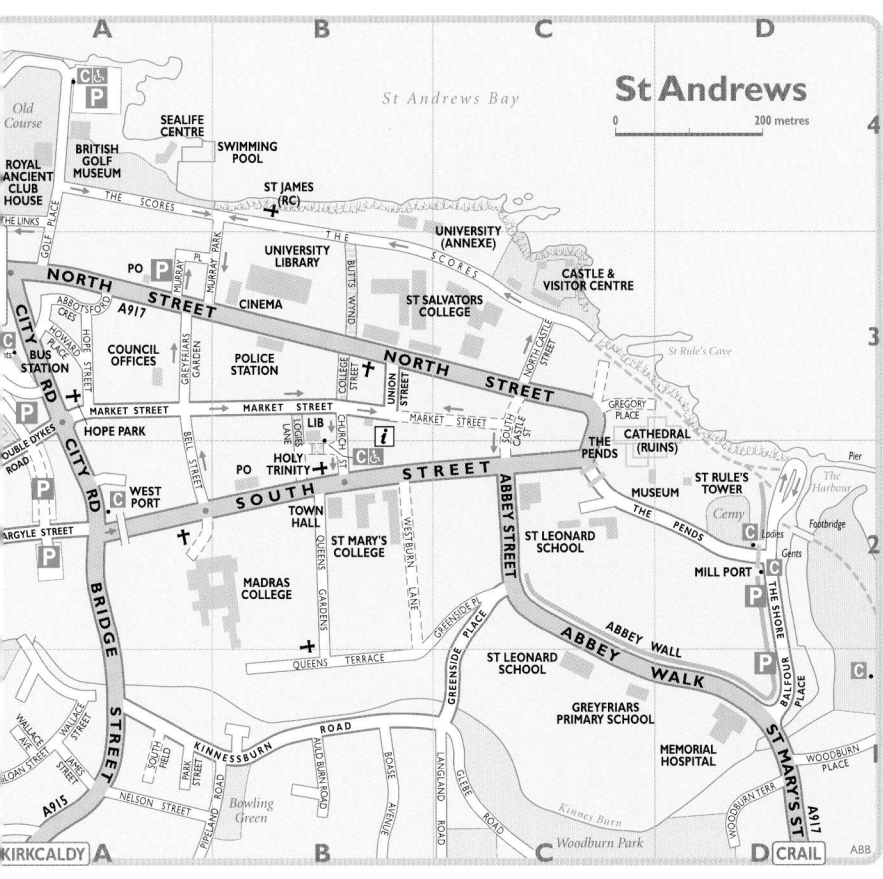

St Andrews

St Andrews is found on atlas page **127**,
grid reference **5116**

Abbey Street	C2
Abbey Walk	C2-C1-D1
Abbotsford Crescent	A3
Argyle Street	A2
Auld Burn Road	B1
Balfour Place	D1
Bell Street	A2-A3
Boase Avenue	B1
Bridge Street	A1-A2
Butts Wynd	B3
Church Street	B2-B3
City Road	A2-A3
College Street	B3
Double Dykes Road	A2-A3
Glebe Road	C1
Golf Place	A3-A4
Greenside Place	B2-C2-C1
Gregory Place	C3
Greyfriars Garden	A3
Hope Street	A3
Howard Place	A3
James Street	A1
Kinnessburn Road	A1-B1
Langland Road	C1
Logies Lane	B2-B3
Market Street	A3-B3-C3
Murray Park	A3-B4
Murray Place	A3
Nelson Street	A1
North Castle Street	C3
North Street	A3-B3-C3
Park Street	A1
Pipeland Road	A1-B1
Queens Gardens	B1-B2
Queens Terrace	B1
St Mary's Street	D1
Sloan Street	A1
South Castle Street	C2-C3
South Field	A1
South Street	A2-B2-C2
The Links	A4
The Pends	C2-D2
The Scores	A4-B4-B3-C3
The Shore	D2
Union Street	B3

Wallace Avenue	A1
Wallace Street	A1
Westburn Lane	B2
Woodburn Place	D1
Woodburn Terrace	D1

outhampton

uthampton is found on atlas page **13**,
d reference **4112**

ove Bar Street	C4-C5-C6	Cambridge Road	C8	East Park Terrace	C5-C6	Kingsbury Road	D8	Orchard Lane	D3	Southampton Street	C7
ert Road North	E3	Canal Walk	C3	East Street	C3-D3	Kingsway	D4-D5	Orchard Place	C2-D2-D3	Southbrook Road	A5
ert Road South	E2	Canton Street	B7	Eddle Street	E2-E3	Landguard Road	A7	Ordnance Road	C7	Southcliff Road	C7-D7-D8
xandra Road	A6	Canute Road	D2-E2	Elm Terrace	E3	Latimer Street	D2	Oxford Avenue	D6-E6	Southern Road	A4-A5
red Street	D7-E7	Captains Place	D2	Empress Road	D8-E8	Leyton Road	E7	Oxford Road	C8	Standford Street	E4
oy Street	B7	Carlton Crescent	B7-C7	Exmoor Road	D6	Lime Street	D3	Oxford Street	D2-D3	Summers Street	E7-F7
dersons Road	E3	Carlton Place	B7-C7	Fanshawe Street	D7	Liverpool Street	C7-C8	Padwell Road	C8-D8	Terminus Terrace	D2
glesea Terrace	E3	Carlton Road	B7-B8	Fitzhugh Place	B8	London Road	C6-C7	Paget Street	E3	The Avenue	C7-C8
chers Road	A7-A8-B8-C8	Castle Street	D8	Fitzhugh Street	B5	Lower Alfred Street	E7	Palmerston Road	C4-C5	The Polygon	B6
gyle Road	D6-E6	Castle Way	B4-C4-C3-C2	Floating Bridge Road	E2-F2	Lower Banister Street	C6-C7	Park Walk	C5	The Square	C5
cupart Street	D5	Cedar Road	D8	Frederick Street	D7	Lower Canal Walk	A2	Parsonage Road	E6	Thornbury Avenue	A7-A8
lum Road	C6-C7	Central Bridge	D3-E3-E2	French Street	C2	Lyon Street	C7-D7-E7	Peel Street	E5-F6	Town Quay	C2
gusta Road	D8	Central Station Bridge	A5	Golden Grove	D5-E5-E4	Mandela Way	A6	Platform Road	C2-D2	Trinity Road	D5-D6
gustine Road	E6	Channel Way	E2	Graham Road	D6-E6	Marine Parade	E3-E4-E5	Porters Lane	C2	Union Road	E7-F7
k of the Walls	C2-C3	Chapel Road	D3-D4-E4-E3	Graham Street	F6	Maritime Walk	E1	Portland Street	C4	Upper Banister Street	B7-C7
ister Gardens	B8	Charlotte Place	C6	Granville Street	E3-E4	Market Place	C3	Portland Terrace	B4-B5	Upper Bugle Street	C3
ister Road	B8-C8	Civic Centre Road	B5-C5	Grosvenor Square	B6	Marsh Lane	D3	Pound Tree Road	C4	Victoria Street	E5
gate Street	C4	Clausentum Road	D8	Hamtun Street	C3	Maryfield	D3	Princes Street	F6	Vincents Walk	C4
h Street	C8-D8	Clifford Street	D5	Handel Road	B6	Mayfair Gardens	B8	Quayside Road	F8	Waterloo Terrace	C6
dford Place	B7-B6-C6	Clovelly Road	D6-E6	Handel Terrace	A6-B6	Melbourne Street	E4	Queens Terrace	D2	West Marland Road	C5
levue Road	C7	Coleman Street	D4-E4	Hanover Buildings	C4	Methuen Street	C7-C8	Queensway	C2-C3	West Park Road	B5
videre Road	E5-F5	College Street	D3	Harborough Road	B7	Middle Street	C8-D8	Radcliffe Road	E6-E7	West Quay Road	A4-B4-B3
videre Terrace	F6	Commercial Road	A5-A6-B6-C6	Hartington Road	E5-E6-E7	Millbank Street	F6-F7	Ranelagh Gardens	B8	West Street	C3
keley Road	B7	Cook Street	D4	Havelock Road	B5-B6	Milton Road	A7-B7	Raven Road	D6-D7	Western Esplanade	A5-B5-B4-B3
nard Street	C3-D3	Cossack Green	C5-D4	Hawkswood Road	F8	Mordaunt Road	C8-D8	Richmond Street	D3	Westrow Gardens	B8
vois Valley Road	D8	Court Road	B8	Henstead Road	B7	Morris Road	A6-B6	Roberts Road	A6	Westrow Road	A8-B8
cerne Road West	F8	Coventry Road	B7	Herbert Walker Avenue	B2-B3	Mount Pleasant Road	D8-D7-E7	Rochester Street	E5-F5	William Street	F6
ckberry Terrace	D8	Cranbury Avenue	D7-E7	High Street	C2-C3-C4	Mountbatten Way	A5	Rockstone Lane	C7-D7	Wilson Street	E5-E6
chynden Terrace	A5-B5	Cranbury Place	C7-D7	Hill Farm Road	A7	Neptune Way	D2	Rockstone Place	C7	Wilton Avenue	A7-B7
nd Street	F6	Cromwell Road	B7-B8	Hill Lane	A6-A7-A8	New Road	C5-D5	Royal Crescent Road	E2	Winchester Street	C7
ghton Road	B8-C8	Crosshouse Road	E3-F3	Holt Road	B7	Newcombe Road	B6-B7	St Albans Road	E6	Winkle Street	C2
ntons Terrace	D6-D7	Cumberland Place	B6-C6	Houndwell Place	C4-D4	Nichols Road	D6	St Andrews Road	C6-D6-D5	Winton Street	C5-D5
annia Road	E5-E6	Darwin Road	A8	Howard Road	A7	North Front	C5-D5	St Marks Road	D5-D6	Wyndham Place	A5
con Street	C2	Denzil Avenue	D7-E7	Imperial Road	E7-E8	Northam Bridge	F7-F8	St Mary Street	D3-D4-D5	York Close	F6
ntons Road	D5-D6	Derby Road	E5-E6-E7	Itchen Bridge	E2-F2	Northam Road	D5-E5-E6-F7	St Marys Road	D5-D6-D7		
ad Green	D5	Devonshire Road	B6-B7	James Street	D4-E4	Northbrook Road	D5-D6	St Michaels Street	C3		
nswick Place	C6	Dorset Street	C6-C7	John Street	D2	Northlands Gardens	A8	Salisbury Street	C6-C7		
nswick Square	C2-C3	Dover Street	C8-D8	Kenilworth Road	B7	Northlands Road	A8	Saltmarsh Road	E2		
gle Street	B2-C2-C3	Duke Street	D3	Kent Street	F6	Northumberland Road	E5-E6-E7	Sandhurst Road	A6-B6		
lar Street	D7-E7	Durnford Road	E6	King Street	D3	Ocean Way	D1-E1-E2	Shirley Road	A5-A6		
rlington Road	A6-A7	Earls Road	D8	Kings Park Road	C6-C7	Ogle Road	B4-C4	Silverdale Road	A8		
rton Road	A7	Eastgate Street	C3	Kings Park Road	C6-C7	Onslow Road	D7	South Front	C4-D4		

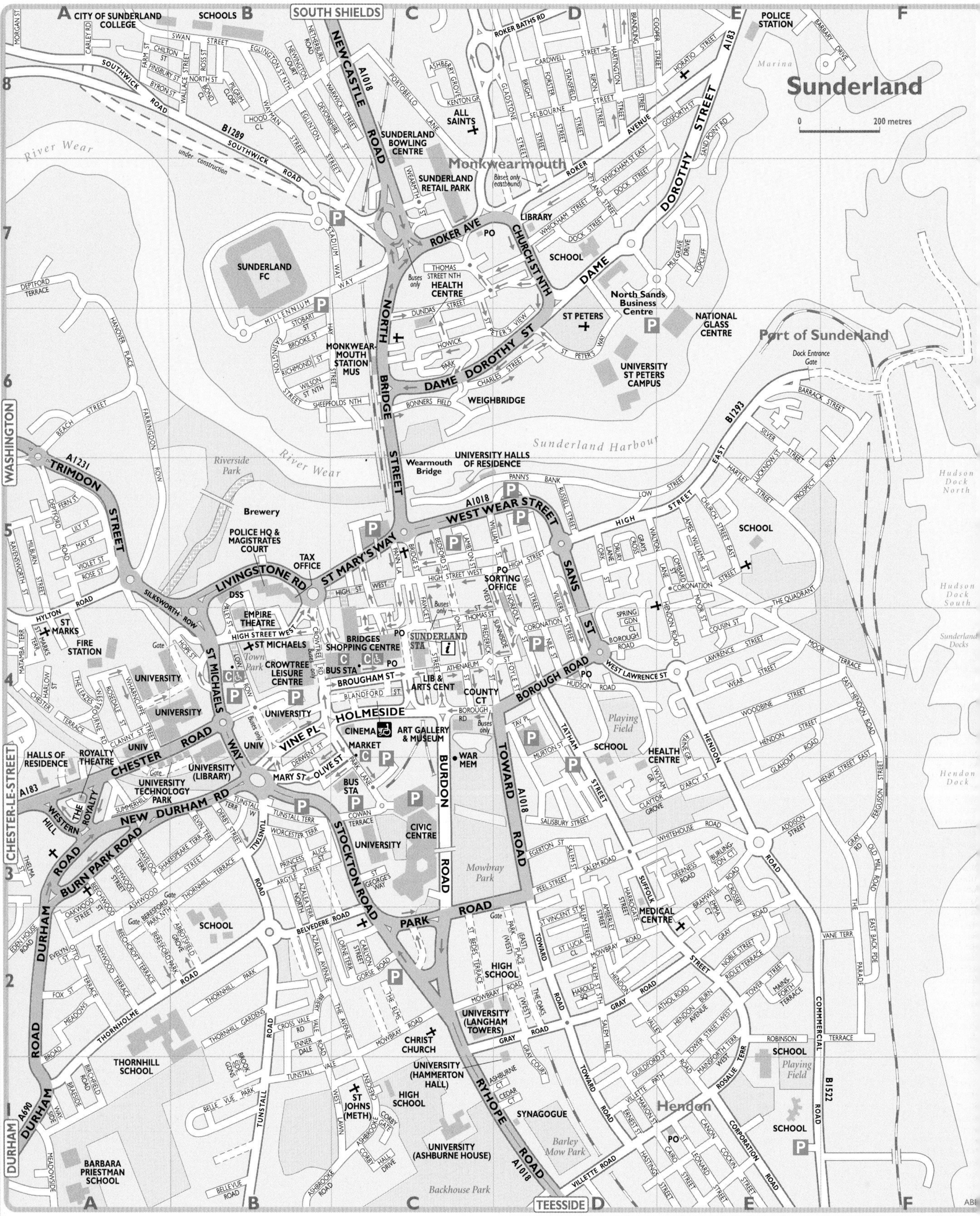

220

Sunderland

CITY OF SUNDERLAND COLLEGE
SCHOOLS
SOUTH SHIELDS
POLICE STATION

River Wear

Monkwearmouth

SUNDERLAND BOWLING CENTRE
SUNDERLAND RETAIL PARK
ALL SAINTS
ROKER AVE
PO
LIBRARY
SCHOOL
DAME
DOROTHY STREET
Marina

SUNDERLAND FC
MONKWEAR-MOUTH STATION MUS
HEALTH CENTRE
ST PETERS
North Sands Business Centre
NATIONAL GLASS CENTRE
Port of Sunderland

SOUTHWICK ROAD
B1289
SOUTHWICK ROAD
under construction
NEWCASTLE RD
A1018
NORTH BRIDGE STREET
DAME DOROTHY ST
WEIGHBRIDGE
UNIVERSITY ST PETERS CAMPUS
Dock Entrance Gate

WASHINGTON
TRIMDON STREET
A1231
Riverside Park
River Wear
Brewery
Wearmouth Bridge
UNIVERSITY HALLS OF RESIDENCE
Sunderland Harbour
BARRACK STREET
Hudson Dock North

POLICE HQ & MAGISTRATES COURT
TAX OFFICE
ST MARY'S WAY
WEST WEAR STREET
SORTING OFFICE
PO
SCHOOL
B1293
Hudson Dock South

LIVINGSTONE RD
DSS
EMPIRE THEATRE
ST MARKS
FIRE STATION
HIGH STREET WEST
ST MICHAELS
BRIDGES SHOPPING CENTRE
BUS STA
SUNDERLAND STA
LIB & ARTS CENT
SANS ST
BOROUGH ROAD
PO
WEST LAWRENCE ST
HEALTH CENTRE
Sunderland Docks

HALLS OF RESIDENCE
ROYALTY THEATRE
CHESTER ROAD
UNIVERSITY
CROWTREE LEISURE CENTRE
VINE PL
BROUGHAM ST
HOLMESIDE
CINEMA
MARKET
ART GALLERY & MUSEUM
WAR MEM
Playing Field
SCHOOL
HENDON
Hendon Dock

CHESTER-LE-STREET
A183
THE ROYALTY
NEW DURHAM RD
BURN PARK ROAD
UNIVERSITY TECHNOLOGY PARK
UNIVERSITY (LIBRARY)
MARY ST
OLIVE ST
BUS STA
COWAN TERRACE
CIVIC CENTRE
BURDON ROAD
TOWARD ROAD
A1018
MEDICAL CENTRE

DURHAM ROAD
STOCKTON ROAD
BELVEDERE ROAD
PARK ROAD
Mowbray Park
CHRIST CHURCH
HIGH SCHOOL
UNIVERSITY (LANGHAM TOWERS)

THORNHOLME
THORNHILL SCHOOL
THORNHILL GARDENS
UNIVERSITY (HAMMERTON HALL)
HIGH SCHOOL
RYHOPE ROAD
SYNAGOGUE
Barley Mow Park
SCHOOL
Playing Field
B1522

DURHAM ROAD
A690
BARBARA PRIESTMAN SCHOOL
ST JOHNS (METH)
UNIVERSITY (ASHBURNE HOUSE)
A1018
Backhouse Park
TEESSIDE
Villette Park
CORPORATION ROAD

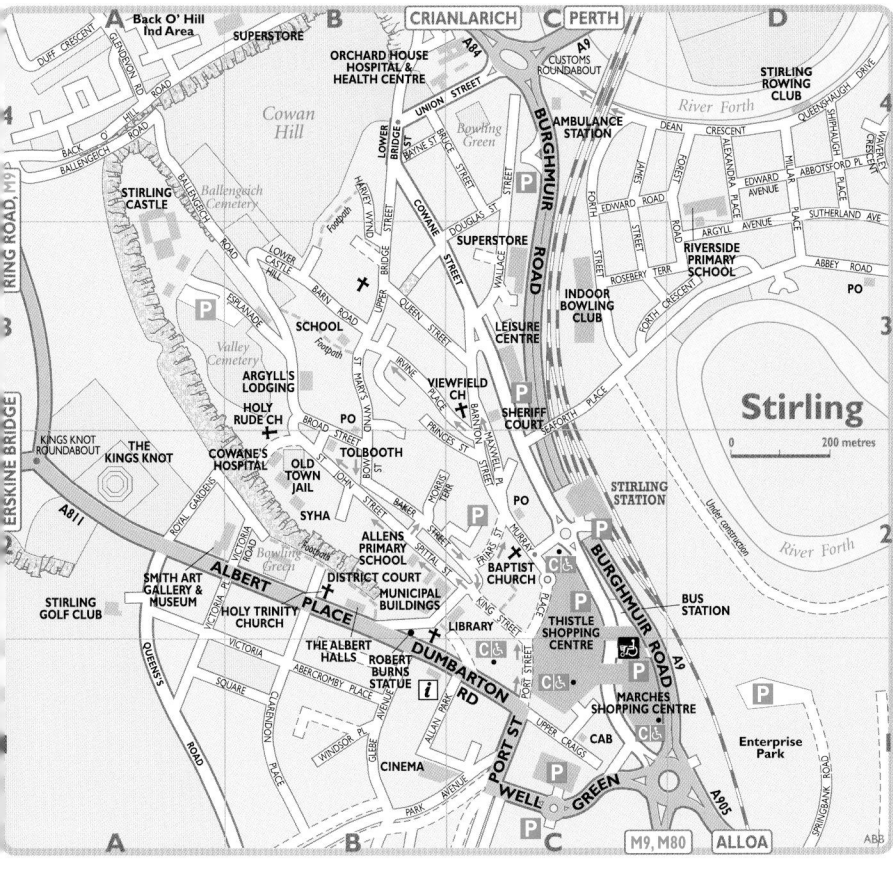

Stirling

Stirling is found on atlas page 116,
grid reference 7993

Abbey Road	D3	Queen Street	B3-C3
Abbotsford Place	D4	Queenshaugh Drive	D4
Abercromby Place	B1	Queen's Road	A1-A2
Albert Place	A2-B2	Rosebery Terrace	C3-D3
Alexandra Place	D4	Royal Gardens	A2
Allan Park	B1-C1	St John Street	B2
Argyll Avenue	D3-D4	St Mary's Wynd	B2-B3
Back O' Hill Road	A4-B4	Seaforth Place	C2-C3
Baker Street	B2-C2	Shiphaugh Place	D4
Ballengeich Road	A4-A3-B3	Spittal Street	B2-C2
Barn Road	B3	Springbank Road	D1
Barnton Street	C2-C3	Sutherland Avenue	D4
Bayne Street	B4	Union Street	B4-C4
Bow Street	B2	Upper Bridge Street	B3-B4
Broad Street	B2-B3	Upper Craigs	C1
Bruce Street	B4-C4	Victoria Place	A2-B2
Burghmuir Road	C4-C2-D1	Victoria Road	B2
Clarendon Place	B1-B2	Victoria Square	A1-B1
Cowane Street	B4-B3-C3	Wallace Street	C3-C4
Dean Crescent	C4-D4	Waverley Crescent	D4
Douglas Street	B3-C4	Well Green	C1
Duff Crescent	A4	Windsor Place	B1
Dumbarton Road	B1-C1		
Edward Avenue	D4		
Edward Road	C4		
Esplanade	A3-B3		
Forest Road	D3-D4		
Forth Crescent	C3-D3		
Forth Street	C3-C4		
Friars Street	C2		
Glebe Avenue	B1		
Glendevon Road	A4		
Harvey Wynd	B3-B4		
Irvine Place	B3-C2		
James Street	C3-C4		
King Street	C1-C2		
Lower Bridge Street	B4		
Lower Castle Hill	B3		
Maxwell Place	C2-C3		
Millar Place	D3-D4		
Morris Terrace	B2		
Murray Place	C2		
Park Avenue	B1-C1		
Port Street	C1		
Princes Street	B3-B2-C2		

221

Sunderland

Sunderland is found on atlas page 96,
grid reference 3957

Abbotsfield Grove	B2	Burn Park Road	A3	East Hendon Road	F4	Horatio Street	E8	Portobello Lane	C7-C8	The Elms	C2
Addison Street	E3	Byron Street	A8-B8	Eden House Road	A2	Howick Park	C6	Princess Street	B3	The Leazes	A4
Alice Street	B3	Cairo Street	E1	Egerton Street	D3	Hudson Street	D4	Prospect Row	E5-F6	The Oaks West	D2
Amberley Street	D2-D3	Canon Cockin Street	E1	Eglinton Street	B8-C7	Hylton Road	A4-A5	Raine Grove	E4	The Parade	E3-F2
Argyle Street	B3-C3	Cardwell Street	D8	Eglinton Street North	B8	James Williams Street	E5	Ravensworth Street	A4-A5	The Quadrant	E5
Ashberry Grove	C8	Carley Road	A8	Elmwood Street	A3	John Street	C4-C5	Richmond Street	B6	The Royalty	A3
Ashbrooke Crescent	C1	Carlyon Street	C2	Elvin Terrace	B3	Kenton Grove	C8	Ridley Terrace	E2	Thelma Street	A3
Ashbrooke Road	B1-C1	Cedar Court	D1	Emma Court	E2-E3	Lambton Street	C5	Ripon Street	D8	Thomas Street North	C7
Ashburne Court	C1-C2	Charles Street	C6-D6	Ennerdale	B2	Lawrence Street	E4	Robinson Terrace	E2-F2	Thornhill Gardens	B2
Ashwood Street	A2-B3	Chester Road	A3-B4	Ernest Street	D1	Lily Street	A5	Roker Avenue	C7-E8	Thornhill Park	B2
Ashwood Terrace	A2	Chester Terrace	A4	Evelyn Street	A2	Livingstone Road	B5	Roker Baths Road	D8	Thornhill Terrace	B3
Athenaeum Street	C4-D4	Chilton Street	A8-B8	Farm Street	A8	Lombard Street	E5	Rosalie Terrace	E1-E2	Thornholme Road	A1-B2
Azalea Terrace Avenue	B2	Church Street East	E5	Farringdon Row	A5-A6	Lorne Terrace	C2	Rose Street	A5	Topcliff	E7
Azalea Terrace North	B2	Clanny Street	A4	Fawcett Street	C4-C5	Low Row	B4	Rosedale Street	A4	Toward Road	D1-D4
Barbary Drive	E8-F8	Clayton Grove	D3-E3	Ferguson Street	F3	Low Street	D5-E6	Ross Street	B8	Tower Street	E2
Beach Street	A6	Commercial Road	E1-E2	Fern Street	A5	Lucknow Street	E5-E6	Russell Street	D5	Tower Street West	E2
Bedford Street	C5	Cooper Street	E8	Finsbury Street	A8-B8	Mainsforth Terrace	E2	Ryhope Road	C2-D1	Trimdon Street	A5-A6
Beechcroft Terrace	A2	Corby Gate	C1	Forster Street	D7-D8	Mainsforth Terrace West	E1-E2	St Bedes Terrace	C2	Tunstall Road	B1-B3
Beechwood Street	A2-A3	Corby Hall Drive	C1	Fox Street	A2	Marion Street	D1	St George's Way	C3	Tunstall Terrace	B3
Belle Vue Park	B1	Cork Street	D5	Foyle Street	D4	Mary Street	B3	St Leonard Street	E1	Tunstall Terrace West	B3
Belvedere Road	B2-C3	Coronation Street	D4-E5	Frederick Street	C4-D4	Matamba Terrace	A4	St Lucia Close	D2	Tunstall Vale	B1-C2
Beresford Park North	A2-B3	Corporation Road	E1	George Street	D5	May Street	A5	St Marks Terrace	A4	Vane Terrace	F2
Beresford Road	A2-B2	Cousin Street	E4	Gladstone Street	D7-D8	Meadowside	A1	St Mary's Way	B5-C5	Villette Path	D1-E1
Birchfield Road	A1	Cowan Terrace	C3	Glaholm Road	E3-E4	Milburn Street	A5	St Michael's Way	B3-B4	Villette Road	D1-E1
Black Road	B7-C7	Crossby Court	E3	Gorse Road	C2	Millennium Way	B6-B7-C7	St Peter's View	C7-D7	Villiers Street	D4-D5
Blandford Street	C4	Cross Vale Road	B2	Gosforth Street	E8	Moor Street	E4-E5	St Peter's Way	D6-D7	Vine Place	B3-B4
Bond Close	B8	Crowtree Road	B4	Gray Court	D1-D2	Moor Terrace	E4-F4	St Thomas Street	C4-D4	Violet Street	A5
Bonners Field	C6	D'Arcy Street	E3	Gray Road	C2-E3-F3	Mowbray Road	C2-E2	St Vincent Street	D2	Wallace Street	B8
Borough Road	C4-E4	Dame Dorothy Street	D6-E8	Grays Cross	D5	Mulgrave Drive	E7	Salem Hill	D2	Walton Lane	D5-E5
Braeside	A1	Deerness Road	E3	Guildford Street	D1-E2	Murton Street	D3-D4	Salem Road	D3	Warren Street	E6
Bramwell Road	E2-E3	Deptford Road	A5	Gunton Street	B8-C7	Netherburn Road	B8	Salem Street	D2-D3	Warwick Street	B8-C8
Brandling Street	D8	Deptford Terrace	A7	Hanover Place	A6-A7	New Durham Road	A3-B3	Salem Street South	D2	Wayman Street	B8-C7
Bridge Street	C5	Derby Street	B3	Harold Square	D2	Newington Court	B8	Salisbury Street	D3	Wayside	A1
Briery Vale Road	B1-B2	Derwent Street	B3-C3	Hartington Street	D8	Nile Street	D4-D5	Sand Point Road	E7-E8	Wear Street	E4
Bright Street	D7-D8	Devonshire Street	B8-C7	Harlow Street	A4	Noble Street	E2	Sans Street	D4-D5	Wearmouth Street	C7
Broad Meadows	A1-A2	Dock Street	D7-E8	Harrogate Street	D2-D3	Norfolk Street	D4-D5	Selbourne Street	D8	West Lawn	B1-C1
Brooke Street	B6	Drury Lane	D5	Hartley Street	E5-E6	North Bridge Street	C5-C7	Shakespeare Terrace	A3-B3	West Lawrence Street	D4-E4
Brookside Gardens	B1-B2	Dundas Street	C6-C7	Hastings Road	D1-E1	North Street	B8	Sheepfolds North	B6-C6	West Sunniside	C5-D4
Brougham Street	B4-C4	Durham Road	A1-A3	Havelock Terrace	A3	Old Mill Road	F3	Silksworth Row	A5-B4	West Wear Street	C5-D5
Burdon Road	C2-C4	Easington Street	B6	Hay Street	C6-C7	Olive Street	B3-C4	Silver Street	E5-E6	Westbourne Road	A3-A4
Burlington Court	E3	East Back Poe	F2	Hendon Burn Avenue	D2-E2	Osman Terrace	D3-E3	Southwick Road	A8-C7	Western Hill	A3
		East Barrack Street	D5-F6	Hendon Road	E2-E5	Otto Terrace	A2	Spring Garden Close	D4	Wharncliffe Street	A4
				Hendon Street	E4-F4	Paley Street	B4-B5	Stadium Way	B7-C7	Whickham Street	D7-D8
				Hendon Valley Road	D2-E1	Pann's Bank	C5-D5	Stansfield Street	D7-D8	Whitehouse Road	D3-E3
				Henry Street East	E3-F4	Pann Lane	C5	Stobart Street	B6-B7	Wilson Street North	B6
				High Street	B5-D5	Park Lane	C3-C4	Stockton Road	B3-C2	Woodbine Street	E4-F4
				High Street West	B4-B5-C5	Park Place West	D2	Summerhill	A3	Worcester Terrace	B3
				Holmside	C4	Park Road	C2-D3	Swan Street	A8-B8	Wreath Quay Road	B6-C7
				Hood Close	B8	Peel Street	D3	Tavistock Place	D4	Wylam Grove	E3
				Hope Street	A4-B4	Pilgrim Close	B8	The Avenue	B2-C2	Zetland Street	D7

222

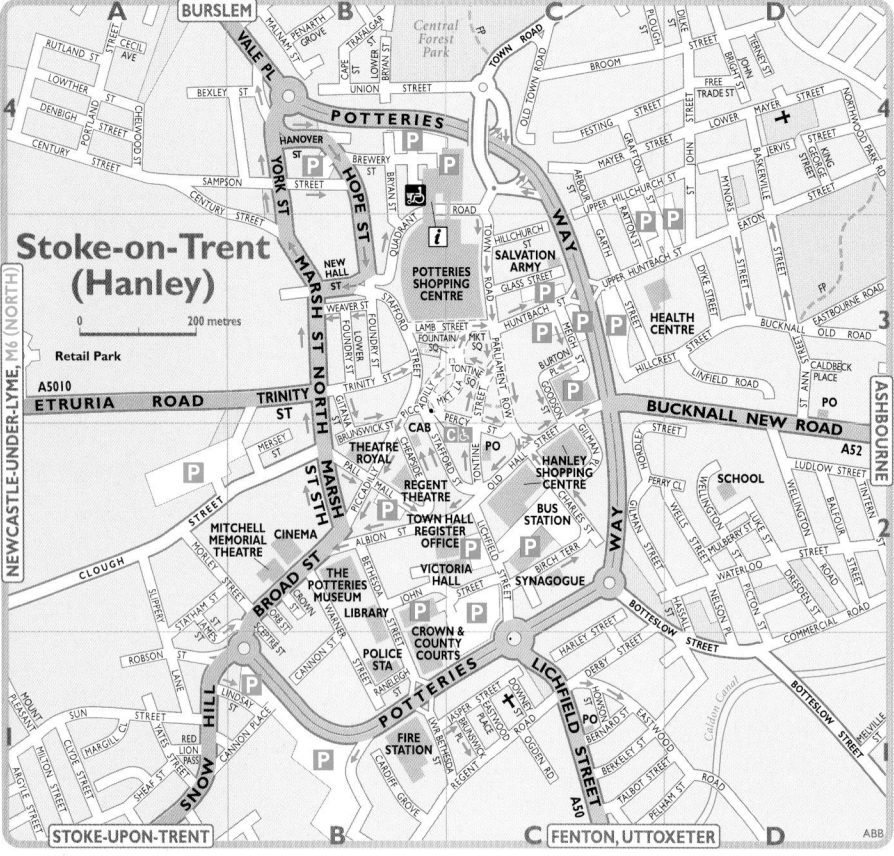

Stoke-on-Trent (Hanle

Stoke-on-Trent (Hanley) is found on atlas page **72**, grid reference **8847**

Albion Street	B2	Market Lane	B3-
Baskerville Street	D3-D4	Market Square	
Bethesda Street	B1-B2	Marsh Street North	B2-
Birch Terrace	C2	Marsh Street South	
Botteslow Street	C2-D1	Mayer Street	C4-
Brewery Street	B4	Meigh Street	
Broad Street	B2	Mersey Street	
Broom Street	C4-D4	Morley Street	A2-
Brunswick Street	B2	New Hall Street	
Bryan Street	B3-B4	Northwood Park Road	
Bucknall New Road	C3-D3-D2	Old Hall Street	C2-
Bucknall Old Road	D3	Old Town Road	
Burton Place	C3	Pall Mall	
Cannon Place	A1-B1	Parliament Row	
Cannon Street	B1	Percy Street	C2-
Century Street	A4-B3	Piccadilly	B2-
Charles Street	C2	Portland Street	
Cheapside	B2	Potteries Way	B1-C2-C4-
Clough Street	A2-B2	Quadrant Road	B3-B4-
Clyde Street	A1	Regent Road	B1-
Commercial Road	D1-D2	Sampson Street	A4
Derby Street	C1-C2	Sheaf Street	
Dresden Street	D2	Slippery Lane	A1-
Eastwood Road	C1-D1	Snow Hill	
Eaton Street	D3-D4	St Ann Street	
Etruria Road	A3	St John Street	D3-
Festing Street	C4-D4	Stafford Street	B3-B2-
Foundry Street	B3	Sun Street	
Fountain Square	B3-C3	Talbot Street	C1-
Garth Street	C3	Tontine Square	
Gilman Street	C2-D2	Tontine Street	C2-
Glass Street	C3	Town Road	C3-
Goodson Street	C3	Trafalgar Street	
Harley Street	C1-C2	Trinity Street	
Hillcrest Street	C3-D3	Union Street	B4-
Hope Street	B3-B4	Upper Hillchurch Street	C3-
Huntbach Street	C3	Upper Huntbach Street	C3-
Jasper Street	B1-C1	Vale Place	
John Street	B2-C2	Warner Street	B1-
Lamb Street	B3-C3	Waterloo Street	
Lichfield Street	C1-C2	Wellington Road	
Lower Bethesda Street	B1-C1	Wells Street	
Lower Foundry Street	B3	Yates Street	
Lower Mayer Street	D4	York Street	B3-
Lowther Street	A4		
Ludlow Street	D2		

Stratford-upon-Avon

Stratford-upon-Avon is found on atlas page **48**, grid reference **2055**

Albany Road	A3	Shreeves Walk	C2-
Alcester Road	A3-A4	Southern Lane	B1-B2-C
Arden Street	A3-A4-B4	Station Road	
Avonbank Paddock	B1	Swans Nest Lane	D1-E
Banbury Road	D1-D2	Tiddington Road	E
Birmingham Road	B4	Tyler Street	C
Bridge Foot	C3-D2	Union Street	C
Bridge Street	C3	Warwick Crescent	
Bridge Way	C3-D3	Warwick Road	D
Broad Street	A2	Waterside	
Broad Walk	A2	Wellesbourne Grove	
Bull Street	A1-A2	West Street	A1-A
Chapel Lane	B2-C2	Windsor Street	
Chapel Street	B2	Wood Street	E
Chestnut Walk	A2		
Church Street	A2-B2		
Clopton Bridge	D2		
College Lane	A1		
College Street	A1-B1		
Ely Street	A3-B3-B2		
Evesham Place	A2		
Great William Street	B4-C4		
Greenhill Street	A3-B3		
Grove Road	A2-A3		
Guild Street	B4-C3		
Henley Street	B3-B4		
High Street	B3		
Holtom Street	A1		
John Street	C3-C4		
Lock Close	C4		
Mansell Street	A4-B4		
Meer Street	B3		
Mulberry Street	B4-C4		
Narrow Lane	A1		
New Broad Street	A1		
Old Town	A2-B1		
Paddock Place	A1		
Payton Street	C3-C4		
Rother Road	A2-A3-B3		
St Gregory's Road	C4-D4		
Sanctus Street	A1		
Scholars Lane	A2-B2		
Shakespeare Street	B4		
Sheep Street	B2-C2		
Shipston Road	D1		

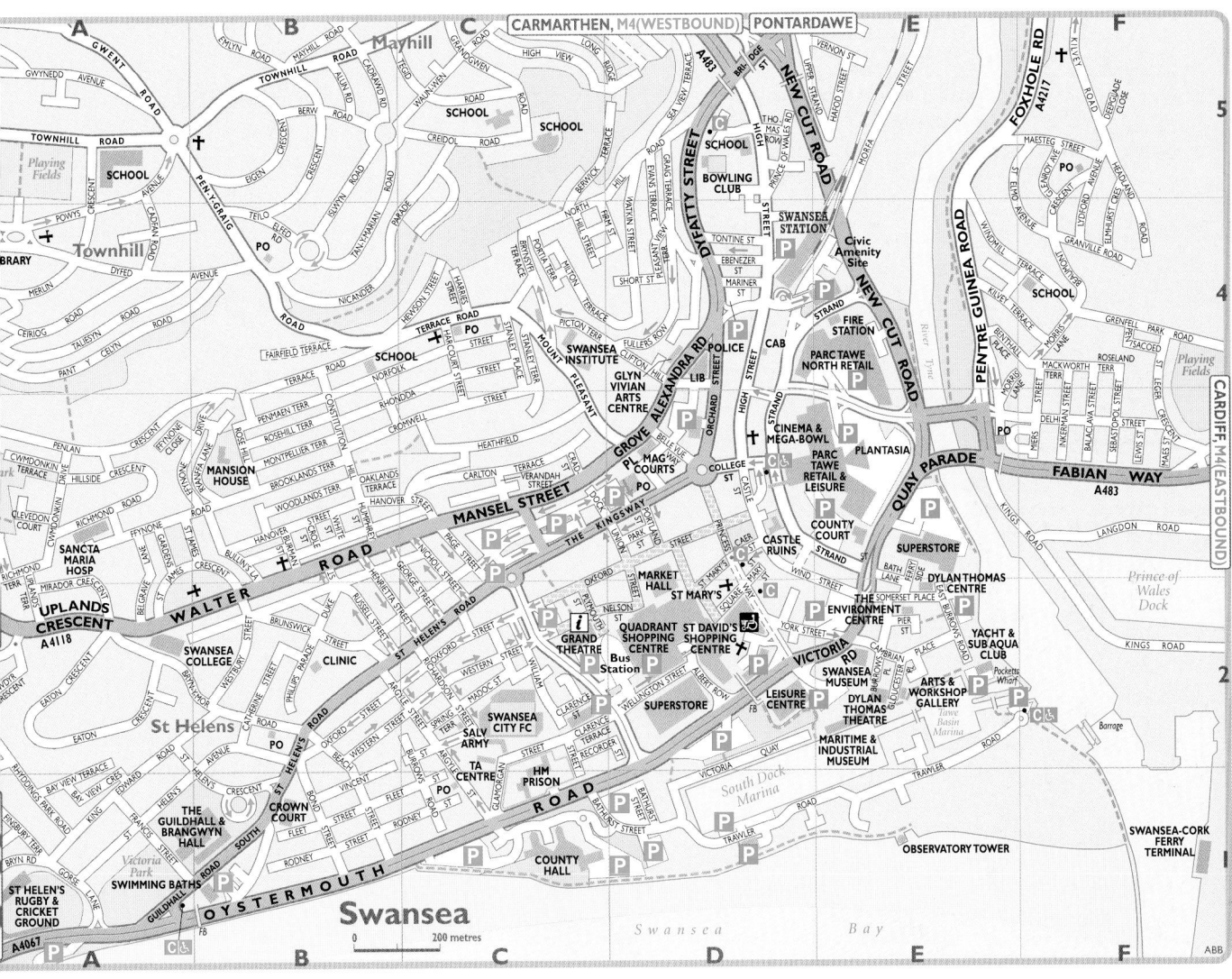

Swansea

Swansea is found on atlas page **32**,
grid reference **6592**

bert Row	D2	Ceiriog Road	A4	Fleet Street	B1-C1	Langdon Road	F3	Phillips Parade	B2	Stanley Place	C4
exandra Road	D3-D4	Clarence Street	C2	Foxhole Road	E5-F5	Lewis Street	F3	Picton Terrace	C4-D4	Stanley Terrace	C4
un Road	B5	Clarence Terrace	C2-D2	Francis Street	A1	Long Ridge	C5-D5	Pier Street	E2	Strand	E4-D4-D3-E3
gyle Street	B2-C2-C1	Clevedon Court	A3	Fullers Row	D4	Lydford Avenue	F4-F5	Pleasant View Terrace	D4	Taliesyn Road	A4
aclava Street	F3-F4	Clifton Hill	D4	George Street	B3-C3-C2	Mackworth Terrace	F4	Plymouth Street	C2	Tan-Y-Marian Road	B5-B5
th Lane	E2-E3	College Street	D3	Glamorgan Street	C1-C2	Madoc Street	C2	Portia Terrace	C4	Tegid Road	B5-C5
thurst Street	C1-D1	Constitution Hill	B3-B4	Glenroy Avenue	F5	Maes Street	F3	Portland Street	D3	Teilo Crescent	B4-B5
View Crescent	A1-A2	Craddock Street	C3	Gloucester Place	E2	Maesteg Street	F5	Powys Avenue	A4-A5	Terrace Road	B3-B4-C4
y View Terrace	A1-A2	Creidol Road	C5	Gorse Lane	A1	Mansel Street	C3	Prince of Wales Road	D5	The Kingsway	C3-D3
ach Street	B1-B2	Crole Street	B3	Graig Terrace	D4-D5	Mariner Street	D4	Princess Way	D2-D3	Thomas Row	D5
aumont Crescent	F4-F5	Cromwell Street	B3-C3-C4	Grandgwen Road	C5	Mayhill Road	B5	Quay Parade	E3	Tontine Street	D4
grave Lane	A2-A3	Cwmdonkin Drive	A3	Granville Road	F4	Merlin Crescent	A4-A5	Recorder Street	C2-D2	Townhill Road	A5-B5-C5
lle Vue Way	D3	Cwmdonkin Terrace	A3	Grenfell Park Road	F4	Miers Street	F3-F4	Rhondda Street	B3-C3-C4	Trawler Road	D1-E1-E2
nthall Place	E4-F4	Deepglade Close	F5	Grove Place	D3	Milton Terrace	C4-D4	Rhyddings Park Road	A1-A2	Union Street	D2-D3
rw Road	B5	Delhi Street	E3-F3	Guildhall Road South	A1-B1	Mirador Crescent	A2-A3	Richardson Street	C2	Uplands Crescent	A2
rwick Terrace	C4-C5-D5	Duke Street	B2-B3	Gwdyr Crescent	A2	Montpellier Terrace	B3	Richmond Road	A3	Uplands Terrace	A2-A3
nd Street	B1-B2	Dyfatty Street	D4-D5	Gwent Road	A5	Morfa Street	E4-E5	Richmond Terrace	A3	Upper Strand	D5-E5
dge Street	D5	Dyfed Avenue	A4-B4	Gwynedd Avenue	A5	Morris Lane	E3-E4-F4	Rodney Street	B1-C1	Verandah Street	C3
ooklands Terrace	B3	East Burrows Road	E2	Hafod Street	E5	Mount Pleasant	C4-C3-D3	Rose Hill	B3	Vernon Street	E5
unswick Street	B2	Eaton Crescent	A2	Hanover Street	B3-C3	Nelson Street	C2-D2	Rosehill Terrace	B3	Victoria Quay	D1-D2
yn Road	A1	Ebenezer Street	D4	Harcourt Street	C3-C4	New Cut Road	D5-E5-E4-E3	Roseland Terrace	F4	Victoria Road	D2-E2
yn-Y-Mor Road	A2-B2	Eigen Crescent	B5	Harries Street	C4	Nicander Parade	B4-C4-C5	Russell Street	B2	Vincent Street	B1-B2-C2
ynsyfi Terrace	C4	Elfed Road	B4	Headland Road	F4-F5	Nicholl Street	C2-C3	Ryanffa Lane	B3	Walter Road	A2-B2-B3
llin's Lane	B3	Elmhurst Crescent	F4-F5	Heathfield	C3	Norfolk Street	B4-C4	St Elmo Avenue	F5-E5-F4	Watkin Street	D4-D5
rman Street	B3	Emlyn Road	B5	Henrietta Street	B3-B2-C2	North Hill Road	C4-C5-D5	St Helen's Avenue	A1-B2	Waun-Wen Road	C5
rrows Place	E2	Evans Terrace	D4-D5	Hewson Street	B4-C4	Oaklands Terrace	B3	St Helen's Crescent	A2-B1	Wellington Street	D2
rrows Road	C1-C2	Fabian Way	F3	High Street	D3-D4-D5	Orchard Street	D3-D4	St Helen's Road	B1-B2-C2	Westbury Street	B2
adfan Road	A4-A5	Fairfield Terrace	B4	High View	C5	Oxford Street	B2-C2-C3-D3	St James Crescent	A2-A3-B3-B2	Western Street	B2-C2
adrawd Road	B5	Ferry Side	E2-E3	Hill Street	C4	Oystermouth Road	A1-B1-C1-D2	St James Gardens	A3-B3	White Street	B3
aer Street	D3	Ffynone Close	A3	Hillside Crescent	A3	Page Street	C3	St Leger Crescent	F3-F4	William Street	C1-C2
ambrian Place	E2	Ffynone Drive	A3-B3	Humphrey Street	B3	Pant Y Celyn Road	A4-B4	St Mary Street	D2-D3	Wind Street	D3-E2
arlton Terrace	C3	Ffynone Road	A3-B3	Inkerman Street	F3-F4	Park Street	D3	St Mary's Square	D2-D3	Windmill Terrace	E5-E4-F4
astle Street	D3	Finsbury Terrace	A1	Islwyn Road	B4-B5	Pen-Y-Graig Road	A5-B5-B4	Sea View Terrace	D5	Woodlands Terrace	B3
atherine Street	B2	Firm Street	C4-D4	Kilvey Road	F5	Penlan Crescent	A3-B3-B4	Sebastopol Street	F3-F4	York Street	D2-E2
				Kilvey Terrace	E4-F4	Penmaen Terrace	B3	Short Street	D4		
				King Edward Road	A1-A2-B2	Penmaen Terrace	B3	Somerset Place	E2		
				Kings Road	E3-F3-F2	Pentre Guinea Road	E3-E4	Spring Terrace	C2		

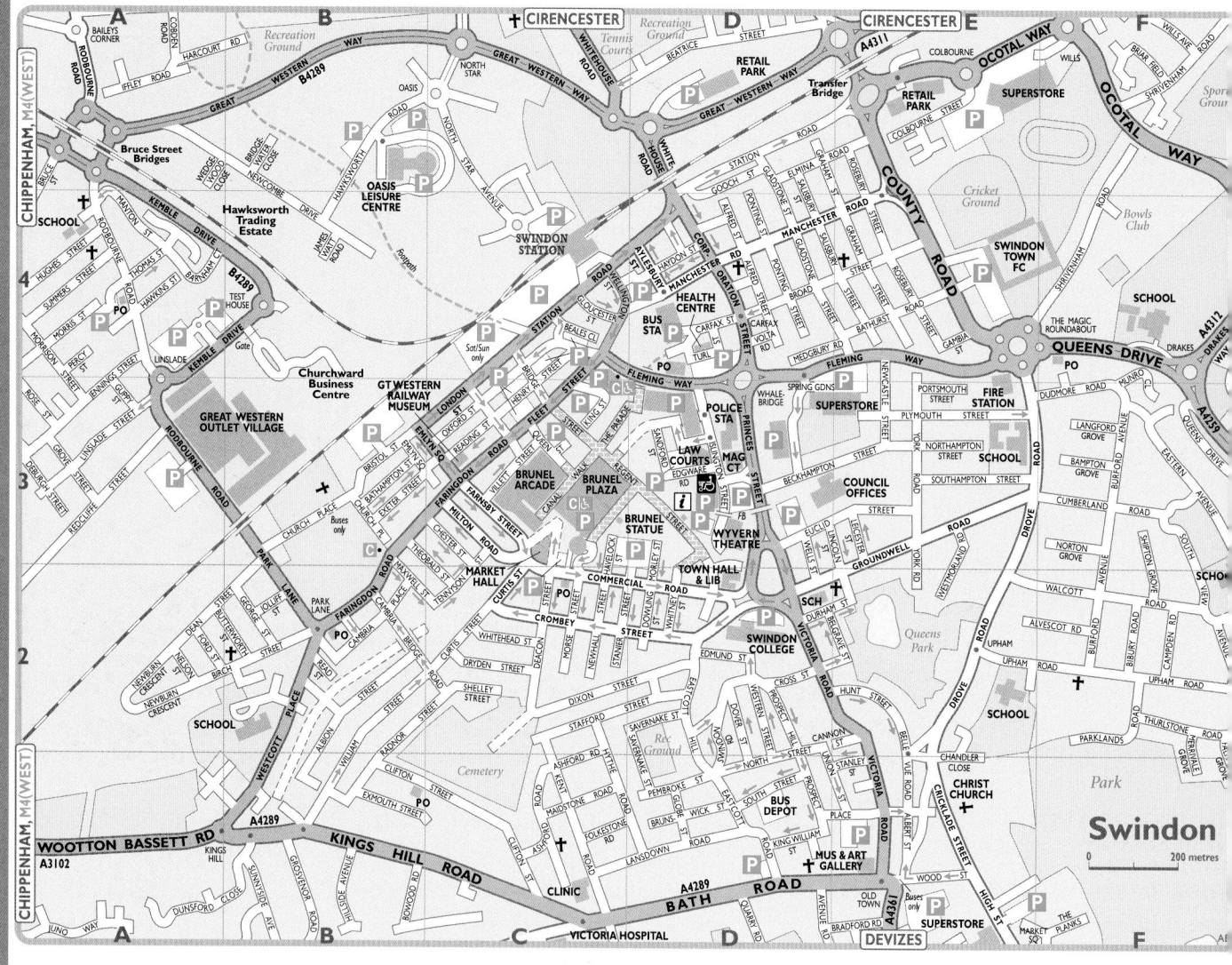

Swindon

Swindon is found on atlas page **36**,
grid reference **1484**

Albert Street	E1	Cambria Bridge Road	B2-C2	
Albion Street	B1-B2	Cambria Place	B2	
Alfred Street	D4	Campden Road	F2	
Alvescot Road	E2-F2	Canal Walk	C3	
Ashford Road	C1-C2	Cannon Street	E2	
Avenue Road	D1	Carfax Street	D4	
Aylesbury Street	D4	Chandler Close	E1-E2	
Bampton Grove	F3	Chester Street	C3	
Barnham Court	A4	Church Place	B3	
Bath Road	C1-D1-E1	Clifton Street	B1-C1	
Bathampton Street	B3	Cobden Road	A5	
Bathurst Road	E4	Colbourne Street	E5	
Beales Close	C4	Commercial Road	C2-D2	
Beatrice Street	C5-D5	Corporation Street	D4	
Beckhampton Street	D3-E3	County Road	E4-E5	
Belgrave Street	D2-E2	Cricklade Street	E1	
Belle Vue Road	E1-E2	Crombey Street	C2-D2	
Bibury Road	F2	Cross Street	D2	
Birch Street	A2-B2	Cumberland Road	F3	
Bowood Road	B1	Curtis Street	C2-C3	
Bradford Road	D1-E1	Deacon Street	C2-C3	
Briar Field	F5	Dean Street	A2-B2	
Bridge Street	C3-C4	Deburgh Street	A3	
Bridgewater Close	B5	Dixon Street	C2-D2	
Bristol Street	B3	Dover Street	D1-D2	
Broad Street	D4-E4	Dowling Street	D2	
Bruce Street	A4-A5	Drakes Way	F4	
Brunswick Street	D1	Drove Road	E2-E3-E4	
Burford Avenue	F2-F3	Dryden Street	C2	
Butterworth Street	A2-B2	Dudmore Road	F3-F4	

Dunsford Close	A1-B1	High Street	E1
Durham Street	D2-E2	Hillside Avenue	B1
Eastcott Hill	D1-D2	Hughes Street	A4
Eastcott Road	D1	Hunt Street	E2
Eastern Avenue	F3	Hythe Road	C2-C1-D1
Edgware Road	D3	Iffley Road	A5
Edmund Street	D2	Islington Street	D3
Elmina Road	D5-E5	James Watt Road	B4
Emlyn Square	B3-C3	Jennings Street	A3-A4
Euclid Street	D3-E3	Jolliff Street	B2
Exeter Street	B3	Juno Way	A1
Exmouth Street	B1-C1	Kemble Drive	A3-A4-A5-B4
Falmouth Grove	F1-F2	Kent Road	C1
Faringdon Road	B2-B3-C3	King Street	C3
Farnsby Street	C3	King William Street	D1
Fleet Street	C3-C4	Kings Hill Road	B1-C1
Fleming Way	C4-D3-D4-E4	Langford Grove	F3
Folkestone Road	C1	Lansdown Road	C1-D1
Ford Street	A2	Leicester Street	E3
Gambia Street	E4	Lincoln Street	D3-E3
George Street	B2	Linslade Street	A3
Gladstone Street	D5-D4-E4	London Street	C3-C4
Globe Street	D1	Maidstone Road	C1
Gloucester Street	C4	Manchester Road	D4-E4
Gooch Street	D4-D5	Manton Street	A4
Graham Street	D5-E4	Market Square	E1-F1
Great Western Way	A5-B5-C5-D5	Maxwell Street	B3-B2-C2
Grosvenor Road	B1	Medgbury Road	D4-E4
Groundwell Road	D2-E2-E3	Merrivale Grove	F1-F2
Grove Street	A3	Milton Road	C3
Guppy Street	A3	Morley Street	D2-D3
Harcourt Road	A5-B5	Morris Street	A4
Havelock Street	C2-C3	Morrison Street	A3-A4
Hawkins Street	A4	Morse Street	C2
Hawksworth Road	B4-B5	Munro Close	F3-F4
Haydon Street	D4	Nelson Street	A2
Henry Street	C3-C4	Newburn Crescent	A2

Newcastle Street	E3-E4	South View Avenue	F2
Newcombe Drive	A5-B5-B4	Southampton Street	
Newhall Street	C2	Stafford Street	C2
North Star Avenue	C4-C5	Stanier Street	C2
North Street	D1-D2	Stanley Street	
Northampton Street	E3	Station Road	C4-D4
Norton Grove	F3	Summers Street	
Ocotal Way	E5-F5-F4	Sunnyside Avenue	
Oxford Street	C3	Swindon Road	D1
Park Lane	B2-B3	Tennyson Street	C2
Parklands Road	F2	The Parade	
Pembroke Street	D1	The Planks	
Percy Street	A4	Theobald Street	B3
Plymouth Street	E3	Thomas Street	
Ponting Street	D4	Thurlstone Road	
Portsmouth Street	E3	Turl Street	
Princes Street	D3	Union Street	E1
Prospect Hill	D2	Upham Road	E2
Prospect Place	D1-E1	Victoria Road	D2-E2
Quarry Road	D1	Villett Street	
Queen Street	C3	Volta Road	
Queens Drive	F3-F4	Walcott Road	E2
Radnor Street	B1-B2-C2	Wedgewood Close	
Read Street	B2	Wellington Street	
Reading Street	C3	Wells Street	D2
Redcliffe Street	A2-A3	Westcott Place	B1
Regent Street	C3-D3	Western Street	
Rodbourne Road	A5-A4-A3-B3	Westmorland Road	E2
Rose Street	A3	Whitehead Street	
Rosebury Street	E4-E5	Whitehouse Road	C5
Salisbury Street	D5-D4-E4	Whitney Street	
Sandford Street	D3	William Street	B1
Savernake Street	D1-D2	Wills Avenue	
Shelley Street	C2	Wood Street	
Shipton Grove	F2-F3	Wootton Bassett Road	
Shrivenham Road	E4-F4-F5	York Road	E2-E3
South Street	D1		

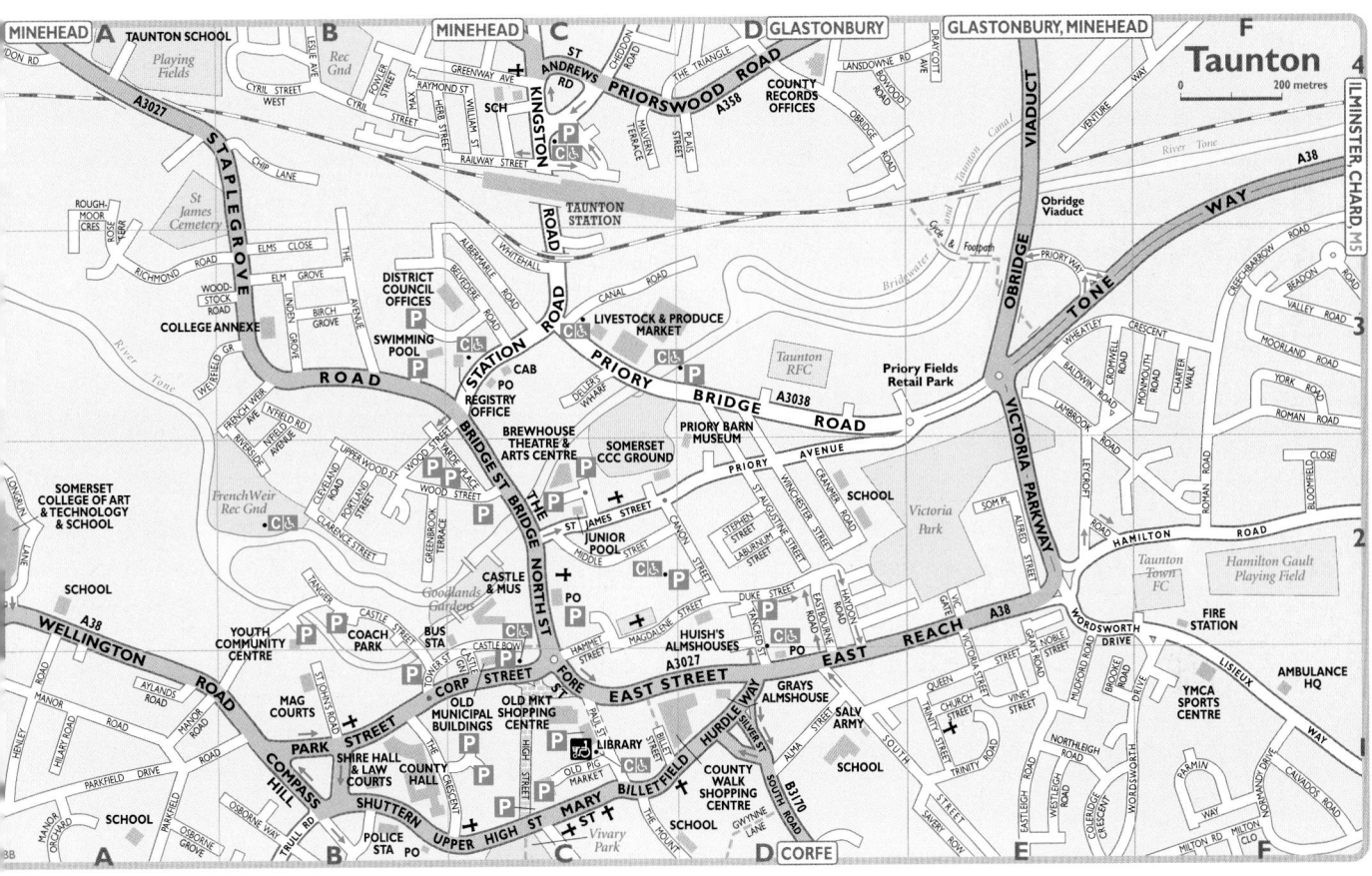

aunton

aunton is found on atlas page **20**,
d reference **2224**

ermarle Road	B4-C3	Elms Close	B3	Obridge Road	D4	The Mount	C1
red Street	E2	Fore Street	C2-C1	Obridge Viaduct	E3-E4	The Triangle	C4-D4
na Street	D1	Fowler Street	B4	Old Pig Market	C1	Tone Way	E3-F3-F4
ands Road	A1	French Weir Avenue	B3	Osborne Grove	A1-B1	Tower Street	B1-C1
dwin Road	E3	Grays Road	E1-E2	Osborne Way	B1	Trinity Road	E1
adon Road	F3	Greenbrook Terrace	B2	Park Street	B1	Trinity Street	E1
vedere Road	B3-C3	Greenway Avenue	B4-C4	Parkfield Drive	A1	Trull Road	B1
et Street	C1	Gwynne Lane	D1	Parkfield Road	A1	Upper High Street	B1-C1
etfield	C1-D1	Hamilton Road	E2-F2	Parmin Way	F1	Upper Wood Street	B3-B2
don Road	A4	Hammet Street	C1-C2	Paul Street	C1	Valley Road	F3
ch Grove	B3	Henley Road	A1-A2	Plais Street	D4	Venture Way	E4-F4
omfield Close	F2	Herbert Street	B4-C4	Portland Street	B2	Victoria Gate	E2
wood Road	D4	High Street	C1	Priorswood Road	C4-D4	Victoria Parkway	E3-E2
dge Street	C3-C2	Hilary Road	A1	Priory Avenue	D2-D3	Victoria Street	E2-E1
ooke Road	E1-E2	Hurdle Way	D1	Priory Bridge Road	C3-D3	Viney Street	E1
vados Road	F1	Kingston Road	C4	Priory Way	E3	Weirfield Green	A3-B3
nal Road	C3-D3	Laburnum Street	D2	Queen Street	D1-E1-E2	Wellington Road	A2-A1-B1
non Street	C2-D2	Lambrook Road	E3-E2-F2	Railway Street	C4	Westgate Street	B1
stle Bow	C2	Lansdowne Road	D4-E4	Raymond Street	B4-C4	Westleigh Road	E1
stle Green	C1	Leslie Avenue	B4	Richmond Road	A3-B3	Wheatley Crescent	E3-F3
stle Street	B2-B1	Leycroft Road	E3-E2	Riverside	B3-B2	Whitefield	C3
arter Walk	F3	Linden Grove	B3	Roman Road	F2-F3	Whitehall	C3
eddon Road	C4	Lisieux Way	F2-F1	Rose Terrace	A3-A4	William Street	C4
urch Street	E1	Longrun Lane	A2-A3	Roughmoor Crescent	A3-A4	Winchester Street	D2
arence Street	B2	Magdalene Street	C2-D2	St Andrews Road	C4	Wood Street	C2-B2-B3-C3
eveland Road	B2	Malvern Terrace	C4	St Augustine Street	D3-D2	Woodstock Road	A3-B3
leridge Crescent	E1	Manor Orchard	A1	St James Street	C2	Wordsworth Drive	E1-F1-F2-E2
mpass Hill	B1	Manor Road	A1	St John's Road	B1	Yarde Place	B3-C2
rporation Street	B1-C1	Mary Street	C1	Savery Row	E1	York Road	F3
anmer Road	D2	Max Street	B4	Shuttern	B1		
eechbarrow Road	F3-F4	Middle Street	C2	Silver Street	D1		
omwell Road	E3	Milton Close	F1	Somerset Place	E2		
ril Street	B4	Milton Road	F1	South Road	D1		
ril Street West	B4	Monmouth Road	E3-F3	South Street	D1-E1		
ril's Wharf	C3	Moorland Road	F3	Staplegrove Road	A4-B4-B3		
aycott Avenue	E4	Mudford Road	E1-E2	Station Road	C3-C4		
ke Street	D2	Noble Street	E2	Stephen Street	D2		
st Reach	D1-D2-E2	Normandy Drive	F1	Tancred Street	D2-D1		
st Street	C1-D1	North Street	C2	Tangier	B2		
stbourne Road	D2	Northfield Avenue	B2-B3	The Avenue	B4-B3		
stleigh Road	E1	Northfield Road	B3	The Bridge	C2		
n Grove	B3	Northleigh Road	E1	The Crescent	B1-C1		

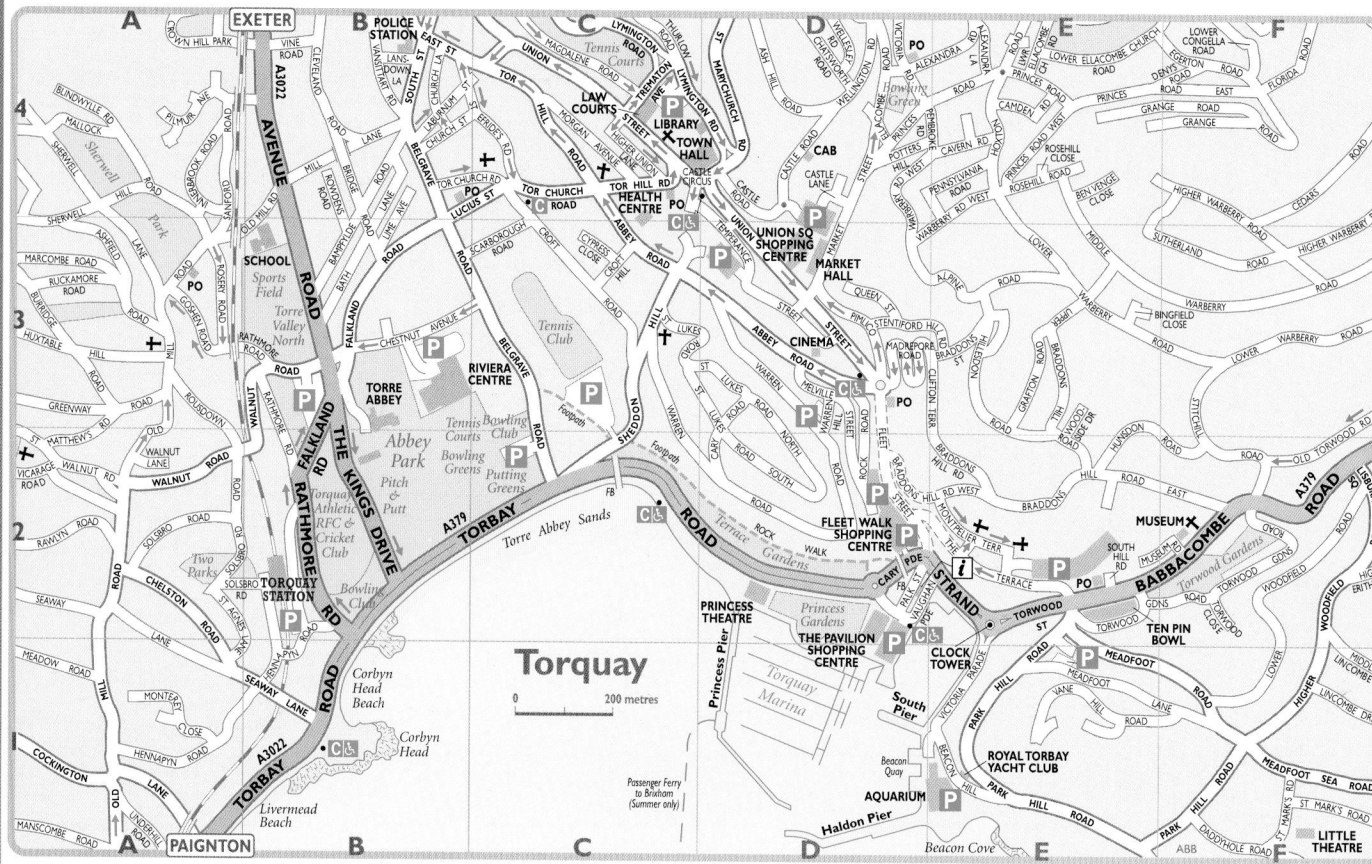

Torquay

Torquay is found on atlas page **7**,
grid reference **9164**

Abbey Road	C4-C3-D3	Denys Road	F4	Middle Lincombe Road	F1-F2	Sherwell Lane	A3-A4
Alexandra Lane	E4	East Street	B4	Middle Warberry Road	E4-E3-F3	Solsbro Road	A2-B2
Alexandra Road	D4-E4	Egerton Road	E4-F4	Mill Lane	B4	South Hill Road	E2
Alpine Road	D3-E3	Ellacombe Road	D4	Monterey Close	A1	South Street	B4
Ash Hill Road	D4	Falkland Road	B2-B3	Montpelier Terrace	E2	Stentiford Hill Road	D3-E3
Ashfield Road	A3	Fleet Street	D2-D3	Morgan Avenue	C4	Stitchill Road	F2-F3
Avenue Road	B3-B4	Florida Road	F4	Museum Road	E2-F2	Strand	E2
Babbacombe Road	E2-F2	Goshen Road	A3	Old Mill Road	A1-A3-B3-B4	Sutherland Road	F4-E4-E3-F3
Bampfylde Road	B3-B4	Grafton Road	E3	Old Torwood Road	F2-F3	Temperance Street	D4-D3
Bath Lane	B3-B4	Grange Road	E4-F4	Palk Street	D2	The Kings Drive	B2-B3
Beacon Hill	E1	Greenway Road	A3	Park Hill Road	E2-E1-F1	The Terrace	D2-E2
Belgrave Road	B4-B3-C3-C2	Hennapyn Road	A1-B1-B2	Pembroke Road	D4-E4	Thurlow Road	C4
Ben Venge Close	E4	Higher Erith Road	F2	Pennsylvania Road	D4-E4	Tor Church Road	B4-C4
Bingfield Close	E3	Higher Union Lane	C4	Pilmuir Avenue	A4	Tor Hill Road	C4
Blindwylle Road	A4	Higher Warberry Road	E4-F4-F3	Pimlico	D3	Torbay Road	A1-B1-C2-D2
Braddons Hill Road	E2	Higher Woodfield Road	F1-F2	Potters Hill	D4	Torwood Close	F2
Braddons Hill Road East	E2-F2	Hillesdon Road	E2-E3	Princes Road	D4-E4	Torwood Gardens Road	E2-F2
Braddons Hill Road West	D2-E2	Hoxton Road	E4	Princes Road East	E4-F4	Torwood Street	E2
Braddons Street	E3	Hunsdon Road	E2-E3-F3-F2	Princes Road West	E4	Trematon Avenue	C4
Bridge Road	B3-B4	Huxtable Hill	A3	Queen Street	D3	Uncombe Drive	F1
Burridge Road	A3	Innerbrook Road	A4	Rathmore Road	A3-B3-B2	Underhill Road	A1
Camden Road	E4	Laburnum Street	B4	Rawlyn Road	A2	Union Street	C4-D4-D3
Cary Parade	D2	Lansdown Lane	B4	Rock Road	D2-D3	Upper Braddons Hill Road	E2-E3
Cary Road	D2-D3	Lime Avenue	B3-B4	Rosehill Close	E4	Vane Hill Road	E1-F1
Castle Circus	C4-D4	Lisburn Square	F2	Rosehill Road	E4	Vansittart Road	B4
Castle Lane	D4	Lower Congela Road	E4	Rosery Road	A3	Vaughan Parade	D2-E2
Castle Road	D4	Lower Ellacombe Ch Road	E4-F4	Rousdown Road	A2-A3	Vicarage Road	A2
Cavern Road	E4	Lower Warberry Road	E4-E3-F3	Rowdens Road	B3-B4	Victoria Parade	E1-E2
Cedars Road	F4	Lower Woodfield Road	F1-F2	Ruckamore Road	A3	Victoria Road	D4
Chatsworth Road	D4	Lucius Street	B4-C4	St Agnes Lane	A2-B2-A1	Vine Road	B4
Chelston Road	A1-A2	Lymington Road	C4-D4	St Efrides Road	B4-C4	Walnut Lane	A2
Chestnut Avenue	B3-C3	Madrepore Road	D3	St Lukes Road	C3-D3	Walnut Road	A2-B2-B3
Church Lane	B4	Magdalene Road	C4	St Lukes Road North	C3-D3-D2	Warberry Road West	D4-E3-E4
Church Street	B4	Mallock Road	A4	St Lukes Road South	C3-D3-D2	Warren Hill	D3
Cleveland Road	B4	Manscombe Road	A1	St Mark's Road	F1	Warren Road	C3-C2-D2-D3
Clifton Terrace	E3	Marcombe Road	A3	St Marychurch Road	D4	Wellesley Road	D4
Cockington Lane	A1	Market Street	D3-D4	St Matthew's Road	A2-A3	Wellington Road	D4
Croft Hill	C3	Meadfoot Lane	E1-F1	Sanford Road	A3-A4	Woodside Drive	E3
Croft Road	C3-C4	Meadfoot Road	E2-E1-F1	Scarborough Road	B3-C3		
Crown Hill Park	A4	Meadfoot Sea Road	F1	Seaway Lane	A2-A1-B1		
Cypress Close	C3	Meadow Road	A1	Sheddon Hill	C2-C3		
Daddyhole Road	F1	Melville Street	D2-D3	Sherwell Hill	A3-A4		

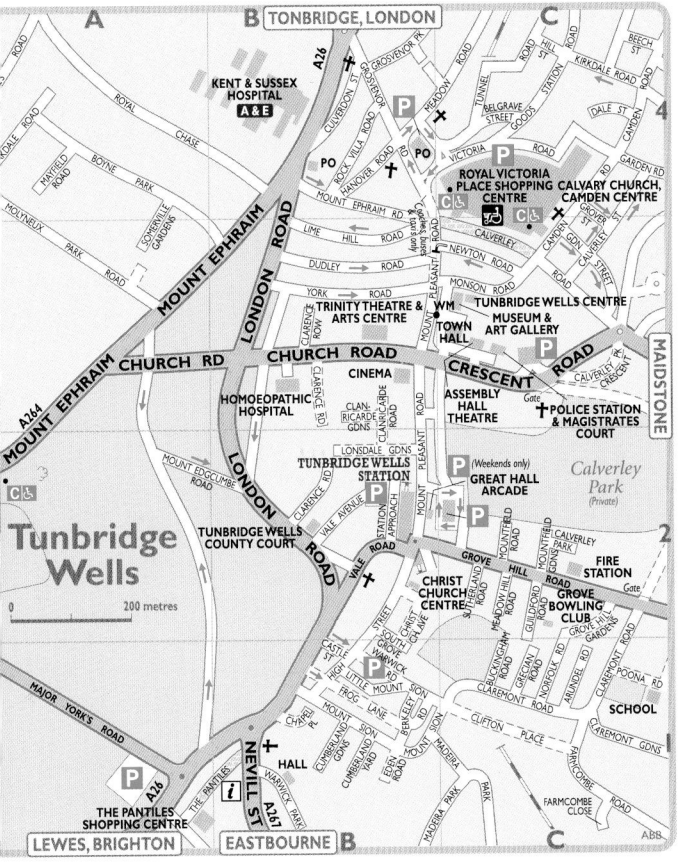

Tunbridge Wells

Tunbridge Wells is found on atlas page **16**,
grid reference **5839**

Arundel Road	C1	Hill Street	C4
Beech Street	C4	Kirkdale Road	C4
Belgrave Street	C4	Lansdowne Square	C3
Berkeley Road	B1	Lime Hill Road	B3
Boyne Park	A4-B3	Little Mount Sion	B1
Buckingham Road	C1	London Road	B2-B3-B4
Calverley Street	C3-C4	Lonsdale Gardens	B2
Calverley Park	C2	Madeira Park	B1-C1
Calverley Park Crescent	C3	Major York's Road	A1
Calverley Road	C3	Mayfield Road	A4
Camden Road	C3-C4	Meadow Hill Road	C2
Castle Street	B1	Meadow Road	B4-C4
Chapel Place	B1	Molyneux Park Road	A3-A4
Christ Church Avenue	B2	Monson Road	C3
Church Road	A3-B3	Mount Edgcumbe Road	A2-B2
Clanricarde Gardens	B3	Mount Ephraim	A2-A3-B3-B4
Clanricarde Road	B2-B3	Mount Ephraim Road	B4
Claremont Gardens	C1	Mount Pleasant Road	B2-B3-C3-B4
Claremont Road	C1-C2	Mount Sion	B1-C1
Clarence Road	B2-B3	Mountfield Gardens	C2
Clarence Row	B3	Mountfield Road	C2
Clifton Place	C1	Nevill Street	B1
Crescent Road	B3-C3	Newton Road	C3
Culverden Street	B4	Norfolk Road	C1
Cumberland Gardens	B1	Oakdale Road	A4
Cumberland Yard	B1	Poona Road	C1
Dale Street	C4	Rock Villa Road	B4
Dudley Road	B3	Royal Chase	A4-B4
Earl's Road	A4	Somerville Gardens	A3-A4
Eden Road	B1	South Grove	B1-B2
Farmcombe Close	C1	Station Approach	B2
Farmcombe Road	C1	Sutherland Road	C2
Frog Lane	B1	The Pantiles	A1-B1
Garden Road	C4	Tunnel Road	C4
Garden Street	C3	Vale Avenue	B2
Goods Station Road	C4	Vale Road	B2
Grecian Road	C1	Victoria Road	B4-C4
Grosvenor Park	B4	Warwick Park	B1
Grosvenor Road	B4	Warwick Road	B1
Grove Hill Gardens	C2	York Road	B3
Grove Hill Road	B2-C2		
Grover Street	C3-C4		
Guildford Road	C2		
Hanover Road	B4		
High Street	B1-B2		

Warwick

Warwick is found on atlas page **48**,
grid reference **2865**

Albert Street	A4	St Nicholas Church Street	B2-C3
Archery Fields	C1	Saltisford	A3-A4
Back Lane	A2	Sharpe Close	B4
Banbury Road	B2-C1	Smith Street	B2-C3
Barrack Street	A3	Spring Pool	A4
Bartlett Close	C3	Station Avenue	C4
Bowling Green Street	A2	Station Road	C4
Bridge Brooke Close	B1-C1	Swan Street	A2
Bridge End	B1-C1	The Butts	A3-B2
Brook Street	A2	The Paddocks	C3
Cape Road	A3-A4	Theatre Street	A3
Castle Close	A1	Victoria Street	A3-A4
Castle Hill	B2	Vine Street	B4
Castle Lane	A2-B2	West Street	A1-A2
Castle Street	A2-B2	Woodcote Road	C4
Cattel Road	A4		
Chapel Street	B3		
Cherry Street	C3-C4		
Church Street	A2		
Coten End	C3		
Coventry Road	C3-C4		
Deerpark Drive	A4		
Edward Street	A3-A4		
Gerrard Street	B2-B3		
Guy Street	C3-C4		
Guys Cliffe Terrace	C4		
High Street	A2		
Jury Street	A2-B2		
Lakin Road	C4		
Market Place	A3		
Market Street	A2		
Mill Street	B2		
Myton Road	C1		
New Street	A2-A3		
Northgate Street	A3		
Old Square	A3		
Packmore Street	B4-C4		
Paradise Street	B4-C4		
Park View	B3		
Parkes Street	A3		
Priory Mews	A3		
Priory Road	A3-C3		
Roe Close	B4		
St John's Court	C3		
St Johns	C3		

227

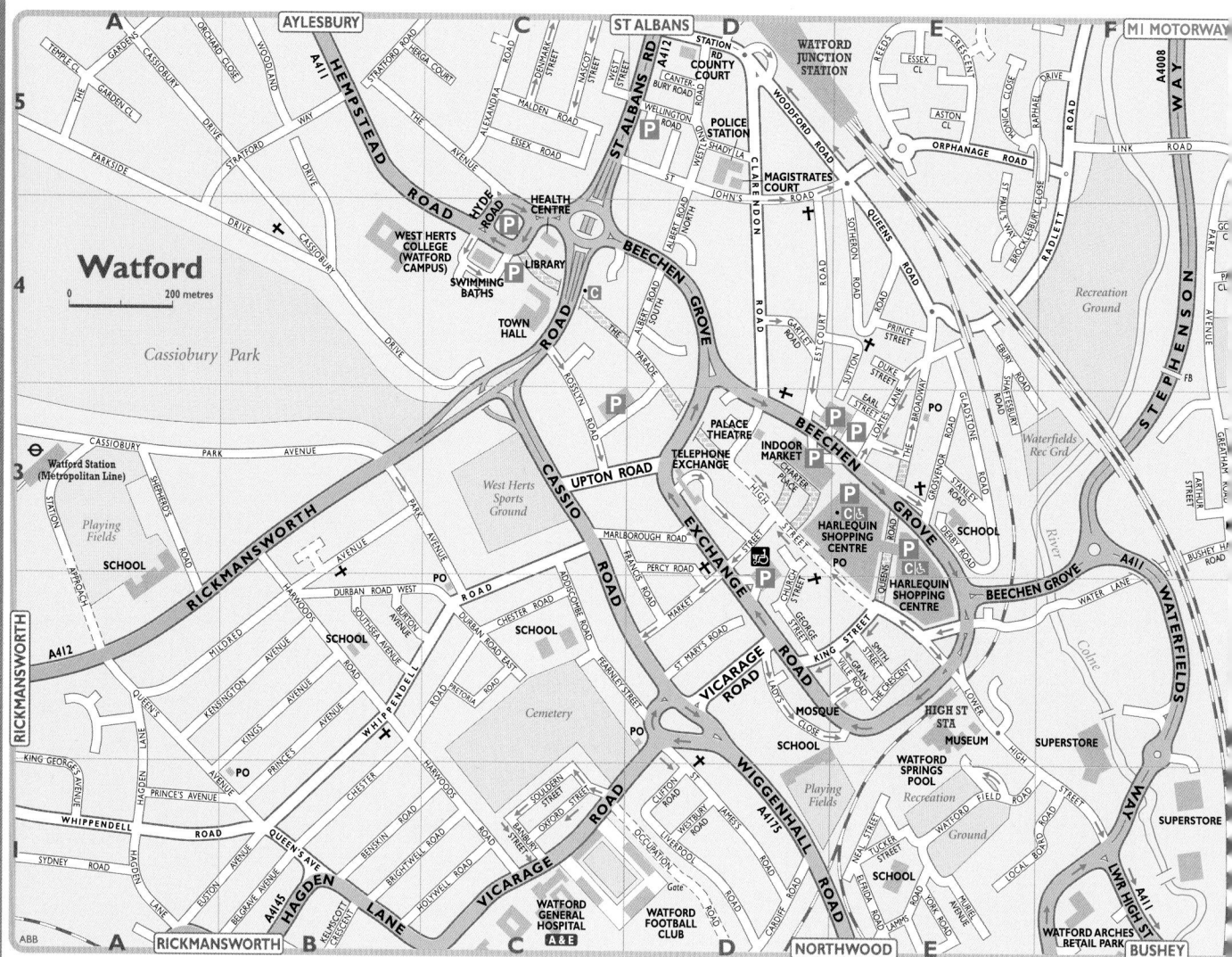

Watford

Watford is found on atlas page **26**,
grid reference **1196**

Addiscombe Road	C2-C3	Ebury Road	E4-F3	Lamms Road	E1	Raphael Drive	E5-F5	Tucker Street	E1
Albert Road North	D4-D5	Elfrida Road	E1	Link Road	F5	Reeds Crescent	E5	Upton Road	C3-D3
Albert Road South	D4	Essex Close	E5	Liverpool Road	D1	Rickmansworth Road	A2-B3-C4	Vicarage Road	C1-D1-D2
Alexandra Road	C5	Essex Road	C5	Loates Lane	E3-E4	Rosslyn Road	C3-C4	Water Lane	F2-F3
Arthur Street	F3	Estcourt Road	D3-D4	Local Board Road	D1	Shady Lane	D5	Waterfields Way	F1-F2-F3
Aston Close	E5	Euston Avenue	A1-B1	Lower High Street	E2-F1	Shaftesbury Road	E3-E4	Watford Field Road	E1-F1
Banbury Street	C1	Exchange Road	D3-D2	Malden Road	D1	Shepherd's Road	A2-A3	Wellington Road	D5
Beechen Grove	C4-D3-E2-F3	Fearnley Street	C2-D2	Market Street	D2-D3	Smith Street	E2	West Street	C5
Belgrave Avenue	B1	Francis Road	C3-D3-D2	Marlborough Road	C3-D3	Sotheron Road	E4-E5	Westbury Road	D1
Benskin Road	B1-C1	Garden Close	A5	Mildred Avenue	A2-B2-B3	Souldern Street	C1	Westland Road	D5
Brightwell Road	B1-C1	Gartlet Road	D4	Monica Close	E5	Southsea Avenue	B2	Whippendell Road	A1-B1-B2-C3
Brocklesbury Close	E4-E5-F5	George Street	D2	Muriel Avenue	E1	St Albans Road	C5-D5	Wiggenhall Road	D2-D1-E1
Burton Avenue	B2-C2	Gladstone Road	E3-E4	Nascot Street	C5	St James's Road	D1-D2	Woodford Road	D5-E5
Bushey Hall Road	F3	Golf Close	F4	Neal Street	E1	St John's Road	C5-D5	Woodland Drive	B4-B5
Canterbury Road	D5	Granville Road	E2	Occupation Road	C1-D1	St Mary's Road	D2	York Road	E1
Cardiff Road	D1	Greatham Road	F3	Orchard Close	A5-B5	St Paul's Way	E4-E5		
Cassio Road	C3-C2-D2	Grosvenor Road	E3	Orphanage Road	E5-F5	Stanley Road	E3		
Cassiobury Drive	A5-B5-B4-C4	Hagden Lane	A2-A1-B1	Oxford Street	C1	Station Approach	A2-A3		
Cassiobury Park Avenue	A3-B3	Harwoods Road	B3-B2-C1	Park Avenue	B3-C3-C2	Station Road	D5		
Charter Place	D3	Hempstead Road	B5-C4	Park Avenue	F4-F5	Stephenson Way	F3-F4-F5		
Chester Road	B1-B2-C2	Herga Court	B5-C5	Park Close	F4	Stratford Road	D5		
Church Street	D2-D3	High Street	D3	Parkside Drive	A5-A4-B4	Stratford Way	A4-A5-B5		
Clarendon Road	D3-D4-D5	Holywell Road	B1-C1	Percy Road	D2-D3	Sutton Road	E3-E4		
Clifton Road	D1	Hyde Road	C4	Pretoria Road	C2	Sydney Road	A1		
Denmark Street	C5	Kelmscott Crescent	B1	Prince Street	E4	Temple Close	A5		
Derby Road	E3	Kensington Avenue	A2-B2	Prince's Avenue	A1-B1-B2	The Avenue	B5-C5		
Duke Street	E4	King George's Avenue	A1-A2	Queen's Avenue	A2-A1-B1	The Broadway	E3-E4		
Durban Road East	C2	King Street	D2-E2	Queens Road	E2-E3	The Crescent	E2		
Durban Road West	B2-C2	Kings Avenue	A1-B1-B2	Queens Road	E4-E5	The Gardens	A5		
Earl Street	E3	Lady's Close	D2-E2	Radlett Road	E4-F4-F5	The Parade	C4-D4		

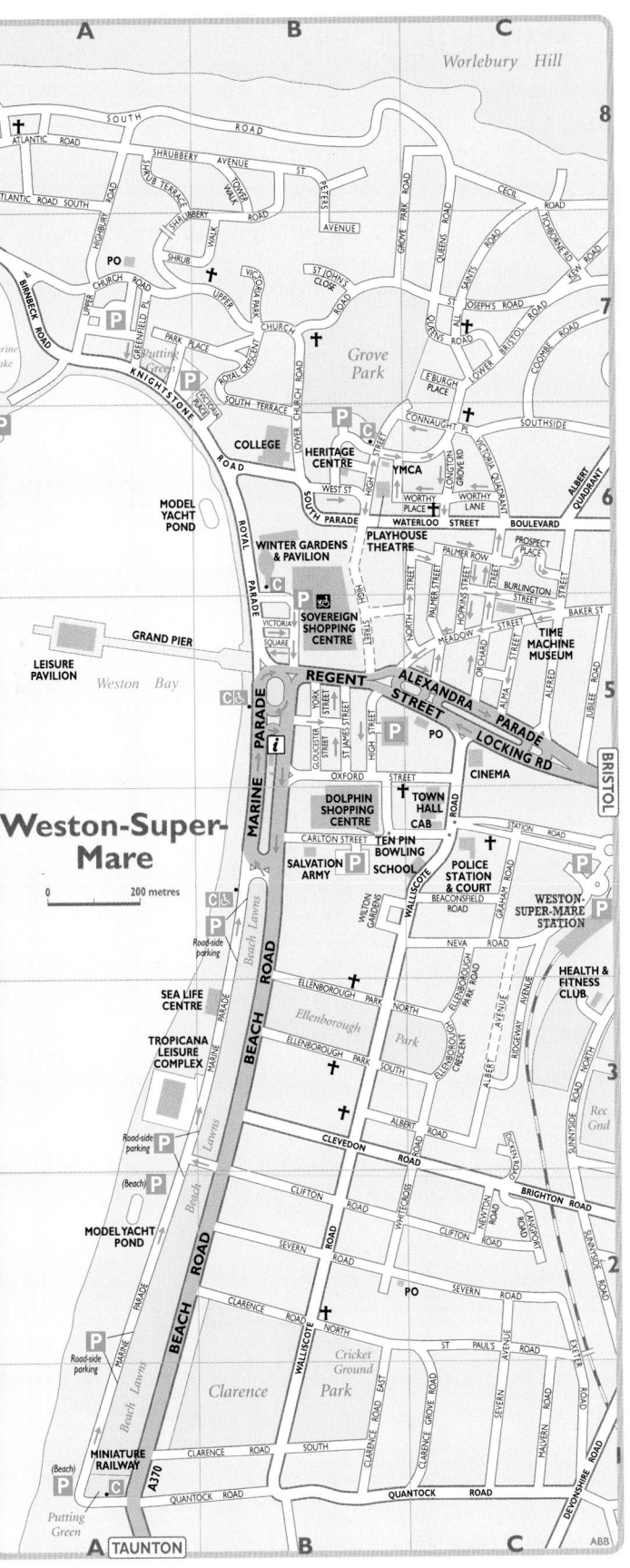

Weston-Super-Mare

Weston-Super-Mare is found on atlas page **21**, grid reference **3260**

Albert Avenue	C3-C4
Albert Quadrant	C6
Albert Road	B3-C3
Alexandra Parade	B5-C5
Alfred Street	C5-C6
All Saints Road	C7-C8
Alma Street	C5
Atlantic Road	A8
Atlantic Road South	A8
Baker Street	C5
Beach Road	A1-A2-B3-B5
Beaconsfield Road	C4
Birnbeck Road	A7
Brighton Road	C2
Burlington Street	C5
Carlton Street	B4
Cecil Road	C8
Clarence Grove Road	B1-C1-B2
Clarence Road East	B1-B2
Clarence Road North	A2-B2
Clarence Road South	A1-B1
Clevedon Road	B3-C2
Clifton Road	B2-C2
Connaught Place	B6-C6
Coombe Road	C6-C7
Devonshire Road	C1
Dicken Road	C2-C3
Edinburgh Place	C7
Ellenborough Crescent	C3
Ellenborough Park North	B4-B3-C3
Ellenborough Park Road	C3-C4
Ellenborough Park South	B3-C3
Exeter Road	C1-C2
Gloucester Street	B5
Graham Road	C4
Greenfield Place	A7
Grove Park Road	B7-B8
High Street	B5-B6
Highbury Road	A7-A8
Hopkins Street	C5-C6
Jubilee Road	C5
Kew Road	C7
Knightstone Road	A7-A6-B6
Langport Road	C2
Locking Road	C5
Longton Grove Road	C6
Lower Bristol Road	C7
Lower Church Road	B6-B7
Malvern Road	C1
Marine Parade	A1-A3-B3-B5
Meadow Street	B5-C5
Neva Road	B4-C4
Newton Road	C2
North Street	B6-B5-C5
Orchard Street	C5-C6
Oxford Street	B5-C5
Palmer Row	C6
Palmer Street	C5-C6
Park Place	A7-B7
Prospect Place	C6
Quantock Road	A1-B1-C1
Queens Road	C7-C8
Regent Street	B5-C5
Ridgeway Avenue	C3-C4
Royal Crescent	B7
Royal Parade	B5-B6
St James Street	B5
St John's Close	B7
St Joseph's Road	C7
St Paul's Road	C2
St Peters Avenue	B7-B8
Severn Avenue	C1-C2
Severn Road	A2-B2-C2
Shrub Terrace	A8
Shrub Walk	A7-B7
Shrubbery Avenue	A8-B8
Shrubbery Road	A7-B7-B8
South Parade	B6
South Road	A8-B8
South Terrace	B6-B7
Southside	C6
Station Road	C4
Sunnyside Road	C2
Sunnyside Road North	C2-C3
Tichborne Road	C7
Tower Walk	B8
Upper Church Road	A7-B7
Victoria Park	B7
Victoria Place	B6-B7
Victoria Quadrant	C6
Victoria Square	B5
Walliscote Road	B1-B4-C4-C5
Waterloo Street Boulevard	B6-C6
West Street	B6
Whitecross Road	B2-B3-C3
Wilton Gardens	B4
Worthy Lane	C6
Worthy Place	B6-C6
York Street	B5

230

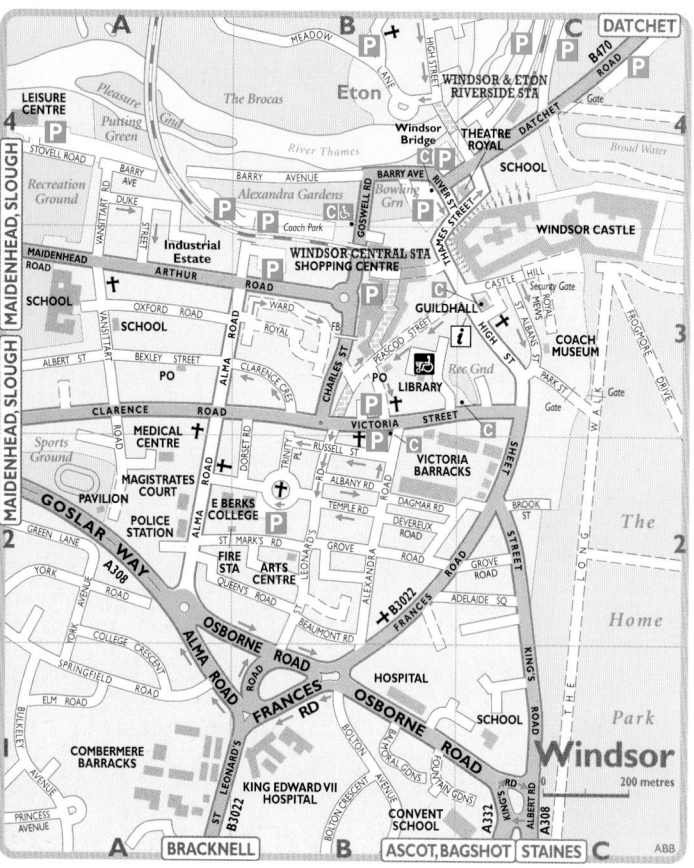

Windsor

Windsor is found on atlas page **26**,
grid reference **9576**

Adelaide Square	B2-C2	Royal Mews	C3
Albany Road	B2	Russell Street	B2
Albert Road	C1	St Albans Street	C3
Albert Street	A3	St Leonard's Road	A1-B1-B2-B3
Alexandra Road	B1-B2-B3	St Mark's Road	A2-B2
Alma Road	B1-B2-B3	Sheet Street	C2-C3
Arthur Road	A3-B3	Springfield Road	A1-A2
Balmoral Gardens	B1	Stovell Road	A4
Barry Avenue	A4-B4	Temple Road	B2
Beaumont Road	B2	Thames Street	B3-C4
Bexley Street	A3	The Long Walk	C1-C2-C3
Bolton Avenue	B1	Trinity Place	B2-B3
Bolton Crescent	B1	Vansittart Road	A2-A3-A4
Brook Street	C2	Victoria Street	B3-C3
Bulkeley Avenue	A1	Ward Royal	B3
Castle Hill	C3	York Avenue	A1-A2
Charles Street	B3	York Road	A2
Clarence Crescent	B3		
Clarence Road	A3-B3		
College Crescent	A1-A2		
Dagmar Road	B2		
Datchet Road	C4		
Devereux Road	B2		
Dorset Road	B2-B3		
Duke Street	A3-A4		
Elm Road	A1		
Fountain Gardens	B1-C1		
Frances Road	B1-B2-C2		
Frogmore Drive	C3		
Goslar Way	A2		
Goswell Road	B3-B4		
Green Lane	A2		
Grove Road	B2-C2		
High Street (Eton)	B4		
High Street (Windsor)	C3		
King's Road	C1-C2		
Maidenhead Road	A3		
Meadow Lane	A4-B4		
Osborne Road	A2-B2-B1-C1		
Oxford Road	A3		
Park Street	C3		
Peascod Street	B3		
Princess Avenue	A1		
Queen's Road	A2-B2		
River Street	B4		

Worcester

Worcester is found on atlas page **47**,
grid reference **8554**

All Saints Road	A3	Pheasant Street	C3-C4
Angel Place	B3	Pierpoint Street	B4
Angel Row	B3	Pump Street	B2-C2
Angel Street	B3	Queen Street	B3-C3
Arboretum Road	B4-C4	St Martin's Gate	C3
Bank Street	B3	St Nicholas Street	B3
Bath Road	C1	St Paul's Street	C2-C3
Bridge Street	A2-B3	St Swithun's Street	B3
Brittania Road	B4	Sansome Place	B4-C4
Broad Street	B3	Sansome Street	B3
Castle Street	A4-B4	Sansome Walk	B4
Charles Street	C2	Severn Street	B1
Church Street	B3	Severn Terrace	A4
City Walls Road	C1-C2-C3	Shaw Street	B3
College Precinct	B1	Sidbury	C1
College Street	B1-B2	South Parade	A2-B2
Copenhagen Street	B2	Southfield Street	B4-C4
Croft Road	A3-A4	Spring Gardens	C2-C3
Deansway	B2-B3	Taylor's Lane	B4
Derby Road	C1	The Butts	A3-B3
Dolday	A3	The Cross	B3
East Street	C4	The Shambles	B2-B3
Easy Row	A4	Trinity Street	B3
Edgar Street	B1-C1	Union Street	C2
Farrier Street	B3-B4	Westbury Street	C4
Foregate	B3	Wyld's Lane	C1
Foregate Street	B3-B4		
Foundry Street	C2		
Garden Street	C2		
George Street	C3		
Grand Stand Road	A3		
Hamilton Road	C1		
High Street	B2-B3		
Infirmary Walk	A4-B4-B3		
King Street	B1-C1		
Love's Grove	A4		
Lowesmoor	C3-C4		
Lowesmoor Place	C4		
Lowesmoor Terrace	C4		
Middle Street	C4		
New Road	A2		
New Street	C2-C3		
North Quay	A2-A3		
Padmore Street	C3-C4		
Park Street	C1-C2		

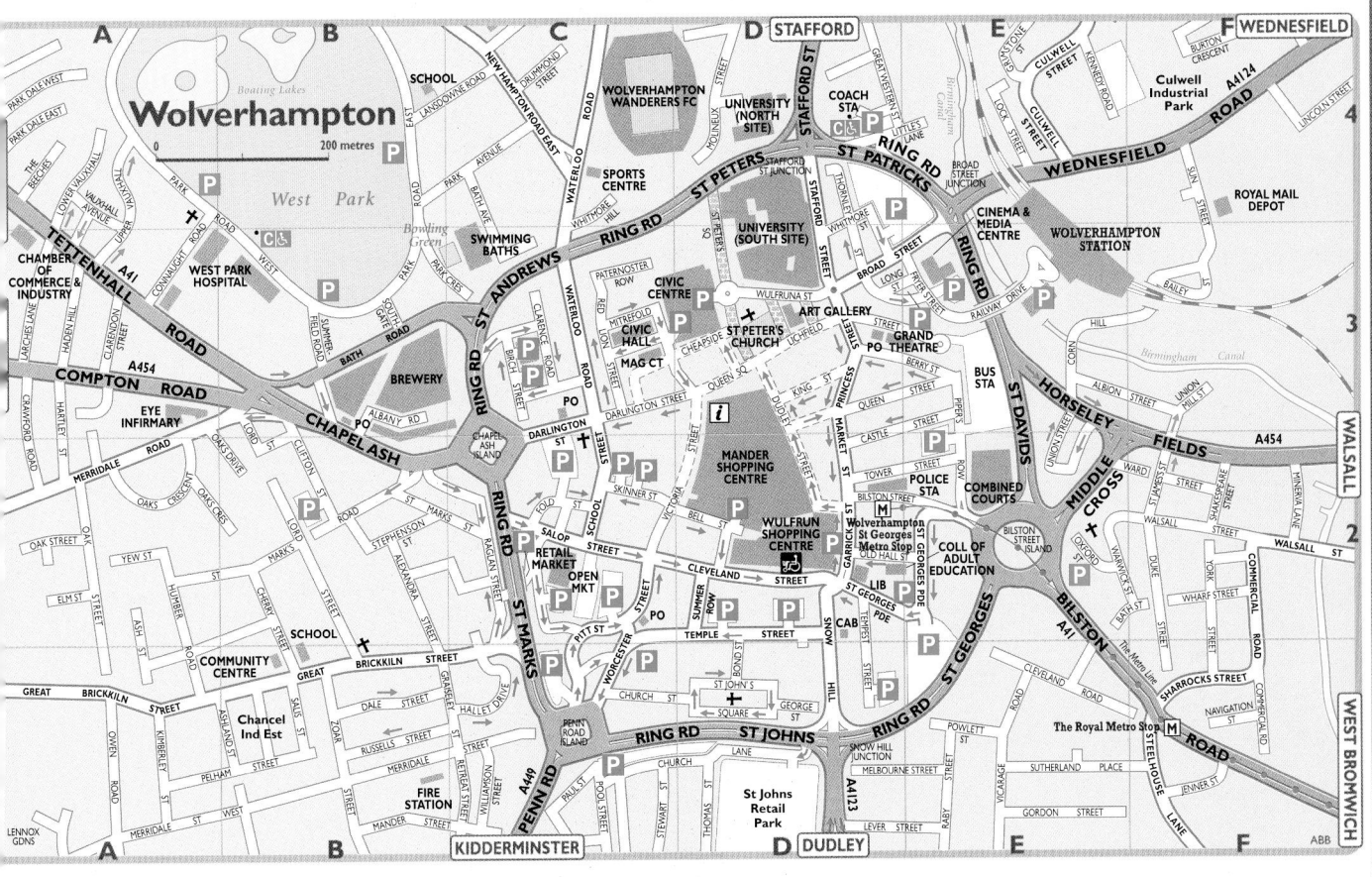

Wolverhampton

Wolverhampton is found on atlas page **60**,
grid reference **9198**

Albany Road	B3	Elm Street	A2	Minerva Lane	F2
Albion Street	E3-F3	Fold Street	C2	Mitrefold	C3
Alexandra Street	B1-B2	Fryer Street	E3	Molineux Street	D4
Ash Street	A1-A2	Garrick Street	D2	Navigation Street	F1
Ashland Street	B1	George Street	D1	New Hampton Road East	C4
Bailey Street	F3	Gordon Street	E1	Oak Street	A1-A2
Berry Avenue	C3-C4	Gramstone Street	E4	Oaks Crescent	A2-B2
Bath Road	B3-C3	Greasely Street	B1-C1	Oaks Drive	A3-A2-B2
Bath Street	E2-F2	Great Brick Kiln Street	A1-B1-C1	Old Hall Street	D2-E2
Bell Street	D2	Great Western Street	D4	Owen Road	A1
Berry Street	D3-E3	Haden Hill	A3	Oxford Street	E2
Bilston Road	E2-E1-F1	Hallet Drive	C1	Park Avenue	B4-C4
Bilston Street	D2-E2	Hartley Street	A2-A3	Park Crescent	B3-C3
Birch Street	C3	Herbert Street	D4	Park Dale East	A4
Bond Street	D1	Horseley Fields	E3-E2-F2	Park Dale West	A4
Broad Street	D3-E3	Humber Road	A1-A2	Park Road East	B3-B4
Burton Crescent	F4	Jenner Street	F1	Park Road West	B3-B4-A4
Castle Street	D2-D3-C3	Kennedy Road	E4	Paternoster Row	C3
Chapel Ash	B3-B2	Kimberley Street	A1	Paul Street	C1
Cheapside	D3	King Street	D3	Pelham Street	A1-B1
Cherry Street	B1-B2	Laburnum Street	A1-B2	Penn Road	E2-E3
Church Lane	C1-D1	Lansdowne Road	B4-C4	Piper's Row	E2-E3
Church Street	C1-D1	Larches Lane	A3	Pitt Street	C2
Clarence Road	C3	Lennox Gardens	A1	Pool Street	C1
Clarendon Street	A3	Lever Street	D1-E1	Powlett Street	E1
Cleveland Road	E1-F1	Lichfield Street	D3-E3	Princess Street	D3
Cleveland Street	C2-D2	Lincoln Street	F4	Queen Street	D3-E3
Clifton Street	B2-B3	Little's Lane	D4-E4	Queen Square	D3
Commercial Road	F1-F2	Lock Street	E4	Raby Street	E1
Compton Road	A3-B3	Long Street	D3-E3	Raglan Street	C2
Connaught Road	A3-A4	Lord Street	B1-B2-B3	Railway Drive	E3
Corn Hill	E3-F3	Lower Vauxhall	A4	Red Lion Street	C3
Crawford Road	A2-A3	Mander Street	B1-C1	Retreat Street	C1
Culwell Street	E4	Market Street	D2-D3	Ring Road St Andrews	C3
Dale Street	B1	Melbourne Street	D1-E1	Ring Road St Davids	E2-E3
Darlington Square	C2-C3-D3	Merridale Road	A2-A3-B3	Ring Road St Georges	D1-E1-E2
Drummond Street	C4	Merridale Street	B1-C1	Ring Road St Johns	C1-D1
Dudley Street	D2-D3	Merridale Street West	A1-B1	Ring Road St Marks	C1-C2
Duke Street	F1-F2	Middle Cross	E2	Ring Road St Patricks	D4-E4

Ring Road St Peters	C3-C4-D4	Warwick Street	E2-F2
Russell Street	B1	Waterloo Road	C3-C4
St Georges Parade	D2-E2	Wednesfield Road	E4-F4
St James's Street	F2	Wharf Street	F2
St John's Square	D1	Whitmore Hill	C4
St Mark's Road	A2-B2	Whitmore Street	D3-D4
St Marks Street	B2-C2	Williamson Street	C1
St Peter's Square	D3-D4	Worcester Street	C1-C2
Salisbury Street	B1	Wulfruna Street	D3
Salop Street	C2	Yew Street	A2
School Street	C2-C3	York Street	F1-F2
Sharrocks Street	F1	Zoar Street	B1
Shakespeare Street	F2		
Skinner Street	C2		
Snow Hill	D1-D2		
Southgate	B3		
Stafford Street	D3-D4		
Steelhouse Lane	F1		
Stephenson Street	B2		
Stewart Street	C1		
Summer Row	D2		
Summerfield Road	B3		
Sun Street	F3-F4		
Sutherland Place	E1-F1		
Tempest Street	D1-D2		
Temple Street	D1-D2-C1-C2		
Tettenhall Road	A4-A3-B3		
The Beeches	A4		
Thomas Street	D1		
Thornley Street	D3-D4		
Tower Street	D2-E2		
Union Mill Street	F3		
Union Street	E2-E3		
Upper Vauxhall Avenue	A3-A4		
Vauxhall Avenue	A4		
Vicarage Road	E1		
Victoria Street	C2-D2-D3		
Walsall Street	E2-F2		
Ward Street	E2-F2		

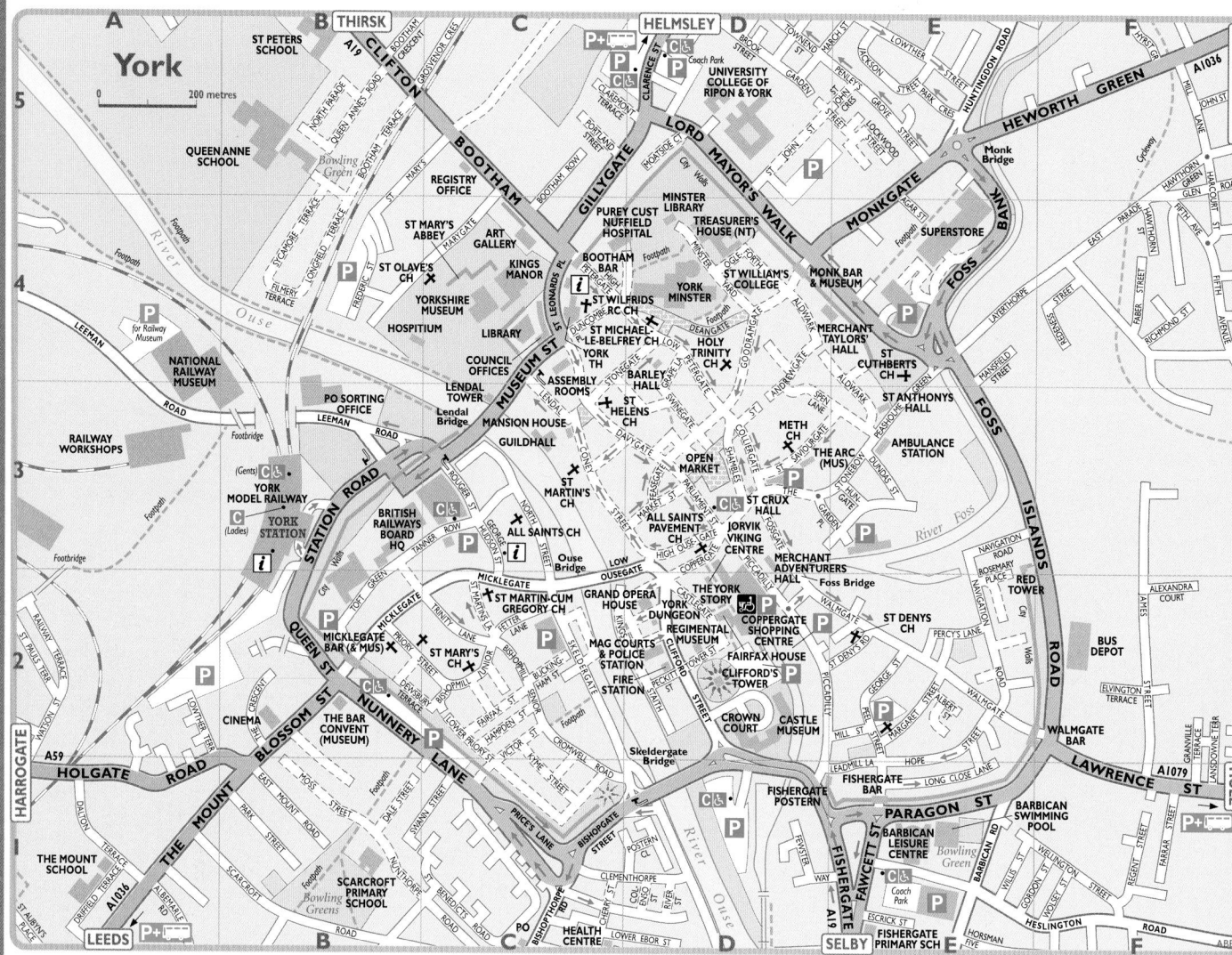

York

York is found on atlas page **83**,
grid reference **6051**

Agar Street	E4	Davygate	C3-D3	Goodramgate	D3-D4	Lockwood Street	E5	Park Crescent	E5	St Mary's	B4-B5-C
Albemarle Road	A1	Deangate	D4	Gordon Street	E1-F1	Long Close Lane	E1	Park Street	B1	St Pauls Terrace	B1
Albert Street	E2	Dewsbury Terrace	B2-C2	Granville Terrace	F1-F2	Longfield Terrace	B4	Parliament Street	D3	St Saviourgate	D3-
Aldwark	D4-E4-E3	Driffield Terrace	A1	Grape Lane	D4	Lord Mayor's Walk	D4-D5	Peasholme Green	E3-E4	Scarcroft Road	A1-
Alexandra Court	F2	Duncombe Place	C4	Grosvenor Crescent	B5-C5	Low Ousegate	C2-D3	Peckitt Street	D2	Shambles	D
Barbican Road	E1	Dundas Street	E3	Hampden Street	C2	Low Petergate	D3-D4	Peel Street	E2	Skeldergate	D
Bishopgate Street	C1-D1	East Mount Road	B1	Harcourt Street	F4-F5	Lower Ebor Street	C1-D1	Penley's Grove Street	D5-E5	Spen Lane	D
Bishopmill Junior	C2	East Parade	F4	Hawthorn Green	F5	Lower Priory Street	C2	Percy's Lane	E2	Station Road	B2-I
Bishopmill Senior	C2	Elvington Terrace	F2	Hawthorn Street	F4	Lowther Street	E5	Piccadilly	D1-D2-D3	Stonegate	C3-C4-D
Bishopthorpe Road	C1	Escrick Street	E1	Heslington Road	E1-F1	Lowther Terrace	A2	Portland Street	C5	Swann Street	B1-
Blossom Street	B1-B2	Faber Street	F4	Heworth Green	E5-F5	Mansfield Street	E4	Postern Close	D1	Swinegate	D
Bootham Crescent	B5	Fairfax Street	C2	High Ousegate	D3	March Street	D5-E5	Price's Lane	C1	Sycamore Terrace	B4-
Bootham Row	C4-C5	Farrar Street	F1	High Petergate	C4	Margaret Street	E2	Priory Street	B2-C2	Tanner Row	B3-C
Bootham Terrace	B5	Fawcett Street	E1	Holgate Road	A1-B1	Market Street	D3	Queen Anne's Road	B5	The Crescent	B
Brook Street	D5	Feasegate	D3	Hope Street	E1-E2	Marygate	B4-C4-C5	Queen Street	B2	The Mount	A1-B
Buckingham Street	C2	Fetter Lane	C2	Horsman Five	E1	Micklegate	B2-C2	Railway Terrace	A2	The Stonebow	D3-I
Castlegate	D2	Fewster Way	D1-E1	Hungate	E3	Mill Lane	F5	Redeness Street	F4	Toft Green	C
Cherry Street	C1	Fifth Avenue	F4	Huntingdon Road	E5	Mill Street	E2	Regent Street	F1	Tower Street	D
Claremont Terrace	C5-D5	Filmery Terrace	B4	Hyrst Green	F5	Minster Yard	D4	Richmond Street	F4	Townend Street	D
Clarence Street	D5	Fishergate	D1-E1	Jackson Street	E5	Moatside Court	D5	River Street	D1	Trinity Lane	C
Clementhorpe	C1-D1	Foss Bank	E4-E5	James Street	F1-F2-F3	Monkgate	D4-E4-E5	Rosemary Place	E2-E3	Victor Street	D
Clifford Street	D2	Foss Islands Road	E4-E3-F3-F2	John Street	F5	Moss Street	B1	Rougier Street	C3	Walmgate	D2-E2-
Clifton Bootham	B5-C5-C4	Fossgate	D3	Kings Staith	C2-D2	Museum Street	C3-C4	St Andrew Gate	D3-D4	Watson Street	A
Colenso Street	D1	Frederic Street	B4	Kyme Street	C1-C2	Navigation Road	E2-E3	St Aubyn's Place	A1	Wellington Street	E1-
Colliergate	D3	Garden Place	D3-E3	Lansdowne Terrace	F1-F2	North Parade	B5	St Benedicts Road	C1	Willis Street	E
Coney Street	C3-D3	Garden Street	D5-E5	Lawrence Street	F1-F2	North Street	C2	St Denys Road	E2	Wolsey Street	E
Coppergate	D2-D3	George Hudson Street	C2-C3	Layerthorpe	E4-F4	Nunnery Lane	B2-C2-C1	St John Crescent	E5		
Cromwell Road	C1-C2	George Street	E2	Leadmill Lane	E1-E2	Nunthorpe Road	B1-C1	St John Street	D5		
Dale Street	B1	Gillygate	C4-C5-D5	Leeman Road	A4-A3-B3	Ogle Forth	D4	St Leonards Place	C4		
Dalton Terrace	A1	Glen Road	F5	Lendal	C3-C4	Paragon Street	E1	St Martins Lane	C2		

ports and airports

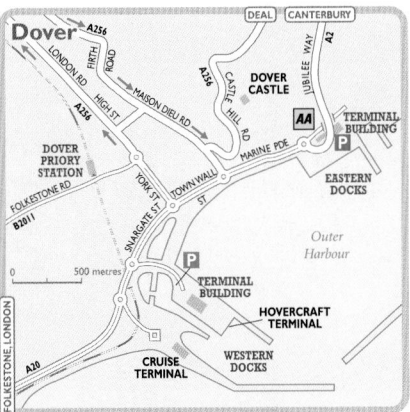

Pay-on-return parking is available at the Dover Eastern Docks and pay-and-display at the Hovercraft Terminal.
For further information tel: 01304 241427
Other long-stay parking facilities are available with a collection and delivery service.
For details tel: 01304 201227

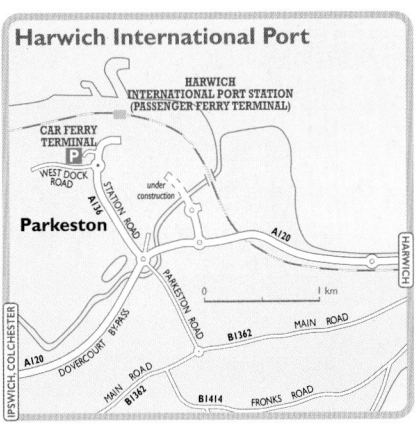

Open-air parking is available at the terminal.
For charge details tel: 01255 242000
Further parking is available 5 miles from Harwich International Port with a collection and delivery service.
For charge details tel: 01255 870217

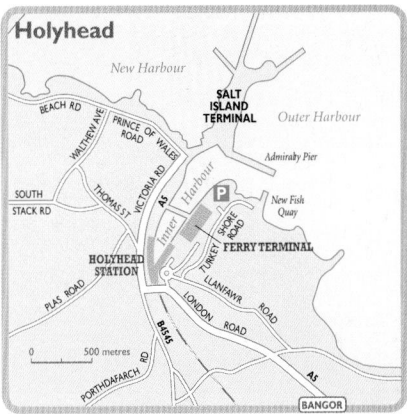

Open-air pay-and-display parking is available close to the Ferry Terminal.
For charge details tel: 01407 762304 or 606732

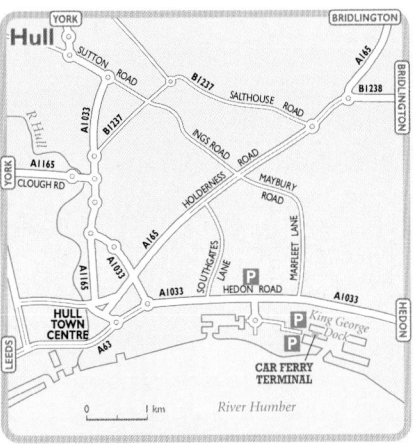

Free open-air parking is available at King George Dock (left at owners' risk).
Tel: 01482 795141
Undercover parking is also available.
For charge details tel: 01482 781021

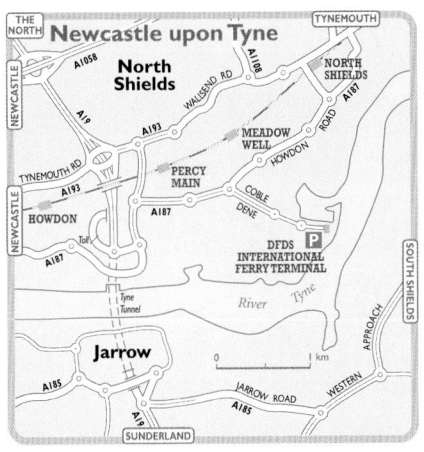

Open-air secure parking is available at the DFDS International Ferry Terminal, Royal Quays.
For charge details tel: 0191 296 0202

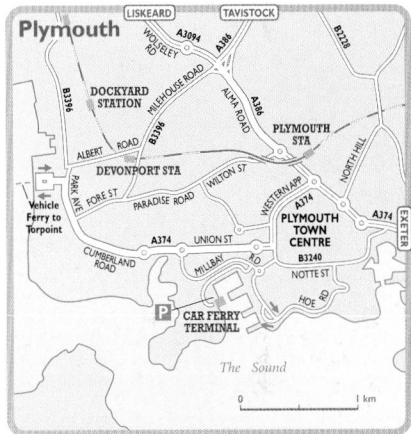

Free open-air parking is available outside the terminal building.
Tel: 0990 360360

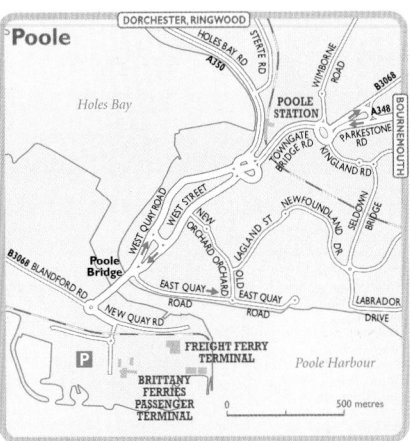

Open-air parking for 600 vehicles is available adjacent to the Ferry Terminal.
For charge details tel: 01202 440220

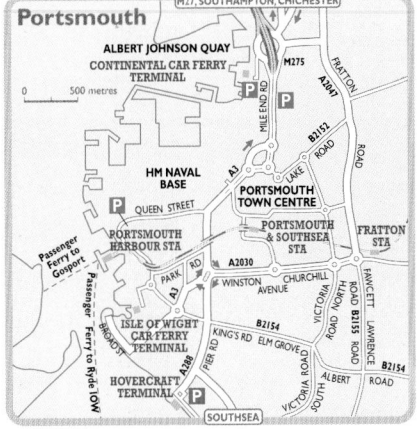

Secure parking facilities are available at the Continental Car Ferry Terminal and long-stay parking off Mile End Rd.
For charge details tel: 023 9275 1261
Pay-and-display parking is available opposite the Hovercraft Terminal.
Multi-storey parking is available close to the Isle of Wight Passenger Ferry Terminal.
For charge details tel: 023 9282 3153

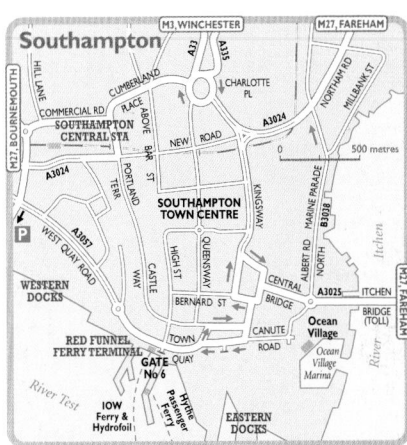

Covered or fenced compound parking for 2,000 vehicles is available within the Western Docks with a collection and delivery service.
For charge details tel: 023 8022 8001/2/3

major airports

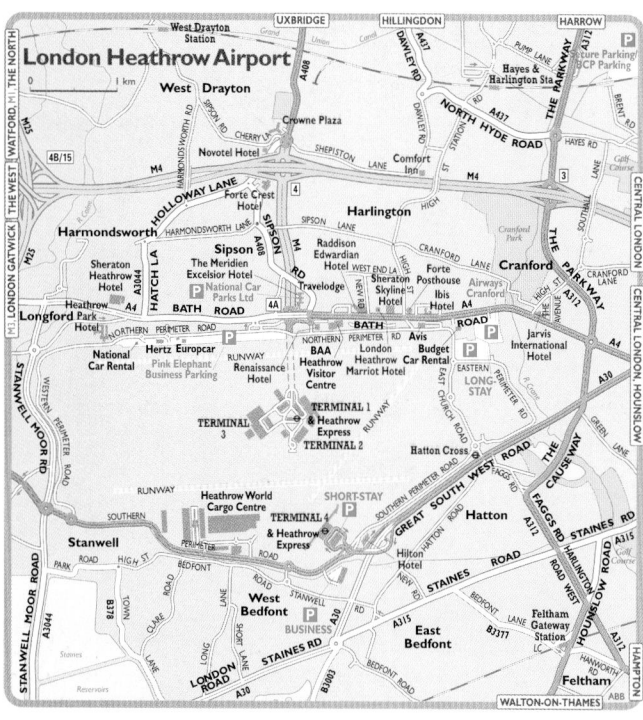

London Heathrow Airport – 16 miles west of London

Telephone: 020 8759 4321 or visit www.baa.co.uk
Parking: short-stay, long-stay and business parking is available.
For charge details tel: 0345 405000
Public Transport: coach, bus, rail and London Underground.
There are several 4-star and 3-star hotels within easy reach of the airport.
Car hire facilities are available.

London Gatwick Airport – 35 miles south of London

Telephone: 01293 535353 or visit www.baa.co.uk
Parking: short and long-stay parking is available at both the North and South terminals.
For charge details tel: 0345 405000
Public Transport: coach, bus and rail.
There are several 4-star and 3-star hotels within easy reach of the airport.
Car hire facilities are available.

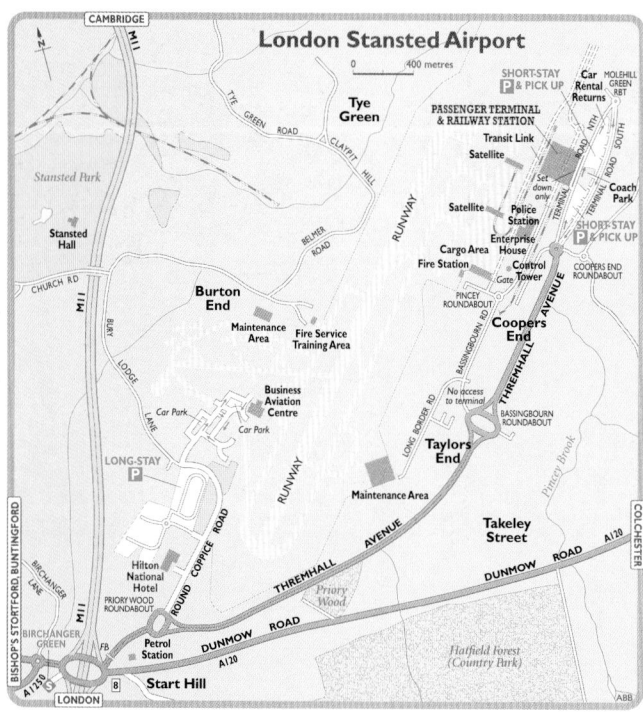

London Stansted Airport – 36 miles north-east of London

Telephone: 01279 680500 or visit www.baa.co.uk
Parking: short and long-stay open-air parking is available.
For charge details tel: 01279 681192
Public Transport: coach, bus and direct rail link to London on the 'Stansted Skytrain'.
There is one 3-star hotel within easy reach of the airport.
Car hire facilities are available.

London Luton Airport – 33 miles north of London

Telephone: 01582 405100 or visit www.london-luton.com
Parking: short and long-stay open-air parking is available.
For charge details tel: 01582 395249
Public Transport: coach, bus and rail.
There is one 2-star hotel at the airport and two 3-star hotels within easy reach of the airport.
Car hire facilities are available.

234

major airports

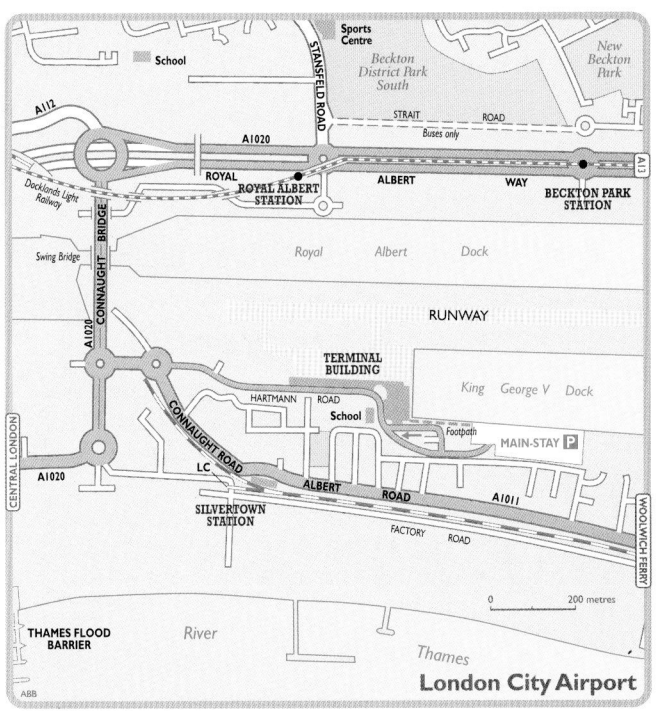

London City Airport – 7 miles east of London

Telephone: 020 7646 0088 or visit www.londoncityairport.com
Parking: open-air parking is available.
For charge details tel: 020 7646 0088
Public Transport: shuttle-bus service into London (Liverpool Street). Easy access to the rail network and the London Underground.
There are 5-star, 4-star and 3-star hotels within easy reach of the airport.
Car hire facilities are available.

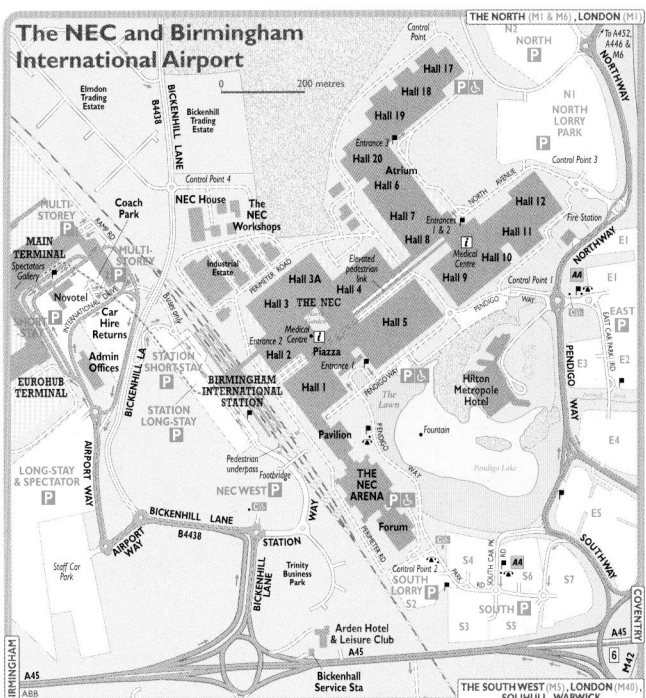

Birmingham International Airport – 8 miles east of Birmingham

Telephone: 0121 767 5511 (Main Terminal), 0121 767 7502 (Eurohub Terminal) or visit www.bhx.co.uk
Parking: short and long-stay parking is available. For charge details tel: 0121 767 7861
Public Transport: shuttle-bus service to Birmingham International railway station and the NEC.
There is one 3-star hotel adjacent to the airport and several 4 and 3-star hotels within easy reach of the airport. Car hire facilities are available.

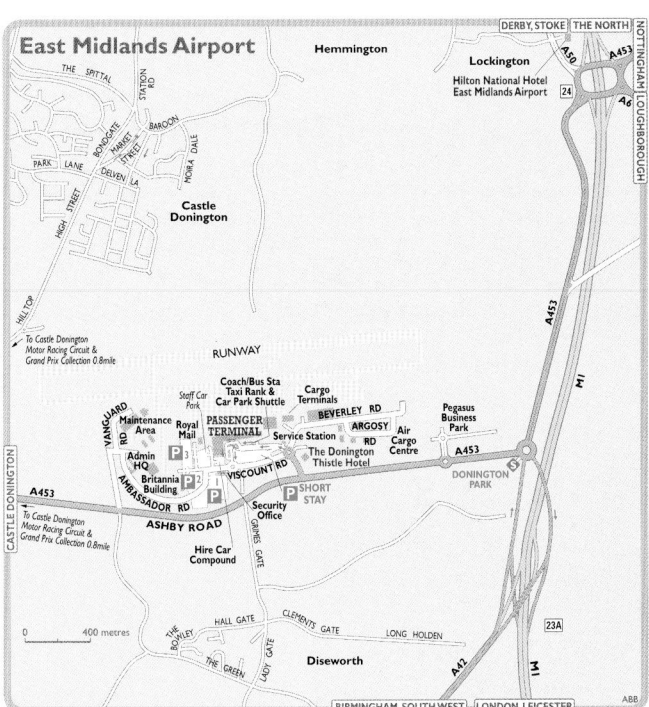

East Midlands Airport – 15 miles south-west of Nottingham, next to the M1 at junctions 23A and 24

Telephone: 01332 852852 or visit www.eastmidsairport.co.uk
Parking: short and long-stay parking is available.
For charge details tel: 0800 128128
Public Transport: bus and coach services to major towns and cities in the East Midlands.
There is one 4-star hotel and several 3-star hotels within easy reach of the airport.
Car hire facilities are available.

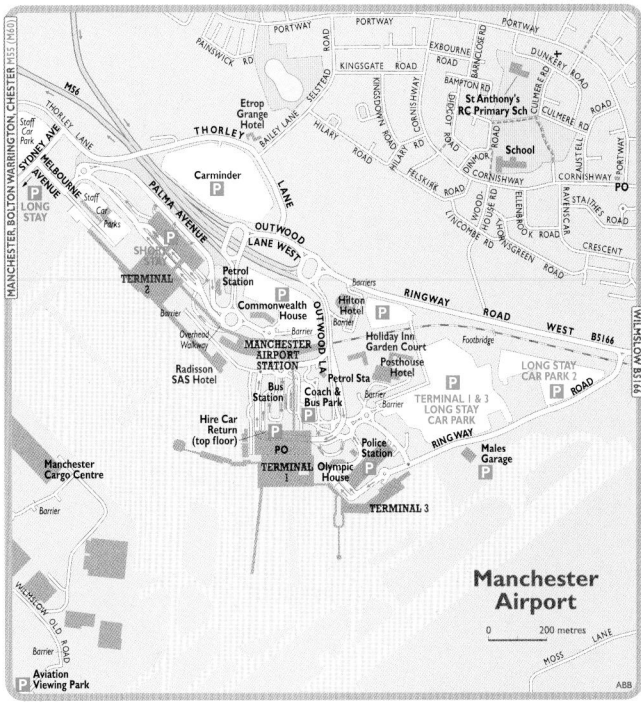

Manchester Airport – 10 miles south of Manchester

Telephone: 0161 489 3000 or visit www.manairport.co.uk
Parking: short and long-stay parking is available. For charge details tel: 0161 489 3723
Public Transport: bus, coach and rail. Manchester airport railway station connects with the rail network.
There is one 4-star hotel and several 3-star hotels within easy reach of the airport.
Car hire facilities are available.

major airports

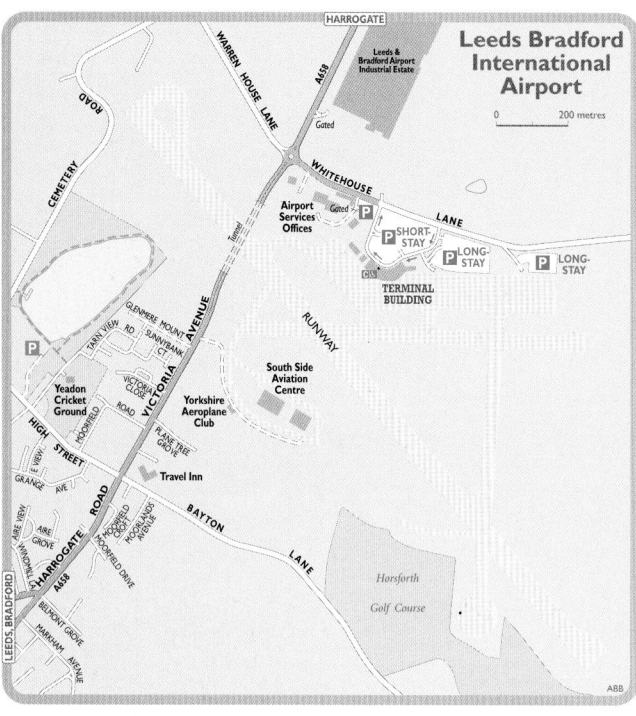

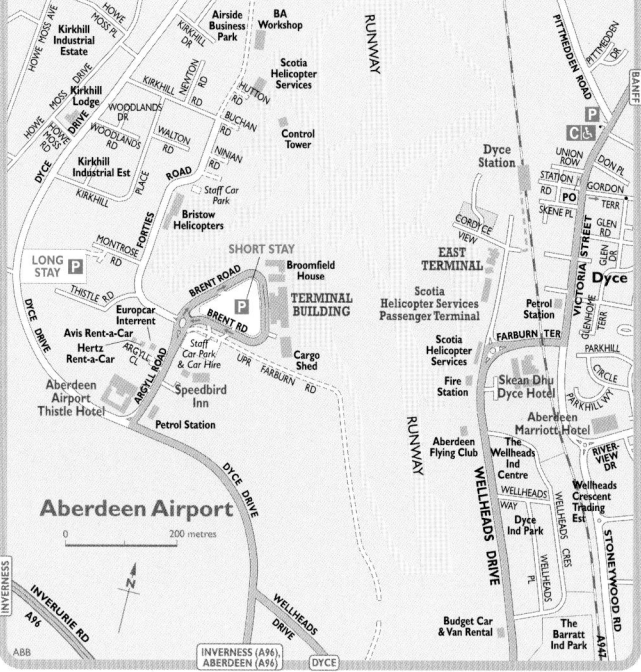

Leeds Bradford International Airport – 7 miles north-east of Bradford and 9 miles north-west of Leeds

Telephone: 0113 250 9696 or visit www.lbia.co.uk
Parking: short and long-stay parking is available.
Public Transport: bus from Leeds and Bradford.
There are several 4-star and 3-star hotels within easy reach of the airport.
Car hire facilities are available.

Aberdeen Airport – 7 miles north-west of Aberdeen

Telephone: 01224 722331 or visit www.baa.co.uk
Parking: open-air parking is available.
For charge details tel: 01224 722331 ext 5142
Public Transport: regular bus to central Aberdeen.
There are several 4-star and 3-star hotels within easy reach of the airport.
Car hire facilities are available.

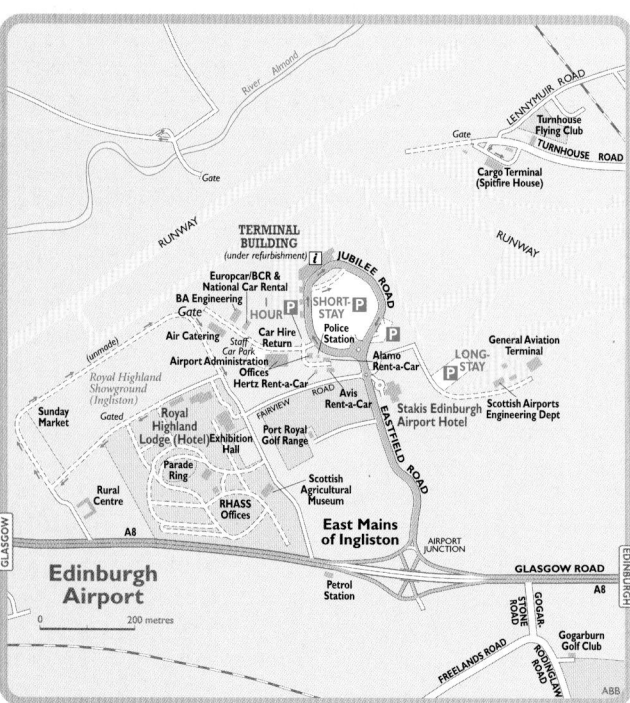

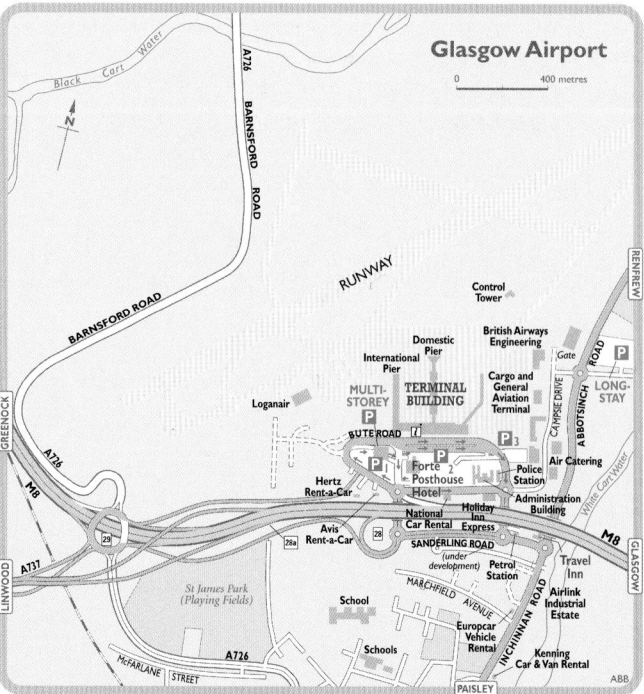

Edinburgh Airport – 7 miles west of Edinburgh

Telephone: 0131 333 1000 or visit www.baa.co.uk
Parking: open-air parking is available.
For charge details tel: 0131 344 3197
Public Transport: regular bus services operate between central Edinburgh and Glasgow.
There is one 4-star hotel and several 3-star hotels within easy reach of the airport.
Car hire facilities are available.

Glasgow Airport – 8 miles west of Glasgow

Telephone: 0141 887 1111 or visit www.baa.co.uk
Parking: short and long-stay parking is available, mostly open-air.
For charge details tel: 0141 889 2751
Public Transport: regular coach services operate between central Glasgow and Edinburgh.
There are several 3-star hotels within easy reach of the airport.
Car hire facilities are available.

the Channel Tunnel

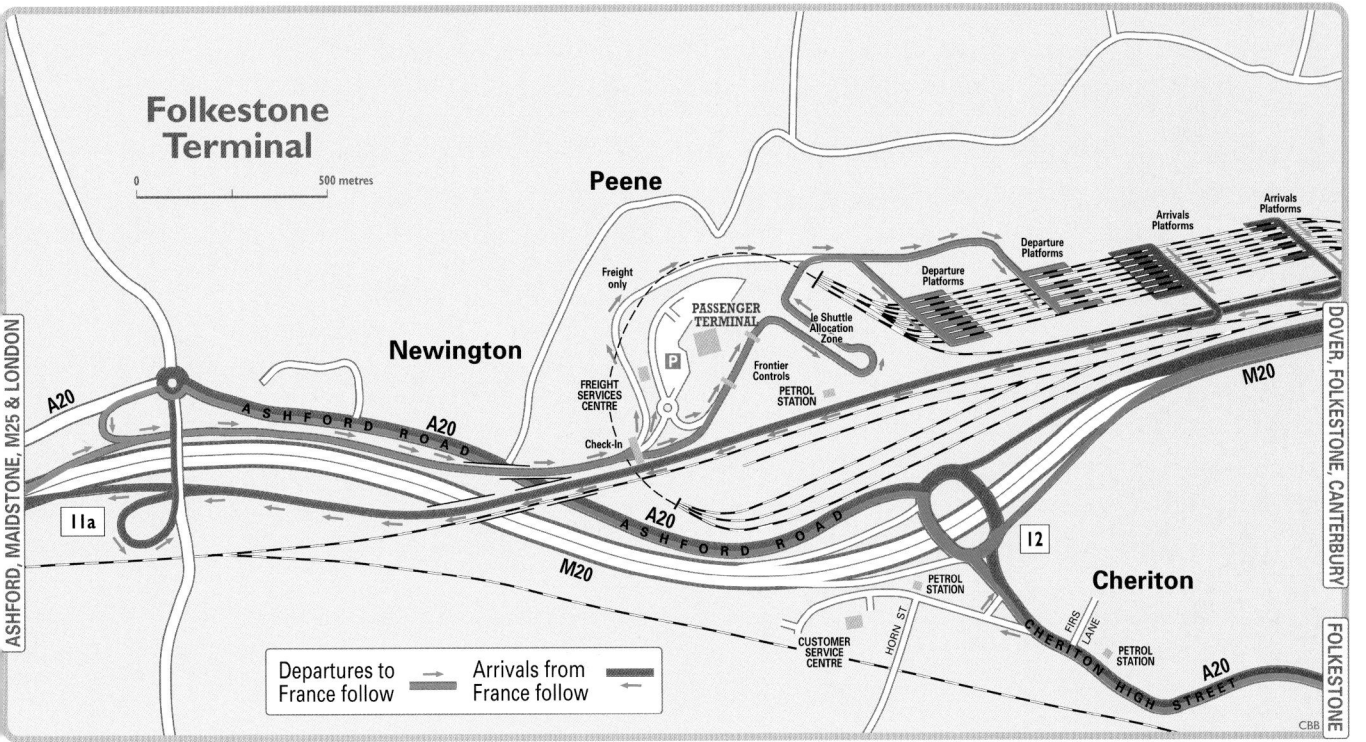

Folkestone Terminal

0   500 metres

Peene

Newington

ASHFORD, MAIDSTONE, M25 & LONDON

A20

A20   ASHFORD ROAD

11a

M20

A20   ASHFORD ROAD

Freight only

PASSENGER TERMINAL

FREIGHT SERVICES CENTRE

Check-In

le Shuttle Allocation Zone

Frontier Controls

PETROL STATION

Departure Platforms

Departure Platforms

Arrivals Platforms

Arrivals Platforms

M20

DOVER, FOLKESTONE, CANTERBURY

FOLKESTONE

12

Cheriton

PETROL STATION

FIRS LANE

CHERITON HIGH STREET

PETROL STATION

A20

HORN ST

CUSTOMER SERVICE CENTRE

CBB

Departures to France follow →   Arrivals from France follow ←

Services to Europe

The Eurotunnel Shuttle service for cars, cars towing caravans and trailers, motorcycles, coaches and HGV vehicles runs between terminals at Folkestone and Calais/Coquelles.
It takes just over one hour to travel from the M20 motorway in Kent, via the Channel Tunnel, to the A16 autoroute in France. The service runs 24 hours a day, every day of the year. Call the Eurotunnel Call Centre (tel: 0990 353535) or visit www.eurotunnel.com for the latest ticket and travel information.

There are up to four departures per hour at peak times, with the journey in the tunnel from platform to platform taking just 35 minutes (45 minutes at night). Travellers pass through British and French frontier controls on departure, saving time on the other side of the Channel. Each terminal has bureaux de change, restaurants and a variety of shops. In Calais/Coquelles, the Cité de l'Europe contains numerous shops and restaurants, hotels and a hypermarket.

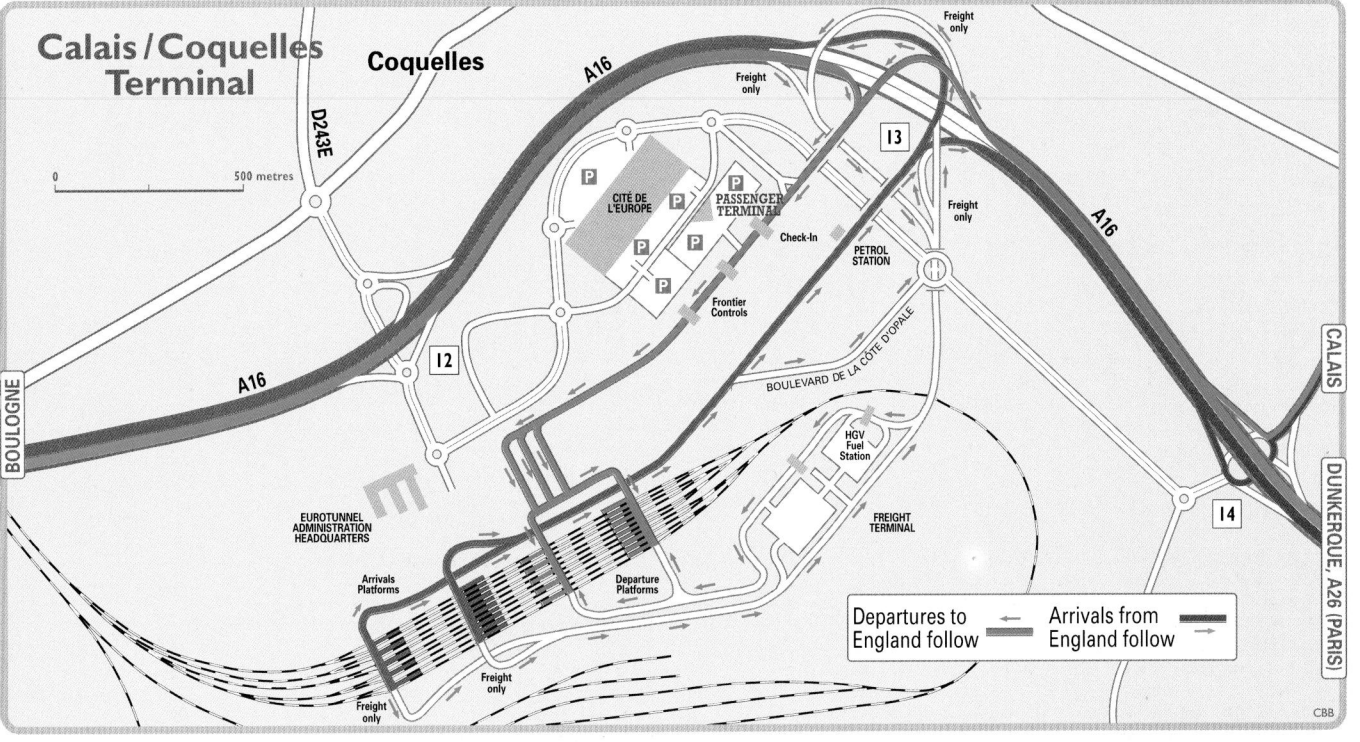

Calais/Coquelles Terminal

Coquelles

A16

0   500 metres

BOULOGNE

D243E

A16

12

CITÉ DE L'EUROPE

P   P   P   P   P

PASSENGER TERMINAL

Check-In

Frontier Controls

PETROL STATION

Freight only

Freight only

Freight only

Freight only

13

A16

CALAIS

DUNKERQUE, A26 (PARIS)

14

BOULEVARD DE LA CÔTE D'OPALE

HGV Fuel Station

FREIGHT TERMINAL

EUROTUNNEL ADMINISTRATION HEADQUARTERS

Arrivals Platforms

Departure Platforms

Freight only

Freight only

Departures to England follow ←   Arrivals from England follow →

CBB

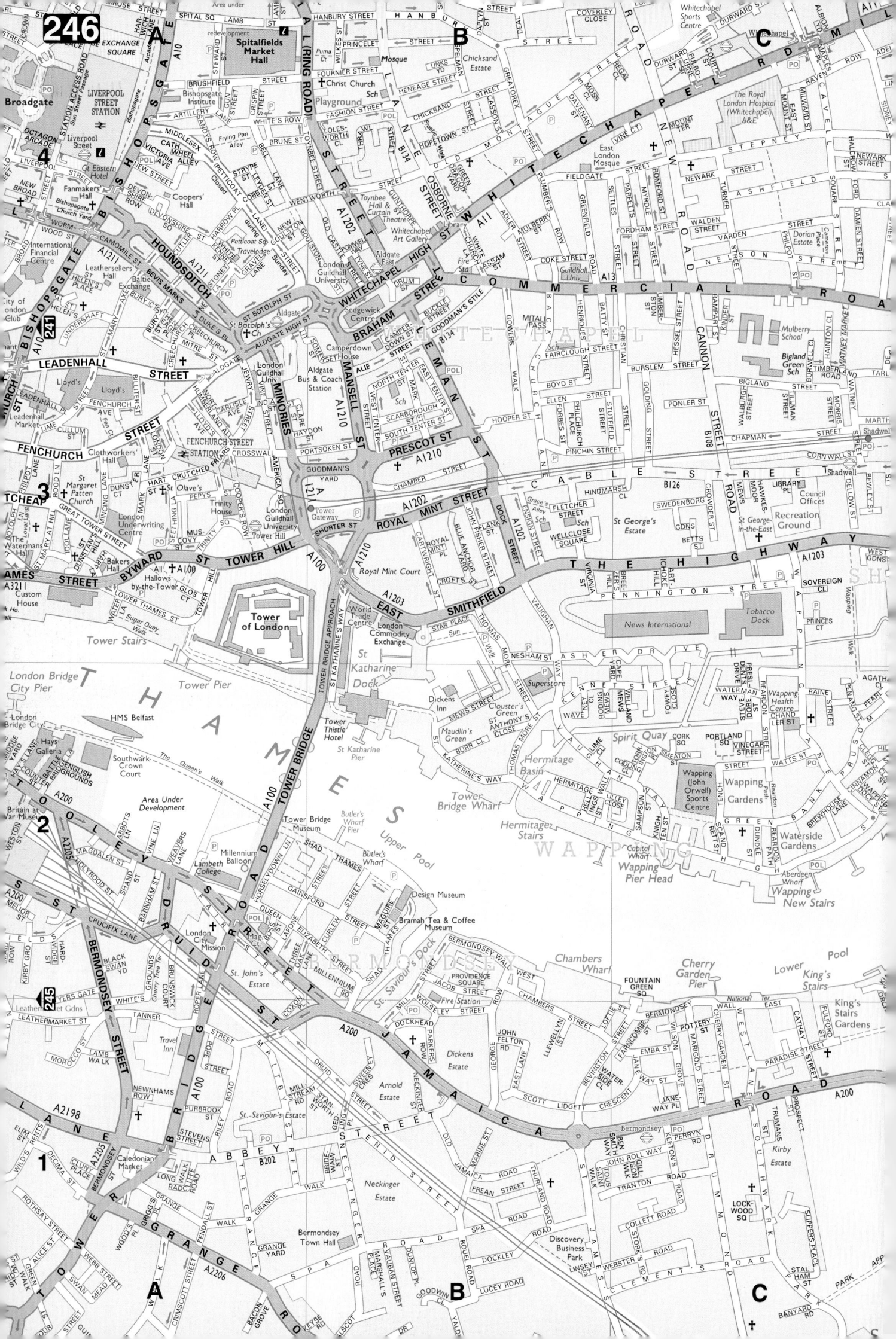

Central London street index

In the index the street names are listed in alphabetical order and written in full, but may be abbreviated on the map. Postal codes are listed where information is available. Each entry is followed by its map page number in bold type, and an arbitrary letter and grid reference number. For example, for Exhibition Road SW7 **242** C3, turn to page 242. The letter 'C' refers to the grid square located at the bottom of the page; the figure '3' refers to the grid square located at the left-hand side of the page. Exhibition Road is found within the intersecting square. SW7 is the postcode. A proportion of street names and their references are also followed by the name of another street in italics. These entries do not appear on the map due to insufficient space but can be located adjacent to the name of the road in italics.

A

bey Orchard Street SW1 ... **244** B3
bey Street SE1 ... **246** A1
bots Gardens W8 ... **242** A3
St Mary's Place
bots Lane SE1 ... **246** A2
bots Walk W8 ... **242** A3
St Mary's Place
botshade Road SE16 ... **247** E2
church Lane EC4 ... **241** F1
ercorn Close NW8 ... **238** B4
ercorn Place NW8 ... **238** B4
erdeen Place NW8 ... **238** C3
erdour Street SE1 ... **245** F2
ingdon Road W8 ... **242** A3
ingdon Street SW1 ... **244** B3
ingdon Villas W8 ... **242** A3
hilles Way W1 ... **243** E4
kroyd Drive E3 ... **247** F4
ton Walk SE16 ... **247** F2
am and Eve Court W1 ... **239** E1
Oxford Street
am And Eve Mews W8 ... **242** A3
am Street W8 ... **240** B1
am's Row W1 ... **239** E1
ams Place E14 ... **248** A4
dington Street SE1 ... **244** C3
dle Hill EC4 ... **241** E1
dle Street EC4 ... **241** E2
elaide Street WC2 ... **240** B1
William IV Street
elina Grove E1 ... **246** D4
eline Street SE16 ... **240** B2
elphi Terrace WC2 ... **240** B1
Adams Street
ler Street E1 ... **246** B4
miral Place SE16 ... **247** E2
miral Way W9 ... **238** A3
mirals Way E14 ... **248** A3
par Street W1 ... **238** C3
rian Mews SW10 ... **242** A1
ar Street WC2 ... **240** B1
atha Close E1 ... **246** C2
don Street SE1 ... **241** D3
nes Street E1 ... **247** F4
nstey Street SE16 ... **247** D1
Brunel Road
Street E1 ... **240** A1
aska Street SE1 ... **244** C4
bany Mews SE5 ... **245** E1
bany Road SE5 ... **245** E1
bany Street NW1 ... **239** F4
batross Way SE16 ... **247** D1
bemarle Street W1 ... **239** F1
bemarle Way EC1 ... **240** C3
Clerkenwell Road
bert Court SW7 ... **242** C3
bert Embankment SE1 ... **244** B1
bert Gardens E1 ... **247** D3
bert Hall Mansions SW7 ... **242** C3
bert Mews W8 ... **242** B3
bert Place W8 ... **242** B3
berta Street SE17 ... **245** D1
bion Close W2 ... **239** D1
bion Mews W2 ... **239** D1
bion Place EC1 ... **241** D3
bion Street SE16 ... **247** D1
bion Street W2 ... **239** D1
bion Way EC1 ... **241** E2
bion Yard E1 ... **246** C4
dburgh Mews W1 ... **239** E2
Marylebone Lane
denham Street NW1 ... **240** A4
dermanbury EC2 ... **241** E2
dermanbury Square EC2 ... **241** E2
Aldermanbury
derney Street SW1 ... **243** F2
dersgate Street EC1 ... **241** E3
dford Street W1 ... **239** E1
dgate EC3 ... **246** A3
dgate High Street EC3 ... **246** A3
dsworth Close W9 ... **238** A3
dwych WC2 ... **240** C1
exander Place SW7 ... **242** C2
exander Square SW3 ... **242** C2
exander Street W2 ... **238** A2
ford Place N1 ... **241** E4
fred Mews W1 ... **240** A3
fred Place W1 ... **240** A3
fred Road W2 ... **238** A2
ice Street SE1 ... **245** F3
ie Street E1 ... **246** B3
l Hallows Lane EC4 ... **241** F1
l Soul's Place W1 ... **239** F2
Langham Street
len Street W8 ... **242** A3
lington Street W1 ... **243** F3
lsop Place NW1 ... **239** D3
ma Square NW8 ... **238** B4
pha Grove E14 ... **248** A3
pha Place SW3 ... **243** D1
sace Road SE17 ... **245** F1
scot Road SE1 ... **246** B1
vey Street SE17 ... **245** F2
mbassador Square E14 ... **248** B2
mbergate Street SE17 ... **245** D1
mberley Road W9 ... **238** A3
mbrosden Avenue SW1 ... **244** A3
melia Street SE17 ... **245** E2
men Corner EC4 ... **241** D2
men Court EC4 ... **241** D2
merica Square EC3 ... **246** A3
merica Street SE1 ... **245** E4
moy Place E14 ... **247** F3
mpton Place WC1 ... **240** C4

Ampton Street WC1 ... **240** C4
Amsterdam Road E14 ... **248** C2
Amwell Street EC1 ... **240** C4
Anderson Road SW3 ... **243** D2
Andrew Borde Street WC2 ... **240** B2
Charing Cross Road
Angel Court EC2 ... **241** F2
Angel Court SW1 ... **244** A4
King Street
Angel Passage EC4 ... **241** F1
Angel Place SE1 ... **245** E4
Angel Street EC1 ... **241** E2
Ann Moss Way SE16 ... **247** D1
Annsdell Street W8 ... **242** A3
Antill Terrace E1 ... **247** D4
Apothecary Street EC4 ... **241** D2
New Bridge Street
Appold Street EC2 ... **241** F3
Apple Tree Yard SW1 ... **240** A1
Aquinas Street SE1 ... **245** D4
Arbour Square E1 ... **247** D4
Archangel Street SE16 ... **247** E1
Archer Street W1 ... **240** A1
Arden Crescent E14 ... **248** A2
Argent Street E14 ... **245** E4
Loman Street
Argyle Square WC1 ... **240** B4
Argyle Street WC1 ... **240** B4
Argyle Walk WC1 ... **240** B4
Argyll Road W8 ... **242** A3
Argyll Street W1 ... **239** F2
Arlington Street SW1 ... **243** F4
Arlington Way EC1 ... **241** D4
Arne Street WC2 ... **240** B2
Arneway Street SW1 ... **244** A2
Arnhem Place E14 ... **248** A2
Arnside Street SE17 ... **245** E1
Arthur Street EC4 ... **241** F1
Artichoke Hill E1 ... **246** C3
Artillery Lane E1 ... **246** A4
Artillery Passage E1 ... **246** A4
Artillery Lane
Artillery Row SW1 ... **244** A3
Artizan Street E1 ... **246** A4
Harrow Place
Arundel Street WC2 ... **240** C1
Ashbridge Street NW8 ... **238** C3
Ashburn Gardens SW7 ... **242** B2
Ashburn Mews SW7 ... **242** B2
Ashburn Place SW7 ... **242** B2
Ashby Street EC1 ... **241** D4
Ashdown Walk E14 ... **248** A2
Asher Drive E1 ... **246** B3
Ashfield Street E1 ... **246** C4
Ashfield Yard E1 ... **247** D4
Ashfield Street
Ashland Place W1 ... **238** E3
Ashley Place SW1 ... **243** F3
Ashmill Street NW1 ... **238** C3
Ashworth Road W9 ... **238** A4
Aske Street N1 ... **241** F4
Asolando Drive SE17 ... **245** E2
King & Queen Street
Aspen Way E14 ... **248** B4
Assam Street E1 ... **246** B4
Assembly Passage E1 ... **247** D4
Aste Street E14 ... **248** B3
Astell Street SW3 ... **243** D2
Aston Street E14 ... **247** E4
Astwood Mews SW7 ... **242** B2
Atherstone Mews SW7 ... **242** B2
Atterbury Street SW1 ... **244** B2
Attneave Street WC1 ... **240** C4
Aubrey Place NW8 ... **238** B4
Auckland Street SE11 ... **244** C1
Augustus Street NW1 ... **239** F4
Aulton Place SE11 ... **245** D1
Austin Friars EC2 ... **241** F2
Austin Friars Square EC2 ... **241** F2
Austin Friars
Austral Street SE11 ... **245** D2
Ave Maria Lane EC4 ... **241** E2
Aveline Street SE11 ... **244** C1
Avery Row W1 ... **239** F1
Avis Square E1 ... **247** E4
Avon Place SE1 ... **245** E3
Avonmouth Street SE1 ... **245** E3
Aybrook Street W1 ... **239** E2
Aylesbury Road SE17 ... **245** F1
Aylesbury Street EC1 ... **241** D3
Aylesford Street SW1 ... **244** A1
Aylward Street E1 ... **247** D4
Ayres Street SE1 ... **245** E4

B

Babmaes Street SW1 ... **244** A4
Jermyn Street
Bacchus Walk N1 ... **241** F4
Bache's Street N1 ... **241** F4
Back Church Lane E1 ... **246** B4
Back Hill EC1 ... **241** D3
Bacon Grove SE1 ... **246** A1
Baffin Way E14 ... **248** C4
Bainbridge Street WC1 ... **240** B2
Baker Street W1 & NW1 ... **239** D3
Baker's Mews W1 ... **239** E2
Baker's Row EC1 ... **241** F3
Baker's Yard EC1 ... **241** D3
Baker's Row
Bakers Hall Court EC3 ... **246** A3
Harp Lane
Balcombe Street NW1 ... **239** D3
Balderton Street W1 ... **239** E1
Baldwin Street EC1 ... **241** F4

Baldwin's Gardens EC1 ... **240** C3
Balfe Street N1 ... **240** B4
Balfour Mews W1 ... **239** E1
Balfour Place W1 ... **239** E1
Balfour Street SE17 ... **245** F2
Ballast Quay SE10 ... **248** C1
Balneil Gate SW1 ... **244** A1
Baltic Street East EC1 ... **241** E3
Baltic Street West EC1 ... **241** E3
Balvaird Place SW1 ... **244** B2
Bancroft Road E1 ... **244** C1
Bank End SE1 ... **245** E4
Bankside SE1 ... **245** E4
Bankside Jetty SE1 ... **241** E1
Banner Street EC1 ... **241** E3
Banyard Road SE16 ... **246** C1
Barbon Close WC1 ... **240** C3
Barge House Street SE1 ... **241** D1
Bark Place W2 ... **238** A1
Barkston Gardens SW5 ... **242** A2
Barleycorn Way E14 ... **247** F3
Barlow Place W1 ... **239** F1
Barlow Street SE17 ... **245** F2
Barnaby Place SW7 ... **242** C2
Barnardo Street E1 ... **247** D3
Barnby Street NW1 ... **240** A4
Barnes Street E14 ... **247** E4
Barnfield Place E14 ... **248** A2
Barnham Street SE1 ... **246** A2
Barnsdale Avenue E14 ... **248** A2
Barnwood Close W9 ... **238** A3
Baron's Place SE1 ... **245** D3
Barque Mews SE8 ... **248** A1
Barrett Street W1 ... **239** E2
Barrie Street W2 ... **238** B1
Barrow Hill Road NW8 ... **238** C4
St Johns Wood High Street
Barter Street WC1 ... **240** B2
Barth Lane EC2 ... **241** F2
Bartholomew Close EC1 ... **241** E2
Bartholomew Square EC1 ... **241** E3
Bartholomew Street SE1 ... **245** F2
Barton Street SW1 ... **244** B3
Basil Street SW3 ... **243** D3
Basinghall Avenue EC2 ... **241** E2
Basinghall Street EC2 ... **241** E2
Bastwick Street EC1 ... **241** E3
Bate Street E14 ... **247** F3
Bateman Street W1 ... **240** A2
Bateman's Buildings W1 ... **240** A2
Bateman Street
Bath Court EC1 ... **240** C3
Warner Street
Bath Place N1 ... **241** F4
Bath Street EC1 ... **241** E4
Bath Terrace SE1 ... **245** E3
Bathurst Mews W2 ... **238** C1
Bathurst Street W2 ... **238** C1
Battle Bridge Lane SE1 ... **245** F4
Batty Street E1 ... **246** B4
Bayley Street WC1 ... **240** A2
Baylis Road SE1 ... **244** C3
Bayswater Road W2 ... **238** A1
Baythorne Street E3 ... **247** F4
Beaconsfield Road SE17 ... **245** F1
Beak Street W1 ... **240** A1
Bear Alley EC4 ... **241** D2
Farringdon Street
Bear Gardens SE1 ... **241** E1
Bear Lane SE1 ... **245** D4
Bear Street WC2 ... **240** B1
Cranbourn Street
Beatrice Place W8 ... **242** A2
Beauchamp Place SW3 ... **243** D3
Beauchamp Street EC1 ... **241** D3
Brooke Street
Beaufort Gardens SW3 ... **243** D3
Beaufort Street SW3 ... **242** B1
Beaumont Mews W1 ... **239** E2
Beaumont Place W1 ... **240** A3
Beaumont Street W1 ... **239** E3
Beccles Street E14 ... **247** F3
Beckway Street SE17 ... **245** F2
Bedale Street SE1 ... **245** E4
Borough High Street
Bedford Avenue WC1 ... **240** B2
Bedford Court WC2 ... **240** B1
Bedford Gardens W8 ... **242** A4
Bedford Place WC1 ... **240** B3
Bedford Row WC1 ... **240** C3
Bedford Square WC1 ... **240** B2
Bedford Street WC2 ... **240** B1
Bedford Way WC1 ... **240** B3
Bedfordbury WC2 ... **240** B1
Bedser Close SE11 ... **244** C1
Beech Street EC2 ... **241** E3
Beeston Place SW1 ... **243** F3
Bekesbourne Street E14 ... **247** E3
Belgrave Mews North SW1 ... **243** E3
Belgrave Mews South SW1 ... **243** E3
Belgrave Mews West SW1 ... **243** E3
Belgrave Place SW1 ... **243** E3
Belgrave Road SW1 ... **243** F2
Belgrave Square SW1 ... **243** E3
Belgrave Street E1 ... **247** E3
Belgrove Street WC1 ... **240** B4
Bell Lane E1 ... **246** A4
Bell Street NW1 ... **238** C3
Bell Yard WC2 ... **240** C2
Bellamy Close E14 ... **248** A3
Manilla Street
Belvedere Buildings SE1 ... **245** E3
Belvedere Road SE1 ... **244** C4
Ben Jonson Road E1 ... **247** E4
Ben Smith Way SE16 ... **246** C1
Benbow Street SE8 ... **248** A1
Bendall Mews W1 ... **239** D3
Bennet's Hill EC4 ... **241** E1
Castle Baynard Street
Benson Quay E1 ... **247** D3
Bentinck Mews W1 ... **239** E2
Marylebone Lane

Bentinck Street W1 ... **239** E2
Bere Street E1 ... **247** E3
Bergen Square SE16 ... **247** E1
Bering Square E14 ... **248** A1
Maritime Quay
Berkeley Gardens W8 ... **242** A4
Berkeley Mews W1 ... **239** D2
Berkeley Square W1 ... **239** F1
Berkeley Street W1 ... **239** F1
Bermondsey Square SE1 ... **246** A2
Long Lane
Bermondsey Street SE1 ... **246** A2
Bermondsey Wall East SE16 ... **246** B1
Bermondsey Wall West SE16 ... **246** B1
Bernard Street WC1 ... **240** B3
Berners Mews W1 ... **240** A2
Berners Street W1 ... **240** A2
Berry Street EC1 ... **241** E3
Berryfield Road SE17 ... **245** E1
Berwick Street W1 ... **240** A2
Bessborough Gardens SW1 ... **244** B2
Bessborough Place SW1 ... **244** A1
Bessborough Street SW1 ... **244** A1
Betterton Street WC2 ... **240** B2
Betts Street E1 ... **246** C3
Bevenden Street N1 ... **241** F4
Beverston Mews W1 ... **239** D2
Bevin Close SE16 ... **247** E2
Bevin Way WC1 ... **240** C4
Bevington Street SE16 ... **246** B1
Bevis Marks EC3 ... **246** A4
Bewley Street E1 ... **246** C3
Bickenhall Street W1 ... **239** D3
Bidborough Street WC1 ... **240** B4
Biddulph Road W9 ... **238** A4
Bigland Street E1 ... **246** C3
Billiter Square EC3 ... **246** A3
Fenchurch Avenue
Billiter Street EC3 ... **246** A3
Billson Street E14 ... **248** C2
Bina Gardens SW5 ... **242** B2
Bingham Place W1 ... **239** E3
Binney Street W1 ... **239** E1
Birchfield Street E14 ... **247** E3
Birchin Lane EC3 ... **241** F1
Bird Street W1 ... **239** E2
Birdcage Walk SW1 ... **244** A3
Birkenhead Street WC1 ... **240** B4
Bishop's Court EC4 ... **241** D2
Old Bailey
Bishop's Court WC2 ... **240** C2
Chancery Lane
Bishop's Terrace SE11 ... **245** D2
Bishops Bridge Road W2 ... **238** B2
Bishopsgate EC2 ... **241** F2
Bishopsgate Arcade EC2 ... **246** A4
Bishopsgate Churchyard EC2 ... **241** F2
Bittern Street SE1 ... **245** E3
Black Prince Road SE1 & SE11 ... **244** C2
Black Swan Yard SE1 ... **246** A2
Blackall Street EC2 ... **241** F3
Blackburne's Mews W1 ... **239** E1
Blackfriars Bridge EC4 & SE1 ... **241** D1
Blackfriars Lane EC4 ... **241** D1
Blackfriars Passage EC4 ... **241** D1
Blackfriars Road SE1 ... **245** D4
Blacklands Terrace SW3 ... **243** D2
Blackwall Tunnel E14 & SE10 ... **248** C4
Blackwood Street SE17 ... **245** F1
Blandford Square NW1 ... **239** D3
Blandford Street W1 ... **239** E2
Blasker Walk E14 ... **248** A1
Bleeding Heart Yard EC1 ... **241** D2
Greville Street
Blenheim Street W1 ... **239** F1
New Bond Street
Bletchley Street N1 ... **241** E4
Blithfield Street W8 ... **242** A3
Blomfield Road W9 ... **238** A3
Blomfield Street EC2 ... **241** F2
Blomfield Villas W2 ... **238** B2
Bloomburg Street SW1 ... **243** F2
Vauxhall Bridge Road
Bloomfield Place W1 ... **239** F1
Bourdon Street
Bloomfield Terrace SW1 ... **243** E2
Bloomsbury Court WC1 ... **240** B2
High Holborn
Bloomsbury Place WC1 ... **240** B3
Southampton Row
Bloomsbury Square WC1 ... **240** B2
Bloomsbury Street WC1 ... **240** B2
Bloomsbury Way WC1 ... **240** B2
Blount Street E14 ... **247** E3
Blue Anchor Yard E1 ... **246** B3
Blue Ball Yard SW1 ... **244** A4
St James's Street
Blyth Close E14 ... **248** C2
Boardwalk Place E14 ... **248** B4
Bolsover Street W1 ... **239** F3
Bolt Court EC4 ... **241** D2
Bolton Gardens SW5 ... **242** A2
Bolton Gardens Mews SW10 ... **242** B1
Bolton Street W1 ... **243** F4
Boltons Place SW10 ... **242** B2
Bond Way SW8 ... **244** B1
Bonding Yard Walk SE16 ... **247** E1
Bonhill Street EC2 ... **241** F3
Bonnington Square SW8 ... **244** C1
Booker Close E14 ... **247** F4
Boot Street N1 ... **241** F4
Booth's Place W1 ... **239** F2
Wells Street
Boreas Walk N1 ... **241** E4
Nelson Place
Borough High Street SE1 ... **245** E3
Borough Road SE1 ... **245** E3
Borrett Close SE17 ... **245** E1
Borthwick Street SE8 ... **248** A1
Boscobel Place SW1 ... **243** E2
Boscobel Street NW8 ... **238** C3

Boss Street SE1 ... **246** A2
Boston Place NW1 ... **238** D3
Boswell Court WC1 ... **240** B3
Boswell Street
Boswell Street WC1 ... **240** B3
Botolph Lane EC3 ... **241** F1
Bott's Mews W2 ... **238** A2
Boulcott Street E1 ... **247** E3
Boundary Lane SE17 ... **245** E1
Boundary Road SE1 ... **245** D4
Bourdon Street W1 ... **239** F1
Bourlet Close W1 ... **239** F2
Bourne Street SW1 ... **243** E2
Bourne Terrace W2 ... **238** A2
Bouverie Street EC4 ... **241** D1
Bow Lane EC4 ... **241** E1
Bow Street WC2 ... **240** B2
Bowden Street SE11 ... **245** D1
Bower Street E1 ... **247** D3
Bowling Green Lane EC1 ... **241** D3
Bowling Green Place SE1 ... **245** F4
Newcomen Street
Bowling Green Street SE11 ... **244** C1
Bowling Green Walk N1 ... **241** F4
Boyd Street E1 ... **246** B3
Boyfield Street SE1 ... **245** D3
Boyle Street W1 ... **239** F1
Savile Row
Boyson Road SE17 ... **245** E1
Brackley Street EC1 ... **241** E3
Brad Street SE1 ... **245** D4
Braden Street W9 ... **238** A3
Bradenham Close SE17 ... **245** F1
Braganza Street SE17 ... **245** D1
Braham Street E1 ... **246** B3
Bramerton Street SW3 ... **242** C1
Bramham Gardens SW5 ... **242** A2
Branch Road E14 ... **247** E3
Brandon Street SE17 ... **245** E2
Brangton Road SE11 ... **244** C1
Brass Tally Alley SE16 ... **247** E1
Bray Crescent SE16 ... **247** D2
Bray Place SW3 ... **243** D2
Bread Street EC4 ... **241** E1
Bream's Buildings EC ... **240** C2
Brechin Place SW7 ... **242** B2
Breezer's Hill E1 ... **246** C3
Bremner Road SW7 ... **242** B3
Brendon Street W1 ... **239** D2
Brenton Street E14 ... **247** E4
Bressenden Place SW1 ... **243** F3
Brettell Street SE17 ... **245** F1
Brewer Street W1 ... **240** A1
Brewers' Green SW1 ... **244** A3
Caxton Street
Brewhouse Lane E1 ... **246** C2
Brewhouse Walk SE16 ... **247** E2
Brick Court WC2 ... **240** C2
Middle Temple Lane
Brick Street W1 ... **243** E4
Bride Lane EC4 ... **241** D2
Bridewain Street SE1 ... **246** B1
Bridewell Place EC4 ... **241** D1
Bridford Mews W1 ... **239** F3
Bridge House Quay E14 ... **248** C1
Bridge Place SW1 ... **243** F2
Bridge Street SW1 ... **244** B3
Bridge Yard SE1 ... **245** F4
Bridgeport Place E14 ... **246** B2
Kennet Street
Bridgewater Square EC2 ... **241** E3
Beech Street
Bridgewater Street EC2 ... **241** E3
Beech Street
Bridgeway Street NW1 ... **240** A2
Bridle Lane W1 ... **240** A1
Bridstow Place W2 ... **238** A2
Brightlingsea Place E14 ... **247** F3
Brill Place NW1 ... **240** A4
Briset Street EC1 ... **241** D3
Bristol Gardens W9 ... **238** A3
Bristol Mews W9 ... **238** A3
Britannia Road E14 ... **248** A2
Britannia Street WC1 ... **240** C4
Britannia Walk N1 ... **241** F4
Britten Street SW3 ... **242** C1
Britton Street EC1 ... **241** D3
Broad Court WC2 ... **240** B2
Broad Sanctuary SW1 ... **244** B3
Broad Walk W2 ... **243** E4
Broadbent Street W1 ... **239** F1
Broadley Street NW8 ... **238** C4
Broadley Terrace NW1 ... **239** D3
Broadstone Place W1 ... **239** E2
Broadwall SE1 ... **245** D4
Broadway SW1 ... **244** A3
Broadwick Street W1 ... **240** A1
Brockham Street SE1 ... **245** E3
Brodlove Lane E1 ... **247** D3
Bromley Street E1 ... **247** E4
Brompton Place SW3 ... **243** D3
Brompton Road SW3 ... **243** D3
Brompton Square SW3 ... **242** C3
Bronti Close SE17 ... **245** E1
Brook Drive SE11 ... **245** D2
Brook Gate W1 ... **239** D1
Brook Mews North W2 ... **238** B1
Brook Street W1 ... **239** E1
Brook Street W2 ... **238** C1
Brook's Mews W1 ... **239** F1
Brooke Street EC1 ... **241** D2
Brooke's Court EC1 ... **240** C3
Brooke's Market EC1 ... **241** D2
Brooke Street
Brown Hart Gardens W1 ... **239** E1
Brown Street W1 ... **239** D2
Browning Close W9 ... **238** B3
Browning Street SE17 ... **245** E2
Brownlow Mews WC1 ... **240** C3
Brownlow Street WC1 ... **240** C2
Brune Street E1 ... **246** A4

Brunel Road SE16 ...... 247 D1
Brunswick Gardens W8 ...... 242 A4
Brunswick Mews W1 ...... 239 D2
Brunswick Place N1 ...... 241 F4
Brunswick Quay SE16 ...... 247 D3
Brunswick Square WC1 ...... 240 B3
Brunton Place E14 ...... 247 E3
Brushfield Street E1 ...... 246 A4
Bruton Lane W1 ...... 239 F1
Bruton Place W1 ...... 239 F1
Bruton Street W1 ...... 239 F1
Bryan Road SE16 ...... 247 F2
Bryanston Mews East W1 ...... 239 D2
Bryanston Mews West W1 ...... 239 D2
Bryanston Place W1 ...... 239 D2
Bryanston Square W1 ...... 239 D2
Bryanston Street W1 ...... 239 D2
Buck Hill Walk W2 ...... 238 C1
Buck Street WC2 ...... 240 B1
Buckingham Gate SW1 ...... 243 F3
Buckingham Palace Road SW1 ...... 243 F2
Buckingham Place SW1 ...... 243 F3
Buckland Street N1 ...... 241 F4
Buckle Street E1 ...... 246 B4
Bucklersbury EC4 ...... 241 E2
Bucknall Street WC2 ...... 240 B2
Buckters Rents SE16 ...... 247 D3
Budge's Walk W2 ...... 238 B4
Bulleid Way SW1 ...... 243 F2
Bulstrode Place W1 ...... 239 E2
    Marylebone Lane
Bulstrode Street W1 ...... 239 E2
Bunhill Row EC1 ...... 241 F3
Bunhouse Place SW1 ...... 243 E2
Burbage Close SE1 ...... 245 F3
Burdett Street SE1 ...... 245 D3
Burge Street SE1 ...... 245 F3
Burgess Street E14 ...... 247 F4
Burgon Street EC4 ...... 241 E2
    Carter Lane
Burleigh Street WC2 ...... 240 B1
Burlington Arcade W1 ...... 239 F1
Burlington Gardens W1 ...... 239 F1
Burne Street NW1 ...... 238 C3
Burnsall Street SW3 ...... 243 D1
Burnside Close SE16 ...... 247 E2
Burr Close E1 ...... 246 B2
Burrell Street SE1 ...... 245 D4
Burrells Wharf Square E14 ...... 248 A1
Burrows Mews SE1 ...... 245 D4
Bursar Street SE1 ...... 246 A2
    Tooley Street
Burslem Street E1 ...... 246 C3
Burton Grove SE17 ...... 245 F1
Burton Street WC1 ...... 240 B4
Burwell Close E1 ...... 246 C3
Burwood Place W2 ...... 239 D2
Bury Close SE16 ...... 247 E2
Bury Court EC3 ...... 246 A4
Bury Place WC1 ...... 240 B2
Bury Street EC3 ...... 246 A3
Bury Street SW1 ...... 244 A4
Bury Walk SW3 ...... 242 C2
Bush Lane EC4 ...... 241 E1
Bushell Street E1 ...... 246 B2
    Wapping High Street
Butcher Row E1 ...... 247 E3
Bute Street SW7 ...... 242 C1
Butler Place SW1 ...... 243 F3
    Buckingham Gate
Butterfield Close SE16 ...... 246 C1
Buttesland Street N1 ...... 241 F4
Byelands Close SE16 ...... 247 E2
Byfield Close SE16 ...... 247 F2
Byng Place WC1 ...... 240 A3
Byng Street E14 ...... 248 A3
Byward Street EC3 ...... 246 A3
Bywater Place SE16 ...... 247 E3
Bywater Street SW3 ...... 243 D2

C

Cabbell Street NW1 ...... 238 C2
Cable Street E1 ...... 246 B3
Cabot Square E14 ...... 248 A4
Cadiz Street SE17 ...... 245 E1
Cadogan Gardens SW3 ...... 243 D2
Cadogan Gate SW1 ...... 243 E2
Cadogan Lane SW1 ...... 243 E3
Cadogan Square SW1 ...... 243 D2
Cadogan Street SW3 ...... 243 D2
Cahill Street EC1 ...... 241 E3
    Dufferin Street
Cahir Street E14 ...... 248 A2
Cale Street SW3 ...... 242 C2
Caleb Street SE1 ...... 245 E4
    Marshalsea Road
Caledonia Street N1 ...... 240 B4
Caledonian Road N1 & N7 ...... 240 B4
Caledonian Wharf E14 ...... 248 C2
Callingham Close E14 ...... 247 F4
Callow Street SW3 ...... 242 B1
Calthorpe Street WC1 ...... 240 C4
Camberwell Road SE5 ...... 245 E1
Cambridge Circus WC2 ...... 240 B1
Cambridge Gate NW1 ...... 239 F3
Cambridge Gate Mews NW1 ...... 239 F4
    Albany Street
Cambridge Place W8 ...... 242 B3
Cambridge Road NW6 ...... 238 A4
Cambridge Square W2 ...... 238 C2
Cambridge Street SW1 ...... 243 F2
Cambridge Terrace Mews NW1 ...... 239 F4
    Chester Gate
Camdenhurst Street E14 ...... 247 E4
Camera Place SW10 ...... 242 B1
Cameron Place E1 ...... 246 C4
Camomile Street EC3 ...... 246 A4
Campden Grove W8 ...... 242 A4
Campden Hill Road W8 ...... 242 A3
Camperdown Street E1 ...... 246 B3
Canada Square E14 ...... 248 B4
Canada Street SE16 ...... 247 E1
Canal Street SE5 ...... 245 F1
Candover Street W1 ...... 239 F2
    Foley Street
Canning Passage W8 ...... 242 B3
Canning Place W8 ...... 242 B3
Cannon Beck Road SE16 ...... 247 D2
Cannon Drive E14 ...... 247 F3
Cannon Row SW1 ...... 244 B3
Cannon Street EC4 ...... 241 E2
Cannon Street Road E1 ...... 246 C4
Canterbury Place SE17 ...... 245 E2
Canvey Street SE1 ...... 245 E4
Cape Yard E1 ...... 246 B3
Capland Street NW8 ...... 238 C3
Capper Street WC1 ...... 240 A3
Capstan Square E14 ...... 248 C3
Capstan Way SE16 ...... 247 E2
Caravel Close E14 ...... 248 A3
Carbis Road E14 ...... 247 F4
Carburton Street W1 ...... 239 F3

Cardale Street E14 ...... 248 B3
    Plevina Street
Cardigan Street SE11 ...... 244 C1
Cardington Street NW1 ...... 240 A4
Carey Lane EC2 ...... 241 E2
Carey Street WC2 ...... 240 C2
Carlisle Avenue EC3 ...... 246 A3
Carlisle Lane SE1 ...... 244 C3
Carlisle Place SW1 ...... 243 F2
Carlisle Street W1 ...... 240 A2
Carlos Place W1 ...... 239 E1
Carlton Gardens SW1 ...... 244 A4
Carlton House Terrace SW1 ...... 244 A4
Carlton Vale NW6 ...... 238 A4
Carlyle Square SW3 ...... 242 C1
Carmelite Street EC4 ...... 241 D1
Carnaby Street W1 ...... 240 A1
Caroline Place Mews W2 ...... 238 A1
Caroline Place W2 ...... 238 A1
Caroline Street E1 ...... 247 E3
Caroline Terrace SW1 ...... 243 E2
Carpenter Street W1 ...... 239 E1
Carr Street E14 ...... 247 E4
Carrick Mews SE8 ...... 248 A1
Carrington Street W1 ...... 243 E4
    Shepherd Street
Carter Lane EC4 ...... 241 E2
Carter Place SE17 ...... 245 F1
Carter Street SE17 ...... 245 E1
Carteret Street SW1 ...... 244 A3
Carthusian Street EC1 ...... 241 E3
Cartier Circle E14 ...... 248 B4
Carting Lane WC2 ...... 240 C1
Cartwright Gardens WC1 ...... 240 B4
Cartwright Street E1 ...... 246 B3
Casson Street E1 ...... 246 B4
Castalia Square E14 ...... 248 B3
Castellain Road W9 ...... 238 A3
Castle Baynard Street EC4 ...... 241 E1
Castle Lane SW1 ...... 244 A3
Castle Yard SE1 ...... 245 D4
Castlebrook Close SE11 ...... 245 D2
    Brook Drive
Castlereagh Street W1 ...... 239 D2
Castor Lane E14 ...... 248 A4
Catesby Street SE17 ...... 245 F2
Cathay Street SE16 ...... 246 C1
Cathcart Road SW10 ...... 242 B1
Cathedral Piazza SW1 ...... 243 F3
Cathedral Street SE1 ...... 245 F4
    Winchester Walk
Catherine Place SW1 ...... 243 F3
Catherine Street WC2 ...... 240 C1
Catherine Wheel Alley E1 ...... 246 A4
Catherine Wheel Yard SW1 ...... 244 A4
    Little St James's Street
Cato Street W1 ...... 239 D2
Caton Street W1 ...... 240 C2
Causton Street SW1 ...... 244 A2
Cavell Street E1 ...... 246 C4
Cavendish Avenue NW8 ...... 238 C4
Cavendish Close NW8 ...... 238 C4
Cavendish Mews North W1 ...... 239 F3
    Hallam Street
Cavendish Mews South W1 ...... 239 F2
    Hallam Street
Cavendish Place W1 ...... 239 F2
Cavendish Square W1 ...... 239 F2
Caversham Street SW3 ...... 243 D1
Caxton Street SW1 ...... 244 A3
Cayton Place EC1 ...... 241 E4
    Cayton Street
Cayton Street EC1 ...... 241 E4
Cecil Court WC2 ...... 240 B1
    St Martin's Lane
Centaur Street SE1 ...... 244 C3
Central Street EC1 ...... 241 E4
Chadwell Street EC1 ...... 241 D4
Chadwick Street SW1 ...... 244 A3
Chagford Street NW1 ...... 239 D3
Chalton Street NW1 ...... 240 A4
Chamber Street E1 ...... 246 B3
Chambers Street SE16 ...... 246 B1
Chancel Street SE1 ...... 245 D4
Chancellor Passage E14 ...... 248 A4
    South Colonnade
Chancery Lane WC2 ...... 240 C2
Chandler Street E1 ...... 246 C2
Chandos Place WC2 ...... 240 B1
Chandos Street W1 ...... 239 F2
Chantry Square W8 ...... 242 A3
Chapel Court SE1 ...... 245 E4
Chapel House Street E14 ...... 248 B1
Chapel Place W1 ...... 239 F2
Chapel Side W2 ...... 238 A1
Chapel Street NW1 ...... 238 C2
Chapel Street SW1 ...... 243 E3
Chapman Street E1 ...... 246 C3
Chapter Road SE17 ...... 245 E1
Chapter Street SW1 ...... 244 A2
Chapter Terrace SE17 ...... 245 D1
Chargrove Close SE16 ...... 247 D2
Charing Cross Road WC2 ...... 240 B1
Charles II Street SW1 ...... 244 A4
Charles Square N1 ...... 241 F4
Charles Street W1 ...... 243 E4
Charleston Street SE17 ...... 245 E2
Charlie Chaplin Walk SE1 ...... 244 C4
    Waterloo Road
Charlotte Place SW1 ...... 243 F2
    Wilton Road
Charlotte Road EC2 ...... 241 F4
Charlotte Street W1 ...... 240 A3
Charlwood Street SW1 ...... 244 A1
Charnwood Gardens E14 ...... 248 A2
Chart Street N1 ...... 241 F4
Charterhouse Square EC1 ...... 241 E3
Charterhouse Street EC1 ...... 241 D2
Chaseley Street E14 ...... 247 E4
Chatham Street SE17 ...... 245 F2
Cheapside EC4 ...... 241 E2
Chelsea Bridge SW1 & SW8 ...... 243 E1
Chelsea Bridge Road SW1 ...... 243 E1
Chelsea Embankment SW3 ...... 243 D1
Chelsea Manor Gardens SW3 ...... 243 D1
Chelsea Manor Street SW3 ...... 243 D1
Chelsea Park Gardens SW3 ...... 242 C1
Cheltenham Terrace SW3 ...... 243 D2
Chenies Mews WC1 ...... 240 A3
Chenies Street WC1 ...... 240 A3
Cheniston Gardens W8 ...... 242 A3
Chepstow Place W2 ...... 238 A1
Chepstow Road W2 ...... 238 A2
Chequer Street EC1 ...... 241 E3
Cherbury Street N1 ...... 241 F4
Cherry Garden Street SE16 ...... 246 C1
Cherry Tree Terrace SE1 ...... 246 A2
Chesham Place SW1 ...... 243 E3
Chesham Street SW1 ...... 243 E3
Chester Close North NW1 ...... 239 F4
Chester Close South NW1 ...... 239 F4
Chester Court NW1 ...... 239 F4
    Albany Street
Chester Gate NW1 ...... 239 F4
Chester Mews SW1 ...... 243 E3
Chester Place NW1 ...... 239 F4

Chester Row SW1 ...... 243 E2
Chester Square SW1 ...... 243 E2
Chester Street SW1 ...... 243 E3
Chester Terrace NW1 ...... 239 F4
Chester Way SE11 ...... 245 D2
Chesterfield Gardens W1 ...... 243 E4
Chesterfield Hill W1 ...... 239 E1
Chesterfield Street W1 ...... 243 E4
Cheval Place SW7 ...... 243 D3
Cheval Street E14 ...... 248 A3
Cheyne Gardens SW3 ...... 242 D1
Cheyne Walk SW3 & SW10 ...... 242 C1
Chicheley Street SE1 ...... 244 C4
Chichester Parade E14 ...... 248 C2
Chichester Rents WC2 ...... 240 C2
    Chancery Lane
Chichester Road W2 ...... 238 A3
Chichester Street SW1 ...... 244 A1
Chicksand Street E1 ...... 246 B4
Chigwell Hill E1 ...... 246 C3
    The Highway
Child's Place SW5 ...... 242 A2
Child's Street SW5 ...... 242 A2
Chiltern Street W1 ...... 239 E3
Chilworth Mews W2 ...... 238 B2
Chilworth Street W2 ...... 238 B2
Chipka Street E14 ...... 248 B3
Chiswell Street EC1 ...... 241 E3
Chitty Street W1 ...... 240 A3
Christchurch Street SW3 ...... 243 D1
Christian Court SE16 ...... 247 E3
Christian Street E1 ...... 246 C3
Christopher Close SE16 ...... 246 D1
Christopher Street EC2 ...... 241 F3
Chudleigh Street E1 ...... 247 E4
Chumleigh Street SE5 ...... 245 F1
Church Place SW1 ...... 243 F4
    Piccadilly
Church Street NW8 ...... 238 C3
Church Yard Row SE11 ...... 245 D2
Churchill Gardens Road SW1 ...... 243 F1
Churchill Place E14 ...... 248 B4
Churchway NW1 ...... 240 A4
Churton Street SW1 ...... 244 A2
Cinnamon Street E1 ...... 246 C2
Circus Mews W1 ...... 239 D3
    Enford Street
Circus Place EC2 ...... 241 F2
    Finsbury Circus
Circus Road NW8 ...... 238 C4
Cirencester Street W2 ...... 238 A3
Citadel Place SE11 ...... 244 C2
City Garden Row N1 ...... 241 E4
City Road N1 ...... 241 F3
Clabon Mews SW1 ...... 243 D2
Clack Street SE16 ...... 247 D1
Claire Place E14 ...... 248 A3
Clanricarde Gardens W2 ...... 238 A1
Clare Market WC2 ...... 240 C2
Claremont Close N1 ...... 241 D4
Claremont Square N1 ...... 241 D4
Clarence Gardens NW1 ...... 239 F4
Clarence Mews SE16 ...... 247 D2
Clarendon Close W2 ...... 238 C1
Clarendon Gardens W9 ...... 238 B3
Clarendon Place W2 ...... 238 C1
Clarendon Road W11 ...... 243 F1
Clarendon Street SW1 ...... 243 F1
Clarendon Terrace W9 ...... 238 B3
Clareville Grove SW7 ...... 242 B2
Clareville Street SW7 ...... 242 B2
Clarges Mews W1 ...... 243 E4
Clarges Street W1 ...... 243 F4
Clark Street E1 ...... 246 C4
Clark's Orchard SE16 ...... 246 C1
Claude Street E14 ...... 248 A2
Clave Street E1 ...... 246 C2
Claverton Street SW1 ...... 244 A1
Clay Street W1 ...... 239 D2
Clayton Street SE11 ...... 244 C1
Clearbrook Way E1 ...... 247 D4
Clearwell Drive W9 ...... 238 A3
Cleaver Square SE11 ...... 245 D1
Cleaver Street SE11 ...... 245 D1
Clegg Street E1 ...... 246 C2
Clemence Street E14 ...... 247 F4
Clement's Inn WC2 ...... 240 C2
Clement's Road SE16 ...... 246 C1
Clements Lane EC4 ...... 241 F1
Clenston Mews W1 ...... 239 D2
Clere Street EC2 ...... 241 F3
Clerkenwell Close EC1 ...... 241 D3
Clerkenwell Green EC1 ...... 241 D3
Clerkenwell Road EC1 ...... 240 C3
Cleveland Gardens W2 ...... 238 B2
Cleveland Mews W1 ...... 239 F3
Cleveland Place SW1 ...... 244 A4
    King Street
Cleveland Row SW1 ...... 244 A4
Cleveland Square W2 ...... 238 B2
Cleveland Street W1 ...... 239 F3
Cleveland Terrace W2 ...... 238 B2
Clifford Street W1 ...... 239 F1
Clifton Gardens W9 ...... 238 B3
Clifton Place W2 ...... 238 C1
Clifton Place W9 ...... 238 B3
Clifton Street EC2 ...... 241 F3
Clifton Villas W9 ...... 238 B3
Clink Street SE1 ...... 245 E4
Clipper Close SE16 ...... 247 D2
    Kinburn Street
Clipstone Mews W1 ...... 239 F3
Clipstone Street W1 ...... 239 F3
Cliveden Place SW1 ...... 243 E2
Cloak Lane EC4 ...... 241 E1
Cloth Fair EC1 ...... 241 E2
Cloth Street EC1 ...... 241 E2
Clunbury Street N1 ...... 241 F4
    Cherbury Street
Cluny Place SE1 ...... 245 F3
Coach & Horses Yard W1 ...... 239 F1
    Old Burlington Street
Cobb Street E1 ...... 246 A4
Cobourg Street NW1 ...... 240 A4
Cock Lane EC1 ...... 241 D2
Cockpit Yard WC1 ...... 240 C3
Cockspur Street SW1 ...... 244 B4
Codling Close E1 ...... 246 C1
Coin Street SE1 ...... 245 D4
Coke Street E1 ...... 246 B4
Colbeck Mews SW7 ...... 242 B2
Colchester Street E1 ...... 246 B4
Coldbath Square EC1 ...... 240 C3
Coldharbour E14 ...... 248 C4
Cole Street SE1 ...... 245 E3
Colebrooke Row N1 ...... 241 D4
Coleherne Mews SW10 ...... 242 A1
Coleherne Road SW10 ...... 242 A1
Coleman Street EC2 ...... 241 E2
Coley Street WC1 ...... 240 C3
College Hill EC4 ...... 241 E1
    College Street
College Street EC4 ...... 241 E1
Collett Road SE16 ...... 246 C1
Collier Street N1 ...... 240 C4
Collingham Gardens SW5 ...... 242 A2
Collingham Place SW5 ...... 242 A2
Collingham Road SW5 ...... 242 A2
Collinson Street SE1 ...... 245 E3

Colnbrook Street SE1 ...... 245 D3
Colombo Street SE1 ...... 245 D4
Colonnade WC1 ...... 240 B3
Colworth Grove SE17 ...... 245 E2
Commercial Road E1 & E14 ...... 246 B4
Commercial Street E1 ...... 246 A4
Compton Passage EC1 ...... 241 D3
Compton Place WC1 ...... 240 B3
Compton Street EC1 ...... 241 D3
Comus Place SE17 ...... 245 F2
Concert Hall Approach SE1 ...... 244 C4
Conder Street E14 ...... 247 E4
Conduit Mews W2 ...... 238 C4
    Salmon Lane
Conduit Place W2 ...... 238 C2
Conduit Street W1 ...... 239 F1
Congreve Street SE17 ...... 245 F2
Connaught Place W2 ...... 239 D1
Connaught Square W2 ...... 239 D1
Connaught Street W2 ...... 238 C2
Cons Street SE1 ...... 245 D4
Constitution Hill SW1 ...... 243 E3
Content Street SE17 ...... 245 E2
Conway Street W1 ...... 239 F3
Cook's Road E15 ...... 245 D1
Cookham Crescent SE16 ...... 247 D2
Coombs Street N1 ...... 241 E4
Cooper Close SE1 ...... 245 D3
Cooper's Row EC3 ...... 246 A3
Cope Place W8 ...... 242 A3
Copeland Drive E14 ...... 248 B2
Copenhagen Place E14 ...... 247 F3
Copley Close SE17 ...... 245 D1
Copperfield Street SE1 ...... 245 E4
Copthall Avenue EC2 ...... 241 F2
Coptic Street WC1 ...... 240 B2
Coral Street SE1 ...... 245 D3
Coram Street WC1 ...... 240 B3
Cord Way E14 ...... 248 A3
Cork Square E1 ...... 246 C2
Cork Street W1 ...... 239 F1
Corlett Street NW1 ...... 238 C3
    Bell Street
Corner House Street WC2 ...... 244 B4
    Northumberland Street
Cornhill EC3 ...... 241 F2
Cornwall Gardens SW7 ...... 242 B3
Cornwall Gardens Walk SW7 ...... 242 A2
Cornwall Mews South SW7 ...... 242 B2
Cornwall Mews West SW7 ...... 242 A2
Cornwall Road SE1 ...... 244 C4
Cornwall Terrace NW1 ...... 239 E3
Cornwood Drive E1 ...... 247 D4
Coronet Street N1 ...... 241 F4
Corporation Row EC1 ...... 241 D3
Corsham Street N1 ...... 241 F4
Cosmo Place WC1 ...... 240 B3
Cosser Street SE1 ...... 244 C3
Cosway Street NW1 ...... 239 D3
Cotham Street SE17 ...... 245 E2
Cottage Place SW3 ...... 242 C3
Cottesloe Mews SE1 ...... 245 D3
Cottesmore Gardens W8 ...... 242 B3
Cottingham Close SE11 ...... 245 D2
Cottington Street SE11 ...... 245 D2
Cottons Lane SE1 ...... 245 F4
Counter Street SE1 ...... 245 F4
County Street SE1 ...... 245 E2
Court Street E1 ...... 246 C4
Courtenay Square SE11 ...... 244 C1
Courtenay Street SE11 ...... 244 C1
Courtfield Gardens SW5 ...... 242 A2
Courtfield Road SW7 ...... 242 B2
Cousin Lane EC4 ...... 241 F1
Coventry Street W1 ...... 240 A1
Coverley Close E1 ...... 246 B4
Cowcross Street EC1 ...... 241 D3
Cowley Street SW1 ...... 244 B3
Cowper Street EC2 ...... 241 F3
Coxon Place SE1 ...... 246 A1
Crace Street NW1 ...... 240 A4
Crail Row SE17 ...... 245 F2
Cramer Street W1 ...... 239 E2
Crampton Street SE17 ...... 245 E2
Cranbourn Street WC2 ...... 240 B1
Crane Street SE10 ...... 248 C1
Cranford Street E1 ...... 247 E3
Cranley Gardens SW7 ...... 242 B2
Cranley Mews SW7 ...... 242 B2
Cranley Place SW7 ...... 242 C2
Cranmer Court SW3 ...... 243 D2
Cranwood Street EC1 ...... 241 F4
Craven Hill W2 ...... 238 B1
Craven Hill Gardens W2 ...... 238 B1
Craven Hill Mews W2 ...... 238 B1
Craven Road W2 ...... 238 B1
Craven Street WC2 ...... 240 B1
Craven Terrace W2 ...... 238 B1
Crawford Passage EC1 ...... 241 D3
Crawford Place W1 ...... 239 D2
Crawford Street W1 ...... 239 D2
Creasy Street SE1 ...... 245 F3
    Swan Mead
Creechurch Lane EC3 ...... 246 A3
Creechurch Place EC3 ...... 246 A3
Creed Lane EC4 ...... 241 D2
Crescent EC3 ...... 246 A3
    America Square
Crescent Place SW3 ...... 243 D2
Crescent Row EC1 ...... 241 E3
Cresswell Place SW10 ...... 242 B1
Cressy Place E1 ...... 247 D4
Crestfield Street WC1 ...... 240 B4
Cricketers' Court SE11 ...... 245 D1
    Kennington Park Road
Crimscott Street SE1 ...... 246 A1
Cripplegate Street EC1 ...... 239 E3
    Viscount Street
Crispin Street E1 ...... 246 A4
Crofts Street E1 ...... 246 B3
Cromer Street WC1 ...... 240 B3
Crompton Street W2 ...... 238 B3
Cromwell Crescent SW5 ...... 242 A2
Cromwell Mews SW7 ...... 242 C2
Cromwell Place SW7 ...... 242 C2
Cromwell Road SW7 & SW5 ...... 242 A1
Crondall Street N1 ...... 241 F4
Crosby Row SE1 ...... 245 F3
Crosby Square EC3 ...... 241 F2
    Great St Helen's
Cross Keys Close W1 ...... 239 E2
    Marylebone Lane
Cross Lane EC3 ...... 246 A3
    St Dunstan's Hill
Crosslet Street SE17 ...... 245 F2
Crosswall EC3 ...... 246 A3
Crowder Street E1 ...... 246 C3
Crown Court WC2 ...... 240 B2
Crown Office Row EC4 ...... 241 D1
Crown Passage SW1 ...... 244 A4
Crown Place EC2 ...... 241 F3
Crucifix Lane SE1 ...... 246 A2
Cruikshank Street WC1 ...... 240 C4
Crutched Friars EC3 ...... 246 A3
Cuba Street E14 ...... 248 A4
Cubitt Steps E14 ...... 248 A4
Cubitt Street WC1 ...... 240 C4
Cubitts Yard WC2 ...... 240 B1
    James Street
Culford Gardens SW3 ...... 243 D2

Culling Road SE16 247
Cullum Street EC3 246
Culross Street W1 239
Culworth Street NW8 238
Cumberland Gardens WC1 240
    Great Percy Street
Cumberland Gate W1 & W2 239
Cumberland Market NW1 239
Cumberland Street SW1 243
Cumberland Terrace NW1 239
Cumberland Terrace Mews NW1 239
    Albany Street
Cumming Street N1 240
Cundy Street SW1 243
Cunningham Place NW8 238
Cureton Street SW1 244
Curlew Street SE1 246
Cursitor Street EC4 240
Curzon Gate W1 243
Curzon Place W1 243
Curzon Street W1 243
Cuthbert Street W2 238
Cutler Street E1 246
Cutlers Square E14 248
Cyclops Mews E14 248
Cynthia Street N1 240
Cypress Place W1 240
Cyrus Street EC1 241
Czar Street SE8 248

D

D'Arblay Street W1 240
D'Oyley Street SW1 243
Da Gama Place E14 248
    Maritime Quay
Dacre Street SW1 244
Dalgleish Street E14 247
Dallington Street EC1 241
Damien Street E1 246
Dane Street WC1 240
Dante Road SE11 245
Daplyn Street E1 246
Dark House Walk EC3 241
Dartford Street SE17 245
Dartmouth Street SW1 244
Darwin Street SE17 245
Date Street SE17 245
Davenant Street E1 246
Daventry Street NW1 238
Davidge Street SE1 245
Davies Mews W1 239
Davies Street W1 239
Dawes Street SE17 245
Dawson Place W2 238
De Laune Street SE17 245
De Vere Gardens W8 242
De Walden Street W1 239
    Westmorland Street
Deacon Way SE17 245
Deal Porters Way SE16 247
Deal Street E1 246
Dean Bradley Street SW1 244
Dean Close SE16 247
Dean Farrar Street SW1 244
Dean Ryle Street SW1 244
Dean Stanley Street SW1 244
    Millbank
Dean Street W1 240
Dean Trench Street SW1 244
Dean's Buildings SE17 245
Dean's Court EC4 241
    Carter Lane
Dean's Mews W1 239
Deancross Street E1 246
Deanery Street W1 243
Decima Street SE1 245
Deck Close SE16 247
Defoe Close SE16 247
Delamere Terrace W2 238
Delaware Road W9 238
Dellow Street E1 246
Delverton Road SE17 245
Denbigh Street SW1 244
Denman Street W1 240
Denmark Place WC2 240
    Charing Cross Road
Denmark Street WC2 240
Denning Close NW8 238
Denny Crescent SE11 245
Denny Street SE11 245
Denyer Street SW3 243
Deptford Green SE8 248
Derby Gate SW1 244
Derby Street W1 243
Dering Street W1 239
Deverell Street SE1 245
Devereux Court WC2 240
    Strand
Devonport Street E1 247
Devonshire Close W1 239
Devonshire Mews South W1 239
Devonshire Mews West W1 239
Devonshire Mews W1 239
Devonshire Place W8 242
    St Mary's Place
Devonshire Place Mews W1 239
Devonshire Row EC2 246
Devonshire Square EC2 246
Devonshire Street W1 239
Devonshire Terrace W2 238
Diadem Court W1 240
    Dean Street
Dickens Square SE1 245
Dilke Street SW3 243
Dingle Gardens E14 248
Dingley Place EC1 241
Dingley Road EC1 241
Disney Place SE1 245
Disney Street SE1 245
    Redcross Way
Distaff Lane EC4 241
Distin Street SE11 245
Dixon's Alley SE16 246
    West Lane
Dock Hill Avenue SE16 247
Dock Street E1 246
Dockers Tanner Road E14 248
Dockhead SE1 246
Dockley Road SE16 246
Dod Street E14 247
Doddington Grove SE17 245
Doddington Place SE17 245
Dodson Street SE1 245
Dolben Street SE1 245
Dolland Street SE11 244
Dolphin Close SE16 247
Dombey Street WC1 240
Domingo Street EC1 241
    Old Street
Dominion Street EC2 241
Donegal Street N1 240
Donne Place SW3 243
Doon Street SE1 244

...ra Street E14 ... 247 F4
...ic Way NW1 ... 240 A4
...rrington Street EC1 ... 241 D3
Brooke Street
...rset Close NW1 ... 239 D3
...rset Mews SW1 ... 243 E3
...rset Rise EC4 ... 241 D1
...rset Square NW1 ... 239 D3
...rset Street NW1 ... 239 D2
...ughty Street WC1 ... 240 C3
...ughty Avenue W1 ... 240 C3
...uglas Mews NW1 ... 244 A2
Douglas Street
...uglas Street SW1 ... 244 A2
...uro Place W8 ... 242 B3
...ve Mews SW5 ... 242 B2
...ve Walk SW1 ... 243 E2
...vehouse Street SW3 ... 242 C1
...ver Street SW1 ... 239 F1
...wgate Hill EC4 ... 241 F1
...wn Street W1 ... 243 E4
...wnfield Close W9 ... 238 A3
...wning Street SW1 ... 244 B4
...wnton Road SE16 ... 247 E2
...yce Street EC1 ... 245 E4
...aco Street SE17 ... 245 E1
...ake Street WC1 ... 240 C2
...awdock Road SE10 ... 248 C4
...aycott Avenue SW3 ... 243 D2
...aycott Place SW3 ... 243 D2
...aycott Terrace SW3 ... 243 D2
...ayson Mews W8 ... 242 A3
...ayton Gardens SW10 ... 242 B1
...uid Street SE1 ... 246 A2
...um Street E1 ... 246 B4
...ummond Crescent NW1 ... 240 A4
...ummond Gate SW1 ... 244 A1
...ummond Road SE16 ... 246 C1
...ummond Street NW1 ... 239 F3
...ury Lane WC2 ... 240 B2
...yden Court SE11 ... 245 D2
...chess Mews W1 ... 239 F2
...chess Street W1 ... 239 F2
...chy Street SE1 ... 245 D4
...ck Lane W1 ... 240 A2
...dley Street W1 ... 238 B2
...dmaston Mews SW3 ... 242 C2
...fferin Street EC1 ... 241 E3
...four's Place W1 ... 240 A4
...gard Way SE11 ... 245 D2
Renfrew Road
...ke of Wellington Place SW1 ... 243 E3
...ke of York Street SW1 ... 240 A1
...ke Street W1 ... 239 E2
...ke Street Hill SE1 ... 245 F4
...ke's Lane W8 ... 242 A4
...ke's Place EC3 ... 246 A4
...ke's Road WC1 ... 240 B4
...ke's Yard W1 ... 239 E2
Duke Street
...ncannon Street WC2 ... 240 B1
...ndee Street E1 ... 246 C2
...ndee Wharf E14 ... 247 F3
...nelm Street W1 ... 247 D4
...nlop Place SE16 ... 246 B1
...nraven Street W1 ... 239 E1
...nstable Mews W1 ... 239 E3
...nster Court EC3 ... 246 A3
...nsterville Way SE1 ... 245 F3
...plex Ride SW1 ... 243 E3
...pont Street E1 ... 247 E4
...rham House Street WC2 ... 240 B1
...rham Row E1 ... 247 E4
...rham Street SE11 ... 244 C1
...rham Terrace W2 ... 238 A2
...rward Street W1 ... 246 C4
...rweston Street W1 ... 239 D2
Crawford Street
...thie Street E14 ... 248 C4
...ott Street W1 ... 240 B2
...sart Street EC2 ... 241 F3

E

...gle Court EC1 ... 241 D3
...gle Place SW1 ... 244 A4
Piccadilly
...gle Street WC2 ... 240 C2
...dley Crescent SW5 ... 242 A1
...l Street E1 ... 241 F3
...'s Court Gardens SW5 ... 242 A2
...'s Court Square SW5 ... 242 A1
...lham Street WC2 ... 240 B2
...ls Court Road W8 ... 242 A2
...lstoke Street EC1 ... 241 D4
Spencer Street
...rnshaw Street WC2 ... 240 B2
...sley's Mews W1 ... 239 E2
Wigmore Street
...st Arbour Street E1 ... 247 D4
...st Ferry Road E14 ... 248 B2
...st Harding Street EC4 ... 241 D2
...st India Dock Wall Road E14 ... 241 D2
...st Lane SE16 ... 246 B1
...st Mount Street E1 ... 246 C4
...st Road N1 ... 241 F4
...st Smithfield E1 ... 246 B3
...st Street SE17 ... 245 E1
...st Tenter Street E1 ... 246 B3
...stbourne Mews W2 ... 238 B2
...stbourne Terrace W2 ... 238 B2
...stcastle Street W1 ... 240 A2
...stcheap EC3 ... 241 F1
...stney Street SE10 ... 248 C1
...ston Street WC1 ... 240 C3
...on Gate SW1 ... 243 E2
...on Mews North SW1 ... 243 E2
...on Mews South SW1 ... 243 E2
...on Place SW1 ... 243 E2
...on Square SW1 ... 243 E2
...on Terrace SW1 ... 243 E2
...bisham Drive SW8 ... 244 C1
...enezer Street N1 ... 241 F4
...ury Bridge SW1 ... 243 E2
...ury Bridge Road SW1 ... 243 E1
...ury Mews SW1 ... 243 E2
...ury Mews East SW1 ... 243 E2
...ury Square SW1 ... 243 E2
...ury Street SW1 ... 243 E2
...cleston Bridge SW1 ... 243 F2
...cleston Mews SW1 ... 243 E3
...cleston Place SW1 ... 243 E2
...cleston Square SW1 ... 243 F2
...cleston Square Mews SW1 ... 243 F2
...cleston Street SW1 ... 243 E2
...brooke Road W9 ... 238 A3
...ge Street W8 ... 242 A4
...gware Road W2 ... 238 C3
...ward Mews NW1 ... 239 F4
...ward Mews W1 ... 239 E2
...erton Crescent SW3 ... 243 D2
...erton Street SW3 ... 242 C2
...erton Terrace SW3 ... 243 D2

Elba Place SE17 ... 245 E2
Eldon Road W8 ... 242 A4
Eldon Street EC2 ... 241 F2
Eleanor Close SE16 ... 247 D2
Elephant and Castle SE1 ... 245 D2
Elephant Lane SE16 ... 246 C2
Elephant Road SE17 ... 245 D2
Elf Row E1 ... 247 D3
Elgar Street SE16 ... 247 F1
Elgin Mews North W9 ... 238 A4
Elgin Mews South W9 ... 238 A4
Elia Street N1 ... 241 D4
Elim Street SE1 ... 245 F3
Eliot Mews NW8 ... 238 B4
Elizabeth Bridge SW1 ... 243 F2
Elizabeth Close W9 ... 238 B3
Elizabeth Square SE16 ... 247 E3
Elizabeth Street SW1 ... 243 E2
Ellen Street E1 ... 246 B3
Elliott Road SE9 ... 245 D2
Ellis Street SW1 ... 243 E2
Elm Park Gardens SW10 ... 242 C1
Elm Park Lane SW3 ... 242 B1
Elm Park Road SW3 ... 242 B1
Elm Place SW7 ... 242 C1
Elm Street WC1 ... 240 C3
Elm Tree Close NW8 ... 238 C4
Elm Tree Road NW8 ... 238 C4
Elmfield Way W9 ... 238 A3
Elmos Road SE16 ... 247 E1
Elms Mews W2 ... 238 C1
Elnathan Mews W9 ... 238 A3
Elsa Street E1 ... 247 E4
Elsted Street SE17 ... 245 F2
Elvaston Mews SW7 ... 242 B3
Elvaston Place SW7 ... 242 B3
Elverton Street SW1 ... 244 A2
Ely Place EC1 ... 241 D2
Elystan Place SW3 ... 243 D2
Elystan Street SW3 ... 242 C2
Emba Street SE16 ... 246 C1
Embankment Gardens SW3 ... 243 D1
Embankment Place WC2 ... 244 B4
Emerald Street WC1 ... 240 C3
Emerson Street SE1 ... 245 E4
Emery Hill Street SW1 ... 244 A2
Emery Street SE1 ... 245 D3
Emmett Street E14 ... 247 F3
Emperor's Gate SW7 ... 242 B2
Empire Wharf Road E14 ... 248 C2
Empress Place SW6 ... 242 A1
Empress Street SE17 ... 245 E1
Endell Street WC2 ... 240 B2
Endsleigh Gardens WC1 ... 240 A3
Endsleigh Place WC1 ... 240 A3
Endsleigh Street WC1 ... 240 A3
Enford Street W1 ... 239 D3
English Grounds SE1 ... 246 A2
Enid Street SE16 ... 246 B1
Ennismore Garden Mews SW7 ... 242 C3
Ennismore Gardens SW7 ... 242 C3
Ennismore Mews SW7 ... 242 C3
Ennismore Street SW7 ... 242 C3
Ensign Street E1 ... 246 B3
Ensor Mews SW7 ... 242 B1
Epping Close E14 ... 248 A2
Epworth Street EC2 ... 241 F3
Erasmus Street SW1 ... 244 B2
Errol Street EC1 ... 241 E3
Essendine Road W9 ... 238 A4
Essex Street WC2 ... 240 C1
Esterbrooke Street SW1 ... 244 A2
Ethel Street SE17 ... 245 E2
Europa Place EC1 ... 241 E4
Euston Road NW1 ... 239 F3
Euston Square NW1 ... 240 A4
Euston Street NW1 ... 240 A4
Evelyn Gardens SW7 ... 244 B1
Evelyn Walk N1 ... 241 F4
Evelyn Yard W1 ... 240 A2
Gresse Street
Eversholt Street NW1 ... 240 A4
Ewer Street SE1 ... 245 E4
Exchange Place EC2 ... 246 A4
Exchange Square EC2 ... 246 A4
Exeter Street WC2 ... 240 B1
Exhibition Road SW7 ... 242 C3
Exmouth Market EC1 ... 241 D3
Exmouth Street E1 ... 247 D4
Exon Street SE17 ... 245 F2
Exton Street SE1 ... 244 C4
Eyre Street Hill EC1 ... 241 D3

F

Factory Place E14 ... 248 B1
Ferry Street
Fair Street SE1 ... 246 A2
Fairclough Street E1 ... 246 B3
Falcon Close SE1 ... 245 E4
Falcon Way E14 ... 248 B2
Falconberg Mews W1 ... 240 A2
Sutton Row
Falmouth Road SE1 ... 245 E3
Fann Street EC1 ... 241 E3
Fanshaw Street N1 ... 241 F4
Fareham Street W1 ... 240 B1
Dean Street
Farm Street W1 ... 239 E1
Farmer Street W8 ... 242 A4
Farncombe Street SE16 ... 246 C1
Farnell Mews SW5 ... 242 A1
Farnham Place SE1 ... 245 E4
Farnham Royal SE11 ... 244 C3
Farrance Street E14 ... 247 F3
Farrier Street NW10 ... 242 B1
Farringdon Lane EC1 ... 241 D3
Farringdon Road EC1 ... 240 C3
Farringdon Street EC4 ... 241 D2
Farrins Rents SE16 ... 247 E2
Farrow Place SE16 ... 247 E1
Farthing Street SE1 ... 246 B1
Wolseley Street
Farthing Fields E1 ... 246 C2
Raine Street
Fashion Street E1 ... 246 B4
Faunce Street SE17 ... 245 D1
Fawcett Street SW10 ... 242 B1
Feather's Place SE10 ... 248 C1
Featherstone Street EC1 ... 241 F3
Felstead Gardens E14 ... 248 B1
Fen Court EC3 ... 246 A3
Fenchurch Avenue EC3 ... 246 A3
Fenchurch Buildings EC3 ... 241 F1
Fenchurch Street
Fenchurch Place EC3 ... 241 F1
Fenchurch Street
Fenchurch Street EC3 ... 246 A3
Fendall Street SE1 ... 246 A1
Fenning Street SE1 ... 245 F4
St Thomas Street
Fennings Circus SE1 ... 240 A2
Ferguson Close E14 ... 248 A2

Fernsbury Street WC1 ... 240 C4
Ferry Street E14 ... 248 B1
Fetter Lane EC4 ... 241 D2
Field Street WC1 ... 240 C4
Fieldgate Street E1 ... 246 B4
Fielding Street SE17 ... 245 E1
Finborough Road SW10 ... 242 A1
Finch Lane EC3 ... 241 F2
Finland Street SE16 ... 247 E1
Finsbury Avenue EC2 ... 241 F2
Finsbury Circus EC2 ... 241 F2
Finsbury Market EC2 ... 241 F3
Finsbury Pavement EC2 ... 241 F3
Finsbury Square EC2 ... 241 F3
Finsbury Street EC2 ... 241 F3
First Street SW3 ... 243 D2
Firtree Close SE16 ... 247 E2
Fish Street Hill EC3 ... 241 F1
Fish Wharf EC3 ... 241 F1
Fisher Street WC1 ... 240 C2
Fisherman's Walk E14 ... 248 A4
Fishermans Place SE16 ... 247 E2
Fisherton Street NW8 ... 238 C3
Fitzalan Street SE11 ... 244 C2
Fitzhardinge Street W1 ... 239 E2
Fitzmaurice Place W1 ... 239 F1
Fitzroy Square W1 ... 239 F3
Fitzroy Street W1 ... 239 F3
Flamborough Street E14 ... 247 E3
Flank Street E1 ... 246 B3
Flaxman Terrace WC1 ... 240 A4
Fleet Square WC1 ... 240 C4
Fleet Street EC4 ... 241 D2
Fleming Road SE17 ... 245 D1
Fletcher Street E1 ... 246 B3
Flint Street SE17 ... 245 F2
Flitcroft Street WC2 ... 240 B2
Flood Street SW3 ... 243 D1
Flood Walk SW3 ... 243 D1
Floral Street WC2 ... 240 B1
Flower and Dean Walk E1 ... 246 B4
Thrawl Street
Foley Street W1 ... 239 F2
Folly Wall E14 ... 248 C3
Forbes Street E1 ... 246 B3
Ford Square E1 ... 246 C4
Fordham Street E1 ... 246 C4
Fore Street EC2 ... 241 E2
Fore Street Avenue EC2 ... 241 E2
Formosa Street W9 ... 238 A3
Forset Street W1 ... 239 D2
Forsyth Gardens SE17 ... 245 D1
Fort Street E1 ... 246 A4
Artillery Lane
Fortune Street EC1 ... 241 E3
Foscote Mews W9 ... 238 A3
Foster Lane EC2 ... 241 E2
Foubert's Place W1 ... 239 F1
Foulis Terrace SW7 ... 242 C2
Foundry Close SE16 ... 247 E2
Fountain Green Square SE16 ... 246 C1
Fournier Street E1 ... 246 B4
Fowey Close E1 ... 246 C2
Fox and Knot Street EC1 ... 241 E2
Charterhouse Square
Frampton Street NW8 ... 238 C3
Francis Close E14 ... 248 C2
Francis Street SW1 ... 244 A2
Franklin's Row SW3 ... 243 D1
Frazier Street SE1 ... 244 C3
Frean Street SE16 ... 246 B1
Frederick Close W2 ... 239 D1
Frederick Road SE17 ... 245 E1
Frederick Square SE16 ... 247 E3
Frederick Street WC1 ... 240 C4
Fredericks Row EC1 ... 241 D4
Goswell Road
Fremantle Street SE17 ... 245 F2
French Ordinary Court EC3 ... 246 A3
Hart Street
Friar Street EC4 ... 241 E2
Carter Lane
Friars Mead E14 ... 248 B2
Friday Street EC4 ... 241 E1
Friend Street EC1 ... 241 D4
Frigate Mews SE8 ... 248 A1
Frith Street W1 ... 240 A2
Frobisher Passage E14 ... 248 A4
North Collonade
Frobisher Passage E14 ... 248 A4
Frostic Walk E1 ... 246 B4
Frying Pan Alley E1 ... 246 A4
Fulbourne Street E1 ... 246 C4
Fulford Street SE16 ... 246 C1
Fulham Road
Fulham Road SW3, SW6 & SW10 ... 242 C1
Fulwood Place WC1 ... 240 C2
Furnival Street EC4 ... 241 D2
Fynes Street SW1 ... 244 A2

G

Gabriels Wharf SE1 ... 245 D4
Gainsford Street SE1 ... 246 A2
Galbraith Street E14 ... 254
Galen Place WC1 ... 240 B2
Galleon Close SE16 ... 247 D2
Kinburn Street
Galleons View E14 ... 248 C3
Galway Street EC1 ... 241 E4
Gambia Street SE1 ... 245 D4
Ganton Street W1 ... 240 A1
Garbutt Place W1 ... 239 E2
Gard Street EC1 ... 241 E4
Garden Mews W2 ... 238 A1
Garden Road NW8 ... 238 B4
Garden Row SE1 ... 245 D3
Garden Street E1 ... 247 E4
Gardeners Lane EC4 ... 241 E1
High Timber Street
Garford Street E14 ... 247 F3
Garlick Hill EC4 ... 241 E1
Garnault Mews EC1 ... 241 D4
Garnet Street E1 ... 247 D3
Garrett Street EC1 ... 241 E3
Garrick Street WC2 ... 240 B1
Garter Way SE16 ... 247 D1
Garway Road W2 ... 238 A2
Gaselee Street E14 ... 248 C4
Gasholder Place SE11 ... 244 C1
Gaspar Close SW5 ... 242 B2
Gaspar Mews SW5 ... 242 B2
Gate Street WC2 ... 240 C2
Gateway SE17 ... 245 E1
Gatliff Road SW1 ... 243 E1
Gaunt Street SE1 ... 245 E3
Gavel Street SE17 ... 245 F2
Gayfere Street SW1 ... 244 B3
Gaywood Street SE1 ... 245 D3
Gaza Street SE17 ... 245 D1
Gedling Place SE1 ... 246 B1
Gee Street EC1 ... 241 E3
Gees Court W1 ... 239 E2

George Mathers Road SE11 ... 245 D2
George Mews NW1 ... 240 A4
George Row SE16 ... 246 B1
George Street SW1 ... 239 D2
George Yard EC3 ... 241 F1
George Yard W1 ... 239 E1
Gerald Road SW1 ... 243 E2
Geraldine Street SE11 ... 245 D3
Gerrard Place W1 ... 240 B1
Gerrard Street
Gerrard Street W1 ... 240 A1
Gerridge Street SE1 ... 245 D3
Gibson Road SE11 ... 245 D3
Gilbert Place WC1 ... 240 B2
Gilbert Road SE11 ... 245 D2
Gilbert Street W1 ... 239 E1
Gildea Street W1 ... 239 F2
Gill Street E14 ... 247 F3
Gillingham Street SW1 ... 243 F2
Gillison Walk SE16 ... 246 C1
Gilpin Close W2 ... 238 B2
Porteus Road
Gilston Road SW10 ... 242 B1
Giltspur Street EC1 ... 241 E2
Gladstone Street SE1 ... 245 D3
Glamis Place E1 ... 247 D3
Glamis Road E1 ... 247 D3
Glangarnock Avenue E14 ... 248 C2
Glasgow Terrace SW1 ... 243 F1
Glasshill Street SE1 ... 245 E3
Glasshouse Fields E1 ... 247 D3
Glasshouse Street W1 ... 240 A1
Glasshouse Walk SE11 ... 244 B1
Glebe Place SW3 ... 242 C1
Gledhow Gardens SW5 ... 242 B2
Glenaffric Avenue E14 ... 248 C2
Glendower Place SW7 ... 242 C2
Glengall Grove E14 ... 248 B3
Glenworth Avenue E14 ... 248 C2
Globe Pond Road SE16 ... 247 E2
Globe Street SE1 ... 245 E3
Gloucester Arcade SW7 ... 242 B2
Gloucester Court EC3 ... 246 A3
Gloucester Gate Mews NW1 ... 240 F4
Albany Street
Gloucester Mews W2 ... 238 B2
Gloucester Mews West W2 ... 238 B2
Gloucester Park SW7 ... 242 B2
Gloucester Place NW1 & W1 ... 239 D3
Gloucester Place Mews W1 ... 239 D2
Gloucester Road SW7 ... 242 B2
Gloucester Square W2 ... 238 C2
Gloucester Street SW1 ... 243 F1
Gloucester Terrace W2 ... 238 B2
Gloucester Walk W8 ... 242 A4
Gloucester Way EC1 ... 241 D4
Glyn Street SE11 ... 244 C1
Goat Street SE1 ... 246 A2
Lafone Street
Godfrey Street SW3 ... 243 D2
Goding Street SE11 ... 244 B1
Godliman Street EC4 ... 241 E1
Golden Lane EC1 ... 241 E3
Golden Square W1 ... 240 A1
Golding Street E1 ... 246 C3
Gomm Road SE16 ... 247 D1
Goodge Place W1 ... 240 A2
Goodge Street W1 ... 240 A2
Goodhart Place E14 ... 247 E3
Goodman's Stile E1 ... 246 B4
Goodman's Yard E1 ... 246 B3
Goodwin Close SE16 ... 246 B1
Gophir Lane EC4 ... 241 F1
Bush Lane
Gordon Place W8 ... 242 A4
Gordon Square WC1 ... 240 A3
Gordon Street WC1 ... 240 A3
Gore Street SW7 ... 242 B3
Goring Street E1 ... 246 A4
Bevis Marks
Gosfield Street W1 ... 239 F2
Goslett Yard WC2 ... 240 B2
Goswell Road EC1 ... 241 D4
Gough Square EC4 ... 241 D2
Gough Street WC1 ... 240 C3
Goulston Street E1 ... 246 B4
Gower Mews WC1 ... 240 A2
Gower Place WC1 ... 240 A3
Gower Street WC1 ... 240 A3
Gowers Walk E1 ... 246 B3
Grace's Alley E1 ... 246 B3
Gracechurch Street EC3 ... 241 F1
Graces Mews NW8 ... 238 B4
Grafton Mews W1 ... 239 F3
Grafton Place NW1 ... 240 A4
Grafton Street W1 ... 239 F1
Grafton Way W1 ... 239 F3
Graham Street N1 ... 241 E4
Graham Terrace SW1 ... 243 E2
Granby Terrace NW1 ... 239 F4
Grand Avenue EC1 ... 241 E2
Grand Junction Wharf N1 ... 241 E4
Grange Court WC2 ... 240 C2
Grange Road SE1 ... 246 A1
Grange Walk SE1 ... 246 A1
Grange Yard SE1 ... 246 A1
Grant's Quay Wharf EC3 ... 241 F1
Grantully Road W9 ... 238 A4
Granville Place W1 ... 239 E2
Granville Road NW6 ... 238 A4
Granville Square WC1 ... 240 C4
Granville Street WC1 ... 240 C4
Granville Square
Grape Street WC2 ... 240 B2
Gravel Lane E1 ... 246 A4
Gray Street SE1 ... 245 D3
Gray's Inn Place WC1 ... 240 C2
Gray's Inn Road WC1 ... 240 B4
Great Castle Street W1 ... 239 F2
Great Central Street NW1 ... 239 D3
Great Chapel Street W1 ... 240 A2
Great College Street SW1 ... 239 D1
Seymour Street
Great Cumberland Place W1 ... 239 D2
Great Dover Street SE1 ... 245 F3
Great Eastern Street EC2 ... 241 F3
Great George Street SW1 ... 244 B3
Great Guildford Street SE1 ... 245 E4
Great James Street WC1 ... 240 C3
Great Marlborough Street W1 ... 239 F2
Great Maze Pond SE1 ... 245 F4
Great New Street EC4 ... 241 D2
Great Newport Street WC2 ... 240 B1
Charing Cross Road
Great Ormond Street WC1 ... 240 C3
Great Percy Street WC1 ... 240 C4
Great Peter Street SW1 ... 244 A3
Great Portland Street W1 ... 239 F3
Great Pulteney Street W1 ... 240 A1
Great Queen Street WC2 ... 240 B2
Great Russell Street WC1 ... 240 B2
Great Scotland Yard SW1 ... 244 B4
Great Smith Street SW1 ... 244 B3
Great St Helen's EC3 ... 241 F2
Great St Thomas Apostle EC4 ... 241 E1
Queen Street
Great Suffolk Street SE1 ... 245 E3
Great Sutton Street EC1 ... 241 E3
Great Swan Alley EC2 ... 241 F2

Great Tower Street EC3 ... 246 A3
Great Trinity Lane EC4 ... 241 E1
Garlick Hill
Great Turnstile WC1 ... 240 B2
High Holborn
Great Winchester Street EC2 ... 241 F2
Great Windmill Street W1 ... 240 A1
Greatorex Street E1 ... 246 B4
Greek Street W1 ... 240 B2
Green Bank E1 ... 246 C2
Green Dragon Yard E1 ... 246 B4
Green Street W1 ... 239 E1
Green Walk SE1 ... 245 F3
Green Yard WC1 ... 240 C3
Greenacre Square SE16 ... 247 E2
Greenberry Street NW8 ... 238 C4
Greencoat Place SW1 ... 244 A2
Greencoat Row SW1 ... 244 A2
Greenfield Road E1 ... 246 B4
Greenham Close SE1 ... 245 D3
Greenwell Street W1 ... 239 F3
Greenwich Park Street SE10 ... 248 C1
Greenwich View Place E14 ... 248 C3
Greet Street SE1 ... 245 D4
Gregory Place W8 ... 242 A3
Greig Terrace SE17 ... 245 E1
Grenade Street E14 ... 247 F3
Grendon Street NW8 ... 238 C3
Grenville Place SW7 ... 242 B2
Grenville Street WC1 ... 240 B3
Gresham Street EC2 ... 241 E2
Gresse Street W1 ... 240 A2
Greville Street EC1 ... 241 D2
Greycoat Place SW1 ... 244 A3
Greycoat Street SW1 ... 244 A2
Greystoke Place EC4 ... 241 D2
Fetter Lane
Griggs Place SE1 ... 246 A1
Groom Place SW1 ... 243 E3
Grosvenor Crescent SW1 ... 243 E3
Grosvenor Crescent Mews SW1 ... 243 E3
Grosvenor Gardens SW1 ... 243 F3
Grosvenor Gate W1 ... 239 E1
Park Lane
Grosvenor Hill W1 ... 239 F1
Grosvenor Place SW1 ... 243 E3
Grosvenor Road SW1 ... 243 F1
Grosvenor Square W1 ... 239 E1
Grosvenor Street W1 ... 239 E1
Grosvenor Wharf Road E14 ... 248 C2
Grove End Road NW8 ... 238 B4
Grove Gardens NW8 ... 239 D4
Grove Hall Court NW8 ... 238 B4
Guildhall Buildings EC2 ... 241 E2
Basinghall Street
Guildhall Yard EC2 ... 241 E2
Guildhouse Street SW1 ... 243 F2
Guilford Place WC1 ... 240 B3
Guilford Street
Guilford Street WC1 ... 240 B3
Guinness Square SE1 ... 245 F2
Gulliver Street SE16 ... 247 F1
Gulston Walk SW3 ... 243 D2
Gun Street E1 ... 246 A4
Gunthorpe Street E1 ... 246 B4
Gunwhale Close SE16 ... 247 E2
Guthrie Street SW3 ... 242 C2
Gutter Lane EC2 ... 241 E2
Guy Street SE1 ... 245 F3
Gwynne Place WC1 ... 240 C4

H

Haberdasher Street N1 ... 241 F4
Hainton Close E1 ... 246 C3
Halcrow Street E1 ... 246 C4
Half Moon Court EC1 ... 241 E2
Bartholomew Close
Half Moon Street W1 ... 243 F4
Halkin Place SW1 ... 243 E3
Halkin Street SW1 ... 243 E3
Hall Gate NW8 ... 238 B4
Hall Place W2 ... 238 C3
Hall Road NW8 ... 238 B4
Hall Street EC1 ... 241 D4
Hallam Mews W1 ... 239 F3
Hallam Street W1 ... 239 F3
Halley Place E14 ... 247 E4
Halley Street E14 ... 247 E4
Halsey Mews SW3 ... 243 D2
Halsey Street SW3 ... 243 D2
Hamilton Close NW8 ... 238 B4
Hamilton Close SE16 ... 247 E1
Hamilton Gardens NW8 ... 238 B4
Hamilton Place W1 ... 243 E4
Hamilton Square SE1 ... 245 F3
Hamilton Terrace NW8 ... 238 B4
Hammett Street EC3 ... 246 A3
America Square
Hampstead Road NW1 ... 239 F4
Hampton Street SE1 & SE17 ... 245 E2
Hanbury Street E1 ... 246 B4
Handel Street WC1 ... 240 B3
Hankey Place SE1 ... 245 F3
Hannibal Road E1 ... 247 D4
Hanover Place WC2 ... 240 B1
Long Acre
Hanover Square W1 ... 239 F2
Hanover Street W1 ... 239 F2
Hanover Terrace NW1 ... 239 D4
Hanover Terrace Mews NW1 ... 239 D4
Hans Crescent SW1 ... 243 D3
Hans Place SW1 ... 243 D3
Hans Road SW3 ... 243 D3
Hans Street SW1 ... 243 D3
Hanson Street W1 ... 239 F2
Hanway Place W1 ... 240 A2
Hanway Street W1 ... 240 A2
Harbet Road W2 ... 238 C2
Harbinger Road E14 ... 248 B2
Harbour Exchange Square E14 ... 248 B3
Harcourt Street W1 ... 239 D2
Harcourt Terrace SW10 ... 242 B1
Harding Close SE17 ... 245 E1
Hardinge Lane E1 ... 247 D3
Hardinge Street
Hardinge Street E1 ... 247 D3
Hardwick Street EC1 ... 241 D4
Hardwicke Mews WC1 ... 240 C4
Lloyd Baker Street
Hardwidge Street SE1 ... 245 F4
Harewood Avenue NW1 ... 239 D3
Harewood Place W1 ... 239 F2
Harley Gardens SW10 ... 242 B1
Harley Place W1 ... 239 E2
Harley Street W1 ... 239 E3
Harleyford Road SE11 ... 244 C1
Harmsworth Mews SE11 ... 245 D2
West Square
Harmsworth Street SE17 ... 245 D1
Harp Alley EC4 ... 241 D2
Farringdon Street
Harp Lane EC3 ... 246 A3
Harper Road SE1 ... 245 E3

251

Harpur Street WC1 .... 240 C3
Harriet Street SW1 .... 243 D3
Harriet Walk SW1 .... 243 D3
Harrington Gardens SW7 ...... 242 B2
Harrington Road SW7 .... 242 C2
Harrington Street NW1 .... 239 F4
Harrison Street WC1 .... 240 B4
Harrow Place E1 .... 246 A4
Harrow Road
  W2, W9, W10 & NW10 .... 238 B3
Harrow Road Bridge W2 .... 238 B2
Harrowby Street W1 .... 239 D2
Hart Street EC3 .... 246 A3
Harwich Lane EC2 .... 246 A4
Harwood Row NW1 .... 239 D3
Hasker Street SW3 .... 243 D2
Hastings Street WC1 .... 240 B4
Hatfields SE1 .... 245 D4
Hatherley Grove W2 .... 238 A2
Hatherley Street SW1 .... 244 A2
Hatteraick Street SE16 .... 247 D2
Hatton Garden EC1 .... 241 D3
Hatton Place EC1 .... 241 D3
Hatton Place EC1 .... 241 D3
Hatton Street NW8 .... 238 C3
Hatton Wall EC1 .... 241 D3
Haunch of Venison Yard W1 .. 238 C1
  Brook Street
Havannah Street E14 .... 248 A3
Havering Street E1 .... 247 D3
Haverstock Street N1 .... 241 E4
Hawkesmoor Mews E1 .... 246 C3
Hay Hill W1 .... 239 F1
Hay's Lane SE1 .... 245 F4
Hay's Mews W1 .... 239 F1
Hayes Place NW1 .... 239 D3
Hayles Street SE11 .... 245 D2
Haymarket SW1 .... 240 A1
Hayne Street EC1 .... 241 E3
Hayward's Place EC1 .... 241 D3
Headfort Place SW1 .... 243 E3
Heathcote Street WC1 .... 240 C3
Heckford Street E1 .... 247 E3
Heddon Street W1 .... 239 F1
Hedger Street SE11 .... 245 D2
Heiron Street SE17 .... 245 D1
Helena Square SE16 .... 247 E3
Hellings Street E1 .... 246 B2
Helmet Row EC1 .... 241 E3
Helsinki Square SE16 .... 247 E2
Hemp Walk SE17 .... 245 F2
Henderson Drive NW8 .... 238 C3
Heneage Lane EC3 .... 246 A4
Heneage Place EC3 .... 246 A4
Heneage Street E1 .... 246 B4
Henniker Mews SW3 .... 242 B1
Henrietta Close SE8 .... 248 A1
Henrietta Place W1 .... 239 E2
Henrietta Street WC2 .... 240 B1
Henriques Street E1 .... 246 B4
Henshaw Street SE17 .... 245 F2
Herald's Place SE11 .... 245 D2
Herbal Hill EC1 .... 241 D3
Herbrand Street WC1 .... 240 B3
Hercules Road SE1 .... 244 C3
Hereford Road W2 .... 238 A2
Hereford Square SW7 .... 242 B2
Hermes Street N1 .... 240 C4
Hermit Street EC1 .... 241 D4
Hermitage Street W2 .... 238 C2
Hermitage Wall E1 .... 246 B2
Heron Place SE16 .... 247 D2
Heron Quays E14 .... 248 A4
Herrick Street SW1 .... 244 B2
Hertford Street W1 .... 243 E4
Hertsmere Road E14 .... 248 A4
Hesper Mews SW5 .... 242 A2
Hesperus Crescent E14 .... 248 B2
Hessel Street E1 .... 246 C3
Heygate Street SE17 .... 245 E2
Hickin Street E14 .... 248 B3
Hide Place SW1 .... 244 A2
High Holborn WC1 .... 240 B2
High Timber Street EC4 .... 241 E1
Highbridge SE10 .... 248 C1
Hildyard Road SW6 .... 242 A1
Hill Road W9 .... 238 B4
Hill Street W1 .... 239 F1
Hillery Close SE17 .... 245 F2
Hilliard's Court E1 .... 246 C2
Hillingdon Street SE5 & SE17 ... 245 E1
  Pelier Street
Hind Court EC4 .... 241 D2
Hinde Street W1 .... 239 E2
Hindmarsh Close E1 .... 246 B3
Hobart Place SW1 .... 243 F3
Hogarth Court EC3 .... 241 F1
  Fenchurch Street
Hogarth Place SW5 .... 242 A2
Hogarth Road SW5 .... 242 A2
Holbein Mews SW1 .... 243 E2
Holbein Place SW1 .... 243 E2
Holborn EC1 .... 241 D2
Holborn Circus EC1 .... 241 D2
Holborn Viaduct EC1 .... 241 D2
Holford Street WC1 .... 240 C4
Holford Street WC1 .... 240 C4
Holland Street SE1 .... 245 D4
Holland Street W8 .... 242 A3
Hollen Street W1 .... 240 A2
  Wardour Street
Holles Street W1 .... 239 F2
Holley Mews SW10 .... 242 B1
  Drayton Gardens
Hollywood Mews SW10 .... 242 B1
Hollywood Road SW10 .... 242 B1
Holyoak Road SE11 .... 245 D2
Holyoake Court SE16 .... 247 E2
Holyrood Street SE1 .... 246 A2
Holywell Row EC2 .... 241 F3
Homer Drive E14 .... 248 A2
Homer Row W1 .... 239 D2
Homer Street W1 .... 239 D2
Honduras Street EC1 .... 241 E3
  Old Street
Hooper Street E1 .... 246 B3
Hop Gardens WC2 .... 240 B1
  St Martin's Lane
Hope Wharf SE16 .... 247 D2
Hopetown Street E1 .... 246 B4
Hopkins Street W1 .... 240 A1
Hopton Street SE1 .... 245 D4
Hopwood Road SE17 .... 245 F1
Horatio Place E14 .... 248 C4
Horley Crescent SE16 .... 247 D2
  Marlow Way
Hornton Place W8 .... 242 A3
Hornton Street W8 .... 242 A3
Horse Guards Avenue SW1 ... 244 B4
Horse Guards Road SW1 ...... 244 B4
Horse Ride SW1 .... 243 F3
Horseferry Road E14 .... 247 E3
Horseferry Road SW1 .... 244 B3
Horselydown Lane SE1 .... 246 A2
Horseshoe Close E14 .... 248 B2
Hosier Lane EC1 .... 241 D2
Hoskins Street SE10 .... 248 C1
Hothfield Place SE16 .... 247 D1
Hotspur Street SE11 .... 244 C2

Houghton Street WC2 .... 240 C1
Houndsditch EC3 .... 246 A4
Howard Place SW1 .... 240 A2
  Carlisle Street
Howell Walk SE1 .... 245 E2
Howick Place SW1 .... 244 A3
Howland Street W1 .... 240 A3
Howland Way SE16 .... 247 E1
Howley Place W2 .... 238 B3
Hoxton Market N1 .... 241 F4
Hoxton Square N1 .... 241 F4
Huddart Street E3 .... 247 F4
Hudson's Place SW1 .... 243 F2
Huggin Hill EC4 .... 241 E1
Hugh Street SW1 .... 243 F2
Hull Close SE16 .... 247 E2
Hull Street EC1 .... 241 E4
Hunt's Court WC2 .... 240 B1
Hunter Close SE1 .... 245 F3
  Prioress Street
Hunter Street WC1 .... 240 B3
Huntley Street WC1 .... 240 A3
Huntsman Street SE17 .... 245 F2
Huntsworth Mews NW1 .... 239 D3
Hutching's Street E14 .... 248 A3
Hutton Street EC4 .... 241 D1
Hyde Park Corner W1 .... 243 E4
Hyde Park Crescent W2 .... 238 C2
Hyde Park Gardens W2 .... 238 C1
Hyde Park Gardens Mews W2 ... 238 C1
Hyde Park Gate SW7 .... 242 B3
Hyde Park Square W2 .... 238 C2
Hyde Park Street W2 .... 238 C2

I

Idol Lane EC3 .... 246 A3
Ifield Road SW10 .... 242 A1
Ilchester Gardens W2 .... 238 A1
Iliffe Street SE17 .... 245 E2
India Street EC3 .... 246 A3
India Street EC3 .... 246 A3
  Montreal Place
Indescon Court E14 .... 248 A3
India Street EC3 .... 246 A3
  Paradise Street
Ingestre Place W1 .... 240 A1
Inglebert Street EC1 .... 241 D4
Inglewood Close E14 .... 248 A2
Ingram Close SE11 .... 244 C2
Inigo Place WC2 .... 240 B1
  Bedford Street
Inner Temple Lane EC4 .... 241 D2
Inverness Gardens W8 .... 242 A4
  Palace Garden Terrace
Inverness Mews W2 .... 238 B1
Inverness Place W2 .... 238 B1
Inverness Terrace W2 .... 238 B1
Invicta Plaza SE1 .... 245 D4
Inville Road SE17 .... 245 F1
Ireland Yard EC4 .... 241 D1
  St Andrew's Hill
Ironmonger Lane EC2 .... 241 E2
Ironmonger Place E14 .... 248 A2
Ironmonger Row EC1 .... 241 E4
Ironside Close SE16 .... 247 D2
Irving Street WC2 .... 240 B1
Isambard Place SE16 .... 247 D2
Island Row E14 .... 247 F3
Iverna Court W8 .... 242 A3
Iverna Gardens W8 .... 242 A3
Ives Street SW3 .... 243 D2
Ivor Place NW1 .... 239 D3
Ixworth Place SW3 .... 242 C2

J

Jacob Street SE1 .... 246 B2
Jamaica Road SE1 & SE16 ... 246 B1
Jamaica Street E1 .... 247 D4
James Street W1 .... 239 E2
James Street WC2 .... 240 B1
  Long Acre
Jameson Street W8 .... 242 A4
Janet Street E14 .... 248 A3
Janeway Street SE16 .... 246 C1
Janeway Street SE16 .... 246 C1
Jardine Road E1 .... 247 E3
Jay Mews SW7 .... 242 B3
Jermyn Street SW1 .... 244 A4
Jerome Crescent NW8 .... 238 C3
Jewry Street EC3 .... 246 A3
Joan Street SE1 .... 245 D4
Jockey's Fields WC1 .... 240 C3
John Adams Street WC2 ...... 240 B1
John Aird Court W2 .... 238 B3
John Carpenter Street EC4 ... 241 D1
John Felton Road SE16 .... 246 B1
John Fisher Street E1 .... 246 B3
John Islip Street SW1 .... 244 B2
John Maurice Close SE17 .... 245 F2
John Princes Street W1 .... 239 F2
John Roll Way SE16 .... 246 C1
John Street WC1 .... 240 C3
John's Mews WC1 .... 240 C3
Johnson Street E1 .... 247 D3
Johnson's Place SW1 .... 244 A1
Joiner Street SE1 .... 245 F4
Jonathan Street SE11 .... 244 C2
Jonathan Street SE11 .... 244 C2
  Bourdon Street
Jubilee Crescent E14 .... 248 C3
Jubilee Street SW3 .... 243 D2
Jubilee Street E1 .... 247 D4
Judd Street WC1 .... 240 B4
Julian Place E14 .... 248 B1
Junction Mews W2 .... 238 C2
Juxon Street SE11 .... 244 C2

K

Katherine Close SE16 .... 247 D2
Kean Street WC2 .... 240 C2
Keel Close SE16 .... 247 E2
Keeley Street WC2 .... 240 C2
Keeton's Road SE16 .... 246 C1
Kelso Place W8 .... 242 A3
Kemble Street WC2 .... 240 C2
Kempsford Gardens SW5 ..... 242 A1
Kempsford Road SE11 .... 245 D2
Kempton Court E1 .... 246 C4
  Durward Street
Kendal Street W2 .... 239 C2

Kendall Place W1 .... 239 D2
Kendrick Mews SW7 .... 242 C2
Kendrick Place SW7 .... 242 C2
  Reece Mews
Kennet Street E1 .... 246 B2
Kenning Street SE16 .... 247 D2
Kennings Way SE11 .... 245 D2
  Borough High Street
Kennington Green SE11 .... 245 D1
Kennington Grove SE11 .... 244 C1
Kennington Lane SE11 .... 244 C1
Kennington Oval SE11 .... 244 C1
Kennington Park Gardens SE11 ... 245 D1
Kennington Park Place SE11 ... 245 D1
Kennington Park Road SE11 ... 245 D1
Kennington Road SE1 & SE11 ... 244 C3
Kenrick Place W1 .... 239 E2
Kensington Church Street W8 ... 242 A3
Kensington Church Walk W8 ... 242 A3
Kensington Court W8 .... 242 A3
Kensington Court Place W8 ... 242 A3
Kensington Gardens Square W2 ... 238 A2
Kensington Gate W8 .... 242 B3
Kensington Gore SW7 .... 242 B3
Kensington High Street
  W8 & W14 .... 242 A3
Kensington Mall W8 .... 242 A4
Kensington Palace Gardens W8 ... 242 A4
Kensington Road W8 & SW7 ... 242 A3
Kensington Square W8 .... 242 A3
Kent Passage NW1 .... 239 D4
Kent Terrace NW1 .... 239 D4
Kenton Street WC1 .... 239 B3
Kenway Road SW5 .... 242 A2
Keppel Row SE1 .... 245 E4
Keppel Street WC1 .... 240 B3
Keyse Road SE1 .... 246 B1
Keystone Crescent N1 .... 240 B4
Keyworth Street SE1 .... 245 D3
Kilburn Park Road NW6 .... 238 A4
Kildare Gardens W2 .... 238 A2
Kildare Terrace W2 .... 238 A2
Kimbolton Row SW3 .... 242 C2
  Fulham Road
Kinburn Street SE16 .... 247 D2
Kinder Street E1 .... 246 C3
King and Queen Street SE17 ... 245 E2
King Charles Street SW1 ...... 244 B3
King David Lane E1 .... 247 D3
King Edward III Mews SE16 ... 246 C1
  Paradise Street
King Edward Street EC1 .... 241 E2
King Edward Walk SE1 .... 245 D3
King James Street SE1 .... 245 E3
King Square EC1 .... 241 E4
King Street EC2 .... 241 E2
King Street SW1 .... 244 A4
King Street WC2 .... 240 B1
King William Street EC4 .... 241 F1
King's Bench Walk EC4 .... 241 D1
King's Cross Road WC1 .... 240 C4
King's Mews WC1 .... 240 C3
King's Road SW3, SW6 & SW10 ... 243 D1
King's Scholars' Passage SW1 ... 243 F2
King's Stairs Close SE16 ...... 246 C2
Kingfield Street E14 .... 248 B2
Kinghorn Street EC1 .... 241 E3
Kinglake Street SE17 .... 245 F2
Kingly Court W1 .... 240 A1
Kingly Street W1 .... 239 F1
Kings Arms Yard EC2 .... 241 F2
Kings Bench Street SE1 .... 245 D3
Kingscote Street EC4 .... 241 D1
Kingsway WC2 .... 240 C2
Kinnerton Street SW1 .... 243 E3
Kipling Street SE1 .... 245 F4
Kirby Grove SE1 .... 245 F3
Kirby Street EC1 .... 241 D3
Knaresborough Place SW5 ... 242 A2
Knight's Walk SE11 .... 245 D2
Knighten Street E1 .... 246 C2
Knightrider Street EC4 .... 241 E1
  Godliman Street
Knightsbridge SW1 & SW7 ... 243 D3
Knightsbridge Green SW1 .... 243 D3
  Brompton Road
Knox Street W1 .... 239 D3
Kramer Mews SW5 .... 242 A1
Kynance Mews SW7 .... 242 B3

L

Lackington Street EC2 .... 241 F3
Lafone Street SE1 .... 246 A2
Lagado Mews SE16 .... 247 E2
Lamb Street E1 .... 246 A4
Lamb Walk SE1 .... 245 F3
Lamb's Conduit Street WC1 ... 240 C3
Lamb's Passage EC1 .... 241 F3
Lambeth Bridge SW1 & SE11 ... 244 B2
Lambeth High Street SE1 ..... 244 C2
Lambeth Hill EC4 .... 241 E1
Lambeth Palace Road SE1 ... 244 C2
Lambeth Road SE1 .... 244 C2
Lambeth Walk SE11 .... 244 C2
Lamlash Street SE11 .... 245 D2
Lanark Place W9 .... 238 B3
Lanark Road W9 .... 238 A4
Lanark Square E14 .... 248 B3
Lancaster Drive E14 .... 248 B4
Lancaster Gate W2 .... 238 B1
Lancaster Mews W2 .... 238 B1
Lancaster Place WC2 .... 240 C1
Lancaster Street SE1 .... 245 D3
Lancaster Terrace W2 .... 238 C1
Lancaster Walk W2 .... 238 B1
Lancelot Place SW7 .... 243 D3
Lancing Street NW1 .... 240 A4
Landon Place SW1 .... 243 D3
Landon's Close E14 .... 248 B4
Langdale Street SE17 .... 245 E1
Langford Close E8 .... 241 F2
Langham Place W1 .... 239 F2
Langham Street W1 .... 239 F2
Langley Lane SW8 .... 244 B1
Langley Street WC2 .... 240 B1
Langton Close WC1 .... 240 C3
Lansdowne Row W1 .... 239 F1
Lansdowne Terrace WC1 ...... 240 B3
Lant Street SE1 .... 245 E3
Lanterns Court E14 .... 248 A3
Larcom Street SE17 .... 245 E2
Lassell Street SE10 .... 248 C1
Lauderdale Road W9 .... 238 A4
Launcelot Street SE1 .... 244 C3
  Lower Marsh
Launceston Place W8 .... 242 B3
Launch Street E14 .... 248 B3
Laurence Pountney Lane EC4 ... 241 F1
Lavender Close SW3 .... 242 C1
Lavender Road SE16 .... 247 E2
Laverton Place SW5 .... 242 A2
Lavington Street SE1 .... 245 E4
Law Street SE1 .... 245 F3
Lawn House Close E14 .... 248 B3

Lawn Lane SW8 .... 244 B1
Lawrence Lane EC2 .... 241 E2
  Trump Street
Lawrence Street SW3 .... 242 C1
Laxton Place NW1 .... 239 F3
Laystall Street EC1 .... 240 C3
Layton's Buildings SE1 .... 245 E4
  Borough High Street
Leadenhall Place EC3 .... 241 F1
Leadenhall Street EC3 .... 241 F2
Leake Street SE1 .... 244 C3
Leather Lane EC1 .... 241 D3
Leathermarket Court SE1 ..... 245 F3
  Leathermarket Street
Leathermarket Street SE1 .... 245 F3
Lecky Street SW7 .... 242 C2
Leerdam Drive E14 .... 248 C2
Lees Place W1 .... 239 E1
Leicester Court WC2 .... 240 B1
  Cranbourn Street
Leicester Place WC2 .... 240 A1
  Lisle Street
Leicester Square WC2 .... 240 B1
Leigh Hunt Street SE1 .... 245 E3
Leinster Gardens W2 .... 238 B1
Leinster Mews W2 .... 238 B1
Leinster Place W2 .... 238 B1
Leinster Square W2 .... 238 A2
Leinster Terrace W2 .... 238 B1
Leman Street E1 .... 246 B3
Lennox Gardens SW1 .... 243 D2
Lennox Gardens Mews SW1 ... 243 D2
Leonard Street EC2 .... 241 F3
Leopold Estate E3 .... 247 F4
Leroy Street SE1 .... 245 F2
Lever Street EC1 .... 241 E4
Leverett Street SW3 .... 243 D2
  Mossop Street
Lewisham Street SW1 .... 244 B3
Lexham Gardens W8 .... 242 A2
Lexham Mews W8 .... 242 A2
Lexham Walk W8 .... 242 A2
  Lexington Street
Lexington Street W1 .... 240 A1
Leyden Street E1 .... 246 A4
Leydon Close SE16 .... 247 E2
Library Place E1 .... 246 C3
Library Street SE1 .... 245 D3
Lighterman Mews E1 .... 247 E4
Lightermans Road E14 .... 248 A3
Lilestone Street NW8 .... 238 C3
Lilley Close SE1 .... 246 B2
Lillie Yard SW6 .... 242 A1
Lillie Close E1 .... 246 B2
Lime Close E3 .... 241 F1
Lime Street Passage EC3 ..... 241 F1
  Lime Street
Limeburner Lane EC4 .... 241 D2
Limeharbour E14 .... 248 B3
Limehouse Causeway E14 .... 247 F3
Limehouse Link Tunnel E14 ... 247 E3
Limerston Street SW10 .... 242 B1
Lincoln Street SW3 .... 243 D2
Lincoln's Inn Fields WC2 ..... 240 C2
Linden Gardens W2 .... 238 A1
Linden Mews W2 .... 238 A1
Lindley Street E1 .... 246 C4
Lindsay Square SW1 .... 244 B2
Lindsey Street EC1 .... 241 E3
Linhope Street NW1 .... 239 D3
Links Yard E1 .... 246 B4
Linsey Street SE16 .... 246 B1
Lipton Road E1 .... 247 D3
Lisle Street W1 .... 240 A1
Lisson Grove NW1 & NW8 ... 238 C3
Lisson Street NW1 .... 238 C3
Litchfield Street WC2 .... 240 B1
Little Argyll Street W1 .... 244 A2
  Regent Street
Little Britain EC1 .... 241 E2
Little Chester Street SW1 ..... 243 E3
Little College Street SW1 ..... 244 B3
Little Dorrit Close SE1 .... 245 E4
Little Edward Street NW1 ..... 239 F4
Little George Street SW1 ...... 244 B3
  Great George Street
Little London Court SE1 .... 246 B1
  Mill Street
Little Marlborough Street W1 ... 239 F1
  Kingly Street
Little New Street EC4 .... 241 D2
  New Street Square
Little Newport Street WC2 .... 240 B1
Little Portland Street W1 ...... 239 F2
Little Russell Street WC1 ..... 240 B2
Little Sanctuary SW1 .... 244 B3
  Broad Sanctuary
Little Smith Street SW1 .... 244 B3
Little Somerset Street E1 ..... 244 A3
Little St James's Street SW1 ... 244 A4
Little Titchfield Street W1 ..... 239 F2
Little Trinity Lane EC4 .... 241 E1
Liverpool Grove SE17 .... 245 E1
Liverpool Street EC2 .... 241 F2
Livingstone Place E14 .... 248 B1
Livonia Street W2 .... 240 A2
Lizard Street EC1 .... 241 E4
Llewellyn Street SE16 .... 246 B1
Lloyd Baker Street WC1 ...... 240 C4
Lloyd Square WC1 .... 240 C4
Lloyd Street WC1 .... 240 C4
Lloyd's Avenue EC3 .... 246 A3
Lloyd's Row EC1 .... 241 D4
Lockesfield Place E14 .... 248 B1
Locksley Street E14 .... 247 F4
Lockwood Square SE16 .... 247 D1
Lodge Road NW8 .... 238 C4
Loftie Street SE16 .... 246 B1
Lolesworth Close E1 .... 246 B4
Lollard Street SE11 .... 244 C2
Loman Street SE1 .... 245 E4
Lomas Street E1 .... 246 C4
Lombard Court EC4 .... 241 F1
Lombard Lane EC4 .... 241 D1
  Temple Lane
London Bridge EC4 & SE1 ... 241 F1
London Bridge Street SE1 .... 245 F4
London Road EC3 .... 245 D3
London Street EC3 .... 246 A3
London Street W2 .... 238 C2
London Wall EC2 .... 241 E2
Long Acre WC2 .... 240 B1
Long Lane EC1 .... 241 E3
Long Lane SE1 .... 245 F3
Long Walk SE1 .... 246 A1
Long Yard WC1 .... 240 C3
Longford Street NW1 .... 239 F3
Longridge Road SW5 .... 242 A2
Longville Road SE11 .... 245 D2
Lord Hill's Bridge W2 .... 238 A2
Lord Hill's Road W2 .... 238 A2
Lord North Street SW1 .... 244 B3
Lordship Place SW3 .... 242 C1
  Lawrence Street
Lorenzo Street WC1 .... 240 C4
Lorrimore Road SE17 .... 245 E1
Lorrimore Square SE17 .... 245 E1
Lothbury EC2 .... 241 F2
Loughborough Street SE11 ... 244 C1

Lovat Lane EC3 241
Love Lane EC3 241
Lovegrove Walk E14 248
Lovell Place SE16 247
Lovers' Walk W1 243
Lowell Street E14 247
Lower Belgrave Street SW1 .. 243
Lower Grosvenor Place SW1 . 243
Lower James Street W1 240
Lower John Street W1 240
Lower Marsh SE1 247
Lower Road SE8 & SE16 247
Lower Robert Street WC2 240
  Savoy Place
Lower Sloane Street SW1 243
Lower Thames Street EC3 241
Lowndes Place SW1 243
Lowndes Square SW1 243
Lowndes Street SW1 243
Lowood Street E1 246
  Bewley Street
Loxham Street WC1 240
  Cromer Street
Lucan Place SW3 242
Lucerne Mews W8 242
Lucey Road SE16 246
Ludgate Broadway EC4 241
  Pilgrim Street
Ludgate Circus EC4 241
Ludgate Square EC4 241
Luke Street EC2 241
Lukin Street E1 247
Lumley Street W1 239
  Brown Hart Garden
Lupus Street SW1 243
Luralda Gardens E14 248
Luton Street NW8 238
Luxborough Street W1 239
Lyall Street SW1 243
Lygon Place SW1 243
Lynch Walk SE8 248
Lyons Place NW8 238
Lytham Street SE17 245

M

Mabledon Place WC1 240
Macclesfield Road EC1 241
Mackenzie Walk E14 248
Macklin Street WC2 240
Mackworth Street NW1 239
Macleod Street SE17 245
Maconochies Road E14 248
Macquarie Way E14 248
Maddock Way SE17 245
Maddox Street W1 239
Magdalen Street SE1 246
Magee Street SE11 245
Magellan Place E14 248
  Maritime Quay
Maguire Street SE1 246
Mahogany Close SE16 247
Maida Avenue W2 238
Maida Vale W9 238
Maiden Lane WC2 240
Maiden Lane SE1 245
Makins Street SW3 243
Malabar Street E14 248
Malet Street WC1 240
Mallord Street SW3 242
Mallory Street NW8 238
Mallow Street EC1 241
Maltby Street SE1 246
Maltravers Street WC2 240
Managers Street E14 248
Manchester Grove E14 248
Manchester Road E14 248
Manchester Square W1 239
Manchester Street W1 239
Manciple Street SE1 245
Mandarin Street E14 248
Mandeville Place W1 239
Manette Street W1 240
Manilla Street E14 248
Manningford Close EC1 241
Manningtree Street E1 246
  Commercial Road
Manor Place SE17 245
Manresa Road SW3 242
Mansell Street E1 246
Mansfield Mews W1 239
  Mansfield Street
Mansfield Street W1 239
Mansion House Place EC4 ... 241
  St Swithun's Lane
Manson Mews SW7 242
Manson Place SW7 242
Maple Leaf Square SE16 247
Maples Place E1 246
Marble Arch W1 239
Marchmont Street WC1 240
Margaret Court W1 239
  Margaret Street
Margaret Street W1 239
Margaretta Terrace SW3 242
Margery Street WC1 240
Marigold Street SE16 246
Mariners Mews E14 248
Maritime Quay E14 248
Marjorie Mews E1 247
Mark Lane EC3 246
Market Court E14 247
  Oxford Street
Market Mews W1 243
Market Place W1 239
Markham Place SW3 243
  Elystan Place
Markham Square SW3 243
Markham Street SW3 243
Marlborough Close SE17 245
Marlborough Road SW1 244
Marlborough Street SW3 242
Marloes Road W8 242
Marlow Way SE16 247
Marne Street W10 246
Maroon Street E14 247
Marsh Street E14 248
Marsh Wall E14 248
Marshall Street W1 240
Marshall's Place SE16 246
Marshalsea Road SE1 245
Marsham Street SW1 244
Marshfield Street E14 248
Marsland Close SE17 245
Martha Street E1 247
Martin Lane EC4 241
  Martin's Lane
Martlett Court WC2 240
Marylands Road W9 238
Marylebone High Street W1 .. 239
Marylebone Lane W1 239
Marylebone Mews W1 239

arylebone Road NW1 ... 239 D3
rylebone Street W1 ... 239 E2
ryle Way SE1 ... 244 C2
son Street SE17 ... 245 F3
son's Arms Mews W1 ... 239 F1
Maddox Street
son's Place EC1 ... 241 E4
son's Street W1 ... 239 E2
Duke Street
ssinger Street SE17 ... 245 F2
st House Terrace E14 ... 248 A2
ester's Street E1 ... 247 E4
stmaker Road E14 ... 248 A2
lock Street E1 ... 247 E4
thew Parker Street SW1 ... 244 B3
unsel Street SW1 ... 244 A2
y's Court WC2 ... 240 B1
St Martin's Lane
fair Place W1 ... 243 F4
flower Street SE16 ... 247 D1
ynards Quay E1 ... 246 C3
Auley Close SE1 ... 244 C3
Cleod's Mews SW7 ... 242 B2
ad Row SE1 ... 245 D3
adcroft Road SE11 ... 245 D1
adow Row SE1 ... 245 E2
ard Street W1 ... 240 A2
cklenburgh Street WC1 ... 240 C3
cklenburgh Square WC1 ... 240 C3
cklenburgh Street WC1 ... 240 C3
Mecklenburgh Square
dway Street SW1 ... 244 A2
bury Terrace NW1 ... 239 D3
lcombe Place NW1 ... 239 D3
lcombe Street NW1 ... 239 D3
lina Place NW8 ... 238 B4
lior Place SE1 ... 245 F4
Snowsfields
llish Street E14 ... 248 A3
lon Place W8 ... 242 A4
Kensington Church Street
lton Street NW1 ... 240 A4
mel Court EC1 ... 241 E3
Baltic Street
pham Street SE1 ... 244 C4
rcator Place E14 ... 248 A1
Napier Avenue
rcer Street WC2 ... 240 B1
redith Street EC1 ... 241 D4
ridian Place E14 ... 248 B3
rlin Street W1 ... 241 D4
rmaid Court SE1 ... 245 F4
rmaid Court SE16 ... 247 F2
rmaid Row SE1 ... 245 F3
rrick Street SE1 ... 245 E3
rrington Road SW6 ... 242 A1
thley Street SE17 ... 245 E1
ws Street SE1 ... 246 B2
ymott Street SE1 ... 245 D4
Lawber Street N1 ... 241 E4
ddle Street EC4 ... 241 E2
ddle Temple Lane EC4 ... 240 C2
ddle Yard SE1 ... 245 F4
ddlesex Street E1 ... 246 A4
ddleton Drive SE16 ... 247 E2
ddleton Drive ... 240 A3
Tottenham Court Road
lhope Street WC1 ... 240 B4
lland Street E14 ... 248 B1
lland Road NW1 ... 240 B4
dship Close SE16 ... 247 E2
borne Grove SW10 ... 242 B1
cote Street SE1 ... 245 D3
e End Road E1 ... 246 C4
es Street SW8 ... 244 B1
ford Lane WC2 ... 240 C1
k Street E2 ... 241 E2
k Yard SE1 ... 247 D3
l Place E14 ... 247 F3
l Street E1 ... 246 B1
l Street W1 ... 239 F1
lbank SW1 ... 244 B2
lennium Drive E14 ... 248 C2
lennium Square SE1 ... 246 B2
lharbour E14 ... 248 A3
ligan Street E14 ... 247 F3
lman Street WC1 ... 240 C3
lstream Road SW1 ... 246 A1
lwall Dock Road E14 ... 248 A3
ner Street SW3 ... 243 D2
ton Court EC2 ... 241 F3
verton Street SE11 ... 245 D1
ward Street E1 ... 246 C4
ncing Lane EC3 ... 246 A3
nera Mews SW1 ... 243 E2
nories EC3 ... 246 A3
n Street SE1 ... 245 E3
randa Close E1 ... 246 C4
tchell Street EC1 ... 241 E3
tre Road SE1 ... 245 D3
tre Square EC3 ... 246 A3
Mitre Street
lyneux Street W1 ... 239 D2
nck Street SW1 ... 244 B3
ncorvo Close SW7 ... 242 C3
nkton Street SE11 ... 245 D2
nkwell Square EC2 ... 241 E2
nmouth Road W2 ... 238 A2
nmouth Street WC2 ... 240 B1
ntagu Mansions W1 ... 239 D3
ntagu Mews North W1 ... 239 D2
ntagu Mews South W1 ... 239 D2
ntagu Mews West W1 ... 239 D2
ntagu Place W1 ... 239 D2
ntagu Row W1 ... 239 D2
ntagu Square W1 ... 239 D2
ntagu Street W1 ... 239 D2
ntague Close SE1 ... 245 F4
ntague Place WC1 ... 240 B3
ntague Place EC1 ... 241 E2
ntague Street WC1 ... 240 B3
ntford Place SE1 ... 244 C1
ntpelier Mews SW7 ... 243 D3
ntpelier Place SW7 ... 243 D3
ntpelier Street SW7 ... 243 D3
ntpelier Square SW7 ... 243 D3
ntpelier Street SW7 ... 243 D3
ntpelier Walk SW7 ... 243 D3
ntreal Place WC2 ... 240 C1
ntrose Court SW7 ... 242 C3
ntrose Place SW1 ... 243 E3
nument Street EC3 ... 241 F1
nza Street SE17 ... 245 D2
odkee Street SE16 ... 247 D1
or Lane EC2 ... 241 F2
or Place EC2 ... 241 F2
Moorfields
ore Street SW3 ... 240 A1
Old Compton Street
orfields EC2 ... 241 F2
orgate EC2 ... 241 F2
ra Street E1 ... 241 E4
recombe Close SE1 ... 247 D4
recombe Street SE17 ... 245 E2
reland Street EC1 ... 241 E4
reton Place SW1 ... 244 A2

Moreton Street SW1 ... 244 A2
Moreton Terrace SW1 ... 244 A1
Morley Street SE1 ... 245 D3
Morocco Street SE1 ... 245 F3
Morpeth Terrace SW1 ... 243 F2
Morris Street E1 ... 246 C3
Morshead Road W9 ... 238 A4
Mortimer Market WC1 ... 240 A3
Capper Street
Mortimer Street W1 ... 239 F2
Morton Mews SW5 ... 242 A2
Earl's Court Gardens
Morwell Street WC1 ... 240 A2
Moscow Place W2 ... 238 A1
Moscow Road W2 ... 238 A1
Moss Close E1 ... 246 B4
Mossop Street SW3 ... 243 D2
Motcomb Street SW1 ... 243 E2
Mount Pleasant WC1 ... 240 C3
Mount Row W1 ... 239 E1
Mount Street W1 ... 239 E1
Mount Terrace E1 ... 246 C4
Moxon Street W1 ... 239 E2
Mozart Terrace SW1 ... 243 E2
Muirfield Crescent E14 ... 248 B3
Mulberry Street E1 ... 246 B4
Mulberry Walk SW3 ... 242 C1
Mulready Street NW8 ... 238 C3
Mulvaney Way SE1 ... 245 F3
Mumford Court EC2 ... 241 E2
Milk Street
Mundy Street N1 ... 241 F4
Munster Square NW1 ... 239 F4
Munton Road SE17 ... 245 E2
Murphy Street SE1 ... 244 C3
Murray Grove N1 ... 241 E4
Musbury Street E1 ... 247 D4
Muscovy Street EC3 ... 246 A3
Museum Street WC1 ... 240 B2
Myddelton Passage EC1 ... 241 D4
Myddelton Square EC1 ... 241 D4
Myddelton Street EC1 ... 241 D4
Mylne Street EC1 ... 241 D4
Myrdle Street E1 ... 246 C4
Myrtle Walk N1 ... 241 F4

N

Naoroji Street WC1 ... 240 C4
Napier Avenue E14 ... 248 A1
Narrow Street E14 ... 247 E1
Nash Place E14 ... 248 A4
Nash Street NW1 ... 239 F4
Nassau Street W1 ... 239 F2
Nathaniel Close E1 ... 246 B4
Throwl Street
National Terrace SE16 ... 246 C1
Bermondsey Wall East
Neal Street E2 ... 240 B2
Wilton Road
Neathouse Place SW1 ... 243 F2
Nebraska Street SE1 ... 245 E3
Neckinger SE1 ... 246 B1
Neckinger Street SE1 ... 246 B1
Nelson Court SE16 ... 247 D2
Nelson Passage EC1 ... 241 E4
Mora Street
Nelson Place N1 ... 241 E4
Nelson Square SE1 ... 245 D4
Nelson Street E1 ... 246 C4
Nelson Terrace N1 ... 241 D4
Nelson Walk SE16 ... 247 F2
Neptune Street SE16 ... 247 D1
Nesham Street E1 ... 246 B3
Netherton Grove SW10 ... 242 B1
Netley Street NW1 ... 239 F4
Nevern Place SW5 ... 242 A2
Nevern Square SW5 ... 242 A2
Neville Court EC4 ... 241 D2
Neville Street SW7 ... 242 C2
Neville Terrace SW7 ... 242 C1
New Bond Street W1 ... 239 F1
New Bridge Street EC4 ... 241 D2
New Broad Street EC2 ... 241 F2
New Burlington Mews W1 ... 246 A3
Hart Street
New Burlington Place W1 ... 239 F1
New Burlington Street W1 ... 239 F1
New Cavendish Street W1 ... 239 E2
New Change EC4 ... 241 E2
New Compton Street WC2 ... 240 B2
New Crane Place E1 ... 247 D2
New Fetter Lane EC4 ... 241 D2
New Globe Walk SE1 ... 245 E4
New Goulston Street E1 ... 246 A4
New Kent Road SE1 ... 245 E2
New King Street SE8 ... 248 A1
New North Place EC2 ... 241 F3
New North Road N1 ... 241 F4
New North Street WC1 ... 240 C3
New Oxford Street WC1 ... 240 B2
New Quebec Street W1 ... 239 D2
New Ride SW7 ... 242 C3
New Road E1 ... 246 C4
New Row WC2 ... 240 B1
New Spring Gardens Walk SE11 ... 244 B1
Goding Street
New Square WC2 ... 240 C2
New Street EC2 ... 246 A4
New Street Square EC4 ... 241 D2
New Turnstile WC1 ... 240 B2
High Holborn
New Union Close E14 ... 248 C3
New Union Street EC2 ... 241 E2
Newark Street E1 ... 246 C4
Newburgh Street W1 ... 240 F1
Foubert's Place
Newburn Street SE11 ... 244 C1
Newbury Street EC1 ... 241 E2
Newcastle Place W2 ... 238 C3
Newcomen Street SE1 ... 245 F4
Newell Street E14 ... 247 F3
Newgate Street EC1 ... 241 D2
Newington Butts SE1 & SE11 ... 245 D2
Newington Causeway SE1 ... 245 E3
Newlands Quay E1 ... 247 D3
Newman Street W1 ... 240 A2
Newman's Row WC2 ... 240 C2
Lincoln's Inn Fields
Newnham Terrace SE1 ... 244 C3
Newnhams Row SE1 ... 246 A1
Newport Place WC2 ... 240 B1
Newport Street SE11 ... 244 C2
Newton Road W2 ... 238 A2
Newton Street WC2 ... 240 B2
Nicholas Lane EC4 ... 241 F1
Nicholson Street SE1 ... 245 D4
Nightingale Place SW10 ... 242 B1
Nile Street N1 ... 241 E4
Nine Elms Lane SW8 ... 244 A1
Noble Street EC2 ... 241 E2
Noel Street W1 ... 240 A2
Norbiton Road E14 ... 247 F4
Norfolk Crescent W2 ... 238 C2

Norfolk Place W2 ... 238 C2
Norfolk Square W2 ... 238 C2
Norman Street EC1 ... 241 E4
Norris Street SW1 ... 240 A1
North Audley Street W1 ... 239 E1
North Bank NW8 ... 238 C4
North Colonnade E14 ... 248 A4
North Crescent WC1 ... 240 A3
North Flockton Street SE16 ... 246 B1
Chambers Street
North Gower Street NW1 ... 240 A4
North Mews WC1 ... 240 C3
North Ride W2 ... 238 C1
North Row W1 ... 239 E1
North Tenter Street E1 ... 246 B3
North Terrace SW3 ... 242 C2
North Wharf Road W2 ... 238 B2
Northampton Road EC1 ... 241 D3
Northampton Row EC1 ... 241 D3
Exmouth Market
Northampton Square EC1 ... 241 D4
Northburg Street EC1 ... 241 E4
Northchurch SE17 ... 245 F2
Northdown Street N1 ... 240 C4
Northington Street WC1 ... 240 C3
Northumberland Alley EC3 ... 246 A3
Northumberland Avenue WC2 ... 244 B4
Northumberland Street WC2 ... 240 B1
Northwick Close NW8 ... 238 C3
Northwick Terrace NW8 ... 238 B3
Northy Street E14 ... 247 E3
Norton Folgate E1 ... 246 A4
Norway Gate SE16 ... 247 E1
Norway Place E14 ... 247 F3
Norwich Street EC4 ... 241 D2
Notting Hill Gate W11 ... 238 A1
Nottingham Place W1 ... 239 E3
Nottingham Street W1 ... 239 E3
Nugent Terrace NW8 ... 238 B4

O

O'Leary Square E1 ... 247 D4
O'Meara Street SE1 ... 245 E4
Oak Lane E14 ... 247 F3
Oak Tree Road NW8 ... 238 C4
Oakden Street SE11 ... 245 D2
Oakfield Street SW10 ... 242 B1
Oakington Road W9 ... 238 A3
Oakley Crescent EC1 ... 241 E4
Oakley Gardens SW3 ... 243 D1
Oakley Street SW3 ... 242 C1
Oat Lane EC2 ... 241 E2
Observatory Gardens W8 ... 242 A4
Observatory Mews E14 ... 248 C2
Storers Quay
Occupation Road SE17 ... 245 E1
Ocean Street E1 ... 247 E4
Ocean Wharf E14 ... 248 A3
Octagon Arcade EC2 ... 241 F3
Octagon Court SE16 ... 247 E1
Odessa Street SE16 ... 247 F1
Ogle Street W1 ... 239 F2
Old Bailey EC4 ... 241 D2
Old Bond Street W1 ... 239 F1
Old Broad Street EC2 ... 241 F2
Old Brompton Road SW5 & SW7 ... 242 A1
Old Burlington Street W1 ... 239 F1
Old Castle Street E1 ... 246 B4
Old Cavendish Street W1 ... 239 F2
Old Church Road E1 ... 247 D4
Old Church Street SW3 ... 242 C1
Old Compton Street W1 ... 240 A1
Old Court Place W8 ... 242 A3
Old Fleet Lane EC4 ... 241 D2
Old Gloucester Street WC1 ... 240 B3
Old Jamaica Road SE16 ... 246 B1
Old Jewry EC2 ... 241 F2
Old Marylebone Road NW1 ... 239 D2
Old Mitre Court EC4 ... 241 D2
Fleet Street
Old Montagu Street E1 ... 246 B4
Old North Street WC1 ... 240 C3
Theobalds Road
Old Palace Yard SW1 ... 244 B3
Old Paradise Street SE11 ... 244 C2
Old Park Lane W1 ... 243 E4
Old Pye Street SW1 ... 244 A3
Old Quebec Street W1 ... 239 D2
Old Queen Street SW1 ... 244 A3
Old Square WC2 ... 240 C2
Old Street EC1 ... 241 E3
Old Theatre Court SE1 ... 244 E4
Park Street
Old Woolwich Road SE10 ... 248 C1
Oldbury Place W1 ... 239 E3
Olivers Yard EC1 ... 241 F3
Olliffe Street E14 ... 248 C2
Olney Road SE7 ... 245 E1
Olympia Mews W2 ... 238 B1
Omega Close E14 ... 248 A3
Omega Street SE16 ... 247 E1
Ongar Road SW6 ... 242 A1
Onslow Gardens SW7 ... 242 B2
Onslow Mews SW7 ... 242 C2
Onslow Square SW7 ... 242 C2
Onslow Street EC1 ... 241 D3
Ontario Street SE1 ... 245 E3
Ontario Way E14 ... 248 A4
Opal Street SE11 ... 245 D2
Orange Place SE16 ... 247 D1
Orange Street WC2 ... 240 B1
Orb Street SE17 ... 245 F2
Orchard Street W1 ... 239 E2
Orchardson Street NW8 ... 238 C3
Orde Hall Street WC1 ... 240 C3
Orient Street SE11 ... 245 D2
Orme Court W2 ... 238 A1
Orme Lane W2 ... 238 A1
Orme Square W2 ... 238 A1
Ormond Yard SW1 ... 240 A1
Ormonde Gate SW3 ... 243 D1
Orsett Street SE11 ... 244 C2
Orsett Terrace W2 ... 238 B2
Orton Street E1 ... 246 B2
Wapping High Street
Osbert Street SW1 ... 244 A2
Osborne Street E1 ... 246 B4
Oslo Square SE16 ... 247 E1
Osnaburgh Street NW1 ... 239 F3
Osnaburgh Terrace NW1 ... 239 F3
Albany Street
Ossington Buildings W1 ... 239 E2
Moxon Street
Ossington Street W2 ... 238 A1
Osulston Street NW1 ... 240 A4
Osten Mews SW7 ... 242 B2
Oswin Street SE11 ... 245 D2
Othello Close SE1 ... 245 D1
Otto Street SE17 ... 244 C1
Oval Way SE11 ... 244 C1
Ovex Close E14 ... 248 C3

Ovington Gardens SW3 ... 243 D3
Ovington Square SW3 ... 243 D3
Ovington Street SW3 ... 243 D2
Owen Street EC1 ... 241 D4
Oxendon Street SW1 ... 240 A1
Coventry Street
Oxford Circus W1 ... 239 F2
Regent Street
Oxford Square W2 ... 238 C2
Oxford Street W1 ... 239 E1
Oyster Row E1 ... 247 D3
Oystergate Walk EC4 ... 241 F1

P

Paddington Green W2 ... 238 C3
Paddington Street W1 ... 239 E3
Page Street SW1 ... 244 B2
Pageant Crescent SE16 ... 247 F2
Pageant Steps SE16 ... 247 E2
Pageantmaster Court EC4 ... 241 D2
Ludgate Hill
Paget Street EC1 ... 241 D4
Pakenham Street WC1 ... 240 C3
Palace Avenue W8 ... 242 A4
Palace Court W2 ... 238 A1
Palace Gardens Mews W8 ... 242 A4
Palace Gardens Terrace W8 ... 242 A4
Palace Gate W8 ... 242 B3
Palace Street SW1 ... 243 F2
Pall Mall SW1 ... 244 A4
Pall Mall East SW1 ... 240 B1
Pall Mall Place SW1 ... 244 A4
Palmer Street SW1 ... 244 A3
Pancras Lane EC4 ... 241 E2
Panton Street SW1 ... 240 A1
Paradise Street SE16 ... 246 C1
Paradise Walk SW3 ... 243 D1
Paragon Mews SE1 ... 245 F2
Searles Road
Pardoner Street SE1 ... 245 F3
Parfetts Street E1 ... 246 C4
Paris Garden SE1 ... 245 D4
Park Approach SE16 ... 246 C1
Park Crescent W1 ... 239 E3
Park Crescent Mews East W1 ... 239 E3
Park Crescent Mews West W1 ... 239 E3
Park Lane W1 ... 239 E1
Park Place SW1 ... 243 F4
Park Place E14 ... 248 A4
Park Place Villas W2 ... 238 B3
Park Road NW1 & NW8 ... 239 D4
Park Row SE10 ... 248 C1
Park Square East NW1 ... 239 F3
Park Square Mews W1 ... 239 E3
Harley Street
Park Square West NW1 ... 239 E3
Park Street SE1 ... 245 E4
Park Street W1 ... 239 E1
Park Walk SW10 ... 242 B1
Park West Place W2 ... 239 D2
Parker Street WC2 ... 240 B2
Parkers Row SE1 ... 246 B1
Parliament Square SW1 ... 244 B3
Parliament Street SW1 ... 244 B4
Parnham Street E14 ... 247 E4
Parry Street SW8 ... 244 B1
Parsonage Street E14 ... 248 C2
Pasley Close SE17 ... 245 E2
Passmore Street SW1 ... 243 E2
Pastor Street SE11 ... 245 D2
Pater Street W8 ... 242 A3
Paternoster Row EC4 ... 241 E2
Paternoster Square EC4 ... 241 E2
Paul Julius Close E14 ... 248 C4
Paul Street EC2 ... 241 F3
Paul's Walk EC4 ... 241 E1
Paultons Square SW3 ... 242 C1
Paveley Street NW8 ... 238 C4
Pavilion Road SW1 ... 243 D2
Pavilion Street SW1 ... 243 D2
Peabody Avenue SW1 ... 243 F1
Peacock Street SE17 ... 245 E2
Pear Tree Court EC1 ... 241 D3
Pear Tree Street EC1 ... 241 E3
Pearl Street E1 ... 246 C2
Pearman Street SE1 ... 245 D3
Peartree Lane E1 ... 247 D3
Peerless Street EC1 ... 241 E4
Pelham Crescent SW7 ... 242 C2
Pelham Place SW7 ... 242 C2
Pelham Street SW7 ... 242 C2
Pelier Street SE17 ... 245 E1
Pelling Street E14 ... 247 F4
Pemberton Row EC4 ... 241 D2
Pembridge Gardens W2 ... 238 A1
Pembridge Mews W2 ... 238 A1
Pembridge Road W11 ... 238 A1
Pembridge Square W2 ... 238 A1
Pembroke Mews W8 ... 242 A2
Earls Court Road
Penang Street E1 ... 246 C2
Penfold Place NW1 ... 238 C3
Penfold Street NW1 & NW8 ... 238 C3
Pennant Mews W8 ... 242 A2
Pennington Street E1 ... 246 C3
Penrose Grove SE17 ... 245 E1
Penrose Street SE17 ... 245 E1
Penryn Street NW1 ... 240 A4
Penton Place SE17 ... 245 D2
Penton Rise WC1 ... 240 C4
Pentonville Road N1 ... 240 C4
Pepper Street SE1 ... 245 E4
Pepper Street E14 ... 248 B3
Pepys Street EC3 ... 246 A3
Percival Street EC1 ... 241 D3
Percy Circus WC1 ... 240 C4
Percy Street W1 ... 240 A2
Perkin's Rents SW1 ... 244 A3
Perkins Square SE1 ... 245 E4
Perry's Place W1 ... 240 A2
Perryn Road SE16 ... 246 C1
Peter Street W1 ... 240 A1
Peter's Hill EC4 ... 241 E2
Peter's Lane EC1 ... 241 D3
Petersham Lane SW7 ... 242 B3
Petersham Mews SW7 ... 242 B3
Petersham Place SW7 ... 242 B3
Peto Place NW1 ... 239 E3
Petticoat Lane E1 ... 246 A4
Petticoat Square E1 ... 246 A4
Petty France SW1 ... 244 A3
Petyward SW3 ... 243 D2
Phelp Street SE17 ... 245 F1
Phene Street SW3 ... 243 D1
Philchurch Place E1 ... 246 B3
Phillimore Walk W8 ... 242 A3
Philpot Lane EC3 ... 241 F1
Philpot Street E1 ... 246 C4
Phipp Street EC2 ... 241 F3
Phoenix Place WC1 ... 240 C3
Phoenix Road NW1 ... 240 A4
Phoenix Street WC2 ... 240 B2
Charing Cross Road

Piccadilly W1 ... 243 F4
Piccadilly Arcade SW1 ... 244 A4
Piccadilly
Piccadilly Circus W1 ... 240 A1
Piccadilly Place W1 ... 240 A1
Vine Street
Pickard Street EC1 ... 241 E4
Pickford Wharf N1 ... 241 E4
Pickwick Street SE1 ... 245 E3
Picton Place W1 ... 239 E2
Pier Street E14 ... 248 C2
Piggot Street E14 ... 247 F3
Pilgrim Street EC4 ... 241 D2
Pilgrimage Street SE1 ... 245 F3
Pimlico Road SW1 ... 243 E2
Pinchin Street E1 ... 246 B3
Pindar Street EC2 ... 241 F3
Pindock Mews W9 ... 238 A3
Pine Street EC1 ... 241 D3
Pitfield Street N1 ... 241 F4
Pitsea Place E1 ... 247 D4
Pitsea Street E1 ... 247 D4
Pitt Street W8 ... 242 A3
Pitt's Head Mews W1 ... 243 E4
Pixley Street E14 ... 247 F4
Platina Street EC2 ... 241 F3
Playhouse Yard EC4 ... 241 D1
Plevina Street E14 ... 248 B3
Pleydell Street EC4 ... 241 D1
Bouverie Street
Plough Place EC4 ... 241 D2
Fetter Lane
Plover Way SE16 ... 247 E1
Plumber's Row E1 ... 246 B4
Plumtree Court EC4 ... 241 D2
Plymouth Wharf E14 ... 248 C2
Plympton Street NW8 ... 238 C3
Pocock Street SE1 ... 245 D3
Pointers Close E14 ... 248 B1
Poland Street W1 ... 240 A2
Pollen Street W1 ... 239 F1
Pollitt Drive NW8 ... 238 C3
Polygon Road NW1 ... 240 A4
Pomwell Way E1 ... 246 B4
Pond Place SW3 ... 242 C2
Ponler Street E1 ... 246 C3
Ponsonby Place SW1 ... 244 B2
Ponsonby Terrace SW1 ... 244 B2
Pont Street SW1 ... 243 D3
Pont Street Mews SW1 ... 243 D3
Poolmans Street SE16 ... 247 D2
Poonah Street E1 ... 247 D3
Pope Street SE1 ... 246 A1
Poplar Place W2 ... 238 A1
Poppins Court EC4 ... 241 D2
Fleet Street
Porchester Gardens W2 ... 238 A1
Porchester Place W2 ... 239 D2
Porchester Road W2 ... 238 A2
Porchester Square W2 ... 238 A2
Porchester Terrace W2 ... 238 B1
Porlock Street SE1 ... 245 F3
Porter Street W1 ... 239 E3
Porter Street SE1 ... 245 E4
Porteus Road W2 ... 238 B2
Portland Mews W1 ... 240 A2
D'Arblay Street
Portland Place W1 ... 239 F2
Portland Square E1 ... 246 C2
Portland Street SE17 ... 245 F1
Portman Close W1 ... 239 E2
Portman Mews South W1 ... 239 E2
Portman Square W1 ... 239 E2
Portman Street W1 ... 239 E2
Portpool Lane EC1 ... 240 C3
Portsea Place W2 ... 239 D2
Portsmouth Street WC2 ... 240 C2
Portugal Street
Portsoken Street EC3 ... 246 B3
Portugal Street WC2 ... 240 C2
Potier Street SE1 ... 245 F3
Pottery Street SE16 ... 246 C1
Poultry EC2 ... 241 E2
Praed Street W2 ... 238 C2
Pratt Walk SE11 ... 244 C2
Premier Place E14 ... 248 A4
Prescot Street E1 ... 246 B3
President Street EC1 ... 241 E4
Central Street
Presidents Drive E1 ... 246 C2
Prestage Way E14 ... 248 C4
Prestons Road E14 ... 248 C4
Prestwood Street N1 ... 241 E4
Wenlock Road
Price's Street SE1 ... 245 D4
Prideaux Place WC1 ... 240 C4
Primrose Hill EC4 ... 241 D1
Hutton Street
Primrose Street EC2 ... 246 A4
Prince Albert Road NW1 & NW8 ... 238 C4
Prince Consort Road SW7 ... 242 C3
Prince of Wales Terrace W8 ... 242 B1
Kensington Road
Prince's Gardens SW7 ... 242 C3
Prince's Gate SW7 ... 242 C3
Prince's Gate Mews SW7 ... 242 C3
Prince's Mews W2 ... 238 A1
Prince's Square W2 ... 238 A1
Princelet Street E1 ... 246 B4
Princes Arcade SW1 ... 244 A4
Piccadilly
Princes Circus WC2 ... 240 B2
Princes Court E1 ... 246 C3
Princes Riverside Road SE16 ... 247 E2
Princes Street EC2 ... 241 F2
Princes Street W1 ... 239 F2
Princess Street SE1 ... 245 D3
Princeton Street WC1 ... 240 C2
Printer Street EC4 ... 241 D2
Prioress Street SE1 ... 245 F3
Priory Walk SW10 ... 242 B1
Procter Street WC1 ... 240 C2
Prospect Place E1 ... 247 D2
Prospect Street SE16 ... 246 C1
Providence Court W1 ... 239 E1
Providence Square SE1 ... 246 B2
Provost Street N1 ... 241 F4
Prusom Street E1 ... 246 C2
Pudding Lane EC3 ... 241 F1
Puddle Dock EC4 ... 241 D2
Puma Court E1 ... 246 B4
Purbrook Street SE1 ... 246 A1

Q

Quarley Way SE15 ... 239 D2
New Quebec Street
Quebec Way SE16 ... 247 E1
Queen Anne Mews W1 ... 239 F2
Chandos Street
Queen Anne Street W1 ... 239 E2
Queen Anne's Gate SW1 ... 244 A3
Queen Elizabeth Street SE1 ... 246 A2

254

Queen Square WC1 .... 240 B3
Queen Street EC4 .... 241 E1
Queen Street W1 .... 241 F4
Queen Street Place EC4 .... 241 E1
Queen Victoria Street EC4 .... 241 D1
Queen's Gardens SW1 .... 243 F3
Queen's Gardens W2 .... 238 B1
Queen's Gate SW7 .... 242 B2
Queen's Gate Gardens SW7 ...... 242 B2
Queen's Gate Mews SW7 .... 242 B3
Queen's Gate Place SW7 .... 242 B2
Queen's Gate Place Mews SW7 .. 242 B2
Queen's Gate Terrace SW7 .... 242 B3
Queen's Mews W2 .... 238 A1
Queen's Row SE17 .... 245 D2
Queen's Walk SW1 .... 243 F3
Queenhithe EC4 .... 241 E1
Queensberry Mews West SW7 .... 242 B2
Queensberry Place SW7 .... 239 F4
Harrington Street
Queensborough Terrace W2 .... 238 B1
Queensway W2 .... 238 A2
Quick Street N1 .... 241 D4

R

Rabbit Row W8 .... 242 A4
Raby Street E14 .... 247 E4
Radcliffe Road SE1 .... 246 A1
Radcot Street SE11 .... 245 D1
Radley Court SE16 .... 247 E2
Radley Mews W8 .... 242 A2
Radnor Mews W2 .... 238 C2
Radnor Place W2 .... 238 C2
Radnor Street EC1 .... 241 D3
Radnor Walk SW3 .... 243 D1
Railway Approach SE1 .... 245 F4
Railway Avenue SE16 .... 247 D3
Rainbow Avenue E14 .... 248 B1
Raine Street E1 .... 246 C2
Rainsford Street W2 .... 238 C2
Ralston Street SW3 .... 243 D1
Ramillies Place W1 .... 239 F2
Ramillies Street W1 .... 240 A2
Rampart Street E1 .... 246 C4
Rampayne Street SW1 .... 244 A2
Ramsey Mews SW3 .... 242 C1
Randall Road SE11 .... 244 C2
Randall Row SE11 .... 244 C2
Randolph Avenue W9 .... 238 A4
Randolph Crescent W9 .... 238 B3
Randolph Mews W9 .... 238 B3
Randolph Road W9 .... 238 B3
Ranelagh Bridge W2 .... 238 B2
Ranelagh Grove SW1 .... 243 E2
Ranelagh Road SW1 .... 244 A1
Ranston Street NW1 .... 238 C3
Raphael Street SW7 .... 243 D3
Ratcliff Grove EC1 .... 241 E4
Ratcliffe Cross Street E1 .... 247 E3
Ratcliffe Lane E14 .... 247 E3
Rathbone Place W1 .... 240 A2
Raven Row E1 .... 246 C4
Ravensdon Street SE11 .... 245 D1
Ravent Road SE11 .... 244 C2
Ravey Street EC2 .... 241 F3
Rawlings Street SW3 .... 243 D2
Rawstorne Place EC1 .... 241 D4
Rawstorne Street
Rawstorne Street EC1 .... 241 D4
Ray Street EC1 .... 240 C3
Reardon Path E1 .... 246 C2
Reardon Street E1 .... 246 C2
Rebecca Terrace SE16 .... 247 D1
Rectory Square E1 .... 247 E4
Red Lion Row SE17 .... 245 E1
Red Lion Square WC1 .... 240 C2
Red Lion Street WC1 .... 240 C2
Redan Place W2 .... 238 A2
Redburn Street SW3 .... 243 D1
Redcastle Close E1 .... 247 D3
Redcliffe Gardens SW10 & SW5 .. 242 A1
Redcliffe Mews SW10 .... 242 B1
Redcliffe Place SW10 .... 242 B1
Redcliffe Road SW10 .... 242 B1
Redcliffe Square SW10 .... 242 A1
Redcliffe Street SW10 .... 242 A1
Redcross Way SE1 .... 245 E4
Rede Place W2 .... 238 A1
Redesdale Street SW3 .... 243 D1
Redfield Lane SW5 .... 242 A2
Redhill Street NW1 .... 239 F4
Redman's Road E1 .... 247 D4
Redmead Lane E1 .... 246 B2
Wapping High Street
Redriff Road SE16 .... 247 E1
Redwood Close SE16 .... 247 E2
Reece Mews SW7 .... 242 C1
Reedworth Street SE11 .... 245 D2
Reeves Mews W1 .... 239 E1
Regal Close E1 .... 246 C4
Regan Way N1 .... 241 F4
Regency Street SW1 .... 244 A2
Regent Square WC1 .... 240 B4
Regent Street W1 & SW1 .... 239 F2
Regnart Buildings NW1 .... 240 A4
Euston Street
Relton Mews SW7 .... 243 D3
Remington Street N1 .... 241 D4
Remnant Street WC2 .... 240 C2
Kingsway
Renforth Street SE16 .... 247 D1
Renfrew Road SE11 .... 245 D2
Rennie Street SE1 .... 241 D1
Rephidim Street SE1 .... 245 F3
Repton Street E14 .... 247 E4
Reston Place SW7 .... 242 B3
Reveley Close SE16 .... 247 E1
Rex Place W1 .... 239 E1
Rhodeswell Road E14 .... 247 E4
Rich Lane SW5 .... 242 A1
Rich Street E14 .... 247 F3
Richard's Place SW3 .... 243 D2
Richbell Place WC1 .... 240 C3
Emerald Street
Richmond Buildings W1 .... 240 A2
Dean Street
Richmond Mews W1 .... 240 A2
Richmond Terrace SW1 .... 244 B4
Rickett Street SW6 .... 242 A1
Ridgmount Gardens WC1 .... 240 A3
Ridgmount Street WC1 .... 240 A3
Riding House Street W1 .... 239 F2
Riley Road SE1 .... 246 A1
Ringwood Gardens E14 .... 248 A2
Risborough Street SE1 .... 245 E4
Risdon Street SE16 .... 247 D1
River Barge Close E14 .... 248 C3
River Street EC1 .... 241 D4
Riverside Walk SE1 .... 244 C4
Rivington Street EC2 .... 241 F3
Robert Adam Street W1 .... 239 E2
Robert Close W9 .... 238 B3

Robert Dashwood Way SE17 ..... 245 E2
Robert Street NW1 .... 239 F4
Robert Street WC2 .... 240 B1
Roberts Place EC1 .... 241 D3
Bowling Green Lane
Robinson Street SW3 .... 243 D1
Flood Street
Rochester Row SW1 .... 244 A2
Rochester Street SW1 .... 244 A2
Rockingham Street SE1 .... 245 E3
Rocliffe Street N1 .... 241 E4
Roding Mews E1 .... 246 B2
Rodmarton Street W1 .... 239 D2
Rodney Place SE17 .... 245 E2
Rodney Road SE17 .... 245 E2
Roffey Street E14 .... 248 B3
Roger Street WC1 .... 240 C3
Roland Gardens SW7 .... 242 B1
Roland Way SE17 .... 245 F1
Roland Way SW7 .... 242 B1
Rolls Buildings EC4 .... 241 D2
Rolls Passage EC4 .... 240 C2
Romford Street E1 .... 246 C4
Romilly Street W1 .... 240 A1
Romney Mews W1 .... 239 E3
Chiltern Street
Romney Street SW1 .... 244 B2
Ronald Street E1 .... 247 D3
Rood Lane EC3 .... 241 F1
Rope Street SE16 .... 247 E1
Ropemaker Road SE16 .... 247 E1
Ropemaker Street EC2 .... 241 F3
Ropemaker's Fields E14 .... 247 F3
Roper Lane SE1 .... 246 A1
Rosary Gardens SW7 .... 242 B2
Roscoe Street EC1 .... 241 E3
Rose & Crown Yard SW1 .... 244 A4
King Street
Rose Alley SE1 .... 245 E4
Rose Street WC2 .... 240 B1
Rosebery Avenue EC1 .... 240 C3
Rosemoor Street SW3 .... 243 D2
Roserton Street E14 .... 248 B3
Rosoman Place EC1 .... 241 D4
Rosoman Street
Rosoman Street EC1 .... 241 D4
Rossmore Road NW1 .... 239 D3
Rotary Street SE1 .... 245 D3
Rotherhithe Street SE16 .... 247 D2
Rotherhithe Tunnel Approach
E14 .... 247 E3
Rotherhithe Tunnel Approach
SE16 .... 247 F1
Rothsay Street SE1 .... 245 F3
Rotten Row SW7 & SW1 .... 242 C4
Rotterdam Drive E14 .... 248 C2
Rouel Road SE16 .... 246 B1
Roupell Street SE1 .... 245 D4
Rowington Close W2 .... 238 A3
Roxby Place SW6 .... 242 A1
Roy Square E14 .... 247 F3
Royal Avenue SW3 .... 243 D1
Royal Exchange Buildings EC3 ... 241 F2
Cornhill
Royal Hospital Road SW3 .... 243 D1
Royal Mint Place E1 .... 246 B3
Royal Mint Street E1 .... 246 B3
Royal Oak Yard SE1 .... 246 A1
Royal Opera Arcade SW1 .... 244 A4
Royal Road SE1 .... 245 D1
Royal Street SE1 .... 244 C3
Rudolf Place SW8 .... 244 B1
Rudolph Road NW6 .... 238 A4
Rufus Street N1 .... 241 F4
Rugby Street WC1 .... 240 C3
Rugg Street E14 .... 247 F3
Rum Close E1 .... 246 C3
Rupack Street SE16 .... 247 D1
Rupert Street W1 .... 240 A1
Rushworth Street SE1 .... 245 D3
Russell Court SW1 .... 244 A4
Cleveland Row
Russell Place SE16 .... 247 E1
Russell Square WC1 .... 240 B3
Russell Street WC2 .... 240 C1
Russia Dock Road SE16 .... 247 E2
Russia Row EC2 .... 241 E2
Russia Walk SE16 .... 247 E1
Rutherford Street SW1 .... 244 A2
Rutland Gardens SW7 .... 243 D3
Rutland Gate SW7 .... 242 C3
Rutland Gate Mews SW7 .... 242 C3
Rutland Gate
Rutland Mews East SW7 .... 242 C3
Ennismore Street
Rutland Mews South SW7 .... 242 C3
Ennismore Street
Rutland Place SW7 .... 241 E3
Rutland Street SW7 .... 242 C3
Rysbrack Street SW3 .... 243 D3

S

Sackville Street W1 .... 240 A1
Saddle Yard W1 .... 243 E4
Saffron Hill EC1 .... 241 D3
Saffron Street EC1 .... 241 D3
Sage Street E1 .... 246 C3
Sage Way WC1 .... 240 C4
Sail Street SE11 .... 244 C2
St Agnes Place SE11 .... 245 D1
St Alban's Grove W8 .... 242 A3
St Alban's Street SW1 .... 240 A1
St Albans Mews W2 .... 238 C3
Saint Street SE1 .... 245 E4
St Alphage Garden EC2 .... 241 E2
St Andrew Street EC4 .... 241 D2
St Andrew's Hill EC4 .... 241 D1
St Ann's Lane SW1 .... 244 A3
St Ann's Row E14 .... 247 F3
St Ann's Street SW1 .... 244 B3
St Anne Street E14 .... 247 F3
St Anne's Court W1 .... 240 A2
St Anselm's Place W1 .... 239 E1
St Anthony's Close E1 .... 246 B2
St Barnabas Street SW1 .... 243 E2
St Botolph Street EC3 .... 246 A4
St Bride Street EC4 .... 241 D2
St Catherines Mews SW3 .... 243 D2
Milner Street
St Chad's Place WC1 .... 240 B4
St Chad's Street WC1 .... 240 B4
St Christoper's Place W1 .... 239 E2
St Clare Street EC3 .... 246 A3
St Clement's Lane WC2 .... 240 C2
St Clements Court EC4 .... 241 F1
St Cross Street EC1 .... 241 D3
St David's Square E14 .... 248 B1
St Dunstan's Court EC4 .... 241 D2
Fleet Street
St Dunstan's Lane EC3 .... 241 F1
St Mary at Hill
St Dunstans Alley EC3 .... 246 A3
St Dunstans Hill
St Dunstans Hill EC3 .... 246 A3
St Ermins Hill SW1 .... 244 A3

St George Street W1 .... 239 F1
St George's Circus SE1 .... 245 D3
St George's Court EC4 .... 241 D2
St George's Drive SW1 .... 243 E2
St George's Mews SE1 .... 245 D3
St George's Road SE1 .... 245 D3
St George's Square SW1 .... 244 A1
St George's Square E14 .... 247 E3
St George's Square Mews SW1 .. 244 A1
St Georges Fields W2 .... 239 D1
St Giles High Street WC2 .... 240 B2
St Helen's Place EC3 .... 241 F2
St Helena Street WC1 .... 240 C4
St James's Court SW1 .... 244 A3
St James's Market SW1 .... 240 A1
Haymarket
St James's Place SW1 .... 243 F3
St James's Road SE1 & SE16 .... 246 B1
St James's Row EC1 .... 241 D3
St James's Walk
St James's Square SW1 .... 244 A4
St James's Street SW1 .... 244 A4
St James's Walk EC1 .... 241 D3
St John Street EC1 .... 241 D4
St John's Lane EC1 .... 241 D3
St John's Place EC1 .... 241 D3
St John's Square EC1 .... 241 D3
St John's Villas W8 .... 242 A3
St Mary's Place
St John's Wood High Street
NW8 .... 238 C4
St John's Wood Road NW8 .... 238 C3
St Katherine's Row EC3 .... 241 F1
Fenchurch Street
St Katherine's Way E1 .... 246 B2
St Lawrence Street E14 .... 248 C4
St Leonard's Terrace SW3 .... 243 D1
St Loo Avenue SW3 .... 243 D1
St Luke's Close EC1 .... 241 E3
St Luke's Street SW3 .... 242 C1
St Margaret's Lane W8 .... 242 A3
St Margaret's Street SW1 .... 244 B3
St Mark Street E1 .... 246 B3
St Martin's Court WC2 .... 240 B1
St Martin's Lane
St Martin's Lane WC2 .... 240 B1
St Martin's Place WC2 .... 240 B1
St Martin's Street WC2 .... 240 B1
St Martin's-le-Grand EC1 .... 241 E2
St Mary at Hill EC3 .... 241 F1
St Mary Axe EC3 .... 246 A3
St Mary's Gardens SE11 .... 245 D2
St Mary's Gate W8 .... 242 A3
St Mary's Mansions W2 .... 238 B3
St Mary's Place W8 .... 242 A3
St Mary's Square W2 .... 238 C3
St Mary's Terrace W2 .... 238 B3
St Mary's Walk SE11 .... 245 D2
St Marychurch Street SE16 .... 247 D1
St Matthew Street SW1 .... 244 A3
St Michael's Street W2 .... 238 C2
St Olav's Square SE16 .... 247 D1
Lower Road
St Oswald's Place SE11 .... 244 C1
St Paul's Avenue SE16 .... 247 E2
St Paul's Churchyard EC4 .... 241 E2
St Paul's Terrace SE17 .... 245 E1
St Paul's Way E3 .... 247 F4
St Peter's Place W9 .... 238 A3
St Petersburgh Mews W2 .... 238 A1
St Petersburgh Place W2 .... 238 A1
St Stephen's Crescent W2 .... 238 A2
St Stephen's Gardens W2 .... 238 A2
St Stephen's Mews W2 .... 238 A2
St Swithin's Lane EC4 .... 241 F1
St Thomas Street SE1 .... 245 F4
St Vincent Street W1 .... 239 E2
Salamanca Place SE1 .... 244 C2
Salamanca Street SE1 & SE11 .. 244 C2
Salem Road W2 .... 238 A1
Salisbury Close SE17 .... 245 F2
Salisbury Court EC4 .... 241 D2
Salisbury Place W1 .... 239 D3
Salisbury Square EC4 .... 241 D2
Salisbury Court
Salisbury Street NW8 .... 238 C3
Salmon Lane E14 .... 247 E4
Salter Road SE16 .... 247 E1
Salter Street E14 .... 247 F3
Samford Street NW8 .... 238 C3
Sampson Street E1 .... 246 C2
Sancroft Street SE11 .... 244 C2
Sanctuary Street SE1 .... 245 E4
Marshalsea Road
Sandell Street SE1 .... 245 D4
Sandland Street WC1 .... 240 C2
Sandpiper Close SE16 .... 247 F2
Sandwich Street WC1 .... 240 B4
Sandys Row E1 .... 246 A4
Sans Walk EC1 .... 241 D3
Sardinia Street WC2 .... 240 C2
Saunders Court E14 .... 247 F3
Limehouse Causeway
Saunders Ness Road E14 .... 248 C2
Savage Gardens EC3 .... 246 A3
Pepys Street
Savernake Street E14 .... 248 C4
Savile Row W1 .... 239 F1
Savoy Buildings WC2 .... 240 C1
Savoy Court WC2 .... 240 C1
Savoy Way
Savoy Hill WC2 .... 240 C1
Savoy Street
Savoy Place WC2 .... 240 B1
Savoy Row WC2 .... 240 C1
Savoy Street
Savoy Steps WC2 .... 240 C1
Savoy Way
Savoy Street WC2 .... 240 C1
Savoy Way WC2 .... 240 C1
Sawyer Street SE1 .... 245 E4
Scala Street W1 .... 240 A2
Scandrett Street E1 .... 246 C2
Scarborough Street E1 .... 246 B3
Scarsdale Place W8 .... 242 A3
Scarsdale Villas W8 .... 242 A3
School House Lane E1 .... 247 D3
Schooner Close SE16 .... 247 E1
Schooner Close E14 .... 248 C2
Scoresby Street SE1 .... 245 D4
Scotswood Street EC1 .... 240 D3
Sans Walk
Scott Ellis Gardens NW8 .... 238 B4
Scott Lidgett Crescent SE16 ..... 246 B1
Scott Russell Place E14 .... 248 B1
Scovell Road SE1 .... 245 E3
Scrutton Street EC2 .... 241 F3
Seagrave Road SW6 .... 242 A1
Searles Road SE1 .... 245 F2
Seaton Close SE11 .... 245 D1
Sebastian Street EC1 .... 241 D4
Secker Street SE1 .... 245 D4
Sedan Way SE17 .... 245 F2
Sedding Street SW1 .... 243 E2
Sloane Square
Seddon Street WC1 .... 240 C4
Sedley Place W1 .... 239 F2
Woodstock Street
Seething Lane EC3 .... 246 A3
Sekforde Street EC1 .... 241 D3
Selbie Street E14 .... 248 C2
Selsdon Way E14 .... 248 B2

Selsey Street E14 .... 247 F4
Selwood Terrace SW7 .... 242 C1
Selwood Place SW7 .... 242 C1
Semley Place SW1 .... 243 E2
Senrab Street E1 .... 247 D4
Senior Street W2 .... 238 A3
Serpentine Road W2 .... 242 C1
Serle Street WC2 .... 240 C2
Seth Street SE16 .... 247 D1
Settles Street E1 .... 246 C4
Seven Dials WC2 .... 240 B2
Seville Street SW1 .... 243 D3
Knightsbridge
Sevington Street W9 .... 238 A3
Seward Street EC1 .... 241 E3
Sextant Avenue E14 .... 248 C2
Seymour Mews W1 .... 239 E2
Seymour Place W1 .... 239 D2
Seymour Street W2 .... 239 D1
Seymour Walk SW10 .... 242 B1
Seyssel Street E14 .... 248 C2
Shad Thames SE1 .... 246 A2
Shadwell Pier Head E1 .... 247 D3
Shadwell Place E1 .... 246 C3
Shaftesbury Avenue W1 & WC2 .. 240 A1
Shaftesbury Mews W8 .... 242 A2
Shafto Mews SW1 .... 243 D3
Shand Street SE1 .... 246 A2
Sharsted Street SE17 .... 245 D1
Shawfield Street SW3 .... 243 D1
Portugal Street
Sheffield Street WC2 .... 240 C2
Sheffield Terrace W8 .... 242 A4
Shelmerdine Close E3 .... 247 F4
Shelton Street WC2 .... 240 B2
Shepherd Market W1 .... 243 E4
Shepherd Street W1 .... 243 E4
Shepherd's Place W1 .... 239 E1
Shepherd's Walk N1 .... 241 E4
Shepherdess Walk
Shepherdess Walk N1 .... 241 E4
Sheraton Street W1 .... 240 A2
Wardour Street
Sherlock Mews W1 .... 239 E3
Sherwood Gardens E14 .... 248 A2
Sherwood Street W1 .... 240 A1
Shillibeer Place W1 .... 239 D2
Ship Yard E14 .... 248 A1
Shipwright Road SE16 .... 247 E1
Shirland Road W9 .... 238 A3
Shoe Lane EC4 .... 241 D2
Short Street SE1 .... 245 D4
Short's Gardens WC2 .... 240 B2
Shorter Street E1 .... 246 B3
Shoulder of Mutton Alley E14 ... 247 F2
Shouldham Street W1 .... 239 D2
Shroton Street NW1 .... 238 C3
Sicilian Avenue WC1 .... 240 B2
Vernon Place
Siddons Lane NW1 .... 239 D3
Sidford Place SE1 .... 244 C2
Sidmouth Street WC1 .... 240 C4
Sidney Square E1 .... 247 D4
Sidney Street E1 .... 246 C4
Silex Street SE1 .... 245 D3
Silk Street EC2 .... 241 E3
Silver Walk SE16 .... 247 F2
Silvester Street SE1 .... 245 E3
Simpson's Road E14 .... 248 B1
Singer Street EC2 .... 241 F3
Sise Lane EC4 .... 241 E2
Pancras Lane
Skinner Street EC1 .... 241 D3
Skinners Lane EC4 .... 241 F4
Queen Street
Sleaford Street SW8 .... 240 B4
Slingsby Place WC2 .... 240 B1
Slippers Place SE16 .... 246 C1
Sloane Avenue SW3 .... 243 D2
Sloane Court East SW3 .... 243 E2
Sloane Court West SW3 .... 243 E1
Sloane Gardens SW1 .... 243 E2
Sloane Square SW1 .... 243 E2
Sloane Street SW1 .... 243 D3
Sloane Terrace SW1 .... 243 E2
Sly Street E1 .... 246 C3
Cannon Street Road
Smart's Place WC2 .... 240 B2
Smeaton Street E1 .... 246 C2
Smith Close SE16 .... 247 D1
Smith Square SW1 .... 244 B3
Smith Street SW3 .... 243 D1
Smith Terrace SW3 .... 243 D1
Smithfield Street EC1 .... 241 D2
Smithy Street E1 .... 247 D4
Snow Hill EC1 .... 241 D2
Snowsfields SE1 .... 245 F4
Soho Square W1 .... 240 A2
Soho Street W1 .... 240 A2
Somerford Way SE16 .... 247 E1
Somers Crescent W2 .... 238 C2
Somers Mews W2 .... 238 C2
Sondes Street SE17 .... 245 F1
Sophia Square SE16 .... 247 E3
South Audley Street W1 .... 239 E1
South Bolton Gardens SW5 ...... 242 B1
South Carriage Drive
SW1 & SW7 .... 242 C3
South Collonnade E14 .... 248 A4
South Crescent WC1 .... 240 A2
Store Street
South Eaton Place SW1 .... 243 E2
South End W8 .... 242 A3
South End Row W8 .... 242 A3
South Lambeth Place SW8 .... 244 B1
South Molton Lane W1 .... 239 E1
South Molton Street W1 .... 239 E2
South Parade SW3 .... 242 C1
South Place EC2 .... 241 F3
South Street W1 .... 243 E4
South Tenter Street E1 .... 246 B3
South Terrace SW7 .... 242 C2
South Wharf Road W2 .... 238 C2
Southall Place SE1 .... 245 F3
Long Lane
Southampton Buildings WC2 ..... 240 C2
Southampton Place WC1 .... 240 B2
Southampton Row WC1 .... 240 B3
Southampton Street WC2 .... 240 B1
Southsea Street SE16 .... 247 F1
Southwark Bridge EC4 & SE1 .... 241 E1
Southwark Bridge Road SE1 ..... 245 E3
Southwark Park Road SE16 .... 246 C1
Southwark Street SE1 .... 245 D4
Southwell Gardens SW7 .... 242 B2
Southwick Street W2 .... 238 C2
Hyde Park Crescent
Sovereign Close E1 .... 246 C3
Spa Road SE16 .... 246 B1
Spanish Place W1 .... 239 E2
Spear Mews SW5 .... 242 A2
Spelman Street E1 .... 246 B4
Spence Close SE16 .... 247 F1
Spencer Place EC1 .... 241 D4
Spencer Street EC1 .... 241 D4
Spert Street E14 .... 247 E3
Spindrift Avenue E14 .... 248 A2
Spital Square E1 .... 246 A4
Spital Street E1 .... 246 B4
Sprimont Place SW3 .... 243 D2

Spring Gardens SW1 244
Spring Mews W1 239
Spring Street W2 238
Spur Road SW1 243
Spur Road SE1 245
Lower Marsh
Spurgeon Street SE1 245
Squire Gardens NW8 238
Stable Yard Road SW1 244
Stables Way SE11 244
Stacey Street WC2 240
Staff Street EC1 241
Vince Street
Stafford Place SW1 243
Stag Place SW1 243
Stainer Street SE1 245
Staining Lane EC2 241
Stalbridge Street NW1 238
Stalham Street SE16 246
Stamford Street SE1 245
Stanford Road W8 242
Stanford Street SW1 244
Stanhope Gardens SW7 242
Stanhope Gate W1 243
Hertford Street
Stanhope Mews East SW7 242
Stanhope Mews South SW7 242
Stanhope Mews West SW7 242
Stanhope Place W2 242
Stanhope Street NW1 239
Stanhope Terrace W2 238
Stannary Place SE11 245
Stannary Street SE11 245
Stanworth Street SE1 246
Staple Inn Buildings WC1 240
Staple Street SE1 245
Staples Close SE16 247
Star Place E1 246
Star Street W2 238
Star Yard WC2 240
Starboard Way E14 248
Starcross Street NW1 240
Station Acces Road EC2 241
Stave Yard Road SE16 247
Stead Street SE17 245
Stebondale Street E14 248
Stedham Place WC1 240
New Oxford Street
Steedman Street SE17 245
Steel's Lane E1 247
Steelyard Passage EC4 241
Steers Way SE16 247
Stephen Mews W1 240
Gresse Street
Stephen Street W1 240
Stephen's Row EC4 241
Walbrook
Stephenson Way NW1 240
Stepney Causeway E1 247
Stepney Green E1 247
Stepney High Street E1 247
Stepney Way E1 246
Sterling Street SW7 243
Montpelier Place
Sterry Street SE1 245
Stevedore Street E1 246
Stevens Street SE1 246
Steward Street E1 246
Stewart Street E14 248
Stewart's Grove SW3 242
Stillington Street SW1 244
Stockholm Way E1 246
Vaughan Way
Stocks Place E14 247
Stone Buildings WC2 240
Chancery Lane
Stone Hall Gardens W8 242
Stone Hall Place W8 242
Stone Hall Gardens
Stone Stairs E1 247
Stonecutter Street EC4 241
Stones End Street SE1 245
Stoney Lane E1 246
Stoney Street SE1 245
Stopford Road SE17 245
Store Street WC1 240
Storers Quay E14 248
Storey's Gate SW1 244
Stork's Road SE16 246
Stoughton Close SE11 244
Stourcliffe Street W1 239
Strafford Street E14 248
Strand WC2 240
Stratford Avenue W8 242
Stratford Place W1 239
Stratford Road W8 242
Strathearn Place W2 238
Hyde Park Square
Strathmore Gardens W8 238
Palace Gardens Terrace
Stratton Street W1 243
Strattondale Street E14 248
Streatham Street WC1 240
Dyott Street
Strutton Ground SW1 244
Strype Street E1 246
Stukeley Street WC2 240
Sturge Street SE1 245
Sturgeon Road SE17 245
Sturt Street N1 241
Stutfield Street E1 246
Sudeley Street N1 241
Sudrey Street SE1 245
Suffolk Lane EC4 241
Suffolk Place SW1 240
Suffolk Street
Suffolk Street SW1 240
Sugar Quay Walk EC3 246
Sullivan Road SE11 245
Summercourt Road E1 247
Summers Street EC1 241
Back Hill
Sumner Place SW7 242
Sumner Place Mews SW7 242
Sumner Street SE1 245
Sun Street EC2 241
Sun Street Passage EC2 241
Sun Walk E1 246
Sunderland Terrace W2 238
Sunningdale Gardens W8 242
Stratford Road
Surrenale Place W9 238
Surrey Quays Road SE16 247
Surrey Row SE1 245
Surrey Square SE17 245
Surrey Street WC2 240
Surrey Water Road SE16 247
Sussex Gardens W2 238
Sussex Place NW1 239
Sussex Place W2 238
Sussex Square W2 238
Sussex Street SW1 243
Sutherland Avenue W9 238
Sutherland Row SW1 243
Sutherland Street
Sutherland Square SE17 245
Sutherland Street SW1 243
Sutherland Walk SE17 245
Sutton Row W1 240
Swallow Street W1 240

van Lane
Zoar Street
255

n Lane EC4 241 F1
n Mead SE1 245 F3
n Road SE16 247 D2
n Street SE1 245 E3
n Walk SW3 243 D1
den Gate SE16 247 E1
denborg Gardens E1 246 C3
eney Crescent SE1 246 B1
nton Street WC1 240 C4
s Court WC2 240 B1
eicester Square
more Street EC1 241 E3
ld Street
ney Close SW3 242 C2
ney Mews SW3 242 C2
ney Street SW3 242 C2
ons Street SW3 243 D2

T

ard Street SE1 245 F3
ernacle Street EC2 241 F3
nbrook Street SW1 244 A2
bing Street E14 248 B2
worth Street E1 246 B4
Chicksand Street
ot Square W2 238 C2
ot Yard SE1 245 F4
s Street EC4 241 D1
eraire Street SE16 247 D2
worth Street SW6 241 A1
kerton Street WC1 240 B4
Cromer Street
ner Street SE1 246 A1
ow Street N1 241 E4
bert Walk E1 247 D3
ing Street E1 246 C3
ver Road SE17 245 E1
im Street SE17 245 F2
nton Mews NW1 239 D3
Balcombe Street
nton Place NW1 239 D3
stock Place WC1 240 B3
stock Square WC1 240 B3
stock Street WC2 240 B1
ton Street WC1 240 A3
 Close SE11 245 D2
k Close SE16 247 E2
worth Square SW3 243 D1
egraph Place E14 248 A2
egraph Street EC2 241 F2
nple Avenue EC4 241 D1
nple Lane EC4 241 A2
nple Place WC2 240 C1
npleton Place SW5 241 D1
ch Street E1 246 C2
ison Court W1 239 F2
Regent Street
ison Way SE1 244 C4
nis Street SE1 245 F3
ter Ground E1 246 A4
White's Row
terden Street W1 239 F2
minus Place SW1 243 F3
ackeray Street W8 242 A3
alia Close SE10 248 C1
ame Road SE16 247 E2
ames Circle E14 248 A2
ames Link SE16 247 D2
ames Street SE10 248 B1
anet Street WC1 240 B4
avies Inn EC4 241 D2
ayer Street W1 239 E2
e Boltons SW10 242 B1
e Broad Walk NW1 239 E4
e Broad Walk W8 242 B4
e Cut SE1 245 D4
e Dial Walk W8 242 B4
e Economist Plaza SW1 244 A4
Bury Street
e Flower Walk SW7 242 B3
e Grange SE1 246 A1
e Highway E1 & E14 246 C3
e Limes W2 238 A1
e Little Boltons SW10 & SW5 241 B1
e Mall SW1 244 A4
e Mitre E14 247 F3
e Piazza WC2 240 B1
e Quarterdeck E14 248 A3
e Vale SW3 242 C1
eed Street SE1 245 D4
eobald Street SE1 245 F2
New Kent Road
eobold's Road WC1 240 C3
ermopylae Gate E14 248 B2
eseus Walk N1 241 E4
Rocliffe Street
irleby Road SE1 244 A3
istle Grove SW10 242 B1
omas Doyle Street SE1 245 D3
omas More Street E1 246 B2
omas Place W8 242 A3
St Mary's Place
omas Road E14 247 F4
oresby Street N1 241 E4
orney Street SW1 244 B2
orngate Road W9 238 A3
ornton Place W1 239 D3
rale Street SE1 245 E4
rawl Street E1 246 B4
readneedle Street EC2 241 F2
ree Colt Street E14 247 F3
ree Cranes Walk EC4 241 E1
ree Kings Yard W1 239 E1
ree Oak Lane SE1 246 A2
rogmorton Avenue EC2 241 F2
rogmorton Street EC2 241 F2
rush Street SE17 245 E1
urland Road SE16 246 B1
urloe Close SW7 242 C2
urloe Place SW7 242 C2
urloe Place Mews SW7 242 C2
urloe Square SW7 242 C2
urloe Street SW7 242 C2
urlow Street SE17 245 F2
ler Road E14 248 A3
lman Street E1 246 C3
ney Street W1 243 E3
nber Street EC1 241 E3
nberland Road E1 246 C3
nberpond Road SE16 247 E2
nsley Road E1 247 D4
Tinworth Street SE11 244 B2
Titchborne Row W2 238 C2
Tite Street SW3 243 D1
Tiverton Street SE1 245 E3
Tivoli Court SE16 247 F2
Tobago Street E14 248 A3
Tokenhouse Yard EC2 241 F2
Tolmers Square NW1 240 A3
Tonbridge Street WC1 240 B4
Took's Court EC4 240 C2
Tooley Street SE1 246 A2
Topham Street EC1 241 D3
Tor Gardens W8 242 A4
Torquay Street W2 238 A2
Torrens Street EC1 241 D4
Torres Square E14 248 A1
Maritime Quay
Torrington Place E1 246 C1
Torrington Place WC1 240 A3
Tothill Street SW1 244 A3
Tottenham Court Road W1 240 A3
Tottenham Street W1 240 A3
Toulmin Street SE1 245 E3
Toussaint Walk SE16 246 B1
Tower Bridge E1 & SE1 246 A2
Tower Bridge Approach E1 246 B2
Tower Bridge Road SE1 246 A1
Tower Court WC2 240 B1
Monmouth Street
Tower Hill EC3 246 A3
Tower Hill Terrace EC3 246 A3
Gloucester Close
Tower Street WC2 240 B1
Townley Street SE17 245 E2
Townsend Street SE17 245 F2
Toynbee Street E1 246 B4
Tracey Street SE11 244 C2
Trafalgar Gardens E1 247 E4
Trafalgar Gardens W8 242 A3
South End Row
Trafalgar Grove SE10 248 C1
Trafalgar Road SE10 248 C1
Trafalgar Square WC2 240 B1
Trafalgar Street SE17 245 F1
Trafalgar Way E14 248 B4
Transom Square E14 248 B1
Tranton Road SE16 246 C1
Trebeck Street W1 243 E4
Curzon Street
Trebovir Road SW5 242 A2
Tregunter Road SW10 242 B1
Trenchard Street SE10 248 C1
Tresham Crescent NW8 238 C4
Treveris Street SE1 245 D4
Bear Lane
Trevithick Street SE8 248 A1
Trevor Place SW7 243 D3
Trevor Square SW7 243 D3
Trevor Street SW7 243 D3
Trinidad Street E14 247 F3
Trinity Church Square SE1 245 E3
Trinity Place EC3 246 A3
Trinity Square
Trinity Square EC3 246 A3
Trinity Street SE1 245 E3
Trio Place SE1 245 E3
Triton Square NW1 239 F3
Troon Street E1 247 E4
Trumans Street SE16 246 C1
Trump Street EC2 241 E2
Tryon Street SW3 243 D2
Tudor Street EC4 241 D1
Tufton Street SW1 244 B3
Tunley Green E14 247 F4
Tunnel Avenue SE10 248 C3
Tunnel Road SE16 247 D2
Turk's Row SW3 243 E1
Turner Street E1 246 C4
Turnmill Street EC1 241 D3
Turpentine Lane SW1 243 F1
Turquand Street SE17 245 E2
Twine Court E1 246 C3
Twyford Place WC2 240 C2
Kingsway
Tyers Gate SE1 245 F3
Tyers Street SE11 244 C1
Tyers Terrace SE11 244 C1
Tyne Street E1 246 B4
Tysoe Street EC1 241 D4

U

Udall Street SW1 244 A2
Ufford Street SE1 245 D3
Ulster Place NW1 239 E3
Umberston Street E1 246 C4
Undershaft EC3 241 F2
Underwood Row N1 241 E4
Shepherdess Walk
Underwood Street N1 241 E4
Undine Road E14 248 B2
Union Street SE1 245 D4
University Street WC1 240 A3
Upbrook Mews W2 238 B2
Upper Belgrave Street SW1 243 E3
Upper Berkeley Street W1 239 D2
Upper Brook Street W1 239 E1
Upper Cheyne Row SW3 242 C1
Upper Grosvenor Street W1 239 E1
Upper Ground SE1 241 D1
Upper Harley Street NW1 239 E3
Upper James Street W1 240 A1
Upper John Street W1 240 A1
Upper Marsh SE1 244 C3
Upper Montagu Street W1 239 D3
Upper St Martin's Lane WC2 240 B1
Upper Tachbrook Street SW1 244 A2
Upper Thames Street EC4 241 E1
Upper Wimpole Street W1 239 E3
Upper Woburn Place WC1 240 B3

V

Valcan Square E14 248 A2
Vale Close W9 238 B4
Valentine Place SE1 245 D3
Valentine Row SE1 245 D3
Vandon Passage SW1 244 A3
Vandon Street SW1 244 A3
Vandy Street EC2 241 F3
Vane Street SW1 244 A2
Vantage Mews E14 248 C4
Managers Street
Varden Street E1 246 C4
Varndell Street NW1 239 F4
Vauban Street SE16 246 B1
Vaughan Street SE16 247 F1
Vaughan Way E1 246 B2
Vauxhall Bridge SW1 & SE1 244 B2
Vauxhall Bridge Road SW1 243 F2
Vauxhall Grove SW8 244 B1
Vauxhall Street SE11 244 C1
Vauxhall Walk SE11 244 C2
Venables Street NW8 238 C3
Vere Street W1 239 E2
Vernon Place WC1 240 B2
Vernon Rise WC1 240 C4
Vernon Square WC1 240 C4
Penton Rise
Vernon Street W14 240 C4
Verulam Street WC1 240 C3
Vestry Street N1 241 F4
Vicarage Court W8 242 A4
Vicarage Gardens W8 242 A4
Vicarage Gate W8 242 A4
Victoria Avenue EC2 246 A4
Victoria Embankment
SW1, WC2 & EC4 240 C1
Victoria Grove W8 242 B3
Victoria Road W8 242 B3
Victoria Street SW1 243 F3
Victory Place SE17 245 F2
Victory Place E14 247 E3
Victory Way SE16 247 E1
Vigo Street W1 240 A1
Villa Street SE17 245 F1
Villiers Street WC2 240 B1
Vince Street EC1 241 F4
Vincent Close SE16 247 E1
Vincent Square SW1 244 A2
Vincent Street SW1 244 A2
Vine Court E1 246 C4
Vine Lane SE1 246 A2
Vine Street EC3 246 A3
Vine Street W1 240 A1
Vine Street Bridge EC1 241 D3
Farringdon Lane
Vinegar Street E1 246 C2
Vinegar Yard SE1 245 F4
St Thomas Street
Vineyard Walk EC1 241 D3
Pine Street
Vintner's Place EC4 241 E1
Violet Hill NW8 238 B4
Virgil Place W1 239 D2
Seymour Place
Virgil Street SE1 244 C3
Virginia Street E1 246 B3
Viscount Street EC1 241 E3

W

Wadding Street SE17 245 E2
Waithman Street EC4 241 D2
Pilgrim Street
Wakefield Mews WC1 240 B4
Wakefield Street
Wakefield Street WC1 240 B4
Wakeling Street E14 247 E3
Wakley Street EC1 241 D4
Walbrook EC4 241 F1
Walburgh Street E1 246 C3
Walcorde Avenue SE17 245 E2
Walcot Square SE11 245 D2
Walden Street E1 246 C4
Waley Street E1 247 E4
Wallgrave Road SW5 242 A2
Wallwood Street E14 247 F4
Walmer Street W1 239 D3
Seymour Place
Walnut Tree Walk SE11 244 C2
Walpole Street SW3 243 D2
Walter Terrace E1 247 E4
Walton Place SW3 243 D3
Walton Street SW3 243 D2
Walton's Mews W1 239 D2
Walworth Place SE17 245 E1
Walworth Road SE1 & SE17 245 E2
Wansey Street SE17 245 E2
Wapping Dock Street E1 246 C2
Wapping High Street E1 246 B2
Wapping Lane E1 246 C3
Wapping Walk E1 246 C3
Wapping Wall E1 247 D2
Wardour Street W1 240 A2
Warner Street EC1 240 C3
Warren Street W1 239 F3
Warrington Crescent W9 238 B3
Warrington Gardens W9 238 B3
Warwick Avenue W9 238 A3
Warwick Court WC1 240 C2
Warwick Crescent W2 238 B3
Warwick House Street SW1 244 B4
Warwick Lane EC4 241 E2
Warwick Passage EC4 241 D2
Warwick Square
Warwick Place W9 238 B3
Warwick Row SW1 243 F3
Warwick Square SW1 243 F2
Warwick Square EC4 241 D2
Warwick Street W1 240 A1
Warwick Way SW1 243 F2
Water Lane EC3 246 A3
Watergate EC4 241 D2
New Brodge Street
Watergate Street SE8 248 A1
Watergate Walk WC2 240 B1
Villiers Street
Wateridge Close E14 248 A2
West Ferry Road
Waterloo Bridge WC2 & SE1 240 C1
Waterloo Place SW1 244 A4
Waterloo Road SE1 244 C4
Waterman Way E1 246 C2
Waterman's Walk EC4 241 F1
Waterside Close SE16 246 B1
Watling Street EC4 241 E2
Watney Market E1 246 C4
Watney Street E1 246 C3
Watson's Street SE8 246 C2
Watts Way SW7 242 C3
Waveney Close E1 246 B2
Waverton Street W1 243 E4
Weavers Lane SE1 246 A2
Webb Street SE1 245 F3
Webber Row SE1 245 D3
Webber Street SE1 245 D3
Webster Road SE16 246 C1
Weighouse Street W1 239 E1
Welbeck Street W1 239 E2
Welbeck Way W1 239 E2
Well Court EC4 241 E1
Queen Street
Welland Mews E1 246 C1
Wellclose Square E1 246 B3
Wellclose Street E1 246 C3
The Highway
Weller Street SE1 245 E3
Wellesley Street E1 247 D4
Wellesley Terrace N1 241 E4
Wellington Place NW8 238 C4
Wellington Road NW8 238 C4
Wellington Square SW3 243 D1
Wellington Street WC2 240 C1
Wells Mews W1 240 A2
Wells Square WC1 240 C4
Wells Street W1 239 F2
Wendover SE17 245 F1
Wenlock Road N1 241 E4
Wenlock Street N1 241 E4
Wentworth Market E1 246 B4
Wentworth Street
Wentworth Street E1 246 B4
Werrington Street NW1 240 A4
Wesley Close SE17 245 D2
Wesley Street W1 239 E2
Weymouth Street
West Arbour Street E1 247 D4
West Central Street WC1 240 B2
West Eaton Place SW1 243 E2
West Ferry Road E14 248 A3
West Gardens E1 246 C3
West Halkin Street SW1 243 E3
West India Avenue E14 248 A4
West India Dock Road E14 247 F3
West Lane SE16 246 C1
West Mews SW1 243 F2
Warwick Way
West Poultry Avenue EC1 241 D2
West Smithfield
West Road SW4 243 D1
West Smithfield EC1 241 D2
West Square SE11 245 D2
West Street WC2 240 B1
West Tenter Street E1 246 B3
Westbourne Crescent W2 238 B1
Westbourne Gardens W2 238 A2
Westbourne Grove W2 & W11 238 A2
Westbourne Grove Terrace W2 238 A2
Westbourne Park Road
W2 & W11 238 A1
Westbourne Park Villas W2 238 A1
Westbourne Street W2 238 C1
Westbourne Terrace W2 238 B2
Westbourne Terrace Mews W2 238 B2
Westbourne Terrace Road W2 238 B2
Westcott Road SE17 245 D1
Western Place SE16 247 D2
Westferry Circus E14 248 A4
Westgate Terrace SW10 242 A1
Westland Place N1 241 F4
Westminster Bridge SW1 & SE1 244 B3
Westminster Bridge Road SE1 244 F3
Westmoreland Place SW1 243 F1
Westmoreland Road SE17 245 E1
Westmoreland Street W1 239 E2
Westmoreland Terrace SW1 243 F1
Weston Rise WC1 240 C4
Weston Street SE1 245 F3
Westport Street E1 247 E4
Westway W12 238 B2
Wetherby Gardens SW5 242 B2
Wetherby Mews SW5 242 A2
Earls Court Road
Wetherby Place SW7 242 B2
Weymouth Mews W1 239 F2
Weymouth Street W1 239 E2
Wharf Road N1 241 E4
Wharfedale Street SW10 242 A1
Wharton Street WC1 240 C4
Wheat Sheaf Close E14 248 A2
Wheatley Street W1 239 E2
Marylebone Street
Whetstone Park WC2 240 C2
Whidborne Street WC1 240 B4
Whiskin Street EC1 241 D4
Whitcomb Street WC2 240 A1
White Church Lane E1 246 B4
White Hart Street SE11 245 D2
White Horse Lane E1 247 E4
White Horse Mews SE1 245 D3
White Horse Road E1 247 E3
White Horse Street W1 243 F4
White Kennet Street E1 246 A4
White Lion Hill EC4 241 E1
White's Grounds SE1 246 A1
White's Row E1 246 A4
Whiteadder Way E14 248 B2
Whitechapel High Street E1 246 B4
Whitechapel Road E1 246 B4
Whitecross Place EC2 241 F3
Whitecross Street EC1 241 E3
Whitefriars Street EC4 241 D2
Whitehall SW1 244 B4
Whitehall Court SW1 244 B4
Whitehall Place SW1 244 B4
Whitehaven Street NW8 238 C3
Whitehead's Grove SW3 243 D2
Whitfield Place W1 240 A3
Whitfield Street
Whitfield Street W1 240 A3
Whitgift Street SE11 244 C2
Whittaker Street SW1 243 E2
Whittington Avenue EC3 241 F2
Leadenhall Street
Whittlesey Street SE1 245 D4
Wickham Street SE11 244 C1
Wicklow Street WC1 240 C4
Widegate Street E1 246 A4
Middlesex Street
Widley Road W9 238 A4
Wigmore Place W1 239 E2
Wigmore Street W1 239 E2
Wilbraham Place SW1 243 E2
Wilcox Place SW1 244 A3
Wild Court WC2 240 C2
Wild Street WC2 240 B2
Wild's Rents SE1 245 F3
Wilfred Street SW1 243 F3
Wilkes Street E1 246 B4
William IV Street WC2 240 B1
William Mews SW1 243 E3
William Road NW1 239 F4
William Square SE16 247 E3
William Street SW1 243 D3
Willoughby Passage E14 248 A4
Willoughby Street WC1 240 B2
Streatham Street
Willow Place SW1 244 A2
Willow Street EC2 241 F3
Wilmington Square WC1 241 D4
Wilmington Street WC1 241 D4
Wilson Grove SE16 246 C1
Wilson Street EC2 241 F2
Wilson's Place E14 247 F3
Wilton Crescent SW1 243 E3
Wilton Mews SW1 243 E3
Wilton Place SW1 243 E3
Wilton Road SW1 243 F2
Wilton Row SW1 243 E3
Wilton Street SW1 243 E3
Wilton Terrace SW1 243 E3
Wimpole Mews W1 239 E2
Wimpole Street W1 239 E2
Winchester Close SE17 245 D2
Winchester Square SE1 245 F4
Winchester Walk
Winchester Street SW1 243 F2
Winchester Walk SE1 245 F4
Wincott Street SE11 245 D2
Windmill Row SE11 245 D1
Windmill Street W1 240 A2
Windmill Walk SE1 245 D4
Windrose Close SE16 247 D2
Windsor Terrace N1 241 E4
Wine Close E1 246 C2
Wine Office Court EC4 241 D2
Winnett Street W1 240 A1
Rupert Street
Winsland Mews W2 238 C2
Winsland Street W2 238 C2
Winsley Street W1 240 A2
Winterton Place SW10 242 B1
Woburn Place WC1 240 B3
Woburn Square WC1 240 B3
Woburn Walk WC1 240 B3
Upper Woburn Place
Wolfe Crescent SE16 247 D1
Wolseley Street SE1 246 B1
Wood Street EC2 241 E2
Wood's Mews W1 239 E1
Wood's Place SE1 246 A1
Woodbridge Street EC1 241 D3
Woodchester Square W2 238 A3
Woodfall Street SW3 243 D1
Woodland Crescent SE16 247 D1
Woodstock Mews W1 239 E2
Westmoreland Street
Woodstock Street W1 239 F2
Woolaston Close SE1 245 E2
Wooler Street SE17 245 F1
Wooster Place SE1 245 F2
Wootton Street SE1 245 D4
Worgan Street SE11 244 C2
Wormwood Street EC2 241 F2
Worship Street EC2 241 F3
Wren Landing E14 248 A4
Wren Street WC1 240 C3
Wright's Lane W8 242 A3
Wyatt Close SE16 247 F1
Wybert Street NW1 239 F3
Laxton Place
Wyclif Street EC1 241 D4
Wymering Road W9 238 A4
Wynan Road E14 248 B1
Wyndham Mews W1 239 D2
Wyndham Place W1 239 D2
Wyndham Street W1 239 D2
Wyndham Yard W1 239 D2
Wynnstay Gardens W8 242 A3
Wynyard Terrace SE11 244 C1
Wynyatt Street EC1 241 D4
Wythburn Place W1 239 D2

Y

Yabsley Street E14 248 C4
Yardley Street WC1 240 C4
Yarmouth Place W1 243 E4
Yeoman's Row SW3 243 D3
York Buildings WC2 240 B1
York Gate NW1 239 E3
York House Place W8 242 A4
York Road SE1 244 C3
York Square E14 247 E4
York Street W1 239 D3
York Terrace East NW1 239 E3
York Terrace West NW1 239 E3
Yorkshire Road E14 247 E3
Young Street W8 242 A3

Z

Zoar Street SE1 245 E4

London district

0   1   2 miles

0   1   2   3 kilometres

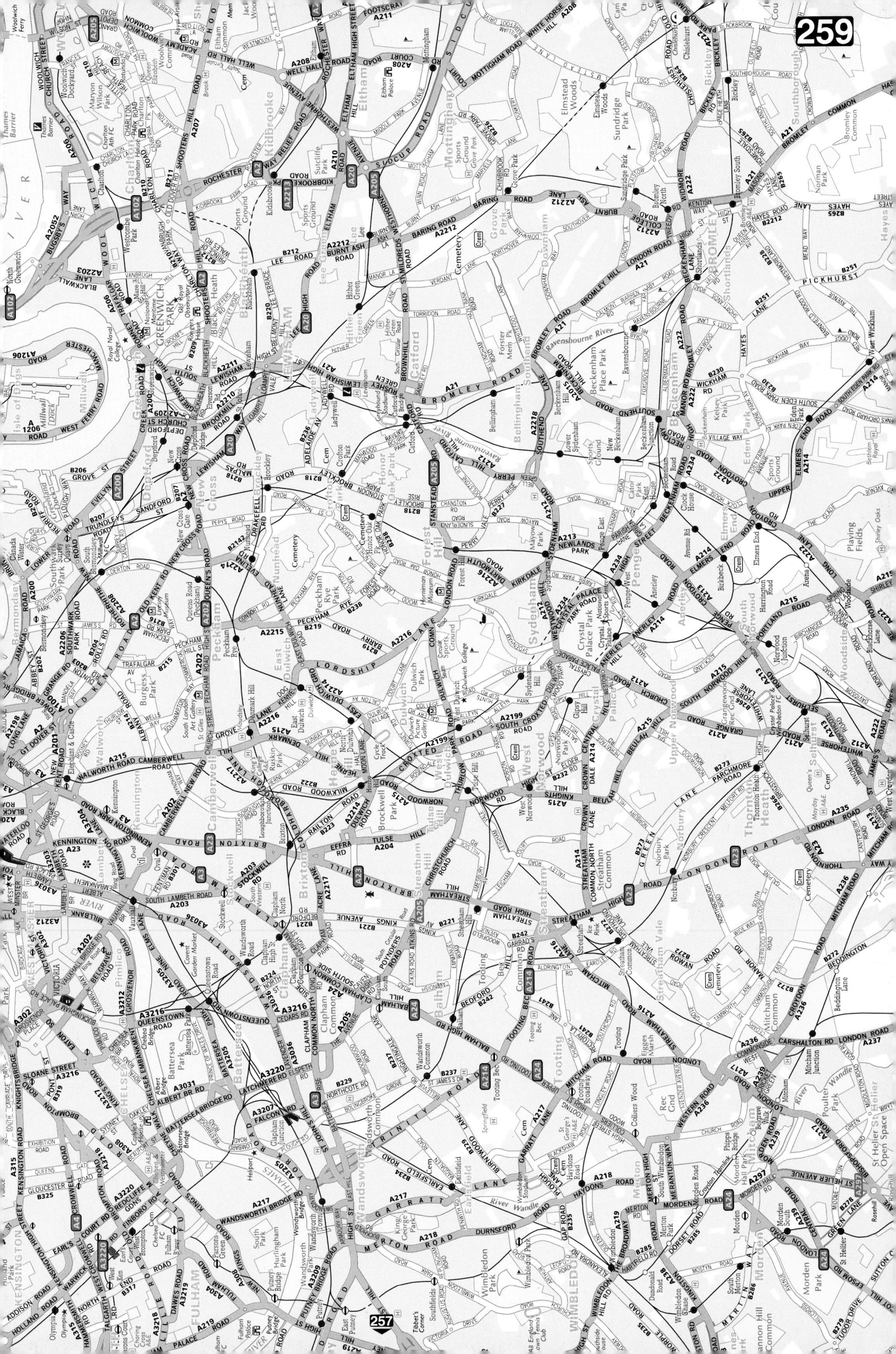

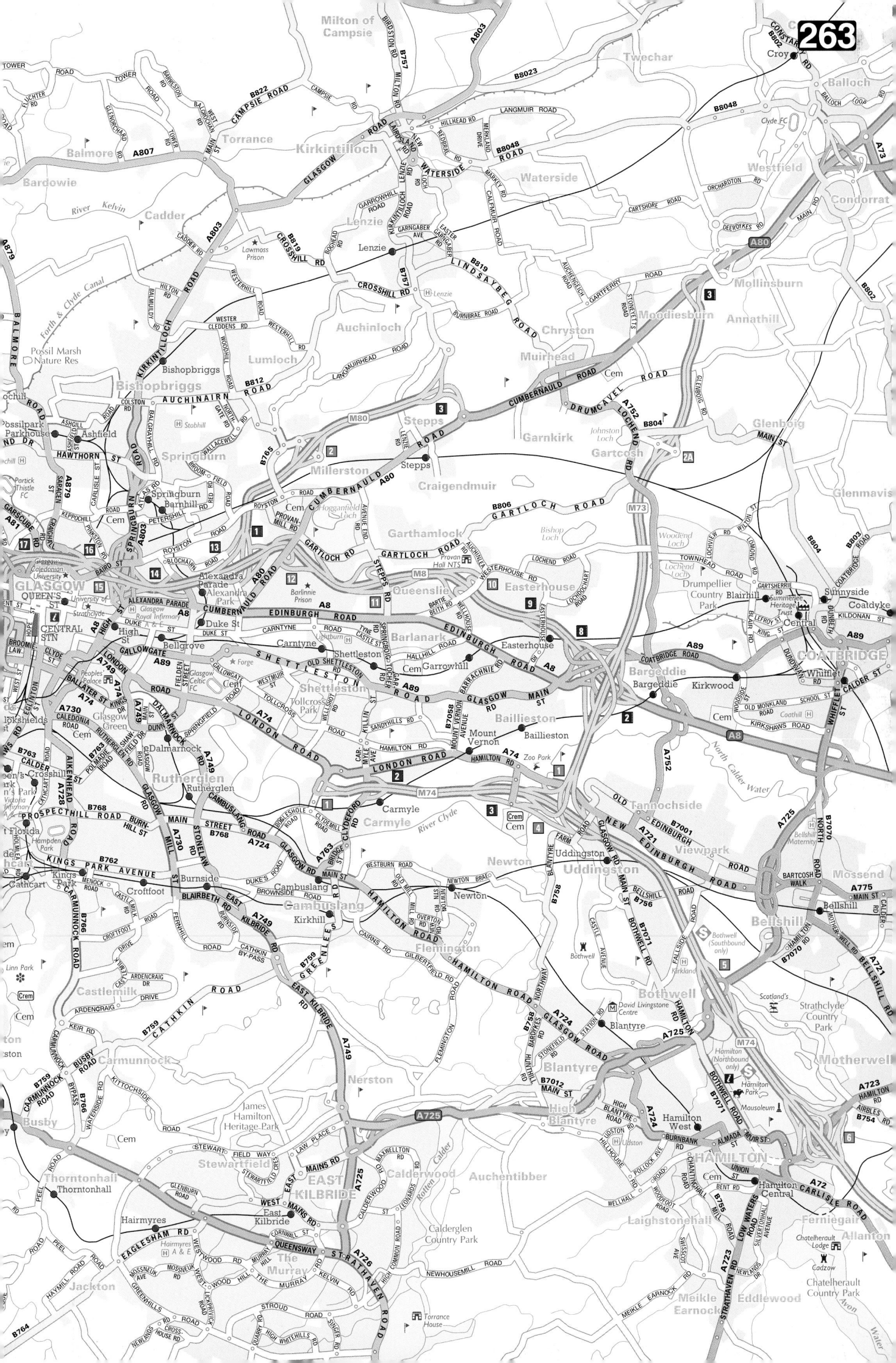

Manchester district

Tyne & Wear district

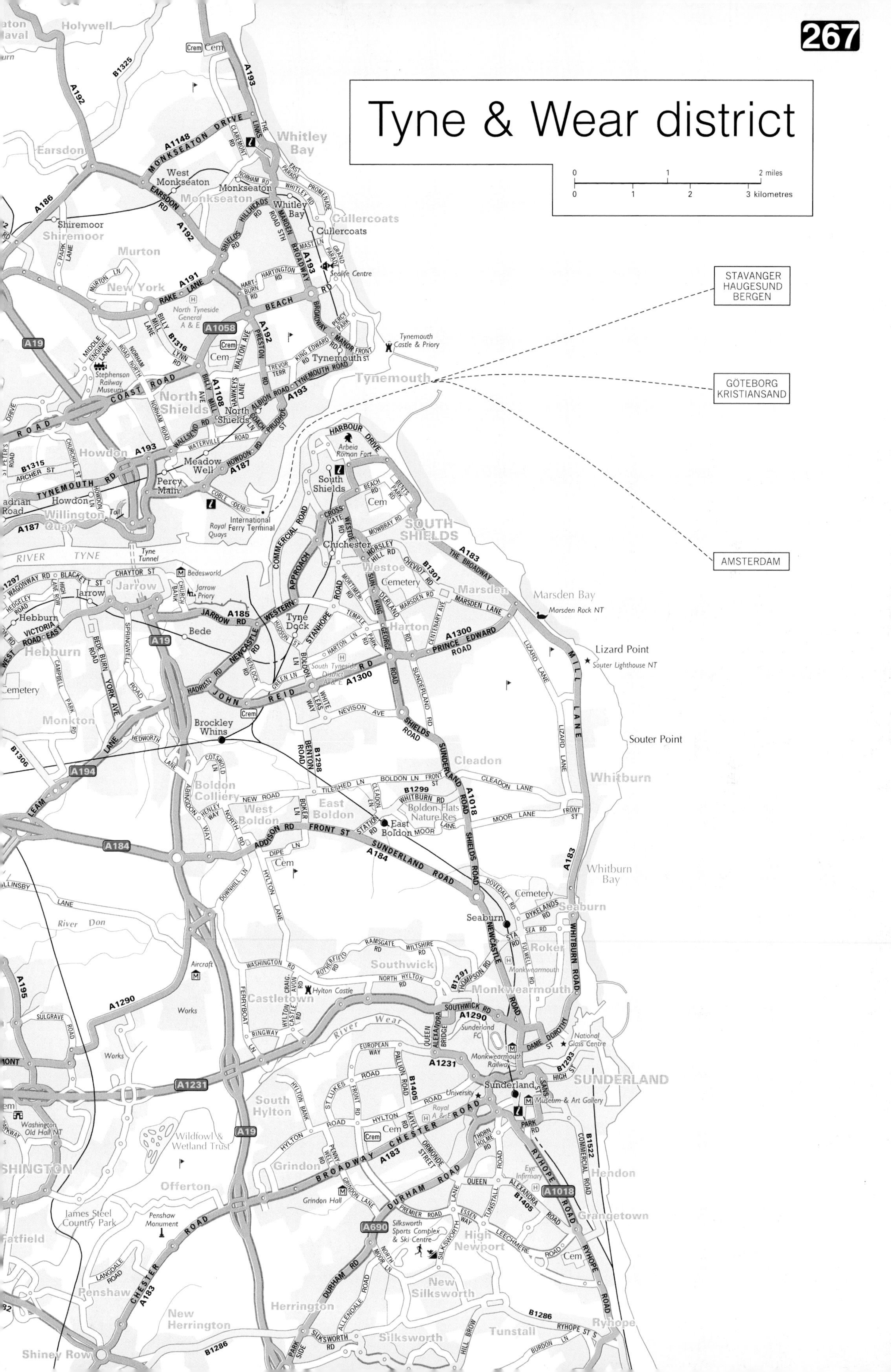

Holywell
Earsdon
Shiremoor
Murton
New York
West Monkseaton
Earsdon
Monkseaton
Whitley Bay
Cullercoats
Sealife Centre
North Shields
Meadow Well
Percy Main
Howdon
Willington Quay
Howdon
Tynemouth
Tynemouth Castle & Priory
Stephenson Railway Museum
North Tyneside General A & E
Arbeia Roman Fort
South Shields
SOUTH SHIELDS
Chichester
Westoe
Harbour Drive
Bedesworld
Jarrow
Jarrow Priory
Hebburn
Bede
Tyne Dock
Harton
Marsden
Marsden Bay
Marsden Rock NT
Lizard Point
Souter Lighthouse NT
Prince Edward Road
Brockley Whins
Monkton
Boldon Colliery
West Boldon
East Boldon
Cleadon
Souter Point
Whitburn
East Boldon Moor
Boldon Flats Nature Res
Southwick
Hylton Castle
Castletown
Seaburn
Roker
Monkwearmouth
Whitburn Bay
Sunderland FC
Sunderland Bridge
Monkwearmouth Railway
National Glass Centre
SUNDERLAND
University
Royal A & E Road
Museum & Art Gallery
South Hylton
Washington Old Hall NT
Wildfowl & Wetland Trust
Grindon
Grindon Hall
Eye Infirmary
Hendon
Grangetown
James Steel Country Park
Penshaw Monument
Silksworth Sports Complex & Ski Centre
High Newport
Offerton
Fatfield
Shiney Row
Penshaw
New Herrington
Herrington
New Silksworth
Silksworth
Tunstall
Ryhope

River Tyne
River Don
River Wear

A19 A184 A194 A1231 A1290 A195 A690 A183 A1018

index to place names

England

5	Beds	Bedfordshire
6	Berks	Berkshire
10	Bristl	Bristol
11	Bucks	Buckinghamshire
13	Cambs	Cambridgeshire
17	Ches	Cheshire
22	Cnwll	Cornwall
23	Cumb	Cumbria
25	Derbys	Derbyshire
26	Devon	Devon
27	Dorset	Dorset
30	Dur	Durham
35	E R Yk	East Riding of Yorkshire
36	E Susx	East Sussex
37	Essex	Essex
41	Gloucs	Gloucestershire
42	Gt Lon	Greater London
43	Gt Man	Greater Manchester
46	Hants	Hampshire
47	Herefs	Herefordshire
48	Herts	Hertfordshire
53	IOW	Isle of Wight
54	IOS	Isles of Scilly
56	Kent	Kent
57	Lancs	Lancashire
58	Leics	Leicestershire
59	Lincs	Lincolnshire
60	Mersyd	Merseyside
67	Norfk	Norfolk
70	N York	North Yorkshire
71	Nhants	Northamptonshire
72	Nthumb	Northumberland
73	Notts	Nottinghamshire
75	Oxon	Oxfordshire
81	Rutlnd	Rutland
83	Shrops	Shropshire
84	Somset	Somerset
87	S York	South Yorkshire
88	Staffs	Staffordshire
90	Suffk	Suffolk
91	Surrey	Surrey
94	T & W	Tyne & Wear
96	Warwks	Warwickshire
100	W Mids	West Midlands
101	W Susx	West Sussex
102	W York	West Yorkshire
103	Wilts	Wiltshire
104	Worcs	Worcestershire

Wales

7	Blae G	Blaenau Gwent
9	Brdgnd	Bridgend
12	Caerph	Caerphilly
14	Cardif	Cardiff
15	Carmth	Carmarthenshire
16	Cerdgn	Ceredigion
21	Conwy	Conwy
24	Denbgs	Denbighshire
40	Flints	Flintshire
45	Gwynd	Gwynedd
51	IOA	Isle of Anglesey
61	Myr Td	Merthyr Tydfil
63	Mons	Monmouthshire
65	Neath	Neath Port Talbot
66	Newpt	Newport
76	Pembks	Pembrokeshire
78	Powys	Powys
80	Rhondd	Rhondda Cynon Taff
92	Swans	Swansea
93	Torfn	Torfaen
95	V Glam	Vale of Glamorgan
105	Wrexhm	Wrexham

Scotland

1	Aber C	Aberdeen City
2	Abers	Aberdeenshire
3	Angus	Angus
4	Ag & B	Argyll & Bute
8	Border	Borders (Scottish)
18	C Edin	City of Edinburgh
19	C Glas	City of Glasgow
20	Clacks	Clackmannanshire
28	D & G	Dumfries & Galloway
29	Dund C	Dundee City
31	E Ayrs	East Ayrshire
32	E Duns	East Dunbartonshire
33	E Loth	East Lothian
34	E Rens	East Renfrewshire
38	Falk	Falkirk
39	Fife	Fife
49	Highld	Highland
50	Inver	Inverclyde
62	Mdloth	Midlothian
64	Moray	Moray
68	N Ayrs	North Ayrshire
69	N Lans	North Lanarkshire
74	Ork	Orkney Islands
77	P & K	Perth & Kinross
79	Rens	Renfrewshire
82	Shet	Shetland Islands
85	S Ayrs	South Ayrshire
86	S Lans	South Lanarkshire
89	Stirlg	Stirling
97	W Isls	Western Isles
98	W Duns	West Dunbartonshire
99	W Loth	West Lothian

The Channel Islands & Isle of Man

44	Guern	Guernsey
55	Jersey	Jersey
52	IOM	Isle of Man

Each place name entry in this index is identified with its County, County Borough or Council Area name. These are shown in *italics*, and can be identified using the key map belo A list of the abbreviated forms used is shown on the left.

To locate a place name in the atlas turn to the map page indicated in bold type in the index and use the 4-figure grid reference.

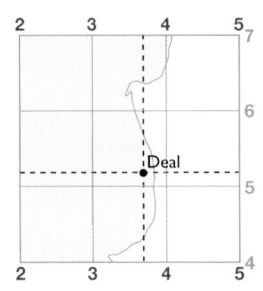

Example:

Deal *Kent* **29** 3752

Turn to page **29**

Find **3** along the bottom or top of the page

Move a further **7** tenths of the square to the right (easting

Find **5** up the side of the page

Move a further **2** tenths up (northing)

Deal will be found where the easting and northing intersec

The National Grid two-letter prefixes are also shown on the map pages to denote the 100km square, e.g. Deal TR3752

100 places of interest are indexed in red.

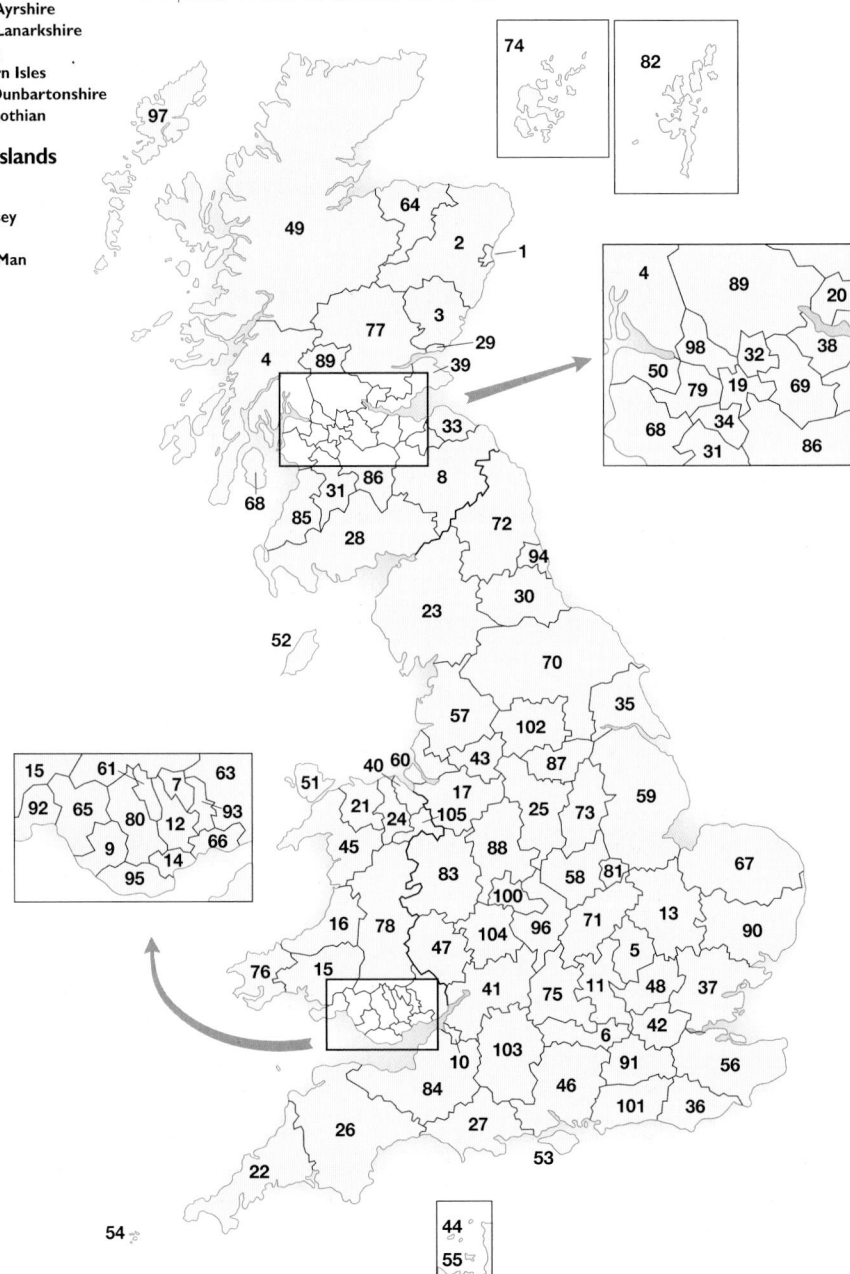

A

Chill Highld ... 128 2705
Kettleby Leics ... 63 7223
Lench Worcs ... 47 0151
bas Combe Somset ... 22 7022
berley Worcs ... 47 7567
berley Common Worcs ... 47 7467
berton Essex ... 41 0019
berton Worcs ... 47 9953
berwick Nthumb ... 111 1313
bess Roding Essex ... 40 5711
bey Devon ... 9 1410
bey Dore Herefs ... 46 3830
bey Green Staffs ... 72 9757
bey Hill Somset ... 10 2718
beydale S York ... 74 3281
bey Village Lancs ... 81 6422
beystead Lancs ... 81 5654
bot's Chair Derbys ... 74 0290
bot's Salford Warwks ... 48 0650
botrule Border ... 110 6113
bots Bickington Devon ... 18 3813
bots Bromley Staffs ... 73 0724
bots Deuglie P & K ... 126 1111
bots Langley Herts ... 26 0901
bots Leigh Somset ... 34 5474
bots Morton Worcs ... 48 0255
bots Ripton Cambs ... 52 2377
bots Worthy Hants ... 24 4932
botsbury Dorset ... 10 5785
botsham Devon ... 18 4226
botskerswell Devon ... 7 8568
botsleigh Devon ... 7 8048
botsley Cambs ... 52 2256
botstone Hants ... 24 5634
botswood Hants ... 23 3623
bott Street Dorset ... 11 9800
botts Ann Hants ... 23 3243
cott Shrops ... 46 3978
don Shrops ... 59 5786
enhall Gloucs ... 35 6717
er Clydach Powys ... 33 1021
er-arad Carmth ... 31 3140
er-banc Cerdgn ... 31 3541
er-giar Carmth ... 44 5040
er-Magwr Cerdgn ... 43 6673
er-meurig Cerdgn ... 44 5656
er-nant Rhondd ... 33 0103
eraeron Cerdgn ... 42 4562
eraman Rhondd ... 33 0100
erangell Gwynd ... 57 8410
erarder Highld ... 140 6225
erargie P & K ... 126 1615
erarth Cerdgn ... 42 4763
eravon Neath ... 32 7489
erbargoed Caerph ... 33 1500
erbeeg Blae G ... 33 2002
ercairny P & K ... 125 9222
ercanaid Myr Td ... 33 0503
ercarn Pembks ... 33 2194
ercastle Pembks ... 30 8533
ercegir Powys ... 57 8001
erchalder Lodge Highld ... 131 3403
erchirder Abers ... 142 6252
ercoed Cerdgn ... 44 6757
ercraf Powys ... 33 8212
ercregan Neath ... 33 8496
ercwmboi Rhondd ... 33 0299
ercych Pembks ... 31 2441
ercynon Rhondd ... 33 0794
erdalgie P & K ... 125 0720
erdare Rhondd ... 33 0002
erdaron Gwynd ... 56 1726
erdeen Aber C ... 135 9306
erdeen Airport ... 135 8712
erdesach Gwynd ... 68 4251
erdour Fife ... 117 1985
erdulais Neath ... 32 7799
erdyfi Gwynd ... 43 6196
eredw Powys ... 45 0847
ereiddy Pembks ... 30 7931
ererch Gwynd ... 56 3936
erfan Myr Td ... 33 0700
erfeldy P & K ... 125 8549
erffraw IOA ... 68 3569
erffrwd Cerdgn ... 43 6878
erford W York ... 83 4337
erfoyle Stirlg ... 115 5200
ergarw Brdgnd ... 33 9184
ergarwed Neath ... 33 8102
ergavenny Mons ... 34 2914
ergele Conwy ... 70 9477
ergorlech Carmth ... 44 5833
ergwesyn Powys ... 45 8552
ergwili Carmth ... 31 4320
ergwydol Powys ... 57 7903
ergwynfi Neath ... 33 8995
ergwyngregyn Gwynd ... 69 6572
ergwynolwyn Gwynd ... 57 6806
erhafesp Powys ... 58 0792
erhosan Powys ... 43 8197
erkenfig Brdgnd ... 33 8984
erlady E Loth ... 118 4679
erlemno Angus ... 127 5255
erllefenni Powys ... 57 7609
erllynfi Powys ... 45 1737
erlour Moray ... 141 2642
ermorddu Flints ... 71 3056
ermule Powys ... 58 1694
ernant Carmth ... 31 3323
ernethy P & K ... 126 1816
ernyte P & K ... 126 2531
erporth Cerdgn ... 42 2651
ersoch Gwynd ... 56 3127
ersychan Torfn ... 34 2603
erthin V Glam ... 33 0074
ertillery Blae G ... 33 2104
ertridwr Caerph ... 33 1289
ertridwr Powys ... 58 0319
ertysswg Caerph ... 33 1305

Aberuthven P & K ... 125 9615
Aberyscir Powys ... 45 9929
Aberystwyth Cerdgn ... 43 5881
Abingdon Oxon ... 37 4997
Abinger Surrey ... 14 1145
Abinger Hammer Surrey ... 14 0947
Abington Nhants ... 50 7861
Abington S Lans ... 108 9323
Abington Pigotts Cambs ... 39 3044
Ablington Gloucs ... 36 1007
Ablington Wilts ... 23 1546
Abney Derbys ... 74 1980
Above Church Staffs ... 73 0150
Aboyne Abers ... 134 5298
Abram Gt Man ... 78 6001
Abriachan Highld ... 139 5535
Abridge Essex ... 27 4696
Abson Gloucs ... 35 7074
Abthorpe Nhants ... 49 6446
Aby Lincs ... 77 4078
Acaster Malbis N York ... 83 5845
Acaster Selby N York ... 83 5741
Accott Devon ... 19 6432
Accrington Lancs ... 81 7628
Acha Ag & B ... 120 1854
Acha Mor W Isls ... 152 3029
Achahoish Ag & B ... 113 7877
Achalader P & K ... 126 1245
Achaleven Ag & B ... 122 9233
Achanalt Highld ... 139 2661
Achandunie Highld ... 146 6472
Achany Highld ... 146 5602
Acharacle Highld ... 121 6767
Acharn Highld ... 122 7050
Acharn P & K ... 124 7543
Achavanich Highld ... 151 1842
Achduart Highld ... 145 0403
Achfary Highld ... 148 2939
Achiltibuie Highld ... 144 0208
Achinhoan Ag & B ... 105 7516
Achintee Highld ... 138 9441
Achintraid Highld ... 138 8438
Achmelvich Highld ... 148 0524
Achmore Highld ... 138 8533
Achmore W Isls ... 152 3029
Achnacarnin Highld ... 148 0432
Achnacarry Highld ... 131 1787
Achnacloich Highld ... 129 5908
Achnaconeran Highld ... 139 4118
Achnacroish Ag & B ... 122 8541
Achnadrish Lodge Ag & B ... 121 4652
Achnafauld P & K ... 125 3741
Achnagarron Highld ... 146 6870
Achnaha Highld ... 128 4668
Achnahaird Highld ... 144 0013
Achnairn Highld ... 146 5512
Achnalea Highld ... 130 8561
Achnamara Ag & B ... 113 7887
Achnasheen Highld ... 138 1658
Achnashellach Station Highld ... 138 0048
Achnastank Moray ... 141 2733
Achosnich Highld ... 121 4467
Achranich Highld ... 122 7047
Achreamie Highld ... 150 0166
Achriabhach Highld ... 131 1468
Achriesgill Highld ... 148 2554
Achtoty Highld ... 149 6762
Achurch Nhants ... 51 0283
Achvaich Highld ... 146 7194
Ackergill Highld ... 151 3553
Acklam N York ... 97 4817
Acklam N York ... 90 7861
Ackleton Shrops ... 60 7698
Acklington Nthumb ... 103 2301
Ackton W York ... 83 4121
Ackworth Moor Top W York ... 83 4316
Acle Norfk ... 67 4010
Acock's Green W Mids ... 61 1283
Acol Kent ... 29 3067
Acomb N York ... 83 5651
Acomb Nthumb ... 102 9366
Aconbury Herefs ... 46 5133
Acre Lancs ... 81 7924
Acrefair Wrexhm ... 70 2743
Acresford Derbys ... 61 2913
Acton Ches ... 71 6352
Acton Dorset ... 11 9978
Acton Gt Lon ... 26 2080
Acton Staffs ... 72 8241
Acton Suffk ... 54 8945
Acton Worcs ... 47 8467
Acton Beauchamp Herefs ... 47 6850
Acton Bridge Ches ... 71 5975
Acton Burnell Shrops ... 59 5302
Acton Green Herefs ... 47 6950
Acton Park Wrexhm ... 71 3451
Acton Pigott Shrops ... 59 5402
Acton Round Shrops ... 59 6395
Acton Scott Shrops ... 59 4589
Acton Trussell Staffs ... 72 9318
Acton Turville Gloucs ... 35 8080
Adbaston Staffs ... 72 7627
Adber Dorset ... 21 5920
Adbolton Notts ... 62 5938
Adderbury Oxon ... 49 4735
Adderley Shrops ... 72 6640
Adderstone Nthumb ... 111 1330
Addiewell W Loth ... 117 9962
Addingham W York ... 82 0749
Addington Bucks ... 49 7428
Addington Gt Lon ... 27 3664
Addington Kent ... 28 6559
Addiscombe Gt Lon ... 27 3366
Addlestone Surrey ... 26 0564
Addlestonemoor Surrey ... 26 0565
Addlethorpe Lincs ... 77 5468
Adeney Shrops ... 72 6918
Adeyfield Herts ... 38 0708
Adfa Powys ... 58 0601
Adforton Herefs ... 46 4071
Adisham Kent ... 29 2253
Adlestrop Gloucs ... 48 2426
Adlingfleet E R Yk ... 84 8421
Adlington Ches ... 79 9180
Adlington Lancs ... 81 6013
Admaston Shrops ... 59 6313
Admaston Staffs ... 73 0423

Admington Warwks ... 48 2045
Adsborough Somset ... 20 2729
Adscombe Somset ... 20 1837
Adstock Bucks ... 49 7329
Adstone Nhants ... 49 5951
Adswood Gt Man ... 79 8888
Adversane W Susx ... 14 0723
Advie Highld ... 141 1334
Adwalton W York ... 82 2328
Adwell Oxon ... 37 6999
Adwick Le Street S York ... 83 5308
Adwick upon Dearne S York ... 83 4701
Ae D & G ... 100 9889
Ae Bridgend D & G ... 100 0186
Affetside Gt Man ... 81 7513
Affleck Abers ... 142 5540
Affpuddle Dorset ... 11 8093
Affric Lodge Highld ... 138 1822
Afon-wen Flints ... 70 1371
Afton Devon ... 7 8462
Afton IOW ... 12 3486
Agglethorpe N York ... 89 0885
Aigburth Mersyd ... 78 3886
Aike E R Yk ... 84 0446
Aiketgate Cumb ... 94 4846
Aikhead Cumb ... 93 2349
Aikton Cumb ... 93 2753
Ailby Lincs ... 77 4376
Ailey Herefs ... 46 3348
Ailsworth Cambs ... 64 1198
Ainderby Quernhow N York ... 89 3480
Ainderby Steeple N York ... 89 3392
Aingers Green Essex ... 41 1120
Ainsdale Mersyd ... 80 3112
Ainsdale-on-Sea Mersyd ... 80 2912
Ainstable Cumb ... 94 5246
Ainsworth Gt Man ... 79 7610
Ainthorpe N York ... 90 7007
Aintree Mersyd ... 78 3898
Ainville W Loth ... 117 1063
Aird Ag & B ... 113 7600
Aird D & G ... 98 0960
Aird W Isls ... 152 5635
Aird a Mhulaidh W Isls ... 152 1810
Aird Asaig W Isls ... 152 1222
Aird Dhubh Highld ... 137 7040
Aird of Kinloch Ag & B ... 121 5228
Aird of Sleat Highld ... 129 5900
Aird Uig W Isls ... 152 0533
Airdeny Ag & B ... 122 9929
Airdrie N Lans ... 116 7565
Airdriehill N Lans ... 116 7867
Airds Bay Ag & B ... 122 9932
Airds of Kells D & G ... 99 6770
Airidh a bhruaich W Isls ... 152 2417
Airieland D & G ... 99 7556
Airlie Angus ... 126 3150
Airmyn E R Yk ... 84 7224
Airntully P & K ... 125 0935
Airor Highld ... 129 7205
Airth Falk ... 116 9087
Airton N York ... 88 9059
Aisby Lincs ... 76 8692
Aisby Lincs ... 64 0138
Aisgill Cumb ... 88 7797
Aish Devon ... 7 6960
Aish Devon ... 7 8458
Aisholt Somset ... 20 1935
Aiskew N York ... 89 2788
Aislaby Dur ... 89 4012
Aislaby N York ... 90 8608
Aislaby N York ... 90 7785
Aisthorpe Lincs ... 76 9480
Aith Shet ... 153 3455
Akeld Nthumb ... 111 9529
Akeley Bucks ... 49 7037
Akenham Suffk ... 54 1449
Albaston Devon ... 6 4270
Alberbury Shrops ... 59 3614
Albourne W Susx ... 15 2516
Albourne Green W Susx ... 15 2616
Albrighton Shrops ... 59 4918
Albrighton Shrops ... 60 8004
Alburgh Norfk ... 55 2687
Albury Herts ... 39 4324
Albury Oxon ... 37 6505
Albury Surrey ... 14 0447
Albury End Herts ... 39 4223
Albury Heath Surrey ... 14 0646
Alby Hill Norfk ... 67 1934
Alcaig Highld ... 139 5657
Alcaston Shrops ... 59 4587
Alcester Warwks ... 48 0857
Alcester Lane End W Mids ... 61 0780
Alciston E Susx ... 16 5005
Alcombe Wilts ... 35 8169
Alconbury Cambs ... 52 1875
Alconbury Weston Cambs ... 52 1777
Aldborough N York ... 89 4066
Aldborough Norfk ... 66 1834
Aldbourne Wilts ... 36 2676
Aldbrough E R Yk ... 85 2438
Aldbrough St John N York ... 89 2011
Aldbury Herts ... 38 9612
Aldcliffe Lancs ... 87 4660
Aldclune P & K ... 132 8964
Aldeburgh Suffk ... 55 4656
Aldeby Norfk ... 67 4493
Aldenham Herts ... 26 1498
Alder Moor Staffs ... 73 2226
Alderbury Wilts ... 23 1827
Aldercar Derbys ... 62 4447
Alderford Norfk ... 66 1218
Alderholt Dorset ... 12 1212
Alderley Gloucs ... 35 7690
Alderley Edge Ches ... 79 8478
Aldermans Green W Mids ... 61 3683
Aldermaston Berks ... 24 5965
Alderminster Warwks ... 48 2348
Aldershot Hants ... 25 8650
Alderton Gloucs ... 47 0033
Alderton Nhants ... 49 7446
Alderton Shrops ... 59 4924
Alderton Suffk ... 55 3441
Alderton Wilts ... 35 8482
Alderwasley Derbys ... 73 3053
Aldfield N York ... 89 2669
Aldford Ches ... 71 4159

Aldgate Rutlnd ... 63 9804
Aldham Essex ... 40 9126
Aldham Suffk ... 54 0545
Aldingbourne W Susx ... 14 9205
Aldingham Cumb ... 86 2870
Aldington Kent ... 29 0736
Aldington Worcs ... 48 0644
Aldington Corner Kent ... 29 0636
Aldivalloch Moray ... 141 3526
Aldochlay Ag & B ... 115 3591
Aldon Shrops ... 46 4379
Aldoth Cumb ... 92 1448
Aldreth Cambs ... 53 4473
Aldridge W Mids ... 61 0500
Aldringham Suffk ... 55 4461
Aldro N York ... 90 8162
Aldsworth Gloucs ... 36 1509
Aldsworth W Susx ... 14 7608
Aldunie Moray ... 141 3626
Aldwark Derbys ... 74 2257
Aldwark N York ... 89 4663
Aldwick W Susx ... 14 9198
Aldwincle Nhants ... 51 0081
Aldworth Berks ... 37 5579
Alexandria W Duns ... 115 3979
Aley Somset ... 20 1838
Alfardisworthy Devon ... 18 2911
Alfington Devon ... 9 1197
Alfold Surrey ... 14 0333
Alfold Bars W Susx ... 14 0333
Alfold Crossways Surrey ... 14 0333
Alford Abers ... 142 5715
Alford Lincs ... 77 4575
Alford Somset ... 21 6032
Alfreton Derbys ... 74 4155
Alfrick Worcs ... 47 7453
Alfrick Pound Worcs ... 47 7452
Alfriston E Susx ... 16 5103
Algarkirk Lincs ... 64 2935
Alhampton Somset ... 21 6234
Alkborough Lincs ... 84 8821
Alkerton Gloucs ... 35 7705
Alkerton Oxon ... 48 3743
Alkham Kent ... 29 2542
Alkington Shrops ... 71 5339
Alkmonton Derbys ... 73 1838
All Cannings Wilts ... 23 0661
All Saints South Elmham Suffk ... 55 3482
All Stretton Shrops ... 59 4595
Allaleigh Devon ... 7 8053
Allanaquoich Abers ... 133 1291
Allanbank N Lans ... 116 8458
Allanton Border ... 119 8654
Allanton N Lans ... 116 8457
Allanton S Lans ... 116 7454
Allaston Gloucs ... 35 6304
Allbrook Hants ... 13 4521
Allen End Warwks ... 61 1696
Allen's Green Herts ... 39 4516
Allendale Nthumb ... 95 8355
Allenheads Nthumb ... 95 8645
Allensford Dur ... 95 0750
Allensmore Herefs ... 46 4635
Allenton Derbys ... 62 3732
Aller Devon ... 19 7625
Aller Somset ... 21 4029
Allerby Cumb ... 92 0839
Allercombe Devon ... 9 0494
Allerford Somset ... 20 9046
Allerston N York ... 90 8782
Allerthorpe E R Yk ... 84 7847
Allerton Mersyd ... 78 3987
Allerton W York ... 82 1134
Allerton Bywater W York ... 83 4227
Allerton Mauleverer N York ... 89 4157
Allesley W Mids ... 61 3080
Allestree Derbys ... 62 3439
Allet Common Cnwll ... 3 7948
Allexton Leics ... 51 8100
Allgreave Ches ... 72 9767
Allhallows Kent ... 28 8377
Allhallows-on-Sea Kent ... 40 8478
Alligin Shuas Highld ... 137 8357
Allimore Green Staffs ... 72 8519
Allington Dorset ... 10 4693
Allington Kent ... 28 7557
Allington Lincs ... 63 8540
Allington Wilts ... 35 8975
Allington Wilts ... 23 0663
Allington Wilts ... 23 2039
Allithwaite Cumb ... 87 3876
Alloa Clacks ... 116 8892
Allonby Cumb ... 92 0842
Allostock Ches ... 79 7471
Alloway S Ayrs ... 106 3318
Allowenshay Somset ... 10 3913
Allscott Shrops ... 59 6113
Allscott Shrops ... 60 7396
Alltami Flints ... 70 2665
Alltchaorunn Highld ... 123 1951
Alltmawr Powys ... 45 0746
Alltwalis Carmth ... 31 4431
Alltwen Neath ... 32 7303
Alltyblaca Cerdgn ... 44 5245
Allweston Dorset ... 11 6614
Allwood Green Suffk ... 54 0472
Almeley Herefs ... 46 3351
Almeley Wootton Herefs ... 46 3352
Almer Dorset ... 11 9199
Almholme S York ... 83 5608
Almington Staffs ... 72 7034
Almodington W Susx ... 14 8297
Almondbank P & K ... 125 0625
Almondbury W York ... 82 1614
Almondsbury Gloucs ... 34 6084
Alne N York ... 90 4965
Alnesbourn Priory Suffk ... 55 1940
Alness Highld ... 146 6569
Alnham Nthumb ... 111 9810
Alnmouth Nthumb ... 111 2410
Alnwick Nthumb ... 111 1813
Alperton Gt Lon ... 26 1883
Alphamstone Essex ... 54 8735
Alpheton Suffk ... 54 8750
Alphington Devon ... 9 9190
Alpington Norfk ... 67 2901
Alport Derbys ... 74 2264
Alpraham Ches ... 71 5859

Alresford Essex ... 41 0621
Alrewas Staffs ... 61 1614
Alsager Ches ... 72 7955
Alsagers Bank Staffs ... 72 7948
Alsop en le Dale Derbys ... 73 1554
Alston Cumb ... 94 7146
Alston Devon ... 10 3002
Alston Sutton Somset ... 21 4151
Alstone Gloucs ... 47 9832
Alstone Somset ... 21 3146
Alstone Green Staffs ... 72 8518
Alstonefield Staffs ... 73 1355
Alswear Devon ... 19 7222
Alt Gt Man ... 79 9403
Altandhu Highld ... 144 9812
Altarnun Cnwll ... 5 2281
Altass Highld ... 146 5000
Altcreich Ag & B ... 122 6938
Altgaltraig Ag & B ... 114 0473
Altham Lancs ... 81 7732
Althorne Essex ... 40 9198
Althorpe Lincs ... 84 8309
Altnabreac Station Highld ... 150 0045
Altnacraig Ag & B ... 122 8429
Altnaharra Highld ... 149 5635
Altofts W York ... 83 3823
Alton Derbys ... 74 3664
Alton Hants ... 24 7139
Alton Staffs ... 73 0741
Alton Wilts ... 23 1546
Alton Barnes Wilts ... 23 1062
Alton Pancras Dorset ... 11 7002
Alton Priors Wilts ... 23 1162
Alton Towers ... 73 0743
Altrincham Gt Man ... 79 7687
Altskeith Hotel Stirlg ... 124 4602
Alva Clacks ... 116 8897
Alvah Abers ... 142 6760
Alvanley Ches ... 71 4974
Alvaston Derbys ... 62 3833
Alvechurch Worcs ... 60 0272
Alvecote Warwks ... 61 2404
Alvediston Wilts ... 22 9723
Alveley Shrops ... 60 7584
Alverdiscott Devon ... 19 5225
Alverstoke Hants ... 13 6098
Alverstone IOW ... 13 5785
Alverthorpe W York ... 82 3121
Alverton Notts ... 63 7942
Alves Moray ... 141 1362
Alvescot Oxon ... 36 2704
Alveston Gloucs ... 35 6388
Alveston Warwks ... 48 2356
Alvingham Lincs ... 77 3691
Alvington Gloucs ... 34 6000
Alwalton Cambs ... 64 1396
Alwinton Nthumb ... 110 9106
Alwoodley W York ... 82 2840
Alwoodley Gates W York ... 82 3140
Alyth P & K ... 126 2448
Amber Hill Lincs ... 76 2346
Amber Row Derbys ... 74 3856
Ambergate Derbys ... 74 3451
Amberley Gloucs ... 35 8501
Amberley W Susx ... 14 0213
Ambirstone E Susx ... 16 5911
Amble Nthumb ... 103 2604
Amblecote W Mids ... 60 8985
Ambler Thorn W York ... 82 0929
Ambleside Cumb ... 87 3704
Ambleston Pembks ... 30 0025
Ambrosden Oxon ... 37 6019
Amcotts Lincs ... 84 8514
America Cambs ... 53 4378
Amersham Bucks ... 26 9597
Amersham on the Hill Bucks ... 26 9798
Amerton Staffs ... 73 9927
Amesbury Wilts ... 23 1541
Amhuinnsuidhe W Isls ... 152 0408
Amington Staffs ... 61 2304
Amisfield Town D & G ... 100 0082
Amlwch IOA ... 68 4492
Ammanford Carmth ... 32 6212
Amotherby N York ... 90 7473
Ampfield Hants ... 13 4023
Ampleforth N York ... 90 5878
Ampney Crucis Gloucs ... 36 0601
Ampney St Mary Gloucs ... 36 0802
Ampney St Peter Gloucs ... 36 0801
Amport Hants ... 23 3044
Ampthill Beds ... 38 0337
Ampton Suffk ... 54 8671
Amroth Pembks ... 31 1608
Amulree P & K ... 125 8936
Amwell Herts ... 39 1613
An T-ob W Isls ... 152 0286
Anaheilt Highld ... 130 8162
Ancaster Lincs ... 63 9843
Anchor Shrops ... 58 1785
Ancroft Nthumb ... 111 9945
Ancrum Border ... 110 6224
Ancton W Susx ... 14 9800
Anderby Lincs ... 77 5275
Andersea Somset ... 21 3333
Andersfield Somset ... 20 2434
Anderson Dorset ... 11 8797
Anderton Ches ... 79 6475
Anderton Cnwll ... 6 4351
Andover Hants ... 23 3645
Andoversford Gloucs ... 35 0219
Andreas IOM ... 158 4199
Anelog Gwynd ... 56 1527
Anerley Gt Lon ... 27 3369
Anfield Mersyd ... 78 3692
Angarrack Cnwll ... 2 5838
Angarrick Cnwll ... 3 7937
Angelbank Shrops ... 46 5776
Angersleigh Somset ... 20 1918
Angerton Cumb ... 93 2257
Angle Pembks ... 30 8603
Angmering W Susx ... 14 0604
Angram N York ... 88 8899
Angram N York ... 83 5248
Angrouse Cnwll ... 2 6619
Anick Nthumb ... 102 9465
Ankerville Highld ... 147 8174
Ankle Hill Leics ... 63 7518
Anlaby E R Yk ... 84 0328

Anmer *Norfk* — **65** 7429
Anmore *Hants* — **13** 6611
Anna Valley *Hants* — **23** 3543
Annan *D & G* — **101** 1966
Annaside *Cumb* — **86** 0986
Annat *Highld* — **138** 8954
Annathill *N Lans* — **116** 7270
Annbank *S Ayrs* — **106** 4023
Anne Hathaway's Cottage — **48** 1854
Annesley *Notts* — **75** 5053
Annesley Woodhouse *Notts* — **75** 4953
Anfield Plain *Dur* — **96** 1651
Anniesland *C Glas* — **115** 5368
Annitsford *T & W* — **103** 2674
Annscroft *Shrops* — **59** 4507
Ansdell *Lancs* — **80** 3428
Ansford *Somset* — **21** 6433
Ansley *Warwks* — **61** 3091
Anslow *Staffs* — **73** 2125
Anslow Gate *Staffs* — **73** 1924
Anslow Lees *Staffs* — **73** 2024
Ansteadbrook *Surrey* — **14** 9332
Anstey *Hants* — **24** 7240
Anstey *Herts* — **39** 4033
Anstey *Leics* — **62** 5508
Anstruther *Fife* — **127** 5703
Ansty *W Susx* — **15** 2923
Ansty *Warwks* — **61** 4083
Ansty *Wilts* — **22** 9526
Ansty Cross *Dorset* — **11** 7603
Anthill Common *Hants* — **13** 6312
Anthonys *Surrey* — **26** 0161
Anthorn *Cumb* — **93** 1958
Antingham *Norfk* — **67** 2533
Anton's Gowt *Lincs* — **77** 3047
Antony *Cnwll* — **5** 4054
Antrobus *Ches* — **79** 6480
Antron *Cnwll* — **2** 6327
Anvil Corner *Devon* — **18** 3704
Anvil Green *Kent* — **29** 1049
Anwick *Lincs* — **76** 1150
Anwoth *D & G* — **99** 5856
Aperfield *Gt Lon* — **27** 4158
Apes Dale *Worcs* — **60** 9972
Apethorpe *Nhants* — **51** 0295
Apeton *Staffs* — **72** 8518
Apley *Lincs* — **76** 1075
Apperknowle *Derbys* — **74** 3878
Apperley *Gloucs* — **47** 8628
Apperley Bridge *W York* — **82** 1937
Apperley Dene *Nthumb* — **95** 0558
Appersett *N York* — **88** 8690
Appin *Ag & B* — **122** 9346
Appleby *Lincs* — **84** 9614
Appleby Magna *Leics* — **61** 3109
Appleby Parva *Leics* — **61** 3008
Appleby Street *Herts* — **39** 3304
Appleby-in-Westmorland *Cumb* — **94** 6820
Applecross *Highld* — **137** 7144
Appledore *Devon* — **18** 4630
Appledore *Devon* — **9** 0814
Appledore *Kent* — **17** 9529
Appledore Heath *Kent* — **17** 9630
Appleford *Oxon* — **37** 5293
Applegarth Town *D & G* — **100** 1084
Applehaigh *S York* — **83** 3512
Appleshaw *Hants* — **23** 3048
Applethwaite *Cumb* — **93** 2825
Appleton *Ches* — **78** 5186
Appleton *Ches* — **79** 6184
Appleton *Oxon* — **37** 4401
Appleton Roebuck *N York* — **83** 5542
Appleton Thorn *Ches* — **79** 6383
Appleton Wiske *N York* — **89** 3804
Appleton-le-Moors *N York* — **90** 7387
Appleton-le-Street *N York* — **90** 7373
Appletreehall *Border* — **109** 5117
Appletreewick *N York* — **88** 0560
Appley *Somset* — **20** 0721
Appley Bridge *Lancs* — **78** 5209
Apse Heath *IOW* — **13** 5583
Apsley End *Beds* — **38** 1232
Apuldram *W Susx* — **14** 8403
Arabella *Highld* — **147** 8076
Arbirlot *Angus* — **127** 6040
Arboll *Highld* — **147** 8781
Arborfield *Berks* — **24** 7567
Arborfield Cross *Berks* — **24** 7666
Arbourthorne *S York* — **74** 3785
Arbroath *Angus* — **127** 6441
Arbuthnott *Abers* — **135** 7975
Arcadia *Kent* — **28** 8836
Archdeacon Newton *Dur* — **96** 2517
Archencarroch *W Duns* — **115** 4182
Archiestown *Moray* — **141** 2244
Archirondel *Jersey* — **158** 0000
Arclid Green *Ches* — **72** 7861
Ardanaiseig Hotel *Ag & B* — **123** 0824
Ardaneaskan *Highld* — **137** 8335
Ardarroch *Highld* — **137** 8339
Ardbeg *Ag & B* — **104** 4146
Ardbeg *Ag & B* — **114** 0766
Ardbeg *Ag & B* — **114** 1583
Ardcharnich *Highld* — **145** 1788
Ardchiavaig *Ag & B* — **121** 3518
Ardchonnel *Ag & B* — **122** 9812
Ardchullarie More *Stirlg* — **124** 5813
Arddarroch *Ag & B* — **114** 2494
Arddleen *Powys* — **58** 2616
Ardechive *Highld* — **131** 1490
Ardeer *N Ayrs* — **106** 2740
Ardeley *Herts* — **39** 3027
Ardelve *Highld* — **138** 8627
Arden *Ag & B* — **115** 3684
Ardens Grafton *Warwks* — **48** 1154
Ardentallen *Ag & B* — **122** 8324
Ardentinny *Ag & B* — **114** 1887
Ardentraive *Ag & B* — **114** 0374
Ardeonaig Hotel *Stirlg* — **124** 6735
Ardersier *Highld* — **140** 7855
Ardessie *Highld* — **145** 0689
Ardfern *Ag & B* — **122** 8004
Ardgay *Highld* — **146** 5990
Ardgour *Highld* — **130** 0163
Ardgowan *Inver* — **114** 2073
Ardhallow *Ag & B* — **114** 1674
Ardhasig *W Isls* — **152** 1202

Ardheslaig *Highld* — **137** 7855
Ardindrean *Highld* — **145** 1588
Ardingly *W Susx* — **15** 3429
Ardington *Oxon* — **36** 4388
Ardington Wick *Oxon* — **36** 4389
Ardlamont *Ag & B* — **114** 9865
Ardleigh *Essex* — **41** 0529
Ardleigh Heath *Essex* — **41** 0530
Ardler *P & K* — **126** 2642
Ardley *Oxon* — **49** 5427
Ardley End *Essex* — **39** 5214
Ardlui *Ag & B* — **123** 3115
Ardlussa *Ag & B* — **113** 6487
Ardmaddy *Ag & B* — **123** 0837
Ardmair *Highld* — **145** 1097
Ardmaleish *Ag & B* — **114** 0768
Ardminish *Ag & B* — **104** 6448
Ardmolich *Highld* — **129** 7172
Ardmore *Ag & B* — **115** 3178
Ardmore *Highld* — **146** 7086
Ardnadam *Ag & B* — **114** 1780
Ardnagrask *Highld* — **139** 5249
Ardnarff *Highld* — **138** 8935
Ardnastang *Highld* — **130** 8061
Ardno *Ag & B* — **123** 1508
Ardochy Lodge Hotel *Highld* — **131** 2002
Ardpatrick *Ag & B* — **113** 7559
Ardrishaig *Ag & B* — **113** 8585
Ardross *Highld* — **146** 6174
Ardsley *Barns* — **83** 3805
Ardsley East *W York* — **82** 3025
Ardslignish *Highld* — **121** 5661
Ardtalla *Ag & B* — **112** 4654
Ardtoe *Highld* — **129** 6270
Arduaine *Ag & B* — **122** 7910
Ardullie *Highld* — **139** 5862
Ardvasar *Highld* — **129** 6303
Ardvorlich *P & K* — **124** 6322
Ardvourlie *W Isls* — **152** 1810
Ardwell *D & G* — **98** 1045
Ardwick *Gt Man* — **79** 8597
Areley Kings *Worcs* — **60** 7970
Arevegaig *Highld* — **129** 6568
Arford *Hants* — **14** 8236
Argoed *Caerph* — **33** 1799
Argoed *Shrops* — **59** 3220
Argoed Mill *Powys* — **45** 9963
Argos Hill *E Susx* — **16** 5728
Aribruach *W Isls* — **152** 2417
Aridhglas *Ag & B* — **120** 3123
Arileod *Ag & B* — **120** 1655
Arinagour *Ag & B* — **120** 2257
Ariogan *Ag & B* — **122** 8627
Arisaig *Highld* — **129** 6586
Arisaig House *Highld* — **129** 6984
Arkendale *N York* — **89** 3861
Arkesden *Essex* — **39** 4834
Arkholme *Lancs* — **87** 5871
Arkle Town *N York* — **88** 0001
Arkleby *Cumb* — **92** 1439
Arkleton *D & G* — **101** 3791
Arkley *Gt Lon* — **26** 2295
Arksey *S York* — **83** 5807
Arkwright Town *Derbys* — **74** 4271
Arle *Gloucs* — **47** 9223
Arlecdon *Cumb* — **92** 0418
Arlescote *Warwks* — **48** 3848
Arlesey *Beds* — **39** 1936
Arleston *Shrops* — **60** 6610
Arley *Ches* — **79** 6680
Arley *Warwks* — **61** 2890
Arlingham *Gloucs* — **35** 7010
Arlington *Devon* — **19** 6140
Arlington *E Susx* — **16** 5407
Arlington *Gloucs* — **36** 1006
Arlington Beccott *Devon* — **19** 6241
Armadale *Highld* — **150** 7864
Armadale *Highld* — **129** 6303
Armadale *W Loth* — **116** 9368
Armaside *Cumb* — **92** 1527
Armathwaite *Cumb* — **94** 5046
Arminghall *Norfk* — **67** 2504
Armitage *Staffs* — **73** 0715
Armitage Bridge *W York* — **82** 1313
Armley *W York* — **82** 2833
Armscote *Warwks* — **48** 2444
Armshead *Staffs* — **72** 9348
Armston *Nhants* — **51** 0685
Armthorpe *S York* — **83** 6204
Arnabost *Ag & B* — **120** 2159
Arnaby *Cumb* — **86** 1884
Arncliffe *N York* — **88** 9371
Arncliffe Cote *N York* — **88** 9470
Arncroach *Fife* — **127** 5105
Arndilly House *Moray* — **141** 2847
Arne *Dorset* — **11** 9788
Arnesby *Leics* — **50** 6192
Arnfield *Derbys* — **79** 0197
Arngask *P & K* — **126** 1410
Arnisdale *Highld* — **130** 8410
Arnish *Highld* — **137** 5948
Arniston *Mdloth* — **118** 3362
Arnol *W Isls* — **152** 3148
Arnold *E R Yk* — **85** 1241
Arnold *Notts* — **62** 5645
Arnprior *Stirlg* — **116** 6194
Arnside *Cumb* — **87** 4578
Aros *Ag & B* — **121** 5645
Arowry *Wrexhm* — **71** 4639
Arrad Foot *Cumb* — **86** 3080
Arram *E R Yk* — **84** 0344
Arrathorne *N York* — **89** 2393
Arreton *IOW* — **13** 5386
Arrina *Highld* — **137** 7458
Arrington *Cambs* — **52** 3250
Arrochar *Ag & B* — **123** 2904
Arrow *Warwks* — **48** 0856
Arrowfield Top *Worcs* — **61** 0374
Arscott *Shrops* — **59** 4307
Artafallie *Highld* — **140** 6349
Arthington *W York* — **82** 2644
Arthingworth *Nhants* — **50** 7581
Arthog *Gwynd* — **57** 6414
Arthrath *Abers* — **143** 9636
Arthursdale *W York* — **83** 3737
Artrochie *Abers* — **143** 0031
Arundel *W Susx* — **14** 0106

Asby *Cumb* — **92** 0620
Ascog *Ag & B* — **114** 1062
Ascot *Berks* — **25** 9268
Ascott *Warwks* — **48** 3234
Ascott Earl *Oxon* — **36** 3018
Ascott-under-Wychwood *Oxon* — **36** 3018
Asenby *N York* — **89** 3975
Asfordby *Leics* — **63** 7019
Asfordby Hill *Leics* — **63** 7219
Asgarby *Lincs* — **64** 1145
Asgarby *Lincs* — **77** 3366
Ash *Devon* — **19** 5208
Ash *Devon* — **7** 8349
Ash *Dorset* — **11** 8610
Ash *Kent* — **27** 6064
Ash *Kent* — **29** 2858
Ash *Somset* — **20** 2822
Ash *Somset* — **21** 4720
Ash *Surrey* — **25** 9051
Ash Green *Surrey* — **25** 9049
Ash Green *Warwks* — **61** 3384
Ash Magna *Shrops* — **71** 5739
Ash Mill *Devon* — **19** 7823
Ash Parva *Shrops* — **71** 5739
Ash Priors *Somset* — **20** 1529
Ash Street *Suffk* — **54** 0146
Ash Thomas *Devon* — **9** 0010
Ash Vale *Surrey* — **25** 8951
Ashampstead *Berks* — **37** 5676
Ashampstead Green *Berks* — **37** 5677
Ashbocking *Suffk* — **54** 1754
Ashbocking Green *Suffk* — **54** 1854
Ashbourne *Derbys* — **73** 1746
Ashbrittle *Somset* — **20** 0521
Ashburnham Place *E Susx* — **16** 6814
Ashburton *Devon* — **7** 7570
Ashbury *Devon* — **5** 5098
Ashbury *Oxon* — **36** 2685
Ashby *Lincs* — **84** 8908
Ashby by Partney *Lincs* — **77** 4266
Ashby cum Fenby *Lincs* — **77** 2500
Ashby de la Launde *Lincs* — **76** 0555
Ashby Folville *Leics* — **63** 7012
Ashby Magna *Leics* — **50** 5690
Ashby Parva *Leics* — **50** 5288
Ashby Puerorum *Lincs* — **77** 3271
Ashby St Ledgers *Nhants* — **50** 5768
Ashby St Mary *Norfk* — **67** 3202
Ashby-de-la-Zouch *Leics* — **62** 3516
Ashchurch *Gloucs* — **47** 9233
Ashcombe *Devon* — **9** 9179
Ashcombe *Somset* — **21** 3361
Ashcott *Somset* — **21** 4336
Ashdon *Essex* — **53** 5842
Ashe *Hants* — **24** 5350
Asheldham *Essex* — **41** 9701
Ashen *Essex* — **53** 7442
Ashendon *Bucks* — **37** 7014
Asheridge *Bucks* — **38** 9304
Ashfield *Hants* — **12** 3619
Ashfield *Herefs* — **46** 5923
Ashfield *Stirlg* — **124** 7803
Ashfield *Suffk* — **55** 2062
Ashfield Green *Suffk* — **53** 7655
Ashfield Green *Suffk* — **55** 2573
Ashfields *Shrops* — **72** 7026
Ashfold Crossways *W Susx* — **15** 2328
Ashford *Devon* — **19** 5335
Ashford *Devon* — **7** 6948
Ashford *Kent* — **28** 0142
Ashford *Surrey* — **26** 0771
Ashford Bowdler *Shrops* — **46** 5170
Ashford Carbonel *Shrops* — **46** 5270
Ashford Hill *Hants* — **24** 5562
Ashford in the Water *Derbys* — **74** 1969
Ashgill *S Lans* — **116** 7850
Ashill *Devon* — **9** 0611
Ashill *Norfk* — **66** 8804
Ashill *Somset* — **10** 3217
Ashingdon *Essex* — **40** 8693
Ashington *Dorset* — **11** 0098
Ashington *Nthumb* — **103** 2687
Ashington *Somset* — **21** 5621
Ashington *W Susx* — **15** 1315
Ashkirk *Border* — **109** 4722
Ashleworth *Gloucs* — **47** 8125
Ashleworth Quay *Gloucs* — **47** 8125
Ashley *Cambs* — **53** 6961
Ashley *Ches* — **79** 7784
Ashley *Devon* — **19** 6511
Ashley *Dorset* — **12** 1304
Ashley *Gloucs* — **35** 9394
Ashley *Hants* — **23** 3831
Ashley *Hants* — **12** 2595
Ashley *Kent* — **29** 3048
Ashley *Nhants* — **50** 7990
Ashley *Staffs* — **72** 7636
Ashley *Wilts* — **22** 8268
Ashley Green *Bucks* — **38** 9705
Ashley Heath *Dorset* — **12** 1204
Ashley Moor *Herefs* — **46** 4767
Ashmansworth *Hants* — **24** 4157
Ashmansworthy *Devon* — **18** 3418
Ashmead Green *Gloucs* — **35** 7699
Ashmill *Devon* — **5** 3995
Ashmore *Dorset* — **11** 9117
Ashmore Green *Berks* — **24** 5069
Ashorne *Warwks* — **48** 3057
Ashover *Derbys* — **74** 3463
Ashover Hay *Derbys* — **74** 3460
Ashperton *Herefs* — **46** 6441
Ashprington *Devon* — **7** 8157
Ashreigney *Devon* — **19** 6313
Ashridge Park *Herts* — **38** 9912
Ashstead *Surrey* — **26** 1857
Ashton *Cambs* — **64** 1005
Ashton *Ches* — **71** 5069
Ashton *Cnwll* — **2** 6028
Ashton *Cnwll* — **5** 3468
Ashton *Devon* — **8** 8584
Ashton *Hants* — **13** 5419
Ashton *Herefs* — **46** 5164
Ashton *Inver* — **114** 2377
Ashton *Nhants* — **49** 7849
Ashton *Nhants* — **51** 0588

Ashton *Somset* — **21** 4149
Ashton Common *Wilts* — **22** 8958
Ashton Hill *Wilts* — **22** 9057
Ashton Keynes *Wilts* — **36** 0494
Ashton under Hill *Worcs* — **47** 9937
Ashton upon Mersey *Gt Man* — **79** 7892
Ashton Watering *Somset* — **21** 5369
Ashton-in-Makerfield *Gt Man* — **78** 5798
Ashton-under-Lyne *Gt Man* — **79** 9399
Ashurst *Hants* — **12** 3310
Ashurst *Kent* — **16** 5138
Ashurst *W Susx* — **15** 1715
Ashurstwood *W Susx* — **15** 4136
Ashwater *Devon* — **5** 3895
Ashwell *Herts* — **39** 2639
Ashwell *Rutlnd* — **63** 8613
Ashwell *Somset* — **10** 3616
Ashwell End *Herts* — **39** 2540
Ashwellthorpe *Norfk* — **66** 1497
Ashwick *Somset* — **21** 6348
Ashwicken *Norfk* — **65** 7018
Ashwood *Staffs* — **60** 8688
Askam in Furness *Cumb* — **86** 2177
Aske Hall *N York* — **89** 1703
Askern *S York* — **83** 5613
Askerswell *Dorset* — **10** 5292
Askett *Bucks* — **38** 8105
Askham *Cumb* — **94** 5123
Askham *Notts* — **75** 7374
Askham Bryan *N York* — **83** 5548
Askham Richard *N York* — **83** 5347
Asknish *Ag & B* — **114** 9391
Askrigg *N York* — **88** 9491
Askwith *N York* — **82** 1648
Aslackby *Lincs* — **64** 0830
Aslacton *Norfk* — **54** 1590
Aslockton *Notts* — **63** 7440
Asney *Somset* — **21** 4636
Aspall *Suffk* — **54** 1664
Aspatria *Cumb* — **92** 1441
Aspenden *Herts* — **39** 3528
Aspenshaw *Derbys* — **79** 0187
Asperton *Lincs* — **64** 2637
Aspley *Staffs* — **72** 8133
Aspley Guise *Beds* — **38** 9335
Aspley Heath *Beds* — **38** 9334
Aspley Heath *Warwks* — **61** 0970
Aspull *Gt Man* — **78** 6108
Aspull Common *Gt Man* — **79** 6498
Asselby *E R Yk* — **84** 7127
Asserby *Lincs* — **77** 4977
Asserby Turn *Lincs* — **77** 4477
Assington *Suffk* — **54** 9338
Assington Green *Suffk* — **53** 7751
Astbury *Ches* — **72** 8461
Astcote *Nhants* — **49** 6753
Asterley *Shrops* — **59** 3707
Asterton *Shrops* — **59** 3991
Asthall *Oxon* — **36** 2811
Asthall Leigh *Oxon* — **36** 3013
Astle *Highld* — **146** 7391
Astley *Gt Man* — **79** 7000
Astley *Shrops* — **59** 5218
Astley *W York* — **83** 3828
Astley *Warwks* — **61** 3189
Astley *Worcs* — **47** 7867
Astley Abbots *Shrops* — **60** 7096
Astley Bridge *Gt Man* — **81** 7111
Astley Cross *Worcs* — **47** 8069
Astley Green *Gt Man* — **79** 7099
Astley Town *Worcs* — **47** 7968
Aston *Berks* — **37** 7884
Aston *Ches* — **71** 5578
Aston *Ches* — **71** 6146
Aston *Derbys* — **71** 1783
Aston *Flints* — **71** 3067
Aston *Herefs* — **46** 4662
Aston *Herefs* — **46** 4671
Aston *Herts* — **39** 2722
Aston *Oxon* — **36** 3403
Aston *S York* — **75** 4685
Aston *Shrops* — **59** 5328
Aston *Shrops* — **59** 6109
Aston *Shrops* — **60** 8093
Aston *Staffs* — **72** 5541
Aston *Staffs* — **72** 8823
Aston *Staffs* — **72** 9130
Aston *W Mids* — **61** 0888
Aston Abbotts *Bucks* — **38** 8420
Aston Botterell *Shrops* — **59** 6384
Aston Cantlow *Warwks* — **48** 1460
Aston Clinton *Bucks* — **38** 8812
Aston Crews *Herefs* — **47** 6723
Aston Cross *Gloucs* — **47** 9433
Aston End *Herts* — **39** 2724
Aston Fields *Worcs* — **47** 9669
Aston Flamville *Leics* — **50** 4692
Aston Heath *Ches* — **71** 5678
Aston Ingham *Herefs* — **47** 6823
Aston juxta Mondrum *Ches* — **72** 6456
Aston le Walls *Nhants* — **49** 4950
Aston Magna *Gloucs* — **48** 1935
Aston Munslow *Shrops* — **59** 5186
Aston on Clun *Shrops* — **59** 3981
Aston Pigott *Shrops* — **59** 3305
Aston Rogers *Shrops* — **59** 3406
Aston Rowant *Oxon* — **37** 7299
Aston Sandford *Bucks* — **37** 7507
Aston Somerville *Worcs* — **48** 0438
Aston Subedge *Gloucs* — **48** 1441
Aston Tirrold *Oxon* — **37** 5586
Aston Upthorpe *Oxon* — **37** 5586
Aston-Eyre *Shrops* — **59** 6594
Aston-upon-Trent *Derbys* — **62** 4129
Astonlane *Shrops* — **59** 6494
Astrop *Nhants* — **49** 5036
Astrope *Herts* — **38** 8914
Astwick *Beds* — **39** 2138
Astwith *Derbys* — **75** 4464
Astwood *Bucks* — **38** 9547
Astwood *Worcs* — **47** 9365
Astwood Bank *Worcs* — **48** 0462
Aswarby *Lincs* — **64** 0639
Aswardby *Lincs* — **77** 3570
Atch Lench *Worcs* — **48** 0350
Atcham *Shrops* — **59** 5409
Athelhampton *Dorset* — **11** 7694

Athelington *Suffk* — **55** 21..
Athelney *Somset* — **21** 34..
Athelstaneford *E Loth* — **118** 53..
Atherfield Green *IOW* — **13** 4..
Atherington *Devon* — **19** 59..
Atherington *W Susx* — **14** 0..
Atherstone *Somset* — **10** 3..
Atherstone *Warwks* — **61** 3..
Atherstone on Stour *Warwks* — **48** 2..
Atherton *Gt Man* — **79** 67..
Atley Hill *N York* — **89** 2..
Atlow *Derbys* — **73** 2..
Attadale *Highld* — **138** 9..
Attenborough *Notts* — **62** 5..
Atterby *Lincs* — **76** 97..
Attercliffe *S York* — **74** 37..
Atterley *Shrops* — **59** 65..
Atterton *Leics* — **61** 33..
Attleborough *Norfk* — **66** 04..
Attleborough *Warwks* — **61** 33..
Attlebridge *Norfk* — **66** 1..
Attleton Green *Suffk* — **53** 7..
Atwick *E R Yk* — **85** 1..
Atworth *Wilts* — **22** 8..
Auberrow *Herefs* — **46** 4..
Aubourn *Lincs* — **76** 9..
Auchedly *Abers* — **143** 8..
Auchenblae *Abers* — **135** 7..
Auchenbowie *Stirlg* — **116** 7..
Auchencairn *D & G* — **92** 7..
Auchencairn *D & G* — **100** 9..
Auchencairn *N Ayrs* — **105** 0..
Auchencrow *Border* — **119** 8..
Auchendinny *Mdloth* — **117** 2..
Auchengray *S Lans* — **117** 9..
Auchenhalrig *Moray* — **141** 3..
Auchenheath *S Lans* — **108** 8..
Auchenhessnane *D & G* — **100** 8..
Auchenlochan *Ag & B* — **114** 9..
Auchenmade *N Ayrs* — **115** 3..
Auchenmalg *D & G* — **98** 2..
Auchentiber *N Ayrs* — **115** 3..
Auchindrain *Ag & B* — **145** 19..
Auchininna *Abers* — **142** 66..
Auchinleck *E Ayrs* — **107** 55..
Auchinloch *N Lans* — **116** 66..
Auchinstarry *N Lans* — **116** 7..
Auchintore *Highld* — **130** 0..
Auchiries *Abers* — **143** 0..
Auchlee *Abers* — **135** 8..
Auchleven *Abers* — **142** 6..
Auchlochan *S Lans* — **107** 7..
Auchlossan *Abers* — **134** 5..
Auchlyne *Stirlg* — **124** 5..
Auchmillan *E Ayrs* — **107** 5..
Auchmithie *Angus* — **127** 6..
Auchmuirbridge *Fife* — **126** 2..
Auchnacree *Angus* — **134** 4..
Auchnagatt *Abers* — **143** 9..
Auchnarrow *Moray* — **141** 2..
Auchnotteroch *D & G* — **98** 9..
Auchroisk *Moray* — **141** 3..
Auchterarder *P & K* — **125** 9..
Auchteraw *Highld* — **131** 3..
Auchterblair *Highld* — **140** 9..
Auchtercairn *Highld* — **144** 8..
Auchterderran *Fife* — **117** 2..
Auchterhouse *Angus* — **126** 3..
Auchterless *Abers* — **142** 7..
Auchtermuchty *Fife* — **126** 2..
Auchterneed *Highld* — **139** 4..
Auchtertool *Fife* — **117** 2..
Auchtertyre *Highld* — **138** 84..
Auchtubh *Stirlg* — **124** 5..
Auckengill *Highld* — **151** 3..
Auckley *S York* — **75** 6..
Audenshaw *Gt Man* — **79** 9..
Audlem *Ches* — **72** 6..
Audley *Staffs* — **72** 7..
Audley End — **39** 5..
Audley End *Essex* — **39** 5..
Audley End *Essex* — **54** 8..
Audley End *Suffk* — **54** 8..
Audmore *Staffs* — **72** 8..
Audnam *W Mids* — **60** 8..
Aughertree *Cumb* — **93** 2..
Aughton *E R Yk* — **84** 7..
Aughton *Lancs* — **78** 3..
Aughton *Lancs* — **87** 5..
Aughton *S York* — **75** 4..
Aughton *Wilts* — **23** 2..
Aughton Park *Lancs* — **78** 4..
Auldearn *Highld* — **140** 9..
Aulden *Herefs* — **46** 4..
Auldgirth *D & G* — **100** 9..
Auldhouse *S Lans* — **116** 6..
Ault a' chruinn *Highld* — **138** 9..
Ault Hucknall *Derbys* — **75** 4..
Aultbea *Highld* — **144** 8..
Aultgrishin *Highld* — **144** 7..
Aultguish Inn *Highld* — **145** 3..
Aultmore *Moray* — **142** 4..
Aultnagoire *Highld* — **139** 5..
Aultnamain Inn *Highld* — **146** 6..
Aunby *Lincs* — **64** 0..
Aunk *Devon* — **9** 0..
Aunsby *Lincs* — **64** 0..
Aust *Gloucs* — **34** 5..
Austendike *Lincs* — **64** 2..
Austerfield *S York* — **75** 6..
Austerlands *Gt Man* — **79** 9..
Austhorpe *W York* — **83** 3..
Austonley *W York* — **82** 1..
Austrey *Warwks* — **61** 2..
Austwick *N York* — **88** 7..
Authorpe *Lincs* — **77** 3..
Authorpe Row *Lincs* — **77** 5..
Avebury *Wilts* — **36** 1..
Avebury Trusloe *Wilts* — **36** 0..
Aveley *Essex* — **27** 5..
Avening *Gloucs* — **35** 8..
Averham *Notts* — **75** 7..
Aveton Gifford *Devon* — **7** 6..
Aviemore *Highld* — **132** 8..
Avington *Berks* — **23** 3..
Avoch *Highld* — **140** 7..
Avon *Dorset* — **12** 1..

von Dassett
Batford
271

on Dassett Warwks 49 4150
onbridge Falk 116 9172
onmouth Bristl 34 5178
onwick Devon 7 7158
oridge Hants 12 3224
kley Gloucs 34 5985
liscombe Devon 9 1301
re Gloucs 35 7008
sworth Notts 62 4844
oorough Worcs 60 8579
oridge Somset 21 4354
ord Hants 24 6043
ord Wilts 36 2370
minster Devon 10 2998
mouth Devon 10 2591
ton Flints 70 1080
cliffe Dur 96 2822
don Nthumb 103 0065
burton Gloucs 34 6101
e Cumb 94 7149
esbeare Devon 9 0392
esbury Bucks 38 8213
esby Lincs 85 2007
esford Kent 28 7359
esham Kent 29 2452
estone Leics 50 5700
estone Park Leics 50 5800
merton Norfk 66 1839
sham Norfk 67 1926
ton Gloucs 47 6537
worth Gloucs 36 1021
nestrey Herefs 46 4265
nho Nhants 49 5133
ot Green Herts 39 2214
ot St Lawrence Herts 39 1916
ot St Peter Herts 39 2115
S Ayrs 106 3321
sgarth N York 88 0088
shford Devon 9 0415
side Cumb 87 3983
ston Rutlnd 51 8600
thorpe Roding Essex 40 5815
ton Border 119 9260
erley N York 89 2574

B

bbacombe Devon 7 9265
bbington Notts 62 4943
bbinswood Shrops 59 3329
obs Green Herts 39 3916
ocary Somset 21 5628
bel Carmth 44 8235
oel Green Suffk 53 7348
oell Flints 70 1573
oeny Devon 7 6775
oington Somset 22 7051
block Hythe Oxon 36 4304
braham Cambs 53 5150
bworth Notts 75 6880
chau IOA 68 4383
che Shrops 59 4681
cheldre Powys 58 2492
chelor's Bump E Susx 17 8412
ck o' th' Brook Staffs 73 0751
ck of Keppoch Highld 129 6587
ck Street Suffk 53 7458
ckaland Ork 153 5630
ckbarrow Cumb 87 3584
cke Carmth 31 2615
ckfolds Abers 143 0252
ckford Ches 71 3971
ckford Cross Ches 71 3873
ckies Highld 147 8302
cklass Highld 151 2053
ckwell Somset 21 4968
ckworth T & W 103 3072
con's End W Mids 61 1888
consthorpe Norfk 66 1236
cton Herefs 46 3732
cton Norfk 67 3433
cton Suffk 54 0567
cton Green Suffk 54 0365
cup Lancs 81 8622
dachro Highld 137 7873
dbury Wilts 36 1980
dby Nhants 49 5658
dcall Highld 148 1541
dcall Highld 148 2455
dcaul Highld 144 0291
ddeley Edge Staffs 72 9150
ddeley Green Staffs 72 9151
ddesley Clinton Warwks 61 2072
ddesley Ensor Warwks 61 2798
ddidarrach Highld 145 0822
ddingsgill Border 117 1254
denscoth Abers 142 6938
denyon Abers 141 3319
dgall Cnwll 5 2486
dgeney Cambs 65 4397
dger Shrops 60 7699
dger's Cross Cnwll 2 4833
dgers Mount Kent 27 4962
dgeworth Gloucs 35 9019
dgworth Somset 21 3952
dharlick Cnwll 5 2686
dicaul Highld 137 7529
dingham Suffk 55 3068
dlesmere Kent 28 0153
dlieu Border 108 0518
dlipster Highld 151 2448
dluachrach Highld 144 9994
dninish Highld 147 7594
drallach Highld 145 0691
dsey Worcs 48 0743
dshot Lea Surrey 25 8648
dsworth W York 83 4614
dwell Ash Suffk 54 9868
dwell Green Suffk 54 0169
g Enderby Lincs 77 3571
gber Dorset 11 7513
Bagby N York 89 4680
Bagendon Gloucs 35 0106
Bagginswood Shrops 60 6881
Baggrow Cumb 93 1741
Bagh a Chaisteil W Isls 152 6698
Bagh a Tuath W Isls 152 7003
Bagham Kent 29 0753
Bagillt Flints 70 2175
Baginton Warwks 61 3474
Baglan Neath 32 7492
Bagley Shrops 59 4027
Bagley Somset 21 4645
Bagley W York 82 2235
Bagmore Hants 24 6544
Bagnall Staffs 72 9250
Bagnor Berks 24 4569
Bagot Shrops 46 5873
Bagshot Surrey 25 9063
Bagshot Wilts 23 3165
Bagstone Gloucs 35 6987
Bagthorpe Notts 75 4651
Bagworth Leics 62 4408
Bagwy Llydiart Herefs 46 4426
Baildon W York 82 1539
Baildon Green W York 82 1439
Baile a Mhanaich W Isls 152 7755
Baile Ailein W Isls 152 2920
Baile Mor Ag & B 120 2824
Bailey Green Hants 13 6627
Baileyhead Cumb 101 5179
Bailiff Bridge W York 82 1425
Baillieston C Glas 116 6764
Bailrigg Lancs 87 4858
Bainbridge N York 88 9390
Bainshole Abers 142 6035
Bainton Cambs 64 0906
Bainton E R Yk 84 9652
Bainton Oxon 49 5827
Baintown Fife 126 3503
Bairnkine Border 110 6515
Baker Street Essex 40 6381
Baker's End Herts 39 3917
Bakewell Derbys 74 2168
Bala Gwynd 58 9235
Balallan W Isls 152 2920
Balbeg Highld 139 4431
Balbeggie P & K 126 1629
Balblair Highld 139 5145
Balblair Highld 140 7066
Balby S York 75 5600
Balcary D & G 92 8149
Balchraggan Highld 139 5343
Balchreick Highld 148 1960
Balcombe W Susx 15 3130
Balcombe Lane W Susx 15 3132
Balcomie Links Fife 127 6209
Baldersby N York 89 3578
Baldersby St James N York 89 3676
Balderstone Gt Man 79 9010
Balderstone Lancs 81 6332
Balderton Notts 75 8151
Baldhu Cnwll 3 7743
Baldinnie Fife 127 4211
Baldinnies P & K 125 0216
Baldock Herts 39 2434
Baldovie Dund C 127 4533
Baldrine IOM 158 4281
Baldslow E Susx 17 8013
Baldwin IOM 158 3581
Baldwin's Gate Staffs 72 7939
Baldwin's Hill Surrey 15 3839
Baldwinholme Cumb 93 3351
Bale Norfk 66 0136
Baledgarno P & K 126 2730
Balemartine Ag & B 120 9841
Balerno C Edin 117 1666
Balfarg Fife 126 2803
Balfield Angus 134 5468
Balfour Ork 153 4716
Balfron Stirlg 115 5489
Balgaveny Abers 142 6540
Balgavies Angus 127 5451
Balgonar Fife 117 0293
Balgowan D & G 98 1142
Balgowan Highld 132 6494
Balgown Highld 136 3868
Balgracie D & G 98 9860
Balgray Angus 126 4038
Balgray S Lans 108 8824
Balham Gt Lon 27 2873
Balhary P & K 126 2646
Balholmie P & K 126 1436
Baligill Highld 150 8565
Balintore Angus 133 2859
Balintore Highld 147 8675
Balintraid Highld 146 7370
Balivanich W Isls 152 7755
Balk N York 89 4780
Balkeerie Angus 126 3244
Balkholme E R Yk 84 7828
Ball Green Staffs 72 8952
Ball Haye Green Staffs 72 9856
Ball Hill Hants 24 4163
Ball's Green Gloucs 35 8699
Ballabeg IOM 158 2570
Ballachulish Highld 130 0858
Ballafesson IOM 158 2070
Ballakilpheric IOM 158 2271
Ballamodha IOM 158 2773
Ballanlay Ag & B 114 0462
Ballantrae S Ayrs 98 0882
Ballards Gore Essex 40 9092
Ballards Green Warwks 61 2791
Ballasalla IOM 158 2870
Ballater Abers 134 3695
Ballaugh IOM 158 3493
Ballchraggan Highld 147 7675
Ballencrieff E Loth 118 4878
Ballevullin Ag & B 120 9546
Ballidon Derbys 73 2054
Balliekine N Ayrs 105 8739
Balliemore Ag & B 114 1099
Balligmorrie S Ayrs 106 2290
Ballimore Ag & B 114 9283
Ballimore Stirlg 124 5317
Ballindalloch Moray 141 1636
Ballindean P & K 126 2529
Ballingdon Essex 54 8640
Ballinger Common Bucks 38 9103
Ballingham Herefs 46 5731
Ballingry Fife 117 1797
Ballinluig P & K 125 9752
Ballinshoe Angus 126 4153
Ballintuim P & K 126 1055
Balloch Highld 140 7247
Balloch N Lans 116 7374
Balloch P & K 125 8419
Balloch S Ayrs 106 3295
Balloch W Duns 115 3982
Ballogie Abers 134 5795
Balls Cross W Susx 14 9826
Balls Green E Susx 16 4936
Ballygown Ag & B 121 4343
Ballygrant Ag & B 112 3966
Ballyhaugh Ag & B 120 1758
Ballymenoch Ag & B 115 3086
Ballymichael N Ayrs 105 9231
Balmacara Highld 137 8028
Balmaclellan D & G 99 6579
Balmae D & G 99 6844
Balmaha Stirlg 115 4290
Balmalcolm Fife 126 3208
Balmangan D & G 99 6445
Balmedie Abers 143 9618
Balmer Heath Shrops 59 4434
Balmerino Fife 126 3524
Balmerlawn Hants 12 3003
Balmoral Castle Grounds 133 2594
Balmore E Duns 115 5973
Balmuchy Highld 147 8678
Balmuir Angus 127 5648
Balmule Fife 117 2088
Balmullo Fife 127 4220
Balnacoil Lodge Highld 147 8011
Balnacra Highld 138 9846
Balnacroft Abers 133 2894
Balnafoich Highld 140 6835
Balnaguard P & K 125 9451
Balnahard Ag & B 121 4534
Balnahard Ag & B 112 4199
Balnain Highld 139 4430
Balnakeil Highld 149 3968
Balnapaling Highld 147 7969
Balne N York 83 5918
Balquharn P & K 125 0235
Balquhidder Stirlg 124 5320
Balsall Common W Mids 61 2376
Balsall Heath W Mids 61 0784
Balsall Street W Mids 61 2276
Balscote Oxon 48 3942
Balsham Cambs 53 5850
Baltasound Shet 153 6208
Baltasound Airport 153 6207
Balterley Staffs 72 7650
Balterley Green Staffs 72 7650
Balterley Heath Staffs 72 7450
Baltersan D & G 99 4261
Baltonsborough Somset 21 5434
Balvarran P & K 133 0761
Balvicar Ag & B 122 7616
Balvraid Highld 129 8416
Balvraid Highld 140 8231
Balwest Cnwll 2 5930
Bamber Bridge Lancs 81 5625
Bamber's Green Essex 40 5722
Bamburgh Nthumb 111 1734
Bamburgh Castle 111 1835
Bamff P & K 126 2251
Bamford Derbys 74 2083
Bamford Gt Man 81 8612
Bampton Cumb 94 5118
Bampton Devon 20 9522
Bampton Oxon 36 3103
Bampton Grange Cumb 94 5218
Banavie Highld 130 1177
Banbury Oxon 49 4540
Banc-y-ffordd Carmth 31 4037
Bancffosfelen Carmth 32 4811
Banchory Abers 135 6995
Banchory-Devenick Abers 135 9002
Bancycapel Carmth 31 4214
Bancyfelin Carmth 31 3218
Bandirran P & K 126 2030
Bandrake Head Cumb 86 3187
Banff Abers 142 6863
Bangor Gwynd 69 5772
Bangor's Green Lancs 78 3709
Bangor-is-y-coed Wrexhm 71 3845
Bangors Cnwll 18 2099
Bangrove Suffk 54 9372
Banham Norfk 54 0687
Bank Hants 12 2807
Bank Ground Cumb 86 3196
Bank Newton N York 81 9053
Bank Street Worcs 47 6362
Bank Top Lancs 78 5207
Bank Top W York 82 1024
Bankend D & G 100 0268
Bankfoot P & K 125 0635
Bankglen E Ayrs 107 5912
Bankhead Aber C 135 9009
Bankhead S Lans 116 9844
Banknock Falk 116 7779
Banks Cumb 101 5664
Banks Lancs 80 3920
Banks Green Worcs 47 9967
Bankshill D & G 101 1982
Banningham Norfk 67 2129
Bannister Green Essex 40 6920
Bannockburn Stirlg 116 8190
Banstead Surrey 27 2559
Bantham Devon 7 6643
Banton N Lans 116 7480
Banwell Somset 21 3959
Bapchild Kent 28 9263
Bapton Wilts 22 9938
Bar Hill Cambs 52 3863
Barabhas W Isls 152 3649
Barassie S Ayrs 106 3232
Barbaraville Highld 146 7472
Barber Booth Derbys 74 1184
Barber Green Cumb 87 3982
Barbieston S Ayrs 107 4317
Barbon Cumb 87 6282
Barbridge Ches 71 6156
Barbrook Devon 19 7147
Barby Nhants 50 5470
Barcaldine Ag & B 122 9641
Barcheston Warwks 48 2639
Barclose Cumb 101 4462
Barcombe E Susx 15 4114
Barcombe Cross E Susx 15 4115
Barcroft W York 82 0437
Barden N York 89 1493
Barden Park Kent 16 5746
Bardfield End Green Essex 40 6231
Bardfield Saling Essex 40 6826
Bardney Lincs 76 1269
Bardon Leics 62 4412
Bardon Mill Nthumb 102 7764
Bardowie E Duns 115 5873
Bardown E Susx 16 6629
Bardrainney Inver 115 3373
Bardsea Cumb 86 3074
Bardsey W York 83 3643
Bardsley Gt Man 79 9201
Bardwell Suffk 54 9473
Bare Lancs 87 4564
Bareppa Cnwll 3 7729
Barewood Herefs 46 3856
Barfad D & G 98 3266
Barford Norfk 66 1107
Barford Warwks 48 2760
Barford St John Oxon 49 4433
Barford St Martin Wilts 23 0531
Barford St Michael Oxon 49 4332
Barfrestone Kent 29 2650
Bargate Derbys 62 3546
Bargeddie N Lans 116 6964
Bargoed Caerph 33 1599
Bargrennan D & G 98 3577
Barham Cambs 52 1375
Barham Kent 29 2050
Barham Suffk 54 1451
Barholm Lincs 64 0810
Barkby Leics 63 6309
Barkby Thorpe Leics 63 6309
Barkers Green Shrops 59 5228
Barkestone-le-Vale Leics 63 7734
Barkham Berks 25 7766
Barking Gt Lon 27 4484
Barking Suffk 54 0753
Barking Tye Suffk 54 0652
Barkingside Gt Lon 27 4489
Barkisland W York 82 0519
Barkla Shop Cnwll 3 7350
Barkston Lincs 63 9341
Barkston Ash N York 83 4936
Barkway Herts 39 3835
Barlanark C Glas 116 6664
Barlaston Staffs 72 8938
Barlavington W Susx 14 9716
Barlborough Derbys 75 4777
Barlby N York 83 6333
Barlestone Leics 62 4205
Barley Herts 39 4038
Barley Lancs 81 8240
Barley Hole S York 74 3697
Barleycroft End Herts 39 4327
Barleythorpe Rutlnd 63 8409
Barling Essex 40 9389
Barlings Lincs 76 0774
Barlochan D & G 92 8157
Barlow Derbys 74 3474
Barlow N York 83 6428
Barlow T & W 96 1561
Barmby Moor E R Yk 84 7748
Barmby on the Marsh E R Yk 83 6928
Barmer Norfk 66 8133
Barming Heath Kent 28 7255
Barmollack Ag & B 105 8043
Barmouth Gwynd 57 6116
Barmpton Dur 96 3118
Barmston E R Yk 91 1659
Barnaby Green Suffk 55 4780
Barnacarry Ag & B 114 0094
Barnack Cambs 64 0705
Barnacle Warwks 61 3884
Barnard Castle Dur 95 0516
Barnard Gate Oxon 36 4010
Barnardiston Suffk 53 7148
Barnbarroch D & G 92 8456
Barnburgh S York 83 4803
Barnby Suffk 55 4789
Barnby Dun S York 83 6109
Barnby in the Willows Notts 76 8552
Barnby Moor Notts 75 6684
Barncorkrie D & G 98 0935
Barnes Gt Lon 26 2276
Barnes Street Kent 16 6447
Barnet Gt Lon 26 2496
Barnet Gate Gt Lon 26 2195
Barnetby le Wold Lincs 84 0509
Barney Norfk 66 9932
Barnham Suffk 54 8779
Barnham W Susx 14 9503
Barnham Broom Norfk 66 0807
Barnhead Angus 135 6657
Barnhill Ches 71 4854
Barnhill Dund C 127 4731
Barnhill Moray 141 1457
Barnhills D & G 98 9871
Barningham Dur 89 0810
Barningham Suffk 54 9676
Barnoldby le Beck Lincs 85 2303
Barnoldswick Lancs 81 8746
Barns Green W Susx 14 1226
Barnsdale Bar N York 83 5014
Barnsley Gloucs 36 0704
Barnsley S York 83 3406
Barnsley Shrops 60 7592
Barnsole Kent 29 2756
Barnstaple Devon 19 5633
Barnston Essex 40 6419
Barnston Mersyd 78 2783
Barnstone Notts 63 7335
Barnt Green Worcs 60 0173
Barnton C Edin 117 1874
Barnton Ches 71 6375
Barnwell All Saints Nhants 51 0484
Barnwell St Andrew Nhants 51 0584
Barnwood Gloucs 35 8518
Baron's Cross Herefs 46 4758
Barons Wood Devon 8 7003
Baronwood Cumb 94 5143
Barr S Ayrs 106 2794
Barra Airport 152 7005
Barrachan D & G 99 3649
Barrapoll Ag & B 120 9442
Barras Cumb 88 8312
Barrasford Nthumb 102 9173
Barrets Green Ches 71 5859
Barrhead E Rens 115 4958
Barrhill S Ayrs 98 2382
Barrington Cambs 52 3849
Barrington Somset 10 3818
Barripper Cnwll 2 6338
Barrmill N Ayrs 115 3651
Barrnacarry Bay Ag & B 122 8122
Barrock Highld 151 2570
Barrow Gloucs 47 8824
Barrow Lancs 81 7338
Barrow Rutlnd 63 8815
Barrow Shrops 59 6500
Barrow Somset 22 7231
Barrow Suffk 53 7663
Barrow Bridge Gt Man 81 6811
Barrow Burn Nthumb 110 8610
Barrow Gurney Somset 21 5268
Barrow Haven Lincs 84 0622
Barrow Hill Derbys 74 4275
Barrow Island Cumb 86 1968
Barrow Nook Lancs 78 4402
Barrow Street Wilts 22 8330
Barrow upon Soar Leics 62 5717
Barrow upon Trent Derbys 62 3528
Barrow Vale Somset 21 6460
Barrow's Green Ches 78 5287
Barrow's Green Ches 72 6857
Barrow-in-Furness Cumb 86 2068
Barrow-upon-Humber Lincs 84 0620
Barroway Drove Norfk 65 5703
Barrowby Lincs 63 8736
Barrowden Rutlnd 51 9400
Barrowford Lancs 81 8539
Barry Angus 127 5334
Barry V Glam 20 1268
Barry Island V Glam 20 1166
Barsby Leics 63 6911
Barsham Suffk 55 3989
Barston W Mids 61 2078
Bartestree Herefs 46 5640
Barthol Chapel Abers 143 8133
Bartholomew Green Essex 40 7221
Barthomley Ches 72 7652
Bartley Hants 12 3012
Bartley Green W Mids 60 0081
Bartlow Cambs 53 5845
Barton Cambs 52 4055
Barton Ches 71 4454
Barton Cumb 94 4826
Barton Devon 7 9167
Barton Gloucs 48 0925
Barton Herefs 46 2957
Barton Lancs 78 3509
Barton Lancs 80 5137
Barton N York 89 2208
Barton Oxon 37 5507
Barton Warwks 48 1051
Barton Bendish Norfk 65 7105
Barton End Gloucs 35 8498
Barton Green Staffs 73 1717
Barton Hartshorn Bucks 49 6430
Barton Hill N York 90 7064
Barton in Fabis Notts 62 5132
Barton in the Beans Leics 62 3906
Barton Mills Suffk 53 7173
Barton Seagrave Nhants 51 8877
Barton St David Somset 21 5432
Barton Stacey Hants 24 4341
Barton Town Devon 19 6840
Barton Turf Norfk 67 3522
Barton upon Irwell Gt Man 79 7697
Barton Waterside Lincs 84 0222
Barton-le-Clay Beds 38 0830
Barton-le-Street N York 90 7274
Barton-le-Willows N York 90 7163
Barton-on-Sea Hants 12 2393
Barton-on-the-Heath Warwks 48 2532
Barton-under-Needwood Staffs 73 1818
Barton-upon-Humber Lincs 84 0221
Barugh S York 82 3108
Barugh Green S York 82 3107
Barvas W Isls 152 3649
Barway Cambs 53 5575
Barwell Leics 50 4496
Barwick Devon 8 5907
Barwick Herts 39 3819
Barwick Somset 10 5513
Barwick in Elmet W York 83 4037
Baschurch Shrops 59 4221
Bascote Warwks 48 4063
Bascote Heath Warwks 48 3962
Base Green Suffk 54 0163
Basford Green Staffs 72 9851
Bashall Eaves Lancs 81 6943
Bashall Town Lancs 81 7142
Bashley Hants 12 2496
Basildon Berks 37 6078
Basildon Essex 40 7189
Basingstoke Hants 24 6352
Baslow Derbys 74 2572
Bason Bridge Somset 21 3446
Bassaleg Newpt 34 2786
Bassendean Border 110 6245
Bassenthwaite Cumb 93 2332
Bassett Hants 13 4216
Bassingbourn Cambs 39 3343
Bassingfield Notts 62 6137
Bassingham Lincs 76 9060
Bassingthorpe Lincs 63 9628
Bassus Green Herts 39 3025
Basted Kent 27 6055
Baston Lincs 64 1113
Bastwick Norfk 67 4217
Batch Somset 21 3255
Batchworth Herts 26 0694
Batchworth Heath Herts 26 0792
Batcombe Dorset 10 6103
Batcombe Somset 22 6938
Bate Heath Ches 79 6879
Batford Herts 38 1415

Bath
Birchgro
272

Bath *Somset* 22 7464
Bath Side *Essex* 41 2532
Bathampton *Somset* 22 7766
Bathealton *Somset* 20 0823
Batheaston *Somset* 22 7767
Bathford *Somset* 22 7866
Bathgate *W Loth* 117 9768
Bathley *Notts* 75 7759
Bathpool *Cnwll* 5 2874
Bathpool *Somset* 20 2526
Bathville *W Loth* 116 9367
Bathway *Somset* 21 5952
Batley *W York* 82 2224
Batsford *Gloucs* 48 1833
Batson *Devon* 7 7339
Batt's Corner *Surrey* 25 8140
Battersby *N York* 90 5907
Battersea *Gt Lon* 27 2776
Battisborough Cross *Devon* 6 5948
Battisford *Suffk* 54 0554
Battisford Tye *Suffk* 54 0354
Battle *E Susx* 17 7515
Battle *Powys* 45 0130
Battle of Britain Memorial Flight 77 2256
Battleborough *Somset* 21 3450
Battledown *Gloucs* 35 9621
Battledykes *Angus* 127 4555
Battlefield *Shrops* 59 5117
Battlesbridge *Essex* 40 7894
Battlesden *Beds* 38 9628
Battleton *Somset* 20 9127
Battlies Green *Suffk* 54 9064
Battramsley Cross *Hants* 12 3198
Battyeford *W York* 82 1920
Baughton *Worcs* 47 8841
Baughurst *Hants* 24 5860
Baulds *Abers* 134 6093
Baulking *Oxon* 36 3191
Baumber *Lincs* 76 2274
Baunton *Gloucs* 35 0104
Baveney Wood *Shrops* 60 6979
Baverstock *Wilts* 23 0332
Bawburgh *Norfk* 66 1508
Bawdeswell *Norfk* 66 0420
Bawdrip *Somset* 21 3439
Bawdsey *Suffk* 55 3440
Bawtry *S York* 75 6493
Baxenden *Lancs* 81 7726
Baxter's Green *Suffk* 53 7557
Baxterley *Warwks* 61 2896
Bay *Highld* 136 2654
Bay Horse *Lancs* 80 4952
Bayble *W Isls* 152 5231
Baybridge *Hants* 13 5223
Baybridge *Nthumb* 95 9550
Baycliff *Cumb* 86 2872
Baydon *Wilts* 36 2878
Bayford *Herts* 39 3108
Bayford *Somset* 22 7229
Bayhead *W Isls* 152 7468
Bayley's Hill *Kent* 27 5151
Baylham *Suffk* 54 1051
Baynard's Green *Oxon* 49 5429
Baysdale Abbey *N York* 90 6206
Baysham *Herefs* 46 5727
Bayston Hill *Shrops* 59 4808
Baythorne End *Essex* 53 7242
Bayton *Worcs* 60 6973
Bayton Common *Worcs* 60 7173
Bayworth *Oxon* 37 4901
Beach *Gloucs* 35 7071
Beachampton *Bucks* 49 7736
Beachamwell *Norfk* 65 7505
Beachborough *Kent* 29 1638
Beachley *Gloucs* 34 5591
Beacon *Devon* 9 1805
Beacon End *Essex* 40 9524
Beacon Hill *E Susx* 16 5030
Beacon Hill *Kent* 17 8232
Beacon Hill *Notts* 75 8153
Beacon Hill *Surrey* 14 8736
Beacon's Bottom *Bucks* 37 7895
Beaconsfield *Bucks* 26 9490
Beadlam *N York* 90 6584
Beadlow *Beds* 38 1038
Beadnell *Nthumb* 111 2229
Beaford *Devon* 19 5515
Beal *N York* 83 5325
Beal *Nthumb* 111 0642
Bealbury *Cnwll* 5 3766
Bealsmill *Cnwll* 5 3576
Beam Hill *Staffs* 73 2325
Beamhurst *Staffs* 73 0536
Beaminster *Dorset* 10 4701
Beamish *Dur* 96 2253
Beamsley *N York* 82 0752
Bean *Kent* 27 5872
Beanacre *Wilts* 22 9066
Beanley *Nthumb* 111 0818
Beardon *Devon* 5 5184
Beardwood *Lancs* 81 6629
Beare *Devon* 9 9901
Beare Green *Surrey* 15 1742
Bearley *Warwks* 48 1860
Bearley Cross *Warwks* 48 1761
Bearpark *Dur* 96 2343
Bearsden *W Duns* 115 5372
Bearsted *Kent* 28 8055
Bearstone *Shrops* 72 7239
Bearwood *Dorset* 12 0496
Bearwood *W Mids* 60 0286
Beattock *D & G* 108 0802
Beauchamp Roding *Essex* 40 5809
Beauchief *S York* 74 3381
Beaudesert *Warwks* 48 1565
Beaufort *Blae G* 33 1611
Beaulieu *Hants* 12 3802
Beaulieu House 13 3802
Beauly *Highld* 139 5246
Beaumaris *IOA* 69 6076
Beaumont *Cumb* 93 3459
Beaumont *Essex* 41 1624
Beaumont *Jersey* 158 0000
Beaumont Hill *Dur* 96 2918
Beausale *Warwks* 61 2470
Beauworth *Hants* 13 5726
Beaver *Kent* 28 0040
Beaver Green *Kent* 28 0041
Beaworthy *Devon* 18 4699
Beazley End *Essex* 40 7429
Bebington *Mersyd* 78 3383
Bebside *Nthumb* 103 2781
Beccles *Suffk* 55 4289
Becconsall *Lancs* 80 4523
Beck Foot *Cumb* 87 6196
Beck Hole *N York* 90 8202
Beck Row *Suffk* 53 6977
Beck Side *Cumb* 86 2382
Beck Side *Cumb* 87 3780
Beckbury *Shrops* 60 7601
Beckenham *Gt Lon* 27 3769
Beckering *Lincs* 76 1280
Beckermet *Cumb* 86 0106
Beckett End *Norfk* 65 7798
Beckfoot *Cumb* 92 0949
Beckfoot *Cumb* 86 1600
Beckfoot *Cumb* 86 1989
Beckford *Worcs* 47 9736
Beckhampton *Wilts* 23 0868
Beckingham *Lincs* 76 8753
Beckingham *Notts* 75 7789
Beckington *Somset* 22 8051
Beckjay *Shrops* 46 3977
Beckley *E Susx* 17 8523
Beckley *Hants* 12 2296
Beckley *Oxon* 37 5611
Becks *W York* 82 0345
Beckside *Cumb* 87 6187
Beckton *Gt Lon* 27 4381
Beckwithshaw *N York* 82 2653
Becontree *Gt Lon* 27 4786
Becquet Vincent *Jersey* 158 0000
Bedale *N York* 89 2688
Bedburn *Dur* 95 0931
Bedchester *Dorset* 11 8517
Beddau *Rhondd* 33 0585
Beddgelert *Gwynd* 69 5948
Beddingham *E Susx* 16 4407
Beddington *Gt Lon* 27 3065
Beddington Corner *Gt Lon* 27 2866
Bedfield *Suffk* 55 2166
Bedfield Little Green *Suffk* 55 2365
Bedford *Beds* 38 0449
Bedgebury Cross *Kent* 17 7134
Bedham *W Susx* 14 0122
Bedhampton *Hants* 13 7006
Bedingfield *Suffk* 54 1768
Bedingfield Green *Suffk* 54 1866
Bedingfield Street *Suffk* 54 1768
Bedlam *N York* 89 2661
Bedlam Lane *Kent* 28 8845
Bedlington *Nthumb* 103 2681
Bedlinog *Myr Td* 33 0901
Bedminster *Bristl* 34 5871
Bedminster Down *Bristl* 34 5770
Bedmond *Herts* 38 0903
Bednall *Staffs* 72 9517
Bedrule *Border* 110 6017
Bedstone *Shrops* 46 3676
Bedwas *Caerph* 33 1789
Bedwellty *Caerph* 33 1600
Bedworth *Warwks* 61 3687
Bedworth Woodlands *Warwks* 61 3487
Beeby *Leics* 63 6608
Beech *Hants* 24 6938
Beech *Staffs* 72 8538
Beech Hill *Berks* 24 6964
Beechingstoke *Wilts* 23 0859
Beedon *Berks* 37 4878
Beedon Hill *Berks* 37 4877
Beeford *E R Yk* 85 1253
Beeley *Derbys* 74 2667
Beelsby *Lincs* 85 2001
Beenham *Berks* 24 5868
Beenham's Heath *Berks* 25 8375
Beeny *Cnwll* 4 1192
Beer *Devon* 9 2289
Beer *Somset* 21 4031
Beer Hackett *Dorset* 10 6011
Beercrocombe *Somset* 21 3220
Beesands *Devon* 7 8140
Beesby *Lincs* 77 4680
Beeson *Devon* 7 8140
Beeston *Beds* 52 1648
Beeston *Ches* 71 5358
Beeston *Norfk* 66 9015
Beeston *Notts* 62 5236
Beeston *W York* 82 2830
Beeston Regis *Norfk* 66 1642
Beeswing *D & G* 100 8969
Beetham *Cumb* 87 4979
Beetham *Somset* 10 2712
Beetley *Norfk* 66 9718
Began *Cardif* 34 2283
Begbroke *Oxon* 37 4614
Begdale *Cambs* 65 4506
Begelly *Pembks* 31 1107
Beggar's Bush *Powys* 46 2664
Beggarington Hill *W York* 82 2724
Beguildy *Powys* 45 1979
Beighton *Norfk* 67 3808
Beighton *S York* 75 4483
Beighton Hill *Derbys* 73 2951
Bein Inn *P & K* 126 1513
Beith *N Ayrs* 115 3553
Bekesbourne *Kent* 29 1955
Bekesbourne Hill *Kent* 29 1856
Belaugh *Norfk* 67 2818
Belbroughton *Worcs* 60 9277
Belchalwell *Dorset* 11 7909
Belchalwell Street *Dorset* 11 7909
Belchamp Otten *Essex* 54 8041
Belchamp St Paul *Essex* 53 7942
Belchamp Walter *Essex* 54 8240
Belchford *Lincs* 77 2975
Belford *Nthumb* 111 1034
Belgrave *Leics* 62 5906
Belhaven *E Loth* 118 6678
Belhelvie *Abers* 143 9417
Belhinnie *Abers* 142 4627
Bell Bar *Herts* 39 2505
Bell Busk *N York* 81 9056
Bell End *Worcs* 60 9477
Bell Heath *Worcs* 60 9477
Bell Hill *Hants* 13 7324
Bell o' th' Hill *Ches* 71 5245
Bellabeg *Abers* 134 3513
Bellamore *Herefs* 46 3840
Bellanoch *Ag & B* 113 7992
Bellasize *E R Yk* 84 8227
Bellaty *Angus* 133 2359
Belle Vue *Cumb* 93 3756
Belle Vue *W York* 83 3419
Belleau *Lincs* 77 4078
Bellerby *N York* 89 1192
Bellever *Devon* 8 6577
Bellfield *S Lans* 108 8234
Bellfield *S Lans* 108 9620
Bellingdon *Bucks* 38 9405
Bellingham *Nthumb* 102 8383
Belloch *Ag & B* 105 6737
Bellochantuy *Ag & B* 104 6632
Bellows Cross *Dorset* 12 0613
Bells Cross *Suffk* 54 1552
Bells Yew Green *E Susx* 16 6135
Bellshill *N Lans* 116 7360
Bellshill *Nthumb* 111 1230
Bellside *N Lans* 116 8058
Bellsquarry *W Loth* 117 0465
Belluton *Somset* 21 6164
Belmesthorpe *Rutlnd* 64 0410
Belmont *Gt Lon* 27 2562
Belmont *Lancs* 81 6715
Belmont *S Ayrs* 106 3419
Belmont *Shet* 153 5600
Belnacraig *Abers* 141 3716
Belowda *Cnwll* 4 9661
Belper *Derbys* 62 3447
Belper Lane End *Derbys* 74 3349
Belph *Derbys* 75 5475
Belsay *Nthumb* 103 0978
Belses *Border* 110 5725
Belsford *Devon* 7 7659
Belsize *Herts* 26 0300
Belstead *Suffk* 54 1241
Belstone *Devon* 8 6293
Belthorn *Lancs* 81 7124
Beltinge *Kent* 29 1967
Beltingham *Nthumb* 102 7863
Beltoft *Lincs* 84 8006
Belton *Leics* 62 4420
Belton *Lincs* 84 7806
Belton *Lincs* 63 9339
Belton *Norfk* 67 4802
Belton *Rutlnd* 63 8101
Beltring *Kent* 28 6747
Belvedere *Gt Lon* 27 4978
Belvoir *Leics* 63 8133
Belvoir Castle 63 8233
Bembridge *IOW* 13 6488
Bemersley Green *Staffs* 72 8854
Bemerton *Wilts* 23 1230
Bempton *E R Yk* 91 1972
Ben Rhydding *W York* 82 1347
Benacre *Suffk* 55 5184
Benbecula Airport 152 7855
Benbuie *D & G* 107 7196
Benderloch *Ag & B* 122 9038
Benenden *Kent* 17 8033
Benfieldside *Dur* 95 0952
Bengates *Norfk* 67 3027
Bengeworth *Worcs* 48 0443
Benhall Green *Suffk* 55 3961
Benhall Street *Suffk* 55 3561
Benholm *Abers* 135 8069
Beningbrough *N York* 90 5257
Benington *Herts* 39 2923
Benington *Lincs* 77 3946
Benington Sea End *Lincs* 65 4145
Benllech *IOA* 68 5182
Benmore *Ag & B* 114 1385
Bennacott *Cnwll* 5 2992
Bennan *N Ayrs* 105 9921
Bennet Head *Cumb* 93 4423
Bennetland *E R Yk* 84 8228
Bennett End *Bucks* 37 7897
Benniworth *Lincs* 76 2081
Benover *Kent* 28 7048
Benson *Oxon* 37 6291
Bentfield Green *Essex* 39 5025
Benthall *Shrops* 60 6602
Bentham *Gloucs* 35 9116
Benthoul *Aber C* 135 8003
Bentlawn *Shrops* 59 3301
Bentley *E R Yk* 84 0136
Bentley *Hants* 25 7844
Bentley *S York* 83 5605
Bentley *Suffk* 54 1136
Bentley *Warwks* 61 2895
Bentley Heath *Herts* 27 2599
Bentley Heath *W Mids* 61 1675
Benton *Devon* 19 6536
Bentpath *D & G* 101 3190
Bentwichen *Devon* 19 7333
Bentworth *Hants* 24 6640
Benvie *Angus* 126 3231
Benville *Dorset* 10 5303
Benwick *Cambs* 52 3490
Beoley *Worcs* 48 0669
Beoraidbeg *Highld* 129 6793
Bepton *W Susx* 14 8618
Berden *Essex* 39 4629
Bere Alston *Devon* 6 4466
Bere Ferrers *Devon* 6 4563
Bere Regis *Dorset* 11 8494
Berea *Pembks* 30 7930
Berepper *Cnwll* 2 6523
Bergh Apton *Norfk* 67 3001
Berhill *Somset* 21 4436
Berinsfield *Oxon* 37 5795
Berkeley *Gloucs* 35 6899
Berkeley Heath *Gloucs* 35 6999
Berkeley Road *Gloucs* 35 7200
Berkhamsted *Herts* 38 9907
Berkley *Somset* 22 8049
Berkswell *W Mids* 61 2479
Bermondsey *Gt Lon* 27 3479
Bernera *Highld* 129 8020
Bernice *Ag & B* 114 1391
Bernisdale *Highld* 136 4050
Berrick Prior *Oxon* 37 6294
Berrick Salome *Oxon* 37 6293
Berriedale *Highld* 147 1222
Berrier *Cumb* 93 3929
Berriew *Powys* 58 1801
Berrington *Nthumb* 111 0043
Berrington *Shrops* 59 5206
Berrington *Worcs* 46 5767
Berrington Green *Worcs* 46 5766
Berrow *Somset* 20 2951
Berrow *Worcs* 47 7934
Berrow Green *Worcs* 47 7458
Berry Brow *W York* 82 1314
Berry Cross *Devon* 18 4714
Berry Down Cross *Devon* 19 5743
Berry Hill *Gloucs* 34 5712
Berry Hill *Pembks* 30 0640
Berry Pomeroy *Devon* 7 8261
Berry's Green *Gt Lon* 27 4359
Berryhillock *Moray* 142 5054
Berryhillock *Moray* 142 5060
Berrynarbor *Devon* 19 5646
Bersham *Wrexhm* 71 3049
Berthengam *Flints* 70 1179
Berwick *E Susx* 16 5105
Berwick Bassett *Wilts* 36 0973
Berwick Hill *Nthumb* 103 1775
Berwick St James *Wilts* 23 0739
Berwick St John *Wilts* 22 9422
Berwick St Leonard *Wilts* 22 9233
Berwick-upon-Tweed *Nthumb* 119 9953
Bescaby *Leics* 63 8126
Bescar *Cumb* 80 3913
Besford *Shrops* 59 5525
Besford *Worcs* 47 9144
Besom Hill *Gt Man* 79 9508
Bessacarr *S York* 75 6100
Bessels Leigh *Oxon* 37 4501
Besses o' th' Barn *Gt Man* 79 8005
Bessingby *E R Yk* 91 1566
Bessingham *Norfk* 66 1636
Bestbeech Hill *E Susx* 16 6231
Besthorpe *Norfk* 66 0595
Besthorpe *Notts* 75 8264
Beswick *E R Yk* 84 0147
Betchcott *Shrops* 59 4398
Betchworth *Surrey* 26 2150
Beth Chatto Garden 41 0624
Bethania *Cerdgn* 43 5763
Bethania *Gwynd* 57 7044
Bethel *Gwynd* 68 5265
Bethel *Gwynd* 70 9839
Bethel *IOA* 68 3970
Bethel *Powys* 58 1021
Bethersden *Kent* 28 9240
Bethesda *Gwynd* 69 6266
Bethesda *Pembks* 31 0918
Bethlehem *Carmth* 44 6825
Bethnal Green *Gt Lon* 27 3482
Betley *Staffs* 72 7548
Betsham *Kent* 27 6071
Betteshanger *Kent* 29 3152
Bettiscombe *Dorset* 10 3900
Bettisfield *Wrexhm* 59 4635
Betton *Shrops* 72 6936
Betton Strange *Shrops* 59 5009
Bettws *Newpt* 34 2890
Bettws Bledrws *Cerdgn* 44 5952
Bettws Cedewain *Powys* 58 1296
Bettws Evan *Cerdgn* 42 3047
Bettws-Newydd *Mons* 34 3606
Bettyhill *Highld* 150 7061
Betws *Brdgnd* 33 9086
Betws *Carmth* 32 6311
Betws Garmon *Gwynd* 69 5357
Betws Gwerfil Goch *Denbgs* 70 0346
Betws-y-coed *Conwy* 69 7956
Betws-yn-Rhos *Conwy* 69 9073
Beulah *Cerdgn* 42 2846
Beulah *Powys* 45 9251
Bevendean *E Susx* 15 3306
Bevercotes *Notts* 75 6972
Beverley *E R Yk* 84 0339
Beverstone *Gloucs* 35 8694
Bevington *Gloucs* 35 6596
Bewaldeth *Cumb* 93 2034
Bewcastle *Cumb* 101 5674
Bewdley *Worcs* 60 7875
Bewerley *N York* 89 1565
Bewholme *E R Yk* 85 1649
Bewlbridge *Kent* 16 6834
Bexhill *E Susx* 17 7407
Bexley *Gt Lon* 27 4973
Bexleyheath *Gt Lon* 27 4875
Bexleyhill *W Susx* 14 9125
Bexon *Kent* 28 8959
Bexwell *Norfk* 65 6303
Beyton *Suffk* 54 9363
Beyton Green *Suffk* 54 9363
Bhaltos *W Isls* 152 0936
Bhatarsaigh *W Isls* 152 6394
Bibstone *Gloucs* 35 6991
Bibury *Gloucs* 36 1106
Bicester *Oxon* 49 5823
Bickenhill *W Mids* 61 1882
Bicker *Lincs* 64 2237
Bicker Bar *Lincs* 64 2438
Bicker Gauntlet *Lincs* 64 2139
Bickershaw *Gt Man* 79 6201
Bickerstaffe *Lancs* 78 4404
Bickerton *Ches* 71 5052
Bickerton *Devon* 7 8139
Bickerton *N York* 83 4550
Bickerton *Nthumb* 103 9900
Bickford *Staffs* 60 8814
Bickington *Devon* 19 5332
Bickington *Devon* 7 8072
Bickleigh *Devon* 9 9407
Bickleigh *Devon* 6 5262
Bickleton *Devon* 19 5030
Bickley *Ches* 71 5348
Bickley *Gt Lon* 27 4268
Bickley *N York* 91 9191
Bickley *Worcs* 47 6371
Bickley Moss *Ches* 71 5448
Bicknacre *Essex* 40 7802
Bicknoller *Somset* 20 1139
Bicknor *Kent* 28 8658
Bickton *Hants* 12 1412
Bicton *Herefs* 46 4764
Bicton *Shrops* 59 4415
Bicton *Shrops* 59 2
Bidborough *Kent* 16 5
Bidden *Hants* 24 7
Biddenden *Kent* 28 8
Biddenden Green *Kent* 28 8
Biddenham *Beds* 38 0
Biddestone *Wilts* 35 8
Biddisham *Somset* 21 3
Biddlesden *Bucks* 49 6
Biddlestone *Nthumb* 111 9
Biddulph *Staffs* 72 8
Biddulph Moor *Staffs* 72 9
Bideford *Devon* 18 4
Bidford-on-Avon *Warwks* 48 1
Bidston *Mersyd* 78 2
Bielby *E R Yk* 84 7
Bieldside *Aber C* 135 8
Bierley *IOW* 13 5
Bierton *Bucks* 38 8
Big Balcraig *D & G* 99 3
Big Carlae *D & G* 107 6
Big Pit Blaenavon 34 2
Big Sand *Highld* 144 7
Bigbury *Devon* 7 6
Bigbury-on-Sea *Devon* 7 6
Bigby *Lincs* 84 0
Biggar *Cumb* 86 1
Biggar *S Lans* 108 0
Biggin *Derbys* 73 2
Biggin *Derbys* 74 1
Biggin *N York* 83 5
Biggin Hill *Gt Lon* 27 4
Biggin Hill Airport 27 4
Biggleswade *Beds* 39 1
Bigholms *D & G* 101 3
Bighouse *Highld* 150 8
Bighton *Hants* 24 6
Bigland Hall *Cumb* 87 3
Biglands *Cumb* 93 2
Bignor *W Susx* 14 9
Bigrigg *Cumb* 92 0
Bilborough *Notts* 62 5
Bilbrook *Somset* 20 0
Bilbrook *Staffs* 60 8
Bilbrough *N York* 83 5
Bilbster *Highld* 151 2
Bildershaw *Dur* 96 2
Bildeston *Suffk* 54 9
Billacott *Cnwll* 5 2
Billericay *Essex* 40 6
Billesdon *Leics* 63 7
Billesley *Warwks* 48 1
Billingborough *Lincs* 64 1
Billinge *Mersyd* 78 5
Billingford *Norfk* 66 01
Billingford *Norfk* 54 1
Billingham *Dur* 97 4
Billinghay *Lincs* 76 1
Billingley *S York* 83 4
Billingshurst *W Susx* 14 0
Billingsley *Shrops* 60 7
Billington *Beds* 38 9
Billington *Lancs* 81 7
Billington *Staffs* 72 8
Billockby *Norfk* 67 4
Billy Row *Dur* 96 1
Bilsborrow *Lancs* 80 5
Bilsby *Lincs* 77 4
Bilsham *W Susx* 14 97
Bilsington *Kent* 17 0
Bilsthorpe *Notts* 75 6
Bilsthorpe Moor *Notts* 75 65
Bilston *Mdloth* 117 2
Bilston *W Mids* 60 95
Bilstone *Leics* 62 36
Bilting *Kent* 28 05
Bilton *E R Yk* 85 16
Bilton *N York* 83 47
Bilton *N York* 89 31
Bilton *Nthumb* 111 22
Bilton *Warwks* 50 48
Bilton Banks *Nthumb* 111 20
Binbrook *Lincs* 76 20
Binchester Blocks *Dur* 96 22
Bincombe *Dorset* 11 68
Binegar *Somset* 21 61
Bines Green *W Susx* 15 18
Binfield *Berks* 25 84
Binfield Heath *Oxon* 37 74
Bingfield *Nthumb* 102 97
Bingham *Notts* 63 70
Bingham's Melcombe *Dorset* 11 77
Bingley *W York* 82 10
Bings *Shrops* 59 53
Binham *Norfk* 66 98
Binley *Hants* 24 42
Binley *W Mids* 61 37
Binnegar *Dorset* 11 88
Binniehill *Falk* 116 85
Binns Farm *Moray* 141 31
Binscombe *Surrey* 25 96
Binsey *Oxon* 37 49
Binstead *Hants* 25 77
Binstead *IOW* 13 58
Binsted *W Susx* 14 98
Binton *Warwks* 48 14
Bintree *Norfk* 66 01
Binweston *Shrops* 59 30
Birch *Essex* 40 94
Birch *Gt Man* 79 85
Birch Close *Dorset* 11 88
Birch Cross *Staffs* 73 12
Birch Green *Essex* 40 94
Birch Green *Herts* 39 29
Birch Green *Worcs* 47 86
Birch Heath *Ches* 71 54
Birch Hill *Ches* 71 51
Birch Vale *Derbys* 74 02
Birch Wood *Somset* 9 24
Bircham Newton *Norfk* 65 77
Bircham Tofts *Norfk* 65 77
Birchanger *Essex* 39 51
Birchencliffe *W York* 82 12
Bircher *Herefs* 46 47
Birchfield *W Mids* 61 07
Birchgrove *Cardif* 33 16
Birchgrove *E Susx* 15 40
Birchgrove *Swans* 32 70

rchington
Bosoughan
273

chington Kent 29 3069
chley Heath Warwks 61 2894
chmoor Green Beds 38 9534
chover Derbys 74 2362
chwood Ches 79 6591
chyfield Herefs 47 6453
cotes Notts 75 6369
d End W Mids 60 0194
d Street Suffk 54 0052
dbrook Essex 53 7041
dforth N York 90 4875
dham W Susx 14 8200
dingbury Warwks 50 4368
dlip Gloucs 35 9214
doswald Cumb 102 6166
ds Edge W York 82 2007
ds Green Essex 40 5808
dsall N York 90 8165
dsgreen Shrops 60 7785
dsmoorgate Dorset 10 3900
dwell S York 83 3401
dwood Gloucs 35 7418
gham Border 110 7939
ichin Highld 147 7592
kacre Lancs 81 5714
kby N York 89 3202
kdale Mersyd 80 3214
kenbog Abers 142 5365
kenhead Mersyd 78 3288
kenhills Abers 142 7445
kenshaw W York 82 2028
khall Abers 134 3493
khill Angus 126 3534
khill D & G 109 2015
kholme Lincs 63 9623
kin N York 83 5326
ks W York 82 2626
kshaw Nthumb 102 7765
ley Herefs 46 4553
ley Carr S York 74 3392
ling Kent 28 6860
ling Nthumb 111 2406
ling Gap E Susx 16 5596
lingham Worcs 47 9343
mingham W Mids 61 0786
mingham Airport 61 1883
mingham Museum & Art Gallery 61 0786
nam P & K 125 0341
ness Abers 143 9933
se Abers 134 5697
semore Abers 134 5297
stall Leics 62 5909
stall W York 82 2225
stwith N York 89 2359
thorpe Lincs 64 1033
tley Herefs 46 3639
tley Nthumb 102 8778
tley T & W 96 2756
rts Street Worcs 47 7836
sbrooke Rutlnd 51 8889
scathorpe Lincs 76 2284
scovey Cnwll 3 0552
sh Mill Devon 19 7425
sham Berks 26 8485
shampton Worcs 47 9951
shop Auckland Dur 96 2028
shop Burton E R Yk 84 9839
shop Middleham Dur 96 3231
shop Monkton N York 89 3266
shop Norton Lincs 76 9832
shop Sutton Somset 21 5859
shop Thornton N York 89 2563
shop Wilton E R Yk 84 7955
shop's Castle Shrops 59 3288
shop's Caundle Dorset 11 6913
shop's Cleeve Gloucs 47 9627
shop's Frome Herefs 47 6648
shop's Green Essex 40 6217
shop's Green Hants 24 5063
shop's Itchington Warwks 48 3857
shop's Norton Gloucs 47 8424
shop's Nympton Devon 19 7523
shop's Offley Staffs 72 7729
shop's Stortford Herts 39 4821
shop's Sutton Hants 24 6032
shop's Tachbrook Warwks 48 3161
shop's Tawton Devon 19 5729
shop's Waltham Hants 13 5517
shop's Wood Staffs 60 8309
shopbridge Lincs 76 0391
shopbriggs E Duns 116 6070
shopmill Moray 141 2163
shops Cannings Wilts 23 0364
shops Gate Surrey 25 9871
shops Hull Somset 20 2024
shops Lydeard Somset 20 1729
shopsbourne Kent 29 1852
shopsteignton Devon 7 9073
shopstoke Hants 13 4619
shopston Swans 32 5789
shopstone Bucks 38 8010
shopstone E Susx 16 4701
shopstone Herefs 46 4143
shopstone Kent 29 2068
shopstone Wilts 23 0625
shopstone Wilts 36 2483
shopstrow Wilts 22 8943
shopswood Somset 10 2612
shopsworth Bristl 21 5768
shopthorpe N York 83 5947
shopton Dur 96 3621
shopton Rens 115 4371
shopton Warwks 48 1956
shton Newpt 34 3887
shton Staffs 73 0220
sley Gloucs 35 9005
sley Surrey 25 9559
sley Camp Surrey 25 9357
spham Lancs 80 3140
spham Green Lancs 80 4813
ssoe Cnwll 3 7741
sterne Hants 12 1401
tchet Green Kent 27 5654
tchfield Lincs 63 9828
ttadon Devon 19 5441
ttaford Devon 7 6656
ttering Norfk 66 9417
Bitterley Shrops 46 5677
Bitterne Hants 13 4513
Bitteswell Leics 50 5385
Bitton Gloucs 35 6869
Bix Oxon 37 7284
Blaby Leics 50 5697
Black Bourton Oxon 36 2804
Black Callerton T & W 103 1769
Black Car Norfk 66 0995
Black Corner W Susx 15 2939
Black Corries Highld 123 2956
Black Crofts Ag & B 122 9234
Black Cross Cnwll 4 9060
Black Dog Devon 19 8009
Black Heddon Nthumb 103 0775
Black Lane Gt Man 79 7708
Black Lane Ends Lancs 81 9243
Black Moor W York 82 2939
Black Notley Essex 40 7620
Black Pill Swans 32 6190
Black Street Suffk 55 5186
Black Tar Pembks 30 9909
Black Torrington Devon 18 4605
Blackadder Border 119 8452
Blackawton Devon 7 8051
Blackbank Warwks 61 3586
Blackbeck Cumb 86 0207
Blackborough Devon 9 0909
Blackborough End Norfk 65 6615
Blackboys E Susx 16 5220
Blackbrook Derbys 62 3347
Blackbrook Staffs 72 7638
Blackbrook Surrey 15 1846
Blackburn Abers 135 8212
Blackburn Lancs 81 6827
Blackburn S York 74 3992
Blackburn W Loth 117 9865
Blackcraig E Ayrs 107 6308
Blackden Heath Ches 79 7871
Blackdog Abers 135 9513
Blackdown Devon 5 5079
Blackdown Dorset 10 3903
Blackdyke Cumb 92 1452
Blackenall Heath W Mids 60 0002
Blacker S York 83 3309
Blacker Hill S York 83 3602
Blackfen Gt Lon 27 4674
Blackfield Hants 13 4402
Blackford Cumb 101 3961
Blackford P & K 125 8908
Blackford Somset 21 4147
Blackford Somset 21 6526
Blackford Bridge Gt Man 79 8007
Blackfordby Leics 62 3217
Blackgang IOW 13 4876
Blackhall C Edin 117 1975
Blackhall Dur 97 4638
Blackhall Colliery Dur 97 4539
Blackhaugh Border 109 4238
Blackheath Essex 40 0021
Blackheath Gt Lon 27 3876
Blackheath Suffk 55 4274
Blackheath Surrey 14 0346
Blackheath W Mids 60 9786
Blackhill Abers 143 0039
Blackhill Abers 143 0755
Blackhill Abers 143 0843
Blackhill Dur 95 0851
Blackhill of Clackriach Abers 143 9246
Blackhorse Devon 9 9893
Blackhorse Hill E Susx 17 7714
Blackjack Lincs 64 2639
Blackland Somset 19 8336
Blackland Wilts 22 0168
Blacklaw D & G 108 0408
Blackley Gt Man 79 8502
Blacklunans P & K 133 1460
Blackmarstone Herefs 46 5038
Blackmill Brdgnd 33 9386
Blackmoor Hants 14 7733
Blackmoor Somset 21 4661
Blackmoorfoot W York 82 0913
Blackmore Essex 40 6001
Blackmore End Essex 40 7430
Blackmore End Herts 39 1716
Blackness Falk 117 0579
Blacknest Berks 25 9568
Blacknest Hants 25 7941
Blacko Lancs 81 8541
Blackpool Devon 7 8547
Blackpool Devon 7 8174
Blackpool Lancs 80 3036
Blackpool Airport 80 3131
Blackpool Gate Cumb 101 5377
Blackridge W Loth 116 8967
Blackrock Cnwll 2 6534
Blackrock Mons 33 2112
Blackrock Mons 34 5188
Blackrod Gt Man 78 6110
Blacksboat Moray 141 1838
Blackshaw D & G 100 0465
Blackshaw Head W York 82 9527
Blacksmith's Green Suffk 54 1465
Blacksnape Lancs 81 7121
Blackstone W Susx 15 2316
Blackthorn Oxon 37 6219
Blackthorpe Suffk 54 9063
Blacktoft E R Yk 84 8324
Blacktop Aber C 135 8604
Blackwall Derbys 73 2549
Blackwater Cnwll 3 7346
Blackwater Hants 25 8459
Blackwater IOW 13 5086
Blackwater Somset 10 2615
Blackwaterfoot N Ayrs 105 9028
Blackwell Cumb 93 4053
Blackwell Derbys 74 1272
Blackwell Derbys 75 4458
Blackwell Dur 89 2713
Blackwell Warwks 48 2443
Blackwell Worcs 60 9972
Blackwellsend Green Gloucs 47 7825
Blackwood Caerph 33 1797
Blackwood D & G 100 9087
Blackwood S Lans 116 7844
Blackwood Hill Staffs 72 9255
Blacon Ches 71 3868
Bladbean Kent 29 1847
Bladnoch D & G 99 4254
Bladon Oxon 37 4514
Bladon Somset 21 4220
Blaen Dyryn Powys 45 9336
Blaen-y-Coed Carmth 31 3427
Blaen-y-cwm Blae G 33 1311
Blaen-y-cwm Rhondd 33 9298
Blaenannerch Cerdgn 42 2448
Blaenau Ffestiniog Gwynd 57 7045
Blaenavon Torfn 34 2508
Blaenffos Pembks 31 1937
Blaengarw Brdgnd 33 9092
Blaengeuffardd Cerdgn 43 6480
Blaengwrach Neath 33 8605
Blaengwynfi Neath 33 8996
Blaenllechau Rhondd 33 0097
Blaenpennal Cerdgn 43 6264
Blaenplwyf Cerdgn 43 5775
Blaenporth Cerdgn 42 2648
Blaenrhondda Rhondd 33 9299
Blaenwaun Carmth 31 2327
Blaenycwm Cerdgn 43 8275
Blagdon Devon 7 8561
Blagdon Somset 20 2118
Blagdon Somset 21 5059
Blagdon Hill Somset 9 2117
Blagill Cumb 94 7347
Blaguegate Lancs 78 4506
Blaich Highld 130 0376
Blain Highld 129 6769
Blaina Blae G 33 2008
Blair Atholl P & K 132 8665
Blair Drummond Stirlg 116 7399
Blair's Ferry Ag & B 114 9869
Blairgowrie P & K 126 1745
Blairingone P & K 117 9896
Blairlogie Stirlg 116 8396
Blairmore Ag & B 114 1983
Blairmore Highld 148 1959
Blairnamarrow Moray 141 2015
Blaisdon Gloucs 35 7017
Blake End Essex 40 7023
Blakebrook Worcs 60 8276
Blakedown Worcs 60 8878
Blakeley Lane Staffs 72 9746
Blakemere Ches 71 5571
Blakemere Herefs 46 3641
Blakemore Devon 7 7660
Blakeney Gloucs 35 6707
Blakeney Norfk 66 0243
Blakenhall Ches 72 7247
Blakenhall W Mids 60 9197
Blakeshall Worcs 60 8381
Blakesley Nhants 49 6250
Blanchland Nthumb 95 9650
Bland Hill N York 82 2053
Blandford Camp Dorset 11 9107
Blandford Forum Dorset 11 8806
Blandford St Mary Dorset 11 8805
Blanefield Stirlg 115 5479
Blankney Lincs 76 0660
Blantyre S Lans 116 6957
Blar a' Chaorainn Highld 130 1066
Blargie Highld 132 6094
Blarmachfoldach Highld 130 0969
Blashford Hants 12 1506
Blaston Leics 51 8095
Blatherwycke Nhants 51 9795
Blawith Cumb 86 2888
Blawquhairn D & G 99 6282
Blaxhall Suffk 55 3656
Blaxton S York 75 6700
Blaydon T & W 103 1863
Bleadney Somset 21 4845
Bleadon Somset 21 3456
Bleak Street Somset 22 7631
Blean Kent 29 1260
Bleasby Lincs 76 1384
Bleasby Notts 75 7149
Bleasdale Lancs 81 5945
Bleatarn Cumb 94 7313
Bleathwood Herefs 46 5570
Blebocraigs Fife 127 4214
Bleddfa Powys 45 2068
Bledington Gloucs 36 2422
Bledlow Bucks 37 7702
Bledlow Ridge Bucks 37 7997
Bleet Wilts 22 8958
Blegbie E Loth 118 4861
Blencarn Cumb 94 6331
Blencogo Cumb 93 1947
Blendworth Hants 13 7113
Blennerhasset Cumb 93 1741
Bletchingdon Oxon 37 5018
Bletchingley Surrey 27 3250
Bletchley Bucks 38 8633
Bletchley Shrops 59 6233
Bletherston Pembks 31 0721
Bletsoe Beds 51 0258
Blewbury Oxon 37 5385
Blickling Norfk 66 1728
Blidworth Notts 75 5956
Blidworth Bottoms Notts 75 5954
Blindburn Nthumb 110 8210
Blindcrake Cumb 92 1434
Blindley Heath Surrey 15 3645
Blisland Cnwll 4 1073
Bliss Gate Worcs 60 7472
Blissford Hants 12 1713
Blisworth Nhants 49 7253
Blithbury Staffs 73 0819
Blitterlees Cumb 92 1052
Blo Norton Norfk 54 0179
Blockley Gloucs 48 1634
Blofield Norfk 67 3309
Bloomfield Border 110 5824
Blore Staffs 72 7234
Blore Staffs 73 1349
Blounts Green Staffs 73 0732
Blowick Mersyd 80 3516
Bloxham Oxon 49 4336
Bloxholm Lincs 76 0653
Bloxwich W Mids 60 9902
Bloxworth Dorset 11 8894
Blubberhouses N York 82 1655
Blue Anchor Cnwll 4 9157
Blue Anchor Somset 20 0243
Blue Bell Hill Kent 28 7462
Blue John Cavern 74 1384
Blundellsands Mersyd 78 3099
Blundeston Suffk 67 5297
Blunham Beds 52 1551
Blunsdon St Andrew Wilts 36 1389
Bluntington Worcs 60 9074
Bluntisham Cambs 52 3674
Blunts Cnwll 5 3463
Blunts Green Warwks 48 1468
Blurton Staffs 72 8941
Blyborough Lincs 76 9394
Blyford Suffk 55 4276
Blymhill Staffs 60 8112
Blymhill Lawn Staffs 60 8211
Blyth Notts 75 6287
Blyth Nthumb 103 3181
Blyth Bridge Border 117 1345
Blythburgh Suffk 55 4475
Blythe Border 110 5849
Blythe Bridge Staffs 72 9541
Blythe End Warwks 61 2190
Blythe Marsh Staffs 72 9640
Blyton Lincs 76 8594
Bo'ness Falk 117 0081
Boar's Head Gt Man 78 5708
Boarhills Fife 127 5613
Boarhunt Hants 13 6008
Boarley Kent 28 7659
Boars Hill Oxon 37 4902
Boarsgreave Lancs 81 8420
Boarshead E Susx 16 5332
Boarstall Bucks 37 6214
Boasley Cross Devon 5 5093
Boat of Garten Highld 140 9319
Boath Highld 146 5774
Bobbing Kent 28 8865
Bobbington Staffs 60 8090
Bobbingworth Essex 39 5305
Bocaddon Cnwll 4 1858
Bochym Cnwll 2 6920
Bocking Essex 40 7623
Bocking Churchstreet Essex 40 7525
Bockleton Worcs 46 5961
Boconnoc Cnwll 4 1460
Boddam Abers 143 1342
Boddam Shet 153 3915
Boddington Gloucs 47 8925
Bodedern IOA 68 3380
Bodelwyddan Denbgs 70 0075
Bodenham Herefs 46 5350
Bodenham Wilts 23 1626
Bodenham Moor Herefs 46 5450
Bodewryd IOA 68 4090
Bodfari Denbgs 70 0970
Bodffordd IOA 68 4277
Bodfuan Gwynd 56 3237
Bodham Norfk 66 1240
Bodiam E Susx 17 7825
Bodiam Castle 17 7825
Bodicote Oxon 49 4538
Bodieve Cnwll 4 9973
Bodinnick Cnwll 3 1352
Bodle Street Green E Susx 16 6514
Bodmin Cnwll 4 0667
Bodnant Garden 69 8072
Bodney Norfk 66 8298
Bodorgan IOA 68 3867
Bodrean Cnwll 3 8448
Bodsham Green Kent 29 1045
Bodwen Cnwll 4 0360
Bodymoor Heath Warwks 61 1996
Bogallan Highld 140 6350
Bogbrae Abers 143 0335
Boghall Mdloth 117 2465
Boghall W Loth 117 9867
Boghead S Lans 107 7742
Boghead Farm Moray 141 3559
Bogmoor Moray 141 3563
Bogmuir Abers 135 6471
Bogniebrae Abers 142 5945
Bognor Regis W Susx 14 9399
Bogroy Highld 140 9022
Bogue D & G 99 6481
Bohetherick Devon 5 4167
Bohortha Cnwll 3 8532
Bohuntine Highld 131 2983
Bojewyan Cnwll 2 3934
Bokiddick Cnwll 4 0562
Bolam Dur 96 1922
Bolam Nthumb 103 1082
Bolberry Devon 7 6939
Bold Heath Mersyd 78 5389
Boldmere W Mids 61 1194
Boldon Colliery T & W 96 3462
Boldre Hants 12 3198
Boldron Dur 95 0314
Bole Notts 75 7987
Bole Hill Derbys 74 3374
Bolehill Derbys 73 2955
Bolenowe Cnwll 2 6738
Bolham Devon 9 9515
Bolham Water Devon 9 1612
Bolingey Cnwll 3 7653
Bollington Ches 79 9377
Bollington Cross Ches 79 9277
Bollow Gloucs 35 7413
Bolney W Susx 15 2622
Bolnhurst Beds 51 0859
Bolshan Angus 127 6252
Bolsover Derbys 75 4770
Bolster Moor W York 82 0815
Bolsterstone S York 74 2696
Boltby N York 90 4886
Boltenstone Abers 134 4110
Bolter End Bucks 37 7992
Bolton Cumb 94 6323
Bolton E Loth 118 5070
Bolton E R Yk 84 7752
Bolton Gt Man 79 7108
Bolton Nthumb 111 1013
Bolton Abbey N York 82 0754
Bolton Bridge N York 82 0653
Bolton by Bowland Lancs 81 7849
Bolton Hall N York 88 0789
Bolton le Sands Lancs 87 4867
Bolton Low Houses Cumb 93 2344
Bolton New Houses Cumb 93 2444
Bolton Percy N York 83 5341
Bolton Town End Lancs 87 4867
Bolton Upon Dearne S York 83 4502
Bolton-on-Swale N York 89 2599
Boltonfellend Cumb 101 4768
Boltongate Cumb 93 2340
Bolventor Cnwll 4 1876
Bomarsund Nthumb 103 2684
Bomere Heath Shrops 59 4719
Bonar Bridge Highld 146 6191
Bonawe Ag & B 122 0033
Bonby Lincs 84 0015
Boncath Pembks 31 2038
Bonchester Bridge Border 110 5812
Bonchurch IOW 13 5778
Bond's Green Herefs 46 3554
Bondleigh Devon 8 6505
Bonds Lancs 80 4944
Bone Cnwll 2 4632
Bonehill Devon 8 7277
Bonehill Staffs 61 1902
Boney Hay Staffs 61 0410
Bonhill W Duns 115 3979
Boningale Shrops 60 8202
Bonjedward Border 110 6522
Bonkle N Lans 116 8457
Bonnington Angus 127 5739
Bonnington Kent 17 0535
Bonnybank Fife 126 3503
Bonnybridge Falk 116 8279
Bonnykelly Abers 143 8653
Bonnyrigg Mdloth 117 3065
Bonnyton Angus 126 3338
Bonsall Derbys 74 2758
Bonshaw Tower D & G 101 2472
Bont Mons 57 3819,
Bont-Dolgadfan Powys 57 8800
Bontddu Gwynd 57 6718
Bonthorpe Lincs 77 4872
Bontnewydd Cerdgn 43 6165
Bontnewydd Gwynd 68 4859
Bontuchel Denbgs 70 0857
Bonvilston V Glam 33 0673
Bonwm Denbgs 70 1042
Bonymaen Swans 32 6795
Boode Devon 19 5037
Boohay Devon 7 8952
Booker Bucks 37 8391
Booley Shrops 59 5625
Boon Border 110 5745
Boon Hill Staffs 72 8150
Boorley Green Hants 13 5014
Boosbeck N York 97 6617
Boose's Green Essex 40 8431
Boot Cnwll 5 2697
Boot Cumb 86 1700
Boot Street Suffk 55 2248
Booth E R Yk 84 7326
Booth W York 82 0427
Booth Green Ches 79 9280
Booth Town W York 82 0926
Boothby Graffoe Lincs 76 9859
Boothby Pagnell Lincs 63 9730
Boothstown Gt Man 79 7200
Boothville Nhants 50 7864
Bootle Cumb 86 1088
Bootle Mersyd 78 3495
Boots Green Ches 79 7572
Booze N York 88 0102
Boraston Shrops 46 6169
Bordeaux Guern 158 0000
Borden Kent 28 8862
Borden W Susx 14 8324
Border Cumb 92 1654
Bordley N York 88 9465
Bordon Hants 14 8035
Bordon Camp Hants 14 7936
Boreham Essex 40 7609
Boreham Wilts 22 8944
Boreham Street E Susx 16 6611
Borehamwood Herts 26 1996
Boreland D & G 100 1691
Boreraig Highld 136 1853
Boreston Devon 7 7653
Boreton Ches 59 5106
Borgh W Isls 152 4055
Borgh W Isls 152 6501
Borgie Highld 149 6759
Borgue D & G 99 6248
Borgue Highld 151 1326
Borley Essex 54 8443
Borley Green Essex 54 8442
Borley Green Suffk 54 9960
Borneskitaig Highld 136 3770
Borness D & G 99 6145
Borough Green Kent 27 6157
Boroughbridge N York 89 3966
Borras Head Wrexhm 71 3653
Borrowash Derbys 62 4234
Borrowby N York 97 7715
Borrowby N York 89 4289
Borrowdale Cumb 93 2514
Borrowstoun Falk 117 9980
Borstal Kent 28 7366
Borth Cerdgn 43 6090
Borth-y-Gest Gwynd 57 5637
Borthwickbrae Border 109 4113
Borthwickshiels Border 109 4315
Borve Highld 136 4448
Borve W Isls 152 4055
Borve W Isls 152 6501
Borve W Isls 152 0394
Borwick Lancs 87 5272
Borwick Lodge Cumb 87 3499
Borwick Rails Cumb 86 1879
Bosavern Cnwll 2 3730
Bosbury Herefs 47 6943
Boscarne Cnwll 4 0367
Boscastle Cnwll 4 0990
Boscombe Dorset 12 1191
Boscombe Wilts 23 2038
Boscoppa Cnwll 3 0353
Bosham W Susx 14 8003
Bosham Hoe W Susx 14 8102
Bosherston Pembks 30 9694
Boskednan Cnwll 2 4434
Boskenna Cnwll 2 4223
Bosley Ches 72 9165
Bosoughan Cnwll 4 8760

274

Bossall N York 90 7160
Bossiney Cnwll 4 0688
Bossingham Kent 29 1548
Bossington Somset 19 8947
Bostock Green Ches 79 6769
Boston Lincs 64 3343
Boston Spa W York 83 4245
Boswarthan Cnwll 2 4433
Boswinger Cnwll 3 9841
Botallack Cnwll 2 3732
Botanic Gardens 115 5666
Botany Bay Gt Lon 27 2999
Botcheston Leics 62 4804
Botesdale Suffk 54 0475
Bothal Nthumb 103 2386
Bothampstead Berks 37 5076
Bothamsall Notts 75 6773
Bothel Cumb 93 1838
Bothenhampton Dorset 10 4791
Bothwell S Lans 116 7058
Botley Bucks 26 9802
Botley Hants 13 5113
Botley Oxon 37 4806
Botolph Claydon Bucks 49 7324
Botolph's Bridge Kent 17 1233
Botolphs W Susx 15 1909
Bottesford Leics 63 8038
Bottesford Lincs 84 8906
Bottisham Cambs 53 5460
Bottom o' th' Moor Gt Man 81 6511
Bottom of Hutton Lancs 80 4827
Bottomcraig Fife 126 3724
Bottoms Cnwll 2 3824
Bottoms W York 81 9321
Botts Green Warwks 61 2492
Botusfleming Cnwll 5 4061
Botwnnog Gwynd 56 2631
Bough Beech Kent 16 4847
Boughrood Powys 45 1239
Boughspring Gloucs 34 5597
Boughton Cambs 52 1965
Boughton Nhants 50 7565
Boughton Norfk 65 7002
Boughton Notts 75 6768
Boughton Aluph Kent 28 0246
Boughton End Beds 38 9838
Boughton Green Kent 28 7650
Boughton Malherbe Kent 28 8849
Boughton Monchelsea Kent 28 7650
Boughton Street Kent 28 0559
Boulby N York 97 7618
Boulder Clough W York 82 0323
Bouldnor IOW 12 3789
Bouldon Shrops 59 5485
Boulge Suffk 55 2552
Boulmer Nthumb 111 2614
Boulston Pembks 30 9712
Boultham Lincs 76 9669
Bourn Cambs 52 3256
Bourne Lincs 64 0920
Bourne End Beds 38 9644
Bourne End Beds 51 0160
Bourne End Bucks 26 8987
Bourne End Herts 38 0206
Bournebridge Essex 27 5094
Bournebrook W Mids 61 0483
Bournemouth Dorset 12 0890
Bournemouth Airport 12 1198
Bournes Green Essex 40 9186
Bournes Green Gloucs 35 9104
Bournheath Worcs 60 9574
Bournstream Gloucs 35 7494
Bournville W Mids 61 0481
Bourton Dorset 22 7630
Bourton Oxon 36 2386
Bourton Shrops 59 5996
Bourton Somset 21 3864
Bourton Wilts 23 0464
Bourton on Dunsmore Warwks 50 4370
Bourton-on-the-Hill Gloucs 48 1732
Bourton-on-the-Water Gloucs 36 1620
Bousd Ag & B 120 2563
Boustead Hill Cumb 93 2959
Bouth Cumb 86 3285
Bouthwaite N York 89 1271
Bouts Worcs 48 0359
Bovain Stirlg 124 5430
Boveney Berks 26 9377
Boveridge Dorset 12 0514
Bovey Tracey Devon 8 8178
Bovingdon Herts 38 0103
Bovingdon Green Bucks 37 8386
Bovinger Essex 39 5205
Bovington Dorset 11 8288
Bovington Camp Dorset 11 8389
Bovington Tank Museum 11 8388
Bow Cumb 93 3356
Bow Devon 8 7201
Bow Devon 7 8156
Bow Gt Lon 27 3683
Bow Ork 153 3693
Bow Brickhill Bucks 38 9034
Bow Lee Gt Man 79 8406
Bow of Fife Fife 126 3212
Bow Street Cerdgn 43 6285
Bow Street Norfk 66 0198
Bowbank Dur 95 9423
Bowbridge Gloucs 35 8505
Bowburn Dur 96 3037
Bowcombe IOW 13 4786
Bowd Devon 9 1090
Bowden Border 109 5530
Bowden Devon 7 8449
Bowden Hill Wilts 22 9367
Bowdon Gt Man 79 7686
Bower Highld 151 2362
Bower Ashton Bristl 34 5671
Bower Hinton Somset 10 4517
Bower House Tye Suffk 54 9840
Bower's Row W York 83 4028
Bowerchalke Wilts 23 0223
Bowerhill Wilts 22 9162
Bowermadden Highld 151 2464
Bowers Staffs 72 8135
Bowers Gifford Essex 40 7588
Bowershall Fife 117 0991
Bowes Dur 95 9913
Bowgreave Lancs 80 4943

Bowhouse D & G 100 0165
Bowithick Cnwll 4 1882
Bowker's Green Lancs 78 4004
Bowland Border 109 4540
Bowland Bridge Cumb 87 4189
Bowley Herefs 46 5452
Bowley Town Herefs 46 5352
Bowlhead Green Surrey 25 9138
Bowling W Duns 115 4373
Bowling W York 82 1731
Bowling Bank Wrexhm 71 3948
Bowling Green Worcs 47 8251
Bowmanstead Cumb 86 3096
Bowmore Ag & B 112 3159
Bowness-on-Solway Cumb 101 2262
Bowness-on-
    Windermere Cumb 87 4097
Bowriefauld Angus 127 5147
Bowscale Cumb 93 3531
Bowsden Nthumb 111 9941
Bowston Cumb 87 4996
Bowthorpe Norfk 66 1709
Box Gloucs 35 8600
Box Wilts 22 8268
Box End Beds 38 0049
Box Hill Surrey 26 1951
Box's Shop Cnwll 18 2101
Boxbush Gloucs 35 6720
Boxbush Gloucs 35 7413
Boxford Berks 24 4271
Boxford Suffk 54 9640
Boxgrove W Susx 14 9007
Boxley Kent 28 7758
Boxmoor Herts 38 0406
Boxted Essex 41 9933
Boxted Suffk 54 8251
Boxted Cross Essex 41 0032
Boxted Heath Essex 41 0031
Boxwell Gloucs 35 8192
Boxworth Cambs 52 3464
Boxworth End Cambs 52 3667
Boyden End Suffk 53 7355
Boyden Gate Kent 29 2265
Boylestone Derbys 73 1835
Boyndie Abers 142 6463
Boyndlie Abers 143 9162
Boynton E R Yk 91 1367
Boys Hill Dorset 11 6710
Boysack Angus 127 6249
Boythorpe Derbys 74 3869
Boyton Cnwll 5 3292
Boyton Suffk 55 3747
Boyton Wilts 22 9539
Boyton Cross Essex 40 6409
Boyton End Suffk 53 7244
Bozeat Nhants 51 9058
Braaid IOM 158 3276
Brabling Green Suffk 55 2964
Brabourne Kent 29 1041
Brabourne Lees Kent 29 0840
Brabstermire Highld 151 3169
Bracadale Highld 136 3538
Braceborough Lincs 64 0713
Bracebridge Heath Lincs 76 9867
Bracebridge Low Fields Lincs 76 9666
Braceby Lincs 64 0135
Bracewell Lancs 81 8648
Brackenfield Derbys 74 3759
Brackenthwaite Cumb 93 2946
Brackenthwaite N York 82 2851
Bracklesham W Susx 14 8096
Brackletter Highld 131 1882
Brackley Nhants 49 5837
Brackley Hatch Nhants 49 6441
Bracknell Berks 25 8769
Braco P & K 125 8309
Bracobrae Moray 142 5053
Bracon Ash Norfk 66 1899
Bracora Highld 129 7192
Bracorina Highld 129 7292
Bradaford Devon 5 3994
Bradbourne Derbys 73 2052
Bradbury Dur 96 3128
Bradden Nhants 49 6448
Braddock Cnwll 4 1662
Bradeley Staffs 72 8851
Bradenham Bucks 37 8297
Bradenstoke Wilts 35 0079
Bradfield Berks 24 6072
Bradfield Devon 9 0509
Bradfield Essex 41 1430
Bradfield Norfk 67 2733
Bradfield S York 74 2692
Bradfield Combust Suffk 54 8957
Bradfield Green Ches 72 6859
Bradfield Heath Essex 41 1430
Bradfield St Clare Suffk 54 9057
Bradfield St George Suffk 54 9059
Bradford Cnwll 4 1175
Bradford Devon 18 4207
Bradford Nthumb 111 1532
Bradford Nthumb 103 0679
Bradford W York 82 1632
Bradford Abbas Dorset 10 5813
Bradford Leigh Wilts 22 8362
Bradford Peverell Dorset 11 6593
Bradford-on-Avon Wilts 22 8261
Bradford-on-Tone Somset 20 1722
Bradiford Devon 19 5534
Brading IOW 13 6087
Bradley Ches 71 5377
Bradley Derbys 73 2246
Bradley Hants 24 6341
Bradley Lincs 85 2406
Bradley N York 88 0380
Bradley Staffs 72 8717
Bradley W Mids 60 9595
Bradley W York 82 1720
Bradley Worcs 47 9860
Bradley Wrexhm 71 3253
Bradley Green Ches 71 5045
Bradley Green Somset 20 2538
Bradley Green Warwks 61 2800
Bradley Green Worcs 47 9862
Bradley in the Moors Staffs 73 0541
Bradley Stoke Gloucs 34 6181
Bradmore Notts 62 5830

Bradney Somset 21 3338
Bradninch Devon 19 6133
Bradnop Staffs 73 0155
Bradnor Green Herefs 46 2957
Bradpole Dorset 10 4894
Bradshaw Gt Man 81 7312
Bradshaw W York 82 0514
Bradshaw W York 82 0729
Bradstone Devon 5 3880
Bradwall Green Ches 72 7563
Bradwell Bucks 38 8340
Bradwell Derbys 74 1781
Bradwell Devon 19 5042
Bradwell Essex 40 8122
Bradwell Norfk 67 5003
Bradwell Waterside Essex 41 9907
Bradwell-on-Sea Essex 41 0006
Bradworthy Devon 18 3214
Brae Highld 140 6662
Brae Shet 153 3568
Brae Roy Lodge Highld 131 3391
Braeface Falk 116 7880
Braehead Angus 127 6952
Braehead D & G 99 4152
Braehead S Lans 117 9550
Braemar Abers 133 1591
Braemore Highld 150 0829
Braemore Highld 145 2079
Braes of Coul Angus 133 2857
Braes of Enzie Moray 142 3957
Braeside Inver 114 2374
Braeswick Ork 153 6137
Braevallich Ag & B 122 9507
Brafferton Dur 96 2921
Brafferton N York 89 4370
Brafield-on-the-Green Nhants 51 8258
Bragar W Isls 152 2947
Bragbury End Herts 39 2621
Braidwood S Lans 116 8448
Brailsford Derbys 73 2541
Brailsford Green Derbys 73 2541
Brain's Green Gloucs 35 6609
Braintree Essex 40 7523
Braiseworth Suffk 54 1371
Braishfield Hants 23 3725
Braithwaite Cumb 93 2323
Braithwaite W York 82 0341
Braithwell S York 75 5394
Braken Hill W York 83 4126
Bramber W Susx 15 1810
Brambridge Hants 13 4721
Bramcote Notts 62 5037
Bramcote Warwks 61 4088
Bramdean Hants 24 6128
Bramerton Norfk 67 2904
Bramfield Herts 39 2915
Bramfield Suffk 55 3973
Bramford Suffk 54 1246
Bramhall Gt Man 79 8984
Bramham W York 83 4242
Bramhope W York 82 2543
Bramley Derbys 74 4079
Bramley Hants 24 6559
Bramley S York 75 4892
Bramley Surrey 25 0044
Bramley W York 82 2435
Bramley Corner Hants 24 6359
Bramley Green Hants 24 6658
Bramley Head N York 89 1258
Bramling Kent 29 2256
Brampford Speke Devon 9 9298
Brampton Cambs 52 2170
Brampton Cumb 101 5361
Brampton Cumb 94 6723
Brampton Lincs 76 8479
Brampton Norfk 67 2223
Brampton S York 83 4101
Brampton Suffk 55 4381
Brampton Abbotts Herefs 46 6026
Brampton Ash Nhants 50 7987
Brampton Bryan Herefs 46 3772
Brampton-en-le-Morthen S York 75 4887
Bramshall Staffs 73 0532
Bramshaw Hants 12 2615
Bramshill Hants 24 7461
Bramshott Hants 14 8432
Bramwell Somset 21 4329
Bran End Essex 40 6525
Branault Highld 128 5269
Brancaster Norfk 65 7743
Brancaster Staithe Norfk 66 7944
Brancepeth Dur 96 2237
Branchill Moray 141 0852
Brand End Lincs 64 3745
Brand Green Gloucs 47 7328
Branderburgh Moray 141 2371
Brandesburton E R Yk 85 1147
Brandeston Suffk 55 2460
Brandis Corner Devon 18 4104
Brandiston Norfk 66 1421
Brandon Dur 96 2340
Brandon Lincs 76 9048
Brandon Nthumb 111 0417
Brandon Suffk 53 7886
Brandon Warwks 50 4176
Brandon Bank Norfk 53 6289
Brandon Creek Norfk 65 6091
Brandon Parva Norfk 66 0708
Brandsby N York 90 5872
Brandy Wharf Lincs 76 0196
Brane Cnwll 2 4028
Branksome Dorset 12 0492
Branksome Park Dorset 12 0590
Bransbury Hants 24 4242
Bransby Lincs 76 8978
Branscombe Devon 9 1988
Bransford Worcs 47 7952
Bransgore Hants 12 1897
Bransholme E R Yk 85 1033
Bransley Shrops 47 6575
Branson's Cross Worcs 61 0970
Branston Leics 63 8129
Branston Lincs 76 0166
Branston Staffs 73 2221
Branston Booths Lincs 76 0668
Branstone IOW 13 5583
Brant Broughton Lincs 76 9154

Brantham Suffk 54 1034
Branthwaite Cumb 92 0525
Branthwaite Cumb 93 2937
Brantingham E R Yk 84 9429
Branton Nthumb 111 0416
Branton S York 83 6401
Branton Green N York 89 4362
Branxton Nthumb 110 8937
Brassey Green Ches 71 5260
Brassington Derbys 73 2254
Brasted Kent 27 4755
Brasted Chart Kent 27 4653
Brathens Abers 135 6798
Bratoft Lincs 77 4764
Brattleby Lincs 76 9481
Bratton Shrops 59 6413
Bratton Somset 20 9446
Bratton Wilts 22 9152
Bratton Clovelly Devon 5 4691
Bratton Fleming Devon 19 6437
Bratton Seymour Somset 22 6729
Braughing Herts 39 3925
Braughing Friars Herts 39 4124
Braunston Nhants 50 5466
Braunston Rutlnd 63 8306
Braunstone Leics 62 5502
Braunton Devon 18 4836
Brawby N York 90 7378
Brawdy Pembks 30 8524
Brawl Highld 150 8166
Braworth N York 90 5007
Bray Berks 26 9079
Bray Shop Cnwll 5 3374
Bray's Hill E Susx 16 6714
Braybrooke Nhants 50 7684
Braydon Wilts 36 0488
Braydon Brook Wilts 35 9891
Braydon Side Wilts 35 0185
Brayford Devon 19 6834
Braystones Cumb 86 0106
Braythorn N York 82 2449
Brayton N York 83 6030
Braywick Berks 26 8979
Braywoodside Berks 26 8775
Brazacott Cnwll 5 2691
Breach Kent 28 8465
Breach Kent 29 1947
Breachwood Green Herts 39 1522
Breaden Heath Shrops 59 4436
Breadsall Derbys 62 3639
Breadstone Gloucs 35 7000
Breadward Herefs 46 2854
Breage Cnwll 2 6128
Breakachy Highld 139 4644
Brealangwell Lodge Highld 146 5192
Bream Gloucs 34 6005
Breamore Hants 12 1517
Brean Somset 20 2956
Breanais W Isls 152 9925
Brearley W York 82 0225
Brearton N York 89 3261
Breascleit W Isls 152 2135
Breasclete W Isls 152 2135
Breaston Derbys 62 4533
Brechfa Carmth 44 5230
Brechin Angus 134 6060
Breckles Norfk 66 9594
Breckonside D & G 100 8489
Brecon Powys 45 0428
Bredbury Gt Man 79 9291
Brede E Susx 17 8218
Bredenbury Herefs 46 6056
Bredfield Suffk 55 2653
Bredgar Kent 28 8860
Bredhurst Kent 28 7962
Bredon Worcs 47 9236
Bredon's Hardwick Worcs 47 9135
Bredon's Norton Worcs 47 9339
Bredwardine Herefs 46 3344
Breedon on the Hill Leics 62 4022
Breich W Loth 117 9560
Breightmet Gt Man 79 7409
Breighton E R Yk 84 7033
Breinton Herefs 46 4739
Bremhill Wilts 35 9773
Bremridge Devon 19 6929
Brenchley Kent 28 6741
Brendon Devon 18 3607
Brendon Devon 19 7748
Brendon Hill Somset 20 0234
Brenfield Ag & B 113 8482
Brenish W Isls 152 9925
Brenkley T & W 103 2175
Brent Eleigh Suffk 54 9448
Brent Knoll Somset 21 3350
Brent Mill Devon 7 6959
Brent Pelham Herts 39 4330
Brentford Gt Lon 26 1777
Brentingby Leics 63 7816
Brentwood Essex 27 5993
Brenzett Kent 17 0027
Brenzett Green Kent 17 0128
Brereton Staffs 73 0516
Brereton Green Ches 72 7764
Brereton Heath Ches 72 8065
Brereton Hill Staffs 73 0515
Bressingham Norfk 54 0780
Bressingham Common Norfk 54 0981
Bretby Derbys 73 2922
Bretford Warwks 50 4477
Bretforton Worcs 48 0943
Bretherdale Head Cumb 87 5705
Bretherton Lancs 80 4720
Brettabister Shet 153 4857
Brettenham Norfk 54 9383
Brettenham Suffk 54 9654
Bretton Derbys 74 2078
Bretton Flints 71 3563
Brewer Street Surrey 27 3251
Brewers End Essex 39 5521
Brewood Staffs 60 8808
Briantspuddle Dorset 11 8193
Brick End Essex 40 5725
Brick Houses S York 74 3081
Brickendon Herts 39 3208
Bricket Wood Herts 26 1202
Brickkiln Green Essex 40 7331
Bricklehampton Worcs 47 9742

Bride IOM 158 4481
Bridekirk Cumb 92 1132
Bridell Pembks 31 1174
Bridestowe Devon 5 5148
Brideswell Abers 142 5716
Bridford Devon 8 8186
Bridge Cnwll 2 6743
Bridge Kent 29 1853
Bridge End Beds 38 0055
Bridge End Cumb 93 3742
Bridge End Cumb 86 1808
Bridge End Devon 7 6943
Bridge End Dur 95 0235
Bridge End Essex 40 6744
Bridge End Lincs 64 1436
Bridge End Nthumb 102 8936
Bridge End Surrey 39 4688
Bridge Green Essex 39 4686
Bridge Hewick N York 89 3371
Bridge of Alford Abers 142 5648
Bridge of Allan Stirlg 116 7998
Bridge of Avon Moray 141 1830
Bridge of Avon Moray 141 1439
Bridge of Balgie P & K 124 5746
Bridge of Brown Highld 141 1118
Bridge of Cally P & K 126 1351
Bridge of Canny Abers 135 6599
Bridge of Craigisla Angus 126 2552
Bridge of Dee D & G 99 7360
Bridge of Don Aber C 135 9407
Bridge of Dulsie Highld 140 9342
Bridge of Dye Abers 135 6586
Bridge of Earn P & K 126 1318
Bridge of Ericht P & K 131 5268
Bridge of Feugh Abers 135 7096
Bridge of Forss Highld 150 0369
Bridge of Gairn Abers 134 3597
Bridge of Gaur P & K 124 5057
Bridge of Marnoch Abers 142 5950
Bridge of Orchy Ag & B 123 2946
Bridge of Tilt P & K 132 8765
Bridge of Tynet Moray 141 3864
Bridge of Walls Shet 153 2751
Bridge of Weir Rens 115 3965
Bridge Reeve Devon 19 6613
Bridge Sollers Herefs 46 4142
Bridge Street Suffk 54 8749
Bridge Trafford Ches 71 5371
Bridge Yate Gloucs 35 6874
Bridgefoot Cumb 92 0528
Bridgehampton Somset 21 5624
Bridgehill Dur 95 0951
Bridgehouse Gate N York 89 1564
Bridgemary Hants 13 5802
Bridgemere Ches 72 7145
Bridgend Abers 142 5182
Bridgend Ag & B 112 3362
Bridgend Angus 134 5360
Bridgend Brdgnd 33 9080
Bridgend Cerdgn 42 1748
Bridgend Cumb 93 4017
Bridgend D & G 108 0708
Bridgend Devon 6 6546
Bridgend Fife 126 3916
Bridgend Moray 141 3720
Bridgend P & K 126 1225
Bridgend W Loth 117 0475
Bridgend of Lintrathen Angus 126 2854
Bridgerule Devon 18 2703
Bridges Shrops 59 3996
Bridgetown Devon 5 3385
Bridgetown Somset 20 9233
Bridgham Norfk 54 9685
Bridgnorth Shrops 60 7193
Bridgtown Staffs 60 9807
Bridgwater Somset 20 2937
Bridlington E R Yk 91 1866
Bridport Dorset 10 4692
Bridstow Herefs 46 5824
Brierfield Lancs 81 8435
Brierley Gloucs 35 6215
Brierley Herefs 46 4955
Brierley W York 83 4011
Brierley Hill W Mids 60 9186
Brierton Dur 97 4732
Briery Cumb 93 2825
Brig o'Turk Stirlg 124 5306
Brigg Lincs 84 0007
Briggate Norfk 67 3129
Briggswath N York 90 8608
Brigham Cumb 92 0887
Brigham Cumb 93 2823
Brigham E R Yk 85 0778
Brighouse W York 82 1423
Brighstone IOW 13 4282
Brightgate Derbys 74 2659
Brighthampton Oxon 36 3803
Brightholmlee Derbys 74 2892
Brightley Devon 8 6092
Brightling E Susx 16 6821
Brightlingsea Essex 41 0816
Brighton Cnwll 3 9053
Brighton E Susx 15 3104
Brighton le Sands Mersyd 78 3099
Brightons Falk 116 9277
Brightor Cnwll 5 3563
Brightwalton Berks 36 4279
Brightwalton Green Berks 36 4279
Brightwalton Holt Berks 36 4178
Brightwell Suffk 55 2543
Brightwell Baldwin Oxon 37 6595
Brightwell Upperton Oxon 37 6555
Brightwell-cum-Sotwell Oxon 37 5790
Brignall Dur 95 0712
Brigsley Lincs 85 2501
Brigsteer Cumb 87 4889
Brigstock Nhants 51 9485
Brill Bucks 37 6513
Brill Cnwll 3 7221
Brilley Herefs 46 2649
Brimfield Herefs 46 5267
Brimfield Cross Herefs 46 5367
Brimington Derbys 74 4072
Brimley Devon 8 8077
Brimpsfield Gloucs 35 9312
Brimpton Berks 24 5564
Brimscombe Gloucs 35 8702

Place	Page	Grid
rimstage Mersyd	78	3082
ncliffe S York	74	3284
nd E R Yk	84	7430
ndham Somset	21	5139
ndister Shet	153	2857
ndle Lancs	81	5924
ineton Staffs	60	8013
inghurst Leics	51	8492
ngton Cambs	51	0875
ningham Norfk	66	0434
nkely Notts	75	7153
nkhill Lincs	77	3773
inkley Cambs	53	6354
inklow Warwks	50	4379
inkworth Wilts	35	0184
inscall Lancs	81	6221
inscombe Somset	21	4251
insea Somset	21	4461
insley Notts	75	4548
insop Herefs	46	4444
insworth S York	74	4289
inton Neath	66	0335
inyan Ork	153	4327
isco Cumb	93	4252
isley Norfk	66	9421
islington Bristl	35	6270
issenden Green Kent	28	9439
istol Bristl	34	5972
istol Airport	21	5065
istol Zoo	34	5773
iston Norfk	66	0632
isworthy Devon	6	5665
itania Lancs	81	8821
itford Wilts	23	1627
ithdir Caerph	33	1401
ithdir Gwynd	57	7618
itish Torfn	34	2503
itish Legion Village Kent	28	7257
iton Ferry Neath	32	7394
itwell Salome Oxon	37	6792
ixham Devon	7	9255
ixton Devon	6	5552
ixton Gt Lon	27	3175
ixton Deverill Wilts	22	8638
ixworth Nhants	50	7470
ize Norton Oxon	36	2907
ize Norton Airport	36	2905
oad Alley Worcs	47	8867
oad Blunsdon Wilts	36	1491
oad Campden Gloucs	48	1537
oad Carr W York	82	0919
oad Chalke Wilts	23	0325
oad Clough Lancs	81	8623
oad Ford Kent	28	7139
oad Green Essex	40	8823
oad Green Suffk	53	7859
oad Green Worcs	47	7556
oad Green Worcs	60	9970
oad Haven Pembks	30	8613
oad Hill Cambs	53	5976
oad Hinton Wilts	36	1075
oad Laying Hants	24	4362
oad Marston Worcs	48	1446
oad Meadow Staffs	72	8348
oad Oak Cumb	86	1194
oad Oak E Susx	17	8219
oad Oak E Susx	16	6022
oad Oak Hants	24	7551
oad Oak Herefs	34	4821
oad Oak Kent	29	1761
oad Oak Mersyd	78	5395
oad Road Suffk	55	2676
oad Street E Susx	17	8616
oad Street Essex	39	5516
oad Street Kent	28	7672
oad Street Kent	28	8356
oad Street Wilts	23	1059
oad Street Green Essex	40	8509
oad Town Wilts	36	0977
oad's Green Essex	40	6912
oadbottom Gt Man	79	9993
oadbridge W Susx	14	8105
oadbridge Heath W Susx	15	1431
oadclyst Devon	9	9897
oadfield Inver	115	3373
oadfield Pembks	31	1303
oadford Highld	129	6423
oadford Bridge W Susx	14	0921
oadgairhill Border	109	2010
oadgate Lancs	64	3610
oadgrass Green Suffk	54	9663
oadhaugh Border	119	8655
oadheath Gt Man	79	7689
oadheath Worcs	47	6665
oadhembury Devon	9	1004
oadhempston Devon	7	8066
oadholme Notts	76	8874
oadland Row E Susx	17	8319
oadlay Carmth	31	3709
oadley Essex	39	4207
oadley Gt Man	81	8816
oadley Moray	142	3961
oadley Common Essex	39	4207
oadmayne Dorset	11	7286
oadmere Hants	24	6247
oadmoor Gloucs	35	6415
oadmoor Pembks	31	0906
oadnymett Devon	8	7001
oadoak Dorset	10	4396
oadoak Gloucs	35	6912
oadoak Wrexhm	71	3658
oadstairs Kent	29	3967
oadstone Dorset	11	0095
oadstone Mons	34	5102
oadstone Shrops	59	5499
oadwas Worcs	47	7555
oadwater Herts	39	2422
oadwater W Susx	15	1404
oadwaters Worcs	60	8477
oadway Carmth	31	2910
oadway Carmth	31	3808
oadway Pembks	30	8713
oadway Somset	10	3215
oadway Suffk	55	3979
oadwell Gloucs	48	0393
oadwell Gloucs	34	5811
oadwell Gloucs	48	2027
oadwell Oxon	36	2504
Broadwell Warwks	50	4565
Broadwey Dorset	11	6683
Broadwindsor Dorset	10	4302
Broadwood Kelly Devon	8	6106
Broadwoodwidger Devon	5	4189
Brobury Herefs	46	3444
Brochel Highld	137	5846
Brock Lancs	80	5140
Brock's Green Hants	24	5061
Brockamin Worcs	47	7753
Brockbridge Hants	13	6118
Brockdish Norfk	55	2179
Brockencote Worcs	60	8873
Brockenhurst Hants	12	3002
Brocketsbrae S Lans	108	8239
Brockford Green Suffk	54	1265
Brockford Street Suffk	54	1167
Brockhall Nhants	49	6362
Brockhampton Gloucs	47	9326
Brockhampton Gloucs	36	0322
Brockhampton Hants	13	7106
Brockhampton Herefs	46	5931
Brockhampton Green Dorset	11	7106
Brockholes W York	82	1510
Brockhurst Derbys	74	3364
Brockhurst W York	50	4683
Brocklebank Cumb	93	3042
Brocklesby Lincs	85	1311
Brockley Somset	21	4666
Brockley Suffk	54	8371
Brockley Green Suffk	53	7247
Brockley Green Suffk	54	8254
Brockleymoor Cumb	94	4937
Brockmoor W Mids	60	9088
Brockscombe Devon	5	4695
Brockton Shrops	59	3104
Brockton Shrops	60	7103
Brockton Shrops	59	3285
Brockton Shrops	59	5794
Brockton Shrops	72	8131
Brockweir Gloucs	34	5401
Brockwood Park Hants	13	6226
Brockworth Gloucs	35	8916
Brocton Cnwll	4	0168
Brocton Staffs	72	9619
Brodick N Ayrs	105	0135
Brodie Moray	140	9757
Brodsworth S York	83	5007
Brogaig Highld	136	4767
Brogborough Beds	38	9638
Broken Cross Ches	79	6873
Broken Cross Ches	79	8973
Brokenborough Wilts	35	9189
Brokerswood Wilts	22	8352
Bromborough Mersyd	78	3582
Brome Suffk	54	1376
Brome Street Suffk	54	1576
Bromeswell Suffk	55	3050
Bromfield Cumb	93	1746
Bromfield Shrops	46	4876
Bromham Beds	38	0051
Bromham Wilts	22	9665
Bromley Gt Lon	27	4069
Bromley S York	74	3298
Bromley Shrops	60	7395
Bromley W Mids	60	9088
Bromley Common Gt Lon	27	4266
Bromley Cross Essex	41	0627
Bromlow Shrops	59	3201
Brompton N York	28	7668
Brompton N York	89	3796
Brompton N York	91	9482
Brompton Shrops	59	5408
Brompton Ralph Somset	20	0832
Brompton Regis Somset	20	9531
Brompton-on-Swale N York	89	2199
Bromsash Herefs	47	6524
Bromsberrow Gloucs	47	7433
Bromsberrow Heath Gloucs	47	7333
Bromsgrove Worcs	60	9670
Bromstead Heath Staffs	72	7917
Bromyard Herefs	47	6554
Bromyard Downs Herefs	47	6655
Bronaber Gwynd	57	7131
Bronant Cerdgn	43	6467
Broncroft Shrops	59	5486
Brongest Cerdgn	42	3245
Bronington Wrexhm	71	4839
Bronllys Powys	45	1434
Bronwydd Carmth	31	4123
Bronydd Powys	45	2245
Bronygarth Shrops	58	2637
Brook Carmth	31	2609
Brook Hants	12	2714
Brook Hants	23	3429
Brook IOW	13	3983
Brook Kent	29	0644
Brook Surrey	14	9237
Brook Surrey	14	0546
Brook End Beds	51	0763
Brook End Beds	52	1547
Brook End Bucks	38	9244
Brook End Cambs	51	0773
Brook Hill Hants	12	2714
Brook House Denbgs	70	0765
Brook Street Essex	27	5793
Brook Street Kent	17	9333
Brook Street Suffk	54	8248
Brook Street W Susx	15	3026
Brooke Norfk	67	2899
Brooke Rutlnd	63	8405
Brookfield Rens	115	4164
Brookhampton Oxon	37	6098
Brookhampton Somset	21	6327
Brookhouse Lancs	87	5464
Brookhouse S York	75	5188
Brookhouse Green Ches	72	8161
Brookhouses Derbys	74	0388
Brookland Kent	17	9926
Brooklands Gt Man	79	7890
Brookmans Park Herts	39	2404
Brooks Powys	58	1499
Brooks End Kent	29	2967
Brooks Green W Susx	14	1224
Brooksby Leics	63	6715
Brookthorpe Gloucs	35	8312
Brookville Norfk	65	7396
Brookwood Surrey	25	9557
Broom Beds	39	1742
Broom Dur	96	2441
Broom S York	75	4491
Broom Warwks	48	0853
Broom Green Norfk	66	9823
Broom Hill Dorset	12	0302
Broom Hill Notts	62	5447
Broom Hill S York	83	4102
Broom Hill Worcs	60	9175
Broom Street Kent	28	0462
Broom's Green Gloucs	47	7132
Broome Norfk	67	3591
Broome Shrops	59	4080
Broome Worcs	60	9078
Broome Park Nthumb	111	1012
Broomedge Ches	79	7085
Broomer's Corner W Susx	14	1220
Broomershill W Susx	14	0619
Broomfield Essex	40	7010
Broomfield Kent	28	8452
Broomfield Kent	29	1966
Broomfield Somset	20	2232
Broomfields Shrops	59	4217
Broomfleet E R Yk	84	8727
Broomhall Surrey	25	9566
Broomhaugh Nthumb	103	0261
Broomhill Nthumb	103	2401
Broomhill Green Ches	71	6247
Broomley Nthumb	103	0360
Broomsthorpe Norfk	66	8428
Brora Highld	147	9103
Broseley Shrops	60	6701
Brotherhouse Bar Lincs	64	2614
Brotherlee Dur	95	9237
Brothertoft Lincs	77	2746
Brotherton N York	83	4825
Brotton N York	97	6819
Broubster Highld	150	0359
Brough Cumb	95	7914
Brough Derbys	74	1882
Brough E R Yk	84	9326
Brough Highld	151	2273
Brough Notts	76	8458
Brough Shet	153	5665
Brough Lodge Shet	153	5892
Brough Sowerby Cumb	95	7912
Broughall Shrops	71	5741
Broughton Border	108	1136
Broughton Bucks	38	8413
Broughton Bucks	38	8939
Broughton Cambs	52	2878
Broughton Flints	71	3363
Broughton Gt Man	79	8201
Broughton Hants	23	3033
Broughton Lancs	80	5234
Broughton Lincs	84	9608
Broughton N York	82	9451
Broughton N York	90	7673
Broughton Nhants	51	8375
Broughton Oxon	49	4138
Broughton Staffs	72	7634
Broughton V Glam	33	9270
Broughton Astley Leics	50	5292
Broughton Beck Cumb	86	2882
Broughton Gifford Wilts	22	8763
Broughton Green Worcs	47	9561
Broughton Hackett Worcs	47	9254
Broughton Mains D & G	99	4545
Broughton Mills Cumb	86	2290
Broughton Moor Cumb	92	0633
Broughton Poggs Oxon	36	2303
Broughton Tower Cumb	86	2187
Broughton-in-Furness Cumb	86	2187
Broughty Ferry Dund C	127	4630
Brow End Cumb	86	2674
Brow-of-the-Hill Norfk	65	6819
Brown Candover Hants	24	5739
Brown Edge Lancs	80	3614
Brown Edge Staffs	72	9053
Brown Heath Ches	71	4564
Brown Lees Ches	72	8756
Brown Street Suffk	54	0663
Brown's Green W Mids	61	0591
Brownber Cumb	87	7005
Brownheath Shrops	59	4629
Brownhill Abers	143	8640
Brownhills Fife	127	5215
Brownhills W Mids	61	0405
Brownieside Nthumb	111	1623
Browninghill Green Hants	24	5859
Brownlow Heath Ches	72	8360
Brownrigg Cumb	92	0420
Brownrigg Cumb	92	1652
Browns Hill Gloucs	35	8802
Brownsham Devon	18	2826
Brownsover Warwks	50	5177
Brownston Devon	7	6952
Browston Green Norfk	67	4901
Broxa N York	91	9491
Broxbourne Herts	39	3606
Broxburn E Loth	119	6977
Broxburn W Loth	117	0872
Broxfield Nthumb	111	2016
Broxted Essex	40	5727
Broxton Ches	71	4754
Broxwood Herefs	46	3654
Broyle Side E Susx	16	4513
Bruan Highld	151	3139
Bruar P & K	132	8265
Brucefield Highld	147	9386
Bruchag Ag & B	114	1157
Bruera Ches	71	4360
Bruern Abbey Oxon	36	2620
Bruichladdich Ag & B	112	2661
Bruisyard Suffk	55	3266
Bruisyard Street Suffk	55	3365
Brumby Lincs	84	8909
Brund Staffs	74	1061
Brundall Norfk	67	3308
Brundish Suffk	55	2769
Brundish Street Suffk	55	2671
Brunnion Cnwll	2	5036
Brunslow Shrops	59	3684
Bruntcliffe W York	82	2526
Brunthwaite W York	82	0546
Bruntingthorpe Leics	50	6089
Brunton Fife	126	3220
Brunton Nthumb	111	2024
Brunton Wilts	23	2456
Brushford Somset	20	9225
Brushford Barton Devon	8	6707
Bruton Somset	22	6835
Bryan's Green Worcs	47	8868
Bryanston Dorset	11	8607
Bryant's Bottom Bucks	26	8599
Brydekirk D & G	101	1870
Brymbo Wrexhm	71	2953
Brympton Somset	10	5115
Bryn Ches	71	6072
Bryn Gt Man	78	5600
Bryn Neath	33	8192
Bryn Shrops	59	2985
Bryn Du IOA	68	3472
Bryn Gates Lancs	78	5901
Bryn Golau Rhondd	33	0088
Bryn Saith Marchog Denbgs	70	0750
Bryn-coch Neath	32	7499
Bryn-Eden Gwynd	57	7129
Bryn-Henllan Pembks	30	0139
Bryn-mawr Gwynd	56	2433
Bryn-newydd Denbgs	70	1842
Bryn-penarth Powys	58	1004
Bryn-y-bal Flints	70	2564
Bryn-y-Maen Conwy	69	8376
Bryn-yr-Eos Wrexhm	71	2840
Brynaman Carmth	32	7114
Brynberian Pembks	31	1035
Brynbryddan Neath	32	7792
Bryncae Rhondd	33	9982
Bryncethin Brdgnd	33	9183
Bryncir Gwynd	56	4844
Bryncroes Gwynd	56	2231
Bryncrug Gwynd	57	6103
Bryneglwys Denbgs	70	1447
Brynfields Wrexhm	71	3044
Brynford Flints	70	1774
Bryngwran IOA	68	3577
Bryngwyn Mons	34	3309
Bryngwyn Powys	45	1849
Brynhoffnant Cerdgn	42	3351
Bryning Lancs	80	4029
Brynithel Blae G	33	2101
Brynmawr Blae G	33	1911
Brynmenyn Brdgnd	33	9084
Brynmill Swans	32	6392
Brynna Rhondd	33	9883
Brynrefail Gwynd	69	5562
Brynrefail IOA	68	4836
Brynsadler Rhondd	33	0280
Brynsiencyn IOA	68	4867
Brynteg IOA	68	4982
Bualintur Highld	128	4020
Buarth-draw Flints	70	1779
Bubbenhall Warwks	61	3672
Bubwith E R Yk	84	7136
Buchanan Smithy Stirlg	115	4689
Buchanhaven Abers	143	1447
Buchanty P & K	125	9328
Buchany Stirlg	124	7102
Buchlyvie Stirlg	115	5793
Buck's Cross Devon	18	3522
Buck's Mills Devon	18	3523
Buckabank Cumb	93	3749
Buckden Cambs	52	1967
Buckden N York	88	9477
Buckenham Norfk	67	3505
Buckerell Devon	9	1200
Buckfast Devon	7	7467
Buckfastleigh Devon	7	7366
Buckhaven Fife	118	3598
Buckholt Mons	34	5016
Buckhorn Weston Dorset	22	7524
Buckhurst Hill Essex	27	4194
Buckie Moray	142	4265
Buckingham Bucks	49	6933
Buckland Bucks	38	8812
Buckland Devon	7	6743
Buckland Gloucs	48	0835
Buckland Hants	12	3196
Buckland Herts	39	3533
Buckland Kent	29	3042
Buckland Oxon	36	3498
Buckland Surrey	26	2150
Buckland Brewer Devon	18	4220
Buckland Common Bucks	38	9207
Buckland Dinham Somset	22	7551
Buckland Filleigh Devon	18	4609
Buckland in the Moor Devon	7	7273
Buckland Monachorum Devon	6	4968
Buckland Newton Dorset	11	6805
Buckland Ripers Dorset	11	6582
Buckland St Mary Somset	10	2613
Buckland-Tout-Saints Devon	7	7645
Bucklebury Berks	24	5570
Bucklers Hard Hants	13	4000
Bucklesham Suffk	55	2441
Buckley Flints	70	2763
Buckley Green Warwks	48	1567
Buckley Mountain Flints	70	2765
Bucklow Hill Ches	79	7383
Buckminster Leics	63	8722
Bucknall Lincs	85	1768
Bucknall Staffs	72	9047
Bucknell Oxon	49	5625
Bucknell Shrops	46	3574
Buckpool Moray	142	4165
Bucks Green W Susx	14	0833
Bucks Hill Herts	26	0500
Bucks Horn Oak Hants	25	8041
Bucksburn Aber C	135	8909
Buckshead Cnwll	3	8346
Buckton E R Yk	91	1872
Buckton Herefs	46	3873
Buckton Nthumb	111	0838
Buckworth Cambs	52	1476
Budby Notts	75	6169
Budd's Titson Cnwll	18	2401
Buddileigh Staffs	72	7449
Buddon Angus	127	5232
Bude Cnwll	18	2105
Budge's Shop Cnwll	5	3259
Budlake Devon	9	9800
Budle Nthumb	111	1535
Budleigh Salterton Devon	9	0682
Budlett's Common E Susx	16	4723
Budock Water Cnwll	3	7831
Buerton Ches	72	6843
Bugbrooke Nhants	49	6757
Bugford Devon	7	8350
Buglawton Ches	72	8763
Bugle Cnwll	4	0158
Bugley Dorset	22	7824
Bugthorpe E R Yk	90	7757
Buildwas Shrops	59	6204
Builth Road Powys	45	0353
Builth Wells Powys	45	0350
Bulbourne Herts	38	9313
Bulbridge Wilts	23	0830
Bulby Lincs	64	0526
Buldoo Highld	150	0067
Bulford Wilts	23	1643
Bulford Barracks Wilts	23	1843
Bulkeley Ches	71	5354
Bulkington Warwks	61	3986
Bulkington Wilts	22	9458
Bulkworthy Devon	18	3914
Bull Bay IOA	68	4294
Bull's Green Herts	39	2717
Bull's Green Norfk	67	4194
Bullamore N York	89	3994
Bullbridge Derbys	74	3552
Bullbrook Berks	25	8869
Bullen's Green Herts	39	2105
Bulley Gloucs	35	7619
Bullgill Cumb	92	0938
Bullinghope Herefs	46	5136
Bullington Hants	24	4541
Bullington Lincs	76	0877
Bullington End Bucks	38	8145
Bullockstone Kent	29	1665
Bulmer Essex	54	8440
Bulmer N York	90	6967
Bulmer Tye Essex	54	8438
Bulphan Essex	40	6385
Bulstone Devon	9	1789
Bulstrode Herts	26	0302
Bulstrode Park Bucks	26	9888
Bulverhythe E Susx	17	7708
Bulwark Abers	143	9345
Bulwell Notts	62	5343
Bulwick Nhants	51	9694
Bumble's Green Essex	39	4005
Bunacaimb Highld	129	6588
Bunarkaig Highld	131	1887
Bunbury Ches	71	5657
Bunbury Heath Ches	71	5558
Bunchrew Highld	140	6246
Buncton W Susx	15	1413
Bundalloch Highld	138	8927
Bunessan Ag & B	121	3821
Bungay Suffk	55	3389
Bunker's Hill Lincs	77	2653
Bunnahabhain Ag & B	112	4173
Bunny Notts	62	5829
Buntait Highld	139	4030
Buntingford Herts	39	3629
Bunwell Norfk	66	1292
Bunwell Street Norfk	66	1193
Bupton Derbys	73	2237
Burbage Derbys	74	0472
Burbage Leics	50	4492
Burbage Wilts	23	2262
Burcher Herefs	46	3360
Burchett's Green Berks	26	8481
Burchett's Green E Susx	16	6631
Burcombe Wilts	23	0730
Burcot Oxon	37	5695
Burcote Shrops	60	7495
Burcott Bucks	38	8415
Burcott Bucks	38	8823
Burdale N York	90	8762
Bures Essex	54	9034
Burford Oxon	36	2512
Burford Shrops	46	5868
Burg Ag & B	121	3845
Burgates Hants	14	7728
Burge End Herts	38	1432
Burgess Hill W Susx	15	3218
Burgh Suffk	55	2351
Burgh by Sands Cumb	93	3259
Burgh Castle Norfk	67	4805
Burgh Heath Surrey	26	2457
Burgh Hill E Susx	17	7226
Burgh le Marsh Lincs	77	5065
Burgh next Aylsham Norfk	67	2125
Burgh on Bain Lincs	76	2186
Burgh St Margaret Norfk	67	4413
Burgh St Peter Norfk	67	4693
Burghclere Hants	24	4761
Burghead Moray	141	1168
Burghfield Berks	24	6668
Burghfield Common Berks	24	6566
Burghill Herefs	46	4844
Burghwallis S York	83	5311
Burham Kent	28	7262
Buriton Hants	13	7419
Burland Ches	71	6153
Burlawn Cnwll	4	9970
Burleigh Berks	25	9169
Burleigh Gloucs	35	8601
Burlescombe Devon	9	0716
Burleston Dorset	11	7794
Burlestone Devon	7	8248
Burley Hants	12	2102
Burley Rutlnd	63	8810
Burley Shrops	59	4881
Burley Gate Herefs	46	5947
Burley in Wharfedale W York	82	1646
Burley Lawn Hants	12	2103
Burley Street Hants	12	2004
Burley Wood Head W York	82	1544
Burleydam Ches	71	6042
Burlingham Green Norfk	67	3610
Burlingjobb Powys	46	2558
Burlington Shrops	60	7711
Burlton Shrops	59	4526
Burmarsh Kent	17	1032
Burmington Warwks	48	2637
Burn N York	83	5928
Burn Cross S York	74	3496
Burn Naze Lancs	80	3443

C

Burn of Cambus *Stirlg* 124 7102
Burnage *Gt Man* 79 8692
Burnaston *Derbys* 73 2832
Burnbanks *Cumb* 94 5016
Burnbrae *N Lans* 116 8759
Burnby *E R Yk* 84 8346
Burndell *W Susx* 14 9802
Burnden *Gt Man* 79 7207
Burnedge *Gt Man* 79 9110
Burneside *Cumb* 87 5095
Burneston *N York* 89 3084
Burnett *Somset* 22 6665
Burnfoot *Border* 109 4113
Burnfoot *Border* 109 5116
Burnfoot *D & G* 100 7911
Burnfoot *D & G* 101 3388
Burnfoot *D & G* 101 3996
Burnfoot *P & K* 125 9904
Burnham *Bucks* 26 9282
Burnham *Lincs* 84 0516
Burnham Deepdale *Norfk* 66 8044
Burnham Green *Herts* 39 2616
Burnham Market *Norfk* 66 8342
Burnham Norton *Norfk* 66 8343
Burnham Overy *Norfk* 66 8442
Burnham Overy Staithe *Norfk* 66 8444
Burnham Thorpe *Norfk* 66 8541
Burnham-on-Crouch *Essex* 40 9496
Burnham-on-Sea *Somset* 20 3049
Burnhaven *Abers* 143 1244
Burnhead *D & G* 100 8695
Burnhervie *Abers* 142 7319
Burnhill Green *Staffs* 60 7800
Burnhope *Dur* 96 1948
Burnhouse *N Ayrs* 115 3850
Burniston *N York* 91 0193
Burnley *Lancs* 81 8432
Burnmoor *Dur* 96 3051
Burnmouth *Border* 119 9560
Burnopfield *Dur* 96 1757
Burnrigg *Cumb* 94 4856
Burnsall *N York* 88 0361
Burnside *Angus* 127 5650
Burnside *Angus* 134 4259
Burnside *Fife* 126 1608
Burnside *Moray* 147 1769
Burnside *W Loth* 117 0575
Burnside of Duntrune *Angus* 127 4434
Burnt Heath *Essex* 41 0627
Burnt Hill *Berks* 24 5774
Burnt Houses *Dur* 96 1223
Burnt Oak *E Susx* 16 5126
Burnt Yates *N York* 89 2561
Burntcommon *Surrey* 26 0354
Burntheath *Derbys* 73 2431
Burnthouse *Cnwll* 3 7636
Burntisland *Fife* 117 2385
Burntwood *Staffs* 61 0509
Burntwood Green *Staffs* 61 0608
Burnville *Devon* 5 4982
Burnworthy *Somset* 9 1915
Burpham *Surrey* 26 0152
Burpham *W Susx* 14 0308
Burradon *Nthumb* 111 9806
Burradon *T & W* 103 2772
Burrafirth *Shet* 153 6113
Burras *Cnwll* 2 6734
Burraton *Cnwll* 5 4167
Burraton *Devon* 6 6153
Burravoe *Shet* 153 5180
Burrells *Cumb* 94 6718
Burrelton *P & K* 126 2037
Burridge *Devon* 19 5735
Burridge *Devon* 10 3106
Burridge *Hants* 13 5110
Burrill *N York* 89 2387
Burringham *Lincs* 84 8309
Burrington *Devon* 19 6416
Burrington *Herefs* 46 4472
Burrington *Somset* 21 4859
Burrough End *Cambs* 53 6255
Burrough Green *Cambs* 53 6355
Burrough on the Hill *Leics* 63 7510
Burrow *Lancs* 87 6174
Burrow *Somset* 20 9342
Burrow Bridge *Somset* 21 3550
Burrowhill *Surrey* 25 9762
Burrows Cross *Surrey* 14 0846
Burry *Swans* 32 4590
Burry Port *Carmth* 32 4400
Burrygreen *Swans* 32 4591
Burscough *Lancs* 78 4310
Burscough Bridge *Lancs* 80 4412
Bursea *E R Yk* 84 8033
Burshill *E R Yk* 85 0948
Bursledon *Hants* 13 4809
Burslem *Staffs* 72 8649
Burstall *Suffk* 54 0944
Burstock *Dorset* 10 4202
Burston *Norfk* 54 1383
Burston *Staffs* 72 9330
Burstow *Surrey* 15 3141
Burstwick *E R Yk* 85 2227
Burtersett *N York* 88 8999
Burtholme *Cumb* 101 5463
Burthorpe Green *Suffk* 53 7764
Burthwaite *Cumb* 93 4149
Burthy *Cnwll* 3 9155
Burtle Hill *Somset* 21 3843
Burtoft *Lincs* 64 2635
Burton *Ches* 71 3174
Burton *Ches* 71 5063
Burton *Dorset* 11 6891
Burton *Dorset* 12 1694
Burton *Lincs* 76 9574
Burton *Nthumb* 111 1833
Burton *Pembks* 30 9805
Burton *Somset* 20 1944
Burton *Somset* 10 5313
Burton *Wilts* 35 8179
Burton *Wilts* 22 8232
Burton Agnes *E R Yk* 91 1062
Burton Bradstock *Dorset* 10 4889
Burton Coggles *Lincs* 63 9725
Burton Constable Hall 85 1836
Burton Dassett *Warwks* 48 3991
Burton End *Essex* 39 5323
Burton End *Suffk* 53 6645

Burton Fleming *E R Yk* 91 0871
Burton Green *Warwks* 61 2675
Burton Green *Wrexhm* 71 3458
Burton Hastings *Warwks* 50 4189
Burton in Lonsdale *N York* 87 6572
Burton Joyce *Notts* 63 6443
Burton Latimer *Nhants* 51 9074
Burton Lazars *Leics* 63 7716
Burton Leonard *N York* 89 3263
Burton on the Wolds *Leics* 62 5821
Burton Overy *Leics* 50 6798
Burton Pedwardine *Lincs* 64 1142
Burton Pidsea *E R Yk* 85 2431
Burton Salmon *N York* 83 4927
Burton upon Stather *Lincs* 84 8717
Burton upon Trent *Staffs* 73 2323
Burton's Green *Essex* 40 8226
Burton-in-Kendal *Cumb* 87 5376
Burtonwood *Ches* 78 5692
Burwardsley *Ches* 71 5156
Burwarton *Shrops* 59 6185
Burwash *E Susx* 16 6724
Burwash Common *E Susx* 16 6323
Burwash Weald *E Susx* 16 6523
Burwell *Cambs* 53 5866
Burwell *Lincs* 77 3579
Burwen *IOA* 68 4293
Burwick *Ork* 153 4484
Bury *Cambs* 52 2883
Bury *Gt Man* 81 8011
Bury *Somset* 20 9427
Bury *W Susx* 14 0113
Bury End *Beds* 38 1235
Bury End *Bucks* 26 9697
Bury Green *Herts* 39 4521
Bury St Edmunds *Suffk* 54 8554
Burythorpe *N York* 90 7964
Busby *E Rens* 115 5756
Buscot *Wilts* 36 2298
Bush *Abers* 135 7565
Bush *Cnwll* 18 2307
Bush Bank *Herefs* 46 4551
Bush Green *Norfk* 55 2187
Bush Green *Suffk* 54 9157
Bush Hill Park *Gt Lon* 27 3385
Bushbury *W Mids* 60 9202
Bushby *Leics* 63 6503
Bushey *Herts* 26 1395
Bushey Heath *Herts* 26 1494
Bushley *Worcs* 47 8734
Bushley Green *Worcs* 47 8634
Bushmead *Beds* 52 1160
Bushton *Wilts* 36 0677
Busk *Cumb* 94 6042
Buslingthorpe *Lincs* 76 0785
Bussage *Gloucs* 35 8803
Bussex *Somset* 21 3535
Butcher Hill *W York* 81 9322
Butcher's Cross *E Susx* 16 5525
Butcombe *Somset* 21 5161
Butleigh *Somset* 21 5233
Butleigh Wootton *Somset* 21 5035
Butler's Cross *Bucks* 38 8407
Butler's Hill *Notts* 75 5448
Butlers Marston *Warwks* 48 3250
Butley *Suffk* 55 3650
Butley High Corner *Suffk* 55 3849
Butt Green *Ches* 72 6651
Butt Lane *Staffs* 72 8254
Butt's Green *Essex* 40 7603
Buttercrambe *N York* 90 7358
Butterdean *Border* 119 7964
Butterknowle *Dur* 95 1025
Butterleigh *Devon* 9 9708
Butterley *Derbys* 74 4051
Buttermere *Cumb* 93 1717
Buttermere *Wilts* 23 3461
Butters Green *Staffs* 72 8150
Buttershaw *W York* 82 1329
Butterstone *P & K* 125 0645
Butterton *Staffs* 72 8242
Butterton *Staffs* 73 0076
Butterwick *Dur* 96 3830
Butterwick *Lincs* 64 3845
Butterwick *N York* 90 7277
Butterwick *N York* 91 9871
Buttington *Powys* 58 2408
Buttonbridge *Shrops* 60 7379
Buttonoak *Shrops* 60 7578
Buttsash *Hants* 13 4206
Buttsbear Cross *Cnwll* 18 2604
Buxhall *Suffk* 54 0057
Buxhall Fen Street *Suffk* 54 0059
Buxted *E Susx* 16 4923
Buxton *Derbys* 74 0572
Buxton *Norfk* 67 2322
Buxton Heath *Norfk* 66 1821
Bwlch *Powys* 33 1522
Bwlch-y-cibau *Powys* 58 1717
Bwlch-y-Ddar *Powys* 58 1722
Bwlch-y-ffridd *Powys* 58 0795
Bwlch-y-groes *Pembks* 31 2436
Bwlch-y-sarnau *Powys* 45 0374
Bwlchgwyn *Wrexhm* 70 2653
Bwlchllan *Cerdgn* 44 5758
Bwlchnewydd *Carmth* 31 3624
Bwlchtocyn *Gwynd* 56 3125
Bwlchyfadfa *Cerdgn* 42 4349
Bwlchymyrdd *Swans* 32 5798
Byermoor *T & W* 96 1857
Byers Garth *Dur* 96 3140
Byers Green *Dur* 96 2233
Byfield *Nhants* 49 5152
Byfleet *Surrey* 26 0661
Byford *Herefs* 46 3942
Bygrave *Herts* 39 2636
Byker *T & W* 103 2764
Bylchau *Conwy* 70 9762
Byley *Ches* 79 7269
Bynea *Carmth* 32 5499
Byrewalls *Border* 110 6642
Byrness *Nthumb* 102 7602
Bystock *Devon* 9 0283
Bythorn *Cambs* 51 0575
Byton *Herefs* 46 3764
Bywell *Nthumb* 103 0461
Byworth *W Susx* 14 9821

Cabbacott *Devon* 18 4021
Cabourne *Lincs* 85 1401
Cabrach *Ag & B* 112 4964
Cabrach *Moray* 141 3826
Cabus *Lancs* 80 4948
Cackle Street *E Susx* 16 4526
Cackle Street *E Susx* 16 6919
Cackle Street *E Susx* 17 8218
Cadbury *Devon* 9 9105
Cadbury Barton *Devon* 19 6917
Cadder *E Duns* 116 6072
Caddington *Beds* 38 0619
Caddonfoot *Border* 109 4535
Cade Street *E Susx* 16 6020
Cadeby *Leics* 62 4202
Cadeby *S York* 75 5100
Cadeleigh *Devon* 9 9108
Cadgwith *Cnwll* 3 7214
Cadham *Fife* 126 2801
Cadishead *Gt Man* 79 7091
Cadle *Swans* 32 6296
Cadley *Lancs* 80 5231
Cadley *Wilts* 23 2006
Cadley *Wilts* 23 2453
Cadmore End *Bucks* 37 7882
Cadnam *Hants* 12 3013
Cadney *Lincs* 84 0103
Cadole *Flints* 70 2062
Cadoxton V Glam* 20 1269
Cadoxton Juxta-Neath *Neath* 32 7598
Cadsden *Bucks* 38 8204
Cadwst *Denbgs* 58 0225
Cae'r bryn *Carmth* 32 5913
Cae'r-bont *Powys* 32 8011
Caeathro *Gwynd* 68 5051
Caehopkin *Powys* 33 8212
Caenby *Lincs* 76 9909
Caenby Corner *Lincs* 76 9689
Caeo *Carmth* 44 6740
Caer Farchell *Pembks* 30 7927
Caerau *Brdgnd* 33 8694
Caerau *Cardif* 33 1375
Caerdeon *Gwynd* 57 6518
Caergeiliog *IOA* 68 3178
Caergwrle *Flints* 71 3057
Caerhun *Conwy* 69 7770
Caerlanrig *Border* 109 3904
Caerleon *Newpt* 34 3490
Caernarfon *Gwynd* 68 4862
Caernarfon Airport 68 4359
Caernarfon Castle 68 4762
Caerphilly *Caerph* 33 1587
Caersws *Powys* 58 0392
Caerwedros *Cerdgn* 42 3755
Caerwent *Mons* 34 4790
Caerwys *Flints* 70 1272
Caerynwch *Gwynd* 57 7617
Caggle Street *Mons* 34 3717
Caim *IOA* 69 6280
Cairinis *W Isls* 152 8260
Cairnbaan *Ag & B* 113 8390
Cairnbulg *Abers* 143 0365
Cairncross *Border* 119 8963
Cairncurran *Inver* 115 3170
Cairndow *Ag & B* 123 1810
Cairneyhill *Fife* 117 0486
Cairnfield House *Moray* 142 4162
Cairngarroch *D & G* 98 0549
Cairngrassie *Abers* 135 9095
Cairnie *Abers* 142 4844
Cairnorrie *Abers* 143 8641
Cairnryan *D & G* 98 0668
Cairnty *Moray* 141 3352
Caister-on-Sea *Norfk* 67 5112
Caistor *Lincs* 85 1101
Caistor St Edmund *Norfk* 67 2303
Cake Street *Norfk* 54 0690
Cakebole *Worcs* 60 8772
Calais Street *Suffk* 54 9739
Calanais *W Isls* 152 2133
Calbourne *IOW* 13 4286
Calceby *Lincs* 77 3875
Calcot *Berks* 24 6671
Calcot *Flints* 70 1674
Calcot *Gloucs* 36 0810
Calcot Row *Berks* 24 6671
Calcots *Moray* 141 2563
Calcott *Kent* 29 1762
Calcott *Shrops* 59 4413
Calcutt *N York* 83 3455
Calcutt *Wilts* 36 1193
Caldbeck *Cumb* 93 3240
Caldbergh *N York* 89 0965
Caldecote *Cambs* 52 1488
Caldecote *Cambs* 52 3456
Caldecote *Herts* 39 2338
Caldecote *Nhants* 49 6851
Caldecote Highfields *Cambs* 52 3559
Caldecott *Nhants* 51 9868
Caldecott *Oxon* 37 4996
Caldecott *Rutlnd* 51 8693
Caldecotte *Bucks* 38 8935
Calder Bridge *Cumb* 86 0306
Calder Grove *W York* 82 3016
Calder Vale *Lancs* 80 5345
Calderbank *N Lans* 116 7663
Calderbrook *Gt Man* 82 9418
Caldercruix *N Lans* 116 8167
Caldermill *S Lans* 107 6641
Caldermore *Gt Man* 81 9316
Calderwood *S Lans* 116 6555
Caldicot *Mons* 34 4888
Caldwell *N York* 89 1613
Caldy *Mersyd* 78 2285
Caledfwlch *Carmth* 44 6525
Calendra *Cnwll* 3 9240
Calenick *Cnwll* 3 8243
Calford Green *Suffk* 53 7045
Calfsound *Ork* 153 5738
Calgary *Ag & B* 121 3751
Califer *Moray* 141 0857
California *Falk* 116 9076

California *Norfk* 67 5115
California Cross *Devon* 7 7053
Calke *Derbys* 62 3721
Callakille *Highld* 137 6955
Callander *Stirlg* 124 6207
Callanish *W Isls* 152 2133
Callaughton *Shrops* 59 6197
Callestick *Cnwll* 3 7750
Calligarry *Highld* 129 6203
Callington *Cnwll* 5 3669
Callow *Herefs* 46 4934
Callow End *Worcs* 47 8350
Callow Hill *Wilts* 36 0384
Callow Hill *Worcs* 60 7573
Callow Hill *Worcs* 47 0164
Callows Grave *Worcs* 46 5967
Calmore *Hants* 12 3414
Calmsden *Gloucs* 36 0508
Calne *Wilts* 35 9971
Calow *Derbys* 74 4071
Calshot *Hants* 13 4701
Calstock *Cnwll* 6 4368
Calstone Wellington *Wilts* 23 0268
Calthorpe *Norfk* 66 1831
Calthorpe Street *Norfk* 67 4025
Calthwaite *Cumb* 93 4640
Calton *N York* 88 9059
Calton *Staffs* 73 1049
Calton Green *Staffs* 73 1049
Calveley *Ches* 71 5958
Calver *Derbys* 74 2374
Calver Hill *Herefs* 46 3748
Calver Sough *Derbys* 74 2374
Calverhall *Shrops* 59 6037
Calverleigh *Devon* 9 9214
Calverley *W York* 82 2036
Calvert *Bucks* 49 6824
Calverton *Bucks* 38 7939
Calverton *Notts* 75 6149
Calvine *P & K* 132 8065
Calvo *Cumb* 92 1453
Calzeat *Border* 108 1135
Cam *Gloucs* 35 7599
Camas Luinie *Highld* 138 9428
Camas na Platform *Highld* 130 7660
Camasachoirce *Highld* 130 7561
Camasine *Highld* 130 7561
Camastianavaig *Highld* 137 5099
Camault Muir *Highld* 139 5040
Camber *E Susx* 17 9618
Camberley *Surrey* 25 8860
Camberwell *Gt Lon* 27 3276
Camblesforth *N York* 83 6425
Cambo *Nthumb* 103 0285
Cambois *Nthumb* 103 3083
Camborne *Cnwll* 2 6440
Cambourne *Cambs* 52 3159
Cambridge *Cambs* 53 4558
Cambridge *Gloucs* 35 7403
Cambridge Airport 53 4858
Cambrose *Cnwll* 2 6845
Cambus *Clacks* 116 8594
Cambus o' May *Abers* 134 4198
Cambusavie Platform *Highld* 147 7696
Cambusbarron *Stirlg* 116 7792
Cambuskenneth *Stirlg* 116 8094
Cambuslang *S Lans* 116 6460
Cambuswallace *S Lans* 108 0438
Camden Town *Gt Lon* 27 2883
Cameley *Somset* 21 6157
Camelford *Cnwll* 4 1083
Camelon *Falk* 116 8680
Camer's Green *Worcs* 47 7735
Camerory *Highld* 141 0131
Camerton *Cumb* 92 0330
Camerton *Somset* 22 6857
Camghouran *P & K* 124 5556
Camieston *Border* 110 5730
Cammachmore *Abers* 135 9195
Cammeringham *Lincs* 76 9402
Camore *Highld* 147 7889
Campbeltown *Ag & B* 105 7120
Camperdown *T & W* 103 2772
Cample *D & G* 100 8993
Campmuir *Angus* 126 2137
Camps *W Loth* 117 0968
Camps End *Cambs* 53 6142
Campsall *S York* 83 5413
Campsea Ash *Suffk* 55 3356
Campton *Beds* 38 1238
Camptown *Border* 110 6813
Camrose *Cnwll* 30 9220
Camserney *P & K* 125 8149
Camusnagaul *Highld* 145 0689
Camusnagaul *Highld* 130 0874
Camusteel *Highld* 137 7042
Camusterrach *Highld* 137 7141
Canada *Hants* 12 2818
Canal Foot *Cumb* 86 3177
Canaston Bridge *Pembks* 30 0615
Candacraig *Abers* 134 3499
Candle Street *Suffk* 54 0374
Candlesby *Lincs* 77 4567
Candover Green *Shrops* 59 5005
Candyburn *Border* 108 0741
Cane End *Oxon* 37 6779
Canewdon *Essex* 40 9094
Canford Bottom *Dorset* 12 0300
Canford Cliffs *Dorset* 12 0589
Canford Heath *Dorset* 12 0293
Canford Magna *Dorset* 12 0398
Canhams Green *Suffk* 54 0565
Canisbay *Highld* 151 3472
Canklow *S York* 74 4291
Canley *W Mids* 61 3077
Cann *Dorset* 22 8721
Cannich *Highld* 139 3331
Canning Town *Gt Lon* 27 4081
Cannington *Somset* 20 2539
Cannock *Staffs* 60 9810
Cannock Wood *Staffs* 61 0412
Cannon Bridge *Herefs* 46 4340
Canon Frome *Herefs* 47 6443
Canon Pyon *Herefs* 46 4548
Canonbie *D & G* 101 3976
Canons Ashby *Nhants* 49 5750
Canonstown *Cnwll* 2 5335
Canterbury *Kent* 29 1457

Canterbury Cathedral 29 14
Cantley *Norfk* 67 37
Cantley *S York* 83 62
Cantlop *Shrops* 59 52
Canton *Cardif* 33 16
Cantraywood *Highld* 140 78
Cantsfield *Lancs* 87 62
Canvey Island *Essex* 40 75
Canwick *Lincs* 76 98
Canworthy Water *Cnwll* 5 22
Caol *Highld* 130 11
Caolas Scalpaigh *W Isls* 152 21
Caoles *Ag & B* 120 08
Caonich *Highld* 130 06
Capel *Kent* 16 63
Capel *Surrey* 15 17
Capel Bangor *Cerdgn* 43 65
Capel Betws Lleucu *Cerdgn* 44 60
Capel Coch *IOA* 68 46
Capel Curig *Conwy* 69 72
Capel Cynon *Cerdgn* 42 38
Capel Dewi *Carmth* 32 47
Capel Dewi *Cerdgn* 31 45
Capel Garmon *Conwy* 69 81
Capel Green *Suffk* 55 36
Capel Gwyn *Carmth* 32 46
Capel Gwyn *IOA* 68 34
Capel Gwynfe *Carmth* 32 72
Capel Hendre *Carmth* 32 59
Capel Isaac *Carmth* 44 59
Capel Iwan *Carmth* 31 29
Capel le Ferne *Kent* 29 25
Capel Llanilltern *Cardif* 33 09
Capel Mawr *IOA* 68 41
Capel Seion *Cerdgn* 43 63
Capel St Andrew *Suffk* 55 37
Capel St Mary *Suffk* 54 08
Capel Trisant *Cerdgn* 43 71
Capel-Dewi *Cerdgn* 43 62
Capel-y-ffin *Powys* 46 25
Capel-y-graig *Gwynd* 69 54
Capelles *Guern* 158 00
Capeluchaf *Gwynd* 68 43
Capelulo *Conwy* 69 74
Capenhurst *Ches* 71 36
Capernwray *Lancs* 87 53
Capheaton *Nthumb* 103 03
Caplaw *E Rens* 115 44
Capon's Green *Suffk* 55 28
Cappercleuch *Border* 109 24
Capstone *Kent* 28 78
Capton *Devon* 7 83
Capton *Somset* 20 08
Caputh *P & K* 125 08
Car Colston *Notts* 63 71
Caradon Town *Cnwll* 5 29
Carbeth Inn *Stirlg* 115 52
Carbis *Cnwll* 4 00
Carbis Bay *Cnwll* 2 52
Carbost *Highld* 136 37
Carbost *Highld* 136 42
Carbrook *S York* 74 38
Carbrooke *Norfk* 66 94
Carburton *Notts* 75 61
Carclaze *Cnwll* 3 02
Carclew *Cnwll* 3 78
Carcroft *S York* 83 54
Cardenden *Fife* 117 21
Cardeston *Shrops* 59 39
Cardewlees *Cumb* 93 35
Cardhu *Moray* 141 19
Cardiff *Cardif* 33 18
Cardiff Airport 20 07
Cardigan *Cerdgn* 42 17
Cardinal's Green *Cambs* 53 64
Cardington *Beds* 38 08
Cardington *Shrops* 59 50
Cardinham *Cnwll* 4 12
Cardrain *D & G* 98 12
Cardrona *Border* 109 30
Cardross *Ag & B* 115 34
Cardryne *D & G* 98 11
Cardurnock *Cumb* 93 17
Careby *Lincs* 64 02
Careston *Angus* 134 52
Carew *Pembks* 30 04
Carew Cheriton *Pembks* 30 04
Carew Newton *Pembks* 30 04
Carey *Herefs* 46 57
Carfin *N Lans* 116 75
Carfraemill *Border* 118 50
Cargate Green *Norfk* 67 39
Cargen *D & G* 100 96
Cargenbridge *D & G* 100 95
Cargill *P & K* 126 15
Cargo *Cumb* 93 36
Cargreen *Cnwll* 6 43
Cargurrel *Cnwll* 3 87
Carham *Nthumb* 110 79
Carhampton *Somset* 20 04
Carharrack *Cnwll* 3 73
Carie *P & K* 124 62
Carinish *W Isls* 152 82
Carisbrooke *IOW* 13 48
Cark *Cumb* 87 36
Carkeel *Cnwll* 5 41
Carlabhagh *W Isls* 152 20
Carland Cross *Cnwll* 3 85
Carlbury *Dur* 96 21
Carlby *Lincs* 64 04
Carlcroft *Nthumb* 110 83
Carlecotes *S York* 82 17
Carleen *Cnwll* 2 61
Carlesmoor *N York* 89 20
Carleton *Cumb* 93 45
Carleton *Cumb* 94 53
Carleton *Cumb* 86 01
Carleton *Lancs* 80 33
Carleton *N York* 82 97
Carleton *W York* 83 46
Carleton Forehoe *Norfk* 66 09
Carleton Rode *Norfk* 66 10
Carleton St Peter *Norfk* 67 34
Carlidnack *Cnwll* 3 77
Carlin How *N York* 97 71
Carlincraig *Abers* 142 64
Carlincott *Somset* 22 69
Carlisle *Cumb* 93 39

rlisle Airport	101 4860	Castell Conwy	69 7669	Caulcott Beds	38 0042	Chalgrove Oxon	37 6396	Charlton Marshall Dorset	11 9004
rloggas Cnwll	4 8765	Castell-y-bwch Torfn	34 2792	Caulcott Oxon	49 5024	Chalk Kent	28 6773	Charlton Musgrove Somset	22 7229
rlops Border	117 1656	Casterton Lancs	87 6279	Cauldcots Angus	127 6547	Chalk End Essex	40 6310	Charlton on the Hill Dorset	11 8903
rloway W Isls	152 2043	Castle Cnwll	4 0958	Cauldhame Stirlg	116 6493	Chalkhouse Green Berks	37 7178	Charlton-all-Saints Wilts	23 1723
rlton Beds	51 9555	Castle Acre Norfk	66 8115	Cauldmill Border	109 5315	Chalkway Somset	10 3707	Charlton-on-Otmoor Oxon	37 5616
rlton Cambs	53 6452	Castle Ashby Nhants	51 8659	Cauldon Staffs	73 0749	Chalkwell Kent	28 8963	Charlwood Hants	24 6731
rlton Dur	96 3921	Castle Bolton N York	88 0391	Cauldon Lowe Staffs	73 0747	Challaborough Devon	7 6544	Charlwood Surrey	15 2441
rlton Leics	62 3904	Castle Bromwich W Mids	61 1489	Cauldwell Derbys	73 2517	Challacombe Devon	19 6640	Charminster Dorset	11 6792
rlton N York	88 0684	Castle Bytham Lincs	63 9818	Caulkerbush D & G	92 9257	Challoch D & G	99 3867	Charmouth Dorset	10 3693
rlton N York	90 6086	Castle Caereinion Powys	58 1605	Caulside D & G	101 4480	Challock Kent	28 0050	Charndon Bucks	49 6724
rlton N York	83 6423	Castle Camps Cambs	53 6242	Caundle Marsh Dorset	11 6713	Chalmington Dorset	10 5900	Charney Bassett Oxon	36 3804
rlton Notts	62 6041	Castle Carrock Cumb	94 5455	Caunsall Worcs	60 8581	Chalton Beds	38 0326	Charnock Green Lancs	81 5516
rlton S York	83 3610	Castle Cary Somset	21 6432	Caunton Notts	75 7460	Chalton Beds	52 1450	Charnock Richard Lancs	81 5515
rlton Suffk	55 3764	Castle Combe Wilts	35 8477	Causeway Hants	13 7422	Chalton Hants	13 7315	Charsfield Suffk	55 2556
rlton W York	83 3327	Castle Donington Leics	62 4427	Causeway End Cumb	87 4885	Chalvey Berks	26 9679	Chart Corner Kent	28 7950
rlton Colville Suffk	55 5189	Castle Douglas D & G	99 7662	Causeway End D & G	99 4260	Chalvington E Susx	16 5109	Chart Hill Kent	28 7949
rlton Curlieu Leics	50 6997	Castle Eaton Wilts	36 1496	Causeway End Essex	40 6819	Chambers Green Kent	28 9243	Chart Sutton Kent	28 8049
rlton Green Cambs	53 6451	Castle Eden Dur	96 4238	Causewayend S Lans	108 0336	Chandler's Cross Herts	26 0698	Charter Alley Hants	24 5958
rlton Husthwaite N York	90 4976	Castle End Cambs	64 1208	Causewayhead Cumb	92 1253	Chandler's Ford Hants	13 4319	Charterhall Border	110 7647
rlton in Lindrick Notts	75 5883	Castle Frome Herefs	47 6645	Causewayhead Stirlg	116 8095	Chandlers Cross Worcs	47 7758	Charterhouse Somset	21 4965
rlton Miniott N York	89 3991	Castle Gate Cnwll	2 4934	Causey Park Nthumb	103 1794	Channel's End Beds	51 1056	Chartershall Stirlg	116 7990
rlton Scroop Lincs	63 9445	Castle Green Cumb	87 5392	Causey Park Bridge Nthumb	103 1804	Chantry Somset	22 7146	Charterville Allotments Oxon	36 3110
rlton-in-Cleveland N York	90 5004	Castle Green Surrey	25 9761	Causeyend Abers	143 9419	Chantry Suffk	54 1443	Chartham Kent	29 1054
rlton-le-Moorland Lincs	76 9058	Castle Gresley Derbys	73 2717	Cavendish Suffk	54 8046	Chapel Cumb	93 2231	Chartham Hatch Kent	29 1056
rlton-on-Trent Notts	75 7963	Castle Hedingham Essex	53 7835	Cavenham Suffk	53 7670	Chapel Fife	117 2593	Chartridge Bucks	38 9303
rluddon Cnwll	3 0255	Castle Hill Kent	28 6942	Caversfield Oxon	49 5825	Chapel Allerton Somset	21 4050	Chartway Street Kent	28 8350
rluke S Lans	116 8450	Castle Hill N York	54 1446	Caversham Berks	24 7274	Chapel Allerton W York	82 3037	Charwelton Nhants	49 5356
rlyon Bay Cnwll	3 0552	Castle Kennedy D & G	98 1159	Caverswall Staffs	72 9542	Chapel Amble Cnwll	4 9975	Chase Terrace Staffs	61 0309
rmacoup S Lans	107 7927	Castle Lachlan Ag & B	114 0195	Caverton Mill Border	110 7425	Chapel Brampton Nhants	50 7266	Chasetown Staffs	61 0408
rmarthen Carmth	31 4120	Castle Morris Pembks	30 9031	Cavil E R Yk	84 7730	Chapel Chorlton Staffs	72 8137	Chastleton Oxon	48 2429
rmel Carmth	32 5816	Castle O'er D & G	101 2492	Cawdor Highld	140 8450	Chapel Cross E Susx	16 6120	Chasty Devon	18 3402
rmel Flints	70 1676	Castle Pulverbatch Shrops	59 4202	Cawkwell Lincs	77 2879	Chapel End Beds	38 0512	Chatburn Lancs	81 7614
rmel Gwynd	68 4954	Castle Rising Norfk	65 6624	Cawood N York	83 5737	Chapel End Beds	51 1058	Chatcull Staffs	72 7934
rmichael S Lans	108 9238	Castle Street W York	82 9524	Cawsand Cnwll	6 4350	Chapel End Cambs	52 1282	Chatham Caerph	33 2188
rminowe Cnwll	2 6623	Castle Stuart Highld	140 7449	Cawston Norfk	66 1323	Chapel End Warwks	61 3393	Chatham Kent	28 7567
rmunnock C Glas	115 5957	Castlebay W Isls	152 6608	Cawston Warwks	50 4773	Chapel Field Gt Man	79 7906	Chatham Green Essex	40 7115
rmyle C Glas	116 6462	Castlebythe Pembks	30 0229	Cawthorn N York	90 7788	Chapel Green Warwks	61 2785	Chathill Nthumb	111 1827
rmyllie Angus	127 5442	Castlecary Falk	116 7878	Cawthorne S York	82 2808	Chapel Green Warwks	49 4660	Chatley Worcs	47 8561
rn Brea Cnwll	2 6841	Castleford W York	83 4225	Cawton N York	90 6476	Chapel Haddlesey N York	83 5826	Chatsworth House	74 2570
rn-gorm Highld	138 9520	Castlehill Border	109 2135	Caxton Cambs	52 3058	Chapel Hill Abers	143 0635	Chattenden Kent	28 7572
rnaby E R Yk	91 1465	Castlehill Highld	151 1968	Caxton End Cambs	52 3157	Chapel Hill Lincs	76 2054	Chatter End Essex	39 4725
rnbee Fife	127 5206	Castlehill W Duns	115 3875	Caxton Gibbet Cambs	52 2960	Chapel Hill Mons	34 5399	Chatteris Cambs	52 3995
rnbo P & K	125 0503	Castlemartin Pembks	30 9198	Caynham Shrops	46 5573	Chapel Hill N York	83 3446	Chatterton Lancs	81 7918
rnbrogie Abers	143 8527	Castlemilk C Glas	115 5958	Caythorpe Lincs	76 9348	Chapel Lawn Shrops	46 3176	Chattisham Suffk	54 0942
rndu Highld	138 8827	Castlemorton Worcs	47 7937	Caythorpe Notts	63 6845	Chapel le Dale N York	88 7377	Chatto Border	110 7717
rnduff S Lans	116 6646	Castlerigg	93 2823	Cayton N York	91 0583	Chapel Leigh Somset	20 1229	Chatton Nthumb	111 0528
rne Cnwll	3 7724	Castleside Dur	95 0748	Ceann a Bhaigh W Isls	152 7468	Chapel Milton Derbys	74 0581	Chaul End Beds	38 0521
rne Cnwll	3 9138	Castlethorpe Bucks	38 8044	Ceannacroc Lodge Highld	131 2211	Chapel of Garioch Abers	142 7124	Chawleigh Devon	19 7112
rne Cnwll	4 9558	Castlethorpe Lincs	84 9807	Cearsiadar W Isls	152 3320	Chapel Rossan D & G	98 1044	Chawley Oxon	37 4604
rnell E Ayrs	107 4731	Castleton Border	101 5109	Ceciliford Mons	34 5003	Chapel Row E Susx	24 5769	Chawston Beds	52 1556
rnewas Cnwll	4 8569	Castleton Derbys	74 1582	Cefn Newpt	34 2788	Chapel Row Berks	24 5524	Chawton Hants	24 7037
rnforth Lancs	87 4970	Castleton Gt Man	79 8810	Cefn Berain Conwy	70 9909	Chapel Row E Susx	40 7900	Chaxhill Gloucs	35 7414
rnhedryn Pembks	30 8027	Castleton N York	90 6807	Cefn Byrle Powys	33 8311	Chapel St Leonards Lincs	77 5672	Chazey Heath Oxon	37 6977
rnhell Green Cnwll	2 6137	Castleton Newpt	34 2523	Cefn Canel Powys	58 2331	Chapel Stile Cumb	86 3205	Cheadle Gt Man	79 8688
rnie Abers	135 8005	Castletown Dorset	11 6874	Cefn Coch Powys	58 1026	Chapel Town Cnwll	3 8855	Cheadle Staffs	73 0043
rnkie Cnwll	2 7134	Castletown Highld	151 1967	Cefn Cribwr Brdgnd	33 8582	Chapel-en-le-Frith Derbys	74 0580	Cheadle Heath Gt Man	79 8688
rnkiet Cnwll	3 7852	Castletown IOM	158 2667	Cefn Cross Brdgnd	33 8682	Chapelbridge Cambs	64 2993	Cheadle Hulme Gt Man	79 8786
rno Powys	58 9696	Castletown T & W	96 3658	Cefn Mably Caerph	34 2283	Chapelend Way Essex	53 7039	Cheam Gt Lon	26 2463
rnoch Highld	130 8696	Castley N York	82 2646	Cefn-brith Conwy	70 9350	Chapelgate Lincs	65 4124	Cheapside Berks	25 9469
rnock Fife	117 0489	Castor Norfk	66 9597	Cefn-bryn-brain Carmth	32 7413	Chapelhall N Lans	116 7862	Chearsley Bucks	37 7110
rnon Downs Cnwll	3 7940	Castor Cambs	64 1298	Cefn-coed-y-cymmer Myr Td	33 0318	Chapelhope Border	109 2318	Chebsey Staffs	72 8528
rnousie Abers	142 6650	Caswell Bay Swans	32 5907	Cefn-ddwysarn Gwynd	70 9638	Chapelknowe D & G	101 3173	Checkendon Oxon	37 6683
rnoustie Angus	127 5534	Cat and Fiddle Ches	79 0072	Cefn-Einion Shrops	58 2886	Chapels Cumb	86 2383	Checkley Ches	72 7346
rnwath S Lans	117 9846	Cat's Ash Newpt	34 3790	Cefn-mawr Wrexhm	70 2842	Chapelton Angus	127 6247	Checkley Staffs	73 0237
rnyorth Cnwll	2 3733	Catacol N Ayrs	105 9149	Cefn-y-bedd Wrexhm	71 3156	Chapelton Devon	19 5726	Checkley Green Ches	72 7245
rol Green W Mids	61 2577	Catbrook Mons	34 5102	Cefn-y-pant Carmth	31 1925	Chapelton S Lans	116 6848	Chedburgh Suffk	53 7967
rpalla Cnwll	3 9654	Catch Flints	70 2070	Cefneithin Carmth	32 5513	Chapeltown Lancs	81 7315	Cheddar Somset	21 4553
rperby N York	88 0089	Catchall Cnwll	2 4228	Cefngorwydd Powys	45 9045	Chapeltown Moray	141 2320	Cheddington Bucks	38 9217
rr Gt Man	81 7816	Catchem's Corner W Mids	61 2576	Cefnpennar Rhondd	33 0300	Chapeltown S York	74 3596	Cheddleton Staffs	72 9752
rr S York	75 5090	Catchgate Dur	96 1652	Ceint IOA	68 4875	Chapmans Well Devon	5 3593	Cheddleton Heath Staffs	72 9853
rr Gate W York	82 3123	Catcliffe S York	74 4288	Cellan Cerdgn	44 6149	Chapmanslade Wilts	22 8247	Cheddon Fitzpaine Somset	20 2427
rr Shield Nthumb	95 8047	Catcomb Wilts	35 0076	Cellardyke Fife	127 5704	Chapmore End Herts	39 3216	Chedglow Wilts	35 9493
rr Vale Derbys	75 4669	Catcott Somset	21 3939	Cellarhead Staffs	72 9547	Chappel Essex	40 8928	Chedgrave Norfk	67 3699
rradale Ag & B	105 8138	Catcott Burtle Somset	21 4043	Celleron Cumb	94 4925	Charaton Cnwll	5 3009	Chedington Dorset	10 4805
rrbridge Highld	140 9022	Catel Guern	158 0000	Celynen Caerph	33 2195	Chard Somset	10 3208	Chediston Suffk	55 3577
rrbrook Gt Man	79 9800	Caterham Surrey	27 3455	Cemaes IOA	68 3793	Chard Junction Somset	10 3404	Chediston Green Suffk	55 3578
rrefour Jersey	158 0000	Catfield Norfk	67 3821	Cemmaes Powys	57 8406	Chardleigh Green Somset	10 3110	Chedworth Gloucs	36 0512
rreglefn IOA	68 3889	Catfield Common Norfk	67 4021	Cemmaes Road Powys	57 8104	Chardstock Devon	10 3004	Chedzoy Somset	21 3437
rrhouse Lincs	84 7706	Catford Gt Lon	27 3773	Cenarth Cerdgn	31 2641	Charfield Gloucs	35 7292	Cheesden Gt Man	81 8216
rrick Ag & B	114 9006	Catforth Lancs	80 4735	Cerbyd Pembks	30 8227	Chargrove Gloucs	35 9219	Cheeseman's Green Kent	28 0338
rrick Castle Ag & B	114 1904	Cathcart C Glas	115 5860	Ceres Fife	126 4011	Charing Kent	28 9549	Cheetham Hill Gt Man	79 8401
rriden Falk	117 0181	Cathedine Powys	45 1425	Cerne Abbas Dorset	11 6601	Charing Heath Kent	28 9249	Cheetwood Gt Man	79 8399
rrington Gt Man	79 7492	Catherine Slack W York	82 0928	Cerney Wick Gloucs	36 0796	Charing Hill Kent	28 9560	Cheldon Devon	19 7313
rrington Lincs	77 3155	Catherine-de-Barnes W Mids	61 1780	Cerrigceinwen IOA	68 4274	Charingworth Gloucs	48 1939	Chelford Ches	79 8174
rrington Mdloth	117 3160	Catherington Hants	13 6914	Cerrigydrudion Conwy	70 9548	Charlbury Oxon	36 3519	Chellaston Derbys	62 3730
rrismerry Cnwll	4 0158	Catherston Leweston Dorset	10 3694	Cess Norfk	67 4417	Charlcombe Somset	22 7467	Chellington Beds	51 9555
rrog Conwy	69 7647	Catherton Shrops	47 6578	Ceunant Gwynd	69 5361	Charlcutt Wilts	35 9875	Chelmarsh Shrops	60 7288
rrog Denbgs	70 1043	Catisfield Hants	13 5506	Chaceley Gloucs	47 8530	Charlecote Warwks	48 2656	Chelmick Shrops	59 4791
rron Falk	116 8882	Catley Herefs	47 6844	Chacewater Cnwll	3 7544	Charles Devon	19 6832	Chelmondiston Suffk	55 2037
rron Moray	141 2241	Catley Lane Head Gt Man	81 8715	Chackmore Bucks	49 6835	Charles Tye Suffk	54 0252	Chelmorton Derbys	74 1169
rron Bridge Stirlg	116 7483	Catlodge Highld	132 6392	Chacombe Nhants	49 4944	Charleshill Surrey	25 8944	Chelmsford Essex	40 7007
rronbridge D & G	100 8698	Catlow Lancs	81 8836	Chadbury Worcs	47 0146	Charleston Angus	126 3845	Chelmsley Wood W Mids	61 1837
rronshore Falk	116 8993	Catlowdy Cumb	101 4576	Chadderton Gt Man	79 9005	Charlestown Aber C	135 9300	Chelsea Gt Lon	27 2778
rrow Hill Mons	34 4390	Catmere End Essex	39 4939	Chadderton Fold Gt Man	79 9006	Charlestown Cnwll	3 0351	Chelsfield Gt Lon	27 4864
rruth House Inver	115 3566	Catmore Berks	37 4679	Chaddesden Derbys	62 3836	Charlestown Derbys	74 0392	Chelsham Surrey	27 3758
rrutherstown D & G	100 1071	Caton Devon	7 7872	Chaddesley Corbett Worcs	60 8973	Charlestown Dorset	11 6579	Chelston Somset	20 1521
rrville Dur	96 3043	Caton Lancs	87 5364	Chaddlehanger Devon	5 4678	Charlestown Fife	117 0683	Chelsworth Suffk	54 9748
rrycoats Hall Nthumb	102 9279	Caton Green Lancs	87 5565	Chaddleworth Berks	36 4178	Charlestown Gt Man	79 8100	Cheltenham Gloucs	35 9422
rsaig Ag & B	121 5421	Cator Court Devon	8 6877	Chadlington Oxon	36 3321	Charlestown Highld	144 8174	Chelveston Nhants	51 9969
rse Gray Angus	127 4553	Catrine E Ayrs	107 5225	Chadshunt Warwks	48 3493	Charlestown Highld	140 6448	Chelvey Somset	21 4668
rseriggan D & G	98 3167	Catsfield E Susx	17 7213	Chadwell Leics	63 7824	Charlestown W York	82 9726	Chelwood Somset	21 6361
rsethorn D & G	92 9959	Catsfield Stream E Susx	17 7113	Chadwell Shrops	60 7814	Charlestown W York	82 1638	Chelwood Common E Susx	15 4128
rshalton Gt Lon	27 2764	Catsgore Somset	21 5025	Chadwell End Beds	51 0865	Charlesworth Derbys	79 0002	Chelwood Gate E Susx	15 4120
rsington Derbys	73 2553	Catsham Somset	21 5533	Chadwell Heath Gt Lon	27 4888	Charlinch Somset	20 2338	Chelworth Wilts	35 9604
rskey Ag & B	104 6508	Catshill Worcs	60 9573	Chadwell St Mary Essex	40 6478	Charlton Gt Lon	27 4178	Chelworth Lower Green Wilts	36 0892
rsluith D & G	99 4854	Catstree Shrops	60 7496	Chadwick Worcs	47 8369	Charlton Hants	23 3547	Chelworth Upper Green Wilts	36 0893
rsphairn D & G	107 5693	Cattadale Ag & B	105 6710	Chadwick End W Mids	61 2073	Charlton Herts	39 1728	Cheney Longville Shrops	59 4284
rstairs S Lans	116 9345	Cattal N York	83 4454	Chadwick Green Mersyd	78 5299	Charlton Nhants	49 5335	Chenies Bucks	26 0198
rstairs Junction S Lans	117 9545	Cattawade Suffk	41 1033	Chaffcombe Somset	10 3510	Charlton Nthumb	102 8184	Chepstow Mons	34 5393
rswell Marsh Oxon	36 3299	Catterall Lancs	80 4942	Chafford Hundred Essex	40 6079	Charlton Oxon	36 4098	Chequerbent Gt Man	79 6706
rter's Clay Hants	23 3024	Catterick N York	89 2397	Chagford Devon	8 7087	Charlton Shrops	59 5911	Chequers Corner Norfk	65 4908
rters Green Essex	39 5110	Catterick Bridge N York	89 2299	Chailey E Susx	15 3919	Charlton Somset	20 2296	Cherhill Wilts	36 0370
rterton Oxon	36 2806	Catterick Garrison N York	89 1897	Chainbridge Cambs	27 4200	Charlton Somset	21 6343	Cherington Gloucs	35 9698
rterway Heads Dur	95 0451	Catterlen Cumb	94 4833	Chainhurst Kent	28 7248	Charlton Somset	22 6652	Cherington Warwks	48 2996
rthew Cnwll	3 0056	Catterline Abers	135 8678	Chalbury Dorset	12 0206	Charlton Surrey	26 0899	Cheriton Devon	19 7346
rthorpe N York	89 3083	Catterton N York	83 5145	Chalbury Common Dorset	12 0206	Charlton W Susx	14 8812	Cheriton Hants	24 5828
rtington Nthumb	103 0204	Catteshall Surrey	25 9844	Chaldon Surrey	27 3155	Charlton Wilts	22 9002	Cheriton Kent	29 2007
rtledge Derbys	74 3276	Catthorpe Leics	50 5578	Chaldon Herring or		Charlton Wilts	35 9588	Cheriton Swans	32 4593
rtmel Cumb	87 3878	Cattishall Suffk	54 8865	East Chaldon Dorset	11 7963	Charlton Wilts	23 1156	Cheriton Bishop Devon	8 7793
rtmel Fell Cumb	87 4188	Cattishall Suffk	54 8865	Chale IOW	13 4877	Charlton Worcs	60 8371	Cheriton Fitzpaine Devon	9 8606
rway Cumb	32 4606	Catton N York	89 3678	Chale Green IOW	13 4879	Charlton Worcs	47 0015	Cheriton or	
rwinley Cumb	101 4072	Catton Norfk	67 2312	Chalfont Common Bucks	26 0092	Charlton Abbots Gloucs	48 0324	Stackpole Elidor Pembks	30 9887
ashe's Green Gloucs	35 8205	Catwick E R Yk	85 1345	Chalfont St Giles Bucks	26 9893	Charlton Adam Somset	21 5328	Cherrington Shrops	72 6619
ashmoor Dorset	11 9713	Catworth Cambs	51 0873	Chalfont St Peter Bucks	26 0090	Charlton Hill Shrops	59 5807	Cherry Burton E R Yk	84 9841
assington Oxon	37 4511	Caudle Green Gloucs	35 9410	Chalford Gloucs	35 8903	Charlton Horethorne Somset	22 6663	Cherry Hinton Cambs	53 4866
assop Colliery Dur	96 3438			Chalford Oxon	37 7200	Charlton Kings Gloucs	35 9621	Cherry Orchard Worcs	47 8553
astallack Cnwll	2 4525			Chalford Wilts	22 8650	Charlton Mackrell Somset	21 5328	Cherry Willingham Lincs	76 0272
				Chalgrave Beds	38 0127			Chertsey Surrey	26 0466

278

Cheselbourne Dorset 11 7699
Chesham Bucks 26 9601
Chesham Gt Man 81 8012
Chesham Bois Bucks 26 9699
Cheshunt Herts 27 3502
Chesley Kent 28 8563
Cheslyn Hay Staffs 60 9707
Chessetts Wood Warwks 61 1873
Chessington Surrey 26 1863
Chessington
    World of Adventure 26 1962
Chester Ches 71 4066
Chester Cathedral 71 4066
Chester Moor Dur 96 2649
Chester Zoo 71 4170
Chester-le-Street Dur 96 2751
Chesterblade Somset 22 6641
Chesterfield Derbys 74 3871
Chesterfield Staffs 61 0905
Chesterhill Mdloth 118 3764
Chesters Border 110 6022
Chesters Border 110 6210
Chesterton Cambs 64 1295
Chesterton Cambs 53 4660
Chesterton Gloucs 35 0100
Chesterton Oxon 37 5621
Chesterton Shrops 60 7897
Chesterton Staffs 72 8349
Chesterton Green Warwks 48 3558
Chesterwood Nthumb 102 8364
Chestfield Kent 29 1365
Chestnut Street Kent 28 8763
Cheston Devon 7 6858
Cheswardine Shrops 72 7130
Cheswell Shrops 72 7116
Cheswick Nthumb 111 0346
Cheswick Green W Mids 61 1376
Chetnole Dorset 10 6008
Chettiscombe Devon 9 9814
Chettisham Cambs 53 5483
Chettle Dorset 11 9513
Chetton Shrops 60 6690
Chetwode Bucks 49 6429
Chetwynd Shrops 72 7321
Chetwynd Aston Shrops 72 7517
Cheveley Cambs 53 6861
Chevening Kent 27 4857
Cheverton IOW 13 4583
Chevington Suffk 53 7859
Chevington Drift Nthumb 103 2598
Chevithorne Devon 9 9715
Chew Magna Somset 21 5763
Chew Moor Gt Man 79 6607
Chew Stoke Somset 21 5561
Chewton Keynsham Somset 21 6566
Chewton Mendip Somset 21 5953
Chichacott Devon 8 6096
Chicheley Bucks 38 9046
Chichester W Susx 14 8604
Chickerell Dorset 11 6480
Chickering Suffk 55 2176
Chicklade Wilts 22 9134
Chickward Herefs 46 2853
Chidden Hants 13 6517
Chiddingfold Surrey 14 9635
Chiddingly E Susx 16 5414
Chiddingstone Kent 16 5045
Chiddingstone Causeway Kent 16 5246
Chideock Dorset 10 4292
Chidham W Susx 14 7903
Chidswell W York 82 2623
Chieveley Berks 24 4774
Chignall Smealy Essex 40 6611
Chignall St James Essex 40 6610
Chigwell Essex 27 4494
Chigwell Row Essex 27 4693
Chilbolton Hants 23 3940
Chilcomb Hants 24 5028
Chilcombe Dorset 10 5291
Chilcompton Somset 21 6451
Chilcote Leics 61 2811
Child Okeford Dorset 11 8312
Child's Ercall Shrops 72 6625
Childer Thornton Ches 71 3677
Childrey Oxon 36 3687
Childswickham Worcs 48 0738
Childwall Mersyd 78 4189
Childwick Bury Herts 38 1410
Childwick Green Herts 38 1410
Chilfrome Dorset 10 5898
Chilgrove W Susx 14 8314
Chilham Kent 29 0853
Chilhampton Wilts 23 0933
Chilla Devon 18 4402
Chillaton Devon 5 4381
Chillenden Kent 29 2753
Chillerton IOW 13 4883
Chillesford Suffk 55 3852
Chillingham Nthumb 111 0525
Chillington Devon 7 7942
Chillington Somset 10 3811
Chilmark Wilts 22 9732
Chilmington Green Kent 28 9840
Chilson Oxon 36 3119
Chilsworthy Cnwll 5 4172
Chilsworthy Devon 18 3206
Chiltern Green Beds 38 1319
Chilthorne Domer Somset 21 5219
Chilton Bucks 37 6811
Chilton Devon 9 8604
Chilton Dur 96 2829
Chilton Kent 29 2743
Chilton Oxon 37 4885
Chilton Suffk 54 8842
Chilton Candover Hants 24 5940
Chilton Cantelo Somset 21 5722
Chilton Foliat Wilts 36 3170
Chilton Polden Somset 21 3740
Chilton Street Suffk 53 7546
Chilton Trinity Somset 20 2939
Chilwell Notts 62 5135
Chilworth Hants 13 4018
Chilworth Surrey 14 0347
Chimney Oxon 36 3501
Chineham Hants 24 6555
Chingford Gt Lon 27 3894
Chinley Derbys 74 0482
Chinnor Oxon 37 7501

Chipchase Castle Nthumb 102 8775
Chipnall Shrops 72 7231
Chippenham Cambs 53 6669
Chippenham Wilts 35 9173
Chipperfield Herts 26 0401
Chipping Herts 39 3531
Chipping Lancs 81 6243
Chipping Campden Gloucs 48 1539
Chipping Hill Essex 40 8215
Chipping Norton Oxon 48 3127
Chipping Ongar Essex 39 5503
Chipping Sodbury Gloucs 35 7282
Chipping Warden Nhants 49 4948
Chipstable Somset 20 0427
Chipstead Kent 27 5056
Chipstead Surrey 27 2756
Chirbury Shrops 58 2698
Chirk Wrexhm 71 2837
Chirnside Border 119 8766
Chirnsidebridge Border 119 8556
Chirton Wilts 23 0757
Chisbury Wilts 23 2766
Chiselborough Somset 10 4614
Chiseldon Wilts 36 1880
Chiselhampton Oxon 37 5999
Chisholme Border 109 4112
Chislehurst Gt Lon 27 4470
Chislet Kent 29 2264
Chisley W York 82 0028
Chiswell Green Herts 38 1304
Chiswick Gt Lon 26 2078
Chiswick End Cambs 52 3745
Chisworth Derbys 79 9991
Chitcombe E Susx 17 8120
Chithurst W Susx 14 8423
Chittering Cambs 53 4969
Chitterne Wilts 22 9843
Chittlehamholt Devon 19 6520
Chittlehampton Devon 19 6325
Chittlehampton Devon 19 6511
Chittoe Wilts 22 9566
Chivelstone Devon 7 7838
Chivenor Devon 19 5034
Chlenry D & G 98 1260
Chobham Surrey 25 9762
Cholderton Wilts 23 2242
Cholesbury Bucks 38 9307
Chollerford Nthumb 102 9170
Chollerton Nthumb 102 9372
Cholmondeston Ches 71 6359
Cholsey Oxon 37 5886
Cholstrey Herefs 46 4659
Chop Gate N York 90 5599
Choppington Nthumb 103 2484
Chopwell T & W 95 1158
Chorley Ches 71 5751
Chorley Lancs 81 5817
Chorley Shrops 60 6983
Chorley Staffs 61 0710
Chorleywood Herts 26 0396
Chorleywood West Herts 26 0296
Chorlton Ches 72 7250
Chorlton Lane Ches 71 4547
Chorlton-cum-Hardy Gt Man 79 8193
Choulton Shrops 59 3788
Chowley Ches 71 4756
Chrishall Essex 39 4439
Chrisswell Inver 114 2274
Christ's Hospital W Susx 15 1428
Christchurch Cambs 65 4906
Christchurch Dorset 12 1592
Christchurch Gloucs 34 5613
Christchurch Mons 34 3489
Christian Malford Wilts 35 9678
Christleton Ches 71 4465
Christmas Common Oxon 37 7193
Christon Somset 21 3757
Christon Bank Nthumb 111 2123
Christow Devon 8 8385
Chuck Hatch E Susx 16 4733
Chudleigh Devon 9 8679
Chudleigh Knighton Devon 8 8477
Chulmleigh Devon 19 6814
Chunal Derbys 74 0390
Church Lancs 81 7429
Church Aston Shrops 72 7317
Church Brampton Nhants 50 7165
Church Brough Cumb 95 7913
Church Broughton Derbys 73 2033
Church Cove Cnwll 2 7012
Church Crookham Hants 25 8051
Church Eaton Staffs 72 8417
Church End Beds 38 9832
Church End Beds 38 9921
Church End Beds 38 0334
Church End Beds 51 0558
Church End Beds 51 1058
Church End Beds 39 1937
Church End Cambs 51 0873
Church End Cambs 52 2082
Church End Cambs 52 3278
Church End Cambs 53 4857
Church End Essex 40 6223
Church End Essex 40 7228
Church End Essex 40 7316
Church End Gt Lon 26 2490
Church End Hants 24 6756
Church End Herts 38 1011
Church End Herts 39 2630
Church End Herts 39 4422
Church End Lincs 64 2234
Church End Lincs 77 4295
Church End Warwks 61 2400
Church End Warwks 61 2992
Church Enstone Oxon 48 3725
Church Fenton N York 83 5136
Church Green Devon 9 1796
Church Gresley Derbys 73 2918
Church Hanborough Oxon 36 4213
Church Hill Ches 72 6465
Church Hill Staffs 60 0011
Church Houses N York 90 6697
Church Knowle Dorset 11 9481
Church Laneham Notts 75 8176
Church Langton Leics 50 7293
Church Lawford Warwks 50 4576
Church Lawton Staffs 72 8255
Church Leigh Staffs 73 0235

Church Lench Worcs 48 0251
Church Mayfield Staffs 73 1544
Church Minshull Ches 72 6660
Church Norton W Susx 14 8795
Church Preen Shrops 59 5498
Church Pulverbatch Shrops 59 4303
Church Stowe Nhants 49 6357
Church Street Essex 53 7943
Church Street Kent 28 7174
Church Street Suffk 55 4883
Church Stretton Shrops 59 4593
Church Town Lincs 84 7806
Church Village Rhondd 33 0885
Church Warsop Notts 75 5668
Church Wilne Derbys 62 4431
Churcham Gloucs 35 7618
Churchbridge Staffs 60 9808
Churchdown Gloucs 35 8819
Churchend Essex 41 0093
Churchfield W Mids 60 0192
Churchgate Herts 27 3402
Churchgate Street Essex 39 4811
Churchill Devon 19 5940
Churchill Devon 10 2902
Churchill Oxon 48 2824
Churchill Somset 21 4459
Churchill Worcs 60 8879
Churchill Worcs 47 9253
Churchinford Somset 9 2112
Churchover Warwks 50 5180
Churchstanton Somset 9 1914
Churchstoke Powys 58 2794
Churchtown Cnwll 7 7145
Churchthorpe Lincs 77 3297
Churchtown Derbys 74 2662
Churchtown Devon 19 6744
Churchtown Lancs 80 3240
Churchtown Lancs 80 4843
Churchtown Mersyd 80 3618
Churnsike Lodge Nthumb 102 6617
Churston Ferrers Devon 7 9056
Churt Surrey 25 8538
Churton Ches 71 4156
Churwell W York 82 2729
Chwilog Gwynd 56 4338
Chyandour Cnwll 2 4731
Chyanvounder Cnwll 2 6522
Chyeowling Cnwll 3 7941
Chysauster 2 4734
Chyvarloe Cnwll 2 6523
Cil Powys 58 1701
Cilcain Flints 70 1765
Cilcennin Cerdgn 44 5260
Cilcewydd Powys 58 2204
Cilfrew Neath 32 7700
Cilfynydd Rhondd 33 0891
Cilgerran Pembks 31 1942
Cilgwyn Carmth 44 7429
Cilgwyn Gwynd 68 4953
Ciliau-Aeron Cerdgn 44 5057
Cilmaengwyn Neath 32 7405
Cilmery Powys 45 0051
Cilrhedyn Pembks 31 2834
Cilsan Carmth 32 5922
Ciltalgarth Gwynd 57 8940
Cilycwm Carmth 44 7539
Cimla Neath 32 7696
Cinder Hill W Mids 60 9294
Cinderford Gloucs 35 6514
Cippenham Berks 26 9580
Cirencester Gloucs 35 0201
Citadilla N York 89 2299
City Gt Lon 27 3231
City V Glam 33 9878
City Airport 27 4280
City Dulas IOA 68 4687
Clabhach Ag & B 120 1858
Clachaig Ag & B 114 1181
Clachan Ag & B 122 7819
Clachan Ag & B 122 8543
Clachan Ag & B 113 7556
Clachan Highld 137 5436
Clachan Mor Ag & B 120 9847
Clachan na Luib W Isls 152 8163
Clachan of Campsie E Duns 116 6079
Clachan-a-Luib W Isls 152 8163
Clachan-Seil Ag & B 122 7718
Clachaneasy D & G 98 3574
Clachnaharry Highld 140 6446
Clachtoll Highld 148 0427
Clackavoid P & K 133 1463
Clackmannan Clacks 116 9191
Clackmarras Moray 141 2458
Clacton-on-Sea Essex 41 1715
Cladich Ag & B 123 0921
Cladswell Worcs 48 0558
Claggan Highld 122 7049
Claigan Highld 136 2354
Clandown Somset 22 6855
Clanfield Hants 13 6916
Clanfield Oxon 36 2801
Clannaborough Devon 8 7402
Clanville Hants 23 3148
Clanville Somset 21 6233
Claonaig Ag & B 113 8656
Clap Hill Kent 28 0537
Clapgate Dorset 11 0102
Clapgate Herts 39 4424
Clapham Beds 38 0352
Clapham Devon 9 8987
Clapham Gt Lon 27 2975
Clapham N York 88 7469
Clapham W Susx 14 0906
Clapham Folly Beds 38 0252
Clappersgate Cumb 87 3603
Clapton Somset 10 4106
Clapton Somset 21 6453
Clapton-in-Gordano Somset 34 4774
Clapton-on-the-Hill Gloucs 36 1617
Clapworthy Devon 19 6724
Clarach Cerdgn 43 6084
Claravale T & W 103 1364
Clarbeston Pembks 30 0521
Clarbeston Road Pembks 30 0121
Clarborough Notts 75 7383
Clare Suffk 53 7745
Clarebrand D & G 99 7665
Clarencefield D & G 100 0968

Clareton N York 89 3959
Clarewood Nthumb 103 0169
Clarilaw Border 109 5218
Clark's Green Surrey 15 1739
Clarken Green Hants 24 5651
Clarkston E Rens 115 5757
Clashmore Highld 148 0331
Clashmore Highld 146 7489
Clashnessie Highld 148 0530
Clashnoir Moray 141 2222
Clathy P & K 125 9920
Clathymore P & K 125 0121
Clatt Abers 142 5326
Clatter Powys 58 9994
Clatterford End Essex 40 6113
Clatworthy Somset 20 0531
Claughton Lancs 80 5342
Claughton Lancs 87 5566
Claughton Mersyd 78 3088
Clavelshay Somset 20 2531
Claverdon Warwks 48 1965
Claverham Somset 21 4566
Clavering Essex 39 4731
Claverley Shrops 60 7993
Claverton Somset 22 7864
Claverton Down Somset 22 7763
Clawdd-coch V Glam 33 0577
Clawdd-newydd Denbgs 70 0852
Clawthorpe Cumb 87 5377
Clawton Devon 18 3599
Claxby Lincs 76 1194
Claxby Lincs 77 4571
Claxton N York 90 6959
Claxton Norfk 67 3303
Clay Common Suffk 55 4681
Clay Coton Nhants 50 5976
Clay Cross Derbys 74 3963
Clay End Herts 39 3024
Claybrooke Magna Leics 50 4988
Claydon Oxon 49 4549
Claydon Suffk 54 1349
Claygate D & G 101 3979
Claygate Kent 28 7144
Claygate Surrey 26 1563
Claygate Cross Kent 27 6155
Clayhall Gt Lon 27 4390
Clayhanger Devon 20 0222
Clayhanger W Mids 61 0404
Clayhidon Devon 9 1615
Clayhill E Susx 17 8323
Clayhill Hants 12 3006
Clayhithe Cambs 53 5064
Clayock Highld 151 1659
Claypit Hill Cambs 52 3554
Claypits Gloucs 35 7606
Claypole Lincs 76 8449
Claythorpe Lincs 77 4178
Clayton S York 83 4507
Clayton W Susx 15 2914
Clayton W York 82 1231
Clayton Green Lancs 81 5723
Clayton West W York 82 2510
Clayton-le-Moors Lancs 81 7530
Clayton-le-Woods Lancs 81 5622
Clayworth Notts 75 7387
Cleadale Highld 128 4789
Cleadon T & W 96 3862
Clearbrook Devon 6 5265
Clearwell Gloucs 34 5608
Clearwell Meend Gloucs 34 5808
Cleasby N York 89 2512
Cleat Ork 153 4584
Cleatlam Dur 95 1118
Cleator Cumb 92 0113
Cleator Moor Cumb 92 0115
Cleckheaton W York 82 1825
Clee St Margaret Shrops 59 5684
Cleedownton Shrops 59 5880
Cleehill Shrops 46 5975
Cleekhimin N Lans 116 7658
Cleestanton Shrops 46 5779
Cleethorpes Lincs 85 3008
Cleeton St Mary Shrops 46 6178
Cleeve Oxon 37 6081
Cleeve Somset 21 4666
Cleeve Hill Gloucs 47 9827
Cleeve Prior Worcs 48 0849
Cleghornie E Loth 118 5983
Clehonger Herefs 46 4437
Cleish P & K 117 0998
Cleland N Lans 116 7958
Clement Street Kent 27 5370
Clement's End Beds 38 0214
Clenamacrie Ag & B 122 9228
Clench Common Wilts 23 1765
Clenchwarton Norfk 65 5920
Clenerty Abers 142 7760
Clent Worcs 60 9279
Cleobury Mortimer Shrops 60 6675
Cleobury North Shrops 59 6286
Cleongart Ag & B 105 6734
Clephanton Highld 140 8150
Clerkhill D & G 101 2697
Cleuch-head D & G 108 8200
Clevancy Wilts 36 0575
Clevedon Somset 34 4171
Cleveley Oxon 48 3923
Cleveleys Lancs 80 3143
Clevelode Worcs 47 8347
Cleverton Wilts 35 9785
Clewer Somset 21 4451
Cley next the Sea Norfk 66 0444
Cliburn Cumb 94 5824
Cliddesden Hants 24 6349
Cliff Warwks 61 2197
Cliff End E Susx 17 8813
Cliffe Dur 96 2115
Cliffe Kent 28 7376
Cliffe Lancs 81 7333
Cliffe N York 83 6631
Cliffe Woods Kent 28 7373
Clifford Herefs 46 2445
Clifford W York 83 4344
Clifford Chambers Warwks 48 1952
Clifford's Mesne Gloucs 47 7023
Cliffsend Kent 29 3464
Clifton Beds 39 1639
Clifton Bristl 34 5773

Clifton Cumb ...... 94 5...
Clifton Derbys ...... 73 1...
Clifton Gt Man ...... 79 7...
Clifton Lancs ...... 80 4...
Clifton N York ...... 82 1...
Clifton N York ...... 83 5...
Clifton Notts ...... 62 5...
Clifton Nthumb ...... 103 20...
Clifton Oxon ...... 49 4...
Clifton S York ...... 75 5...
Clifton W York ...... 82 1...
Clifton Worcs ...... 47 8...
Clifton Campville Staffs ...... 61 25...
Clifton Dykes Cumb ...... 44 5...
Clifton Hampden Oxon ...... 37 5...
Clifton Reynes Bucks ...... 38 9...
Clifton
    Dunsmore Warwks ...... 50 5...
Clifton upon Teme Worcs ...... 47 7...
Cliftonville Kent ...... 29 3...
Climping W Susx ...... 14 9...
Clink Somset ...... 22 7...
Clint N York ...... 89 26...
Clint Green Norfk ...... 66 0...
Clinterty Aber C ...... 135 8...
Clintmains Border ...... 110 6...
Clipiau Gwynd ...... 57 8...
Clippesby Norfk ...... 67 4...
Clipsham Rutlnd ...... 63 9...
Clipston Nhants ...... 50 7...
Clipston Notts ...... 63 6...
Clipstone Beds ...... 38 9...
Clipstone Notts ...... 75 5...
Clitheroe Lancs ...... 81 74...
Clive Shrops ...... 59 5...
Clixby Lincs ...... 85 09...
Cloatley Wilts ...... 35 98...
Clocaenog Denbgs ...... 70 08...
Clochan Moray ...... 142 40...
Clochtow Angus ...... 127 48...
Clock Face Mersyd ...... 78 52...
Cloddiau Powys ...... 58 20...
Clodock Herefs ...... 46 32...
Cloford Somset ...... 22 72...
Clola Abers ...... 143 00...
Clophill Beds ...... 38 03...
Clopton Nhants ...... 51 06...
Clopton Suffk ...... 55 22...
Clopton Corner Suffk ...... 55 22...
Clopton Green Suffk ...... 53 76...
Clopton Green Suffk ...... 54 97...
Clos du Valle Guern ...... 158 0...
Closeburn D & G ...... 100 8...
Closeburnmill D & G ...... 100 8...
Closeclark IOM ...... 158 27...
Closworth Somset ...... 10 56...
Clothall Herts ...... 39 27...
Clotton Ches ...... 71 52...
Cloudesley Bush Warwks ...... 50 46...
Clough Gt Man ...... 79 94...
Clough Foot W York ...... 81 91...
Clough Head N York ...... 82 09...
Cloughton N York ...... 91 01...
Cloughton Newlands N York ...... 91 00...
Clousta Shet ...... 153 30...
Clova Angus ...... 134 32...
Clovelly Devon ...... 18 31...
Clovenfords Border ...... 109 45...
Clovulin Highld ...... 130 00...
Clow Bridge Lancs ...... 81 82...
Clowne Derbys ...... 75 48...
Clows Top Worcs ...... 60 71...
Cloy Wrexhm ...... 71 39...
Cluanie Inn Highld ...... 130 07...
Cluanie Lodge Highld ...... 130 09...
Clubworthy Cnwll ...... 5 27...
Clugston D & G ...... 98 35...
Clun Shrops ...... 59 30...
Clunas Highld ...... 140 88...
Clunbury Shrops ...... 59 37...
Clune Highld ...... 140 79...
Clunes Highld ...... 131 19...
Clungunford Shrops ...... 46 39...
Clunie Abers ...... 142 63...
Clunie P & K ...... 126 10...
Clunton Shrops ...... 59 33...
Cluny Fife ...... 117 24...
Clutton Ches ...... 71 46...
Clutton Somset ...... 21 62...
Clutton Hill Somset ...... 21 63...
Clwt-y-bont Gwynd ...... 69 57...
Clydach Mons ...... 34 22...
Clydach Swans ...... 32 68...
Clydach Vale Rhondd ...... 33 97...
Clydebank W Duns ...... 115 49...
Clydey Pembks ...... 31 25...
Clyffe Pypard Wilts ...... 36 07...
Clynder Ag & B ...... 114 24...
Clynderwen Carmth ...... 31 12...
Clyne Neath ...... 32 80...
Clynnog-fawr Gwynd ...... 68 41...
Clyro Powys ...... 45 21...
Clyst Honiton Devon ...... 9 98...
Clyst Hydon Devon ...... 9 03...
Clyst St George Devon ...... 9 98...
Clyst St Lawrence Devon ...... 9 02...
Clyst St Mary Devon ...... 9 97...
Cnoc W Isls ...... 152 49...
Cnwch Coch Cerdgn ...... 43 67...
Coad's Green Cnwll ...... 5 29...
Coal Aston Derbys ...... 74 36...
Coal Pool W Mids ...... 60 01...
Coal Street Suffk ...... 55 23...
Coalbrookdale Shrops ...... 60 66...
Coalbrookvale Blae G ...... 33 19...
Coalburn S Lans ...... 108 81...
Coalburns T & W ...... 96 15...
Coalcleugh Nthumb ...... 95 80...
Coaley Gloucs ...... 35 77...
Coalfell Cumb ...... 94 59...
Coalhill Essex ...... 40 75...
Coalmoor Shrops ...... 60 66...
Coalpit Heath Gloucs ...... 35 67...
Coalpit Hill Staffs ...... 72 82...
Coalport Shrops ...... 60 69...
Coalsnaughton Clacks ...... 116 91...
Coaltown of Balgonie Fife ...... 117 29...
Coaltown of Wemyss Fife ...... 118 32...

oalville Leics 62 4214
anwood Nthumb 94 6859
at Somset 21 4520
atbridge N Lans 116 7385
atdyke N Lans 116 7465
ate Wilts 23 0462
ate Wilts 36 1882
ates Cambs 64 3097
ates Gloucs 35 9701
ates Lincs 75 8181
ates Lincs 76 9083
ates W Susx 14 9917
atham N York 97 5925
atham Mundeville Dur 96 2820
bbaton Devon 19 6126
berley Gloucs 35 9616
bhall Common Herefs 46 4535
bham Kent 28 6768
bham Surrey 26 1060
blers Green Essex 40 6819
bnash Herefs 46 4560
bo Guern 158 0000
bridge Staffs 72 8747
burby Abers 143 9164
ck & End Suffk 53 7253
ck Alley Derbys 74 4170
ck Bank Wrexhm 71 3545
ck Bevington Warwks 48 0552
ck Bridge Abers 133 2509
ck Clarks Essex 40 8102
ck Green Essex 40 6919
ck Marling E Susx 17 8718
ck Street Kent 28 7850
ckayne N York 90 6198
ckayne Hatley Beds 52 2649
ckburnspath Border 119 7770
ckenzie and
Port Seton E Loth 118 4075
cker Bar Lancs 80 5022
cker Brook Lancs 81 7425
ckerham Lancs 80 4651
ckermouth Cumb 92 1230
ckernhoe Green Herts 38 1223
ckersdale W York 82 2329
ckett Swans 32 6394
ckfield Dur 96 1224
ckfield Suffk 54 9054
ckfosters Gt Lon 27 2796
cking N York 14 8717
cking Causeway W Susx 14 8819
ckington Devon 7 8963
cklake Somset 21 4449
ckle Park Nthumb 103 2091
ckley Beck Cumb 86 2501
ckley Cley Norfk 66 7904
ckpole Green Berks 37 7981
cks Cnwll 3 7652
ckshutford Shrops 59 5885
ckshutt Shrops 59 4328
ckthorpe Norfk 66 9842
ckwells Cnwll 2 5234
ckwood Devon 9 9780
ckwood Somset 20 2242
ckyard Derbys 74 0479
ckyard Herefs 46 4133
ddenham Suffk 54 1354
ddington Ches 71 4555
ddington Herefs 47 7142
ddington Notts 76 8354
ddford St Mary Wilts 22 9739
ddford St Peter Wilts 22 9639
adicote Herts 39 2118
admore Hill W Susx 14 0520
adnor Derbys 74 4149
adrington Gloucs 35 7278
adsall Staffs 60 8603
adsall Wood Staffs 60 8404
aed Morgan Mons 34 3511
aed Talon Flints 70 2659
aed Ystumgwern Gwynd 57 5824
aed-y-Bryn Cerdgn 42 3545
aed-y-caerau Newpt 34 3491
aed-y-paen Mons 34 3398
aed-yr-ynys Powys 33 1520
aedana IOA 68 4382
aedely Rhondd 33 0285
aedkernew Newpt 34 2783
aedpoeth Wrexhm 70 2851
aedway Powys 59 3315
aelbren Powys 33 8511
affinswell Devon 7 8968
affle End Beds 51 0159
afton Devon 9 9680
afton Hackett Worcs 60 0075
agan V Glam 33 1771
agenhoe Nhants 51 8260
agges Oxon 36 3609
aggeshall Essex 40 8522
aggin's Mill E Susx 16 5927
aignafearn Highld 140 7018
ailacriech Abers 134 3296
ailantogle Stirlg 124 5907
aillore Highld 136 3537
ailtry Highld 131 3506
aity Brdgnd 33 9281
al W Isls 152 4739
alaboll Highld 146 5610
alan Cnwll 4 8661
alaton Raleigh Devon 9 0787
albost Highld 136 2148
alburn N York 89 1999
albury Hants 12 3410
alby Cumb 94 6620
alby IOM 158 2370
alby Norfk 67 2231
alchester Essex 41 9925
old Ash Berks 24 5169
old Ashby Nhants 50 6576
old Ashton Gloucs 35 7572
old Aston Gloucs 36 1219
old Blow Pembks 31 1212
old Brayfield Bucks 38 9252
old Cotes N York 88 7171
old Greens Herefs 47 6842
old Hanworth Lincs 76 0383
old Harbour Herts 38 1415
old Harbour Oxon 37 6379

Cold Harbour Wilts 22 8645
Cold Hatton Shrops 59 6221
Cold Hatton Heath Shrops 59 6321
Cold Hesleden Dur 96 4146
Cold Hiendley W York 83 3714
Cold Higham Nhants 49 6653
Cold Kirby N York 90 5384
Cold Newton Leics 63 7106
Cold Northcott Cnwll 5 2086
Cold Norton Essex 40 8500
Cold Overton Leics 63 8010
Cold Weston Shrops 59 5583
Coldbackie Highld 149 6160
Coldbeck Cumb 88 7204
Coldean E Susx 15 3308
Coldeast Devon 7 8174
Colden W York 82 9628
Colden Common Hants 13 4822
Coldfair Green Suffk 55 4360
Coldham Cambs 65 4303
Coldharbour Cnwll 3 7548
Coldharbour Devon 9 0612
Coldharbour Gloucs 34 5503
Coldharbour Surrey 15 1443
Coldingham Border 119 9065
Coldmeece Staffs 72 8532
Coldred Kent 29 2747
Coldridge Devon 8 6907
Coldstream Border 110 8439
Coldwaltham W Susx 14 0216
Coldwell Herefs 46 4235
Coldwells Abers 143 9538
Cole Somset 22 6733
Cole End Warwks 61 2089
Cole Green Herts 39 2811
Cole Green Herts 39 4330
Cole Henley Hants 24 4651
Cole's Cross Devon 7 7746
Colebatch Shrops 59 3287
Colebrook Devon 9 0006
Colebrook Devon 6 5457
Colebrooke Devon 8 7699
Coleby Lincs 84 9919
Coleby Lincs 76 9760
Coleford Devon 8 7701
Coleford Gloucs 34 5710
Coleford Somset 22 6848
Coleford Water Somset 20 1133
Colegate End Norfk 55 1987
Colehill Dorset 12 0201
Coleman Green Herts 39 1812
Coleman's Hatch E Susx 16 4433
Colemere Shrops 59 4332
Colemore Hants 24 7030
Colemore Green Shrops 60 7197
Colenden P & K 126 1029
Coleorton Leics 62 4017
Colerne Wilts 35 8271
Coles Green Dorset 10 3902
Coles Green Suffk 54 1041
Colesbourne Gloucs 35 0013
Colesden Beds 52 1255
Coleshill Bucks 26 9495
Coleshill Oxon 36 2393
Coleshill Warwks 61 2089
Colestocks Devon 9 0900
Coley Somset 21 5855
Colgate W Susx 15 2332
Colinsburgh Fife 127 4703
Colinton C Edin 117 2168
Colintraive Ag & B 114 0374
Colkirk Norfk 66 9126
Collace P & K 126 2032
Collafirth Shet 153 3482
Collaton Devon 7 7139
Collaton Devon 7 7952
Collaton St Mary Devon 7 8660
College Green Somset 21 5736
College of Roseisle Moray 141 1466
College Town Berks 25 8560
Collessie Fife 126 2813
Colleton Mills Devon 19 6615
Collier Row Gt Lon 27 5091
Collier Street Kent 28 7145
Collier's End Herts 39 3720
Collier's Green Kent 17 7822
Colliers Green Kent 28 7538
Colliery Row T & W 96 3249
Collieston Abers 143 0328
Collin D & G 100 0276
Collingbourne Ducis Wilts 23 2453
Collingbourne Kingston Wilts 23 2355
Collingham Notts 76 8262
Collingham W York 83 3945
Collington Herefs 47 6460
Collingtree Nhants 49 7555
Collins Green Ches 78 5594
Collins Green Worcs 47 7457
Colliston Angus 127 6045
Colliton Devon 9 0804
Collyweston Nhants 63 9902
Colmonell S Ayrs 98 1485
Colmworth Beds 51 1058
Coln Rogers Gloucs 36 0809
Coln St Aldwyns Gloucs 36 1405
Coln St Dennis Gloucs 36 0810
Colnbrook Berks 26 0277
Colne Cambs 52 3775
Colne Lancs 81 8939
Colne Bridge W York 82 1720
Colne Edge Lancs 81 8841
Colne Engaine Essex 40 8430
Colney Norfk 66 1807
Colney Heath Herts 39 2005
Colney Street Herts 26 1502
Colpy Abers 142 6432
Colquhar Border 109 3341
Colquite Cnwll 4 0570
Colscott Devon 18 3614
Colsterdale N York 89 1381
Colsterworth Lincs 63 9324
Colston Bassett Notts 63 7033
Colt Hill Hants 24 7551
Colt's Hill Kent 16 6443
Coltfield Moray 141 1163
Coltishall Norfk 67 2719
Colton Cumb 86 3185
Colton N York 83 5444

Colton Norfk 66 1009
Colton Staffs 73 0420
Colton W York 83 3732
Columbjohn Devon 9 9699
Colva Powys 45 1952
Colvend D & G 92 8654
Colwall Herefs 47 7542
Colwall Nthumb 102 9575
Colwich Staffs 73 0121
Colwick Notts 62 6140
Colwinston V Glam 33 9375
Colworth W Susx 14 9103
Colwyn Bay Conwy 69 8578
Colyford Devon 10 2592
Colyton Devon 9 2494
Combe Berks 23 3760
Combe Devon 7 7238
Combe Devon 7 8448
Combe Herefs 46 3463
Combe Oxon 36 4116
Combe Almer Dorset 11 9597
Combe Common Surrey 14 9436
Combe Down Somset 22 7662
Combe Fishacre Devon 7 8465
Combe Florey Somset 20 1531
Combe Hay Somset 22 7359
Combe Martin Devon 19 5846
Combe Raleigh Devon 9 1502
Combe St Nicholas Somset 10 3011
Combeinteignhead Devon 7 9071
Comberbach Ches 79 6477
Comberford Staffs 61 1907
Comberton Cambs 52 3856
Comberton Herefs 46 4968
Combpyne Devon 10 2892
Combridge Staffs 73 0907
Combrook Warwks 48 3051
Combs Derbys 74 0478
Combs Suffk 54 0456
Combs Ford Suffk 54 0457
Combwich Somset 20 2542
Comers Abers 135 6707
Comhampton Worcs 47 8367
Commercial Pembks 31 1416
Commercial End Cambs 53 5563
Commins Coch Powys 57 8402
Common Edge Lancs 80 3232
Common End Cumb 92 0022
Common Moor Cnwll 5 2469
Common Platt Wilts 36 1186
Common Side Derbys 74 3375
Commondale N York 90 6610
Commonside Ches 71 5473
Commonside Derbys 73 2441
Commonwood Shrops 59 4828
Commonwood Wrexhm 71 3753
Compass Somset 20 2934
Compstall Gt Man 79 9690
Compstonend D & G 99 6652
Compton Berks 37 5280
Compton Devon 7 8664
Compton Hants 23 3529
Compton Hants 13 4625
Compton Staffs 60 8284
Compton Surrey 25 9546
Compton W Susx 14 7714
Compton Wilts 23 1351
Compton Abbas Dorset 22 8618
Compton Abdale Gloucs 36 0516
Compton Bassett Wilts 36 0372
Compton Beauchamp Oxon 36 2786
Compton Bishop Somset 21 3955
Compton Chamberlayne Wilts 23 0229
Compton Dando Somset 21 6464
Compton Dundon Somset 21 4932
Compton Durville Somset 10 4117
Compton Greenfield Gloucs 34 5681
Compton Martin Somset 21 5447
Compton Pauncefoot Somset 21 6426
Compton Valence Dorset 10 5993
Compton Verney Warwks 48 3152
Comrie Fife 117 0289
Comrie P & K 124 7722
Conaglen House Highld 130 0268
Conchra Highld 138 8827
Concraigie P & K 125 0944
Conder Green Lancs 80 4556
Conderton Worcs 47 9637
Condicote Gloucs 48 1528
Condorrat N Lans 116 7373
Condover Shrops 59 4905
Coney Hill Gloucs 35 8517
Coney Weston Suffk 54 9578
Coneyhurst Common W Susx 14 1023
Coneysthorpe N York 90 7171
Coneythorpe W York 89 3958
Conford Hants 14 8233
Congdon's Shop Cnwll 5 2878
Congerstone Leics 62 3605
Congham Norfk 65 7123
Conghurst Kent 17 7628
Congl-y-wal Gwynd 57 7041
Congleton Ches 72 8562
Congresbury Somset 21 4363
Congreve Staffs 60 9013
Conheath D & G 100 9969
Conicavel Moray 140 9853
Coningsby Lincs 76 2257
Conington Cambs 52 1885
Conington Cambs 52 3266
Conisbrough S York 75 5098
Conisholme Lincs 77 4095
Coniston Cumb 86 3097
Coniston E R Yk 85 1535
Coniston Cold N York 81 9054
Conistone N York 88 9867
Connah's Quay Flints 71 2969
Connel Ag & B 122 9134
Connel Park E Ayrs 107 6012
Connor Downs Cnwll 2 5939
Cononley N York 82 9846
Conon Bridge Highld 139 5455
Cononley N York 82 9846
Consall Staffs 72 9848
Consett Dur 95 1051
Constable Burton N York 89 1690
Constable Lee Lancs 81 8123
Constantine Cnwll 3 7230
Constantine Bay Cnwll 4 8774

Contin Highld 139 4556
Conwy Conwy 69 7877
Conyer Kent 28 9664
Conyer's Green Suffk 54 8867
Cooden E Susx 17 7107
Cook's Green Essex 41 1818
Cookbury Devon 18 4006
Cookbury Wick Devon 18 3905
Cookham Berks 26 8985
Cookham Dean Berks 26 8685
Cookham Rise Berks 26 8885
Cookhill Warwks 48 0558
Cookley Suffk 55 3475
Cookley Worcs 60 8480
Cookley Green Oxon 37 6900
Cookney Abers 135 8693
Cooks Green Suffk 54 9753
Cooksbridge E Susx 15 4013
Cooksey Green Worcs 47 9069
Cookshill Staffs 72 9443
Cooksland Cnwll 4 0867
Cooksmill Green Essex 40 6306
Cookson Green Ches 71 5774
Cookson's Green Dur 96 2933
Coolham W Susx 14 1122
Cooling Kent 28 7575
Cooling Street Kent 28 7474
Coombe Cnwll 2 6242
Coombe Cnwll 3 8340
Coombe Devon 8 8384
Coombe Devon 7 9373
Coombe Devon 9 1091
Coombe Gloucs 35 7694
Coombe Hants 13 6620
Coombe Wilts 23 1450
Coombe Bissett Wilts 23 1026
Coombe Cellars Devon 7 9072
Coombe Cross Hants 13 6620
Coombe End Somset 20 0329
Coombe Hill Gloucs 47 8826
Coombe Keynes Dorset 11 8484
Coombe Pafford Devon 7 9166
Coombe Street Somset 22 7631
Coombes W Susx 15 1808
Coombes-Moor Herefs 46 3663
Coombeswood W Mids 60 9785
Cooper Street Kent 29 3060
Cooper Turning Gt Man 79 6308
Cooper's Corner Kent 16 4849
Cooperhill Moray 141 9953
Coopers Green E Susx 16 4723
Coopers Green Herts 39 1909
Coopersale Common Essex 27 4702
Coopersale Street Essex 27 4701
Cootham W Susx 14 0714
Cop Street Kent 29 3060
Copdock Suffk 54 1242
Copford Green Essex 40 9222
Copgrove N York 89 3463
Copister Shet 153 4879
Cople Beds 38 1048
Copley Dur 95 0825
Copley Gt Man 79 9798
Copley W York 82 0822
Coplow Dale Derbys 74 1679
Copmanthorpe N York 83 5646
Copmere End Staffs 72 8029
Copp Lancs 80 4239
Coppathorne Cnwll 18 2000
Coppenhall Staffs 72 9019
Coppenhall Moss Ches 72 7058
Copperhouse Cnwll 2 5637
Coppicegate Shrops 60 7379
Coppingford Cambs 52 1679
Coppins Corner Kent 28 9448
Copplestone Devon 8 7702
Coppull Lancs 81 5614
Coppull Moor Lancs 81 5512
Copsale W Susx 15 1724
Copster Green Lancs 81 6733
Copston Magna Warwks 50 4588
Copt Heath W Mids 61 1777
Copt Hewick N York 89 3471
Copt Oak Leics 62 4812
Copthall Green Essex 27 4201
Copthorne Cnwll 5 2692
Copthorne W Susx 15 3139
Copy's Green Norfk 66 9439
Copythorne Hants 12 3014
Coram Street Suffk 54 0042
Corbets Tey Gt Lon 27 5685
Corbiere Jersey 158 0000
Corbridge Nthumb 103 9964
Corby Nhants 51 8988
Corby Glen Lincs 63 0024
Corby Hill Cumb 94 4857
Cordon N Ayrs 105 0230
Cordwell Derbys 74 3176
Coreley Shrops 46 6173
Cores End Bucks 26 9087
Corfe Somset 20 2319
Corfe Castle Dorset 11 9681
Corfe Mullen Dorset 11 9886
Corfton Shrops 59 4985
Corgarff Abers 133 2708
Corhampton Hants 13 6120
Corks Pond Kent 28 6540
Corley Warwks 61 3085
Corley Ash Warwks 61 2986
Corley Moor Warwks 61 2884
Cormuir Angus 134 3066
Cornard Tye Suffk 54 9041
Corndon Devon 8 6955
Corner Row Lancs 80 4134
Corney Cumb 86 1191
Cornforth Dur 96 3134
Cornhill Abers 142 5858
Cornhill-on-Tweed Nthumb 110 8639
Cornholme W York 81 9126
Cornish Hall End Essex 53 6836
Cornoigmore Ag & B 120 9846
Cornriggs Dur 95 8411
Cornsay Dur 96 1443
Cornsay Colliery Dur 96 1663
Corntown Highld 139 5556
Corntown V Glam 33 9177
Cornwell Oxon 48 2720
Cornwood Devon 6 6059

Cornworthy Devon 7 8255
Corpach Highld 130 0976
Corpusty Norfk 66 1129
Corrachree Abers 134 4604
Corran Cnwll 3 9946
Corran Highld 130 8409
Corran Highld 130 0263
Corrany IOM 158 4689
Corrie D & G 101 2086
Corrie N Ayrs 105 0242
Corriecravie N Ayrs 105 9223
Corriegills N Ayrs 105 0335
Corriegour Lodge Hotel Highld 131 2692
Corriemoille Highld 139 3663
Corrimony Highld 139 3730
Corringham Essex 40 7083
Corringham Lincs 76 8691
Corris Gwynd 57 7508
Corris Uchaf Gwynd 57 7408
Corrow Ag & B 114 1800
Corry Highld 137 6424
Cors-y-Gedol Gwynd 57 6022
Corscombe Devon 8 6296
Corscombe Dorset 10 5105
Corse Gloucs 47 7826
Corse Lawn Gloucs 47 8330
Corsham Wilts 35 8770
Corsindae Abers 135 6808
Corsley Wilts 22 8246
Corsley Heath Wilts 22 8245
Corsock D & G 99 7576
Corston Somset 22 6965
Corston Wilts 35 9283
Corstorphine C Edin 117 1972
Cortachy Angus 134 3959
Corton Suffk 67 5497
Corton Wilts 22 9340
Corton Denham Somset 21 6322
Coruanan Lodge Highld 130 0668
Corwen Denbgs 70 0743
Coryates Dorset 10 6285
Coryton Devon 5 4583
Coryton Essex 40 7382
Cosby Leics 50 5495
Coseley W Mids 60 9494
Cosford Shrops 60 8005
Cosgrove Nhants 38 7942
Cosham Hants 13 6505
Cosheston Pembks 30 0003
Coshieville P & K 124 7749
Cossall Notts 62 4842
Cossall Marsh Notts 62 4842
Cossington Leics 62 6013
Cossington Somset 21 3540
Costessey Norfk 66 1711
Costock Notts 62 5726
Coston Leics 63 8422
Coston Norfk 66 0506
Cote Oxon 36 3502
Cote Somset 21 3444
Cotebrook Ches 71 5765
Cotehill Cumb 93 4650
Cotes Cumb 87 4886
Cotes Leics 62 5520
Cotes Staffs 72 8434
Cotes Heath Staffs 72 8334
Cotesbach Leics 50 5382
Cotgrave Notts 63 6435
Cothal Abers 143 8715
Cotham Notts 63 7947
Cothelstone Somset 20 1831
Cotherstone Dur 95 0119
Cothill Oxon 37 4699
Cotleigh Devon 9 2002
Cotmanhay Derbys 62 4543
Coton Cambs 52 4058
Coton Nhants 50 6771
Coton Shrops 59 5334
Coton Staffs 72 8120
Coton Staffs 72 9731
Coton Staffs 61 1804
Coton Clanford Staffs 72 8723
Coton Hayes Staffs 72 9832
Coton Hill Shrops 59 4813
Coton in the Clay Staffs 73 1628
Coton in the Elms Derbys 73 2415
Coton Park Derbys 73 2617
Cott Devon 7 7861
Cottage End Hants 24 4143
Cottam E R Yk 91 9964
Cottam Lancs 80 5032
Cottam Notts 75 8179
Cottenham Cambs 53 4467
Cotterdale N York 88 8393
Cottered Herts 39 3129
Cotteridge W Mids 61 0480
Cotterstock Nhants 51 0490
Cottesbrooke Nhants 50 7173
Cottesmore Rutlnd 63 9013
Cottingham E R Yk 84 0432
Cottingham Nhants 51 8490
Cottingley W York 82 1137
Cottisford Oxon 49 5831
Cotton Suffk 54 0666
Cotton End Beds 38 0845
Cotton Tree Lancs 81 9039
Cottown Abers 142 5026
Cottown Abers 142 7615
Cottown of Gight Abers 143 8140
Cotts Devon 6 4365
Cotwall Shrops 59 6017
Cotwalton Staffs 72 9234
Couch's Mill Cnwll 4 1459
Coughton Herefs 34 5921
Coughton Warwks 48 0860
Coulaghailtor Ag & B 113 7165
Coulags Highld 138 9645
Coulderton Cumb 86 9808
Coull Abers 134 5102
Coulport Ag & B 114 2187
Coulsdon Gt Lon 27 2959
Coulston Wilts 22 9554
Coulter S Lans 108 0234
Coultershaw Bridge W Susx 14 9719
Coultings Somset 20 2241
Coulton N York 90 6373
Coultra Fife 126 3523

280

Cound Shrops 59 5505
Coundlane Shrops 59 5705
Coundon Dur 96 2309
Coundon Grange Dur 96 2228
Countersett N York 88 9187
Countess Wilts 23 1542
Countess Cross Essex 40 8631
Countess Wear Devon 9 9489
Countesthorpe Leics 50 5885
Countisbury Devon 19 7449
Coup Green Lancs 81 5927
Coupar Angus P & K 126 2239
Coupland Cumb 94 7118
Coupland Nthumb 110 9330
Cour Ag & B 105 8248
Courance D & G 100 0590
Court Henry Carmth 32 5522
Court-at-Street Kent 17 0905
Courteachan Highld 129 6897
Courteenhall Nhants 49 7653
Courtsend Essex 41 0293
Courtway Somset 20 2033
Cousland Mdloth 118 3708
Cousley Wood E Susx 16 6533
Cove Ag & B 114 2282
Cove Border 119 7771
Cove Devon 20 9619
Cove Hants 25 8555
Cove Highld 144 8191
Cove Bay Aber C 135 9501
Cove Bottom Suffk 55 4979
Covehithe Suffk 55 5282
Coven Staffs 60 9106
Coven Lawn Staffs 60 9005
Coveney Cambs 53 4832
Covenham
  St Bartholomew Lincs 77 3394
Covenham St Mary Lincs 77 3394
Coventry W Mids 61 3378
Coventry Airport 61 3574
Coverack Cnwll 3 7818
Coverack Bridges Cnwll 2 6630
Coverham N York 89 1086
Covington Cambs 51 0570
Covington S Lans 108 9739
Cow Green Suffk 54 0505
Cow Honeybourne Worcs 48 1143
Cowan Bridge Lancs 87 6376
Cowbeech E Susx 16 6114
Cowbit Lincs 64 2518
Cowbridge V Glam 33 9974
Cowdale Derbys 74 0771
Cowden Kent 16 4640
Cowden Pound Kent 16 4642
Cowden Station Kent 16 4741
Cowdenbeath Fife 117 1691
Cowers Lane Derbys 73 3046
Cowes IOW 13 4996
Cowesby N York 89 4689
Cowesfield Green Wilts 23 2503
Cowfold W Susx 15 2122
Cowgill Cumb 88 7506
Cowhill Gloucs 34 6091
Cowie Stirlg 116 8389
Cowlam E R Yk 91 9665
Cowley Derbys 74 3376
Cowley Devon 9 9005
Cowley Gloucs 35 9614
Cowley Gt Lon 26 0582
Cowley Oxon 37 5304
Cowley Oxon 49 6628
Cowling Lancs 81 5917
Cowling N York 82 9643
Cowling N York 89 2387
Cowlinge Suffk 53 7154
Cowmes W York 82 1815
Cowpe Lancs 81 8320
Cowpen Nthumb 103 2981
Cowpen Bewley Dur 97 4824
Cowplain Hants 13 6810
Cowshill Dur 95 8540
Cowslip Green Somset 21 4861
Cowthorpe N York 83 4252
Cox Common Suffk 55 4032
Coxall Shrops 46 3774
Coxbench Derbys 62 3743
Coxbridge Somset 21 5436
Coxford Cnwll 4 1696
Coxford Norfk 66 8509
Coxgreen Staffs 60 8086
Coxheath Kent 28 7451
Coxhoe Dur 96 3106
Coxley Somset 21 5343
Coxley W York 82 2717
Coxley Wick Somset 21 5243
Coxpark Cnwll 5 4072
Coxtie Green Essex 27 5696
Coxwold N York 90 5377
Coychurch Brdgnd 33 9379
Coylton S Ayrs 107 4219
Coylumbridge Highld 132 9111
Coytrahen Brdgnd 33 8885
Crab Orchard Dorset 12 0806
Crabbs Cross Worcs 48 0465
Crabtree E Susx 15 2125
Crabtree Green Wrexhm 71 3344
Crackenthorpe Cumb 94 6622
Crackington Haven Cnwll 4 1496
Crackley Staffs 72 8300
Crackley Warwks 61 2903
Crackleybank Shrops 60 7611
Crackpot N York 88 9796
Cracoe N York 88 9780
Craddock Devon 9 0812
Cradle End Herts 39 4521
Cradley Herefs 47 7347
Cradley W Mids 60 9485
Cradoc Powys 45 0130
Crafthole Cnwll 5 3654
Crafton Bucks 38 8819
Crag Foot Lancs 87 4873
Cragg Hill W York 82 2437
Cragg Vale W York 82 0003
Craggan Highld 141 0226
Craghead Dur 96 2150
Crai Powys 45 8924

Craibstone Moray 142 4959
Craichie Angus 127 5047
Craig Angus 127 6956
Craig Highld 138 0349
Craig Llangiwg Neath 32 7204
Craig Penllyn V Glam 33 9717
Craig's End Essex 53 7137
Craig-y-Duke Neath 32 7002
Craig-y-nos Powys 33 8415
Craigbank E Ayrs 107 5911
Craigburn Border 117 2354
Craigcefnparc Swans 32 6702
Craigcleuch D & G 101 3486
Craigdam Abers 143 8430
Craigdhu Ag & B 122 8205
Craigearn Abers 142 7214
Craigellachie Moray 141 2844
Craigend P & K 126 1120
Craigend Rens 115 4670
Craigendoran Ag & B 115 3181
Craighlaw D & G 98 3061
Craighouse Ag & B 113 5267
Craigie P & K 126 1143
Craigie S Ayrs 107 4232
Craigiefold Abers 143 9165
Craigley D & G 99 7658
Craiglockhart C Edin 117 2271
Craiglug Moray 141 3355
Craigmillar C Edin 117 3071
Craignant Shrops 58 2535
Craigneston D & G 107 7587
Craigneuk N Lans 116 7765
Craigneuk N Lans 116 7756
Craignure Ag & B 122 7236
Craigo Angus 135 6864
Craigrothie Fife 126 3810
Craigton Aber C 135 8301
Craigton Angus 127 5138
Craigton E Rens 115 4994
Craigton of Airlie Angus 126 3230
Crail Fife 127 6107
Crailing Border 110 6824
Craiselound Lincs 75 7698
Crakehall N York 89 2499
Crakehill N York 89 4273
Crakemarsh Staffs 73 0936
Crambe N York 90 7364
Cramlington Nthumb 103 2676
Cramond C Edin 117 1976
Cramond Bridge C Edin 117 1775
Cranage Ches 79 7568
Cranberry Staffs 72 8235
Cranborne Dorset 12 0513
Cranbrook Kent 28 7776
Cranbrook Common Kent 28 7838
Crane Moor S York 82 3001
Crane's Corner Norfk 66 9113
Cranfield Beds 38 9542
Cranford Devon 18 3421
Cranford Gt Lon 26 1076
Cranford St Andrew Nhants .. 51 9277
Cranford St John Nhants 51 9276
Cranham Gloucs 35 8913
Cranham Gt Lon 27 5787
Cranhill Warwks 48 1253
Crank Mersyd 78 5099
Cranleigh Surrey 14 0539
Cranmer Green Suffk 54 0171
Cranmore IOW 13 3990
Cranmore Somset 22 6643
Cranoe Leics 50 7695
Cransford Suffk 55 3164
Cranshaws Border 118 6861
Cranstal IOM 158 4602
Cranswick E R Yk 84 0252
Crantock Cnwll 4 7960
Cranwell Lincs 76 0349
Cranwich Norfk 65 7704
Cranworth Norfk 66 9804
Craobh Haven Ag & B 122 7907
Crapstone Devon 6 5067
Crarae Ag & B 114 9897
Crask Inn Highld 149 5224
Crask of Aigas Highld 139 4642
Craster Nthumb 111 2519
Craswall Herefs 46 2735
Crateford Staffs 60 9009
Cratfield Suffk 55 3175
Crathes Abers 135 7596
Crathes Castle 135 7397
Crathie Abers 133 2695
Crathie Highld 132 5793
Crathorne N York 89 4407
Craven Arms Shrops 59 4382
Crawcrook T & W 103 1363
Crawford Lancs 78 4902
Crawford S Lans 108 9520
Crawfordjohn S Lans 108 8823
Crawick D & G 107 7811
Crawley Hants 24 4285
Crawley Oxon 36 3412
Crawley W Susx 15 2636
Crawley Down W Susx 15 3437
Crawleyside Dur 95 9940
Crawshawbooth Lancs 81 8125
Crawton Abers 135 8779
Craxe's Green Essex 40 9419
Cray N York 88 9419
Cray's Pond Oxon 37 6380
Crayford Gt Lon 27 5175
Crayke N York 90 5670
Craymere Beck Norfk 66 0631
Crays Hill Essex 40 7192
Craythorne Staffs 73 2426
Craze Lowman Devon 9 9814
Crazies Hill Oxon 37 7980
Creacombe Devon 18 3219
Creag Ghoraidh W Isls 152 7948
Creagan Inn Ag & B 122 9744
Creagorry W Isls 152 7948
Creaguaineach Lodge Highld 131 3008
Creamore Bank Shrops 59 5150
Creaton Nhants 50 7071
Creca D & G 101 2219
Credenhill Herefs 46 4543
Crediton Devon 8 8300
Creebank D & G 98 3477

Creebridge D & G 99 4165
Creech Heathfield Somset 20 2727
Creech St Michael Somset 20 2725
Creed Cnwll 3 9347
Creedy Park Devon 8 8301
Creekmouth Gt Lon 27 4581
Creeting St Mary Suffk 54 0956
Creeton Lincs 64 0120
Creetown D & G 99 4759
Cregneash IOM 158 1867
Cregny Baa IOM 158 3981
Cregrina Powys 45 1252
Creich Fife 126 3221
Creigiau Cardif 33 0781
Crelly Cnwll 2 6732
Cremyll Cnwll 6 4553
Cressage Shrops 59 5904
Cressbrook Derbys 74 1673
Cresselly Pembks 30 0606
Cressex Bucks 26 8442
Cressing Essex 40 7920
Cresswell Nthumb 103 2903
Cresswell Pembks 30 0506
Cresswell Staffs 72 9739
Creswell Derbys 75 5274
Creswell Green Staffs 61 0710
Cretingham Suffk 55 2260
Cretshengan Ag & B 113 7166
Crew Green Powys 59 3215
Crewe Ches 71 4253
Crewe Ches 72 7056
Crewe Green Ches 72 7255
Crewkerne Somset 10 4409
Crews Hill Herefs 35 6722
Crews Hill Station Herts 27 3000
Crewton Derbys 62 3733
Crianlarich Stirlg 123 3825
Cribbs Causeway Gloucs 34 5780
Cribyn Cerdgn 44 5250
Criccieth Gwynd 56 4938
Crich Derbys 74 3454
Crich Carr Derbys 74 3354
Crich Common Derbys 74 3553
Crichton Mdloth 118 3862
Crick Mons 34 4890
Crick Nhants 50 5872
Crickadarn Powys 45 0942
Cricket St Thomas Somset 10 3708
Crickheath Shrops 59 2922
Crickhowell Powys 33 2118
Cricklade Wilts 36 0993
Cricklewood Gt Lon 26 2385
Cridling Stubbs N York 83 5221
Crieff P & K 125 8621
Criggan Cnwll 4 0160
Criggion Powys 59 2915
Crigglestone W York 82 3116
Crimble Gt Man 81 8611
Crimond Abers 143 9542
Crimplesham Norfk 65 6503
Crimscote Warwks 48 2347
Crinaglack Highld 139 4340
Crindledyke N Lans 116 8366
Cringleford Norfk 67 1905
Cringles N York 82 0448
Crinow Pembks 31 1214
Cripp's Corner E Susx 17 7721
Cripplesease Cnwll 2 5006
Cripplestyle Dorset 12 0812
Crizeley Herefs 46 4532
Croachy Highld 140 6527
Croanford Cnwll 4 0371
Crochmore House D & G 100 8977
Crock Street Somset 10 3213
Crockenhill Kent 27 5067
Crocker End Oxon 37 7086
Crocker's Ash Herefs 34 5316
Crockerhill W Susx 14 9206
Crockernwell Devon 8 7592
Crockerton Wilts 22 8642
Crocketford D & G 100 8372
Crockey Hill N York 83 6246
Crockham Hill Kent 27 4450
Crockhurst Street Kent 16 6245
Crockleford Heath Essex 41 0426
Croes-goch Pembks 30 8330
Croes-lan Cerdgn 42 3844
Croes-y-mwyalch Torfn 34 3092
Croes-y-pant Mons 34 3104
Croeserw Neath 33 8795
Croesor Gwynd 57 6344
Croesyceiliog Carmth 31 4016
Croesyceiliog Torfn 34 3096
Croft Ches 79 6393
Croft Devon 5 5296
Croft Leics 50 5195
Croft Lincs 77 5061
Croft Michael Cnwll 2 6637
Croft-on-Tees Dur 89 2809
Croftamie Stirlg 115 4785
Crofton Cumb 93 3050
Crofton W York 83 3817
Crofton Wilts 23 2562
Crofts D & G 99 7365
Crofts Moray 141 3806
Crofts Bank Gt Man 79 7695
Crofts of Dipple Moray 141 3259
Crofts of Savoch Abers 143 0460
Crofty Swans 32 5294
Crogen Gwynd 58 0036
Croggan Ag & B 122 7027
Croglin Cumb 94 5747
Croick Highld 146 4591
Cromarty Highld 140 7867
Crombie Fife 117 0584
Cromdale Highld 141 0728
Cromer Herts 39 2928
Cromer Norfk 67 2242
Cromford Derbys 73 2956
Cromhall Gloucs 35 6990
Cromhall Common Gloucs 35 6989
Cromor W Isls 152 4021
Crompton Fold Gt Man 79 9409
Cromwell Notts 75 7961
Cronberry E Ayrs 107 6022
Crondall Hants 25 7948
Cronk-y-Voddy IOM 158 3085

Cronkbourne IOM 158 3677
Cronton Mersyd 78 4988
Crook Cumb 87 4695
Crook Dur 96 1635
Crook Inn Border 108 1026
Crook of Devon P & K 117 0400
Crookdake Cumb 93 1943
Crooke Gt Man 78 5507
Crooked End Gloucs 35 6217
Crooked Holme Cumb 101 5161
Crooked Soley Wilts 36 3172
Crookedholm E Ayrs 107 4537
Crookes S York 74 3287
Crookhall Dur 95 1150
Crookham Berks 24 5464
Crookham Nthumb 110 9138
Crookham Village Hants 25 7752
Crooklands Cumb 87 5383
Cropper Derbys 73 2335
Cropredy Oxon 49 4646
Cropston Leics 62 5510
Cropthorne Worcs 47 9945
Cropton N York 90 7589
Cropwell Bishop Notts 63 6835
Cropwell Butler Notts 63 6837
Cros W Isls 152 5061
Crosbie N Ayrs 114 2149
Crosbost W Isls 152 3924
Crosby Cumb 92 0738
Crosby IOM 158 3279
Crosby Lincs 84 8912
Crosby Mersyd 78 3198
Crosby Garret Cumb 88 7209
Crosby Ravensworth Cumb .. 94 6214
Crosby Villa Cumb 92 0939
Croscombe Somset 21 5944
Crosemere Shrops 59 4329
Crosland Edge W York 82 1012
Crosland Hill W York 82 1114
Cross Somset 21 4154
Cross Ash Mons 34 4019
Cross Coombe Cnwll 3 7251
Cross End Beds 51 0658
Cross End Essex 54 8534
Cross Flatts W York 82 1040
Cross Gates W York 83 3534
Cross Green Devon 5 3888
Cross Green Staffs 60 9105
Cross Green Suffk 54 8353
Cross Green Suffk 54 8955
Cross Green Suffk 54 9852
Cross Hands Carmth 32 5612
Cross Hands Pembks 31 0712
Cross Hill Derbys 74 4148
Cross Hills N York 82 0145
Cross Houses Shrops 59 5307
Cross Houses Shrops 60 6991
Cross in Hand E Susx 16 5521
Cross Inn Cerdgn 42 3957
Cross Inn Cerdgn 43 5464
Cross Inn Pembks 31 1005
Cross Inn Rhondd 33 0582
Cross Keys Ag & B 115 3385
Cross Keys Wilts 35 8711
Cross Lane IOW 13 5089
Cross Lane Head Shrops 60 7195
Cross Lanes Cnwll 2 6921
Cross Lanes Cnwll 3 7642
Cross Lanes N York 90 5364
Cross Lanes Wrexhm 71 3746
Cross o' th' hands Derbys 73 2846
Cross Oak Powys 45 1023
Cross of Jackston Abers 142 7432
Cross Roads Powys 45 9756
Cross Street Suffk 54 1876
Cross Town Ches 79 7578
Cross-at-Hand Kent 28 7846
Crossaig Ag & B 113 8351
Crossapol Ag & B 120 9943
Crossbush W Susx 14 0306
Crosscanonby Cumb 92 0739
Crossdale Street Norfk 67 2239
Crossens Mersyd 80 3720
Crossford Fife 117 0786
Crossford S Lans 116 8246
Crossgate Cnwll 5 3488
Crossgate Lincs 64 2426
Crossgate Staffs 72 9437
Crossgatehall E Loth 118 3669
Crossgates E Ayrs 115 3741
Crossgates Fife 117 1488
Crossgates N York 91 0284
Crossgates Powys 45 0864
Crossgill Lancs 87 5563
Crosshands Carmth 31 1923
Crosshands E Ayrs 107 4830
Crosshill Fife 117 1796
Crosshill S Ayrs 106 3206
Crosshouse E Ayrs 106 3908
Crosskeys Caerph 34 2292
Crosskirk Highld 150 0369
Crosslands Cumb 87 3489
Crosslanes Shrops 59 3218
Crosslee Rens 115 4006
Crossley W York 82 2021
Crossmichael D & G 99 7366
Crosspost W Susx 15 2502
Crossroads Abers 134 5607
Crossroads Abers 135 7594
Crosston Angus 127 5256
Crossway Mons 34 4419
Crossway Pembks 31 1542
Crossway Powys 45 0558
Crossway Green Mons 34 5294
Crossway Green Worcs 47 8468
Crossways Dorset 11 7788
Crosswell Pembks 31 1236
Crosthwaite Cumb 87 4391
Croston Lancs 80 4818
Crostwick Norfk 67 2515
Crostwight Norfk 67 3429
Crouch Kent 28 0530
Crouch Kent 27 6155
Crouch End Gt Lon 27 3088
Crouch Hill Dorset 11 7010
Croucheston Wilts 23 0625
Crough House Green Kent 16 4346
Croughton Nhants 49 5433

Crovie Abers .... 143 8?
Crow Hants 12 15
Crow Edge S York 82 18
Crow End Cambs 52 32
Crow Green Essex 27 57
Crow Hill Herefs 47 63
Crow's Green Essex 40 69
Crow's Nest Cnwll 5 26
Crowan Cnwll 2 64
Crowborough E Susx 16 5
Crowborough Town E Susx .. 16 5
Crowcombe Somset 20 14
Crowdecote Derbys 74 10
Crowden Derbys 74 08
Crowden Devon 18 44
Crowdhill Hants 13 45
Crowdleham Kent 27 56
Crowell Oxon 37 74
Crowfield Nhants .... 49 6?
Crowfield Suffk 54 14
Crowfield Green Suffk 54 14
Crowgate Street Norfk 67 3
Crowhill E Loth 119 73
Crowhole Derbys 74 33
Crowhurst E Susx 17 75
Crowhurst Surrey 15 38
Crowhurst Lane End Surrey .. 15 3?
Crowland Lincs 64 24
Crowland Suffk .... 54 0?
Crowlas Cnwll .... 2 5?
Crowle Lincs .... 84 7?
Crowle Worcs .... 47 9?
Crowle Green Worcs .... 47 9?
Crowmarsh Gifford Oxon 37 6
Crown Corner Suffk 55 25
Crownhill Devon 6 48
Crownpits Surrey 25 97
Crownthorpe Norfk 66 08
Crowntown Cnwll .... 2 6?
Crows-an-Wra Cnwll 2 32
Crowshill Norfk 66 95
Crowsnest Shrops 59 36
Crowthorne Berks 25 84
Crowton Ches 71 57
Croxall Staffs 61 15
Croxby Lincs 76 18
Croxdale Dur 96 26
Croxden Staffs 73 06
Croxley Green Herts 26 07
Croxton Cambs 52 24
Croxton Lincs 85 09
Croxton Norfk 66 98
Croxton Norfk 54 87
Croxton Staffs 72 82
Croxton Green Ches 71 55
Croxton Kerrial Leics 63 83
Croxtonbank Staffs 72 78
Croy Highld 140 79
Croy N Lans 116 72
Croyde Devon 18 44
Croyde Bay Devon 18 44
Croydon Cambs 52 31
Croydon Gt Lon 27 32
Crubenmore Highld 132 67
Cruckmeole Shrops 59 43
Cruckton Shrops 59 43
Cruden Bay Abers 143 08
Crudgington Shrops 59 63
Crudwell Wilts .... 35 9?
Crug Powys 45 19
Crug-y-byddar Powys 58 16
Crugmeer Cnwll .... 4 9?
Crugybar Carmth 44 65
Crumlin Caerph 33 21
Crumplehorn Cnwll 5 20
Crumpsall Gt Man 79 84
Crundale Kent 29 07
Crundale Pembks 30 97
Crunwear Pembks 31 18
Cruwys Morchard Devon 19 87
Crux Easton Hants 24 42
Cruxton Dorset 10 60
Crwbin Carmth 32 47
Cryers Hill Bucks 26 87
Crymmych Pembks 31 18
Crynant Neath 32 79
Crystal Palace Gt Lon 27 33
Cuaig Highld 137 70
Cuan Ferry Village Ag & B .. 122 75
Cubbington Warwks 48 34
Cubert Cnwll 4 78
Cubley S York 82 24
Cublington Bucks 38 84
Cublington Herefs 46 40
Cuckfield W Susx 15 30
Cucklington Somset 22 75
Cuckney Notts 75 56
Cuckold's Green Kent 28 82
Cuckoo Bridge Lincs 64 20
Cuckoo's Corner Hants 24 74
Cuckoo's Nest Ches 71 38
Cuddesdon Oxon 37 59
Cuddington Bucks 37 73
Cuddington Ches 71 59
Cuddington Heath Ches 71 47
Cuddy Hill Lancs 80 49
Cudham Gt Lon 27 44
Cudliptown Devon 5 52
Cudnell Dorset 12 06
Cudworth S York 83 38
Cudworth Somset 10 38
Cudworth Common S York ... 83 40
Cuerden Green Lancs 81 55
Cuerdley Cross Ches 78 54
Cufaude Hants 24 65
Cuffley Herts 39 30
Cuil Highld 122 99
Culbokie Highld 140 60
Culbone Somset 19 84
Culburnie Highld 139 49
Culcabock Highld 140 68
Culcharry Highld 140 85
Culcheth Ches 79 66
Culdrain Abers 142 51
Culduie Highld 137 71
Culford Suffk 54 83
Culgaith Cumb 94 60
Culham Oxon 37 50

lkein
Dittisham
281

kein *Highld* 148 0333
kein Drumbeg *Highld* 148 1133
kerton *Gloucs* 35 9395
en *Moray* 142 5167
ercoats *T & W* 103 3570
erlie *Abers* 135 7603
icudden *Highld* 140 6463
ingworth *W York* 82 0636
ipool House *Ag & B* 122 7413
ivoe *Shet* 153 5402
oden *Highld* 140 7246
ompton *Devon* 9 0207
n Davy *Devon* 9 1215
mington *Shrops* 59 4982
mstock *Devon* 9 1013
nacraig *Highld* 145 0603
naightrie *D & G* 92 7750
naknock *Highld* 137 5162
pho *Suffk* 55 2149
rain *Highld* 146 5794
ross *Fife* 117 9886
roy *S Ayrs* 106 3114
salmond *Abers* 142 6532
scadden *D & G* 99 4748
shabbin *D & G* 98 3051
swick *Shet* 153 2745
tercullen *Abers* 143 9223
ts *Aber C* 135 8903
verstone Green *Kent* 27 6362
verthorpe *Lincs* 64 0240
worth *Nhants* 49 5446
zean Castle 106 2310
nbernauld *N Lans* 116 7674
nbernauld Village *N Lans* 116 7676
nberworth *Lincs* 77 5073
ndivock *Cumb* 93 3448
ninestown *Abers* 143 8050
nledge *Border* 119 7956
nmersdale *Cumb* 93 3953
nmertrees *D & G* 100 1366
nmingston *Moray* 141 1368
nnock *E Ayrs* 107 5620
nnor *Oxon* 37 4504
nrew *Cumb* 94 5550
nrue *D & G* 100 0686
nwhinton *Cumb* 93 4552
nwhitton *Cumb* 94 5052
ndall *N York* 89 4272
nninghamhead *N Ayrs* 106 3741
oar *Fife* 126 3714
oar Muir *Fife* 126 3613
pernham *Hants* 23 3622
bar *Derbys* 74 2574
bridge *Hants* 13 5211
bridge *Oxon* 36 3308
dridge *Hants* 13 5213
dworth *Warwks* 61 1792
land *Somset* 10 2717
ridge *Berks* 24 4972
rie *C Edin* 117 1867
ry Mallet *Somset* 21 3221
ry Rivel *Somset* 21 3925
teis Corner *Kent* 28 8539
tisden Green *Kent* 28 7440
rtisknowle *Devon* 7 7353
ry *Cnwll* 2 6721
shnie *Abers* 134 5211
shuish *Somset* 20 1930
sop *Herefs* 46 2441
tcloy *D & G* 99 4534
tcombe *Somset* 20 9339
tgate *Gt Man* 81 8614
thill *Highld* 147 7587
tiau *Gwynd* 57 6317
tler's Green *Essex* 40 5930
tmadoc *Cnwll* 4 0963
tmere *Cnwll* 5 3260
tnall Green *Worcs* 47 8868
tsdean *Gloucs* 48 0830
tsyke *W York* 83 4224
tthorpe *Derbys* 74 3473
ttivett *Cnwll* 5 3662
xham *Oxon* 37 6695
xton *Kent* 28 7066
xwold *Lincs* 85 1701
m *Blae G* 33 1805
m *Denbgs* 70 0677
m Capel *Carmth* 32 4502
m Crawnon *Powys* 33 1419
m Dulais *Swans* 32 6103
m Irfon *Powys* 45 8549
m Morgan *Carmth* 31 2934
m Penmachno *Conwy* 69 7547
m-bach *Carmth* 32 4801
m-celyn *Blae G* 33 2008
m-Cewydd *Gwynd* 57 8713
m-cou *Cerdgn* 31 2942
m-Ifor *Carmth* 44 6625
m-Llinau *Powys* 57 8408
m-y-glo *Carmth* 32 5513
m-y-glo *Gwynd* 69 5562
mafan *Neath* 32 7791
maman *Rhondd* 33 0099
mann *Carmth* 44 5847
mavon *Torfn* 34 2706
mbach *Carmth* 31 2526
mbach *Powys* 45 1639
mbach *Rhondd* 33 0201
mbach Llechrhyd *Powys* 45 0254
mbelan *Powys* 58 9481
mbran *Torfn* 34 2994
mbrwyno *Cerdgn* 43 7180
mcarn *Caerph* 34 2293
mcarvan *Mons* 34 4707
mdare *Rhondd* 33 9803
mdu *Carmth* 44 6330
mdu *Powys* 45 1823
mdu *Swans* 32 6494
mduad *Carmth* 31 3731
mdwr *Carmth* 44 7132
mergyr *Cerdgn* 43 7982
mfelin *Brdgnd* 33 8589
mfelin *Myr Td* 33 0901
mfelin Boeth *Carmth* 31 1919
mfelin Mynach *Carmth* 31 2224
mfelinfach *Caerph* 33 1891
mffrwd *Carmth* 31 4217
mgiedd *Powys* 32 7911
Cwmgorse *Carmth* 32 7010
Cwmgwili *Carmth* 32 5710
Cwmgwrach *Neath* 33 8604
Cwmhiraeth *Carmth* 31 3437
Cwmisfael *Carmth* 32 4915
Cwmllynfell *Neath* 32 7412
Cwmmawr *Carmth* 32 5312
Cwmparc *Rhondd* 33 9495
Cwmpengraig *Carmth* 31 3536
Cwmpennar *Rhondd* 33 0300
Cwmrhos *Powys* 45 1824
Cwmrhydyceirw *Swans* 32 6699
Cwmsychbant *Cerdgn* 44 4746
Cwmtillery *Blae G* 33 2105
Cwmyoy *Mons* 46 2923
Cwmystwyth *Cerdgn* 43 7874
Cwrt *Gwynd* 32 6800
Cwrt-newydd *Cerdgn* 44 4947
Cwrt-y-gollen *Powys* 34 2317
Cyfronydd *Powys* 58 1408
Cylibebyll *Neath* 32 7404
Cymer *Neath* 33 8695
Cymmer *Rhondd* 33 0290
Cynghordy *Carmth* 44 8040
Cynheidre *Carmth* 32 4907
Cynonville *Neath* 33 8395
Cynwyd *Denbgs* 70 0541
Cynwyl Elfed *Carmth* 31 3727

D

Daccombe *Devon* 7 9068
Dacre *Cumb* 93 4526
Dacre *N York* 89 1960
Dacre Banks *N York* 89 1962
Daddry Shield *Dur* 95 8937
Dadford *Bucks* 49 6638
Dadlington *Leics* 61 4097
Dafen *Carmth* 32 5201
Daffy Green *Norfk* 66 9609
Dagenham *Gt Lon* 27 5084
Daglingworth *Gloucs* 35 9905
Dagnall *Bucks* 38 9916
Dagworth *Suffk* 54 0361
Dailly *S Ayrs* 106 2701
Dainton *Devon* 7 8566
Dairsie *Fife* 126 4117
Daisy Hill *Gt Man* 79 6504
Daisy Hill *W York* 82 2728
Dalabrog *W Isls* 152 7521
Dalavich *Ag & B* 122 9612
Dalbeattie *D & G* 100 8361
Dalbury *Derbys* 73 2634
Dalby *IOM* 158 2178
Dalby *Lincs* 77 4169
Dalby *N York* 90 6371
Dalcapon *P & K* 125 9754
Dalchalm *Highld* 147 9105
Dalchreichart *Highld* 131 2812
Dalchruin *P & K* 124 7116
Dalcrue *P & K* 125 0427
Dalderby *Lincs* 77 2565
Dalditch *Devon* 9 0483
Dale *Cumb* 94 5443
Dale *Derbys* 62 4338
Dale *Pembks* 30 8005
Dale Bottom *Cumb* 93 2921
Dale End *Derbys* 74 2161
Dale End *N York* 82 9645
Dale Hill *E Susx* 16 7030
Dalehouse *N York* 97 7717
Dalgarven *N Ayrs* 115 2846
Dalgety Bay *Fife* 117 1683
Dalgig *E Ayrs* 107 5512
Dalginross *P & K* 124 7721
Dalguise *P & K* 125 9847
Dalhalvaig *Highld* 150 8954
Dalham *Suffk* 53 7261
Daliburgh *W Isls* 152 7521
Dalkeith *Mdloth* 118 3367
Dallas *Moray* 141 1252
Dallinghoo *Suffk* 55 2655
Dallington *E Susx* 16 6519
Dallington *Nhants* 49 7362
Dallow *N York* 89 1971
Dalmally *Ag & B* 123 1627
Dalmary *Stirlg* 115 5195
Dalmellington *E Ayrs* 107 4705
Dalmeny *C Edin* 117 1477
Dalmigavie *Highld* 140 7319
Dalmigavie Lodge *Highld* 140 7523
Dalmore *Highld* 140 6668
Dalmuir *W Duns* 115 4871
Dalnabreck *Highld* 129 7069
Dalnacardoch *P & K* 132 7270
Dalnahaitnach *Highld* 140 8519
Dalnaspidal *P & K* 132 6473
Dalnawillan Lodge *Highld* 150 0340
Daloist *P & K* 124 7857
Dalqueich *P & K* 125 0804
Dalquhairn *S Ayrs* 106 3296
Dalreavoch Lodge *Highld* 147 7508
Dalry *N Ayrs* 115 2949
Dalrymple *E Ayrs* 106 3514
Dalserf *S Lans* 116 7950
Dalsmeran *Ag & B* 104 6413
Dalston *Cumb* 93 3650
Dalston *Gt Lon* 27 3384
Dalswinton *D & G* 100 9385
Dalton *Cumb* 87 5476
Dalton *D & G* 100 1173
Dalton *Lancs* 78 4908
Dalton *N York* 89 1108
Dalton *N York* 89 4376
Dalton *Nthumb* 103 1172
Dalton *S York* 75 4594
Dalton Magna *S York* 75 4692
Dalton Parva *S York* 75 4593
Dalton Piercy *Dur* 97 4631
Dalton-in-Furness *Cumb* 86 2274
Dalton-le-Dale *Dur* 96 4048
Dalton-on-Tees *N York* 89 2907
Dalveen *D & G* 108 8806
Dalveich *Stirlg* 124 6124
Dalwhinnie *Highld* 132 6384
Dalwood *Devon* 9 2400
Dam Green *Norfk* 54 0485
Damask Green *Herts* 39 2529
Damerham *Hants* 12 1016
Damgate *Norfk* 67 4009
Dan-y-Parc *Powys* 34 2217
Danaway *Kent* 28 8663
Danbury *Essex* 40 7805
Danby *N York* 90 7008
Danby Bottom *N York* 90 6904
Danby Wiske *N York* 89 3398
Dandaleith *Moray* 141 2846
Danderhall *Mdloth* 117 3069
Dane End *Herts* 39 3321
Dane Hills *Leics* 62 5604
Dane Street *Kent* 28 0552
Danebridge *Ches* 72 9665
Danegate *E Susx* 16 5633
Danehill *E Susx* 15 4027
Danemoor Green *Norfk* 66 0505
Danesford *Shrops* 60 7391
Danesmoor *Derbys* 74 4063
Daniel's Water *Kent* 28 9541
Danshillock *Abers* 142 7157
Danskine *E Loth* 118 5667
Danthorpe *E R Yk* 85 2532
Danzey Green *Warwks* 48 1269
Dapple Heath *Staffs* 73 0425
Darby Green *Hants* 25 8360
Darcy Lever *Gt Man* 79 7308
Daren-felen *Mons* 34 2212
Darenth *Kent* 27 5671
Daresbury *Ches* 78 5882
Darfield *S York* 83 4104
Darfoulds *Notts* 75 5578
Dargate *Kent* 29 0861
Darite *Cnwll* 5 2569
Darland *Kent* 28 7865
Darland *Wrexhm* 71 3757
Darlaston *Staffs* 72 8835
Darlaston *W Mids* 60 9796
Darlaston Green *W Mids* 60 9797
Darley *N York* 89 2059
Darley Abbey *Derbys* 62 3538
Darley Bridge *Derbys* 74 2661
Darley Dale *Derbys* 74 2663
Darley Green *Warwks* 61 1874
Darley Head *N York* 89 1959
Darleyhall *Herts* 38 1422
Darlingscott *Warwks* 48 2342
Darlington *Dur* 89 2814
Darliston *Shrops* 59 5733
Darlton *Notts* 75 7773
Darnford *Staffs* 61 1308
Darnick *Border* 109 5334
Darowen *Powys* 57 8201
Darra *Abers* 142 7447
Darracott *Cnwll* 18 2811
Darracott *Devon* 18 2317
Darracott *Devon* 18 4739
Darras Hall *Nthumb* 103 1570
Darrington *W York* 83 4820
Darsham *Suffk* 55 4169
Darshill *Somset* 21 6144
Dartford *Kent* 27 5474
Dartington *Devon* 7 7862
Dartmeet *Devon* 7 6773
Dartmouth *Devon* 7 8751
Darton *S York* 82 3110
Darvel *E Ayrs* 107 5637
Darwell Hole *E Susx* 16 6919
Darwen *Lancs* 81 6922
Datchet *Berks* 26 9877
Datchworth *Herts* 39 2619
Datchworth Green *Herts* 39 2718
Daubhill *Gt Man* 79 7007
Dauntsey *Wilts* 35 9782
Dauntsey Green *Wilts* 35 9981
Dava *Highld* 141 0038
Davenham *Ches* 79 6571
Davenport *Gt Man* 79 9088
Davenport Green *Ches* 79 8379
Davenport Green *Gt Man* 79 8086
Daventry *Nhants* 49 5762
David Street *Kent* 27 6464
Davidson's Mains *C Edin* 117 2175
Davidstow *Cnwll* 4 1587
Davington *D & G* 109 2302
Davington Hill *Kent* 28 0161
Daviot *Abers* 142 7428
Daviot *Highld* 140 7239
Daviot House *Highld* 140 7240
Davis's Town *E Susx* 16 5217
Davoch of Grange *Moray* 142 4751
Davyhulme *Gt Man* 79 7595
Daw End *W Mids* 61 0300
Daw's House *Cnwll* 5 3182
Dawesgreen *Surrey* 15 2147
Dawley *Shrops* 60 6808
Dawlish *Devon* 9 9576
Dawlish Warren *Devon* 9 9778
Dawn *Conwy* 69 8672
Daws Green *Somset* 20 1921
Daws Heath *Essex* 40 8188
Dawsmere *Lincs* 65 4430
Day Green *Ches* 72 7757
Daybrook *Notts* 62 5744
Dayhills *Staffs* 72 9532
Dayhouse Bank *Worcs* 60 9678
Daylesford *Gloucs* 48 2425
Ddol *Flints* 70 1471
Ddol-Cownwy *Powys* 58 0117
Deal *Kent* 29 3752
Dean *Cumb* 92 0725
Dean *Devon* 19 6245
Dean *Devon* 19 7048
Dean *Devon* 7 7364
Dean *Dorset* 11 9715
Dean *Hants* 24 4431
Dean *Hants* 13 5619
Dean *Lancs* 81 8525
Dean *Oxon* 36 3422
Dean *Somset* 22 6743
Dean Bottom *Kent* 27 5868
Dean Court *Oxon* 37 4705
Dean End *Dorset* 11 9717
Dean Head *S York* 74 2600
Dean Prior *Devon* 7 7363
Dean Row *Ches* 79 8781
Dean Street *Kent* 28 7453
Deanburnhaugh *Border* 109 3911
Deancombe *Devon* 7 7264
Deane *Gt Man* 79 6907
Deane *Hants* 24 5450
Deanhead *W York* 82 0415
Deanland *Dorset* 22 9918
Deanlane End *W Susx* 13 7412
Deanraw *Nthumb* 102 8162
Deans *W Loth* 117 0369
Deanscales *Cumb* 92 0926
Deanshanger *Nhants* 49 7639
Deanshaugh *Moray* 141 3550
Deanston *Stirlg* 124 7101
Dearham *Cumb* 92 0736
Dearnley *Gt Man* 81 9215
Debach *Suffk* 55 2454
Debden *Essex* 53 5533
Debden *Essex* 27 4496
Debden Green *Essex* 40 5831
Debenham *Suffk* 54 1763
Deblin's Green *Worcs* 47 8148
Dechmont *W Loth* 117 0370
Dechmont Road *W Loth* 117 0269
Deddington *Oxon* 49 4631
Dedham *Essex* 41 0533
Dedham Heath *Essex* 41 0531
Dedworth *Berks* 26 9476
Deene *Nhants* 51 9492
Deenethorpe *Nhants* 51 9591
Deepcar *S York* 74 2897
Deepcut *Surrey* 25 9057
Deepdale *Cumb* 88 7184
Deepdale *N York* 88 8979
Deeping Gate *Lincs* 64 1509
Deeping St James *Lincs* 64 1609
Deeping St Nicholas *Lincs* 64 2115
Deerhurst *Gloucs* 47 8730
Deerhurst Walton *Gloucs* 47 8828
Deerton Street *Kent* 28 9762
Defford *Worcs* 47 9143
Defynnog *Powys* 45 9227
Deganwy *Conwy* 69 7779
Degnish *Ag & B* 122 7812
Deighton *N York* 89 3801
Deighton *N York* 83 6244
Deighton *W York* 82 1519
Deiniolen *Gwynd* 69 5763
Delabole *Cnwll* 4 0683
Delamere *Ches* 71 5668
Delfrigs *Abers* 143 9620
Dell Quay *W Susx* 14 8302
Delley *Devon* 19 5424
Delliefure *Highld* 141 0730
Delly End *Oxon* 36 3513
Delmonden Green *Kent* 17 7330
Delnashaugh Inn *Moray* 141 1835
Delny *Highld* 146 7372
Delph *Gt Man* 82 9807
Delves *Dur* 95 1149
Delvine *P & K* 126 1240
Dembleby *Lincs* 64 0437
Demelza *Cnwll* 4 9763
Den of Lindores *Fife* 126 2616
Denaby *S York* 75 4899
Denaby Main *S York* 75 4999
Denbies *Surrey* 26 1450
Denbigh *Denbgs* 70 0566
Denbrae *Fife* 126 3818
Denbury *Devon* 7 8268
Denby *Derbys* 62 3946
Denby Bottles *Derbys* 62 3846
Denby Dale *W York* 82 2208
Denchworth *Oxon* 36 3891
Dendron *Cumb* 86 2470
Denel End *Beds* 38 0335
Denfield *P & K* 125 9517
Denford *Nhants* 51 9976
Dengie *Essex* 41 9802
Denham *Bucks* 26 0487
Denham *Suffk* 53 7561
Denham *Suffk* 55 1974
Denham End *Suffk* 53 7663
Denham Green *Bucks* 26 0488
Denham Green *Suffk* 55 1974
Denhead *Abers* 143 9952
Denhead *Fife* 127 4613
Denhead of Gray *Dund C* 126 3531
Denholm *Border* 110 5718
Denholme *W York* 82 0734
Denholme Clough *W York* 82 0732
Denio *Gwynd* 56 3635
Denmead *Hants* 13 6512
Denmore *Aber C* 135 9411
Denne Park *W Susx* 15 1628
Dennington *Suffk* 55 2867
Denny *Falk* 116 8082
Dennyloanhead *Falk* 116 8080
Denshaw *Gt Man* 82 9710
Denside *Abers* 135 8095
Densole *Kent* 29 2141
Denston *Suffk* 53 7652
Denstone *Staffs* 73 0940
Denstroude *Kent* 29 1061
Dent *Cumb* 87 7086
Denton *Cambs* 52 1587
Denton *Dur* 96 2118
Denton *E Susx* 16 4502
Denton *Gt Man* 79 9295
Denton *Kent* 28 6673
Denton *Kent* 29 2147
Denton *Lincs* 63 8632
Denton *N York* 82 1448
Denton *Nhants* 51 8358
Denton *Norfk* 55 2788
Denton *Oxon* 37 5902
Denver *Norfk* 65 6001
Denwick *Nthumb* 111 2014
Deopham *Norfk* 66 0400
Deopham Green *Norfk* 66 0499
Depden *Suffk* 53 7857
Depden Green *Suffk* 53 7756
Deptford *Gt Lon* 27 3777
Deptford *Wilts* 22 0138
Derby *Derbys* 62 3536
Derby *Devon* 19 5633
Derbyhaven *IOM* 158 2867
Derculich *P & K* 125 8852
Dereham *Norfk* 66 9913
Deri *Caerph* 33 1201
Derril *Devon* 18 3003
Derringstone *Kent* 29 2049
Derrington *Staffs* 72 8922
Derriton *Devon* 18 3303
Derry Hill *Wilts* 35 9670
Derrythorpe *Lincs* 84 8208
Dersingham *Norfk* 65 6830
Dervaig *Ag & B* 121 4352
Derwen *Denbgs* 70 0750
Derwen Fawr *Carmth* 44 5722
Derwenlas *Powys* 57 7298
Derwydd *Carmth* 32 6117
Desborough *Nhants* 51 8083
Desford *Leics* 62 4703
Deskford *Moray* 142 5061
Detchant *Nthumb* 111 0836
Detling *Kent* 28 7958
Deuxhill *Shrops* 60 6987
Devauden *Mons* 34 4898
Devil's Bridge *Cerdgn* 43 7376
Deviock *Cnwll* 5 3155
Devitts Green *Warwks* 61 2790
Devizes *Wilts* 22 0061
Devonport *Devon* 6 4554
Devonside *Clacks* 116 9196
Devoran *Cnwll* 3 7939
Dewarton *Mdloth* 118 3763
Dewlish *Dorset* 11 7798
Dewsbury *W York* 82 2421
Dewsbury Moor *W York* 82 2321
Deytheur *Powys* 58 2317
Dial *Somset* 21 5366
Dial Green *W Susx* 14 9227
Dial Post *W Susx* 15 1519
Dibberford *Dorset* 10 4504
Dibden *Hants* 13 4008
Dibden Purlieu *Hants* 13 4106
Dickens Heath *W Mids* 61 1176
Dickleburgh *Norfk* 54 1682
Didbrook *Gloucs* 48 0531
Didcot *Oxon* 37 5290
Didcot Railway Centre 37 5290
Diddington *Cambs* 52 1965
Diddlebury *Shrops* 59 5085
Didley *Herefs* 46 4532
Didling *W Susx* 14 8318
Didmarton *Gloucs* 35 8287
Didsbury *Gt Man* 79 8491
Didworthy *Devon* 7 6862
Digby *Lincs* 76 0854
Digg *Highld* 136 4668
Diggle *Gt Man* 82 0007
Digmoor *Lancs* 78 4905
Digswell *Herts* 39 2415
Digswell Water *Herts* 39 2514
Dihewyd *Cerdgn* 44 4855
Dilham *Norfk* 67 3325
Dilhorne *Staffs* 72 9743
Dillington *Cambs* 52 1365
Dilston *Nthumb* 102 9763
Dilton *Wilts* 22 8548
Dilton Marsh *Wilts* 22 8449
Dilwyn *Herefs* 46 4154
Dimple *Derbys* 74 2960
Dimple *Gt Man* 81 7015
Dinas *Carmth* 31 2730
Dinas *Cnwll* 4 9274
Dinas *Gwynd* 56 2735
Dinas *Pembks* 30 0138
Dinas *Rhondd* 33 0091
Dinas Dinlle *Gwynd* 68 4356
Dinas Powys *V Glam* 33 1571
Dinas-Mawddwy *Gwynd* 57 8515
Dinder *Somset* 21 5744
Dinedor *Herefs* 46 5336
Dingestow *Mons* 34 4510
Dingle *Mersyd* 78 3687
Dingleden *Kent* 17 8131
Dingley *Nhants* 50 7787
Dingwall *Highld* 139 5458
Dinham *Mons* 34 4792
Dinmael *Conwy* 70 0044
Dinnet *Abers* 134 4598
Dinnington *S York* 75 5285
Dinnington *Somset* 10 4012
Dinnington *T & W* 103 2073
Dinorwic *Gwynd* 69 5961
Dinton *Bucks* 37 7610
Dinton *Wilts* 22 0131
Dinwoodie *D & G* 100 1190
Dinworthy *Devon* 18 3015
Dipford *Somset* 20 2021
Dipley *Hants* 24 7457
Dippen *Ag & B* 105 7937
Dippen *N Ayrs* 105 0422
Dippenhall *Surrey* 25 8146
Dippermill *Devon* 18 4406
Dippertown *Devon* 5 4284
Dipple *Moray* 141 3258
Dipple *S Ayrs* 106 2002
Diptford *Devon* 7 7256
Dipton *Dur* 96 1554
Diptonmill *Nthumb* 102 9361
Dirleton *E Loth* 118 5184
Dirt Pot *Nthumb* 95 8545
Discoed *Powys* 46 2764
Diseworth *Leics* 62 4524
Dishforth *N York* 89 3873
Disley *Ches* 79 9784
Diss *Norfk* 54 1180
Disserth *Powys* 45 0358
Distington *Cumb* 92 0023
Ditchampton *Wilts* 23 0831
Ditchburn *Nthumb* 111 1320
Ditcheat *Somset* 21 6236
Ditchingham *Norfk* 67 3391
Ditchley *Oxon* 36 3820
Ditchling *E Susx* 15 3215
Ditherington *Shrops* 59 5014
Ditteridge *Wilts* 35 8169
Dittisham *Devon* 7 8655

Place	Page	Ref
Ditton Ches	78	4986
Ditton Kent	28	7158
Ditton Green Cambs	53	6558
Ditton Priors Shrops	59	6089
Dixton Gloucs	47	9830
Dixton Mons	34	5113
Dizzard Cnwll	4	1698
Dobcross Gt Man	82	9906
Dobroyd Castle W York	81	9323
Dobwalls Cnwll	5	2165
Doccombe Devon	8	7786
Dochgarroch Highld	140	6140
Dockenfield Surrey	25	8240
Docker Lancs	87	5774
Docking Norfk	65	7636
Docklow Herefs	46	5657
Dockray Cumb	93	2649
Dockray Cumb	93	3921
Dod's Leigh Staffs	73	0134
Dodbrooke Devon	7	7444
Dodd's Green Ches	71	6043
Doddinghurst Essex	27	5999
Doddington Cambs	52	4090
Doddington Kent	28	9357
Doddington Lincs	76	8970
Doddington Nthumb	111	9932
Doddington Shrops	46	6176
Doddiscombsleigh Devon	8	8586
Doddshill Norfk	65	6930
Doddy Cross Cnwll	5	3062
Dodford Nhants	49	6160
Dodford Worcs	60	9373
Dodington Gloucs	35	7580
Dodington Somset	20	1740
Dodleston Ches	71	3661
Dodscott Devon	19	5419
Dodside E Rens	115	5053
Dodworth S York	82	3105
Dodworth Bottom S York	83	3204
Dodworth Green S York	82	3004
Doe Bank W Mids	61	1197
Doe Lea Derbys	75	4666
Dog Village Devon	9	9896
Dogdyke Lincs	76	2055
Dogley Lane W York	82	1813
Dogmersfield Hants	25	7852
Dogridge Wilts	36	0887
Dogsthorpe Cambs	64	1901
Dol-for Powys	57	8106
Dol-gran Carmth	31	4334
Dolanog Powys	58	0612
Dolau Powys	45	1467
Dolaucothi Carmth	44	6640
Dolbenmaen Gwynd	56	5043
Doley Shrops	72	7429
Dolfach Powys	58	9101
Dolfor Powys	58	1087
Dolgarrog Conwy	69	7767
Dolgellau Gwynd	57	7217
Dolgoch Gwynd	57	6504
Doll Highld	147	8803
Dollar Clacks	117	9698
Dollarfield Clacks	117	9697
Dolley Green Powys	46	2865
Dollwen Cerdgn	43	6881
Dolphin Flints	70	1973
Dolphinholme Lancs	80	5253
Dolphinton S Lans	117	1046
Dolton Devon	19	5712
Dolwen Conwy	69	8874
Dolwyddelan Conwy	69	7352
Dolybont Cerdgn	43	6288
Dolyhir Powys	46	2457
Domgay Powys	58	2818
Donaldson's Lodge Nthumb	110	8741
Doncaster S York	83	5703
Doncaster Carr S York	83	5801
Donhead St Andrew Wilts	22	9124
Donhead St Mary Wilts	22	9024
Donibristle Fife	117	1688
Doniford Somset	20	0842
Donington Lincs	64	2035
Donington on Bain Lincs	76	2382
Donington Southing Lincs	64	2034
Donisthorpe Leics	61	3113
Donkey Street Kent	17	1032
Donkey Town Surrey	25	9360
Donnington Berks	24	4668
Donnington Gloucs	48	1928
Donnington Herefs	47	7034
Donnington Shrops	59	5708
Donnington Shrops	60	7114
Donnington W Susx	14	8501
Donnington Wood Shrops	60	7012
Donyatt Somset	10	3314
Doomsday Green W Susx	15	1929
Doonfoot S Ayrs	106	3219
Doonholm S Ayrs	106	3317
Dorback Lodge Highld	141	0114
Dorchester Dorset	11	6990
Dorchester Oxon	37	5794
Dordon Warwks	61	2500
Dore S York	74	3181
Dores Highld	140	5934
Dorking Surrey	15	1649
Dorking Tye Suffk	54	9236
Dormans Land Surrey	15	4041
Dormans Park Surrey	15	3940
Dormington Herefs	46	5840
Dormston Worcs	47	9857
Dorn Gloucs	48	2034
Dorney Bucks	26	9378
Dornie Highld	138	8826
Dornoch Highld	147	7989
Dornock D & G	101	2366
Dorrery Highld	150	0754
Dorridge W Mids	61	1775
Dorrington Lincs	76	0852
Dorrington Shrops	59	4702
Dorrington Shrops	72	7340
Dorsington Warwks	48	1349
Dorstone Herefs	46	3141
Dorton Bucks	36	6814
Dosthill Staffs	61	2199
Dottery Dorset	10	4595
Doublebois Cnwll	5	1964
Doughton Gloucs	35	8791
Douglas IOM	158	3775
Douglas S Lans	108	8330
Douglas and Angus Dund C	127	4233
Douglas Castle S Lans	108	8431
Douglas Pier Ag & B	114	1999
Douglas Water S Lans	108	8736
Douglas West S Lans	108	8231
Douglastown Angus	126	4147
Doulting Somset	21	6443
Dounby Ork	153	2920
Doune Highld	146	4400
Doune Stirlg	116	7201
Dounepark S Ayrs	106	1897
Dounie Highld	146	5690
Dousland Devon	6	5369
Dovaston Shrops	59	3521
Dove Green Notts	75	4652
Dove Holes Derbys	74	0777
Dovenby Cumb	92	0933
Dover Gt Man	78	6000
Dover Kent	29	3241
Dover Castle	29	3241
Dovercourt Essex	41	2431
Doverdale Worcs	47	8666
Doveridge Derbys	73	1133
Doversgreen Surrey	15	2548
Dowally P & K	125	0048
Dowbridge Lancs	80	4331
Dowdeswell Gloucs	35	0019
Dowlais Myr Td	33	0607
Dowland Devon	19	5610
Dowlish Ford Somset	10	3513
Dowlish Wake Somset	10	3712
Down Ampney Gloucs	36	0096
Down Hatherley Gloucs	35	8622
Down St Mary Devon	8	7404
Down Thomas Devon	6	5050
Downacarey Devon	5	3790
Downderry Cnwll	5	3154
Downe Gt Lon	27	4361
Downend Berks	37	4775
Downend Gloucs	35	6577
Downend Gloucs	35	8398
Downend IOW	13	5387
Downfield Dund C	126	3932
Downgate Cnwll	5	2871
Downgate Cnwll	5	3672
Downham Essex	40	7296
Downham Gt Lon	27	3871
Downham Lancs	81	7844
Downham Nthumb	110	8633
Downham Market Norfk	65	6103
Downhead Somset	21	5625
Downhead Somset	22	6645
Downhill Cnwll	4	8669
Downholland Cross Lancs	78	3606
Downholme N York	89	1197
Downies Abers	135	9294
Downing Flints	70	1578
Downley Bucks	26	8495
Downside Somset	21	6244
Downside Somset	21	6450
Downside Surrey	26	1057
Downton Hants	12	2693
Downton Wilts	12	1821
Downton on the Rock Herefs	46	4273
Dowsby Lincs	64	1129
Dowsdale Lincs	64	2810
Dowsland Green Essex	40	8724
Doxey Staffs	72	8923
Doynton Gloucs	35	7274
Draethen Caerph	34	2287
Draffan S Lans	116	7945
Dragonby Lincs	84	9014
Dragons Green W Susx	15	1423
Drakeholes Notts	75	7090
Drakelow Worcs	60	8180
Drakemyre N Ayrs	115	2950
Drakes Broughton Worcs	47	9248
Drakes Cross Worcs	61	0876
Drakewalls Cnwll	6	4270
Draughton N York	82	0352
Draughton Nhants	50	7676
Drax N York	83	6726
Drax Hales N York	83	6725
Draycot Foliat Wilts	36	1777
Draycote Warwks	50	4470
Draycott Derbys	62	4433
Draycott Gloucs	48	1835
Draycott Shrops	60	8093
Draycott Somset	21	4751
Draycott Somset	21	5521
Draycott Worcs	47	8548
Draycott in the Clay Staffs	73	1528
Draycott in the Moors Staffs	72	9840
Drayford Devon	19	7813
Draynes Cnwll	5	2169
Drayton Hants	13	6705
Drayton Leics	51	8392
Drayton Lincs	64	2439
Drayton Norfk	66	1813
Drayton Oxon	49	4241
Drayton Oxon	37	4894
Drayton Somset	21	4024
Drayton Worcs	60	9075
Drayton Bassett Staffs	61	1900
Drayton Beauchamp Bucks	38	9011
Drayton Manor Park	61	1901
Drayton Parslow Bucks	38	8328
Drayton St Leonard Oxon	37	5996
Drebley N York	88	0559
Dreemskerry IOM	158	4791
Dreen Hill Pembks	30	9214
Drefach Carmth	31	3538
Drefach Carmth	32	5213
Drefach Cerdgn	44	4945
Drefach Carmth	31	3637
Dreghorn N Ayrs	106	3538
Drellingore Kent	29	2441
Drem E Loth	118	5079
Dresden Staffs	72	9142
Drewsteignton Devon	8	7391
Driby Lincs	77	3874
Driffield E R Yk	91	0257
Driffield Gloucs	36	0799
Driffield Cross Roads Gloucs	36	0698
Drift Cnwll	2	4328
Drigg Cumb	86	0699
Drighlington W York	82	2228
Drimnin Highld	121	5554
Drimpton Dorset	10	4104
Drimsallie Highld	130	9578
Dringhoe E R Yk	85	1454
Dringhouses N York	83	5849
Drinkstone Suffk	54	9561
Drinkstone Green Suffk	54	9660
Drinsey Nook Notts	76	8773
Drive End Dorset	10	5808
Driver's End Herts	39	2220
Drointon Staffs	73	0226
Droitwich Worcs	47	8963
Dron P & K	126	1416
Dronfield Derbys	74	3578
Dronfield Woodhouse Derbys	74	3378
Drongan E Ayrs	107	4418
Dronley Angus	126	3435
Droop Dorset	11	7508
Dropping Well S York	74	3994
Droxford Hants	13	6018
Droylsden Gt Man	79	9097
Druid Denbgs	70	0443
Druids Heath W Mids	61	0502
Druidston Pembks	30	8616
Druimachoish Highld	123	1446
Druimarbin Highld	130	0770
Druimdrishaig Ag & B	113	7301
Druimindarroch Highld	129	6884
Drum Ag & B	114	9276
Drum P & K	117	0400
Drumalbin S Lans	108	9038
Drumbeg Highld	148	1232
Drumblade Abers	142	5840
Drumbreddon D & G	98	0843
Drumbuie Highld	137	7730
Drumburgh Cumb	93	2659
Drumburn D & G	92	8854
Drumchapel C Glas	115	5270
Drumchastle P & K	132	6858
Drumclog S Lans	107	6438
Drumeldrie Fife	127	4403
Drumelzier Border	108	1334
Drumfearn Highld	129	6716
Drumfrennie Abers	135	7298
Drumguish Highld	132	7900
Drumhead Abers	134	6092
Drumin Moray	141	1830
Drumjohn D & G	107	5297
Drumlamford S Ayrs	98	2876
Drumlasie Abers	135	6405
Drumleaning Cumb	93	2751
Drumlemble Ag & B	104	6619
Drumlithie Abers	135	7880
Drummoddie D & G	99	3845
Drummore D & G	98	1336
Drummuir Moray	141	3843
Drumnadrochit Highld	139	5030
Drumnagorrach Moray	142	5252
Drumpark D & G	100	8779
Drumrunie Lodge Highld	145	1604
Drumshang S Ayrs	106	2514
Drumuie Highld	136	4546
Drumuillie Highld	140	9420
Drumvaich Stirlg	124	6704
Drunzie P & K	126	1308
Druridge Nthumb	103	2796
Drury Flints	71	2964
Dry Doddington Lincs	63	8546
Dry Drayton Cambs	52	3861
Dry Sandford Oxon	37	4600
Dry Street Essex	40	6986
Drybeck Cumb	94	6615
Drybridge Moray	142	4362
Drybridge N Ayrs	106	3536
Drybrook Gloucs	35	6417
Dryburgh Border	110	5932
Drym Cnwll	2	6133
Drymen Stirlg	115	4788
Drymuir Abers	143	9046
Drynoch Highld	136	4031
Dryslwyn Carmth	32	5520
Dryton Shrops	59	5806
Dubford Abers	143	7963
Dublin Suffk	54	1669
Duchally Highld	145	3817
Duck End Beds	38	0048
Duck End Cambs	52	2464
Duck End Essex	40	6526
Duck End Essex	53	6833
Duck's Cross Beds	52	1156
Duckend Green Essex	40	7223
Duckington Ches	71	4851
Ducklington Oxon	36	3507
Duddingston C Edin	117	2872
Duddington Nhants	51	9800
Duddlestone Somset	20	2321
Duddleswell E Susx	16	4628
Duddlewick Shrops	59	6583
Duddo Nthumb	110	9342
Duddon Ches	71	5164
Duddon Bridge Cumb	86	1988
Dudleston Shrops	71	3438
Dudleston Heath Shrops	59	3736
Dudley T & W	103	2573
Dudley W Mids	60	9490
Dudley Hill W York	82	1830
Dudley Port W Mids	60	9691
Dudnill Shrops	47	6474
Dudsbury Dorset	12	0798
Dudswell Herts	38	9609
Duffield Derbys	62	3443
Duffryn Neath	33	8495
Dufftown Moray	141	3240
Duffus Moray	141	1668
Dufton Cumb	94	6825
Duggleby N York	90	8767
Duirinish Highld	137	7831
Duisdalemore Highld	129	7013
Duisky Highld	130	0076
Duke Street Suffk	54	0742
Dukestown Blae G	33	1410
Dukinfield Gt Man	79	9397
Dulas IOA	68	4789
Dulcote Somset	21	5644
Dulford Devon	9	0706
Dull P & K	125	8049
Dullatur N Lans	116	7476
Dullingham Cambs	53	6357
Dullingham Ley Cambs	53	6456
Dulnain Bridge Highld	141	9925
Duloe Beds	52	1560
Duloe Cnwll	5	2358
Dulverton Somset	20	9127
Dulwich Gt Lon	27	3373
Dumbarton W Duns	115	3975
Dumbleton Gloucs	47	0135
Dumfries D & G	100	9776
Dumgoyne Stirlg	115	5283
Dummer Hants	24	5846
Dumpton Kent	29	3966
Dun Angus	135	6659
Dunalastair P & K	132	7158
Dunan Ag & B	114	1571
Dunan Highld	137	5828
Dunan P & K	124	4757
Dunaverty Ag & B	105	6807
Dunball Somset	21	3141
Dunbar E Loth	118	6778
Dunbeath Highld	151	1629
Dunbeg Ag & B	122	8833
Dunblane Stirlg	116	7801
Dunbog Fife	126	2817
Dunbridge Hants	23	3226
Duncanston Highld	139	5856
Duncanstone Abers	142	5726
Dunchideock Devon	9	8787
Dunchurch Warwks	50	4871
Duncote Nhants	49	6750
Duncow D & G	100	9683
Duncrievie P & K	126	1309
Duncton W Susx	14	9617
Dundee Dund C	126	4030
Dundee Airport	126	3728
Dundon Somset	21	4832
Dundonald S Ayrs	106	3634
Dundonnell Highld	145	0987
Dundraw Cumb	93	2149
Dundreggan Highld	131	3214
Dundrennan D & G	99	7447
Dundry Somset	21	5666
Dunecht Abers	135	7509
Dunfermline Fife	117	0987
Dunfield Gloucs	36	1497
Dunford Bridge S York	82	1502
Dungate Kent	28	9159
Dungavel S Lans	107	6537
Dunge Wilts	22	8954
Dungworth S York	74	2789
Dunham Notts	75	8074
Dunham Town Gt Man	79	7387
Dunham Woodhouses Gt Man	79	7287
Dunham-on-the-Hill Ches	71	4772
Dunhampstead Worcs	47	9160
Dunhampton Worcs	47	8466
Dunholme Lincs	76	0279
Dunino Fife	127	5311
Dunipace Falk	116	8083
Dunkeld P & K	125	0242
Dunkerton Somset	22	7159
Dunkeswell Devon	9	1407
Dunkeswick W York	82	3047
Dunkirk Ches	71	3872
Dunkirk Gloucs	35	7885
Dunkirk Kent	29	0759
Dunkirk Staffs	72	8152
Dunkirk Wilts	22	9962
Dunlappie Angus	134	5867
Dunley Hants	24	4553
Dunley Worcs	47	7869
Dunlop E Ayrs	115	4049
Dunmaglass Highld	140	5922
Dunmere Cnwll	4	0467
Dunmore Falk	116	8989
Dunn Street Kent	28	7961
Dunnet Highld	151	2171
Dunnichen Angus	127	5048
Dunning P & K	125	0114
Dunnington E R Yk	85	1551
Dunnington N York	83	6652
Dunnington Warwks	48	0654
Dunnockshaw Lancs	81	8127
Dunoon Ag & B	114	1776
Dunphail Moray	141	0048
Dunragit D & G	98	1557
Duns Border	119	7853
Duns Tew Oxon	49	4528
Dunsa Derbys	74	2470
Dunsby Lincs	64	1026
Dunscar Gt Man	81	7113
Dunscore D & G	100	8684
Dunscroft S York	83	6409
Dunsdale N York	97	6019
Dunsden Green Oxon	37	7377
Dunsdon Devon	18	3008
Dunsfold Surrey	14	0035
Dunsford Devon	8	8189
Dunshalt Fife	126	2410
Dunshillock Abers	143	9848
Dunsill Notts	75	4661
Dunsley N York	90	8511
Dunsley Staffs	60	8583
Dunsmore Bucks	38	8605
Dunsop Bridge Lancs	81	6649
Dunstable Beds	38	0122
Dunstall Staffs	73	1820
Dunstall Common Worcs	47	8843
Dunstall Green Suffk	53	7460
Dunstan Nthumb	111	2419
Dunstan Steads Nthumb	111	2422
Dunster Somset	20	9943
Dunston Lincs	76	0662
Dunston Norfk	67	2202
Dunston Staffs	72	9217
Dunston T & W	96	2362
Dunstone Devon	6	5951
Dunstone Devon	7	7175
Dunsville S York	83	6407
Dunswell E R Yk	85	0735
Dunsyre S Lans	117	0748
Dunterton Devon	5	3779
Dunthrop Oxon	48	3528
Duntisbourne Abbots Gloucs	35	9607
Duntisbourne Rouse Gloucs	35	9…
Duntish Dorset	11	6…
Duntocher W Duns	115	4…
Dunton Beds	39	2…
Dunton Bucks	38	8…
Dunton Norfk	66	8…
Dunton Bassett Leics	50	5…
Dunton Green Kent	27	4…
Dunton Wayletts Essex	40	6…
Duntulm Highld	136	4…
Dunure S Ayrs	106	2…
Dunvant Swans	32	5…
Dunvegan Highld	136	2…
Dunwich Suffk	55	4…
Dunwood Staffs	72	9…
Durdar Cumb	93	4…
Durgan Cnwll	3	7…
Durham Dur	96	2…
Durham Cathedral	96	2…
Durisdeer D & G	108	8…
Durisdeermill D & G	108	8…
Durkar W York	82	3…
Durleigh Somset	20	2…
Durley Hants	13	5…
Durley Wilts	23	2…
Durley Street Hants	13	5…
Durlock Kent	29	2…
Durlock Kent	29	3…
Durlow Common Gloucs	47	6…
Durmgley Angus	127	4…
Durn Gt Man	82	9…
Durness Highld	149	4…
Duror Highld	122	9…
Durran Ag & B	122	9…
Durrington W Susx	14	1…
Durrington Wilts	23	1…
Durris Abers	135	7…
Dursley Gloucs	35	7…
Dursley Cross Gloucs	35	6…
Durston Somset	20	2…
Durweston Dorset	11	8…
Duston Nhants	49	7…
Duthil Highld	140	9…
Dutlas Powys	45	2…
Duton Hill Essex	40	6…
Dutson Cnwll	5	3…
Dutton Ches	71	5…
Duxford Cambs	53	4…
Duxford Oxon	36	3…
Duxford Aircraft Museum	53	4…
Dwygyfylchi Conwy	69	7…
Dwyran IOA	68	4…
Dyce Aber C	135	8…
Dyer's End Essex	53	7…
Dyfatty Carmth	32	4…
Dyffryn Gwynd	57	6…
Dyffryn Brdgnd	33	8…
Dyffryn Myr Td	33	0…
Dyffryn V Glam	33	0…
Dyffryn Ardudwy Gwynd	57	5…
Dyffryn Castell Cerdgn	43	7…
Dyffryn Cellwen Neath	33	8…
Dyke Lincs	64	1…
Dyke Moray	140	9…
Dykehead Angus	126	2…
Dykehead Angus	134	3…
Dykehead N Lans	116	8…
Dykehead Stirlg	115	5…
Dykelands Abers	135	7…
Dykends Angus	133	2…
Dykeside Abers	142	7…
Dylife Powys	43	8…
Dymchurch Kent	17	1…
Dymock Gloucs	47	7…
Dyrham Gloucs	35	7…
Dysart Fife	117	3…
Dyserth Denbgs	70	0…

E

Place	Page	Ref
Eachway Worcs	60	9…
Eachwick Nthumb	103	1…
Eagland Hill Lancs	80	4…
Eagle Lincs	76	8…
Eagle Barnsdale Lincs	76	8…
Eagle Moor Lincs	76	8…
Eaglescliffe Dur	96	4…
Eaglesfield Cumb	92	0…
Eaglesfield D & G	101	2…
Eaglesham E Rens	115	5…
Eagley Gt Man	81	7…
Eairy IOM	158	2…
Eakley Lanes Bucks	38	8…
Eakring Notts	75	6…
Ealand Lincs	84	7…
Ealing Gt Lon	26	1…
Eals Nthumb	94	6…
Eamont Bridge Cumb	94	5…
Earby Lancs	81	9…
Earcroft Lancs	81	6…
Eardington Shrops	60	7…
Eardisland Herefs	46	4…
Eardisley Herefs	46	3…
Eardiston Shrops	59	3…
Eardiston Worcs	47	6…
Earith Cambs	52	3…
Earl Shilton Leics	50	4…
Earl Soham Suffk	55	2…
Earl Sterndale Derbys	74	0…
Earl Stonham Suffk	54	1…
Earl's Croome Worcs	47	8…
Earl's Green Suffk	54	0…
Earle Nthumb	111	9…
Earlestown Mersyd	78	5…
Earley Berks	24	7…
Earlham Norfk	67	1…
Earlish Highld	136	3…
Earls Barton Nhants	51	8…
Earls Colne Essex	40	8…
Earls Common Worcs	47	9…

sditton Shrops 47 6275
sdon W Mids 61 3278
sferry Fife 118 4800
sfield Gt Lon 27 2573
sford Abers 143 8334
sheaton W York 82 2621
ston Border 110 5738
ston E Ayrs 106 4035
sswood Surrey 15 2749
sswood Warwks 61 1174
sswood Common Mons 34 4594
nley W Susx 14 8196
nshaw Bridge Lancs 80 5222
sdon Nthumb 103 1993
sdon T & W 103 3272
sham Norfk 55 3288
swick N York 90 6157
sham N York 14 9309
cham W Susx 14 9309
chcott Gloucs 35 6585
sby N York 90 5708
dale Ag & B 122 7417
ebourne W Susx 14 9023
eenhall Warwks 50 4679
ening Surrey 25 9443
ngton Bucks 37 6810
ngton Dur 96 4143
ngton E R Yk 85 3919
ngton N York 97 7417
ngton Nthumb 111 1234
ngton Oxon 37 6697
ngton Colliery Dur 96 4344
ngton Lane T & W 96 3646
ngwold N York 90 5269
ple Street Kent 29 2652
sie and Nevay Angus 126 3344
: Aberthaw V Glam 20 0366
: Allington Devon 7 7748
: Anstey Devon 19 8626
: Anton Hants 23 3747
: Appleton N York 89 2395
: Ashey IOW 13 5888
: Ashling W Susx 14 8107
: Aston Hants 24 4445
: Ayton N York 91 9985
: Balsdon Cnwll 5 2898
: Bank Blae G 33 2105
: Barkwith Lincs 76 1681
: Barming Kent 28 7254
: Barnby N York 90 8212
: Barnet E Loth 27 2795
: Barns E Loth 119 7176
: Barsham Norfk 66 9133
: Beckham Norfk 66 1639
: Bedfont Gt Lon 26 0873
: Bergholt Suffk 54 0734
: Bierley W York 82 1929
t Bilney Norfk 66 9519
t Blatchington E Susx 16 4800
t Bloxworth Dorset 11 8894
t Boldon T & W 96 3661
t Boldre Hants 12 3700
t Bolton Nthumb 111 1216
t Bower Somset 21 3237
t Bradenham Norfk 66 9308
t Brent Somset 21 3451
t Bridgford Notts 63 6943
t Briscoe Dur 95 9719
t Buckland Devon 19 6831
t Budleigh Devon 9 0684
t Burnham Bucks 26 9584
t Burton Dorset 11 8287
t Butsfield Dur 95 1145
t Butterwick Lincs 84 8306
t Calder W Loth 117 0867
t Carleton Norfk 66 1701
t Carlton Nhants 51 8389
t Carlton W York 82 2143
t Challow Oxon 36 3888
t Charleton Devon 7 7642
t Chelborough Dorset 10 5505
t Chevington Nthumb 103 2699
t Chiltington E Susx 15 3715
t Chinnock Somset 10 4913
t Chisenbury Wilts 23 1452
t Cholderton Hants 23 2945
t Clandon Surrey 26 0651
t Claydon Bucks 49 7325
t Clevedon Somset 34 4171
t Coker Somset 10 5412
t Combe Somset 20 1631
t Compton Somset 21 6141
t Cornworthy Devon 7 8455
t Cote Cumb 92 1255
t Cottingham E R Yk 84 7042
t Cowes IOW 13 5095
t Cowick E R Yk 83 6620
t Cowton N York 89 3003
t Cramlington Nthumb 103 2776
t Cranmore Somset 22 6743
t Creech Dorset 11 9382
t Curthwaite Cumb 93 3348
t Dean E Susx 16 5598
t Dean Gloucs 35 6520
t Dean Hants 23 2726
t Dean W Susx 14 9012
t Down Devon 19 6041
t Drayton Notts 75 7775
t Dulwich Gt Lon 27 3375
t Dundry Somset 21 5766
t Ella E R Yk 84 0539
t End Beds 38 9642
t End Beds 51 1055
t End Beds 38 9344
t End E R Yk 85 1931
t End E R Yk 85 2927
t End Essex 39 4210
t End Hants 24 4161
t End Hants 12 3696
t End Herts 39 4527
t End Kent 17 8335
t End Kent 28 9673
t End Oxon 36 3915
t End Somset 34 4770
t End Somset 22 6746
t Everleigh Wilts 23 2053
t Farleigh Kent 28 7353
t Farndon Nhants 50 7184
t Ferry Lincs 75 8199

East Firsby Lincs 76 0085
East Ford Suffk 54 1035
East Fortune E Loth 118 5479
East Garforth W York 83 4133
East Garston Berks 36 3576
East Ginge Oxon 37 4486
East Goscote Leics 63 6413
East Grafton Wilts 23 2560
East Green Suffk 55 4065
East Grimstead Wilts 23 2227
East Grinstead W Susx 15 3938
East Guldeford E Susx 17 9321
East Haddon Nhants 50 6668
East Hagbourne Oxon 37 5288
East Halton Lincs 85 1319
East Ham Gt Lon 27 4283
East Hanney Oxon 36 4193
East Hanningfield Essex 40 7701
East Hardwick W York 83 4618
East Harling Norfk 54 9986
East Harlsey N York 89 4299
East Harnham Wilts 23 1428
East Harptree Somset 21 5655
East Hartburn Dur 96 4217
East Hartford Nthumb 103 2679
East Harting W Susx 14 7919
East Hatch Wilts 22 9228
East Hatley Cambs 52 2850
East Hauxwell N York 89 1693
East Haven Angus 127 5836
East Heckington Lincs 64 1944
East Hedleyhope Dur 96 1540
East Helmsdale Highld 147 0315
East Hendred Oxon 37 4588
East Heslerton N York 91 9276
East Hewish Somset 21 4064
East Hoathly E Susx 16 5216
East Holme Dorset 11 8986
East Horrington Somset 21 5846
East Horsley Surrey 26 0952
East Horton Nthumb 111 0330
East Howe Dorset 12 0795
East Huntington N York 83 6155
East Huntspill Somset 21 3445
East Hyde Beds 38 1217
East Ilkerton Devon 19 7147
East Ilsley Berks 37 4980
East Keal Lincs 77 3863
East Kennett Wilts 23 1167
East Keswick W York 83 3644
East Kilbride S Lans 116 6354
East Kimber Devon 5 4998
East Kirkby Lincs 77 3362
East Knighton Dorset 11 8185
East Knowstone Devon 19 8423
East Knoyle Wilts 22 8830
East Kyloe Nthumb 111 0639
East Lambrook Somset 10 4318
East Langdon Kent 29 3346
East Langton Leics 50 7292
East Laroch Highld 130 0858
East Lavant W Susx 14 8608
East Lavington W Susx 14 9416
East Layton N York 89 1509
East Leake Notts 62 5526
East Learmouth Nthumb 110 8637
East Leigh Devon 8 6905
East Leigh Devon 7 6852
East Leigh Devon 7 7657
East Lexham Norfk 66 8517
East Linton E Loth 118 5577
East Liss Hants 14 7827
East Lockinge Oxon 36 4287
East Lound Lincs 75 7899
East Lulworth Dorset 11 8682
East Lutton N York 91 9469
East Lydeard Somset 20 1829
East Lydford Somset 21 5731
East Malling Kent 28 7056
East Malling Heath Kent 28 6955
East Marden W Susx 14 8014
East Markham Notts 75 7373
East Martin Hants 12 0719
East Marton N York 81 9050
East Meon Hants 13 6822
East Mere Devon 9 9916
East Mersea Essex 41 0414
East Midlands Airport 62 4626
East Molesey Surrey 26 1467
East Morden Dorset 11 9194
East Morton D & G 108 8800
East Morton W York 82 0942
East Ness N York 90 6978
East Newton E R Yk 85 2638
East Norton Leics 50 7800
East Ogwell Devon 7 8370
East Orchard Dorset 11 8317
East Ord Nthumb 119 9751
East Panson Devon 5 3692
East Parley Dorset 12 1097
East Peckham Kent 28 6648
East Pennar Pembks 30 9602
East Pennard Somset 21 5597
East Perry Cambs 52 1566
East Portlemouth Devon 7 7538
East Prawle Devon 7 7836
East Preston W Susx 14 0602
East Pulham Dorset 11 7209
East Putford Devon 18 3616
East Quantoxhead Somset 20 1143
East Rainham Kent 28 8267
East Rainton T & W 96 3347
East Ravendale Lincs 76 2399
East Raynham Norfk 66 8825
East Rigton N York 83 3743
East Rolstone Somset 21 3962
East Rounton N York 89 4203
East Rudham Norfk 66 8228
East Runton Norfk 67 1942
East Ruston Norfk 67 3437
East Saltoun E Loth 118 4767
East Scrafton N York 89 0884
East Sheen Gt Lon 26 2075
East Shefford Berks 36 3874
East Sleekburn Nthumb 103 2883
East Somerton Norfk 67 4719
East Stockwith Lincs 75 7804
East Stoke Dorset 11 8686

East Stoke Notts 75 7549
East Stour Dorset 22 8022
East Stourmouth Kent 29 2662
East Stowford Devon 19 6326
East Stratton Hants 24 5440
East Studdal Kent 29 3149
East Sutton Kent 28 8349
East Taphouse Cnwll 4 1863
East Thirston Nthumb 89 1900
East Tilbury Essex 28 6877
East Tisted Hants 24 7032
East Torrington Lincs 76 1483
East Tuddenham Norfk 66 0711
East Tytherley Hants 23 2929
East Tytherton Wilts 35 9674
East Village Devon 8 8405
East Wall Shrops 59 5293
East Walton Norfk 65 7416
East Water Somset 21 5530
East Week Devon 8 6692
East Wellow Hants 12 3020
East Wemyss Fife 118 3497
East Whitburn W Loth 117 9665
East Wickham Gt Lon 27 4677
East Williamston Pembks 31 0904
East Winch Norfk 65 6916
East Winterslow Wilts 23 2434
East Wittering W Susx 14 7997
East Witton N York 89 1486
East Woodburn Nthumb 102 9086
East Woodhay Hants 24 4061
East Woodlands Somset 22 7944
East Worldham Hants 24 7538
East Wretham Norfk 54 9190
East Youlstone Devon 18 2715
East-the-Water Devon 18 4526
Eastbourne Dur 89 3013
Eastbourne E Susx 16 6199
Eastbridge Suffk 55 4566
Eastbrook V Glam 33 1671
Eastburn W York 82 0144
Eastbury Berks 36 3477
Eastbury Herts 26 1092
Eastby N York 82 0154
Eastchurch Kent 28 9871
Eastcombe Gloucs 35 8904
Eastcote Gt Lon 26 1088
Eastcote Nhants 49 6853
Eastcote W Mids 61 1979
Eastcott Cnwll 18 2515
Eastcott Wilts 23 0255
Eastcourt Wilts 35 9792
Eastcourt Wilts 23 2361
Eastdown Devon 7 8249
Eastend Essex 40 9492
Eastend S Lans 108 9537
Easter Balmoral Abers 133 2694
Easter Compton Gloucs 34 5782
Easter Dalziel Highld 140 7550
Easter Howgate Mdloth 117 2463
Easter Kinkell Highld 139 5755
Easter Moniack Highld 139 5543
Easter Ord Abers 135 8304
Easter Pitkierie Fife 127 5606
Easter Skeld Shet 153 3144
Easter Softlaw Border 110 7532
Eastergate W Susx 14 9405
Easterhouse C Glas 116 6865
Eastern Green W Mids 61 2879
Easterton Wilts 23 0254
Eastertown Somset 21 3454
Eastfield N Lans 116 8964
Eastfield N York 91 0484
Eastgate Dur 95 9538
Eastgate Lincs 64 1019
Eastgate Norfk 66 1423
Eastham Mersyd 78 3680
Eastham Ferry Mersyd 78 3661
Easthampstead Berks 25 8667
Easthampton Herefs 46 4063
Eastheath Berks 25 7967
Easthope Shrops 59 5695
Easthorpe Essex 40 9121
Easthorpe Notts 75 7053
Eastington Devon 19 7408
Eastington Gloucs 36 1213
Eastington Gloucs 35 7705
Eastlands D & G 100 8172
Eastleach Martin Gloucs 36 2004
Eastleach Turville Gloucs 36 1905
Eastleigh Devon 18 4827
Eastleigh Hants 13 4519
Eastling Kent 28 9656
Eastmoor Norfk 65 7303
Eastney Hants 13 6698
Eastnor Herefs 47 7237
Eastoft Lincs 84 8016
Easton Berks 24 4172
Easton Cambs 52 1371
Easton Cumb 93 2759
Easton Devon 8 7289
Easton Dorset 11 6971
Easton Hants 24 5132
Easton IOW 12 3486
Easton Lincs 63 9326
Easton Norfk 66 1310
Easton Somset 21 5147
Easton Suffk 55 2858
Easton Wilts 35 8970
Easton Grey Wilts 35 8887
Easton Maudit Nhants 51 8858
Easton on the Hill Nhants 64 0104
Easton Royal Wilts 23 2060
Easton-in-Gordano Somset 34 5175
Eastpeek Devon 5 3494
Eastrea Cambs 64 2997
Eastriggs D & G 101 2466
Eastrington E R Yk 84 7929
Eastrop Wilts 36 2092
Eastry Kent 29 3054
Eastshaw W Susx 14 8724
Eastville Bristl 35 6174
Eastville Lincs 77 4056
Eastwell Leics 63 7728
Eastwick Herts 39 4311
Eastwood Essex 40 8688
Eastwood Notts 62 4646
Eastwood W York 82 9726

Eastwood End Cambs 65 4292
Eathorpe Warwks 48 3969
Eaton Ches 71 5763
Eaton Ches 72 8765
Eaton Leics 63 7928
Eaton Norfk 67 2006
Eaton Notts 75 7077
Eaton Oxon 37 4403
Eaton Shrops 59 3789
Eaton Shrops 59 5089
Eaton Bishop Herefs 46 4439
Eaton Bray Beds 38 9720
Eaton Constantine Shrops 59 5906
Eaton Ford Beds 52 1759
Eaton Green Beds 38 9621
Eaton Hastings Oxon 36 2598
Eaton Mascott Shrops 59 5305
Eaton Socon Cambs 52 1759
Eaton upon Tern Shrops 72 6523
Eaves Brow Ches 79 6393
Eaves Green W Mids 61 2682
Ebberston N York 91 8982
Ebbesborne Wake Wilts 22 9924
Ebbw Vale Blae G 33 1609
Ebchester Dur 95 1055
Ebdon Somset 21 3664
Ebford Devon 9 9887
Ebley Gloucs 35 8205
Ebnal Ches 71 4948
Ebnall Herefs 46 4758
Ebrington Gloucs 48 1840
Ebsworthy Town Devon 5 5090
Ecchinswell Hants 24 4959
Ecclaw Border 119 7568
Ecclefechan D & G 101 1974
Eccles Border 110 7641
Eccles Gt Man 79 7798
Eccles Kent 28 7360
Eccles on Sea Norfk 67 4128
Eccles Road Norfk 54 0189
Ecclesall S York 74 3284
Ecclesfield S York 74 3593
Eccleshall Staffs 72 8329
Eccleshill W York 82 1736
Ecclesmachan W Loth 117 0573
Eccleston Ches 71 4162
Eccleston Lancs 80 5217
Eccleston Mersyd 78 4895
Eccleston Green Lancs 80 5216
Echt Abers 135 7405
Eckford Border 110 7026
Eckington Derbys 75 4379
Eckington Worcs 47 9241
Ecton Nhants 51 8263
Ecton Staffs 74 0958
Edale Derbys 74 1285
Eday Airport 153 5634
Edburton W Susx 15 2311
Edderside Cumb 92 1045
Edderton Highld 146 7084
Eddington Kent 29 1867
Eddleston Border 117 2447
Eddlewood S Lans 116 7153
Eden Mount Cumb 87 4077
Eden Park Gt Lon 27 3667
Edenbridge Kent 16 4446
Edenfield Lancs 81 8019
Edenhall Cumb 94 5632
Edenham Lincs 64 0621
Edensor Derbys 74 2469
Edentaggart Ag & B 115 3293
Edenthorpe S York 83 6206
Edern Gwynd 56 2739
Edgarley Somset 21 5238
Edgbaston W Mids 61 0684
Edgcombe Cnwll 2 7133
Edgcott Bucks 37 6722
Edgcott Somset 19 8438
Edge Gloucs 35 8409
Edge Shrops 59 3908
Edge End Gloucs 34 5913
Edge Green Ches 71 4851
Edgebolton Shrops 59 5721
Edgefield Norfk 66 0934
Edgefield Green Norfk 66 0934
Edgefold Gt Man 79 7005
Edgehill Warwks 48 3747
Edgerley Shrops 59 3518
Edgerton W York 82 1317
Edgeside Lancs 81 8322
Edgeworth Gloucs 35 9406
Edgeworthy Devon 19 8413
Edgiock Worcs 48 0461
Edgmond Shrops 72 7119
Edgmond Marsh Shrops 72 7120
Edgton Shrops 59 3885
Edgware Gt Lon 26 1991
Edgworth Lancs 81 7416
Edial Staffs 61 0808
Edinbane Highld 136 3450
Edinburgh C Edin 117 2573
Edinburgh Airport 117 1473
Edinburgh Castle 117 2573
Edinburgh Zoo 117 2173
Edingale Staffs 61 2111
Edingham D & G 100 8363
Edingley Notts 75 6655
Edingthorpe Norfk 67 3132
Edingthorpe Green Norfk 67 3031
Edington Border 119 8955
Edington Nthumb 103 1582
Edington Somset 21 3839
Edington Wilts 22 9253
Edington Burtle Somset 21 3943
Edingworth Somset 21 3653
Edith Weston Rutlnd 63 9205
Edithmead Somset 21 3249
Edlesborough Bucks 38 9719
Edlingham Nthumb 111 1109
Edlington Lincs 76 2371
Edmond Castle Cumb 94 4968
Edmondsham Dorset 12 0611
Edmondsley Dur 96 2349
Edmondthorpe Leics 63 8517
Edmonton Cnwll 4 9672
Edmonton Gt Lon 27 3492
Edmundbyers Dur 95 0150

Ednam Border 110 7337
Ednaston Derbys 73 2341
Edradynate P & K 125 8751
Edrom Border 119 8255
Edstaston Shrops 59 5132
Edstone Warwks 48 1861
Edvin Loach Herefs 47 6658
Edwalton Notts 62 5935
Edwardstone Suffk 54 9442
Edwardsville Myr Td 33 0896
Edwinsford Carmth 44 6334
Edwinstowe Notts 75 6266
Edworth Beds 39 2241
Edwyn Ralph Herefs 47 6457
Edzell Angus 134 6068
Efail Isaf Rhondd 33 0844
Efail-fach Neath 32 7895
Efail-Rhyd Powys 58 1626
Efailnewydd Gwynd 56 3535
Efailwen Carmth 31 1325
Efenechtyd Denbgs 70 1155
Effgill D & G 101 3092
Effingham Surrey 26 1153
Efflinch Staffs 73 1816
Efford Devon 9 8901
Egbury Hants 24 4352
Egdean W Susx 14 9920
Egerton Gt Man 81 7014
Egerton Kent 28 9147
Eggbuckland Devon 6 5057
Eggesford Devon 19 6811
Eggington Beds 38 9525
Egginton Derbys 73 2628
Egglescliffe Dur 89 4113
Eggleston Dur 95 9923
Egham Surrey 25 0071
Egham Wick Surrey 25 9870
Eginswell Devon 7 8866
Egleton Rutlnd 63 8707
Eglingham Nthumb 111 1019
Egloshayle Cnwll 4 0072
Egloskerry Cnwll 5 2786
Eglwys Cross Wrexhm 71 4740
Eglwys-Brewis V Glam 20 0068
Eglwysbach Conwy 69 8070
Eglwysfach Cerdgn 43 6996
Eglwyswrw Pembks 31 1438
Egmanton Notts 75 7368
Egremont Cumb 86 0110
Egremont Mersyd 78 3192
Egton N York 90 8006
Egton Bridge N York 90 8004
Eight and Forty E R Yk 84 8529
Eight Ash Green Essex 40 9425
Eilanreach Highld 129 8018
Elan Village Powys 45 9364
Elberton Gloucs 34 6088
Elbridge W Susx 14 9101
Elburton Devon 6 5353
Elcombe Wilts 36 1280
Elcot Berks 36 3999
Elder Street Essex 53 5734
Eldernell Cambs 64 3298
Eldersfield Worcs 47 7931
Elderslie Rens 115 4463
Eldmire N York 89 4274
Eldon Dur 96 2328
Eldwick W York 82 1240
Elfhill Abers 135 8085
Elford Nthumb 111 1831
Elford Staffs 61 1810
Elgin Moray 141 2162
Elgol Highld 128 5213
Elham Kent 29 1744
Elie Fife 118 4900
Elilaw Nthumb 111 9708
Elim IOA 68 3564
Eling Hants 12 3612
Elkesley Notts 75 6975
Elkstone Gloucs 35 9612
Ella Abers 142 6459
Ellacombe Devon 7 9164
Ellanbeich Ag & B 122 7417
Elland W York 82 1120
Elland Lower Edge W York 82 1221
Ellary Ag & B 113 7376
Ellastone Staffs 73 1143
Ellel Lancs 80 4856
Ellemford Border 119 7260
Ellen's Green Surrey 14 0935
Ellenborough Cumb 92 0435
Ellenbrook Gt Man 79 7201
Ellenhall Staffs 72 8426
Ellerbeck N York 89 4396
Ellerby N York 90 7914
Ellerdine Heath Shrops 59 6122
Ellerhayes Devon 9 9702
Elleric Ag & B 123 0448
Ellerker E R Yk 84 9229
Ellers N York 82 0043
Ellerton E R Yk 84 7039
Ellerton N York 89 2598
Ellerton Shrops 72 7125
Ellesborough Bucks 38 8306
Ellesmere Shrops 59 3934
Ellesmere Port Ches 71 4076
Ellicombe Somset 20 9844
Ellingham Hants 12 1408
Ellingham Norfk 67 3592
Ellingham Nthumb 111 1725
Ellingstring N York 89 1783
Ellington Cambs 52 1611
Ellington Nthumb 103 2791
Ellington Thorpe Cambs 52 1670
Elliots Green Somset 22 7945
Ellisfield Hants 24 6446
Ellishader Highld 137 5065
Ellistown Leics 62 4310
Ellon Abers 143 9530
Ellonby Cumb 93 4235
Ellough Suffk 55 4486
Elloughton E R Yk 84 9428
Ellwood Gloucs 34 5908
Elm Cambs 65 4707
Elm Green Essex 40 7705
Elm Grove Norfk 67 4803
Elm Park Gt Lon 27 5385
Elmbridge Worcs 47 9068

Elmdon
Feshiebridge

284

Elmdon Essex 39 4639
Elmdon W Mids 61 1783
Elmdon Heath W Mids 61 1680
Elmer W Susx 14 9800
Elmer's Green Lancs 78 5006
Elmers End Gt Lon 27 3668
Elmesthorpe Leics 50 4696
Elmhurst Staffs 61 1112
Elmley Castle Worcs 47 9841
Elmley Lovett Worcs 47 8769
Elmore Gloucs 35 7815
Elmore Back Gloucs 35 7616
Elms Green Worcs 47 7266
Elmscott Devon 18 2321
Elmsett Suffk 54 0546
Elmstead Heath Essex 41 0622
Elmstead Market Essex 41 0624
Elmstead Row Essex 41 0621
Elmsted Court Kent 29 1144
Elmstone Kent 29 2660
Elmstone Hardwicke Gloucs 47 9125
Elmswell E R Yk 91 9958
Elmswell Suffk 54 9964
Elmton Derbys 75 5073
Elphin Highld 145 2111
Elphinstone E Loth 118 3970
Elrick Abers 135 8106
Elrig D & G 98 3247
Elrington Nthumb 102 8563
Elsdon Nthumb 102 9393
Elsecar S York 74 3899
Elsenham Essex 39 5326
Elsfield Oxon 37 5410
Elsham Lincs 84 0312
Elsick House Abers 135 8894
Elsing Norfk 66 0516
Elslack N York 81 9349
Elson Hants 13 6002
Elson Shrops 59 3735
Elsrickle S Lans 108 0643
Elstead Surrey 25 9043
Elsted W Susx 14 8119
Elsthorpe Lincs 64 0623
Elstob Dur 96 3323
Elston Lancs 81 5932
Elston Notts 63 7647
Elston Wilts 23 0644
Elstone Devon 19 6716
Elstow Beds 38 0546
Elstree Herts 26 1795
Elstronwick E R Yk 85 2232
Elswick Lancs 80 4238
Elswick T & W 103 2263
Elsworth Cambs 52 3163
Elterwater Cumb 86 3204
Eltham Gt Lon 27 4274
Eltisley Cambs 52 2759
Elton Cambs 51 0893
Elton Ches 71 4575
Elton Derbys 74 2260
Elton Dur 96 4017
Elton Gloucs 35 7014
Elton Gt Man 81 7911
Elton Herefs 46 4570
Elton Notts 63 7638
Elton Green Ches 71 4574
Eltringham Nthumb 103 0762
Elvanfoot S Lans 108 9517
Elvaston Derbys 62 4032
Elveden Suffk 54 8280
Elvetham Hall Hants 25 7856
Elvingston E Loth 118 4674
Elvington Kent 29 2750
Elvington N York 84 7047
Elwell Devon 19 6631
Elwick Dur 97 4532
Elwick Nthumb 111 1136
Elworth Ches 72 7361
Elworthy Somset 20 0834
Ely Cambs 53 5480
Ely Cardif 33 1476
Emberton Bucks 38 8849
Embleton Cumb 92 1629
Embleton Dur 96 4129
Embleton Nthumb 111 2322
Embo Highld 147 8192
Embo Street Highld 147 8091
Emborough Somset 21 6151
Embsay N York 82 0053
Emery Down Hants 12 2808
Emley W York 82 2413
Emley Moor W York 82 2313
Emmbrook Berks 25 8069
Emmer Green Berks 37 7276
Emmett Carr Derbys 75 4577
Emmington Oxon 37 7402
Emneth Cambs 65 4807
Emneth Hungate Norfk 65 5107
Empingham Rutlnd 63 9408
Empshott Hants 24 7531
Empshott Green Hants 24 7431
Emsworth Hants 13 7406
Enborne Berks 24 4365
Enborne Row Hants 24 4463
Enchmarsh Shrops 59 5096
Enderby Leics 50 5399
Endmoor Cumb 87 5384
Endon Staffs 72 9253
Endon Bank Staffs 72 9253
Enfield Gt Lon 27 3597
Enfield Lock Gt Lon 27 3698
Enfield Wash Gt Lon 27 3598
Enford Wilts 23 1351
Engine Common Gloucs 35 6984
England's Gate Herefs 46 5451
Englefield Berks 24 6272
Englefield Green Surrey 25 9971
Englesea brook Ches 72 7551
English Bicknor Gloucs 34 5815
English Frankton Shrops 59 4529
Englishcombe Somset 22 7162
Engollan Cnwll 4 8670
Enham-Alamein Hants 23 3649
Enmore Somset 20 2435
Enmore Green Dorset 22 8523
Ennerdale Bridge Cumb 92 0615
Enniscaven Cnwll 4 9659
Enochdhu P & K 133 0662
Ensay Ag & B 121 3648
Ensbury Dorset 12 0896
Ensdon Shrops 59 4017
Ensis Devon 19 5626
Enson Staffs 72 9328
Enstone Oxon 48 3724
Enterkinfoot D & G 108 8504
Enterpen N York 89 4605
Enville Staffs 60 8286
Enys Cnwll 3 7836
Eolaigearraidh W Isls 152 7007
Epney Gloucs 35 7611
Epperstone Notts 75 6548
Epping Essex 27 4502
Epping Green Essex 39 4305
Epping Green Herts 39 2906
Epping Upland Essex 39 4404
Eppleby N York 89 1713
Eppleworth E R Yk 84 0131
Epsom Surrey 26 2160
Epwell Oxon 48 3540
Epworth Lincs 84 7803
Epworth Turbary Lincs 84 7603
Erbistock Wrexhm 71 3541
Erdington W Mids 61 1191
Eridge Green E Susx 16 5535
Eridge Station E Susx 16 5434
Erines Ag & B 113 8575
Erisey Cnwll 2 7117
Eriska Ag & B 122 9043
Eriswell Suffk 53 7278
Erith Gt Lon 27 5177
Erlestoke Wilts 22 9653
Ermington Devon 6 6353
Erpingham Norfk 67 1931
Erriottwood Kent 28 9459
Errogie Highld 139 5622
Errol P & K 126 2422
Erskine Rens 115 4770
Ervie D & G 98 0067
Erwarton Suffk 55 2234
Erwood Powys 45 0942
Eryholme N York 89 3208
Eryrys Denbgs 70 2057
Escalls Cnwll 2 3627
Escomb Dur 96 1830
Escott Somset 20 0937
Escrick N York 83 6242
Esgair Carmth 31 3728
Esgair Cerdgn 43 5868
Esgairgeiliog Powys 57 7606
Esgerdawe Carmth 44 6140
Esgyryn Conwy 69 8078
Esh Dur 96 1944
Esh Winning Dur 96 1942
Esher Surrey 26 1364
Esholt W York 82 1840
Eshott Nthumb 103 2097
Eshton N York 81 9356
Eskadale Highld 139 4540
Eskbank Mdloth 118 3266
Eskdale Green Cumb 86 1400
Eskdalemuir D & G 101 2597
Eskett Cumb 92 0516
Eskham Lincs 77 3698
Eskholme S York 83 6317
Esperley Lane Ends Dur 96 1324
Esprick Lancs 80 4036
Essendine Rutlnd 64 0412
Essendon Herts 39 2708
Essich Highld 140 6439
Essington Staffs 60 9603
Esslemont Abers 143 9229
Eston N York 97 5418
Etal Nthumb 110 9339
Etchilhampton Wilts 23 0460
Etchingham E Susx 17 7126
Etchinghill Kent 29 1639
Etchinghill Staffs 73 0218
Etchingwood E Susx 16 5022
Etherdwick E R Yk 85 2337
Etling Green Norfk 66 0113
Etloe Gloucs 35 6806
Eton Berks 26 9677
Eton Wick Berks 26 9478
Etruria Staffs 72 8647
Etteridge Highld 132 6892
Ettersgill Dur 95 8829
Ettiley Heath Ches 72 7360
Ettingshall W Mids 60 9396
Ettington Warwks 48 2749
Etton Cambs 64 1406
Etton E R Yk 84 9743
Ettrick Border 109 2714
Ettrickbridge Border 109 3824
Ettrickhill Border 109 2514
Etwall Derbys 73 2631
Eudon George Shrops 60 6888
Euston Suffk 54 8979
Euximoor Drove Cambs 65 4898
Euxton Lancs 81 5519
Evancoyd Powys 46 2663
Evanton Highld 140 6066
Evedon Lincs 76 0947
Evelith Shrops 60 7405
Evelix Highld 147 7790
Evenjobb Powys 46 2662
Evenley Oxon 49 5834
Evenlode Gloucs 48 2129
Evenwood Dur 96 1524
Evenwood Gate Dur 96 1624
Evercreech Somset 21 6438
Everingham E R Yk 84 8042
Everleigh Wilts 23 2053
Everley N York 91 9788
Eversfield Devon 5 4792
Eversholt Beds 38 9833
Evershot Dorset 10 5704
Eversley Hants 25 7762
Eversley Cross Hants 25 7961
Everthorpe E R Yk 84 9031
Everton Beds 52 2051
Everton Hants 12 2894
Everton Mersyd 78 3491
Everton Notts 75 6990
Evertown D & G 101 3576
Evesbatch Herefs 47 6948
Evesham Worcs 48 0344
Evington Leics 62 6203
Ewden Village S York 74 2796
Ewdness Shrops 60 7396
Ewell Surrey 26 2262
Ewell Minnis Kent 29 2643
Ewelme Oxon 37 6491
Ewen Gloucs 35 0097
Ewenny V Glam 33 9077
Ewerby Lincs 76 1247
Ewerby Thorpe Lincs 76 1347
Ewesley Nthumb 103 0591
Ewhurst Surrey 14 0940
Ewhurst Green E Susx 17 7924
Ewhurst Green Surrey 14 0939
Ewloe Flints 71 3066
Ewloe Green Flints 71 2966
Ewood Lancs 81 6725
Ewood Bridge Lancs 81 7920
Eworthy Devon 5 4495
Ewshot Hants 25 8149
Ewyas Harold Herefs 46 3828
Exbourne Devon 8 6002
Exbury Hants 13 4200
Exceat E Susx 16 5199
Exebridge Somset 20 9324
Exelby N York 89 2987
Exeter Devon 9 9292
Exeter Airport 9 9993
Exford Somset 19 8538
Exfordsgreen Shrops 59 4505
Exhall Warwks 48 1055
Exhall Warwks 61 3485
Exlade Street Oxon 37 6581
Exley Head W York 82 0440
Exminster Devon 9 9487
Exmouth Devon 9 0081
Exning Suffk 53 6265
Exted Kent 29 1744
Exton Devon 9 9886
Exton Hants 13 6120
Exton Rutlnd 63 9211
Exton Somset 20 9233
Exwick Devon 9 9093
Eyam Derbys 74 2176
Eydon Nhants 49 5449
Eye Cambs 64 2202
Eye Herefs 46 4964
Eye Suffk 54 1473
Eye Green Cambs 64 2303
Eye Kettleby Leics 63 7316
Eyemouth Border 119 9464
Eyeworth Beds 52 2545
Eyhorne Street Kent 28 8354
Eyke Suffk 55 3151
Eynesbury Cambs 52 1859
Eynsford Kent 27 5465
Eynsham Oxon 36 4309
Eype Dorset 10 4491
Eyre Highld 136 4153
Eythorne Kent 29 2849
Eyton Herefs 46 4761
Eyton Shrops 59 3714
Eyton Shrops 59 4422
Eyton Shrops 59 3787
Eyton Wrexhm 71 3544
Eyton on Severn Shrops 59 5706
Eyton upon the Weald Moors Shrops 72 6515

F

Faccombe Hants 23 3857
Faceby N York 90 4903
Fachwen Powys 58 0316
Facit Lancs 81 8819
Fackley Notts 75 4761
Faddiley Ches 71 5852
Fadmoor N York 90 6789
Faerdre Swans 32 6901
Fagwyr Swans 32 6702
Faifley W Duns 115 4973
Failand Somset 34 5171
Failford S Ayrs 107 4626
Failsworth Gt Man 79 8901
Fair Oak Hants 13 4918
Fair Oak Green Hants 24 6660
Fairbourne Gwynd 57 6113
Fairburn N York 83 4727
Fairfield Derbys 74 0673
Fairfield Kent 17 9626
Fairfield Worcs 60 9475
Fairford Gloucs 36 1501
Fairford Park Gloucs 36 1501
Fairgirth D & G 92 8756
Fairhaven Lancs 80 3227
Fairlie N Ayrs 114 2054
Fairlight E Susx 17 8511
Fairmile Devon 9 0897
Fairmile Surrey 26 1161
Fairnilee Border 109 4532
Fairoak Staffs 72 7632
Fairseat Kent 27 6261
Fairstead Essex 40 7616
Fairstead Norfk 67 2823
Fairwarp E Susx 16 4626
Fairwater Cardif 33 1477
Fairy Cross Devon 18 4024
Fakenham Norfk 66 9229
Fakenham Magna Suffk 54 9176
Fala Mdloth 118 4460
Fala Dam Mdloth 118 4361
Falcondale Cerdgn 44 5649
Falcut Nhants 49 5942
Faldingworth Lincs 76 0684
Faldouet Jersey 158 0000
Falfield Gloucs 35 6893
Falkenham Suffk 55 2939
Falkirk Falk 116 8880
Falkland Fife 126 2507
Fallgate Derbys 74 3561
Fallin Stirlg 116 8391
Falloden Nthumb 111 1922
Fallowfield Gt Man 79 8593
Fallowfield Nthumb 102 9268
Falls of Blarghour Ag & B 122 9913
Falmer E Susx 15 3508
Falmouth Cnwll 3 8032
Falnash Border 109 3905
Falsgrave N York 91 0288
Falstone Nthumb 102 7287
Fanagmore Highld 148 1749
Fancott Beds 38 0127
Fanellan Highld 139 4942
Fangdale Beck N York 90 5694
Fangfoss E R Yk 84 7653
Fanmore Ag & B 121 4144
Fannich Lodge Highld 139 2266
Fans Border 110 6140
Far Bletchley Bucks 38 8533
Far Cotton Nhants 49 7559
Far End Cumb 86 3098
Far Forest Worcs 60 7275
Far Green Gloucs 35 7700
Far Moor Gt Man 78 5204
Far Oakridge Gloucs 35 9203
Far Sawrey Cumb 87 3795
Far Thorpe Lincs 77 2674
Farcet Cambs 64 2094
Farden Shrops 46 5775
Fareham Hants 13 5606
Farewell Staffs 61 0811
Farforth Lincs 77 3178
Faringdon Oxon 36 2895
Farington Lancs 80 5325
Farkhill P & K 125 0435
Farlam Cumb 94 5558
Farleigh Devon 7 7553
Farleigh Somset 21 5069
Farleigh Surrey 27 3760
Farleigh Hungerford Somset 22 8057
Farleigh Wallop Hants 24 6247
Farlesthorpe Lincs 77 4774
Farleton Cumb 87 5380
Farleton Lancs 87 5767
Farley Derbys 74 2962
Farley Staffs 73 0644
Farley Wilts 23 2229
Farley Green Suffk 53 7353
Farley Green Surrey 14 0545
Farley Hill Berks 24 7464
Farleys End Gloucs 35 7614
Farlington Hants 13 6805
Farlington N York 90 6167
Farlow Shrops 59 6380
Farm Town Leics 62 3916
Farmborough Somset 22 6660
Farmbridge End Essex 40 6211
Farmcote Gloucs 48 0628
Farmcote Shrops 60 7791
Farmers Carmth 44 6444
Farmington Gloucs 36 1315
Farmoor Oxon 37 4506
Farms Common Cnwll 2 6734
Farmtown Moray 142 5051
Farnachty Moray 142 4261
Farnah Green Derbys 62 3347
Farnborough Berks 36 4381
Farnborough Gt Lon 27 4464
Farnborough Hants 25 8753
Farnborough Warwks 49 4349
Farnborough Park Hants 25 8755
Farnborough Street Hants 25 8756
Farncombe Surrey 25 9744
Farndish Beds 51 9263
Farndon Ches 71 4154
Farndon Notts 75 7651
Farnell Angus 127 6255
Farnham Dorset 11 9515
Farnham Essex 39 4724
Farnham N York 89 3460
Farnham Suffk 55 3660
Farnham Surrey 25 8346
Farnham Common Bucks 26 9585
Farnham Green Essex 39 4625
Farnham Royal Bucks 26 9583
Farningham Kent 27 5467
Farnley N York 82 2148
Farnley W York 82 2532
Farnley Tyas W York 82 1612
Farnsfield Notts 75 6456
Farnworth Ches 78 5187
Farnworth Gt Man 79 7306
Farr Highld 150 7163
Farr Highld 140 6833
Farr Highld 132 8203
Farraline Highld 139 5621
Farringdon Devon 9 0191
Farrington Gurney Somset 21 6355
Farsley W York 82 2135
Farther Howegreen Essex 40 8401
Farthing Green Kent 28 8146
Farthing Street Gt Lon 27 4262
Farthinghoe Nhants 49 5339
Farthingloe Kent 29 2940
Farthingstone Nhants 49 6154
Fartown W York 82 1518
Fartown W York 82 2233
Farway Street Devon 9 1895
Fasnacloich Ag & B 122 0247
Fasnakyle Highld 139 3128
Fassfern Highld 130 0278
Fatfield T & W 96 2954
Faugh Cumb 94 5154
Fauld Staffs 73 1728
Fauldhouse W Loth 116 9360
Faulkbourne Essex 40 7917
Faulkland Somset 22 7354
Fauls Shrops 59 5832
Faversham Kent 28 0161
Fawdington N York 89 4372
Fawdon Nthumb 111 0315
Fawfieldhead Staffs 74 0763
Fawkham Green Kent 27 5865
Fawler Oxon 36 3717
Fawley Berks 36 3981
Fawley Bucks 37 7586
Fawley Hants 13 4503
Fawley Chapel Herefs 46 5929
Fawnog Flints 70 2466
Fawsley Nhants 49 5
Faxfleet E R Yk 84 8
Faygate W Susx 15 2
Fazakerley Mersyd 78 3
Fazeley Staffs 61 2
Fearby N York 89 1
Fearn Highld 147 8
Fearnan P & K 124 7
Fearnbeg Highld 137 7
Fearnhead Ches 79 6
Fearnmore Highld 137 7
Fearnoch Ag & B 114 9
Featherstone Staffs 60 9
Featherstone W York 83 4
Feckenham Worcs 47 0
Feering Essex 40 8
Feetham N York 88 9
Feizor N York 88 7
Felbridge Surrey 15 3
Felbrigg Norfk 67 2
Felcourt Surrey 15 3
Felday Surrey 14 1
Felden Herts 38 0
Felin Fach Cerdgn 44 5
Felin gwm Isaf Carmth 44 5
Felin gwm Uchaf Carmth 44 5
Felin-newydd Powys 45 1
Felindre Carmth 32 5
Felindre Carmth 44 7
Felindre Carmth 31 3
Felindre Cerdgn 44 5
Felindre Powys 58 1
Felindre Powys 45 1
Felindre Swans 32 6
Felindre Farchog Pembks 31 1
Felinfach Powys 45 0
Felinfoel Carmth 32 5
Felixkirk N York 89 4
Felixstowe Suffk 55 3
Felixstowe Ferry Suffk 55 3
Felkington Nthumb 110 9
Felkirk W York 83 3
Fell Foot Cumb 86 2
Fell Lane W York 82 0
Fell Side Cumb 93 3
Felling T & W 96 2
Felmersham Beds 51 9
Felmingham Norfk 67 2
Felpham W Susx 14 9
Felsham Suffk 54 9
Felsted Essex 40 6
Feltham Gt Lon 26 1
Felthamhill Gt Lon 26 0
Felthorpe Norfk 66 1
Felton Herefs 46 5
Felton Nthumb 103 1
Felton Somset 21 5
Felton Butler Shrops 59 3
Feltwell Norfk 53 7
Fen Ditton Cambs 53 4
Fen Drayton Cambs 52 3
Fen End Lincs 64 2
Fen End W Mids 61 2
Fen Street Norfk 66 9
Fen Street Suffk 54 1
Fenay Bridge W York 82 1
Fence Lancs 81 8
Fence S York 75 4
Fencehouses T & W 96 3
Fencote N York 89 2
Fencott Oxon 37 5
Fendike Corner Lincs 77 4
Fenham Nthumb 111 0
Feniscliffe Lancs 81 6
Feniscowles Lancs 81 6
Feniton Devon 9 1
Fenn Green Shrops 60 7
Fenn Street Kent 28 7
Fenny Bentley Derbys 73 1
Fenny Bridges Devon 9 1
Fenny Compton Warwks 49 4
Fenny Drayton Leics 61 3
Fenny Stratford Bucks 38 8
Fenrother Nthumb 103 1
Fenstanton Cambs 52 3
Fenstead End Suffk 54 8
Fenton Cambs 52 3
Fenton Cumb 94 5
Fenton Lincs 76 8
Fenton Lincs 76 8
Fenton Notts 75 7
Fenton Nthumb 111 9
Fenton Staffs 72 8
Fenton Barns E Loth 118 5
Fenwick E Ayrs 107 4
Fenwick Nthumb 111 0
Fenwick Nthumb 103 0
Fenwick S York 83 5
Feock Cnwll 3 8
Feolin Ferry Ag & B 112 4
Fergushill N Ayrs 106 3
Feriniquarrie Highld 136 1
Fermain Bay Guern 158 0
Fern Angus 134 4
Ferndale Rhondd 33 9
Ferndown Dorset 12 0
Ferness Moray 140 9
Fernham Oxon 36 2
Fernhill Heath Worcs 47 8
Fernhurst W Susx 14 8
Fernie Fife 126 3
Ferniegair S Lans 116 7
Fernilea Highld 136 3
Fernilee Derbys 79 0
Ferny Common Herefs 46 3
Ferrensby N York 89 3
Ferriby Sluice Lincs 84 9
Ferrindonald Highld 129 6
Ferring W Susx 14 0
Ferry Point Highld 146 7
Ferrybridge W York 83 4
Ferryden Angus 127 7
Ferryhill Dur 96 2
Ferryside Carmth 31 3
Ferrytown Highld 146 7
Fersfield Norfk 54 0
Fersit Highld 131 3
Feshiebridge Highld 132 8

...cham Surrey ... 26 1455
...erangus Abers ... 143 9850
...ercairn Abers ... 135 6573
...cott Oxon ... 49 5428
...ston N York ... 82 1954
... Rhos Cerdgn ... 43 7368
...fach Carmth ... 32 6321
...d-y-Brenin Carmth ... 44 6344
...wyddog Gwynd ... 33 2018
...tiniog Gwynd ... 57 7042
...tiniog Railway ... 57 6541
...dd-las Denbgs ... 70 1264
...rest Carmth ... 32 5704
...rest Mons ... 34 2820
...rest Fach Swans ... 32 6295
...rest Goch Neath ... 32 7401
...trasol Cerdgn ... 42 3747
...h Flints ... 70 2855
...non-Oer Cerdgn ... 44 5353
...anonddewi Cerdgn ... 42 3852
...anongroyw Flints ... 70 1382
... Lodge Highld ... 149 4528
...leshole Surrey ... 27 3860
...lington Gloucs ... 47 9231
...lington Somset ... 20 2140
...leford Dorset ... 11 8013
...llers Green Cnwll ... 3 8155
...llers Hamlet Essex ... 27 4701
...d Staffs ... 73 0233
...d Broughton Cumb ... 87 3881
...d Dalling Norfk ... 66 0038
...d Head Leics ... 62 4909
...dhead Cumb ... 93 4539
... Keith Moray ... 142 4250
...head Magdalen Dorset ... 22 7821
...head Neville Dorset ... 11 7610
...head St Quintin Dorset ... 11 7710
...eld Berks ... 26 9076
...eld Oxon ... 36 2418
...eld Staffs ... 23 1450
...eldean Wilts ... 23 1547
...nds Wilts ... 35 9388
...y Norfk ... 67 4613
...y N York ... 91 1180
...rave Bucks ... 38 8648
...ins Oxon ... 36 2304
...eigh Devon ... 19 6627
...eigh Devon ... 19 7410
...ngham Lincs ... 76 9485
...ongley Warwks ... 61 2887
...ore Hill Hants ... 13 6627
...on Gloucs ... 34 6079
...ber E R Yk ... 91 8960
...avon Angus ... 127 4956
...cham Norfk ... 65 6806
...hampstead Berks ... 25 7963
...charn Ag & B ... 122 9003
...chdean Hants ... 13 7312
...chingfield Essex ... 40 6832
...chley Gt Lon ... 27 2690
...dern Moray ... 73 3030
...dhorn Moray ... 141 0364
...dhorn Bridge Highld ... 140 8027
...do Gask P & K ... 125 0019
...dochty Moray ... 142 4667
...don Abers ... 135 9397
...don W Susx ... 14 1208
...don Mains Abers ... 140 6060
...drack House Abers ... 134 6004
...edon Nhants ... 51 9172
...eshade Nhants ... 51 9798
...gal Street Suffk ... 55 2169
...gask P & K ... 126 1619
...gest Bucks ... 37 7791
...ghall N York ... 89 1889
...gland Cumb ... 93 2557
...gland D & G ... 107 7517
...glesham Surrey ... 29 3353
...grinhoe Essex ... 41 0220
...kle Green Essex ... 53 7040
...kle Street S York ... 74 3099
...larig Stirlg ... 124 5733
...mere P & K ... 49 6332
...nart P & K ... 124 5157
...ningham Suffk ... 54 0669
...ningley S York ... 75 6799
...sbay W Isls ... 152 0786
...stall Worcs ... 60 9770
...sthwaite Cumb ... 87 3687
...stock Oxon ... 36 3616
...stown Ork ... 153 3513
...try Abers ... 142 7554
...try Stirlg ... 116 6186
...zean Abers ... 134 5993
...nnport Ag & B ... 120 3023
...nnsbhagh W Isls ... 152 0786
... Tree Dur ... 96 1434
...bank Cumb ... 87 6293
...beck S York ... 75 5688
...by N York ... 89 2686
...by N York ... 90 7466
...grove Gt Man ... 81 9113
...sby N York ... 77 4562
...sdown Dorset ... 23 2133
...hbourne IOW ... 13 5592
...hbourne W Susx ... 14 8304
...hbourne Roman Palace ... 14 8305
...hburn Dur ... 96 3632
...hcross Clacks ... 116 8995
...her W Susx ... 14 8700
...her's Pond Hants ... 13 4820
...her's Row Lancs ... 80 4148
...herford Abers ... 142 6735
...herrow E Loth ... 118 3472
...herstreet W Susx ... 14 9431
...herton Highld ... 140 7451
...herton S Ayrs ... 106 2717
...herton la Mere Wilts ... 22 0038
...herwick Staffs ... 61 1708
...hery Estate Berks ... 26 9940
...nguard Pembks ... 30 9537
...hlake S York ... 83 6513
...hleigh Devon ... 8 5405
...hmere End Lincs ... 64 2837
...hnish Pier Ag & B ... 121 6542
...hpond Bottom Dorset ... 10 3698
...hponds Bristl ... 35 6375
...hpool Gt Man ... 79 8009

Fishtoft Lincs ... 64 3642
Fishtoft Drove Lincs ... 77 3148
Fishwick Lancs ... 81 5629
Fiskavaig Highld ... 136 3334
Fiskerton Lincs ... 76 0471
Fiskerton Notts ... 75 7351
Fitling E R Yk ... 85 2534
Fittleton Wilts ... 23 1449
Fittleworth W Susx ... 14 0019
Fitton End Cambs ... 65 4313
Fitz Shrops ... 59 4417
Fitzhead Somset ... 20 1228
Fitzroy Somset ... 20 1927
Fitzwilliam W York ... 83 4115
Five Ash Down E Susx ... 16 4723
Five Ashes E Susx ... 16 5525
Five Bells Somset ... 20 0642
Five Bridges Herefs ... 47 6446
Five Lanes Mons ... 34 4490
Five Oak Green Kent ... 16 6445
Five Oaks Jersey ... 158 0000
Five Oaks W Susx ... 14 0928
Five Roads Carmth ... 32 4805
Five Wents Kent ... 28 8050
Fivecrosses Ches ... 71 5276
Fivehead Somset ... 21 3522
Fivelanes Cnwll ... 5 2280
Flack's Green Essex ... 40 7614
Flackwell Heath Bucks ... 26 8909
Fladbury Worcs ... 47 9946
Fladdabister Shet ... 153 4332
Flagg Derbys ... 74 1368
Flamborough E R Yk ... 91 2270
Flamingo Land Theme Park ... 90 7880
Flamstead Herts ... 38 0714
Flansham W Susx ... 14 9601
Flanshaw W York ... 82 3020
Flappit Spring W York ... 82 0536
Flasby N York ... 82 9456
Flash Staffs ... 74 0266
Flashader Highld ... 136 3453
Flaunden Herts ... 26 0100
Flawborough Notts ... 63 7842
Flawith N York ... 90 4865
Flax Bourton Somset ... 21 5069
Flaxby N York ... 89 3957
Flaxley Gloucs ... 35 6815
Flaxmere Ches ... 71 5572
Flaxpool Somset ... 20 1435
Flaxton N York ... 90 6762
Fleckney Leics ... 50 6493
Flecknoe Warwks ... 49 5163
Fledborough Notts ... 75 8072
Fleet Dorset ... 10 6330
Fleet Hants ... 13 7201
Fleet Hants ... 25 8053
Fleet Lincs ... 64 3823
Fleet Hargate Lincs ... 65 3925
Fleetend Hants ... 13 5006
Fleetwood Lancs ... 80 3348
Flemingston V Glam ... 20 0169
Flemington S Lans ... 116 6559
Flempton Suffk ... 54 8169
Fletcher Green Kent ... 16 5334
Fletchersbridge Cnwll ... 4 1065
Fletchertown Cumb ... 93 2042
Fletching E Susx ... 16 4223
Fleur-de-lis Caerph ... 33 1696
Flexbury Cnwll ... 18 2107
Flexford Surrey ... 25 9350
Flimby Cumb ... 92 0233
Flimwell E Susx ... 17 7131
Flint Flints ... 70 2472
Flint Mountain Flints ... 70 2470
Flint's Green W Mids ... 61 2680
Flintham Notts ... 63 7445
Flinton E R Yk ... 85 2136
Flishinghurst Kent ... 28 7537
Flitcham Norfk ... 65 7326
Flitton Beds ... 38 0535
Flitwick Beds ... 38 0334
Flixborough Lincs ... 84 8714
Flixborough Stather Lincs ... 84 8614
Flixton Gt Man ... 79 7494
Flixton N York ... 91 0479
Flixton Suffk ... 55 3186
Flockton W York ... 82 2314
Flockton Green W York ... 82 2515
Flodden Nthumb ... 110 9285
Flodigarry Highld ... 136 4671
Flookburgh Cumb ... 87 3675
Flordon Norfk ... 66 1897
Flore Nhants ... 49 6460
Flotterton Nthumb ... 103 9902
Flowers Green E Susx ... 16 6311
Flowton Suffk ... 54 0846
Flushdyke W York ... 82 2820
Flushing Cnwll ... 3 8034
Fluxton Devon ... 9 0883
Flyford Flavell Worcs ... 47 9755
Fobbing Essex ... 40 7183
Fochabers Moray ... 141 3458
Fochriw Caerph ... 33 1005
Fockerby Lincs ... 84 8519
Foddington Somset ... 21 5729
Foel Powys ... 58 9911
Foel y Dyffryn Brdgnd ... 33 8504
Foelgastell Carmth ... 32 5414
Foggathorpe E R Yk ... 84 7537
Fogo Border ... 110 7649
Fogwatt Moray ... 141 2356
Foindle Highld ... 148 1948
Folda Angus ... 133 1963
Fole Staffs ... 73 0437
Foleshill W Mids ... 61 3582
Foliejon Park Berks ... 25 8974
Folke Dorset ... 11 6613
Folkestone Kent ... 29 2336
Folkingham Lincs ... 64 0733
Folkington E Susx ... 16 5603
Folksworth Cambs ... 52 1489
Folkton N York ... 91 0579
Folla Rule Abers ... 142 7332
Follifoot N York ... 83 3452
Folly Gate Devon ... 8 5708
Folly Hill Surrey ... 25 8348
Fonmon V Glam ... 20 0467
Font-y-gary V Glam ... 20 0566

Fonthill Bishop Wilts ... 22 9333
Fonthill Gifford Wilts ... 22 9231
Fontmell Magna Dorset ... 11 8616
Fontmell Parva Dorset ... 11 8214
Fontwell W Susx ... 14 9407
Foolow Derbys ... 74 1976
Foots Cray Gt Lon ... 27 4770
Forbestown Abers ... 134 3513
Forcett N York ... 89 1712
Ford Ag & B ... 122 8603
Ford Bucks ... 37 7709
Ford Derbys ... 74 4080
Ford Devon ... 18 4124
Ford Devon ... 6 6160
Ford Devon ... 7 7940
Ford Gloucs ... 48 0829
Ford Nthumb ... 110 9437
Ford Shrops ... 59 4113
Ford Somset ... 20 0958
Ford Somset ... 21 5993
Ford Staffs ... 73 0653
Ford W Susx ... 14 9903
Ford Wilts ... 35 8475
Ford Wilts ... 23 1632
Ford End Essex ... 40 6716
Ford Green Lancs ... 80 4746
Ford Heath Shrops ... 59 4011
Ford Street Somset ... 20 1518
Ford's Green Suffk ... 54 0666
Forda Devon ... 8 5390
Fordcombe Kent ... 16 5240
Fordell Fife ... 117 1508
Forden Powys ... 58 2201
Forder Devon ... 8 6789
Forder Green Devon ... 7 7967
Fordham Cambs ... 53 6370
Fordham Essex ... 40 9228
Fordham Norfk ... 65 6199
Fordham Heath Essex ... 40 9426
Fordingbridge Hants ... 12 1414
Fordon E R Yk ... 91 0475
Fordoun Abers ... 135 7475
Fordstreet Essex ... 40 9226
Fordton Devon ... 8 8399
Fordwells Oxon ... 36 3013
Fordwich Kent ... 29 1859
Fordyce Abers ... 142 5563
Forebridge Staffs ... 72 9322
Foremark Derbys ... 62 3336
Forest N York ... 89 2700
Forest Becks Lancs ... 81 7851
Forest Chapel Ches ... 79 9772
Forest Gate Gt Lon ... 27 4085
Forest Green Surrey ... 14 1241
Forest Hall Cumb ... 87 5401
Forest Hall T & W ... 103 2769
Forest Head Cumb ... 94 5857
Forest Hill Gt Lon ... 27 3672
Forest Hill Oxon ... 37 5807
Forest Lane Head N York ... 83 3356
Forest Lodge Ag & B ... 123 2742
Forest Mill Clacks ... 117 9664
Forest Row E Susx ... 16 4234
Forest Side IOW ... 13 4809
Forest Town Notts ... 75 5662
Forest-in-Teesdale Dur ... 95 8630
Forestburn Gate Nthumb ... 103 0696
Forestside W Susx ... 14 7612
Forfar Angus ... 127 4550
Forgandenny P & K ... 125 0818
Forge Powys ... 57 7639
Forge Hammer Torfn ... 34 2895
Forge Side Torfn ... 34 2408
Forgie Moray ... 141 3864
Forgieside Moray ... 142 4013
Forgue Abers ... 142 6145
Forhill Worcs ... 61 0575
Formby Mersyd ... 78 3006
Forncett End Norfk ... 66 1493
Forncett St Mary Norfk ... 66 1694
Forncett St Peter Norfk ... 66 1693
Fornham All Saints Suffk ... 54 8367
Fornham St Martin Suffk ... 54 8567
Fornside Cumb ... 93 3220
Forres Moray ... 141 0358
Forsbrook Staffs ... 72 9641
Forse Highld ... 151 2234
Forse House Highld ... 151 2135
Forshaw Heath Warwks ... 61 0873
Forsinard Highld ... 150 8942
Forston Dorset ... 11 6695
Fort Augustus Highld ... 131 3709
Fort Hommet Guern ... 158 0000
Fort le Marchant Guern ... 158 0000
Fort William Highld ... 130 1074
Forteviot P & K ... 125 0517
Forth S Lans ... 116 9453
Forthampton Gloucs ... 47 8532
Fortingall P & K ... 124 7347
Fortnighty Highld ... 140 9350
Forton Hants ... 24 4143
Forton Lancs ... 80 4851
Forton Shrops ... 59 4316
Forton Somset ... 10 3307
Forton Staffs ... 72 7521
Fortrie Abers ... 142 6645
Fortrose Highld ... 140 7256
Fortuneswell Dorset ... 11 6873
Forty Green Bucks ... 26 9291
Forty Hill Gt Lon ... 27 3398
Forward Green Suffk ... 54 1099
Fosbury Wilts ... 23 3157
Foscot Oxon ... 36 2421
Foscote Nhants ... 49 6546
Fosdyke Lincs ... 64 3133
Fosdyke Bridge Lincs ... 64 3232
Foss P & K ... 132 7858
Foss-y-ffin Cerdgn ... 42 4460
Fossebridge Gloucs ... 36 0711
Foster Street Essex ... 39 4809
Fosterhouses S York ... 83 6514
Foston Derbys ... 73 1931
Foston Leics ... 50 6094
Foston Lincs ... 63 8542
Foston N York ... 90 6965
Foston on the Wolds E R Yk ... 85 1055
Fotherby Lincs ... 77 3191

Fothergill Cumb ... 92 0234
Fotheringhay Nhants ... 51 0593
Foul End Warwks ... 61 2494
Foul Mile E Susx ... 16 6215
Foulbridge Cumb ... 93 4248
Foulby W York ... 83 3917
Foulden Border ... 119 9355
Foulden Norfk ... 65 7699
Foulridge Lancs ... 81 8942
Foulsham Norfk ... 66 0334
Fountainhall Border ... 118 4249
Four Ashes Staffs ... 60 9108
Four Ashes Staffs ... 60 8087
Four Ashes Suffk ... 54 0010
Four Ashes W Mids ... 61 1575
Four Cabots Guern ... 158 0000
Four Crosses Powys ... 58 2618
Four Crosses Staffs ... 60 9509
Four Elms Kent ... 16 4648
Four Foot Somset ... 21 5833
Four Forks Somset ... 20 2336
Four Gates Gt Man ... 79 6407
Four Gotes Cambs ... 65 4516
Four Lane End S York ... 82 2702
Four Lane Ends Ches ... 71 5561
Four Lanes Cnwll ... 2 6838
Four Marks Hants ... 24 6735
Four Mile Bridge IOA ... 68 2778
Four Oaks E Susx ... 17 8524
Four Oaks Gloucs ... 47 6928
Four Oaks W Mids ... 61 1008
Four Oaks W Mids ... 61 2400
Four Points Berks ... 37 5519
Four Roads Carmth ... 32 4409
Four Shire Stone Warwks ... 48 2232
Four Throws Kent ... 17 7729
Four Wents Kent ... 27 6251
Fourlanes End Ches ... 72 8059
Fourpenny Highld ... 147 8054
Fourstones Nthumb ... 102 8867
Fovant Wilts ... 22 0008
Foveran Abers ... 143 9723
Fowey Cnwll ... 3 1261
Fowley Common Ches ... 79 6795
Fowlhall Kent ... 28 6946
Fowlis Angus ... 126 3233
Fowlis Wester P & K ... 125 9224
Fowlmere Cambs ... 53 4215
Fownhope Herefs ... 46 5834
Fox Corner Surrey ... 25 9664
Fox Hatch Essex ... 27 5798
Fox Street Essex ... 41 0027
Foxbar Rens ... 115 4561
Foxcombe Devon ... 5 4807
Foxcote Gloucs ... 35 0118
Foxcote Somset ... 22 7155
Foxdale IOM ... 158 2778
Foxearth Essex ... 54 8314
Foxendown Kent ... 27 6646
Foxfield Cumb ... 86 2185
Foxham Wilts ... 35 9777
Foxhills Hants ... 12 3411
Foxhole Cnwll ... 3 9654
Foxhole Swans ... 32 6664
Foxholes N York ... 91 0173
Foxhunt Green E Susx ... 16 5417
Foxley Nhants ... 49 6451
Foxley Norfk ... 66 0422
Foxley Wilts ... 35 8996
Foxley Green Wilts ... 35 8995
Foxlydiate Worcs ... 47 0167
Foxt Staffs ... 73 0348
Foxton Cambs ... 52 4148
Foxton Dur ... 96 3624
Foxton Leics ... 50 7089
Foxton N York ... 89 4296
Foxup N York ... 88 8676
Foxwist Green Ches ... 71 6268
Foxwood Shrops ... 47 6276
Foy Herefs ... 46 5928
Foyers Highld ... 139 4921
Foynesfield Highld ... 140 8953
Fraddam Cnwll ... 2 5834
Fraddon Cnwll ... 4 9158
Fradley Staffs ... 61 1513
Fradswell Staffs ... 73 9931
Fraisthorpe E R Yk ... 91 1511
Framfield E Susx ... 16 4920
Framingham Earl Norfk ... 67 2202
Framingham Pigot Norfk ... 67 2703
Framlingham Suffk ... 55 2863
Frampton Dorset ... 10 6295
Frampton Lincs ... 64 3239
Frampton Cotterell Gloucs ... 35 6682
Frampton Mansell Gloucs ... 35 9202
Frampton on Severn Gloucs ... 35 7407
Frampton West End Lincs ... 64 3041
Framsden Suffk ... 55 1959
Framwellgate Moor Dur ... 96 2644
Frances Green Lancs ... 81 6236
Franche Worcs ... 60 8278
Frandley Ches ... 71 6379
Frankaborough Devon ... 5 3991
Frankby Mersyd ... 78 2486
Frankfort Norfk ... 67 3004
Franklands Gate Herefs ... 46 5346
Frankley Worcs ... 60 9990
Franksbridge Powys ... 45 1156
Frankton Warwks ... 50 4270
Frant E Susx ... 16 5835
Fraserburgh Abers ... 143 9966
Frating Essex ... 41 0722
Frating Green Essex ... 41 0823
Fratton Hants ... 13 6500
Freathy Cnwll ... 5 3952
Freckenham Suffk ... 53 6672
Freckleton Lancs ... 80 4329
Freebirch Derbys ... 74 3072
Freeby Leics ... 63 8010
Freefolk Hants ... 24 4848
Freehay Staffs ... 73 0241
Freeland Oxon ... 36 4112
Freethorpe Norfk ... 67 4005
Freethorpe Common Norfk ... 67 4004
Freiston Lincs ... 64 3743
Fremington Devon ... 19 5132
Fremington N York ... 88 0499
French Street Kent ... 27 4532

Frenchay Gloucs ... 35 6377
Frenchbeer Devon ... 8 6785
French P & K ... 132 8258
Frensham Surrey ... 25 8441
Freshfield Mersyd ... 78 2907
Freshford Somset ... 22 7860
Freshwater IOW ... 12 3487
Freshwater Bay IOW ... 12 3485
Freshwater East Pembks ... 30 0198
Fressingfield Suffk ... 55 2677
Freston Suffk ... 54 1638
Freswick Highld ... 151 3667
Fretherne Gloucs ... 35 7210
Frettenham Norfk ... 67 2417
Freuchie Fife ... 126 2806
Freystrop Pembks ... 30 9511
Friar Waddon Dorset ... 11 6486
Friar's Gate E Susx ... 16 4933
Friars' Hill N York ... 90 7455
Friday Bridge Cambs ... 65 4604
Friday Street E Susx ... 16 6203
Friday Street Suffk ... 55 2459
Friday Street Suffk ... 55 3351
Friday Street Suffk ... 55 3760
Friday Street Surrey ... 14 1245
Fridaythorpe E R Yk ... 90 8759
Friden Derbys ... 74 1660
Friendly W York ... 82 0534
Friern Barnet Gt Lon ... 27 2892
Friesland Bay Ag & B ... 120 1954
Friesthorpe Lincs ... 76 0663
Frieston Lincs ... 63 9347
Frieth Bucks ... 37 7990
Friezeland Notts ... 75 4750
Frilford Oxon ... 37 4497
Frilsham Berks ... 24 5473
Frimley Surrey ... 25 8757
Frimley Green Surrey ... 25 8856
Frindsbury Kent ... 28 7469
Fring Norfk ... 65 7334
Fringford Oxon ... 49 6029
Frinsted Kent ... 28 8957
Frinton-on-Sea Essex ... 41 2320
Friockheim Angus ... 127 5949
Friog Gwynd ... 57 6112
Frisby on the Wreake Leics ... 63 6917
Friskney Lincs ... 77 4655
Friskney Eaudike Lincs ... 77 4755
Friston E Susx ... 16 5598
Friston Suffk ... 55 4160
Fritchley Derbys ... 74 3552
Frith Bank Lincs ... 77 3147
Frith Common Worcs ... 47 6919
Fritham Hants ... 12 2314
Frithelstock Devon ... 18 4619
Frithelstock Stone Devon ... 18 4518
Frithend Hants ... 25 8039
Frithsden Herts ... 38 0109
Frithville Lincs ... 77 3150
Frittenden Kent ... 28 8140
Frittiscombe Devon ... 7 8043
Fritton Norfk ... 67 4600
Fritton Norfk ... 67 2203
Fritwell Oxon ... 49 5229
Frizinghall W York ... 82 1435
Frizington Cumb ... 92 0316
Frocester Gloucs ... 35 7803
Frodesley Shrops ... 59 5101
Frodsham Ches ... 71 5177
Frog End Cambs ... 52 3946
Frog End Cambs ... 53 5358
Frog Pool Worcs ... 47 8065
Frogden Border ... 110 7628
Froggatt Derbys ... 74 2476
Froghall Staffs ... 73 0247
Frogham Hants ... 12 1612
Frogham Kent ... 29 2550
Frogmore Devon ... 7 7742
Frognall Lincs ... 64 1610
Frogpool Cnwll ... 3 7540
Frogwell Cnwll ... 5 3468
Frolesworth Leics ... 50 5090
Frome Somset ... 22 7747
Frome St Quintin Dorset ... 10 5902
Frome Whitfield Dorset ... 11 6991
Fromes Hill Herefs ... 47 6846
Fron Denbgs ... 70 0696
Fron Gwynd ... 56 3539
Fron Gwynd ... 68 5054
Fron Powys ... 58 2203
Fron Powys ... 58 1797
Fron Isaf Wrexhm ... 70 2740
Fron-goch Gwynd ... 70 9039
Froncysyllte Denbgs ... 70 2760
Frostenden Suffk ... 55 4781
Frosterley Dur ... 95 0237
Froxfield Beds ... 38 9733
Froxfield Wilts ... 23 2968
Froxfield Green Hants ... 13 7025
Fryern Hill Hants ... 13 4320
Fryerning Essex ... 40 6300
Fryton N York ... 90 6874
Fuinary Highld ... 121 6246
Fulbeck Lincs ... 76 9450
Fulbourn Cambs ... 53 5256
Fulbrook Oxon ... 36 2513
Fulflood Hants ... 24 4730
Fulford N York ... 83 6149
Fulford Somset ... 20 2029
Fulford Staffs ... 72 9537
Fulham Gt Lon ... 27 2576
Fulking W Susx ... 15 2411
Full Sutton E R Yk ... 84 7455
Fullaford Devon ... 19 6838
Fullarton N Ayrs ... 106 3238
Fuller Street Essex ... 40 7416
Fuller Street Kent ... 27 5646
Fuller's End Essex ... 39 5335
Fuller's Moor Ches ... 71 4954
Fullerton Hants ... 23 3709
Fulletby Lincs ... 77 2973
Fullready Warwks ... 48 2846
Fullwood E Ayrs ... 115 4450
Fulmer Bucks ... 26 9985
Fulmodeston Norfk ... 66 9930
Fulnetby Lincs ... 76 0979
Fulney Lincs ... 64 2623
Fulstone W York ... 82 1709

Fulstow Lincs 77 3297
Fulwell Oxon 36 3722
Fulwood Lancs 80 5431
Fulwood Notts 75 4757
Fulwood S York 74 3085
Fulwood Somset 20 2120
Fundenhall Norfk 66 1596
Funtington W Susx 14 8008
Funtley Hants 13 5608
Funtullich P & K 124 7526
Furley Devon 10 2604
Furnace Ag & B 114 0200
Furnace Carmth 32 5001
Furnace Cerdgn 43 6895
Furnace End Warwks 61 2491
Furner's Green E Susx 15 4126
Furness Vale Derbys 79 0083
Furneux Pelham Herts 39 4327
Further Quarter Kent 28 8939
Furtho Nhants 49 7743
Furze Platt Berks 26 8782
Furzehill Devon 19 7245
Furzehill Dorset 11 0101
Furzehills Lincs 77 2572
Furzeley Corner Hants 13 6510
Furzley Hants 12 2816
Fyfett Somset 9 2314
Fyfield Essex 40 5707
Fyfield Hants 23 2946
Fyfield Oxon 36 4298
Fyfield Wilts 23 1468
Fyfield Wilts 23 1760
Fyfield Bavant Wilts 22 0125
Fyfield Wick Oxon 36 4197
Fylingthorpe N York 91 9404
Fyning W Susx 14 8123
Fyvie Abers 142 7637

286

G

Gabroc Hill E Ayrs 115 4550
Gaddesby Leics 63 6813
Gaddesden Row Herts 38 0512
Gadfa IOA 68 4689
Gadgirth S Ayrs 106 4022
Gadlas Shrops 59 3737
Gaer Powys 33 1721
Gaer-llwyd Mons 34 4496
Gaerwen IOA 68 4871
Gagingwell Oxon 48 4025
Gailey Staffs 60 9110
Gailes N Ayrs 106 3235
Gainford Dur 96 1716
Gainsborough Lincs 75 8189
Gainsford End Essex 53 7235
Gairloch Highld 144 8076
Gairlochy Highld 131 1784
Gairneybridge P & K 117 1398
Gaisby S York 82 1536
Gaisgill Cumb 87 6305
Gaitsgill Cumb 93 3846
Galashiels Border 109 4936
Galgate Lancs 80 4855
Galhampton Somset 21 6329
Gallanach Ag & B 122 8326
Gallantry Bank Ches 71 5153
Gallatown Fife 117 2994
Galley Common Warwks 61 3091
Galleywood Essex 40 7003
Gallovie Highld 132 5589
Gallowfauld Angus 127 4342
Gallowhill P & K 126 1635
Gallows Green Essex 40 9226
Gallows Green Worcs 47 9362
Gallowstree Common Oxon 37 6980
Galltair Highld 129 8120
Gally Hill Hants 25 8051
Gallypot Street E Susx 16 4735
Galmpton Devon 7 6940
Galmpton Devon 7 8856
Galphay N York 89 2572
Galston E Ayrs 107 5036
Galton Dorset 11 7785
Gamballs Green Staffs 74 0367
Gambles Green Essex 40 7614
Gamblesby Cumb 94 6039
Gamelsby Cumb 93 2552
Gamesley Gt Man 79 0194
Gamlingay Cambs 52 2452
Gamlingay Cinques Cambs 52 2352
Gamlingay Great Heath Beds 52 2151
Gammersgill N York 88 0582
Gamrie Abers 143 7962
Gamston Notts 75 7176
Gamston Notts 62 5937
Ganarew Herefs 34 5216
Ganavan Bay Ag & B 122 8632
Gang Cnwll 5 3068
Ganllwyd Gwynd 57 7324
Gannachy Angus 134 5970
Ganstead E R Yk 85 1434
Ganthorpe N York 90 6870
Ganton N York 91 9977
Ganwick Corner Herts 27 2599
Gappah Devon 9 8677
Garbity Moray 141 3152
Garboldisham Norfk 54 0081
Garchory Abers 134 3010
Garden City Flints 71 3269
Garden Village Derbys 74 2698
Gardeners Green Berks 25 8266
Gardenstown Abers 143 8064
Garderhouse Shet 153 3347
Gardham E R Yk 84 9542
Gare Hill Somset 22 7840
Garelochhead Ag & B 114 2491
Garford Oxon 36 4296
Garforth W York 83 4033
Garforth Bridge W York 83 3932
Gargrave N York 81 9354

Gargunnock Stirlg 116 7094
Garizim Conwy 69 6975
Garlic Street Norfk 55 2183
Garlieston D & G 99 4746
Garlinge Kent 29 3369
Garlinge Green Kent 29 1152
Garmond Abers 143 8052
Garmondsway Dur 96 3434
Garmouth Moray 141 3364
Garmston Shrops 59 6006
Garn Gwynd 56 2834
Garn-Dolbenmaen Gwynd 56 4943
Garnant Carmth 32 6713
Garnett Bridge Cumb 87 5299
Garnkirk N Lans 116 6768
Garnswllt Swans 32 6209
Garrabost W Isls 152 5133
Garragie Lodge Highld 130 4315
Garras Cnwll 2 7023
Garreg Gwynd 57 6141
Garrigill Cumb 94 7441
Garriston N York 89 1592
Garroch D & G 99 5981
Garrochtrie D & G 98 1138
Garrochty Ag & B 114 0953
Garros Highld 136 4962
Garrowby Hall E R Yk 90 7957
Garsdale Cumb 88 7489
Garsdale Head Cumb 88 7891
Garsdon Wilts 35 9687
Garshall Green Staffs 72 9633
Garsington Oxon 37 5802
Garstang Lancs 80 4945
Garston Herts 26 1100
Garston Mersyd 78 4084
Gartachossan Ag & B 112 3461
Gartcosh N Lans 116 6967
Garth Brdgnd 33 8690
Garth Denbgs 70 2542
Garth Mons 34 3492
Garth Powys 45 9549
Garth Powys 46 2772
Garth Penrhyncoch Cerdgn 43 6484
Garth Row Cumb 87 5297
Garthamlock C Glas 116 6566
Garthbrengy Powys 45 0433
Gartheli Cerdgn 44 5856
Garthmyl Powys 58 1999
Garthorpe Leics 63 8320
Garthorpe Lincs 84 8418
Garths Cumb 87 5489
Gartly Abers 142 5232
Gartmore Stirlg 115 5297
Gartness N Lans 116 7864
Gartness Stirlg 115 5086
Gartocharn W Duns 115 4286
Garton E R Yk 85 2635
Garton-on-the-Wolds E R Yk 91 9759
Gartymore Highld 147 0114
Garvald E Loth 118 5870
Garvan Highld 130 9777
Garvard Ag & B 112 3791
Garve Highld 139 3961
Garvestone Norfk 66 0027
Garvock Inver 114 2570
Garway Herefs 34 4522
Garway Common Herefs 34 4622
Garway Hill Herefs 46 4425
Garyvard W Isls 152 3619
Gasper Wilts 22 7633
Gastard Wilts 22 8868
Gasthorpe Norfk 54 9781
Gaston Green Essex 39 4917
Gatcombe IOW 13 4985
Gate Burton Lincs 76 8382
Gate Helmsley N York 83 6955
Gatebeck Cumb 87 5485
Gateford Notts 75 5781
Gateforth N York 83 5628
Gatehead E Ayrs 106 3936
Gatehouse Nthumb 102 7889
Gatehouse of Fleet D & G 99 5956
Gateley Norfk 66 9624
Gatenby N York 89 3287
Gates Heath Ches 71 4760
Gatesgarth Cumb 93 1915
Gateshaw Border 110 7722
Gateshead T & W 96 2562
Gateside Angus 127 4344
Gateside E Rens 115 4858
Gateside Fife 126 1809
Gateside N Ayrs 115 3653
Gateslack D & G 108 8902
Gathurst Gt Man 78 5407
Gatley Gt Man 79 8488
Gatton Surrey 27 2752
Gattonside Border 109 5435
Gatwick Airport 15 2740
Gaufron Powys 45 9968
Gaulby Leics 50 6900
Gauldry Fife 126 3723
Gauldswell P & K 126 2151
Gaulkthorn Lancs 81 7526
Gaultree Norfk 65 4907
Gaunt's Common Dorset 12 0205
Gaunt's End Essex 39 5525
Gaunton's Bank Ches 71 5647
Gautby Lincs 76 1772
Gavinton Border 119 7652
Gawber S York 83 3207
Gawcott Bucks 49 6831
Gawsworth Ches 79 8969
Gawthorpe W York 82 2721
Gawthorpe W York 87 6687
Gawthwaite Cumb 86 2784
Gay Bowers Essex 40 7904
Gay Street W Susx 14 0820
Gaydon Warwks 48 3653
Gayhurst Bucks 38 8446
Gayle N York 88 8688
Gayles N York 89 1207
Gayton Mersyd 78 2780
Gayton Nhants 49 7054
Gayton Norfk 65 7219
Gayton Staffs 72 9828
Gayton le Marsh Lincs 77 4284
Gayton Thorpe Norfk 65 7418

Gaywood Norfk 65 6320
Gazeley Suffk 53 7264
Gear Cnwll 3 7224
Gearraidh Bhaird W Isls 152 3619
Geary Highld 136 2661
Gedding Suffk 54 9457
Geddinge Kent 29 2346
Geddington Nhants 51 8983
Gedling Notts 62 6142
Gedney Lincs 65 4024
Gedney Broadgate Lincs 65 4022
Gedney Drove End Lincs 65 4629
Gedney Dyke Lincs 65 4126
Gedney Hill Lincs 64 3311
Gee Cross Gt Man 79 9593
Geeston Rutlnd 63 9803
Geldeston Norfk 67 3991
Gelli Rhondd 33 9794
Gelli Torfn 34 2792
Gellifor Denbgs 70 1262
Gelligaer Caerph 33 1396
Gelligroes Caerph 33 1794
Gelligron Neath 32 7104
Gellilydan Gwynd 57 6839
Gellinudd Neath 32 7303
Gelly Carmth 31 0819
Gellyburn P & K 125 0939
Gellywen Carmth 31 2723
Gelston D & G 92 7758
Gelston Lincs 63 9145
Gembling E R Yk 91 1057
Gentleshaw Staffs 61 0511
George Green Bucks 26 9981
George Nympton Devon 19 7023
Georgefield D & G 101 2991
Georgeham Devon 18 4639
Georgetown Blae G 33 1508
Georgia Cnwll 2 4836
Georth Ork 153 3625
Gerlan Gwynd 69 6366
Germansweek Devon 5 4394
Germoe Cnwll 2 5829
Gerrans Cnwll 3 8735
Gerrards Cross Bucks 26 0088
Gestingthorpe Essex 54 8138
Geufforddd Powys 58 2114
Gib Hill Ches 79 6477
Gibraltar Lincs 77 5558
Gibsmere Notts 75 7148
Giddeahall Wilts 35 8674
Giddy Green Dorset 11 8386
Gidea Park Gt Lon 27 5290
Gidleigh Devon 8 6788
Giffnock E Rens 115 5658
Gifford E Loth 118 5368
Giffordtown Fife 126 2811
Giggleswick N York 88 8063
Gilberdyke E R Yk 84 8329
Gilbert Street Hants 24 6432
Gilbert's Cross Staffs 60 8187
Gilbert's End Worcs 47 8342
Gilchriston E Loth 118 4865
Gilcrux Cumb 92 1138
Gildersome W York 82 2429
Gildingwells S York 75 5585
Gilesgate Moor Dur 96 2942
Gileston V Glam 20 0166
Gilfach Caerph 33 1598
Gilfach Goch Brdgnd 33 9790
Gilfachrheda Cerdgn 42 4158
Gilgarran Cumb 92 0323
Gill Cnwll 93 4429
Gill's Green Kent 17 7532
Gillamoor N York 90 6889
Gillan Cnwll 3 7825
Gillen Highld 136 2659
Gillesbie D & G 100 1691
Gilling East N York 90 6176
Gilling West N York 89 1805
Gillingham Dorset 22 8026
Gillingham Kent 28 7768
Gillingham Norfk 67 4191
Gillock Highld 151 2159
Gillow Heath Staffs 72 8858
Gills Highld 151 3272
Gilmanscleuch Border 109 3321
Gilmerton C Edin 117 2868
Gilmerton P & K 125 8823
Gilmonby Dur 95 9912
Gilmorton Leics 50 5787
Gilsland Nthumb 102 6366
Gilson Warwks 61 1989
Gilstead W York 82 1239
Gilston Herts 39 4413
Gilston Mdloth 118 4456
Giltbrook Notts 62 4845
Gilwern Mons 34 2414
Gimingham Norfk 67 2836
Ginclough Ches 79 9576
Gingers Green E Susx 16 6212
Gipping Suffk 54 0763
Gipsey Bridge Lincs 77 2849
Girdle Toll N Ayrs 106 3440
Girlington W York 82 1334
Girlsta Shet 153 4250
Girsby N York 89 3508
Girtford Beds 52 1649
Girthon D & G 99 6053
Girton Cambs 53 4262
Girton Notts 75 8265
Girvan S Ayrs 106 1897
Gisburn N York 81 8248
Gisleham Suffk 55 5188
Gislingham Suffk 54 0771
Gissing Norfk 54 1485
Gittisham Devon 9 1398
Gladestry Powys 45 2355
Gladsmuir E Loth 118 4573
Glais Swans 32 7000
Glaisdale N York 90 7705
Glamis Angus 126 3846
Glan-Duar Carmth 44 5243
Glan-Dwyfach Gwynd 56 4843
Glan-rhyd Powys 32 7809
Glan-y-don Flints 70 1679
Glan-y-llyn Rhondd 33 1183
Glan-y-nant Powys 58 9384

Glan-yr-afon Gwynd 70 9140
Glan-yr-afon Gwynd 70 0142
Glan-yr-afon IOA 69 6080
Glan-yr-afon Swans 32 6305
Glanaber Gwynd 69 6351
Glanafon Pembks 30 9617
Glandford Norfk 66 0441
Glandwr Pembks 31 1928
Glandyfi Cerdgn 43 6996
Glangrwyney Powys 34 2416
Glanllynfi Brdgnd 33 8690
Glanmule Powys 58 1690
Glanrhyd Pembks 31 1442
Glanton Nthumb 111 0714
Glanton Pike Nthumb 111 0514
Glanvilles Wootton Dorset 11 6708
Glapthorn Nhants 51 0290
Glapwell Derbys 75 4766
Glasbury Powys 45 1739
Glascoed Denbgs 70 9973
Glascoed Mons 34 3301
Glascote Staffs 61 2203
Glascwm Powys 45 1552
Glasfryn Conwy 70 9250
Glasgow C Glas 115 5865
Glasgow Airport 115 4766
Glasgow
   Art Gallery & Museum 115 5865
Glasinfryn Gwynd 69 5868
Glasnacardoch Bay Highld 129 6795
Glasnakille Highld 128 5313
Glaspwll Powys 43 7397
Glass Houghton W York 83 4324
Glassenbury Kent 28 7536
Glasserton D & G 99 4237
Glassford S Lans 116 7247
Glasshouse Gloucs 35 7021
Glasshouse Hill Gloucs 35 7020
Glasshouses N York 89 1764
Glasson Cumb 101 2560
Glasson Lancs 80 4456
Glassonby Cumb 94 5738
Glasterlaw Angus 127 5951
Glaston Rutlnd 51 8900
Glastonbury Somset 21 5038
Glatton Cambs 52 1586
Glazebrook Ches 79 6992
Glazebury Ches 79 6797
Glazeley Shrops 60 7088
Gleadless S York 83 3787
Gleadsmoss Ches 79 8168
Gleaston Cumb 86 2570
Glebe Highld 139 5118
Gledhow W York 82 3137
Gledpark D & G 99 6250
Gledrid Shrops 59 3036
Glemsford Suffk 54 8348
Glen Auldyn IOM 158 4393
Glen Clunie Lodge Abers 133 1383
Glen Maye IOM 158 2319
Glen Mona IOM 158 4588
Glen Nevis House Highld 130 1272
Glen Parva Leics 50 5798
Glen Trool Lodge D & G 99 4080
Glen Vine IOM 158 3378
Glenallachie Highld 141 2641
Glenancross Highld 129 6691
Glenaros House Ag & B 121 5544
Glenbarr Ag & B 105 6736
Glenbarry Abers 142 5554
Glenbeg Highld 121 5862
Glenbeg Highld 141 0028
Glenbervie Abers 135 7680
Glenboig N Lans 116 7268
Glenborrodale Highld 121 6061
Glenbranter Ag & B 114 1197
Glenbreck Border 108 0521
Glenbrittle House Highld 128 4121
Glenbuck E Ayrs 107 7429
Glencally Angus 134 3562
Glencaple D & G 100 9968
Glencarron Lodge Highld 138 0650
Glencarse P & K 126 1921
Glenceitlein Highld 123 1548
Glencoe Highld 130 1058
Glencothe Border 108 0829
Glencraig Fife 117 1894
Glencrosh D & G 107 7689
Glendale Highld 136 1749
Glenderuel Ag & B 114 9983
Glendevon P & K 125 9904
Glendoe Lodge Highld 131 4009
Glendoick P & K 126 2022
Glenduckie Fife 126 2818
Gleneagles P & K 125 9208
Gleneagles Hotel P & K 125 9111
Glenegedale Ag & B 112 3351
Glenelg Highld 129 8119
Glenerney Moray 141 0146
Glenfarg P & K 126 1310
Glenfeshie Lodge Highld 132 8493
Glenfield Leics 62 5406
Glenfinnan Highld 130 9080
Glenfintaig Lodge Highld 131 2286
Glenfoot P & K 126 1815
Glenfyne Lodge Ag & B 123 2215
Glengarnock N Ayrs 115 3252
Glengolly Highld 151 1065
Glengorm Castle Ag & B 121 4457
Glengrasco Highld 136 4444
Glenholm Border 108 1033
Glenhoul D & G 107 6187
Glenisla Angus 133 2160
Glenkin Ag & B 114 1280
Glenkindie Abers 142 4314
Glenlivet Moray 141 1929
Glenlochar D & G 99 7364
Glenlomond P & K 126 1704
Glenluce D & G 98 1957
Glenmassen Ag & B 114 1088
Glenmavis N Lans 116 7567
Glenmore Highld 136 4340
Glenmore Lodge Highld 133 9709
Glenquiech Angus 134 4261
Glenralloch Ag & B 113 8569
Glenridding Cumb 93 3817
Glenrosa Fife 117 2700
Glenshee P & K 125 9834

Glenshera Lodge Highld .... 132 5...
Glenstriven Ag & B .... 114 0...
Glentham Lincs .... 76 0...
Glentromie Lodge Highld ...... 132 7...
Glentrool Village D & G .... 98 3...
Glentruim House Highld .... 132 6...
Glentworth Lincs .... 76 9...
Glenuig Highld .... 129 6...
Glenure Ag & B .... 123 0...
Glenurquhart Highld .... 140 7...
Glenvarragill Highld .... 136 4...
Glenwhilly D & G .... 98 1...
Glespin S Lans .... 108 8...
Glewstone Herefs .... 34 5...
Glinton Cambs .... 64 1...
Glooston Leics .... 50 7...
Glororum Nthumb .... 111 1...
Glossop Derbys .... 74 0...
Gloster Hill Nthumb .... 103 2...
Gloucester Gloucs .... 35 8...
Gloucestershire Airport .... 35 8...
Glusburn N York .... 82 0...
Glutt Lodge Highld .... 150 0...
Gluvian Cnwll .... 4 9...
Glympton Oxon .... 36 4...
Glyn Ceiriog Wrexhm .... 70 2...
Glyn-Neath Neath .... 33 8...
Glynarthen Cerdgn .... 42 3...
Glyncorrwg Neath .... 33 8...
Glynde E Susx .... 16 4...
Glyndebourne E Susx .... 16 4...
Glyndyfrdwy Denbgs .... 70 1...
Glyntaff Rhondd .... 33 0...
Glyntawe Powys .... 33 8...
Glynteg Carmth .... 31 3...
Gnosall Staffs .... 72 8...
Gnosall Heath Staffs .... 72 8...
Goadby Leics .... 50 7...
Goadby Marwood Leics .... 63 7...
Goat Lees Kent .... 28 0...
Goatacre Wilts .... 35 0...
Goatfield Ag & B .... 114 0...
Goatham Green E Susx .... 17 8...
Goathill Dorset .... 11 6...
Goathland N York .... 90 8...
Goathurst Somset .... 20 2...
Goathurst Common Kent .... 27 4...
Gobowen Shrops .... 59 3...
Godalming Surrey .... 25 9...
Godameavy Devon .... 6 5...
Goddard's Corner Suffk .... 55 2...
Goddard's Green Kent .... 28 7...
Godford Cross Devon .... 9 1...
Godington Bucks .... 49 6...
Godley Gt Man .... 79 9...
Godmanchester Cambs .... 52 2...
Godmanstone Dorset .... 11 6...
Godmersham Kent .... 28 0...
Godney Somset .... 21 4...
Godolphin Cross Cnwll .... 2 6...
Godre'r-graig Neath .... 32 7...
Godshill Hants .... 12 1...
Godshill IOW .... 13 5...
Godstone Staffs .... 73 0...
Godstone Surrey .... 27 3...
Godsworthy Devon .... 5 5...
Godwinscroft Hants .... 12 1...
Goetre Mons .... 34 3...
Goff's Oak Herts .... 27 3...
Gofilon Mons .... 34 2...
Gogar C Edin .... 117 1...
Goginan Cerdgn .... 43 6...
Golan Gwynd .... 57 5...
Golant Cnwll .... 3 1...
Golberdon Cnwll .... 5 3...
Golborne Gt Man .... 78 6...
Golcar W York .... 82 0...
Gold Hill Cambs .... 65 5...
Gold Hill Dorset .... 11 8...
Goldcliff Newpt .... 34 3...
Golden Cross E Susx .... 16 5...
Golden Green Kent .... 16 6...
Golden Grove Carmth .... 32 5...
Golden Hill Pembks .... 30 9...
Golden Pot Hants .... 24 7...
Golden Valley Derbys .... 74 4...
Goldenhill Staffs .... 72 8...
Golders Green Gt Lon .... 26 2...
Goldfinch Bottom Berks .... 24 5...
Goldhanger Essex .... 40 9...
Golding Shrops .... 59 5...
Goldington Beds .... 38 0...
Golds Green W Mids .... 60 9...
Goldsborough N York .... 90 8...
Goldsborough N York .... 83 3...
Goldsithney Cnwll .... 2 5...
Goldstone Kent .... 29 2...
Goldstone Shrops .... 72 7...
Goldsworth Surrey .... 25 9...
Goldthorpe S York .... 83 4...
Goldworthy Devon .... 18 3...
Golford Kent .... 28 7...
Golford Green Kent .... 28 7...
Golfa Clwyd .... 00 0...
Gollanfield Highld .... 140 8...
Gollinglith Foot N York .... 89 1...
Golly Wrexhm .... 71 3...
Golsoncott Somset .... 20 0...
Golspie Highld .... 147 8...
Gomeldon Wilts .... 23 1...
Gomersal W York .... 82 2...
Gomshall Surrey .... 14 0...
Gonalston Notts .... 63 6...
Gonerby Hill Foot Lincs .... 63 9...
Gonfirth Shet .... 153 3...
Good Easter Essex .... 40 6...
Gooderstone Norfk .... 65 7...
Goodleigh Devon .... 19 6...
Goodmanham E R Yk .... 84 8...
Goodmayes Gt Lon .... 27 4...
Goodnestone Kent .... 28 2...
Goodnestone Kent .... 29 2...
Goodrich Herefs .... 34 5...
Goodrich Castle .... 34 5...
Goodrington Devon .... 7 8...
Goodshaw Lancs .... 81 8...
Goodshaw Fold Lancs .... 81 8...
Goodstone Devon .... 7 7...
Goodwick Pembks .... 30 9...

oodworth Clatford

Grove Vale

287

odworth Clatford Hants 23 3642
odyers End Warwks 61 3385
ole E R Yk 84 7423
ole Fields E R Yk 84 7520
om's Hill Worcs 47 0154
onbell Cnwll 3 7249
onhavern Cnwll 3 7853
onvrea Cnwll 2 7149
ose Green Essex 41 1327
ose Green Essex 41 1325
ose Green Gloucs 35 6774
ose Green Gt Man 78 5603
ose Green Kent 27 6451
ose Green Kent 28 8437
ose Green W Susx 14 1118
ose Pool Herefs 46 4636
osecruives Abers 135 7583
oseford Devon 8 6792
oseham Cnwll 18 2316
osehill Green Worcs 47 9361
osemoor Somset 20 9635
osey Oxon 36 3591
osnargh Lancs 81 5536
ostrey Ches 79 7770
rddinog Conwy 69 6773
rdon Border 110 6443
rdon Arms Hotel Border 109 3025
rdonstown Abers 142 5656
rdonstown Abers 142 7138
re Powys 46 2558
re Pit Essex 40 8719
re Street Kent 29 2765
rebridge Mdloth 118 3461
refield Cambs 64 4112
res Wilts 23 1158
rey Jersey 158 0000
ring Oxon 37 6080
ring Heath Oxon 37 6579
ring-by-Sea W Susx 14 1102
rleston on Sea Norfk 67 5204
rrachie Abers 142 7358
rran Cnwll 3 9942
rran Haven Cnwll 3 0141
rran High Lanes Cnwll 3 9843
rrig Cerdgn 31 4142
rs Cerdgn 43 6277
rse Hill Wilts 36 1586
rsedd Flints 70 1576
rseinon Swans 32 5998
rseybank Derbys 73 2953
rsgoch Cerdgn 44 4850
rslas Carmth 32 5713
rsley Gloucs 47 6925
rsley Common Gloucs 47 6825
rst Hill Worcs 60 7373
rstage Ches 71 6172
rstan Highld 139 3862
rstello Ches 71 3562
rsty Hill Staffs 73 1028
rten Ag & B 122 7432
rthleck Highld 139 5420
rton Gt Man 79 8896
sbeck Suffk 54 1555
sberton Lincs 64 2331
sberton Clough Lincs 64 1929
sfield Essex 40 7829
sford Devon 9 1097
sforth Cumb 86 0603
sforth T & W 103 2368
sland Green Ches 71 5758
sling Street Somset 21 5433
smore Herts 39 1827
spel End Staffs 60 8993
spel Green W Susx 14 9431
sport Hants 13 6099
ssard's Green Beds 38 9643
ssington Gloucs 35 7302
swick Nthumb 111 0644
tham Notts 62 5330
therington Gloucs 47 9529
tton Somset 20 2428
udhurst Kent 28 7237
ulceby Lincs 77 2579
urdas Abers 142 7741
urdie Angus 126 3532
urdon Abers 135 8270
urock Inver 114 2477
van C Glas 115 5465
veton Devon 7 7546
wdall E R Yk 83 6222
wer Highld 139 5058
werton Swans 32 5896
wkhall Fife 117 0589
wthorpe E R Yk 84 7654
xhill E R Yk 85 1844
xhill Lincs 85 1021
abhair W Isls 152 3915
aby Lincs 64 0929
ade Cnwll 2 7114
adeley Green Ches 71 5851
affham W Susx 14 9217
afham Cambs 52 1669
afham Surrey 14 0241
afton Herefs 46 4936
afton N York 89 4163
afton Oxon 36 2600
afton Shrops 59 4319
afton Worcs 46 5761
afton Worcs 47 9837
afton Flyford Worcs 47 9655
afton Regis Nhants 49 7546
afton Underwood Nhants 51 9280
afty Green Kent 28 8748
aianrhyd Denbgs 70 2156
aig Conwy 69 8071
aig Denbgs 70 0872
aig-fechan Denbgs 70 1454
ain Kent 28 8876
ains Bar Gt Man 79 9608
ainsby Lincs 77 2799
ainthorpe Lincs 77 3896
ampound Cnwll 3 9348
ampound Road Cnwll 3 9150
amsdal W Isls 152 8155
amsdale W Isls 152 8155
anborough Bucks 49 7625
anby Notts 63 7536
and Chemins Jersey 158 0000
Grand Prix
Collection Donington 62 4225
Grandborough Warwks 50 4966
Grandes Rocques Guern 158 0000
Grandtully P & K 125 9153
Grange Cumb 93 2517
Grange Kent 28 7968
Grange Mersyd 78 2286
Grange P & K 126 2625
Grange Crossroads Moray 142 4754
Grange Gate Dorset 11 9182
Grange Hall Moray 141 0660
Grange Hill Gt Lon 27 4492
Grange Moor W York 82 2215
Grange of Lindores Fife 126 2516
Grange Villa Dur 96 2352
Grange-over-Sands Cumb 87 4077
Grangehall S Lans 108 9642
Grangemill Derbys 74 2457
Grangemouth Falk 116 9281
Grangepans Falk 117 0181
Grangetown N York 97 5420
Grangetown T & W 96 4154
Gransmoor E R Yk 91 1259
Gransmore Green Essex 40 6922
Granston Pembks 30 8934
Grantchester Cambs 53 4355
Grantham Lincs 63 9135
Granton C Edin 117 2376
Grantown-on-Spey Highld 141 0328
Grantsfield Herefs 46 5260
Grantshouse Border 119 8065
Grappenhall Ches 79 6486
Grasby Lincs 85 0804
Grasmere Cumb 86 3307
Grass Green Essex 53 7338
Grasscroft Gt Man 82 9704
Grassendale Mersyd 78 3985
Grassgarth Cumb 93 3444
Grassington N York 88 0063
Grassmoor Derbys 74 4067
Grassthorpe Notts 75 7967
Grateley Hants 23 2741
Gratwich Staffs 73 0231
Graveley Cambs 52 2563
Graveley Herts 39 2327
Gravelly Hill W Mids 61 1090
Gravelsbank Shrops 59 3300
Graveney Kent 28 0562
Gravesend Kent 28 6574
Gravir W Isls 152 3915
Grayingham Lincs 76 9396
Grayrigg Cumb 87 5796
Grays Essex 27 6177
Grayshott Hants 14 8735
Grayson Green Cumb 92 9925
Grayswood Surrey 14 9134
Graythorpe Dur 97 5227
Grazeley Berks 24 6966
Greasbrough S York 74 4195
Greasby Mersyd 78 2587
Greasley Notts 62 4846
Great Abington Cambs 53 5348
Great Addington Nhants 51 9675
Great Alne Warwks 48 1259
Great Altcar Lancs 78 3305
Great Amwell Herts 39 3712
Great Asby Cumb 94 6713
Great Ashfield Suffk 54 9967
Great Ayton N York 90 5610
Great Baddow Essex 40 7304
Great Badminton Gloucs 35 8082
Great Bardfield Essex 40 6730
Great Barford Beds 52 1351
Great Barr W Mids 61 0495
Great Barrington Gloucs 36 2113
Great Barrow Ches 71 4768
Great Barton Suffk 54 8967
Great Barugh N York 90 7479
Great Bavington Nthumb 102 9880
Great Bealings Suffk 55 2348
Great Bedwyn Wilts 23 2764
Great Bentley Essex 41 1021
Great Billing Nhants 51 8162
Great Bircham Norfk 65 7732
Great Blakenham Suffk 54 1150
Great Blencow Cumb 93 4532
Great Bolas Shrops 72 6421
Great Bookham Surrey 26 1354
Great Bosullow Cnwll 2 4133
Great Bourton Oxon 49 4545
Great Bowden Leics 50 7488
Great Bradley Suffk 53 6753
Great Braxted Essex 40 8614
Great Bricett Suffk 54 0350
Great Brickhill Bucks 38 9030
Great Bridge W Mids 60 9892
Great Bridgeford Staffs 72 8827
Great Brington Nhants 50 6665
Great Bromley Essex 41 0826
Great Broughton Cumb 92 0731
Great Broughton N York 90 5405
Great Budworth Ches 79 6677
Great Burdon Dur 96 3116
Great Burstead Essex 40 6892
Great Busby N York 90 5205
Great Canfield Essex 40 5918
Great Carlton Lincs 77 4085
Great Casterton Rutlnd 63 0008
Great Chalfield Wilts 22 8563
Great Chart Kent 28 9841
Great Chatwell Staffs 60 7914
Great Chell Staffs 72 8652
Great Chesterford Essex 39 5042
Great Cheverell Wilts 22 9854
Great Chishill Cambs 39 4238
Great Clacton Essex 41 1716
Great Cliffe W York 82 3015
Great Clifton Cumb 92 0429
Great Coates Lincs 85 2309
Great Comberton Worcs 47 9542
Great Comp Kent 27 6356
Great Corby Cumb 93 4754
Great Cornard Suffk 54 8840
Great Cowden E R Yk 85 2342
Great Coxwell Oxon 36 2693
Great Cransley Nhants 51 8376
Great Cressingham Norfk 66 8501
Great Crosthwaite Cumb 93 2524
Great Cubley Derbys 73 1638
Great Dalby Leics 63 7414
Great Doddington Nhants 51 8864
Great Doward Herefs 34 5416
Great Dunham Norfk 66 8714
Great Dunmow Essex 40 6222
Great Durnford Wilts 23 1338
Great Easton Essex 40 6025
Great Easton Leics 51 8492
Great Eccleston Lancs 80 4240
Great Edstone N York 90 7083
Great Ellingham Norfk 66 0196
Great Elm Somset 22 7449
Great Englebourne Devon 7 7756
Great Everdon Nhants 49 5957
Great Eversden Cambs 52 3653
Great Finborough Suffk 54 0158
Great Fransham Norfk 66 8913
Great Gaddesden Herts 38 0211
Great Gidding Cambs 52 1183
Great Givendale E R Yk 84 8153
Great Glemham Suffk 55 3361
Great Glen Leics 50 6597
Great Gonerby Lincs 63 8938
Great Gransden Cambs 52 2655
Great Green Cambs 39 2844
Great Green Norfk 55 2889
Great Green Suffk 54 9155
Great Green Suffk 54 9365
Great Habton N York 90 7576
Great Hale Lincs 64 1442
Great Hallingbury Essex 39 5119
Great Harrowden Nhants 51 8770
Great Harwood Lancs 81 7332
Great Haseley Oxon 37 6401
Great Hatfield E R Yk 85 1842
Great Haywood Staffs 73 9922
Great Heck N York 83 5920
Great Henny Essex 54 8637
Great Hinton Wilts 22 9059
Great Hockham Norfk 66 9592
Great Holland Essex 41 2019
Great Horkesley Essex 41 9731
Great Hormead Herts 39 4029
Great Horton W York 82 1431
Great Horwood Bucks 49 7731
Great Houghton Nhants 50 7958
Great Houghton S York 83 4206
Great Hucklow Derbys 74 1777
Great Kelk E R Yk 91 1058
Great Kimble Bucks 38 8205
Great Kingshill Bucks 26 8797
Great Langdale Cumb 86 2906
Great Langton N York 89 2996
Great Leighs Essex 40 7217
Great Limber Lincs 85 1308
Great Linford Bucks 38 8542
Great Livermere Suffk 54 8871
Great Longstone Derbys 74 2071
Great Lumley Dur 96 2949
Great Lyth Shrops 59 4507
Great Malvern Worcs 47 7746
Great Maplestead Essex 54 8034
Great Marton Lancs 80 3235
Great Massingham Norfk 66 7922
Great Melton Norfk 66 1206
Great Meols Mersyd 78 2390
Great Milton Oxon 37 6202
Great Missenden Bucks 26 8901
Great Mitton Lancs 81 7138
Great Mongeham Kent 29 3551
Great Moulton Norfk 54 1690
Great Munden Herts 39 3524
Great Musgrave Cumb 94 7613
Great Ness Shrops 59 3919
Great Notley Essex 40 7421
Great Nurcott Somset 20 9036
Great Oak Mons 34 3810
Great Oakley Essex 41 1927
Great Oakley Nhants 51 8785
Great Offley Herts 38 1427
Great Ormside Cumb 94 7017
Great Orton Cumb 93 3254
Great Ouseburn N York 89 4461
Great Oxendon Nhants 50 7383
Great Oxney Green Essex 40 6606
Great Pattenden Kent 28 7344
Great Paxton Cambs 52 2063
Great Plumpton Lancs 80 3833
Great Plumstead Norfk 67 3010
Great Ponton Lincs 63 9230
Great Potheridge Devon 19 5114
Great Preston W York 83 4029
Great Purston Nhants 49 5139
Great Raveley Cambs 52 2581
Great Rissington Gloucs 36 1917
Great Rollright Oxon 48 3231
Great Rudbaxton Pembks 30 9620
Great Ryburgh Norfk 66 9527
Great Ryle Nthumb 111 0212
Great Ryton Shrops 59 4803
Great Saling Essex 40 6925
Great Salkeld Cumb 94 5536
Great Sampford Essex 53 6435
Great Sankey Ches 78 5688
Great Saredon Staffs 60 9508
Great Saughall Ches 71 3669
Great Saxham Suffk 53 7862
Great Shefford Berks 36 3875
Great Shelford Cambs 53 4651
Great Smeaton N York 89 3404
Great Snoring Norfk 66 9434
Great Somerford Wilts 35 9682
Great Soudley Shrops 72 7229
Great Stainton Dur 96 3322
Great Stambridge Essex 40 8991
Great Staughton Cambs 52 1264
Great Steeping Lincs 77 4364
Great Stoke Bristl 35 6280
Great Stonar Kent 29 3359
Great Strickland Cumb 94 5522
Great Stukeley Cambs 52 2274
Great Sturton Lincs 76 2176
Great Sutton Ches 71 3775
Great Sutton Shrops 59 5183
Great Swinburne Nthumb 102 9375
Great Tew Oxon 48 4028
Great Tey Essex 40 8925
Great Torrington Devon 18 4919
Great Tosson Nthumb 103 0200
Great Totham Essex 40 8611
Great Totham Essex 40 8713
Great Tows Lincs 76 2290
Great Urswick Cumb 86 2674
Great Wakering Essex 40 9487
Great Waldingfield Suffk 54 9144
Great Walsingham Norfk 66 9437
Great Waltham Essex 40 6913
Great Warford Ches 79 8177
Great Warley Essex 27 5890
Great Washbourne Gloucs 47 9834
Great Weeke Devon 8 7187
Great Weldon Nhants 51 9289
Great Welnetham Suffk 54 8759
Great Wenham Suffk 54 0738
Great Whittington Nthumb 103 0070
Great Wigborough Essex 41 9615
Great Wilbraham Cambs 53 5557
Great Wishford Wilts 23 0735
Great Witchingham Norfk 66 1020
Great Witcombe Gloucs 35 9114
Great Witley Worcs 47 7566
Great Wolford Warwks 48 2534
Great Wratting Essex 53 6848
Great Wymondley Herts 39 2128
Great Wyrley Staffs 60 9907
Great Wytheford Shrops 59 5719
Great Yarmouth Norfk 67 5207
Great Yeldham Essex 53 7638
Greatfield Wilts 36 0785
Greatford Lincs 64 0811
Greatgate Staffs 73 0539
Greatham Dur 97 4927
Greatham Hants 14 7730
Greatham W Susx 14 0415
Greatstone-on-Sea Kent 17 0822
Greatworth Nhants 49 5542
Grebby Lincs 77 4368
Greeba IOM 158 3081
Green Denbgs 70 0668
Green Bank Cumb 87 3780
Green Cross Surrey 14 8637
Green Down Somset 21 5753
Green End Beds 38 0147
Green End Beds 51 0864
Green End Beds 51 1063
Green End Beds 52 1252
Green End Cambs 52 2274
Green End Cambs 52 3856
Green End Cambs 53 4668
Green End Cambs 53 4861
Green End Cambs 52 1683
Green End Herts 39 2630
Green End Herts 39 3222
Green End Herts 39 3333
Green End Warwks 61 2686
Green Hammerton N York 83 4556
Green Head Cumb 93 3649
Green Heath Staffs 60 9913
Green Hill Wilts 36 0686
Green Lane Devon 8 7877
Green Lane Warwks 48 0664
Green Moor S York 74 2899
Green Oak E R Yk 84 8127
Green Ore Somset 21 5750
Green Quarter Cumb 87 4603
Green Street E Susx 17 7611
Green Street Gloucs 35 8915
Green Street Herts 39 4521
Green Street Herts 26 1998
Green Street Worcs 47 8749
Green Street Green Gt Lon 27 4563
Green Street Green Kent 27 5870
Green Tye Herts 39 4418
Greenburn W Loth 116 9360
Greencroft Hall Dur 96 1549
Greenend Oxon 36 3221
Greenfield Ag & B 114 2490
Greenfield Beds 38 0534
Greenfield Flints 70 1977
Greenfield Gt Man 82 9904
Greenfield Highld 131 2000
Greenfield Oxon 37 7191
Greenford Gt Lon 26 1482
Greengairs N Lans 116 7870
Greengates W York 82 1937
Greengill Cumb 92 1037
Greenhalgh Lancs 80 4035
Greenham Berks 24 4865
Greenham Somset 20 0820
Greenhaugh Nthumb 102 7987
Greenhead Nthumb 102 6565
Greenheys Gt Man 79 7104
Greenhill D & G 100 1079
Greenhill Falk 116 8279
Greenhill Herefs 47 7248
Greenhill Kent 29 1666
Greenhill S Lans 108 9332
Greenhillocks Derbys 74 4049
Greenhithe Kent 27 5875
Greenholm E Ayrs 107 5437
Greenholme Cumb 87 5905
Greenhouse Border 109 5523
Greenhow Hill N York 89 1164
Greenland Highld 151 2367
Greenland S York 74 3988
Greenlands Bucks 37 7785
Greenlaw Border 110 7146
Greenlea D & G 100 0375
Greenloaning P & K 125 8307
Greenmoor Hill Oxon 37 6481
Greenmount Gt Man 81 7714
Greenock Inver 115 2876
Greenodd Cumb 86 3182
Greens Norton Nhants 49 6649
Greensgate Norfk 66 1015
Greenshields S Lans 108 0243
Greenside T & W 96 1362
Greenside W York 82 1716
Greenstead Essex 41 0125
Greenstead Green Essex 40 8227
Greensted Essex 39 5403
Greenstreet Green Suffk 54 0349
Greenway Gloucs 47 7033
Greenway Somset 21 3124
Greenway V Glam 33 0573
Greenway Worcs 60 7470
Greenwich Gt Lon 27 3877
Greet Gloucs 48 0230
Greete Shrops 46 5770
Greetham Lincs 77 3070
Greetham Rutlnd 63 9214
Greetland W York 82 0821
Gregson Lane Lancs 81 5926
Greinton Somset 21 4136
Grenaby IOM 158 2672
Grendon Nhants 51 8760
Grendon Warwks 61 2799
Grendon Green Herefs 46 5957
Grendon Underwood Bucks 37 6820
Grenofen Devon 6 4971
Grenoside S York 74 3393
Greosabhagh W Isls 152 1593
Gresford Wrexhm 71 3454
Gresham Norfk 66 1638
Greshornish
House Hotel Highld 136 3454
Gressenhall Norfk 66 9615
Gressenhall Green Norfk 66 9616
Gressingham Lancs 87 5769
Gresty Green Ches 72 7053
Greta Bridge Dur 95 0813
Gretna D & G 101 3167
Gretna Green D & G 101 3168
Gretton Gloucs 47 0030
Gretton Nhants 51 8994
Gretton Shrops 59 5195
Grewelthorpe N York 89 2376
Grey Friars Suffk 55 4770
Grey Green Lincs 84 7807
Greygarth N York 89 1872
Greylake Somset 21 3833
Greyrigg D & G 100 0888
Greys Green Oxon 37 7182
Greysouthen Cumb 92 0729
Greystoke Cumb 93 4430
Greystone Angus 127 5343
Greywell Hants 24 7151
Gribb Dorset 10 3703
Gribthorpe E R Yk 84 7635
Griff Warwks 61 3689
Griffithstown Torfn 34 2998
Griffydam Leics 62 4118
Griggs Green Hants 14 8231
Grimeford Village Lancs 81 6112
Grimesthorpe S York 74 3689
Grimethorpe S York 83 4109
Grimley Worcs 47 8360
Grimmet S Ayrs 106 3210
Grimoldby Lincs 77 3988
Grimpo Shrops 59 3526
Grimsargh Lancs 81 5834
Grimsby Lincs 85 2710
Grimscote Nhants 49 6553
Grimscott Cnwll 18 2606
Grimshader W Isls 152 4025
Grimshaw Lancs 81 7024
Grimshaw Green Lancs 80 4912
Grimsthorpe Lincs 64 0422
Grimston E R Yk 85 2735
Grimston Leics 63 6821
Grimston Norfk 65 7222
Grimston Hill Notts 75 6865
Grimstone Dorset 10 6394
Grimstone End Suffk 54 9368
Grinacombe Moor Devon 5 4191
Grindale E R Yk 91 1271
Grindle Shrops 60 7503
Grindleford Derbys 74 2477
Grindleton Lancs 81 7545
Grindley Brook Shrops 71 5242
Grindlow Derbys 74 1877
Grindon Dur 96 3925
Grindon Nthumb 110 9144
Grindon Staffs 73 0854
Grindon T & W 96 3555
Grindon Hill Nthumb 102 8268
Grindonrigg Nthumb 110 9243
Gringley on the Hill Notts 75 7390
Grinsdale Cumb 93 3758
Grinshill Shrops 59 5223
Grinton N York 88 0498
Griomaisiader W Isls 152 4025
Griomsaigh W Isls 152 8457
Grishipoll Ag & B 120 1859
Grisling Common E Susx 16 4322
Gristhorpe N York 91 0981
Griston Norfk 66 9499
Gritley Ork 153 5504
Grittenham Wilts 36 0382
Grittleton Wilts 35 8580
Grizebeck Cumb 86 2384
Grizedale Cumb 86 3394
Groby Leics 62 5207
Groes Conwy 70 0064
Groes-faen Rhondd 33 0680
Groes-Wen Caerph 33 1286
Groesffordd Gwynd 56 2739
Groesffordd Marli Denbgs 70 0073
Groesllwyd Powys 58 2111
Groeslon Gwynd 68 4755
Groeslon Gwynd 68 5260
Grogarry W Isls 152 7739
Grogport Ag & B 105 8144
Groigearraidh W Isls 152 7739
Gromford Suffk 55 3858
Gronant Flints 70 0983
Groombridge E Susx 16 5337
Grosebay W Isls 152 1593
Grosmont Mons 46 4024
Grosmont N York 90 8305
Grotton Suffk 54 9641
Grotton Gt Man 79 9604
Grouville Jersey 158 0000
Grove Bucks 38 9122
Grove Dorset 11 6972
Grove Kent 29 2362
Grove Notts 75 7479
Grove Oxon 36 4090
Grove Pembks 30 9900
Grove Green Kent 28 7856
Grove Park Gt Lon 27 4072
Grove Vale W Mids 61 0394

288

Grovenhurst Kent 28 7140
Grovesend Gloucs 35 6589
Grovesend Swans 32 5900
Grubb Street Kent 27 5869
Gruinard Highld 144 9489
Gruinart Ag & B 112 2966
Grula Highld 136 3826
Gruline Ag & B 121 5440
Grumbla Cnwll 2 4029
Grundisburgh Suffk 55 2251
Gruting Shet 153 2749
Gualachulain Highld 123 1145
Guanockgate Lincs 64 3710
Guardbridge Fife 127 4518
Guarlford Worcs 47 8145
Guay P & K 125 0049
Guernsey Airport 158 0000
Guestling Green E Susx 17 8513
Guestling Thorn E Susx 17 8516
Guestwick Norfk 66 0626
Guide Lancs 81 7025
Guide Bridge Gt Man 79 9297
Guide Post Nthumb 103 2585
Guilden Down Shrops 59 3082
Guilden Morden Cambs 39 2744
Guilden Sutton Ches 71 4468
Guildford Surrey 25 9949
Guildstead Kent 28 8262
Guildtown P & K 126 1331
Guilsborough Nhants 50 6772
Guilsfield Powys 58 2211
Guilton Kent 29 2858
Guiltreehill S Ayrs 106 3610
Guineaford Devon 19 5537
Guisborough N York 97 6015
Guiseley W York 82 1942
Guist Norfk 66 0025
Guiting Power Gloucs 48 0924
Gullane E Loth 118 4882
Gulling Green Suffk 54 8256
Gulval Cnwll 2 4831
Gulworthy Devon 6 4572
Gumfreston Pembks 31 1001
Gumley Leics 50 6889
Gummow's Shop Cnwll 4 8657
Gun Green Kent 17 7731
Gun Hill E Susx 16 5614
Gun Hill Warwks 61 2899
Gunby E R Yk 84 7035
Gunby Lincs 63 9121
Gunby Lincs 77 4666
Gundleton Hants 24 6133
Gunn Devon 19 6333
Gunnerside N York 88 9598
Gunnerton Nthumb 102 9074
Gunness Lincs 84 8411
Gunnislake Cnwll 6 4371
Gunnista Shet 153 5043
Gunthorpe Cambs 64 1802
Gunthorpe Norfk 66 0134
Gunthorpe Notts 63 6844
Gunton Suffk 67 5395
Gunville IOW 13 4788
Gunwalloe Cnwll 2 6522
Gupworthy Somset 20 9734
Gurnard IOW 13 4795
Gurnett Ches 79 9271
Gurney Slade Somset 21 6249
Gurnos Powys 32 7709
Gushmere Kent 28 0457
Gussage All Saints Dorset 11 0010
Gussage St Andrew Dorset 11 9714
Gussage St Michael Dorset 11 9811
Guston Kent 29 3244
Gutcher Shet 153 5499
Guthrie Angus 127 5650
Guy's Marsh Dorset 22 8420
Guyhirn Cambs 65 4003
Guyhirn Gull Cambs 65 3904
Guyzance Nthumb 103 2103
Gwaenysgor Flints 70 0781
Gwalchmai IOA 68 3876
Gwastadnant Gwynd 69 6157
Gwaun-Cae-Gurwen Carmth 32 6911
Gwbert on Sea Cerdgn 42 1650
Gwealavellan Cnwll 2 6041
Gwealeath Cnwll 2 6922
Gweek Cnwll 2 7026
Gwehelog Mons 34 3804
Gwenddwr Powys 45 0643
Gwendreath Cnwll 3 7217
Gwennap Cnwll 3 7340
Gwenter Cnwll 3 7417
Gwernaffield Flints 70 2065
Gwernesney Mons 34 4101
Gwernogle Carmth 44 5333
Gwernymynydd Flints 70 2162
Gwersyllt Wrexhm 71 3153
Gwespyr Flints 70 1183
Gwindra Cnwll 3 9552
Gwinear Cnwll 2 5937
Gwithian Cnwll 2 5841
Gwredog IOA 68 4085
Gwrhay Caerph 33 1899
Gwyddelwern Denbgs 70 0746
Gwyddgrug Carmth 44 4635
Gwynfryn Wrexhm 70 2552
Gwystre Powys 45 0665
Gwytherin Conwy 69 8761
Gyfelia Wrexhm 71 3245
Gyrn-goch Gwynd 68 4048

H

Habberley Shrops 59 3903
Habberley Worcs 60 8177
Habergham Lancs 81 8033
Habertoft Lincs 77 5069
Habin W Susx 14 8022
Habrough Lincs 85 1413
Hacconby Lincs 64 1025

Haceby Lincs 64 0236
Hacheston Suffk 55 3059
Hack Green Ches 72 6448
Hackbridge Gt Lon 27 2865
Hackenthorpe S York 74 4183
Hackford Norfk 66 0502
Hackforth N York 89 2492
Hackland Ork 153 3920
Hackleton Nhants 51 8055
Hacklinge Kent 29 3454
Hackman's Gate Worcs 60 8978
Hackness N York 91 9790
Hackness Somset 21 3345
Hackney Gt Lon 27 3484
Hackthorn Lincs 76 9982
Hackthorpe Cumb 94 5423
Hacton Gt Lon 27 5585
Hadden Border 110 7836
Haddenham Bucks 37 7308
Haddenham Cambs 53 4675
Haddington E Loth 118 5173
Haddington Lincs 76 9162
Haddiscoe Norfk 67 4497
Haddo Abers 143 8337
Haddon Cambs 64 1392
Hade Edge W York 82 1444
Hadfield Derbys 74 0296
Hadham Cross Herts 39 4218
Hadham Ford Herts 39 4321
Hadleigh Essex 40 8187
Hadleigh Suffk 54 0242
Hadleigh Heath Suffk 54 9941
Hadley Shrops 60 6711
Hadley Worcs 47 8564
Hadley End Staffs 73 1320
Hadley Wood Gt Lon 27 2698
Hadlow Kent 27 6350
Hadlow Down E Susx 16 5324
Hadnall Shrops 59 5220
Hadstock Essex 53 5644
Hadzor Worcs 47 9162
Haffenden Quarter Kent 28 8840
Hafod-y-bwch Wrexhm 71 3147
Hafod-y-coed Blae G 34 2200
Hafodunos Conwy 69 8666
Hafodyrynys Caerph 34 2298
Haggate Lancs 81 8735
Haggbeck Cumb 101 4773
Haggerston Nthumb 111 0443
Haggington Hill Devon 19 5547
Haggs Falk 116 7879
Hagley Herefs 46 5641
Hagley Worcs 60 9180
Hagmore Green Suffk 54 9539
Hagnaby Lincs 77 3462
Hagnaby Lincs 77 4879
Hagworthingham Lincs 77 3469
Haigh Gt Man 78 6009
Haighton Green Lancs 81 5634
Hail Weston Cambs 52 1662
Haile Cumb 86 0308
Hailes Gloucs 48 0430
Hailey Herts 39 3710
Hailey Oxon 37 6485
Hailey Oxon 36 3512
Hailsham E Susx 16 5909
Hainault Gt Lon 27 4591
Hainford Norfk 67 2218
Hainton Lincs 76 1884
Hainworth W York 82 0638
Haisthorpe E R Yk 91 1264
Hakin Pembks 30 8905
Halam Notts 75 6754
Halbeath Fife 117 1288
Halberton Devon 9 0112
Halcro Highld 151 2360
Hale Ches 78 4782
Hale Cumb 87 5019
Hale Gt Man 79 7786
Hale Hants 12 1818
Hale Somset 22 7427
Hale Surrey 25 8448
Hale Bank Ches 78 4784
Hale Green E Susx 16 5514
Hale Nook Lancs 80 3944
Hale Street Kent 28 6749
Halebarns Gt Man 79 7985
Hales Norfk 67 3797
Hales Staffs 72 7134
Hales Green Derbys 73 1841
Hales Place Kent 29 1459
Halesgate Lincs 64 3226
Halesowen W Mids 60 9683
Halesville Essex 40 9092
Halesworth Suffk 55 3877
Halewood Mersyd 78 4585
Halford Devon 7 8174
Halford Shrops 59 4383
Halford Warwks 48 2645
Halfpenny Cumb 87 5387
Halfpenny Green Staffs 60 8291
Halfpenny Houses N York 89 2284
Halfway Berks 24 4068
Halfway Carmth 44 6440
Halfway Carmth 44 8232
Halfway S York 75 4381
Halfway Bridge W Susx 14 9321
Halfway House Shrops 59 3411
Halfway Houses Kent 28 9372
Halifax W York 82 0925
Halkirk Highld 151 1359
Halkyn Flints 70 2171
Hall E Rens 115 4154
Hall Cliffe W York 82 2918
Hall Cross Lancs 80 4230
Hall Dunnerdale Cumb 86 2195
Hall End Beds 38 0045
Hall End Beds 38 0737
Hall End W Mids 60 0092
Hall Glen Falk 116 8978
Hall Green W Mids 61 1181
Hall's Green Essex 39 4108
Hall's Green Herts 39 2728
Hallam Fields Derbys 62 4739
Halland E Susx 16 4916
Hallaton Leics 50 7896
Hallatrow Somset 21 6357

Hallbankgate Cumb 94 5859
Hallbeck Cumb 87 6288
Hallen Gloucs 34 5580
Hallfield Gate Derbys 74 3958
Hallgarth Dur 96 3243
Hallin Highld 136 2558
Halling Kent 28 7063
Hallington Lincs 77 3085
Hallington Nthumb 102 9875
Halliwell Gt Man 79 6910
Halloughton Notts 75 6951
Hallow Worcs 47 8258
Hallow Heath Worcs 47 8259
Hallsands Devon 7 8138
Hallthwaites Cumb 86 1885
Halltoft End Lincs 64 3645
Hallworthy Cnwll 4 1787
Hallyne Border 109 1940
Halmer End Staffs 72 7948
Halmond's Frome Herefs 47 6747
Halmore Gloucs 35 7002
Halnaker W Susx 14 9007
Halsall Lancs 78 3710
Halse Nhants 49 5640
Halse Somset 20 1428
Halsetown Cnwll 2 5038
Halsham E R Yk 85 2727
Halsinger Devon 19 5138
Halstead Essex 40 8130
Halstead Kent 27 4861
Halstead Leics 63 7505
Halstock Dorset 10 5308
Halsway Somset 20 1337
Haltcliff Bridge Cumb 93 3636
Haltham Lincs 77 2463
Halton Bucks 38 8710
Halton Ches 78 5481
Halton Lancs 87 5064
Halton Nthumb 103 9967
Halton W York 83 3533
Halton Wrexhm 71 3039
Halton East N York 82 0454
Halton Fenside Lincs 77 4263
Halton Gill N York 88 8776
Halton Green Lancs 87 5165
Halton Holegate Lincs 77 4165
Halton Lea Gate Nthumb 94 6458
Halton Quay Cnwll 5 4165
Halton Shields Nthumb 103 0168
Halton West N York 81 8454
Haltwhistle Nthumb 102 7064
Halvergate Norfk 67 4106
Halwell Devon 7 7753
Halwill Devon 18 4299
Halwill Junction Devon 18 4400
Ham Devon 9 2301
Ham Gloucs 35 9721
Ham Gloucs 35 6898
Ham Gt Lon 26 1772
Ham Kent 29 3254
Ham Somset 20 2825
Ham Somset 22 6748
Ham Wilts 23 3262
Ham Common Dorset 22 8125
Ham Green Herefs 47 7544
Ham Green Kent 28 8468
Ham Green Kent 17 8926
Ham Green Somset 34 5375
Ham Green Worcs 47 0163
Ham Hill Kent 28 6960
Ham Street Somset 21 5534
Hamble-le-Rice Hants 13 4806
Hambledon Bucks 37 7886
Hambledon Hants 13 6414
Hambledon Surrey 25 9638
Hambleton Lancs 80 3742
Hambleton N York 83 5530
Hambleton Moss Side Lancs 80 3842
Hambridge Somset 21 3921
Hambrook Gloucs 35 6478
Hambrook W Susx 14 7806
Hameringham Lincs 77 3167
Hamerton Cambs 52 1379
Hamilton S Lans 116 7255
Hamlet Dorset 10 5908
Hamlins E Susx 16 5908
Hammerpot W Susx 14 0605
Hammersmith Gt Lon 26 2378
Hammerwich Staffs 61 0707
Hammerwood E Susx 16 4339
Hammond Street Herts 39 3304
Hammoon Dorset 11 8114
Hamnavoe Shet 153 3735
Hamnavoe Shet 153 4971
Hampden Park E Susx 16 6002
Hampden Row Bucks 26 8501
Hamperden End Essex 40 5730
Hampnett Gloucs 36 0915
Hampole S York 83 5010
Hampreston Dorset 12 0598
Hampsfield Cumb 87 4080
Hampson Green Lancs 80 4954
Hampstead Gt Lon 27 2685
Hampstead Norrey's Berks 37 5276
Hampsthwaite N York 89 2559
Hampt Cnwll 5 3874
Hampton Devon 10 2696
Hampton Gt Lon 26 1369
Hampton Kent 29 1568
Hampton Shrops 60 7486
Hampton Wilts 36 1892
Hampton Worcs 48 0243
Hampton Bishop Herefs 46 5637
Hampton Court
  Palace & Gardens 26 1568
Hampton Fields Gloucs 35 8899
Hampton Green Ches 71 5149
Hampton Heath Ches 71 5049
Hampton in Arden W Mids 61 2080
Hampton Loade Shrops 60 7486
Hampton Lovett Worcs 47 8865
Hampton Lucy Warwks 48 2557
Hampton Magna Warwks 48 2665
Hampton on the Hill Warwks 48 2564
Hampton Poyle Oxon 37 5015
Hampton Wick Gt Lon 26 1769
Hamptworth Wilts 12 2419

Hamrow Norfk 66 9124
Hamsey E Susx 15 4012
Hamsey Green Gt Lon 27 3559
Hamstall Ridware Staffs 73 1019
Hamstead IOW 13 4091
Hamstead W Mids 61 0592
Hamstead Marshall Berks 24 4165
Hamsterley Dur 95 1156
Hamsterley Dur 96 1231
Hamstreet Kent 17 0033
Hamwood Somset 21 3756
Hamworthy Dorset 11 9991
Hanbury Staffs 73 1727
Hanbury Worcs 47 9664
Hanby Lincs 64 0231
Hanchet End Suffk 53 6446
Hanchurch Staffs 72 8441
Hand and Pen Devon 9 0495
Hand Green Ches 71 5460
Handale N York 97 7215
Handbridge Ches 71 4065
Handcross W Susx 15 2629
Handforth Ches 79 8583
Handley Ches 71 4657
Handley Derbys 74 3761
Handley Green Essex 40 6501
Handsacre Staffs 73 0915
Handsworth S York 74 4186
Handsworth W Mids 61 0489
Handy Cross Bucks 26 8590
Hanford Dorset 11 8411
Hanford Staffs 72 8741
Hanging Houghton Nhants 60 7573
Hanging Langford Wilts 23 0337
Hangleton E Susx 15 2607
Hangleton W Susx 14 0803
Hanham Gloucs 35 6472
Hankelow Ches 72 6645
Hankerton Wilts 35 9790
Hankham E Susx 16 6105
Hanley Staffs 72 8847
Hanley Castle Worcs 47 8442
Hanley Child Worcs 47 6565
Hanley Swan Worcs 47 8142
Hanley William Worcs 47 6766
Hanlith N York 88 8961
Hanmer Wrexhm 71 4539
Hannaford Devon 19 6029
Hannah Lincs 77 4979
Hannington Hants 24 5355
Hannington Nhants 51 8170
Hannington Wilts 36 1793
Hannington Wick Wilts 36 1795
Hanscombe End Beds 38 1133
Hanslope Bucks 38 8046
Hanthorpe Lincs 64 0823
Hanwell Gt Lon 26 1579
Hanwell Oxon 49 4343
Hanwood Shrops 59 4409
Hanworth Gt Lon 26 1271
Hanworth Norfk 67 1935
Happendon S Lans 108 8533
Happisburgh Norfk 67 3831
Happisburgh Common Norfk 67 3728
Hapsford Ches 71 4774
Hapton Lancs 81 7931
Hapton Norfk 66 1796
Harberton Devon 7 7758
Harbertonford Devon 7 7856
Harbledown Kent 29 1357
Harborne W Mids 60 0284
Harborough Magna Warwks 50 4879
Harbottle Nthumb 102 9304
Harbourneford Devon 7 7162
Harbours Hill Worcs 47 9565
Harbridge Hants 12 1410
Harbridge Green Hants 12 1410
Harbury Warwks 48 3759
Harby Leics 63 7431
Harby Notts 76 8770
Harcombe Devon 9 8881
Harcombe Devon 9 1590
Harcombe Bottom Devon 10 3395
Harden W Mids 60 0100
Harden W York 82 0838
Hardenhuish Wilts 35 9174
Hardgate Abers 135 7901
Hardgate D & G 100 8167
Hardgate N York 89 2662
Hardgate W Duns 115 5072
Hardham W Susx 14 0317
Hardhorn Lancs 80 3537
Hardingham Norfk 66 0403
Hardingstone Nhants 49 7657
Hardington Somset 22 7452
Hardington Mandeville Somset 10 5111
Hardington Marsh Somset 10 5009
Hardington Moor Somset 10 5112
Hardisworthy Devon 18 2320
Hardley Hants 13 4205
Hardley Street Norfk 67 3701
Hardmead Bucks 38 9347
Hardraw N York 88 8691
Hardsough Lancs 81 7920
Hardstoft Derbys 75 4363
Hardway Hants 13 6001
Hardway Somset 22 7234
Hardwick Bucks 38 8019
Hardwick Cambs 52 3758
Hardwick Lincs 76 8675
Hardwick Nhants 51 8469
Hardwick Norfk 55 2289
Hardwick Oxon 36 3806
Hardwick Oxon 49 5729
Hardwick S York 75 4885
Hardwick W Mids 61 0798
Hardwick Green Worcs 47 8133
Hardwicke Gloucs 35 7912
Hardwicke Gloucs 47 9027
Hardy's Green Essex 40 9320
Hare Croft W York 82 0835
Hare Green Essex 41 1025
Hare Hatch Berks 37 8077
Hare Street Essex 39 4249
Hare Street Essex 27 5300
Hare Street Herts 39 3929
Harebeating E Susx 16 5910
Hareby Lincs 77 3365

Harefield Gt Lon 26 0...
Harehill Derbys 73 1...
Harehills W York 83 3...
Harehope Nthumb 111 0...
Harelaw Border 109 5...
Harelaw D & G 101 4...
Harelaw Dur 96 1...
Hareplain Kent 28 8...
Haresceugh Cumb 94 6...
Harescombe Gloucs 35 8...
Haresfield Gloucs 35 8...
Harestock Hants 24 4...
Harewood W York 83 3...
Harewood End Herefs 46 5...
Harford Devon 6 6...
Hargate Norfk 66 1...
Hargatewall Derbys 74 1...
Hargrave Ches 71 4...
Hargrave Nhants 51 0...
Hargrave Suffk 53 7...
Hargrave Green Suffk 53 7...
Harker Cumb 101 3...
Harkstead Suffk 54 1...
Harlaston Staffs 61 2...
Harlaxton Lincs 63 8...
Harle Syke Lancs 81 8...
Harlech Gwynd 57 5...
Harlescott Shrops 59 4...
Harlesden Gt Lon 26 2...
Harlesthorpe Derbys 75 4...
Harleston Devon 7 7...
Harleston Norfk 55 2...
Harleston Suffk 54 0...
Harlestone Nhants 49 7...
Harley S York 74 3...
Harley Shrops 59 5...
Harlington Beds 38 0...
Harlington Gt Lon 26 0...
Harlington S York 83 4...
Harlosh Highld 136 2...
Harlow Essex 39 4...
Harlow Hill Nthumb 103 0...
Harlthorpe E R Yk 84 7...
Harlton Cambs 52 3...
Harlyn Bay Cnwll 4 8...
Harman's Cross Dorset 11 9...
Harmby N York 89 1...
Harmer Green Herts 39 25...
Harmer Hill Shrops 59 4...
Harmondsworth Gt Lon 26 0...
Harmston Lincs 76 9...
Harnage Shrops 59 5...
Harnham Nthumb 103 0...
Harnhill Gloucs 36 0...
Harold Hill Gt Lon 27 5...
Harold Wood Gt Lon 27 5...
Haroldston West Pembks 30 8...
Haroldswick Shet 153 6...
Harome N York 90 6...
Harpenden Herts 38 1...
Harpford Devon 9 0...
Harpham E R Yk 91 08...
Harpley Norfk 65 7...
Harpley Worcs 47 68...
Harpole Nhants 49 6...
Harpsdale Highld 151 1...
Harpsden Oxon 37 7...
Harpswell Lincs 76 9...
Harpur Hill Derbys 74 0...
Harpurhey Gt Man 79 85...
Harraby Cumb 93 41...
Harracott Devon 19 55...
Harrapool Highld 129 6...
Harrietfield P & K 125 9...
Harrietsham Kent 28 8...
Harringay Gt Lon 27 3...
Harrington Cumb 92 98...
Harrington Lincs 77 36...
Harrington Nhants 50 7...
Harringworth Nhants 51 9...
Harriseahead Staffs 72 86...
Harriston Cumb 92 15...
Harrogate N York 82 30...
Harrold Beds 51 94...
Harrop Dale Gt Man 82 00...
Harrow Gt Lon 26 15...
Harrow Green Suffk 54 86...
Harrow on the Hill Gt Lon 26 15...
Harrow Weald Gt Lon 26 15...
Harrowbarrow Cnwll 5 40...
Harrowden Beds 38 06...
Harrowgate Village Dur 96 29...
Harston Cambs 53 42...
Harston Leics 63 83...
Harswell E R Yk 84 83...
Hart Dur 97 47...
Hart Station Dur 97 48...
Hartburn Nthumb 103 08...
Hartest Suffk 54 83...
Hartfield E Susx 16 47...
Hartford Cambs 52 25...
Hartford Ches 71 63...
Hartford Somset 20 95...
Hartford End Essex 40 68...
Hartfordbridge Hants 25 77...
Hartforth N York 89 16...
Hartgrove Dorset 22 83...
Harthill Ches 71 49...
Harthill N Lans 116 90...
Harthill S York 75 49...
Hartington Derbys 74 12...
Hartington Nthumb 103 02...
Hartland Devon 18 25...
Hartland Quay Devon 18 22...
Hartlebury Worcs 60 84...
Hartlepool Dur 97 50...
Hartley Cumb 88 78...
Hartley Kent 27 60...
Hartley Kent 17 76...
Hartley Nthumb 103 34...
Hartley Green Kent 27 60...
Hartley Green Staffs 72 98...
Hartley Wespall Hants 24 69...
Hartley Wintney Hants 24 76...
Hartlip Kent 28 84...
Hartlip Hill Kent 28 84...
Hartoft End N York 90 74...
Harton N York 90 70...

larton High Bankhill 289

arton Shrops 59 4888
arton T & W 103 3765
artpury Gloucs 47 7924
artshead W York 82 1822
artshead Moor Side W York 82 1625
artshill Staffs 72 8546
artshill Warwks 61 3194
artshorne Derbys 62 3221
artside Nthumb 111 9716
artsop Cumb 93 4013
artswell Somset 20 0827
artwell Nhants 38 7850
artwith N York 89 2161
artwood N Lans 116 8459
artwoodmyres Border 109 4324
arvel Kent 28 6563
arvington Worcs 60 8775
arvington Worcs 48 0549
arwell Notts 75 6891
arwell Oxon 37 4989
arwich Essex 41 2531
arwood Dur 95 8233
arwood Gt Man 79 7410
arwood Nthumb 103 0189
arwood Dale N York 91 9695
arwood Lee Gt Man 81 7411
arworth Notts 75 6191
asbury W Mids 60 9582
ascombe Surrey 25 0039
aselbech Nhants 50 7177
aselbury Plucknett Somset 10 4710
aseley Warwks 48 2367
aseley Green Warwks 48 2369
aseley Knob Warwks 61 2371
aselor Warwks 48 1257
asfield Gloucs 47 8227
asguard Pembks 30 8509
askayne Lancs 78 3508
asketon Suffk 55 2450
asland Derbys 74 3969
asland Green Derbys 74 3968
aslemere Surrey 14 9032
aslingden Lancs 81 7823
aslingden Grane Lancs 81 7522
aslingfield Cambs 52 4052
aslington Ches 72 7355
assall Ches 72 7657
assall Green Ches 72 7858
assell Street Kent 29 0946
assingham Norfk 67 3605
assness Cumb 93 1816
assocks W Susx 15 3015
assop Derbys 74 2272
aste Hill Surrey 14 9032
aster Highld 151 3251
asthorpe Lincs 77 4869
astingleigh Kent 29 0945
astings E Susx 17 8209
astings Somset 10 3116
astingwood Essex 39 4807
astoe Herts 38 9209
aswell Dur 96 3743
aswell Plough Dur 96 3742
atch Beds 52 1547
atch Beauchamp Somset 20 3020
atch End Beds 51 0760
atch End Gt Lon 26 1390
atchet Gate Hants 12 3701
atching Green Herts 38 1312
atchmere Ches 71 5571
atcliffe Lincs 76 2100
atfield Herefs 46 5959
atfield Herts 39 2308
atfield S York 83 6609
atfield Worcs 47 8750
atfield Broad Oak Essex 39 5416
atfield Heath Essex 39 5215
atfield Peverel Essex 40 7911
atfield Woodhouse S York 83 6708
atford Oxon 36 3395
atherden Hants 23 3450
atherleigh Devon 8 5404
athern Leics 62 5022
atherop Gloucs 36 1505
athersage Derbys 74 2381
athersage Booths Derbys 74 2480
atherton Ches 72 6847
atherton Staffs 60 9510
atley St George Cambs 52 2751
att Cnwll 5 4062
attersley Gt Man 79 9894
attingley Hants 24 6437
atton Abers 143 0537
atton Angus 127 4642
atton Ches 78 5982
atton Derbys 73 2130
atton Gt Lon 26 0975
atton Lincs 76 1776
atton Shrops 59 4790
atton Warwks 48 2367
atton Heath Ches 71 4561
atton of Fintray Abers 143 8316
augh E Ayrs 107 4925
augh Lincs 77 4175
augh W York 81 9311
augh Head Nthumb 111 0026
augh of Glass Moray 142 4238
augh of Urr D & G 100 8066
augham Lincs 77 3381
aughhead Inn E Duns 116 6079
aughley Suffk 54 0262
aughley Green Suffk 54 0264
aughton Notts 75 6872
aughton Powys 59 3018
aughton Shrops 59 3726
aughton Shrops 59 5516
aughton Shrops 60 7408
aughton Shrops 60 6896
aughton Staffs 72 8620
aughton Green Gt Man 79 9393
aughton le Skerne Dur 96 3116
aughton Moss Ches 71 5756
aultwick Herts 39 3323
aunton Staffs 61 2310
autes Croix Jersey 158 0000
auxley Nthumb 103 2703
auxton Cambs 53 4452
avannah Ches 72 8664
Havant Hants 13 7106
Haven Herefs 46 4054
Haven Bank Lincs 76 2352
Haven Side E R Yk 85 1827
Havenstreet IOW 13 5690
Havercroft W York 83 3913
Haverfordwest Pembks 30 9515
Haverhill Suffk 53 6745
Haverigg Cumb 86 1578
Havering-atte-Bower Essex 27 5193
Haversham Bucks 38 8242
Haverthwaite Cumb 87 3483
Haverton Hill Dur 97 4822
Havyat Somset 21 4761
Havyatt Somset 21 5338
Hawarden Flints 71 3165
Hawbridge Worcs 47 9049
Hawbush Green Essex 40 7820
Hawcoat Cumb 86 2071
Hawe's Green Norfk 67 2399
Hawen Cerdgn 42 3446
Hawes N York 88 8789
Hawford Worcs 47 8460
Hawick Border 109 5014
Hawk Green Gt Man 79 9687
Hawkchurch Devon 10 3400
Hawkedon Suffk 53 7953
Hawkenbury Kent 28 8045
Hawkeridge Wilts 22 8653
Hawkerland Devon 9 0588
Hawkes End W Mids 61 2982
Hawkesbury Gloucs 35 7686
Hawkesbury Warwks 61 3784
Hawkesbury Upton Gloucs 35 7786
Hawkhill Nthumb 111 2212
Hawkhurst Kent 17 7530
Hawkhurst Common E Susx 16 5217
Hawkinge Kent 29 2139
Hawkley Hants 24 7429
Hawkridge Somset 19 8630
Hawksdale Cumb 93 3648
Hawkshaw Gt Man 81 7615
Hawkshead Cumb 87 3598
Hawkshead Hill Cumb 86 3398
Hawksland S Lans 108 8439
Hawkspur Green Essex 40 6532
Hawkstone Shrops 59 5830
Hawkswick N York 88 9570
Hawksworth Notts 63 7543
Hawksworth W York 82 1641
Hawkwell Essex 40 8591
Hawkwell Nthumb 103 0771
Hawley Hants 25 8657
Hawley Kent 27 5471
Hawling Gloucs 36 0622
Hawnby N York 90 5489
Haworth W York 82 0337
Hawstead Suffk 54 8559
Hawstead Green Suffk 54 8658
Hawthorn Dur 96 4145
Hawthorn Hants 24 6733
Hawthorn Rhondd 33 0987
Hawthorn Hill Berks 25 8773
Hawthorn Hill Lincs 76 2155
Hawthorpe Lincs 64 0427
Hawton Notts 75 7851
Haxby N York 90 6058
Haxby Gates N York 83 6056
Haxey Lincs 75 7799
Haxey Turbary Lincs 84 7501
Haxted Surrey 16 4245
Haxton Wilts 23 1449
Hay Cnwll 3 8651
Hay Cnwll 3 9243
Hay Cnwll 3 9552
Hay Cnwll 4 9770
Hay Green Norfk 65 5418
Hay Street Herts 39 3926
Hay-on-Wye Powys 45 2342
Haydock Mersyd 78 5697
Haydon Dorset 11 6715
Haydon Somset 20 2523
Haydon Somset 22 6853
Haydon Bridge Nthumb 102 8464
Haydon Wick Wilts 36 1387
Haye Cnwll 5 3570
Hayes Gt Lon 26 0980
Hayes Gt Lon 27 4066
Hayes End Gt Lon 26 0882
Hayfield Ag & B 123 0723
Hayfield Derbys 74 0386
Haygate Shrops 59 6410
Hayhillock Angus 127 5242
Hayle Cnwll 2 5537
Hayley Green W Mids 60 9582
Haymoor Green Ches 72 6850
Hayne Devon 9 9515
Hayne Devon 8 7685
Haynes (Church End) Beds 38 0740
Haynes (Northwood End) Beds 38 0941
Haynes (Silver End) Beds 38 1042
Haynes (West End) Beds 38 0640
Hayscastle Pembks 30 8925
Hayscastle Cross Pembks 30 9125
Haysden Kent 16 5745
Hayton Cumb 92 1041
Hayton Cumb 94 5157
Hayton E R Yk 84 8245
Hayton Notts 75 7284
Hayton's Bent Shrops 59 5280
Haytor Vale Devon 8 7777
Haytown Devon 18 3814
Haywards Heath W Susx 15 3324
Haywood Herefs 46 4834
Haywood S York 83 5812
Haywood Oaks Notts 75 6055
Hazards Green E Susx 16 6812
Hazel Grove Gt Man 79 9287
Hazel Street Kent 28 6939
Hazel Stub Suffk 53 6544
Hazelbank S Lans 116 8345
Hazelbury Bryan Dorset 11 7408
Hazeleigh Essex 40 8203
Hazeley Hants 24 7458
Hazelford Notts 75 7249
Hazelhurst Gt Man 79 9600
Hazelslade Staffs 60 0212
Hazelton Walls Fife 126 3322
Hazelwood Derbys 62 3245
Hazlemere Bucks 26 8895
Hazlerigg T & W 103 2372
Hazles Staffs 73 0047
Hazleton Gloucs 36 0718
Heacham Norfk 65 6737
Headbourne Worthy Hants 24 4832
Headbrook Herefs 46 2854
Headcorn Kent 28 8344
Headingley W York 82 2836
Headington Oxon 37 5407
Headlam Dur 96 1818
Headland Dur 97 5234
Headless Cross Worcs 48 0365
Headlesscross N Lans 116 9158
Headley Hants 24 5162
Headley Hants 14 8236
Headley Surrey 26 2054
Headley Down Hants 14 8336
Headley Heath Worcs 61 0676
Headon Notts 75 7476
Heads S Lans 116 7247
Heads Nook Cumb 94 5054
Heage Derbys 74 3750
Healaugh N York 88 0199
Healaugh N York 83 5047
Heald Green Gt Man 79 8485
Heale Devon 19 6446
Heale Somset 20 2420
Heale Somset 21 3825
Healey Lancs 81 8816
Healey N York 89 1780
Healey Nthumb 95 0158
Healey W York 82 2719
Healeyfield Dur 95 0648
Healing Lincs 85 2110
Heamoor Cnwll 2 4631
Heanor Derbys 62 4346
Heanton Punchardon Devon 19 5035
Heapey Lancs 81 5920
Heapham Lincs 76 8788
Hearn Hants 14 8337
Hearts Delight Kent 28 8862
Heasley Mill Devon 19 7332
Heast Highld 129 6417
Heath Derbys 75 4567
Heath W York 83 3520
Heath and Reach Beds 38 9228
Heath Common W Susx 14 0915
Heath End Bucks 26 8898
Heath End Hants 24 4161
Heath End Leics 62 3621
Heath End Surrey 25 8549
Heath End Warwks 48 2360
Heath Green Worcs 61 0771
Heath Hall D & G 100 9979
Heath Hayes & Wimblebury Staffs 60 0110
Heath Hill Shrops 60 7613
Heath House Somset 21 4146
Heath Town W Mids 60 9399
Heathbrook Shrops 59 6228
Heathcote Derbys 74 1460
Heathcote Shrops 72 6528
Heathencote Nhants 49 7147
Heather Leics 62 3910
Heathfield Devon 8 8376
Heathfield E Susx 16 5821
Heathfield N York 89 1367
Heathfield Somset 20 1626
Heathrow Airport 26 0775
Heathstock Devon 9 2402
Heathton Shrops 60 8192
Heatley Gt Man 79 7088
Heatley Staffs 73 0626
Heaton Gt Man 79 6909
Heaton Lancs 87 4460
Heaton Staffs 72 9562
Heaton T & W 103 2666
Heaton W York 82 1335
Heaton Chapel Gt Man 79 8891
Heaton Mersey Gt Man 79 8690
Heaton Norris Gt Man 79 8890
Heaton's Bridge Lancs 80 4011
Heaverham Kent 27 5758
Heaviley Gt Man 79 9088
Heavitree Devon 9 9492
Hebburn T & W 103 3164
Hebden N York 88 0263
Hebden Bridge W York 82 9927
Hebden Green Ches 71 6365
Hebing End Herts 39 3122
Hebron Carmth 31 1827
Hebron IOA 68 4584
Hebron Nthumb 103 1989
Heckfield Hants 24 7260
Heckfield Green Suffk 54 1875
Heckfordbridge Essex 40 9421
Heckington Lincs 64 1444
Heckmondwike W York 82 1824
Heddington Wilts 22 9966
Heddon-on-the-Wall Nthumb 103 1366
Hedenham Norfk 67 3193
Hedge End Hants 13 4912
Hedgerley Bucks 26 9687
Hedgerley Green Bucks 26 9787
Hedging Somset 20 3029
Hedley on the Hill Nthumb 95 0759
Hednesford Staffs 60 9912
Hedon E R Yk 85 1928
Hedsor Bucks 26 9086
Hegdon Hill Herefs 46 5853
Heglibister Shet 153 3851
Heighington Dur 96 2422
Heighington Lincs 76 0269
Heightington Worcs 60 7671
Heiton Border 110 7130
Hele Cnwll 5 2198
Hele Devon 19 5347
Hele Devon 9 9902
Hele Devon 7 7470
Hele Somset 20 1824
Hele Lane Devon 19 7910
Helebridge Cnwll 18 2103
Helensburgh Ag & B 115 2982
Helenton S Ayrs 106 3830
Helford Cnwll 3 7526
Helford Passage Cnwll 3 7626
Helhoughton Norfk 66 8626
Helions Bumpstead Essex 53 6541
Hell Corner Berks 23 3864
Hellaby S York 75 5092
Helland Cnwll 4 0771
Hellandbridge Cnwll 4 0671
Hellescott Cnwll 5 2888
Hellesdon Norfk 67 2010
Hellesveor Cnwll 2 5040
Hellidon Nhants 49 5158
Hellifield N York 81 8556
Hellingly E Susx 16 5812
Hellington Norfk 67 3103
Helm Nthumb 103 1896
Helmdon Nhants 49 5943
Helme W York 82 0912
Helmingham Suffk 54 1857
Helmington Row Dur 96 1835
Helmsdale Highld 147 0315
Helmshore Lancs 81 7821
Helmsley N York 90 6183
Helperby N York 89 4469
Helperthorpe N York 91 9570
Helpringham Lincs 64 1440
Helpston Cambs 64 1205
Helsby Ches 71 4975
Helsey Lincs 77 5172
Helston Cnwll 2 6527
Helstone Cnwll 4 0881
Helton Cumb 94 5021
Helwith N York 88 0702
Helwith Bridge N York 88 8069
Hemblington Norfk 67 3411
Hemel Hempstead Herts 38 0507
Hemerdon Devon 6 5657
Hemingbrough N York 83 6730
Hemingby Lincs 76 2374
Hemingfield S York 83 3801
Hemingford Abbots Cambs 52 2871
Hemingford Grey Cambs 52 2970
Hemingstone Suffk 54 1454
Hemington Nhants 51 0985
Hemington Somset 22 7253
Hemley Suffk 55 2842
Hemlington N York 90 5014
Hempholme E R Yk 85 0850
Hempnall Norfk 67 2494
Hempnall Green Norfk 67 2493
Hempriggs Moray 141 1063
Hempstead Essex 53 6338
Hempstead Kent 28 7964
Hempstead Norfk 66 1037
Hempstead Norfk 67 4028
Hempsted Gloucs 35 8116
Hempton Norfk 66 9129
Hempton Oxon 49 4431
Hemsby Norfk 67 4917
Hemswell Lincs 76 9290
Hemswell Cliff Lincs 76 9489
Hemsworth W York 83 4213
Hemyock Devon 9 1313
Henbury Bristl 34 5678
Henbury Ches 79 8773
Hendersyde Park Border 110 7435
Hendham Devon 7 7450
Hendomen Powys 58 2197
Hendon Gt Lon 26 2389
Hendon T & W 96 4055
Hendra Cnwll 3 7237
Hendra Cnwll 4 0275
Hendre Brdgnd 33 9381
Hendre Flints 70 1867
Hendre Mons 34 4614
Hendy Carmth 32 5803
Heneglwys IOA 68 4276
Henfield W Susx 15 2115
Henford Devon 5 3794
Henghurst Kent 28 9536
Hengoed Caerph 33 1594
Hengoed Powys 45 2253
Hengoed Shrops 58 2833
Hengrave Suffk 54 8268
Henham Essex 39 5428
Henhurst Kent 28 6669
Heniarth Powys 58 1208
Henlade Somset 20 2623
Henley Dorset 11 6904
Henley Gloucs 35 9016
Henley Shrops 59 4588
Henley Shrops 46 5476
Henley Somset 21 4232
Henley Suffk 54 1551
Henley W Susx 14 8925
Henley Green W Mids 61 3681
Henley Park Surrey 25 9352
Henley Street Kent 28 6667
Henley's Down E Susx 17 7312
Henley-in-Arden Warwks 48 1566
Henley-on-Thames Oxon 37 7682
Henllan Cerdgn 31 3540
Henllan Denbgs 70 0268
Henllan Amgoed Carmth 31 1819
Henllys Torfn 34 2691
Henlow Beds 39 1738
Hennock Devon 8 8381
Henny Street Essex 54 8738
Henry's Moat (Castell Hendre) Pembks 30 0427
Henryd Conwy 69 7774
Hensall N York 83 5923
Henshaw Nthumb 102 7664
Hensingham Cumb 92 9816
Henstead Suffk 55 4885
Hensting Hants 13 4922
Henstridge Somset 22 7219
Henstridge Ash Somset 22 7220
Henstridge Marsh Somset 22 7320
Henton Oxon 37 7602
Henton Somset 21 4945
Henwick Worcs 47 8355
Henwood Cnwll 5 2673
Henwood Oxon 37 4602
Heol Senni Powys 45 9223
Heol-las Swans 32 6998
Heol-y-Cyw Brdgnd 33 9484
Hepburn Nthumb 111 0624
Hepple Nthumb 103 9901
Hepscott Nthumb 103 2284
Heptonstall W York 82 9828
Hepworth Suffk 54 9874
Hepworth W York 82 1606
Herbrandston Pembks 30 8707
Hereford Herefs 46 5139
Hereson Kent 29 3865
Heribusta Highld 136 3970
Heriot Border 118 3953
Hermiston C Edin 117 1870
Hermit Hill S York 74 3200
Hermitage Berks 24 5072
Hermitage Border 101 5095
Hermitage Dorset 11 6506
Hermitage Hants 13 7505
Hermon IOA 68 3968
Hermon Pembks 31 2031
Herne Kent 29 1865
Herne Bay Kent 29 1768
Herne Common Kent 29 1765
Herne Hill Gt Lon 27 3274
Herne Pound Kent 28 6654
Herner Devon 19 5826
Hernhill Kent 29 0660
Herodsfoot Cnwll 5 2160
Heronden Kent 29 2954
Herongate Essex 40 6291
Heronsford S Ayrs 98 1283
Heronsgate Herts 26 0294
Herriard Hants 24 6646
Herring's Green Beds 38 0844
Herringfleet Suffk 67 4797
Herringswell Suffk 53 7270
Herringthorpe S York 75 4492
Herrington T & W 96 3453
Hersden Kent 29 2062
Hersham Cnwll 18 2507
Hersham Surrey 26 1164
Herstmonceux E Susx 16 6312
Herston Dorset 11 0178
Herston Ork 153 4191
Hertford Herts 39 3212
Hertford Heath Herts 39 3510
Hertingfordbury Herts 39 3012
Hesket Newmarket Cumb 93 3438
Hesketh Bank Lancs 80 4423
Hesketh Lane Lancs 81 6141
Heskin Green Lancs 80 5315
Hesleden Dur 96 4438
Hesleden N York 88 8874
Hesley S York 75 6194
Hesleyside Nthumb 102 8183
Heslington N York 83 6250
Hessay N York 83 5253
Hessenford Cnwll 5 3057
Hessett Suffk 54 9361
Hessle E R Yk 84 0326
Hessle W York 83 4317
Hest Bank Lancs 87 4666
Hestley Green Suffk 54 1567
Heston Gt Lon 26 1277
Hestwall Ork 153 2618
Heswall Mersyd 78 2681
Hethe Oxon 49 5929
Hethersett Norfk 66 1404
Hethersgill Cumb 101 4767
Hetherside Cumb 101 4366
Hetherson Green Ches 71 5250
Hethpool Nthumb 110 8928
Hett Dur 96 2836
Hetton N York 88 9658
Hetton Steads Nthumb 111 0335
Hetton-le-Hole T & W 96 3547
Heugh Nthumb 103 0873
Heugh Head Border 119 8762
Heughhead Abers 134 3811
Heveningham Suffk 55 3372
Hever Kent 16 4745
Heversham Cumb 87 4983
Hevingham Norfk 67 1921
Hewas Water Cnwll 3 9649
Hewelsfield Gloucs 34 5602
Hewenden W York 82 0736
Hewish Somset 21 4064
Hewish Somset 10 4208
Hewood Dorset 10 3502
Hexham Nthumb 102 9364
Hextable Kent 27 5170
Hexthorpe S York 83 5602
Hexton Herts 38 1030
Hexworthy Cnwll 5 3581
Hexworthy Devon 7 6572
Hey Lancs 81 8843
Hey Houses Lancs 80 3429
Heybridge Essex 40 8508
Heybridge Essex 40 6398
Heybridge Basin Essex 40 8707
Heybrook Bay Devon 6 4949
Heydon Cambs 39 4339
Heydon Norfk 66 1127
Heydour Lincs 63 0039
Heyhead Gt Man 79 8285
Heylipoll Ag & B 120 9743
Heylor Shet 153 2980
Heyrod Gt Man 79 9799
Heysham Lancs 87 4160
Heyshaw N York 89 1761
Heyshott W Susx 14 8917
Heyside Gt Man 79 9307
Heytesbury Wilts 22 9242
Heythrop Oxon 48 3527
Heywood Gt Man 79 8510
Heywood Wilts 22 8753
Hibaldstow Lincs 84 9702
Hickleton S York 83 4805
Hickling Norfk 67 4124
Hickling Notts 63 6928
Hickling Green Norfk 67 4123
Hickling Heath Norfk 67 4022
Hickmans Green Kent 29 0658
Hicks Forstal Kent 29 1863
Hickstead W Susx 15 2620
Hidcote Bartrim Gloucs 48 1742
Hidcote Boyce Gloucs 48 1742
High Ackworth W York 83 4417
High Angerton Nthumb 103 0985
High Ardwell D & G 98 0745
High Auldgirth D & G 100 9187
High Bankhill Cumb 94 5542

High Beach
Hood Gree
290

High Beach Essex 27 4198
High Bentham N York 87 6669
High Bewaldeth Cumb 93 2234
High Bickington Devon 19 6020
High Bickwith N York 88 8076
High Biggins Cumb 87 6078
High Blantyre S Lans 116 6756
High Bonnybridge Falk 116 8379
High Borrans Cumb 87 4300
High Bradley N York 82 0049
High Bray Devon 19 6934
High Brooms Kent 16 5941
High Bullen Devon 19 5320
High Buston Nthumb 111 2308
High Callerton Nthumb 103 1670
High Casterton Cumb 87 6278
High Catton E R Yk 84 7153
High Close N York 96 1715
High Cogges Oxon 36 3709
High Common Norfk 66 9905
High Coniscliffe Dur 96 2215
High Crosby Cumb 93 4559
High Cross Cnwll 3 7429
High Cross E Ayrs 115 4046
High Cross Hants 13 7126
High Cross Herts 39 3618
High Cross W Susx 15 2417
High Cross Warwks 48 2067
High Cross Bank Derbys 73 2817
High Drummore D & G 98 1235
High Dubmire T & W 96 3249
High Easter Essex 40 6214
High Eggborough N York 83 5721
High Ellington N York 89 1983
High Ercall Shrops 59 5917
High Etherley Dur 96 1728
High Ferry Lincs 77 3549
High Flats W York 82 2107
High Garrett Essex 40 7727
High Grange Dur 96 1731
High Grantley N York 89 2369
High Green Cumb 87 4103
High Green Norfk 66 1305
High Green Norfk 54 1689
High Green Norfk 67 2898
High Green S York 74 3397
High Green Shrops 60 7083
High Green Suffk 54 8560
High Green W York 82 2014
High Green Worcs 47 8745
High Halden Kent 28 8937
High Halstow Kent 28 7875
High Ham Somset 21 4231
High Harrington Cumb 92 0025
High Harrogate N York 82 3155
High Haswell Dur 96 3643
High Hatton Shrops 59 6124
High Hawsker N York 91 9207
High Hesket Cumb 93 4744
High Hoyland S York 82 2710
High Hunsley E R Yk 84 9535
High Hurstwood E Susx 16 4926
High Hutton N York 90 7568
High Ireby Cumb 93 2237
High Kilburn N York 90 5179
High Killerby N York 91 0683
High Knipe Cumb 94 5219
High Lands Dur 96 1226
High Lane Gt Man 79 9585
High Lanes Cnwll 2 5637
High Laver Essex 39 5208
High Legh Ches 79 7084
High Leven N York 89 4512
High Littleton Somset 21 6458
High Lorton Cumb 92 1625
High Marnham Notts 75 8070
High Melton S York 83 5001
High Mickley Nthumb 103 0761
High Moorsley T & W 96 3345
High Newport T & W 96 3754
High Newton Cumb 87 4082
High Nibthwaite Cumb 86 2989
High Offley Staffs 72 7826
High Ongar Essex 40 5603
High Onn Staffs 72 8216
High Park Corner Essex 41 0320
High Pennyvenie E Ayrs 107 4907
High Post Wilts 23 1536
High Roding Essex 40 6017
High Row Cumb 93 3535
High Row Cumb 93 3821
High Salter Lancs 87 6062
High Salvington W Susx 14 1206
High Scales Cumb 93 1845
High Seaton Cumb 92 0231
High Shaw N York 88 8691
High Side Cumb 93 2330
High Spen T & W 96 1359
High Stoop Dur 95 1040
High Street Cnwll 3 9653
High Street Kent 17 7430
High Street Suffk 55 4171
High Street Suffk 55 4355
High Throston Dur 97 4833
High Town Staffs 60 9911
High Toynton Lincs 77 2869
High Trewhitt Nthumb 111 0105
High Urpeth Dur 96 2354
High Valleyfield Fife 117 0086
High Warden Nthumb 102 9067
High Westwood Dur 95 1155
High Woolaston Gloucs 34 5899
High Worsall N York 89 3809
High Wray Cumb 87 3799
High Wych Herts 39 4614
High Wycombe Bucks 26 8693
Higham Derbys 74 3859
Higham Kent 16 6048
Higham Kent 28 7171
Higham Lancs 81 8136
Higham S York 82 3107
Higham Suffk 53 7465
Higham Suffk 54 0335
Higham Dykes Nthumb 103 1375
Higham Ferrers Nhants 51 9668
Higham Gobion Beds 38 1032
Higham Hill Gt Lon 27 3590
Higham on the Hill Leics 61 3895
Highampton Devon 18 4804
Highams Park Gt Lon 27 3891
Highbridge Hants 13 4621
Highbridge Somset 21 3247
Highbrook W Susx 15 3630
Highburton W York 82 1813
Highbury Gt Lon 27 3185
Highbury Somset 22 6949
Highclere Hants 24 4359
Highcliffe Dorset 12 2193
Highcross Lancs 80 3437
Higher Alham Somset 22 6741
Higher Ansty Dorset 11 7604
Higher Ballam Lancs 80 3630
Higher Bartle Lancs 80 5033
Higher Berry End Beds 38 9834
Higher Bockhampton Dorset 11 7292
Higher Brixham Devon 7 9155
Higher Burrowton Devon 9 0097
Higher Burwardsley Ches 71 5156
Higher Chillington Somset 10 3810
Higher Clovelly Devon 18 3123
Higher Combe Somset 20 9030
Higher Coombe Dorset 10 5391
Higher Disley Ches 79 9784
Higher Gabwell Devon 7 9169
Higher Halstock Leigh Dorset 10 5107
Higher Harpers Lancs 81 8237
Higher Heysham Lancs 87 4160
Higher Hurdsfield Ches 79 9374
Higher Irlam Gt Man 79 7295
Higher Kingcombe Dorset 10 5400
Higher Kinnerton Flints 71 3261
Higher Melcombe Dorset 11 7402
Higher Muddiford Devon 19 5638
Higher Nyland Dorset 22 7322
Higher Ogden Gt Man 82 9512
Higher Pentire Cnwll 2 6525
Higher Penwortham Lancs 80 5128
Higher Studfold N York 88 8170
Higher Town Cnwll 3 8044
Higher Town Cnwll 4 0061
Higher Town IOS 2 9215
Higher Tregantle Cnwll 5 4052
Higher Walton Ches 78 5985
Higher Walton Lancs 81 5727
Higher Wambrook Somset 10 2908
Higher Waterston Dorset 11 7295
Higher Whatcombe Dorset 11 8301
Higher Wheelton Lancs 81 6022
Higher Whiteleigh Cnwll 5 2494
Higher Whitley Ches 78 6180
Higher Wraxhall Dorset 10 5601
Higher Wych Ches 71 4943
Higherford Lancs 81 8640
Highfield Devon 8 7097
Highfield E R Yk 84 7236
Highfield N Ayrs 115 3150
Highfield T & W 96 1458
Highfields S York 83 5406
Highgate E Susx 16 4234
Highgate Gt Lon 27 2887
Highgate Head Derbys 74 0486
Highgreen Manor Nthumb 102 8091
Highland Wildlife Park 132 8104
Highlane Ches 79 8868
Highlane S York 74 4081
Highlaws Cumb 92 1449
Highleadon Gloucs 47 7623
Highleigh W Susx 14 8498
Highley Shrops 60 7483
Highmoor Cumb 93 2647
Highmoor Oxon 37 7084
Highmoor Cross Oxon 37 7084
Highmoor Hill Mons 34 4689
Highnam Gloucs 35 7817
Highnam Green Gloucs 35 7920
Highridge Somset 21 5567
Highstead Kent 29 2166
Highsted Kent 28 9061
Highstreet Kent 29 0862
Highstreet Green Essex 53 7634
Highstreet Green Surrey 14 9835
Hightae D & G 100 0978
Highter's Heath W Mids 61 0879
Hightown Ches 72 8762
Hightown Hants 12 1704
Hightown Mersyd 78 3003
Hightown Green Suffk 54 9756
Highway Herefs 46 4549
Highway Wilts 36 0474
Highweek Devon 7 8472
Highwood Staffs 73 0931
Highwood Hill Gt Lon 26 2193
Highworth Wilts 36 2092
Hilborough Norfk 66 8130
Hilcote Derbys 75 4558
Hilden Park Kent 16 5747
Hildenborough Kent 16 5648
Hildersham Cambs 53 5448
Hilderstone Staffs 72 9534
Hilderthorpe E R Yk 91 1766
Hilfield Dorset 10 6305
Hilgay Norfk 65 6298
Hill Gloucs 35 6495
Hill Warwks 50 4566
Hill Brow Hants 14 7926
Hill Chorlton Staffs 72 7939
Hill Common Norfk 67 4122
Hill Common Somset 20 1426
Hill Deverill Wilts 22 8640
Hill Dyke Lincs 77 3447
Hill End Dur 95 0136
Hill End Fife 117 0395
Hill End Gloucs 47 9037
Hill Green Kent 28 8362
Hill Head Hants 13 5402
Hill of Beath Fife 117 1590
Hill of Fearn Highld 147 8377
Hill of Tarvit Mansion House 126 3711
Hill Ridware Staffs 73 0817
Hill Side W York 82 1717
Hill Side Worcs 47 7561
Hill Top Dur 95 9924
Hill Top Hants 13 4003
Hill Top S York 74 3992
Hill Top W Mids 60 9993
Hill Top W York 82 0712
Hill Top W York 83 3315
Hillam N York 83 5028
Hillbeck Dur 95 7915
Hillborough Kent 29 2168
Hillbutts Dorset 11 9901
Hillcliffane Derbys 73 2947
Hillcott Wilts 23 1158
Hillend Fife 117 1483
Hillend Mdloth 117 2566
Hillend N Lans 116 8267
Hillend Swans 31 4190
Hillersland Gloucs 34 5614
Hillerton Devon 8 7298
Hillesden Bucks 49 6828
Hillesley Gloucs 35 7689
Hillfarrance Somset 20 1624
Hillgrove W Susx 14 9428
Hillhampton Herefs 46 5847
Hillhead Devon 7 9054
Hillhead S Lans 108 9840
Hillhead of Cocklaw Abers 143 0844
Hillhead of Durno Abers 142 7128
Hilliard's Cross Staffs 61 1511
Hilliclay Highld 151 1764
Hillingdon Gt Lon 26 0782
Hillington C Glas 115 5164
Hillington Norfk 65 7225
Hillis Corner IOW 13 4793
Hillmorton Warwks 50 5373
Hillock Vale Lancs 81 7629
Hillowton D & G 100 7763
Hillpool Worcs 60 8976
Hillpound Hants 13 5715
Hills Town Derbys 75 4869
Hillside Abers 135 9197
Hillside Angus 135 6960
Hillside Devon 7 7060
Hillstreet Hants 12 3416
Hillswick Shet 153 2877
Hilltown Devon 8 5380
Hilltown E Loth 118 3170
Hillwell Shet 153 3714
Hilmarton Wilts 35 0175
Hilperton Wilts 22 8759
Hilperton Marsh Wilts 22 8659
Hilsea Hants 13 6503
Hilston E R Yk 85 2833
Hilston Park Mons 34 4418
Hiltingbury Hants 13 4221
Hilton Border 119 8750
Hilton Cambs 52 2966
Hilton Cumb 94 7320
Hilton Derbys 73 2430
Hilton Dorset 11 7802
Hilton Dur 96 1622
Hilton Highld 147 8776
Hilton N York 89 4611
Hilton Shrops 60 7795
Himbleton Worcs 47 9458
Himley Staffs 60 8891
Hincaster Cumb 87 5084
Hinchley Wood Surrey 26 1565
Hinckley Leics 50 4294
Hinderclay Suffk 54 0276
Hinderwell N York 97 7916
Hindford Shrops 59 3333
Hindhead Surrey 14 8835
Hindle Fold Lancs 81 7332
Hindley Gt Man 78 6104
Hindley Nthumb 95 0459
Hindley Green Gt Man 79 6403
Hindlip Worcs 47 8858
Hindolveston Norfk 66 0329
Hindon Wilts 22 9132
Hindringham Norfk 66 9836
Hingham Norfk 66 0202
Hinksford Staffs 60 8689
Hinnington Shrops 60 7404
Hinstock Shrops 72 6925
Hintlesham Suffk 54 0843
Hinton Gloucs 35 6803
Hinton Gloucs 35 7376
Hinton Hants 12 2195
Hinton Herefs 46 3338
Hinton Shrops 59 4008
Hinton Shrops 59 6582
Hinton Admiral Hants 12 2096
Hinton Ampner Hants 13 6027
Hinton Blewett Somset 21 5956
Hinton Charterhouse Somset 22 7758
Hinton Green Worcs 48 0240
Hinton Marsh Hants 24 5828
Hinton Martell Dorset 11 0106
Hinton on the Green Worcs 48 0240
Hinton Parva Wilts 36 2383
Hinton St George Somset 10 4212
Hinton St Mary Dorset 11 7816
Hinton Waldrist Oxon 36 3799
Hinton-in-the-Hedges Nhants 49 5636
Hints Shrops 46 6174
Hints Staffs 61 1502
Hinwick Beds 51 9361
Hinxhill Kent 28 0442
Hinxton Cambs 53 4945
Hinxworth Herts 39 2340
Hipperholme W York 82 1225
Hipsburn Nthumb 111 2311
Hipswell N York 89 1898
Hirn Abers 135 7200
Hirnant Powys 58 0422
Hirst Nthumb 103 2787
Hirst Courtney N York 83 6124
Hirwaen Denbgs 70 1361
Hirwaun Rhondd 33 9505
Hiscott Devon 19 5426
Histon Cambs 53 4463
Hitcham Suffk 54 9851
Hitcham Causeway Suffk 54 9852
Hitcham Street Suffk 54 9851
Hitchin Herts 39 1829
Hither Green Gt Lon 27 3874
Hittisleigh Devon 8 7395
Hittisleigh Cross Devon 8 7395
Hive E R Yk 84 8230
Hixon Staffs 73 0025
Hoaden Kent 29 2759
Hoar Cross Staffs 73 1323
Hoarwithy Herefs 46 5429
Hoath Kent 29 2064
Hoathly Kent 28 6536
Hobarris Shrops 46 3178
Hobbles Green Suffk 53 7053
Hobbs Cross Essex 27 4799
Hobbs Cross Essex 39 4910
Hobkirk Border 110 5811
Hobland Hall Norfk 67 5001
Hobsick Notts 75 4549
Hobson Dur 96 1756
Hoby Leics 63 6617
Hoccombe Somset 20 1129
Hockering Norfk 66 0713
Hockerton Notts 75 7156
Hockley Ches 79 9383
Hockley Essex 40 8392
Hockley Staffs 61 2200
Hockley W Mids 61 2779
Hockley Heath W Mids 61 1572
Hockliffe Beds 38 9726
Hockwold cum Wilton Norfk 53 7388
Hockworthy Devon 20 0319
Hoddesdon Herts 39 3708
Hoddlesden Lancs 81 7122
Hoddom Cross D & G 101 1773
Hoddom Mains D & G 100 1572
Hodgehill Ches 79 8269
Hodgeston Pembks 30 0399
Hodnet Shrops 59 6128
Hodsall Street Kent 27 6263
Hodsock Notts 75 6185
Hodson Wilts 36 1780
Hodthorpe Derbys 75 5376
Hoe Hants 13 5617
Hoe Norfk 66 9916
Hoe Gate Hants 13 6213
Hoff Cumb 94 6717
Hog Hill E Susx 17 8815
Hogben's Hill Kent 28 0356
Hoggards Green Suffk 54 8856
Hoggeston Bucks 38 8024
Hoggrill's End Warwks 61 2292
Hoghton Lancs 81 6127
Hoghton Bottoms Lancs 81 6227
Hognaston Derbys 73 2350
Hogsthorpe Lincs 77 5372
Holbeach Lincs 64 3624
Holbeach Bank Lincs 64 3527
Holbeach Clough Lincs 64 3526
Holbeach Drove Lincs 64 3212
Holbeach Hurn Lincs 65 3926
Holbeach St Johns Lincs 64 3518
Holbeach St Mark's Lincs 64 3731
Holbeach St Matthew Lincs 65 4132
Holbeck Notts 75 5473
Holbeck Woodhouse Notts 75 5472
Holberrow Green Worcs 48 0259
Holbeton Devon 6 6150
Holborn Gt Lon 27 3181
Holborough Kent 28 7062
Holbrook Derbys 62 3644
Holbrook S York 75 4481
Holbrook Suffk 54 1636
Holbrook Moor Derbys 62 3645
Holburn Nthumb 111 0436
Holbury Hants 13 4303
Holcombe Devon 7 9574
Holcombe Gt Man 81 7816
Holcombe Somset 22 6749
Holcombe Brook Gt Man 81 7815
Holcombe Rogus Devon 20 0518
Holcot Nhants 50 7969
Holden Lancs 81 7749
Holden Gate W York 81 8923
Holdenby Nhants 50 6967
Holder's Green Essex 40 6328
Holdgate Shrops 59 5689
Holdingham Lincs 76 0547
Holditch Dorset 10 3402
Holdsworth W York 82 0829
Hole Devon 18 4206
Hole Park Kent 17 8332
Hole Street W Susx 15 1314
Hole-in-the-Wall Herefs 46 6128
Holehouse Derbys 79 0092
Holemoor Devon 18 4205
Holford Somset 20 1541
Holgate N York 83 5851
Holker Cumb 87 3676
Holkham Norfk 66 8943
Holkham Hall 66 8843
Hollacombe Devon 18 3702
Hollam Somset 20 9232
Holland Fen Lincs 76 2349
Holland Lees Lancs 78 5208
Holland-on-Sea Essex 41 1916
Hollandstoun Ork 153 7553
Hollee D & G 101 2669
Hollesley Suffk 55 3544
Hollicombe Devon 7 8962
Hollies Hill Worcs 60 9377
Hollin Green Ches 71 5952
Hollingbourne Kent 28 8455
Hollingbury E Susx 15 3107
Hollingdon Bucks 38 8727
Hollingthorpe W York 83 3831
Hollington Derbys 73 2239
Hollington Staffs 73 0538
Hollingworth Gt Man 79 0096
Hollinlane Ches 79 8384
Hollins Derbys 74 3271
Hollins Gt Man 79 8107
Hollins Staffs 73 9947
Hollins End S York 74 3883
Hollins Green Ches 79 6990
Hollins Lane Lancs 80 4951
Hollinsclough Staffs 74 0666
Hollinswood Shrops 60 7008
Hollinwood Shrops 59 5136
Hollingrove E Susx 16 6821
Hollocombe Devon 19 6311
Holloway Derbys 74 3256
Holloway Gt Lon 27 3086
Holloway Wilts 22 8730
Hollowell Nhants 50 6971
Hollowmoor Heath Ches 71 4868
Hollows D & G 101 3878
Holly End Norfk 65 4906
Holly Green Worcs 47 86
Hollybush Caerph 33 16
Hollybush E Ayrs 106 39
Hollybush Herefs 47 75
Hollyhurst Ches 71 57
Hollym E R Yk 85 34
Hollywood Worcs 61 08
Holmbridge W York 82 12
Holmbury St Mary Surrey 14 11
Holmbush Cnwll 3 03
Holmcroft Staffs 72 90
Holme Cambs 52 19
Holme Cumb 87 52
Holme Lincs 84 92
Holme N York 89 35
Holme Notts 75 80
Holme W York" 82 11
Holme Chapel Lancs 81 87
Holme Green N York 83 55
Holme Hale Norfk 66 88
Holme Lacy Herefs 46 55
Holme Marsh Herefs 46 34
Holme next the Sea Norfk 65 70
Holme on the Wolds E R Yk 84 96
Holme Pierrepont Notts 62 62
Holme St Cuthbert Cumb 92 10
Holme upon
Spalding Moor E R Yk 84 80
Holmer Herefs 46 50
Holmer Green Bucks 26 90
Holmes Chapel Ches 72 76
Holmes Hill E Susx 16 53
Holmesfield Derbys 74 32
Holmeswood Lancs 80 43
Holmethorpe Surrey 27 28
Holmewood Derbys 75 43
Holmfield W York 82 08
Holmfirth W York 82 14
Holmgate Derbys 74 37
Holmhead E Ayrs 107 56
Holmpton E R Yk 85 36
Holmrook Cumb 86 07
Holmsey Green Suffk 53 69
Holmshurst E Susx 16 64
Holmside Dur 96 21
Holmwrangle Cumb 94 51
Holne Devon 7 70
Holnest Dorset 11 65
Holnicote Somset 20 91
Holsworthy Devon 18 34
Holsworthy Beacon Devon 18 36
Holt Dorset 12 03
Holt Norfk 66 08
Holt Wilts 22 86
Holt Worcs 47 83
Holt Wrexhm 71 40
Holt End Worcs 48 07
Holt Fleet Worcs 47 82
Holt Green Lancs 78 39
Holt Heath Dorset 12 05
Holt Heath Worcs 47 81
Holt Street Kent 29 25
Holtby N York 83 67
Holton Oxon 37 60
Holton Somset 22 68
Holton Suffk 55 40
Holton cum Beckering Lincs 76 11
Holton Heath Dorset 11 94
Holton Hill E Susx 16 66
Holton le Clay Lincs 85 28
Holton le Moor Lincs 76 08
Holton St Mary Suffk 54 05
Holtye E Susx 16 45
Holway Flints 70 18
Holwell Dorset 11 69
Holwell Herts 39 16
Holwell Leics 63 73
Holwell Oxon 36 23
Holwick Dur 95 91
Holworth Dorset 11 76
Holy Cross Worcs 60 92
Holy Island Nthumb 111 12
Holybourne Hants 24 73
Holyfield Essex 39 38
Holyhead IOA 68 24
Holymoorside Derbys 74 33
Holyport Berks 26 89
Holystone Nthumb 102 95
Holytown N Lans 116 76
Holywell Cambs 52 33
Holywell Cnwll 4 76
Holywell Dorset 10 59
Holywell Flints 70 18
Holywell Nthumb 103 31
Holywell Warwks 61 20
Holywell Green W York 82 08
Holywell Lake Somset 20 10
Holywell Row Suffk 53 71
Holywood D & G 100 94
Holywood Village D & G 100 95
Hom Green Herefs 34 58
Homer Shrops 59 61
Homer Green Mersyd 78 34
Homersfield Suffk 55 28
Homescales Cumb 87 55
Homington Wilts 23 12
Honey Hill Kent 29 11
Honey Tye Suffk 54 95
Honeyborough Pembks 30 94
Honeybourne Worcs 48 11
Honeychurch Devon 8 63
Honeystreet Wilts 23 10
Honiley Warwks 61 23
Honing Norfk 67 32
Honingham Norfk 66 10
Honington Lincs 63 94
Honington Suffk 54 91
Honington Warwks 48 26
Honiton Devon 9 16
Honley W York 82 13
Honnington Shrops 72 72
Hoo Kent 29 29
Hoo End Herts 39 18
Hoo Green Ches 79 71
Hoo Meavy Devon 6 52
Hoo St Werburgh Kent 28 78
Hoobrook Worcs 60 83
Hood Green S York 82 310

Hood Hill Insworke

ood Hill S York 74 3697
ooe Devon 6 5052
ooe E Susx 16 6910
oohill Lancs 80 3237
ook Cambs 65 4293
ook Devon 10 3005
ook E R Yk 84 7625
ook Hants 13 5105
ook Hants 24 7254
ook Kent 27 6170
ook Pembks 30 9711
ook Surrey 26 1864
ook Wilts 36 0784
ook Bank Worcs 47 8140
ook End Essex 40 5900
ook Green Kent 16 6535
ook Norton Oxon 48 3533
ook Street Gloucs 35 6799
ook Street Wilts 36 0884
ookagate Shrops 59 4609
ooke Dorset 10 5300
ookgate Staffs 72 7435
ookway Devon 8 8598
ookwood Surrey 15 2643
ooley Surrey 27 2856
ooley Bridge Gt Man 81 8511
ooton Ches 71 3678
ooton Levitt S York 75 5291
ooton Pagnell S York 83 4807
ooton Roberts S York 75 4897
op Pole Lincs 64 1813
opcrofts Holt Oxon 49 4625
ope Derbys 74 1783
ope Devon 7 6740
ope Flints 71 3058
ope Powys 58 2507
ope Shrops 59 3401
ope Shrops 46 5974
ope Staffs 73 1254
ope Bowdler Shrops 59 4792
ope End Green Essex 40 5720
ope Mansell Herefs 35 6219
ope under Dinmore Herefs 46 5052
opehouse Border 109 2916
opeman Moray 147 1469
opesay Shrops 59 3983
opetown W York 83 3923
opgrove N York 83 6354
opperton N York 83 4256
opsford Warwks 50 4284
opstone Shrops 60 7894
Hopton Derbys 73 2653
Hopton Shrops 59 3820
Hopton Staffs 72 9425
Hopton Suffk 54 9979
Hopton Cangeford Shrops 59 5480
Hopton Castle Shrops 46 3678
Hopton on Sea Norfk 67 5299
Hopton Wafers Shrops 47 6376
Hoptonheath Shrops 46 3877
Hopwas Staffs 61 1804
Hopwood Gt Man 79 8609
Hopwood Worcs 61 0375
Horam E Susx 16 5717
Horbling Lincs 64 1135
Horbury W York 82 2918
Horcott Gloucs 36 1500
Horden Dur 96 4440
Horderley Shrops 59 4086
Hordle Hants 12 2795
Hordley Shrops 59 3831
Horeb Carmth 32 4905
Horeb Cerdgn 31 3942
Horfield Bristl 34 5976
Horham Suffk 55 2072
Horkesley Green Essex 41 9831
Horkesley Heath Essex 41 9829
Horkstow Lincs 84 9817
Horley Oxon 49 4144
Horley Surrey 15 2842
Horn Hill Bucks 26 0192
Horn Street Kent 29 1836
Hornblotton Green Somset 21 5833
Hornby Lancs 87 5868
Hornby N York 89 3605
Hornby N York 89 2293
Horncastle Lincs 77 2669
Hornchurch Gt Lon 27 5387
Horncliffe Nthumb 110 9249
Horndean Border 110 9049
Horndean Hants 13 7013
Horndon Devon 5 5280
Horndon on the Hill Essex 40 6683
Horne Surrey 15 3344
Horne Row Essex 40 7704
Horner Somset 20 9045
Horners Green Suffk 54 9641
Horney Common E Susx 16 4525
Horning Norfk 67 3417
Horninghold Leics 51 8097
Horninglow Staffs 73 2425
Horningsea Cambs 53 4962
Horningsham Wilts 22 8141
Horningtoft Norfk 66 9323
Horningtops Cnwll 5 2760
Horns Cross Devon 18 3823
Horns Cross E Susx 17 8222
Hornsbury Somset 10 3310
Hornsby Cumb 94 5150
Hornsbygate Cumb 94 5250
Hornsea E R Yk 85 1947
Hornsey Gt Lon 27 3089
Hornton Oxon 48 3945
Horpit Wilts 36 2183
Horra Shet 153 4693
Horrabridge Devon 6 5169
Horridge Devon 7 7674
Horringer Suffk 54 8261
Horringford IOW 13 5485
Horrocks Fold Gt Man 81 7012
Horrocksford Lancs 81 7543
Horsacott Devon 19 5231
Horsebridge Devon 5 4075
Horsebridge E Susx 16 5811
Horsebridge Hants 23 3430
Horsebridge Shrops 59 3606
Horsebridge Staffs 72 9553
Horsebrook Staffs 60 8810
Horsecastle Somset 21 4265
Horsedown Cnwll 2 6134
Horsegate Lincs 64 1510
Horsehay Shrops 60 6707
Horseheath Cambs 53 6147
Horsehouse N York 88 0480
Horsell Surrey 25 9959
Horseman's Green Wrexhm 71 4441
Horsenden Bucks 37 7902
Horsey Norfk 67 4622
Horsey Somset 21 3239
Horsey Corner Norfk 67 4523
Horsford Norfk 67 1916
Horsforth W York 82 2338
Horsham W Susx 15 1731
Horsham Worcs 47 7358
Horsham St Faith Norfk 67 2115
Horsington Lincs 76 1968
Horsington Somset 22 7023
Horsley Derbys 62 3744
Horsley Gloucs 35 8497
Horsley Nthumb 102 8496
Horsley Nthumb 103 0965
Horsley Cross Essex 41 1227
Horsley Woodhouse Derbys 62 3944
Horsley's Green Bucks 37 7894
Horsley-Gate Derbys 74 3076
Horsleycross Street Essex 41 1228
Horsleyhill Border 109 5319
Horsmonden Kent 28 7040
Horspath Oxon 37 5705
Horstead Norfk 67 2619
Horsted Keynes W Susx 15 3828
Horton Berks 26 0175
Horton Bucks 38 9219
Horton Dorset 12 0307
Horton Gloucs 35 7584
Horton Lancs 81 8550
Horton Nhants 51 8154
Horton Shrops 59 4929
Horton Shrops 60 6814
Horton Somset 10 3214
Horton Staffs 72 9457
Horton Surrey 26 1962
Horton Swans 32 4785
Horton Wilts 23 0463
Horton Cross Somset 10 3315
Horton Green Ches 71 4549
Horton Heath Hants 13 4916
Horton in Ribblesdale N York 88 8071
Horton Kirby Kent 27 5668
Horton-cum-Studley Oxon 37 5912
Horwich Gt Man 81 6311
Horwich End Derbys 79 0080
Horwood Devon 19 5027
Hoscar Lancs 80 4611
Hoscote Border 109 3911
Hose Leics 63 7329
Hosey Hill Kent 27 4553
Hosh P & K 125 8523
Hoswick Shet 153 4123
Hotham E R Yk 84 8934
Hothfield Kent 28 9644
Hoton Leics 62 5722
Hott Nthumb 102 7785
Hough Ches 72 7151
Hough Ches 79 8578
Hough End W York 82 2433
Hough Green Ches 78 4886
Hough-on-the-Hill Lincs 63 9246
Hougham Lincs 63 8844
Houghton Cambs 52 2872
Houghton Cumb 93 4159
Houghton Hants 23 3432
Houghton Nthumb 103 1266
Houghton Pembks 30 9807
Houghton W Susx 14 0111
Houghton Conquest Beds 38 0441
Houghton Gate T & W 96 3051
Houghton Green Ches 79 6291
Houghton Green E Susx 17 9222
Houghton le Side Dur 96 2221
Houghton le Spring T & W 96 3449
Houghton on the Hill Leics 63 6703
Houghton Regis Beds 38 0123
Houghton St Giles Norfk 66 9235
Hound Green Hants 24 7359
Houndslow Border 110 6347
Houndsmoor Somset 20 1225
Houndwood Border 119 8463
Hounslow Gt Lon 26 1375
Hounslow Green Essex 40 6518
Househill Highld 140 8855
Houses Hill W York 82 1916
Housesteads Roman Fort 102 7868
Housieside Abers 143 8926
Houston Rens 115 4066
Houstry Highld 151 1534
Houton Ork 153 3104
Hove E Susx 15 2804
Hove Edge W York 82 1324
Hoveringham Notts 63 6946
Hoveton Norfk 67 3018
Hovingham N York 90 6675
How Caple Herefs 46 6030
How End Beds 38 0340
How Mill Cumb 94 5056
Howbrook S York 74 3298
Howden E R Yk 84 7428
Howden-le-Wear Dur 96 1633
Howe Highld 151 3061
Howe IOM 158 1968
Howe N York 89 3580
Howe Norfk 67 2799
Howe Bridge Gt Man 79 6602
Howe Green Essex 40 7403
Howe of Teuchar Abers 143 7946
Howe Street Essex 40 6914
Howe Street Essex 53 6934
Howegreen Essex 40 8301
Howell Lincs 76 1346
Howes D & G 101 1866
Howey Powys 45 0558
Howgate Mdloth 117 2457
Howgill N York 81 8246
Howick Nthumb 111 2517
Howle Dur 95 0926
Howle Shrops 72 6923
Howle Hill Herefs 34 6020
Howlett End Essex 53 5834
Howley Somset 10 2609
Howmore W Isls 152 7536
Hownam Border 110 7719
Howrigg Cumb 93 3347
Howsham Lincs 84 0404
Howsham N York 90 7362
Howt Green Kent 28 8965
Howtel Nthumb 110 8934
Howton Devon 8 7487
Howton Herefs 46 4129
Howtown Cumb 93 4419
Howwood Rens 115 3960
Hoxne Suffk 54 1777
Hoylake Mersyd 78 2189
Hoyland Common S York 74 3600
Hoyland Nether S York 74 3700
Hoyland Swaine S York 82 2604
Hoyle W Susx 14 9018
Hoyle Mill S York 83 3506
Hubberholme N York 88 9278
Hubberston Pembks 30 8906
Hubbert's Bridge Lincs 64 2643
Huby N York 82 2747
Huby N York 90 5665
Huccaby Devon 7 6673
Hucclecote Gloucs 35 8717
Hucking Kent 28 8458
Hucknall Notts 75 5349
Huddersfield W York 82 1416
Huddington Worcs 47 9457
Hudswell N York 89 1400
Huggate E R Yk 84 8855
Hugglescote Leics 62 4212
Hugh Town IOS 2 9010
Hughenden Valley Bucks 26 8697
Hughley Shrops 59 5698
Huish Devon 19 5311
Huish Wilts 23 1463
Huish Champflower Somset 20 0529
Huish Episcopi Somset 21 4326
Hulberry Kent 27 5265
Hulcote Beds 38 9438
Hulcott Bucks 38 8516
Hulham Devon 9 0183
Hull E R Yk 85 0829
Hulland Derbys 73 2446
Hulland Ward Derbys 73 2546
Hullavington Wilts 35 8981
Hullbridge Essex 40 8095
Hulme Ches 78 6091
Hulme Gt Man 79 8396
Hulme Staffs 72 9345
Hulme End Staffs 74 1059
Hulme Walfield Ches 72 8465
Hulse Heath Ches 79 7283
Hulton Lane Ends Gt Man 79 6905
Hulver Street Norfk 66 9311
Hulver Street Suffk 55 4686
Hulverstone IOW 13 3984
Humber Devon 7 8975
Humber Herefs 46 5356
Humberside Airport 85 0910
Humberston Lincs 85 3105
Humberstone Leics 63 6305
Humberton N York 89 4168
Humbie E Loth 118 4662
Humbleton E R Yk 85 2234
Humbleton Nthumb 111 9728
Humby Lincs 63 0032
Hume Border 110 7041
Humshaugh Nthumb 102 9171
Huna Highld 151 3573
Huncoat Lancs 81 7730
Huncote Leics 50 5197
Hundalee Border 110 6418
Hundall Derbys 74 3876
Hunderthwaite Dur 95 9821
Hundle Houses Lincs 77 2453
Hundleby Lincs 77 3966
Hundleton Pembks 30 9600
Hundon Suffk 53 7348
Hundred Acres Hants 13 5911
Hundred End Lancs 80 4122
Hundred House Powys 45 1154
Hungarton Leics 63 6907
Hungate End Bucks 38 7946
Hunger Hill Lancs 80 5411
Hungerford Berks 23 3368
Hungerford Hants 12 1612
Hungerford Somset 20 0440
Hungerford Newtown Berks 36 3571
Hungerstone Herefs 46 4435
Hungerton Lincs 63 8729
Hungryhatton Shrops 72 6626
Hunmanby N York 91 0977
Hunningham Warwks 48 3767
Hunnington Worcs 60 9681
Hunny Hill IOW 13 4990
Hunsdon Herts 39 4114
Hunsingore N York 83 4253
Hunslet W York 82 3130
Hunsonby Cumb 94 5835
Hunstanton Norfk 65 6740
Hunstanworth Dur 95 9448
Hunsterson Ches 72 6946
Hunston Suffk 54 9768
Hunston W Susx 14 8601
Hunston Green Suffk 54 9866
Hunstrete Somset 21 6462
Hunsworth W York 82 1827
Hunt End Worcs 48 0364
Hunt's Corner Norfk 54 0588
Hunt's Cross Mersyd 78 4385
Hunter's Inn Devon 19 6548
Hunter's Quay Ag & B 114 1879
Huntham Somset 21 3426
Hunthill Lodge Angus 134 4771
Huntingdon Cambs 52 2471
Huntingfield Suffk 55 3374
Huntingford Dorset 22 8030
Huntington Ches 71 4264
Huntington E Loth 118 4874
Huntington Herefs 46 2553
Huntington Herefs 46 4841
Huntington N York 83 6156
Huntington Staffs 60 9712
Huntley Gloucs 35 7219
Huntly Abers 142 5339
Hunton Hants 24 4840
Hunton Kent 28 7149
Hunton N York 89 1892
Hunton Bridge Herts 26 0800
Hunts Green Bucks 38 8903
Hunts Green Warwks 61 1897
Huntscott Somset 20 9144
Huntsham Devon 20 0020
Huntshaw Devon 19 5023
Huntshaw Cross Devon 19 5222
Huntspill Somset 21 3145
Huntstile Somset 20 2633
Huntworth Somset 21 3134
Hunwick Dur 96 1832
Hunworth Norfk 66 0635
Hurcott Somset 10 3916
Hurdcott Wilts 23 1733
Hurdsfield Ches 79 9274
Hurley Berks 37 8283
Hurley Warwks 61 2495
Hurley Bottom Berks 37 8283
Hurley Common Warwks 61 2496
Hurlford E Ayrs 107 4536
Hurlston Green Lancs 80 3911
Hurn Dorset 12 1296
Hurn's End Lincs 77 4249
Hursley Hants 13 4225
Hurst Berks 25 7973
Hurst Dorset 11 7990
Hurst N York 88 0402
Hurst Somset 10 4518
Hurst Green E Susx 17 7327
Hurst Green Essex 41 0916
Hurst Green Lancs 81 6838
Hurst Green Surrey 27 3951
Hurst Hill W Mids 60 9393
Hurst Wickham W Susx 15 2816
Hurstbourne Priors Hants 24 4346
Hurstbourne Tarrant Hants 23 3853
Hurstley Herefs 46 3548
Hurstpierpoint W Susx 15 2716
Hurstway Common Herefs 46 2949
Hurstwood Lancs 81 8831
Hurtiso Ork 153 5001
Hurtmore Surrey 25 9445
Hurworth Burn Dur 96 4033
Hurworth Place Dur 89 2909
Hurworth-on-Tees Dur 89 3009
Hury Dur 95 9519
Husbands Bosworth Leics 50 6484
Husborne Crawley Beds 38 9635
Husthwaite N York 90 5175
Hut Green N York 83 5623
Hutcherleigh Devon 7 7850
Huthwaite N York 90 4801
Huthwaite Notts 75 4659
Huttoft Lincs 77 5176
Hutton Border 119 9053
Hutton Cumb 93 4326
Hutton E R Yk 84 0253
Hutton Essex 40 6395
Hutton Lancs 80 4926
Hutton Somset 21 3558
Hutton Bonville N York 89 3300
Hutton Buscel N York 91 9784
Hutton Conyers N York 89 3273
Hutton Cranswick E R Yk 84 0252
Hutton End Cumb 93 4538
Hutton Hall N York 90 6014
Hutton Hang N York 89 1788
Hutton Henry Dur 96 4236
Hutton Lowcross N York 90 5914
Hutton Magna Dur 89 1212
Hutton Mulgrave N York 90 8309
Hutton Roof Cumb 93 3734
Hutton Roof Cumb 87 5677
Hutton Rudby N York 89 4606
Hutton Sessay N York 89 4776
Hutton Wandesley N York 83 5050
Hutton-le-Hole N York 90 7090
Huxham Devon 9 9497
Huxham Green Somset 21 5936
Huxley Ches 71 5061
Huyton Mersyd 78 4490
Hycemoor Cumb 86 0989
Hyde Gloucs 35 8801
Hyde Gt Man 79 9494
Hyde Hants 12 1612
Hyde End Berks 24 7266
Hyde Heath Bucks 26 9300
Hyde Lea Staffs 72 9120
Hyde Park Corner Somset 20 2832
Hydestile Surrey 25 9640
Hykeham Moor Lincs 76 9366
Hyndford Bridge S Lans 108 9141
Hynish Ag & B 120 9839
Hyssington Powys 59 3194
Hystfield Gloucs 35 6695
Hythe Hants 13 4207
Hythe Kent 29 1634
Hythe Somset 21 4452
Hythe End Berks 26 0172
Hyton Cumb 86 0987

I

Ibberton Dorset 11 7807
Ible Derbys 74 2457
Ibsley Hants 12 1509
Ibstock Leics 62 4009
Ibstone Bucks 37 7593
Ibthorpe Hants 23 3753
Iburndale N York 90 8707
Ibworth Hants 24 5654
Icelton Somset 21 3765
Ickburgh Norfk 66 8195
Ickenham Gt Lon 26 0786
Ickford Bucks 37 6407
Ickham Kent 29 2258
Ickleford Herts 39 1831
Icklesham E Susx 17 8716
Ickleton Cambs 39 4943
Icklingham Suffk 53 7772
Ickornshaw N York 82 9642
Ickwell Green Beds 52 1545
Ickworth 54 8262
Icomb Gloucs 36 2122
Idbury Oxon 36 2319
Iddesleigh Devon 19 5708
Ide Devon 9 8990
Ide Hill Kent 27 4851
Ideford Devon 9 8977
Iden E Susx 17 9123
Iden Green Kent 28 7437
Iden Green Kent 17 8031
Idle W York 82 1737
Idless Cnwll 3 8147
Idlicote Warwks 48 2844
Idmiston Wilts 23 1937
Idridgehay Derbys 73 2849
Idrigill Highld 136 3863
Idstone Oxon 36 2584
Iffley Oxon 37 5203
Ifield W Susx 15 2537
Ifold W Susx 14 0231
Iford Dorset 12 1393
Iford E Susx 15 4007
Ifton Mons 34 4688
Ifton Heath Shrops 59 3237
Ightfield Shrops 71 5938
Ightham Kent 27 5956
Iken Suffk 55 4155
Ilam Staffs 73 1350
Ilchester Somset 21 5222
Ilderton Nthumb 111 0121
Ilford Gt Lon 27 4486
Ilford Somset 10 3617
Ilfracombe Devon 19 5247
Ilkeston Derbys 62 4641
Ilketshall St Andrew Suffk 55 3887
Ilketshall St Margaret Suffk 55 3485
Ilkley W York 82 1147
Illand Cnwll 5 2878
Illey W Mids 60 9881
Illidge Green Ches 72 7963
Illingworth W York 82 0728
Illogan Cnwll 2 6743
Illston on the Hill Leics 50 7099
Ilmer Bucks 37 7605
Ilmington Warwks 48 2143
Ilminster Somset 10 3614
Ilsington Devon 7 7875
Ilsington Dorset 11 7592
Ilston Swans 32 5590
Ilton N York 89 1978
Ilton Somset 10 3517
Imachar N Ayrs 105 8640
Immingham Lincs 85 1814
Immingham Dock Lincs 85 1916
Impington Cambs 53 4463
Ince Ches 71 4576
Ince Blundell Mersyd 78 3203
Ince-in-Makerfield Gt Man 78 5904
Inchbae Lodge Hotel Highld 146 4069
Inchbare Angus 134 6065
Inchberry Moray 141 3055
Inchinnan Rens 115 4769
Inchlaggan Highld 131 1701
Inchmichael P & K 126 2425
Inchnacardoch Hotel Highld 131 3810
Inchnadamph Highld 145 2521
Inchture P & K 126 2728
Inchvuilt Highld 139 2438
Inchyra P & K 126 1820
Indian Queens Cnwll 4 9159
Ingate Place Suffk 55 4288
Ingatestone Essex 40 6499
Ingbirchworth S York 82 2205
Ingerthorpe N York 89 2866
Ingestre Staffs 72 9724
Ingham Lincs 76 9483
Ingham Norfk 67 3926
Ingham Suffk 54 8570
Ingham Corner Norfk 67 3927
Ingleborough Norfk 65 4715
Ingleby Derbys 62 3426
Ingleby Arncliffe N York 89 4400
Ingleby Barwick N York 89 4414
Ingleby Cross N York 89 4500
Ingleby Greenhow N York 90 5706
Ingleigh Green Devon 8 6007
Inglesbatch Somset 22 7061
Inglesham Wilts 36 2098
Ingleston D & G 100 9865
Ingleton Dur 96 1720
Ingleton N York 87 6972
Inglewhite Lancs 80 5439
Ingmire Hall Cumb 87 6391
Ingoe Nthumb 103 0374
Ingoldisthorpe Norfk 65 6832
Ingoldmells Lincs 77 5668
Ingoldsby Lincs 64 0129
Ingram Nthumb 111 0115
Ingrave Essex 40 6291
Ingrow W York 82 0539
Ings Cumb 87 4498
Ingst Gloucs 34 5887
Ingthorpe Lincs 63 9908
Ingworth Norfk 67 1929
Inkberrow Worcs 47 0157
Inkerman Dur 95 1139
Inkhorn Abers 143 9239
Inkpen Berks 23 3664
Inkstack Highld 151 2570
Inmarsh Wilts 22 9460
Innellan Ag & B 114 1570
Innerleithen Border 109 3336
Innerleven Fife 118 3700
Innermessan D & G 98 0862
Innerwick E Loth 119 7273
Innesmill Moray 141 2863
Insch Abers 142 6228
Insh Highld 132 8101
Inskip Lancs 80 4637
Inskip Moss Side Lancs 80 4539
Instow Devon 18 4730
Insworke Cnwll 6 4252

291

Intake Kinerarac
292

Intake *S York* 74 3884
Inver *Abers* 133 2293
Inver *Highld* 147 8682
Inver *P & K* 125 0142
Inver-boyndie *Abers* 142 6664
Inverailort *Highld* 129 7681
Inverallgin *Highld* 138 8457
Inverallochy *Abers* 143 0365
Inveran *Highld* 146 5797
Inveraray *Ag & B* 123 0908
Inverarish *Highld* 137 5535
Inverarity *Angus* 127 4544
Inverarnan *Stirlg* 123 3118
Inverasdale *Highld* 144 8284
Inveravon *Falk* 117 9579
Inverawe *Ag & B* 122 0231
Inverbeg *Ag & B* 115 3497
Inverbervie *Abers* 135 8272
Inverbroom *Highld* 145 1883
Invercreran House Hotel *Ag & B* 122 0146
Inverdruie *Highld* 132 8911
Inveresk *E Loth* 118 3471
Inveresragan *Ag & B* 122 9835
Inverewe Garden 144 8682
Inverey *Abers* 133 0889
Inverfarigaig *Highld* 139 5123
Inverfolla *Ag & B* 122 9544
Invergarry *Highld* 131 3001
Invergeldie *P & K* 124 7327
Invergloy *Highld* 131 2288
Invergordon *Highld* 140 7068
Invergowrie *P & K* 126 3430
Inverguseran *Highld* 129 7407
Inverhadden *P & K* 124 6757
Inverherive Hotel *Stirlg* 123 3626
Inverie *Highld* 129 7600
Inverinan *Ag & B* 122 9917
Inverinate *Highld* 138 9221
Inverkeilor *Angus* 127 6649
Inverkeithing *Fife* 117 1383
Inverkeithny *Abers* 142 6247
Inverkip *Inver* 114 2072
Inverkirkaig *Highld* 145 0719
Inverlael *Highld* 145 1885
Inverlair *Highld* 131 3479
Inverliever Lodge *Ag & B* 122 8905
Inverlochy *Ag & B* 123 1927
Invermark *Angus* 134 4480
Invermarkie *Abers* 142 4239
Invermoriston *Highld* 139 4216
Inverness *Highld* 140 6645
Inverness Dalcross Airport 140 7752
Invernoaden *Ag & B* 114 1297
Inveroran Hotel *Ag & B* 123 2741
Inverquharity *Angus* 134 4057
Inverquhomery *Abers* 143 0146
Inverroy *Highld* 131 2581
Inversanda *Highld* 130 9459
Invershiel *Highld* 138 9319
Invershin *Highld* 146 5796
Invershore *Highld* 151 2435
Inversnaid Hotel *Stirlg* 123 3308
Inverugie *Abers* 143 0948
Inveruglas *Ag & B* 123 3109
Inveruglass *Highld* 132 8000
Inverurie *Abers* 142 7721
Inwardleigh *Devon* 8 5699
Inworth *Essex* 40 8717
Iochdar *W Isls* 152 7646
Iping *W Susx* 14 8522
Ipplepen *Devon* 7 8366
Ipsden *Oxon* 37 6285
Ipstones *Staffs* 73 0149
Ipswich *Suffk* 54 1644
Irby *Mersyd* 78 2584
Irby in the Marsh *Lincs* 77 4663
Irby upon Humber *Lincs* 85 1904
Irchester *Nhants* 51 9265
Ireby *Cumb* 93 2338
Ireby *Lancs* 87 6575
Ireland *Beds* 38 1341
Ireleth *Cumb* 86 2277
Ireshopeburn *Dur* 95 8638
Ireton Wood *Derbys* 73 2847
Irlam *Gt Man* 79 7294
Irnham *Lincs* 64 0226
Iron Acton *Gloucs* 35 6783
Iron Bridge *Cambs* 65 4898
Iron Bridge Museum 60 6603
Iron Cross *Warwks* 48 0552
Ironbridge *Shrops* 60 6703
Ironmacannie *D & G* 99 6675
Irons Bottom *Surrey* 15 2446
Ironville *Derbys* 75 4351
Irstead *Norfk* 67 3620
Irthington *Cumb* 101 4961
Irthlingborough *Nhants* 51 9470
Irton *N York* 91 0184
Irvine *N Ayrs* 106 3238
Isauld *Highld* 150 9865
Isbister *Shet* 153 3790
Isfield *E Susx* 16 4417
Isham *Nhants* 51 8873
Isington *Hants* 25 7842
Islandpool *Worcs* 60 8780
Islay Airport 112 3251
Isle Abbotts *Somset* 21 3520
Isle Brewers *Somset* 21 3621
Isle of Dogs *Gt Lon* 27 3779
Isle of Man Ronaldsway Airport 158 2868
Isle of Whithorn *D & G* 99 4736
Isleham *Cambs* 53 6474
Isleornsay *Highld* 129 7012
Isles of Scilly St Mary's Airport 2 9210
Islesteps *D & G* 100 9672
Islet Village *Guern* 158 0000
Isleworth *Gt Lon* 26 1575
Isley Walton *Leics* 62 4224
Islibhig *W Isls* 152 0029
Islington *Gt Lon* 27 3184
Islip *Nhants* 51 9879
Islip *Oxon* 37 5214
Islivig *W Isls* 152 0029
Isombridge *Shrops* 59 6113
Istead Rise *Kent* 27 6370
Itchen Abbas *Hants* 24 5333
Itchen Stoke *Hants* 24 5532
Itchingfield *W Susx* 15 1328
Itchington *Gloucs* 35 6587
Itteringham *Norfk* 66 1430
Itton *Devon* 8 6899
Itton *Mons* 34 4995
Ivegill *Cumb* 93 4143
Ivelet *N York* 88 9398
Iver *Bucks* 26 0381
Iver Heath *Bucks* 26 0283
Iveston *Dur* 96 1350
Ivinghoe *Bucks* 38 9416
Ivinghoe Aston *Bucks* 38 9517
Ivington *Herefs* 46 4756
Ivington Green *Herefs* 46 4656
Ivy Cross *Dorset* 22 8623
Ivy Hatch *Kent* 27 5854
Ivy Todd *Norfk* 66 8909
Ivybridge *Devon* 6 6356
Ivychurch *Kent* 17 0327
Iwade *Kent* 28 9067
Iwerne Courtney or
Shroton *Dorset* 11 8512
Iwerne Minster *Dorset* 11 8614
Ixworth *Suffk* 54 9370
Ixworth Thorpe *Suffk* 54 9173

J

Jack Green *Lancs* 81 5925
Jack Hill *N York* 82 1951
Jack's Bush *Hants* 23 2636
Jack-in-the-Green *Devon* 9 0195
Jacksdale *Notts* 75 4451
Jackson Bridge *W York* 82 1607
Jackton *S Lans* 115 5952
Jacobs Well *Surrey* 25 0053
Jacobstow *Cnwll* 5 1995
Jacobstowe *Devon* 8 5801
Jameston *Pembks* 30 0598
Jamestown *Highld* 139 4756
Jamestown *W Duns* 115 3981
Janets-town *Highld* 151 3551
Janetstown *Highld* 151 1932
Jardine Hall *D & G* 100 1088
Jarrow *T & W* 103 3364
Jarvis Brook *E Susx* 16 5329
Jasper's Green *Essex* 40 7226
Jawcraig *Falk* 116 8475
Jaywick *Essex* 41 1513
Jealott's Hill *Berks* 25 8673
Jeater Houses *N York* 89 4394
Jedburgh *Border* 110 6420
Jeffreyston *Pembks* 31 0906
Jemimaville *Highld* 140 7165
Jerbourg *Guern* 158 0000
Jersey Airport 158 0000
Jerusalem *Lincs* 76 9170
Jesmond *T & W* 103 2566
Jevington *E Susx* 16 5601
Jingle Street *Mons* 34 4710
Jockey End *Herts* 38 0413
Jodrell Bank *Ches* 79 7970
John o' Groats *Highld* 151 3872
John's Cross *E Susx* 17 7421
Johnby *Cumb* 93 4332
Johnshaven *Abers* 135 7967
Johnson's Street *Norfk* 67 3717
Johnston *Pembks* 30 9310
Johnstone *D & G* 109 2400
Johnstone *Rens* 115 4263
Johnstonebridge *D & G* 100 1092
Johnstown *Carmth* 31 3919
Johnstown *Wrexhm* 71 3046
Joppa *C Edin* 118 3173
Joppa *Cerdgn* 43 5666
Joppa *S Ayrs* 106 4119
Jordans *Bucks* 26 9791
Jordanston *Pembks* 30 9132
Jordanthorpe *S York* 74 3580
Joyden's Wood *Kent* 27 5072
Jubilee Corner *Kent* 28 8447
Jump *S York* 83 3801
Jumper's Town *E Susx* 16 4632
Juniper *Nthumb* 95 9358
Juniper Green *C Edin* 117 1968
Jurby *IOM* 158 3698
Jurston *Devon* 8 6984

K

Kaber *Cumb* 88 7911
Kaimend *S Lans* 117 9945
Kames *Ag & B* 114 9771
Kames *E Ayrs* 107 6926
Kea *Cnwll* 3 8142
Keadby *Lincs* 84 8311
Keal Cotes *Lincs* 77 3660
Kearby Town End *N York* 83 3447
Kearsley *Gt Man* 79 7504
Kearsley *Nthumb* 103 0275
Kearsney *Kent* 29 2844
Kearstwick *Cumb* 87 6079
Kearton *N York* 88 9998
Keasden *N York* 88 7266
Keason *Cnwll* 5 3168
Keaton *Devon* 7 6454
Keckwick *Ches* 78 5783
Keddington *Lincs* 77 3488
Keddington Corner *Lincs* 77 3589
Kedington *Suffk* 53 7046
Kedleston *Derbys* 73 3040
Keelby *Lincs* 85 1610
Keele *Staffs* 72 8045
Keele University *Staffs* 72 8144
Keeley Green *Beds* 38 0046
Keelham *W York* 82 0732
Keeston *Pembks* 30 9019
Keevil *Wilts* 22 9258
Kegworth *Leics* 62 4826
Kehelland *Cnwll* 2 6241
Keig *Abers* 142 6119
Keighley *W York* 82 0541
Keilarsbrae *Clacks* 116 8994
Keillour *P & K* 125 9725
Keiloch *Abers* 133 1891
Keils *Ag & B* 113 5268
Keinton Mandeville *Somset* 21 5430
Keir Mill *D & G* 100 8593
Keirsleywell Row *Nthumb* 94 7751
Keisby *Lincs* 64 0328
Keisley *Cumb* 94 7124
Keiss *Highld* 151 3461
Keith *Moray* 142 4250
Keithick *P & K* 126 2038
Keithock *Angus* 134 6063
Keithtown *Highld* 139 5256
Kelbrook *Lancs* 81 9044
Kelburn *N Ayrs* 114 2156
Kelby *Lincs* 63 0041
Keld *Cumb* 94 5514
Keld *N York* 88 8900
Keld Head *N York* 90 7884
Keldholme *N York* 90 7086
Kelfield *Lincs* 84 8201
Kelfield *N York* 83 5938
Kelham *Notts* 75 7755
Kelhead *D & G* 100 1469
Kellacott *Devon* 5 4088
Kellamergh *Lancs* 80 4029
Kellas *Angus* 127 4535
Kellas *Moray* 141 1654
Kellaton *Devon* 7 8039
Kelleth *Cumb* 87 6605
Kelling *Norfk* 66 0942
Kellington *N York* 83 5524
Kelloe *Dur* 96 3436
Kelloholm *D & G* 107 7411
Kells *Cumb* 92 9616
Kelly *Devon* 5 3981
Kelly Bray *Cnwll* 5 3671
Kelmarsh *Nhants* 50 7379
Kelmscot *Oxon* 36 2499
Kelsale *Suffk* 55 3865
Kelsall *Ches* 71 5268
Kelshall *Herts* 39 3336
Kelsick *Cumb* 93 1950
Kelso *Border* 110 7234
Kelstedge *Derbys* 74 3363
Kelstern *Lincs* 77 2489
Kelsterton *Flints* 70 2770
Kelston *Somset* 22 7067
Keltneyburn *P & K* 124 7749
Kelton *D & G* 100 9970
Kelty *Fife* 117 1494
Kelvedon *Essex* 40 8619
Kelvedon Hatch *Essex* 27 5698
Kelynack *Cnwll* 2 3729
Kemacott *Devon* 19 6647
Kemback *Fife* 126 4115
Kemberton *Shrops* 60 7204
Kemble *Gloucs* 35 9897
Kemble Wick *Gloucs* 35 9895
Kemerton *Worcs* 47 9536
Kemeys Commander *Mons* 34 3404
Kemnay *Abers* 142 7316
Kemp Town *E Susx* 15 3303
Kempe's Corner *Kent* 28 0346
Kempley *Gloucs* 47 6629
Kempley Green *Gloucs* 47 6728
Kemps Green *Warwks* 61 1470
Kempsey *Worcs* 47 8549
Kempsford *Gloucs* 36 1696
Kempshott *Hants* 24 6050
Kempston *Beds* 38 0347
Kempston Hardwick *Beds* 38 0344
Kempton *Shrops* 59 3682
Kemsing *Kent* 27 5558
Kemsley *Kent* 28 9166
Kemsley Street *Kent* 28 8062
Kenardington *Kent* 17 9732
Kenchester *Herefs* 46 4342
Kencot *Oxon* 36 2504
Kendal *Cumb* 87 5192
Kenderchurch *Herefs* 46 4028
Kendleshire *Gloucs* 35 6679
Kenfig *Brdgnd* 32 8081
Kenfig Hill *Brdgnd* 33 8382
Kenidjack *Cnwll* 2 3632
Kenilworth *Warwks* 61 2871
Kenley *Gt Lon* 27 3260
Kenley *Shrops* 59 5500
Kenmore *Highld* 137 7557
Kenmore *P & K* 124 7745
Kenn *Devon* 9 9285
Kenn *Somset* 21 4268
Kennacraig *Ag & B* 113 8262
Kennards House *Cnwll* 5 2883
Kenneggy *Cnwll* 2 5628
Kennerleigh *Devon* 8 8107
Kennessee Green *Mersyd* 78 3801
Kennet *Clacks* 116 9291
Kennethmont *Abers* 142 5428
Kennett *Cambs* 53 7068
Kennford *Devon* 9 9186
Kenninghall *Norfk* 54 0386
Kennington *Kent* 28 0245
Kennington *Oxon* 37 5201
Kennoway *Fife* 126 3502
Kenny *Somset* 10 3117
Kennyhill *Suffk* 53 6679
Kennythorpe *N York* 90 7865
Kenovay *Ag & B* 120 9946
Kensaleyre *Highld* 136 4151
Kensham Green *Kent* 17 8229
Kensington *Gt Lon* 27 2579
Kensworth *Beds* 38 0319
Kensworth Common *Beds* 38 0317
Kent End *Wilts* 36 0594
Kent Green *Ches* 72 8458
Kent Street *E Susx* 17 7816
Kent Street *Kent* 28 6654
Kent's Green *Gloucs* 47 7423
Kent's Oak *Hants* 23 3224
Kentallen *Highld* 122 0057
Kentchurch *Herefs* 46 4125
Kentford *Suffk* 53 7066
Kentisbeare *Devon* 9 0608
Kentisbury *Devon* 19 6243
Kentisbury Ford *Devon* 19 6242
Kentish Town *Gt Lon* 27 2884
Kentmere *Cumb* 87 4504
Kenton *Devon* 9 9583
Kenton *Gt Lon* 26 1788
Kenton *Suffk* 55 1965
Kenton *T & W* 103 2267
Kenton Bankfoot *Nthumb* 103 2069
Kentra *Highld* 129 6569
Kents Bank *Cumb* 87 3975
Kenwick *Shrops* 59 4230
Kenwyn *Cnwll* 3 8145
Kenyon *Ches* 79 6395
Keoldale *Highld* 149 3866
Keppoch *Highld* 138 8924
Kepwick *N York* 89 4690
Keresley *W Mids* 61 3282
Keresley Green *Warwks* 61 3283
Kergilliak *Cnwll* 3 7833
Kernborough *Devon* 7 7941
Kerne Bridge *Herefs* 34 5818
Kerridge *Ches* 79 9376
Kerridge-end *Ches* 79 9475
Kerris *Cnwll* 2 4427
Kerry *Powys* 58 1490
Kerrycroy *Ag & B* 114 1061
Kersall *Notts* 75 7162
Kersbrook *Devon* 9 0683
Kerscott *Devon* 19 6329
Kersey *Suffk* 54 0044
Kersey Tye *Suffk* 54 9843
Kersey Upland *Suffk* 54 9942
Kershader *W Isls* 152 3320
Kershopefoot *Cumb* 101 4782
Kersoe *Worcs* 47 9940
Kerswell *Devon* 9 0806
Kerswell Green *Worcs* 47 8646
Kerthen Wood *Cnwll* 2 5833
Kesgrave *Suffk* 55 2245
Kessingland *Suffk* 55 5286
Kessingland Beach *Suffk* 55 5385
Kestle *Cnwll* 3 9845
Kestle Mill *Cnwll* 4 8459
Keston *Gt Lon* 27 4164
Keswick *Cumb* 93 2623
Keswick *Norfk* 67 2004
Ketsby *Lincs* 77 3676
Kettering *Nhants* 51 8678
Ketteringham *Norfk* 66 1603
Kettins *Angus* 126 2338
Kettle Green *Herts* 39 4118
Kettlebaston *Suffk* 54 9650
Kettlebridge *Fife* 126 3007
Kettlebrook *Staffs* 61 2103
Kettleburgh *Suffk* 55 2660
Kettleholm *D & G* 100 1476
Kettleness *N York* 97 8315
Kettleshulme *Ches* 79 9879
Kettlesing *N York* 82 2256
Kettlesing Bottom *N York* 89 2357
Kettlestone *Norfk* 66 9631
Kettlethorpe *Lincs* 76 8475
Kettletoft *Ork* 153 6538
Kettlewell *N York* 88 9672
Ketton *Rutlnd* 63 9704
Kew *Gt Lon* 26 1876
Kew Gardens 27 1877
Kewstoke *Somset* 21 3363
Kexbrough *S York* 82 3009
Kexby *Lincs* 76 8785
Kexby *N York* 84 7050
Key Green *Ches* 72 8963
Key Green *N York* 90 8004
Key Street *Kent* 28 8764
Key's Toft *Lincs* 77 4858
Keyham *Leics* 63 6706
Keyhaven *Hants* 12 3091
Keyingham *E R Yk* 85 2425
Keymer *W Susx* 15 3115
Keynsham *Somset* 21 6568
Keysoe *Beds* 51 0762
Keysoe Row *Beds* 51 0861
Keyston *Cambs* 51 0475
Keyworth *Notts* 62 6130
Kibbear *Somset* 20 2222
Kibblesworth *T & W* 96 2456
Kibworth Beauchamp *Leics* 50 6893
Kibworth Harcourt *Leics* 50 6894
Kidbrooke *Gt Lon* 27 4176
Kidburngill *Cumb* 92 0621
Kidd's Moor *Norfk* 66 1103
Kiddemore Green *Staffs* 60 8509
Kidderminster *Worcs* 60 8376
Kiddington *Oxon* 49 4123
Kidlington *Oxon* 37 4913
Kidmore End *Oxon* 37 6979
Kidsdale *D & G* 99 4336
Kidsgrove *Staffs* 72 8454
Kidstones *N York* 88 9581
Kidwelly *Carmth* 31 4006
Kiel Crofts *Ag & B* 122 9039
Kielder *Nthumb* 102 6293
Kiells *Ag & B* 112 4168
Kilbarchan *Rens* 115 4063
Kilbeg *Highld* 129 6506
Kilberry *Ag & B* 113 7164
Kilbirnie *N Ayrs* 115 3154
Kilbride *Ag & B* 122 8525
Kilbride *Ag & B* 113 7279
Kilbride *Ag & B* 114 0367
Kilbuiack *Moray* 141 0960
Kilburn *Derbys* 62 3845
Kilburn *Gt Lon* 26 2483
Kilburn *N York* 90 5179
Kilby *Leics* 50 6295
Kilchamaig *Ag & B* 113 8060
Kilchattan *Ag & B* 112 3795
Kilchattan *Ag & B* 114 1054
Kilcheran *Ag & B* 122 8239
Kilchoan *Highld* 121 4863
Kilchoman *Ag & B* 112 2163
Kilchrenan *Ag & B* 122 0322
Kilconquhar *Fife* 127 4802
Kilcot *Gloucs* 47 69
Kilcoy *Highld* 139 57
Kilcreggan *Ag & B* 114 24
Kildale *N York* 90 60
Kildalloig *Ag & B* 105 75
Kildary *Highld* 147 76
Kildavaig *Ag & B* 114 98
Kildavanan *Ag & B* 114 02
Kildonan *Highld* 147 91
Kildonan *N Ayrs* 105 03
Kildonan Lodge *Highld* 147 90
Kildonnan *Highld* 128 48
Kildrochet House *D & G* 98 08
Kildrummy *Abers* 142 46
Kildwick *N York* 82 00
Kilfinan *Ag & B* 114 93
Kilfinnan *Highld* 131 27
Kilford *Denbgs* 70 07
Kilgetty *Pembks* 31 12
Kilgrammie *S Ayrs* 106 25
Kilgwrrwg Common *Mons* 34 47
Kilham *E R Yk* 91 06
Kilham *Nthumb* 110 88
Kilkenneth *Ag & B* 120 94
Kilkenzie *Ag & B* 105 67
Kilkhampton *Cnwll* 18 25
Killamarsh *Derbys* 75 45
Killay *Swans* 32 60
Killearn *Stirlg* 115 52
Killerby *Dur* 96 19
Killerton *Devon* 9 97
Killichonan *P & K* 132 54
Killiechronan *Ag & B* 121 54
Killiecrankie *P & K* 132 91
Killilan *Highld* 138 94
Killin *Stirlg* 124 57
Killinghall *N York* 89 28
Killington *Cumb* 87 61
Killington *Devon* 19 66
Killingworth *T & W* 103 27
Killiow *Cnwll* 3 80
Killivose *Cnwll* 3 80
Killochyett *Border* 118 45
Kilmacolm *Inver* 115 35
Kilmahog *Stirlg* 124 61
Kilmahumaig *Ag & B* 113 78
Kilmaluag *Highld* 136 43
Kilmany *Fife* 126 38
Kilmarnock *E Ayrs* 107 42
Kilmartin *Ag & B* 113 83
Kilmaurs *E Ayrs* 106 41
Kilmelford *Ag & B* 122 85
Kilmersdon *Somset* 22 69
Kilmeston *Hants* 13 58
Kilmichael *Ag & B* 105 69
Kilmichael Glassary *Ag & B* 113 85
Kilmichael of Inverlussa *Ag & B* 113 77
Kilmington *Devon* 10 27
Kilmington *Wilts* 22 77
Kilmington Common *Wilts* 22 77
Kilmington Street *Wilts* 22 78
Kilmorack *Highld* 139 49
Kilmore *Ag & B* 122 88
Kilmore *Highld* 129 650
Kilmory *Ag & B* 113 707
Kilmory *Highld* 128 527
Kilmory *N Ayrs* 105 962
Kilmuir *Highld* 136 254
Kilmuir *Highld* 136 377
Kilmuir *Highld* 140 674
Kilmuir *Highld* 147 757
Kilmun *Ag & B* 114 178
Kiln Green *Berks* 37 817
Kiln Pit Hill *Nthumb* 95 035
Kilnave *Ag & B* 112 287
Kilncadzow *S Lans* 116 884
Kilndown *Kent* 16 703
Kilnhill *Cumb* 93 213
Kilnhouses *Ches* 71 636
Kilnhurst *S York* 75 459
Kilninver *Ag & B* 122 822
Kilnsea *E R Yk* 85 411
Kilnsey *N York* 88 976
Kilnwick *E R Yk* 84 994
Kilnwick Percy *E R Yk* 84 824
Kiloran *Ag & B* 112 399
Kilpatrick *N Ayrs* 105 902
Kilpeck *Herefs* 46 443
Kilpin *E R Yk* 84 772
Kilpin Pike *E R Yk* 84 762
Kilrenny *Fife* 127 570
Kilsby *Nhants* 50 567
Kilspindie *P & K* 126 212
Kilstay *D & G* 98 123
Kilsyth *N Lans* 116 717
Kiltarlity *Highld* 139 504
Kilton *N York* 97 701
Kilton Thorpe *N York* 97 691
Kilvaxter *Highld* 136 386
Kilve *Somset* 20 144
Kilvington *Notts* 63 804
Kilwinning *N Ayrs* 106 304
Kimberley *Norfk* 66 060
Kimberley *Notts* 62 494
Kimberworth *S York* 74 409
Kimble Wick *Bucks* 38 800
Kimblesworth *Dur* 96 254
Kimbolton *Cambs* 51 106
Kimbolton *Herefs* 46 526
Kimcote *Leics* 50 588
Kimmeridge *Dorset* 11 917
Kimmerston *Nthumb* 111 953
Kimpton *Hants* 23 274
Kimpton *Herts* 39 171
Kimworthy *Devon* 18 311
Kinbrace *Highld* 150 863
Kinbuck *Stirlg* 125 790
Kincaple *Fife* 127 461
Kincardine *Fife* 116 938
Kincardine *Highld* 146 608
Kincardine O'Neil *Abers* 134 599
Kinclaven *P & K* 126 153
Kincorth *Aber C* 135 940
Kincorth House *Moray* 141 016
Kincraig *Highld* 132 830
Kincraigie *P & K* 125 984
Kindallachan *P & K* 125 994
Kinerarach *Ag & B* 113 655

ineton

Lamorran

293

neton Gloucs 48 0926
neton Warwks 48 3350
nfauns P & K 126 1622
nfold S Ayrs 106 3634
ng Arthur's Labyrinth 57 7407
ng Sterndale Derbys 74 0972
ng's Acre Herefs 46 4841
ng's Bromley Staffs 73 1216
ng's Cliffe Nhants 51 0097
ng's Coughton Warwks 48 0859
ng's Heath W Mids 61 0781
ng's Hill Warwks 61 3274
ng's Lynn Norfk 65 6120
ng's Mills Guern 158 0000
ng's Moss Lancs 78 5000
ng's Newton Derbys 62 3825
ng's Norton Leics 50 6800
ng's Norton W Mids 61 0579
ng's Nympton Devon 19 6819
ng's Pyon Herefs 46 4450
ng's Somborne Hants 23 3531
ng's Stag Dorset 11 7210
ng's Stanley Gloucs 35 8103
ng's Sutton Oxon 49 4936
ng's Walden Herts 39 1623
ngarth Ag & B 114 0956
ngcausie Abers 135 8699
ngcoed Mons 34 4305
ngerby Lincs 76 0592
ngford Devon 18 2806
ngham Oxon 48 2624
ngholm Quay D & G 100 9773
nghorn Fife 117 2686
nglassie Fife 117 2298
ngoldrum Angus 126 3355
ngoodie P & K 126 3329
ngs Bridge Swans 32 5997
ngs Caple Herefs 46 5528
ngs Green Gloucs 47 7734
ngs Hill Kent 28 6755
ngs Hill W Mids 60 9896
ngs House Hotel Highld 123 2654
ngs Langley Herts 26 0702
ngs Meaburn Cumb 94 6221
ngs Muir Border 109 2539
ngs Newnham Warwks 50 4577
ngs Ripton Cambs 52 2676
ngs Weston Bristl 34 5477
ngs Worthy Hants 24 4932
ingsand Cnwll 6 4350
ingsash Bucks 38 8805
ingsbarns Fife 127 5912
ingsbridge Devon 7 7344
ingsbridge Somset 20 9837
ingsburgh Highld 136 3955
ingsbury Gt Lon 26 1988
ingsbury Warwks 61 2196
ingsbury Episcopi Somset 21 4321
ingsclere Hants 24 5258
ingscote Gloucs 35 8196
ingscott Devon 19 5318
ingscross N Ayrs 105 0428
ingsdon Somset 21 5126
ingsdown Kent 29 3748
ingsdown Wilts 22 8167
ingsdown Wilts 36 1688
ingseat Fife 117 1290
ingsey Bucks 37 7406
ingsfold W Susx 15 1636
ingsford Aber C 135 8506
ingsford E Ayrs 115 4447
ingsford Worcs 60 8181
ingsgate Kent 29 3970
ingshall Street Suffk 54 9161
ingsheanton Devon 19 5537
ingshouse Hotel Stirlg 124 5620
ingshurst W Mids 61 1688
ingside Hill Cumb 92 1551
ingskerswell Devon 7 8767
ingskettle Fife 126 3008
ingsland Dorset 10 4597
ingsland Herefs 46 4461
ingsland IOA 68 2581
ingsley Ches 71 5574
ingsley Hants 25 7838
ingsley Staffs 73 0146
ingsley Green W Susx 14 8930
ingsley Park Nhants 49 7762
ingslow Shrops 60 7998
ingsmead Hants 13 5813
ingsmuir Angus 127 4849
ingsmuir Fife 127 5308
ingsnorth Kent 28 0039
ingstanding W Mids 61 0794
ingsteignton Devon 7 8773
Kingsthorne Herefs 46 4931
Kingsthorpe Nhants 49 7563
ingston Cambs 52 3455
ingston Cnwll 5 3675
ingston Devon 6 6347
ingston Devon 9 0687
ingston Dorset 11 7509
ingston Dorset 11 9579
Kingston E Loth 118 5482
ingston Hants 12 1401
ingston IOW 13 4781
ingston Kent 29 1950
ingston W Susx 14 0802
ingston Bagpuize Oxon 36 4098
ingston Blount Oxon 37 7399
ingston Deverill Wilts 22 8437
ingston Lisle Oxon 36 3287
ingston near Lewes E Susx 15 3908
ingston on Soar Notts 62 5027
ingston on Spey Moray 141 3365
ingston Russell Dorset 10 5791
ingston Seymour Somset 21 4066
ingston St Mary Somset 20 2229
ingston Stert Oxon 37 7200
ingston upon Thames Gt Lon 26 1869
ingstone Herefs 46 4235
ingstone Somset 10 3713
ingstone Staffs 73 0629
ingstone Winslow Oxon 36 2685
ingstown Cumb 93 3959
ingswear Devon 7 8851
ingswells Aber C 135 8606
ingswinford W Mids 60 8888
Kingswood Bucks 37 6919
Kingswood Gloucs 35 6473
Kingswood Gloucs 35 7491
Kingswood Kent 28 8350
Kingswood Powys 58 2302
Kingswood Somset 20 1037
Kingswood Surrey 26 2455
Kingswood Warwks 61 1871
Kingswood Brook Warwks 61 1970
Kingswood Common Herefs 46 2954
Kingswood Common Staffs 60 8302
Kingthorpe Lincs 76 1275
Kington Gloucs 35 6290
Kington Herefs 46 2956
Kington Worcs 47 9956
Kington Langley Wilts 35 9276
Kington Magna Dorset 22 7622
Kington St Michael Wilts 35 9077
Kingussie Highld 132 7500
Kingweston Somset 21 5230
Kinharrachie Abers 143 9231
Kinharvie D & G 100 9266
Kinkell Bridge P & K 125 9316
Kinknockie Abers 143 0041
Kinleith C Edin 117 1866
Kinlet Shrops 60 7180
Kinloch Highld 149 3434
Kinloch Highld 149 5552
Kinloch Highld 128 4099
Kinloch P & K 126 1444
Kinloch P & K 126 2644
Kinloch Hourn Highld 130 9506
Kinloch Rannoch P & K 132 6658
Kinlochard Stirlg 124 4502
Kinlochbervie Highld 148 2256
Kinlocheil Highld 130 9779
Kinlochewe Highld 138 0261
Kinlochlaggan Highld 131 5289
Kinlochleven Highld 131 1861
Kinlochmoidart Highld 129 7072
Kinlochnanuagh Highld 129 7384
Kinloss Moray 141 0661
Kinmel Bay Conwy 70 9880
Kinmuck Abers 143 8119
Kinmundy Abers 143 8817
Kinnabus Ag & B 104 2942
Kinnadie Abers 143 9743
Kinnaird P & K 133 9559
Kinnaird Castle Angus 134 6357
Kinneddar Moray 141 2269
Kinneff Abers 135 8477
Kinnelhead D & G 108 0201
Kinnell Angus 127 6150
Kinnerley Shrops 59 3320
Kinnersley Herefs 46 3449
Kinnersley Worcs 47 8743
Kinnerton Powys 46 2463
Kinnerton Shrops 59 3796
Kinnerton Green Flints 71 3361
Kinnesswood P & K 126 1702
Kinninvie Dur 95 0521
Kinnordy Angus 126 3655
Kinoulton Notts 63 6730
Kinross P & K 126 1102
Kinrossie P & K 126 1832
Kinsbourne Green Herts 38 1016
Kinsey Heath Ches 72 6642
Kinsham Herefs 46 3665
Kinsham Worcs 47 9335
Kinsley W York 83 4114
Kinson Dorset 12 0796
Kintbury Berks 23 3866
Kintessack Moray 141 0060
Kintillo P & K 126 1317
Kinton Herefs 46 4174
Kinton Shrops 59 3719
Kintore Abers 143 7916
Kintour Ag & B 112 4551
Kintra Ag & B 120 3125
Kintraw Ag & B 122 8204
Kinveachy Highld 140 9018
Kinver Staffs 60 8483
Kiplin N York 89 2897
Kippax W York 83 4130
Kippen Stirlg 116 6494
Kippford or Scaur D & G 92 8354
Kipping's Cross Kent 16 6440
Kirbister Ork 153 3607
Kirburd Border 117 1244
Kirby Bedon Norfk 67 2705
Kirby Bellars Leics 63 7117
Kirby Cane Norfk 67 3794
Kirby Corner W Mids 61 2976
Kirby Cross Essex 41 2120
Kirby Fields Leics 62 5203
Kirby Grindalythe N York 91 9067
Kirby Hill N York 89 1406
Kirby Hill N York 89 3968
Kirby Knowle N York 89 4687
Kirby le Soken Essex 41 2121
Kirby Misperton N York 90 7779
Kirby Muxloe Leics 62 5104
Kirby Row Norfk 67 3792
Kirby Sigston N York 89 4194
Kirby Underdale E R Yk 90 8058
Kirby Wiske N York 89 3784
Kirconnel D & G 100 9868
Kirdford W Susx 14 0126
Kirk Highld 151 2859
Kirk Bramwith S York 83 6211
Kirk Deighton N York 83 3950
Kirk Ella E R Yk 84 0129
Kirk Hallam Derbys 62 4540
Kirk Hammerton N York 83 4655
Kirk Ireton Derbys 73 2650
Kirk Langley Derbys 73 2838
Kirk Merrington Dur 96 2631
Kirk Michael IOM 158 3190
Kirk of Shotts N Lans 116 8462
Kirk Sandall S York 83 6108
Kirk Smeaton N York 83 5216
Kirk Yetholm Border 110 8228
Kirkabister Shet 153 4938
Kirkandrews D & G 99 6048
Kirkandrews upon Eden Cumb 93 3558
Kirkbampton Cumb 93 3056
Kirkbean D & G 92 9759
Kirkbride Cumb 93 2256
Kirkbridge N York 89 2590
Kirkbuddo Angus 127 5043
Kirkburn Border 109 2938
Kirkburn E R Yk 84 9855
Kirkburton W York 82 1912
Kirkby Lincs 76 0592
Kirkby Mersyd 78 4099
Kirkby N York 90 5305
Kirkby Fleetham N York 89 2894
Kirkby Green Lincs 76 0857
Kirkby Hall N York 89 2795
Kirkby in Ashfield Notts 75 4856
Kirkby la Thorpe Lincs 76 0946
Kirkby Lonsdale Cumb 87 6178
Kirkby Malham N York 88 8960
Kirkby Mallory Leics 50 4500
Kirkby Malzeard N York 89 2374
Kirkby Mills N York 90 7085
Kirkby on Bain Lincs 77 2462
Kirkby Overblow N York 83 3249
Kirkby Stephen Cumb 88 7708
Kirkby Thore Cumb 94 6325
Kirkby Underwood Lincs 64 0727
Kirkby Wharf N York 83 5041
Kirkby Woodhouse Notts 75 4954
Kirkby-in-Furness Cumb 86 2282
Kirkbymoorside N York 90 6986
Kirkcaldy Fife 117 2892
Kirkcambeck Cumb 101 5368
Kirkchrist D & G 99 6751
Kirkcolm D & G 98 0268
Kirkconnel D & G 107 7311
Kirkconnell D & G 99 6760
Kirkcowan D & G 98 3260
Kirkcudbright D & G 99 6850
Kirkdale Mersyd 78 3493
Kirkfieldbank S Lans 108 8643
Kirkgunzeon D & G 100 8666
Kirkham Lancs 80 4232
Kirkham N York 90 7365
Kirkhamgate W York 82 2922
Kirkharle Nthumb 103 0182
Kirkhaugh Nthumb 94 6949
Kirkheaton Nthumb 103 0177
Kirkheaton W York 82 1818
Kirkhill Highld 139 5545
Kirkhope S Lans 108 9606
Kirkhouse Cumb 94 5759
Kirkhouse Green S York 83 6213
Kirkibost Highld 129 5518
Kirkinch P & K 126 3044
Kirkinner D & G 99 4251
Kirkintilloch E Duns 116 6573
Kirkland Cumb 92 0718
Kirkland Cumb 94 6432
Kirkland D & G 107 7213
Kirkland D & G 100 8190
Kirkland D & G 100 0389
Kirkland Guards Cumb 93 1840
Kirkleatham N York 97 5921
Kirklevington N York 89 4309
Kirkley Suffk 67 5391
Kirklington N York 89 3181
Kirklington Notts 75 6757
Kirklinton Cumb 101 4367
Kirkliston C Edin 117 1274
Kirkmabreck D & G 99 4856
Kirkmaiden D & G 98 1236
Kirkmichael P & K 133 0759
Kirkmichael S Ayrs 106 3408
Kirkmuirhill S Lans 107 7842
Kirknewton Nthumb 110 9130
Kirknewton W Loth 117 1166
Kirkney Abers 142 5132
Kirkoswald Cumb 94 5541
Kirkoswald S Ayrs 106 2407
Kirkpatrick D & G 100 9090
Kirkpatrick IOM 158 2482
Kirkpatrick Durham D & G 100 7870
Kirkpatrick-Fleming D & G 101 2770
Kirksanton Cumb 86 1380
Kirkstall W York 82 2635
Kirkstead Lincs 76 1762
Kirkstile Abers 142 5235
Kirkstile D & G 101 3690
Kirkstone Pass Inn Cumb 87 4007
Kirkstyle Highld 151 3472
Kirkthorpe W York 83 3621
Kirkton Abers 142 6425
Kirkton Abers 143 8243
Kirkton D & G 100 9781
Kirkton Fife 126 3625
Kirkton Highld 137 8227
Kirkton Highld 138 9141
Kirkton P & K 125 9618
Kirkton Manor Border 109 2238
Kirkton of Airlie Angus 126 3151
Kirkton of Auchterhouse Angus 126 3438
Kirkton of Barevan Highld 140 8347
Kirkton of Collace P & K 126 1931
Kirkton of Glenbuchat Abers 141 3715
Kirkton of Logie Buchan Abers 143 9829
Kirkton of Menmuir Angus 134 5364
Kirkton of Monikie Angus 127 5138
Kirkton of Rayne Abers 142 6930
Kirkton of Skene Abers 135 8007
Kirkton of Strathmartine Angus 126 3735
Kirkton of Tealing Angus 126 4038
Kirktown Abers 143 9965
Kirktown Abers 143 0852
Kirktown of Bourtie Abers 143 8025
Kirktown of Fetteresso Abers 135 8486
Kirktown of Mortlach Moray 141 3138
Kirktown of Slains Abers 143 0329
Kirkwall Ork 153 4411
Kirkwall Airport 153 4808
Kirkwhelpington Nthumb 103 9984
Kirmincham Ches 79 8068
Kirmington Lincs 85 1011
Kirmond le Mire Lincs 76 1892
Kirn Ag & B 114 1878
Kirriemuir Angus 126 3853
Kirstead Green Norfk 67 2997
Kirtlebridge D & G 101 2372
Kirtling Cambs 53 6857
Kirtling Green Suffk 53 6855
Kirtlington Oxon 37 4919
Kirtomy Highld 150 7463
Kirton Abers 134 6113
Kirton Lincs 64 3038
Kirton Notts 75 6969
Kirton Suffk 55 2740
Kirton End Lincs 64 2940
Kirton Holme Lincs 64 2642
Kirton in Lindsey Lincs 76 9398
Kirtonhill W Duns 115 3875
Kirwaugh D & G 99 4054
Kishorn Highld 138 8440
Kislingbury Nhants 49 6959
Kite Green Warwks 48 1666
Kitebrook Warwks 48 2431
Kites Hardwick Warwks 50 4768
Kitleigh Cnwll 18 2499
Kitt Green Gt Man 78 5405
Kittisford Somset 20 0822
Kittle Swans 32 5789
Kitts Green W Mids 61 1587
Kittybrewster Aber C 135 9207
Kitwood Hants 24 6633
Kivernoll Herefs 46 4632
Kiveton Park S York 75 4982
Knaith Lincs 75 8284
Knaith Park Lincs 76 8485
Knap Corner Dorset 22 8023
Knaphill Surrey 25 9658
Knaplock Somset 19 8633
Knapp Somset 20 3025
Knapp Hill Hants 13 4023
Knapthorpe Notts 75 7458
Knapton N York 83 5652
Knapton N York 90 8876
Knapton Norfk 67 3034
Knapton Green Herefs 46 4452
Knapwell Cambs 52 3362
Knaresborough N York 89 3557
Knarsdale Nthumb 94 6754
Knaven Abers 143 8943
Knayton N York 89 4387
Knebworth Herts 39 2520
Knedlington E R Yk 84 7327
Kneesall Notts 75 7064
Kneesworth Cambs 39 3444
Kneeton Notts 63 7146
Knelston Swans 32 4688
Knenhall Staffs 72 9237
Knettishall Suffk 54 9780
Knightacott Devon 19 6539
Knightcote Warwks 48 4054
Knightley Staffs 72 8125
Knightley Dale Staffs 72 8123
Knighton Devon 6 5349
Knighton Dorset 10 6111
Knighton Dorset 12 0497
Knighton Leics 62 6001
Knighton Powys 46 2872
Knighton Somset 20 1944
Knighton Staffs 72 7240
Knighton Staffs 72 7527
Knighton Wilts 36 2971
Knighton on Teme Worcs 47 6369
Knightsbridge Gloucs 47 8926
Knightsmill Cnwll 4 0780
Knightwick Worcs 47 7356
Knill Herefs 46 2960
Knipton Leics 63 8231
Knitsley Dur 95 1048
Kniveton Derbys 73 2050
Knock Cumb 94 6727
Knock Highld 129 6709
Knock Moray 142 5452
Knock W Isls 152 4931
Knock Castle N Ayrs 114 1963
Knockally Highld 151 1429
Knockan Highld 145 2110
Knockando Moray 141 1941
Knockbain Highld 139 5543
Knockbain Highld 140 6256
Knockdee Highld 151 1760
Knockdown Wilts 35 8388
Knockeen S Ayrs 106 3195
Knockenkelly N Ayrs 105 0427
Knockentiber E Ayrs 106 4039
Knockhall Kent 27 5974
Knockholt Kent 27 4658
Knockholt Pound Kent 27 4859
Knockin Shrops 59 3322
Knockinlaw E Ayrs 107 4239
Knockmill Kent 27 5761
Knocknain D & G 98 9764
Knocksheen D & G 99 5882
Knockvennie Smithy D & G 99 7571
Knodishall Suffk 55 4262
Knole Somset 21 4825
Knole Park Gloucs 34 5983
Knolls Green Ches 79 8079
Knolton Wrexhm 71 3739
Knook Wilts 22 9341
Knossington Leics 63 8008
Knott End-on-Sea Lancs 80 3548
Knotting Beds 51 0063
Knotting Green Beds 51 0062
Knottingley W York 83 5023
Knotty Green Bucks 26 9392
Knowbury Shrops 46 5775
Knowe D & G 98 3171
Knowehead D & G 107 6090
Knoweside S Ayrs 106 2512
Knowl Green Essex 53 7841
Knowl Hill Berks 37 8279
Knowle Bristl 34 6070
Knowle Devon 18 4938
Knowle Devon 8 7801
Knowle Devon 9 0007
Knowle Devon 9 0582
Knowle Shrops 46 5973
Knowle Somset 20 9643
Knowle W Mids 61 1876
Knowle Cross Devon 9 0397
Knowle Green Lancs 81 6338
Knowle Hill Surrey 25 9966
Knowle St Giles Somset 10 3411
Knowlefield Cumb 93 4057
Knowlton Dorset 12 0209
Knowlton Kent 29 2853
Knowsley Mersyd 78 4395
Knowsley Safari Park 78 4694
Knowstone Devon 19 8323
Knox N York 89 2957
Knox Bridge Kent 28 7840
Knucklas Powys 46 2574
Knuston Nhants 51 9266
Knutsford Ches 79 7578
Knutton Staffs 72 8347
Knypersley Staffs 72 8856
Krumlin W York 82 0518
Kuggar Cnwll 3 7216
Kyle of Lochalsh Highld 137 7627
Kyleakin Highld 137 7526
Kylerhea Highld 129 7820
Kyles Scalpay W Isls 152 2198
Kylesku Highld 148 2233
Kylesmorar Highld 129 8093
Kylestrome Highld 148 2234
Kyloe Nthumb 111 0540
Kynaston Herefs 47 6435
Kynaston Shrops 59 3520
Kynnersley Shrops 72 6716
Kyre Green Worcs 46 6162
Kyre Park Worcs 47 6263
Kyrewood Worcs 46 5967
Kyrle Somset 20 0522

L

L'Ancresse Guern 158 0000
L'Eree Guern 158 0000
L'Etacq Jersey 158 0000
La Bellieuse Guern 158 0000
La Fontenelle Guern 158 0000
La Fosse Guern 158 0000
La Greve Guern 158 0000
La Greve de Lecq Jersey 158 0000
La Hougue Bie Jersey 158 0000
La Houguette Guern 158 0000
La Passee Guern 158 0000
La Pulente Jersey 158 0000
La Rocque Jersey 158 0000
La Rousaillerie Guern 158 0000
La Villette Guern 158 0000
Lacadal W Isls 152 4234
Lacasaigh W Isls 152 3321
Laceby Lincs 85 2106
Lacey Green Bucks 37 8200
Lach Dennis Ches 79 7071
Lackenby N York 97 5619
Lackford Suffk 53 7970
Lackford Green Suffk 53 7970
Lacock Wilts 22 9168
Ladbroke Warwks 49 4158
Ladderedge Staffs 72 9654
Laddingford Kent 28 6948
Lade Bank Lincs 77 3954
Ladock Cnwll 3 8950
Lady Hall Cumb 86 1986
Lady Village Ork 153 6841
Lady's Green Suffk 53 7559
Ladybank Fife 126 3009
Ladycross Cnwll 5 3188
Ladygill S Lans 108 9428
Ladykirk Border 110 8847
Ladyridge Herefs 46 5931
Ladywood W Mids 61 0586
Ladywood Worcs 47 8661
Lag D & G 100 8786
Laga Highld 121 6361
Lagavulin Ag & B 104 4045
Lagg N Ayrs 105 9521
Laggan Highld 131 2997
Laggan Highld 132 6194
Laid Highld 149 4159
Laide Highld 144 9091
Laig Highld 128 4687
Laigh Clunch E Ayrs 115 4647
Laigh Fenwick E Ayrs 107 4542
Laigh Glenmuir E Ayrs 107 6120
Laighstonehall S Lans 116 7054
Laindon Essex 40 6889
Lairg Highld 146 5806
Laisterdyke W York 82 1932
Laithes Cumb 93 4633
Lake Devon 19 5531
Lake Devon 5 5289
Lake Dorset 11 9990
Lake IOW 13 5883
Lake Wilts 23 1339
Lakenheath Suffk 53 7182
Laker's Green Surrey 14 0335
Lakesend Norfk 65 5196
Lakeside Cumb 87 3787
Laleham Surrey 26 0568
Laleston Brdgnd 33 8779
Lamancha Border 117 2052
Lamanva Cnwll 3 7631
Lamarsh Essex 54 8835
Lamas Norfk 67 2423
Lamb Roe Lancs 81 7337
Lambden Border 110 7443
Lamberhurst Kent 28 6736
Lamberhurst Down Kent 16 6735
Lamberton Border 119 9658
Lambeth Gt Lon 27 3178
Lambfair Green Suffk 53 7153
Lambley Notts 63 6345
Lambley Nthumb 94 6658
Lambourn Berks 36 3278
Lambourne End Essex 27 4794
Lambs Green W Susx 15 2136
Lambston Pembks 30 9016
Lamellion Cnwll 5 2463
Lamerton Devon 5 4577
Lamesley T & W 96 2557
Lamington S Lans 108 9731
Lamlash N Ayrs 105 0231
Lamonby Cumb 93 4036
Lamorick Cnwll 4 0364
Lamorna Cnwll 2 4424
Lamorran Cnwll 3 8741

Lampen

Lingwoo

294

Lampen Cnwll 4 1867
Lampeter Cerdgn 44 5747
Lampeter Velfrey Pembks 31 1514
Lamphey Pembks 30 0100
Lamplugh Cumb 92 0820
Lamport Nhants 50 7574
Lamyatt Somset 21 6536
Lana Devon 18 3007
Lana Devon 5 3496
Lanark S Lans 108 8843
Lanarth Cnwll 3 7621
Lancaster Lancs 87 4761
Lancaut Gloucs 34 5396
Lanchester Dur 96 1647
Lancing W Susx 15 1804
Land's End Cnwll 2 3425
Land's End Airport 2 3728
Land-hallow Highld 151 1833
Landbeach Cambs 53 4765
Landcross Devon 18 4523
Landerberry Abers 135 7404
Landford Wilts 12 2519
Landimore Swans 32 4692
Landkey Devon 19 6031
Landkey Town Devon 19 5931
Landore Swans 32 6695
Landrake Cnwll 5 3760
Landscove Devon 7 7766
Landshipping Pembks 30 0211
Landue Cnwll 5 3579
Landulph Cnwll 6 4361
Landwade Suffk 53 6268
Landywood Staffs 60 9805
Lane Cnwll 4 8260
Lane Bottom Lancs 81 8735
Lane End Bucks 37 8091
Lane End Ches 79 6890
Lane End Cnwll 4 0369
Lane End Hants 13 5525
Lane End Kent 27 5671
Lane End Lancs 81 8747
Lane End Wilts 22 8145
Lane End Waberthwaite Cumb 86 1093
Lane Ends Derbys 73 2334
Lane Ends Dur 96 1833
Lane Ends Lancs 81 7930
Lane Ends N York 82 9743
Lane Green Staffs 60 8703
Lane Head Dur 89 1211
Lane Head Gt Man 79 6296
Lane Head W Mids 35 9700
Lane Heads Lancs 80 4339
Lane Side Lancs 81 7922
Laneast Cnwll 5 2283
Laneham Notts 75 8076
Lanehead Dur 95 8441
Lanehead Nthumb 102 7985
Laneshaw Bridge Lancs 81 9240
Langaford Devon 18 4199
Langaller Somset 20 2626
Langar Notts 63 7234
Langbank Rens 115 3873
Langbar N York 82 0951
Langbaurgh N York 90 5511
Langcliffe N York 88 8264
Langdale End N York 91 9391
Langdon Cnwll 5 3089
Langdon Beck Dur 95 8531
Langdown Hants 13 4206
Langdyke Fife 126 3304
Langenhoe Essex 41 0018
Langford Beds 39 1841
Langford Devon 9 0203
Langford Essex 40 8309
Langford Notts 75 8258
Langford Oxon 36 2402
Langford Somset 21 4560
Langford Budville Somset 20 1122
Langford End Beds 52 1753
Langham Dorset 22 7725
Langham Essex 41 0333
Langham Norfk 66 0141
Langham Rutlnd 63 8411
Langham Suffk 54 9769
Langham Moor Essex 41 0131
Langham Wick Essex 41 0231
Langho Lancs 81 7034
Langholm D & G 101 3684
Langland Swans 32 6087
Langlee Border 109 5035
Langley Berks 26 0178
Langley Ches 79 9471
Langley Derbys 62 4445
Langley Gloucs 47 0028
Langley Gt Man 79 8506
Langley Hants 13 4401
Langley Herts 39 2122
Langley Kent 28 8052
Langley Nthumb 102 8261
Langley Oxon 36 2915
Langley Somset 20 0828
Langley W Susx 14 8029
Langley Warwks 48 1962
Langley Burrell Wilts 35 9375
Langley Castle Nthumb 102 8362
Langley Common Derbys 73 2937
Langley Green Derbys 73 2738
Langley Green Essex 40 8722
Langley Green Warwks 48 1962
Langley Lower Green Essex 39 4334
Langley Marsh Somset 20 0729
Langley Mill Derbys 62 4446
Langley Moor Dur 96 2540
Langley Park Dur 96 2145
Langley Street Norfk 67 3601
Langley Upper Green Essex 39 4434
Langleybury Herts 26 0700
Langney E Susx 16 6302
Langold Notts 75 5886
Langore Cnwll 5 2986
Langport Somset 21 4226
Langrick Lincs 77 2648
Langridge Somset 35 7469
Langridge Ford Devon 19 5722
Langrigg Cumb 92 1645
Langrish Hants 13 7023
Langsett S York 74 2100
Langside P & K 125 7913
Langstone Hants 13 7204
Langstone Newpt 34 3789
Langthorne N York 89 2491
Langthorpe N York 89 3867
Langthwaite N York 88 0001
Langtoft E R Yk 91 0066
Langtoft Lincs 64 1212
Langton Dur 96 1619
Langton Lincs 76 2368
Langton Lincs 77 3970
Langton N York 90 7966
Langton by Wragby Lincs 76 1476
Langton Green Kent 16 5439
Langton Green Suffk 54 1474
Langton Herring Dorset 10 6182
Langton Matravers Dorset 11 0078
Langtree Devon 18 4515
Langtree Week Devon 18 4715
Langwathby Cumb 94 5733
Langwell House Highld 147 1122
Langworth Lincs 76 0676
Langworthy Devon 5 4894
Lanhydrock House & Gardens ... 4 0863
Lanivet Cnwll 4 0464
Lanjeth Cnwll 3 9752
Lank Cnwll 4 0875
Lanlivery Cnwll 4 0759
Lanner Cnwll 2 7139
Lanoy Cnwll 5 2977
Lanreath Cnwll 4 1857
Lansallos Cnwll 4 1751
Lanteglos Cnwll 4 0882
Lanteglos Highway Cnwll 3 1453
Lanton Border 110 6221
Lanton Nthumb 110 9231
Lapford Somset 19 7308
Laphroaig Ag & B 104 3845
Lapley Staffs 60 8712
Lapworth Warwks 61 1671
Larachbeg Highld 122 6948
Larbert Falk 116 8582
Larbreck Lancs 80 4040
Largie Abers 142 6131
Largiemore Ag & B 114 9486
Largoward Fife 127 4607
Largs N Ayrs 114 2059
Largybeg N Ayrs 105 0423
Largymore N Ayrs 105 0424
Larkbeare Devon 9 0797
Larkfield Inver 114 2475
Larkfield Kent 28 7058
Larkhall S Lans 116 7651
Larkhill Wilts 23 1244
Larling Norfk 54 9889
Lartington Dur 95 0117
Lasborough Gloucs 35 8294
Lasham Hants 24 6742
Lashbrook Devon 18 4305
Lashenden Kent 28 8440
Lask Edge Staffs 72 9156
Lassodie Fife 117 1292
Lasswade Mdloth 117 3065
Lastingham N York 90 7290
Latcham Somset 21 4447
Latchford Herts 39 3920
Latchford Oxon 37 6501
Latchingdon Essex 40 8800
Latchley Cnwll 5 4173
Latebrook Staffs 72 8453
Lately Common Gt Man 79 6797
Lathbury Bucks 38 8744
Latheron Highld 151 2033
Latheronwheel Highld 151 1832
Lathones Fife 127 4708
Latimer Bucks 26 0099
Latteridge Gloucs 35 6684
Lattiford Somset 22 6926
Latton Wilts 36 0995
Lauder Border 118 5347
Laugharne Carmth 31 3010
Laughterton Lincs 76 8375
Laughton E Susx 16 4913
Laughton Leics 50 6688
Laughton Lincs 76 8497
Laughton Lincs 64 0731
Laughton-en-le-Morthen S York 75 5187
Launcells Cnwll 18 2405
Launcells Cross Cnwll 18 2605
Launceston Cnwll 5 3384
Launton Oxon 37 6022
Laurencekirk Abers 135 7171
Laurieston D & G 99 6864
Laurieston Falk 116 9179
Lavendon Bucks 51 9153
Lavenham Suffk 54 9149
Lavernock V Glam 20 1868
Laversdale Cumb 101 4762
Laverstock Wilts 23 1630
Laverstoke Hants 24 4948
Laverton Gloucs 48 0735
Laverton N York 89 2273
Laverton Somset 22 7753
Lavister Wrexhm 71 3758
Law S Lans 116 8252
Law Hill S Lans 116 8251
Lawers P & K 124 6739
Lawford Essex 41 0831
Lawford Somset 20 1336
Lawgrove P & K 125 0926
Lawhitton Cnwll 5 3582
Lawkland N York 88 7766
Lawkland Green N York 88 7765
Lawley Shrops 60 6608
Lawnhead Staffs 72 8325
Lawrence End Herts 38 1419
Lawrenny Pembks 30 0106
Lawshall Suffk 54 8654
Lawshall Green Suffk 54 8853
Lawton Herefs 46 4459
Laxay W Isls 152 3321
Laxdale W Isls 152 4234
Laxey IOM 158 4384
Laxfield Suffk 55 2972
Laxford Bridge Highld 148 2346
Laxo Shet 153 4463
Laxton E R Yk 84 7925
Laxton Nhants 51 9596
Laxton Notts 75 7267
Laycock W York 82 0341
Layer Breton Essex 40 9417
Layer Marney Essex 40 9217
Layer-de-la-Haye Essex 41 9620
Layham Suffk 54 0240
Layland's Green Berks 23 3866
Laymore Dorset 10 3804
Layter's Green Bucks 26 9890
Laytham E R Yk 84 7439
Laythes Cumb 93 2455
Lazenby N York 97 5719
Lazonby Cumb 94 5439
Le Bigard Guern 158 0000
Le Bourg Guern 158 0000
Le Bourg Jersey 158 0000
Le Gron Guern 158 0000
Le Haguais Jersey 158 0000
Le Hocq Jersey 158 0000
Le Villocq Guern 158 0000
Lea Derbys 74 3257
Lea Herefs 35 6521
Lea Lincs 75 8286
Lea Shrops 59 4108
Lea Shrops 59 3589
Lea Wilts 35 9586
Lea Bridge Derbys 74 3156
Lea Heath Staffs 73 0225
Lea Marston Warwks 61 2093
Lea Town Lancs 80 4730
Lea Yeat Cumb 88 7686
Leachkin Highld 140 6344
Leadburn Mdloth 117 2355
Leaden Roding Essex 40 5913
Leadenham Lincs 76 9452
Leadgate Dur 96 1251
Leadgate Nthumb 95 1159
Leadhills S Lans 108 8815
Leadingcross Green Kent 28 8951
Leadmill Derbys 74 2380
Leafield Oxon 36 3115
Leagrave Beds 38 0523
Leahead Ches 72 6864
Leake N York 89 4390
Leake Common Side Lincs 77 3952
Lealholm N York 90 7607
Lealholm Side N York 90 7607
Lealt Highld 137 5060
Leam Derbys 74 2379
Leamington Hastings Warwks 50 4467
Leamington Spa Warwks 48 3265
Leamonsley Staffs 61 1009
Leamside Dur 96 3146
Leap Cross E Susx 16 5810
Leasgill Cumb 87 4983
Leasingham Lincs 76 0548
Leasingthorne Dur 96 2530
Leatherhead Surrey 26 1656
Leathley N York 82 2347
Leaton Shrops 59 4618
Leaton Shrops 59 6111
Leaveland Kent 28 0053
Leavenheath Suffk 54 9537
Leavening N York 90 7863
Leaves Green Gt Lon 27 4161
Lebberston N York 91 0782
Lechlade Gloucs 36 2199
Lecht Gruinart Ag & B 112 2768
Leck Lancs 87 6476
Leckbuie P & K 124 7040
Leckford Hants 23 3737
Leckhampstead Berks 36 4375
Leckhampstead Bucks 49 7237
Leckhampstead Thicket Berks 36 4276
Leckhampton Gloucs 35 9419
Leckmelm Highld 145 1689
Leckwith V Glam 33 1574
Leconfield E R Yk 84 0143
Ledaig Ag & B 122 9037
Ledburn Bucks 38 9021
Ledbury Herefs 47 7137
Leddington Gloucs 47 6834
Ledgemoor Herefs 46 4150
Ledicot Herefs 46 4162
Ledmore Junction Highld 145 2412
Ledsham Ches 71 3574
Ledsham W York 83 4529
Ledston W York 83 4328
Ledston Luck W York 83 4330
Ledstone Devon 7 7446
Ledwell Oxon 49 4128
Lee Devon 18 4846
Lee Gt Lon 27 3875
Lee Hants 12 3617
Lee Shrops 59 4032
Lee Brockhurst Shrops 59 5427
Lee Chapel Essex 40 6987
Lee Clump Bucks 38 9004
Lee Common Bucks 38 9103
Lee Green Ches 72 6661
Lee Mill Devon 6 5955
Lee Moor Devon 6 5762
Lee Street Surrey 15 2743
Lee-on-the-Solent Hants 13 5600
Leebotwood Shrops 59 4798
Leece Cumb 86 2469
Leedon Beds 38 9325
Leeds Kent 28 8253
Leeds W York 82 2932
Leeds Bradford Airport 82 2241
Leeds Castle 28 8353
Leedstown Cnwll 2 6034
Leek Staffs 72 9856
Leek Wootton Warwks 48 2868
Leeming N York 89 2989
Leeming W York 82 0434
Leeming Bar N York 89 2889
Lees Derbys 73 2637
Lees Gt Man 79 9504
Lees W York 82 0437
Lees Green Derbys 73 2637
Lees Hill Cumb 101 5568
Leesthorpe Leics 63 7813
Leeswood Flints 70 2660
Leetown P & K 126 2121
Leftwich Ches 79 6672
Legbourne Lincs 77 3784
Legburthwaite Cumb 93 3219
Legerwood Border 110 5843
Legoland 26 9474
Legsby Lincs 76 1385
Leicester Leics 62 5804
Leicester Forest East Leics 62 5202
Leigh Devon 19 7212
Leigh Dorset 10 6108
Leigh Gloucs 47 8626
Leigh Gt Man 79 6599
Leigh Kent 16 5446
Leigh Shrops 59 3303
Leigh Surrey 15 2246
Leigh Wilts 36 0692
Leigh Worcs 47 7853
Leigh Beck Essex 40 8183
Leigh Delamere Wilts 35 8879
Leigh Green Kent 17 9033
Leigh Knoweglass S Lans 116 6350
Leigh Park Dorset 12 0299
Leigh Sinton Worcs 47 7750
Leigh upon Mendip Somset 22 6947
Leigh Woods Somset 34 5672
Leigh-on-Sea Essex 40 8286
Leighland Chapel Somset 20 0336
Leighterton Gloucs 35 8290
Leighton N York 89 1679
Leighton Powys 58 2306
Leighton Shrops 59 6105
Leighton Somset 22 7043
Leighton Bromswold Cambs 52 1175
Leighton Buzzard Beds 38 9225
Leinthall Earls Herefs 46 4467
Leinthall Starkes Herefs 46 4369
Leintwardine Herefs 46 4074
Leire Leics 50 5290
Leiston Suffk 55 4462
Leitfie P & K 126 2545
Leith C Edin 117 2776
Leitholm Border 110 7944
Lelant Cnwll 2 5437
Lelley E R Yk 85 2032
Lem Hill Worcs 60 7275
Lemmington Hall Nthumb 111 1211
Lempitlaw Border 110 7832
Lemreway W Isls 152 3711
Lemsford Herts 39 2212
Lenchwick Worcs 48 0347
Lendalfoot S Ayrs 106 1390
Lendrick Stirlg 124 5506
Lendrum Terrace Abers 143 1141
Lenham Kent 28 8952
Lenham Heath Kent 28 9149
Lenie Highld 139 5126
Lennel Border 110 8540
Lennox Plunton D & G 99 6051
Lennoxtown E Duns 116 6277
Lent Bucks 26 9381
Lenton Lincs 64 0230
Lenton Notts 62 5539
Lenwade Norfk 66 0918
Lenzie E Duns 116 6572
Leochel-Cushnie Abers 134 5210
Leominster Herefs 46 4959
Leonard Stanley Gloucs 35 8003
Leoville Jersey 158 0000
Lepe Hants 13 4498
Lephin Highld 136 1749
Leppington N York 90 7661
Lepton W York 82 2015
Lerryn Cnwll 4 1457
Lerwick Shet 153 4741
Les Arquets Guern 158 0000
Les Hubits Guern 158 0000
Les Lohiers Guern 158 0000
Les Murchez Guern 158 0000
Les Nicolles Guern 158 0000
Les Quartiers Guern 158 0000
Les Quennevais Jersey 158 0000
Les Sages Guern 158 0000
Les Villets Guern 158 0000
Lesbury Nthumb 111 2311
Leslie Abers 142 5924
Leslie Fife 126 2501
Lesmahagow S Lans 108 8139
Lesnewth Cnwll 4 1390
Lessingham Norfk 67 3928
Lessonhall Cumb 93 2250
Lestowder Cnwll 3 7924
Leswalt D & G 98 0163
Letchmore Heath Herts 26 1597
Letchworth Herts 39 2232
Letcombe Bassett Oxon 36 3784
Letcombe Regis Oxon 36 3886
Letham Angus 127 5348
Letham Border 110 6708
Letham Falk 116 8986
Letham Fife 126 3014
Letham Grange Angus 127 6345
Lethendy P & K 126 1341
Lethenty Abers 142 5820
Lethenty Abers 143 8140
Letheringham Suffk 55 2757
Letheringsett Norfk 66 0638
Lett's Green Kent 27 4559
Lettaford Devon 8 7084
Letterewe Highld 144 9571
Letterfearn Highld 138 8823
Letterfinlay Lodge Hotel Highld 131 2491
Lettermorar Highld 129 7389
Letters Highld 145 1687
Lettershaw S Lans 108 8920
Letterston Pembks 30 9429
Lettoch Highld 141 0219
Lettoch Highld 141 1032
Letton Herefs 46 3346
Letton Herefs 46 3770
Letty Green Herts 39 2810
Letwell S York 75 5686
Leuchars Fife 127 4521
Leumrabhagh W Isls 152 3711
Leurbost W Isls 152 3725
Levalsa Meor Cnwll 3 0049
Levedale Staffs 72 8916
Level's Green Essex 39 4724
Leven E R Yk 85 1045
Leven Fife 118 3800
Levens Cumb 87 4886
Levens Green Herts 39 3522
Levenshulme Gt Man 79 8794
Levenwick Shet 153 4
Leverburgh W Isls 152 0
Leverington Cambs 65 4
Leverstock Green Herts 38 0
Leverton Lincs 77 4
Levington Suffk 55 2
Levisham N York 90 8
Lew Oxon 36 3
Lewannick Cnwll 5 2
Lewdown Devon 5 4
Lewes E Susx 15 4
Leweston Dorset 10 6
Leweston Pembks 30 9
Lewis Wych Herefs 46 3
Lewisham Gt Lon 27 3
Lewiston Highld 139 5
Lewknor Oxon 37 7
Leworthy Devon 18 3
Leworthy Devon 19 67
Lewson Street Kent 28 96
Lewth Lancs 80 48
Lewtrenchard Devon 5 45
Lexden Essex 41 96
Lexworthy Somset 20 25
Ley Cnwll 4 17
Ley Hill Bucks 26 9
Leybourne Kent 28 68
Leyburn N York 89 11
Leycett Staffs 72 79
Leygreen Herts 39 16
Leyland Lancs 80 54
Leyland Green Mersyd 78 5
Leylodge Abers 135 76
Leys Abers 143 00
Leys Angus 126 25
Leys of Cossans Angus 126 38
Leysdown-on-Sea Kent 28 03
Leysmill Angus 127 60
Leysters Herefs 46 56
Leyton Gt Lon 27 37
Leytonstone Gt Lon 27 39
Lezant Cnwll 5 34
Lezayre IOM 158 42
Lezerea Cnwll 2 68
Lhanbryde Moray 141 27
Libanus Powys 45 99
Libberton S Lans 108 99
Liberton C Edin 117 27
Lichfield Staffs 61 11
Lickey Worcs 60 99
Lickey End Worcs 60 97
Lickey Rock Worcs 60 97
Lickfold W Susx 14 92
Liddaton Green Devon 5 45
Liddesdale Highld 130 77
Liddington Wilts 36 20
Lidgate Derbys 74 30
Lidgate Suffk 53 72
Lidget S York 75 65
Lidgett Notts 75 63
Lidham Hill E Susx 17 83
Lidlington Beds 38 99
Lidsing Kent 28 78
Liff Angus 126 33
Lifford W Mids 61 05
Lifton Devon 5 38
Liftondown Devon 5 36
Lighthazles W York 82 02
Lighthorne Warwks 48 33
Lighthorne Heath Warwks 48 35
Lightwater Surrey 25 93
Lightwood Staffs 72 92
Lightwood Green Ches 71 63
Lightwood Green Wrexhm 71 38
Lilbourne Nhants 50 56
Lilburn Tower Nthumb 111 02
Lilleshall Shrops 72 73
Lilley Berks 37 44
Lilley Herts 38 11
Lilliesleaf Border 109 53
Lillingstone Dayrell Bucks 49 70
Lillingstone Lovell Bucks 49 71
Lillington Dorset 10 62
Lilliput Dorset 12 04
Lilstock Somset 20 16
Lilyhurst Shrops 60 74
Limbrick Lancs 81 60
Limbury Beds 38 07
Lime Street Worcs 47 81
Limebrook Herefs 46 37
Limefield Gt Man 81 80
Limekilnburn S Lans 116 70
Limekilns Fife 117 08
Limerigg Falk 116 85
Limerstone IOW 13 44
Limestone Brae Nthumb 95 79
Limington Somset 21 54
Limmerhaugh E Ayrs 107 61
Limpenhoe Norfk 67 39
Limpley Stoke Wilts 22 78
Limpsfield Surrey 27 40
Limpsfield Chart Surrey 27 42
Linby Notts 75 53
Linchmere W Susx 14 86
Lincluden D & G 100 96
Lincoln Lincs 76 97
Lincomb Worcs 47 82
Lincombe Devon 7 74
Lindal in Furness Cumb 86 24
Lindale Cumb 87 41
Lindfield W Susx 15 34
Lindford Hants 14 80
Lindley W York 82 12
Lindley Green N York 82 22
Lindow End Ches 79 81
Lindridge Worcs 47 67
Lindsell Essex 40 64
Lindsey Suffk 54 97
Lindsey Tye Suffk 54 98
Liney Somset 21 35
Linford Essex 40 67
Linford Hants 12 18
Lingbob W York 82 09
Lingdale N York 97 67
Lingen Herefs 46 36
Lingfield Surrey 15 38
Lingley Green Ches 78 55
Lingwood Norfk 67 35

ınicro

Llangarron

295

ıicro Highld 136 3966
ıkend Worcs 47 8231
ıkenholt Hants 23 3657
ıkhill Kent 17 8127
ıkinhorne Cnwll 5 3173
ıktown Fife 117 2790
ıkwood Moray 142 2361
ıley Shrops 59 3592
ıley Green Herefs 47 6953
ıleygreen Shrops 60 6898
ılithgow W Loth 117 9977
ıshiels Nthumb 110 8906
ısidemore Highld 146 5499
ıslade Beds 38 9125
ıstead Parva Suffk 152 3377
ıstock Cumb 93 4258
ıthurst Worcs 60 9972
ıthwaite W York 82 1014
ıtlaw Border 119 8258
ıtmill Moray 142 5165
ıton Border 110 7726
ıton Cambs 53 5646
ıton Derbys 73 2716
ıton Herefs 47 6625
ıton Kent 28 7550
ıton N York 88 9962
ıton Nthumb 103 2691
ıton W York 83 3946
ıton Heath Derbys 73 2816
ıton Hill Gloucs 47 6624
ıton-on-Ouse N York 90 4860
ıwood Hants 12 1809
ıwood Lincs 76 1186
ıwood Rens 115 4464
ɔnacleit W Isls 152 7849
ɔnal W Isls 152 5263
ɔns Green E Susx 16 5518
ɔhook Hants 14 8431
ɔley Shrops 72 7330
scard Mersyd 78 2991
scombe Somset 19 8732
skeard Cnwll 5 2564
ss Hants 14 7727
ss Forest Hants 14 7828
ssett E R Yk 91 1458
ssington Lincs 76 1083
ston Essex 54 8544
svane Cardif 33 1883
swerry Newpt 34 3487
tcham Norfk 66 8817
tchard Brdgnd 33 9081
tchborough Nhants 49 6354
tchfield Hants 24 4653
therland Mersyd 78 3397
tlington Cambs 39 3142
tlington E Susx 16 5201
ttle Abington Cambs 53 5349
ttle Addington Nhants 51 9673
ttle Airies D & G 99 4248
ttle Almshoe Herts 39 2026
ttle Alne Warwks 48 1461
ttle Altcar Mersyd 78 3006
ttle Amwell Herts 39 3511
ttle Asby Cumb 87 6909
ttle Aston Staffs 61 0900
ttle Atherfield IOW 13 4679
ttle Ayton N York 90 5610
ttle Baddow Essex 40 7707
ttle Badminton Gloucs 35 8084
ttle Bampton Cumb 93 2755
ttle Bardfield Essex 40 6531
ttle Barford Beds 52 1756
ttle Barningham Norfk 66 1333
ttle Barrington Gloucs 36 2012
ttle Barrow Ches 71 4769
ittle Barugh N York 90 7679
ittle Bavington Nthumb 102 9878
ittle Bayton Warwks 61 3585
ttle Bealings Suffk 55 2247
ittle Bedwyn Wilts 23 2866
ttle Bentley Essex 41 1125
ttle Berkhamsted Herts 39 2907
ttle Billing Nhants 51 8061
ttle Billington Beds 38 9322
ttle Birch Herefs 46 5130
ttle Bispham Lancs 80 3141
ttle Blakenham Suffk 54 1048
ttle Blencow Cumb 93 4532
ttle Bloxwich W Mids 60 0003
ittle Bognor W Susx 14 0020
ittle Bolehill Derbys 73 2954
ittle Bollington Ches 79 7286
ittle Bookham Surrey 26 1254
ittle Bourton Oxon 49 4544
ittle Bowden Leics 50 7487
ittle Bradley Suffk 53 6852
ittle Brampton Herefs 46 3061
ittle Brampton Shrops 59 3681
ittle Braxted Essex 40 8314
ittle Brechin Angus 134 5862
ittle Brickhill Bucks 38 9132
ittle Bridgeford Staffs 72 8727
ittle Brington Nhants 49 6663
ittle Bromley Essex 41 0928
ittle Broughton Cumb 92 0731
ittle Budworth Ches 71 5965
ittle Burstead Essex 40 6692
ittle Bytham Lincs 64 0118
ittle Canfield Essex 40 5821
ittle Carlton Lincs 77 3985
ittle Carlton Notts 75 7757
ittle Casterton Rutlnd 64 0109
ittle Catwick E R Yk 85 1244
ittle Catworth Cambs 51 1072
ittle Cawthorpe Lincs 77 3583
ittle Chalfield Wilts 22 8563
ittle Chalfont Bucks 26 9997
ittle Charlinch Somset 20 2437
ittle Chart Kent 28 9446
ittle Chesterford Essex 39 5141
ittle Cheveney Kent 28 7243
ittle Cheverell Wilts 22 9953
ittle Chishill Cambs 39 4137
ittle Clacton Essex 41 1618
ittle Clanfield Oxon 36 2701
ittle Clifton Cumb 92 0528
ittle Coates Lincs 85 2408
ittle Comberton Worcs 47 9643
Little Common E Susx 17 7107
Little Comp Kent 27 6356
Little Compton Warwks 48 2630
Little Corby Cumb 93 4757
Little Cornard Suffk 54 9039
Little Cowarne Herefs 46 6051
Little Coxwell Oxon 36 2893
Little Crakehall N York 89 2390
Little Cransley Nhants 51 8376
Little Cressingham Norfk 66 8700
Little Crosby Mersyd 78 3201
Little Crosthwaite Cumb 93 2327
Little Cubley Derbys 73 1537
Little Dalby Leics 63 7714
Little Dens Abers 143 0643
Little Dewchurch Herefs 46 5231
Little Ditton Cambs 53 6658
Little Doward Herefs 34 5416
Little Downham Cambs 53 5284
Little Driffield E R Yk 91 0058
Little Dunham Norfk 66 8612
Little Dunkeld P & K 125 0342
Little Dunmow Essex 40 6521
Little Durnford Wilts 23 1234
Little Easton Essex 40 6024
Little Eaton Derbys 62 3641
Little Ellingham Norfk 66 0099
Little Elm Somset 22 7146
Little Everdon Nhants 49 5957
Little Eversden Cambs 52 3753
Little Faringdon Oxon 36 2201
Little Fencote N York 89 2893
Little Fenton N York 83 5235
Little Fransham Norfk 66 9011
Little Gaddesden Herts 38 9913
Little Garway Herefs 46 4424
Little Gidding Cambs 52 1282
Little Glemham Suffk 55 3458
Little Gorsley Herefs 47 6924
Little Gransden Cambs 52 2755
Little Green Notts 63 7243
Little Green Somset 22 7248
Little Grimsby Lincs 77 3291
Little Gringley Notts 75 7380
Little Habton N York 90 7477
Little Hadham Herts 39 4322
Little Hale Lincs 64 1441
Little Hallam Derbys 62 4640
Little Hallingbury Essex 39 5017
Little Hanford Dorset 11 8411
Little Harrowden Nhants 51 8771
Little Haseley Oxon 37 6400
Little Hatfield E R Yk 85 1743
Little Hautbois Norfk 67 2521
Little Haven Pembks 30 8512
Little Hay Staffs 61 1102
Little Hayfield Derbys 74 0388
Little Haywood Staffs 73 0021
Little Heath Berks 24 6573
Little Heath Staffs 72 8917
Little Heath W Mids 61 3482
Little Hereford Herefs 46 5568
Little Hermitage Kent 28 7170
Little Horkesley Essex 40 9532
Little Hormead Herts 39 4028
Little Horsted E Susx 16 4718
Little Horton W York 82 1531
Little Horton Wilts 23 0462
Little Horwood Bucks 38 7930
Little Houghton Nhants 51 8059
Little Houghton S York 83 4205
Little Hucklow Derbys 74 1678
Little Hulton Gt Man 79 7203
Little Hungerford Berks 24 5173
Little Hutton N York 89 4576
Little Ingestre Staffs 72 9824
Little Irchester Nhants 51 9066
Little Kelk E R Yk 91 0959
Little Keyford Somset 22 7746
Little Kimble Bucks 38 8207
Little Kineton Warwks 48 3350
Little Kingshill Bucks 26 8999
Little Knox D & G 100 8060
Little Langdale Cumb 86 3103
Little Langford Wilts 23 0436
Little Lashbrook Devon 18 4007
Little Laver Essex 39 5409
Little Leigh Ches 71 6175
Little Leighs Essex 40 7117
Little Lever Gt Man 79 7507
Little Linford Bucks 38 8444
Little Linton Cambs 53 5547
Little Load Somset 21 4724
Little London Bucks 37 6412
Little London Cambs 65 4196
Little London E Susx 16 5620
Little London Essex 39 4729
Little London Essex 53 6835
Little London Gloucs 35 7018
Little London Hants 23 3749
Little London Hants 24 6259
Little London Lincs 64 2321
Little London Lincs 77 3374
Little London Lincs 65 4323
Little London Norfk 65 5621
Little London Powys 58 0488
Little London W York 82 2039
Little Longstone Derbys 74 1871
Little Madeley Staffs 72 7745
Little Malvern Worcs 47 7640
Little Mancot Flints 71 3266
Little Maplestead Essex 54 8234
Little Marcle Herefs 47 6736
Little Marland Devon 18 5012
Little Marlow Bucks 26 8787
Little Massingham Norfk 65 7824
Little Melton Norfk 66 1607
Little Mill Mons 34 3203
Little Milton Oxon 37 6100
Little Missenden Bucks 26 9299
Little Mongeham Kent 29 3351
Little Moor Somset 21 3232
Little Musgrave Cumb 94 7612
Little Ness Shrops 59 4019
Little Neston Ches 71 2976
Little Newcastle Pembks 30 9829
Little Newsham Dur 96 1217
Little Norton Somset 10 4715
Little Norton Staffs 60 0207
Little Oakley Essex 41 2129
Little Oakley Nhants 51 8985
Little Odell Beds 51 9557
Little Offley Herts 38 1328
Little Onn Staffs 72 8315
Little Ormside Cumb 94 7016
Little Orton Cumb 93 3555
Little Ouse Cambs 53 6288
Little Ouseburn N York 89 4460
Little Oxendon Nhants 50 7283
Little Packington Warwks 61 2184
Little Pattenden Kent 28 7445
Little Paxton Cambs 52 1862
Little Petherick Cnwll 4 9172
Little Plumpton Lancs 80 3832
Little Plumstead Norfk 67 3112
Little Ponton Lincs 63 9232
Little Posbrook Hants 13 5304
Little Potheridge Devon 19 5214
Little Preston Nhants 49 5854
Little Preston W York 83 3930
Little Raveley Cambs 52 2579
Little Reedness E R Yk 84 8022
Little Ribston N York 83 3853
Little Rissington Gloucs 36 1819
Little Rollright Oxon 48 2930
Little Rowsley Derbys 74 2566
Little Ryburgh Norfk 66 9628
Little Ryle Nthumb 111 0111
Little Ryton Shrops 59 4803
Little Salkeld Cumb 94 5636
Little Sampford Essex 40 6533
Little Sandhurst Berks 25 8262
Little Saredon Staffs 60 9407
Little Saughall Ches 71 3768
Little Saxham Suffk 54 8063
Little Scatwell Highld 139 3856
Little Sessay N York 89 4674
Little Shelford Cambs 53 4551
Little Silver Devon 9 8601
Little Silver Devon 9 9109
Little Singleton Lancs 80 3739
Little Skipwith N York 83 6538
Little Smeaton N York 83 5216
Little Snoring Norfk 66 9532
Little Sodbury Gloucs 35 7582
Little Sodbury End Gloucs 35 7483
Little Somborne Hants 23 3832
Little Somerford Wilts 35 9684
Little Soudley Shrops 72 7128
Little Stainforth N York 88 8166
Little Stainton Dur 96 3420
Little Stanney Ches 71 4174
Little Staughton Beds 51 1062
Little Steeping Lincs 77 4362
Little Stonham Suffk 54 1160
Little Stretton Leics 50 6600
Little Stretton Shrops 59 4491
Little Strickland Cumb 94 5619
Little Stukeley Cambs 52 2175
Little Sugnall Staffs 72 8031
Little Sutton Ches 71 3776
Little Sutton Shrops 59 5182
Little Swinburne Nthumb 102 9477
Little Sypland D & G 99 7253
Little Tew Oxon 48 3828
Little Tey Essex 40 8923
Little Thetford Cambs 53 5376
Little Thirkleby N York 89 4778
Little Thornage Norfk 66 0538
Little Thornton Lancs 80 3541
Little Thorpe Dur 96 4242
Little Thurlow Suffk 53 6751
Little Thurlow Green Suffk 53 6851
Little Thurrock Essex 27 6277
Little Torrington Devon 18 4916
Little Totham Essex 40 8811
Little Town Ches 79 6494
Little Town Cumb 93 2319
Little Town Lancs 81 6635
Little Twycross Leics 62 3405
Little Urswick Cumb 86 2673
Little Wakering Essex 40 9388
Little Walden Essex 39 5441
Little Waldingfield Suffk 54 9245
Little Walsingham Norfk 66 9337
Little Waltham Essex 40 7012
Little Warley Essex 40 6090
Little Washbourne Gloucs 47 9833
Little Weighton E R Yk 84 9833
Little Weldon Nhants 51 9289
Little Welnetham Suffk 54 8859
Little Welton Lincs 77 3087
Little Wenham Suffk 54 0839
Little Wenlock Shrops 59 6406
Little Weston Somset 21 6225
Little Whitefield IOW 13 5889
Little Whittington Nthumb 102 9869
Little Wilbraham Cambs 53 5458
Little Witcombe Gloucs 35 9115
Little Witley Worcs 47 7863
Little Wittenham Oxon 37 5693
Little Wolford Warwks 48 2635
Little Woodcote Surrey 27 2861
Little Wratting Suffk 53 6847
Little Wymington Beds 51 9565
Little Wymondley Herts 39 2127
Little Wyrley Staffs 60 0105
Little Wytheford Shrops 59 5619
Little Yeldham Essex 53 7839
Littlebeck N York 90 8804
Littleborough Devon 19 8210
Littleborough Gt Man 81 9316
Littleborough Notts 75 8282
Littlebourne Kent 29 2057
Littlebredy Dorset 10 5889
Littlebury Essex 39 5139
Littlebury Green Essex 39 4838
Littlecott Wilts 23 1352
Littledean Gloucs 35 6713
Littledown Hants 23 3457
Littleham Devon 18 4323
Littleham Devon 9 0381
Littlehampton W Susx 14 0201
Littleharle Tower Nthumb 103 0183
Littlehaven W Susx 15 1832
Littlehempston Devon 7 8162
Littlehoughton Nthumb 111 2216
Littlemill Abers 134 3295
Littlemill Highld 140 9150
Littlemoor Derbys 74 3663
Littlemore Oxon 37 5302
Littleover Derbys 62 3334
Littleport Cambs 53 5686
Littleport Bridge Cambs 53 5787
Littler Ches 71 6366
Littlestone-on-Sea Kent 17 0824
Littlethorpe Leics 50 5496
Littlethorpe N York 89 3269
Littleton Angus 126 3350
Littleton Ches 71 4466
Littleton D & G 99 6355
Littleton Dorset 11 8904
Littleton Hants 24 4532
Littleton Somset 21 4930
Littleton Somset 21 5563
Littleton Surrey 25 9847
Littleton Surrey 26 0668
Littleton Drew Wilts 35 8380
Littleton Pannell Wilts 22 0053
Littleton-on-Severn Gloucs 34 5989
Littletown Dur 96 3343
Littletown IOW 13 5390
Littlewick Green Berks 37 8379
Littlewindsor Dorset 10 4304
Littlewood Staffs 60 9807
Littleworth Bucks 38 8823
Littleworth Oxon 36 3197
Littleworth Staffs 72 9323
Littleworth Staffs 60 0111
Littleworth W Susx 15 1920
Littleworth Worcs 47 8850
Littleworth Worcs 47 9962
Littleworth Common Bucks 26 9386
Littleworth End Cambs 52 2266
Littley Green Essex 40 6917
Litton Derbys 74 1675
Litton N York 88 9074
Litton Somset 21 5954
Litton Cheney Dorset 10 5490
Liurbost W Isls 152 3725
Liverpool Mersyd 78 3490
Liverpool Airport 78 4382
Liversedge W York 82 1923
Liverton Devon 7 8075
Liverton N York 97 7115
Liverton Mines N York 97 7117
Liverton Street Kent 28 8750
Livingston W Loth 117 0668
Livingston Village W Loth 117 0366
Lixton Devon 7 6950
Lixwm Flints 70 1671
Lizard Cnwll 2 7012
Llaingoch IOA 68 2382
Llaithddu Powys 58 0680
Llan Powys 57 8800
Llan-y-pwll Wrexhm 71 3752
Llanaber Gwynd 57 6018
Llanaelhaearn Gwynd 56 3844
Llanafan Cerdgn 43 6872
Llanafan-fechan Powys 45 9750
Llanallgo IOA 68 5085
Llanarmon Gwynd 56 4239
Llanarmon Dyffryn Ceiriog Wrexhm 58 1532
Llanarmon-yn-Ial Denbgs 70 1956
Llanarth Cerdgn 42 4257
Llanarth Mons 34 3710
Llanarthne Carmth 32 5320
Llanasa Flints 70 1081
Llanbabo IOA 68 3787
Llanbadarn Fawr Cerdgn 43 6081
Llanbadarn Fynydd Powys 45 0977
Llanbadarn-y-garreg Powys 45 1148
Llanbadoc Mons 34 3799
Llanbadrig IOA 68 3794
Llanbeder Newpt 34 3890
Llanbedr Gwynd 57 5826
Llanbedr Powys 45 1446
Llanbedr Powys 34 2320
Llanbedr-Dyffryn-Clwyd Denbgs 70 1459
Llanbedr-y-Cennin Conwy 69 7669
Llanbedrgoch IOA 68 5180
Llanbedrog Gwynd 56 3231
Llanberis Gwynd 69 5760
Llanbethery V Glam 20 0369
Llanbister Powys 45 1173
Llanblethian V Glam 33 9873
Llanboidy Carmth 31 2123
Llanbradach Caerph 33 1490
Llanbrynmair Powys 57 8902
Llancadle V Glam 20 0368
Llancarfan V Glam 33 0470
Llancayo Mons 34 3603
Llancillo Herefs 46 3625
Llancloudy Herefs 34 4921
Llancynfelyn Cerdgn 43 6492
Llandaff Cardif 33 1577
Llandanwg Gwynd 57 5728
Llandawke Carmth 31 2811
Llanddanielfab IOA 68 4970
Llanddarog Carmth 32 5016
Llanddeiniol Cerdgn 43 5571
Llanddeiniolen Gwynd 69 5465
Llandderfel Gwynd 58 9837
Llanddeusant Carmth 44 7724
Llanddeusant IOA 68 3485
Llanddew Powys 45 0530
Llanddewi Swans 32 4588
Llanddewi Brefi Cerdgn 44 6655
Llanddewi Rhydderch Mons 34 3512
Llanddewi Velfrey Pembks 31 1415
Llanddewi Ystradenni Powys 45 1068
Llanddewi'r Cwm Powys 45 0348
Llanddoget Conwy 69 8063
Llanddona IOA 69 5779
Llanddowror Carmth 31 2514
Llanddulas Conwy 70 9178
Llanddwywe Gwynd 57 5822
Llanddyfnan IOA 68 5078
Llandecwyn Gwynd 57 6337
Llandefaelog Powys 45 0332
Llandefaelog-Trer-Graig Powys 45 1229
Llandefalle Powys 45 1035
Llandegfan IOA 69 5674
Llandegla Denbgs 70 2051
Llandegley Powys 45 1463
Llandegveth Mons 34 3395
Llandegwning Gwynd 56 2629
Llandeilo Carmth 32 6222
Llandeilo Graban Powys 45 0944
Llandeilo'r Fan Powys 45 8934
Llandeloy Pembks 30 8626
Llandenny Mons 34 4104
Llandevaud Newpt 34 4090
Llandevenny Mons 34 4186
Llandinabo Herefs 46 5128
Llandinam Powys 58 0288
Llandissilio Pembks 31 1221
Llandogo Mons 34 5203
Llandough V Glam 33 9972
Llandough V Glam 33 1673
Llandovery Carmth 44 7634
Llandow V Glam 33 9473
Llandre Carmth 44 6741
Llandre Cerdgn 43 6286
Llandre Isaf Pembks 31 1328
Llandrillo Denbgs 58 0337
Llandrillo-yn-Rhos Conwy 69 8380
Llandrindod Wells Powys 45 0561
Llandrinio Powys 58 2817
Llandudno Conwy 69 7882
Llandudno Junction Conwy 69 7977
Llandudwen Gwynd 56 2736
Llandulas Powys 45 8841
Llandwrog Gwynd 68 4555
Llandybie Carmth 32 6115
Llandyfaelog Carmth 31 4111
Llandyfan Carmth 32 6417
Llandyfriog Cerdgn 31 3341
Llandyfrydog IOA 68 4485
Llandygai Gwynd 69 5971
Llandygwydd Cerdgn 31 2443
Llandynan Denbgs 70 1845
Llandyrnog Denbgs 70 1065
Llandyssil Powys 58 1995
Llandysul Cerdgn 31 4140
Llanedeyrn Cardif 33 2181
Llanedi Carmth 32 5806
Llaneglwys Powys 45 0538
Llanegryn Gwynd 57 6005
Llanegwad Carmth 32 5221
Llaneilian IOA 68 4692
Llanelian-yn-Rhos Conwy 69 8676
Llanelidan Denbgs 70 1050
Llanelieu Powys 45 1834
Llanellen Mons 34 3010
Llanelli Carmth 32 5000
Llanelltyd Gwynd 57 7119
Llanelly Mons 34 2314
Llanelwedd Powys 45 0451
Llanenddwyn Gwynd 57 5823
Llanengan Gwynd 56 2926
Llanerch Gwynd 57 8816
Llanerch Powys 59 3093
Llanerchymedd IOA 68 4184
Llanerfyl Powys 58 0309
Llanfachraeth IOA 68 3182
Llanfachreth Gwynd 57 7522
Llanfaelog IOA 68 3373
Llanfaelrhys Gwynd 56 2026
Llanfaenor Mons 34 4317
Llanfaes IOA 69 6077
Llanfaes Powys 45 0328
Llanfaethlu IOA 68 3186
Llanfair Gwynd 57 5728
Llanfair Caereinion Powys 58 1006
Llanfair Clydogau Cerdgn 44 6251
Llanfair Dyffryn Clwyd Denbgs 70 1355
Llanfair Kilgeddin Mons 34 3506
Llanfair P G IOA 68 5271
Llanfair Talhaiarn Conwy 70 9270
Llanfair Waterdine Shrops 45 2376
Llanfair-is-gaer Gwynd 68 5065
Llanfair-Nant-Gwyn Pembks 31 1637
Llanfair-y-Cwmwd IOA 68 4466
Llanfair-yn-Neubwll IOA 68 3076
Llanfairfechan Conwy 69 6874
Llanfairynghornwy IOA 68 3290
Llanfallteg Carmth 31 1520
Llanfallteg West Carmth 31 1419
Llanfarian Cerdgn 43 5877
Llanfechain Powys 58 1920
Llanfechell IOA 68 3791
Llanferres Denbgs 70 1860
Llanfflewyn IOA 68 3588
Llanfigael IOA 68 3282
Llanfihangel Glyn Myfyr Conwy 70 9849
Llanfihangel Nant Bran Powys 45 9434
Llanfihangel Rhydithon Powys 45 1566
Llanfihangel Rogiet Mons 34 4587
Llanfihangel Tal-y-llyn Powys 45 1128
Llanfihangel yn Nhowyn IOA 68 3277
Llanfihangel-ar-Arth Carmth 31 4540
Llanfihangel-nant-Melan Powys 45 1758
Llanfihangel-uwch-Gwili Carmth 32 4922
Llanfihangel-y-Creuddyn Cerdgn 43 6675
Llanfihangel-y-pennant Gwynd 57 5244
Llanfihangel-y-pennant Gwynd 57 6708
Llanfihangel-y-traethau Gwynd 57 5934
Llanfihangel-yng-Ngwynfa Powys 58 0816
Llanfilo Powys 45 1132
Llanfoist Mons 34 2813
Llanfor Gwynd 58 9336
Llanfrechfa Torfn 34 3293
Llanfrothen Gwynd 57 6241
Llanfrynach Powys 45 0725
Llanfwrog Denbgs 70 1157
Llanfwrog IOA 68 3084
Llanfyllin Powys 58 1419
Llanfynydd Carmth 44 5527
Llanfynydd Flints 70 2856
Llanfyrnach Pembks 31 2231
Llangadfan Powys 58 0110
Llangadog Carmth 31 4207
Llangadog Carmth 44 7028
Llangadwaladr IOA 68 3869
Llangadwaladr Powys 58 1830
Llangaffo IOA 68 4468
Llangain Carmth 31 3815
Llangammarch Wells Powys 45 9346
Llangan V Glam 33 9577
Llangarron Herefs 34 5220

Llangasty-Talyllyn Powys ... 45 1326
Llangathen Carmth ... 32 5822
Llangattock Powys ... 33 2117
Llangattock Lingoed Mons ... 34 3620
Llangattock-Vibon-Avel Mons ... 34 4515
Llangedwyn Powys ... 58 1824
Llangefni IOA ... 68 4675
Llangeinor Brdgnd ... 33 9187
Llangeinwen IOA ... 68 4465
Llangeitho Cerdgn ... 44 6259
Llangeler Carmth ... 31 3739
Llangelynin Gwynd ... 57 5707
Llangendeirne Carmth ... 32 4513
Llangennech Carmth ... 32 5601
Llangennith Swans ... 31 4291
Llangenny Powys ... 34 2417
Llangernyw Conwy ... 69 8767
Llangian Gwynd ... 56 2928
Llangiwg Neath ... 32 7205
Llangloffan Pembks ... 30 9032
Llanglydwen Carmth ... 31 1826
Llangoed IOA ... 69 6079
Llangoedmor Cerdgn ... 42 2046
Llangollen Denbgs ... 70 2141
Llangolman Pembks ... 31 1127
Llangors Powys ... 45 1327
Llangovan Mons ... 34 4505
Llangower Gwynd ... 58 9032
Llangranog Cerdgn ... 42 3154
Llangristiolus IOA ... 68 4373
Llangrove Herefs ... 34 5219
Llangua Mons ... 46 3925
Llangunllo Powys ... 45 2171
Llangunnor Carmth ... 31 4320
Llangurig Powys ... 43 9079
Llangwm Conwy ... 70 9644
Llangwm Mons ... 34 4299
Llangwm Pembks ... 30 9909
Llangwm-isaf Mons ... 34 4300
Llangwnnadl Gwynd ... 56 2033
Llangwyfan Denbgs ... 70 1166
Llangwyllog IOA ... 68 4379
Llangwyryfon Cerdgn ... 43 5970
Llangybi Cerdgn ... 44 6053
Llangybi Gwynd ... 56 4341
Llangybi Mons ... 34 3796
Llangyfelach Swans ... 32 6498
Llangynhafal Denbgs ... 70 1263
Llangynidr Powys ... 33 1519
Llangynin Carmth ... 31 2519
Llangynllo Cerdgn ... 42 3544
Llangynog Carmth ... 31 3314
Llangynog Powys ... 58 0526
Llangynwyd Brdgnd ... 33 8588
Llanhamlach Powys ... 45 0926
Llanharan Rhondd ... 33 0083
Llanharry Rhondd ... 33 0080
Llanhennock Mons ... 34 3592
Llanhilleth Blae G ... 33 2100
Llanidan IOA ... 68 4966
Llanidloes Powys ... 58 9584
Llaniestyn Gwynd ... 56 2733
Llanigon Powys ... 45 2139
Llanilar Cerdgn ... 43 6275
Llanilid Rhondd ... 33 9781
Llanina Cerdgn ... 42 4059
Llanio Cerdgn ... 44 6457
Llanishen Cardif ... 33 1781
Llanishen Mons ... 34 4703
Llanllechid Gwynd ... 69 6268
Llanllieonfel Powys ... 45 9350
Llanllowell Mons ... 34 3998
Llanllugan Powys ... 58 0502
Llanllwch Carmth ... 31 3818
Llanllwchaiarn Powys ... 58 1292
Llanllwni Carmth ... 44 4839
Llanllyfni Gwynd ... 68 4751
Llanmadoc Swans ... 32 4493
Llanmaes V Glam ... 20 9769
Llanmartin Newpt ... 34 3989
Llanmerewig Powys ... 58 1593
Llanmihangel V Glam ... 33 9871
Llanmiloe Carmth ... 31 2408
Llanmorlais Swans ... 32 5294
Llannefydd Conwy ... 70 9870
Llannon Carmth ... 32 5308
Llannor Gwynd ... 56 3537
Llanon Cerdgn ... 42 5166
Llanover Mons ... 34 3109
Llanpumsaint Carmth ... 31 4229
Llanrhaeadr-ym-Mochnant Powys ... 58 1226
Llanrhian Pembks ... 30 8231
Llanrhidian Swans ... 32 4992
Llanrhos Conwy ... 69 7980
Llanrhychwyn Conwy ... 69 7761
Llanrhyddlad IOA ... 68 3389
Llanrhystud Cerdgn ... 43 5369
Llanrothal Herefs ... 34 4718
Llanrug Gwynd ... 69 5363
Llanrumney Cardif ... 34 2280
Llanrwst Conwy ... 69 8061
Llansadurnen Carmth ... 31 2810
Llansadwrn Carmth ... 44 6931
Llansadwrn IOA ... 69 5575
Llansaint Carmth ... 31 3808
Llansamlet Swans ... 32 6897
Llansanffraid
  Glan Conwy Conwy ... 69 8076
Llansannan Conwy ... 70 9365
Llansannor V Glam ... 33 9977
Llansantffraed Powys ... 45 1223
Llansantffraed-
  Cwmdeuddwr Powys ... 45 9667
Llansantffraed-in-Elvel Powys ... 45 0954
Llansantffraid Cerdgn ... 42 5167
Llansantffraid-ym-Mechain Powys ... 58 2220
Llansawel Carmth ... 44 6136
Llansilin Powys ... 58 2128
Llansoy Mons ... 34 4402
Llanspyddid Powys ... 45 0128
Llanstadwell Pembks ... 30 9404
Llansteffan Carmth ... 31 3510
Llanstephan Powys ... 45 1141
Llantarnam Torfn ... 34 3093
Llanteg Pembks ... 31 1810
Llanthewy Skirrid Mons ... 34 3416
Llanthony Mons ... 34 2827

Llantilio Pertholey Mons ... 34 3116
Llantilio-Crossenny Mons ... 34 3914
Llantrisant IOA ... 68 3534
Llantrisant Mons ... 34 3996
Llantrisant Rhondd ... 33 0483
Llantrithyd V Glam ... 33 0472
Llantwit Fardre Rhondd ... 33 0886
Llantwit Major V Glam ... 20 9668
Llantysilio Denbgs ... 70 1943
Llanuwchllyn Gwynd ... 57 8730
Llanvaches Newpt ... 34 4391
Llanvair Discoed Mons ... 34 4492
Llanvapley Mons ... 34 3614
Llanvetherine Mons ... 34 3617
Llanveynoe Herefs ... 46 3031
Llanvihangel Crucorney Mons ... 34 3220
Llanvihangel Gobion Mons ... 34 3409
Llanvihangel-
  Ystern-Llewern Mons ... 34 4313
Llanwarne Herefs ... 46 5027
Llanwddyn Powys ... 58 0219
Llanwenarth Mons ... 34 2714
Llanwenog Cerdgn ... 44 4945
Llanwern Newpt ... 34 3688
Llanwinio Carmth ... 31 2626
Llanwnda Gwynd ... 68 4758
Llanwnda Pembks ... 30 9339
Llanwnnen Cerdgn ... 44 5347
Llanwnog Powys ... 58 0293
Llanwonno Rhondd ... 33 0395
Llanwrda Carmth ... 44 7131
Llanwrin Powys ... 57 7803
Llanwrthwl Powys ... 45 9763
Llanwrtyd Powys ... 45 8647
Llanwrtyd Wells Powys ... 45 8846
Llanwyddelan Powys ... 58 0801
Llanyblodwel Shrops ... 58 2323
Llanybri Carmth ... 31 3312
Llanybydder Carmth ... 44 5244
Llanycefn Pembks ... 31 0923
Llanychaer Bridge Pembks ... 30 9835
Llanycrwys Carmth ... 44 6445
Llanymawddwy Gwynd ... 58 9019
Llanymynech Powys ... 58 2621
Llanynghenedl IOA ... 68 3181
Llanynys Denbgs ... 70 1062
Llanyre Powys ... 45 0462
Llanystumdwy Gwynd ... 56 4738
Llanywern Powys ... 45 1028
Llawhaden Pembks ... 31 0717
Llawnt Shrops ... 58 2430
Llawryglyn Powys ... 58 9291
Llay Wrexhm ... 71 3355
Llechcynfarwy IOA ... 68 3880
Llechfaen Powys ... 45 0828
Llechrhyd Caerph ... 33 1009
Llechryd Cerdgn ... 31 2143
Llechylched IOA ... 68 3476
Lledrod Cerdgn ... 43 6470
Llidiardau Gwynd ... 57 8738
Llidiart-y-parc Denbgs ... 70 1143
Llidiartnenog Carmth ... 44 5437
Llithfaen Gwynd ... 56 3542
Lloc Flints ... 70 1376
Llong Flints ... 70 2662
Llowes Powys ... 45 1941
Llwydcoed Rhondd ... 33 9904
Llwydiarth Powys ... 58 0315
Llwyn Denbgs ... 70 0864
Llwyn-drain Pembks ... 31 2634
Llwyn-du Mons ... 34 2816
Llwyn-on Myr Td ... 33 0111
Llwyn-y-brain Carmth ... 31 1914
Llwyn-y-groes Cerdgn ... 44 5956
Llwyncelyn Cerdgn ... 42 4459
Llwyndafydd Cerdgn ... 42 3755
Llwynderw Powys ... 58 2104
Llwyndyrys Gwynd ... 56 3740
Llwyngwril Gwynd ... 57 5909
Llwynhendy Carmth ... 32 5399
Llwynmawr Wrexhm ... 58 2237
Llwynypia Rhondd ... 33 9993
Llyn-y-pandy Flints ... 70 2065
Llynclys Shrops ... 58 2824
Llynfaes IOA ... 68 4178
Llys-y-fran Pembks ... 30 0424
Llysfaen Conwy ... 69 8977
Llyswen Cerdgn ... 44 4661
Llyswen Powys ... 45 1337
Llysworney V Glam ... 33 9673
Llywel Powys ... 45 8630
Load Brook S York ... 74 2788
Loan Falk ... 117 9675
Loanend Nthumb ... 119 9450
Loanhead Mdloth ... 117 2865
Loaningfoot D & G ... 92 9655
Loans S Ayrs ... 106 3431
Lobb Devon ... 18 4737
Lobhillcross Devon ... 5 4686
Loch Baghasdail W Isls ... 152 7919
Loch Euphort W Isls ... 152 8563
Loch Katrine Pier Stirlg ... 124 4907
Loch Maree Hotel Highld ... 144 9170
Loch nam Madadh W Isls ... 152 9169
Lochailort Highld ... 121 6744
Lochaline Highld ... 121 5945
Lochans D & G ... 98 0656
Locharbriggs D & G ... 100 9980
Lochavich Ag & B ... 122 9415
Lochawe Ag & B ... 123 1227
Lochboisdale W Isls ... 152 7919
Lochbuie Ag & B ... 121 6025
Lochcarron Highld ... 138 8939
Lochdon Ag & B ... 122 7233
Lochdonhead Ag & B ... 122 7233
Lochead Ag & B ... 113 7778
Lochearnhead Stirlg ... 124 5823
Lochee Dund C ... 126 3731
Locheilside Station Highld ... 130 9978
Lochend Highld ... 140 5937
Locheport W Isls ... 152 8563
Lochfoot D & G ... 100 8973
Lochgair Ag & B ... 114 9290
Lochgelly Fife ... 117 1893
Lochgilphead Ag & B ... 113 8686
Lochgoilhead Ag & B ... 114 2001
Lochieheads Fife ... 126 2513
Lochill Moray ... 141 2964

Lochindorb Lodge Highld ... 140 9635
Lochinver Highld ... 145 0922
Lochluichart Highld ... 139 3363
Lochmaben D & G ... 100 0882
Lochmaddy W Isls ... 152 9169
Lochore Fife ... 117 1796
Lochranza N Ayrs ... 105 9350
Lochside Abers ... 135 7364
Lochside D & G ... 100 9577
Lochside Highld ... 140 8152
Lochton S Ayrs ... 98 2579
Lochty Angus ... 134 5362
Lochty Fife ... 127 5208
Lochuisge Highld ... 122 7955
Lochwinnoch Rens ... 115 3559
Lochwood D & G ... 100 0896
Lockengate Cnwll ... 4 0361
Lockerbie D & G ... 100 1381
Lockeridge Wilts ... 23 1467
Lockerley Hants ... 23 3025
Locking Somset ... 21 3659
Locking Stumps Ches ... 79 6491
Lockington E R Yk ... 84 9947
Lockington Leics ... 62 4627
Lockleywood Shrops ... 72 6928
Locks Heath Hants ... 13 5107
Locksbottom Gt Lon ... 27 4265
Locksgreen IOW ... 13 4490
Lockton N York ... 90 8489
Loddington Leics ... 63 7902
Loddington Nhants ... 51 8178
Loddiswell Devon ... 7 7248
Loddon Norfk ... 67 3698
Lode Cambs ... 53 5362
Lode Heath W Mids ... 61 1580
Loders Dorset ... 10 4994
Lodge Green W Mids ... 61 2583
Lodsworth W Susx ... 14 9223
Lofthouse N York ... 89 1073
Lofthouse W York ... 83 3325
Lofthouse Gate W York ... 83 3324
Loftus N York ... 97 7218
Logan E Ayrs ... 107 5820
Loganbeck Cumb ... 86 1890
Logansreen N Loth ... 117 9762
Loggerheads Staffs ... 72 7336
Logie Angus ... 135 6963
Logie Fife ... 126 4020
Logie Moray ... 141 0150
Logie Coldstone Abers ... 134 4304
Logie Pert Angus ... 135 6664
Logierait P & K ... 125 9752
Logierieve Abers ... 143 9127
Login Carmth ... 31 1623
Lolworth Cambs ... 52 3664
Lon-las Swans ... 32 7097
Lonbain Highld ... 137 6852
Londesborough E R Yk ... 84 8645
London Gt Lon ... 27 2879
London Apprentice Cnwll ... 3 0049
London Beach Kent ... 28 8836
London Colney Herts ... 39 1803
London End Nhants ... 51 9265
Londonderry N York ... 89 3087
Londonthorpe Lincs ... 63 9537
Londubh Highld ... 144 8680
Lonemore Highld ... 144 7877
Long Ashton Somset ... 34 5570
Long Bank Worcs ... 60 7674
Long Bennington Lincs ... 63 8344
Long Bredy Dorset ... 10 5690
Long Buckby Nhants ... 50 6367
Long Cause Devon ... 7 7961
Long Clawson Leics ... 63 7227
Long Common Hants ... 13 5014
Long Compton Staffs ... 72 8522
Long Compton Warwks ... 48 2832
Long Crendon Bucks ... 37 6908
Long Crichel Dorset ... 11 9710
Long Ditton Surrey ... 26 1766
Long Drax N York ... 83 6828
Long Duckmanton Derbys ... 75 4471
Long Eaton Derbys ... 62 4833
Long Green Ches ... 71 4770
Long Green Worcs ... 47 8433
Long Hanborough Oxon ... 36 4114
Long Hedges Lincs ... 77 3547
Long Itchington Warwks ... 50 4165
Long Lane Shrops ... 59 6315
Long Lawford Warwks ... 50 4776
Long Load Somset ... 21 4623
Long Marston Herts ... 38 8915
Long Marston N York ... 83 5051
Long Marston Warwks ... 48 1548
Long Marton Cumb ... 94 6624
Long Meadow End Shrops ... 59 4181
Long Melford Suffk ... 54 8645
Long Newnton Gloucs ... 35 9192
Long Newton E Loth ... 118 5164
Long Preston N York ... 88 8358
Long Riston E R Yk ... 85 1242
Long Sight Gt Man ... 79 9206
Long Stratton Norfk ... 67 1992
Long Street Bucks ... 38 7947
Long Sutton Hants ... 24 7347
Long Sutton Lincs ... 65 4322
Long Sutton Somset ... 21 4725
Long Thurlow Suffk ... 54 0068
Long Waste Shrops ... 59 6115
Long Whatton Leics ... 62 4723
Long Wittenham Oxon ... 37 5493
Longbenton T & W ... 103 2668
Longborough Gloucs ... 48 1729
Longbridge W Mids ... 60 0177
Longbridge Warwks ... 48 2762
Longbridge Deverill Wilts ... 22 8640
Longburgh Cumb ... 93 3058
Longburton Dorset ... 11 6412
Longcliffe Derbys ... 73 2255
Longcombe Devon ... 7 8359
Longcot Oxon ... 36 2790
Longcroft Cumb ... 93 2158
Longcross Surrey ... 25 9865
Longden Shrops ... 59 4406
Longden Common Shrops ... 59 4305
Longdon Staffs ... 61 0714
Longdon Worcs ... 47 8336
Longdon Green Staffs ... 61 0813

Longdon Heath Worcs ... 47 8338
Longdon upon Tern Shrops ... 59 6115
Longdown Devon ... 9 8691
Longdowns Cnwll ... 3 7434
Longfield Kent ... 27 6069
Longford Derbys ... 73 2137
Longford Gloucs ... 35 8320
Longford Gt Lon ... 26 0576
Longford Kent ... 27 5156
Longford Shrops ... 72 6434
Longford Shrops ... 72 7218
Longford W Mids ... 61 3583
Longforgan P & K ... 126 2929
Longformacus Border ... 119 6957
Longframlington Nthumb ... 103 1300
Longham Dorset ... 12 0698
Longham Norfk ... 66 9416
Longhaven Abers ... 143 1039
Longhirst Nthumb ... 103 2289
Longhope Gloucs ... 35 6918
Longhope Ork ... 153 3190
Longhorsley Nthumb ... 103 1494
Longhoughton Nthumb ... 111 2415
Longlands Cumb ... 93 2636
Longlane Derbys ... 73 2437
Longleat Safari Park ... 22 8143
Longlevens Gloucs ... 35 8519
Longley W York ... 82 0522
Longley W York ... 82 1406
Longley Green Worcs ... 47 7350
Longleys P & K ... 126 2643
Longmanhill Abers ... 142 7642
Longmoor Camp Hants ... 14 7931
Longmorn Moray ... 141 2358
Longmoss Ches ... 79 8974
Longnewton Border ... 110 5827
Longnewton Dur ... 96 3816
Longney Gloucs ... 35 7612
Longniddry E Loth ... 118 4476
Longnor Shrops ... 59 4800
Longnor Staffs ... 74 0864
Longparish Hants ... 24 4345
Longpark Cumb ... 101 4362
Longridge Lancs ... 81 6037
Longridge Staffs ... 72 9015
Longridge W Loth ... 116 9462
Longriggend N Lans ... 116 8270
Longrock Cnwll ... 2 5031
Longsdon Staffs ... 72 9654
Longshaw Common Gt Man ... 78 5302
Longside Abers ... 143 0347
Longslow Shrops ... 72 6535
Longstanton Cambs ... 52 3966
Longstock Hants ... 23 3537
Longstone Pembks ... 31 1409
Longstowe Cambs ... 52 3054
Longstreet Wilts ... 23 1451
Longthorpe Cambs ... 64 1698
Longthwaite Cumb ... 93 4323
Longton Lancs ... 80 4825
Longton Staffs ... 72 9143
Longtown Cumb ... 101 3768
Longtown Herefs ... 46 3229
Longueville Jersey ... 158 0000
Longville in the Dale Shrops ... 59 5393
Longwick Bucks ... 38 7905
Longwitton Nthumb ... 103 0788
Longwood D & G ... 99 7060
Longwood Shrops ... 59 6007
Longwood House Hants ... 13 5324
Longworth Oxon ... 36 3899
Longyester E Loth ... 118 5465
Lonmay Abers ... 143 0159
Lonmore Highld ... 136 2646
Looe Cnwll ... 5 2553
Loose Kent ... 28 7552
Loosebeare Devon ... 8 7105
Loosegate Lincs ... 64 3125
Loosley Row Bucks ... 37 8100
Lootcherbrae Abers ... 142 6053
Lopcombe Corner Wilts ... 23 2535
Lopen Somset ... 10 4214
Loppington Shrops ... 59 4629
Lorbottle Nthumb ... 111 0306
Lordington W Susx ... 14 7809
Lords Wood Kent ... 28 7762
Lordsbridge Norfk ... 65 5712
Lornty P & K ... 126 1746
Loscoe Derbys ... 62 4247
Loscombe Dorset ... 10 4997
Lossiemouth Moray ... 141 2370
Lost Gardens of Heligan ... 3 9946
Lostford Shrops ... 59 6231
Lostock Gralam Ches ... 79 6974
Lostock Green Ches ... 79 6973
Lostock Hall Lancs ... 81 5425
Lostock Hall Fold Gt Man ... 79 6509
Lostock Junction Gt Man ... 79 6708
Lostwithiel Cnwll ... 4 1059
Lothbeg Highld ... 147 9410
Lothersdale N York ... 82 9545
Lothmore Highld ... 147 9611
Loudwater Bucks ... 26 9090
Loughborough Leics ... 62 5319
Loughor Swans ... 32 5698
Loughton Bucks ... 38 8337
Loughton Essex ... 27 4296
Loughton Shrops ... 59 6182
Lound Lincs ... 64 0618
Lound Notts ... 75 6986
Lound Suffk ... 67 5099
Lounston Devon ... 7 7875
Lount Leics ... 62 3819
Louth Lincs ... 77 3287
Love Clough Lancs ... 81 8127
Lovedean Hants ... 13 6812
Lover Wilts ... 12 2120
Loversall S York ... 75 5798
Loves Green Essex ... 40 6404
Lovesome Hill N York ... 89 3699
Loveston Pembks ... 31 0808
Lovington Somset ... 21 5930
Low Ackworth W York ... 83 4517
Low Angerton Nthumb ... 103 0984
Low Barbeth D & G ... 98 0166
Low Barlings Lincs ... 76 0873
Low Bell End N York ... 90 7197
Low Bentham N York ... 87 6469

Low Biggins Cumb ... 87 60
Low Borrowbridge Cumb ... 87 61
Low Bradfield S York ... 74 26
Low Bradley N Ayrs ... 82 00
Low Braithwaite Cumb ... 93 42
Low Burnham Lincs ... 84 78
Low Buston Nthumb ... 111 22
Low Catton E R Yk ... 84 70
Low Coniscliffe Dur ... 89 25
Low Crosby Cumb ... 93 44
Low Dinsdale Dur ... 89 34
Low Eggborough N York ... 83 56
Low Ellington N York ... 89 20
Low Fell T & W ... 96 25
Low Gartachorrans Stirlg ... 115 46
Low Gate Nthumb ... 102 90
Low Gettbridge Cumb ... 94 52
Low Grantley N York ... 89 23
Low Green N York ... 89 20
Low Habberley Worcs ... 60 80
Low Ham Somset ... 21 43
Low Harrogate N York ... 82 29
Low Hawsker N York ... 91 92
Low Hesket Cumb ... 93 46
Low Hill Worcs ... 60 84
Low Hutton N York ... 90 76
Low Knipe Cumb ... 94 51
Low Laithe N York ... 89 19
Low Langton Lincs ... 76 15
Low Leighton Derbys ... 79 00
Low Lorton Cumb ... 92 15
Low Marnham Notts ... 75 80
Low Middleton Nthumb ... 111 10
Low Mill N York ... 90 67
Low Moor Lancs ... 81 73
Low Moor W York ... 82 16
Low Moorsley T & W ... 96 34
Low Mowthorpe N York ... 91 89
Low Newton Cumb ... 87 40
Low Rogerscales Cumb ... 92 14
Low Row Cumb ... 93 19
Low Row Cumb ... 93 35
Low Row Cumb ... 102 58
Low Row N York ... 88 97
Low Salchrie D & G ... 98 03
Low Santon Lincs ... 84 94
Low Street Essex ... 28 66
Low Street Norfk ... 67 34
Low Tharston Norfk ... 66 18
Low Torry Fife ... 117 01
Low Toynton Lincs ... 77 27
Low Valley S York ... 83 40
Low Walworth Dur ... 96 24
Low Wood Cumb ... 87 34
Low Worsall N York ... 89 39
Low Wray Cumb ... 87 37
Lowbands Gloucs ... 47 77
Lowca Cumb ... 92 98
Lowdham Notts ... 63 66
Lowe Shrops ... 59 49
Lowe Hill Staffs ... 73 99
Lower Aisholt Somset ... 20 20
Lower Ansty Dorset ... 11 76
Lower Apperley Gloucs ... 47 85
Lower Arncott Oxon ... 37 60
Lower Ashton Devon ... 8 84
Lower Assendon Oxon ... 37 74
Lower Ballam Lancs ... 80 36
Lower Barewood Herefs ... 46 39
Lower Bartle Lancs ... 80 49
Lower Beeding W Susx ... 15 21
Lower Benefield Nhants ... 51 99
Lower Bentley Worcs ... 47 98
Lower Beobridge Shrops ... 60 78
Lower Birchwood Derbys ... 75 43
Lower Boddington Nhants ... 49 48
Lower Boscaswell Cnwll ... 2 37
Lower Bourne Surrey ... 25 84
Lower Brailes Warwks ... 48 31
Lower Breakish Highld ... 129 67
Lower Bredbury Gt Man ... 79 91
Lower Broadheath Worcs ... 47 81
Lower Brockhampton Manor ... 47 68
Lower Buckenhill Herefs ... 46 60
Lower Bullingham Herefs ... 46 51
Lower Burgate Hants ... 12 15
Lower Burrowton Devon ... 9 00
Lower Burton Herefs ... 46 42
Lower Caldecote Beds ... 52 17
Lower Cam Gloucs ... 35 74
Lower Canada Somset ... 21 35
Lower Catesby Nhants ... 49 55
Lower Chapel Powys ... 45 02
Lower Chicksgrove Wilts ... 22 97
Lower Chute Wilts ... 23 31
Lower Clapton Gt Lon ... 27 34
Lower Clent Worcs ... 60 92
Lower Clopton Warwks ... 48 17
Lower Creedy Devon ... 8 84
Lower Crossings Derbys ... 74 04
Lower Cumberworth W York ... 82 22
Lower Cwmtwrch Powys ... 32 76
Lower Darwen Lancs ... 81 68
Lower Dean Beds ... 51 05
Lower Denby W York ... 82 23
Lower Diabaig Highld ... 137 79
Lower Dicker E Susx ... 16 55
Lower Dinchope Shrops ... 59 45
Lower Down Shrops ... 59 34
Lower Dunsforth N York ... 89 44
Lower Egleton Herefs ... 47 64
Lower Elkstone Staffs ... 74 06
Lower Ellastone Staffs ... 73 11
Lower End Bucks ... 37 68
Lower End Bucks ... 38 92
Lower End Nhants ... 51 86
Lower Everleigh Wilts ... 23 15
Lower Exbury Hants ... 13 42
Lower Eythorne Kent ... 29 24
Lower Failand Somset ... 34 51
Lower Farringdon Hants ... 24 70
Lower Feltham Gt Lon ... 26 07
Lower Fittleworth W Susx ... 14 01
Lower Foxdale IOM ... 158 27
Lower Frankton Shrops ... 59 37
Lower Freystrop Pembks ... 30 95
Lower Froyle Hants ... 24 75
Lower Gabwell Devon ... 7 91

ower Gledfield

Marley

ver Gledfield Highld 146 5890
ver Godney Somset 21 4742
ver Gornal W Mids 60 9191
ver Gravenhurst Beds 38 1035
ver Green Gt Man 79 7098
ver Green Herts 39 1832
ver Green Herts 39 4233
ver Green Kent 16 5640
ver Green Kent 16 6341
ver Green Nhants 51 8159
ver Green Norfk 66 9837
ver Green Staffs 60 9007
ver Green Suffk 53 7465
ver Hacheston Suffk 55 3156
ver Halliford Surrey 26 0866
ver Halstock Leigh Dorset 10 5207
ver Halstow Kent 28 8567
ver Hamworthy Dorset 11 9990
ver Hardres Kent 29 1553
ver Harpton Herefs 46 2760
ver Hartlip Kent 28 8464
ver Hartshay Derbys 74 3851
ver Hartwell Bucks 38 7912
ver Hatton Staffs 72 8236
ver Hawthwaite Cumb 86 2189
ver Hergest Herefs 46 2755
ver Heyford Oxon 49 4824
ver Heysham Lancs 87 4160
ver Higham Kent 28 7172
ver Holbrook Suffk 54 1834
ver Hordley Shrops 59 3929
ver Horncroft W Susx 14 0017
ver Howsell Worcs 47 7848
ver Irlam Gt Man 79 7193
ver Kilburn Derbys 62 3744
ver Kilcott Gloucs 35 7889
ver Killeyan Ag & B 104 2742
ver Kingcombe Dorset 10 5599
ver Kingswood Surrey 26 2453
ver Kinnerton Ches 71 3462
ver Langford Somset 21 4560
ver Largo Fife 126 4102
ver Leigh Staffs 73 0135
ver Lemington Gloucs 48 2134
ver Llanfadog Powys 45 9567
ver Lovacott Devon 19 5227
ver Loxhore Devon 19 6137
ver Lydbrook Gloucs 34 5916
ver Lye Herefs 46 4066
ver Machen Newpt 34 2288
ver Maes-coed Herefs 46 3430
ver Mannington Dorset 12 0604
ver Marston Somset 22 7644
ver Meend Gloucs 34 5504
ver Merridge Somset 20 2034
ver Middleton
Cheney Nhants 49 5041
ver Milton Somset 21 5347
ver Moor W Mids 47 9747
ver Morton Gloucs 35 6491
ver Nazeing Essex 39 3906
ver Norton Warwks 48 2363
ver Nyland Dorset 22 7521
ver Penarth V Glam 20 1869
ver Penn Staffs 60 8796
ver Pennington Hants 12 3193
ver Penwortham Lancs 80 5327
ver Peover Ches 79 7474
ver Place Gt Man 81 9011
ver Pollicott Bucks 37 7013
ver Pond Street Essex 39 4537
ver Quinton Warwks 48 1847
ver Rainham Kent 28 8167
ver Raydon Suffk 54 0338
ver Roadwater Somset 20 0339
ver Salter Lancs 87 6063
ver Seagry Wilts 35 9580
ver Sheering Essex 39 4914
ver Shelton Beds 38 9942
ver Shiplake Oxon 37 7679
ver Shuckburgh Warwks 49 4862
ver Slaughter Gloucs 36 1622
ver Soothill W York 82 2523
ver Soudley Gloucs 35 6609
ver Standen Kent 29 2340
ver Stanton St Quintin Wilts 35 9180
ver Stoke Kent 28 8375
ver Stone Gloucs 35 6794
ver Stonnall Staffs 61 0803
ver Stow Bedon Norfk 66 9694
ver Street Dorset 11 8399
ver Street E Susx 16 7012
ver Street Norfk 67 2635
ver Street Suffk 53 7852
ver Street Suffk 54 1052
ver Stretton Ches 79 6281
ver Stroud Dorset 10 4598
ver Sundon Beds 38 0526
ver Swanwick Hants 13 4909
ver Swell Gloucs 48 1725
ver Tadmarton Oxon 48 4036
ver Tale Devon 9 0601
ver Tean Staffs 73 0138
ver Thurlton Norfk 67 4299
ver Town Cnwll 2 6528
ver Town Devon 7 7172
ver Town Herefs 47 6342
ver Town Pembks 30 9637
ver Trebullett Cnwll 5 3277
ver Tregantle Cnwll 5 3953
ver Treluswell Cnwll 3 7735
ver Tysoe Warwks 48 3445
ver Ufford Suffk 55 2952
ver Upcott Devon 9 8880
ver Upham Hants 13 5219
ver Upnor Kent 28 7571
ver Vexford Somset 20 1135
ver Walton Ches 78 6086
ver Waterston Dorset 11 7395
ver Weare Somset 21 4053
ver Weedon Nhants 49 6259
ver Welson Herefs 46 2950
ver Westmancote Worcs 47 9337
ver Whatcombe Dorset 11 8401
ver Whatley Somset 22 7447
ver Whitley Ches 71 6179
ver Wick Gloucs 35 7096
ver Wick Worcs 47 8352
Lower Wield Hants 24 6340
Lower Wigginton Herts 38 9409
Lower Willingdon E Susx 16 5803
Lower Withington Ches 79 8169
Lower Woodend Bucks 37 8187
Lower Woodford Wilts 23 1235
Lower Wraxhall Dorset 10 5700
Lower Wyche Worcs 47 7743
Lower Wyke W York 82 1525
Lowerhouse Lancs 81 8032
Lowesby Leics 63 7207
Lowestoft Suffk 67 5493
Loweswater Cumb 92 1421
Lowfield Heath W Susx 15 2739
Lowgill Cumb 87 6297
Lowgill Lancs 87 6564
Lowick Cumb 86 2885
Lowick Nhants 51 9881
Lowick Nthumb 111 0139
Lowick Bridge Cumb 86 2986
Lowick Green Cumb 86 2985
Lowlands Dur 96 1325
Lowlands Torfn 34 2996
Lowsonford Warwks 48 1868
Lowther Cumb 94 5323
Lowther Castle Cumb 94 5223
Lowthorpe E R Yk 91 0860
Lowton Devon 8 6604
Lowton Gt Man 78 6197
Lowton Somset 20 1918
Lowton Common Gt Man 79 6397
Lowton St Mary's Gt Man 79 6397
Loxbeare Devon 9 9116
Loxhill Surrey 25 0038
Loxhore Devon 19 6138
Loxhore Cott Devon 19 6138
Loxley Warwks 48 2553
Loxley Green Staffs 73 0630
Loxter Herefs 47 7140
Loxton Somset 21 3755
Loxwood W Susx 14 0331
Loyal Lodge Highld 149 6146
Lubenham Leics 50 7087
Lucas Green Surrey 25 9460
Lucasgate Lincs 77 4147
Luccombe Somset 20 9243
Luccombe Village IOW 13 5879
Lucker Nthumb 111 1530
Luckett Cnwll 5 3873
Lucking Street Essex 54 8134
Luckington Wilts 35 8383
Lucknam Wilts 35 8272
Luckwell Bridge Somset 20 9038
Lucott Somset 19 8645
Lucton Herefs 46 4364
Lucy Cross N York 89 2112
Ludag W Isls 152 7714
Ludborough Lincs 77 2995
Ludbrook Devon 7 6654
Ludchurch Pembks 31 1411
Luddenden W York 82 0426
Luddenden Foot W York 82 0325
Luddenham Court Kent 28 9963
Luddesdown Kent 28 6666
Luddington Lincs 84 8316
Luddington Warwks 48 1652
Luddington
in the Brook Nhants 51 1083
Ludford Lincs 76 1989
Ludford Shrops 46 5174
Ludgershall Bucks 37 6517
Ludgershall Wilts 23 2650
Ludgvan Cnwll 2 5033
Ludham Norfk 67 3818
Ludlow Shrops 46 5175
Ludney Somset 10 3812
Ludwell Wilts 22 9122
Ludworth Dur 96 3641
Luffenhall Herts 39 2928
Luffincott Devon 5 3394
Luffness E Loth 118 4780
Lugar E Ayrs 107 5921
Lugg Green Herefs 46 4462
Luggate Burn E Loth 118 5974
Luggiebank N Lans 116 7672
Lugsdale Ches 78 5285
Lugton E Ayrs 115 4152
Lugwardine Herefs 46 5540
Luib Highld 137 5627
Lulham Herefs 46 4141
Lullington Derbys 61 2412
Lullington E Susx 16 5202
Lullington Somset 22 7851
Lulsgate Bottom Somset 21 5165
Lulsley Worcs 47 7455
Lulworth Camp Dorset 11 8331
Lumb Lancs 81 8324
Lumb W York 82 0221
Lumbutts W York 82 9523
Lumby N York 83 4830
Lumloch E Duns 116 6370
Lumphanan Abers 134 5804
Lumphinnans Fife 117 1792
Lumsden Abers 142 4722
Lunan Angus 127 6851
Lunanhead Angus 127 4752
Luncarty P & K 125 0929
Lund E R Yk 84 9647
Lund N York 83 6532
Lundie Angus 126 2836
Lundie Stirlg 124 7304
Lundin Links Fife 126 4002
Lundin Mill Fife 126 4102
Lundy Green Norfk 67 2392
Lunna Shet 153 4869
Lunsford Kent 28 6959
Lunsford's Cross E Susx 17 7210
Lunt Mersyd 78 3402
Luntley Herefs 46 3955
Luppitt Devon 9 1606
Lupridge Devon 7 7153
Lupset W York 82 3119
Lupton Cumb 87 5581
Lurgashall W Susx 14 9326
Lurley Devon 9 9215
Lusby Lincs 77 3467
Luscombe Devon 7 7957
Luson Devon 6 6050
Luss Ag & B 115 3692
Lusta Highld 136 2656
Lustleigh Devon 8 7881
Luston Herefs 46 4863
Luthermuir Abers 135 6568
Luthrie Fife 126 3319
Lutley Worcs 60 9382
Luton Beds 38 0921
Luton Devon 9 0802
Luton Devon 9 9076
Luton Kent 28 7766
Luton Airport 38 1220
Lutterworth Leics 50 5484
Lutton Devon 6 5959
Lutton Devon 7 6961
Lutton Lincs 65 4325
Lutton Nhants 52 1187
Luxborough Somset 20 9738
Luxulyan Cnwll 4 0558
Luzley Gt Man 79 9600
Lybster Highld 151 2435
Lydbury North Shrops 59 3486
Lydcott Devon 19 6936
Lydd Kent 17 0420
Lydd Airport 17 0621
Lydden Kent 29 2645
Lydden Kent 29 3567
Lyddington Rutlnd 51 8797
Lyde Green Hants 24 7057
Lydeard St Lawrence Somset 20 1332
Lydeway Wilts 23 0557
Lydford Devon 5 5185
Lydford on Fosse Somset 21 5630
Lydgate Gt Man 82 9516
Lydgate W York 81 9225
Lydham Shrops 59 3391
Lydiard Green Wilts 36 0885
Lydiard Millicent Wilts 36 0986
Lydiard Tregoze Wilts 36 1085
Lydiate Mersyd 78 3604
Lydiate Ash Worcs 60 9775
Lydlinch Dorset 11 7413
Lydney Gloucs 35 6303
Lydstep Pembks 31 0898
Lye W Mids 60 9284
Lye Cross Somset 21 4962
Lye Green Bucks 38 9703
Lye Green E Susx 16 5134
Lye Green Warwks 48 1965
Lye Head Worcs 60 7573
Lye's Green Wilts 22 8146
Lyford Oxon 36 3994
Lymbridge Green Kent 29 1244
Lyme Regis Dorset 10 3492
Lyminge Kent 29 1641
Lymington Hants 12 3295
Lyminster W Susx 14 0204
Lymm Ches 79 6887
Lympne Kent 17 1135
Lympsham Somset 21 3354
Lympstone Devon 9 9984
Lynbridge Devon 19 7248
Lynch Somset 20 9047
Lynch Green Norfk 66 1505
Lynchat Highld 132 7801
Lyndhurst Hants 12 3008
Lyndon Rutlnd 63 9004
Lyndon Green W Mids 61 1485
Lyne Border 109 2041
Lyne Surrey 26 0166
Lyne Down Herefs 47 6431
Lyne of Skene Abers 135 7610
Lyneal Shrops 59 4433
Lyneham Devon 8 8579
Lyneham Oxon 36 2720
Lyneham Wilts 35 0278
Lyneham Airport 35 0178
Lyneholmford Cumb 101 5172
Lynemouth Nthumb 103 2991
Lyness Ork 153 3094
Lyng Norfk 66 0617
Lyng Somset 21 3329
Lynhales Herefs 46 3255
Lynmouth Devon 19 7249
Lynn Shrops 72 7815
Lynn Staffs 61 0704
Lynn of Shenval Moray 141 2129
Lynsted Kent 28 9460
Lynstone Cnwll 18 2005
Lynton Devon 19 7249
Lyon's Gate Dorset 11 6505
Lyonshall Herefs 46 3355
Lytchett Matravers Dorset 11 9495
Lytchett Minster Dorset 11 9693
Lyth Highld 151 2762
Lytham Lancs 80 3627
Lytham St Anne's Lancs 80 3427
Lythbank Shrops 59 4607
Lythe N York 90 8413
Lythmore Highld 150 0566

M

Mabe Burnthouse Cnwll 3 7634
Mabie D & G 100 9570
Mablethorpe Lincs 77 5085
Macclesfield Ches 79 9173
Macduff Abers 142 7064
Macharioch Ag & B 105 7309
Machen Caerph 33 2189
Machrie N Ayrs 105 8934
Machrihanish Ag & B 104 6320
Machrins Ag & B 112 3693
Machynlleth Powys 57 7400
Machynys Carmth 32 5198
Mackworth Derbys 62 3137
Macmerry E Loth 118 4372
Maddaford Devon 8 5494
Madderty P & K 125 9522
Maddington Wilts 23 0744
Maddiston Falk 116 9476
Madehurst W Susx 14 9810
Madeley Shrops 60 6904
Madeley Staffs 72 7744
Madeley Heath Staffs 72 7845
Madford Devon 9 1411
Madingley Cambs 52 3960
Madley Herefs 46 4238
Madresfield Worcs 47 8047
Madron Cnwll 2 4531
Maen-y-groes Cerdgn 42 3858
Maenaddwyn IOA 68 4684
Maenan Conwy 69 7965
Maenclochog Pembks 31 0827
Maendy V Glam 33 0076
Maenporth Cnwll 3 7829
Maentwrog Gwynd 57 6640
Maer Cnwll 18 2008
Maer Staffs 72 7938
Maerdy Carmth 44 6527
Maerdy Rhondd 33 9798
Maes-glas Newpt 34 2985
Maesbrook Shrops 59 3021
Maesbury Shrops 59 3026
Maesbury Marsh Shrops 59 3125
Maesgwynne Carmth 31 2024
Maeshafn Denbgs 70 2061
Maesllyn Cerdgn 42 3644
Maesmynis Powys 45 0146
Maesmynis Powys 45 0350
Maesteg Brdgnd 33 8590
Maesybont Carmth 32 5616
Maesycwmmer Caerph 33 1594
Magdalen Laver Essex 39 5108
Maggieknockater Moray 141 3145
Maggots End Essex 39 4827
Magham Down E Susx 16 6011
Maghull Mersyd 78 3703
Magor Mons 34 4286
Maiden Bradley Wilts 22 8038
Maiden Head Somset 21 5666
Maiden Law Dur 96 1749
Maiden Newton Dorset 10 5997
Maiden Wells Pembks 30 9799
Maidenbower W Susx 15 2935
Maidencombe Devon 7 9268
Maidenhayne Devon 10 2795
Maidenhead Berks 26 8980
Maidens S Ayrs 106 2107
Maidens Green Berks 25 8972
Maidenwell Lincs 77 3179
Maidford Nhants 49 6052
Maids Moreton Bucks 49 7035
Maidstone Kent 28 7555
Maidwell Nhants 50 7476
Maindee Newpt 34 3288
Mains of Balhall Angus 134 5163
Mains of Balnakettle Abers 134 6274
Mains of Dalvey Highld 141 1132
Mains of Haulkerton Abers 135 7172
Mainsforth Dur 96 3131
Mainsriddle D & G 92 9456
Mainstone Shrops 58 2787
Maisemore Gloucs 35 8121
Major's Green Worcs 61 1077
Makeney Derbys 62 3544
Malborough Devon 7 7139
Malcoff Derbys 74 0782
Malden Surrey 26 2166
Malden Rushett Gt Lon 26 1761
Maldon Essex 40 8506
Malham N York 88 9063
Mallaig Highld 129 6796
Mallaigvaig Highld 129 6897
Malleny Mills C Edin 117 1665
Mallows Green Essex 39 4726
Malltraeth IOA 68 4068
Mallwyd Gwynd 57 8612
Malmesbury Wilts 35 9387
Malmsmead Somset 19 7947
Malpas Ches 71 4847
Malpas Cnwll 3 8442
Malpas Newpt 34 3090
Malswick Gloucs 47 7324
Maltby Lincs 77 3183
Maltby N York 89 4613
Maltby S York 75 5392
Maltby le Marsh Lincs 77 4681
Malting Green Essex 41 9720
Maltman's Hill Kent 28 9043
Malton N York 90 7871
Malvern Link Worcs 47 7947
Malvern Wells Worcs 47 7742
Malzie D & G 99 3754
Mamble Worcs 60 6871
Mamhilad Mons 34 3003
Manaccan Cnwll 3 7624
Manafon Powys 58 1102
Manais W Isls 152 1089
Manaton Devon 8 7581
Manby Lincs 77 3986
Mancetter Warwks 61 3296
Manchester Gt Man 79 8497
Manchester Airport 79 8184
Mancot Flints 71 3167
Mandally Highld 131 2900
Manderston House 119 8154
Manea Cambs 53 4789
Maney W Mids 61 1195
Manfield N York 89 2113
Mangerton Dorset 10 4995
Mangotsfield Gloucs 35 6676
Mangrove Green Herts 38 1224
Manhay Cnwll 2 6930
Manish W Isls 152 1089
Mankinholes W York 82 9523
Manley Ches 71 5071
Manmoel Caerph 33 1803
Mannel Ag & B 120 9840
Manning's Heath W Susx 15 2028
Manningford Bohune Wilts 23 1357
Manningford Bruce Wilts 23 1358
Manningham W York 82 1435
Mannington Dorset 12 0605
Manningtree Essex 41 1031
Mannofield Aber C 135 9104
Manor Park Gt Lon 27 4285
Manorbier Pembks 30 0697
Manorbier Newton Pembks 30 0400
Manordeilo Carmth 44 6726
Manorhill Border 110 6632
Manorowen Pembks 30 9336
Mansell Gamage Herefs 46 3944
Mansell Lacy Herefs 46 4245
Mansergh Cumb 87 6082
Mansfield E Ayrs 107 6214
Mansfield Notts 75 5361
Mansfield Woodhouse Notts 75 5363
Mansriggs Cumb 86 2980
Manston Dorset 11 8115
Manston Kent 29 3466
Manston W York 83 3634
Manston Airport 29 3365
Manswood Dorset 11 9708
Manthorpe Lincs 63 9137
Manthorpe Lincs 64 0715
Manton Lincs 84 9302
Manton Notts 75 6078
Manton Rutlnd 63 8704
Manton Wilts 23 1768
Manuden Essex 39 4926
Manwood Green Essex 39 5412
Maperton Somset 22 6726
Maple Cross Herts 26 0393
Maplebeck Notts 75 7060
Mapledurham Oxon 37 6776
Mapledurwell Hants 24 6851
Maplehurst W Susx 15 1824
Maplescombe Kent 27 5664
Mapleton Derbys 73 1647
Mapleton Kent 16 4649
Mapperley Derbys 62 4342
Mapperley Park Notts 62 5842
Mapperton Dorset 10 5099
Mappleborough Green Warwks 48 0866
Mappleton E R Yk 85 2243
Mapplewell S York 83 3210
Mappowder Dorset 11 7306
Marazanvose Cnwll 3 7950
Marazion Cnwll 2 5130
Marbury Ches 71 5645
March Cambs 65 4196
March S Lans 108 9914
Marcham Oxon 37 4596
Marchamley Shrops 59 5929
Marchamley Wood Shrops 59 5831
Marchington Staffs 73 1330
Marchington Woodlands Staffs 73 1128
Marchros Gwynd 56 3125
Marchwiel Wrexhm 71 3547
Marchwood Hants 12 3810
Marcross V Glam 20 9269
Marden Herefs 46 5146
Marden Kent 28 7444
Marden Wilts 23 0857
Marden Ash Essex 27 5502
Marden Beech Kent 28 7442
Marden Thorn Kent 28 7642
Mardens Hill E Susx 16 5032
Mardlebury Herts 39 2618
Mardy Mons 34 3015
Marefield Leics 63 7407
Mareham le Fen Lincs 77 2761
Mareham on the Hill Lincs 77 2867
Marehay Derbys 62 3947
Marehill W Susx 14 0618
Maresfield E Susx 16 4624
Marfleet E R Yk 85 1429
Marford Wrexhm 71 3556
Margam Neath 32 7887
Margaret Marsh Dorset 22 8218
Margaret Roding Essex 40 5912
Margaretting Essex 40 6701
Margaretting Tye Essex 40 6800
Margate Kent 29 3571
Margnaheglish N Ayrs 105 0332
Margrie D & G 99 5950
Margrove Park N York 97 6515
Marham Norfk 65 7009
Marhamchurch Cnwll 18 2203
Marholm Cambs 64 1401
Marian-glas IOA 68 5084
Mariansleigh Devon 19 7422
Marine Town Kent 28 9274
Marionburgh Abers 135 7006
Marishader Highld 136 4963
Maristow Devon 6 4764
Maritime Centre 142 4265
Marjoriebanks D & G 100 0883
Mark Somset 21 3847
Mark Causeway Somset 21 3547
Mark Cross E Susx 16 5010
Mark Cross E Susx 16 5831
Mark's Corner IOW 13 4692
Markbeech Kent 16 4742
Markby Lincs 77 4878
Markeaton Derbys 62 3237
Market Bosworth Leics 62 4002
Market Deeping Lincs 64 1310
Market Drayton Shrops 72 6734
Market Harborough Leics 50 7387
Market Lavington Wilts 22 0154
Market Overton Rutlnd 63 8816
Market Rasen Lincs 76 1089
Market Stainton Lincs 76 2279
Market Weighton E R Yk 84 8741
Market Weston Suffk 54 9877
Markfield Leics 62 4809
Markham Caerph 33 1601
Markham Moor Notts 75 7173
Markinch Fife 126 2901
Markington N York 89 2865
Markle E Loth 118 5777
Marks Tey Essex 40 9023
Marksbury Somset 22 6662
Markwell Cnwll 5 3758
Markyate Herts 38 0616
Marl Bank Worcs 47 7840
Marlborough Wilts 23 1868
Marlbrook Herefs 46 5154
Marlbrook Worcs 60 9774
Marlcliff Warwks 48 0950
Marldon Devon 7 8663
Marle Green E Susx 16 5816
Marlesford Suffk 55 3258
Marley Kent 29 1850
Marley Kent 29 3353

Marley Green
Millh
298

Marley Green *Ches* 71 5845
Marley Hill *T & W* 96 2058
Marlingford *Norfk* 66 1309
Marloes *Pembks* 30 7908
Marlow *Bucks* 26 8486
Marlow *Herefs* 46 4076
Marlow Bottom *Bucks* 26 8488
Marlpit Hill *Kent* 16 4347
Marlpits *E Susx* 16 4528
Marlpits *E Susx* 16 7013
Marlpool *Derbys* 62 4345
Marnhull *Dorset* 22 7818
Marple *Gt Man* 79 9588
Marple Bridge *Gt Man* 79 9688
Marr *S York* 83 5105
Marrick *N York* 88 0798
Marros *Carmth* 31 2008
Marsden *T & W* 103 3964
Marsden *W York* 82 0411
Marsden Height *Lancs* 81 8636
Marsett *N York* 88 9085
Marsh *Bucks* 38 8109
Marsh *Devon* 10 2510
Marsh *W York* 82 0235
Marsh Baldon *Oxon* 37 5699
Marsh Chapel *Lincs* 77 3599
Marsh Gibbon *Bucks* 37 6422
Marsh Green *Devon* 9 0493
Marsh Green *Kent* 16 4344
Marsh Green *Shrops* 59 6014
Marsh Green *Staffs* 72 8858
Marsh Lane *Derbys* 74 4079
Marsh Lane *Gloucs* 34 5807
Marsh Street *Somset* 20 9944
Marshall's Heath *Herts* 39 1614
Marshalswick *Herts* 39 1608
Marsham *Norfk* 67 1923
Marshborough *Kent* 29 3057
Marshbrook *Shrops* 59 4489
Marshfield *Gloucs* 35 7873
Marshfield *Newpt* 34 2582
Marshgate *Cnwll* 4 1592
Marshland Green *Gt Man* 79 6899
Marshland St James *Norfk* 65 5209
Marshside *Mersyd* 80 3619
Marshwood *Dorset* 10 3899
Marske *N York* 89 1000
Marske-by-the-Sea *N York* 97 6322
Marston *Ches* 79 6775
Marston *Herefs* 46 3657
Marston *Lincs* 63 8943
Marston *Oxon* 37 5208
Marston *Staffs* 60 8313
Marston *Staffs* 72 9227
Marston *Warwks* 61 2094
Marston *Wilts* 22 9656
Marston Green *W Mids* 61 1785
Marston Jabbet *Warwks* 61 3788
Marston Magna *Somset* 21 5922
Marston Meysey *Wilts* 36 1297
Marston Montgomery *Derbys* 73 1337
Marston Moretaine *Beds* 38 9941
Marston on Dove *Derbys* 73 2329
Marston St Lawrence *Nhants* 49 5341
Marston Stannett *Herefs* 46 5655
Marston Trussell *Nhants* 50 6985
Marstow *Herefs* 34 5518
Marsworth *Bucks* 38 9114
Marten *Wilts* 23 2860
Marthall *Ches* 79 7975
Martham *Norfk* 67 4518
Martin *Hants* 12 0619
Martin *Kent* 29 3447
Martin *Lincs* 76 1259
Martin *Lincs* 77 2466
Martin Dales *Lincs* 76 1762
Martin Drove End *Hants* 12 0520
Martin Hussingtree *Worcs* 47 8860
Martindale *Cumb* 93 4319
Martinhoe *Devon* 19 6648
Martinscroft *Ches* 79 6589
Martinstown *Dorset* 11 6489
Martlesham *Suffk* 55 2547
Martlesham Heath *Suffk* 55 2445
Martletwy *Pembks* 30 0310
Martley *Worcs* 47 7560
Martock *Somset* 21 4619
Marton *Ches* 71 6267
Marton *Ches* 79 8568
Marton *Cumb* 86 2477
Marton *E R Yk* 85 1739
Marton *E R Yk* 91 2069
Marton *Lincs* 76 8381
Marton *N York* 97 5115
Marton *N York* 89 4162
Marton *N York* 90 7383
Marton *Shrops* 58 2802
Marton *Warwks* 48 4068
Marton-le-Moor *N York* 89 3770
Martyr Worthy *Hants* 24 5132
Martyr's Green *Surrey* 26 0857
Marwick *Ork* 153 2324
Marwood *Devon* 19 5437
Mary Tavy *Devon* 5 5079
Marybank *Highld* 139 4853
Maryburgh *Highld* 139 5456
Maryculter *Abers* 135 8599
Marygold *Border* 119 8159
Maryhill *Abers* 143 8245
Maryhill *C Glas* 115 5669
Marykirk *Abers* 135 6865
Maryland *Mons* 34 5105
Marylebone *Gt Lon* 27 2782
Marylebone *Gt Man* 78 5807
Marypark *Moray* 141 1938
Maryport *Cumb* 92 0336
Maryport *D & G* 98 1434
Marystow *Devon* 5 4382
Maryton *Angus* 127 6856
Marywell *Abers* 134 5895
Marywell *Abers* 135 9399
Marywell *Angus* 127 6544
Masham *N York* 89 2280
Mashbury *Essex* 40 6511
Mason *T & W* 103 2073
Masongill *N York* 87 6675
Mastin Moor *Derbys* 75 4575
Matching *Essex* 39 5212
Matching Green *Essex* 39 5311
Matching Tye *Essex* 39 5111
Matfen *Nthumb* 103 0371
Matfield *Kent* 28 6541
Mathern *Mons* 34 5290
Mathon *Herefs* 47 7346
Mathry *Pembks* 30 8832
Matlask *Norfk* 66 1534
Matlock *Derbys* 74 3059
Matlock Bank *Derbys* 74 3060
Matlock Bath *Derbys* 74 2958
Matlock Dale *Derbys* 74 2959
Matson *Gloucs* 35 8515
Matterdale End *Cumb* 93 3923
Mattersey *Notts* 75 6889
Mattersey Thorpe *Notts* 75 6889
Mattingley *Hants* 24 7357
Mattishall *Norfk* 66 0511
Mattishall Burgh *Norfk* 66 0512
Mauchline *E Ayrs* 107 4927
Maud *Abers* 143 9148
Maufant *Jersey* 158 0000
Maugersbury *Gloucs* 48 2025
Maughold *IOM* 158 4991
Mauld *Highld* 139 4038
Maulden *Beds* 38 0538
Maulds Meaburn *Cumb* 94 6216
Maunby *N York* 89 3586
Maund Bryan *Herefs* 46 5650
Maundown *Somset* 20 0628
Mautby *Norfk* 67 4812
Mavesyn Ridware *Staffs* 73 0816
Mavis Enderby *Lincs* 77 3666
Maw Green *Ches* 72 7057
Maw Green *W Mids* 60 0196
Mawbray *Cumb* 92 0846
Mawdesley *Lancs* 80 4914
Mawdlam *Brdgnd* 32 8081
Mawgan *Cnwll* 2 7025
Mawgan Cross *Cnwll* 2 7024
Mawgan Porth *Cnwll* 4 8567
Mawla *Cnwll* 2 7045
Mawnan *Cnwll* 3 7827
Mawnan Smith *Cnwll* 3 7728
Mawthorpe *Lincs* 77 4672
Maxey *Cambs* 64 1208
Maxstoke *Warwks* 61 2386
Maxsted Street *Kent* 29 1244
Maxton *Border* 110 6130
Maxton *Kent* 29 3041
Maxwell Town *D & G* 100 9676
Maxworthy *Cnwll* 5 2593
May Bank *Staffs* 72 8547
May's Green *Oxon* 37 7480
May's Green *Surrey* 26 0957
Mayals *Swans* 32 6089
Maybole *S Ayrs* 106 2909
Maybury *Surrey* 26 0159
Mayes Green *Surrey* 14 1239
Mayfield *E Susx* 16 5826
Mayfield *Mdloth* 118 3565
Mayfield *Staffs* 73 1545
Mayford *Surrey* 25 9956
Mayland *Essex* 40 9201
Maynard's Green *E Susx* 16 5818
Maypole *Kent* 29 2064
Maypole *Mons* 34 4716
Maypole *W Mids* 61 0778
Maypole Green *Norfk* 67 4195
Maypole Green *Suffk* 54 9159
Maypole Green *Suffk* 55 2767
Mead *Devon* 18 2217
Meadgate *Somset* 22 6758
Meadle *Bucks* 38 8005
Meadowfield *Dur* 96 2439
Meadowtown *Shrops* 59 3001
Meadwell *Devon* 5 4081
Meal Bank *Cumb* 87 5495
Mealrigg *Cumb* 92 1345
Mealsgate *Cumb* 93 2042
Meanwood *W York* 82 2837
Mearbeck *N York* 88 8160
Meare *Somset* 21 4541
Meare Green *Somset* 21 3326
Meare Green *Somset* 20 2922
Mearns *E Rens* 115 5455
Mears Ashby *Nhants* 51 8366
Measham *Leics* 62 3311
Meathop *Cumb* 87 4380
Meaux *E R Yk* 85 0839
Meavy *Devon* 6 5467
Medbourne *Leics* 51 8093
Meddon *Devon* 18 2717
Meden Vale *Notts* 75 5870
Medlam *Lincs* 77 3156
Medlar *Lancs* 80 4135
Medmenham *Berks* 37 8084
Medomsley *Dur* 95 1154
Medstead *Hants* 24 6537
Meer Common *Herefs* 46 3652
Meerbrook *Staffs* 72 9860
Meesden *Herts* 39 4332
Meeson *Shrops* 72 6421
Meeth *Devon* 19 5408
Meeting Green *Suffk* 53 7455
Meeting House Hill *Norfk* 67 3028
Meidrim *Carmth* 31 2920
Meifod *Powys* 58 1513
Meigle *P & K* 126 2844
Meikle Carco *D & G* 107 7813
Meikle Earnock *S Lans* 116 7053
Meikle Kilmory *Ag & B* 114 0560
Meikle Obney *P & K* 125 0337
Meikle Wartle *Abers* 142 7230
Meikleour *P & K* 126 1539
Meinciau *Carmth* 32 4610
Meir *Staffs* 72 9342
Meir Heath *Staffs* 72 9240
Melbourn *Cambs* 39 3844
Melbourne *Derbys* 62 3825
Melbourne *E R Yk* 84 7543
Melbury *Devon* 18 3719
Melbury Abbas *Dorset* 22 8820
Melbury Bubb *Dorset* 10 5906
Melbury Osmond *Dorset* 10 5707
Melbury Sampford *Dorset* 10 5705
Melchbourne *Beds* 51 0265
Melcombe Bingham *Dorset* 11 7602
Meldon *Devon* 8 5692
Meldon *Nthumb* 103 1183
Meldon Park *Nthumb* 103 1085
Meldreth *Cambs* 52 3746
Meldrum *Stirlg* 116 7299
Meledor *Cnwll* 3 9254
Melfort *Ag & B* 122 8313
Melgund Castle *Angus* 127 5455
Meliden *Denbgs* 70 0680
Melin Court *Neath* 33 8201
Melin-byrhedyn *Powys* 57 8198
Melin-y-coed *Conwy* 69 8160
Melin-y-ddol *Powys* 58 0807
Melin-y-wig *Denbgs* 70 0448
Melinau *Pembks* 31 1613
Melkinthorpe *Cumb* 94 5525
Melkridge *Nthumb* 102 7364
Melksham *Wilts* 22 9063
Mell Green *Berks* 37 4577
Mellangoose *Cnwll* 2 6826
Mellguards *Cumb* 93 4445
Melling *Lancs* 87 5970
Melling *Mersyd* 78 3800
Melling Mount *Mersyd* 78 4001
Mellington *Powys* 58 2592
Mellis *Suffk* 54 0974
Mellon Charles *Highld* 144 8491
Mellon Udrigle *Highld* 144 8996
Mellor *Gt Man* 79 9888
Mellor *Lancs* 81 6530
Mellor Brook *Lancs* 81 6431
Mells *Somset* 22 7248
Mells *Suffk* 55 4076
Melmerby *Cumb* 94 6137
Melmerby *N York* 88 0785
Melmerby *N York* 89 3376
Melness *Highld* 149 5861
Melon Green *Suffk* 54 8456
Melplash *Dorset* 10 4898
Melrose *Border* 109 5434
Melsetter *Ork* 153 2689
Melsonby *N York* 89 1908
Meltham *W York* 82 1010
Meltham Mills *W York* 82 1110
Melton *E R Yk* 84 9726
Melton *Suffk* 55 2850
Melton Constable *Norfk* 66 0432
Melton Mowbray *Leics* 63 7518
Melton Ross *Lincs* 84 0610
Meltonby *E R Yk* 84 7952
Melvaig *Highld* 144 7486
Melverley *Shrops* 59 3316
Melverley Green *Shrops* 59 3317
Melvich *Highld* 150 8764
Membury *Devon* 10 2803
Memsie *Abers* 143 9762
Memus *Angus* 134 4358
Menabilly *Cnwll* 3 0951
Menagissey *Cnwll* 2 7146
Menai Bridge *IOA* 69 5571
Mendham *Suffk* 55 2782
Mendlesham *Suffk* 54 1065
Mendlesham Green *Suffk* 54 0963
Menheniot *Cnwll* 5 2863
Menithwood *Worcs* 47 7069
Mennock *D & G* 108 8107
Menston *W York* 82 1643
Menstrie *Clacks* 116 8597
Menthorpe *N York* 84 7034
Mentmore *Bucks* 38 9019
Meoble *Highld* 129 7987
Meole Brace *Shrops* 59 4810
Meonstoke *Hants* 13 6119
Meopham *Kent* 27 6466
Meopham Green *Kent* 27 6465
Meopham Station *Kent* 27 6467
Mepal *Cambs* 53 4481
Meppershall *Beds* 38 1336
Mere *Ches* 79 7281
Mere *Wilts* 22 8132
Mere Brow *Lancs* 80 4218
Mere Green *W Mids* 61 1198
Mere Green *Worcs* 47 9562
Mere Heath *Ches* 79 6670
Mereclough *Lancs* 81 8730
Meresborough *Kent* 28 8264
Mereworth *Kent* 28 6553
Meriden *W Mids* 61 2482
Merkadale *Highld* 136 3931
Merley *Dorset* 12 0297
Merlin's Bridge *Pembks* 30 9414
Merrifield *Devon* 7 8147
Merrington *Shrops* 59 4720
Merrion *Pembks* 30 9397
Merriott *Somset* 10 4412
Merrivale *Devon* 6 5475
Merrow *Surrey* 26 0250
Merry Field Hill *Dorset* 12 0201
Merry Hill *Herts* 26 1394
Merry Lees *Leics* 62 4705
Merryhill *W Mids* 60 8897
Merrymeet *Cnwll* 5 2766
Mersham *Kent* 28 0540
Merstham *Surrey* 27 2853
Merston *W Susx* 14 8902
Merstone *IOW* 13 5285
Merther *Cnwll* 3 8644
Merthyr *Carmth* 31 3520
Merthyr Cynog *Powys* 45 9837
Merthyr Dyfan *V Glam* 20 1168
Merthyr Mawr *Brdgnd* 33 8877
Merthyr Tydfil *Myr Td* 33 0406
Merthyr Vale *Myr Td* 33 0799
Merton *Devon* 19 5212
Merton *Gt Lon* 27 2570
Merton *Norfk* 66 9098
Merton *Oxon* 37 5717
Meshaw *Devon* 19 7619
Messing *Essex* 40 8918
Messingham *Lincs* 84 8904
Metfield *Suffk* 55 2980
Metherell *Cnwll* 5 4069
Metherin *Cnwll* 4 1174
Metheringham *Lincs* 76 0661
Methil *Fife* 118 3799
Methilhill *Fife* 126 3500
Methleigh *Cnwll* 2 6226
Methley *W York* 83 3926
Methley Junction *W York* 83 3925
Methlick *Abers* 143 8537
Methven *P & K* 125 0225
Methwold *Norfk* 65 7394
Methwold Hythe *Norfk* 65 7194
Mettingham *Suffk* 55 3689
Metton *Norfk* 67 2037
Mevagissey *Cnwll* 3 0144
Mexborough *S York* 75 4700
Mey *Highld* 151 2872
Meyllteyrn *Gwynd* 56 2332
Meysey Hampton *Gloucs* 36 1100
Miabhig *W Isls* 152 0834
Miavaig *W Isls* 152 0834
Michaelchurch *Herefs* 46 5225
Michaelchurch Escley *Herefs* 46 3134
Michaelchurch-on-Arrow *Powys* 46 2450
Michaelston-le-Pit *V Glam* 33 1572
Michaelstone-y-Fedw *Newpt* 34 2484
Michaelstow *Cnwll* 4 0778
Michelcombe *Devon* 7 6969
Micheldever *Hants* 24 5139
Micheldever Station *Hants* 24 5143
Michelmersh *Hants* 23 3426
Mickfield *Suffk* 54 1361
Mickle Trafford *Ches* 71 4469
Micklebring *S York* 75 5194
Mickleby *N York* 90 8012
Micklefield *W York* 83 4432
Micklefield Green *Herts* 26 0498
Mickleham *Surrey* 26 1653
Mickleover *Derbys* 73 3033
Micklethwaite *Cumb* 93 2850
Micklethwaite *W York* 82 1041
Mickleton *Dur* 95 9623
Mickleton *Gloucs* 48 1643
Mickletown *W York* 83 4027
Mickley *Derbys* 74 3279
Mickley *N York* 89 2576
Mickley Green *Suffk* 54 8457
Mickley Square *Nthumb* 103 0762
Mid Ardlaw *Abers* 143 9463
Mid Beltie *Abers* 134 6200
Mid Bockhampton *Hants* 12 1796
Mid Calder *W Loth* 117 0767
Mid Clyth *Highld* 151 2937
Mid Holmwood *Surrey* 15 1646
Mid Lavant *W Susx* 14 8508
Mid Mains *Highld* 139 4239
Mid Thorpe *Lincs* 77 2672
Mid Yell *Shet* 153 5190
Midbea *Ork* 153 4444
Middle Assendon *Oxon* 37 7385
Middle Aston *Oxon* 49 4726
Middle Barton *Oxon* 49 4325
Middle Chinnock *Somset* 10 4713
Middle Claydon *Bucks* 49 7225
Middle Duntisbourne *Gloucs* 35 9806
Middle Handley *Derbys* 74 4077
Middle Harling *Norfk* 54 9885
Middle Kames *Ag & B* 114 9189
Middle Littleton *Worcs* 48 0847
Middle Madeley *Staffs* 72 7745
Middle Maes-coed *Herefs* 46 3333
Middle Mayfield *Staffs* 73 1444
Middle Mill *Pembks* 30 8026
Middle Quarter *Kent* 28 8938
Middle Rasen *Lincs* 76 0889
Middle Rocombe *Devon* 7 9069
Middle Salter *Lancs* 87 6062
Middle Stoford *Somset* 20 1821
Middle Stoke *Kent* 28 8275
Middle Stoughton *Somset* 21 4249
Middle Street *Gloucs* 35 7704
Middle Taphouse *Cnwll* 4 1763
Middle Town *IOS* 2 8808
Middle Tysoe *Warwks* 48 3444
Middle Wallop *Hants* 23 2937
Middle Winterslow *Wilts* 23 2333
Middle Woodford *Wilts* 23 1136
Middle Yard *Gloucs* 35 8203
Middlebie *D & G* 101 2176
Middlebridge *P & K* 132 8866
Middlecliffe *S York* 83 4305
Middlecott *Devon* 8 7186
Middleham *N York* 89 1287
Middlehill *Cnwll* 5 2869
Middlehill *Wilts* 22 8168
Middlehope *Shrops* 59 4988
Middlemarsh *Dorset* 11 6707
Middlemore *Devon* 6 4973
Middlesbrough *N York* 97 4919
Middlesceugh *Cumb* 93 4041
Middleshaw *Cumb* 87 5588
Middlesmoor *N York* 89 0973
Middlestone *Dur* 96 2531
Middlestone Moor *Dur* 96 2432
Middlestown *W York* 82 2617
Middlethird *Border* 110 6843
Middleton *Ag & B* 120 9443
Middleton *Cumb* 87 6285
Middleton *Derbys* 74 1963
Middleton *Derbys* 73 2755
Middleton *Essex* 54 8639
Middleton *Gt Man* 79 8705
Middleton *Hants* 24 4244
Middleton *Herefs* 46 5469
Middleton *Lancs* 87 4258
Middleton *N Ayrs* 115 3952
Middleton *N York* 82 1249
Middleton *N York* 90 7885
Middleton *Nhants* 51 8489
Middleton *Norfk* 65 6616
Middleton *Nthumb* 111 1035
Middleton *Nthumb* 103 0584
Middleton *P & K* 126 1206
Middleton *Shrops* 59 3129
Middleton *Shrops* 46 5477
Middleton *Suffk* 55 4267
Middleton *Swans* 31 4287
Middleton *W York* 82 3028
Middleton *Warwks* 61 1798
Middleton Cheney *Nhants* 49 4941
Middleton Green *Staffs* 73 9935
Middleton Hall *Nthumb* 111 9825
Middleton Moor *Suffk* 55 4167
Middleton on the Hill *Herefs* 46 5364
Middleton on the Wolds *E R Yk* 84 9449
Middleton One Row *Dur* 89 3
Middleton Priors *Shrops* 59 6
Middleton Quernhow *N York* 89 3
Middleton Scriven *Shrops* 60 6
Middleton St George *Dur* 89 3
Middleton Stoney *Oxon* 49 5
Middleton Tyas *N York* 89 2
Middleton-in-Teesdale *Dur* 95 9
Middleton-on-Leven *N York* 89 4
Middleton-on-Sea *W Susx* 14 9
Middletown *Cumb* 86 9
Middletown *Powys* 59 3
Middletown *Somset* 34 4
Middlewich *Ches* 72 7
Middlewood *Cnwll* 5 2
Middlewood *Herefs* 46 2
Middlewood Green *Suffk* 54 0
Middleyard *E Ayrs* 107 5
Middlezoy *Somset* 21 3
Middridge *Dur* 96 2
Midford *Somset* 22 7
Midge Hall *Lancs* 80 5
Midgeholme *Cumb* 94 6
Midgham *Berks* 24 5
Midgley *W York* 82 0
Midgley *W York* 82 2
Midhopestones *S York* 74 2
Midhurst *W Susx* 14 8
Midlem *Border* 109 5
Midney *Somset* 21 4
Midpark *Ag & B* 114 0
Midsomer Norton *Somset* 22 6
Midtown *Highld* 149 5
Midville *Lincs* 77 3
Midway *Ches* 79 9
Migvie *Abers* 134 4
Milborne Port *Somset* 22 6
Milborne St Andrew *Dorset* 11 8
Milborne Wick *Somset* 22 6
Milbourne *Nthumb* 103 1
Milbourne *Wilts* 35 9
Milburn *Cumb* 94 6
Milbury Heath *Gloucs* 35 6
Milby *N York* 89 4
Milcombe *Oxon* 49 4
Milden *Suffk* 54 9
Mildenhall *Suffk* 53 7
Mildenhall *Wilts* 36 2
Mile Elm *Wilts* 35 9
Mile End *Essex* 41 9
Mile End *Gloucs* 34 5
Mile End *Suffk* 55 3
Mile Oak *E Susx* 15 2
Mile Oak *Kent* 28 6
Mile Oak *Staffs* 61 1
Mile Town *Kent* 28 9
Milebrook *Powys* 46 3
Milebush *Kent* 28 7
Mileham *Norfk* 66 9
Miles Hope *Herefs* 46 5
Miles Platting *Gt Man* 79 8
Milesmark *Fife* 117 0
Milfield *Nthumb* 110 9
Milford *Derbys* 62 3
Milford *Devon* 18 2
Milford *Powys* 58 0
Milford *Staffs* 72 9
Milford *Surrey* 25 9
Milford Haven *Pembks* 30 9
Milford on Sea *Hants* 12 2
Milkwall *Gloucs* 34 5
Mill Bank *W York* 82 0
Mill Brow *Gt Man* 79 9
Mill Common *Norfk* 67 3
Mill Common *Suffk* 55 4
Mill Cross *Devon* 7 7
Mill End *Bucks* 37 7
Mill End *Cambs* 52 3
Mill End *Herts* 39 3
Mill Green *Cambs* 53 6
Mill Green *Essex* 40 6
Mill Green *Herts* 39 2
Mill Green *Lincs* 64 2
Mill Green *Norfk* 54 1
Mill Green *Staffs* 73 0
Mill Green *Suffk* 54 9
Mill Green *Suffk* 54 9
Mill Green *Suffk* 54 1
Mill Green *Suffk* 55 3
Mill Green *W Mids* 61 0
Mill Hill *E Susx* 16 6
Mill Hill *Gt Lon* 26 2
Mill Meece *Staffs* 72 8
Mill of Drummond *P & K* 125 8
Mill of Haldane *W Duns* 115 3
Mill Side *Cumb* 87 4
Mill Street *Kent* 28 6
Mill Street *Norfk* 66 0
Mill Street *Norfk* 66 0
Mill Street *Suffk* 54 0
Millais *Jersey* 158 0
Milland *W Susx* 14 8
Milland Marsh *W Susx* 14 8
Millbeck *Cumb* 93 2
Millbreck *Abers* 143 0
Millbrex *Abers* 143 8
Millbridge *Surrey* 25 8
Millbrook *Beds* 38 0
Millbrook *Cnwll* 6 4
Millbrook *Gt Man* 79 9
Millbrook *Hants* 12 3
Millbrook *Jersey* 158 0
Millbuie *Abers* 135 7
Millburn *S Ayrs* 107 4
Millcombe *Devon* 7 8
Millcorner *E Susx* 17 8
Millcraig *Highld* 146 6
Milldale *Staffs* 73 1
Millend *Gloucs* 34 5
Millend *Gloucs* 35 7
Miller's Dale *Derbys* 74 1
Miller's Green *Essex* 40 5
Millerhill *Mdloth* 118 3
Millers Green *Derbys* 73 2
Millerston *N Lans* 116 6
Millgate *Lancs* 81 8
Millgreen *Shrops* 72 6
Millhalf *Herefs* 46 2

hayes *Devon*	9	2303
head *Lancs*	87	4971
heugh *S Lans*	116	7450
house Ag & B	114	9570
house *Cumb*	93	3637
house Green *S York*	82	2203
housebridge *D & G*	100	1085
houses *S York*	83	4204
houses *S York*	74	3484
iken Park *Rens*	115	4162
in Cross *Pembks*	30	9914
ington *E R Yk*	84	8351
ness *Cumb*	87	5382
om *Cumb*	86	1780
ook *Cnwll*	18	1899
pool *Cnwll*	2	5730
pool *Cnwll*	4	1170
port *N Ayrs*	114	1654
thorpe *Derbys*	74	3167
throp *Cumb*	87	6591
timber *Aber C*	135	8501
town *Abers*	133	2609
town *Abers*	142	4716
town *Cnwll*	4	1057
town *D & G*	101	3375
town *Derbys*	74	3561
town *Devon*	19	5538
town of Campfield *Abers*	135	6500
town of Edinvillie *Moray*	141	2640
town of Learney *Abers*	134	6303
nathort *P & K*	126	1204
ngavie *W Duns*	115	5574
rrow *Gt Man*	81	9212
nthorpe *Cumb*	87	4981
nthorpe *W York*	83	3317
ovaig *Highld*	136	1549
son *Shrops*	47	6472
stead *Kent*	28	9058
ston *Wilts*	23	1645
thorpe *Lincs*	64	1130
thorpe *Nhants*	49	5946
ton *Cambs*	53	4762
ton *Cnwll*	101	5560
ton *D & G*	98	2154
ton *D & G*	100	8470
ton *Derbys*	62	3126
ton *Highld*	151	3451
ton *Highld*	137	7043
ton *Highld*	139	4930
ton *Highld*	139	5749
ton *Highld*	147	7674
ton *Inver*	115	3569
ton *Kent*	28	6674
ton *Moray*	142	5163
ton *Newpt*	34	3688
ton *Notts*	75	7173
ton *Oxon*	49	4535
ton *Oxon*	37	4892
ton *P & K*	133	1357
ton *Pembks*	30	0403
ton *Somset*	21	3462
ton *Somset*	21	4621
ton *Staffs*	72	9050
ton *Stirlg*	115	5001
ton *W Duns*	115	4274
ton Abbas *Dorset*	11	8002
ton Abbot *Devon*	5	4079
ton Bridge *Mdloth*	117	2562
ton Bryan *Beds*	38	9730
ton Clevedon *Somset*	22	6637
ton Combe *Devon*	6	4866
ton Common *Oxon*	37	6503
ton Damerel *Devon*	18	3810
ton End *Gloucs*	35	7110
ton End *Gloucs*	36	1400
ton Ernest *Beds*	51	0156
ton Green *Ches*	71	4658
ton Hill *Oxon*	37	4790
ton Keynes *Bucks*	38	8537
ton Lilbourne *Wilts*	23	1960
ton Malsor *Nhants*	49	7355
ton Morenish *P & K*	124	6135
ton of Auchinhove *Abers*	134	5503
ton of Balgonie *Fife*	118	3200
ton of Buchanan *Stirlg*	115	4490
ton of Campsie *E Duns*	116	6576
ton of Leys *Highld*	140	6942
ton of Tullich *Abers*	134	3897
ton on Stour *Dorset*	22	7928
ton Regis *Kent*	28	9064
ton Street *E Susx*	16	5304
ton-under-Wychwood *Oxon*	36	2618
verton *Somset*	20	1225
verton *Warwks*	48	3166
wich *Staffs*	72	9632
wr *Flints*	70	1974
rard *Ag & B*	114	9796
nchington *Dorset*	11	9614
nchinhampton *Gloucs*	35	8700
drum *Nthumb*	110	8432
drum Mill *Nthumb*	110	8533
nehead *Somset*	20	9646
nera *Wrexhm*	70	2751
afford *Gwynd*	57	5938
ngarryhard *Highld*	129	6869
ningsby *Lincs*	77	3264
nions *Cnwll*	5	2671
nishant *S Ayrs*	106	3314
allyn *Gwynd*	57	8514
nnigaff *D & G*	99	4166
nnis Bay *Kent*	29	2869
nonie *Abers*	142	7760
nskip *N York*	89	3864
nstead *Hants*	12	2811
nstead *W Susx*	14	8520
ster *Kent*	28	9573
ster *Kent*	29	3064
ster Lovell *Oxon*	36	3111
steracres *Nthumb*	95	0156
sterley *Shrops*	59	3705
sterworth *Gloucs*	35	7817
nterne Magna *Dorset*	11	6504
nterne Parva *Dorset*	11	6603
nting *Lincs*	76	1873
ntlaw *Abers*	143	9948
to Border	109	5620
ton *Shrops*	59	4390

Minwear *Pembks*	30	0413
Minworth *W Mids*	61	1691
Mirehouse *Cumb*	92	9715
Mirfield *W York*	82	2019
Miserden *Gloucs*	35	9308
Miskin *Rhondd*	33	0480
Miskin *Rhondd*	33	0498
Misson *Notts*	75	6895
Misterton *Leics*	50	5583
Misterton *Notts*	75	7694
Misterton *Somset*	10	4508
Mistley *Essex*	41	1231
Mistley Heath *Essex*	41	1230
Mitcham *Gt Lon*	27	2768
Mitchel Troy *Mons*	34	4910
Mitcheldean *Gloucs*	35	6618
Mitchell *Cnwll*	3	8554
Mitchellslacks *D & G*	100	9696
Mitford *Nthumb*	103	1786
Mithian *Cnwll*	3	7450
Mitton *Staffs*	72	8815
Mixbury *Oxon*	49	6033
Mixenden *W York*	82	0629
Mixon *Staffs*	74	0457
Moats Tye *Suffk*	54	0455
Mobberley *Ches*	79	7879
Mobberley *Staffs*	73	0041
Moccas *Herefs*	46	3542
Mochdre *Conwy*	69	8278
Mochdre *Powys*	58	0788
Mochrum *D & G*	98	3446
Mockbeggar *Hants*	12	1609
Mockbeggar *Kent*	28	7146
Mockerkin *Cumb*	92	0923
Modbury *Devon*	7	6651
Moddershall *Staffs*	72	9236
Moel Tryfan *Gwynd*	68	5156
Moelfre *IOA*	68	5186
Moelfre *Powys*	58	1828
Moffat *D & G*	108	0805
Mogerhanger *Beds*	52	1449
Moira *Leics*	62	3115
Mol-chlach *Highld*	128	4513
Molash *Kent*	28	0251
Mold *Flints*	70	2363
Moldgreen *W York*	82	1516
Molehill Green *Essex*	40	5624
Molehill Green *Essex*	40	7120
Molescroft *E R Yk*	84	0140
Molesden *Nthumb*	103	1484
Molesworth *Cambs*	51	0775
Molland *Devon*	19	8028
Mollington *Ches*	71	3870
Mollington *Oxon*	49	4447
Mollinsburn *N Lans*	116	7171
Monachty *Cerdgn*	44	5061
Monday Boys *Kent*	28	9045
Mondynes *Abers*	135	7779
Monewden *Suffk*	55	2358
Moneydie *P & K*	125	0629
Moneyrow Green *Berks*	26	8977
Moniaive *D & G*	107	7890
Monifieth *Angus*	127	4932
Monikie *Angus*	127	4938
Monimail *Fife*	126	2914
Monington *Pembks*	42	1344
Monk Bretton *S York*	83	3607
Monk Fryston *S York*	83	5029
Monk Sherborne *Hants*	24	6056
Monk Soham *Suffk*	55	2165
Monk Soham Green *Suffk*	55	2066
Monk Street *Essex*	40	6128
Monk's Gate *W Susx*	15	2027
Monken Hadley *Gt Lon*	26	2497
Monkhide *Herefs*	46	6144
Monkhill *Cumb*	93	3458
Monkhopton *Shrops*	59	6293
Monkland *Herefs*	46	4557
Monkleigh *Devon*	18	4520
Monknash *V Glam*	33	9170
Monkokehampton *Devon*	8	5805
Monks Eleigh *Suffk*	54	9647
Monks Heath *Ches*	79	8474
Monks Horton *Kent*	29	1139
Monks Kirby *Warwks*	50	4683
Monks Risborough *Bucks*	38	8104
Monkseaton *T & W*	103	3472
Monksilver *Somset*	20	0737
Monkspath *W Mids*	61	1376
Monksthorpe *Lincs*	77	4465
Monkswood *Mons*	34	3402
Monkton *Devon*	9	1803
Monkton *Kent*	29	2964
Monkton *S Ayrs*	106	3527
Monkton *T & W*	103	3363
Monkton *V Glam*	33	9270
Monkton Combe *Somset*	22	7762
Monkton Deverill *Wilts*	22	8537
Monkton Farleigh *Wilts*	22	8065
Monkton Heathfield *Somset*	20	2526
Monkton Up Wimborne *Dorset*	11	0113
Monkton Wyld *Dorset*	10	3396
Monkwearmouth *T & W*	96	3958
Monkwood *Hants*	24	6630
Monmore Green *W Mids*	60	9297
Monmouth *Mons*	34	5012
Monnington on Wye *Herefs*	46	3743
Monreith *D & G*	98	3541
Mont Saint *Guern*	158	0000
Montacute *Somset*	10	4916
Montcliffe *Gt Man*	81	6611
Montford *Shrops*	59	4114
Montford Bridge *Shrops*	59	4215
Montgarrie *Abers*	142	5717
Montgarswood *E Ayrs*	107	5227
Montgomery *Powys*	58	2296
Montgreenan *N Ayrs*	106	3343
Monton *Gt Man*	79	7699
Montrose *Angus*	135	7157
Monxton *Hants*	23	3144
Monyash *Derbys*	74	1566
Monymusk *Abers*	142	6815
Monzie *P & K*	125	8725
Moodiesburn *N Lans*	116	6906
Moonzie *Fife*	126	3317
Moor Allerton *W York*	82	3038
Moor Crichel *Dorset*	11	9908
Moor End *Beds*	38	9719

Moor End *Devon*	19	6609
Moor End *E R Yk*	84	8137
Moor End *Lancs*	80	3744
Moor End *N York*	83	6038
Moor End *W York*	82	0528
Moor Green *Herts*	39	3226
Moor Head *W York*	82	2329
Moor Monkton *N York*	83	5156
Moor Row *Cumb*	92	0014
Moor Row *Cumb*	93	2149
Moor Row *Dur*	96	1515
Moor Side *Lancs*	80	4935
Moor Side *Lancs*	80	4334
Moor Side *Lincs*	77	2557
Moor Street *Kent*	28	8265
Moor Street *W Mids*	60	9982
Moorbath *Dorset*	10	4395
Moorby *Lincs*	77	2964
Moorcot *Herefs*	46	3555
Moordown *Dorset*	12	0994
Moore *Ches*	78	5784
Moorend *Gloucs*	35	7303
Moorends *S York*	83	6915
Moorgreen *Hants*	13	4815
Moorgreen *Notts*	62	4847
Moorhall *Derbys*	74	3074
Moorhampton *Herefs*	46	3746
Moorhead *W York*	82	1337
Moorhouse *Cumb*	93	2551
Moorhouse *Cumb*	93	3356
Moorhouse *Notts*	75	7566
Moorhouse *W York*	83	4810
Moorhouse Bank *Surrey*	27	4353
Moorland *Somset*	21	3332
Moorlinch *Somset*	21	3936
Moorsholm *N York*	90	6814
Moorside *Cumb*	86	0701
Moorside *Dorset*	22	7919
Moorside *Gt Man*	79	9407
Moorside *W York*	82	2436
Moorstock *Kent*	29	1038
Moorswater *Cnwll*	5	2364
Moorthorpe *W York*	83	4611
Morangie *Highld*	147	7683
Morar *Highld*	129	6793
Morborne *Cambs*	64	1391
Morchard Bishop *Devon*	8	7707
Morcombelake *Dorset*	10	4094
Morcott *Rutlnd*	51	9200
Morda *Shrops*	58	2827
Morden *Dorset*	11	9195
Morden *Gt Lon*	27	2666
Mordiford *Herefs*	46	5737
Mordon *Dur*	96	3226
More *Shrops*	59	3491
Morebath *Devon*	20	9525
Morebattle *Border*	110	7724
Morecambe *Lancs*	87	4364
Moredon *Wilts*	36	1487
Morefield *Highld*	145	1195
Morehall *Kent*	29	2136
Moreleigh *Devon*	7	7652
Morenish *P & K*	124	6035
Moresby *Cumb*	92	9921
Moresby Parks *Cumb*	92	9919
Morestead *Hants*	13	5025
Moreton *Dorset*	11	8094
Moreton *Essex*	39	5307
Moreton *Herefs*	46	5064
Moreton *Mersyd*	78	2689
Moreton *Oxon*	37	6904
Moreton *Staffs*	72	7817
Moreton *Staffs*	73	1429
Moreton Corbet *Shrops*	59	5623
Moreton Jeffries *Herefs*	46	6048
Moreton Morrell *Warwks*	48	3155
Moreton on Lugg *Herefs*	46	5045
Moreton Paddox *Warwks*	48	3154
Moreton Pinkney *Nhants*	49	5749
Moreton Say *Shrops*	59	6334
Moreton Valence *Gloucs*	35	7809
Moreton-in-Marsh *Gloucs*	48	2032
Moretonhampstead *Devon*	8	7586
Moretonmill *Shrops*	59	5723
Morfa *Cerdgn*	42	3053
Morfa Bychan *Gwynd*	57	5437
Morfa Dinlle *Gwynd*	68	4358
Morfa Glas *Neath*	33	8606
Morfa Nefyn *Gwynd*	56	2840
Morgan's Vale *Wilts*	12	1920
Morganstown *Cardif*	33	1281
Morham *E Loth*	118	5571
Moriah *Cerdgn*	43	6279
Morland *Cumb*	94	6022
Morley *Ches*	79	8282
Morley *Derbys*	62	3940
Morley *Dur*	96	1227
Morley *W York*	82	2627
Morley Green *Ches*	79	8281
Morley St Botolph *Norfk*	66	0799
Mornick *Cnwll*	5	3272
Morningside *C Edin*	117	2470
Morningside *N Lans*	116	8355
Morningthorpe *Norfk*	67	2192
Morpeth *Nthumb*	103	1986
Morphie *Abers*	135	7164
Morrey *Staffs*	73	1218
Morridge Side *Staffs*	73	0254
Morridge Top *Staffs*	74	0365
Morriston *Swans*	32	6697
Morston *Norfk*	66	0043
Mortehoe *Devon*	18	4545
Morthen *S York*	75	4748
Mortimer *Berks*	24	6564
Mortimer Common *Berks*	24	6565
Mortimer West End *Hants*	24	6363
Mortimer's Cross *Herefs*	46	4263
Mortlake *Gt Lon*	26	2075
Morton *Cumb*	93	3854
Morton *Cumb*	93	4539
Morton *Derbys*	74	4060
Morton *IOW*	13	6085

Morton *Lincs*	75	8091
Morton *Lincs*	64	0923
Morton *Norfk*	66	1216
Morton *Notts*	75	7251
Morton *Shrops*	59	2924
Morton Hall *Lincs*	76	8863
Morton Tinmouth *Dur*	96	1821
Morton-on-Swale *N York*	89	3291
Morvah *Cnwll*	2	4035
Morval *Cnwll*	5	2556
Morvich *Highld*	138	9621
Morville *Shrops*	60	6794
Morville Heath *Shrops*	60	6893
Morwellham Quay	6	4570
Morwenstow *Cnwll*	18	2015
Mosborough *S York*	74	4281
Moscow *E Ayrs*	107	4430
Mose *Shrops*	60	7590
Mosedale *Cumb*	93	3532
Moseley *W Mids*	60	9498
Moseley *W Mids*	61	0783
Moseley *Worcs*	47	8159
Moses Gate *Gt Man*	79	7306
Moss Ag & B	120	9544
Moss *S York*	83	5914
Moss *Wrexhm*	71	3053
Moss Bank *Mersyd*	78	5197
Moss Edge *Lancs*	80	4243
Moss End *Ches*	79	6778
Moss Side *Cumb*	93	1952
Moss Side *Lancs*	80	3730
Moss Side *Mersyd*	78	3802
Moss Side *Mersyd*	78	3107
Moss-side *Highld*	140	8555
Mossat *Abers*	142	4719
Mossbank *Shet*	153	4575
Mossbay *Cumb*	92	9927
Mossblown *S Ayrs*	106	4024
Mossbrow *Gt Man*	79	7089
Mossburnford *Border*	110	6616
Mossdale *D & G*	99	6670
Mossdale *E Ayrs*	107	4904
Mossend *N Lans*	116	7460
Mosser Mains *Cumb*	92	1125
Mossley *Ches*	72	8861
Mossley *Gt Man*	82	9701
Mosspaul Hotel *Border*	109	3999
Mosstodloch *Moray*	141	3259
Mossy Lea *Lancs*	80	5312
Mossyard *D & G*	99	5451
Mosterton *Dorset*	10	4505
Moston *Gt Man*	79	8701
Moston *Shrops*	59	5626
Moston Green *Ches*	72	7261
Mostyn *Flints*	70	1580
Motcombe *Dorset*	22	8525
Mothecombe *Devon*	6	6047
Motherby *Cumb*	93	4228
Motherwell *N Lans*	116	7457
Motspur Park *Gt Lon*	26	2267
Mottingham *Gt Lon*	27	4272
Mottisfont *Hants*	23	3226
Mottistone *IOW*	13	4083
Mottram in Longdendale *Gt Man*	79	9995
Mottram St Andrew *Ches*	79	8778
Mouilpied *Guern*	158	0000
Mouldsworth *Ches*	71	5071
Moulin *P & K*	132	9459
Moulsecoomb *E Susx*	15	3307
Moulsford *Oxon*	37	5883
Moulsoe *Bucks*	38	9141
Moultavie *Highld*	146	6371
Moulton *Ches*	79	6569
Moulton *Lincs*	64	3023
Moulton *N York*	89	2303
Moulton *Nhants*	50	7866
Moulton *Suffk*	53	6964
Moulton *V Glam*	33	0770
Moulton Chapel *Lincs*	64	3218
Moulton Seas End *Lincs*	64	3227
Moulton St Mary *Norfk*	67	3907
Mount *Cnwll*	3	7856
Mount *Cnwll*	4	1468
Mount *W York*	82	0917
Mount Ambrose *Cnwll*	2	7043
Mount Bures *Essex*	40	9032
Mount Hawke *Cnwll*	2	7147
Mount Hermon *Cnwll*	2	6915
Mount Lothian *Mdloth*	117	2757
Mount Pleasant *Ches*	72	8456
Mount Pleasant *Derbys*	74	3448
Mount Pleasant *Dur*	96	2634
Mount Pleasant *E Susx*	16	4216
Mount Pleasant *Norfk*	66	9994
Mount Pleasant *Suffk*	53	7347
Mount Pleasant *Worcs*	47	0064
Mount Sorrel *Wilts*	23	0324
Mount Tabor *W York*	82	0527
Mountain *W York*	82	0930
Mountain Ash *Rhondd*	33	0499
Mountain Cross *Border*	117	1547
Mountain Street *Kent*	29	0652
Mountfield *E Susx*	17	7320
Mountgerald House *Highld*	139	5661
Mountjoy *Cnwll*	4	8760
Mountnessing *Essex*	40	6297
Mounton *Mons*	34	5193
Mountsorrel *Leics*	62	5814
Mousehill *Surrey*	25	9441
Mousehole *Cnwll*	2	4626
Mouswald *D & G*	100	0672
Mow Cop *Ches*	72	8557
Mowhaugh *Border*	110	8120
Mowmacre Hill *Leics*	62	5807
Mowsley *Leics*	50	6489
Mowtie *Abers*	135	8388
Moy *Highld*	140	7634
Moy *Highld*	131	4282
Moye *Highld*	138	8818
Moyles Court *Hants*	12	1608
Moylgrove *Pembks*	42	1144
Muasdale *Ag & B*	105	6840
Much Birch *Herefs*	46	5030
Much Cowarne *Herefs*	46	6147
Much Dewchurch *Herefs*	46	4831
Much Hadham *Herts*	39	4219
Much Hoole *Lancs*	80	4723

Much Hoole Town *Lancs*	80	4722
Much Marcle *Herefs*	47	6532
Much Wenlock *Shrops*	59	6299
Muchalls *Abers*	135	9092
Muchelney *Somset*	21	4224
Muchelney Ham *Somset*	21	4423
Muchlarnick *Cnwll*	5	2156
Mucking *Essex*	40	6881
Muckingford *Essex*	40	6779
Muckleburgh Collection	66	1043
Muckleford *Dorset*	10	6393
Mucklestone *Staffs*	72	7237
Muckley *Shrops*	59	6495
Muckton *Lincs*	77	3781
Mud Row *Kent*	28	0072
Muddiford *Devon*	19	5638
Muddles Green *E Susx*	16	5413
Mudeford *Dorset*	12	1892
Mudford *Somset*	21	5719
Mudford Sock *Somset*	21	5519
Mudgley *Somset*	21	4545
Mugdock *Stirlg*	115	5577
Mugeary *Highld*	136	4439
Mugginton *Derbys*	73	2842
Muggintonlane End *Derbys*	73	2844
Muggleswick *Dur*	95	0449
Muir of Fowlis *Abers*	134	5612
Muir of Miltonduff *Moray*	141	1859
Muir of Ord *Highld*	139	5250
Muir of Thorn *P & K*	125	0637
Muirden *Abers*	142	7054
Muirdrum *Angus*	127	5637
Muiresk *Abers*	142	6948
Muirhead *Angus*	126	3434
Muirhead *Fife*	126	2805
Muirhead *N Lans*	116	6869
Muirkirk *E Ayrs*	107	6927
Muirmill *Stirlg*	116	7283
Muirshearlich *Highld*	131	1380
Muirtack *Abers*	143	9937
Muirton *P & K*	125	9211
Muirton Mains *Highld*	139	4553
Muirton of Ardblair *P & K*	126	1643
Muker *N York*	88	9097
Mulbarton *Norfk*	67	1901
Mulben *Moray*	141	3550
Mulfra *Cnwll*	2	4534
Mullacott Cross *Devon*	19	5144
Mullion *Cnwll*	2	6719
Mullion Cove *Cnwll*	2	6617
Mumby *Lincs*	77	5174
Munderfield Row *Herefs*	47	6451
Munderfield Stocks *Herefs*	47	6550
Mundesley *Norfk*	67	3136
Mundford *Norfk*	66	8093
Mundham *Norfk*	67	3397
Mundon Hill *Essex*	40	8602
Mungrisdale *Cumb*	93	3630
Munlochy *Highld*	140	6453
Munnoch *N Ayrs*	114	2548
Munsley *Herefs*	47	6640
Munslow *Shrops*	59	5287
Murchington *Devon*	8	6888
Murcot *Worcs*	48	0640
Murcott *Oxon*	37	5815
Murcott *Wilts*	35	9591
Murkle *Highld*	151	1668
Murlaggan *Highld*	130	0192
Murrell Green *Hants*	24	7455
Murroes *Angus*	127	4635
Murrow *Cambs*	64	3707
Mursley *Bucks*	38	8128
Murston *Kent*	28	9264
Murthill *Angus*	134	4657
Murthly *P & K*	126	1038
Murton *Cumb*	94	7221
Murton *Dur*	96	3847
Murton *N York*	83	6452
Murton *Nthumb*	111	9748
Murton *T & W*	103	3270
Musbury *Devon*	10	2794
Muscoates *N York*	90	6879
Musselburgh *E Loth*	118	3472
Muston *Leics*	63	8237
Muston *N York*	91	0979
Mustow Green *Worcs*	60	8774
Muswell Hill *Gt Lon*	27	2889
Mutehill *D & G*	99	6848
Mutford *Suffk*	55	4888
Muthill *P & K*	125	8717
Mutterton *Devon*	9	0205
Muxton *Shrops*	60	7114
Mybster *Highld*	151	1652
Myddfai *Carmth*	44	7730
Myddle *Shrops*	59	4623
Mydroilyn *Cerdgn*	42	4555
Mylor *Cnwll*	3	8135
Mylor Bridge *Cnwll*	3	8036
Mynachlog ddu *Pembks*	31	1430
Myndd-llan *Flints*	70	1572
Myndtown *Shrops*	59	3989
Mynydd Buch *Cerdgn*	43	7276
Mynydd Isa *Flints*	70	2563
Mynydd Llandygai *Gwynd*	69	6065
Mynydd-bach *Mons*	34	4894
Mynydd-Bach *Swans*	32	6597
Mynyddgarreg *Carmth*	31	4208
Mynytho *Gwynd*	56	3031
Myrebird *Abers*	135	7398
Myredykes *Border*	102	5998
Mytchett *Surrey*	25	8855
Mytholm *W York*	82	9827
Mytholmroyd *W York*	82	0126
Mythop *Lancs*	80	3634
Myton-on-Swale *N York*	89	4366

299

N

Na Buirgh *W Isls*	152	0394
Naast *Highld*	144	8283
Nab's Head *Lancs*	81	6229

Naburn
Newton on the H
300

Naburn N York 83 5945
Naccolt Kent 28 0544
Nackington Kent 29 1554
Nacton Suffk 55 2240
Nafferton E R Yk 91 0559
Nag's Head Gloucs 35 8998
Nailbridge Gloucs 35 6415
Nailsbourne Somset 20 2128
Nailsea Somset 34 4770
Nailstone Leics 62 4106
Nailsworth Gloucs 35 8499
Nairn Highld 140 8856
Nalderswood Surrey 15 2445
Nancegollan Cnwll 2 6332
Nancledra Cnwll 2 4936
Nanhoron Gwynd 56 2731
Nannerch Flints 70 1669
Nanpantan Leics 62 5017
Nanpean Cnwll 3 9556
Nanquidno Cnwll 2 3629
Nanstallon Cnwll 4 0367
Nant Gwynant Gwynd 69 6350
Nant Peris Gwynd 69 6058
Nant-ddu Powys 33 0014
Nant-glas Powys 45 9965
Nant-y-Bwch Blae G 33 1210
Nant-y-caws Carmth 32 4518
Nant-y-derry Mons 34 3306
Nant-y-gollen Shrops 58 2428
Nant-y-moel Brdgnd 33 9392
Nant-y-pandy Conwy 69 6973
Nanternis Cerdgn 42 3756
Nantgaredig Carmth 32 4921
Nantgarw Rhondd 33 1285
Nantglyn Denbgs 70 0061
Nantgwyn Powys 45 9776
Nantlle Gwynd 68 5153
Nantmawr Shrops 58 2524
Nantmel Powys 45 0366
Nantmor Gwynd 57 6046
Nantwich Ches 72 6552
Nantyffyllon Brdgnd 33 8492
Nantyglo Blae G 33 1910
Naphill Bucks 26 8496
Napleton Worcs 47 8648
Nappa N York 81 8553
Napton on the Hill Warwks 49 4661
Narberth Pembks 31 1015
Narborough Leics 50 5497
Narborough Norfk 65 7412
Narkurs Cnwll 5 3255
Nasareth Gwynd 68 4749
Naseby Nhants 50 6978
Nash Bucks 38 7833
Nash Gt Lon 27 4063
Nash Herefs 46 3062
Nash Newpt 34 3483
Nash Shrops 46 6071
Nash End Worcs 60 7781
Nash Lee Bucks 38 8408
Nash Street Kent 27 6469
Nash's Green Hants 24 6745
Nassington Nhants 51 0696
Nastend Gloucs 35 7906
Nasty Herts 39 3524
Nateby Cumb 88 7706
Nateby Lancs 80 4644
National Shire Horse Centre 6 5851
Natland Cumb 87 5289
Naughton Suffk 54 0249
Naunton Gloucs 48 1123
Naunton Worcs 47 8739
Naunton Beauchamp Worcs 47 9652
Navenby Lincs 76 9858
Navestock Essex 27 5397
Navestock Side Essex 27 5697
Navidale House Hotel Highld 147 0316
Navity Highld 140 7864
Nawton N York 90 6584
Nayland Suffk 54 9734
Nazeing Essex 39 4106
Nazeing Gate Essex 39 4105
Neacroft Hants 12 1896
Neal's Green Warwks 61 3384
Neap Shet 153 5058
Near Cotton Staffs 73 0646
Near Sawrey Cumb 87 3795
Neasden Gt Lon 26 2185
Neasham Dur 89 3210
Neath Neath 32 7597
Neatham Hants 24 7440
Neatishead Norfk 67 3420
Nebo Cerdgn 43 5465
Nebo Conwy 69 8355
Nebo Gwynd 68 4850
Nebo IOA 68 4690
Necton Norfk 66 8709
Nedd Highld 148 1331
Nedderton Nthumb 103 2382
Nedging Suffk 54 9948
Nedging Tye Suffk 54 0149
Needham Norfk 55 2281
Needham Market Suffk 54 0855
Needham Street Suffk 53 7265
Needingworth Cambs 52 3472
Neen Savage Shrops 60 6777
Neen Sollars Shrops 60 6672
Neenton Shrops 59 6387
Nefyn Gwynd 56 3040
Neilston E Rens 115 4857
Nelson Caerph 33 1195
Nelson Lancs 81 8638
Nemphlar S Lans 116 8544
Nempnett Thrubwell Somset 21 5260
Nenthall Cumb 94 7545
Nenthead Cumb 94 7743
Nenthorn Border 110 6837
Neopardy Devon 8 7999
Nep Town W Susx 15 2115
Nercwys Flints 70 2360
Nereabolls Ag & B 112 2255
Nerston S Lans 116 6456
Nesbit Nthumb 111 9833
Nesfield N York 82 0949
Ness Ches 71 3076
Ness Botanic Gardens 71 3075
Nesscliffe Shrops 59 3819
Neston Ches 71 2977
Neston Wilts 22 8668
Netchwood Shrops 59 6291
Nether Alderley Ches 79 8476
Nether Blainslie Border 109 5443
Nether Broughton Notts 63 6925
Nether Cerne Dorset 11 6798
Nether Compton Dorset 10 5917
Nether Crimond Abers 143 8222
Nether Dallachy Moray 141 3563
Nether Exe Devon 9 9300
Nether Fingland S Lans 108 9310
Nether Handley Derbys 74 4176
Nether Handwick Angus 126 3641
Nether Haugh S York 74 4196
Nether Headon Notts 75 7477
Nether Heage Derbys 74 3650
Nether Heyford Nhants 49 6658
Nether Howcleugh S Lans 108 0212
Nether Kellet Lancs 87 5068
Nether Kinmundy Abers 143 0543
Nether Langwith Notts 75 5370
Nether Moor Derbys 74 3866
Nether Padley Derbys 74 2478
Nether Poppleton N York 83 5654
Nether Row Cumb 93 3237
Nether Silton N York 89 4592
Nether Skyborry Shrops 46 2873
Nether Stowey Somset 20 1939
Nether Street Essex 40 5812
Nether Wallop Hants 23 3036
Nether Wasdale Cumb 86 1204
Nether Welton Cumb 93 3545
Nether Westcote Gloucs 36 2220
Nether Whitacre Warwks 61 2392
Nether Whitecleuch S Lans 108 8319
Nether Winchendon Bucks 37 7312
Netheravon Wilts 23 1448
Netherbrae Abers 143 7959
Netherburn S Lans 116 7947
Netherbury Dorset 10 4799
Netherby Cumb 101 3971
Netherby N York 83 3346
Nethercleuch D & G 100 1186
Nethercote Warwks 49 5164
Nethercott Devon 18 4839
Nethercott Devon 5 3596
Netherend Gloucs 34 5900
Netherfield E Susx 16 7019
Netherfield Leics 62 5816
Netherfield Notts 62 6140
Netherfield Road E Susx 17 7417
Nethergate Lincs 75 7599
Nethergate Norfk 66 0529
Netherhampton Wilts 23 1029
Netherhay Dorset 10 4105
Netherland Green Staffs 73 1030
Netherlaw D & G 99 7444
Netherley Abers 135 8593
Nethermill D & G 100 0487
Nethermuir Abers 143 9044
Netheroyd Hill W York 82 1419
Netherplace E Rens 115 5255
Netherseal Derbys 61 2812
Netherstreet Wilts 22 9864
Netherthong W York 82 1309
Netherthorpe Derbys 75 4474
Netherton Angus 134 5457
Netherton Devon 7 8971
Netherton Hants 23 3757
Netherton Herefs 46 5226
Netherton N Lans 116 7854
Netherton Nthumb 111 9807
Netherton Oxon 36 4199
Netherton P & K 126 1452
Netherton Shrops 60 7382
Netherton Stirlg 115 5579
Netherton W Mids 60 9488
Netherton W York 82 1213
Netherton W York 82 2816
Netherton Worcs 47 9941
Nethertown Cumb 86 9907
Nethertown Highld 151 3578
Nethertown Lancs 81 7236
Nethertown Staffs 73 1017
Netherurd Border 117 1144
Netherwitton Nthumb 103 0990
Nethy Bridge Highld 141 0020
Netley Hants 13 4508
Netley Marsh Hants 12 3313
Nettacott Devon 9 8999
Nettlebed Oxon 37 6986
Nettlebridge Somset 21 6448
Nettlecombe Dorset 10 5195
Nettlecombe IOW 13 5278
Nettleden Herts 38 0210
Nettleham Lincs 76 0075
Nettlestead Kent 28 6852
Nettlestead Green Kent 28 6850
Nettlestone IOW 13 6290
Nettlesworth Dur 96 2547
Nettleton Lincs 76 1100
Nettleton Wilts 35 8278
Nettleton Shrub Wilts 35 8277
Netton Devon 6 5546
Netton Wilts 23 1336
Neuadd Carmth 32 7021
Neuadd Fawr Carmth 44 7441
Neuadd-ddu Powys 45 9175
Nevendon Essex 40 7591
Nevern Pembks 31 0840
Nevill Holt Leics 51 8193
New Abbey D & G 100 9666
New Aberdour Abers 143 8863
New Addington Gt Lon 27 3763
New Alresford Hants 24 5832
New Alyth P & K 126 2447
New Arram E R Yk 84 0344
New Ash Green Kent 27 6065
New Balderton Notts 75 8152
New Barn Kent 27 6169
New Barnet Gt Lon 27 2695
New Barton Nhants 51 8564
New Bewick Nthumb 111 0620
New Bilton Warwks 50 4875
New Bolingbroke Lincs 77 3057
New Boultham Lincs 76 9670
New Bradwell Bucks 38 8341
New Brampton Derbys 74 3771
New Brancepeth Dur 96 2241
New Bridge N York 90 8085
New Brighton Flints 70 2565
New Brighton Mersyd 78 3093
New Brinsley Notts 75 4550
New Brotton N York 97 6920
New Broughton Wrexhm 71 3151
New Buckenham Norfk 54 0890
New Bury Gt Man 79 7304
New Byth Abers 143 8254
New Costessey Norfk 66 1810
New Cowper Cumb 92 1245
New Crofton W York 83 3817
New Cross Cerdgn 43 6376
New Cross Gt Lon 27 3676
New Cross Somset 21 4119
New Cumnock E Ayrs 107 6213
New Cut E Susx 17 8115
New Deer Abers 143 8847
New Delaval Nthumb 103 2979
New Delph Gt Man 82 9907
New Denham Bucks 26 0484
New Duston Nhants 49 7162
New Earswick N York 83 6155
New Eastwood Notts 62 4646
New Edlington S York 75 5398
New Elgin Moray 141 2261
New Ellerby E R Yk 85 1639
New Eltham Gt Lon 27 4472
New End Worcs 48 0560
New England Cambs 64 1801
New Farnley W York 82 2531
New Ferry Mersyd 78 3385
New Fletton Cambs 64 1997
New Fryston W York 83 4526
New Galloway D & G 99 6377
New Gilston Fife 127 4208
New Grimsby IOS 2 8815
New Hartley Nthumb 103 3076
New Haw Surrey 26 0563
New Hedges Pembks 31 1202
New Herrington T & W 96 3352
New Holkham Norfk 66 8839
New Holland Lincs 85 0823
New Houghton Derbys 75 4965
New Houghton Norfk 66 7927
New Houses Gt Man 78 5502
New Houses N York 88 8073
New Hutton Cumb 87 5691
New Hythe Kent 28 7159
New Inn Carmth 44 4736
New Inn Torfn 34 3099
New Invention Shrops 46 4304
New Lakenham Norfk 67 2307
New Lanark S Lans 108 8842
New Lane Lancs 80 4212
New Lane End Ches 79 6394
New Langholm D & G 101 3684
New Leake Lincs 77 4057
New Leeds Abers 143 9954
New Longton Lancs 80 5025
New Luce D & G 98 1764
New Malden Gt Lon 26 2168
New Marske N York 97 6121
New Marston Oxon 37 5207
New Marton Shrops 59 3334
New Mill Abers 135 7883
New Mill Cnwll 2 4534
New Mill Herts 38 9212
New Mill W York 82 1609
New Mills Cnwll 3 8952
New Mills Derbys 79 0085
New Mills Powys 58 0901
New Milton Hants 12 2495
New Mistley Essex 41 1231
New Moat Pembks 30 0625
New Ollerton Notts 75 6667
New Oscott W Mids 61 0994
New Pitsligo Abers 143 8855
New Polzeath Cnwll 4 9379
New Prestwick S Ayrs 106 3424
New Quay Cerdgn 42 3959
New Quay Essex 41 0223
New Rackheath Norfk 67 2812
New Radnor Powys 45 2161
New Rent Cumb 93 4536
New Ridley Nthumb 95 0559
New Road Side N York 82 9743
New Romney Kent 17 0624
New Rossington S York 75 6198
New Row Cerdgn 43 7273
New Row Lancs 81 6438
New Sauchie Clacks 116 8994
New Sharlston W York 83 3819
New Shoreston Nthumb 111 1932
New Silksworth T & W 96 3853
New Skelton N York 97 6618
New Somerby Lincs 63 9235
New Spilsby Lincs 77 4165
New Springs Gt Man 78 5906
New Stevenston N Lans 116 7659
New Street Herefs 46 3356
New Swannington Leics 62 4215
New Thundersley Essex 40 7789
New Town Beds 52 1945
New Town Dorset 11 9515
New Town Dorset 11 9907
New Town Dorset 22 9918
New Town E Loth 118 4470
New Town E Susx 16 4720
New Town Nhants 51 9677
New Town Wilts 36 2871
New Tredegar Caerph 33 1403
New Trows S Lans 108 8038
New Tupton Derbys 74 3966
New Village E R Yk 84 8530
New Walsoken Cambs 65 4609
New Waltham Lincs 85 2804
New Whittington Derbys 74 3975
New Wimpole Cambs 52 3549
New Winton E Loth 118 4271
New Yatt Oxon 36 3713
New York Lincs 77 2455
New York N York 89 1963
New York T & W 103 3270
Newall W York 82 1946
Newark Cambs 64 2100
Newark Ork 153 7142
Newark-on-Trent Notts 75 7953
Newarthill N Lans 116 7859
Newbarn Kent 29 1540
Newbattle Mdloth 118 3365
Newbie D & G 101 1764
Newbiggin Cumb 93 4729
Newbiggin Cumb 94 5549
Newbiggin Cumb 94 6228
Newbiggin Cumb 86 0994
Newbiggin Cumb 86 2669
Newbiggin Dur 95 9127
Newbiggin Dur 96 1447
Newbiggin N York 88 9591
Newbiggin N York 88 0086
Newbiggin-by-the-Sea Nthumb 103 3087
Newbiggin-on-Lune Cumb 87 7005
Newbigging Angus 126 2841
Newbigging Angus 127 4237
Newbigging Angus 127 4936
Newbigging S Lans 117 0145
Newbold Derbys 74 3672
Newbold Leics 62 4019
Newbold on Avon Warwks 50 4877
Newbold on Stour Warwks 48 2446
Newbold Pacey Warwks 48 2957
Newbold Revel Warwks 50 4580
Newbold Verdon Leics 62 4403
Newborough Cambs 64 2005
Newborough IOA 68 4265
Newborough Staffs 73 1325
Newbottle Nhants 49 5236
Newbottle T & W 96 3351
Newbourne Suffk 55 2743
Newbridge C Edin 117 1272
Newbridge Caerph 33 2097
Newbridge Cerdgn 44 5059
Newbridge Cnwll 2 4231
Newbridge Cnwll 3 7944
Newbridge D & G 100 9479
Newbridge Hants 12 2915
Newbridge IOW 13 4187
Newbridge Oxon 36 4001
Newbridge Pembks 30 9431
Newbridge Wrexhm 71 2841
Newbridge Green Worcs 47 8439
Newbridge on Wye Powys 45 0158
Newbridge-on-Usk Mons 34 3894
Newbrough Nthumb 102 8767
Newbuildings Devon 8 7903
Newburgh Abers 143 9659
Newburgh Abers 143 9925
Newburgh Fife 126 2318
Newburgh Lancs 78 4810
Newburgh Priory N York 90 5476
Newburn T & W 103 1665
Newbury Berks 24 4766
Newbury Somset 22 6949
Newbury Wilts 22 8241
Newbury Park Gt Lon 27 4488
Newby Cumb 94 5921
Newby Lancs 81 8146
Newby N York 90 5012
Newby N York 88 7269
Newby N York 91 0190
Newby Bridge Cumb 87 3686
Newby Cross Cumb 93 3653
Newby East Cumb 93 4758
Newby Head Cumb 94 5821
Newby West Cumb 93 3753
Newby Wiske N York 89 3687
Newcastle Mons 34 4417
Newcastle Shrops 58 2582
Newcastle Airport 103 1871
Newcastle Emlyn Carmth 31 3040
Newcastle upon Tyne T & W 103 2464
Newcastle-under-Lyme Staffs 72 8445
Newcastleton Border 101 4887
Newchapel Pembks 31 2239
Newchapel Staffs 72 8654
Newchapel Surrey 15 3641
Newchurch Blae G 33 1710
Newchurch Herefs 46 3550
Newchurch IOW 13 5685
Newchurch Kent 17 0531
Newchurch Mons 34 4597
Newchurch Powys 45 2150
Newchurch Staffs 73 1423
Newchurch in Pendle Lancs 81 8239
Newcraighall C Edin 118 3272
Newdigate Surrey 15 1942
Newell Green Berks 25 8770
Newenden Kent 17 8327
Newent Gloucs 47 7225
Newfield Dur 96 2033
Newfield Dur 96 2452
Newfield Highld 147 7877
Newfound Hants 24 5851
Newgale Pembks 30 8522
Newgate Norfk 66 0443
Newgate Street Herts 39 3005
Newhall Ches 71 6145
Newhall Derbys 73 2820
Newham Nthumb 111 1728
Newhaven Derbys 74 1660
Newhaven E Susx 16 4401
Newhey Gt Man 82 9411
Newholm N York 90 8610
Newhouse N Lans 116 7961
Newick E Susx 15 4121
Newingreen Kent 29 1236
Newington Kent 28 8564
Newington Kent 29 1837
Newington Oxon 37 6096
Newington Shrops 59 4283
Newington Bagpath Gloucs 35 8194
Newland Cumb 86 3079
Newland E R Yk 84 8029
Newland E R Yk 84 0631
Newland Gloucs 34 5509
Newland N York 83 6824
Newland Oxon 36 3609
Newland Somset 19 8238
Newland Worcs 47 7948
Newlandrig Mdloth 118 3762
Newlands Border 101 5094
Newlands Cumb 93 3439
Newlands Nthumb 95 0855
Newlands of Dundurcas Moray 141 2951
Newlyn Cnwll 2 4
Newlyn East Cnwll 3 8
Newmachar Abers 143 8
Newmains N Lans 116 8
Newman's End Essex 39 5
Newman's Green Suffk 54 8
Newmarket Suffk 53 6
Newmarket W Isls 152 4
Newmill Border 109 4
Newmill Moray 142 4
Newmill of Inshewan Angus 134 4
Newmillerdam W York 83 3
Newmills C Edin 117 1
Newmills Fife 117 0
Newmills Mons 34 5
Newmiln P & K 126 1
Newmilns E Ayrs 107 5
Newnes Shrops 59 3
Newney Green Essex 40 6
Newnham Gloucs 35 6
Newnham Hants 24 7
Newnham Herts 39 2
Newnham Kent 28 9
Newnham Nhants 49 5
Newnham Worcs 47 6
Newnham Paddox Warwks 50 4
Newport Cnwll 5 3
Newport Devon 19 5
Newport Dorset 11 8
Newport E R Yk 84 8
Newport Essex 39 5
Newport Gloucs 35 7
Newport Highld 151 1
Newport IOW 13 5
Newport Newpt 34 3
Newport Norfk 67 5
Newport Pembks 30 0
Newport Shrops 72 7
Newport Pagnell Bucks 38 8
Newport-on-Tay Fife 127 4
Newpound Common W Susx 14 0
Newquay Cnwll 4 8
Newquay Airport 4 8
Newsam Green W York 83 3
Newsbank Ches 72 8
Newseat Abers 142 7
Newsham Lancs 80 5
Newsham N York 89 1
Newsham N York 89 3
Newsham Nthumb 103 3
Newsholme E R Yk 84 7
Newsholme Lancs 81 8
Newstead Border 109 5
Newstead Notts 75 5
Newstead Nthumb 111 1
Newtack Moray 142 4
Newthorpe N York 83 4
Newthorpe Notts 62 4
Newtimber W Susx 15 2
Newtoft Lincs 76 0
Newton Ag & B 114 0
Newton Beds 39 2
Newton Border 110 6
Newton Brdgnd 33 8
Newton Cambs 65 4
Newton Cambs 53 4
Newton Cardif 34 2
Newton Ches 71 4
Newton Ches 71 5
Newton Ches 71 5
Newton Cumb 86 2
Newton Derbys 75 4
Newton Herefs 46 3
Newton Herefs 46 3
Newton Herefs 46 5
Newton Highld 139 5
Newton Highld 140 7
Newton Highld 140 7
Newton Lancs 80 3
Newton Lancs 87 5
Newton Lancs 81 6
Newton Lincs 64 0
Newton Mdloth 118 3
Newton Moray 141 1
Newton Moray 141 3
Newton N York 90 8
Newton Nhants 51 8
Newton Norfk 66 8
Newton Notts 63 6
Newton Nthumb 110 9
Newton Nthumb 103 0
Newton S Lans 116 6
Newton S Lans 108 9
Newton Shrops 59 4
Newton Somset 20 1
Newton Staffs 73 0
Newton Suffk 54 9
Newton W Loth 117 0
Newton W Mids 61 0
Newton W York 83 4
Newton Warwks 50 5
Newton Wilts 23 2
Newton Abbot Devon 7 8
Newton Arlosh Cumb 93 2
Newton Aycliffe Dur 96 2
Newton Bewley Dur 97 4
Newton Blossomville Bucks 38 9
Newton Bromswold Beds 51 9
Newton Burgoland Leics 62 3
Newton by Toft Lincs 76 0
Newton Ferrers Cnwll 5 3
Newton Ferrers Devon 6 5
Newton Ferry W Isls 152 8
Newton Flotman Norfk 67 2
Newton Green Mons 34 5
Newton Harcourt Leics 50 6
Newton Heath Gt Man 79 8
Newton Hill W York 83 3
Newton Kyme N York 83 4
Newton Longville Bucks 38 8
Newton Mearns E Rens 115 5
Newton Morrell N York 89 2
Newton Mountain Pembks 30 9
Newton Mulgrave N York 97 7
Newton of Balcanquhal P & K 126 1
Newton of Balcormo Fife 127 5
Newton on Ouse N York 90 5
Newton on the Hill Shrops 59 4

Newton on Trent Lincs 76 8373
Newton Poppleford Devon 9 0889
Newton Purcell Oxon 49 6230
Newton Regis Warwks 61 2707
Newton Reigny Cumb 93 4731
Newton Row Highld 151 3449
Newton Solney Derbys 73 2825
Newton St Cyres Devon 9 8898
Newton St Faith Norfk 67 2217
Newton St Loe Somset 22 7064
Newton St Petrock Devon 18 4112
Newton Stacey Hants 24 4140
Newton Stewart D & G 99 4065
Newton Toney Wilts 23 2140
Newton Tracey Devon 19 5226
Newton under Roseberry N York 90 5713
Newton Underwood Nthumb 103 1486
Newton upon Derwent E R Yk 84 7149
Newton Valence Hants 24 7232
Newton Wamphray D & G 100 1195
Newton with Scales Lancs 80 4530
Newton-by-the-Sea Nthumb 111 2325
Newton-le-Willows Mersyd 78 5995
Newton-le-Willows N York 89 2189
Newton-on-Rawcliffe N York 90 8090
Newton-on-the-Moor Nthumb 111 1705
Newtongarry Croft Abers 142 5735
Newtongrange Mdloth 118 3364
Newtonhill Abers 135 9193
Newtonloan Mdloth 118 3362
Newtonmill Angus 134 6064
Newtonmore Highld 132 7098
Newtown Blae G 33 1709
Newtown Ches 71 6247
Newtown Ches 72 9060
Newtown Ches 71 5278
Newtown Cnwll 2 5729
Newtown Cnwll 3 7423
Newtown Cnwll 3 1052
Newtown Cnwll 5 2978
Newtown Cumb 92 1048
Newtown Cumb 101 5062
Newtown Cumb 94 5224
Newtown Cumb 101 3862
Newtown D & G 107 7710
Newtown Derbys 79 9984
Newtown Devon 9 0699
Newtown Devon 19 7625
Newtown Dorset 10 4802
Newtown Dorset 12 0393
Newtown Gloucs 35 6702
Newtown Gt Man 78 5604
Newtown Hants 12 2710
Newtown Hants 24 4763
Newtown Hants 13 6013
Newtown Herefs 46 4757
Newtown Herefs 46 5333
Newtown Herefs 46 6145
Newtown Herefs 47 7037
Newtown Highld 131 3504
Newtown IOW 13 4290
Newtown Lancs 80 5118
Newtown Nthumb 111 9631
Newtown Nthumb 103 0300
Newtown Nthumb 103 0425
Newtown Powys 58 1091
Newtown Rhondd 33 0598
Newtown Shrops 59 4222
Newtown Shrops 59 4731
Newtown Somset 10 2712
Newtown Staffs 60 9904
Newtown Wilts 22 9129
Newtown Wilts 23 2963
Newtown Worcs 47 8755
Newtown Worcs 60 9478
Newtown Linford Leics 62 5209
Newtown of Beltrees Rens 115 3758
Newtown St Boswells Border 110 5732
Newtown Unthank Leics 62 4904
Newtyle Angus 126 2941
Newyears Green Gt Lon 26 0788
Newyork Ag & B 122 9611
Nextend Herefs 46 3357
Neyland Pembks 30 9605
Niarbyl IOM 158 2177
Nibley Gloucs 35 6606
Nibley Gloucs 35 6982
Nibley Green Gloucs 35 7396
Nicholashayne Devon 9 1016
Nicholaston Swans 32 5288
Nickies Hill Cumb 101 5367
Nidd N York 89 3060
Nigg Aber C 135 9402
Nigg Highld 147 8071
Nightcott Somset 19 8925
Nimlet Somset 35 7470
Nine Elms Wilts 36 1085
Nine Wells Pembks 30 7924
Ninebanks Nthumb 94 7853
Nineveh Worcs 47 6265
Ninfield E Susx 16 7012
Ningwood IOW 13 3989
Nisbet Border 110 6725
Nisbet Hill Border 119 7950
Niton IOW 13 5076
Nitshill C Glas 115 5260
No Man's Heath Ches 71 5148
No Man's Heath Warwks 61 2808
No Man's Land Cnwll 4 9470
No Man's Land Cnwll 5 2756
Noah's Ark Kent 27 5557
Noak Bridge Essex 40 6990
Noak Hill Essex 27 5494
Noblethorpe W York 82 2805
Nobold Shrops 59 4710
Nobottle Nhants 49 6763
Nocton Lincs 76 0564
Nogdam End Norfk 67 3900
Noke Oxon 37 5413
Nolton Pembks 30 8618
Nolton Haven Pembks 30 8618
Nomansland Devon 19 8313
Nomansland Wilts 12 2517
Noneley Shrops 59 4828
Nonington Kent 29 2552
Nook Cumb 101 4679
Nook Cumb 87 5481

Norbiton Gt Lon 26 1969
Norbreck Lancs 80 3140
Norbridge Herefs 47 7144
Norbury Ches 71 5547
Norbury Derbys 73 1241
Norbury Gt Lon 27 3069
Norbury Shrops 59 3642
Norbury Staffs 72 7823
Norbury Common Ches 71 5548
Norbury Junction Staffs 72 7923
Norchard Worcs 47 8568
Norcott Brook Ches 78 6080
Norcross Lancs 80 3341
Nordelph Norfk 65 5501
Norden Gt Man 81 8614
Nordley Shrops 60 6996
Norham Nthumb 110 9047
Norland Town W York 82 0622
Norley Ches 71 5772
Norleywood Hants 12 3597
Norlington E Susx 16 4413
Norman Cross Cambs 52 1690
Norman's Bay E Susx 16 6805
Norman's Green Devon 9 0503
Normanby Lincs 84 8816
Normanby Lincs 76 9988
Normanby N York 97 5418
Normanby N York 90 7381
Normanby le Wold Lincs 76 1295
Normandy Surrey 25 9351
Normanton Derbys 62 3433
Normanton Leics 63 8140
Normanton Leics 63 9446
Normanton Notts 75 7054
Normanton Rutlnd 63 9305
Normanton W York 83 3822
Normanton Wilts 23 1340
Normanton le Heath Leics 62 3712
Normanton on Soar Notts 62 5122
Normanton on the Wolds Notts 62 6232
Normanton on Trent Notts 75 7868
Normoss Lancs 80 3437
Norney Surrey 25 9444
Norrington Common Wilts 22 8864
Norris Green Cnwll 5 4169
Norristhorpe W York 82 2123
North Anston S York 75 5184
North Aston Oxon 49 4828
North Baddesley Hants 13 3920
North Ballachulish Highld 130 0560
North Barrow Somset 21 6129
North Barsham Norfk 66 9135
North Benfleet Essex 40 7588
North Bersted W Susx 14 9201
North Berwick E Loth 118 5485
North Bitchburn Dur 96 1732
North Blyth Nthumb 103 3082
North Boarhunt Hants 13 6010
North Bockhampton Hants 12 1797
North Bovey Devon 8 7484
North Bradley Wilts 22 8555
North Brentor Devon 5 4881
North Brewham Somset 22 7236
North Bridge Surrey 14 9636
North Brook End Cambs 39 2944
North Buckland Devon 18 4840
North Burlingham Norfk 67 3609
North Cadbury Somset 21 6327
North Carlton Lincs 76 9477
North Carlton Notts 75 5984
North Cave E R Yk 84 8932
North Cerney Gloucs 35 0107
North Chailey E Susx 15 3921
North Charford Hants 12 1919
North Charlton Nthumb 111 1622
North Cheam Gt Lon 26 2365
North Cheriton Somset 22 6925
North Chideock Dorset 10 4294
North Cliffe E R Yk 84 8736
North Clifton Notts 75 8272
North Close Dur 96 2532
North Cockerington Lincs 77 3790
North Connel Ag & B 122 9034
North Cornelly Brdgnd 33 8181
North Corner Cnwll 3 7818
North Corry Highld 122 8353
North Cotes Lincs 77 3400
North Country Cnwll 2 6943
North Cove Suffk 55 4689
North Cowton N York 89 2803
North Crawley Bucks 38 9244
North Cray Gt Lon 27 4872
North Creake Norfk 66 8538
North Curry Somset 21 3125
North Dalton E R Yk 84 9351
North Deighton N York 83 3951
North Duffield N York 83 6837
North Dunham Highld 136 4274
North Elham Kent 29 1844
North Elkington Lincs 77 2890
North Elmham Norfk 66 9820
North Elmsall W York 83 4712
North End Cumb 93 3259
North End Dorset 22 8427
North End E R Yk 85 1941
North End E R Yk 85 2831
North End Essex 40 6618
North End Hants 12 1016
North End Hants 24 5828
North End Hants 13 6502
North End Leics 62 5715
North End Lincs 85 1022
North End Lincs 85 3101
North End Lincs 76 0499
North End Lincs 64 2341
North End Lincs 77 4289
North End Mersyd 78 3004
North End Nhants 51 9668
North End Norfk 66 9992
North End Nthumb 103 1301
North End Somset 21 4266
North End W Susx 14 9703
North End W Susx 14 1109
North Erradale Highld 144 7480
North Evington Leics 62 6204
North Fambridge Essex 40 8597
North Ferriby E R Yk 84 9826
North Frodingham E R Yk 85 1053

North Gorley Hants 12 1611
North Green Norfk 55 2288
North Green Suffk 55 3162
North Green Suffk 55 3966
North Grimston N York 90 8467
North Halling Kent 28 7065
North Hayling Hants 13 7303
North Hazelrigg Nthumb 111 0533
North Heasley Devon 19 7333
North Heath W Susx 14 0621
North Hele Somset 20 0323
North Hill Cnwll 5 2776
North Hillingdon Gt Lon 26 0784
North Hinksey Oxon 37 4905
North Holmwood Surrey 15 1647
North Huish Devon 7 7156
North Hykeham Lincs 76 9465
North Kelsey Lincs 84 0401
North Kessock Highld 140 6548
North Killingholme Lincs 85 1417
North Kilvington N York 89 4285
North Kilworth Leics 50 6183
North Kingston Hants 12 1603
North Kyme Lincs 76 1552
North Landing E R Yk 91 2471
North Lee Bucks 38 8308
North Lees N York 89 2973
North Leigh Kent 29 1347
North Leigh Oxon 36 3813
North Leverton with Habblesthorpe Notts 75 7882
North Littleton Worcs 48 0847
North Lopham Norfk 54 0382
North Luffenham Rutlnd 63 9303
North Marden W Susx 14 8016
North Marston Bucks 37 7722
North Middleton Mdloth 118 3559
North Middleton Nthumb 111 9924
North Milmain D & G 98 0852
North Molton Devon 19 7329
North Moreton Oxon 37 5689
North Mundham W Susx 14 8702
North Muskham Notts 75 7958
North Newbald E R Yk 84 9136
North Newington Oxon 49 4240
North Newnton Wilts 23 1257
North Newton Somset 20 3031
North Nibley Gloucs 35 7495
North Oakley Hants 24 5354
North Ockendon Gt Lon 27 5985
North Ormesby N York 97 5119
North Ormsby Lincs 77 2893
North Otterington N York 89 3689
North Owersby Lincs 76 0594
North Perrott Somset 10 4709
North Petherton Somset 20 2833
North Petherwin Cnwll 5 2789
North Pickenham Norfk 66 8606
North Piddle Worcs 47 9654
North Pool Devon 7 7741
North Poorton Dorset 10 5298
North Poulner Hants 12 1606
North Quarme Somset 20 9236
North Queensferry C Edin 117 1380
North Radworthy Devon 19 7534
North Rauceby Lincs 76 0246
North Reston Lincs 77 3883
North Rigton N York 82 2749
North Ripley Hants 12 1699
North Road Ches 72 8866
North Ronaldsay Airport 153 7554
North Row Cumb 93 2232
North Runcton Norfk 65 6416
North Scale Cumb 86 1869
North Scarle Lincs 76 8466
North Seaton Nthumb 103 2986
North Seaton Colliery Nthumb 103 2986
North Shian Ag & B 122 9143
North Shields T & W 103 3568
North Shoebury Essex 40 9286
North Shore Lancs 80 3037
North Side Cambs 64 2799
North Side Cumb 92 9929
North Skelton N York 97 6718
North Somercotes Lincs 77 4296
North Stainley N York 89 2876
North Stainmore Cumb 95 8314
North Stifford Essex 40 6080
North Stoke Oxon 37 6186
North Stoke Somset 35 7069
North Stoke W Susx 14 0110
North Street Berks 24 6371
North Street Cambs 53 5868
North Street Hants 12 1518
North Street Hants 24 6433
North Street Kent 28 8174
North Street Kent 28 0157
North Sunderland Nthumb 111 2131
North Tamerton Cnwll 5 3197
North Tawton Devon 8 6601
North Third Stirlg 116 7589
North Thoresby Lincs 77 2998
North Tidworth Wilts 23 2349
North Town Berks 26 8882
North Town Devon 19 5109
North Town Somset 21 5642
North Tuddenham Norfk 66 0314
North Walbottle T & W 103 1767
North Walsham Norfk 67 2830
North Walsham Hants 24 5466
North Warnborough Hants 24 7351
North Weald Bassett Essex 39 4904
North Wheatley Notts 75 7585
North Whilborough Devon 8 8766
North Wick Somset 21 5865
North Widcombe Somset 21 5758
North Widcombe Lincs 76 1688
North Wingfield Derbys 74 4065
North Witham Lincs 63 9221
North Wootton Dorset 11 6514
North Wootton Norfk 65 6424
North Wootton Somset 21 5641
North Wraxall Wilts 35 8175
North Wroughton Wilts 36 1431
Northacre Norfk 66 9598
Northall Bucks 38 9520
Northall Green Norfk 66 9914
Northallerton N York 89 3694

Northam Devon 18 4529
Northam Hants 13 4312
Northampton Nhants 49 7560
Northampton Worcs 47 8365
Northaw Herts 27 2702
Northay Somset 10 2811
Northbourne Cambs 64 1507
Northbourne Kent 29 3352
Northbridge Street E Susx 17 7324
Northbrook Hants 24 5139
Northbrook Oxon 37 4922
Northchapel W Susx 14 9529
Northchurch Herts 38 9708
Northcott Devon 9 0912
Northcott Devon 9 1209
Northcott Devon 5 3392
Northcourt Oxon 37 4998
Northdown Kent 29 3770
Northedge Derbys 74 3665
Northend Bucks 37 7392
Northend Warwks 48 3952
Northend Woods Bucks 26 9089
Northenden Gt Man 79 8289
Northfield Aber C 135 9008
Northfield E R Yk 84 0326
Northfield W Mids 60 0279
Northfields Lincs 64 0208
Northfleet Kent 27 6374
Northiam E Susx 17 8324
Northill Beds 52 1446
Northington Gloucs 35 7008
Northington Hants 24 5637
Northlands Lincs 77 3453
Northleach Gloucs 36 1114
Northleigh Devon 19 6034
Northleigh Devon 9 1995
Northlew Devon 19 5099
Northload Bridge Somset 21 4939
Northmoor Oxon 36 4202
Northmoor Somset 20 9028
Northmuir Angus 126 3854
Northney Hants 13 7303
Northolt Gt Lon 26 1384
Northop Flints 70 2468
Northop Hall Flints 70 2667
Northorpe Lincs 76 8997
Northorpe Lincs 64 0917
Northorpe Lincs 64 2036
Northorpe W York 82 2221
Northover Somset 21 4838
Northover Somset 21 5223
Northowram W York 82 1126
Northport Dorset 11 9288
Northrepps Norfk 67 2439
Northton W Isls 152 9989
Northway Somset 20 1329
Northway Swans 32 5889
Northwich Ches 79 6673
Northwick Gloucs 34 5686
Northwick Somset 21 3548
Northwick Worcs 47 8458
Northwold Norfk 65 7597
Northwood Derbys 74 2664
Northwood Gt Lon 26 0990
Northwood IOW 13 4992
Northwood Shrops 59 4633
Northwood Staffs 72 8949
Northwood Green Gloucs 35 7216
Norton Ches 78 5581
Norton Cnwll 4 0869
Norton Dur 96 4421
Norton E Susx 16 4701
Norton Gloucs 47 8524
Norton Herts 39 2334
Norton IOW 12 3488
Norton Mons 34 4420
Norton N York 90 7911
Norton Nhants 49 5963
Norton Notts 75 5771
Norton Powys 46 3067
Norton S York 83 5415
Norton S York 74 3681
Norton Shrops 59 5609
Norton Shrops 60 7200
Norton Shrops 59 4681
Norton Shrops 59 6382
Norton Somset 21 3463
Norton Suffk 54 9565
Norton Swans 32 6188
Norton W Susx 14 9206
Norton Wilts 35 8884
Norton Worcs 47 8751
Norton Worcs 48 0447
Norton Bavant Wilts 22 9043
Norton Bridge Staffs 72 8630
Norton Canes Staffs 60 0107
Norton Canon Herefs 46 3847
Norton Corner Norfk 66 0928
Norton Disney Lincs 76 8859
Norton Ferris Wilts 22 7936
Norton Fitzwarren Somset 20 1925
Norton Green IOW 12 3488
Norton Green IOW 13 0107
Norton Hawkfield Somset 21 5964
Norton Heath Essex 40 6004
Norton in Hales Shrops 72 7038
Norton in the Moors Staffs 72 8951
Norton Lindsey Warwks 48 2263
Norton Little Green Suffk 54 9766
Norton Malreward Somset 21 6064
Norton Mandeville Essex 40 5804
Norton St Philip Somset 22 7755
Norton sub Hamdon Somset 10 4615
Norton Subcourse Norfk 67 4198
Norton Wood Herefs 46 3648
Norton-Juxta-Twycross Leics 61 3207
Norton-le-Clay N York 89 4011
Norwell Notts 75 7761
Norwell Woodhouse Notts 75 7362
Norwich Norfk 67 2308
Norwich Airport 67 2113
Norwich Cathedral 67 2308
Norwick Shet 153 6414
Norwood Clacks 116 8793
Norwood Kent 17 0530
Norwood Surrey 75 4631
Norwood End Essex 40 5608
Norwood Green Gt Lon 26 1378

Norwood Green W York 82 1326
Norwood Hill Surrey 15 2343
Norwoodside Cambs 65 4197
Noseley Leics 50 7398
Noss Mayo Devon 6 5547
Nosterfield N York 89 2780
Nosterfield End Cambs 53 6344
Nostie Highld 138 8527
Notgrove Gloucs 36 1020
Nottage Brdgnd 33 8177
Notter Cnwll 5 3960
Nottingham Notts 62 5739
Nottington Dorset 11 6682
Notton W York 83 3413
Notton Wilts 35 9169
Nottswood Hill Gloucs 35 7018
Nounsley Essex 40 7910
Noutard's Green Worcs 47 8066
Nowton Suffk 54 8660
Nox Shrops 59 4110
Nuffield Oxon 37 6687
Nun Monkton N York 90 5057
Nunburnholme E R Yk 84 8447
Nuncargate Notts 75 5054
Nunclose Cumb 94 4945
Nuneaton Warwks 61 3691
Nuneham Courtenay Oxon 37 5599
Nunhead Gt Lon 27 3475
Nunkeeling E R Yk 85 1449
Nunney Somset 22 7345
Nunney Catch Somset 22 7344
Nunnington Herefs 46 5543
Nunnington N York 90 6679
Nunnykirk Nthumb 103 0793
Nunsthorpe Lincs 85 2607
Nunthorpe N York 83 6050
Nunthorpe N York 97 5314
Nunthorpe Village N York 90 5413
Nunton Wilts 23 1526
Nunwick N York 89 3274
Nunwick Nthumb 102 8774
Nup End Bucks 38 8619
Nupdown Gloucs 35 6395
Nupend Gloucs 35 7806
Nuptow Berks 25 8873
Nursling Hants 12 3716
Nursted Hants 13 7521
Nurserd Wilts 23 0260
Nurton Staffs 60 8399
Nutbourne W Susx 14 7705
Nutbourne W Susx 14 0718
Nutfield Surrey 27 3050
Nuthall Notts 62 5243
Nuthampstead Herts 39 4034
Nuthurst W Susx 15 1925
Nutley E Susx 16 4427
Nutley Hants 24 6044
Nuttal Lane Gt Man 81 7915
Nutwell S York 83 6304
Nybster Highld 151 3663
Nyetimber W Susx 14 8998
Nyewood W Susx 14 8021
Nymet Rowland Devon 19 7108
Nymet Tracey Devon 8 7200
Nympsfield Gloucs 35 8000
Nynehead Somset 20 1422
Nythe Somset 21 4234
Nyton W Susx 14 9305

Oad Street Kent 28 8762
Oadby Leics 50 6200
Oak Cross Devon 8 5399
Oak Tree Dur 89 3613
Oakall Green Worcs 47 8161
Oakamoor Staffs 73 0444
Oakbank W Loth 117 0766
Oakdale Caerph 33 1898
Oake Somset 20 1525
Oaken Staffs 60 8602
Oakenclough Lancs 80 5447
Oakengates Shrops 60 7010
Oakenholt Flints 70 2571
Oakenshaw Dur 96 1937
Oakenshaw W York 82 1727
Oaker Side Derbys 74 2760
Oakerthorpe Derbys 74 3854
Oakford Cerdgn 42 4558
Oakford Devon 20 9121
Oakfordbridge Devon 20 9122
Oakgrove Ches 79 9169
Oakham Rutlnd 63 8608
Oakhanger Ches 72 7754
Oakhanger Hants 14 7635
Oakhill Somset 21 6347
Oakhurst Kent 27 5550
Oakington Cambs 52 4164
Oaklands Powys 45 0450
Oakle Street Gloucs 35 7517
Oakley Beds 51 0153
Oakley Bucks 37 6412
Oakley Dorset 11 0198
Oakley Fife 117 0289
Oakley Hants 24 5650
Oakley Oxon 37 7500
Oakley Suffk 54 1677
Oakley Green Berks 26 9276
Oakley Park Powys 58 9886
Oakridge Gloucs 35 9103
Oaks Dur 96 1525
Oaks Lancs 81 6733
Oaks Shrops 59 4204
Oaks Green Derbys 73 1533
Oaksey Wilts 35 9993
Oakshaw Cumb 101 5176
Oakshott Hants 13 7427
Oakthorpe Leics 61 3212
Oakthorpe Derbys 62 3738
Oakwood Nthumb 102 9465
Oakwoodhill Surrey 15 1337

Place	County	Page	Grid
Oakworth	W York	82	0338
Oare	Kent	28	0063
Oare	Somset	19	7947
Oare	Wilts	23	1563
Oasby	Lincs	63	0039
Oath	Somset	21	3827
Oathlaw	Angus	127	4756
Oatlands Park	Surrey	26	0865
Oban	Ag & B	122	8629
Obley	Shrops	46	3377
Obney	P & K	125	0237
Oborne	Dorset	11	6518
Obthorpe	Lincs	64	0914
Occold	Suffk	54	1570
Occumster	Highld	151	2635
Ochiltree	E Ayrs	107	5021
Ockbrook	Derbys	62	4235
Ocker Hill	W Mids	60	9793
Ockeridge	Worcs	47	7762
Ockham	Surrey	26	0756
Ockle	Highld	129	5570
Ockley	Surrey	15	1440
Ocle Pychard	Herefs	46	5945
Octon	E R Yk	91	0369
Odcombe	Somset	10	5015
Odd Down	Somset	22	7462
Oddingley	Gloucs	47	9159
Oddington	Gloucs	48	2225
Oddington	Oxon	37	5515
Odell	Beds	51	9657
Odham	Devon	18	4703
Odiham	Hants	24	7451
Odsal	W York	82	1529
Odsey	Herts	39	2938
Odstock	Wilts	23	1426
Odstone	Leics	62	3907
Offchurch	Warwks	48	3565
Offenham	Worcs	48	0546
Offerton	T & W	96	3455
Offham	E Susx	15	4012
Offham	Kent	28	6557
Offham	W Susx	14	0208
Offleymarsh	Shrops	72	7829
Offord Cluny	Cambs	52	2267
Offord Darcy	Cambs	52	2266
Offton	Suffk	54	0649
Offwell	Devon	9	1999
Ogbourne Maizey	Wilts	36	1871
Ogbourne St Andrew	Wilts	36	1872
Ogbourne St George	Wilts	36	2074
Ogden	W York	82	0730
Ogle	Nthumb	103	1378
Oglet	Mersyd	78	4481
Ogmore	V Glam	33	8876
Ogmore Vale	Brdgnd	33	9390
Ogmore-by-Sea	V Glam	33	8675
Ogwen Bank	Gwynd	69	6265
Okeford Fitzpaine	Dorset	11	8010
Okehampton	Devon	8	5995
Olchard	Devon	9	8777
Old	Nhants	50	7872
Old Aberdeen	Aber C	135	9407
Old Alresford	Hants	24	5834
Old Auchenbrack	D & G	107	7597
Old Basford	Notts	62	5543
Old Basing	Hants	24	6652
Old Bewick	Nthumb	111	0621
Old Bolingbroke	Lincs	77	3565
Old Bracknell	Berks	25	8668
Old Bramhope	W York	82	2343
Old Brampton	Derbys	74	3371
Old Bridge of Urr	D & G	100	7767
Old Buckenham	Norfk	66	0691
Old Burghclere	Hants	24	4657
Old Byland	N York	90	5585
Old Cassop	Dur	96	3339
Old Castle	Brdgnd	33	9079
Old Churchstoke	Powys	58	2894
Old Clee	Lincs	85	2808
Old Cleeve	Somset	20	0441
Old Clipstone	Notts	75	6064
Old Colwyn	Conwy	69	8678
Old Dailly	S Ayrs	106	2299
Old Dalby	Leics	63	6723
Old Dam	Derbys	74	1179
Old Deer	Abers	143	9747
Old Ditch	Somset	21	5049
Old Edlington	S York	75	5397
Old Eldon	Dur	96	2427
Old Ellerby	E R Yk	85	1637
Old Felixstowe	Suffk	55	3135
Old Fletton	Cambs	64	1997
Old Forge	Herefs	34	5518
Old Furnace	Herefs	46	4923
Old Glossop	Derbys	74	0494
Old Goole	E R Yk	84	7422
Old Grimsby	IOS	2	8915
Old Hall Green	Herts	39	3722
Old Hall Street	Norfk	67	3033
Old Harlow	Essex	39	4711
Old Heath	Essex	41	0122
Old Hunstanton	Norfk	65	6842
Old Hurst	Cambs	52	3077
Old Hutton	Cumb	87	5688
Old Kea	Cnwll	3	8441
Old Kilpatrick	W Duns	115	4672
Old Knebworth	Herts	39	2320
Old Lakenham	Norfk	67	2205
Old Langho	Lancs	81	7035
Old Laxey	IOM	158	4483
Old Leake	Lincs	77	4050
Old Malton	N York	90	7972
Old Micklefield	W York	83	4433
Old Milton	Hants	12	2394
Old Milverton	Warwks	48	2967
Old Newton	Suffk	54	0562
Old Quarrington	Dur	96	3237
Old Radford	Notts	62	5540
Old Radnor	Powys	46	2558
Old Rayne	Abers	142	6728
Old Romney	Kent	17	0325
Old Shoreham	W Susx	15	2006
Old Soar	Kent	27	6254
Old Sodbury	Gloucs	35	7581
Old Somerby	Lincs	63	9633
Old Stratford	Nhants	49	7741
Old Swinford	W Mids	60	9083
Old Tebay	Cumb	87	6105
Old Thirsk	N York	89	4382
Old Town	Cumb	93	4743
Old Town	Cumb	87	5982
Old Town	E Susx	16	5999
Old Town	IOS	2	9110
Old Town	Nthumb	102	8891
Old Trafford	Gt Man	79	8196
Old Tupton	Derbys	74	3865
Old Warden	Beds	38	1343
Old Weston	Cambs	51	0977
Old Wick	Highld	151	3649
Old Windsor	Berks	25	9874
Old Wives Lees	Kent	29	0754
Old Woking	Surrey	26	0157
Old Wolverton	Bucks	38	8041
Old Woods	Shrops	59	4520
Oldany	Highld	148	0932
Oldberrow	Warwks	48	1265
Oldbury	Kent	27	5956
Oldbury	Shrops	60	7192
Oldbury	W Mids	60	9888
Oldbury	Warwks	61	3194
Oldbury Naite	Gloucs	35	6293
Oldbury on the Hill	Gloucs	35	8188
Oldbury-on-Severn	Gloucs	34	6092
Oldcastle	Mons	46	3224
Oldcastle Heath	Ches	71	4745
Oldcotes	Notts	75	5888
Oldfield	W York	82	0037
Oldfield	Worcs	47	8464
Oldford	Somset	22	7850
Oldhall Green	Suffk	54	8956
Oldham	Gt Man	79	9204
Oldhamstocks	E Loth	119	7470
Oldland	Gloucs	35	6771
Oldmeldrum	Abers	143	8127
Oldmill	Cnwll	5	3673
Oldmixon	Somset	21	3358
Oldridge	Devon	8	8296
Oldshoremore	Highld	148	2058
Oldstead	N York	90	5379
Oldwalls	Swans	32	4891
Oldways End	Somset	19	8724
Olive Green	Staffs	73	1118
Oliver	Border	108	0924
Oliver's Battery	Hants	13	4527
Ollaberry	Shet	153	3680
Ollach	Highld	137	5137
Ollerton	Ches	79	7776
Ollerton	Notts	75	6567
Ollerton	Shrops	72	6425
Olmarch	Cerdgn	44	6255
Olmstead Green	Cambs	53	6341
Olney	Bucks	38	8951
Olrig House	Highld	151	1866
Olton	W Mids	61	1382
Olveston	Gloucs	34	6086
Ombersley	Worcs	47	8463
Ompton	Notts	75	6865
Once Brewed	Nthumb	102	7466
Onchan	IOM	158	3978
Onecote	Staffs	73	0455
Onehouse	Suffk	54	0159
Onen	Mons	34	4314
Ongar Street	Herefs	46	3967
Onibury	Shrops	46	4579
Onich	Highld	130	0261
Onllwyn	Neath	33	8410
Onneley	Staffs	72	7542
Onslow Village	Surrey	25	9849
Onston	Ches	71	5873
Openwoodgate	Derbys	62	3647
Orbiston	Moray	141	3057
Orbost	Highld	136	2543
Orby	Lincs	77	4967
Orchard Portman	Somset	20	2421
Orcheston	Wilts	23	0545
Orcop	Herefs	46	4726
Orcop Hill	Herefs	46	4727
Ord	Abers	142	6258
Ordhead	Abers	135	6610
Ordie	Abers	134	4501
Ordiequish	Moray	141	3357
Ordley	Nthumb	95	9459
Ordsall	Notts	75	7079
Ore	E Susx	17	8311
Oreleton Common	Herefs	46	4768
Oreton	Shrops	59	6580
Orford	Ches	78	6190
Orford	Suffk	55	4250
Organford	Dorset	11	9392
Orgreave	Staffs	73	1415
Orlestone	Kent	17	0034
Orleton	Herefs	46	4967
Orleton	Worcs	47	7067
Orlingbury	Nhants	51	8572
Ormathwaite	Cumb	93	2625
Ormesby	N York	97	5317
Ormesby St Margaret	Norfk	67	4914
Ormesby St Michael	Norfk	67	4714
Ormiscaig	Highld	144	8590
Ormiston	E Loth	118	4169
Ormsaigmore	Highld	121	4763
Ormsary	Ag & B	113	7472
Ormskirk	Lancs	78	4108
Ornsby Hill	Dur	96	1648
Oronsay	Ag & B	112	3588
Orphir	Ork	153	3404
Orpington	Gt Lon	27	4666
Orrell	Gt Man	78	5303
Orrell	Mersyd	78	3496
Orrell Post	Gt Man	78	5305
Orrisdale	IOM	158	3292
Orroland	D & G	92	7746
Orsett	Essex	40	6482
Orslow	Staffs	72	8015
Orston	Notts	63	7740
Orthwaite	Cumb	93	2534
Ortner	Lancs	80	5354
Orton	Cumb	87	6208
Orton	Nhants	51	8079
Orton	Staffs	60	8795
Orton Longueville	Cambs	64	1796
Orton Rigg	Cumb	93	3352
Orton Waterville	Cambs	64	1595
Orton-on-the-Hill	Leics	61	3003
Orwell	Cambs	52	3650
Osbaldeston	Lancs	81	6431
Osbaldeston Green	Lancs	81	6432
Osbaldwick	N York	83	6251
Osbaston	Leics	62	4204
Osbaston	Shrops	59	3222
Osborne	IOW	13	5194
Osborne House		13	5195
Osbournby	Lincs	64	0638
Oscroft	Ches	71	5067
Ose	Highld	136	3140
Osgathorpe	Leics	62	4319
Osgodby	Lincs	76	0792
Osgodby	N York	83	6433
Osgodby	N York	91	0584
Oskaig	Highld	137	5438
Oskamull	Ag & B	121	4540
Osmaston	Derbys	73	1943
Osmington	Dorset	11	7283
Osmington Mills	Dorset	11	7381
Osmondthorpe	W York	83	3333
Osmotherley	N York	89	4596
Osney	Oxon	37	4906
Ospringe	Kent	28	0060
Ossett	W York	82	2720
Ossington	Notts	75	7564
Ostend	Essex	40	9397
Osterley	Gt Lon	26	1577
Oswaldkirk	N York	90	6278
Oswaldtwistle	Lancs	81	7327
Oswestry	Shrops	59	2929
Otford	Kent	27	5359
Otham	Kent	28	7953
Otham Hole	Kent	28	8052
Othery	Somset	21	3831
Otley	Suffk	55	2055
Otley	W York	82	2045
Otley Green	Suffk	55	2156
Otter Ferry	Ag & B	114	9384
Otterbourne	Hants	13	4522
Otterburn	N York	88	8857
Otterburn	Nthumb	102	8893
Otterham	Cnwll	4	1690
Otterham Quay	Kent	28	8366
Otterhampton	Somset	20	2443
Otternish	W Isls	152	9079
Ottershaw	Surrey	26	0263
Otterswick	Shet	153	5285
Otterton	Devon	9	0684
Otterwood	Hants	13	4102
Ottery	Devon	6	4475
Ottery St Mary	Devon	9	1095
Ottinge	Kent	29	1642
Ottringham	E R Yk	85	2624
Oughterby	Cumb	93	2955
Oughtershaw	N York	88	8780
Oughterside	Cumb	92	1140
Oughtibridge	S York	74	3093
Oughtrington	Ches	79	6987
Oulston	N York	90	5474
Oulton	Cumb	93	2450
Oulton	Norfk	66	1328
Oulton	Staffs	72	7822
Oulton	Staffs	72	9035
Oulton	W York	83	3628
Oulton Broad	Suffk	67	5192
Oulton Street	Norfk	66	1527
Oundle	Nhants	51	0388
Ounsdale	Staffs	60	8693
Ousby	Cumb	94	6134
Ousden	Suffk	53	7459
Ousefleet	E R Yk	84	8323
Ouston	Dur	96	2554
Out Elmstead	Kent	29	2050
Out Newton	E R Yk	85	3821
Out Rawcliffe	Lancs	80	4041
Outchester	Nthumb	111	1433
Outgate	Cumb	87	3599
Outhgill	Cumb	88	7801
Outhill	Warwks	48	1066
Outlands	Staffs	72	7630
Outlane	W York	82	0817
Outwell	Norfk	65	5103
Outwick	Hants	12	1417
Outwood	Surrey	15	3145
Outwood	W York	83	3323
Outwood Gate	Gt Man	79	7805
Outwoods	Leics	62	4018
Outwoods	Staffs	72	7817
Outwoods	Warwks	61	2484
Ouzlewell Green	W York	83	3326
Ovenden	W York	82	0627
Over	Cambs	52	3770
Over	Ches	71	6365
Over	Gloucs	35	8119
Over	Gloucs	34	5882
Over Burrows	Derbys	73	2639
Over Compton	Dorset	10	5816
Over End	Cambs	51	0893
Over Green	Warwks	61	1694
Over Haddon	Derbys	74	2066
Over Kellet	Lancs	87	5169
Over Kiddington	Oxon	36	4021
Over Monnow	Mons	34	5012
Over Norton	Oxon	48	3128
Over Peover	Ches	79	7873
Over Silton	N York	89	4493
Over Stowey	Somset	20	1838
Over Stratton	Somset	10	4315
Over Tabley	Ches	79	7283
Over Wallop	Hants	23	2838
Over Whitacre	Warwks	61	2590
Over Woodhouse	Derbys	75	4671
Over Worton	Oxon	49	4329
Overbury	Worcs	47	9537
Overcombe	Dorset	11	6982
Overgreen	Derbys	74	3273
Overleigh	Somset	21	4835
Overley	Staffs	73	1515
Overpool	Ches	71	3877
Overscaig Hotel	Highld	149	4123
Overseal	Derbys	73	2915
Oversland	Kent	28	0557
Overstey Green	Warwks	48	0957
Overstone	Nhants	50	7966
Overstrand	Norfk	67	2440
Overstreet	Wilts	23	0637
Overthorpe	Nhants	49	4840
Overton	Aber C	143	8714
Overton	Ches	71	5277
Overton	Hants	24	5149
Overton	Lancs	87	4358
Overton	N York	83	5555
Overton	Shrops	46	5072
Overton	Swans	32	4685
Overton	W York	82	2516
Overton	Wrexhm	71	3741
Overton Bridge	Wrexhm	71	3542
Overton Green	Ches	72	8060
Overtown	N Lans	116	8053
Overtown	W York	83	3516
Overtown	Wilts	36	1579
Overy	Oxon	37	5893
Oving	Bucks	37	7821
Oving	W Susx	14	9004
Ovingdean	E Susx	15	3503
Ovingham	Nthumb	103	0863
Ovington	Dur	89	1314
Ovington	Essex	53	7642
Ovington	Hants	24	5631
Ovington	Norfk	66	9202
Ovington	Nthumb	103	0663
Ower	Hants	12	3216
Ower	Hants	13	4702
Owermoigne	Dorset	11	7685
Owl's Green	Suffk	55	2869
Owlbury	Shrops	59	3191
Owlerton	S York	74	3389
Owlpen	Gloucs	35	7998
Owlsmoor	Berks	25	8462
Owlswick	Bucks	37	7806
Owmby	Lincs	85	0704
Owmby	Lincs	76	0087
Owslebury	Hants	13	5123
Owston	Leics	63	7707
Owston	S York	83	5511
Owston Ferry	Lincs	75	8000
Owstwick	E R Yk	85	2732
Owthorne	E R Yk	85	3328
Owthorpe	Notts	63	6733
Oxborough	Norfk	65	7401
Oxbridge	Dorset	10	4797
Oxcombe	Lincs	77	3177
Oxcroft	Derbys	75	4873
Oxen End	Essex	40	6629
Oxen Park	Cumb	86	3187
Oxenholme	Cumb	87	5389
Oxenhope	W York	82	0334
Oxenpill	Somset	21	4441
Oxenton	Gloucs	47	9531
Oxenwood	Wilts	23	3058
Oxford	Oxon	37	5106
Oxhey	Herts	26	1295
Oxhill	Dur	96	1852
Oxhill	Warwks	48	3146
Oxley	W Mids	60	9001
Oxley Green	Essex	40	9014
Oxley's Green	E Susx	16	6921
Oxlode	Cambs	53	4886
Oxnam	Border	110	6918
Oxnead	Norfk	67	2224
Oxshott	Surrey	26	1460
Oxshott Heath	Surrey	26	1361
Oxspring	S York	82	2601
Oxted	Surrey	27	3852
Oxton	Border	118	4953
Oxton	N York	83	5042
Oxton	Notts	75	6351
Oxwich	Swans	32	4986
Oxwich Green	Swans	32	4985
Oxwick	Norfk	66	9125
Oykel Bridge Hotel	Highld	145	3801
Oyne	Abers	142	6725
Oystermouth	Swans	32	6187
Ozleworth	Gloucs	35	7993

P

Place	County	Page	Grid
Pabail	W Isls	152	5231
Packers Hill	Dorset	11	7110
Packington	Leics	62	3614
Packmoor	Staffs	72	8654
Packmores	Warwks	48	2866
Padanaram	Angus	127	4251
Padbury	Bucks	49	7230
Paddington	Ches	79	6389
Paddington	Gt Lon	27	2681
Paddlesworth	Kent	28	6862
Paddlesworth	Kent	29	1939
Paddock Wood	Kent	28	6744
Paddolgreen	Shrops	59	5032
Padeswood	Flints	70	2762
Padfield	Derbys	74	0296
Padgate	Ches	79	6389
Padhams Green	Essex	40	6497
Padiham	Lancs	81	7933
Padside	N York	89	1659
Padstow	Cnwll	4	9175
Padworth	Berks	24	6166
Page Bank	Dur	96	2335
Pagham	W Susx	14	8897
Paglesham	Essex	40	9293
Paignton	Devon	7	8860
Pailton	Warwks	50	4781
Paine's Cross	E Susx	16	6223
Painleyhill	Staffs	73	0333
Painscastle	Powys	45	1646
Painshawfield	Nthumb	103	0560
Painsthorpe	E R Yk	90	8158
Painswick	Gloucs	35	8609
Painter's Forstal	Kent	28	9958
Paisley	Rens	115	4864
Pakefield	Suffk	55	5390
Pakenham	Suffk	54	9267
Pale	Gwynd	58	9836
Pale Green	Essex	53	6542
Palestine	Hants	23	2...
Paley Street	Berks	26	8...
Palfrey	W Mids	60	0...
Palgrave	Suffk	54	1...
Pallington	Dorset	11	78
Palmers Green	Gt Lon	27	3...
Palmersbridge	Cnwll	5	19
Palmerston	E Ayrs	107	5...
Palmerstown	V Glam	20	13
Palnackie	D & G	92	8
Palnure	D & G	99	45
Palterton	Derbys	75	4...
Pamber End	Hants	24	6...
Pamber Green	Hants	24	6...
Pamber Heath	Hants	24	6...
Pamington	Gloucs	47	9...
Pamphill	Dorset	11	9...
Pampisford	Cambs	53	4...
Panborough	Somset	21	4...
Panbride	Angus	127	5...
Pancrasweek	Devon	18	2...
Pancross	V Glam	20	04
Pandy	Caerph	33	15
Pandy	Gwynd	57	6...
Pandy	Gwynd	57	8...
Pandy	Mons	34	3...
Pandy	Powys	58	9...
Pandy	Wrexhm	57	
Pandy Tudur	Conwy	69	8...
Pandy'r Capel	Denbgs	70	0...
Panfield	Essex	40	7...
Pangbourne	Berks	37	6...
Pangdean	W Susx	15	2...
Panks Bridge	Herefs	47	6...
Pannal	N York	82	2...
Pannal Ash	N York	82	2...
Pannanich Wells Hotel	Abers	134	4...
Pant	Shrops	58	2...
Pant Glas	Gwynd	68	47
Pant Mawr	Powys	43	8...
Pant-ffrwyth	Brdgnd	33	9...
Pant-Gwyn	Carmth	44	5...
Pant-lasau	Swans	32	6...
Pant-pastynog	Denbgs	70	0...
Pant-y-dwr	Powys	45	9...
Pant-y-ffridd	Powys	58	1...
Pant-y-gog	Brdgnd	33	9...
Pant-y-mwyn	Flints	70	1...
Pantasaph	Flints	70	1...
Panteg	Pembks	30	9...
Pantersbridge	Cnwll	4	1...
Pantglas	Powys	43	7...
Panton	Lincs	76	1...
Pantperthog	Gwynd	57	74
Pantyffynnon	Carmth	32	6...
Pantygaseg	Torfn	34	2...
Pantymenyn	Carmth	31	1...
Panxworth	Norfk	67	3...
Papa Westray Airport		153	4...
Papcastle	Cumb	92	1...
Papigoe	Highld	151	3...
Papple	E Loth	118	5...
Papplewick	Notts	75	5...
Papworth Everard	Cambs	52	2...
Papworth St Agnes	Cambs	52	2...
Par	Cnwll	3	07
Paramour Street	Kent	29	2...
Parbold	Lancs	80	4...
Parbrook	Somset	21	5...
Parbrook	W Susx	14	0...
Parc	Gwynd	57	8...
Parc Seymour	Newpt	34	4...
Parcllyn	Cerdgn	42	24
Pardshaw	Cumb	92	0...
Parham	Suffk	55	3...
Park	Abers	135	7...
Park	D & G	100	9...
Park	Nthumb	102	6...
Park Bottom	Cnwll	2	6...
Park Bridge	Gt Man	79	94
Park Corner	Berks	26	8...
Park Corner	E Susx	16	5...
Park Corner	Oxon	37	6...
Park End	Beds	38	9...
Park End	Nthumb	102	8...
Park End	Staffs	72	7...
Park Gate	Hants	13	5...
Park Gate	W York	82	18
Park Gate	Worcs	60	9...
Park Green	Essex	39	6...
Park Green	Suffk	54	13
Park Head	Cumb	94	58
Park Head	Derbys	74	38
Park Hill	Gloucs	34	5...
Park Royal	Gt Lon	26	15
Park Street	Herts	39	14
Park Street	W Susx	14	11
Parkend	Gloucs	34	6...
Parkers Green	Kent	16	61
Parkeston	Essex	41	2...
Parkeston Quay	Essex	41	2...
Parkfield	Cnwll	5	3...
Parkgate	Ches	70	2...
Parkgate	Cumb	93	21
Parkgate	D & G	100	0...
Parkgate	E Susx	17	72
Parkgate	Essex	40	6...
Parkgate	Kent	27	5...
Parkgate	Kent	17	5...
Parkgate	Surrey	15	2...
Parkhall	W Duns	115	48
Parkham	Devon	18	3...
Parkham Ash	Devon	18	3...
Parkhill	Notts	75	6...
Parkhill House	Abers	143	8...
Parkhouse	Mons	34	5...
Parkmill	Swans	32	5...
Parkside	N Lans	116	8...
Parkside	Wrexhm	71	38
Parkstone	Dorset	12	0...
Parley Green	Dorset	12	1...
Parlington	W York	83	4...
Parmoor	Bucks	37	7...
Parndon	Essex	39	4...
Parracombe	Devon	19	6...
Parrog	Pembks	30	0...
Parson Drove	Cambs	64	3...

Place		
...son's Cross S York	74	3492
...son's Heath Essex	41	0226
...sonby Cumb	92	1438
...rick C Glas	115	5467
...ttington Gt Man	79	7191
...tney Lincs	77	4068
...ton Cumb	92	9820
...tridge Green W Susx	15	1919
...trishow Powys	34	2722
...wich Derbys	73	1854
...slow Wood Common Essex	27	5802
...senham Nhants	38	7839
...sfield Hants	14	8234
...ssingford Bridge Essex	27	5097
...ston Cambs	64	1802
...ston Norfk	67	3234
...sturefields Staffs	73	9924
...tchacott Devon	5	4798
...tcham E Susx	15	3008
...tchetts Green Herts	26	1497
...tching W Susx	14	0806
...tchole Devon	19	6142
...tchway Glous	34	6082
...teley Bridge N York	89	1565
...ternoster Heath Essex	40	9115
...teshall Herefs	46	5262
...th of Condie P & K	125	0711
...the Somset	21	3730
...thhead Fife	117	2992
...thhead Mdloth	118	3964
...thlow Warwks	48	1758
...tmore Heath Herts	39	4425
...tna E Ayrs	106	4110
...tney Wilts	23	0758
...trick Brompton N York	89	2190
...tricroft Gt Man	79	7597
...trington E R Yk	85	3122
...trixbourne Kent	29	1855
...tterdale Cumb	93	3915
...ttingham Staffs	60	8299
...ttishall Nhants	49	6754
...ttiswick Green Essex	40	8124
...tton Shrops	59	5895
...tul Cnwll	2	4627
...tul's Dene Wilts	23	1432
...tulerspury Bucks	49	7145
...tull E R Yk	85	1626
...tulton Somset	21	6556
...tunton Herefs	47	6650
...tuperhaugh Nthumb	103	1099
...tve Lane Shrops	72	7616
...tvenham Beds	51	9955
...twlett Somset	20	2942
...twston Nthumb	110	8532
...txford Glous	48	1837
...txton Border	119	9353
...tyden Street Kent	28	9254
...tyhembury Devon	9	0901
...tythorne Lancs	81	8251
...tytoe Herefs	46	4171
...acehaven E Susx	15	4101
...ak Dale Derbys	74	0976
...ak Forest Derbys	74	1179
...ak Hill Lincs	64	2615
...akirk Cambs	64	1606
...anmeanach Highld	129	7180
...arson's Crescent Kent	28	6943
...artree Green Herefs	46	5932
...ase Pottage W Susx	15	2633
...asedown St John Somset	22	7057
...asehill Derbys	74	4049
...aseland Green Norfk	66	0516
...asemore Berks	37	4577
...asenhall Suffk	55	3569
...aslake Surrey	14	0844
...asley Cross Mersyd	78	5294
...asmarsh E Susx	17	8822
...asmarsh Somset	10	3312
...asmarsh Surrey	25	9946
...eat Inn Fife	127	4509
...eathill Abers	143	9366
...eatling Magna Leics	50	5992
...eatling Parva Leics	50	5889
...eaton Shrops	59	5385
...ebmarsh Essex	40	8533
...ebworth Worcs	48	1347
...ecket Well N York	82	9929
...eckforton Ches	71	5356
...eckham Gt Lon	27	3476
...eckleton Leics	62	4701
...edairrfford Powys	58	1124
...edlinge Kent	17	1335
...edmore W Mids	60	9182
...edwell Somset	21	4236
...eebles Border	109	2540
...eel IOM	158	2483
...eel Lancs	80	3531
...eel Common Hants	13	5703
...eene Kent	29	1837
...eening Quarter Kent	17	8828
...eggs Green Leics	62	4117
...egsdon Beds	38	1130
...egswood Nthumb	103	2287
...egwell Kent	29	3664
...einchorran Highld	137	5233
...einlich Highld	136	4158
...elcomb Nhants	30	9218
...elcomb Bridge Pembks	30	9317
...elcomb Cross Pembks	30	9218
...eldon Essex	41	9816
...ell Green E Susx	16	6432
...elsall N York	60	0203
...elsall Wood W Mids	60	0204
...elton Dur	96	2553
...elton Fell Dur	96	2551
...elutho Cumb	92	1249
...elynt Cnwll	5	2055
...emberton Carmth	32	5300
...emberton Gt Man	78	5503
...embles Cross Kent	28	8947
...embrey Carmth	31	4301
...embridge Herefs	46	3958
...embroke Pembks	30	9801
...embroke Dock Pembks	30	9603
...embury Kent	16	6240
...en Rhiwfawr Neath	32	7410
...en-bont Rhydybeddau Cerdgn	43	6783

Place		
Pen-ffordd Pembks	31	0722
Pen-groes-oped Mons	34	3106
Pen-llyn IOA	68	3582
Pen-lon IOA	68	4365
Pen-rhiw Pembks	31	2440
Pen-twyn Caerph	33	2000
Pen-twyn Mons	34	5209
Pen-twyn Torfn	34	2603
Pen-twyn Powys	58	2123
Pen-y-bont Powys	58	2123
Pen-y-bont-fawr Powys	58	0824
Pen-y-bryn Neath	33	8384
Pen-y-bryn Pembks	31	1742
Pen-y-cae Powys	33	8413
Pen-y-cae-mawr Mons	34	4195
Pen-y-cefn Flints	70	1175
Pen-y-clawdd Mons	34	4507
Pen-y-coedcae Rhondd	33	0587
Pen-y-cwn Pembks	30	8523
Pen-y-darren Myr Td	33	0506
Pen-y-fai Brdgnd	33	8981
Pen-y-felin Flints	70	1569
Pen-y-garn Cerdgn	43	6285
Pen-y-Garnedd Powys	58	1023
Pen-y-genffordd Powys	45	1729
Pen-y-graig Gwynd	56	2033
Pen-y-Gwryd Gwynd	69	6655
Pen-y-lan V Glam	33	9976
Pen-y-pass Gwynd	69	6455
Pen-y-stryt Denbgs	70	1952
Pen-yr-Heol Mons	34	4311
Pen-yr-Heolgerrig Myr Td	33	0306
Penair Cnwll	3	8445
Penallt Mons	34	5210
Penally Pembks	31	1199
Penalt Herefs	46	5629
Penare Cnwll	3	9940
Penarth V Glam	33	1871
Penblewin Pembks	31	1216
Penbryn Cerdgn	42	2951
Pencader Carmth	31	4436
Pencaenewydd Gwynd	56	4040
Pencaitland E Loth	118	4468
Pencalenick Cnwll	3	8545
Pencarnisiog IOA	68	3573
Pencarreg Carmth	44	5445
Pencarrow Cnwll	4	1082
Pencelli Powys	45	0925
Penclawdd Swans	32	5495
Pencoed Brdgnd	33	9581
Pencombe Herefs	46	5952
Pencoyd Herefs	46	5126
Pencraig Herefs	34	5620
Pencraig Powys	58	0426
Pendeen Cnwll	2	3834
Penderyn Rhondd	33	9408
Pendine Carmth	31	2208
Pendlebury Gt Man	79	7802
Pendleton Lancs	81	7539
Pendock Worcs	47	7832
Pendoggett Cnwll	4	0279
Pendomer Somset	10	5210
Pendoylan V Glam	33	0576
Pendre Brdgnd	33	9181
Penegoes Powys	57	7600
Penelewey Cnwll	3	8140
Pengam Caerph	33	1597
Pengam Cardif	33	2177
Penge Gt Lon	27	3570
Pengelly Cnwll	3	8551
Pengelly Cnwll	4	0783
Pengorffwysfa IOA	68	4692
Pengover Green Cnwll	5	2765
Pengrugla Cnwll	3	9947
Pengwern Denbgs	70	0276
Penhale Cnwll	2	6918
Penhale Cnwll	4	9057
Penhale Cnwll	4	0860
Penhale Cnwll	5	4153
Penhallow Cnwll	3	7651
Penhalurick Cnwll	2	7038
Penhalvean Cnwll	2	7038
Penhill Wilts	36	1588
Penhow Newpt	34	4290
Penhurst E Susx	16	6916
Peniarth Gwynd	57	6105
Penicuik Mdloth	117	2359
Peniel Carmth	31	4324
Peniel Denbgs	70	0362
Penifiler Highld	136	4841
Peninver Ag & B	105	7524
Penisar Waun Gwynd	69	5563
Penistone S York	82	2403
Penjerrick Cnwll	3	7730
Penkelly Cnwll	4	1854
Penketh Ches	78	5587
Penkill S Ayrs	106	2398
Penkridge Staffs	60	9213
Penlean Cnwll	5	2098
Penley Wrexhm	71	4040
Penllergaer Swans	32	6198
Penllyn V Glam	33	9775
Penmachno Conwy	69	7950
Penmaen Caerph	33	1897
Penmaen Swans	32	5288
Penmaenan Conwy	69	7175
Penmaenmawr Conwy	69	7276
Penmaenpool Gwynd	57	6918
Penmark V Glam	20	0568
Penmon IOA	69	6280
Penmorfa Gwynd	57	5540
Penmynydd IOA	68	5074
Penn Bucks	26	9193
Penn W Mids	60	8895
Penn Street Bucks	26	9295
Pennal Gwynd	57	6900
Pennan Abers	143	8465
Pennant Cerdgn	42	5163
Pennant Denbgs	58	0234
Pennant Powys	43	8897
Pennant-Melangell Powys	58	0226
Pennard Swans	32	5688
Pennerley Shrops	59	3599
Pennicott Devon	9	8701
Pennington Cumb	86	2677
Pennington Hants	12	3195
Pennington Green Gt Man	79	6206
Pennorth Powys	45	1125
Pennsylvania Glous	35	7473

Place		
Penny Bridge Cumb	86	3083
Penny Bridge Pembks	30	0001
Penny Green Notts	75	5475
Penny Hill Lincs	64	3526
Pennycross Ag & B	121	5025
Pennygate Norfk	67	3423
Pennyghael Ag & B	121	5125
Pennyglen S Ayrs	106	2710
Pennymoor Devon	19	8611
Penparc Cerdgn	42	2047
Penparcau Cerdgn	43	5980
Penpedairheol Caerph	33	1497
Penpedairheol Mons	34	3303
Penperlleni Mons	34	3204
Penpethy Cnwll	4	0886
Penpillick Cnwll	3	0856
Penpol Cnwll	3	8139
Penponds Cnwll	2	6339
Penpont Cnwll	4	0874
Penpont D & G	100	8494
Penpont Powys	45	9728
Penquit Devon	7	6454
Penrest Cnwll	5	3377
Penrherber Carmth	31	2938
Penhriw-pal Cerdgn	42	3445
Penrhiwceiber Rhondd	33	0597
Penrhiwllan Cerdgn	31	3641
Penrhos Gwynd	56	3433
Penrhos IOA	68	2781
Penrhos Mons	34	4111
Penrhos Powys	32	8011
Penrhos garnedd Gwynd	69	5670
Penrhyn Bay Conwy	69	8281
Penrhyn Castle	69	6071
Penrhyn-side Conwy	69	8181
Penrhyncoch Cerdgn	43	6384
Penrhyndeudraeth Gwynd	57	6139
Penrice Swans	32	4987
Penrioch N Ayrs	105	8744
Penrith Cumb	94	5130
Penrose Cnwll	4	8770
Penrose Cnwll	5	2589
Penruddock Cumb	93	4227
Penryn Cnwll	3	7834
Pensarn Carmth	31	4119
Pensarn Conwy	70	9578
Pensax Worcs	47	7269
Pensby Mersyd	78	2782
Penselwood Somset	22	7531
Pensford Somset	21	6263
Pensham Worcs	47	9444
Penshaw T & W	96	3253
Penshurst Kent	16	5243
Penshurst Station Kent	16	5246
Pensilva Cnwll	5	2970
Pensnett W Mids	60	9189
Penstone Devon	8	7700
Penstrowed Powys	58	0691
Pentewan Cnwll	3	0147
Pentir Gwynd	69	5766
Pentire Cnwll	4	7961
Pentlepoir Pembks	31	1105
Pentlow Essex	54	8146
Pentlow Street Essex	54	8245
Pentney Norfk	65	7214
Penton Grafton Hants	23	3247
Penton Mewsey Hants	23	3247
Pentonbridge Cumb	101	4476
Pentraeth IOA	68	5278
Pentre Denbgs	70	0862
Pentre Flints	71	3267
Pentre Mons	34	3106
Pentre Powys	58	0685
Pentre Powys	58	1589
Pentre Powys	58	2792
Pentre Rhondd	33	9696
Pentre Shrops	59	3617
Pentre Wrexhm	71	2840
Pentre Bach Cerdgn	44	5547
Pentre Bach Flints	70	2175
Pentre Berw IOA	68	4772
Pentre Ffwrndan Flints	70	2572
Pentre Gwynfryn Gwynd	57	5327
Pentre Halkyn Flints	70	2072
Pentre Hodrey Shrops	46	3277
Pentre Isaf Conwy	70	8871
Pentre Llanrhaeadr Denbgs	70	0863
Pentre Meyrick V Glam	33	9675
Pentre Saron Denbgs	70	0260
Pentre ty gwyn Carmth	44	8135
Pentre'r Felin Conwy	69	8069
Pentre'r-felin Cerdgn	44	6148
Pentre'r-felin Powys	45	9230
Pentre'rbryn Cerdgn	42	3954
Pentre-bach Powys	45	9132
Pentre-bont Conwy	69	7351
Pentre-cagel Cerdgn	31	3340
Pentre-celyn Denbgs	70	1453
Pentre-celyn Powys	57	8805
Pentre-chwyth Swans	32	6794
Pentre-clawdd Shrops	59	2931
Pentre-cwrt Carmth	31	3838
Pentre-dwr Swans	32	6995
Pentre-Gwenlais Carmth	32	6016
Pentre-llwyn-llwyd Powys	45	9654
Pentre-llyn Cerdgn	43	6175
Pentre-llyn-cymmer Conwy	70	9752
Pentre-piod Torfn	34	2601
Pentre-poeth Newpt	34	2888
Pentre-tafarn-y-fedw Conwy	69	8162
Pentrebach Myr Td	33	0604
Pentrebeirdd Powys	58	1813
Pentredwr Denbgs	70	1946
Pentrefelin Gwynd	57	5239
Pentrefelin IOA	68	4392
Pentrefoelas Conwy	69	8751
Pentregalar Pembks	31	1831
Pentregat Cerdgn	42	3551
Pentrich Derbys	74	3852
Pentridge Dorset	12	0317
Pentridge Hill Dorset	12	0317
Pentyrch Cardif	33	1081
Penwithick Cnwll	3	0256
Penwood Hants	24	4461
Penwyllt Powys	33	8515
Penybanc Carmth	44	6123

Place		
Penybont Powys	45	1164
Penycae Wrexhm	70	2745
Penycaerau Gwynd	56	1927
Penyffordd Flints	71	3061
Penygraig Rhondd	33	0090
Penygroes Carmth	32	5813
Penygroes Gwynd	68	4752
Penysarn IOA	68	4590
Penywaun Rhondd	33	9804
Penywern Neath	32	7609
Penzance Cnwll	2	4730
Penzance Heliport	2	4831
Peopleton Worcs	47	9350
Peover Heath Ches	79	7973
Peper Harow Surrey	25	9344
Peplow Shrops	59	6224
Pepper's Green Essex	40	6101
Pepperstock Beds	38	0817
Perceton N Ayrs	106	3540
Percie Abers	134	5992
Percyhorner Abers	143	9665
Perelle Guern	158	0000
Periton Somset	20	9545
Perivale Gt Lon	26	1682
Perkins Village Devon	9	0291
Perkinsville Dur	96	2553
Perlethorpe Notts	75	6470
Perran Wharf Cnwll	3	7738
Perranarworthal Cnwll	3	7738
Perranporth Cnwll	3	7554
Perranuthnoe Cnwll	2	5329
Perranwell Cnwll	3	7739
Perranwell Cnwll	3	7752
Perranzabuloe Cnwll	3	7752
Perrott's Brook Glous	35	0106
Perry W Mids	61	0792
Perry Barr W Mids	61	0791
Perry Green Essex	40	8022
Perry Green Herts	39	4317
Perry Green Wilts	35	9689
Perry Street Somset	10	3305
Pershall Staffs	72	8129
Pershore Worcs	47	9446
Pertenhall Beds	51	0865
Perth P & K	126	1123
Perthy Shrops	59	3633
Perton Herefs	46	5940
Perton Staffs	60	8699
Pertwood Wilts	22	8936
Pet Street Kent	29	0846
Peter Tavy Devon	5	5177
Peter's Green Herts	38	1419
Peterborough Cambs	64	1998
Peterchurch Herefs	46	3438
Peterculter Aber C	135	8300
Peterhead Abers	143	1246
Peterlee Dur	96	4241
Peters Marland Devon	18	4713
Petersfield Hants	13	7423
Petersham Gt Lon	26	1873
Peterston-super-Ely V Glam	33	0876
Peterstone Wentlooge Newpt	34	2679
Peterstow Herefs	46	5624
Petham Kent	29	1251
Petherwin Gate Cnwll	5	2889
Petrockstow Devon	19	5109
Petsoe End Bucks	38	8949
Pett E Susx	17	8714
Pett Bottom Kent	29	1552
Pettaugh Suffk	54	1659
Petterden Angus	127	4240
Pettinain S Lans	108	9543
Pettistree Suffk	55	3055
Petton Devon	20	0124
Petton Shrops	59	4326
Petts Wood Gt Lon	27	4567
Petty France Glous	35	7885
Pettycur Fife	117	2686
Pettymuk Abers	143	9023
Petworth W Susx	14	9721
Pevensey E Susx	16	6405
Pevensey Bay E Susx	16	6504
Pewsey Wilts	23	1660
Pheasant's Hill Bucks	37	7887
Phepson Worcs	47	9459
Philadelphia T & W	96	3352
Philham Devon	18	2522
Philiphaugh Border	109	4327
Phillack Cnwll	2	5638
Philleigh Cnwll	3	8639
Philpot End Essex	40	6118
Philpstoun W Loth	117	0577
Phocle Green Herefs	47	6326
Phoenix Green Hants	24	7555
Phoines Highld	132	7093
Pibsbury Somset	21	4426
Pica Cumb	92	0222
Piccadilly Warwks	61	2398
Piccotts End Herts	38	0409
Pickburn S York	83	5107
Pickering N York	90	7984
Picket Piece Hants	23	3947
Picket Post Hants	12	1906
Pickford W Mids	61	2881
Pickford Green W Mids	61	2781
Pickhill N York	89	3483
Picklescott Shrops	59	4399
Pickmere Ches	79	6977
Pickney Somset	20	1929
Pickstock Shrops	72	7223
Pickup Bank Lancs	81	7122
Pickwell Devon	18	4540
Pickwell Leics	63	7811
Pickworth Lincs	63	9913
Pickworth Lincs	64	0433
Picton Ches	71	4371
Picton Flints	70	1182
Picton N York	89	4107
Picton Ferry Carmth	31	2717
Piddinghoe E Susx	16	4303
Piddington Bucks	37	8094
Piddington Nhants	51	8054
Piddington Oxon	37	6317
Piddlehinton Dorset	11	7197

Place		
Piddletrenthide Dorset	11	7099
Pidley Cambs	52	3377
Pie Corner Herefs	47	6461
Piercebridge Dur	96	2115
Pierowall Ork	153	4348
Piff's Elm Glous	47	9026
Pig Oak Dorset	12	0202
Pig Street Herefs	46	3647
Pigdon Nthumb	103	1588
Pigeon Green Warwks	48	2260
Pikehall Derbys	74	1959
Pilford Dorset	12	0301
Pilgrims Hatch Essex	27	5895
Pilham Lincs	76	8693
Pill Somset	34	5275
Pillaton Cnwll	5	3664
Pillatonmill Cnwll	5	3663
Pillerton Hersey Warwks	48	2948
Pillerton Priors Warwks	48	2947
Pilleth Powys	46	2667
Pilley Hants	12	3298
Pilley S York	74	3300
Pilley Bailey Hants	12	3398
Pillgwenlly Newpt	34	3186
Pillhead Devon	18	4726
Pilling Lancs	80	4048
Pilling Lane Lancs	80	3749
Pilning Glous	34	5684
Pilot Inn Kent	17	0818
Pilsbury Derbys	74	1163
Pilsdon Dorset	10	4199
Pilsgate Cambs	64	0605
Pilsley Derbys	74	2371
Pilsley Derbys	74	4262
Pilson Green Norfk	67	3713
Piltdown E Susx	16	4422
Pilton Devon	19	5534
Pilton Nhants	51	0284
Pilton Rutlnd	63	9102
Pilton Somset	21	5941
Pilton Green Swans	32	4487
Pimlico Lancs	81	7443
Pimlico Nhants	49	6140
Pimperne Dorset	11	9009
Pin Green Herts	39	2525
Pinchbeck Lincs	64	2425
Pinchbeck Bars Lincs	64	1925
Pinchbeck West Lincs	64	2024
Pincheon Green S York	83	6517
Pinchinthorpe N York	90	5714
Pincock Lancs	80	5417
Pindon End Bucks	38	7847
Pinfold Lancs	80	3811
Pinford End Suffk	54	8459
Pinged Carmth	31	4203
Pingewood Berks	24	6699
Pinhoe Devon	9	9694
Pinkett's Booth W Mids	61	2781
Pinkney Wilts	35	9686
Pinley W Mids	61	3577
Pinley Green Warwks	48	2066
Pinminnock S Ayrs	106	1993
Pinmore S Ayrs	106	2091
Pinn Devon	9	1086
Pinner Gt Lon	26	1289
Pinner Green Gt Lon	26	1289
Pinsley Green Ches	71	5846
Pinvin Worcs	47	9549
Pinwherry S Ayrs	98	2086
Pinxton Derbys	75	4554
Pipe and Lyde Herefs	46	5043
Pipe Gate Shrops	72	7340
Pipehill Staffs	61	0907
Piperhill Highld	140	8650
Pipers Pool Cnwll	5	2584
Pipewell Nhants	51	8485
Pippacott Devon	19	5237
Pippin Street Lancs	81	5924
Pipton Powys	45	1637
Pirbright Surrey	25	9455
Pirbright Camp Surrey	25	9356
Pirnie Border	110	6528
Pirnmill N Ayrs	105	8744
Pirton Herts	38	1431
Pirton Worcs	47	8847
Pishill Oxon	37	7389
Pistyll Gwynd	56	3241
Pitagowan P & K	132	8165
Pitblae Abers	143	9864
Pitcairngreen P & K	125	0627
Pitcalnie Highld	147	8072
Pitcaple Abers	142	7225
Pitcarity Angus	134	3365
Pitch Green Bucks	37	7703
Pitch Place Surrey	25	8839
Pitch Place Surrey	25	9852
Pitchcombe Glous	35	8508
Pitchcott Bucks	37	7720
Pitcher Row Lincs	64	2933
Pitchford Shrops	59	5303
Pitchroy Moray	141	1738
Pitcombe Somset	22	6732
Pitcot V Glam	33	8974
Pitcox E Loth	118	6475
Pitfichie Abers	142	6716
Pitglassie Abers	142	6943
Pitgrudy Highld	147	7991
Pitkennedy Angus	127	5454
Pitlessie Fife	126	3309
Pitlochry P & K	133	9358
Pitmachie Abers	142	6728
Pitmain Highld	132	7400
Pitmedden Abers	143	8827
Pitmedden Garden	143	8828
Pitmuies Angus	127	5649
Pitmunie Abers	142	6614
Pitney Somset	21	4528
Pitroddie P & K	126	2125
Pitscottie Fife	126	4112
Pitsea Essex	40	7488
Pitses Gt Man	79	9403
Pitsford Nhants	50	7567
Pitstone Bucks	38	9415
Pitt Devon	9	0316
Pitt Hants	24	4528
Pitt Court Glous	35	7496
Pitt's Wood Kent	16	6149

303

Pittarrow
Pymo
304

Pittarrow Abers 135 7274
Pittenweem Fife 127 5502
Pitteuchar Fife 117 2899
Pittington Dur 96 3244
Pittodrie House Hotel Abers 142 6924
Pitton Wilts 23 2131
Pittulie Abers 143 9567
Pity Me Dur 96 2645
Pityme Cnwll 4 9576
Pivington Kent 28 9146
Pixey Green Suffk 55 2475
Pixham Surrey 26 1750
Plain Street Cnwll 4 9778
Plains N Lans 116 7966
Plaish Shrops 59 5296
Plaistow Derbys 74 3456
Plaistow Gt Lon 27 4082
Plaistow Herefs 47 6939
Plaistow W Susx 14 0030
Plaitford Hants 12 2719
Plank Lane Gt Man 79 6399
Plas Cymyran IOA 68 2975
Plastow Green Hants 24 5361
Platt Kent 27 6257
Platt Bridge Gt Man 78 6002
Platt Lane Shrops 59 5136
Platts Heath Kent 28 8750
Plawsworth Dur 96 2647
Plaxtol Kent 27 6053
Play Hatch Oxon 37 7376
Playden E Susx 17 9221
Playford Suffk 55 2147
Playing Place Cnwll 3 8141
Playley Green Gloucs 47 7631
Plealey Shrops 59 4206
Plean Stirlg 116 8386
Pleasance Fife 126 2312
Pleasington Lancs 81 6426
Pleasley Derbys 75 5064
Pleasleyhill Notts 75 5064
Pleck Dorset 11 7010
Pledgdon Green Essex 40 5626
Pledwick W York 83 3316
Pleinheaume Guern 158 0000
Plemont Jersey 158 0000
Plemstall Ches 71 4570
Plenmeller Nthumb 102 7163
Pleshey Essex 40 6614
Plockton Highld 137 8033
Plowden Shrops 59 3887
Plox Green Shrops 59 3604
Pluckley Kent 28 9245
Pluckley Station Kent 28 9243
Pluckley Thorne Kent 28 9244
Plucks Gutter Kent 29 2663
Plumbland Cumb 92 1539
Plumgarths Cumb 87 4994
Plumley Ches 79 7274
Plumpton Cumb 94 4937
Plumpton Cumb 86 3178
Plumpton E Susx 15 3613
Plumpton Nhants 49 5948
Plumpton End Nhants 49 7245
Plumpton Green E Susx 15 3616
Plumpton Head Cumb 94 5035
Plumstead Gt Lon 27 4478
Plumstead Norfk 66 1334
Plumstead Green Norfk 66 1235
Plumtree Notts 62 6132
Plumtree Green Kent 28 8245
Plungar Leics 63 7634
Plurenden Kent 28 9337
Plush Dorset 11 7102
Plusha Cnwll 5 2580
Plushabridge Cnwll 5 3072
Plwmp Cerdgn 42 3652
Plymouth Devon 6 4754
Plymouth Airport 6 5060
Plympton Devon 6 5456
Plymstock Devon 6 5152
Plymtree Devon 9 0502
Pockley N York 90 6385
Pocklington E R Yk 84 8048
Pode Hole Lincs 64 2121
Podimore Somset 21 5424
Podington Beds 51 9462
Podmore Staffs 72 7835
Point Clear Essex 41 1015
Pointon Lincs 64 1131
Pokesdown Dorset 12 1292
Polapit Tamar Cnwll 5 3389
Polbain Highld 144 9910
Polbathic Cnwll 5 3456
Polbeth W Loth 117 0264
Polbrock Cnwll 4 0169
Poldark Mine 2 6732
Pole Elm Worcs 47 8450
Pole Moor W York 82 0615
Polebrook Nhants 51 0686
Polegate E Susx 16 5804
Polelane Ends Ches 79 6479
Polesworth Warwks 61 2602
Polgigga Cnwll 2 3723
Polglass Highld 144 0307
Polgooth Cnwll 3 9950
Polgown D & G 107 7103
Poling W Susx 14 0404
Poling Corner W Susx 14 0405
Polkerris Cnwll 3 0952
Pollard Street Norfk 67 3332
Pollington E R Yk 83 6119
Polloch Highld 129 7668
Pollokshaws C Glas 115 5661
Pollokshields C Glas 115 5763
Polmassick Cnwll 3 9745
Polmear Cnwll 3 0853
Polmont Falk 116 9378
Polnish Highld 129 7582
Polperro Cnwll 5 2051
Polruan Cnwll 3 1250
Polsham Somset 21 5142
Polstead Suffk 54 9938
Polstead Heath Suffk 54 9940
Poltalloch Ag & B 113 8196
Poltescoe Cnwll 3 7215
Poltimore Devon 9 9696
Polton Mdloth 117 2864
Polwarth Border 119 7450
Polyphant Cnwll 5 2682
Polzeath Cnwll 4 9378
Pomathorn Mdloth 117 2459
Pomeroy Derbys 74 1267
Ponde Powys 45 1037
Ponders End Gt Lon 27 3596
Pondersbridge Cambs 64 2692
Ponsanooth Cnwll 3 7537
Ponsonby Cumb 86 0505
Ponsongath Cnwll 3 7518
Ponsworthy Devon 7 7073
Pont Cyfyng Conwy 69 7357
Pont Dolgarrog Conwy 69 7766
Pont Morlais Carmth 32 5307
Pont Pen-y-benglog Gwynd 69 6560
Pont Rhyd-sarn Gwynd 57 8528
Pont Rhyd-y-cyff Brdgnd 33 8788
Pont Robert Powys 58 1012
Pont Walby Neath 33 8906
Pont-ar-gothi Carmth 32 5021
Pont-ar-Hydfer Powys 45 8627
Pont-ar-llechau Carmth 44 7224
Pont-Ebbw Newpt 34 2985
Pont-faen Powys 45 9934
Pont-Nedd-Fechan Neath 33 9007
Pont-rhyd-y-fen Neath 32 7994
Pont-rug Gwynd 68 5162
Pont-y-blew Wrexhm 71 3138
Pont-y-pant Conwy 69 7554
Pont-yr-hafod Pembks 30 9026
Pont-yr-Rhyl Brdgnd 33 9089
Pontac Jersey 158 0000
Pontamman Carmth 32 6312
Pontantwn Carmth 32 4412
Pontardawe Neath 32 7204
Pontarddulais Swans 32 5903
Pontarsais Carmth 31 4428
Pontblyddyn Flints 70 2760
Pontdolgoch Powys 58 0193
Pontefract W York 83 4521
Ponteland Nthumb 103 1672
Ponterwyd Cerdgn 43 7481
Pontesbury Shrops 59 3906
Pontesbury Hill Shrops 59 3905
Pontesford Shrops 59 4106
Pontfadog Wrexhm 70 2338
Pontfaen Pembks 30 0234
Pontgarreg Cerdgn 42 3353
Pontgarreg Pembks 31 1441
Ponthenry Carmth 32 4709
Ponthir Torfn 34 3292
Ponthirwaun Cerdgn 42 2645
Pontllanfraith Caerph 33 1895
Pontlliw Swans 32 6199
Pontlottyn Caerph 33 1106
Pontlyfni Gwynd 68 4352
Pontnewydd Torfn 34 2896
Pontnewynydd Torfn 34 2701
Pontop Dur 96 1453
Pontrhydfendigaid Cerdgn 43 7366
Pontrhydygroes Cerdgn 43 7472
Pontrhydyrun Torfn 34 2997
Pontrilas Herefs 46 3927
Ponts Green E Susx 16 6715
Pontshaen Cerdgn 42 4446
Pontshill Herefs 35 6421
Pontsticill Powys 33 0511
Pontwelly Carmth 31 4140
Pontyates Carmth 32 4708
Pontyberem Carmth 32 5010
Pontybodkin Flints 70 2759
Pontyclun Rhondd 33 0381
Pontycymer Brdgnd 33 9091
Pontyglasier Pembks 31 1436
Pontygwaith Rhondd 33 0094
Pontygynon Pembks 31 1237
Pontymoel Torfn 34 2900
Pontypool Torfn 34 2800
Pontypool Road Torfn 34 3099
Pontypridd Rhondd 33 0789
Pontywaun Caerph 34 2292
Pooksgreen Hants 12 3710
Pool Cnwll 2 6641
Pool IOS 2 8714
Pool W York 82 2445
Pool Head Herefs 46 5550
Pool of Muckhart Clacks 117 0000
Pool Quay Powys 58 2511
Pool Street Essex 53 7636
Poole Dorset 11 0090
Poole Keynes Gloucs 35 9995
Poolewe Highld 144 8580
Pooley Bridge Cumb 93 4724
Pooley Street Norfk 54 0581
Poolfold Staffs 72 8959
Poolhill Gloucs 47 7229
Pooting's Kent 16 4549
Popham Hants 24 5543
Poplar Gt Lon 27 3780
Poplar Street Suffk 55 4465
Porchbrook Worcs 60 7270
Porchfield IOW 13 4491
Poringland Norfk 67 2701
Porkellis Cnwll 2 6933
Porlock Somset 19 8846
Porlock Weir Somset 19 8647
Port Appin Ag & B 122 9045
Port Askaig Ag & B 112 4369
Port Bannatyne Ag & B 114 0767
Port Carlisle Cumb 101 2461
Port Charlotte Ag & B 112 2558
Port Clarence Dur 97 4921
Port Driseach Ag & B 114 9973
Port e Vallen IOM 158 4792
Port Einon Swans 32 4685
Port Ellen Ag & B 104 3645
Port Elphinstone Abers 142 7720
Port Erin IOM 158 1969
Port Gaverne Cnwll 4 0080
Port Glasgow Inver 115 3274
Port Henderson Highld 137 7573
Port Isaac Cnwll 4 9980
Port Logan D & G 98 0940
Port Mor Highld 128 4279
Port Mulgrave N York 97 7917
Port nan Giuran W Isls 152 5537
Port nan Long W Isls 152 8978
Port Nis W Isls 152 5363
Port of Menteith Stirlg 115 5801
Port of Ness W Isls 152 5363
Port Quin Cnwll 4 9780
Port Ramsay Ag & B 122 8845
Port Soderick IOM 158 3472
Port St Mary IOM 158 2067
Port Sunlight Mersyd 78 3384
Port Talbot Neath 32 7689
Port Tennant Swans 32 6893
Port Wemyss Ag & B 112 1651
Port William D & G 98 3343
Port-an-Eorna Highld 137 7732
Portachoillan Ag & B 113 7557
Portavadie Ag & B 114 9369
Portbury Somset 34 5075
Portchester Hants 13 6105
Porteath Cnwll 4 9679
Portencalzie D & G 98 0171
Portencross N Ayrs 114 1748
Portesham Dorset 10 6085
Portessie Moray 142 4366
Portfield Gate Pembks 30 9215
Portgate Devon 5 4285
Portgordon Moray 142 3964
Portgower Highld 147 0013
Porth Cnwll 4 8362
Porth Rhondd 33 0291
Porth Dinllaen Gwynd 56 2740
Porth Navas Cnwll 3 7527
Porth-y-Waen Shrops 58 2623
Porthallow Cnwll 3 7923
Porthallow Cnwll 5 2251
Porthcawl Brdgnd 33 8177
Porthcothan Cnwll 4 8672
Porthcurno Cnwll 2 3822
Porthgain Pembks 30 8132
Porthgwarra Cnwll 2 3721
Porthill Staffs 72 8448
Porthkea Cnwll 3 8242
Porthkerry V Glam 20 0866
Porthleven Cnwll 2 6225
Porthmadog Gwynd 57 5638
Porthmeor Cnwll 2 4337
Portholland Cnwll 3 9541
Porthoustock Cnwll 3 8021
Porthpean Cnwll 3 0250
Porthtowan Cnwll 2 6947
Porthwgan Wrexhm 71 3846
Porthyrhyd Carmth 32 5215
Portincaple Ag & B 114 2393
Portinfer Jersey 158 0000
Portington E R Yk 84 7831
Portinnisherrich Ag & B 122 9711
Portinscale Cumb 93 2523
Portishead Somset 34 4675
Portknockie Moray 142 4868
Portlethen Abers 135 9196
Portling D & G 92 8753
Portloe Cnwll 3 9339
Portlooe Cnwll 5 2452
Portmahomack Highld 147 9184
Portmellon Cnwll 3 0144
Portmore Hants 12 3397
Portnacroish Ag & B 122 9247
Portnaguran W Isls 152 5537
Portnahaven Ag & B 112 1652
Portnalong Highld 136 3434
Portobello C Edin 117 3073
Portobello T & W 96 2856
Portobello W Mids 60 9598
Porton Wilts 23 1836
Portontown Devon 5 4176
Portpatrick D & G 98 9954
Portreath Cnwll 2 6545
Portree Highld 136 4843
Portscatho Cnwll 3 8735
Portsea Hants 13 6300
Portskerra Highld 150 8765
Portskewett Mons 34 4988
Portslade E Susx 15 2506
Portslade-by-Sea E Susx 15 2605
Portslogan D & G 98 9858
Portsmouth Hants 13 6400
Portsmouth W York 81 9026
Portsonachan Hotel Ag & B 123 0420
Portsoy Abers 142 5866
Portswood Hants 13 4214
Portuairk Highld 128 4368
Portway Herefs 46 4844
Portway Herefs 46 4935
Portway W Mids 60 9787
Portway Worcs 61 0872
Portwrinkle Cnwll 5 3553
Portyerrock D & G 99 4738
Posbury Devon 8 8197
Posenhall Shrops 59 6501
Poslingford Suffk 53 7648
Posso Border 109 2033
Post Green Dorset 11 9593
Postbridge Devon 8 6579
Postcombe Oxon 37 7000
Postling Kent 29 1439
Postwick Norfk 67 2907
Potarch Abers 134 6097
Pothole Cnwll 3 9750
Potsgrove Beds 38 9530
Pott Row Norfk 65 7022
Pott Shrigley Ches 79 9479
Pott's Green Essex 40 9122
Potten End Herts 38 0109
Potten Street Kent 29 2567
Potter Brompton N York 91 9777
Potter Heigham Norfk 67 4119
Potter Row Bucks 26 9002
Potter Somersal Derbys 73 1335
Potter's Cross Staffs 60 8484
Potter's Forstal Kent 28 8946
Potter's Green E Susx 16 5023
Potter's Green Herts 39 3520
Pottergate Street Norfk 66 1591
Potterhanworth Lincs 76 0566
Potterhanworth Booths Lincs 76 0767
Potterne Wilts 22 9958
Potterne Wick Wilts 22 9957
Potters Bar Herts 26 2401
Potters Brook Lancs 80 4852
Potters Crouch Herts 38 1105
Potters Green W Mids 61 3782
Potters Marston Leics 50 4996
Pottersheath Herts 39 2318
Potterspury Nhants 49 7543
Potterton Abers 143 9415
Potterton W York 83 4038
Potthorpe Norfk 66 9422
Pottle Street Wilts 22 8140
Potto N York 89 4703
Potton Beds 52 2249
Poughill Cnwll 18 2207
Poughill Devon 19 8508
Poulner Hants 12 1606
Poulshot Wilts 22 9659
Poulston Devon 7 7754
Poulton Gloucs 36 0901
Poulton Mersyd 78 3091
Poulton Priory Gloucs 36 0900
Poulton-le-Fylde Lancs 80 3439
Pound Bank Worcs 60 7374
Pound Green E Susx 16 5123
Pound Green Suffk 53 7153
Pound Green Worcs 60 7578
Pound Hill W Susx 15 2937
Pound Street Hants 24 4561
Poundffald Swans 32 5694
Poundgate E Susx 16 4928
Poundon Bucks 49 6425
Poundsbridge Kent 16 5341
Poundsgate Devon 7 7072
Poundstock Cnwll 18 2099
Pounsley E Susx 16 5221
Pouton D & G 99 4645
Pouy Street Suffk 55 3570
Povey Cross Surrey 15 2642
Pow Green Herefs 47 7144
Powburn Nthumb 111 0616
Powderham Devon 9 9684
Powerstock Dorset 10 5196
Powfoot D & G 100 1465
Powhill Cumb 93 2355
Powick Worcs 47 8351
Powmill P & K 117 0297
Poxwell Dorset 11 7384
Poyle Surrey 26 0376
Poynings W Susx 15 2611
Poynter's Lane End Cnwll 2 6743
Poyntington Dorset 21 6520
Poynton Ches 79 9283
Poynton Shrops 59 5617
Poynton Green Shrops 59 5618
Poyston Cross Pembks 30 9819
Poystreet Green Suffk 54 9758
Praa Sands Cnwll 2 5828
Pratt's Bottom Gt Lon 27 4762
Praze-an-Beeble Cnwll 2 6335
Predannack Wollas Cnwll 2 6616
Prees Shrops 59 5533
Prees Green Shrops 59 5531
Prees Heath Shrops 71 5538
Prees Higher Heath Shrops 59 5635
Prees Lower Heath Shrops 59 5732
Preesall Lancs 80 3647
Preesgweene Shrops 59 2936
Pren-gwyn Cerdgn 42 4244
Prendwick Nthumb 111 0012
Prenteg Gwynd 57 5841
Prenton Mersyd 78 3086
Prescot Mersyd 78 4692
Prescott Devon 9 0814
Prescott Shrops 59 4220
Prescott Shrops 60 6681
Presnerb Angus 133 1866
Pressen Nthumb 110 8335
Prestatyn Denbgs 70 0682
Prestbury Ches 79 8976
Prestbury Gloucs 47 9723
Presteigne Powys 46 3164
Prestleigh Somset 21 6340
Prestolee Gt Man 79 7505
Preston Border 119 7957
Preston Devon 7 7451
Preston Devon 7 8574
Preston Devon 7 8962
Preston Dorset 11 7083
Preston E Loth 118 5977
Preston E R Yk 85 1830
Preston E Susx 15 3106
Preston Gloucs 47 6834
Preston Gloucs 36 0400
Preston Herts 39 1824
Preston Kent 28 0260
Preston Kent 29 2460
Preston Lancs 80 5329
Preston Nthumb 111 1825
Preston Rutlnd 63 8602
Preston Shrops 59 5211
Preston Somset 20 0935
Preston Suffk 54 9450
Preston Wilts 36 2774
Preston Bagot Warwks 48 1765
Preston Bissett Bucks 49 6529
Preston Bowyer Somset 20 1326
Preston Brockhurst Shrops 59 5324
Preston Brook Ches 78 5680
Preston Candover Hants 24 6041
Preston Capes Nhants 49 5754
Preston Crowmarsh Oxon 37 6190
Preston Deanery Nhants 50 7855
Preston Green Warwks 48 1665
Preston Gubbals Shrops 59 4919
Preston Montford Shrops 59 4314
Preston on Stour Warwks 48 2049
Preston on Tees Dur 96 4315
Preston on the Hill Ches 78 5780
Preston on Wye Herefs 46 3841
Preston Patrick Cumb 87 5483
Preston Plucknett Somset 10 5316
Preston Street Kent 29 2561
Preston upon the
Weald Moors Shrops 72 6815
Preston Wynne Herefs 46 5546
Preston-under-Scar N York 88 0691
Prestonpans E Loth 118 3874
Prestwich Gt Man 79 8104
Prestwick Nthumb 103 1872
Prestwick S Ayrs 106 3525
Prestwick Airport 106 3627
Prestwood Bucks 26 8700
Prestwood Staffs 60 8
Price Town Brdgnd 33 9
Prickwillow Cambs 53 5
Priddy Somset 21 5
Priest Hutton Lancs 87 5
Priestacott Devon 18 4
Priestcliffe Derbys 74 1
Priestcliffe Ditch Derbys 74 1
Priestend Bucks 37 6
Priestland E Ayrs 107 5
Priestley Green W York 82 1
Priestweston Shrops 59 2
Priestwood Green Kent 28 6
Primethorpe Leics 50 5
Primrose Green Norfk 66 0
Primrose Hill Cambs 52 3
Primrose Hill Derbys 75 4
Primrose Hill Lancs 78 3
Primrose Hill W Mids 60 9
Primrosehill Border 119 7
Primsidemill Border 110 8
Princes Gate Pembks 31 1
Princes Risborough Bucks 38 8
Princethorpe Warwks 61 4
Princetown Devon 6 5
Prinsted W Susx 14 7
Prion Denbgs 70 0
Prior Rigg Cumb 101 4
Priors Halton Shrops 46 4
Priors Hardwick Warwks 49 4
Priors Marston Warwks 49 4
Priors Norton Gloucs 47 8
Priory Wood Herefs 46 2
Prisk V Glam 33 0
Priston Somset 22 6
Pristow Green Norfk 54 1
Prittlewell Essex 40 8
Privett Hants 13 6
Prixford Devon 19 5
Probus Cnwll 3 8
Prora E Loth 118 5
Prospect Cumb 92 1
Prospidnick Cnwll 2 6
Protstonhill Abers 143 8
Providence Somset 34 5
Prudhoe Nthumb 103 0
Prussia Cove Cnwll 2 5
Publow Somset 21 6
Puckeridge Herts 39 3
Puckington Somset 10 3
Pucklechurch Gloucs 35 6
Puckrup Gloucs 47 8
Puddinglake Ches 79 7
Puddington Ches 71 3
Puddington Devon 19 8
Puddledock Norfk 66 0
Puddlehill Herts 38 0
Puddletown Dorset 11 7
Puddleston Herefs 46 5
Pudsey W York 82 2
Pulborough W Susx 14 0
Puleston Shrops 72 7
Pulford Ches 71 3
Pulham Dorset 11 7
Pulham Market Norfk 55 1
Pulham St Mary Norfk 55 2
Pullens Green Gloucs 34 6
Pulley Shrops 59 4
Pulloxhill Beds 38 0
Pumpherston W Loth 117 0
Pumsaint Carmth 44 6
Puncheston Pembks 30 0
Puncknowle Dorset 10 5
Punnett's Town E Susx 16 6
Purbrook Hants 13 6
Purbrook Park Hants 13 6
Purfleet Essex 27 5
Puriton Somset 21 3
Purleigh Essex 40 8
Purley Berks 37 6
Purley Gt Lon 27 3
Purlogue Shrops 46 2
Purlpit Wilts 22 8
Purls Bridge Cambs 53 4
Purse Caundle Dorset 11 6
Purshull Green Worcs 60 8
Purslow Shrops 59 3
Purston Jaglin W York 83 4
Purtington Somset 10 3
Purton Gloucs 35 6
Purton Gloucs 35 6
Purton Wilts 36 0
Purton Stoke Wilts 36 0
Pury End Nhants 49 7
Pusey Oxon 36 3
Putley Herefs 47 6
Putley Green Herefs 47 6
Putloe Gloucs 35 7
Putney Gt Lon 26 2
Putron Village Guern 158 0
Putsborough Devon 18 4
Puttenham Herts 38 8
Puttenham Surrey 25 9
Puttock End Essex 54 8
Puttock's End Essex 40 5
Putton Dorset 11 6
Puxley Nhants 49 7
Puxton Somset 21 4
Pwll Carmth 32 4
Pwll Trap Carmth 31 2
Pwll-du Mons 34 2
Pwll-glas Denbgs 70 1
Pwll-y-glaw Neath 32 7
Pwllcrochan Pembks 30 9
Pwllgloyw Powys 45 0
Pwllheli Gwynd 56 3
Pwllmeyric Mons 34 5
Pydew Conwy 69 8
Pye Bridge Derbys 75 4
Pye Corner Herts 39 4
Pye Corner Newpt 34 3
Pye Green Staffs 60 9
Pyecombe W Susx 15 2
Pyle Brdgnd 33 8
Pyleigh Somset 20 1
Pylle Somset 21 6
Pymoor Cambs 53 4
Pymore Dorset 10 4

...ford Surrey ... 26 0358
...ton Oxon ... 37 6896
...chley Nhants ... 51 8674
...worthy Devon ... 18 3102

Q

...abbs Shrops ... 58 2180
...adring Lincs ... 64 2233
...adring Eaudike Lincs ... 64 2433
...ainton Bucks ... 37 7420
...aker's Yard Myr Td ... 33 0995
...arndon Derbys ... 62 3340
...arr Hill IOW ... 13 5792
...arrier's Village Inver ... 115 3666
...arrington Lincs ... 64 0544
...arrington Hill Dur ... 96 3337
...arry Bank W Mids ... 60 9386
...arrybank Ches ... 71 5465
...arrywood Moray ... 141 1763
...arter N Ayrs ... 114 1961
...arter S Lans ... 116 7251
...atford Shrops ... 60 7391
...att Shrops ... 60 7588
...ebec Dur ... 96 1743
...edgeley Gloucs ... 35 8014
...een Adelaide Cambs ... 53 5681
...een Camel Somset ... 21 5924
...een Charlton Somset ... 21 6367
...een Dart Devon ... 19 8316
...een Oak Dorset ... 22 7831
...een Street Kent ... 28 6845
...een Street Wilts ... 35 0287
...een's Bower IOW ... 13 5684
...een's Head Shrops ... 59 3327
...een's Park Beds ... 38 0349
...een's Park Nhants ... 49 7562
...eenborough Kent ... 28 9172
...eenhill Worcs ... 47 8537
...eensbury W York ... 82 1030
...eensferry Flints ... 71 3168
...eenslie C Glas ... 116 6565
...eenzieburn N Lans ... 116 6977
...endon Essex ... 39 5130
...eniborough Leics ... 63 6412
...enington Leics ... 36 1404
...ernmore Lancs ... 87 5160
...ernmore Park Hall Lancs ... 87 5162
...eslett W Mids ... 61 0695
...ethiock Cnwll ... 5 3164
...uick's Green Berks ... 37 5876
...uidenham Norfk ... 54 0287
...uidhampton Hants ... 24 5150
...uidhampton Wilts ... 23 1030
...uina Brook Shrops ... 59 5232
...uinbury End Nhants ... 49 6250
...uinton Nhants ... 49 7754
...uinton W Mids ... 60 9984
...uinton Green Nhants ... 50 7853
...uintrell Downs Cnwll ... 4 8460
...uither Devon ... 5 4481
...uixhall Staffs ... 73 1041
...uixwood Border ... 119 7863
...uoditch Devon ... 5 4097
...uorn Leics ... 62 5616
...uothquan S Lans ... 108 9939
...uoybirray Ork ... 153 5005
...uoyloo Ork ... 153 2420

R

...abbit's Cross Kent ... 28 7847
...ableyheath Herts ... 39 2319
...aby Cumb ... 93 1951
...aby Mersyd ... 71 3179
...achan Mill Border ... 108 1134
...achub Gwynd ... 69 6267
...ackenford Devon ... 19 8518
...ackham W Susx ... 14 0413
...ackheath Norfk ... 67 2814
...acks D & G ... 100 0274
...ackwick Ork ... 153 2099
...adbourne Derbys ... 73 2836
...adcliffe Gt Man ... 79 7806
...adcliffe Nthumb ... 103 2602
...adcliffe on Trent Notts ... 63 6439
...adclive Bucks ... 49 6734
...adcot Oxon ... 36 2899
...addington Somset ... 20 0225
...adernie Fife ... 127 4609
...adford Semele Warwks ... 48 3464
...adlet Somset ... 20 2038
...adlett Herts ... 26 1600
...adley Devon ... 19 7323
...adley Oxon ... 37 5398
...adley Green Essex ... 40 6205
...admore Green Ches ... 71 5955
...adnage Bucks ... 37 7897
...adstock Somset ... 22 6854
...adstone Nhants ... 49 5840
...adway Warwks ... 48 3648
...adway Green Ches ... 72 7754
...adwell Beds ... 51 0057
...adwell Herts ... 39 2335
...adwinter Essex ... 53 6037
...adwinter End Essex ... 53 6139
...adyr Cardif ... 33 1280
...AF College (Cranwell) Lincs ... 76 0049
...afford Moray ... 141 0596
...agdale Leics ... 63 6619
...agdon S Lans ... 59 4591
...aginnis Cnwll ... 2 4625

Raglan Mons ... 34 4107
Ragnall Notts ... 75 8073
Raigbeg Highld ... 140 8128
Rainbow Hill Worcs ... 47 8555
Rainford Mersyd ... 78 4700
Rainham Gt Lon ... 27 5282
Rainham Kent ... 28 8165
Rainhill Mersyd ... 78 4991
Rainhill Stoops Mersyd ... 78 5090
Rainow Ches ... 79 9475
Rainsough Gt Man ... 79 8002
Rainton N York ... 89 3675
Rainworth Notts ... 75 5858
Raisbeck Cumb ... 87 6407
Raise Cumb ... 94 7046
Raisthorpe N York ... 90 8561
Rait P & K ... 126 2226
Raithby Lincs ... 77 3084
Raithby Lincs ... 77 3766
Raithwaite N York ... 90 8611
Rake W Susx ... 14 8027
Rakewood Gt Man ... 82 9414
Ralia Highld ... 132 7097
Ram Carmth ... 44 5846
Ram Hill Gloucs ... 35 6779
Ram Lane Kent ... 28 9646
Ramasaig Highld ... 136 1644
Rame Cnwll ... 3 7233
Rame Cnwll ... 6 4249
Rampisham Dorset ... 10 5602
Rampside Cumb ... 86 2366
Rampton Cambs ... 53 4267
Rampton Notts ... 75 8078
Ramsbottom Gt Man ... 81 7916
Ramsbury Wilts ... 36 2771
Ramscraigs Highld ... 151 1427
Ramsdean Hants ... 13 7022
Ramsdell Hants ... 24 5857
Ramsden Oxon ... 36 3515
Ramsden Worcs ... 47 9246
Ramsden Bellhouse Essex ... 40 7194
Ramsden Heath Essex ... 40 7095
Ramsey Cambs ... 52 2885
Ramsey Essex ... 41 2130
Ramsey IOM ... 158 4594
Ramsey Forty Foot Cambs ... 52 3087
Ramsey Heights Cambs ... 52 2484
Ramsey Island Essex ... 40 9405
Ramsey Mereside Cambs ... 52 2889
Ramsey St Mary's Cambs ... 52 2587
Ramsgate Kent ... 29 3865
Ramsgill N York ... 89 1170
Ramshaw Dur ... 95 9547
Ramsholt Suffk ... 55 3141
Ramshope Nthumb ... 102 7304
Ramshorn Staffs ... 73 0845
Ramsley Devon ... 8 6593
Ramsnest Common Surrey ... 14 9432
Ranby Lincs ... 76 2278
Ranby Notts ... 75 6580
Rand Lincs ... 76 1078
Randwick Gloucs ... 35 8306
Ranfurly Rens ... 115 3865
Rangemore Staffs ... 73 1822
Rangeworthy Gloucs ... 35 6986
Rank's Green Essex ... 40 7418
Rankinston E Ayrs ... 107 4513
Ranksborough Rutlnd ... 63 8311
Rann Lancs ... 81 7124
Rannoch Station P & K ... 124 4257
Ranscombe Somset ... 20 9443
Ranskill Notts ... 75 6587
Ranton Staffs ... 72 8524
Ranton Green Staffs ... 72 8423
Ranworth Norfk ... 67 3514
Raploch Stirlg ... 116 7894
Rapness Ork ... 153 5141
Rapps Somset ... 10 3316
Rascarrel D & G ... 92 7948
Rashfield Ag & B ... 114 1483
Rashwood Worcs ... 47 9165
Raskelf N York ... 90 4971
Rassau Blae G ... 33 1511
Rastrick W York ... 82 1421
Ratagan Highld ... 138 9119
Ratby Leics ... 62 5105
Ratcliffe Culey Leics ... 61 3299
Ratcliffe on Soar Notts ... 62 4928
Ratcliffe on the Wreake Leics ... 63 6314
Ratfyn Wilts ... 23 1642
Rathen Abers ... 143 9960
Rathillet Fife ... 126 3620
Rathmell N York ... 88 8059
Ratho C Edin ... 117 1370
Rathven Moray ... 142 4465
Ratlake Hants ... 13 4123
Ratley Warwks ... 48 3847
Ratling Kent ... 29 2453
Ratlinghope Shrops ... 59 4096
Rattan Row Norfk ... 65 5114
Rattar Highld ... 151 2673
Ratten Row Cumb ... 93 3240
Ratten Row Cumb ... 93 3949
Ratten Row Lancs ... 80 4241
Rattery Devon ... 7 7461
Rattlesden Suffk ... 54 9758
Ratton Village E Susx ... 16 5901
Rattray P & K ... 126 1845
Raughton Cumb ... 93 3947
Raughton Head Cumb ... 93 3745
Raunds Nhants ... 51 9972
Raven Meols Mersyd ... 78 2805
Ravenfield S York ... 75 4895
Ravenglass Cumb ... 86 0896
Ravenhills Green Worcs ... 47 7454
Raveningham Norfk ... 67 3996
Ravenscar N York ... 91 9801
Ravenscliffe Staffs ... 72 8452
Ravensdale IOM ... 158 3536
Ravensden Beds ... 51 0754
Ravenshead Notts ... 75 5654
Ravensmoor Ches ... 71 6150
Ravensthorpe Nhants ... 50 6670
Ravensthorpe W York ... 82 2220
Ravenstone Bucks ... 38 8451
Ravenstone Leics ... 62 4013
Ravenstonedale Cumb ... 88 7203
Ravenstruther S Lans ... 116 9245

Ravensworth N York ... 89 1308
Raw N York ... 91 9305
Rawcliffe E R Yk ... 83 6822
Rawcliffe N York ... 83 5854
Rawcliffe Bridge E R Yk ... 83 6921
Rawdon W York ... 82 2139
Rawling Street Kent ... 28 9059
Rawmarsh S York ... 75 4396
Rawnsley Staffs ... 60 0212
Rawreth Essex ... 40 7893
Rawridge Devon ... 9 2006
Rawtenstall Lancs ... 81 8123
Raydon Suffk ... 54 0438
Raylees Nthumb ... 102 9291
Rayleigh Essex ... 40 8090
Raymond's Hill Devon ... 10 3296
Rayne Essex ... 40 7222
Raynes Park Gt Lon ... 26 2368
Rea Gloucs ... 35 8016
Reach Cambs ... 53 5666
Read Lancs ... 81 7634
Reading Berks ... 24 7173
Reading Street Kent ... 17 9230
Reading Street Kent ... 29 3869
Reagill Cumb ... 94 6017
Rearquhar Highld ... 146 7492
Rearsby Leics ... 63 6514
Rease Heath Shrops ... 72 6454
Reay Highld ... 150 9664
Reculver Kent ... 29 2269
Red Ball Somset ... 9 0017
Red Bull Ches ... 72 8254
Red Cross Cambs ... 53 4754
Red Cross Cnwll ... 18 2605
Red Dial Cumb ... 93 2546
Red Hill Dorset ... 12 0995
Red Hill Warwks ... 48 1356
Red Lodge Suffk ... 53 6970
Red Lumb Gt Man ... 81 8415
Red Rock Gt Man ... 78 5809
Red Roses Carmth ... 31 2011
Red Row T & W ... 103 2599
Red Street Staffs ... 72 8251
Red Wharf Bay IOA ... 68 5281
Redberth Pembks ... 31 0804
Redbourn Herts ... 38 1012
Redbourne Lincs ... 76 9799
Redbrook Gloucs ... 34 5309
Redbrook Wrexhm ... 71 5041
Redbrook Street Kent ... 28 9336
Redburn Highld ... 140 9447
Redburn Nthumb ... 102 7764
Redcar N York ... 97 6024
Redcastle D & G ... 100 8165
Redcastle Highld ... 139 5849
Redding Falk ... 116 9278
Reddingmuirhead Falk ... 116 9177
Reddish Gt Man ... 79 8993
Redditch Worcs ... 48 0467
Rede Suffk ... 54 8055
Redenhall Norfk ... 55 2684
Redenham Hants ... 23 3049
Redesmouth Nthumb ... 102 8682
Redford Abers ... 135 7570
Redford Angus ... 127 5644
Redford W Susx ... 14 8626
Redfordgreen Border ... 109 3616
Redgate Rhondd ... 33 0188
Redgorton P & K ... 125 0828
Redgrave Suffk ... 54 0477
Redhill Abers ... 135 7704
Redhill Herts ... 39 3033
Redhill Somset ... 21 4962
Redhill Surrey ... 27 2750
Redisham Suffk ... 55 4084
Redland Bristl ... 34 5775
Redland Ork ... 153 3724
Redlingfield Suffk ... 54 1870
Redlingfield Green Suffk ... 54 1871
Redlynch Somset ... 22 7033
Redlynch Wilts ... 12 2021
Redmain Cumb ... 92 1333
Redmarley Worcs ... 47 7666
Redmarley D'Abitot Gloucs ... 47 7531
Redmarshall Dur ... 96 3821
Redmile Leics ... 63 7935
Redmire N York ... 88 0491
Redmyre Abers ... 135 7575
Rednal Shrops ... 59 3628
Rednal W Mids ... 60 0076
Redpath Border ... 110 5835
Redpoint Highld ... 137 7368
Redruth Cnwll ... 2 6942
Redstocks Wilts ... 22 9362
Redstone P & K ... 126 1834
Redstone Cross Pembks ... 31 1015
Redvales Gt Man ... 79 8008
Redwick Gloucs ... 34 5846
Redwick Newpt ... 34 4184
Redworth Dur ... 96 2423
Reed Herts ... 39 3636
Reedham Norfk ... 67 4201
Reedness E R Yk ... 84 7923
Reeds Beck Lincs ... 76 2065
Reeds Holme Lancs ... 81 8024
Reepham Lincs ... 76 0473
Reepham Norfk ... 66 1022
Reeth N York ... 88 0399
Reeves Green W Mids ... 61 2677
Regaby IOM ... 158 4397
Reiff Highld ... 144 9614
Reigate Surrey ... 26 2850
Reighton N York ... 91 1375
Reisque Abers ... 143 8819
Reiss Highld ... 151 3354
Rejerrah Cnwll ... 3 7956
Releath Cnwll ... 2 6532
Relubbus Cnwll ... 2 5631
Relugas Moray ... 141 9948
Remenham Berks ... 37 7684
Remenham Hill Berks ... 37 7882
Rempstone Notts ... 62 5724
Rendcomb Gloucs ... 35 0209
Rendham Suffk ... 55 3464
Rendlesham Suffk ... 55 3453
Renfrew Rens ... 115 5067
Renhold Beds ... 38 0952
Renishaw Derbys ... 75 4377

Rennington Nthumb ... 111 2118
Renton W Duns ... 115 3877
Renwick Cumb ... 94 5943
Repps Norfk ... 67 4217
Repton Derbys ... 73 3026
Resaurie Highld ... 140 7045
Rescassa Cnwll ... 3 9842
Rescorla Cnwll ... 3 9848
Resipole Highld ... 121 7264
Reskadinnick Cnwll ... 2 6341
Resolis Highld ... 140 6765
Resolven Neath ... 33 8302
Rest and be thankful Ag & B ... 123 2307
Reston Border ... 119 8862
Restronguet Cnwll ... 3 8136
Reswallie Angus ... 127 5051
Reterth Cnwll ... 4 9463
Retew Cnwll ... 4 9257
Retford Notts ... 75 7081
Retire Cnwll ... 4 0064
Rettendon Essex ... 40 7698
Retyn Cnwll ... 4 8858
Revesby Lincs ... 77 2961
Rew Cnwll ... 7 7570
Rew Devon ... 7 7138
Rew Street IOW ... 13 4794
Rewe Devon ... 9 9499
Rexon Devon ... 5 4188
Reydon Suffk ... 55 4977
Reymerston Norfk ... 66 0206
Reynalton Pembks ... 31 0908
Reynoldston Swans ... 32 4889
Rezare Cnwll ... 5 3677
Rhadyr Mons ... 34 3602
Rhandirmwyn Carmth ... 44 7843
Rhayader Powys ... 45 9768
Rheindown Highld ... 139 5147
Rhes-y-cae Flints ... 70 1871
Rhewl Denbgs ... 70 1060
Rhewl Denbgs ... 70 1714
Rhewl Mostyn Flints ... 70 1580
Rhewl-fawr Flints ... 70 1381
Rhicarn Highld ... 148 0825
Rhiconich Highld ... 148 2552
Rhicullen Highld ... 146 6971
Rhigos Rhondd ... 33 9205
Rhireavach Highld ... 144 0295
Rhives Highld ... 147 8200
Rhiwbina Cardif ... 33 1682
Rhiwbryfdir Gwynd ... 57 6946
Rhiwderyn Newpt ... 34 2687
Rhiwlas Gwynd ... 69 5763
Rhiwinder Rhondd ... 33 0287
Rhiwlas Gwynd ... 69 5765
Rhiwlas Gwynd ... 58 9237
Rhiwlas Powys ... 58 9132
Rhiwsaeson Cardif ... 33 0682
Rhode Somset ... 20 2734
Rhoden Green Kent ... 28 6845
Rhodes Gt Man ... 79 8505
Rhodes Minnis Kent ... 29 1542
Rhodesia Notts ... 75 5679
Rhodiad-y-brenin Pembks ... 30 7627
Rhonehouse D & G ... 99 7459
Rhoose V Glam ... 20 0666
Rhos Carmth ... 31 3835
Rhos Denbgs ... 70 1261
Rhos Neath ... 32 7502
Rhos Powys ... 45 1731
Rhos Haminiog Cerdgn ... 43 5464
Rhos Lligwy IOA ... 68 4886
Rhos-y-brithdir Powys ... 58 1323
Rhos-fawr Gwynd ... 56 3838
Rhos-on-Sea Conwy ... 69 8480
Rhos-y-garth Cerdgn ... 43 6373
Rhos-y-gwaliau Gwynd ... 58 9434
Rhos-y-llan Gwynd ... 56 2337
Rhos-y-meirch Powys ... 46 2769
Rhosbeirio IOA ... 68 3991
Rhoscefnhir IOA ... 68 5276
Rhoscolyn IOA ... 68 2675
Rhoscrowther Pembks ... 30 9002
Rhosesmor Flints ... 70 2168
Rhosgadfan Gwynd ... 68 5067
Rhosgoch IOA ... 68 4089
Rhosgoch Powys ... 45 1847
Rhoshill Pembks ... 31 1940
Rhoshirwaun Gwynd ... 56 2029
Rhoslan Gwynd ... 56 4840
Rhoslefain Gwynd ... 57 5705
Rhosllanerchrugog Wrexhm ... 71 2946
Rhosmaen Carmth ... 44 6423
Rhosmeirch IOA ... 68 4677
Rhosneigr IOA ... 68 3173
Rhosnesni Wrexhm ... 71 3560
Rhosrobin Wrexhm ... 71 3252
Rhossili Swans ... 31 4187
Rhostryfan Gwynd ... 68 4957
Rhostyllen Wrexhm ... 71 3148
Rhosybol IOA ... 68 4288
Rhosygadfa Shrops ... 59 3234
Rhosymedre Wrexhm ... 71 2842
Rhu Ag & B ... 115 2684
Rhuallt Denbgs ... 70 0775
Rhubodach Ag & B ... 114 0273
Rhuddall Heath Ches ... 71 5562
Rhuddlan Cerdgn ... 44 4943
Rhuddlan Denbgs ... 70 0278
Rhulen Powys ... 45 1349
Rhunahaorine Ag & B ... 105 7048
Rhyd Gwynd ... 57 6341
Rhyd-Ddu Gwynd ... 69 5652
Rhyd-lydan Conwy ... 69 8950
Rhyd-uchaf Gwynd ... 58 9037
Rhyd-y pennau Cerdgn ... 43 6385
Rhyd-y-clafdy Gwynd ... 56 3234
Rhyd-y-foel Conwy ... 70 9176
Rhyd-y-groes Gwynd ... 69 5867
Rhyd-y-meirch Mons ... 34 3107
Rhyd-y-sarn Gwynd ... 57 6842
Rhyd-yr-onnen Gwynd ... 57 6102
Rhydargaeau Carmth ... 31 4326
Rhydcymerau Carmth ... 44 5738
Rhydd Worcs ... 47 8345
Rhydding Neath ... 32 7499
Rhydgaled Conwy ... 70 9964
Rhydlanfair Conwy ... 69 8252
Rhydlewis Cerdgn ... 42 3447

Rhydlios Gwynd ... 56 1929
Rhydowen Cerdgn ... 42 4445
Rhydrosser Cerdgn ... 43 5667
Rhydspence Herefs ... 46 2447
Rhydtalog Flints ... 70 2354
Rhydycroesau Shrops ... 58 2430
Rhydyfelin Cerdgn ... 43 5979
Rhydyfelin Rhondd ... 33 0988
Rhydyfro Neath ... 32 7105
Rhydymain Gwynd ... 57 8022
Rhydymwyn Flints ... 70 2066
Rhyl Denbgs ... 70 0081
Rhymney Caerph ... 33 1107
Rhynd P & K ... 126 1520
Rhynie Abers ... 142 4927
Rhynie Highld ... 147 8479
Ribbesford Worcs ... 60 7874
Ribbleton Lancs ... 81 5631
Ribby Lancs ... 80 4031
Ribchester Lancs ... 81 6535
Riber Derbys ... 74 3059
Riby Lincs ... 85 1807
Riccall N York ... 83 6237
Riccarton Border ... 101 5494
Riccarton E Ayrs ... 107 4236
Rich's Holford Somset ... 20 1434
Richards Castle Herefs ... 46 4969
Richings Park Bucks ... 26 0278
Richmond Gt Lon ... 26 1774
Richmond N York ... 89 1701
Richmond S York ... 74 4085
Richmond Fort Guern ... 158 0000
Rickerscote Staffs ... 72 9220
Rickford Somset ... 21 4859
Rickham Devon ... 7 7537
Rickinghall Suffk ... 54 0475
Rickling Essex ... 39 4931
Rickling Green Essex ... 39 5129
Rickmansworth Herts ... 26 0694
Riddell Border ... 109 5124
Riddings Cumb ... 101 4075
Riddings Derbys ... 74 4252
Riddlecombe Devon ... 19 6113
Riddlesden W York ... 82 0742
Ridge Dorset ... 11 9386
Ridge Herts ... 26 2100
Ridge Somset ... 21 5556
Ridge Wilts ... 22 9531
Ridge Green Surrey ... 15 3048
Ridge Lane Warwks ... 61 2994
Ridge Row Kent ... 29 2042
Ridgebourne Powys ... 45 0560
Ridgehill Somset ... 21 5462
Ridgeway Derbys ... 74 3551
Ridgeway Derbys ... 74 4081
Ridgeway Worcs ... 48 0461
Ridgeway Cross Herefs ... 47 7147
Ridgewell Essex ... 53 7340
Ridgewood E Susx ... 16 4719
Ridgmont Beds ... 38 9736
Riding Mill Nthumb ... 103 0161
Ridley Kent ... 27 6164
Ridley Nthumb ... 102 7963
Ridley Green Ches ... 71 5554
Ridlington Norfk ... 67 3430
Ridlington Rutlnd ... 63 8402
Ridlington Street Norfk ... 67 3430
Ridsdale Nthumb ... 102 9084
Rievaulx N York ... 90 5785
Rievaulx Abbey ... 90 5784
Rigg D & G ... 101 2966
Riggend N Lans ... 116 7670
Righoul Highld ... 140 8851
Rigmadon Park Cumb ... 87 6184
Rigsby Lincs ... 77 4375
Rigside S Lans ... 108 8735
Riley Green Lancs ... 81 6225
Rileyhill Staffs ... 61 1114
Rilla Mill Cnwll ... 5 2973
Rillaton Cnwll ... 5 2973
Rillington N York ... 90 8574
Rimington Lancs ... 81 8045
Rimpton Somset ... 21 6121
Rimswell E R Yk ... 85 3128
Rinaston Pembks ... 30 9825
Rindleford Shrops ... 60 7395
Ring o'Bells Lancs ... 78 4510
Ring's End Cambs ... 65 3902
Ringford D & G ... 99 6957
Ringinglow Derbys ... 74 2883
Ringland Norfk ... 66 1313
Ringles Cross E Susx ... 16 4722
Ringlestone Kent ... 28 8755
Ringley Gt Man ... 79 7605
Ringmer E Susx ... 16 4412
Ringmore Devon ... 7 6546
Ringmore Devon ... 7 9272
Ringorm Moray ... 141 2644
Ringsfield Suffk ... 55 4088
Ringsfield Corner Suffk ... 55 4087
Ringshall Bucks ... 38 9814
Ringshall Suffk ... 54 0452
Ringshall Stocks Suffk ... 54 0551
Ringstead Nhants ... 51 9875
Ringstead Norfk ... 65 7040
Ringwood Hants ... 12 1505
Ringwould Kent ... 29 3548
Rinsey Cnwll ... 2 5927
Rinsey Croft Cnwll ... 2 6028
Ripe E Susx ... 16 5110
Ripley Derbys ... 74 3950
Ripley Hants ... 12 1698
Ripley N York ... 89 2860
Ripley Surrey ... 26 0556
Riplingham E R Yk ... 84 9631
Riplington Hants ... 13 6623
Ripon N York ... 89 3171
Rippingale Lincs ... 64 0927
Ripple Kent ... 29 3550
Ripple Worcs ... 47 8737
Ripponden W York ... 82 0319
Risabus Ag & B ... 104 3143
Risbury Herefs ... 46 5455
Risby Lincs ... 84 9114
Risby Suffk ... 54 8066
Risca Caerph ... 34 2391
Rise E R Yk ... 85 1542
Riseden E Susx ... 16 6130

Riseden
St James South Elmha
306

Riseden Kent 28 7036
Risegate Lincs 64 2129
Riseholme Lincs 76 9775
Risehow Cumb 92 0234
Riseley Beds 51 0462
Riseley Berks 24 7263
Rishangles Suffk 54 1668
Rishton Lancs 81 7230
Rishworth W York 82 0318
Rising Bridge Lancs 81 7825
Risley Ches 79 6592
Risley Derbys 62 4535
Risplith N York 89 2468
Rivar Wilts 23 3161
Rivenhall End Essex 40 8316
River Kent 29 2943
River W Susx 14 9323
River Bank Cambs 53 5368
Riverford Highld 139 5454
Riverhead Kent 27 5156
Rivers Corner Dorset 11 7712
Rivington Lancs 81 6214
Roachill Devon 19 8522
Road Ashton Wilts 22 8856
Road Green Norfk 67 2693
Roade Nhants 49 7651
Roadhead Cumb 101 5174
Roadmeetings S Lans 116 8649
Roadside E Ayrs 107 5717
Roadside Highld 151 1560
Roadwater Somset 20 0338
Roag Highld 136 2644
Roan of Craigoch S Ayrs 106 2904
Roast Green Essex 39 4632
Roath Cardif 33 1977
Roberton Border 109 4214
Roberton S Lans 108 9428
Robertsbridge E Susx 17 7423
Roberttown W York 82 1922
Robeston Wathen Pembks 31 0815
Robgill Tower D & G 101 2471
Robin Hill Staffs 72 9057
Robin Hood Lancs 80 5211
Robin Hood W York 83 3227
Robin Hood's Bay N York 91 9505
Robinhood End Essex 53 7036
Roborough Devon 19 5717
Roborough Devon 6 5062
Roby Mersyd 78 4390
Roby Mill Lancs 78 5107
Rocester Staffs 73 1039
Roch Pembks 30 8821
Roch Gate Pembks 30 8720
Rochdale Gt Man 81 8913
Roche Cnwll 4 9860
Rochester Kent 28 7468
Rochester Nthumb 102 8298
Rochford Essex 40 8790
Rochford Worcs 47 6268
Rock Cnwll 4 9375
Rock Neath 32 7893
Rock Nthumb 111 2020
Rock W Susx 14 1213
Rock Worcs 60 7371
Rock Ferry Mersyd 78 3386
Rock Hill Worcs 47 9569
Rockbeare Devon 9 0194
Rockbourne Hants 12 1118
Rockcliffe Cumb 101 3561
Rockcliffe D & G 92 8454
Rockcliffe Cross Cumb 101 3463
Rockend Devon 7 9263
Rockestal Cnwll 2 3722
Rockfield Highld 147 9282
Rockfield Mons 34 4814
Rockford Devon 19 7547
Rockford Hants 12 1607
Rockgreen Shrops 46 5275
Rockhampton Gloucs 35 6593
Rockhead Cnwll 4 0784
Rockhill Shrops 46 2978
Rockingham Nhants 51 8691
Rockland All Saints Norfk 66 9996
Rockland St Mary Norfk 67 3104
Rockland St Peter Norfk 66 9897
Rockley Notts 75 7174
Rockley Wilts 36 1571
Rockliffe Lancs 81 8722
Rockville Ag & B 114 2390
Rockwell End Bucks 37 7988
Rockwell Green Somset 20 1220
Rodborough Gloucs 35 8404
Rodbourne Wilts 36 1485
Rodbourne Wilts 35 9383
Rodd Herefs 46 3262
Roddam Nthumb 111 0220
Rodden Dorset 10 6184
Roddymoor Dur 96 1536
Rode Somset 22 8053
Rode Heath Ches 72 8056
Rode Heath Ches 72 8767
Rodel W Isls 152 0483
Roden Shrops 59 5716
Rodhuish Somset 20 0139
Rodington Shrops 59 5814
Rodington Heath Shrops 59 5814
Rodley Gloucs 35 7411
Rodley W York 82 2236
Rodmarton Gloucs 35 9498
Rodmell E Susx 15 4106
Rodmersham Kent 28 9261
Rodmersham Green Kent 28 9161
Rodney Stoke Somset 21 4849
Rodsley Derbys 73 2040
Rodway Somset 20 2540
Roe Cross Gt Man 79 9896
Roe Green Gt Man 79 7501
Roe Green Herts 39 2107
Roe Green Herts 39 3133
Roecliffe N York 89 3765
Roehampton Gt Lon 26 2273
Roffey W Susx 15 1932
Rogart Highld 146 7202
Rogate W Susx 14 8023
Roger Ground Cumb 87 3597
Rogerstone Newpt 34 2787
Roghadal W Isls 152 0483
Rogiet Mons 34 4587
Roke Oxon 37 6293
Roker T & W 96 4058
Rollesby Norfk 67 4416
Rolleston Leics 50 7300
Rolleston Notts 75 7452
Rolleston Staffs 73 2327
Rolston E R Yk 85 2144
Rolstone Somset 21 3962
Rolvenden Kent 17 8431
Rolvenden Layne Kent 17 8530
Romaldkirk Dur 95 9922
Roman Amphitheatre Caerleon 34 3391
Roman Baths & Pump Room 22 7564
Romanby N York 89 3693
Romanno Bridge Border 117 1647
Romansleigh Devon 19 7220
Romden Castle Kent 28 8941
Romesdal Highld 136 4053
Romford Dorset 12 0709
Romford Gt Lon 27 5188
Romiley Gt Man 79 9490
Romney Street Kent 27 5561
Romsey Hants 12 3521
Romsley Shrops 60 7883
Romsley Worcs 60 9680
Ronachan Ag & B 113 7454
Rookhope Dur 95 9342
Rookley IOW 13 5084
Rookley Green IOW 13 5083
Rooks Bridge Somset 21 3652
Rooks Nest Somset 20 0933
Rookwith N York 89 2086
Roos E R Yk 85 2830
Roose Cumb 86 2269
Roosebeck Cumb 86 2567
Roothams Green Beds 51 0957
Ropley Hants 24 6431
Ropley Dean Hants 24 6232
Ropley Soke Hants 24 6533
Ropsley Lincs 63 9933
Rora Abers 143 0650
Rorrington Shrops 59 3000
Rosarie Moray 141 3850
Roscroggan Cnwll 2 6542
Rose Cnwll 3 7754
Rose Ash Devon 19 7921
Rose Green Essex 40 9028
Rose Green Suffk 54 9337
Rose Green Suffk 54 9744
Rose Green W Susx 14 9099
Rose Hill E Susx 16 4516
Rose Hill Lancs 81 8231
Roseacre Lancs 80 4336
Rosebank S Lans 116 8049
Rosebush Pembks 31 0729
Rosecare Cnwll 4 1695
Rosecliston Cnwll 4 8159
Rosedale Abbey N York 90 7296
Rosehall Highld 146 4702
Rosehearty Abers 143 9267
Rosehill Shrops 59 4715
Roseisle Moray 141 1466
Roselands E Susx 16 6200
Rosemarket Pembks 30 9508
Rosemarkie Highld 140 7357
Rosemary Lane Devon 9 1514
Rosemount P & K 126 1843
Rosenannon Cnwll 4 9566
Rosenithon Cnwll 3 8021
Roser's Cross E Susx 16 5420
Rosevean Cnwll 4 0258
Rosevine Cnwll 3 8736
Rosewarne Cnwll 2 6036
Rosewell Mdloth 117 2862
Roseworth Dur 96 4221
Roseworthy Cnwll 2 6139
Rosgill Cumb 94 5316
Roskhill Highld 136 2744
Roskorwell Cnwll 3 7923
Roskrow Cnwll 3 7635
Rosley Cumb 93 3245
Roslin Mdloth 117 2763
Rosliston Derbys 73 2416
Rosneath Ag & B 114 2583
Ross D & G 99 6444
Ross Nthumb 111 1337
Ross-on-Wye Herefs 46 5923
Rossett Wrexhm 71 3657
Rossett Green N York 82 2952
Rossington S York 75 6298
Rossland Rens 115 4370
Roster Highld 151 2639
Rostherne Ches 79 7483
Rosthwaite Cumb 93 2514
Roston Derbys 73 1340
Rosudgeon Cnwll 2 5529
Rosyth Fife 117 1082
Rothbury Nthumb 103 0501
Rotherby Leics 63 6716
Rotherfield E Susx 16 5529
Rotherfield Greys Oxon 37 7282
Rotherfield Peppard Oxon 37 7182
Rotherham S York 75 4392
Rothersthorpe Nhants 49 7156
Rotherwick Hants 24 7156
Rothes Moray 141 2749
Rothesay Ag & B 114 0864
Rothiebrisbane Abers 142 7437
Rothiemay Moray 142 5548
Rothiemurchus Lodge Highld 133 9407
Rothienorman Abers 142 7235
Rothley Leics 62 5812
Rothley Nthumb 103 0488
Rothmaise Abers 142 6832
Rothwell Lincs 76 1499
Rothwell Nhants 51 8181
Rothwell W York 83 3428
Rothwell Haigh W York 83 3328
Rotsea E R Yk 84 0651
Rottal Lodge Angus 134 3769
Rottingdean E Susx 15 3602
Rottington Cumb 92 9613
Rou Island Cumb 86 2365
Roucan D & G 100 0277
Roud IOW 13 5180
Rough Close Staffs 72 9239
Rough Common Kent 29 1259
Rougham Norfk 66 8320
Rougham Green Suffk 54 9061
Roughlee Lancs 81 8440
Roughley W Mids 61 1399
Roughpark Abers 134 3412
Roughton Lincs 77 2464
Roughton Norfk 67 2136
Roughton Shrops 60 7594
Roughway Kent 27 6153
Round Bush Herts 26 1498
Round Green Beds 38 1022
Round Street Kent 28 6568
Roundbush Essex 40 8501
Roundbush Green Essex 40 5814
Roundham Somset 10 4209
Roundhay W York 83 3337
Rounds Green W Mids 60 9889
Roundstreet Common W Susx 14 0528
Roundway Wilts 22 0163
Roundyhill Angus 126 3750
Rous Lench Worcs 47 0153
Rousdon Devon 10 2991
Rousham Oxon 49 4724
Rout's Green Bucks 37 7898
Routenbeck Cumb 93 1930
Routenburn N Ayrs 114 1961
Routh E R Yk 85 0942
Row Cnwll 4 0976
Row Cumb 94 6234
Row Cumb 87 4589
Row Ash Hants 13 5413
Row Green Essex 40 7420
Row Town Surrey 26 0363
Rowanburn D & G 101 4177
Rowardennan Hotel Stirlg 115 3698
Rowardennan Lodge Stirlg 115 3598
Rowarth Derbys 79 0189
Rowberrow Somset 21 4558
Rowborough IOW 13 4684
Rowde Wilts 22 9762
Rowden Devon 8 6499
Rowen Conwy 69 7671
Rowfield Derbys 73 1948
Rowfoot Nthumb 102 6860
Rowford Somset 20 2327
Rowhedge Essex 41 0221
Rowhook W Susx 14 1234
Rowington Warwks 48 2069
Rowland Derbys 74 2172
Rowland's Castle Hants 13 7310
Rowland's Gill T & W 96 1658
Rowledge Surrey 25 8243
Rowley Dur 95 0848
Rowley E R Yk 84 9732
Rowley Shrops 59 3006
Rowley Green W Mids 61 3483
Rowley Hill W York 82 1914
Rowley Regis W Mids 60 9787
Rowlstone Herefs 46 3727
Rowly Surrey 14 0440
Rowner Hants 13 5801
Rowney Green Worcs 61 0471
Rownhams Hants 12 3817
Rowrah Cumb 92 0518
Rows of Trees Ches 79 8379
Rowsham Bucks 38 8417
Rowsley Derbys 74 2565
Rowstock Oxon 37 4789
Rowston Lincs 76 0856
Rowthorne Derbys 75 4764
Rowton Ches 71 4464
Rowton Shrops 59 3612
Rowton Shrops 59 6119
Rowton Shrops 59 4180
Roxburgh Border 110 6930
Roxby Lincs 84 9116
Roxby N York 97 7616
Roxton Beds 52 1554
Roxwell Essex 40 6408
Roy Bridge Highld 131 2681
Royal Botanic Gardens 117 2475
Royal Oak Dur 96 2023
Royal Oak Lancs 78 4103
Royal's Green Ches 71 6242
Roydhouse W York 82 2112
Roydon Essex 39 4010
Roydon Norfk 65 7023
Roydon Norfk 54 1080
Roydon Hamlet Essex 39 4107
Royston Herts 39 3540
Royston S York 83 3611
Royton Gt Man 79 9107
Rozel Jersey 158 0000
Ruabon Wrexhm 71 3043
Ruaig Ag & B 120 0747
Ruan High Lanes Cnwll 3 9039
Ruan Lanihorne Cnwll 3 8942
Ruan Major Cnwll 2 7016
Ruan Minor Cnwll 2 7115
Ruardean Gloucs 35 6217
Ruardean Hill Gloucs 35 6317
Ruardean Woodside Gloucs 35 6216
Rubery Worcs 60 9977
Rubha Ban W Isls 152 7811
Ruckcroft Cumb 94 5344
Ruckhall Herefs 46 4637
Ruckhall Common Herefs 46 4539
Ruckinge Kent 17 0233
Ruckland Lincs 77 3378
Ruckley Shrops 59 5300
Rudby N York 89 4706
Rudchester Nthumb 103 1167
Ruddington Notts 62 5732
Ruddle Gloucs 35 6811
Ruddlemoor Cnwll 3 0054
Rudford Gloucs 35 7721
Rudge Somset 22 8251
Rudgeway Gloucs 35 6386
Rudgwick W Susx 14 0834
Rudhall Herefs 47 6225
Rudheath Ches 79 6772
Rudley Green Essex 40 8303
Rudloe Wilts 35 8470
Rudry Caerph 33 2086
Rudston E R Yk 91 0967
Rudyard Staffs 72 9557
Ruecastle Border 110 6120
Rufford Lancs 80 4615
Rufforth N York 83 5251
Rug Denbgs 70 0543
Rugby Warwks 50 5075
Rugeley Staffs 73 0418
Ruggaton Devon 19 5545
Ruishton Somset 20 2625
Ruislip Gt Lon 26 0987
Rumbach Moray 141 3852
Rumbling Bridge P & K 117 0199
Rumburgh Suffk 55 3481
Rumby Hill Dur 96 1634
Rumford Cnwll 4 8970
Rumford Falk 116 9377
Rumney Cardif 33 2178
Rumwell Somset 20 1923
Runcorn Ches 78 5182
Runcton W Susx 14 8802
Runcton Holme Norfk 65 6109
Runfold Surrey 25 8647
Runhall Norfk 66 0507
Runham Norfk 67 4610
Runham Norfk 67 5108
Runnington Somset 20 1221
Runsell Green Essex 40 7905
Runshaw Moor Lancs 80 5319
Runswick N York 97 8016
Runtaleave Angus 133 2867
Runwell Essex 40 7594
Ruscombe Berks 37 7976
Rush Green Ches 79 6987
Rush Green Essex 41 1515
Rush Green Gt Lon 27 5187
Rush Green Herts 39 2123
Rush Green Herts 39 3325
Rushall Herefs 47 6435
Rushall Norfk 55 1982
Rushall W Mids 60 0200
Rushall Wilts 23 1255
Rushbrooke Suffk 54 8961
Rushbury Shrops 59 5191
Rushden Herts 39 3031
Rushden Nhants 51 9566
Rushenden Kent 28 9071
Rusher's Cross E Susx 16 6028
Rushett Common Surrey 14 0242
Rushford Devon 5 4576
Rushford Norfk 54 9281
Rushlake Green E Susx 16 6218
Rushmere Suffk 55 4986
Rushmere St Andrew Suffk 55 1946
Rushmoor Surrey 25 8740
Rushock Herefs 46 3058
Rushock Worcs 60 8871
Rusholme Gt Man 79 8594
Rushton Ches 71 5863
Rushton Nhants 51 8482
Rushton Shrops 59 6008
Rushton Spencer Staffs 72 9362
Rushwick Worcs 47 8254
Rushyford Dur 96 2728
Ruskie Stirlg 116 6200
Ruskington Lincs 76 0851
Rusland Cumb 87 3488
Rusper W Susx 15 2037
Ruspidge Gloucs 35 6611
Russ Hill Surrey 15 2240
Russel's Green Suffk 55 2572
Russell Green Essex 40 7413
Russell's Water Oxon 37 7089
Rusthall Kent 16 5639
Rustington W Susx 14 0402
Ruston N York 91 9583
Ruston Parva E R Yk 91 0661
Ruswarp N York 90 8809
Ruthall Shrops 59 5990
Rutherford Border 110 6430
Rutherglen S Lans 116 6161
Ruthernbridge Cnwll 4 0166
Ruthin Denbgs 70 1258
Ruthrieston Aber C 135 9204
Ruthven Abers 142 5046
Ruthven Angus 126 2848
Ruthven Highld 132 7699
Ruthven House Angus 126 3047
Ruthvoes Cnwll 4 9260
Ruthwaite Cumb 93 2336
Ruthwell D & G 100 0967
Ruxley Corner Gt Lon 27 4770
Ruxton Green Herefs 34 5419
Ruyton-XI-Towns Shrops 59 3922
Ryal Nthumb 103 0174
Ryall Dorset 10 4095
Ryall Worcs 47 8640
Ryarsh Kent 28 6660
Rycote Oxon 37 6705
Rydal Cumb 87 3606
Ryde IOW 13 5992
Rye E Susx 17 9220
Rye Cross Worcs 47 7735
Rye Foreign E Susx 17 8922
Rye Harbour E Susx 17 9319
Rye Street Worcs 47 7835
Ryebank Shrops 59 5131
Ryeford Herefs 35 6322
Ryehill E R Yk 85 2225
Ryeish Green Nhants 24 7267
Ryhall Rutlnd 64 0310
Ryhill W York 83 3814
Ryhope T & W 96 4152
Rylah Derbys 75 4667
Ryland Lincs 76 0179
Rylands Notts 62 5335
Rylstone N York 88 9658
Ryme Intrinseca Dorset 10 5810
Ryther N York 83 5539
Ryton N York 90 7975
Ryton Shrops 60 7602
Ryton T & W 103 1564
Ryton Warwks 61 4086
Ryton Woodside T & W 96 1462
Ryton-on-Dunsmore Warwks 61 3874

S

Sabden Lancs 81 7
Sabine's Green Essex 27 5
Sacombe Herts 39 3
Sacombe Green Herts 39 3
Sacriston Dur 96 2
Sadberge Dur 96 3
Saddell Ag & B 105 7
Saddington Leics 50 6
Saddle Bow Norfk 65 6
Saddlescombe W Susx 15 2
Sadgill Cumb 87 4
Saffron Walden Essex 39 5
Sageston Pembks 30 0
Saham Hills Norfk 66 9
Saham Toney Norfk 66 8
Saighton Ches 71 4
St Abbs Border 119 9
St Agnes Border 118 6
St Agnes Cnwll 2 7
St Albans Herts 38 1
St Allen Cnwll 3 8
St Andrew Guern 158 0
St Andrew's Major V Glam 33 1
St Andrews Fife 127 5
St Andrews Well Dorset 10 4
St Ann's D & G 100 0
St Ann's Chapel Cnwll 5 4
St Ann's Chapel Devon 7 6
St Anne's Lancs 80 3
St Anthony Cnwll 3 7
St Anthony's Hill E Susx 16 6
St Arvans Mons 34 5
St Asaph Denbgs 70 0
St Athan V Glam 20 0
St Aubin Jersey 158 0
St Austell Cnwll 3 0
St Bees Cumb 86 9
St Blazey Cnwll 3 0
St Blazey Gate Cnwll 3 0
St Boswells Border 110 5
St Brelade Jersey 158 0
St Brelade's Bay Jersey 158 0
St Breock Cnwll 4 9
St Breward Cnwll 4 0
St Briavels Gloucs 34 5
St Bride's Major V Glam 33 8
St Brides Pembks 30 8
St Brides Netherwent Mons 34 4
St Brides super-Ely V Glam 33 0
St Brides Wentlooge Newpt 34 2
St Budeaux Devon 6 4
St Buryan Cnwll 2 4
St Catherine Somset 35 77
St Catherines Ag & B 123 12
St Chloe Gloucs 35 84
St Clears Carmth 31 2
St Cleer Cnwll 5 24
St Clement Cnwll 3 85
St Clement Jersey 158 0
St Clether Cnwll 5 2
St Colmac Ag & B 114 04
St Columb Major Cnwll 4 91
St Columb Minor Cnwll 4 83
St Columb Road Cnwll 4 91
St Combs Abers 143 05
St Cross South Elmham Suffk 55 29
St Cyrus Abers 135 74
St David's P & K 125 94
St David's Pembks 30 75
St Day Cnwll 3 72
St Decumans Somset 20 06
St Dennis Cnwll 4 95
St Devereux Herefs 46 44
St Dogmaels Cerdgn 42 16
St Dogwells Pembks 30 97
St Dominick Cnwll 5 40
St Donats V Glam 20 93
St Edith's Marsh Wilts 22 97
St Endellion Cnwll 4 99
St Enoder Cnwll 3 89
St Erme Cnwll 3 84
St Erney Cnwll 5 37
St Erth Cnwll 2 55
St Erth Praze Cnwll 2 57
St Ervan Cnwll 4 89
St Ewe Cnwll 3 97
St Fagans Cardif 33 12
St Fagans Welsh Life Museum 33 11
St Fergus Abers 143 09
St Fillans P & K 124 69
St Florence Pembks 31 08
St Gennys Cnwll 4 14
St George Conwy 70 97
St George's V Glam 33 10
St George's Hill Surrey 26 08
St Georges Somset 21 37
St Germans Cnwll 5 36
St Giles in the Wood Devon 19 53
St Giles-on-the-Heath Cnwll 5 36
St Gluvia's Cnwll 3 78
St Harmon Powys 45 98
St Helen Auckland Dur 96 18
St Helena Norfk 66 18
St Helens Cumb 92 02
St Helens E Susx 17 82
St Helens IOW 13 62
St Helens Mersyd 78 51
St Helier Gt Lon 27 25
St Helier Jersey 158 00
St Hilary Cnwll 2 54
St Hilary V Glam 33 01
St Hill Devon 9 09
St Hill W Susx 15 38
St Illtyd Blae G 34 22
St Ippollitts Herts 39 19
St Ishmael's Pembks 30 83
St Issey Cnwll 4 92
St Ive Cnwll 5 31
St Ives Cambs 52 31
St Ives Cnwll 2 51
St Ives Dorset 12 12
St James Norfk 67 27
St James South Elmham Suffk 55 32

St James's End Nhants ... 49 7460
St John Cnwll ... 5 4053
St John Jersey ... 158 0000
St John's IOM ... 158 2781
St John's Chapel Devon ... 19 5329
St John's Chapel Dur ... 95 8837
St John's Fen End Norfk ... 65 5312
St John's Highway Norfk ... 65 5214
St John's Kirk S Lans ... 108 9836
St John's Town of Dalry D & G ... 99 6281
St John's Wood Gt Lon ... 27 2683
St Johns Dur ... 95 0633
St Johns Kent ... 27 5356
St Johns Surrey ... 25 9857
St Johns Worcs ... 47 8454
St Jude's IOM ... 158 3996
St Just Cnwll ... 2 3731
St Just Lane Cnwll ... 3 8535
St Just-in-Roseland Cnwll ... 3 8435
St Katherines Abers ... 142 7834
St Keverne Cnwll ... 3 7921
St Kew Cnwll ... 4 0276
St Kew Highway Cnwll ... 4 0375
St Keyne Cnwll ... 2 5461
St Lawrence Cnwll ... 4 0466
St Lawrence Essex ... 41 9604
St Lawrence IOW ... 13 5376
St Lawrence Jersey ... 158 0000
St Lawrence Kent ... 29 3665
St Leonard's Street Kent ... 28 6756
St Leonards Bucks ... 38 9007
St Leonards Dorset ... 12 1103
St Leonards E Susx ... 17 8009
St Levan Cnwll ... 2 3822
St Lythans V Glam ... 33 1072
St Mabyn Cnwll ... 4 0473
St Madoes P & K ... 126 1921
St Margaret South Elmham Suffk ... 55 3183
St Margaret's at Cliffe Kent ... 29 3544
St Margaret's Hope Ork ... 153 4493
St Margarets Herefs ... 46 3533
St Margarets Herts ... 39 3811
St Marks IOM ... 158 2974
St Martin Cnwll ... 5 2555
St Martin Cnwll ... 3 7323
St Martin Guern ... 158 0000
St Martin Jersey ... 158 0000
St Martin's P & K ... 126 1530
St Martin's Moor Shrops ... 59 3135
St Martins Shrops ... 59 3236
St Mary Jersey ... 158 0000
St Mary Bourne Hants ... 24 4250
St Mary Church V Glam ... 33 0071
St Mary Cray Gt Lon ... 27 4768
St Mary Hill V Glam ... 33 9678
St Mary in the Marsh Kent ... 17 0627
St Mary's Cnwll ... 153 4701
St Mary's Bay Kent ... 17 0827
St Mary's Grove Somset ... 21 4669
St Mary's Hoo Kent ... 28 8076
St Marychurch Devon ... 7 9166
St Maughans Mons ... 34 4617
St Maughans Green Mons ... 34 4717
St Mawes Cnwll ... 3 8433
St Mawgan Cnwll ... 4 8765
St Mellion Cnwll ... 5 3965
St Mellons Cardif ... 34 2281
St Merryn Cnwll ... 4 8874
St Mewan Cnwll ... 3 9951
St Michael Caerhays Cnwll ... 3 9642
St Michael Church Somset ... 20 3030
St Michael Penkevil Cnwll ... 3 8541
St Michael South Elmham Suffk ... 55 3483
St Michael's on Wyre Lancs ... 80 4641
St Michaels Kent ... 17 8835
St Michaels Worcs ... 46 5865
St Minver Cnwll ... 4 9677
St Monans Fife ... 127 5201
St Neot Cnwll ... 4 1868
St Neots Cambs ... 52 1860
St Nicholas Pembks ... 30 9035
St Nicholas V Glam ... 33 0974
St Nicholas at Wade Kent ... 29 2666
St Ninians Stirlg ... 116 7991
St Olaves Norfk ... 67 4599
St Osyth Essex ... 41 1215
St Ouen Jersey ... 158 0000
St Owens Cross Herefs ... 46 5324
St Paul's Walden Herts ... 39 1922
St Pauls Cray Gt Lon ... 27 4768
St Peter Jersey ... 158 0000
St Peter Port Guern ... 158 0000
St Peter's Guern ... 158 0000
St Peter's Kent ... 29 3868
St Peter's Guern ... 158 0000
St Peter's Hill Cambs ... 52 2372
St Petrox Pembks ... 30 9797
St Pinnock Cnwll ... 5 2063
St Quivox S Ayrs ... 106 3723
St Ruan Cnwll ... 2 7115
St Sampson Guern ... 158 0000
St Saviour Guern ... 158 0000
St Saviour Jersey ... 158 0000
St Stephen Cnwll ... 3 9453
St Stephen's Coombe Cnwll ... 3 9451
St Stephens Cnwll ... 5 3285
St Stephens Cnwll ... 5 4158
St Teath Cnwll ... 4 0680
St Tudy Cnwll ... 4 0676
St Twynnells Pembks ... 30 9597
St Veep Cnwll ... 3 1455
St Vigeans Angus ... 127 6443
St Wenn Cnwll ... 4 9664
St Weonards Herefs ... 46 4924
St y-Nyll V Glam ... 33 0977
Saintbury Gloucs ... 48 1139
Salachail Ag & B ... 123 0551
Salcombe Devon ... 7 7439
Salcombe Regis Devon ... 9 1588
Salcott Essex ... 40 9413
Sale Gt Man ... 79 7991
Sale Green Worcs ... 47 9358
Saleby Lincs ... 77 4578
Salehurst E Susx ... 17 7524
Salem Carmth ... 44 6226
Salem Cerdgn ... 43 6684
Salem Gwynd ... 69 5456
Salen Ag & B ... 121 5743
Salen Highld ... 121 6864

Salesbury Lancs ... 81 6832
Salford Beds ... 38 9339
Salford Gt Man ... 79 8197
Salford Oxon ... 48 2828
Salford Priors Warwks ... 48 0751
Salfords Surrey ... 15 2846
Salhouse Norfk ... 67 3114
Saline Fife ... 117 0292
Salisbury Wilts ... 23 1429
Salisbury Cathedral ... 23 1429
Salkeld Dykes Cumb ... 94 5437
Salle Norfk ... 66 1024
Salmonby Lincs ... 77 3273
Salperton Gloucs ... 36 0720
Salph End Beds ... 38 0852
Salsburgh N Lans ... 116 8262
Salt Staffs ... 72 9527
Salt Cotes Cumb ... 93 1853
Salta Cumb ... 92 0845
Saltaire W York ... 82 1438
Saltash Cnwll ... 6 4258
Saltburn Highld ... 146 7270
Saltburn-by-the-Sea N York ... 97 6621
Saltby Leics ... 63 8526
Saltcoats Cumb ... 86 0797
Saltcoats N Ayrs ... 106 2441
Saltcotes Lancs ... 80 3728
Saltdean E Susx ... 15 3802
Salterbeck Cumb ... 92 9926
Salterforth Lancs ... 81 8845
Salterswall Ches ... 71 6266
Salterton Wilts ... 23 1236
Saltfleet Lincs ... 77 4593
Saltfleetby All Saints Lincs ... 77 4593
Saltfleetby St Clement Lincs ... 77 4691
Saltfleetby St Peter Lincs ... 77 4489
Saltford Somset ... 22 6867
Salthouse Norfk ... 66 0743
Saltley W Mids ... 61 1088
Saltmarsh Newpt ... 34 3482
Saltmarshe E R Yk ... 84 7824
Saltney Flints ... 71 3865
Salton N York ... 90 7179
Saltrens Devon ... 18 4522
Saltwick Nthumb ... 103 1780
Saltwood Kent ... 29 1535
Salvington W Susx ... 14 1205
Salwarpe Worcs ... 47 8762
Salwayash Dorset ... 10 4596
Sambourne Warwks ... 48 0662
Sambrook Shrops ... 72 7124
Samlesbury Lancs ... 81 5930
Samlesbury Bottoms Lancs ... 81 6228
Sampford Arundel Somset ... 20 1118
Sampford Brett Somset ... 20 0741
Sampford Courtenay Devon ... 8 6301
Sampford Moor Somset ... 20 1118
Sampford Peverell Devon ... 9 0314
Sampford Spiney Devon ... 6 5372
Samson's Corner Essex ... 41 0818
Samsonlane Ork ... 153 6526
Samuelston E Loth ... 118 4870
Sanaigmore Ag & B ... 112 2370
Sancreed Cnwll ... 2 4129
Sancton E R Yk ... 84 8939
Sand Somset ... 21 4346
Sand Hills W York ... 83 3739
Sand Hole E R Yk ... 84 8137
Sand Hutton N York ... 90 6958
Sand Side Cumb ... 86 2282
Sandaig Highld ... 129 7102
Sandal Magna W York ... 83 3417
Sandale Cumb ... 93 2440
Sandavore Highld ... 128 4784
Sanday Airport ... 153 6740
Sandbach Ches ... 72 7560
Sandbank Ag & B ... 114 1680
Sandbanks Dorset ... 12 0487
Sandend Abers ... 142 5566
Sanderstead Gt Lon ... 27 3461
Sandford Cumb ... 94 7316
Sandford Devon ... 8 8202
Sandford Dorset ... 11 9289
Sandford Hants ... 12 1601
Sandford IOW ... 13 5381
Sandford S Lans ... 107 7143
Sandford Shrops ... 59 3423
Sandford Shrops ... 59 5833
Sandford Somset ... 21 4259
Sandford Orcas Dorset ... 21 6220
Sandford St Martin Oxon ... 49 4226
Sandford-on-Thames Oxon ... 37 5301
Sandgate Kent ... 29 2035
Sandhaven Abers ... 143 9667
Sandhead D & G ... 98 0949
Sandhill S York ... 75 4496
Sandhills Dorset ... 10 5800
Sandhills Dorset ... 11 6810
Sandhills Oxon ... 37 5507
Sandhills Surrey ... 14 9337
Sandhills W Mids ... 61 0604
Sandhoe Nthumb ... 102 9666
Sandhole Ag & B ... 114 0098
Sandholme E R Yk ... 84 8230
Sandholme Lincs ... 64 3337
Sandhurst Berks ... 25 8361
Sandhurst Gloucs ... 47 8223
Sandhurst Kent ... 17 8028
Sandhurst Cross Kent ... 17 7827
Sandhutton N York ... 89 3881
Sandiacre Derbys ... 62 4736
Sandilands Lincs ... 77 5280
Sandiway Ches ... 71 6070
Sandleheath Hants ... 12 1215
Sandleigh Oxon ... 37 4701
Sandley Dorset ... 22 7724
Sandling Kent ... 28 7557
Sandlow Green Ches ... 72 7865
Sandness Shet ... 153 1957
Sandon Essex ... 40 7404
Sandon Herts ... 39 3234
Sandon Staffs ... 72 9429
Sandon Bank Staffs ... 72 9428
Sandown IOW ... 13 5984
Sandplace Cnwll ... 5 2557
Sandridge Herts ... 39 1710
Sandridge Wilts ... 22 9465
Sandringham Norfk ... 65 6928

Sands Bucks ... 26 8493
Sandsend N York ... 90 8612
Sandside Cumb ... 87 4780
Sandtoft Lincs ... 84 7408
Sandway Kent ... 28 8950
Sandwich Kent ... 29 3358
Sandwick Cumb ... 93 4219
Sandwick Shet ... 153 4323
Sandwick W Isls ... 152 4432
Sandwith Cumb ... 92 9614
Sandwith Newtown Cumb ... 92 9814
Sandy Beds ... 52 1649
Sandy Bank Lincs ... 77 2655
Sandy Cross E Susx ... 16 5820
Sandy Cross Herefs ... 47 6757
Sandy Haven Pembks ... 30 8507
Sandy Lane W York ... 82 1135
Sandy Lane Wilts ... 22 9668
Sandy Lane Wrexhm ... 71 4040
Sandy Park Devon ... 8 7189
Sandycroft Flints ... 71 3366
Sandyford D & G ... 101 2093
Sandygate Devon ... 7 8674
Sandygate IOM ... 158 3797
Sandyhills D & G ... 92 8855
Sandylands Lancs ... 87 4263
Sandylane Staffs ... 72 7035
Sandylane Swans ... 32 5589
Sandysike Cumb ... 101 3965
Sandyway Herefs ... 46 4925
Sangobeg Highld ... 149 4266
Sangomore Highld ... 149 4067
Sankey Bridges Ches ... 78 5887
Sankyn's Green Worcs ... 47 7965
Sanna Bay Highld ... 128 4469
Sanndabhaig W Isls ... 152 4432
Sannox N Ayrs ... 105 0145
Sanquhar D & G ... 107 7809
Santon Cumb ... 86 1001
Santon IOM ... 158 3171
Santon Bridge Cumb ... 86 1101
Santon Downham Suffk ... 54 8187
Sapcote Leics ... 50 4893
Sapey Common Herefs ... 47 7064
Sapiston Suffk ... 54 9175
Sapley Cambs ... 52 2474
Sapperton Derbys ... 73 1834
Sapperton Gloucs ... 35 9403
Sapperton Lincs ... 64 0133
Saracen's Head Lincs ... 64 3427
Sarclet Highld ... 151 3443
Sarisbury Hants ... 13 5008
Sarn Brdgnd ... 33 9083
Sarn Gwynd ... 56 2432
Sarn Powys ... 58 9597
Sarn Powys ... 58 2090
Sarn-bach Gwynd ... 56 3026
Sarn-wen Powys ... 58 2718
Sarnau Carmth ... 31 3318
Sarnau Cerdgn ... 42 3150
Sarnau Gwynd ... 70 9639
Sarnau Powys ... 58 2315
Sarnau Powys ... 45 0232
Sarnesfield Herefs ... 46 3750
Saron Carmth ... 31 3737
Saron Carmth ... 32 6012
Saron Gwynd ... 69 5365
Saron Gwynd ... 68 4658
Sarratt Herts ... 26 0499
Sarre Kent ... 29 2565
Sarsden Oxon ... 36 2822
Sarson Hants ... 23 3044
Satley Dur ... 95 1143
Satmar Kent ... 29 2539
Satron N York ... 88 9397
Satterleigh Devon ... 19 6622
Satterthwaite Cumb ... 86 3392
Satwell Oxon ... 37 7083
Sauchen Abers ... 135 7011
Saucher P & K ... 126 1933
Sauchieburn Abers ... 135 6669
Saul Gloucs ... 35 7409
Saundby Notts ... 75 7888
Saundersfoot Pembks ... 31 1304
Saunderton Bucks ... 37 7901
Saunton Devon ... 18 4637
Sausthorpe Lincs ... 77 3868
Saveock Water Cnwll ... 3 7645
Saverley Green Staffs ... 72 9638
Savile Town W York ... 82 2420
Sawbridge Warwks ... 50 5065
Sawbridgeworth Herts ... 39 4814
Sawdon N York ... 91 9485
Sawley Derbys ... 62 4631
Sawley Lancs ... 81 7746
Sawley N York ... 89 2467
Sawston Cambs ... 53 4849
Sawtry Cambs ... 52 1683
Saxby Leics ... 63 8219
Saxby Lincs ... 76 0086
Saxby All Saints Lincs ... 84 9816
Saxelbye Leics ... 63 6921
Saxham Street Suffk ... 54 0861
Saxilby Lincs ... 76 8975
Saxlingham Norfk ... 66 0239
Saxlingham Green Norfk ... 67 2396
Saxlingham Nethergate Norfk ... 67 2297
Saxlingham Thorpe Norfk ... 67 2197
Saxmundham Suffk ... 55 3863
Saxon Street Cambs ... 53 6759
Saxondale Notts ... 63 6839
Saxtead Suffk ... 55 2665
Saxtead Green Suffk ... 55 2564
Saxtead Little Green Suffk ... 55 2466
Saxthorpe Norfk ... 66 1130
Saxton N York ... 83 4736
Sayers Common W Susx ... 15 2618
Scackleton N York ... 90 6472
Scaftworth Notts ... 75 6691
Scagglethorpe N York ... 90 8372
Scalasaig Ag & B ... 112 3993
Scalby E R Yk ... 84 8429
Scalby N York ... 91 0090
Scald End Beds ... 51 0457
Scaldwell Nhants ... 50 7672
Scale Houses Cumb ... 94 5845
Scaleby Cumb ... 101 4463
Scalebyhill Cumb ... 101 4463

Scales Cumb ... 93 3426
Scales Cumb ... 86 2772
Scalesceugh Cumb ... 93 4449
Scalford Leics ... 63 7624
Scaling N York ... 90 7413
Scaling Dam N York ... 90 7412
Scalloway Shet ... 153 4039
Scamblesby Lincs ... 77 2778
Scammonden W York ... 82 0515
Scamodale Highld ... 129 8353
Scampston N York ... 90 8575
Scampton Lincs ... 76 9579
Scaniport Highld ... 140 6239
Scapegoat Hill W York ... 82 0916
Scarborough N York ... 91 0488
Scarcewater Cnwll ... 3 9154
Scarcliffe Derbys ... 75 4968
Scarcroft W York ... 83 3541
Scarcroft Hill W York ... 83 3741
Scarfskerry Highld ... 151 2674
Scargill Dur ... 88 0510
Scarinish Ag & B ... 120 0444
Scarisbrick Lancs ... 80 3713
Scarness Cumb ... 93 2230
Scarning Norfk ... 66 9512
Scarrington Notts ... 63 7341
Scarth Hill Lancs ... 78 4206
Scarthingwell N York ... 83 4937
Scartho Lincs ... 85 2606
Scatsta Airport ... 153 3872
Scawby Lincs ... 84 9605
Scawsby S York ... 83 5404
Scawthorpe S York ... 83 5506
Scawton N York ... 90 5483
Scayne's Hill W Susx ... 15 3623
Scethrog Powys ... 45 1025
Scholar Green Ches ... 72 8357
Scholes Gt Man ... 78 5905
Scholes S York ... 74 3895
Scholes W York ... 82 1507
Scholes W York ... 82 1625
Scholes W York ... 83 3736
Scholes W York ... 83 3825
School Aycliffe Dur ... 96 2523
School Green Ches ... 72 6464
School Green W York ... 82 1132
School House Dorset ... 10 3602
Schoolgreen Berks ... 24 7367
Scissett W York ... 82 2410
Scleddau Pembks ... 30 9434
Sco Ruston Norfk ... 67 2821
Scofton Notts ... 75 6280
Scole Norfk ... 54 1579
Scone P & K ... 126 1226
Sconser Highld ... 137 5132
Scoonie Fife ... 126 3801
Scopwick Lincs ... 76 0757
Scoraig Highld ... 144 0096
Scorborough E R Yk ... 84 0145
Scorrier Cnwll ... 3 7244
Scorriton Devon ... 7 7068
Scorton Lancs ... 80 5048
Scorton N York ... 89 2500
Scot Hay Staffs ... 72 7947
Scot Lane End Gt Man ... 79 6209
Scot's Gap Nthumb ... 103 0386
Scotby Cumb ... 93 4455
Scotch Corner N York ... 89 2105
Scotforth Lancs ... 87 4859
Scothern Lincs ... 76 0377
Scotland Lincs ... 63 0030
Scotland W York ... 82 2340
Scotland Gate T & W ... 103 2584
Scotlandwell P & K ... 126 1801
Scotscalder Station Highld ... 151 0956
Scotsdike Cumb ... 101 3872
Scotsmill Abers ... 142 5618
Scotstoun C Glas ... 115 5267
Scotswood T & W ... 103 2063
Scott Willoughby Lincs ... 64 0537
Scotter Lincs ... 76 8800
Scotterthorpe Lincs ... 84 8701
Scottlethorpe Lincs ... 64 0520
Scotton Lincs ... 76 8899
Scotton N York ... 89 1895
Scotton N York ... 89 3259
Scottow Norfk ... 67 2823
Scoulton Norfk ... 66 9800
Scounslow Green Staffs ... 73 0029
Scourie Highld ... 148 1544
Scourie More Highld ... 148 1443
Scousburgh Shet ... 153 3717
Scouthead Gt Man ... 79 9605
Scrabster Highld ... 151 1070
Scraesburgh Border ... 110 6718
Scrafield Lincs ... 77 3068
Scrainwood Nthumb ... 111 9808
Scrane End Lincs ... 64 3841
Scraptoft Leics ... 63 6405
Scratby Norfk ... 67 5015
Scrayingham N York ... 90 7359
Scrays E Susx ... 17 7619
Scredington Lincs ... 64 0940
Scremby Lincs ... 77 4467
Scremerston Nthumb ... 111 0049
Screveton Notts ... 63 7343
Scrivelsby Lincs ... 77 2766
Scriven N York ... 89 3458
Scrooby Notts ... 75 6590
Scropton Derbys ... 73 1930
Scrub Hill Lincs ... 76 2355
Scruschloch Angus ... 133 2357
Scruton N York ... 89 2992
Scuggate Cumb ... 101 4474
Scullomie Highld ... 149 6161
Sculthorpe Norfk ... 66 8930
Scunthorpe Lincs ... 84 8910
Scurlage Swans ... 32 4687
Sea Somset ... 10 3412
Sea Palling Norfk ... 67 4226
Seaborough Dorset ... 10 4206
Seabridge Staffs ... 72 8343
Seabrook Kent ... 29 1835
Seaburn T & W ... 96 4059
Seacombe Mersyd ... 78 3290
Seacroft Lincs ... 77 5661
Seacroft W York ... 83 3635
Seadyke Lincs ... 64 3236

Seafield Highld ... 136 4743
Seafield W Loth ... 117 0066
Seaford E Susx ... 16 4899
Seaforth Mersyd ... 78 3297
Seagrave Leics ... 62 6117
Seagry Heath Wilts ... 35 9581
Seaham Dur ... 96 4149
Seahouses Nthumb ... 111 2231
Seal Kent ... 27 5556
Seal Sands Dur ... 97 5324
Seale Surrey ... 25 8947
Seamer N York ... 90 4910
Seamer N York ... 91 0183
Seamill N Ayrs ... 114 2047
Searby Lincs ... 85 0705
Seasalter Kent ... 29 0864
Seascale Cumb ... 86 0301
Seathwaite Cumb ... 93 2312
Seathwaite Cumb ... 86 2295
Seatle Cumb ... 87 3783
Seatoller Cumb ... 93 2413
Seaton Cnwll ... 5 3054
Seaton Cumb ... 92 0130
Seaton Devon ... 9 2490
Seaton Dur ... 96 3949
Seaton E R Yk ... 85 1646
Seaton Kent ... 29 2258
Seaton Nthumb ... 103 3276
Seaton Rutlnd ... 51 9098
Seaton Burn T & W ... 103 2373
Seaton Carew Dur ... 97 5229
Seaton Delaval Nthumb ... 103 3075
Seaton Ross E R Yk ... 84 7840
Seaton Sluice Nthumb ... 103 3376
Seatown Dorset ... 10 4291
Seave Green N York ... 90 5500
Seaview IOW ... 13 6291
Seaville Cumb ... 92 1553
Seavington St Mary Somset ... 10 4014
Seavington St Michael Somset ... 10 4015
Sebastopol Torfn ... 34 2998
Sebergham Cumb ... 93 3641
Seckington Warwks ... 61 2507
Sedbergh Cumb ... 87 6591
Sedbury Gloucs ... 34 5493
Sedbusk N York ... 88 8891
Sedge Fen Suffk ... 53 6684
Sedgeberrow Worcs ... 48 0238
Sedgebrook Lincs ... 63 8537
Sedgefield Dur ... 96 3528
Sedgeford Norfk ... 65 7036
Sedgehill Wilts ... 22 8627
Sedgley W Mids ... 60 9193
Sedgley Park Gt Man ... 79 8202
Sedgwick Cumb ... 87 5186
Sedlescombe E Susx ... 17 7818
Sedrup Bucks ... 38 8011
Seed Kent ... 28 9456
Seend Wilts ... 22 9460
Seend Cleeve Wilts ... 22 9360
Seer Green Bucks ... 26 9692
Seething Norfk ... 67 3197
Sefton Mersyd ... 78 3501
Sefton Town Mersyd ... 78 3400
Seghill Nthumb ... 103 2874
Seighford Staffs ... 72 8825
Seion Gwynd ... 69 5466
Seisdon Staffs ... 60 8495
Selattyn Shrops ... 58 2633
Selborne Hants ... 24 7433
Selby N York ... 83 6132
Selham W Susx ... 14 9320
Selhurst Gt Lon ... 27 3267
Selkirk Border ... 109 4728
Sellack Herefs ... 46 5627
Sellafirth Shet ... 153 5198
Sellan Cnwll ... 2 4230
Sellick's Green Somset ... 20 2119
Sellindge Kent ... 29 0938
Selling Kent ... 28 0456
Sells Green Wilts ... 22 9462
Selly Oak W Mids ... 61 0482
Selmeston E Susx ... 16 5007
Selsdon Gt Lon ... 27 3562
Selsey Gloucs ... 35 8303
Selsey W Susx ... 14 8593
Selsfield Common W Susx ... 15 3434
Selside Cumb ... 87 5399
Selside N York ... 88 7875
Selsted Kent ... 29 2144
Selston Notts ... 75 4553
Selworthy Somset ... 20 9246
Semer Suffk ... 54 9946
Semington Wilts ... 22 8960
Semley Wilts ... 22 8926
Sempringham Lincs ... 64 1132
Send Surrey ... 26 0155
Send Marsh Surrey ... 26 0355
Senghenydd Caerph ... 33 1190
Sennen Cnwll ... 2 3525
Sennen Cove Cnwll ... 2 3526
Sennybridge Powys ... 45 9228
Serlby Notts ... 75 6389
Sessay N York ... 89 4575
Setchey Norfk ... 65 6313
Setley Hants ... 12 3000
Seton Mains E Loth ... 118 4275
Settle N York ... 88 8163
Settlingstones Nthumb ... 102 8468
Settrington N York ... 90 8370
Seven Ash Somset ... 20 1533
Seven Kings Gt Lon ... 27 4587
Seven Sisters Neath ... 33 8208
Seven Springs Gloucs ... 35 9617
Seven Star Green Essex ... 40 9325
Seven Wells Gloucs ... 48 1134
Sevenhampton Gloucs ... 36 0321
Sevenhampton Wilts ... 36 2090
Sevenoaks Kent ... 27 5255
Sevenoaks Weald Kent ... 27 5250
Severn Beach Gloucs ... 34 5484
Severn Stoke Worcs ... 47 8644
Sevick End Beds ... 51 0954
Sevington Kent ... 28 0340
Sewards End Essex ... 53 5738
Sewardstonebury Gt Lon ... 27 3995
Sewell Beds ... 38 9922
Sewerby E R Yk ... 91 1968

308

Seworgan Cnwll 2 7030
Sewstern Leics 63 8821
Sexhow N York 89 4706
Sezincote Gloucs 48 1731
Sgiogarstaigh W Isls 152 5461
Shabbington Bucks 37 6606
Shackerstone Leics 62 3706
Shacklecross Derbys 62 4234
Shackleford Surrey 25 9345
Shade N York 81 9323
Shader W Isls 152 3854
Shadforth Dur 96 3440
Shadingfield Suffk 55 4384
Shadoxhurst Kent 28 9737
Shadwell Norfk 54 9383
Shadwell W York 83 3439
Shaftenhoe End Herts 39 4037
Shaftesbury Dorset 22 8623
Shaftholme S York 83 5708
Shafton S York 83 3911
Shafton Two Gates S York 83 3910
Shakespeare's Birthplace 48 1955
Shalbourne Wilts 23 3163
Shalcombe IOW 13 3985
Shalden Hants 24 6941
Shalden Green Hants 24 7043
Shaldon Devon 7 9372
Shalfleet IOW 13 4189
Shalford Essex 40 7229
Shalford Surrey 25 0047
Shalford Green Essex 40 7127
Shallowford Staffs 72 8729
Shalmsford Street Kent 29 0954
Shalstone Bucks 49 6436
Shamley Green Surrey 14 0343
Shandford Angus 134 4962
Shandon Ag & B 114 2586
Shandwick Highld 147 8575
Shangton Leics 50 7196
Shankhouse Nthumb 103 2778
Shanklin IOW 13 5881
Shap Cumb 94 5615
Shapwick Dorset 11 9301
Shapwick Somset 21 4138
Shard End W Mids 61 1588
Shardlow Derbys 62 4330
Shareshill Staffs 60 9406
Sharlston W York 83 3918
Sharlston Common W York 83 3919
Sharman's Cross W Mids 61 1279
Sharnal Street Kent 28 7974
Sharnbrook Beds 51 9959
Sharneyford Lancs 81 8824
Sharnford Leics 50 4891
Sharnhill Green Dorset 11 7105
Sharoe Green Lancs 80 5333
Sharow N York 89 3371
Sharp Green Norfk 67 3820
Sharpenhoe Beds 38 0630
Sharperton Nthumb 102 9503
Sharpness Gloucs 35 6702
Sharpthorne W Susx 15 3732
Sharptor Cnwll 5 2573
Sharpway Gate Worcs 47 9565
Sharrington Norfk 66 0337
Shatterford Worcs 60 7981
Shatterling Kent 29 2658
Shaugh Prior Devon 6 5463
Shave Cross Dorset 10 4198
Shavington Ches 72 6951
Shaw Berks 24 4768
Shaw Gt Man 79 9308
Shaw N York 82 0235
Shaw Wilts 22 8965
Shaw Wilts 36 1185
Shaw Common Gloucs 47 6826
Shaw Green Herts 39 3032
Shaw Green Lancs 80 5218
Shaw Green N York 82 2652
Shaw Hill Lancs 81 5720
Shaw Mills N York 89 2562
Shawbost W Isls 152 6464
Shawbury Shrops 59 5521
Shawclough Gt Man 81 8914
Shawdon Hill Nthumb 111 0813
Shawell Leics 50 5480
Shawford Hants 13 4625
Shawforth Lancs 81 8920
Shawhead D & G 100 8675
Shawsburn S Lans 116 7750
Shear Cross Wilts 22 8642
Shearington D & G 100 0266
Shearsby Leics 50 6290
Shearston Somset 20 2830
Shebbear Devon 18 4409
Shebdon Staffs 72 7625
Shebster Highld 150 0164
Sheddens E Rens 115 5757
Shedfield Hants 13 5613
Sheen Derbys 74 1161
Sheep Hill Dur 96 1757
Sheep-ridge W York 82 1519
Sheepbridge Derbys 74 3674
Sheepscar W York 82 3134
Sheepscombe Gloucs 35 8910
Sheepstor Devon 6 5667
Sheepwash Devon 18 4806
Sheepwash Nthumb 103 2585
Sheepway Somset 34 4976
Sheepy Magna Leics 61 3201
Sheepy Parva Leics 62 3301
Sheering Essex 39 5014
Sheerness Kent 28 9174
Sheerwater Surrey 26 0461
Sheet Hants 13 7524
Sheffield Cnwll 2 4526
Sheffield S York 74 3587
Sheffield Bottom Berks 24 6469
Sheffield City Airport 74 4088
Sheffield Green E Susx 15 4125
Shefford Beds 38 1439
Sheigra Highld 148 1860
Sheinton Shrops 59 6003
Shelderton Shrops 46 4077
Sheldon Derbys 74 1768
Sheldon Devon 9 1208
Sheldon W Mids 61 1584
Sheldwich Kent 28 0156

Sheldwich Lees Kent 28 0156
Shelf W York 82 1228
Shelfanger Norfk 54 1083
Shelfield W Mids 61 0302
Shelfield Warwks 48 1263
Shelfield Green Warwks 48 1261
Shelford Notts 63 6642
Shelford Warwks 50 4288
Shellacres Border 110 8943
Shelley Essex 39 5505
Shelley Suffk 54 0238
Shelley W York 82 2011
Shelley Far Bank W York 82 2010
Shellingford Oxon 36 3193
Shellow Bowells Essex 40 6007
Shelsley Beauchamp Worcs 47 7363
Shelsley Walsh Worcs 47 7263
Shelton Beds 51 0368
Shelton Norfk 67 2291
Shelton Notts 63 7844
Shelton Shrops 59 4613
Shelton Green Norfk 55 2390
Shelton Lock Derbys 62 3730
Shelton Under Harley Staffs 72 8139
Shelve Shrops 59 3399
Shelwick Herefs 46 5242
Shenfield Essex 40 6095
Shenington Oxon 48 3742
Shenley Herts 26 1800
Shenley Brook End Bucks 38 8335
Shenley Church End Bucks 38 8336
Shenleybury Herts 26 1801
Shenmore Herefs 46 3937
Shennanton D & G 98 3363
Shenstone Staffs 61 1004
Shenstone Worcs 60 8673
Shenstone Woodend Staffs 61 1101
Shenton Leics 61 3800
Shepeau Stow Lincs 64 3012
Shephall Herts 39 2623
Shepherd's Bush Gt Lon 26 2380
Shepherd's Green Oxon 37 7183
Shepherds Cnwll 3 8154
Shepherds Patch Gloucs 35 7304
Shepherdswell Kent 29 2647
Shepley W York 82 1909
Shepperdine Gloucs 35 6295
Shepperton Surrey 26 0766
Shepperton Green Surrey 26 0767
Shepreth Cambs 52 3947
Shepshed Leics 62 4819
Shepton Beauchamp Somset 10 4017
Shepton Mallet Somset 21 6143
Shepton Montague Somset 22 6831
Shepway Kent 28 7753
Sheraton Dur 96 4435
Sherborne Dorset 10 6316
Sherborne Gloucs 36 1614
Sherborne Somset 21 5855
Sherborne Causeway Dorset 22 8323
Sherborne St John Hants 24 6255
Sherbourne Warwks 48 2661
Sherburn Dur 96 3142
Sherburn N York 91 9576
Sherburn Hill Dur 96 3342
Sherburn in Elmet N York 83 4933
Shere Surrey 14 0747
Shereford Norfk 66 8829
Sherfield English Hants 23 2922
Sherfield on Loddon Hants 24 6858
Sherfin Lancs 81 7925
Sherford Devon 7 7844
Sherford Dorset 11 9193
Sheriff Hutton N York 90 6566
Sheriffhales Shrops 60 7512
Sheringham Norfk 66 1543
Sherington Bucks 38 8846
Shermanbury W Susx 15 2019
Shernborne Norfk 65 7132
Sherrington Wilts 22 9639
Sherston Wilts 35 8586
Sherwood Notts 62 5643
Shettleston C Glas 116 6464
Shevington Gt Man 78 5408
Shevington Moor Gt Man 78 5410
Shevington Vale Gt Man 78 5309
Sheviock Cnwll 5 3755
Shibden Head W York 82 0928
Shide IOW 13 5088
Shidlaw Nthumb 110 8037
Shiel Bridge Highld 138 9318
Shieldaig Highld 137 8154
Shieldhill D & G 100 0385
Shieldhill Falk 116 8976
Shieldhill House Hotel S Lans 108 0040
Shields N Lans 116 7755
Shielfoot Highld 129 6670
Shielhill Angus 134 4257
Shielhill Inver 114 2472
Shifford Oxon 36 3701
Shifnal Shrops 60 7407
Shilbottle Nthumb 111 1908
Shildon Dur 96 2226
Shillford E Rens 115 4556
Shillingford Devon 20 9824
Shillingford Oxon 37 5992
Shillingford Abbot Devon 9 9088
Shillingford St George Devon 9 9087
Shillingstone Dorset 11 8211
Shillington Beds 38 1234
Shillmoor Nthumb 110 8807
Shilton Oxon 36 2608
Shilton Warwks 61 4084
Shilvinghampton Dorset 10 6284
Shimpling Norfk 54 1583
Shimpling Suffk 54 8651
Shimpling Street Suffk 54 8753
Shincliffe Dur 96 2940
Shiney Row T & W 96 3252
Shinfield Berks 24 7368
Shingay Cambs 52 3046
Shingle Street Suffk 55 3642
Shinnersbridge Devon 7 7862
Shinness Highld 146 5215
Shipbourne Kent 27 5952
Shipbrookhill Ches 79 6771
Shipdham Norfk 66 9507
Shipham Somset 21 4457

Shiphay Devon 7 8965
Shiplake Oxon 37 7678
Shiplake Row Oxon 37 7478
Shiplate Somset 21 3556
Shipley Derbys 62 4444
Shipley Shrops 60 8095
Shipley W Susx 15 1421
Shipley W York 82 1537
Shipley Bridge Surrey 15 3040
Shipley Hatch Kent 28 0038
Shipmeadow Suffk 55 3790
Shippea Hill Station Cambs 53 6484
Shippon Oxon 37 4898
Shipston on Stour Warwks 48 2540
Shipton Bucks 49 7727
Shipton Gloucs 36 0318
Shipton N York 90 5558
Shipton Shrops 59 5692
Shipton Bellinger Hants 23 2345
Shipton Gorge Dorset 10 4991
Shipton Green W Susx 14 8099
Shipton Moyne Gloucs 35 8989
Shipton-on-Cherwell Oxon 37 4716
Shipton-under-Wychwood Oxon 36 2817
Shiptonthorpe E R Yk 84 8543
Shirburn Oxon 37 6995
Shirdley Hill Lancs 80 3612
Shire Cumb 94 6135
Shire Oak W Mids 61 0504
Shirebrook Derbys 75 5267
Shiregreen S York 74 3691
Shirehampton Bristl 34 5376
Shiremoor T & W 103 3171
Shirenewton Mons 34 4793
Shireoaks Notts 75 5580
Shirkoak Kent 17 9435
Shirl Heath Herefs 46 4359
Shirland Derbys 74 4058
Shirlett Shrops 59 6497
Shirley Derbys 73 2141
Shirley Gt Lon 27 3565
Shirley Hants 13 4014
Shirley W Mids 61 1278
Shirrell Heath Hants 13 5714
Shirvan Ag & B 113 8741
Shirwell Devon 19 6037
Shirwell Cross Devon 19 5936
Shiskine N Ayrs 105 9129
Shittlehope Dur 95 0039
Shobdon Herefs 46 4062
Shobley Hants 12 1806
Shobrooke Devon 9 8601
Shoby Leics 63 6820
Shocklach Ches 71 4349
Shocklach Green Ches 71 4349
Shoeburyness Essex 40 9385
Sholden Kent 29 3552
Sholing Hants 13 4511
Shoose Cumb 92 0127
Shoot Hill Shrops 59 4112
Shop Cnwll 18 2214
Shop Cnwll 4 8773
Shop Street Suffk 55 2268
Shopwyke W Susx 14 8805
Shore Gt Man 81 9216
Shoreditch Gt Lon 27 3382
Shoreditch Somset 20 2422
Shoreham Kent 27 5161
Shoreham Airport 15 2005
Shoreham-by-Sea W Susx 15 2105
Shoreswood Nthumb 110 9446
Shorley Hants 13 5726
Shorncote Gloucs 35 0296
Shorne Kent 28 6971
Shorne Ridgeway Kent 28 6970
Short Heath W Mids 60 9700
Short Heath W Mids 61 0992
Shorta Cross Cnwll 5 2857
Shortbridge E Susx 16 4521
Shortfield Common Surrey 25 8442
Shortgate E Susx 16 4915
Shortheath Hants 14 7636
Shortlanesend Cnwll 3 8047
Shortstown Beds 38 0747
Shorwell IOW 13 4583
Shoscombe Somset 22 7156
Shotesham Norfk 67 2499
Shotgate Essex 40 7592
Shotley Suffk 55 2335
Shotley Bridge Dur 95 0953
Shotley Gate Suffk 41 2433
Shotley Street Suffk 55 2335
Shotleyfield Nthumb 95 0553
Shottenden Kent 28 0454
Shottermill Surrey 14 8832
Shottery Warwks 48 1854
Shotteswell Warwks 49 4245
Shottisham Suffk 55 3244
Shottle Derbys 74 3149
Shotton Dur 96 3625
Shotton Dur 96 4139
Shotton Flints 71 3168
Shotton Nthumb 110 8430
Shotton Nthumb 103 2277
Shotton Colliery Dur 96 3491
Shotts N Lans 116 8759
Shotwick Ches 71 3371
Shougle Moray 141 2155
Shouldham Norfk 65 6709
Shouldham Thorpe Norfk 65 6607
Shoulton Worcs 47 8159
Shover's Green E Susx 16 6530
Shraleybrook Staffs 72 7849
Shrawardine Shrops 59 3915
Shrawley Worcs 47 8065
Shreding Green Bucks 26 0280
Shrewley Warwks 48 2167
Shrewsbury Shrops 59 4912
Shrewton Wilts 23 0743
Shripney W Susx 14 9302
Shrivenham Oxon 36 2389
Shropham Norfk 66 9893
Shrub End Essex 41 9723
Shucknall Herefs 46 5842
Shudy Camps Cambs 53 6244
Shurdington Gloucs 35 9218
Shurlock Row Berks 25 8374

Shurnock Worcs 48 0360
Shurrery Highld 150 0458
Shurrery Lodge Highld 150 0456
Shurton Somset 20 2044
Shustoke Warwks 61 2290
Shut Heath Staffs 72 8621
Shute Devon 9 8900
Shute Devon 10 2597
Shutford Oxon 48 3840
Shuthonger Gloucs 47 8935
Shutlanger Nhants 49 7249
Shutt Green Staffs 60 8709
Shutterton Devon 9 9679
Shuttington Warwks 61 2505
Shuttlewood Derbys 75 4673
Shuttlewood Common Derbys 75 4773
Shuttleworth Lancs 81 8017
Siabost W Isls 152 2646
Siadar W Isls 152 3854
Sibbertoft Nhants 50 6882
Sibdon Carwood Shrops 59 4183
Sibford Ferris Oxon 48 3537
Sibford Gower Oxon 48 3537
Sible Hedingham Essex 53 7734
Sibley's Green Essex 40 6128
Sibsey Cnwll 5 2372
Sibsey Lincs 77 3550
Sibsey Fenside Lincs 77 3452
Sibson Cambs 51 0997
Sibson Leics 61 3500
Sibster Highld 151 3253
Sibthorpe Notts 75 7273
Sibthorpe Notts 63 7645
Sibton Suffk 55 3669
Sicklesmere Suffk 54 8760
Sicklinghall N York 83 3648
Sid Cop S York 83 3809
Sidbrook Somset 20 2527
Sidbury Devon 9 1391
Sidbury Shrops 60 6885
Sidcot Somset 21 4257
Sidcup Gt Lon 27 4672
Siddick Cumb 92 0031
Siddington Ches 79 8470
Siddington Gloucs 36 0399
Sidemoor Worcs 60 9571
Sidestrand Norfk 67 2539
Sidford Devon 9 1390
Sidlesham W Susx 14 8599
Sidlesham Common W Susx 14 8599
Sidley E Susx 17 7408
Sidmouth Devon 9 1287
Siefton Shrops 59 4883
Sigford Devon 7 7773
Sigglesthorne E R Yk 85 1545
Sigingstone V Glam 33 9771
Signet Oxon 36 2410
Silchester Hants 24 6261
Sileby Leics 62 6015
Silecroft Cumb 86 1381
Silfield Norfk 66 1299
Silian Cerdgn 44 5751
Silk Willoughby Lincs 64 0542
Silkstead Hants 13 4424
Silkstone S York 82 2805
Silkstone Common S York 82 2904
Silksworth T & W 96 3752
Silloth Cumb 92 1153
Silpho N York 91 9692
Silsden W York 82 0446
Silsoe Beds 38 0835
Silton Dorset 22 7829
Silver End Essex 40 8119
Silver Street Kent 28 8760
Silver Street Somset 21 5432
Silverburn Mdloth 117 2060
Silverdale Lancs 87 4674
Silverdale Staffs 72 8146
Silverdale Green Lancs 87 4674
Silverford Abers 142 7763
Silvergate Norfk 66 1727
Silverlace Green Suffk 55 3160
Silverley's Green Suffk 55 2976
Silverstone Nhants 49 6743
Silverton Devon 9 9502
Silverwell Cnwll 3 7448
Silvington Shrops 47 6279
Simmondley Derbys 74 0293
Simonburn Nthumb 102 8773
Simons Burrow Devon 9 1416
Simonsbath Somset 19 7739
Simonstone Lancs 81 7734
Simonstone N York 88 8791
Simprim Border 110 8445
Simpson Bucks 38 8836
Simpson Cross Pembks 30 8919
Sinclair's Hill Border 119 8150
Sinclairston E Ayrs 107 4716
Sinderby N York 89 3482
Sinderhope Nthumb 95 8451
Sinderland Green Gt Man 79 7389
Sindlesham Berks 25 7769
Single Street Gt Lon 27 4359
Singleborough Bucks 49 7631
Singleton Lancs 80 3838
Singleton W Susx 14 8713
Singlewell Kent 28 6570
Sinkhurst Green Kent 28 8142
Sinnahard Abers 134 4713
Sinnington N York 90 7485
Sinton Worcs 47 8160
Sinton Green Worcs 47 8160
Sipson Gt Lon 26 0777
Sirhowy Blae G 33 1410
Sissinghurst Kent 28 7937
Siston Gloucs 35 6875
Sitcott Devon 5 3691
Sithney Cnwll 2 6328
Sithney Common Cnwll 2 6428
Sithney Green Cnwll 2 6429
Sittingbourne Kent 28 9063
Six Ashes Staffs 60 7988
Six Bells Blae G 34 2202
Six Mile Bottom Cambs 53 5756
Six Rues Jersey 158 0000
Sixhills Lincs 76 1787
Sixmile Cottages Kent 29 1344
Sixpenny Handley Dorset 11 9917

Sizergh Castle 87 49
Sizewell Suffk 55 4
Skaill Ork 153 58
Skares E Ayrs 107 53
Skateraw Abers 135 9
Skateraw E Loth 119 73
Skeabost Highld 136 4
Skeeby N York 89 19
Skeffington Leics 63 74
Skeffling E R Yk 85 37
Skegby Notts 75 49
Skegby Notts 75 78
Skegness Lincs 77 56
Skelberry Highld 147 76
Skelbo Highld 147 79
Skelbo Street Highld 147 79
Skelbrooke S York 83 50
Skeldyke Lincs 64 33
Skellingthorpe Lincs 76 9
Skellorm Green Ches 79 92
Skellow S York 83 53
Skelmanthorpe W York 82 23
Skelmersdale Lancs 78 46
Skelmorlie N Ayrs 114 19
Skelpick Highld 150 72
Skelston D & G 100 82
Skelton Cumb 93 43
Skelton E R Yk 84 74
Skelton N York 89 09
Skelton N York 97 66
Skelton N York 89 36
Skelton N York 83 57
Skelwith Bridge Cumb 87 34
Skendleby Lincs 77 43
Skene House Abers 135 76
Skenfrith Mons 34 45
Skerne E R Yk 84 04
Skerray Highld 149 65
Skerricha Highld 148 23
Skerton Lancs 87 47
Sketchley Leics 50 42
Sketty Swans 32 62
Skewen Neath 32 72
Skewsby N York 90 62
Skeyton Norfk 67 24
Skeyton Corner Norfk 67 25
Skiall Highld 150 02
Skidbrooke Lincs 77 43
Skidbrooke North End Lincs 77 43
Skidby E R Yk 84 01
Skigersta W Isls 152 54
Skilgate Somset 20 98
Skillington Lincs 63 89
Skinburness Cumb 92 12
Skinflats Falk 116 90
Skinidin Highld 136 22
Skinners Green Berks 24 44
Skinningrove N York 97 71
Skipness Ag & B 114 90
Skipper's Bridge Cumb 101 37
Skiprigg Cumb 93 39
Skipsea E R Yk 85 16
Skipsea Brough E R Yk 85 14
Skipton N York 82 98
Skipton-on-Swale N York 89 36
Skipwith N York 83 66
Skirlaugh E R Yk 85 14
Skirling Border 108 07
Skirmett Bucks 37 77
Skirpenbeck E R Yk 84 74
Skirwith Cumb 94 61
Skirwith N York 87 70
Skirza Highld 151 38
Skitby Cumb 101 44
Skittle Green Bucks 37 77
Skulamus Highld 129 66
Skyborry Green Shrops 46 26
Skye Green Essex 40 87
Skye of Curr Highld 141 99
Skyreholme N York 88 06
Slack Derbys 74 33
Slack W York 82 97
Slack Head Cumb 87 47
Slackcote Gt Man 82 97
Slackholme End Lincs 77 53
Slacks of Cairnbanno Abers 143 84
Slad Gloucs 35 87
Slade Devon 19 50
Slade Devon 9 110
Slade Somset 19 83
Slade End Oxon 37 59
Slade Green Kent 27 52
Slade Heath Staffs 60 91
Slade Hooton S York 75 52
Slades Green Worcs 47 81
Sladesbridge Cnwll 4 01
Slaggyford Nthumb 94 67
Slaid Hill W York 83 32
Slaidburn Lancs 81 71
Slaithwaite W York 82 08
Slaley Derbys 74 27
Slaley Nthumb 95 96
Slamannan Falk 116 85
Slapton Bucks 38 93
Slapton Devon 7 82
Slapton Nhants 49 64
Slattocks Gt Man 79 88
Slaugham W Susx 15 25
Slaughterford Wilts 35 84
Slawston Leics 50 78
Sleaford Hants 25 80
Sleaford Lincs 64 06
Sleagill Cumb 94 59
Sleap Shrops 59 48
Sleapford Shrops 59 63
Sleasdairidh Highld 146 64
Sledge Green Worcs 47 81
Sledmere E R Yk 91 93
Sleight Dorset 11 98
Sleightholme Dur 88 55
Sleights N York 90 86
Slepe Dorset 11 92
Slickly Highld 151 29
Sliddery N Ayrs 105 93
Sligachan Highld 136 43
Sligrachan Ag & B 114 17
Slimbridge Gloucs 35 73
Slindon Staffs 72 82
Slindon W Susx 14 96

nfold W Susx	14	1131
ng Gwynd	69	6066
ngsby N York	90	6974
p End Beds	38	0718
p End Herts	39	2837
pton Nhants	51	9579
tting Mill Staffs	73	0217
ockavullin Ag & B	113	8297
ogarie D & G	99	6568
oley Norfk	67	2924
oncombe Devon	8	7386
oothby Lincs	77	4970
ough Berks	26	9879
ough Green Somset	20	2719
ough Green W Susx	15	2826
umbay Highld	138	8938
field Green Surrey	25	9952
yne Lincs	87	4765
mailholm Border	110	6436
nall Dole W Susx	15	2112
nall Heath W Mids	61	1085
nall Hythe Kent	17	8930
nall Wood Hey Lancs	80	3948
nallbridge Gt Man	81	9115
nallbrook Devon	9	8698
nallbrook Gloucs	34	5900
nallburgh Norfk	67	3324
nalldale Derbys	74	0977
nalldale Derbys	74	1781
nalley Derbys	62	4044
nalley Common Derbys	62	4042
nalley Green Derbys	62	4043
nallfield Surrey	15	3143
nallridge Devon	10	3001
nallthorne Staffs	72	8850
nallways N York	89	1111
nallwood Ches	72	8060
nallworth Norfk	54	0080
nannell Hants	23	3749
nardale Cumb	88	7308
narden Kent	28	8742
narden Bell Kent	28	8742
nart's Hill Kent	16	5242
neafield Nthumb	111	0937
nearisay Highld	129	6476
neatharpe Devon	9	1910
neeth Kent	29	0739
neeton Westerby Leics	50	6892
nelthouses N York	89	1964
nerral Highld	151	1733
nestow Staffs	60	8591
nethwick W Mids	60	0287
nethwick Green Ches	72	8063
nisby Derbys	62	3418
nith End Green Worcs	47	7752
nith Green Lancs	80	4955
nith End Herts	39	4037
nith's Green Essex	40	5721
nith's Green Essex	53	6640
nitheclose IOW	13	5391
nithfield Cumb	101	4465
nithies S York	83	3508
nithincott Devon	9	0611
nithsworth Highld	144	7977
nithton Highld	140	7145
nithy Bridge Gt Man	81	9215
nithy Green Ches	79	7474
nithy Green Gt Man	79	8785
nithy Houses Derbys	62	3846
nockington Leics	50	4589
noo Highld	149	4167
nythe's Green Essex	40	9218
nade D & G	100	8485
nailbeach Shrops	59	3702
nailwell Cambs	53	6467
nainton N York	91	9282
naith E R Yk	83	6422
nake Pass Inn Derbys	74	1190
nape N York	89	2684
nape Suffk	55	3959
nape Green Mersyd	80	3813
nape Street Suffk	55	3958
naresbrook Gt Lon	27	4089
narestone Leics	62	3409
narford Lincs	76	0482
nargate Kent	17	9928
nave Kent	17	0129
neachill Worcs	47	9053
nead Powys	59	3192
neath Common Norfk	54	1689
neaton N York	91	8907
neatonthorpe N York	91	9006
nelland Lincs	76	0780
nelson Ches	79	8074
nelston Derbys	73	1543
netterton Norfk	66	9991
nettisham Norfk	65	6834
nibston Leics	62	4114
nig's End Gloucs	47	7828
nitter Nthumb	103	0203
nitterby Lincs	76	9894
nitterfield Warwks	48	2159
nitterton Derbys	74	2760
nittlegarth Cumb	93	2138
nitton Shrops	46	5575
noadhill Kent	28	9442
nodhill Herefs	46	3240
nodland Kent	28	7061
noll Hatch Kent	28	6648
now End Herts	39	4032
now Street Norfk	54	0981
nowden Hill S York	74	2600
nowshill Gloucs	48	0933
noake Hants	13	6611
noar Cardif	33	0983
noar Devon	7	7037
noar Powys	45	9731
noberton Herefs	13	6116
noberton Heath Hants	13	6014
nockbridge Cumb	94	4926
nockburn Dur	89	3406
nodom Denbgs	70	0971
nodylt Bank Shrops	71	3439
noham Cambs	53	5973
noham Cotes Cambs	53	5775
nolas W Isls	152	8074
nolbury Pembks	30	8912
noldon Devon	18	3210
Soldon Cross Devon	18	3210
Soldridge Hants	24	6535
Sole Street Kent	28	6567
Sole Street Kent	29	0949
Solihull W Mids	61	1679
Sollers Dilwyn Herefs	46	4255
Sollers Hope Herefs	46	6132
Sollom Lancs	80	4518
Solva Pembks	30	8024
Solwaybank D & G	101	3077
Somerby Leics	63	7710
Somerby Lincs	84	0606
Somercotes Derbys	74	4253
Somerford Dorset	12	1793
Somerford Keynes Gloucs	35	0195
Somerley W Susx	14	8198
Somerleyton Suffk	67	4897
Somersal Herbert Derbys	73	1335
Somersby Lincs	77	3472
Somersham Cambs	52	3678
Somersham Suffk	54	0848
Somerton Oxon	49	4928
Somerton Somset	21	4928
Somerton Suffk	54	8153
Somerwood Shrops	59	5614
Sompting W Susx	15	1505
Sonning Berks	37	7575
Sonning Common Oxon	37	7180
Sonning Eye Oxon	37	7476
Sontley Wrexhm	71	3347
Sopley Hants	12	1596
Sopworth Wilts	35	8286
Sorbie D & G	99	4346
Sordale Highld	151	1462
Sorisdale Ag & B	120	2763
Sorn E Ayrs	107	5526
Sortat Highld	151	2863
Sosgill Cumb	92	1024
Sotby Lincs	76	2078
Sots Hole Lincs	76	1264
Sotterly Suffk	55	4484
Soughton Flints	70	2466
Soulbury Bucks	38	8826
Soulby Cumb	93	4625
Soulby Cumb	88	7411
Souldern Oxon	49	5231
Souldrop Beds	51	9861
Sound Muir Moray	141	3652
Soundwell Gloucs	35	6575
Sourton Devon	8	5390
Soutergate Cumb	86	2281
South Acre Norfk	66	8114
South Alkham Kent	29	2441
South Allington Devon	7	7938
South Alloa Falk	116	8791
South Ambersham W Susx	14	9120
South Anston S York	75	5183
South Ascot Berks	25	9268
South Ashford Kent	28	0041
South Baddesley Hants	12	3596
South Bank N York	97	5304
South Bank N York	83	5950
South Barrow Somset	21	6028
South Beddington Gt Lon	27	2863
South Beer Cnwll	5	3091
South Benfleet Essex	40	7787
South Bersted W Susx	14	9300
South Bockhampton Dorset	12	1795
South Bowood Dorset	10	4498
South Bramwith S York	83	6211
South Brent Devon	7	6960
South Brewham Somset	22	7236
South Broomhill Nthumb	103	2499
South Burlingham Norfk	67	3807
South Cadbury Somset	21	6325
South Carlton Lincs	76	9476
South Carlton Notts	75	5883
South Cave E R Yk	84	9230
South Cerney Gloucs	36	0497
South Chailey E Susx	15	3918
South Chard Somset	10	3205
South Charlton Nthumb	111	1660
South Cheriton Somset	22	6924
South Church Dur	96	2128
South Cleatlam Dur	96	1218
South Cliffe E R Yk	84	8735
South Clifton Notts	75	8270
South Cockerington Lincs	77	3888
South Cornelly Brdgnd	33	8280
South Cove Suffk	55	4981
South Creake Norfk	66	8536
South Crosland W York	82	1112
South Croxton Leics	63	6810
South Dalton E R Yk	84	9645
South Darenth Kent	27	5669
South Duffield N York	83	6833
South Elkington Lincs	77	2988
South Elmsall W York	83	4711
South End E R Yk	85	3918
South End Hants	12	1015
South End Herefs	47	7444
South End Lincs	85	1120
South End Norfk	54	9990
South Erradale Highld	137	7471
South Fambridge Essex	40	8694
South Fawley Berks	36	3880
South Ferriby Lincs	84	9820
South Field E R Yk	84	0225
South Godstone Surrey	15	3648
South Gorley Hants	12	1610
South Gosforth T & W	103	2467
South Green Essex	41	0319
South Green Essex	40	6893
South Green Kent	28	8560
South Green Norfk	66	0510
South Green Suffk	54	1775
South Gyle C Edin	117	1871
South Hanningfield Essex	40	7497
South Harting W Susx	14	7819
South Hayling Hants	13	7299
South Hazelrigg Nthumb	111	0532
South Heath Bucks	26	9101
South Heighton E Susx	16	4402
South Hetton Dur	96	3845
South Hiendley W York	83	3912
South Hill Cnwll	5	3272
South Hill Somset	21	4726
South Hinksey Oxon	37	5104
South Hole Devon	18	2220
South Holmwood Surrey	15	1744
South Hornchurch Gt Lon	27	5183
South Huish Devon	7	6941
South Hykeham Lincs	76	9364
South Hylton T & W	96	3556
South Kelsey Lincs	76	0498
South Kessock Highld	140	6547
South Killingholme Lincs	85	1416
South Kilvington N York	89	4284
South Kilworth Nhants	50	6081
South Kirkby W York	83	4410
South Knighton Devon	7	8172
South Kyme Lincs	76	1499
South Lawn Oxon	36	2814
South Leigh Oxon	36	3909
South Leverton Notts	75	7881
South Littleton Worcs	48	0746
South Lopham Norfk	54	0481
South Luffenham Rutlnd	63	9301
South Malling E Susx	16	4210
South Marston Wilts	36	1987
South Merstham Surrey	27	2952
South Middleton Nthumb	111	9923
South Milford N York	83	4931
South Milton Devon	7	7042
South Mimms Herts	26	2201
South Molton Devon	19	7125
South Moor Dur	96	1951
South Moreton Oxon	37	5688
South Mundham W Susx	14	8700
South Muskham Notts	75	7957
South Newbald E R Yk	84	9035
South Newington Oxon	48	4033
South Newton Wilts	23	0834
South Normanton Derbys	75	4456
South Norwood Gt Lon	27	3368
South Nutfield Surrey	15	3049
South Ockendon Essex	27	5983
South Ormsby Lincs	77	3675
South Ossett W York	82	2819
South Otterington N York	89	3787
South Owersby Lincs	76	0693
South Park Surrey	15	2448
South Perrott Dorset	10	4706
South Petherton Somset	10	4316
South Petherwin Cnwll	5	3181
South Pickenham Norfk	66	8504
South Pill Cnwll	6	4259
South Pool Devon	7	7740
South Poorton Dorset	10	5297
South Quarme Somset	20	9236
South Queensferry C Edin	117	1378
South Radworthy Devon	19	7432
South Rauceby Lincs	64	0245
South Raynham Norfk	66	8723
South Reddish Gt Man	79	8691
South Reston Lincs	77	4083
South Runcton Norfk	65	6308
South Scarle Notts	76	8463
South Shian Ag & B	122	9042
South Shields T & W	103	3666
South Shore Lancs	80	3033
South Somercotes Lincs	77	4193
South Stainley N York	89	3063
South Stifford Essex	27	5978
South Stoke Lincs	63	9127
South Stoke Oxon	37	5983
South Stoke Somset	22	7461
South Stoke W Susx	14	0209
South Stour Kent	28	0338
South Street Kent	27	6363
South Street Kent	28	0557
South Street Kent	29	1265
South Tarbrax S Lans	117	0353
South Tawton Devon	8	6594
South Thoresby Lincs	77	4076
South Thorpe Dur	95	1013
South Tidworth Wilts	23	2347
South Town Hants	24	6536
South Walsham Norfk	67	3613
South Warnborough Hants	24	7247
South Weald Essex	27	5694
South Weston Oxon	37	7098
South Wheatley Cnwll	5	2492
South Widcombe Somset	21	5856
South Wigston Leics	50	5897
South Willesborough Kent	28	0240
South Willingham Lincs	76	1983
South Wingate Dur	96	4134
South Wingfield Derbys	74	3755
South Witham Lincs	63	9219
South Wonston Hants	24	4636
South Woodham Ferrers Essex	40	8097
South Wootton Norfk	65	6422
South Wraxall Wilts	22	8364
South Zeal Devon	8	6593
Southall Gt Lon	26	1279
Southam Gloucs	47	9725
Southam Warwks	49	4161
Southampton Hants	13	4112
Southampton Airport	13	4516
Southborough Gt Lon	27	4267
Southborough Kent	16	5842
Southbourne Dorset	12	1491
Southbourne W Susx	14	7705
Southbrook Dorset	11	8494
Southburgh Norfk	66	0005
Southburn E R Yk	84	9854
Southchurch Essex	40	9086
Southcott Cnwll	5	1995
Southcott Devon	18	4416
Southcott Devon	8	5495
Southcott Devon	8	7580
Southcott Wilts	23	1659
Southcourt Bucks	38	8112
Southease E Susx	16	4205
Southend Ag & B	105	6908
Southend Wilts	36	1973
Southend Airport	40	8789
Southend-on-Sea Essex	40	8885
Southerndown V Glam	33	8873
Southernden Kent	28	8645
Southerness D & G	92	9754
Southerton Devon	9	0790
Southery Norfk	65	6194
Southfield Falk	116	8472
Southfleet Kent	27	6171
Southford IOW	13	5179
Southgate Gt Lon	27	2994
Southgate Norfk	65	6833
Southgate Norfk	66	8635
Southgate Norfk	66	1324
Southgate Swans	32	5587
Southill Beds	39	1542
Southington Hants	24	5049
Southleigh Devon	9	2093
Southminster Essex	40	9599
Southmoor Oxon	36	3998
Southmuir Angus	126	3852
Southoe Cambs	52	1864
Southolt Suffk	55	1968
Southorpe Cambs	64	0803
Southover Dorset	10	6294
Southover E Susx	16	6525
Southowram W York	82	1123
Southport Mersyd	80	3317
Southrepps Norfk	67	2536
Southrey Lincs	76	1366
Southrop Gloucs	36	1903
Southrope Hants	24	6644
Southsea Hants	13	6599
Southsea Wrexhm	71	3051
Southside Dur	95	1026
Southtown Norfk	67	5106
Southtown Somset	10	3216
Southwaite Cumb	93	4445
Southwark Gt Lon	27	3279
Southwater W Susx	15	1526
Southwater Street W Susx	15	1427
Southway Somset	21	5242
Southwell Dorset	11	6870
Southwell Notts	75	6953
Southwick Hants	13	6208
Southwick Nhants	51	0292
Southwick Somset	21	3646
Southwick T & W	96	3758
Southwick W Susx	15	2405
Southwick Wilts	22	8355
Southwold Suffk	55	5076
Southwood Norfk	67	3905
Southwood Somset	21	5533
Sowe Common W Mids	61	3782
Sower Carr Lancs	80	3743
Sowerby N York	89	4380
Sowerby W York	82	0423
Sowerby Bridge W York	82	0523
Sowerhill Somset	19	8924
Sowhill Torfn	34	2700
Sowley Green Suffk	53	7050
Sowood W York	82	0818
Sowton Devon	6	5065
Soyland Town W York	82	0320
Spa Common Norfk	67	2930
Spain's End Essex	53	6637
Spalding Lincs	64	2422
Spaldington E R Yk	84	7633
Spaldwick Cambs	52	1372
Spalford Notts	76	8369
Spanby Lincs	64	0938
Spanish Green Hants	24	6958
Sparham Norfk	66	0719
Sparhamill Norfk	66	0818
Spark Bridge Cumb	86	3084
Sparket Cumb	93	4325
Sparkford Somset	21	6025
Sparkhill W Mids	61	1083
Sparkwell Devon	6	5557
Sparrow Green Norfk	66	9414
Sparrowpit Derbys	74	0880
Sparrows Green E Susx	16	6332
Sparsholt Hants	24	4331
Sparsholt Oxon	36	3487
Spartylea Cumb	95	8548
Spath Staffs	73	0835
Spaunton N York	90	7289
Spaxton Somset	20	2237
Spean Bridge Highld	131	2281
Spear Hill W Susx	15	1317
Spearywell Hants	23	3127
Speen Berks	24	4567
Speen Bucks	26	8499
Speeton N York	91	1574
Speke Mersyd	78	4383
Speldhurst Kent	16	5541
Spellbrook Herts	39	4817
Spelmonden Kent	28	7037
Spelsbury Oxon	36	3421
Spen W York	82	1925
Spen Green Ches	72	8160
Spencers Wood Berks	24	7166
Spennithorne N York	89	1388
Spennymoor Dur	96	2533
Spernall Warwks	48	0862
Spestos Devon	8	7298
Spetchley Worcs	47	8953
Spetisbury Dorset	11	9102
Spexhall Suffk	55	3780
Spey Bay Moray	141	3565
Speybridge Highld	141	0326
Speyview Moray	141	2541
Spilsby Lincs	77	4066
Spindlestone Nthumb	111	1533
Spinkhill Derbys	75	4578
Spinningdale Highld	146	6789
Spirthill Wilts	35	9976
Spital Berks	26	9675
Spital Mersyd	78	3482
Spital Hill S York	75	6193
Spital in the Street Lincs	76	9690
Spithurst E Susx	16	4217
Spittal E Loth	118	4677
Spittal E R Yk	84	7652
Spittal Highld	151	1654
Spittal Nthumb	119	0051
Spittal Pembks	30	9723
Spittal of Glenmuick Abers	134	3085
Spittal of Glenshee P & K	133	1070
Spittal-on-Rule Border	110	5819
Spittalfield P & K	126	1040
Spixworth Norfk	67	2415
Splatt Cnwll	4	9476
Splatt Cnwll	5	2288
Splatt Devon	8	6005
Splayne's Green E Susx	16	4224
Splottlands Cardif	33	2077
Spodegreen Ches	79	7385
Spofforth N York	83	3651
Spon Green Flints	70	2863
Spondon Derbys	62	4036
Spooner Row Norfk	66	0997
Sporle Norfk	66	8411
Spott E Loth	118	6775
Spottiswoode Border	110	6049
Spratton Nhants	50	7169
Spreakley Surrey	25	8341
Spreyton Devon	8	6996
Spriddlestone Devon	6	5351
Spridlington Lincs	76	0084
Spring Gardens Dur	96	1726
Spring Vale S York	82	2502
Springburn C Glas	116	6068
Springfield D & G	101	3268
Springfield Essex	40	7208
Springfield Fife	126	3411
Springhill Staffs	60	9704
Springhill Staffs	61	0705
Springholm D & G	100	8070
Springside N Ayrs	106	3738
Springthorpe Lincs	76	8789
Springwell T & W	96	2858
Sproatley E R Yk	85	1934
Sproston Green Ches	72	7366
Sprotbrough S York	83	5301
Sproughton Suffk	54	1244
Sprouston Border	110	7535
Sprowston Norfk	67	2512
Sproxton Leics	63	8524
Sproxton N York	90	6181
Sprytown Devon	5	4185
Spurstow Ches	71	5556
Spyway Dorset	10	5293
Square & Compass Pembks	30	8431
Stableford Shrops	60	7598
Stableford Staffs	72	8138
Stacey Bank Derbys	74	2890
Stackhouse N York	88	8165
Stackpole Pembks	30	9896
Stacksford Norfk	54	0590
Stacksteads Lancs	81	8521
Staddiscombe Devon	6	5151
Staddlethorpe E R Yk	84	8328
Staden Derbys	74	0771
Stadhampton Oxon	37	6098
Stadhlaigearraidh W Isls	152	7638
Staffield Cumb	94	5442
Staffin Highld	136	4967
Stafford Staffs	72	9223
Stagsden Beds	38	9848
Stainborough S York	83	3203
Stainburn Cumb	92	0129
Stainburn N York	82	2548
Staincross S York	83	3210
Staindrop Dur	96	1220
Staines Surrey	26	0371
Stainfield Lincs	64	0824
Stainfield Lincs	76	1172
Stainforth N York	88	8267
Stainforth S York	83	6411
Staining Lancs	80	3436
Stainland W York	82	0719
Stainsacre N York	91	9108
Stainsby Derbys	75	4565
Stainton Cumb	93	3657
Stainton Cumb	94	4828
Stainton Cumb	87	5285
Stainton Dur	95	0718
Stainton N York	97	4714
Stainton N York	89	1096
Stainton S York	75	5593
Stainton by Langworth Lincs	76	0677
Stainton le Vale Lincs	76	1794
Stainton with Adgarley Cumb	86	2472
Staintondale N York	91	9998
Stair Cumb	93	2321
Stair E Ayrs	107	4423
Stair Haven D & G	98	2153
Stairfoot S York	83	3705
Staithes N York	97	7818
Stake Pool Lancs	80	4147
Stakeford Nthumb	103	2685
Stakes Hants	13	6808
Stalbridge Dorset	11	7317
Stalbridge Weston Dorset	11	7116
Stalham Norfk	67	3725
Stalham Green Norfk	67	3824
Stalisfield Green Kent	28	9552
Stallen Dorset	10	6016
Stalling Busk N York	88	9186
Stallingborough Lincs	85	1911
Stallington Staffs	72	9439
Stalmine Lancs	80	3745
Stalmine Moss Side Lancs	80	3845
Stalybridge Gt Man	79	9698
Stambourne Essex	53	7238
Stambourne Green Essex	53	6938
Stamford Lincs	64	0307
Stamford Nthumb	111	2219
Stamford Bridge Ches	71	4667
Stamford Bridge E R Yk	84	7155
Stamford Hill Gt Lon	27	3387
Stamfordham Nthumb	103	0771
Stanah Lancs	80	3542
Stanborough Herts	39	2211
Stanbridge Beds	38	9624
Stanbridge Dorset	11	0004
Stanbury W York	82	0137
Stand Gt Man	79	7905
Stand N Lans	116	7668
Standburn Falk	116	9274
Standeford Staffs	60	9107
Standen Kent	28	8540
Standen Street Kent	17	8030
Standerwick Somset	22	8150
Standford Hants	14	8134
Standingstone Cumb	92	0533
Standish Gloucs	35	7908
Standish Gt Man	78	5610
Standish Lower Ground Gt Man	78	5507

310

Standlake Oxon 36 3903
Standon Hants 13 4226
Standon Herts 39 3922
Standon Staffs 72 8135
Standon Green End Herts 39 3620
Standwell Green Suffk 54 1369
Stane N Lans 116 8859
Stanfield Norfk 66 9320
Stanford Beds 39 1640
Stanford Kent 29 1238
Stanford Shrops 59 3313
Stanford Bishop Herefs 47 6851
Stanford Bridge Shrops 72 7024
Stanford Bridge Worcs 47 7265
Stanford Dingley Berks 24 5771
Stanford in the Vale Oxon 36 3493
Stanford le Hope Essex 40 6882
Stanford on Avon Nhants 50 5978
Stanford on Soar Notts 62 5421
Stanford on Teme Worcs 47 7065
Stanford Rivers Essex 27 5301
Stanfree Derbys 75 4773
Stanghow N York 97 6715
Stanground Cambs 64 2097
Stanhill Lancs 81 7227
Stanhoe Norfk 66 8036
Stanhope Border 108 1229
Stanhope Dur 95 9339
Stanhope Bretby Derbys 73 2921
Stanion Nhants 51 9186
Stanklin Worcs 60 8574
Stanley Derbys 62 4140
Stanley Dur 96 1953
Stanley Notts 75 4662
Stanley P & K 126 1033
Stanley Shrops 60 7483
Stanley Staffs 72 9352
Stanley W York 83 3422
Stanley Common Derbys 62 4042
Stanley Crook Dur 96 1637
Stanley Ferry W York 83 3522
Stanley Gate Lancs 78 4405
Stanley Moor Staffs 72 9251
Stanley Pontlarge Gloucs 47 0030
Stanmer E Susx 15 3309
Stanmore Berks 37 4778
Stanmore Gt Lon 26 1692
Stanmore Hants 24 4628
Stannersburn Nthumb 102 7286
Stanningfield Suffk 54 8756
Stanningley W York 82 2234
Stannington Nthumb 103 2179
Stannington S York 74 2987
Stannington Station Nthumb 103 2181
Stansbatch Herefs 46 3461
Stansfield Suffk 53 7852
Stanshope Staffs 73 1253
Stanstead Suffk 54 8449
Stanstead Abbotts Herts 39 3811
Stanstead Street Suffk 54 8448
Stansted Kent 27 6062
Stansted Airport 39 5322
Stansted Mountfitchet Essex 39 5125
Stanton Derbys 73 2718
Stanton Devon 7 7050
Stanton Gloucs 48 0634
Stanton Mons 34 3021
Stanton Nthumb 103 1390
Stanton Staffs 73 1245
Stanton Suffk 54 9673
Stanton Butts Cambs 52 2372
Stanton by Bridge Derbys 62 3726
Stanton by Dale Derbys 62 4637
Stanton Drew Somset 21 5963
Stanton Fitzwarren Wilts 36 1790
Stanton Harcourt Oxon 36 4105
Stanton Hill Notts 75 4760
Stanton in Peak Derbys 74 2364
Stanton Lacy Shrops 46 4978
Stanton Lees Derbys 74 2562
Stanton Long Shrops 59 5791
Stanton on the Wolds Notts 63 6330
Stanton Prior Somset 22 6762
Stanton St Bernard Wilts 23 0961
Stanton St John Oxon 37 5709
Stanton St Quintin Wilts 35 9079
Stanton Street Suffk 54 9566
Stanton under Bardon Leics 62 4610
Stanton upon
Hine Heath Shrops 59 5624
Stanton Wick Somset 21 6162
Stantway Gloucs 35 7313
Stanwardine in the Field Shrops 59 4124
Stanwardine in
the Wood Shrops 59 4227
Stanway Essex 40 9424
Stanway Gloucs 48 0632
Stanway Green Essex 40 9523
Stanway Green Suffk 55 2470
Stanwell Surrey 26 0574
Stanwell Moor Surrey 26 0474
Stanwick Nhants 51 9771
Stanwix Cumb 93 4057
Staoinebrig W Isls 152 7532
Stape N York 90 7994
Stapehill Dorset 12 0500
Stapeley Ches 72 6749
Stapenhill Staffs 73 2521
Staple Kent 29 2756
Staple Somset 20 1141
Staple Cross Devon 20 0320
Staple Cross E Susx 17 7822
Staple Fitzpaine Somset 10 2618
Staple Hill Worcs 60 9773
Staplefield W Susx 15 2728
Stapleford Cambs 53 4751
Stapleford Herts 39 3117
Stapleford Leics 63 8018
Stapleford Lincs 76 8857
Stapleford Notts 62 4837
Stapleford Wilts 23 0737
Stapleford Abbotts Essex 27 5194
Stapleford Tawney Essex 27 5099
Staplegrove Somset 20 2126
Staplehay Somset 20 2121
Staplehurst Kent 28 7843
Staplers IOW 13 5189
Staplestreet Kent 29 0660

Staplet Cumb 101 5071
Stapleton Herefs 46 3265
Stapleton Leics 50 4398
Stapleton N York 89 2612
Stapleton Shrops 59 4704
Stapleton Somset 21 4621
Stapley Somset 9 1913
Staploe Beds 52 1560
Staplow Herefs 47 6941
Star Fife 126 3103
Star Pembks 31 2434
Star Somset 21 4358
Starbeck N York 83 3255
Starbotton N York 88 9574
Starcross Devon 9 9781
Stareton Warwks 61 3371
Starkholmes Derbys 74 3058
Starling Gt Man 79 7710
Starlings Green Essex 39 4631
Starr's Green E Susx 17 7615
Starston Norfk 55 2384
Start Devon 7 8044
Startforth Dur 95 0415
Startley Wilts 35 9482
Statenborough Kent 29 3155
Statham Ches 79 6787
Stathe Somset 21 3728
Stathern Leics 63 7731
Station Town Dur 96 4036
Staughton Green Cambs 52 1365
Staughton Highway Cambs 52 1364
Staunton Gloucs 34 5512
Staunton Gloucs 47 7829
Staunton Green Herefs 46 3661
Staunton in the Vale Notts 63 8043
Staunton on Arrow Herefs 46 3660
Staunton on Wye Herefs 46 3644
Staveley Cumb 87 3786
Staveley Cumb 87 4698
Staveley Derbys 75 4374
Staveley N York 89 3662
Staverton Devon 7 7964
Staverton Gloucs 47 8923
Staverton Nhants 49 5361
Staverton Wilts 22 8560
Staverton Bridge Gloucs 35 8722
Stawell Somset 21 3738
Stawley Somset 20 0622
Staxigoe Highld 151 3852
Staxton N York 91 0179
Staylittle Cerdgn 43 6489
Staylittle Powys 43 8891
Staynall Lancs 80 3643
Staythorpe Notts 75 7554
Stead W York 82 1446
Stean N York 89 0973
Steane Nhants 49 5538
Stearsby N York 90 6171
Steart Somset 20 2745
Stebbing Essex 40 6624
Stebbing Green Essex 40 6823
Stebbing Park Essex 40 6524
Stechford W Mids 61 1287
Stede Quarter Kent 28 8738
Stedham W Susx 14 8622
Steel Nthumb 95 9458
Steel Cross E Susx 16 5331
Steel Green Cumb 86 1679
Steel Heath Shrops 59 5436
Steele Road Border 101 5293
Steelend Fife 117 0392
Steen's Bridge Herefs 46 5357
Steep Hants 13 7425
Steep Lane W York 82 0223
Steephill IOW 13 5477
Steeple Dorset 11 9080
Steeple Essex 40 9303
Steeple Ashton Wilts 22 9056
Steeple Aston Oxon 49 4725
Steeple Barton Oxon 49 4424
Steeple Bumpstead Essex 53 6841
Steeple Claydon Bucks 49 7026
Steeple Gidding Cambs 52 1381
Steeple Langford Wilts 23 0337
Steeple Morden Cambs 39 2842
Steeton W York 82 0344
Stein Highld 136 2656
Stelling Minnis Kent 29 1447
Stembridge Somset 21 4220
Stenalees Cnwll 3 0156
Stenhouse D & G 100 8093
Stenhousemuir Falk 116 8783
Stenigot Lincs 77 2480
Stenscholl Highld 136 4767
Stenton E Loth 118 6274
Steornabhagh W Isls 152 4232
Stepaside Pembks 31 1407
Stepney Gt Lon 27 3681
Stepping Hill Gt Man 79 9187
Steppingley Beds 38 0035
Stepps N Lans 116 6568
Sternfield Suffk 55 3861
Sterridge Devon 19 5545
Stert Wilts 23 0259
Stetchworth Cambs 53 6459
Steven's Crouch E Susx 17 7115
Stevenage Herts 39 2325
Stevenston N Ayrs 106 2742
Steventon Hants 24 5441
Steventon Oxon 37 4691
Steventon End Essex 53 5942
Stevington Beds 51 9853
Stewartby Beds 38 0142
Stewartfield S Lans 116 6255
Stewarton E Ayrs 115 4245
Stewkley Bucks 38 8526
Stewley Somset 10 3118
Stewton Lincs 77 3587
Steyne Cross IOW 13 6487
Steyning W Susx 15 1711
Steynton Pembks 30 9107
Stibb Cnwll 18 2210
Stibb Cross Devon 18 4314
Stibb Green Wilts 23 2262
Stibbard Norfk 66 9828
Stibbington Cambs 51 0898
Stichill Border 110 7138

Sticker Cnwll 3 9750
Stickford Lincs 77 3560
Sticklepath Devon 8 6494
Sticklepath Somset 20 0436
Stickling Green Essex 39 4732
Stickney Lincs 77 3457
Stiff Street Kent 28 8761
Stiffkey Norfk 66 9742
Stifford's Bridge Herefs 47 7347
Stile Bridge Kent 28 7547
Stileway Somset 21 4641
Stilligarry W Isls 152 7638
Stillingfleet N York 83 5940
Stillington Dur 96 3723
Stillington N York 90 5867
Stilton Cambs 52 1689
Stinchcombe Gloucs 35 7298
Stinsford Dorset 11 7091
Stiperstones Shrops 59 3600
Stirchley Shrops 60 6907
Stirchley W Mids 61 0581
Stirling Abers 143 1242
Stirling Stirlg 116 7993
Stirtloe Cambs 52 1966
Stirton N York 82 9752
Stisted Essex 40 8024
Stitchcombe Wilts 36 2369
Stithians Cnwll 3 7336
Stivichall W Mids 61 3376
Stixwould Lincs 76 1765
Stoak Ches 71 4273
Stobo Border 109 1837
Stoborough Dorset 11 9286
Stoborough Green Dorset 11 9285
Stobs Castle Border 109 5008
Stobswood Nthumb 103 2195
Stock Essex 40 6998
Stock Somset 21 4561
Stock Green Worcs 47 9859
Stock Wood Worcs 47 0058
Stockbridge Hants 23 3535
Stockbriggs S Lans 107 7936
Stockbury Kent 28 8461
Stockcross Berks 24 4368
Stockdale Cnwll 3 7837
Stockdalewath Cumb 93 3845
Stocker's Hill Kent 28 9650
Stockerston Leics 51 8397
Stocking Herefs 47 6230
Stocking Green Bucks 38 8047
Stocking Pelham Herts 39 4529
Stockingford Warwks 61 3391
Stockland Devon 9 2404
Stockland Bristol Somset 20 2443
Stockland Green Kent 16 5642
Stockleigh English Devon 8 8506
Stockleigh Pomeroy Devon 9 8703
Stockley Wilts 22 9967
Stockley Hill Herefs 46 3738
Stocklinch Somset 10 3817
Stockmoor Herefs 46 3954
Stockport Gt Man 79 8990
Stocksbridge S York 74 2698
Stocksfield Nthumb 103 0561
Stockstreet Essex 40 8222
Stockton Herefs 46 5261
Stockton Norfk 67 3894
Stockton Shrops 58 2601
Stockton Shrops 72 7716
Stockton Shrops 60 7299
Stockton Warwks 49 4363
Stockton Wilts 22 9838
Stockton Brook Staffs 72 9151
Stockton Heath Ches 78 6185
Stockton on Teme Worcs 47 7167
Stockton on the Forest N York 83 6556
Stockton-on-Tees Dur 96 4419
Stockwell Gloucs 35 9414
Stockwell End W Mids 60 8900
Stockwell Heath Staffs 73 0521
Stockwood Bristl 21 6368
Stockwood Dorset 10 5906
Stodday Lancs 87 4658
Stodmarsh Kent 29 2260
Stody Norfk 66 0535
Stoer Highld 148 0328
Stoford Somset 10 5613
Stoford Wilts 23 0835
Stogumber Somset 20 0937
Stogursey Somset 20 2042
Stoke Devon 18 2324
Stoke Hants 24 4051
Stoke Hants 13 7202
Stoke Kent 28 8274
Stoke W Mids 61 3778
Stoke Abbott Dorset 10 4500
Stoke Albany Nhants 51 8088
Stoke Ash Suffk 54 1170
Stoke Bardolph Notts 63 6441
Stoke Bliss Worcs 47 6563
Stoke Bruerne Nhants 49 7449
Stoke by Clare Suffk 53 7443
Stoke Canon Devon 9 9398
Stoke Charity Hants 24 4839
Stoke Climsland Cnwll 5 3674
Stoke Cross Herefs 47 6250
Stoke D'Abernon Surrey 26 1258
Stoke Doyle Nhants 51 0286
Stoke Dry Rutlnd 51 8596
Stoke Edith Herefs 46 6040
Stoke End Warwks 61 1797
Stoke Farthing Wilts 23 0525
Stoke Ferry Norfk 65 7000
Stoke Fleming Devon 7 8648
Stoke Gabriel Devon 7 8657
Stoke Gifford Gloucs 35 6279
Stoke Golding Leics 61 3997
Stoke Goldington Bucks 38 8348
Stoke Green Bucks 26 9882
Stoke Hammond Bucks 38 8829
Stoke Heath Shrops 72 6529
Stoke Heath W Mids 61 3681
Stoke Heath Worcs 47 9468
Stoke Holy Cross Norfk 67 2301
Stoke Lacy Herefs 47 6249
Stoke Lyne Oxon 49 5628
Stoke Mandeville Bucks 38 8310
Stoke Newington Gt Lon 27 3386

Stoke Orchard Gloucs 47 9128
Stoke Poges Bucks 26 9783
Stoke Pound Worcs 47 9667
Stoke Prior Herefs 46 5256
Stoke Prior Worcs 47 9467
Stoke Rivers Devon 19 6335
Stoke Rochford Lincs 63 9127
Stoke Row Oxon 37 6884
Stoke St Gregory Somset 21 3427
Stoke St Mary Somset 20 2622
Stoke St Michael Somset 22 6646
Stoke St Milborough Shrops 59 5682
Stoke sub Hamdon Somset 10 4717
Stoke Talmage Oxon 37 6799
Stoke Trister Somset 22 7428
Stoke upon Tern Shrops 59 6328
Stoke Wake Dorset 11 7606
Stoke Wharf Worcs 47 9567
Stoke-by-Nayland Suffk 54 9836
Stoke-on-Trent Staffs 72 8847
Stoke-upon-Trent Staffs 72 8745
Stokeford Dorset 11 8687
Stokeham Notts 75 7876
Stokeinteignhead Devon 7 9170
Stokenchurch Bucks 37 7696
Stokenham Devon 7 8042
Stokesay Shrops 59 4381
Stokesay Castle 59 4381
Stokesby Norfk 67 4310
Stokesley N York 90 5208
Stolford Somset 20 2345
Ston Easton Somset 21 6253
Stondon Massey Essex 27 5800
Stone Bucks 37 7812
Stone Gloucs 35 6895
Stone Kent 27 5774
Stone Kent 17 9427
Stone S York 75 5589
Stone Somset 21 5834
Stone Staffs 72 9034
Stone Worcs 60 8675
Stone Allerton Somset 21 3951
Stone Bridge Corner Cambs 64 2700
Stone Chair W York 82 1227
Stone Cross E Susx 16 5128
Stone Cross E Susx 16 6104
Stone Cross E Susx 16 6431
Stone Cross Kent 16 5239
Stone Cross Kent 28 0236
Stone Cross Kent 29 3257
Stone Hill S York 83 6809
Stone House Cumb 88 7685
Stone Street Kent 27 5754
Stone Street Suffk 54 9639
Stone Street Suffk 54 0143
Stone Street Suffk 55 3882
Stone-edge-Batch Somset 34 4671
Stonea Cambs 65 4593
Stonebridge Norfk 54 9290
Stonebridge Somset 21 3859
Stonebridge W Mids 61 2182
Stonebroom Derbys 74 4059
Stonecross Green Suffk 54 8257
Stonecrouch Kent 16 7033
Stoneferry E R Yk 85 1031
Stonefield Castle Hotel Ag & B 113 8671
Stonegate E Susx 16 6628
Stonegate N York 90 7708
Stonegrave N York 90 6577
Stonehall Worcs 47 8848
Stonehaugh Nthumb 102 7976
Stonehaven Abers 135 8786
Stonehenge 23 1142
Stonehill Green Gt Lon 27 5070
Stonehouse Ches 71 5070
Stonehouse D & G 100 8268
Stonehouse Devon 6 4654
Stonehouse Gloucs 35 8005
Stonehouse Nthumb 94 6958
Stonehouse S Lans 116 7546
Stoneleigh Warwks 61 3372
Stoneley Green Ches 71 6151
Stonely Cambs 52 1167
Stoner Hill Hants 13 7225
Stones Green Essex 41 1626
Stonesby Leics 63 8224
Stonesfield Oxon 36 3917
Stonestreet Green Kent 29 0637
Stonethwaite Cumb 93 2613
Stonewells Moray 141 2865
Stonewood Kent 27 5972
Stoney Cross Hants 12 2611
Stoney Middleton Derbys 74 2375
Stoney Stanton Leics 50 4994
Stoney Stoke Somset 22 7032
Stoney Stratton Somset 21 6539
Stoney Stretton Shrops 59 3809
Stoneybridge W Isls 152 7532
Stoneybridge Worcs 60 9476
Stoneyburn W Loth 117 9862
Stoneygate Leics 62 6002
Stoneyhills Essex 40 9597
Stoneykirk D & G 98 0853
Stoneywood Aber C 135 8811
Stoneywood Falk 116 7982
Stonham Aspal Suffk 54 1359
Stonnall Staffs 61 0603
Stonor Oxon 37 7388
Stonton Wyville Leics 50 7395
Stony Cross Herefs 46 5466
Stony Cross Herefs 47 7247
Stony Houghton Derbys 75 4966
Stony Stratford Bucks 38 7840
Stonyford Hants 12 3215
Stonywell Staffs 61 0712
Stoodleigh Devon 19 6532
Stoodleigh Devon 20 9218
Stopham W Susx 14 0219
Stopsley Beds 38 1023
Stoptide Cnwll 3 9475
Storeton Mersyd 78 3084
Storeyard Green Herefs 47 7144
Stormy Corner Lancs 78 4707
Stornoway W Isls 152 4232
Stornoway Airport 152 4632
Storridge Herefs 47 7548
Storrington W Susx 14 0814
Storth Cumb 87 4779

Storwood E R Yk 84 71..
Stotfield Moray 141 22..
Stotfold Beds 39 21..
Stottesdon Shrops 60 67..
Stoughton Leics 63 64..
Stoughton Surrey 25 98..
Stoughton W Susx 14 80..
Stoul Highld 129 75..
Stoulton Worcs 47 90..
Stour Provost Dorset 22 79..
Stour Row Dorset 22 82..
Stourbridge W Mids 60 89..
Stourpaine Dorset 11 86..
Stourport-on-Severn Worcs 60 81..
Stourton Staffs 60 86..
Stourton W York 83 32..
Stourton Warwks 48 29..
Stourton Wilts 22 77..
Stourton Caundle Dorset 11 71..
Stout Somset 21 43..
Stove Shet 153 42..
Stoven Suffk 55 44..
Stow Border 118 45..
Stow Lincs 76 88..
Stow Bardolph Norfk 65 620.
Stow Bedon Norfk 66 95..
Stow Longa Cambs 51 10..
Stow Maries Essex 40 83..
Stow-cum-Quy Cambs 53 52..
Stow-on-the-Wold Gloucs 48 192.
Stowbridge Norfk 65 60..
Stowe Gloucs 34 56..
Stowe Shrops 46 31..
Stowe by Chartley Staffs 73 00..
Stowehill Nhants 49 64..
Stowell Somset 22 68..
Stowey Somset 21 59..
Stowford Devon 5 43..
Stowford Devon 19 65..
Stowford Devon 5 43..
Stowford Devon 9 11..
Stowlangtoft Suffk 54 95..
Stowmarket Suffk 54 04..
Stowting Kent 29 12..
Stowting Common Kent 29 12..
Stowupland Suffk 54 07..
Straanruie Moray 141 99..
Strachan Abers 135 67..
Strachur Ag & B 114 09..
Stracthro Hospital Angus 134 62..
Stradbroke Suffk 55 237.
Stradbrook Wilts 22 91..
Stradishall Suffk 53 75..
Stradsett Norfk 65 66..
Stragglethorpe Lincs 76 91..
Stragglethorpe Notts 63 65..
Straight Soley Wilts 36 31..
Straiton Mdloth 117 276.
Straiton S Ayrs 106 38..
Straloch Abers 143 86..
Straloch P & K 133 04..
Stramshall Staffs 73 07..
Strang IOM 158 35..
Strangford Herefs 46 58..
Stranraer D & G 98 05..
Strata Florida Cerdgn 43 74..
Stratfield Mortimer Berks 24 66..
Stratfield Saye Hants 24 68..
Stratfield Turgis Hants 24 69..
Stratford Beds 52 174.
Stratford Gt Lon 27 388.
Stratford St Andrew Suffk 55 356.
Stratford St Mary Suffk 54 043.
Stratford sub Castle Wilts 23 133.
Stratford Tony Wilts 23 092.
Stratford-upon-Avon Warwks 48 205.
Strath Highld 144 797.
Strath Highld 145 082.
Strathan Highld 149 576.
Strathan Highld 116 704.
Strathaven S Lans 116 704.
Strathblane Stirlg 115 567.
Strathcanaird Highld 145 150.
Strathcarron Station Highld 138 944.
Strathcoil Ag & B 122 683.
Strathdon Abers 134 351.
Strathkinness Fife 127 451.
Strathloanhead W Loth 116 927.
Strathmashie House Highld 132 589.
Strathmiglo Fife 126 210.
Strathpeffer Highld 139 486.
Strathtay P & K 125 915.
Strathwhillan N Ayrs 105 023.
Strathy Highld 150 846.
Strathy Inn Highld 150 836.
Strathyre Stirlg 124 561.
Stratton Cnwll 18 230.
Stratton Dorset 11 659.
Stratton Gloucs 35 010.
Stratton Audley Oxon 49 602.
Stratton St Margaret Wilts 36 178.
Stratton St Michael Norfk 67 209.
Stratton Strawless Norfk 67 222.
Stratton-on-the-Fosse Somset 22 665.
Stravithie Fife 127 531.
Stream Somset 20 04..
Streat E Susx 15 351.
Streatham Gt Lon 27 307.
Streatley Beds 38 072.
Streatley Berks 37 598.
Street Devon 9 188.
Street Lancs 80 525.
Street N York 90 730.
Street Somset 21 483.
Street Ashton Warwks 50 458.
Street Dinas Shrops 71 333.
Street End E Susx 16 602.
Street End Kent 29 145.
Street End W Susx 14 859.
Street Gate T & W 96 215.
Street Houses N York 97 741.
Street Houses N York 83 524.
Street Lane Derbys 74 384.
Street on the Fosse Somset 21 623.
Streethay Staffs 61 141.
Streetlam N York 89 309.
Streetly W Mids 61 089.
Streetly End Cambs 53 614.
Strefford Shrops 59 418.

elitz P & K 126 1836
elley Notts 62 5141
ensall N York 90 6360
ensham Worcs 47 9140
etcholt Somset 20 2943
ete Devon 7 8446
etford Gt Man 79 7994
etford Herefs 46 4455
etford Herefs 46 5257
ethall Essex 39 4839
etham Cambs 53 5174
ettington W Susx 14 8907
etton Ches 71 4452
etton Ches 79 6282
etton Derbys 74 3961
etton Rutlnd 63 9415
etton Staffs 60 8811
etton Staffs 73 2526
etton en le Field Leics 61 3011
etton Grandison Herefs 47 6344
etton Heath Shrops 59 3610
etton on Fosse Warwks 48 2238
etton Sugwas Herefs 46 4642
etton under Fosse Warwks 50 4581
etton Westwood Shrops 59 5998
etton-on-Dunsmore Warwks 61 4072
richen Abers 143 9455
rines Gt Man 79 9786
ringston Somset 20 1742
rixton Nhants 51 9061
roat Gloucs 34 5797
romeferry Highld 138 8634
romness Ork 153 2508
ronachlachar Stirlg 123 4010
ronafian Ag & B 114 0281
ronchrubie Highld 145 2419
rone Ag & B 114 1980
rone Highld 131 1481
ronenaba Highld 131 2084
ronmilchan Ag & B 123 1528
ronsay Airport 153 6329
rontian Highld 130 8161
rood Kent 28 7268
rood Kent 17 8532
rood Green Surrey 15 2048
rood Green W Susx 14 0224
roud Gloucs 35 8505
roud Lincs 13 7223
roud Green Essex 40 8590
roud Green Gloucs 35 8007
roude Surrey 25 0068
roxton Lincs 63 9030
ruan Highld 136 3438
ruan P & K 132 8065
rubby Lincs 77 4582
rumpshaw Norfk 67 3407
rutherhill S Lans 116 7649
ruthers Fife 126 3709
ruy Highld 139 4040
ryd-y-Facsen IOA 68 3383
ryt-issa Wrexhm 70 2845
uartfield Abers 143 9745
ubbers Green W Mids 61 0401
ubbington Hants 13 5503
ubbins N York 81 7918
ubbs Green Norfk 67 2598
ubhampton Dorset 11 9113
ubley Derbys 74 3378
ubshaw Cross Gt Man 78 5809
ubton Lincs 76 8748
uchbury Nhants 49 5643
uckton Hants 12 1613
ud Green Berks 26 8877
udfold N York 88 8169
udham Beds 38 0215
udholme Cumb 93 2556
udland Dorset 12 0382
udley Warwks 48 0764
udley Wilts 35 9671
udley Common Warwks 48 0664
udley Roger N York 89 2970
udley Royal N York 89 2770
ump Cross Cambs 39 5044
untney Cambs 53 5578
urbridge Staffs 72 8330
urgate Lincs 76 8888
urmer Essex 53 6943
urminster Common Dorset 11 7812
urminster Marshall Dorset 11 9500
urminster Newton Dorset 11 7814
urry Kent 29 1760
urton Nhants 84 9604
urton by Stow Lincs 76 8980
urton le Steeple Notts 75 7883
utton Suffk 54 1377
utton Suffk 83 4841
utton Suffk 54 1534
yal Ches 79 8383
ydd Lancs 81 6536
ynie Moray 141 3360
yrrup Notts 75 6090
ccoth Ag & B 123 2905
ckley Worcs 47 7251
ckley Green Worcs 47 7253
dborough Nhants 51 9682
dbourne Suffk 55 4153
dbrook Lincs 63 9744
dbrook Mons 34 5087
dbrooke Lincs 76 0376
dbury Derbys 73 1631
dbury Gt Lon 26 1685
dbury Suffk 54 8741
dden Gt Man 81 8812
ddie Highld 140 6554
ddington Worcs 47 8463
dgrove Gloucs 35 9308
ffield N York 91 9890
ffield Norfk 67 2232
gdon Shrops 59 6015
gnall Staffs 72 7931
gwas Pool Herefs 46 4541
isnish Highld 129 5816
lby IOM 158 3304
lgrave Nhants 49 5544
lgrave Manor 49 5645
lham Berks 24 6474

Sulhamstead Berks 24 6368
Sulhamstead Abbots Berks 24 6467
Sulhamstead Bannister Berks 24 6368
Sullington W Susx 14 0913
Sullom Shet 153 3573
Sullom Voe Shet 153 4075
Sully V Glam 20 1568
Sumburgh Airport 153 3810
Summer Heath Bucks 37 7490
Summer Hill Wrexhm 71 3153
Summerbridge N York 89 2062
Summercourt Cnwll 3 8856
Summerfield Norfk 65 7538
Summerfield Worcs 60 8473
Summerhouse Dur 96 2019
Summerlands Cumb 87 5386
Summerley Derbys 74 3778
Summersdale W Susx 14 8606
Summerseat Gt Man 81 7914
Summertown Oxon 37 5009
Summit Gt Man 79 9109
Summit N York 82 9418
Sunbiggin N York 87 6608
Sunbury Surrey 26 1168
Sundaywell D & G 100 8284
Sunderland Ag & B 112 2464
Sunderland Cumb 93 1735
Sunderland Lancs 80 4255
Sunderland T & W 96 3957
Sunderland Bridge Dur 96 2637
Sundhope Border 109 3325
Sundon Park Beds 38 0525
Sundridge Kent 27 4855
Sunk Island E R Yk 85 2619
Sunningdale Berks 25 9567
Sunninghill Surrey 25 9367
Sunningwell Oxon 37 4900
Sunniside Dur 96 1438
Sunniside T & W 96 2059
Sunny Bank Lancs 81 7720
Sunny Brow Dur 96 1934
Sunnyhill Derbys 62 3432
Sunnyhurst Lancs 81 6722
Sunnylaw Stirlg 116 7998
Sunnymead Oxon 37 5009
Sunton Wilts 23 2454
Surbiton Gt Lon 26 1867
Surfleet Lincs 64 2528
Surfleet Seas End Lincs 64 2628
Surlingham Norfk 67 3106
Surrex Essex 40 8722
Sustead Norfk 66 1837
Susworth Lincs 84 8302
Sutcombe Devon 18 3411
Sutcombemill Devon 18 3411
Suton Norfk 66 0999
Sutterby Lincs 77 3872
Sutterton Lincs 64 2835
Sutton Beds 52 2247
Sutton Cambs 51 0998
Sutton Cambs 53 4479
Sutton Devon 8 7202
Sutton Devon 7 7042
Sutton E Susx 16 4999
Sutton Gt Lon 27 2564
Sutton Kent 29 3349
Sutton Mersyd 78 5393
Sutton N York 83 4925
Sutton N York 67 3823
Sutton Notts 75 6784
Sutton Notts 63 7637
Sutton Oxon 36 4106
Sutton Pembks 30 9115
Sutton S York 83 5512
Sutton Shrops 59 3527
Sutton Shrops 59 5010
Sutton Shrops 72 6631
Sutton Staffs 60 7386
Sutton Staffs 72 7622
Sutton Staffs 55 3046
Sutton W Susx 14 9715
Sutton at Hone Kent 27 5569
Sutton Bassett Nhants 50 7790
Sutton Benger Wilts 35 9478
Sutton Bingham Somset 10 5410
Sutton Bonington Notts 62 5024
Sutton Bridge Lincs 65 4721
Sutton Cheney Leics 50 4100
Sutton Coldfield W Mids 61 1295
Sutton Courtenay Oxon 37 5094
Sutton Crosses Lincs 65 4321
Sutton Fields Notts 62 4926
Sutton Grange N York 89 2873
Sutton Green Oxon 36 4107
Sutton Green Surrey 25 0054
Sutton Green Wrexhm 71 4048
Sutton Howgrave N York 89 3179
Sutton in Ashfield Notts 75 4958
Sutton in the Elms Leics 50 5193
Sutton Lane Ends Ches 79 9270
Sutton Maddock Shrops 60 7201
Sutton Mallet Somset 21 3736
Sutton Mandeville Wilts 22 9828
Sutton Manor Mersyd 78 5190
Sutton Marsh Herefs 46 5544
Sutton Montis Somset 21 6224
Sutton on Sea Lincs 77 5281
Sutton on the Hill Derbys 73 2333
Sutton on Trent Notts 75 7965
Sutton Poyntz Dorset 11 7083
Sutton Scotney Hants 24 4639
Sutton St Edmund Lincs 64 3613
Sutton St James Lincs 65 3918
Sutton St Nicholas Herefs 46 5245
Sutton Street Kent 28 8055
Sutton upon Derwent E R Yk 84 7047
Sutton Valence Kent 28 8149
Sutton Veny Wilts 22 9041
Sutton Waldron Dorset 11 8615
Sutton Weaver Ches 71 5479
Sutton Wick Oxon 37 4894
Sutton Wick Somset 21 5759
Sutton-in-Craven N York 82 0043
Sutton-on-Hull E R Yk 85 1232
Sutton-on-the-Forest N York 90 5864
Sutton-under-Brailes Warwks 48 3037
Sutton-under-Whitestonecliffe N York 90 4882

Swaby Lincs 77 3877
Swadlincote Derbys 73 2919
Swaffham Norfk 66 8108
Swaffham Bulbeck Cambs 53 5562
Swaffham Prior Cambs 53 5764
Swafield Norfk 67 2832
Swainby N York 89 4701
Swainshill Herefs 46 4641
Swainsthorpe Norfk 67 2101
Swainswick Somset 22 7668
Swalcliffe Oxon 48 3737
Swalecliffe Kent 29 1367
Swallow Lincs 85 1703
Swallow Beck Lincs 76 9467
Swallow Nest S York 75 4585
Swallowcliffe Wilts 22 9627
Swallowfield Berks 24 7264
Swallows Cross Essex 40 6198
Swampton Hants 24 4150
Swan Green Ches 79 7373
Swan Street Essex 40 8927
Swan Village W Mids 60 9892
Swanage Dorset 12 0378
Swanbourne Bucks 38 8026
Swanbridge V Glam 20 1667
Swancote Shrops 60 7494
Swanland E R Yk 84 9928
Swanley Kent 27 5168
Swanley Village Kent 27 5369
Swanmore Hants 13 5716
Swannington Leics 62 4116
Swannington Norfk 66 1319
Swanpool Garden Suburb Lincs 76 9569
Swanscombe Kent 27 6074
Swansea Swans 32 6592
Swansea Airport 32 5691
Swanton Abbot Norfk 67 2625
Swanton Morley Norfk 66 0117
Swanton Novers Norfk 66 0231
Swanton Street Kent 28 8759
Swanwick Derbys 74 4053
Swanwick Hants 13 5109
Swarby Lincs 64 0440
Swardeston Norfk 67 2002
Swarkestone Derbys 62 3728
Swarland Nthumb 103 1602
Swarland Estate Nthumb 103 1603
Swarraton Hants 24 5636
Swartha W York 82 0546
Swarthmoor Cumb 86 2777
Swaton Lincs 64 1337
Swavesey Cambs 52 3668
Sway Hants 12 2798
Swayfield Lincs 63 9922
Swaythling Hants 13 4416
Sweet Green Worcs 47 6462
Sweetham Devon 9 8899
Sweethaws E Susx 16 5028
Sweetlands Corner Kent 28 7845
Sweets Cnwll 4 1595
Sweetshouse Cnwll 4 0861
Swefling Suffk 55 3463
Swepstone Leics 62 3610
Swerford Oxon 48 3731
Swettenham Ches 72 8067
Swffryd Blae G 33 2198
Swift's Green Kent 28 8744
Swilland Suffk 54 1852
Swillbrook Lancs 80 4834
Swillington W York 83 3830
Swimbridge Devon 19 6230
Swimbridge Newland Devon 19 6030
Swinbrook Oxon 36 2812
Swincliffe N York 89 2458
Swincliffe W York 82 2027
Swincombe Devon 19 6941
Swinden N York 81 8554
Swinderby Lincs 76 8663
Swindon Gloucs 47 9325
Swindon Nthumb 102 9799
Swindon Staffs 60 8690
Swindon Wilts 36 1484
Swine E R Yk 85 1335
Swinefleet E R Yk 84 7621
Swineford Gloucs 35 6969
Swineshead Beds 51 0565
Swineshead Lincs 64 2340
Swineshead Bridge Lincs 64 2242
Swiney Highld 151 2335
Swinford Leics 50 5679
Swinford Oxon 37 4408
Swingfield Minnis Kent 29 2142
Swingfield Street Kent 29 2343
Swingleton Green Suffk 54 9647
Swinhoe Nthumb 111 2128
Swinhope Lincs 76 2196
Swinithwaite N York 88 0489
Swinmore Common Herefs 47 6741
Swinscoe Staffs 73 1247
Swinside Cumb 93 2421
Swinstead Lincs 64 0122
Swinthorpe Lincs 76 0680
Swinton Border 110 8347
Swinton Gt Man 79 7701
Swinton N York 89 2179
Swinton N York 90 7573
Swinton S York 75 4599
Swithland Leics 62 5512
Swordale Highld 139 5765
Swordland Highld 129 7891
Swordly Highld 150 7463
Sworton Heath Ches 79 6884
Swyddffynnon Cerdgn 43 6966
Swynnerton Staffs 72 8535
Swyre Dorset 10 5288
Sychant Powys 58 2025
Sychnant Powys 45 9777
Sychtyn Powys 58 9907
Sydallt Flints 71 3055
Syde Gloucs 35 9511
Sydenham Gt Lon 27 3671
Sydenham Oxon 37 7301
Sydenham Damerel Devon 5 4176
Sydenhurst Surrey 14 9534
Syderstone Norfk 66 8332
Sydling St Nicholas Dorset 10 6399
Sydmonton Hants 24 4651
Sydnal Lane Shrops 60 8005

Syerston Notts 63 7447
Sygun Copper Mine 69 6048
Syke Gt Man 81 8915
Sykehouse S York 83 6316
Syleham Suffk 55 2078
Sylen Carmth 32 5106
Symbister Shet 153 5462
Symington S Ayrs 106 3831
Symington S Lans 108 9935
Symonds Yat Herefs 34 5515
Symondsbury Dorset 10 4493
Sympson Green W York 82 1838
Synderford Dorset 10 3803
Synod Inn Cerdgn 42 4054
Syre Highld 149 6943
Syreford Gloucs 35 0220
Syresham Nhants 49 6241
Syston Leics 62 6211
Syston Lincs 63 9240
Sytchampton Worcs 47 8466
Sywell Nhants 51 8267

T

Tabley Hill Ches 79 7379
Tackley Oxon 37 4719
Tacolneston Norfk 66 1495
Tadcaster N York 83 4843
Taddington Derbys 74 1471
Taddington Gloucs 48 0831
Taddiport Devon 18 4818
Tadley Hants 24 6061
Tadlow Cambs 52 2847
Tadmarton Oxon 48 3937
Tadwick Somset 35 7470
Tadworth Surrey 26 2257
Tafarn-y-bwlch Pembks 31 0834
Tafarn-y-Gelyn Denbgs 70 1961
Tafarnaubach Blae G 33 1210
Taff's Well Cardif 33 1283
Tafolwern Powys 57 8902
Tai'r Bull Powys 45 9925
Taibach Neath 32 7788
Tain Highld 151 2266
Tain Highld 147 7781
Tairbeart W Isls 152 1500
Takeley Essex 40 5621
Takeley Street Essex 39 5421
Tal-y-Bont Conwy 69 7668
Tal-y-bont Gwynd 57 5921
Tal-y-bont Gwynd 69 6070
Tal-y-Cafn Conwy 69 7871
Tal-y-coed Mons 34 4115
Tal-y-garn Rhondd 33 0379
Tal-y-llyn Gwynd 57 7109
Tal-y-Waun Torfn 34 2604
Talachddu Powys 45 0833
Talacre Flints 70 1183
Talaton Devon 9 0699
Talbenny Pembks 30 8411
Talbot Green Rhondd 33 0382
Talbot Village Dorset 12 0793
Taleford Devon 9 0997
Talerddig Powys 58 9300
Talgarreg Cerdgn 42 4251
Talgarth Powys 45 1533
Taliesin Cerdgn 43 6591
Talisker Highld 136 3230
Talke Staffs 72 8253
Talke Pits Staffs 72 8353
Talkin Cumb 94 5557
Talla Linnfoots Border 108 1320
Talladale Highld 144 9170
Tallaminnock S Ayrs 106 4098
Tallarn Green Wrexhm 71 4444
Tallentire Cumb 92 1035
Talley Carmth 44 6332
Tallington Lincs 64 0908
Tallwrn Wrexhm 71 2947
Talmine Highld 149 5863
Talog Carmth 31 3325
Talsarn Cerdgn 44 5456
Talsarnau Gwynd 57 6135
Talskiddy Cnwll 4 9165
Talwrn IOA 68 4877
Talwrn Wrexhm 71 3847
Talybont-on-Usk Powys 33 1122
Talysarn Gwynd 68 4952
Talywern Powys 57 8200
Tamer Lane End Gt Man 79 6401
Tamerton Foliot Devon 6 4761
Tamworth Staffs 61 2003
Tamworth Green Lincs 64 3842
Tan Hill N York 88 8906
Tan Office Green Suffk 53 7858
Tan-y-Bwlch Gwynd 57 6540
Tan-y-fron Conwy 70 9540
Tan-y-fron Wrexhm 71 2952
Tan-y-Grisiau Gwynd 57 6945
Tan-y-groes Cerdgn 42 2849
Tancred N York 89 4558
Tancredston Pembks 30 8826
Tandridge Surrey 27 3750
Tanfield Dur 96 1855
Tanfield Lea Dur 96 1853
Tangiers Pembks 30 9518
Tangley Hants 23 3252
Tangmere W Susx 14 9006
Tangusdale W Isls 152 6500
Tankerness Ork 153 5109
Tankersley S York 74 3499
Tankerton Kent 29 1166
Tannach Highld 151 3247
Tannachie Abers 135 7884
Tannadice Angus 134 4758
Tanner's Green Worcs 61 0874
Tannington Suffk 55 2467
Tannochside N Lans 116 7061
Tansley Derbys 74 3259
Tansor Nhants 51 0590

Tantobie Dur 96 1754
Tanton N York 90 5210
Tanwood Worcs 60 9074
Tanworth in Arden Warwks 61 1170
Taobh Tuath W Isls 152 9989
Taplow Bucks 26 9182
Tarbert Ag & B 113 6551
Tarbert Ag & B 113 6668
Tarbert W Isls 152 1500
Tarbet Ag & B 123 3104
Tarbet Highld 148 1649
Tarbet Highld 129 7992
Tarbock Green Mersyd 78 4687
Tarbolton S Ayrs 107 4327
Tarbrax S Lans 117 0255
Tardebigge Worcs 47 9969
Tarfside Angus 134 4879
Tarland Abers 134 4804
Tarleton Lancs 80 4520
Tarlscough Lancs 80 4314
Tarlton Gloucs 35 9599
Tarnock Somset 21 3752
Tarns Cumb 92 1248
Tarnside Cumb 87 4390
Tarporley Ches 71 5562
Tarr Somset 19 8632
Tarr Somset 20 1030
Tarrant Crawford Dorset 11 9203
Tarrant Gunville Dorset 11 9213
Tarrant Hinton Dorset 11 9311
Tarrant Keyneston Dorset 11 9204
Tarrant Launceston Dorset 11 9409
Tarrant Monkton Dorset 11 9408
Tarrant Rawston Dorset 11 9306
Tarrant Rushton Dorset 11 9305
Tarring Neville E Susx 16 4403
Tarrington Herefs 46 6140
Tarskavaig Highld 129 5810
Tarves Abers 143 8631
Tarvie P & K 133 0164
Tarvin Ches 71 4966
Tarvin Sands Ches 71 4967
Tasburgh Norfk 67 1996
Tasley Shrops 60 6894
Taston Oxon 36 3521
Tatenhill Staffs 73 2021
Tathall End Bucks 38 8246
Tatham Lancs 87 6069
Tathwell Lincs 77 3182
Tatsfield Surrey 27 4156
Tattenhall Ches 71 4858
Tatterford Norfk 66 8628
Tattersett Norfk 66 8429
Tattershall Lincs 76 2157
Tattershall Bridge Lincs 76 1956
Tattershall Thorpe Lincs 76 2159
Tattingstone Suffk 54 1337
Tattingstone White Horse Suffk 54 1338
Tatworth Somset 10 3205
Tauchers Moray 141 3749
Taunton Somset 20 2224
Taverham Norfk 66 1613
Taverners Green Essex 40 5618
Tavernspite Pembks 31 1812
Tavistock Devon 6 4874
Taw Green Devon 8 6597
Tawstock Devon 19 5529
Taxal Derbys 79 0079
Taychreggan Hotel Ag & B 123 0421
Tayinloan Ag & B 105 6946
Taynton Gloucs 35 7222
Taynton Oxon 36 2313
Taynuilt Ag & B 122 0031
Tayport Fife 127 4628
Tayvallich Ag & B 113 7487
Tealby Lincs 76 1590
Team Valley T & W 103 2459
Teangue Highld 129 6609
Teanord Highld 140 5964
Tebay Cumb 87 6104
Tebworth Beds 38 9926
Tedburn St Mary Devon 8 8194
Teddington Gloucs 47 9633
Teddington Gt Lon 26 1670
Tedstone Delamere Herefs 47 6958
Tedstone Wafer Herefs 47 6759
Teesport N York 97 5423
Teesside Airport 89 3713
Teesside Park N York 97 4618
Teeton Nhants 50 6970
Teffont Evias Wilts 22 9931
Teffont Magna Wilts 22 9932
Tegryn Pembks 31 2233
Teigh Rutlnd 63 8615
Teigncombe Devon 8 6787
Teigngrace Devon 7 8574
Teignmouth Devon 7 9473
Teindside Border 109 4408
Telford Shrops 60 6908
Tellisford Somset 22 8055
Telscombe E Susx 15 4003
Telscombe Cliffs E Susx 15 4001
Tempar P & K 124 6857
Templand D & G 100 0886
Temple Cnwll 4 1473
Temple Midloth 117 3158
Temple Balsall W Mids 61 2076
Temple Bar Cerdgn 44 5354
Temple Cloud Somset 21 6257
Temple End Suffk 53 6650
Temple Ewell Kent 29 2844
Temple Grafton Warwks 48 1255
Temple Guiting Gloucs 48 0928
Temple Hirst N York 83 6024
Temple Normanton Derbys 74 4167
Temple of Fiddes Abers 135 8080
Temple Pier Highld 139 5330
Tenwood Sowerby Cumb 94 6127
Templecombe Somset 22 7022
Templeton Devon 19 8813
Templeton Pembks 31 1111
Templetown Dur 95 1050
Tempsford Beds 52 1653
Ten Mile Bank Norfk 65 5996
Tenbury Wells Worcs 46 5968
Tenby Pembks 31 1300
Tendring Essex 41 1424
Tendring Green Essex 41 1325

312

Place	County	Page	Grid
Tomdoun	Highld	131	1500
Tomich	Highld	146	6005
Tomich	Highld	139	3027
Tomich	Highld	139	5348
Tomich	Highld	146	6971
Tomintoul	Moray	141	1619
Tomlow	Warwks	49	4563
Tomnacross	Highld	139	5141
Tomnavoulin	Moray	141	2126
Tompkin	Staffs	72	9451
Ton	Mons	34	3301
Ton	Mons	34	3695
Ton-teg	Rhondd	33	0986
Tonbridge	Kent	16	5846
Tondu	Brdgnd	33	8984
Tonedale	Somset	20	1321
Tong	Kent	28	9556
Tong	Shrops	60	7907
Tong	W York	82	2230
Tong Green	Kent	28	9853
Tong Norton	Shrops	60	7908
Tong Street	W York	82	1930
Tonge	Leics	62	4223
Tongham	Surrey	25	8848
Tongland	D & G	99	6954
Tongue	Highld	149	5956
Tongue End	Lincs	64	1518
Tongwynlais	Cardif	33	1382
Tonna	Neath	32	7798
Tonwell	Herts	39	3316
Tonypandy	Rhondd	33	9991
Tonyrefail	Rhondd	33	0188
Toot Baldon	Oxon	37	5600
Toot Hill	Essex	27	5102
Toot Hill	Hants	12	3818
Toothill	Wilts	36	1183
Tooting	Gt Lon	27	2771
Tooting Bec	Gt Lon	27	2872
Top End	Beds	51	0362
Top of Hebers	Gt Man	79	8607
Top-y-rhos	Flints	70	2558
Topcliffe	N York	89	3976
Topcroft	Norfk	67	2693
Topcroft Street	Norfk	67	2691
Topham	S York	83	6217
Toppesfield	Essex	53	7437
Toppings	Gt Man	81	7213
Toprow	Norfk	66	1698
Topsham	Devon	9	9688
Torbeg	N Ayrs	105	8929
Torboll	Highld	147	7599
Torbreck	Highld	140	6441
Torbryan	Devon	7	8266
Torcastle	Highld	131	1378
Torcross	Devon	7	8241
Tore	Highld	140	6052
Torfrey	Cnwll	3	1154
Torinturk	Ag & B	113	8164
Torksey	Lincs	76	8378
Tormarton	Gloucs	35	7678
Tormore	N Ayrs	105	8932
Tornagrain	Highld	140	7650
Tornaveen	Abers	134	6106
Torness	Highld	139	5326
Tornewton	Devon	7	8167
Toronto	Dur	96	1930
Torosay Castle	Ag & B	122	7335
Torpenhow	Cumb	93	2039
Torphichen	W Loth	117	9672
Torphins	Abers	134	6202
Torpoint	Cnwll	6	4355
Torquay	Devon	7	9164
Torquhan	Border	118	4448
Torr	Devon	6	5851
Torran	Highld	137	5949
Torrance	E Duns	116	6173
Torranyard	N Ayrs	115	3544
Torre	Somset	20	0439
Torridon	Highld	138	9055
Torridon House	Highld	138	8657
Torrisdale	Ag & B	105	7936
Torrisdale	Highld	149	6761
Torrish	Highld	147	9718
Torrisholme	Lancs	87	4563
Torrobull	Highld	146	5904
Torry	Aber C	135	9405
Torryburn	Fife	117	0286
Tortan	Worcs	60	8472
Torteval	Guern	158	0000
Torthorwald	D & G	100	0378
Tortington	W Susx	14	0004
Tortworth	Gloucs	35	7093
Torvaig	Highld	136	4944
Torver	Cumb	86	2894
Torwood	Falk	116	8385
Torwoodlee	Border	109	4738
Torworth	Notts	75	6586
Toscaig	Highld	137	7138
Toseland	Cambs	52	2462
Tosside	N York	81	7656
Tostock	Suffk	54	9563
Totaig	Highld	136	2050
Tote	Highld	136	4149
Tote	Highld	137	5160
Tote Hill	W Susx	14	8624
Tothill	Lincs	77	4181
Totland	IOW	12	3287
Totley	S York	74	3079
Totley Brook	S York	74	3180
Totnes	Devon	7	8060
Toton	Notts	62	5034
Totronald	Ag & B	120	1656
Totscore	Highld	136	3866
Tottenham	Gt Lon	27	3390
Tottenhill	Norfk	65	6411
Totteridge	Gt Lon	26	2494
Totternhoe	Beds	38	9821
Tottington	Gt Man	81	7712
Tottleworth	Lancs	81	7331
Totton	Hants	12	3613
Touchen End	Berks	26	8776
Toulston	N York	83	4543
Toulton	Somset	20	1931
Toulvaddie	Highld	147	8880
Tovil	Kent	28	7554
Tow Law	Dur	95	1138
Towan	Cnwll	4	8774
Towan	Cnwll	3	0148
Toward	Ag & B	114	1368
Toward Quay	Ag & B	114	1167
Towcester	Nhants	49	6948
Towednack	Cnwll	2	4838
Towersey	Oxon	37	7305
Towie	Abers	134	4312
Town End	Cambs	65	4195
Town End	Cumb	86	2692
Town End	Cumb	87	3406
Town End	Cumb	94	6325
Town End	Cumb	87	3687
Town End	Cumb	87	4483
Town Green	Lancs	78	4005
Town Green	Norfk	67	3612
Town Head	Cumb	87	4103
Town Head	N York	88	8258
Town Head	N York	82	1748
Town Kelloe	Dur	96	3536
Town Lane	Gt Man	79	6999
Town Littleworth	E Susx	15	4117
Town of Lowdon	Mersyd	78	6196
Town Row	E Susx	16	5630
Town Street	Suffk	53	7785
Town Yetholm	Border	110	8128
Townend	W Duns	115	3976
Towngate	Cumb	94	5246
Towngate	Lincs	64	1310
Townhead	Cumb	92	0735
Townhead	Cumb	94	6334
Townhead	D & G	100	0088
Townhead	S Ayrs	82	1602
Townhead of Greenlaw	D & G	99	7464
Townhill	Fife	117	1089
Townlake	Devon	5	4074
Towns End	Hants	24	5659
Townsend	Somset	10	3614
Townshend	Cnwll	2	5932
Townwell	Gloucs	35	7090
Towthorpe	E R Yk	91	8962
Towthorpe	N York	90	6258
Towton	N York	83	4839
Towyn	Conwy	70	9779
Toxteth	Mersyd	78	3588
Toy's Hill	Kent	27	4651
Toynton All Saints	Lincs	77	3963
Toynton Fen Side	Lincs	77	3961
Toynton St Peter	Lincs	77	4063
Trabboch	E Ayrs	107	4421
Trabbochburn	E Ayrs	107	4621
Traboe	Cnwll	3	7421
Tracebridge	Somset	20	0621
Tradespark	Highld	140	8656
Traethsaith	Cerdgn	42	2851
Trallong	Powys	45	9629
Tramway Museum		74	3455
Tranent	E Loth	118	4072
Tranmere	Mersyd	78	3187
Trannack	Cnwll	2	5633
Trantelbeg	Highld	150	8952
Trantlemore	Highld	150	8953
Tranwell	Nthumb	103	1883
Trap's Green	Warwks	48	1069
Trapp	Carmth	32	6518
Traprain	E Loth	118	5975
Trapshill	Berks	23	3763
Trash Green	Berks	24	6569
Traveller's Rest	Devon	19	6127
Trawden	Lancs	81	9138
Trawscoed	Cerdgn	43	6672
Trawsfynydd	Gwynd	57	7035
Tre Aubrey	V Glam	33	0372
Tre'r-ddol	Cerdgn	43	6692
Tre-gagle	Mons	34	5207
Tre-Gibbon	Rhondd	33	9905
Tre-groes	Cerdgn	42	4044
Tre-Mostyn	Flints	70	1479
Trealaw	Rhondd	33	0092
Treales	Lancs	80	4332
Tre-Vaughan	Carmth	31	3921
Tre-wyn	Mons	34	3222
Trearddur Bay	IOA	68	2579
Treaslane	Highld	136	3953
Treator	Cnwll	4	9075
Trebanog	Rhondd	33	0190
Trebanos	Neath	32	7103
Trebartha	Cnwll	5	2677
Trebarvah	Cnwll	2	7130
Trebarwith	Cnwll	4	0586
Trebeath	Cnwll	5	2587
Trebehor	Cnwll	2	3724
Trebelzue	Cnwll	4	8464
Trebetherick	Cnwll	4	9378
Treborough	Somset	20	0136
Trebudannon	Cnwll	4	8961
Trebullett	Cnwll	5	3278
Treburgett	Cnwll	4	0579
Treburick	Cnwll	4	8971
Treburley	Cnwll	5	3577
Treburrick	Cnwll	4	8670
Trebyan	Cnwll	4	0763
Trecastle	Powys	45	8829
Trecogo	Cnwll	5	3080
Trecott	Devon	8	6300
Trecwn	Pembks	30	9632
Trecynon	Rhondd	33	9903
Tredaule	Cnwll	5	2381
Tredavoe	Cnwll	2	4528
Tredegar	Blae G	33	1408
Tredethy	Cnwll	4	0672
Tredington	Gloucs	47	9029
Tredington	Warwks	48	2543
Tredinnick	Cnwll	4	9270
Tredinnick	Cnwll	4	0459
Tredinnick	Cnwll	4	1666
Tredinnick	Cnwll	5	2357
Tredinnick	Cnwll	5	2957
Tredomen	Powys	45	1231
Tredrissi	Pembks	31	0742
Tredrizzick	Cnwll	4	9577
Tredunhock	Mons	34	3794
Tredustan	Powys	45	1332
Treen	Cnwll	2	4337
Treen	Cnwll	2	3923
Treesmill	Cnwll	3	0855
Treeton	S York	75	4387
Trefasser	Pembks	30	8938
Trefdraeth	IOA	68	4170
Trefecca	Powys	45	1431
Trefeglwys	Powys	58	9690
Trefenter	Cerdgn	43	6068
Treffgarne	Pembks	30	9523
Treffgarne Owen	Pembks	30	8625
Trefforest	Rhondd	33	0858
Treffynnon	Pembks	30	8528
Trefil	Blae G	33	1212
Trefilan	Cerdgn	44	5456
Trefin	Pembks	30	8432
Treflach Wood	Shrops	58	2625
Trefnannau	Powys	58	2316
Trefnant	Denbgs	70	0570
Trefonen	Shrops	58	2526
Trefor	Gwynd	56	3746
Trefor	IOA	68	3780
Treforda	Cnwll	4	0988
Trefrew	Cnwll	4	1084
Trefriw	Conwy	69	7863
Tregadillett	Cnwll	5	2983
Tregaian	IOA	68	4580
Tregare	Mons	34	4110
Tregarne	Cnwll	3	7823
Tregaron	Cerdgn	44	6759
Tregarth	Gwynd	69	6067
Tregaswith	Cnwll	4	8962
Tregatta	Cnwll	4	0587
Tregawne	Cnwll	4	0066
Tregear	Cnwll	3	8650
Tregeare	Cnwll	5	2486
Tregeiriog	Wrexhm	58	1733
Tregele	IOA	68	3592
Tregellist	Cnwll	4	0177
Tregenna	Cnwll	3	8743
Tregenna	Cnwll	4	0973
Tregeseal	Cnwll	2	3731
Tregew	Cnwll	3	8034
Tregidden	Cnwll	3	7523
Tregiddle	Cnwll	2	6723
Tregidgeo	Cnwll	3	9647
Tregiskey	Cnwll	3	0146
Treglemais	Pembks	30	8229
Tregole	Cnwll	5	1998
Tregolls	Cnwll	3	7535
Tregonce	Cnwll	4	9373
Tregonetha	Cnwll	4	9563
Tregony	Cnwll	3	9244
Tregoodwell	Cnwll	4	1183
Tregoose	Cnwll	2	6823
Tregoss	Cnwll	4	9660
Tregowris	Cnwll	3	7722
Tregoyd	Powys	45	1937
Tregrehan Mills	Cnwll	3	0453
Tregullon	Cnwll	4	0664
Tregunna	Cnwll	4	9673
Tregunnon	Cnwll	5	2283
Tregurrian	Cnwll	4	8565
Tregustick	Cnwll	4	9486
Tregynon	Powys	58	0998
Trehafod	Rhondd	33	0290
Trehan	Cnwll	5	4058
Treharris	Myr Td	33	0996
Treharrock	Cnwll	4	0178
Trehemborne	Cnwll	4	8773
Treherbert	Carmth	44	5847
Treherbert	Rhondd	33	9498
Trehunist	Cnwll	5	3263
Trekelland	Cnwll	5	3480
Trekenner	Cnwll	5	3478
Treknow	Cnwll	4	0586
Trelan	Cnwll	3	7418
Trelash	Cnwll	4	1890
Trelassick	Cnwll	3	8752
Trelawne	Cnwll	5	2154
Trelawnyd	Flints	70	0979
Treleague	Cnwll	3	7821
Treleaver	Cnwll	3	7716
Trelech	Carmth	31	2830
Trelech a'r Betws	Carmth	31	3026
Treleddyd-fawr	Pembks	30	7528
Trelew	Cnwll	3	8135
Trelewis	Myr Td	33	1096
Treligga	Cnwll	4	0484
Trelights	Cnwll	4	9979
Trelill	Cnwll	4	0478
Trelinnoe	Cnwll	5	3181
Trelion	Cnwll	3	9252
Trelissick	Cnwll	3	8339
Trelissick Garden		3	8339
Trelleck	Mons	34	5005
Trelleck Grange	Mons	34	4901
Trelogan	Flints	70	1180
Trelonk	Cnwll	3	8941
Trelow	Cnwll	4	8961
Trelowarren	Cnwll	2	7124
Trelowia	Cnwll	5	2182
Treluggan	Cnwll	3	8838
Trelystan	Powys	58	2503
Tremadog	Gwynd	57	5640
Tremail	Cnwll	4	1686
Tremain	Cerdgn	42	2248
Tremaine	Cnwll	5	2389
Tremar	Cnwll	5	2568
Trematon	Cnwll	5	3959
Trembraze	Cnwll	5	2565
Tremeirchion	Denbgs	70	0873
Tremethick Cross	Cnwll	2	4430
Tremollett	Cnwll	5	2975
Tremore	Cnwll	4	0164
Trenance	Cnwll	3	8022
Trenance	Cnwll	4	8568
Trenance	Cnwll	4	9270
Trenance	Cnwll	2	6716
Trenarren	Cnwll	3	0348
Trencreek	Cnwll	4	8260
Trencreek	Cnwll	4	1896
Trendeal	Cnwll	3	8952
Trendrine	Cnwll	2	4739
Treneague	Cnwll	4	9871
Trenear	Cnwll	2	6731
Treneglos	Cnwll	5	2088
Trenerth	Cnwll	2	6035
Trenewan	Cnwll	4	1753
Trenewth	Cnwll	4	0778
Trengune	Cnwll	4	1893
Treninnick	Cnwll	4	8760
Trenowah	Cnwll	4	7959
Trenoweth	Cnwll	3	7533
Trent	Dorset	10	5918
Trent Port	Lincs	76	8381
Trent Vale	Staffs	72	8643
Trentham	Staffs	72	8740
Trentishoe	Devon	19	6448
Trentlock	Derbys	62	4831
Treoes	V Glam	33	9478
Treorchy	Rhondd	33	9597
Trequite	Cnwll	4	0377
Trerhyngyll	V Glam	33	0077
Trerulefoot	Cnwll	5	3358
Tresaith	Cerdgn	3	7431
Tresawle	Cnwll	3	8846
Tresco Heliport		2	8914
Trescott	Staffs	60	8597
Trescowe	Cnwll	2	5731
Tresean	Cnwll	4	7858
Tresham	Gloucs	35	7991
Tresillian	Cnwll	3	8646
Tresinney	Cnwll	4	1081
Treskinnick Cross	Cnwll	5	2098
Treslea	Cnwll	4	1368
Tresmeer	Cnwll	5	2387
Tresparrett	Cnwll	4	1491
Tressait	P & K	132	8160
Tresta	Shet	153	6653
Tresta	Shet	153	6090
Treswell	Notts	75	7879
Treswithian	Cnwll	2	6241
Trethawle	Cnwll	5	2662
Trethevey	Cnwll	4	0789
Trethewey	Cnwll	2	3823
Trethomas	Caerph	33	1868
Trethosa	Cnwll	3	9454
Trethurgy	Cnwll	3	0355
Tretio	Pembks	30	7829
Tretire	Herefs	45	5123
Tretower	Powys	33	1821
Treuddyn	Flints	70	2557
Trevadlock	Cnwll	5	2679
Trevague	Cnwll	5	2379
Trevalga	Cnwll	4	0890
Trevalyn	Wrexhm	71	3856
Trevanger	Cnwll	4	9677
Trevanson	Cnwll	4	9773
Trevarrack	Cnwll	2	4731
Trevarren	Cnwll	4	9160
Trevarrian	Cnwll	4	8566
Trevarrick	Cnwll	3	9843
Trevarth	Cnwll	3	7240
Trevaughan	Carmth	31	2015
Treveal	Cnwll	2	4740
Treveal	Cnwll	4	7858
Treveighan	Cnwll	4	0779
Trevellas Downs	Cnwll	3	7452
Trevelmond	Cnwll	5	2063
Trevemper	Cnwll	4	8159
Treveneague	Cnwll	2	5432
Treveor	Cnwll	3	9841
Treverbyn	Cnwll	3	9659
Treverbyn	Cnwll	4	0157
Treverva	Cnwll	3	7531
Trevescan	Cnwll	2	3524
Trevethin	Torfn	34	2801
Trevia	Cnwll	4	0983
Trevigro	Cnwll	5	3369
Trevilla	Cnwll	3	8239
Trevilledor	Cnwll	4	8867
Trevilson	Cnwll	3	8455
Treviscoe	Cnwll	3	9455
Treviskey	Cnwll	3	9340
Trevissick	Cnwll	3	0248
Trevithal	Cnwll	2	4626
Trevithick	Cnwll	4	8862
Trevithick	Cnwll	3	9645
Trevivian	Cnwll	4	1785
Trevoll	Cnwll	4	8358
Trevone	Cnwll	4	8975
Trevor	Denbgs	70	2742
Trevorgans	Cnwll	2	4025
Trevorrick	Cnwll	4	8672
Trevorrick	Cnwll	4	9273
Trevose	Cnwll	4	8576
Trew	Cnwll	2	6129
Trewalder	Cnwll	4	0782
Trewalkin	Powys	45	1531
Trewarlett	Cnwll	5	3380
Trewarmett	Cnwll	4	0686
Trewarthenick	Cnwll	3	9044
Trewassa	Cnwll	4	1486
Trewavas	Cnwll	2	5926
Treween	Cnwll	5	2182
Trewellard	Cnwll	2	3733
Trewen	Cnwll	5	2583
Trewen	Cnwll	4	1190
Trewennack	Cnwll	2	6728
Trewent	Pembks	30	0197
Trewern	Powys	58	2811
Trewetha	Cnwll	4	0080
Trewethern	Cnwll	4	0076
Trewidland	Cnwll	5	2559
Trewillis	Cnwll	3	7818
Trewince	Cnwll	3	8633
Trewint	Cnwll	4	1072
Trewint	Cnwll	5	2180
Trewint	Cnwll	5	2963
Trewirgie	Cnwll	3	8845
Trewithian	Cnwll	3	8737
Trewoodloe	Cnwll	5	3271
Trewoofe	Cnwll	2	4425
Trewoon	Cnwll	2	6683
Trewoon	Cnwll	3	9952
Treworga	Cnwll	3	8649
Treworlas	Cnwll	3	8938
Treworld	Cnwll	4	1190
Treworthal	Cnwll	3	8673
Treyarnon	Cnwll	4	8673
Treyford	W Susx	14	8218
Triangle	W York	82	0422
Trickett's Cross	Dorset	12	0800
Triermain	Cumb	102	5966
Triffleton	Pembks	30	9724
Trillacott	Cnwll	5	2689
Trimdon	Dur	96	3634
Trimdon Colliery	Dur	96	3735
Trimdon Grange	Dur	96	3635
Trimingham	Norfk	67	2838
Trimley	Suffk	55	2737
Trimley Lower Street	Suffk	55	2636
Trimpley	Worcs	60	7978
Trims Green	Herts	39	4717
Trimsaran	Carmth	32	4504
Trimstone	Devon	19	5043
Trinafour	P & K	132	7264
Trinant	Caerph	33	2099
Tring	Herts	38	9211
Tring Wharf	Herts	38	9212
Tringford	Herts	38	9113
Trinity	Angus	134	6061
Trinity	Jersey	158	0000
Trinity Gask	P & K	125	9618
Triscombe	Somset	20	9237
Triscombe	Somset	20	1535
Trislaig	Highld	130	0874
Trispen	Cnwll	3	8450
Tritlington	Nthumb	103	2092
Troan	Cnwll	4	8957
Trochry	P & K	125	9740
Troedrhiwfuwch	Caerph	33	1204
Troedyraur	Cerdgn	42	3245
Troedyrhiw	Myr Td	33	0702
Trofarth	Conwy	69	8571
Trois Bois	Jersey	158	0000
Troon	Cnwll	2	6638
Troon	S Ayrs	106	3230
Tropical World Roundhay Park		83	3238
Troston	Suffk	54	8972
Troswell	Cnwll	5	2592
Trotshill	Worcs	47	8855
Trottiscliffe	Kent	27	6460
Trotton	W Susx	14	8322
Trough Gate	Lancs	81	8821
Troughend	Nthumb	102	8692
Troutbeck	Cumb	93	3927
Troutbeck	Cumb	87	4002
Troutbeck Bridge	Cumb	87	4000
Troway	Derbys	74	3879
Trowbridge	Wilts	22	8558
Trowell	Notts	62	4839
Trowle Common	Wilts	22	8458
Trowse Newton	Norfk	67	2406
Troy	W York	82	2439
Trudoxhill	Somset	22	7443
Trull	Somset	20	2122
Trumfleet	S York	83	6011
Trumpan	Highld	136	2261
Trumpet	Herefs	47	6539
Trumpington	Cambs	53	4454
Trumpsgreen	Surrey	25	9967
Trunch	Norfk	67	2834
Trunnah	Lancs	80	3442
Truro	Cnwll	3	8244
Truro Cathedral		3	8145
Truscott	Cnwll	5	2985
Trusham	Devon	8	8582
Trusley	Derbys	73	2535
Trusthorpe	Lincs	77	5183
Trysull	Staffs	60	8594
Tubney	Oxon	36	4399
Tuckenhay	Devon	7	8156
Tuckhill	Shrops	60	7888
Tuckingmill	Cnwll	2	6540
Tuckingmill	Wilts	22	9329
Tuckton	Dorset	12	1492
Tucoyse	Cnwll	3	9465
Tuddenham	Suffk	53	7371
Tuddenham	Suffk	55	1948
Tudeley	Kent	16	6245
Tudhoe	Dur	96	2535
Tudorville	Herefs	45	5922
Tudweiliog	Gwynd	56	2436
Tuesley	Surrey	25	9642
Tuffley	Gloucs	35	8314
Tufton	Hants	24	4546
Tufton	Pembks	30	0428
Tugby	Leics	63	7601
Tugford	Shrops	59	5587
Tughall	Nthumb	111	2126
Tullibody	Clacks	116	8595
Tullich	Highld	140	6328
Tullich	Highld	147	8576
Tulliemet	P & K	125	0052
Tulloch	Abers	143	8031
Tulloch	Stirlg	124	5120
Tulloch Station	Highld	131	3580
Tullochgorm	Ag & B	114	9695
Tullybeagles Lodge	P & K	125	0136
Tullynessle	Abers	142	5519
Tulse Hill	Gt Lon	27	3172
Tumble	Carmth	32	5411
Tumbler's Green	Essex	40	8025
Tumby	Lincs	76	2359
Tumby Woodside	Lincs	77	2757
Tummel Bridge	P & K	132	7659
Tunbridge Wells	Kent	16	5839
Tundergarth	D & G	101	1780
Tungate	Norfk	67	2629
Tunstall	E R Yk	85	3031
Tunstall	Kent	28	8961
Tunstall	Lancs	87	6073
Tunstall	N York	89	2196
Tunstall	Norfk	67	4107
Tunstall	Staffs	72	7727
Tunstall	Staffs	72	8651
Tunstall	Suffk	55	3655
Tunstall	T & W	96	3953
Tunstead	Derbys	74	1074
Tunstead	Norfk	67	2921
Tunstead Milton	Derbys	79	0180
Tunworth	Hants	24	6748
Tupsley	Herefs	46	5340
Tur Langton	Leics	50	7194
Turgis Green	Hants	24	6959
Turkdean	Gloucs	36	1017
Turleigh	Wilts	22	8060
Turleygreen	Shrops	60	7685
Turn	Lancs	81	8118
Turnastone	Herefs	46	3536
Turnberry	S Ayrs	106	2005

314

Turnchapel *Devon*	**6**	4953
Turnditch *Derbys*	**73**	2946
Turner Green *Lancs*	**81**	6030
Turner's Green *E Susx*	**16**	6319
Turner's Green *Warwks*	**48**	1969
Turner's Hill *W Susx*	**15**	3435
Turners Puddle *Dorset*	**11**	8393
Turnford *Herts*	**39**	3604
Turnhouse *C Edin*	**117**	1674
Turnworth *Dorset*	**11**	8207
Turriff *Abers*	**142**	7250
Turton Bottoms *Gt Man*	**81**	7315
Turves *Cambs*	**64**	3396
Turvey *Beds*	**38**	9452
Turville *Bucks*	**37**	7691
Turville Heath *Bucks*	**37**	7490
Turweston *Bucks*	**49**	6037
Tushielaw Inn *Border*	**109**	3017
Tushingham cum Grindley *Ches*	**71**	5246
Tutbury *Staffs*	**73**	2128
Tutnall *Worcs*	**60**	9970
Tutshill *Gloucs*	**34**	5494
Tuttington *Norfk*	**67**	2227
Tutwell *Cnwll*	**5**	3875
Tuxford *Notts*	**75**	7471
Twatt *Ork*	**153**	2724
Twatt *Shet*	**153**	3253
Twechar *E Duns*	**116**	6975
Tweedmouth *Nthumb*	**119**	9952
Tweedsmuir *Border*	**108**	1024
Twelve Oaks *E Susx*	**16**	6820
Twelveheads *Cnwll*	**3**	7542
Twenty *Lincs*	**64**	1520
Twerton *Somset*	**22**	7264
Twickenham *Gt Lon*	**26**	1673
Twigworth *Gloucs*	**35**	8422
Twineham *W Susx*	**15**	2519
Twineham Green *W Susx*	**15**	2520
Twinhoe *Somset*	**22**	7559
Twinstead *Essex*	**54**	8636
Twitchen *Devon*	**19**	7930
Twitchen *Shrops*	**46**	3779
Twitham *Kent*	**29**	2656
Two Bridges *Devon*	**6**	6174
Two Dales *Derbys*	**74**	2763
Two Gates *Staffs*	**61**	2101
Two Mile Oak Cross *Devon*	**7**	8468
Two Pots *Devon*	**19**	5344
Two Waters *Herts*	**38**	0505
Twycross *Leics*	**62**	3304
Twycross Zoo	**61**	3105
Twyford *Berks*	**37**	7976
Twyford *Bucks*	**49**	6626
Twyford *Hants*	**13**	4824
Twyford *Leics*	**63**	7210
Twyford *Lincs*	**63**	9323
Twyford *Norfk*	**66**	0123
Twyford Common *Herefs*	**46**	5135
Twyn-carno *Caerph*	**33**	1108
Twyn-y-Sheriff *Mons*	**34**	4005
Twyn-yr-Odyn *V Glam*	**33**	1173
Twynholm *D & G*	**99**	6654
Twyning *Gloucs*	**47**	8936
Twyning Green *Gloucs*	**47**	9036
Twynllanan *Carmth*	**44**	7524
Twywell *Nhants*	**51**	9578
Ty'n-dwr *Denbgs*	**70**	2341
Ty'n-y-brdynk *Rhondd*	**33**	0087
Ty'n-y-coedcae *Caerph*	**33**	1988
Ty'n-y-Groes *Conwy*	**69**	7771
Ty-nant *Conwy*	**70**	9944
Ty-nant *Gwynd*	**58**	9026
Tyberton *Herefs*	**46**	3839
Tyburn *W Mids*	**61**	1391
Tycroes *Carmth*	**32**	6010
Tycrwyn *Powys*	**58**	1018
Tydd Gote *Lincs*	**65**	4518
Tydd St Giles *Cambs*	**65**	4216
Tydd St Mary *Lincs*	**65**	4418
Tye *Hants*	**13**	7302
Tye Green *Essex*	**39**	5424
Tye Green *Essex*	**53**	5935
Tye Green *Essex*	**40**	7821
Tyersal *W York*	**82**	1932
Tyldesley *Gt Man*	**79**	6802
Tyler Hill *Kent*	**29**	1461
Tyler's Green *Essex*	**39**	5005
Tylers Green *Bucks*	**26**	9093
Tylers Green *Surrey*	**27**	3552
Tylorstown *Rhondd*	**33**	0095
Tylwch *Powys*	**58**	9780
Tyn-y-nant *Rhondd*	**33**	0685
Tyndrum *Stirlg*	**123**	3230
Tynemouth *T & W*	**103**	3669
Tynewydd *Rhondd*	**33**	9398
Tyninghame *E Loth*	**118**	6179
Tynron *D & G*	**100**	8093
Tynygongl *IOA*	**68**	5092
Tynygraig *Cerdgn*	**43**	6969
Tyringham *Bucks*	**38**	8547
Tyseley *W Mids*	**61**	1184
Tythegston *Brdgnd*	**33**	8578
Tytherington *Ches*	**79**	9175
Tytherington *Gloucs*	**35**	6688
Tytherington *Somset*	**22**	7644
Tytherington *Wilts*	**22**	9141
Tytherleigh *Devon*	**10**	3103
Tytherton Lucas *Wilts*	**35**	9474
Tywardreath *Cnwll*	**3**	0854
Tywardreath Highway *Cnwll*	**3**	0755
Tywyn *Conwy*	**69**	7878
Tywyn *Gwynd*	**57**	5800

U

Ubbeston Green *Suffk*	**55**	3271
Ubley *Somset*	**21**	5258
Uckerby *N York*	**89**	2402
Uckfield *E Susx*	**16**	4721
Uckinghall *Worcs*	**47**	8637

Uckington *Gloucs*	**47**	9124
Uckington *Shrops*	**59**	5709
Uddingston *S Lans*	**116**	6960
Uddington *S Lans*	**108**	8633
Udimore *E Susx*	**17**	8719
Udny Green *Abers*	**143**	8726
Udny Station *Abers*	**143**	9024
Uffcott *Wilts*	**36**	1277
Uffculme *Devon*	**9**	0612
Uffington *Lincs*	**64**	0507
Uffington *Oxon*	**36**	3089
Uffington *Shrops*	**59**	5313
Ufford *Cambs*	**64**	0903
Ufford *Suffk*	**55**	2952
Ufton *Warwks*	**48**	3762
Ufton Nervet *Berks*	**24**	6367
Ugadale *Ag & B*	**105**	7828
Ugborough *Devon*	**7**	6755
Uggeshall *Suffk*	**55**	4480
Ugglebarnby *N York*	**90**	8707
Ughill *Derbys*	**74**	2590
Ugley *Essex*	**39**	5228
Ugley Green *Essex*	**39**	5227
Ugthorpe *N York*	**90**	7911
Uig *Ag & B*	**120**	1654
Uig *Highld*	**136**	1952
Uig *Highld*	**136**	3963
Uig *W Isls*	**152**	0533
Uigshader *Highld*	**136**	4346
Uisken *Ag & B*	**121**	3919
Ulbster *Highld*	**151**	3241
Ulcat Row *Cumb*	**93**	4022
Ulceby *Lincs*	**85**	1014
Ulceby *Lincs*	**77**	4272
Ulceby Cross *Lincs*	**77**	4173
Ulceby Skitter *Lincs*	**85**	1215
Ulcombe *Kent*	**28**	8448
Uldale *Cumb*	**93**	2437
Uley *Gloucs*	**35**	7898
Ulgham *Nthumb*	**103**	2392
Ullapool *Highld*	**145**	1294
Ullenhall *Warwks*	**48**	1267
Ullenwood *Gloucs*	**35**	9416
Ulleskelf *N York*	**83**	5239
Ullesthorpe *Leics*	**50**	5087
Ulley *S York*	**75**	4687
Ullingswick *Herefs*	**46**	5949
Ullock *Cumb*	**92**	0724
Ulpha *Cumb*	**86**	1993
Ulpha *Cumb*	**87**	4581
Ulrome *E R Yk*	**85**	1656
Ulsta *Shet*	**153**	4680
Ulting Wick *Essex*	**40**	8009
Ulverley Green *W Mids*	**61**	1382
Ulverston *Cumb*	**86**	2878
Ulwell *Dorset*	**12**	0280
Umachan *Highld*	**137**	6050
Umberleigh *Devon*	**19**	6023
Unapool *Highld*	**148**	2333
Under Burnmouth *Border*	**101**	4783
Under River *Kent*	**27**	5552
Underbarrow *Cumb*	**87**	4692
Undercliffe *W York*	**82**	1834
Underdale *Shrops*	**59**	5013
Underley Hall *Cumb*	**87**	6179
Underling Green *Kent*	**28**	7546
Underwood *Notts*	**75**	4750
Undley *Suffk*	**53**	6981
Undy *Mons*	**34**	4386
Union Mills *IOM*	**158**	3577
Union Street *E Susx*	**16**	7031
Unstone *Derbys*	**74**	3777
Unstone Green *Derbys*	**74**	3776
Unsworth *Gt Man*	**79**	8207
Unthank *Cumb*	**93**	3948
Unthank *Cumb*	**93**	4536
Unthank *Cumb*	**94**	6040
Unthank *Derbys*	**74**	3075
Unthank *Nthumb*	**111**	9848
Unthank End *Cumb*	**93**	4535
Up Cerne *Dorset*	**11**	6502
Up Exe *Devon*	**9**	9402
Up Holland *Lancs*	**78**	5205
Up Marden *W Susx*	**14**	7913
Up Mudford *Somset*	**10**	5718
Up Nately *Hants*	**24**	6951
Up Somborne *Hants*	**23**	3932
Up Sydling *Dorset*	**10**	6201
Upavon *Wilts*	**23**	1354
Upchurch *Kent*	**28**	8467
Upcott *Devon*	**19**	5838
Upcott *Devon*	**19**	7529
Upcott *Herefs*	**46**	3250
Upcott *Somset*	**20**	9025
Updown Hill *Surrey*	**25**	9363
Upend *Cambs*	**53**	7058
Upgate *Norfk*	**66**	1318
Upgate Street *Norfk*	**66**	0992
Upgate Street *Norfk*	**67**	2891
Uphall *Dorset*	**10**	5502
Uphall *W Loth*	**117**	0671
Upham *Devon*	**19**	8808
Upham *Hants*	**13**	5320
Uphampton *Herefs*	**46**	3963
Uphampton *Worcs*	**47**	8364
Uphill *Somset*	**21**	3158
Uplawmoor *E Rens*	**115**	4355
Upleadon *Gloucs*	**47**	7527
Upleatham *N York*	**97**	6319
Uplees *Kent*	**28**	0064
Uploders *Dorset*	**10**	5093
Uplowman *Devon*	**9**	0115
Uplyme *Devon*	**10**	3293
Upminster *Gt Lon*	**27**	5686
Upottery *Devon*	**9**	2007
Uppaton *Devon*	**5**	4380
Upper & Lower Stondon *Beds*	**38**	1435
Upper Affcot *Shrops*	**59**	4486
Upper Ardchronie *Highld*	**146**	6183
Upper Arley *Worcs*	**60**	7680
Upper Arncott *Oxon*	**37**	6117
Upper Astrop *Nhants*	**49**	5137
Upper Basildon *Berks*	**37**	5976
Upper Batley *W York*	**82**	2325
Upper Beeding *W Susx*	**15**	1910
Upper Benefield *Nhants*	**51**	9789
Upper Bentley *Worcs*	**47**	9966

Upper Bighouse *Highld*	**150**	8856
Upper Birchwood *Derbys*	**75**	4355
Upper Boat *Rhondd*	**33**	1086
Upper Boddington *Nhants*	**49**	4852
Upper Borth *Cerdgn*	**43**	6088
Upper Brailes *Warwks*	**48**	3039
Upper Breakish *Highld*	**129**	6823
Upper Breinton *Herefs*	**46**	4640
Upper Broadheath *Worcs*	**47**	8056
Upper Broughton *Notts*	**63**	6826
Upper Bucklebury *Berks*	**24**	5468
Upper Burgate *Hants*	**12**	1516
Upper Bush *Kent*	**28**	6966
Upper Caldecote *Beds*	**52**	1645
Upper Canada *Somset*	**21**	3658
Upper Canterton *Hants*	**12**	2612
Upper Catesby *Nhants*	**49**	5259
Upper Catshill *Worcs*	**60**	9674
Upper Chapel *Powys*	**45**	0040
Upper Cheddon *Somset*	**20**	2328
Upper Chicksgrove *Wilts*	**22**	9529
Upper Chute *Wilts*	**23**	2953
Upper Clapton *Gt Lon*	**27**	3487
Upper Clatford *Hants*	**23**	3543
Upper Clynnog *Gwynd*	**56**	4646
Upper Coberley *Gloucs*	**35**	9816
Upper Cokeham *W Susx*	**15**	1605
Upper Cotton *Staffs*	**73**	0547
Upper Cound *Shrops*	**59**	5505
Upper Cudworth *S York*	**83**	3909
Upper Cumberworth *W York*	**82**	2008
Upper Cwmtwrch *Powys*	**32**	7511
Upper Dallachy *Moray*	**141**	3662
Upper Deal *Kent*	**29**	3651
Upper Dean *Beds*	**51**	0467
Upper Denby *W York*	**82**	2207
Upper Denton *Cumb*	**102**	6165
Upper Dicker *E Susx*	**16**	5509
Upper Dinchope *Shrops*	**59**	4583
Upper Dounreay *Highld*	**150**	0065
Upper Dovercourt *Essex*	**41**	2330
Upper Drumbane *Stirlg*	**124**	6606
Upper Dunsforth *N York*	**89**	4463
Upper Eashing *Surrey*	**25**	9543
Upper Egleton *Herefs*	**47**	6344
Upper Elkstone *Staffs*	**74**	0558
Upper Ellastone *Staffs*	**73**	1043
Upper End *Derbys*	**74**	0875
Upper Enham *Hants*	**23**	3650
Upper Ethie *Highld*	**140**	7662
Upper Farmcote *Shrops*	**60**	7791
Upper Farringdon *Hants*	**24**	7135
Upper Framilode *Gloucs*	**35**	7510
Upper Froyle *Hants*	**24**	7543
Upper Godney *Somset*	**21**	4842
Upper Gravenhurst *Beds*	**38**	1136
Upper Green *Berks*	**23**	3763
Upper Green *Essex*	**53**	5935
Upper Green *Mons*	**34**	3818
Upper Green *Suffk*	**53**	7464
Upper Grove Common *Herefs*	**46**	5526
Upper Hackney *Derbys*	**74**	2861
Upper Hale *Surrey*	**25**	8349
Upper Halliford *Surrey*	**26**	0968
Upper Halling *Kent*	**28**	6964
Upper Hambleton *Rutlnd*	**63**	9007
Upper Hardres Court *Kent*	**29**	1550
Upper Hardwick *Herefs*	**46**	4057
Upper Hartfield *E Susx*	**16**	4634
Upper Hartshay *Derbys*	**74**	3850
Upper Hatherley *Gloucs*	**35**	9220
Upper Hatton *Staffs*	**72**	8237
Upper Haugh *S York*	**74**	4297
Upper Hayton *Shrops*	**59**	5181
Upper Heaton *W York*	**82**	1719
Upper Helmsley *N York*	**83**	6956
Upper Hergest *Herefs*	**46**	2654
Upper Heyford *Nhants*	**49**	6659
Upper Heyford *Oxon*	**49**	4925
Upper Hill *Herefs*	**46**	4753
Upper Hockenden *Kent*	**27**	5069
Upper Hopton *W York*	**82**	1918
Upper Howsell *Worcs*	**47**	7848
Upper Hulme *Staffs*	**73**	0160
Upper Ifold *Surrey*	**14**	0033
Upper Inglesham *Wilts*	**36**	2096
Upper Kilcott *Gloucs*	**35**	7988
Upper Killay *Swans*	**32**	5892
Upper Kinchrackie *Ag & B*	**123**	1627
Upper Lambourn *Berks*	**36**	3080
Upper Landywood *Staffs*	**60**	9805
Upper Langford *Somset*	**21**	4659
Upper Langwith *Derbys*	**75**	5169
Upper Largo *Fife*	**127**	4203
Upper Leigh *Staffs*	**73**	0136
Upper Ley *Gloucs*	**35**	7217
Upper Littleton *Somset*	**21**	5564
Upper Longdon *Staffs*	**61**	0614
Upper Ludstone *Shrops*	**60**	8095
Upper Lybster *Highld*	**151**	2537
Upper Lydbrook *Gloucs*	**34**	6015
Upper Lyde *Herefs*	**46**	4944
Upper Lye *Herefs*	**46**	3965
Upper Maes-coed *Herefs*	**46**	3334
Upper Midhope *Derbys*	**74**	2199
Upper Milton *Worcs*	**60**	8172
Upper Minety *Wilts*	**35**	0091
Upper Moor *Worcs*	**47**	9747
Upper Moor Side *W York*	**82**	2430
Upper Mulben *Moray*	**141**	3551
Upper Netchwood *Shrops*	**59**	6092
Upper Nobut *Staffs*	**73**	0335
Upper Norwood *W Susx*	**14**	9317
Upper Padley *Derbys*	**74**	2478
Upper Pennington *Hants*	**12**	3095
Upper Pickwick *Wilts*	**35**	8571
Upper Pollicott *Bucks*	**37**	7013
Upper Pond Street *Essex*	**39**	4636
Upper Poppleton *N York*	**83**	5553
Upper Quinton *Warwks*	**48**	1846
Upper Ratley *Hants*	**23**	3223
Upper Rochford *Worcs*	**47**	6367
Upper Ruscoe *D & G*	**99**	5661
Upper Sapey *Herefs*	**47**	6863
Upper Seagry *Wilts*	**35**	9480
Upper Shelton *Beds*	**38**	9843
Upper Sheringham *Norfk*	**66**	1441

Upper Shuckburgh *Warwks*	**49**	5061
Upper Skelmorlie *N Ayrs*	**114**	2067
Upper Slaughter *Gloucs*	**48**	1523
Upper Soudley *Gloucs*	**35**	6510
Upper Spond *Herefs*	**46**	3152
Upper Standen *Kent*	**29**	2139
Upper Staploe *Beds*	**52**	1459
Upper Stepford *D & G*	**100**	8681
Upper Stoke *Norfk*	**67**	2502
Upper Stowe *Nhants*	**49**	6456
Upper Street *Hants*	**12**	1518
Upper Street *Norfk*	**67**	3217
Upper Street *Norfk*	**67**	3616
Upper Street *Norfk*	**54**	1779
Upper Street *Suffk*	**53**	7851
Upper Street *Suffk*	**54**	1050
Upper Street *Suffk*	**54**	1434
Upper Strensham *Worcs*	**47**	8939
Upper Sundon *Beds*	**38**	0428
Upper Swell *Gloucs*	**48**	1726
Upper Tankersley *S York*	**74**	3499
Upper Tasburgh *Norfk*	**67**	2095
Upper Tean *Staffs*	**73**	0139
Upper Threapwood *Ches*	**71**	4345
Upper Town *Derbys*	**73**	2351
Upper Town *Derbys*	**74**	2361
Upper Town *Dur*	**95**	0737
Upper Town *Herefs*	**46**	5848
Upper Town *Somset*	**21**	5265
Upper Town *Suffk*	**54**	9267
Upper Tumble *Carmth*	**32**	5411
Upper Tysoe *Warwks*	**48**	3343
Upper Ufford *Suffk*	**55**	2952
Upper Upham *Wilts*	**36**	2277
Upper Upnor *Kent*	**28**	7570
Upper Victoria *Angus*	**127**	5336
Upper Vobster *Somset*	**22**	7049
Upper Wardington *Oxon*	**49**	4945
Upper Weald *Bucks*	**38**	8037
Upper Weedon *Nhants*	**49**	6258
Upper Wellingham *E Susx*	**16**	4313
Upper Weston *Somset*	**22**	7267
Upper Weybread *Suffk*	**55**	2379
Upper Wick *Worcs*	**47**	8252
Upper Wield *Hants*	**24**	6238
Upper Winchendon *Bucks*	**37**	7414
Upper Woodford *Wilts*	**23**	1237
Upper Wootton *Hants*	**24**	5754
Upper Wraxall *Wilts*	**35**	8074
Upper Wyche *Worcs*	**47**	7643
Upperby *Cumb*	**93**	4153
Upperglen *Highld*	**136**	3151
Uppermill *Gt Man*	**82**	9905
Upperthong *W York*	**82**	1208
Upperthorpe *Derbys*	**75**	4580
Upperthorpe *Lincs*	**84**	7500
Upperton *W Susx*	**14**	9522
Uppertown *Derbys*	**74**	3264
Uppertown *Highld*	**151**	3576
Upperup *Gloucs*	**36**	0496
Upperwood *Derbys*	**73**	2956
Uppincott *Devon*	**9**	9006
Uppingham *Rutlnd*	**51**	8699
Uppington *Dorset*	**12**	0206
Uppington *Shrops*	**59**	5909
Upsall *N York*	**89**	4586
Upsettlington *Border*	**110**	8846
Upshire *Essex*	**27**	4101
Upstreet *Kent*	**29**	2263
Upthorpe *Suffk*	**54**	9772
Upton *Berks*	**26**	9779
Upton *Bucks*	**37**	7711
Upton *Cambs*	**64**	1000
Upton *Cambs*	**52**	1778
Upton *Ches*	**71**	4069
Upton *Ches*	**78**	5087
Upton *Cnwll*	**18**	2004
Upton *Cnwll*	**5**	2772
Upton *Cumb*	**93**	3139
Upton *Devon*	**9**	0902
Upton *Devon*	**7**	7043
Upton *Dorset*	**11**	7483
Upton *Dorset*	**11**	9893
Upton *E R Yk*	**85**	1454
Upton *Hants*	**23**	3555
Upton *Hants*	**12**	3716
Upton *Leics*	**61**	3699
Upton *Lincs*	**76**	8686
Upton *Mersyd*	**78**	2788
Upton *Nhants*	**49**	7159
Upton *Norfk*	**67**	3912
Upton *Notts*	**75**	7354
Upton *Notts*	**75**	7476
Upton *Oxon*	**36**	2312
Upton *Oxon*	**37**	5187
Upton *Pembks*	**30**	0204
Upton *Somset*	**20**	9928
Upton *Somset*	**21**	4526
Upton *W York*	**83**	4713
Upton *Warwks*	**48**	1257
Upton *Wilts*	**22**	8731
Upton Bishop *Herefs*	**47**	6527
Upton Cheyney *Gloucs*	**35**	6970
Upton Cressett *Shrops*	**59**	6592
Upton Crews *Herefs*	**47**	6427
Upton Cross *Cnwll*	**5**	2872
Upton End *Beds*	**38**	1234
Upton Grey *Hants*	**24**	6948
Upton Heath *Ches*	**71**	4169
Upton Hellions *Devon*	**8**	8403
Upton Lovell *Wilts*	**22**	9440
Upton Magna *Shrops*	**59**	5512
Upton Noble *Somset*	**22**	7139
Upton Pyne *Devon*	**9**	9198
Upton Scudamore *Wilts*	**22**	8647
Upton Snodsbury *Worcs*	**47**	9454
Upton St Leonards *Gloucs*	**35**	8615
Upton upon Severn *Worcs*	**47**	8540
Upton Warren *Worcs*	**47**	9267
Upwaltham *W Susx*	**14**	9413
Upware *Cambs*	**53**	5470
Upwell *Norfk*	**65**	4902
Upwey *Dorset*	**11**	6685
Upwood *Cambs*	**52**	2582
Urchfont *Wilts*	**23**	0357
Urdimarsh *Herefs*	**46**	5248

Ure Bank *N York*	**89**	317
Urlay Nook *Dur*	**89**	401
Urmston *Gt Man*	**79**	769
Urquhart *Moray*	**141**	286
Urra *N York*	**90**	560
Urray *Highld*	**139**	505
Usan *Angus*	**127**	725
Ushaw Moor *Dur*	**96**	224
Usk *Mons*	**34**	370
Usselby *Lincs*	**76**	099
Usworth *T & W*	**96**	305
Utkinton *Ches*	**71**	556
Utley *W York*	**82**	054
Uton *Devon*	**8**	829
Utterby *Lincs*	**77**	309
Uttoxeter *Staffs*	**73**	093
Uwchmynydd *Gwynd*	**56**	152
Uxbridge *Gt Lon*	**26**	058
Uyeasound *Shet*	**153**	590
Uzmaston *Pembks*	**30**	971

V

Vale *Guern*	**158**	000
Vale of Rheidol Railway	**43**	588
Valley *IOA*	**68**	292
Valley End *Surrey*	**25**	956
Valley Truckle *Cnwll*	**4**	098
Valtos *Highld*	**137**	516
Valtos *W Isls*	**152**	093
Van *Caerph*	**33**	168
Vange *Essex*	**40**	718
Varteg *Torfn*	**34**	260
Vatsetter *Shet*	**153**	536
Vatten *Highld*	**136**	284
Vaynor *Myr Td*	**33**	04
Vazon Bay *Guern*	**158**	000
Velindre *Powys*	**45**	183
Vellow *Somset*	**20**	093
Velly *Devon*	**18**	292
Venn *Cnwll*	**18**	260
Venn *Devon*	**7**	854
Venn Ottery *Devon*	**9**	089
Venngreen *Devon*	**18**	371
Vennington *Shrops*	**59**	330
Venny Tedburn *Devon*	**8**	829
Venterdon *Cnwll*	**5**	367
Ventnor *IOW*	**13**	567
Venton *Devon*	**6**	595
Vernham Dean *Hants*	**23**	335
Vernham Street *Hants*	**23**	345
Vernolds Common *Shrops*	**59**	478
Verwood *Dorset*	**12**	086
Veryan *Cnwll*	**3**	915
Veryan Green *Cnwll*	**3**	914
Vickerstown *Cumb*	**86**	186
Victoria *Blae G*	**33**	170
Victoria *Cnwll*	**4**	986
Victoria *S York*	**82**	170
Vidlin *Shet*	**153**	476
Viewfield *Moray*	**141**	286
Viewpark *N Lans*	**116**	706
Vigo *Kent*	**27**	636
Ville la Bas *Jersey*	**158**	000
Villiaze *Guern*	**158**	000
Vinehall Street *E Susx*	**17**	752
Vines Cross *E Susx*	**16**	591
Virginia Water *Surrey*	**25**	006
Virginstow *Devon*	**5**	379
Virley *Essex*	**40**	94
Vobster *Somset*	**22**	704
Voe *Shet*	**153**	406
Vowchurch *Herefs*	**46**	363
Vulcan Village *Lancs*	**78**	589

W

Wackerfield *Dur*	**96**	152
Wacton *Norfk*	**66**	179
Wadborough *Worcs*	**47**	90
Waddesdon *Bucks*	**37**	74
Waddeton *Devon*	**7**	87
Waddicar *Mersyd*	**78**	399
Waddingham *Lincs*	**76**	989
Waddington *Lancs*	**81**	734
Waddington *Lincs*	**76**	97
Waddon *Devon*	**9**	887
Waddon *Dorset*	**10**	62
Wadebridge *Cnwll*	**4**	99
Wadeford *Somset*	**10**	31
Wadenhoe *Nhants*	**51**	01
Wadesmill *Herts*	**39**	36
Wadhurst *E Susx*	**16**	64
Wadshelf *Derbys*	**74**	31
Wadswick *Wilts*	**22**	84
Wadworth *S York*	**75**	56
Waen *Denbgs*	**70**	06
Waen *Denbgs*	**70**	10
Waen *Powys*	**58**	23
Waen Fach *Powys*	**58**	20
Waen-pentir *Gwynd*	**69**	57
Waen-wen *Gwynd*	**69**	57
Wagbeach *Shrops*	**59**	36
Wainfelin *Torfn*	**34**	27
Wainfleet All Saints *Lincs*	**77**	49
Wainfleet Bank *Lincs*	**77**	47
Wainford *Norfk*	**55**	34
Wainhouse Corner *Cnwll*	**4**	18
Wains Hill *Somset*	**34**	39
Wainscott *Kent*	**28**	74
Wainstalls *W York*	**82**	04
Waitby *Cumb*	**88**	75
Waithe *Lincs*	**77**	28
Wake Green *W Mids*	**61**	09

Wakefield

West Chisenbury

Wakefield W York 83 3320
Wakerley Nhants 51 9599
Wakes Colne Essex 40 8928
Wal-wen Flints 70 2076
Wal-wen Flints 70 2076
Walberswick Suffk 55 4974
Walberton W Susx 14 9705
Walbottle T & W 103 1666
Walbutt D & G 99 7468
Walby Cumb 101 4460
Walcombe Somset 21 5546
Walcot Lincs 84 8720
Walcot Lincs 64 0635
Walcot Shrops 59 5912
Walcot Shrops 59 3485
Walcot Warwks 48 1358
Walcot Wilts 36 1684
Walcot Green Norfk 54 1280
Walcote Leics 50 5683
Walcott Lincs 76 1356
Walcott Norfk 67 3532
Walden N York 88 0082
Walden Head N York 88 9880
Walden Stubbs N York 83 5516
Walderslade Kent 28 7663
Walderton W Susx 14 7910
Walditch Dorset 10 4892
Waldley Derbys 73 1236
Waldridge Dur 96 2549
Waldringfield Suffk 55 2845
Waldron E Susx 16 5419
Wales S York 75 4882
Wales Somset 21 5824
Walesby Lincs 76 1392
Walesby Notts 75 6870
Walford Herefs 46 3872
Walford Herefs 34 5820
Walford Shrops 59 4320
Walford Staffs 72 8133
Walford Heath Shrops 59 4419
Walgherton Ches 72 6948
Walgrave Nhants 51 8071
Walhampton Hants 12 3396
Walk Mill Lancs 81 8729
Walkden Gt Man 79 7302
Walker T & W 103 2864
Walker Fold Lancs 81 6741
Walker's Green Herefs 46 5247
Walker's Heath W Mids 61 0578
Walkerburn Border 109 3637
Walkeringham Notts 75 7792
Walkerith Lincs 75 7892
Walkern Herts 39 2826
Walkerton Fife 126 2301
Walkford Dorset 12 2194
Walkhampton Devon 6 5369
Walkington E R Yk 84 9936
Walkley S York 74 3388
Walkwood Worcs 48 0364
Wall Cnwll 2 6036
Wall Nthumb 102 9168
Wall Staffs 61 1006
Wall End Cumb 86 2383
Wall End Herefs 46 4457
Wall Heath W Mids 60 8889
Wall Houses Nthumb 103 0368
Wall under Haywood Shrops 59 5092
Wallacetown S Ayrs 106 2703
Wallacetown S Ayrs 106 3422
Wallands Park E Susx 15 4010
Wallasey Mersyd 78 2992
Wallend Kent 28 8775
Waller's Green Herefs 47 6739
Wallhead Cumb 101 4660
Wallingford Oxon 37 6089
Wallington Gt Lon 27 2864
Wallington Hants 13 5806
Wallington Herts 39 2933
Wallington Heath W Mids 60 9903
Wallis Pembks 30 0125
Wallisdown Dorset 12 0694
Walliswood W Susx 14 1138
Walls Shet 153 2449
Wallsend T & W 103 2966
Wallthwaite Cumb 93 3526
Wallyford E Loth 118 3671
Walmer Kent 29 3750
Walmer Bridge Lancs 80 4724
Walmersley Gt Man 81 8013
Walmestone Kent 29 2559
Walmley W Mids 61 1393
Walmley Ash W Mids 61 1492
Walmsgate Lincs 77 3677
Walpole Somset 20 3042
Walpole Suffk 55 3674
Walpole Cross Keys Norfk 65 5119
Walpole Highway Norfk 65 5114
Walpole St Andrew Norfk 65 5017
Walpole St Peter Norfk 65 5016
Walrow Somset 21 3447
Walsall W Mids 60 0198
Walsall Wood W Mids 61 0403
Walsden W York 81 9321
Walsgrave on Sowe W Mids 61 3881
Walsham le Willows Suffk 54 0071
Walshaw Gt Man 81 7711
Walshaw W York 82 9731
Walshford N York 83 4153
Walsoken Norfk 65 4710
Walston S Lans 117 0545
Walsworth Herts 39 1930
Walter's Ash Bucks 37 8398
Walters Green Kent 16 5140
Walterston V Glam 33 0671
Walterstone Herefs 46 3425
Waltham Kent 29 1048
Waltham Lincs 85 2603
Waltham Abbey Essex 27 3800
Waltham Chase Hants 13 5614
Waltham Cross Herts 27 3600
Waltham on the Wolds Leics 63 8024
Waltham St Lawrence Berks 37 8276
Waltham's Cross Essex 40 6930
Walton Bucks 38 8936
Walton Cambs 64 1702
Walton Cumb 101 5264
Walton Derbys 74 3568
Walton Leics 50 5987
Walton Powys 46 2559
Walton Shrops 59 5818
Walton Shrops 46 4679
Walton Somset 21 4636
Walton Staffs 72 8528
Walton Staffs 72 8932
Walton Suffk 55 2935
Walton W Susx 14 8104
Walton W York 83 3516
Walton W York 83 4447
Walton Warwks 48 2853
Walton Cardiff Gloucs 47 9032
Walton East Pembks 30 0223
Walton Elm Dorset 11 7717
Walton Grounds Nhants 49 5135
Walton on the Hill Surrey 26 2255
Walton on the Naze Essex 41 2522
Walton on the Wolds Leics 62 5919
Walton Park Somset 34 4172
Walton West Pembks 30 8612
Walton-in-Gordano Somset 34 4273
Walton-le-Dale Lancs 81 5628
Walton-on-Thames Surrey 26 1066
Walton-on-the-Hill Staffs 72 9520
Walton-on-Trent Derbys 73 2118
Walwen Flints 70 1771
Walwick Nthumb 102 9070
Walworth Dur 96 2318
Walworth Gt Lon 27 3277
Walworth Gate Dur 96 2320
Walwyn's Castle Pembks 30 8711
Wambrook Somset 10 2907
Wampool Cumb 93 2454
Wanborough Surrey 25 9348
Wanborough Wilts 36 2082
Wandon End Herts 38 1322
Wandsworth Gt Lon 27 2574
Wangford Suffk 55 4679
Wanlip Leics 62 5910
Wanlockhead D & G 108 8712
Wannock E Susx 16 5703
Wansford Cambs 64 0799
Wansford E R Yk 84 0656
Wanshurst Green Kent 28 7645
Wanstead Gt Lon 27 4088
Wanstrow Somset 22 7141
Wanswell Gloucs 35 6801
Wantage Oxon 36 3988
Wants Green Worcs 47 7557
Wapley Gloucs 35 7179
Wappenbury Warwks 48 3769
Wappenham Nhants 49 6245
Warbleton E Susx 16 6018
Warborough Oxon 37 5993
Warboys Cambs 52 3080
Warbreck Lancs 80 3238
Warbstow Cnwll 5 2090
Warburton Gt Man 79 7089
Warcop Cumb 94 7415
Ward End W Mids 61 1188
Ward Green Suffk 54 0464
Warden Kent 28 0271
Warden Nthumb 102 9166
Warden Law T & W 96 3649
Warden Street Beds 38 1244
Wardhedges Beds 38 0635
Wardington Oxon 49 4846
Wardle Ches 71 6156
Wardle Gt Man 81 9116
Wardley Gt Man 79 7602
Wardley Rutlnd 51 8300
Wardley T & W 96 3061
Wardlow Derbys 74 1874
Wardsend Ches 79 9382
Wardy Hill Cambs 53 4782
Ware Herts 39 3514
Ware Street Kent 28 7956
Wareham Dorset 11 9287
Warehorne Kent 17 9832
Waren Mill Nthumb 111 1434
Warenford Nthumb 111 1328
Warenton Nthumb 111 1030
Wareside Herts 39 3915
Waresley Cambs 52 2554
Waresley Worcs 60 8470
Warfield Berks 25 8872
Warfleet Devon 7 8750
Wargate Lincs 64 2330
Wargrave Berks 37 7978
Warham Herefs 46 4838
Warham All Saints Norfk 66 9541
Warham St Mary Norfk 66 9441
Wark Nthumb 110 8238
Wark Nthumb 102 8577
Warkleigh Devon 19 6422
Warkton Nhants 51 8979
Warkworth Nhants 49 4840
Warkworth Nthumb 111 2406
Warlaby N York 89 3491
Warland W York 82 9420
Warleggan Cnwll 4 1569
Warleigh Somset 22 7964
Warley Town W York 82 0524
Warlingham Surrey 27 3658
Warmanbie D & G 101 1969
Warmbrook Derbys 73 2853
Warmfield W York 83 3720
Warmingham Ches 72 7061
Warmington Nhants 51 0790
Warmington Warwks 49 4147
Warminster Wilts 22 8745
Warmley Gloucs 35 6673
Warmsworth S York 75 5400
Warmwell Dorset 11 7585
Warndon Worcs 47 8856
Warnford Hants 13 6223
Warnham W Susx 15 1533
Warnham Court W Susx 15 1533
Warningcamp W Susx 14 0307
Warninglid W Susx 15 2426
Warren Ches 79 8870
Warren Pembks 30 9397
Warren Row Berks 37 8180
Warren Street Kent 28 9252
Warren's Green Herts 39 2628
Warrenby N York 97 5825
Warrenhill S Lans 108 9438
Warrington Bucks 51 8953
Warrington Ches 78 6088
Warriston C Edin 117 2575
Warsash Hants 13 4906
Warslow Staffs 74 0858
Warsop Notts 75 5667
Warsop Vale Notts 75 5467
Warter E R Yk 84 8750
Warter Priory E R Yk 84 8449
Warthermaske N York 89 2078
Warthill N York 83 6755
Wartling E Susx 16 6509
Wartnaby Leics 63 7123
Warton Lancs 80 4128
Warton Lancs 87 4972
Warton Nthumb 103 0002
Warton Warwks 61 2803
Warwick Cumb 93 4656
Warwick Warwks 48 2865
Warwick Bridge Cumb 93 4756
Warwick Castle 48 2864
Warwicksland Cumb 101 4577
Wasbister Ork 153 3932
Wasdale Head Cumb 86 1808
Wash Derbys 74 0682
Wash Devon 7 7665
Washall Green Herts 39 4430
Washaway Cnwll 4 0369
Washbourne Devon 7 7954
Washbrook Somset 21 4250
Washbrook Suffk 54 1142
Washfield Devon 9 9315
Washfold N York 88 0502
Washford Somset 20 0541
Washford Pyne Devon 19 8111
Washingborough Lincs 76 0170
Washington T & W 96 3155
Washington W Susx 14 1112
Washwood Heath W Mids 61 1088
Wasing Berks 24 5764
Waskerley Dur 95 0445
Wasperton Warwks 48 2658
Wasps Nest Lincs 76 0764
Wass N York 90 5579
Watchet Somset 20 0743
Watchfield Oxon 36 2490
Watchfield Somset 21 3446
Watchgate Cumb 87 5398
Watchill Cumb 93 1842
Watcombe Devon 7 9267
Watendlath Cumb 93 2716
Water Devon 8 7580
Water Lancs 81 8425
Water Eaton Oxon 37 5112
Water Eaton Staffs 60 9011
Water End Beds 38 0637
Water End Beds 38 1047
Water End Beds 38 1051
Water End E R Yk 84 7938
Water End Essex 53 5840
Water End Herts 38 0310
Water End Herts 39 2304
Water Fryston W York 83 4726
Water Newton Cambs 51 1097
Water Orton Warwks 61 1790
Water Stratford Bucks 49 6534
Water Street Neath 32 8083
Water Yeat Cumb 86 2889
Water's Nook Gt Man 79 6605
Waterbeach Cambs 53 4965
Waterbeach W Susx 14 8908
Waterbeck D & G 101 2477
Watercombe Dorset 11 7585
Waterden Norfk 66 8836
Waterend Cumb 92 1122
Waterfall Staffs 73 0851
Waterfoot Lancs 81 8321
Waterfoot S Lans 115 5655
Waterford Herts 39 3114
Watergate Cnwll 4 1181
Waterhead Cumb 87 3703
Waterhead E Ayrs 107 5411
Waterheads Border 117 2451
Waterhouses Dur 96 1841
Waterhouses Staffs 73 0850
Wateringbury Kent 28 6853
Waterlane Gloucs 35 9204
Waterloo Cnwll 4 1072
Waterloo Derbys 74 4163
Waterloo Dorset 11 0193
Waterloo Herefs 46 3447
Waterloo Highld 129 6623
Waterloo Mersyd 78 3298
Waterloo N Lans 116 8154
Waterloo Norfk 67 2219
Waterloo P & K 125 0537
Waterloo Pembks 30 9803
Waterloo Cross Devon 9 0514
Waterloo Port Gwynd 68 4964
Waterlooville Hants 13 6809
Watermillock Cumb 93 4422
Waterperry Oxon 37 6206
Waterrow Somset 20 0525
Waters Upton Shrops 59 6319
Watersfield W Susx 14 0115
Waterside Bucks 26 9600
Waterside Cumb 93 2245
Waterside E Ayrs 107 4308
Waterside E Ayrs 107 4843
Waterside E Duns 116 6773
Waterside Lancs 81 7123
Waterside S York 83 6714
Waterstein Highld 136 1348
Waterstock Oxon 37 6305
Waterston Pembks 30 9305
Watford Herts 26 1196
Watford Nhants 50 6069
Wath N York 89 1467
Wath N York 89 3277
Wath upon Dearne S York 75 4300
Watlington Norfk 65 6111
Watlington Oxon 37 6894
Watnall Notts 62 5046
Watten Highld 151 2454
Wattisfield Suffk 54 0074
Wattisham Suffk 54 0151
Watton Dorset 10 4591
Watton E R Yk 84 0150
Watton Norfk 66 9100
Watton Green Norfk 66 9201
Watton-at-Stone Herts 39 3019
Wattons Green Essex 27 5295
Wattston N Lans 116 7770
Wattstown Rhondd 33 0193
Wattsville Caerph 33 2091
Wauldby E R Yk 84 9629
Waulkmill Abers 135 6492
Waunarlwydd Swans 32 6095
Waunfawr Cerdgn 43 6081
Waunfawr Gwynd 68 5259
Waungron Swans 32 5901
Waunlwyd Blae G 33 1806
Wavendon Bucks 38 9137
Waverbridge Cumb 93 2249
Waverton Ches 71 4663
Waverton Cumb 93 2247
Wawne E R Yk 85 0936
Waxham Norfk 67 4426
Waxholme E R Yk 85 3229
Way Kent 29 3265
Way Village Devon 19 8810
Way Wick Somset 21 3862
Waye Devon 7 7771
Wayford Somset 10 4006
Waytown Dorset 10 4797
Weacombe Somset 20 1140
Weald Oxon 36 3002
Wealdstone Gt Lon 26 1589
Weardley W York 82 2944
Weare Somset 21 4152
Weare Giffard Devon 18 4721
Wearhead Dur 95 8539
Wearne Somset 21 4228
Weasdale Cumb 87 6903
Weasenham All Saints Norfk 66 8421
Weasenham St Peter Norfk 66 8522
Weaste Gt Man 79 8098
Weatheroak Hill Worcs 61 0674
Weaverham Ches 71 6174
Weaverslake Staffs 73 1319
Weaverthorpe N York 91 9670
Webb's Heath Gloucs 35 6873
Webbington Somset 21 3855
Webheath Worcs 48 0266
Webton Herefs 46 4136
Wedderlairs Abers 143 8532
Wedding Hall Fold N York 82 9445
Weddington Kent 29 2959
Weddington Warwks 61 3693
Wedhampton Wilts 23 0557
Wedmore Somset 21 4347
Wednesbury W Mids 60 9895
Wednesfield W Mids 60 9400
Weecar Notts 75 8266
Weedon Bucks 38 8118
Weedon Nhants 49 6359
Weedon Lois Nhants 49 6046
Weeford Staffs 61 1403
Week Devon 19 5727
Week Devon 19 7316
Week Devon 7 7862
Week Somset 20 9133
Week St Mary Cnwll 5 2397
Weeke Devon 8 7606
Weeke Hants 24 4630
Weekley Nhants 51 8881
Weel E R Yk 84 0639
Weeley Essex 41 1422
Weeley Heath Essex 41 1520
Weem P & K 125 8449
Weeping Cross Staffs 72 9421
Weethley Warwks 48 0555
Weeting Norfk 53 7788
Weeton E R Yk 85 3520
Weeton Lancs 80 3834
Weeton N York 82 2847
Weetwood W York 82 2737
Weir Lancs 81 8625
Weir Quay Devon 6 4365
Weirbrook Shrops 59 3424
Welbeck Abbey Notts 75 5574
Welborne Norfk 66 0610
Welbourn Lincs 76 9654
Welburn N York 90 7267
Welbury N York 89 3902
Welby Lincs 63 9738
Welches Dam Cambs 53 4686
Welcombe Devon 18 2318
Weldon Bridge Nthumb 103 1398
Welford Berks 24 4073
Welford Nhants 50 6480
Welford-on-Avon Warwks 48 1452
Welham Leics 50 7692
Welham Notts 75 7281
Welham Green Herts 39 2305
Well Hants 24 7646
Well Lincs 77 4473
Well N York 89 2681
Well End Bucks 26 8888
Well End Herts 26 2098
Well Fold W York 82 2024
Well Head Herts 39 1727
Well Hill Kent 27 4963
Well Town Devon 9 9009
Welland Worcs 47 7940
Welland Stone Worcs 47 8138
Wellbank Angus 127 4737
Wellbury Herts 38 1329
Wellesbourne Warwks 48 2855
Wellesbourne
Mountford Warwks 48 2755
Wellhouse Berks 24 5272
Welling Gt Lon 27 4675
Wellingborough Nhants 51 8967
Wellingham Norfk 66 8722
Wellingore Lincs 76 9856
Wellington Cumb 86 0704
Wellington Herefs 46 4948
Wellington Shrops 59 6511
Wellington Somset 20 1320
Wellington Heath Herefs 47 7140
Wellington Marsh Herefs 46 4946
Wellow IOW 12 3888
Wellow Notts 75 6766
Wellow Somset 22 7458
Wellpond Green Herts 39 4122
Wells Somset 21 5445
Wells Green Ches 72 6853
Wells Head W York 82 0833
Wells-next-the-sea Norfk 66 9143
Wellsborough Leics 62 3602
Wellstye Green Essex 40 6318
Welltree P & K 125 9622
Wellwood Fife 117 0988
Welney Norfk 65 5293
Welsh Bicknor Herefs 34 5917
Welsh End Shrops 59 5135
Welsh Frankton Shrops 59 3533
Welsh Hook Pembks 30 9327
Welsh Newton Herefs 34 5017
Welsh St Donats V Glam 33 0276
Welshampton Shrops 59 4335
Welshpool Powys 58 2207
Welton Cumb 93 3544
Welton E R Yk 84 9627
Welton Lincs 76 0179
Welton Nhants 50 5865
Welton le Marsh Lincs 77 4768
Welton le Wold Lincs 77 2787
Welwick E R Yk 85 3421
Welwyn Herts 39 2316
Welwyn Garden City Herts 39 2312
Wem Shrops 59 5128
Wembdon Somset 20 2837
Wembley Gt Lon 26 1885
Wembury Devon 6 5248
Wembworthy Devon 19 6609
Wemyss Bay Inver 114 1969
Wenallt Cerdgn 43 6771
Wendens Ambo Essex 39 5136
Wendlebury Oxon 37 5619
Wendling Norfk 66 9312
Wendover Bucks 38 8607
Wendron Cnwll 2 6731
Wendy Cambs 52 3247
Wenfordbridge Cnwll 4 0875
Wenhaston Suffk 55 4275
Wennington Cambs 52 2379
Wennington Gt Lon 27 5381
Wennington Lancs 87 6170
Wensley Derbys 74 2661
Wensley N York 89 0989
Wentbridge W York 83 4817
Wentnor Shrops 59 3892
Wentworth Cambs 53 4878
Wentworth S York 74 3898
Wentworth Castle S York 83 3202
Wenvoe V Glam 33 1272
Weobley Herefs 46 4051
Weobley Marsh Herefs 46 4151
Wepham W Susx 14 0408
Wereham Norfk 65 6801
Wergs Staffs 60 8700
Wern Gwynd 57 5439
Wern Powys 58 9612
Wern Powys 58 2513
Wern Powys 33 1217
Wern Shrops 58 2734
Wern-y-gaer Flints 70 2068
Werneth Low Gt Man 79 9592
Wernffrwd Swans 32 5194
Werrington Cambs 64 1603
Werrington Cnwll 5 3287
Werrington Staffs 72 9447
Wervin Ches 71 4271
Wesham Lancs 80 4133
Wessington Derbys 74 3757
West Aberthaw V Glam 20 0266
West Acre Norfk 65 7815
West Allerdean Nthumb 111 9646
West Alvington Devon 7 7243
West Amesbury Wilts 23 1341
West Anstey Devon 19 8527
West Appleton N York 89 2294
West Ashby Lincs 77 2672
West Ashling W Susx 14 8107
West Ashton Wilts 22 8755
West Auckland Dur 96 1826
West Ayton N York 91 9884
West Bagborough Somset 20 1733
West Balsdon Cnwll 5 2798
West Bank Blae G 33 2105
West Bank Ches 78 5183
West Barkwith Lincs 76 1580
West Barnby N York 90 8212
West Barns E Loth 118 6578
West Barsham Norfk 66 9033
West Bay Dorset 10 4690
West Beckham Norfk 66 1439
West Bedfont Surrey 26 0674
West Bergholt Essex 40 9527
West Bexington Dorset 10 5386
West Bilney Norfk 65 7115
West Blatchington E Susx 15 2707
West Boldon T & W 96 3561
West Bourton Dorset 22 7629
West Bowling W York 82 1630
West Brabourne Kent 29 0842
West Bradenham Norfk 66 9108
West Bradford Lancs 81 7444
West Bradley Somset 21 5536
West Bretton W York 82 2813
West Bridgford Notts 62 5836
West Briscoe Dur 95 9619
West Bromwich W Mids 60 0091
West Buccleuch Hotel Border 109 3214
West Buckland Devon 19 6531
West Buckland Somset 20 1720
West Burton N York 88 0186
West Burton W Susx 14 9914
West Butsfield Dur 95 1044
West Butterwick Lincs 84 8305
West Byfleet Surrey 26 0461
West Cairngaan D & G 98 1231
West Caister Norfk 67 5011
West Calder W Loth 117 0163
West Camel Somset 21 5724
West Chaldon Dorset 11 7782
West Challow Oxon 36 3688
West Charleton Devon 7 7542
West Chelborough Dorset 10 5405
West Chevington Nthumb 103 2297
West Chiltington W Susx 14 0818
West Chinnock Somset 10 4613
West Chisenbury Wilts 23 1352

315

316

West Clandon Surrey 26 04 52
West Cliffe Kent 29 34 44
West Coker Somset 10 51 13
West Combe Devon 7 76 62
West Compton Somset 21 59 42
West Compton Abbas Dorset .. 10 56 94
West Cottingwith N York 83 69 42
West Cowick E R Yk 83 64 21
West Cross Swans 32 61 89
West Curry Cnwll 5 28 93
West Curthwaite Cumb 93 32 49
West Dean W Susx 14 86 12
West Dean Wilts 23 25 26
West Deeping Lincs 64 10 08
West Derby Mersyd 78 39 93
West Dereham Norfk 65 65 00
West Down Devon 19 51 42
West Drayton Gt Lon 26 05 79
West Drayton Notts 75 70 74
West Dunnet Highld 151 21 71
West Ella E R Yk 84 00 29
West End Beds 51 98 53
West End Berks 37 82 75
West End Berks 25 86 71
West End Caerph 33 21 95
West End Cambs 52 31 68
West End Cumb 93 32 58
West End E R Yk 84 91 30
West End E R Yk 85 18 30
West End E R Yk 85 26 27
West End Gloucs 35 71 88
West End Hants 13 46 14
West End Hants 24 63 35
West End Herts 39 26 08
West End Herts 39 33 06
West End Lancs 81 73 28
West End Lincs 77 35 98
West End N York 89 14 57
West End N York 83 51 40
West End Norfk 66 90 09
West End Nthumb 67 50 11
West End Oxon 37 58 86
West End Somset 21 45 69
West End Somset 22 67 34
West End Surrey 25 94 61
West End Surrey 26 12 63
West End W Susx 15 20 16
West End W York 82 22 38
West End Wilts 22 91 24
West End Wilts 35 97 77
West End Wilts 22 98 24
West End Green Hants 24 66 61
West Ewell Surrey 26 20 63
West Farleigh Kent 28 71 52
West Farndon Nhants 49 52 51
West Felton Shrops 59 34 25
West Firle E Susx 16 47 07
West Firsby Lincs 76 97 84
West Flotmanby N York 91 07 79
West Garforth W York 83 39 32
West Ginge Oxon 37 44 86
West Grafton Wilts 23 24 60
West Green Hants 24 74 56
West Grimstead Wilts 23 20 26
West Grinstead W Susx 15 18 22
West Haddlesey N York 83 56 26
West Haddon Nhants 50 63 71
West Hagbourne Oxon 37 51 87
West Hagley Worcs 60 90 80
West Hallam Derbys 62 43 41
West Hallam Common Derbys .. 62 42 41
West Halton Lincs 84 90 20
West Ham Gt Lon 27 39 83
West Handley Derbys 74 39 77
West Hanney Oxon 36 40 92
West Hanningfield Essex 40 73 99
West Harnham Wilts 23 13 29
West Harptree Somset 21 55 56
West Harting W Susx 14 78 20
West Hatch Somset 20 28 21
West Hatch Wilts 22 92 27
West Haven Angus 127 57 35
West Head Norfk 65 57 05
West Heath Hants 24 58 58
West Heath W Mids 60 02 77
West Helmsdale Highld 147 01 15
West Hendred Oxon 37 44 88
West Heslerton N York 91 91 76
West Hewish Somset 21 39 63
West Hill Devon 9 07 94
West Hoathly W Susx 15 36 32
West Holme Dorset 11 88 85
West Horndon Essex 40 62 88
West Horrington Somset 21 57 47
West Horsley Surrey 26 07 52
West Horton Nthumb 111 02 30
West Hougham Kent 29 26 40
West Howe Dorset 12 06 95
West Howetown Somset 20 91 34
West Huntingtower P & K 125 07 24
West Huntspill Somset 20 30 44
West Hyde Beds 38 11 17
West Hyde Herts 26 03 91
West Hythe Kent 17 12 34
West Ilkerton Devon 19 70 46
West Illsley Berks 37 47 82
West Itchenor W Susx 14 79 01
West Keal Lincs 77 36 63
West Kennett Wilts 23 11 68
West Kilbride N Ayrs 114 20 48
West Kingsdown Kent 27 57 61
West Kington Wilts 35 80 77
West Kirby Mersyd 78 21 86
West Knapton N York 90 87 75
West Knighton Dorset 11 73 87
West Knoyle Wilts 22 86 32
West Lambrook Somset 10 41 18
West Langdon Kent 29 32 47
West Laroch Highld 130 07 58
West Lavington W Susx 14 89 20
West Lavington Wilts 22 00 52
West Layton N York 89 14 10
West Leake Notts 62 52 26
West Learmouth Nthumb 110 84 37
West Lees N York 89 47 02
West Leigh Devon 8 68 05
West Leigh Devon 7 75 57
West Leigh Somset 20 12 30

West Lexham Norfk 66 84 17
West Lilling N York 90 64 65
West Linton Border 117 15 51
West Littleton Gloucs 35 76 75
West Lockinge Oxon 36 41 87
West Lulworth Dorset 11 82 80
West Lutton N York 91 93 69
West Lydford Somset 21 56 31
West Lyn Devon 19 72 48
West Lyng Somset 21 31 28
West Lynn Norfk 65 61 20
West Malling Kent 28 67 57
West Malvern Worcs 47 76 46
West Marden W Susx 14 77 13
West Markham Notts 75 72 72
West Marsh Lincs 85 25 09
West Marton N York 81 89 50
West Melbury Dorset 22 87 20
West Melton S York 83 42 01
West Meon Hants 13 64 23
West Meon Hut Hants 13 65 26
West Meon Woodlands Hants .. 13 64 26
West Mersea Essex 41 01 12
West Mickley Nthumb 103 06 61
West Midlands Safari Park 60 80 75
West Milton Dorset 10 50 96
West Minster Kent 28 90 73
West Molesey Surrey 26 13 68
West Monkton Somset 20 26 28
West Moors Dorset 12 08 02
West Morden Dorset 11 90 95
West Morriston Border 110 60 40
West Morton W York 82 09 42
West Mudford Somset 21 56 20
West Ness N York 90 68 79
West Newbiggin Dur 96 35 18
West Newton E R Yk 85 20 37
West Newton Norfk 65 69 28
West Newton Somset 20 28 29
West Norwood Gt Lon 27 31 71
West Ogwell Devon 7 82 70
West Orchard Dorset 11 82 16
West Overton Wilts 23 12 67
West Panson Devon 5 34 91
West Parley Dorset 12 08 96
West Peckham Kent 27 64 52
West Pelton Dur 96 23 53
West Pennard Somset 21 54 38
West Pentire Cnwll 4 77 60
West Perry Cambs 52 14 66
West Porlock Somset 19 87 47
West Prawle Devon 7 76 37
West Pulham Dorset 11 70 08
West Putford Devon 18 36 16
West Quantoxhead Somset 20 11 41
West Raddon Devon 9 89 02
West Rasen Lincs 76 06 89
West Ravendale Lincs 76 22 99
West Raynham Norfk 66 87 25
West Retford Notts 75 69 81
West Rounton N York 89 41 03
West Row Suffk 53 67 75
West Rudham Norfk 66 81 27
West Runton Norfk 66 18 42
West Saltoun E Loth 118 46 67
West Sandford Devon 8 81 02
West Sandwick Shet 153 45 88
West Scrafton N York 88 07 83
West Sleekburn Nthumb 103 28 84
West Somerton Norfk 67 46 20
West Stafford Dorset 11 72 89
West Stockwith Notts 75 78 95
West Stoke W Susx 14 82 08
West Stonesdale N York 88 88 01
West Stoughton Somset 21 41 48
West Stour Dorset 22 78 22
West Stourmouth Kent 29 25 62
West Stow Suffk 54 81 71
West Stowell Wilts 23 13 61
West Stratton Hants 24 52 40
West Street Kent 28 73 76
West Street Kent 28 90 54
West Street Kent 29 32 54
West Street Suffk 54 98 71
West Tanfield N York 89 26 78
West Taphouse Cnwll 4 14 63
West Tarbert Ag & B 113 84 67
West Tarring W Susx 14 11 03
West Thirston Nthumb 103 18 99
West Thorney W Susx 14 76 02
West Thorpe Notts 62 62 25
West Thurrock Essex 27 58 77
West Tilbury Essex 40 66 78
West Tisted Hants 24 65 29
West Torrington Lincs 76 13 81
West Town Hants 13 71 99
West Town Herefs 46 43 61
West Town Somset 21 48 68
West Town Somset 21 51 60
West Town Somset 21 53 35
West Town Somset 22 70 42
West Tytherley Hants 23 27 29
West Walton Norfk 65 46 13
West Walton Highway Norfk .. 65 49 13
West Wellow Hants 12 28 19
West Wembury Devon 6 52 49
West Wemyss Fife 118 32 94
West Wick Somset 21 37 61
West Wickham Cambs 53 61 49
West Wickham Gt Lon 27 36 66
West Williamston Pembks 30 03 05
West Winch Norfk 65 63 16
West Winterslow Wilts 23 23 31
West Wittering W Susx 14 78 98
West Witton N York 88 05 88
West Woodburn Nthumb 102 89 87
West Woodhay Berks 23 39 63
West Woodlands Somset 22 77 43
West Woodside Cumb 93 30 49
West Worldham Hants 24 74 36
West Worthing W Susx 15 13 02
West Wratting Essex 53 60 52
West Wycombe Bucks 37 82 94
West Wylam Nthumb 103 10 63
West Yatton Wilts 35 85 75
West Yoke Kent 27 60 65
West Youlstone Cnwll 18 26 15

Westbere Kent 29 19 61
Westborough Lincs 63 85 44
Westbourne Dorset 12 07 91
Westbourne W Susx 13 75 07
Westbrook Berks 24 42 72
Westbrook Kent 29 34 70
Westbrook Wilts 22 95 65
Westbury Bucks 49 62 35
Westbury Shrops 59 35 09
Westbury Wilts 22 87 51
Westbury Leigh Wilts 22 86 49
Westbury on Severn Gloucs 35 71 14
Westbury-on-Trym Bristl 34 57 77
Westbury-sub-Mendip Somset .. 21 50 49
Westby Lancs 80 38 31
Westcombe Somset 22 67 39
Westcote Gloucs 36 21 20
Westcott Bucks 37 71 16
Westcott Devon 9 02 04
Westcott Somset 19 87 20
Westcott Surrey 15 14 48
Westcourt Wilts 23 22 61
Westcott Barton Oxon 49 43 25
Westdean E Susx 16 52 99
Westdown Camp Wilts 23 04 47
Westdowns Cnwll 4 05 82
Wested Kent 27 51 66
Westend Gloucs 35 78 07
Westend Town Nthumb 102 78 65
Westenhanger Kent 29 12 37
Wester Drumashie Highld 140 60 32
Wester Ochiltree W Loth 117 03 74
Wester Pitkierie Fife 127 55 05
Westerdale Highld 151 12 51
Westerdale N York 90 66 05
Westerfield Suffk 54 17 47
Westergate W Susx 14 93 05
Westerham Kent 27 44 54
Westerhope T & W 103 19 66
Westerland Devon 7 86 62
Westerleigh Gloucs 35 69 79
Westerton Angus 127 64 54
Westerton W Susx 14 88 07
Westfield E Susx 17 81 15
Westfield Highld 150 06 64
Westfield N Lans 116 72 73
Westfield Norfk 66 99 09
Westfield Somset 22 67 53
Westfield W Loth 116 94 72
Westfield Sole Kent 28 77 61
Westfields Dorset 11 72 06
Westfields Herefs 46 49 41
Westfields of Rattray P & K .. 126 17 46
Westford Somset 20 12 20
Westgate Dur 95 90 38
Westgate Lincs 84 77 07
Westgate Norfk 66 97 40
Westgate Hill W York 82 20 29
Westgate on Sea Kent 29 32 70
Westgate Street Norfk 67 19 21
Westhall Suffk 55 42 80
Westham Dorset 11 66 79
Westham E Susx 16 64 04
Westham Somset 21 40 46
Westhampnett W Susx 14 88 06
Westhay Somset 21 43 42
Westhide Herefs 46 58 43
Westhill Abers 135 83 07
Westholme Somset 21 57 41
Westhope Herefs 46 46 51
Westhope Shrops 59 47 86
Westhorp Nhants 49 51 52
Westhorpe Lincs 64 22 31
Westhorpe Suffk 54 04 68
Westhoughton Gt Man 79 65 06
Westhouse N York 87 67 73
Westhouses Derbys 74 41 57
Westhumble Surrey 26 16 51
Westlake Devon 6 62 53
Westland Green Herts 39 42 22
Westleigh Devon 18 47 28
Westleigh Devon 9 06 17
Westleton Suffk 55 43 69
Westley Shrops 59 36 07
Westley Suffk 54 82 64
Westley Waterless Cambs 53 61 56
Westlington Bucks 37 76 10
Westlinton Cumb 101 39 64
Westmarsh Kent 29 27 61
Westmeston E Susx 15 33 13
Westmill Herts 39 36 27
Westminster Gt Lon 27 29 79
Westmuir Angus 126 36 52
Westnewton Cumb 92 13 44
Westoe T & W 103 37 65
Weston Berks 36 39 73
Weston Ches 78 50 80
Weston Ches 72 73 52
Weston Devon 9 14 00
Weston Devon 9 16 88
Weston Dorset 11 68 71
Weston Hants 13 72 21
Weston Herefs 46 36 56
Weston Herts 39 25 30
Weston Lincs 64 29 24
Weston N York 82 14 47
Weston Nhants 49 58 46
Weston Notts 75 76 67
Weston Shrops 59 60 93
Weston Shrops 59 29 27
Weston Shrops 46 32 73
Weston Somset 22 72 66
Weston Staffs 72 97 26
Weston Beggard Herefs 46 58 41
Weston by Welland Nhants .. 50 77 91
Weston Colley Hants 24 50 39
Weston Colville Cambs 53 61 53
Weston Corbett Hants 24 68 46
Weston Coyney Staffs 72 93 43
Weston Favell Nhants 50 79 62
Weston Green Cambs 53 62 52
Weston Heath Shrops 60 77 13
Weston Hills Lincs 64 27 20
Weston in Arden Warwks 61 38 86
Weston Jones Staffs 72 76 24

Weston Longville Norfk 66 11 15
Weston Lullingfields Shrops 59 42 24
Weston Patrick Hants 24 69 46
Weston Rhyn Shrops 58 28 35
Weston Subedge Gloucs 48 12 41
Weston Turville Bucks 38 85 10
Weston under Penyard Herefs .. 35 63 22
Weston under
  Wetherley Warwks 48 36 69
Weston Underwood Bucks 38 86 50
Weston Underwood Derbys 73 29 42
Weston-in-Gordano Somset 34 44 74
Weston-on-the-Green Oxon 37 53 18
Weston-Super-Mare Somset 21 32 60
Weston-under-Lizard Staffs 60 80 10
Weston-under-Redcastle Shrops .. 59 56 29
Weston-upon-Trent Derbys 62 40 27
Westonbirt Gloucs 35 85 89
Westoning Beds 38 03 32
Westoning Woodend Beds 38 02 32
Westonzoyland Somset 21 35 34
Westow N York 90 75 65
Westpeek Devon 5 34 93
Westport Somset 21 38 20
Westquarter Falk 116 91 78
Westra V Glam 33 14 70
Westray Airport 153 46 51
Westridge Green Berks 37 56 79
Westrigg W Loth 116 90 67
Westrop Wilts 36 20 93
Westruther Border 110 63 49
Westry Cambs 65 40 98
Westthorpe Derbys 75 45 79
Westward Cumb 93 27 44
Westward Ho! Devon 18 43 29
Westwell Kent 28 99 47
Westwell Oxon 36 22 09
Westwell Leacon Kent 28 96 47
Westwick Cambs 53 42 65
Westwick Dur 95 07 15
Westwick Norfk 67 27 26
Westwood Devon 9 01 99
Westwood Kent 27 60 70
Westwood Kent 29 36 67
Westwood Notts 75 45 51
Westwood Nthumb 102 77 65
Westwood Wilts 22 80 59
Westwood Heath W Mids 61 27 76
Westwoodside Lincs 75 74 00
Wetham Green Kent 28 84 68
Wetherby W York 83 40 48
Wetherden Suffk 54 00 62
Wetheringsett Suffk 54 12 66
Wethersfield Essex 40 71 31
Wetherup Street Suffk 54 14 64
Wetley Rocks Staffs 72 96 49
Wettenhall Ches 71 62 61
Wetton Staffs 73 10 55
Wetwang E R Yk 91 93 59
Wetwood Staffs 72 77 33
Wexcombe Wilts 23 27 58
Wexham Bucks 26 98 82
Wexham Street Bucks 26 98 83
Weybourne Norfk 66 11 42
Weybread Suffk 55 24 80
Weybread Street Suffk 55 24 79
Weybridge Surrey 26 07 64
Weycroft Devon 10 30 99
Weydale Highld 151 15 64
Weyhill Hants 23 31 46
Weymouth Dorset 11 67 79
Whaddon Bucks 38 80 34
Whaddon Cambs 52 35 46
Whaddon Gloucs 35 83 13
Whaddon Gloucs 35 84 06
Whaddon Wilts 22 88 61
Whaddon Wilts 23 19 26
Whale Cumb 94 52 21
Whaley Derbys 75 51 71
Whaley Bridge Derbys 79 01 80
Whaley Thorns Derbys 75 52 71
Whaligoe Highld 151 31 40
Whalley Lancs 81 73 36
Whalley Banks Lancs 81 73 35
Whalton Nthumb 96 13 18
Whaplode Lincs 64 32 24
Whaplode Drove Lincs 64 32 13
Wharf Warwks 49 43 52
Wharfe N York 88 78 69
Wharles Lancs 80 44 35
Wharley End Beds 38 94 42
Wharncliffe Side S York 74 29 94
Wharram-le-Street N York 90 86 65
Wharton Ches 72 66 66
Wharton Herefs 46 50 55
Whashton N York 89 15 06
Whashton Green N York 89 14 05
Whasset Cumb 87 50 80
Whatcote Warwks 48 29 44
Whateley Warwks 61 22 99
Whatfield Suffk 54 02 46
Whatley Somset 10 36 07
Whatley Somset 22 73 47
Whatley's End Gloucs 35 65 81
Whatlington E Susx 17 76 18
Whatsole Street Kent 29 11 44
Whatstandwell Derbys 74 33 54
Whatton Notts 63 74 39
Whauphill D & G 99 40 49
Whaw N York 88 98 04
Wheal Rose Cnwll 2 71 44
Wheatacre Norfk 67 46 94
Wheatfield Oxon 37 68 99
Wheathampstead Herts 39 17 14
Wheathill Shrops 59 62 82
Wheathill Somset 21 58 30
Wheatley Hants 25 78 40
Wheatley Oxon 37 59 05
Wheatley W York 82 07 26
Wheatley Hill Dur 96 37 38
Wheatley Hills S York 83 59 04
Wheatley Lane Lancs 81 83 37
Wheaton Aston Staffs 60 85 12
Wheatsheaf Wrexhm 71 34 53
Wheddon Cross Somset 20 92 38
Wheel Inn Cnwll 2 69 21
Wheelbarrow Town Kent 29 14 45

Wheeler's Green Oxon 24 76 7
Wheeler's Street Kent 28 84 4
Wheelerend Common Bucks .. 37 80 9
Wheelerstreet Surrey 25 94 4
Wheelock Ches 72 75 5
Wheelock Heath Ches 72 75 5
Wheelton Lancs 81 60 2
Wheldale W York 83 45 2
Wheldrake N York 83 68 4
Whelford Gloucs 36 16 9
Whelpley Hill Bucks 38 99 0
Whelpo Cumb 93 31 3
Whelston Flints 70 20 7
Whempstead Herts 39 32 2
Whenby N York 90 63 6
Whepstead Suffk 54 83 5
Wherstead Suffk 42 14 0
Wherwell Hants 23 38 4
Wheston Derbys 74 13 7
Whetsted Kent 28 66 4
Whetstone Gt Lon 27 26 9
Whetstone Leics 50 55 9
Wheyrigg Cumb 93 19 4
Whicham Cumb 86 13 8
Whichford Warwks 48 31 3
Whickham T & W 96 20 6
Whiddon Devon 18 47 9
Whiddon Down Devon 8 69 9
Whight's Corner Suffk 54 12 4
Whigstreet Angus 127 48 4
Whilton Nhants 49 63 0
Whimble Devon 18 35 0
Whimple Devon 9 04 9
Whimpwell Green Norfk 67 38 2
Whin Lane End Lancs 80 39 4
Whinburgh Norfk 66 00 0
Whinnie Liggate D & G 99 72 5
Whinnow Cumb 93 30 5
Whinny Hill Dur 96 38 1
Whinnyfold Abers 143 07 3
Whippingham IOW 13 51 9
Whipsnade Beds 38 01 1
Whipsnade Wild Animal Park 38 00 1
Whipton Devon 9 94 9
Whirlow S York 74 31 8
Whisby Lincs 76 90 6
Whissendine Rutlnd 63 82 1
Whissonsett Norfk 66 91 2
Whistlefield Ag & B 114 23 9
Whistlefield Inn Ag & B 114 14 6
Whistley Green Berks 25 79 2
Whiston Mersyd 78 47 9
Whiston Nhants 51 84 6
Whiston S York 75 44 8
Whiston Staffs 60 89 1
Whiston Staffs 73 03 4
Whiston Cross Shrops 60 79 0
Whiston Eaves Staffs 73 04 4
Whitacre Fields Warwks 78 46 6
Whitbeck Cumb 86 11 8
Whitbourne Herefs 47 72 5
Whitburn T & W 96 40 6
Whitburn W Loth 116 94 0
Whitby Ches 71 39 7
Whitby N York 91 89 9
Whitbyheath Ches 71 39 7
Whitchester Border 119 71 8
Whitchurch Bucks 38 80 2
Whitchurch Cardif 33 15 7
Whitchurch Devon 6 49 7
Whitchurch Hants 24 46 4
Whitchurch Herefs 34 55 5
Whitchurch Oxon 37 63 7
Whitchurch Pembks 30 80 1
Whitchurch Shrops 71 53 4
Whitchurch Somset 21 61 8
Whitchurch
  Canonicorum Dorset 10 39 9
Whitchurch Hill Oxon 37 63 7
Whitcombe Dorset 11 71 8
Whitcot Shrops 59 37 8
Whitcott Keysett Shrops 58 27 7
White Ball Somset 20 10 1
White Chapel Lancs 81 55 4
White Chapel Worcs 48 07 6
White Colne Essex 40 87 3
White Coppice Lancs 81 61 1
White Cross Cnwll 2 68 3
White End Worcs 47 78 3
White Kirkley Dur 95 02 3
White Lackington Dorset 11 71 0
White Ladies Aston Worcs 47 92 5
White Mill Carmth 32 46 6
White Notley Essex 40 78 2
White Ox Mead Somset 22 72 6
White Pit Lincs 77 37 7
White Roding Essex 40 56 0
White Stake Lancs 80 51 1
White Stone Herefs 46 56 6
White Waltham Berks 26 85 7
White-le-Head Dur 96 16 8
Whiteacre Kent 29 11 4
Whiteacre Heath Warwks 61 22 9
Whiteash Green Essex 40 79 3
Whitebirk Lancs 81 70 5
Whitebridge Highld 139 48 8
Whitebrook Mons 34 53 8
Whitecairns Abers 143 92 5
Whitechapel Gt Lon 27 33 8
Whitechurch Pembks 31 15 6
Whitecliffe Gloucs 34 56 9
Whitecraig E Loth 118 34 3
Whitecroft Gloucs 35 62 5
Whitecrook D & G 98 16 6
Whitecross Cnwll 2 52 9
Whitecross Cnwll 4 96 7
Whitecross Falk 117 96 7
Whiteface Highld 146 70 7
Whitefarland N Ayrs 105 86 7
Whitefaulds S Ayrs 106 29 1
Whitefield Devon 19 70 9
Whitefield Gt Man 79 80 8
Whitefield Somset 20 07 7
Whitefield Lane End Mersyd .. 78 45 9
Whiteford Abers 142 71 9
Whitegate Ches 71 62 6
Whitehall Hants 24 74 7

Vhitehall Wood Street

317

hitehall Ork 153 6528
hitehall W Susx 15 1321
hitehaven Cumb 92 9718
hitehill Hants 14 7934
hitehill Kent 28 0059
hitehill Leics 62 4211
hitehills Abers 142 6565
hitehouse Abers 142 6114
hitehouse Ag & B 113 8161
hitehouse Common W Mids 61 1397
hitekirk E Loth 118 5981
hitelackington Somset 10 3815
hiteley Hants 13 5209
hiteley Bank IOW 13 5581
hiteley Green Ches 79 9278
hiteley Village Surrey 26 0962
hitemans Green W Susx 15 3025
hitemire Moray 140 9854
hitemoor Cnwll 4 9757
hitemoor Derbys 62 3647
hitemoor Notts 62 5441
hitemoor Staffs 72 8861
hitenap Hants 12 3620
hiteness Shet 153 3844
hiteoak Green Oxon 36 3414
hiteparish Wilts 23 2423
hiterashes Abers 143 8523
hiterow Highld 151 3648
hiterow Moray 141 0257
hiteshill Gloucs 35 8406
hitesmith E Susx 16 5213
hitestaunton Somset 10 2810
hitestone Devon 9 8694
hitestone Cross Devon 9 8993
hitestreet Green Suffk 54 9739
hitewall Corner N York 90 7969
hiteway Gloucs 35 9110
hiteway Somset 22 7264
hitewell Lancs 81 6646
hiteworks Devon 6 6171
hitfield Gloucs 35 6791
hitfield Kent 29 3045
hitfield Nhants 49 6039
hitfield Nthumb 94 7857
hitfield Hall Nthumb 94 7756
hitford Devon 10 2595
hitford Flints 70 1478
hitgift E R Yk 84 8122
hitgreave Staffs 72 9028
hithorn D & G 99 4440
hiting Bay N Ayrs 105 0425
hitkirk W York 83 3633
hitland Carmth 31 1916
hitlaw Border 109 5012
hitletts S Ayrs 106 3623
hitley Berks 24 7270
hitley N York 83 5620
hitley S York 74 3494
hitley Wilts 22 8866
hitley Bay T & W 103 3571
hitley Chapel Nthumb 95 9257
hitley Heath Staffs 72 8126
hitley Lower W York 82 2217
hitley Row Kent 27 4952
hitlock's End W Mids 61 1076
hitminster Gloucs 35 7708
hitmore Dorset 12 0609
hitmore Staffs 72 8140
hitnage Devon 9 0215
hitnash Warwks 48 3263
hitney-on-Wye Herefs 46 2747
hitrigg Cumb 93 2038
hitrigg Cumb 93 2257
hitrigglees Cumb 93 2457
hitsbury Hants 12 1219
hitsford Devon 19 6633
hitsome Border 119 8650
hitson Newpt 34 3883
hitstable Kent 29 1066
hitstone Cnwll 5 2698
hittingham Nthumb 111 0611
hittingslow Shrops 59 4388
hittington Derbys 74 3875
hittington Gloucs 35 0120
hittington Lancs 87 6075
hittington Norfk 65 7199
hittington Shrops 59 3231
hittington Staffs 61 1508
hittington Staffs 60 8682
hittington Warwks 61 2999
hittington Worcs 47 8753
hittington Moor Derbys 74 3773
hittle-le-Woods Lancs 81 5821
hittlebury Nhants 49 6943
hittlesey Cambs 64 2697
hittlesford Cambs 53 4748
hittlestone Head Lancs 81 7119
hitton Dur 96 3822
hitton Lincs 84 9024
hitton Nthumb 103 0501
hitton Powys 46 2767
hitton Shrops 46 5772
hitton Suffk 54 1447
hittonditch Wilts 36 2872
hittonstall Nthumb 95 0757
hitway Hants 24 4559
hitwell Derbys 75 5276
hitwell Herts 39 1820
hitwell IOW 13 5277
hitwell N York 89 2899
hitwell Rutlnd 63 9208
hitwell Street Norfk 66 1022
hitwell-on-the-Hill N York 90 7265
hitwick Leics 62 4315
hitwood W York 83 4024
hitworth Lancs 81 8818
hixall Shrops 59 5134
hixley N York 89 4458
horlton Dur 95 1014
horlton N York 90 4802
hyle Herefs 46 5561
hyteleafe Surrey 27 3358
bdon Gloucs 34 5797
bsey W York 82 1430
btoft Warwks 50 4887
chenford Worcs 47 7860
chling Kent 28 9256
ck Devon 9 1704
Wick Dorset 12 1591
Wick Gloucs 35 7072
Wick Highld 151 3650
Wick Somset 20 2144
Wick Somset 21 4026
Wick V Glam 33 9271
Wick W Susx 14 0203
Wick Wilts 12 1621
Wick Worcs 47 9645
Wick Airport 151 3652
Wick End Beds 38 9850
Wick St Lawrence Somset 21 3665
Wicken Cambs 53 5770
Wicken Nhants 49 7439
Wicken Bonhunt Essex 39 4933
Wickenby Lincs 76 0982
Wicker Street Green Suffk 54 9742
Wickersley S York 75 4791
Wickford Essex 40 7493
Wickham Berks 36 3971
Wickham Hants 13 5711
Wickham Bishops Essex 40 8412
Wickham Green Berks 24 4072
Wickham Green Suffk 54 0969
Wickham Heath Berks 24 4169
Wickham Market Suffk 55 3055
Wickham Skeith Suffk 54 0969
Wickham St Paul Essex 54 8336
Wickham Street Suffk 53 7654
Wickham Street Suffk 54 0869
Wickhambreaux Kent 29 2158
Wickhambrook Suffk 53 7554
Wickhamford Worcs 48 0641
Wickhampton Norfk 67 4205
Wicklewood Norfk 66 0702
Wickmere Norfk 66 1733
Wickstreet E Susx 16 5308
Wickwar Gloucs 35 7288
Widdington Essex 39 5331
Widdop Lancs 81 9233
Widdrington Nthumb 103 2595
Widdrington Station T & W 103 2493
Wide Open T & W 103 2472
Widecombe in the Moor Devon 8 7176
Widegates Cnwll 5 2858
Widemouth Bay Cnwll 18 2002
Widford Essex 40 6904
Widford Herts 39 4216
Widford Oxon 36 2712
Widham Wilts 36 0988
Widmer End Bucks 26 8896
Widmerpool Notts 63 6327
Widmore Gt Lon 27 4268
Widnes Ches 78 5184
Widworthy Devon 9 2199
Wigan Gt Man 78 5805
Wigborough Somset 10 4415
Wiggaton Devon 9 1093
Wiggenhall St Germans Norfk 65 5914
Wiggenhall St Mary Magdalen Norfk 65 5911
Wiggenhall St Mary the Virgin Norfk 65 5813
Wiggens Green Essex 53 6642
Wiggenstall Staffs 74 0960
Wiggington Shrops 59 3335
Wigginton Herts 38 9310
Wigginton N York 90 6058
Wigginton Oxon 48 3833
Wigginton Staffs 61 2006
Wigglesworth N York 81 8156
Wiggold Gloucs 36 0404
Wiggonby Cumb 93 2952
Wiggonholt W Susx 14 0616
Wighill N York 83 4746
Wighton Norfk 66 9439
Wightwick Staffs 60 8698
Wigley Derbys 74 3171
Wigley Hants 12 3217
Wigmore Herefs 46 4169
Wigmore Kent 28 7964
Wigsley Notts 76 8570
Wigsthorpe Nhants 51 0482
Wigston Leics 50 6198
Wigston Fields Leics 50 6000
Wigston Parva Leics 50 4689
Wigthorpe Notts 75 5983
Wigtoft Lincs 64 2636
Wigton Cumb 93 2548
Wigtown D & G 99 4355
Wigtwizzle S York 74 2495
Wike W York 83 3342
Wilbarston Nhants 51 8188
Wilberfoss E R Yk 84 7350
Wilburton Cambs 53 4775
Wilby Nhants 51 8666
Wilby Norfk 54 0389
Wilby Suffk 55 2472
Wilcot Wilts 23 1360
Wilcott Shrops 59 3718
Wilcrick Newpt 34 4088
Wilday Green Derbys 74 3274
Wildboarclough Ches 79 9868
Wilden Beds 51 0955
Wilden Worcs 60 8272
Wildhern Hants 23 3550
Wildhill Herts 39 2606
Wildmanbridge S Lans 116 8253
Wildmoor Worcs 60 9575
Wildsworth Lincs 75 8097
Wilford Notts 62 5637
Wilkesley Ches 71 6241
Wilkhaven Highld 147 9486
Wilkieston W Loth 117 1268
Wilkin's Green Herts 39 1907
Wilksby Lincs 77 2862
Willand Devon 9 0310
Willards Hill E Susx 17 7124
Willaston Ches 71 3377
Willaston Ches 72 6852
Willen Bucks 38 8741
Willenhall W Mids 60 9798
Willenhall W Mids 61 3676
Willerby E R Yk 84 0230
Willerby N York 91 0079
Willersey Gloucs 48 1039
Willersley Herefs 46 3147
Willesborough Kent 28 0441
Willesborough Lees Kent 28 0342
Willesden Gt Lon 26 2284
Willesleigh Devon 19 6033
Willesley Wilts 35 8588
Willett Somset 20 1033
Willey Shrops 60 6799
Willey Warwks 50 4984
Willey Green Surrey 25 9351
Williamscot Oxon 49 4845
Williamstown Rhondd 33 0090
Willian Herts 39 2230
Willicote Warwks 48 1849
Willingale Essex 40 5907
Willingdon E Susx 16 5902
Willingham Cambs 52 4070
Willingham by Stow Lincs 76 8784
Willingham Green Cambs 53 6254
Willington Beds 52 1150
Willington Derbys 73 2928
Willington Dur 96 1935
Willington Kent 28 7853
Willington Warwks 48 2639
Willington Corner Ches 71 5266
Willington Quay T & W 103 3267
Willitoft E R Yk 84 7434
Williton Somset 20 0840
Willoughby Lincs 77 4771
Willoughby Warwks 50 5167
Willoughby Hills Lincs 64 3545
Willoughby Waterleys Leics 50 5792
Willoughby-on-the-Wolds Notts 63 6325
Willoughton Lincs 76 9293
Willow Green Ches 71 6076
Willows Green Essex 40 7219
Willsbridge Gloucs 35 6670
Willsworthy Devon 8 5381
Willtown Somset 21 3924
Wilmcote Warwks 48 1658
Wilmington Devon 9 2199
Wilmington E Susx 16 5404
Wilmington Kent 27 5372
Wilmington Somset 22 6962
Wilmslow Ches 79 8481
Wilnecote Staffs 61 2200
Wilpshire Lancs 81 6832
Wilsden W York 82 0936
Wilsford Lincs 63 0042
Wilsford Wilts 23 1057
Wilsford Wilts 23 1339
Wilsham Devon 19 7548
Wilshaw W York 82 1109
Wilsill N York 89 1864
Wilsley Green Kent 28 7736
Wilsley Pound Kent 28 7837
Wilson Herefs 46 5523
Wilson Leics 62 4024
Wilsontown S Lans 116 9455
Wilstead Beds 38 0643
Wilsthorpe Lincs 64 0913
Wilstone Herts 38 9014
Wilstone Green Herts 38 9013
Wilton Cumb 86 0311
Wilton Herefs 46 5824
Wilton N York 97 5819
Wilton N York 90 8582
Wilton Wilts 23 0931
Wilton Wilts 23 2661
Wilton Dean Border 109 4914
Wimbish Essex 53 5936
Wimbish Green Essex 53 6035
Wimbledon Gt Lon 26 2370
Wimblington Cambs 65 4192
Wimboldsley Ches 72 6962
Wimborne Minster Dorset 11 0199
Wimborne St Giles Dorset 12 0311
Wimbotsham Norfk 65 6205
Wimpstone Warwks 48 2148
Wincanton Somset 22 7128
Winceby Lincs 77 3268
Wincham Ches 79 6775
Winchburgh W Loth 117 0975
Winchcombe Gloucs 48 0228
Winchelsea E Susx 17 9017
Winchelsea Beach E Susx 17 9116
Winchester Hants 24 4829
Winchet Hill Kent 28 7340
Winchfield Hants 24 7654
Winchmore Hill Bucks 26 9395
Winchmore Hill Gt Lon 27 3194
Wincle Ches 72 9566
Wincobank S York 74 3891
Winder Cumb 92 0417
Windermere Cumb 87 4098
Winderton Warwks 48 3240
Windhill Highld 139 5348
Windlehurst Gt Man 79 9586
Windlesham Surrey 25 9364
Windmill Cnwll 4 8974
Windmill Derbys 74 1677
Windmill Hill E Susx 16 6412
Windmill Hill Somset 10 3116
Windrush Gloucs 36 1913
Windsole Abers 142 5560
Windsor Berks 26 9576
Windsor Castle 26 9877
Windsor Green Suffk 54 8954
Windsoredge Gloucs 35 8400
Windy Arbour Warwks 61 2971
Windy Hill Wrexhm 71 3054
Windygates Fife 118 3400
Windyharbour Ches 79 8270
Wineham W Susx 15 2320
Winestead E R Yk 85 2924
Winewall Lancs 81 9140
Winfarthing Norfk 54 1085
Winford IOW 13 5584
Winford Somset 21 5464
Winforton Herefs 46 2946
Winfrith Newburgh Dorset 11 8084
Wing Bucks 38 8822
Wing Rutlnd 63 8903
Wingate Dur 96 4036
Wingates Gt Man 79 6507
Wingates Nthumb 103 0995
Wingerworth Derbys 74 3867
Wingfield Beds 38 0026
Wingfield Suffk 55 2277
Wingfield Wilts 22 8256
Wingfield Green Suffk 55 2177
Wingham Kent 29 2457
Wingmore Kent 29 1946
Wingrave Bucks 38 8719
Winkburn Notts 75 7058
Winkfield Berks 25 9072
Winkfield Row Berks 25 8971
Winkfield Street Berks 25 8972
Winkhill Staffs 73 0651
Winkhurst Green Kent 16 4949
Winkleigh Devon 19 6308
Winksley N York 89 2571
Winkton Dorset 12 1696
Winlaton T & W 96 1762
Winlaton Mill T & W 96 1860
Winless Highld 151 3054
Winllan Powys 58 2221
Winmarleigh Lancs 80 4647
Winnall Hants 24 4829
Winnall Worcs 47 8167
Winnersh Berks 25 7870
Winnington Ches 79 6474
Winscales Cumb 92 0226
Winscombe Somset 21 4257
Winsford Ches 72 6566
Winsford Somset 20 9034
Winsham Devon 19 5038
Winsham Somset 10 3706
Winshill Staffs 73 2623
Winshwen Swans 32 6896
Winskill Cumb 94 5834
Winslade Hants 24 6548
Winsley Wilts 22 7960
Winslow Bucks 49 7727
Winson Gloucs 36 0808
Winsor Hants 12 3114
Winster Cumb 87 4193
Winster Derbys 74 2460
Winston Dur 96 1416
Winston Suffk 54 1861
Winston Green Suffk 54 1761
Winstone Gloucs 35 9509
Winswell Devon 18 4913
Winterborne Came Dorset 11 7088
Winterborne Clenston Dorset 11 8303
Winterborne Herringston Dorset 11 6888
Winterborne Houghton Dorset 11 8204
Winterborne Kingston Dorset 11 8697
Winterborne Monkton Dorset 11 6787
Winterborne Stickland Dorset 11 8304
Winterborne Tomson Dorset 11 8897
Winterborne Whitechurch Dorset 11 8300
Winterborne Zelston Dorset 11 8997
Winterbourne Berks 24 4572
Winterbourne Gloucs 35 6480
Winterbourne Abbas Dorset 10 6190
Winterbourne Bassett Wilts 36 0974
Winterbourne Dauntsey Wilts 23 1734
Winterbourne Earls Wilts 23 1734
Winterbourne Gunner Wilts 23 1735
Winterbourne Monkton Wilts 36 0971
Winterbourne Steepleton Dorset 10 6289
Winterbourne Stoke Wilts 23 0741
Winterbrook Oxon 37 6088
Winterburn N York 88 9358
Winteringham Lincs 84 9221
Winterley Ches 72 7457
Wintersett W York 83 3815
Winterslow Wilts 23 2332
Winterton Lincs 84 9218
Winterton-on-Sea Norfk 67 4919
Winthorpe Lincs 77 5665
Winthorpe Notts 75 8156
Winton Cumb 88 7810
Winton Dorset 12 0893
Winton E Susx 16 5103
Winton N York 89 4196
Wintringham N York 90 8873
Winwick Cambs 51 1080
Winwick Ches 78 6092
Winwick Nhants 50 6273
Wirksworth Derbys 73 2854
Wirswall Ches 71 5444
Wisbech Cambs 65 4609
Wisbech St Mary Cambs 65 4208
Wisborough Green W Susx 14 0525
Wiseman's Bridge Pembks 31 1406
Wiseton Notts 75 7189
Wishanger Gloucs 35 9109
Wishaw N Lans 116 7955
Wishaw Warwks 61 1794
Wisley Surrey 26 0659
Wisley Gardens 26 0657
Wispington Lincs 76 2071
Wissenden Kent 28 9041
Wissett Suffk 55 3679
Wissington Norfk 65 6697
Wissington Suffk 40 9533
Wistanstow Shrops 59 4385
Wistanswick Shrops 72 6629
Wistaston Ches 72 6853
Wistaston Green Ches 72 6854
Wisterfield Ches 79 8371
Wiston Pembks 30 0218
Wiston S Lans 108 9532
Wiston W Susx 15 1414
Wistow Cambs 52 2780
Wistow Leics 50 6495
Wistow N York 83 5935
Wiswell Lancs 81 7437
Witcham Cambs 53 4680
Witchampton Dorset 11 9806
Witchford Cambs 53 5078
Witcombe Somset 21 4721
Witham Essex 40 8214
Witham Friary Somset 22 7441
Witham on the Hill Lincs 64 0516
Withcall Lincs 77 2883
Withdean E Susx 15 3007
Witherenden Hill E Susx 16 6426
Witheridge Devon 19 8014
Witherley Leics 61 3297
Withern Lincs 77 4282
Withernsea E R Yk 85 3427
Withernwick E R Yk 85 1940
Withersdale Street Suffk 55 2680
Withersfield Essex 53 6548
Witherslack Cumb 87 4384
Witherslack Hall Cumb 87 4385
Withiel Cnwll 4 9965
Withiel Florey Somset 20 9833
Withielgoose Cnwll 4 0065
Withington Gloucs 35 0215
Withington Gt Man 79 8492
Withington Herefs 46 5643
Withington Shrops 59 5713
Withington Staffs 73 0335
Withington Green Ches 79 8071
Withington Marsh Herefs 46 5544
Withleigh Devon 9 9012
Withnell Lancs 81 6322
Withy Mills Somset 22 6657
Withybed Green Worcs 60 0172
Withybrook Warwks 50 4383
Withycombe Somset 20 0141
Withyditch Somset 22 6959
Withyham E Susx 16 4935
Withypool Somset 19 8435
Withywood Bristl 21 5667
Witley Surrey 25 9439
Witnesham Suffk 54 1751
Witney Oxon 36 3510
Wittering Cambs 64 0502
Wittersham Kent 17 9027
Witton Norfk 67 3109
Witton Norfk 67 3331
Witton W Mids 61 0790
Witton Gilbert Dur 96 2345
Witton Green Norfk 67 4102
Witton le Wear Dur 96 1431
Witton Park Dur 96 1730
Wiveliscombe Somset 20 0827
Wivelrod Hants 24 6738
Wivelsfield E Susx 15 3420
Wivelsfield Green E Susx 15 3519
Wivelsfield Station W Susx 15 3219
Wivenhoe Essex 41 0321
Wivenhoe Cross Essex 41 0423
Wiveton Norfk 66 0442
Wix Essex 41 1628
Wix Green Essex 41 1728
Wixford Warwks 48 0854
Wixhill Shrops 59 5528
Wixoe Essex 53 7143
Woburn Beds 38 9433
Woburn Abbey 38 9632
Woburn Sands Bucks 38 9235
Wokefield Park Berks 24 6765
Woking Surrey 25 0058
Wokingham Berks 25 8168
Wolborough Devon 7 8570
Wold Newton E R Yk 91 0473
Wold Newton Lincs 77 2496
Woldingham Surrey 27 3755
Wolf Hills Nthumb 94 7258
Wolf's Castle Pembks 30 9526
Wolfclyde S Lans 108 0236
Wolferlow Herefs 47 6661
Wolferton Norfk 65 6528
Wolfhampcote Warwks 50 5265
Wolfhill P & K 126 1533
Wolfsdale Pembks 30 9321
Wollaston Nhants 51 9062
Wollaston Shrops 59 3212
Wollaton Notts 62 5239
Wolleigh Devon 8 8080
Wollerton Shrops 59 6130
Wollescote W Mids 60 9283
Wolseley Bridge Staffs 73 0220
Wolsingham Dur 95 0737
Wolstanton Staffs 72 8548
Wolstenholme Gt Man 81 8414
Wolston Warwks 50 4175
Wolsty Cumb 92 1050
Wolvercote Oxon 37 4910
Wolverhampton W Mids 60 9198
Wolverley Shrops 59 4731
Wolverley Worcs 60 8379
Wolverton Bucks 38 8141
Wolverton Hants 24 5558
Wolverton Kent 29 2642
Wolverton Warwks 48 2062
Wolverton Wilts 22 7831
Wolverton Common Hants 24 5659
Wolvesnewton Mons 34 4599
Wolvey Warwks 50 4387
Wolvey Heath Warwks 50 4388
Wolviston Dur 97 4525
Wombleton N York 90 6683
Wombourne Staffs 60 8793
Wombwell S York 83 4002
Womenswold Kent 29 2250
Womersley N York 83 5319
Wonastow Mons 34 4810
Wonersh Surrey 14 0145
Wonford Devon 9 9491
Wonson Devon 8 6789
Wonston Hants 24 4739
Wooburn Bucks 26 9087
Wooburn Green Bucks 26 9188
Wooburn Moor Bucks 26 9189
Wood Bevington Warwks 48 0554
Wood Burcot Nhants 49 6946
Wood Dalling Norfk 66 0827
Wood Eaton Staffs 72 8417
Wood End Beds 38 0046
Wood End Beds 51 0866
Wood End Cambs 52 3675
Wood End Gt Lon 26 1081
Wood End Herts 39 3225
Wood End W Mids 60 9400
Wood End Warwks 61 1171
Wood End Warwks 61 2498
Wood End Warwks 61 2987
Wood Enderby Lincs 77 2764
Wood Green Gt Lon 27 3090
Wood Hayes W Mids 60 9402
Wood Lane Shrops 59 4132
Wood Lane Staffs 72 8149
Wood Norton Norfk 66 0127
Wood Row W York 83 3827
Wood Street Norfk 67 3722

318

Wood Street *Surrey* 25 9550
Wood Top *Lancs* 81 5643
Wood Walton *Cambs* 52 2180
Wood's Corner *E Susx* 16 6619
Wood's Green *E Susx* 16 6333
Woodale *N York* 88 0279
Woodall *S York* 75 4880
Woodbastwick *Norfk* 67 3315
Woodbeck *Notts* 75 7777
Woodborough *Notts* 63 6347
Woodborough *Wilts* 23 1159
Woodbridge *Devon* 9 1895
Woodbridge *Dorset* 22 8518
Woodbridge *Suffk* 55 2649
Woodbury *Devon* 9 0087
Woodbury Salterton *Devon* 9 0189
Woodchester *Gloucs* 35 8302
Woodchurch *Kent* 17 9434
Woodchurch *Mersyd* 78 2786
Woodcombe *Somset* 20 9546
Woodcote *Gt Lon* 27 2962
Woodcote *Oxon* 37 6482
Woodcote *Shrops* 72 7615
Woodcote Green *Worcs* 60 9172
Woodcott *Hants* 24 4354
Woodcroft *Gloucs* 34 5495
Woodcutts *Dorset* 11 9717
Woodditton *Cambs* 53 6559
Woodeaton *Oxon* 37 5312
Wooden *Pembks* 31 1105
Woodend *Highld* 130 7861
Woodend *Nhants* 49 6149
Woodend *Staffs* 73 1726
Woodend *W Loth* 116 9269
Woodend *W Susx* 14 8108
Woodend Green *Essex* 39 5528
Woodfalls *Wilts* 12 1920
Woodford *Devon* 7 7950
Woodford *Gloucs* 35 6995
Woodford *Gt Lon* 27 4191
Woodford *Gt Man* 79 8882
Woodford *Nhants* 51 9676
Woodford Bridge *Gt Lon* 27 4291
Woodford Halse *Nhants* 49 5452
Woodford Wells *Gt Lon* 27 4093
Woodgate *Devon* 9 1015
Woodgate *Norfk* 66 8915
Woodgate *Norfk* 66 0215
Woodgate *W Mids* 60 9982
Woodgate *W Susx* 14 9304
Woodgate *Worcs* 47 9666
Woodgreen *Hants* 12 1717
Woodgreen *Oxon* 36 3610
Woodhall *Lincs* 76 2267
Woodhall *N York* 88 9790
Woodhall Hill *W York* 82 2035
Woodhall Spa *Lincs* 76 1963
Woodham *Bucks* 37 7018
Woodham *Dur* 96 2826
Woodham *Surrey* 26 0462
Woodham Ferrers *Essex* 40 7999
Woodham Mortimer *Essex* 40 8104
Woodham Walter *Essex* 40 8007
Woodhead *Abers* 142 7838
Woodhill *Somset* 21 3527
Woodhorn *Nthumb* 103 2988
Woodhorn Demesne *Nthumb* 103 3088
Woodhouse *Leics* 62 5314
Woodhouse *S York* 74 4284
Woodhouse *W York* 82 2935
Woodhouse *W York* 83 3821
Woodhouse Eaves *Leics* 62 5214
Woodhouse Green *Staffs* 72 9162
Woodhouse Mill *S York* 75 4385
Woodhouselee *Mdloth* 117 2364
Woodhouselees *D & G* 101 3975
Woodhouses *Cumb* 93 3252
Woodhouses *Gt Man* 79 9100
Woodhouses *Staffs* 61 0709
Woodhouses *Staffs* 73 1518
Woodhuish *Devon* 7 9152
Woodhurst *Cambs* 52 3176
Woodingdean *E Susx* 15 3505
Woodkirk *W York* 82 2725
Woodland *Abers* 143 8723
Woodland *Devon* 7 7968
Woodland *Devon* 6 6256
Woodland *Dur* 95 0726
Woodland *Kent* 29 1441
Woodland *S Ayrs* 106 1795
Woodland Head *Devon* 8 7796
Woodland Street *Somset* 21 5337
Woodland View *S York* 74 3188
Woodlands *Abers* 135 7895
Woodlands *Dorset* 12 0509
Woodlands *Hants* 12 3211
Woodlands *Kent* 27 5660
Woodlands *N York* 83 3254
Woodlands *S York* 83 5308
Woodlands *Somset* 20 1640
Woodlands Park *Berks* 26 8678
Woodlands St Mary *Berks* 36 3375
Woodleigh *Devon* 7 7349
Woodlesford *W York* 83 3629
Woodley *Berks* 25 7773
Woodley *Gt Man* 79 9392
Woodmancote *Gloucs* 47 9727
Woodmancote *Gloucs* 35 0008
Woodmancote *Gloucs* 35 7597
Woodmancote *W Susx* 14 7707
Woodmancote *W Susx* 15 2314
Woodmancote *Worcs* 47 9142
Woodmancott *Hants* 24 5642
Woodmansey *E R Yk* 84 0538
Woodmansgreen *W Susx* 14 8627
Woodmansterne *Surrey* 27 2759
Woodmanton *Devon* 9 0186
Woodmarsh *Wilts* 22 8555
Woodmill *Staffs* 73 1320
Woodminton *Wilts* 22 0022
Woodnesborough *Kent* 29 3157
Woodnewton *Nhants* 51 0394
Woodnook *Notts* 75 4752

Woodplumpton *Lancs* 80 4934
Woodrising *Norfk* 66 9803
Woodrow *Worcs* 60 8975
Woodseaves *Shrops* 72 6831
Woodseaves *Staffs* 72 7925
Woodsend *Wilts* 36 2176
Woodsetts *S York* 75 5483
Woodsford *Dorset* 11 7590
Woodside *Berks* 25 9371
Woodside *Cumb* 92 0434
Woodside *Essex* 39 4704
Woodside *Fife* 127 4207
Woodside *Gt Lon* 27 3467
Woodside *Hants* 12 3294
Woodside *Herts* 39 2406
Woodside *P & K* 126 2037
Woodside Green *Kent* 28 9053
Woodstock *Oxon* 37 4416
Woodstock *Pembks* 30 0325
Woodthorpe *Derbys* 75 4574
Woodthorpe *Leics* 62 5417
Woodthorpe *Lincs* 77 4380
Woodton *Norfk* 67 2994
Woodtown *Devon* 18 4123
Woodvale *Mersyd* 78 3010
Woodville *Derbys* 62 3118
Woodwall Green *Staffs* 72 7831
Woody Bay *Devon* 19 6748
Woodyates *Dorset* 12 0219
Woofferton *Shrops* 46 5268
Wookey *Somset* 21 5145
Wookey Hole *Somset* 21 5347
Wool *Dorset* 11 8486
Woolacombe *Devon* 18 4643
Woolage Green *Kent* 29 2349
Woolage Village *Kent* 29 2350
Woolaston *Gloucs* 34 5899
Woolaston Common *Gloucs* 34 5801
Woolavington *Somset* 21 3441
Woolbeding *W Susx* 14 8722
Woolbrook *Devon* 9 1289
Woolcotts *Somset* 20 9631
Wooldale *W York* 82 1508
Wooler *Nthumb* 111 9927
Woolfardisworthy *Devon* 18 3321
Woolfardisworthy *Devon* 19 8208
Woolfold *Gt Man* 81 7811
Woolfords *S Lans* 117 0056
Woolhampton *Berks* ...... 24 '5766
Woolhanger *Devon* 19 6945
Woolhope *Herefs* 46 6135
Woolland *Dorset* 11 7707
Woollard *Somset* 21 6364
Woollensbrook *Herts* 39 3609
Woolley *Cambs* 52 1574
Woolley *Cnwll* 18 2516
Woolley *Derbys* 74 3760
Woolley *Somset* 22 7468
Woolley *W York* 83 3212
Woolley Bridge *Derbys* 79 0194
Woolley Green *Berks* 26 8480
Woolmer Green *Herts* 39 2518
Woolmere Green *Worcs* 47 9663
Woolmerston *Somset* 20 2833
Woolminstone *Somset* 10 4108
Woolpack *Kent* 28 8537
Woolpit *Suffk* 54 9762
Woolpit Green *Suffk* 54 9761
Woolscott *Warwks* 50 5068
Woolsgrove *Devon* 8 7902
Woolsington *T & W* 103 1870
Woolstaston *Shrops* 59 4498
Woolsthorpe *Lincs* 63 8333
Woolsthorpe-by-
  Colsterworth *Lincs* 63 9224
Woolston *Ches* 79 6489
Woolston *Devon* 7 7141
Woolston *Devon* 7 7150
Woolston *Hants* 13 4310
Woolston *Shrops* 59 3224
Woolston *Shrops* 59 4287
Woolston *Somset* 20 0939
Woolston *Somset* 21 6527
Woolston Green *Devon* 7 7766
Woolstone *Bucks* 38 8738
Woolstone *Gloucs* 47 9630
Woolstone *Oxon* 36 2987
Woolton *Mersyd* 78 4286
Woolton Hill *Hants* 24 4361
Woolverstone *Suffk* 54 1738
Woolverton *Somset* 22 7953
Woolwich *Gt Lon* 27 4478
Woonton *Herefs* 46 3552
Woonton *Herefs* 46 5562
Wooperton *Nthumb* 111 0420
Woore *Shrops* 72 7342
Wootten Green *Suffk* 55 2372
Wootton *Beds* 38 0044
Wootton *Hants* 12 2498
Wootton *Herefs* 46 3252
Wootton *IOW* 13 5392
Wootton *Kent* 29 2246
Wootton *Lincs* 85 0815
Wootton *Nhants* 49 7656
Wootton *Oxon* 37 4419
Wootton *Oxon* 37 4701
Wootton *Shrops* 59 3327
Wootton *Staffs* 72 8227
Wootton *Staffs* 73 1044
Wootton Bassett *Wilts* 36 0682
Wootton Bridge *IOW* 13 5492
Wootton Broadmead *Beds* 38 0243
Wootton Common *IOW* 13 5391
Wootton Courtenay *Somset* 20 9343
Wootton Fitzpaine *Dorset* 10 3695
Wootton Rivers *Wilts* 23 1962
Wootton St Lawrence *Hants* 24 5953
Wootton Wawen *Warwks* 48 1563
Worcester *Worcs* 47 8555
Worcester Park *Gt Lon* 26 2165
Wordsley *W Mids* 60 8987
Worfield *Shrops* 60 7595

Worgret *Dorset* 11 9087
Workhouse End *Beds* 38 1052
Workington *Cumb* 92 0028
Worksop *Notts* 75 5879
Worlaby *Lincs* 84 0113
Worlaby *Lincs* 77 3476
World's End *Berks* 37 4877
Worlds End *Bucks* 38 8509
Worlds End *Hants* 13 6311
Worlds End *W Susx* 15 3220
Worle *Somset* 21 3562
Worleston *Ches* 72 6556
Worlingham *Suffk* 55 4489
Worlington *Devon* 19 7713
Worlington *Suffk* 53 6973
Worlingworth *Suffk* 55 2368
Wormald Green *N York* 89 3065
Wormbridge *Herefs* 46 4230
Wormegay *Norfk* 65 6611
Wormelow Tump *Herefs* 46 4930
Wormhill *Derbys* 74 1274
Wormhill *Herefs* 46 4239
Wormingford *Essex* 40 9332
Worminghall *Bucks* 37 6308
Wormington *Gloucs* 48 0336
Worminster *Somset* 21 5743
Wormit *Fife* 126 4026
Wormleighton *Warwks* 49 4553
Wormley *Herts* 39 3605
Wormley *Surrey* 25 9438
Wormley Hill *S York* 83 6616
Wormleybury *Herts* 39 3506
Wormshill *Kent* 28 8857
Wormsley *Herefs* 46 4247
Worplesdon *Surrey* 25 9753
Worrall *S York* 74 3092
Worrall Hill *Gloucs* 34 6014
Worsbrough *S York* 83 3602
Worsbrough Bridge *S York* 83 3503
Worsbrough Dale *S York* 83 3604
Worsley *Gt Man* 79 7500
Worsley Mesnes *Gt Man* 78 5703
Worstead *Norfk* 67 3025
Worsthorne *Lancs* 81 8732
Worston *Devon* 6 5953
Worston *Lancs* 81 7742
Worth *Kent* 29 3355
Worth *Somset* 21 5144
Worth *W Susx* 15 3036
Worth Abbey *Surrey* 15 3134
Worth Matravers *Dorset* 11 9777
Wortham *Suffk* 54 0877
Worthen *Shrops* 59 3204
Worthenbury *Wrexhm* 71 4146
Worthing *Norfk* 66 9919
Worthing *W Susx* 15 1403
Worthington *Leics* 62 4020
Worthybrook *Mons* 34 4711
Worting *Hants* 24 5952
Wortley *S York* 74 3099
Wortley *W York* 82 2732
Worton *N York* 88 9589
Worton *Wilts* 22 9757
Wortwell *Norfk* 55 2784
Wotherton *Shrops* 58 2800
Wothorpe *Cambs* 64 0205
Wotter *Devon* 6 5661
Wotton *Surrey* 14 1247
Wotton Underwood *Bucks* 37 6815
Wotton-under-Edge *Gloucs* 35 7593
Woughton on the Green *Bucks* 38 8737
Wouldham *Kent* 28 7164
Woundale *Shrops* 60 7793
Wrabness *Essex* 41 1731
Wrafton *Devon* 18 4935
Wragby *Lincs* 76 1378
Wragby *W York* 83 4116
Wramplingham *Norfk* 66 1106
Wrangaton *Devon* 7 6758
Wrangbrook *W York* 83 4913
Wrangle *Lincs* 77 4250
Wrangle Common *Lincs* 77 4253
Wrangle Lowgate *Lincs* 77 4451
Wrangway *Somset* 20 1218
Wrantage *Somset* 20 3022
Wrawby *Lincs* 84 0108
Wraxall *Somset* 34 4971
Wraxall *Somset* 21 6036
Wray *Lancs* 87 6067
Wray Castle *Cumb* 87 3700
Wraysbury *Berks* 25 0074
Wrayton *Lancs* 87 6172
Wrea Green *Lancs* 80 3931
Wreaks End *Cumb* 86 2286
Wreay *Cumb* 93 4348
Wreay *Cumb* 93 4423
Wrecclesham *Surrey* 25 8244
Wrekenton *T & W* 96 2759
Wrelton *N York* 90 7696
Wrenbury *Ches* 71 5947
Wrench Green *N York* 91 9689
Wreningham *Norfk* 66 1698
Wrentham *Suffk* 55 4982
Wrenthorpe *W York* 82 3122
Wrentnall *Shrops* 59 4203
Wressle *E R Yk* 84 7131
Wressle *Lincs* 84 9709
Wrestlingworth *Beds* 52 2547
Wretton *Norfk* 65 6900
Wrexham *Wrexhm* 71 3350
Wribbenhall *Worcs* 60 7975
Wrickton *Shrops* 59 6486
Wright's Green *Essex* 39 5017
Wrightington Bar *Lancs* 80 5313
Wrinehill *Staffs* 72 7547
Wrington *Somset* 21 4762
Wringworthy *Cnwll* 5 2658
Writhlington *Somset* 22 6954
Writtle *Essex* 40 6706
Wrockwardine *Shrops* 59 6212
Wroot *Lincs* 84 7103
Wrose *W York* 82 1636
Wrotham *Kent* 27 6158

Wrotham Heath *Kent* 27 6357
Wrottesley *Staffs* 60 8200
Wroughton *Wilts* 36 1480
Wroxall *IOW* 13 5579
Wroxall *Warwks* 61 2271
Wroxeter *Shrops* 59 5608
Wroxham *Norfk* 67 3017
Wroxton *Oxon* 49 4141
Wyaston *Derbys* 73 1842
Wyatt's Green *Essex* 40 5999
Wyberton East *Lincs* 64 3240
Wyberton West *Lincs* 64 3142
Wyboston *Beds* 52 1656
Wybunbury *Ches* 72 6949
Wych Cross *E Susx* 15 4131
Wychbold *Worcs* 47 9266
Wychnor *Staffs* 73 1715
Wyck *Hants* 24 7539
Wyck Rissington *Gloucs* 36 1821
Wycliffe *Dur* 95 1114
Wycoller *Lancs* 81 9339
Wycomb *Leics* 63 7724
Wycombe Marsh *Bucks* 26 8892
Wyddial *Herts* 39 3731
Wye *Kent* 28 0546
Wyesham *Mons* 34 5211
Wyfordby *Leics* 63 7918
Wyke *Devon* 9 8799
Wyke *Devon* 10 2996
Wyke *Dorset* 22 7926
Wyke *Shrops* 59 6402
Wyke *Surrey* 25 9251
Wyke *W York* 82 1526
Wyke Champflower *Somset* 22 6634
Wyke Regis *Dorset* 11 6677
Wykeham *N York* 90 8175
Wykeham *N York* 91 9683
Wyken *Shrops* 60 7695
Wyken *W Mids* 61 3780
Wykey *Shrops* 59 3824
Wykin *Leics* 61 4095
Wylam *Nthumb* 103 1164
Wylde Green *W Mids* 61 1294
Wylye *Wilts* 22 0037
Wymeswold *Leics* 62 6023
Wymington *Beds* 51 9564
Wymondham *Leics* 63 8418
Wymondham *Norfk* 66 1001
Wyndham Brdgnd 33 9392
Wynford Eagle *Dorset* 10 5896
Wynyard Park *Dur* 96 4326
Wyre Piddle *Worcs* 47 9647
Wysall *Notts* 62 6027
Wyson *Herefs* 46 5267
Wythall *Worcs* 61 0774
Wytham *Oxon* 37 4708
Wythburn *Cumb* 93 3214
Wythenshawe *Gt Man* 79 8386
Wythop Mill *Cumb* 93 1729
Wyton *Cambs* 52 2772
Wyton *E R Yk* 85 1733
Wyverstone *Suffk* 54 0468
Wyverstone Street *Suffk* 54 0367
Wyville *Lincs* 63 8729

Y

Y Felinheli *Gwynd* 68 5267
Y Ferwig *Cerdgn* 42 1849
Y Ffor *Gwynd* 56 3939
Y Gyffylliog *Denbgs* 70 0557
Y Maerdy *Conwy* 70 0144
Y Nant *Wrexhm* 71 2850
Y Rhiw *Gwynd* 56 2227
Yaddlethorpe *Lincs* 84 8806
Yafford *IOW* 13 4481
Yafforth *N York* 89 3494
Yalberton *Devon* 7 8658
Yalding *Kent* 28 6950
Yanwath *Cumb* 94 5127
Yanworth *Gloucs* 36 0713
Yapham *E R Yk* 84 7851
Yapton *W Susx* 14 9703
Yarborough *Somset* 21 3857
Yarbridge *IOW* 13 6086
Yarburgh *Lincs* 77 3592
Yarcombe *Devon* 9 2408
Yard *Devon* 19 7721
Yardley *W Mids* 61 1386
Yardley Gobion *Nhants* 49 7644
Yardley Hastings *Nhants* 51 8657
Yardley Wood *W Mids* 61 1079
Yardro *Powys* 45 2258
Yarford *Somset* 20 2029
Yarkhill *Herefs* 46 6042
Yarley *Somset* 21 5044
Yarlington *Somset* 21 6529
Yarlsber *N York* 87 7072
Yarm *N York* 89 4112
Yarmouth *IOW* 12 3589
Yarnacott *Devon* 19 6230
Yarnbrook *Wilts* 22 8654
Yarner *Devon* 9 7778
Yarnfield *Staffs* 72 8632
Yarnscombe *Devon* 19 5623
Yarnton *Oxon* 37 4711
Yarpole *Herefs* 46 4764
Yarrow *Border* 109 3528
Yarrow *Somset* 21 3746
Yarrow Feus *Border* 109 3325
Yarrowford *Border* 109 4030
Yarsop *Herefs* 46 4047
Yarwell *Nhants* 51 0697
Yate *Gloucs* 35 7081
Yateley *Hants* 25 8161

Yatesbury *Wilts* 36 06
Yattendon *Berks* 24 55
Yatton *Herefs* 46 43
Yatton *Herefs* 47 63
Yatton *Somset* 21 43
Yatton Keynell *Wilts* 35 86
Yaverland *IOW* 13 61
Yawl *Devon* 10 31
Yawthorpe *Lincs* 76 89
Yaxham *Norfk* 66 00
Yaxley *Cambs* 64 18
Yaxley *Suffk* 54 12
Yazor *Herefs* 46 40
Yeading *Gt Lon* 26 11
Yeadon *W York* 82 20
Yealand Conyers *Lancs* 87 50
Yealand Redmayne *Lancs* 87 50
Yealand Storrs *Lancs* 87 49
Yealmbridge *Devon* 6 58
Yealmpton *Devon* 6 58
Yearby *N York* 97 59
Yearngill *Cumb* 92 14
Yearsley *N York* 90 58
Yeaton *Shrops* 59 43
Yeaveley *Derbys* 73 18
Yeavering *Nthumb* 110 93
Yedingham *N York* 91 89
Yelford *Oxon* 36 36
Yelland *Devon* 18 49
Yelling *Cambs* 52 26
Yelvertoft *Nhants* 50 59
Yelverton *Devon* 6 52
Yelverton *Norfk* 67 29
Yenston *Somset* 22 71
Yeo Mill *Somset* 19 84
Yeo Vale *Devon* 18 42
Yeoford *Devon* 8 78
Yeolmbridge *Cnwll* 5 31
Yeovil *Somset* 10 55
Yeovil Marsh *Somset* 10 54
Yeovilton *Somset* 21 54
Yeovilton Fleet
  Air Arm Museum 21 55
Yerbeston *Pembks* 30 06
Yesnaby *Ork* 153 22
Yetlington *Nthumb* 111 02
Yetminster *Dorset* 10 59
Yetson *Devon* 7 80
Yettington *Devon* 9 05
Yetts o' Muckhart *Clacks* 117 00
Yew Green *Warwks* 48 23
Yews Green *W York* 82 09
Yielden *Beds* 51 01
Yieldingtree *Worcs* 60 89
Yieldshields *S Lans* 116 87
Yiewsley *Gt Lon* 26 06
Ynysboeth *Rhondd* 33 06
Ynysddu *Caerph* 33 17
Ynysforgan Swans 32 67
Ynyshir *Rhondd* 33 02
Ynyslas *Cerdgn* 43 61
Ynysmaerdy *Rhondd* 33 03
Ynysmeudwy *Neath* 32 73
Ynystawe *Swans* 32 68
Ynyswen *Powys* 33 83
Ynyswen *Rhondd* 33 95
Ynysybwl *Rhondd* 33 05
Ynysmaengwyn *Gwynd* 57 59
Yockenthwaite *N York* 88 90
Yockleton *Shrops* 59 39
Yokefleet *E R Yk* 84 81
Yoker *C Glas* 115 50
York *Lancs* 81 71
York *N York* 83 6C
York Minster 83 6C
York Town *Surrey* 25 8E
Yorkletts *Kent* 29 06
Yorkley *Gloucs* 35 63
Yorton Heath *Shrops* 59 5C
Youlgreave *Derbys* 74 2C
Youlthorpe *E R Yk* 84 76
Youlton *N York* 90 49
Young's End *Essex* 40 73
Youngsbury *Herts* 39 36
Yoxall *Staffs* 73 14
Yoxford *Suffk* 55 35
Yoxford Little Street *Suffk* 55 38
Ysbyty Cynfyn *Cerdgn* 43 75
Ysbyty Ifan *Conwy* 69 84
Ysbyty Ystwyth *Cerdgn* 43 73
Ysceifiog *Flints* 70 15
Ysgubor-y-Coed *Cerdgn* 43 68
Ystalyfera *Powys* 32 76
Ystrad *Rhondd* 33 98
Ystrad Aeron *Cerdgn* 44 52
Ystrad Ffin *Carmth* 44 78
Ystrad Meurig *Cerdgn* 43 70
Ystrad Mynach *Caerph* 33 14
Ystradfellte *Powys* 33 93
Ystradgynlais *Powys* 32 75
Ystradowen *V Glam* 33 00
Ystumtuen *Powys* 43 73
Ythanbank *Abers* 143 90
Ythanwells *Abers* 142 63
Ythsie *Abers* 143 88

Z

Zeal Monachorum *Devon* 8 72
Zeals *Wilts* 22 78
Zelah *Cnwll* 3 81
Zennor *Cnwll* 2 45
Zoar *Cnwll* 3 70
Zouch *Notts* 62 50

distances and journey times

The distances between towns on the mileage chart are given to the nearest mile, and are measured along the normal AA-recommended routes. It should be noted that AA-recommended routes do not necessarily follow the shortest distance between places but are based on the quickest travelling time, making maximum use of motorways and dual carriageways.

These times are average off-peak journey times based on normal AA-recommended routes. The times given do not take into account rest breaks, fuel stops or any unforeseen traffic delays, and therefore should be used as a guide only.

Example: Glasgow to Norwich, a journey of 379 miles taking approximately 7 hours 31 minutes.

journey times

(Diagonal triangular mileage and journey-time chart with place names along the diagonal: Aberdeen, Aberystwyth, Barnstaple, Birmingham, Brighton, Bristol, Cambridge, Cardiff, Carlisle, Carmarthen, Dorchester, Dover, Edinburgh, Exeter, Fort William, Glasgow, Gloucester, Guildford, Hereford, Holyhead, Hull, Inverness, Kendal, Leeds, Lincoln, Liverpool, Maidstone, Manchester, Middlesbrough, Newcastle, Northampton, Norwich, Nottingham, Oxford, Penzance, Perth, Peterborough, Plymouth, Portsmouth, Preston, Salisbury, Sheffield, Shrewsbury, Southampton, Stoke-on-Trent, Stranraer, Taunton, Wick, York, LONDON.)

distances